THE DEAD SEA SCROLLS

Hebrew, Aramaic, and Greek Texts

with English Translations

Volume 5A

Thanksgiving Hymns and Related Documents

The Princeton Dead Sea Scrolls Project

Editor: James H. Charlesworth
Associate Editors: Henry W. Morisada Rietz
and Loren L. Johns

Graphic Concordance
to the Dead Sea Scrolls

The Dead Sea Scrolls
Hebrew, Aramaic, and Greek Texts with English Translations

1. Rule of the Community and Related Documents

2. Damascus Document, War Scroll, and Related Documents

3. Damascus Document II,
Some Works of the Torah, and Related Documents

4A: Pseudepigraphic and Non-Masoretic Psalms and Prayers

4B: Angelic Liturgy: Songs of the Sabbath Sacrifice

5A: Thanksgiving Hymns and Related Documents

5B: Hymns and Related Documents

6A: Targum on Job, Parabiblical, and Related Documents

6B: Pesharim, Other Commentaries, and Related Documents

7: Temple Scroll and Related Documents

8A: Genesis Apocryphon and Related Documents

8B: New Jerusalem, Wisdom Texts, and Related Documents

9A: Visions, Testaments, Qumran Greek Fragments, and Other Documents

9B: Copper Scroll, Priestly Texts, and Other Documents

10: Biblical Apocrypha and Pseudepigrapha

Lexical Concordance to the Dead Sea Scrolls

THE PRINCETON DEAD SEA SCROLLS PROJECT

Sponsored by the Foundation on Judaism and Christian Origins

THE DEAD SEA SCROLLS

Hebrew, Aramaic, and Greek Texts with English Translations

Volume 5A

Thanksgiving Hymns and Related Documents

edited by

JAMES H. CHARLESWORTH

and

HENRY W. MORISADA RIETZ, Associate Editor
and LOREN L. JOHNS, Associate Editor

with

LEA BERKUZ, HERMANN LICHTENBERGER, DORON MENDELS, CASEY D. ELLEDGE, GARY A. RENDSBURG, JOSEPH L. TRAFTON,

along with

BLAKE A. JURGENS, BRADY A. BEARD, and JOLYON G. R. PRUSZINSKI

WESTMINSTER
JOHN KNOX PRESS
LOUISVILLE · KENTUCKY

First edition
Published by Westminster John Knox Press
Louisville, Kentucky

22 23 24 25 26 27 28 29 30 31—10 9 8 7 6 5 4 3 2 1

Library of Congress Cataloging-in-Publication Data is on file
at the Library of Congress, Washington, D.C.

ISBN 9780664267728 (paperback)
ISBN 9781646982608 (ebook)

Most Westminster John Knox Press books are available at special quantity discounts when purchased in bulk by corporations, organizations, and special-interest groups. For more information, please email SpecialSales@wjkbooks.com.

This edition of the *Hodayot* is dedicated to

THE VERY REV. DR. IAIN TORRANCE, KT, AND MORAG

PROF. DR. MARTIN HENGEL AND MARIANA

REV. DR. PROFESSOR HERMANN LICHTENBERGER AND DORIS

and

PROFESSOR DR. DORON MENDELS AND DR. MICHAL DAYAGI-MENDELS,

Devoted Friends, Esteemed Scholars, and Life Companions,

Known to me as Iain, Martin, Hermann, Doron, and Mulki

Table of Contents

Contents

The Princeton Dead Sea Scrolls Project

List of Contributors

JAMES F. ARMSTRONG (deceased)
Princeton Theological Seminary,
Princeton, New Jersey

JOSEPH M. BAUMGARTEN (deceased)
Baltimore Hebrew College,
Baltimore, Maryland

BRADY ALAN BEARD
Princeton Theological Seminary,
Princeton, New Jersey

LEA BERKUZ
Ramat Hasharon,
Israel

GEORGE J. BROOKE
University of Manchester,
Manchester, England

MAGEN BROSHI (deceased)
Shrine of the Book (Emeritus),
Jerusalem, Israel

JAMES H. CHARLESWORTH
Princeton Theological Seminary
(Emeritus),
Princeton, New Jersey

CARSTEN CLAUSSEN
Ludwig-Maximilians-Universität
München,
Munich, Germany

JOHN J. COLLINS
Yale University,
New Haven, Connecticut

FRANK M. CROSS JR. (deceased)
Harvard University,
Cambridge, Massachusetts

MICHAEL T. DAVIS
Princeton Theological Seminary,
Princeton, New Jersey

DEVORAH DIMANT
University of Haifa,
Haifa, Israel

JEAN DUHAIME
Université de Montréal,
Montreal, Quebec, Canada

LORENZO DITOMMASO
Concordia University,
Montreal, Quebec, Canada

JULIE A. DUNCAN
Garrett-Evangelical Theological
Seminary,
Evanston, Illinois

CASEY D. ELLEDGE
Gustavus Adolphus College,
St. Peter, Minnesota

ELDON J. EPP
Case Western Reserve University
(Emeritus),
Cleveland, Ohio

JOSEPH A. FITZMYER
Catholic University of America
(Emeritus),
Washington, D.C.

PETER W. FLINT (deceased)
Dead Sea Scrolls Institute,
Langley, British Columbia, Canada

DAVID N. FREEDMAN (deceased)
University of Michigan,
Ann Arbor, Michigan

ANDREW D. GROSS
The Catholic University of America,
Washington, District of Columbia

DANIEL M. GURTNER
Southern Baptist Theological Semi-
nary,
Louisville, Kentucky

MAURYA P. HORGAN
The Scriptorium,
Denver, Colorado

LARRY HURTADO (deceased)
University of Edinburgh,
Edinburgh, Scotland

LOREN L. JOHNS
Anabaptist Mennonite Biblical Sem-
inary (retired),
Elkhart, Indiana

BLAKE A. JURGENS
Princeton Theological Seminary,
Princeton, New Jersey

JOHN KAMPEN
Methodist Theological School in
Ohio,
Delaware, Ohio

ROBERT A. KUGLER
Gonzaga University,
Spokane, Washington

HERMANN LICHTENBERGER
University of Tübingen,
Tübingen, Germany

DANIEL A. MACHIELA
McMaster University,
Hamilton, Ontario, Canada

P. KYLE MCCARTER JR.
Johns Hopkins University,
Baltimore, Maryland

DORON MENDELS
Hebrew University,
Jerusalem, Israel

JACOB MILGROM (deceased)
University of California (Emeritus),
Berkeley, California

ROLAND E. MURPHY, O. Carm. (deceased)
Duke University,
Durham, North Carolina

CAROL A. NEWSOM
Emory University,
Atlanta, Georgia

LIDIJA NOVAKOVIC
Baylor University,
Waco, Texas

YOSEF OFER
Hebrew University,
Jerusalem, Israel

DENNIS T. OLSON
Princeton Theological Seminary,
Princeton, New Jersey

STEPHEN J. PFANN
University of the Holy Land,
Jerusalem, Israel

JOLYON G. R. PRUSZINSKI
Princeton University,
Princeton, New Jersey

ELISHA QIMRON
Ben Gurion University of the Negev,
Beer-Sheva, Israel

MICHAEL C. RAND
The Academy of the Hebrew Language,
Jerusalem, Israel

GARY A. RENDSBURG
Rutgers University,
New Brunswick, New Jersey

HENRY W. MORISADA RIETZ
Grinnell College,
Grinnell, Iowa

J. J. M. ROBERTS
Princeton Theological Seminary
(Emeritus),
Princeton, New Jersey

JAMES A. SANDERS (deceased)
Ancient Biblical Manuscript Center
(Emeritus),
Claremont, California

LAWRENCE H. SCHIFFMAN
New York University,
New York, New York

EILEEN M. SCHULLER
McMaster University,
Hamilton, Ontario, Canada

DANIEL R. SCHWARTZ
Hebrew University,
Jerusalem, Israel

ALAN F. SEGAL (deceased)
Barnard College,
New York, New York

BRENT A. STRAWN
Duke University,
Durham, North Carolina

LOREN T. STUCKENBRUCK
University of Munich,
Munich, Germany

SHEMARYAHU TALMON (deceased)
Hebrew University (Emeritus),
Jerusalem, Israel

EMANUEL TOV
Hebrew University (Emeritus),
Jerusalem, Israel

JOSEPH L. TRAFTON
Western Kentucky University,
Bowling Green, Kentucky

EUGENE ULRICH
University of Notre Dame,
Notre Dame, Indiana

JAMES C. VANDERKAM
University of Notre Dame,
Notre Dame, Indiana

MOSHE WEINFELD (deceased)
Hebrew University,
Jerusalem, Israel

RICHARD E. WHITAKER
Princeton Theological Seminary
(Emeritus),
Princeton, New Jersey

SIDNIE A. WHITE CRAWFORD
University of Nebraska-Lincoln,
Lincoln, Nebraska

ADELA YARBRO COLLINS
Yale University,
New Haven, Connecticut

ADA YARDENI (deceased)
Hebrew University,
Jerusalem, Israel

BRUCE ZUCKERMAN
University of Southern California,
Los Angeles, California

Preface

The Princeton Dead Sea Scrolls Project was launched in 1985. The Project has benefited from scholarly societies, libraries, museums, foundations, and philanthropists. The Computer Committee, the Board of Editorial Advisors, the Editor's assistants, and especially the subeditors have labored to make this series the critical and comprehensive edition of the nonbiblical Dead Sea Scrolls, with texts (and an *apparatus criticus*), English translations, introductions, and composite text (when possible).

Societies, Libraries, and Museums. Many assume that the Dead Sea Scrolls are preserved in the Shrine of the Book and the Rockefeller Museum. *Most* of the Dead Sea Scrolls are in these two locations, but some are preserved in other places. The Editor appreciates each institution that (or individual who) preserves Dead Sea Scrolls and fragments or the *Damascus Document* and has made them available for study and imaging. The Editor also is grateful to institutions and individuals who have provided improved photographs or digital images of the Scrolls. The project is indebted to the following:

The ASOR Ancient Manuscript Committee,
The Albright Institute,
The Israel Department of Antiquities and Museums,
The Shrine of the Book,
The Rockefeller Museum,
The Museum of the Studium Biblicum Franciscanum, Jerusalem,
The Antiquities Department of the Hashemite Kingdom of Jordan,
The Bibliothèque Nationale,
The University of Cambridge Library,
The Musée Terre Sainte, Paris,
The Ancient Biblical Manuscript Center,
The West Semitic Research Project,
Kodansha Ltd.,
The Huntington Library, and
Archbishop Mar Athanasius Y. Samuel.

Foundations, Institutions, and Philanthropists. The Project has received funding and support from numerous sources. Its success has been made possible by funding from the Alexander von Humboldt Stiftung, Lady Davis Foundation (The Hebrew University), the Foundation on Judaism and Christian Origins, the Institute for Semitic Studies, the Henry Luce Foundation, the Edith C. Blum Foundation, Inc., Frank and Roberta Furbush Fund, Anabaptist Mennonite Biblical Seminary, and Grinnell College. Special appreciations are also expressed to Frances M. and Wilbur H. Friedman, Dan Hales, Dr. John Hoffmann, Linda Wall, and Tom and Ann Cousins for their generous support.

Computer Committee, Board of Editorial Advisors, and Assistants. When the Project began, a special Computer Committee recommended that the Project work with the IBYCUS Computer System and develop software for the preparation of Semitic texts with appropriate sigla in order to present the exotic forms found in the Dead Sea Scrolls. James F. Armstrong served as chair. The other members were D. Packard, R. E. Whitaker, J. J. M. Roberts, and the Editor. The Princeton Project now uses Nota Bene for Windows to produce the near-camera-ready copy for introductions, texts, and translations.

The Editor has been guided by a Board of Editorial Advisors: F. M. Cross, J. A. Sanders, D. N. Freedman, and S. Talmon. J. Strugnell offered valuable advice and insight. The Board advised the Editor about which documents should be included in early volumes and which should be published later, due to the state of research on unpublished fragments. The Board also suggested scholars to serve as subeditors.

In the Princeton Qumran Laboratory many editorial assistants have helped Charlesworth edit volume 5A by entering all texts into Nota Bene. They also helped by correcting entries, checking readings, and aligning all translations. These assistants include Lea Berkuz, Brandon Lee Allen, Blake A. Jurgens, Brady Alan Beard, Sarah Kay Duke, Mitchell Esswein, Aaron T. Neff, Charles Ashby Neterer, Felipe Alejandro Ocampo, Justin Lee Pannkuk, Jolyon G. R. Pruszinski, Jon David Shearer III, Rachel Erin Stuart, and Aron M. Tillema.

Subeditors. The Project is dependent on the expertise and cooperation of the specialists who prepared the critical texts and translations. The two main criteria employed in selecting a scholar for this work are proven expertise in Qumran research, especially on the document to be assigned, and demonstrated skill with English. The team of subeditors is from the U.S.A., Canada, Germany, France, Great Britain, and Israel (see the List of Contributors).

Finally a personal note: The dedication of all concerned has been encouraging. The enthusiasm of the subeditors, especially the dedicated assistants, helped me in ways that are known only to editors of massive and seemingly impossible projects.

Rietz, Johns, and I are grateful for the assistance from Westminster John Knox. Thanks especially to Daniel Braden and the Westminster John Knox staff for their commitment to making this Project an example of state-of-the-art publishing. To all mentioned above, and to many others, we are both indebted and grateful.

James H. Charlesworth, Editor and President, Foundation on Judaism and Christian Origins Princeton, New Jersey 30 May 2021

Henry W. M. Rietz, Associate Editor Grinnell College Grinnell, Iowa

Foreword
(with Signa and Sigla)

The Princeton Dead Sea Scrolls Project was established to make available the first comprehensive and critical edition of texts, translations, and introductions to all the Dead Sea Scrolls that are not copies of biblical books (that is, documents collected in the *Biblia Hebraica*). Hence, the documents composed at Qumran, as well as the Jewish writings composed elsewhere but found in the eleven Qumran caves, are collected in this series. Volume 10 in the series is devoted to Qumran versions of documents considered to be part of the biblical Apocrypha and Pseudepigrapha.

All Qumran sectarian documents are translated so that technical terms are rendered in the same manner (see the Consistency Chart following the Foreword). On the one hand, the Editor and his staff (in consultation with the Board of Advisors) had to decide how to translate *termini technici*; for example, we voted against "the Teacher of Righteousness," in favor of "the Righteous Teacher,"[1] and against *Yaḥad* in favor of "Community." On the other hand, words or phrases with more than one meaning had to be translated consistently, yet with some variety, so as to reflect the literary context or social setting.

Obviously, each introduction must be tailored both for the corpus and for the idiosyncrasies of the document under consideration. When the document is extensive, introductions can be organized according to an accepted pattern and a recognized order. For the convenience of the reader the guidelines for introductions may be summarized as follows:

Texts. The contributor presents all textual evidence for the document and discusses the material state of the manuscript(s).

Contents. This section describes the nature of the composition and its general content and character.

Original Language. The scholar discusses the language of composition.

Date. After assessing the date of the earliest witness to a document, the subeditor discusses the probable date of composition.

Provenience. Not all of the documents found in the Qumran Caves were composed at Qumran. Some were composed there; but others were written elsewhere in Palestine (in Jerusalem or perhaps somewhere in Galilee), and perhaps derive from documents (not merely traditions) that took initial shape in Babylon or elsewhere. In light of these insights the specialist discusses the provenience of the document.

History. This section attempts to discern the history or historical episodes reflected in the scroll or necessary to comprehend it.

Theology. The expert discusses the major theological ideas and symbols in the writing.

Relation to the Hebrew Bible. The contributor assesses how, if at all, the document is related to books in the *Biblia Hebraica* (and perhaps to the versions of it extant before 70 C.E.).

Relation to Other Jewish Writings. The scholar discusses possible links to other Jewish writings, especially the *Books of Enoch, Jubilees,* and the earliest portions of the *Testaments of the Twelve Patriarchs.* The specialist also reflects on how the document helps us reconstruct Early Judaism (or types of Judaism during the period of the Second Temple).

Relation to the New Testament. The specialist discusses the significant ties with the documents collected into the New Testament and with the figures (like John the Baptist), symbolic language, or world view mentioned or preserved in these documents. Finally, the contributor presents an assessment of how the document may affect the reconstruction of Christian Origins.

Working with the Editor and his assistants, the subeditors reproduce as accurately as possible the texts of the manuscripts. Contributors use the best available photographs. When necessary, the manuscripts are rephotographed or digitized for their use. Whenever feasible, the contributors consult the actual manuscripts. Initial, medial, and final forms of consonants in anomalous positions are reproduced in the transcription precisely as seen on a scroll. The following signa, sigla, and script are employed in the transcriptions of texts:

א̇	= essentially certain reading of a damaged character[2]
א̥	= uncertain reading of a damaged character
̥	= illegible character
א̣, א̣, א	= deletion by a scribe[3]
אשר אין	= deletion by a scribe
א\ו/ל,ו/ל	= supralinear correction by a scribe
◇	= emendation proposed by subeditor (used only in the composite texts)
[ ]	= lacuna

---

[1] The *môrēh haṣ-ṣedeq* was not one who taught "righteousness"; he was the right teacher to whom God had revealed all mysteries (cf. 1QpHab 7.4-5).

[2] The dot added by a transcriber is always above the character.

[3] A scribe's use of a single dot over a character is indicated in a footnote to distinguish it from the sign for an essentially certain reading of a damaged character.

‏בני א]ור[‏	= restoration of lacuna
⟦ ⟧	= join between fragments
( )	= area of erasure
‏(העם)‏	= area of erasure with legible character or characters
⌐	= separating mark supplied by scribe in margin
‏ו,י‏	= a *waw* which could be a *yodh* (or a *yodh* a *waw*)
vac, vacat	= uninscribed surface[4]
⸕	= end of line mark supplied by scribe in margin of CD
𐤉𐤄𐤅𐤄	= Palaeo-Hebrew script for ‏יהוה‏
𐤀𐤋	= Palaeo-Hebrew script for ‏אל‏
𐤀𐤋𐤄𐤉𐤌	= Palaeo-Hebrew script for ‏אלוהים‏
𐤀𐤋𐤉	= Palaeo-Hebrew script for ‏אלי‏
𐤀	= Ligature (only for CD) signifying ‏אל‏
. . . .	= Signifies ‏יהוה‏
✗	= Palaeo-Hebrew ‏ת‏

Only obvious restorations of lacunae are attempted in the text and are circumscribed by brackets [ ]. In the composite text, these probable restorations of words or phrases are included in the diplomatic text, usually anchored by at least one extant letter. More speculative restorations are relegated to the notes. Restorations are based on comparisons with similar passages in the Qumran corpus; the *GC* serves as our guide.

When appropriate, more extensive restorations of passages from the Hebrew Bible are made according to the Qumran biblical manuscripts, the Aleppo Codex, Codex Leningradensis, or the Masoretic Text. In the case of documents which are attested in multiple manuscript witnesses, a critical apparatus is employed.[5] Whenever possible, each manuscript witness is presented separately with its own critical apparatus or textual notes. In exceptional instances, a composite text is reconstructed from the fragments of various manuscript witnesses.

Finally, the translators present in English the literal *meaning* of the Hebrew, Aramaic, or Greek. They avoid free idiomatic renderings. The following signs are employed in the translations:

[...]	= lacuna[6]
Sons of Li[ght...]	= restoration of lacuna
(God)	= additional words necessary for meaningful English
⟨⟩	= emendation proposed by subeditor (used only in the composite texts)
°	= illegible consonant
(vacat)	= uninscribed surface

Italics are used to transliterate consonants or forms that are not translatable.[7]

J. H. Charlesworth
Princeton, New Jersey

---

[4] This term is demanded by the ambiguity of many fragments. To avoid the intrusiveness of a Latin term in a Semitic (or Greek) manuscript, we use vacat sparingly. Aligning the text so as to clarify an uninscribed surface, especially when the line is indented, serves the intended purpose without intruding editorially into the transcription.

[5] Underlined footnote numbers indicate significant textual variants between manuscripts. In the apparatus, cf. is used to refer to similar, though not necessarily overlapping material.

[6] Elipses indicate various lengths.

[7] Transliteration of Hebrew characters are according to the *SBL Handbook of Style*. Since *śîn* and *šîn* are not distinct forms in the manuscripts, both are rendered as *š* in the translation. However, they may be distinguished in the notes. When relevant, vocalizations appear in the notes following the conventions of the Society of Biblical Literature.

Consistency Chart

The Princeton Dead Sea Scrolls Project primarily intends to present an improved critical text – with an *apparatus criticus* where appropriate and possible – to all the nonbiblical documents found in the eleven Qumran caves (that means all the documents not collected within the *Biblia Hebraica*). The translation provided is dependent on the text and is an aid to comprehending it; hence, it is as literal as good English will allow. Notes to the translation indicate other possible renderings, clarify how a word or phrase has been previously translated, or draw attention to a variant reading in another copy of the document.

Two principles have been followed so as to present a faithful and coherent translation. First, the meaning of a word must be discerned within its context; that is, within the cluster of contiguous words, and within the flow of the document (or a section of it). Previously, translations of Qumran Hebrew were prepared in light of Biblical Hebrew; now, however, the subeditors have decades of experience in reading and translating Qumran Hebrew in over 900 documents. Second, technical terms must be translated uniformly and consistently throughout the extensive corpus. The following list of terms clarify the decisions obtained from the Editor's dialogues with the subeditors and with the Board of Editorial Advisors (words in parentheses indicate examples of how the word or words have been translated in nontechnical contexts).

אביונים	Poor Ones
אודכה אדוני כי	I thank you, O Lord, because
איש הכזב	the Man of the Lie
אלים	divine beings
אסף	gather
ארץ	earth, land
בינה	discernment
בית קודש	House of Holiness
בליעל	Belial
בני אהרון	Sons of Aaron
בני אור	Sons of Light
בני אמת	Sons of Truth
בני השחר	Sons of the Dawn
בני חושך	Sons of Darkness
בני צדוק	Sons of Zadok
בני צדק	Sons of Righteousness
גורל	lot
דביר	inner room
דעת	knowledge
הדרך	the Way, the way
חוק	statute, boundary; (assigned)
חטא	sin
חכמה	wisdom
חסד	mercy

טובים	Good Ones
יום הכפורים	Day of Atonement
יום המשפט	Day of Judgment
יום נקם	Day of Vengeance
היחד	the Community; (community, common, each other, together, one, unity)
יעד	be summoned; (appointed)
הכוהן הרשע	the Wicked Priest
הכתיאים	the Kittim
מבקר	Examiner
מועד	appointed time, holy day, season; (meeting, feast, festival)
מורה הצדק	Righteous Teacher
מטע	planting
מטיף הכזב	Spouter of the Lie
מעין	fountain
מעשים	works; (workmanship)
מצוותיו	his ordinances
מקור	spring; (discharge – 1QM 7.6)
משכיל	Master
משפט	judgment, precept; (justice)
נגלות	revealed, revealed (laws)
נפש	soul, being; (life, human being, self)
נצר	shoot
נקמה	(time of) vengeance
סוד	foundation, assembly, principle
עדה	congregation, Congregation
עול	deceit
עון	iniquity
עצה	counsel, the council, the Council
העת, עת	time, the Endtime; (now, age, continually)
פקיד	Overseer
צדקות, צדק	righteous, righteous deeds
צדיקים	Righteous Ones
קדושי קדושים	Most Holy Ones
קדושימ	Holy Ones
קהל	assemble, assembly
קץ	Endtime, end, time
רוח קודש	Holy Spirit; (holy spirit)
הרבים	the Many
רז	mystery
תבל	world
תורה	Torah
תירוש	new wine
תכון	norm, measure
תמים, תם	perfect, perfectly; (perfection, continually, always, every, complete)
תמימים	Perfect Ones
תעודה	fixed times, convocation, distinction; (testimony, instruction)

Abbreviations

Modern Publications

AASOR	*Annual of the American Schools of Oriental Research*
AB	Anchor Bible
ABD	Freedman, D. N., ed. *The Anchor Bible Dictionary*, 6 vols. New York, 1992.
Abegg and Wacholder, *PEUPDSS*	Abegg, M. G. and B.-Z. Wacholder, eds. *A Preliminary Edition of the Unpublished Dead Sea Scrolls*, 4 vols. Washington, D. C., 1991–96.
ABRL	Anchor Bible Reference Library
AcOr	*Acta orientalia*
AGAJU	Arbeiten zur Geschichte des antiken Judentums und des Urchristentums
AHDSS	Schiffman, L. H., ed. *Archaeology and History in the Dead Sea Scrolls: The New York University Conference in Memory of Yigael Yadin.* JSOT/ ASOR Monograph Series 2; JSPS 8; Sheffield, 1990.
AJSL	*American Journal of Semitic Languages and Literatures*
ALBO	Analecta lovaniensia biblica et orientalia
ALUOS	*Annual of Leeds University Oriental Society*
ANRW	Haase, W., and H. Temporini, eds. *Aufstieg und Niedergang der römischen Welt.* Berlin, New York, 1979–.
ANTI	Arbeiten zum Neuen Testament und Judentum
AO	Analecta Orientalia
AOT	Altorientalische Texte zum Alten Testament
APAT	Kautzsch, E., ed. *Die Apokryphen und Pseudepigraphen des Alten Testaments*, 2 vols. Tübingen, 1900.
APOT	Charles, R. H., ed. *The Apocrypha and Pseudepigrapha of the Old Testament in English*, 2 vols. Oxford, 1913.
ArOr	*Archiv Orientální*
ASOR	American Schools of Oriental Research
ATR	*Anglican Theological Review*
BA	*Biblical Archaeologist*
BAGD	Bauer, W., W. F. Arndt, and F. W. Gingrich, eds. *A Greek-English Lexicon of the New Testament and Other Early Christian Literature*, 2nd ed., rev. and aug. F. W. Gingrich and F. W. Danker. Chicago, 1979.
BAR	*Biblical Archaeology Review*
BASOR	*Bulletin of the American Schools of Oriental Research*
BASORSS	*Bulletin of the American Schools of Oriental Research* Supplementary Studies
BDB	Brown, F., S. R. Driver, and C.A. Briggs, eds. *A Hebrew and English Lexicon of the Old Testament.* Oxford, 1907.

BDSS	Charlesworth, J. H., ed. *The Bible and the Dead Sea Scrolls*, 3 vols. Waco, Texas, 2006.
BETL	Bibliotheca Ephemeridum Theologicarum Lovaniensium, Paris and Leuven
BH	Biblical Hebrew
BHS	*Biblia Hebraica Stuttgartensia*
BHT	Beiträge zur historischen Theologie
Bib	Biblica
BibOr	Biblica et orientalia
BIOSCS	*Bulletine of the International Organization for the Septuagint and Cognate Studies*
BJRL	*Bulletin of the John Rylands Library*
BJRULM	*Bulletin of the John Rylands University Library of Manchester*
BN	Catalogue général des livres imprimés de la bibliothèque nationale
BR	*Biblical Research*
Broshi, *DRR*	Broshi, M., ed. *The Damascus Document Reconsidered.* Jerusalem, 1992.
BSO(A)S	*Bulletin of the School of Oriental and African Studies*
BWANT	Beiträge zur Wissenschaft vom Alten und Neuen Testament
BZ	*Biblische Zeitschrift*
BZAW	*Beihefte zur ZAW*
BZNW	*Beihefte zur ZNW*
BZRG	Beihefte der Zeitschrift für Religions- und Geistesgeschichte
Carmignac, *Règle*	Carmignac, J. *La Règle de la Guerre des Fils de Lumière contre les Fils e Ténèbres.* Paris, 1958.
CBQ	*Catholic Biblical Quarterly*
CBQMS	Catholic Biblical Quarterly Monograph Series
CCWJCW	Cambridge Commentaries on Writings of the Jewish and Christian World 200 BC to AD 200
CDSS	Vermes, G. *The Complete Dead Sea Scrolls in English: Revised Edition.* New York and London, 2004.
CEJL	Commentaries on Early Jewish Literature
CIJ	Frey, J. B., ed. *Corpvs inscriptionvm ivdaicarvm.* Vatican City, 1936–52.
CIS	*Corpus inscriptionum semiticarum.* Paris, 1881.
COL	Christian Origins Library
CPJ	Tcherikover, A., ed. *Corpus papyrorum Judaicarum*, 3 vols. Cambridge, MA, 1957–64.
CQS	Companion to the Qumran Scrolls
CRAI	Comptes rendus de l'Académie des inscriptions et belles-lettres
CRB	Cahiers de la Revue biblique
CRINT	Compendia Rerum Iudaicarum ad Novum Testamentum

Cross, *AL*	Cross, F. M. *The Ancient Library of Qumran and Modern Biblical Studies*, 3rd ed. Minneapolis, 1995.
Cross, "Dating"	Cross, F. M. "Excursus on the Dating of the Copper Document," DJD 3; pp. 217–21.
Cross, "Development"	Cross, F. M. "The Development of the Jewish Scripts," in *The Bible and The Ancient Near East: Essays in Honor of William Foxwell Albright*, ed. G. E. Wright. Garden City, New York, 1961; pp. 133–202.
CTSRIR	College Theological Society Resources in Religion
DBSup	*Dictionnaire de la Bible, Supplément*
DCH	Clines, D. J. A., ed. *Dictionary of Classical Hebrew*, 3 vols. Sheffield, 1993–96.
Delcor, *Ancien*	*Delcor, M. Religion d'Israel et proche orient ancien*. Leiden, 1976.
Delcor, *Hymnes*	Delcor, M. *Les Hymnes de Qumrân (Hodayot)*. Paris, 1962.
de Vaux, *Archaeology*	de Vaux, R. *Archaeology and the Dead Sea Scrolls*, rev. ed. in an English translation. London, 1973.
DISO	Jean, C.-F. and J. Hoftijzer, eds. *Dictionnaire des inscriptions sémitiques de l'ouest*. Leiden, 1965.
DJD	Discoveries in the Judaean Desert
DNWSI	Hoftijzer, J. and K. Jongeling, eds. *Dictionary of North West Semitic Inscriptions*, 2 vols. Leiden, 1995.
DSD	*Dead Sea Discoveries*
DSPS	Sanders, J. A. *Dead Sea Psalms Scroll*. Ithaca, 1967.
DSSAFY	Flint, P. W., and J. C. VanderKam, eds. *The Dead Sea Scrolls After Fifty Years*, 2 vols. Leiden, 1998–99.
DSSEL (2006)	*The Dead Sea Scrolls Electronic Library* [revised edition of 2006]. Provo and Leiden, 1991–2006.
DSSR	D. W. Parry and E. Tov, eds. *The Dead Sea Scrolls Reader*, 6 vols. Leiden, Boston: Brill, 2004–2005.
Dupont-Sommer, *EE*	Dupont-Sommer, A. *Les Écrits Esséniens découverts près de la Mer Morte*, 4th ed. Bibliothèque historique; Paris, 1980.
EcInt	Dupont-Sommer, A., M. Philonenko, et al., eds. *La Bible ecrits intertestamentaires*. [Paris] 1987.
EJT	Early Judaism and Its Literature
EncBibl	Encyclopaedia Biblica, Jerusalem
EncJud	Wigoder, G., ed. *The Encyclopedia of Judaism*. New York and London, 1989.
EncyDSS	Schiffman, L. H., and J. C. VanderKam, eds. *Encyclopedia of the Dead Sea Scrolls*, 2 vols. Oxford, 2000.
ETL	*Ephemerides Theologicae Lovanienses*
EvT	*Evangelische Theologie*
ExpT	*Expository Times*
FB	Forschung zur Bibel
Fifty Years	Schiffman, L. H., E. Tov, and J. C. VanderKam, eds. *The Dead Sea Scrolls: Fifty Years after Their Discovery* [*Jerusalem Congress*]. Jerusalem, 2000.
Fitzmyer, *Apocryphon*	Fitzmyer, J. A. *The Genesis Apocryphon of Qumran Cave I*, Rome, 1966.
Fitzmyer, *Tools*	Fitzmyer, J. A. *The Dead Sea Scrolls: Major Publications and Tools for Study,* rev. ed. SBLRBS 20; Atlanta, 1990.
FRLANT	Forschungen zur Religion und Literatur des Alten und Neuen Testaments
Gaster, *DSS*	Gaster, T. H. *The Dead Sea Scriptures: In English Translation with Introduction and Notes,* 3rd ed. New York, 1976.
GC	Charlesworth, J. H., et al., eds. *Graphic Concordance to the Dead Sea Scrolls*. Tübingen and Louisville, 1991.
GKC	Kautzsch, E., ed. *Gesenius' Hebrew Grammar,* 2nd ed., rev. A. E. Cowley. Oxford, 1910.
GNMM	*Good News for Modern Man*
HALAT	Koehler, L., and W. Baumgartner, eds. *Hebräisches und aramäisches Lexikon zum Alten Testament,* 2 vols. Leiden 1967–95.
HAR	*Hebrew Annual Review*
HAT	Handbuch zum Alten Testament
HDR	Harvard Dissertations in Religion
Hen	*Henoch*
Hengel, *JudHell*	Hengel, M. *Judaism and Hellenism: Studies in their Encounter in Palestine during the Early Hellenistic Period*, 2 vols., trans. J. Bowden. Philadelphia, 1974.
HNT	Handbuch zum Neuen Testament
Horgan, *Pesharim*	*Horgan, M. P. Pesharim: Qumrân Interpretations of Biblical Books*. CBQMS 8; Washington, D.C., 1979.
HR	*History of Religions*
HSCPh	Harvard Studies in Classical Philology
HSM	Harvard Semitic Monographs
HSS	Harvard Semitic Studies
HTR	*Harvard Theological Review*
HTS	Harvard Theological Studies
HUCA	*Hebrew Union College Annual*
IDB	Buttrick, G. A., ed. *Interpreter's Dictionary of the Bible,* 5 vols. Nashville, 1962.
IDBS	Crim, K., et al., eds. *The Interpreter's Dictionary of the Bible, Supplementary Volume.* Nashville, 1976.
IEJ	*Israel Exploration Journal*
JAAR	*Journal of the American Academy of Religion*
JANES	*Journal of the Ancient Near Eastern Society of Columbia University*
JAOS	*Journal of the America Oriental Society*
Jastrow, *Dictionary*	Jastrow, M. A. *Dictionary of the Targumim, the Talmud Babli and Yerushalmi, and the Midrashic Literature*, 2 vols. New York, 1950, reprinted in Israel.
JB	*Jerusalem Bible*
JBL	*Journal of Biblical Literature*

JDS	Charlesworth, J. H., ed. *John and the Dead Sea Scrolls.* COL; New York, 1990.
JDSer	Judean Desert Series
JDSS	Charlesworth, J. H., et al. *Jesus and the Dead Sea Scrolls.* ABRL; New York, 1992.
Jeremias, *Lehrer*	*Jeremias, G. Der Lehrer der Gerechtigkeit.* SUNT 2; Göttingen, 1963.
JJS	*Journal of Jewish Studies*
JNES	*Journal of Near Eastern Studies*
JNSL	*Journal of Northwest Semitic Languages*
Joüon-Muraoka	Joüon, P. and T. Muraoka. *A Grammar of Biblical Hebrew,* 2 vols. Subsidia Biblica 14. Rome, 1991.
JQR	*Jewish Quarterly Review*
JR	*Journal of Religion*
JSHRZ	Jüdische Schriften aus hellenistisch römischer Zeit. Gütersloh, 1973–.
JSJ	*Journal for the Study of Judaism*
JSJSup	Journal for the Study of Judaism Supplements
JSNT	*Journal for the Study of the New Testament*
JSOT	*Journal for the Study of the Old Testament*
JSOTSup	Journal for the Study of the Old Testament Supplement Series
JSP	*Journal for the Study of the Pseudepigrapha*
JSPS	Journal for the Study of the Pseudepigrapha Supplement Series
JSS	*Journal of Semitic Studies*
JSSR	*Journal for the Scientific Study of Religion*
JThC	*Journal for Theology and the Church*
JTS	*Journal of Theological Studies*
KB	Koehler, L. and W. Baumgartner, *Lexicon in Veteris Testamenti Libros* and *Supplementum.* Leiden, 1985.
Knibb, *Qumran*	*Knibb, M. A. The Qumran Community.* CCWJCW 2; Cambridge, 1987.
Lampe	Lampe, G. W. H., ed. *A Patristic Greek Lexicon.* Oxford, 1961.
LD	Lectio divina
Leaney, *Rule*	Leaney, A. R. C. *The Rule of the Community and Its Meaning.* NTL; London, 1966.
LibCong	Sussmann, A. and R. Peled, eds. *Scrolls from the Dead Sea: An Exhibition of Scrolls and Archaeological Artifacts from the Collections of the Israel Antiquities Authority.* Washington, 1993.
Licht, *RS*	Licht, J. *The Rule Scroll: A Scroll from the Wilderness of Judea.* Jerusalem, 1965. [Hebrew]
Licht, *TS*	Licht, J. *The Thanksgiving Scroll.* Jerusalem, 1957. [Hebrew]
Lichtenberger, *Menschenbild*	*Lichtenberger, H. Studien zum Menschenbild in Texten der Aumrangemeinde.* SUNT 15; Göttingen, 1980.
Lohse, *Texte*	Lohse, E., ed. *Die Texte aus Qumran.* Darmstadt, 1981.
LSJM	Liddell, H. G. and R. Scott. *A Greek-English Lexicon,* 9th ed., rev. H. S. Jones and R. McKenzie. Oxford, 1940 with a Supplement of 1968.

LSTS	Library of Second Temple Studies
Maier,	Maier, J. *Die Tempelrolle vom Toten Meer und das "Neue Jerusalem,"* 3rd ed. UTB 829; Munich, 1997.
Maier/Schubert, *Qumran*	Maier, J. and K. Schubert. *Die Qumran Essener* and *Die Qumran Essener: Die Texte vom Toten Meer,* 3 vols. UTB 1862, 1863, 1916; Munich, 1995–1996.
Manual	Fitzmyer, J. A., and D. J. Harrington, *A Manual of Palestinian Aramaic Texts.* BO 34. Rome, 1994 [2nd reprint].
MHUC	Monographs of the Hebrew Union College
Milik, *Books*	*Milik, J. T. with M. Black. The Books of Enoch: Aramaic Fragments of Qumrân Cave 4.* Oxford, 1976.
MNTC	Moffatt New Testament Commentary
MQ	Moraldi, L., ed. *I Manoscritti di Qumrân.* Turin, 1971.
Muraoka	Muraoka, T. *A Grammar of Qumran Aramaic.* Ancient Near Eastern Studies 38. Leuven and Walpole, MA, 2011.
NEAEHL	Stern, E., ed. *New Encyclopedia of Archaeological Excavations in the Holy Land,* 4 vols. New York, 1993.
NEB	*New English Bible*
Newsom, *Songs*	Newsom, C. *Songs of the Sabbath Sacrifice: A Critical Edition.* HSS 27; Atlanta, 1985.
NHS	Nag Hammadi Studies
NKBE	Koehler, L. and W. Baumgartner, eds., rev. W. Baumgartner and J. J. Stamm, trans. and ed. M. E. J. Richardson. *The Hebrew and Aramaic Lexicon of the Old Testament: The New Koehler-Baumgartner in English,* 5 vols. Leiden/New York/Boston/Köln, 1994–2000.
NovT	*Novum Testamentum*
NRSV	*New Revised Standard Version*
NRT	*Nouvelle Revue Théologique*
NTL	New Testament Library
NTS	*New Testament Studies*
NTTS	New Testament Tools and Studies
OEANE	Meyers, E., ed. *The Oxford Encyclopedia of Archaeology in the Near East,* 5 vols. Oxford, 1997.
Of Scribes	Attridge, H. W., J. J. Collins, T. H. Tobin, eds. *Of Scribes and Scrolls: Studies on the Hebrew Bible, Intertestamental Judaism, and Christian Origins.* CTSRIR 5; Lanham, Maryland, 1990.
OTP	Charlesworth, J. H., ed. *The Old Testament Pseudepigrapha,* 2 vols. New York, 1983, 1985.
OTS	Oudtestamentische Studiën
PAAJR	*Proceedings of the American Academy for Jewish Research*
PDS	Murphy-O'Connor, J. and J. H. Charlesworth, eds. *Paul and the Dead Sea Scrolls.* COL; New York, 1990.
PEQ	*Palestine Exploration Quarterly*
PFES	Publications of the Finnish Exegetical Society

PhotogEd	Charlesworth, J. H., *et al. Rule of the Community: Photographic Multi-Language Edition.* New York, 1996.
Pouilly, *Règle*	*Pouilly, J. La Règle de la Communauté de Qumrân. CRB 17; Paris, 1976.*
Proof	*Prooftexts: A Journal of Jewish Literary History*
PTSDSSP	Princeton Theological Seminary Dead Sea Scrolls Project
QBONT	Cryer, F. H. and T. L. Thompson, eds. *Qumran Between the Old and New Testaments.* JSOT-Sup 290; Copenhagen International Seminar 6; Sheffield, 1998.
Qimron, *HDSS*	*Qimron, E. The Hebrew of the Dead Sea Scrolls.* HSS 29; Atlanta, 1986.
Qumrân	Delcor, M., ed. *Qumrân: Sa piété, sa théologie et son milieu.* BETL 46; Paris and Leuven, 1978.
Qumran	Grözinger, K. E. et al., eds. *Qumran.* Wege der Forschung 410; Darmstadt, 1981.
Rabin, *QumSt*	Rabin, C. *Qumran Studies.* New York, 1957.
Rabin, ed. *ZadDoc*	Rabin, C. *The Zadokite Documents*, 2nd rev. ed. Oxford, 1958.
RB	*Revue biblique*
Reed, *Catalogue*	*Reed, S. A. and M. J. Lundberg with M. B.* Phelps, eds. *The Dead Sea Scrolls Catalogue: Documents, Photographs and Museum Inventory Numbers.* SBLRBS 32; Atlanta, 1994.
Reed, *Inventory*	Reed, S. *Dead Sea Scroll Inventory Project: Lists of Documents, Photographs and Museum Plates.* Claremont, 1993.
ReScRel	*Recherches de Science Religieuse*
Reymond	Reymond, E. D. *Qumran Hebrew.* Atlanta, 2014.
RGG	*Die Religion in Geschichte und Gegenwart*
RHPR	*Revue d'histoire et de philosophie religieuses*
RHR	*Revue de l'histoire des religions*
RivB	*Rivista Biblica Italiana*
RQ	*Revue de Qumran*
RSV	*Revised Standard Version*
SAOC	Studies in Ancient Oriental Civilization
SBL	Society of Biblical Literature
SBLDS	Society of Biblical Literature Dissertation Series
SBLMS	Society of Biblical Literature Monograph Series
SBLRBS	Society of Biblical Literature Resources for Biblical Study
SBLSS	Society of Biblical Literature Symposium Series
SBT	Studies in Biblical Theology
ScEs	*Science et Esprit*
Schuller, *PsPsalms*	Schuller, E. M. *Non-Canonical Psalms from Qumran: A Pseudepigraphic Collection.* HSS 28; Atlanta, 1986.
Schürer, *HJP*	Schürer, E. *The History of the Jewish People in the Age of Jesus Christ.* Rev. ed. by G. Vermes, F. Millar, and M. Goodman, 3 vols. Edinburgh, 1973–87.
ScrHie	Scripta Hierosolymitana
SCS	Septuagint and Cognate Studies
SDSS	Studies in the Dead Sea Scrolls and Related Literature
SEA	*Svensk exegetisk Årsbok*
Sekine, DSS	Sekine, M., ed. *The Dead Sea Scrolls.* Tokyo, 1979.
Sem	*Semitica*
ShaTalmon	Fishbane, M. and E. Tov, eds. *"Sha'arei Talmon" Studies in the Bible, Qumran, and the Ancient Near East Presented to Shemaryahu Talmon.* Winona Lake, Indiana, 1992.
SJLA	Studies in Judaism in Late Antiquity
SJT	*Scottish Journal of Theology*
SNT	Stendahl, K., ed. *The Scrolls and the New Testament.* New introduction by J. H. Charlesworth; COL; New York, 1992.
SNTS MS	*Studiorum Novi Testamenti Societas* Monograph Series
Sokoloff, *Dictionary*	Sokoloff, M. *A Dictionary of Jewish Palestinian Aramaic of the Byzantine Period.* Dictionaries of Talmud, Midrash and Targum 2; Ramat-Gan, 1990.
Sokoloff, *Targum*	Sokoloff, M. *The Targum to Job from Qumrân Cave XI.* Ramat-Gan, 1974.
ST	*Studia Theologica*
STDJ	Studies on the Texts of the Desert of Judah
StNT	*Studien zum Neuen Testament*
SUNT	Studien zur Umwelt des Neuen Testaments
SVTP	Studia in Veteris Testamenti Pseudepigrapha
Talmon, *King*	Talmon, S. *King, Cult and Calendar in Ancient Israel.* Jerusalem, 1986.
Talmon, *World*	Talmon, S. *The World of Qumran from Within.* Jerusalem, 1989.
TANAKH	*TANAKH: A New Translation of the Holy Scriptures According to the Traditional Hebrew Text.* Philadelphia, New York and Jerusalem, 5746, 1985.
TAPA	Transactions and Proceedings, American Philological Association.
TBN	Themes in Biblical Narrative
TDNT	Kittel, G. and G. Friedrich, eds. *Theological Dictionary of the New Testament*, 10 vols., trans. G. W. Bromiley. Grand Rapids, Michigan and London, 1964–76.
TDOT	Botterweck, G. J. and H. Ringgren, eds. *Theological Dictionary of the Old Testament*, 6 vols., trans. D. E. Green. Grand Rapids, Michigan, 1974–.
TdQ	Carmignac, J., P. Guilbert, É. Cothenet and H. Lignée. *Les textes de Qumran traduits et annotés*, 2 vols. Paris, 1961, 1963.
Textus	*Textus*
Thesaurus Syriacus	Payne Smith, R. *Thesaurus Syriacus*, 2 vols. Oxford, 1879–1901; reprinted Hildesheim, 1981.

ThRu	*Theologische Rundschau*
ThWQ	Fabry, H.–J. and U. Dahmen, eds. *Theologisches Wörterbuch zu den Qumrantexte,* 3 vols. Stuttgart, 2011-2016.
TICP	Travaux de l'Institut Catholique de Paris
TLZ	*Theologische Literaturzeitung*
Tov, *Companion Volume*	Tov, E. with S. J. Pfann, eds. *Companion Volume to the Dead Sea Scrolls Microfiche Edition,* 2nd rev. ed. Leiden, 1995.
Tov, *Microfiche*	Tov, E., ed. *The Dead Sea Scrolls on Microfiche.* Leiden, 1993.
Tov, *Revised Lists*	Tov, E. *Revised List of the Texts from the Judean Desert.* Leiden, Boston: Brill, 2010.
Tov, *Scribal Practices*	Tov, E. *Scribal Practices and Approaches Reflected in the Texts Found in the Judean Desert.* STDJ 54, Leiden, Boston: Brill, 2004.
TS	*Theological Studies*
TSAJ	Texts and Studies in Ancient Judaism
TWNT	Kittel, G. and G. Friedrich, eds. *Theologisches Wörterbuch zum Neuen Testament,* 10 vols. Stuttgart, 1932–1979.
TZ	*Theologische Zeitschrift*
USQR	*Union Seminary Quarterly Review*
UTB	Uni-Taschenbücher
VC	*Vigiliae christianae*
Vermes, *DSS*	Vermes, G. *The Dead Sea Scrolls in English,* 4th ed. London and New York, 1995.
VT	*Vetus Testamentum*
VTSup	Vetus Testamentum Supplements
Wernberg-Møller, *Manual*	Wernberg-Møller, P. *The Manual of Discipline: Translated and Annotated with an Introduction.* STDJ 1; Leiden, 1957.
Wise, *Temple*	Wise, M. O. *A Critical Study of the Temple Scroll from Qumrân Cave 11.* SAOC 49; Chicago, 1990.
WMANT	Wissenschaftliche Monographien zum Alten und Neuen Testament.
WO	Waltke, B. K. and M. O'Connor. *An Introduction to Biblical Hebrew Syntax.* Winona Lake, Indiana, 1990.
WUNT	Wissenschaftliche Untersuchungen zum Neuen Testament
WZ Leipzig	Wissenschaftliche Zeitschrift der Karl-Marx Universität Leipzig
WZKM	*Weiner Zeitschift für die Kunde des Morgenlandes*
Yadin, *Message*	Yadin, Y. *The Message of the Scrolls.* New Introduction by J. H. Charlesworth; COL; New York, 1992.
Yadin, *Temple*	Yadin, Y. *The Temple Scroll,* 3 vols. with Supplementary Plates. Jerusalem, 1983.
ZAW	*Zeitschrift für die alttestamentliche Wissenschaft*
ZKT	*Zeitschrift für katholische Theologie*
ZNW	*Zeitwchrift für die neutestamentliche Wissenschaft*
ZTK	*Zeitschrift für Theologie und Kirche*

Additional Abbreviations

ab.	above
add.	added/addition
alt.	alternative
appar.	apparently
assump.	assumption
beg.	beginning
betw.	between
BH	Biblical Hebrew
bl.	below
bot.	bottom
c.	circa
cf.	compare
ch., chs.	chapter, chapters
cit.	citation
col., cols.	column, columns
cons.	consistent
Cop.	Coptic
corr.	corrected/correction/correctly
cpr.	corruption
d.leather	defect in the leather
del.	deletion/deleted
diff.	different/differ
eras.	erasure/erased
ET	English translation
Eth.	Ethiopic
excl.	excluding/excluded
extd.	extended
frg., frgs.	fragment, fragments
Gk.	Greek
HB	Hebrew Bible
Heb.	Hebrew
impf.	imperfect
impv.	imperative
incons.	inconsistent
init.	initially
(in mg.)	letter or word written in the margin
inter.	interlinear
l., ll.	line, lines
Lat.	Latin
lt.	left
lit.	literally
ltr., ltrs.	letter, letters
LXX	Septuagint
mg.	margin
MH	Mishnaic Hebrew
MS, MSS	Manuscript, Manuscripts
msg.	missing
MT	Masoretic Text
n., nn.	note, notes
NT	New Testament
OG	Old Greek
orig.	original/originally
OT	Old Testament
p., pp.	page, pages
part.	participle
pass.	passive

pf.	perfect
pl.	plural
Pl., Pls.	plate, plates
poss.	possible/possibly
prob.	probably
prps.	perhaps
pt., pts.	part, parts
QH	Qumran Hebrew
rdg., rdgs.	reading, readings
recop.	recopying
repet.	repetition
rest.	restoration
rt	right
sg.	singular
sim.	similar
sp.	space
supral.	supralinear
synt.	syntactically
Syr.	Syriac
vert.	vertical
vs., vss.	verse, verses
writ.	writing/written

Ancient Documents

Bible and Apocrypha

Gen	Genesis
Ex	Exodus
Lev	Leviticus
Num	Numbers
Deut	Deuteronomy
Josh	Joshua
Judg	Judges
Ruth	Ruth
1Sam	1 Samuel
2Sam	2 Samuel
1Kgs	1 Kings
2Kgs	2 Kings
1Chr	1 Chronicles
2Chr	2 Chronicles
Ezra	Ezra
Neh	Nehemiah
Esth	Esther
Job	Job
Ps(s)	Psalm(s)
Prov	Proverbs
Eccl, Qoh	Ecclesiastes, Qohelet
Song	Song of Songs
Isa	Isaiah
Jer	Jeremiah
Lam	Lamentations
Ezek	Ezekiel
Dan	Daniel
Hos	Hosea
Joel	Joel
Amos	Amos
Obad	Obadiah

Jonah	Jonah
Micah	Micah
Nah	Nahum
Hab	Habakkuk
Zeph	Zephaniah
Hag	Haggai
Zech	Zechariah
Mal	Malachi
2Ezra	2 Ezra
Tob	Tobit
Jdt	Judith
AddEsth	Additions to Esther
WisSol	Wisdom of Solomon
Sir	Sirach
1Bar	1 Baruch
LetJer	Letter of Jeremiah
PrAzar	Prayer of Azariah
Sus	Susanna
Bel	Bel and the Dragon
1Mac	1 Maccabees
2Mac	2 Maccabees
Mt	Matthew
Mk	Mark
Lk	Luke
Jn	John
Acts	Acts
Rom	Romans
1Cor	1 Corinthians
2Cor	2 Corinthians
Gal	Galatians
Eph	Ephesians
Phil	Philippians
Col	Colossians
1Thes	1 Thessalonians
2Thes	2 Thessalonians
1Tim	1 Timothy
2Tim	2 Timothy
Tit	Titus
Phlm	Philemon
Heb	Hebrews
Jas	James
1Pet	1 Peter
2Pet	2 Peter
1Jn	1 John
2Jn	2 John
3Jn	3 John
Jude	Jude
Rev	Revelation

Pseudepigrapha

All abbreviations are according to *OTP*.

Philo

Abr	*De Abrahamo*
Cher	*De Cherubim*
Conf	*De Confusione Linguarum*

Ebr	*De Ebrietate*	*Life*	*Life of Josephus*
Flacc	*In Flaccum*	*War*	*Jewish Wars*
Gaium	*De Legatione ad Gaium*		
Heres	*Quis Rerum divinarum Heres*	Rabbinics	
Migr	*De Migratione Abrahami*		
Mut	*De Mutatione Nominum*	ARN	Abot de-Rabbi Nathan
OpDe	*Opificio Mundi*	b.	Babylonian Talmud (before a rabbinic text)
Post	*De Posteritate Caini*	Ber	Berakot
Praem	*De Praemiis et Poenis*	GenR	Bereshit Rabbah
Quaes Ex I–II	*Quaestiones et Solutiones in Exodus I–II*	Hag	Hagigah
Quod Det	*Quod Deterius Potiori insidiari solet*	m.	Mishnah (before a rabbinic text)
Quod Deus	*Quod Deus immutabilis sit*	Meg	Megillah
Sacr	*De Sacrificiis Abelis et Caini*	Sanh	Sanhedrin
Somn I–II	*De Somniis I–II*	SifDeut	Sifre Deuteronomy
Spec Leg I–IV	*De Specialibus Legibus I–IV*	Sot.	Sotah
Virt	*De Virtutibus*	t.	Tosephta (before a rabbinic text)
Vita Mos I–II	*De Vita Mosis I–II*	*TK*	Lieberman, S., ed. *Tosefta Kifshutah*. New York, 1955–.
		TargPsJon	Targum Pseudo-Jonathan
Josephus		y.	Jerusalem Talmud (before a rabbinic text)
Ant	*Jewish Antiquities*		
Apion	*Against Apion*		

General Introduction

The Dead Sea Scrolls as Primary Sources for Second Temple Judaism and a Clarified Perception of Christian Origins

JAMES H. CHARLESWORTH

Scholars as well as those who are not research specialists on the Dead Sea Scrolls might appreciate a brief introduction to this collection. The following introduction thus attempts to summarize the position of most Qumran experts. Many of the thoughts mentioned now will be developed in the introductions to the documents in this corpus; they will be supported in various ways in the texts, translations, and notes.

The Dead Sea Scrolls have revolutionized scholars' understanding of Early Judaism (Second Temple Judaism) and Early Christianity (Christian Origins). Prior to their discovery, scholars tended to reconstruct pre-70 Judaism in terms of the opening of *Aboth*, according to which Moses received Torah from Sinai, committed it to Joshua, he to the elders, the elders to the prophets, and the prophets to the men of the so-called great Synagogue. Three things were imperative: be deliberate in judgment, train many disciples, and *construct a fence around Torah.* Accordingly, Early Judaism was considered to be monolithic, orthodox, and isolated ("fenced-off") from the rest of the world. This depiction of Early Judaism was constructed out of improper analyses of the Mishnah, the New Testament, and Josephus.

Since the discovery of the Dead Sea Scrolls in 1947, and their subsequent intensive study beginning in the early fifties, scholars have come to affirm that this reconstruction does not reflect the complexities of Judaism before the destruction of the Temple in 70 CE. Now, we know – thanks to exhaustive research on the transmission of the tractates in the Mishnah – that the Mishnah was shaped by post-70 Jewish concerns, and was codified by Judah the Prince shortly after 200 CE. It thus embodies the struggle of Hillel's group of Pharisaism first against the Zealots of 66–70 (the first Jewish revolt against Rome) and then against the zealous warriors who from 132 to 136 CE. followed Simon Bar Kosiba (whom Akiba may have hailed as the "Messiah"). Hillel's followers (the House of Hillel) also had to struggle for self-identification and survival against the "Christians" (who made apocalyptic and increasingly exclusivistic claims about their Messiah, Jesus of Nazareth). Furthermore, the Hillelites had to struggle over the meaning of Torah against their fellow Pharisees, notably the followers of Shammai. The Mishnah (and the later Tosephta and Talmudim) nevertheless preserve early traditions and thus provide valuable information regarding religious life in pre-70 Judaism, especially in the Temple cult. Rabbinic literature, therefore, should be read as an edited and expanded record of Early Judaism.

The New Testament was another main source for reconstructing the Judaism of Jesus' day. Today, however, scholars have been forced to admit that passages preserved in this canon of scripture are sometimes anti-Jewish, and received their present shape because of many social pressures and needs, including the struggle for self-definition against other Jewish groups. Hence, Paul and the authors of Matthew and John, for example, do not present us with reliable records of what Judaism was like when Hillel was a Rabbi and Jesus was an eschatological prophet from Galilee. Rather, the New Testament documents represent the attempts of some Jews (and also a few Gentiles) to establish and convert others to their own proclamations. Many of the sayings of Jesus preserved in the canon, therefore, reflect the polemical ambience of the period from circa 30 (the date of Jesus' crucifixion) to 100 CE (the probable date of the final form of the latest gospel, the Gospel of John). The New Testament does provide invaluable data regarding the life and teachings of Jesus, as well as life in Galilee and in Jerusalem when the Temple was the economic and religious center for millions of Jews living in the Hellenistic world. The New Testament gospels, however, are not objective biographies of Jesus, and the New Testament documents, with the exception of Paul's authentic letters, reached their definitive form after 70, perhaps decades later, and often in places far removed from ancient Palestine.

Finally, before 1947 many specialists considered Josephus to be a reliable and unbiased historian of Jewish thought and history prior to 100 CE. It was commonly accepted by almost all that he correctly depicted the Judaism of Hillel's and Jesus' time as quadrifurcated into four "sects" like the Greek philosophical schools: Pharisees (the dominant sect), the Sadducees, the Essenes, and the Zealots. Now scholars widely affirm that Josephus' report is biased and at times unrepresentative. There were not "four sects"; and they were not modeled after the Greeks. There were certainly more than 20 groups, and it is unwise (without careful definition) simply to continue to use the sociologically loaded term "sect." Josephus, however, is a reliable source regarding the topography of ancient Palestine, the mood of Palestinian Jews before the War of 66–70, the movement and success of Roman troops, and the general concerns and fears of Jews. Even so, he surely shaped his presentation of

Judaism, especially Jewish thought, to win the admiration of his Roman readers, especially the Roman establishment and the Emperor, who paid him an annual stipend.

Now, thanks to the discovery of the Dead Sea Scrolls, we have Jewish documents that are not in any way altered by thoughts, redactions, or additions that date after 68 CE, the year when the Qumran Community was burned by Roman soldiers. All the Dead Sea Scrolls antedate 68 (with the exception of the *Copper Scroll*). They were once held and studied by Jews contemporaneous with Hillel and Jesus. Some of the Jewish documents found in the Qumran caves were composed by Jews who lived in the Qumran Community from circa 100 BCE to 68 CE. Other documents were composed elsewhere and were brought to the Community. Some of them (e.g. 1En) contain compositions that may antedate the third century BCE.

Established scholars around the world affirm the indispensability of archaeology and palaeography (which is not simply an art but is also a science which can date a document within plus or minus 50 years). Using these methods scholars can demonstrate that the Qumran Community is where some of the Dead Sea Scrolls were composed and studied. The Dead Sea Scrolls contain allusions to history; hence, it is possible to reconstruct the origins of the Qumranites. They were priests who left the Temple around 150 BCE because of factions within the priestly circles in Jerusalem. They eventually went into the wilderness of Judaea and found at Qumran an abandoned Israelite ruin, perhaps an old border fort. They built communal buildings at this site. Later, the group became a Community and the architectural complex was considerably expanded. There were many incentives for the move from the Temple to the wilderness: the corruption of the Temple cult by priests who compromised Torah in face of Greek influences from Syria, the conviction that the Righteous Teacher (probably of the lineage of Aaron and Zadok, King David's high priest) alone had been given special powers and revelations by God, the allegiance to a different lunar-solar calendar, and especially the profession of halakot different from the priestly establishment (cf. 4QMMT). The clarion words of Isaiah 40:3 were interpreted to mean that the Qumranites were to heed the Voice and prepare *in the wilderness* the way of the Lord.

Over the next nearly two hundred years converts came to Qumran from many of the Jewish groups that were scattered over the land of Israel (probably including the precursors of the Sadducees and Pharisees). After a period of initiation lasting at least two years the novitiates became full members of the Community. The Community existed until the spring of 68 CE. At that time the Roman legions, under the direction of Vespasian (the future emperor of Rome), had just conquered the last holdouts in Galilee and quelled all resistance in the environs of Jericho. Qumran is less than 15 kilometers or 10 miles south of Jericho.

Today, most experts recognize that the Qumran library was not a genizah or a depository of scrolls that belonged to only one group of Jews. Rather, experts affirm that the eleven caves – especially Cave IV – preserved documents from a variety of Jewish groups and constituted an early Jewish library. In this Jewish library were preserved all the books of the TANAK or "Old Testament" (with the exception that Esther has not been recognized among the tiny fragments), some of the Apocrypha (esp. *Tobit*) and the Pseudepigrapha (esp. the *Books of Enoch* and *Jubilees*), writings peculiar to and composed at the Qumran Community (notably 1QS, 1QSa, 1QSb, 1QH, 1QM, MMT and the *Pesharim*), and documents written elsewhere by other related groups or subgroups (viz. *Prayer of Jonathan, Second Ezekiel, Copper Scroll*).

This ancient library contained early Jewish writings of different genres. Hence, the corpus of this series is divided into the following categories: Rules, Hymns, Liturgies, Targumim, Commentaries, Apocryphal Works, Miscellanea, and Biblical Apocrypha and Pseudepigrapha.

One final caveat: As early Jewish writings must not be interpreted as if they represent a normative system, so Qumran ideas must not be pressed into a unified system. The documents in this corpus demonstrate many competing ordinances regarding purification and cleansing, different types of calendars (variations of the lunar-solar calendar), and contrasting rules (the *Rule of the Community* was clearly a late "vulgate" text that incorporates different documents with various textual histories – a theory confirmed by the fragments of the document preserved in Cave IV). Most of these clashing concepts, explanations, exhortations, and rules existed at Qumran, if not simultaneously, then at least during the extended history of its existence from perhaps 100 BCE to 68 CE. Therefore, it is prudent to discuss diverse ideas at Qumran and within the thought-world of an Essense.

Qumranites seemed to refer to themselves as "the Poor Ones," members of "the Way," the "Sons of Righteousness," "the Most Holy Ones," and notably the "Sons of Light." All others – including Jews and especially ruling priests in the Temple – were the "Sons of Darkness." As the Qumranites developed their special ordinances, cosmic speculations, and rules they were influenced by the books in the TANAK or Hebrew Bible (especially Isaiah, Deuteronomy, and the Psalms), some so-called extracanonical works (like the *Books of Enoch* and *Jubilees*), and previously hitherto unknown writings (notably the *Moses Apocryphon*, the *Psalms of Joshua, Pseudo-Ezekiel*, the *Temple Scroll*, and *Some Works of the Torah*).

The Dead Sea Scrolls present data that are fundamental for any reconstruction of Early Judaism and Early Christianity. They disclose a variety of creative issues, perspectives, and concerns that were current in many Jewish circles before the destructions of 66–74 CE. Most important among these are innovative prescriptions and provisions for ritual purification, the impossibility of obtaining forgiveness except through God's "mercy," speculations on the nature of the human and the origin of evil in the world, and the presence and efficaciousness of good angels. Probably unique to Qumran – at least in terms of development – are the following concepts: The paradigmatic cosmic dualism centered in the opposition between the Angel of Light and the demonic power of the evil angels, notably Belial, who is probably identical (in some scrolls) with the Angel of Darkness; the development of the concept of the Holy Spirit *from* God (which obviously influenced the development of Christian proclamations and social identity); the cosmic hymnic celebrations at twilight (in the evening praying for protection from the darkness, and in the morning participating in the bringing of light [the sun] back to God's created order); the clarifications of the importance of the lunar-solar calendar with the special feast days, the weeks, the Sabbaths, the months, and the yearly celebration (perhaps the Day of Atonement); the descriptions of the heavens above filled with angels chanting praises to God (the Creator); the eschatological expectations for God's visitation (the Day of Judgment); and the joyous time when the Messiah or the Messiahs of Aaron and Israel will appear.

The Qumran Community was in existence during the time of Jesus' ministry; but there is no reference to him or to any of his disciples. There is no reason to be surprised by this fact. There were many groups within Early Judaism, and the Dead Sea Scrolls do not mention any known first-century Rabbi or Jewish leader. It is not the alleged direct influence from the Dead Sea Scrolls upon any New Testament document that is significant (with the probable exception of the Gospel of John which seems to be influenced by the thoughts preserved in a unique way in the Dead Sea Scrolls). What is paradigmatically important is this internationally acknowledged insight: The Dead Sea Scrolls reveal ideas once considered unique to "Christianity" and this discovery proves that Early Christianity was for many years one of the groups (probably a sect) within Judaism. Now, the milieu – the intellectual and social matrix – of earliest "Christianity" is coming into view. The importance of the Dead Sea Scrolls, however, must always remain firmly grounded in the invaluable and precious insights preserved in them. The Dead Sea Scrolls were once held, studied, and revered by Jews who lived in an erudite and deeply religious Community that eked out an existence on the northwestern shores of the Dead Sea, waiting for the fulfillment of God's promises found in Scriptures which we share with the Qumranites.

Qumran and Masada

Why should manuscripts found on Masada be included in the Princeton edition of the Dead Sea Scrolls? First, it is imperative to include all ancient witnesses to a text in a critical edition; some of these manuscripts have been found in the Qumran caves and some on Masada. Second, it is now clear that almost all, or all, of the manuscripts found on Masada were taken there by Qumranites sometime about June 68 CE when the Roman army conquered Jericho and its surrounding area, including Qumran.[1] Third, the *Angelic Liturgy* has been found only in Qumran Caves (4Q400–4Q407, 11Q17) and on Masada (Mas1k).[2] Fourth, *A Joseph Apocryphon* (Mas1045–1350 and 1375) found on Masada was copied in the first century BCE and thus was probably not copied on Masada. Fifth, the manuscript evidence of *A Joseph Apocryphon* (Mas1045–1350 and 1375) reveals parallels and orthography associated with the Qumran Scribal School.[3] Sixth, while a Jew may have conceivably prepared animal skins for scrolls on Masada, on this desert fortress there is no evidence of a scriptorium for the copying of scrolls. Seventh, the Qumran and Masada corpora show characteristics that distinguish them from the manuscripts found elsewhere in the Judean desert. Finally, it is evident that those on Masada did not gather their manuscripts into a central location or locations, as at Qumran; thus they were probably only studied or used liturgically on Masada. Consequently, most of the Masada texts were probably taken to Masada from Qumran (or other Essene locations). I thus agree with Yadin, Talmon, and Tov that the Masada texts were taken to Masada by refugees from Qumran.

---

[1] See the comments by E. Tov in "A Qumran Origin for the Masada Non-Biblical Texts?" DSD 7 (2000) 57–73. Tov suggests that "all the texts found on Masada were imported from Qumran," observing similar scribal practices, such as guide dots and rulings, large inscribed areas, number of columns per sheet, paragraphing systems, superscriptions, and special layout of the poetical texts.

[2] See volume 4B.

[3] See volume 8A. Note the insights and data in E. Tov, "The Hebrew Texts from Masada," *Scribal Practices*, pp. 317–22. See especially p. 322 on which Tov summarizes the data to support the assumption "that all the texts found at Masada were imported from Qumran... ."

The Thanksgiving Hymns (*Hodayot*)
1QH[a], 1Q35 (1QH[b]), 4Q427–4Q432 (4QH[a]–4QH[f])

JAMES H. CHARLESWORTH with LEA BERKUZ[1]

with HERMANN LICHTENBERGER and DORON MENDELS

Introduction

The *Thanksgiving Hymns,* the *Hôdāyôt* (הודיות), contain about 35 poems, hymns, or psalms that were composed and edited during the second and first centuries BCE.[2] The precise number of compositions cannot be determined due to the fragmentary state of all eight witnesses (*Chart 3: The Number of Hymns and Titles*).[3]

The name "Thanksgiving Hymns" was derived from the *incipit* of most of the hymns: "I thank you, O Lord, because (אודכה אודך אדוני כי or אודך כי אדוני כי)."[4] This "Hodayot formula" is usually preceded by a *vacat*. The collection placards the perspective of the Qumranites, since the key note of Qumran piety is jubilation.[5] This attitude of praise is remarkable as is the relatively new *incipit* in biblical literature: "I thank you, O Lord, because." This formula clarifies that honor and praise cannot be diminished even in the face of suffering and persecution, as the Community and its leader experienced, especially at its beginning. Those who are in the Community are "those who have the knowledge (to be) in the Community of exultation" (19.17). Praise and thanksgiving define the *Yaḥad* (Community).

Thanksgiving is appropriate since the Sons of Light are sustained by their election and hope. Note especially these passages:

And I walk continuously in unfathomable uprightness
so that I know that there exists hope for (him)
whom you fashioned from dust for the eternal assembly.
(11.21–22)

And I know that there is hope in your [lov]ing-kindnesses
and expectation in the abundance of your

---

[1] In 1962, I began working on the *Thanksgiving Hymns* under John Strugnell at Duke University. After over a decade of focusing on the publication of the *Old Testament Pseudepigrapha*, I again focused on the *Thanksgiving Hymns*. In 1983–1984 in Tübingen, I worked with Hermann Lichtenberger (Stegemannn's protégé) and Doron Mendels (the former head of the History Department at Hebrew University). Lichtenberger assisted me with a provisional draft of the Hebrew text of 1QH[a]; Mendels provided a draft translation of that early text. Eventually, I needed to begin again with the publication of DJD 40, Qimron's edition, better images (some taken for my research), and computer technology. Over the past five years, I have been assisted by Lea Berkuz on the text and translation of the *Thanksgiving Hymns* and by my editorial assistants in Princeton, namely Blake Jurgens, Mitchell Esswein, and Brady Beard. The latter two helped me notably with the charts. Each of these scholars or assistants has been of inestimable help as I prepared this volume. I thank Wipf and Stock Publishers and Cascade Books for permission to base this translation of the *Thanksgiving Hymns* on my *The Qumran Psalter: The Thanksgiving Hymns Among the Dead Sea Scrolls* (Eugene, 2014).

[2] See the chart that clarifies the order, number, and title of each composition.

[3] I use the titles the *Thanksgiving Hymns* and the *Hodayot*; the former is the English translation of the latter. E. M. Schuller chooses to refer to the compositions in the *Thanksgiving Hymns* or *Hodayot* as "psalms." See Schuller, "Prayer, Hymnic, and Liturgical Texts from Qumran," in *The Com-

munity of the Renewed Covenant, edited by E. Ulrich and J. C. VanderKam (Notre Dame, 1994) pp. 153–71; and Schuller, "Recent Scholarship on the *Hodayot* 1993-2010," *Currents in Biblical Research* 10 (2011) 122.

[4] Since this introduction is to the *Thanksgiving Hymns* or all eight witnesses (not just 1QH[a]), texts and translations are cited according to our Composite Text. In the notes, I draw attention to the most important publications and seek to avoid the error of thinking the best work is the most recent publication.

[5] Thanksgiving Hymns (1QH[a], 1Q35 (1QH[b]), 4Q427–4Q432 (4QH[a]–4QH[f]).

power, because no one is justified in your
judg[me]nts; and (no one) w[ins] your lawsuit.
(17.14–15)

These poems or psalms are uniquely related to the Qumran *Yaḥad* and are attested in eight separate manuscripts found in Qumran Caves I and IV.[6]

Since the discovery of the Qumran Scrolls in the late 1940s, gifted scholars have attempted to provide accurate and detailed information concerning the *Thanksgiving Hymns*, the poetic jewel in the Qumran corpus.[7] These creations are treasures left to us by the geniuses within Second Temple Judaism. Central to many of the poems is the confession that humans cannot present before God any form of righteousness as an offering. Only God's continuing loving-kindnesses and righteousness, and especially unmerited forgiveness, allow humans to move toward perfection and acceptance before the awesome God.

1. Discovery, Publication, and Reconstruction

The only extensively preserved copy of the *Thanksgiving Hymns*, 1QH^a, was discovered by Bedouin in Cave I in the early winter of 1947. On 29 November 1947, Eleazar Lipa Sukenik purchased two substantial manuscripts which were recovered from Qumran. One manuscript is a collection of poems, hymns, and psalms written on leather; it is now known as 1QH^a. It was first published in 1948 and in 1955 under the title מגילת ההודיות (*The Scroll of Thanksgiving*).[8]

While uncertainty often surrounds the cave in which a scroll might have been found, it is clear that two copies of the *Hoda-*

yot had been placed in Cave I, a natural limestone cave on the northwest of the Dead Sea. Three sheets of 1QH^a and then about 70 fragments were found in this cave.[9] Two small fragments of 1QH^a were found later by archaeologists in Cave I, proving the claims of the Bedouins that the cave in which they found the portions of 1QH^a was Cave I.[10] Of the eight witnesses, the best preserved manuscript is 1QH^a.[11]

While 1QH^a is extant, intermittently, in full columns, 1QH^b is preserved in only two fragments. The first copy of the *Hoda-yot* may have been placed in a jar and the second only thrown into the cave by Qumranites in 68 CE. It is also possible that the Bedouin took most of 1QH^b and used it to repair sandals or let it deteriorate.[12] As E. Tov states: "It is unclear why some scrolls are better preserved than others."[13]

Sukenik's early attempts to organize these fragments were primarily concerned with rapidly publishing all the available material rather than constructing a definitive restoration of the text.[14] His initial work was followed in 1957 by J. Licht's

---

[6] None of these scrolls is an opisthograph [a text written on both sides of the leather or papyrus].

[7] For a list of commentaries on the *Hodayot*, see the selected bibliography at the end of the introduction.

[8] E. L. Sukenik, *The Dead Sea Scrolls of the Hebrew University* (Jerusalem, 1955). The *Thanksgiving Hymns* were published in Hebrew by Sukenik in אוצר המגילות הגנוזות - שבידי האוניברסטה העברית (Jerusalem, 1954). It is imperative to contextualize the study of the *Hodayot*. Y. Yadin, who published Sukenik's diary, noted: "[T]he first three scrolls were bought by my father for Israel on 29th November, 1947, the very day on which the United Nations voted for the re-creation of the Jewish state in Israel after two thousand years;" Y. Yadin, *The Message of the Scrolls* (New York, 1957) p. 14. As Sukenik read words put on leather 2000 years previously when Israel was a great nation, he heard the announcement that the United Nations had voted to establish the State of Israel. Amid terrible violence, the loss of his son, Matti, and having to negotiate in "the sickening presence of the barbed wire," Sukenik, after saying the *Hagomel*, thought "Were it not for the *Genizah*, the year would have been intolerable for me;" Sukenik, *The Dead Sea Scrolls of the Hebrew University*, p. 17. Sukenik dedicated his volume to the memory of Mattitiahu Sukenik. By "*Genizah*" Sukenik meant the Qumran Scrolls.

[9] Notably, see Yadin, *The Message of the Scrolls*, p. 105. Yadin calls his brother "Mati" (p. 24).

[10] Sukenik, *The Dead Sea Scrolls of the Hebrew University*, pp. 7–39; see esp. p. 18 and 39 [the discovery of 1QH^b by Harding and de Vaux]. For images of 1QH^a before unrolling, see Fig. 14 and Fig. 15, and partially unrolled in Fig. 16 and Fig. 17. For a good image of 1QH^b, see Fig. 30. The attitude to such small fragments is given by Sukenik: "The writing in these fragments is too slight to be of intrinsic interest" (p. 39). Hence, many fragments, especially when difficult to read, were ignored. Mansoor did not include the fragments. We have included all fragments and discerned readings on each.

[11] The textile that covered 1QH^a has been found and published by M. Bélis. It is TQ1; Bélis chose to examine "the finest linen" (no. 1 in DJD 1) and "was amazed at the result" (email to Charlesworth on Feb. 2, 2015). That is, Bélis discovered that the fine linen of TQ1 was chosen to cover 1QH^a. It is possible to establish the original folding and to discern that the scroll was damaged before it was enrolled in the linen. See Bélis, "Les textiles de Qumrân: Catalogue et commentaires," in *Khirbet Qumrân et Aïn Feshkha, II: Études d'anthropolgie, de physique et de chimie - Studies of Anthropology, Physics and Chemistry*, edited by J.-B. Humbert and J. Cunneweg (Novum Testamentum et Orbis Antiquus, Series Archaeologica 3; Fribourg and Göttingen, 2003) pp. 207–76; see esp. "TQ1 et Hodayot" on pp. 234–37.

[12] Since 1968, many Bedouin near Bethlehem have told me that they first estimated the smelly leather rolls were not valuable, so they repaired their sandals with them.

[13] E. Tov, *Scribal Practices and Approaches Reflected in the Texts Found in the Judean Desert* (Leiden and Boston, 2004) p. 108.

[14] Sukenik organized the fragments of 1QH^a according to the transition between the first scribe and the second scribe and according to the position of the large holes in the manuscript. See *The Dead Sea Scrolls of the Hebrew University*, p. 38.

groundbreaking commentary on the *Thanksgiving Hymns* which continued to follow Sukenik's initial configuration of the numerous columns and fragments. And, for the first time, Licht provided informed reconstructions.[15]

Interpreting the *Thanksgiving Hymns* demands a vast knowledge of the concepts in all the scrolls composed or definitively edited at Qumran.[16] Licht rightly contended that the ruins at Qumran represent a Jewish establishment with installations that could be identified as a *mikveh* (ברכת טבילה), a dining room (חדר אכילה), and a scrollery (חדר כתיבה).[17] He also knew that Jewish coins and a cemetery were discovered at the site.[18]

Though most early scholars, like Licht, did not criticize Sukenik's initial arrangement of the Hymns,[19] later scholars sought to make more coherent sense of the manuscript. In 1962, H. Stegemann reconfigured the order of Sukenik's initial reconstruction, moving Sukenik's cols. 1–12 to the middle of the manuscript as they were the best preserved of the columns, suggesting a place towards the center of the rolled scroll.[20]

Thus, for example, Sukenik's cols. 1–12 became Stegemann's cols. 9–20 and Sukenik's cols. 13–16 became Stegemann's cols. 5–8.[21] Stegemann also concluded that two fragments taken from Cave I (now known as 1QH[b] [1Q35]) were not consistent with the original document, suggesting they represent a second copy of the work.[22]

Stegemann's research was advanced through the work of J. Strugnell. Concentrating on the unpublished *Hodayot* and *Hodayot-Like* fragments of Cave IV (4Q427–432; 4Q433; 4Q433a; 4Q440), Strugnell confirmed many of Stegemann's restorations.[23] Prior to Strugnell's precise study, scholars such as Licht knew of the existence of these Cave IV fragments but did not use them extensively in their research due to their unpublished status.[24] The restorations which were made by the joint effort of Stegemann and Strugnell, aided by the Cave IV fragments, was affirmed through the independent work of É. Puech whose 1988 publication yielded many of the same restorations suggested by Stegemann and Strugnell.[25] Due to his health, Strugnell proceeded to pass on his still-unpublished work on the Cave IV fragments to E. M. Schuller in 1989, who finally published the fragments in 1999.[26] Stegemann continued to work on the *Thanksgiving Hymns* until his death in 2005. With the help of C. A. Newsom, Schuller completed the extensive work of Stegemann, publishing the DJD edition in 2009.[27]

---

[15] J. Licht, מגילת ההודיות (Jerusalem, 1957).

[16] In 1994, Schuller reported that "the study of prayer and hymnic materials in the Dead Sea Scrolls is still in a very preliminary stage;" Schuller, "Prayer, Hymnic, and Liturgical Texts from Qumran," p. 160. Since 1994, a vast amount of research has been published on the poems, hymns, and psalms found in the Qumran caves; but, focus has been on editing texts. There is still much to be done on commentaries and on attempts to present an overview that includes more than a few selected compositions.

[17] Licht, מגילת ההודיות, p. 4.

[18] Licht cites his dependence on R. de Vaux's preliminary report in *RB* (1953) 83ff., and 540ff.

[19] Examples include M. Martin, *The Scribal Character of the Dead Sea Scrolls*, 2 vols. (Bibliothèque du Muséon 44 and 45; Louvain, 1958) and S. Holm-Nielsen, *Hodayot: Psalms from Qumran* (ATDan 2; Aarhus, 1960). J. Carmignac agreed with much of Sukenik's research, but proposed (incorrectly) that Sukenik's manuscript was two different scrolls; see "Remarques sur le texte des hymnes de Qumrân," *Bib* 39 (1958) 139–55; see esp. p. 146.

[20] H. Stegemann's initial work on the *Thanksgiving Hymns* is his unpublished dissertation *Rekonstruktion der Hodajot: Ursprüngliche Gestalt und kritisch bearbeiteter Text der Hymnenrolle aus Höhle 1 von Qumran* (Ph.D. diss., Heidelberg, 1963). Also see Stegemann, "The Material Reconstruction of 1QHodayot," in *Fifty Years*, edited by L. H. Schiffman, E. Tov, and J. C. VanderKam (Jerusalem, 2000) pp. 272–84. Also see Stegemann, "The Number of Psalms in 1QHodayot[a] and Some of Their Sections," in *Liturgical Perspectives: Prayer and Poetry in Light of the Dead Sea Scrolls* (STDJ 48; Leiden, 2003) pp. 191–234. The edition of Stegemann's work was completed by E. M. Schuller, following Stegemann's death in 2005. See H. Stegemann, with E. M. Schuller and C. A. Newsom, and in consultation with J. C. VanderKam and M. Brady, *1QHodayot[a]* with Incorporation of *1QHodayot[b]* and

4QHodayot[a-f] (DJD 40; Oxford, 2009) see esp. pp. 26–42. The text and translation were republished in D. W. Parry and E. Tov, eds., *DSSR* (Leiden and Boston, 2014) vol. 2, pp. 269–351 [1QH[a]] and 352–53 [1QH[b]].

[21] Intermittently throughout this introduction and in the notes to the texts and to the translations of all the witnesses to the *Thanksgiving Hymns*, one will find more on Stegemann's improvement of Sukenik's superb, pioneering work.

[22] These were first published by J. T. Milik, "1Q35, Recueil de cantiques d'action de grâces (1QH)," in *Qumran Cave I* (DJD 1; Oxford, 1955) pp. 136–38, Pl. 31.

[23] See Stegemann with Schuller, DJD 40, pp. 3–4. Strugnell worked extensively with these fragments, first announcing their existence in "Le travail d'édition des fragments manuscrits de Qumrân," *RB* 63 (1956) 64. Also see Strugnell and Schuller, "Further Hodayot Manuscripts from Qumran?," in *Antikes Judentum und frühes Christentum: Festschrift für Hartmut Stegemann zum 65. Gerburtstag*, edited by B. Kollmann, W. Reinbold, and A. Steudel (BZNW 97; Berlin, 1999) pp. 51–72.

[24] Licht, מגילת ההודיות, p. 4.

[25] É. Puech, "Quelques aspects de la restauration du Rouleau des Hymnes (1QH)," *JJS* 39 (1988) 38–55.

[26] E. M. Schuller, "Hodayot," *Qumran Cave 4.XX, Poetical and Liturgical Texts, Part 2* (DJD 29; Oxford, 1999) pp. 69–254, Pls. 4–16, 28.

[27] Stegemann with E. M. Schuller and C. A. Newsom, *1QHodayot[a]* (DJD 40; Oxford, 2009). In the notes, we have referred to this marvelous and detailed work as DJD, otherwise the notes

As a summary, it is helpful to learn from Schuller's organization of research on the *Thanksgiving Hymns* into three periods. In light of our own research, we may discern these as follows: The first period is from 1947 to 1961;[28] it is the beginning of this research and highlighted by the publications of Sukenik and Licht. The second period is from 1962 to 1992; in 1962, Stegemenn completed his dissertation and discerned the probable order of 1QHᵃ. Subsequently, Strugnell prepared provisional editions of the Cave IV witnesses to the *Hodayot*, Puech discerned how to reconstruct 1QHᵃ, and many monographs were published, notably those of Becker, Jeremias, Kuhn, Lichtenberger, Schulz, and Osten-Sacken.[29] The third period extends from 1993 to the present; in 1993, Schuller published a preliminary edition of the fragments of the *Hodayot* found in Cave IV. Schuller is certainly correct to note that publications on the *Thanksgiving Hymns* have increased markedly since 1993.

1QHᵃ and Its Handle-Sheet. É. Puech judged that col. 1 is actually col. 9 and that, therefore, eight columns are lost at the beginning.[30] No one can be certain how much is lost at the beginning; we, however, have followed the insights of Stegemann who was certain that three columns are lost (and that may include the handle-sheet).[31] Thus, more than two hymns or po-

ems were probably lost from the beginning of 1QHᵃ. This information helps us search for the handle-sheet of 1QHᵃ.[32]

In 1990, Stegemann, focusing on 1QHᵃ, reported that he found the handle-sheet. It had not been published because supposedly no consonants were visible.[33] Ten years later,[34] Stegemann referred again to the still unpublished handle-sheet, mentioning that what remained of the sheet resided in the Shrine of the Book and can been seen on photograph SHR 4285. Stegemann's perspicacious identification of the handle-sheet prefixed to 1QHᵃ has guided his and our restoration of the column order of 1QHᵃ.[35]

Further information regarding the handle-sheet of 1QHᵃ is now available. Before presenting that information, we should first review what is known about handle-sheets; that is, the opening or concluding sheets of a scroll so it can be held. Handle-sheets have been discerned for numerous manuscripts, especially the one at the beginning of 4Q471, the main source for the *Self-Glorification Hymn*,[36] and those found in Cave XI.[37] The remains of many more handle-sheets may never be detected among the unidentified fragments, because handle-

would be cumbersome (Strugnell's name should have been included) and an abbreviation should be brief.

[28] Schuller gives different dates to the three periods: 1947–1965, 1965–1993, and 1993 to the present. But choosing 1962 enables us to highlight the work of Becker and the dissertation of Stegemann. See Schuller, "Recent Scholarship on the *Hodayot* 1993–2010," 119–62.

[29] In "Recent Scholarship on the *Hodayot* 1993–2010," Schuller reports that, between 1965 and 1993, there "was much less interest in the *Hodayot* and relatively few books or even articles appeared" (p. 120). I am impressed by the publications of so many outstanding monographs from 1965 to 1993 related to the *Hodayot*, notably those emanating from the Qumran *Forschungsgemeinschaft* in Göttingen. My 1970 article in *Revue Biblique* showed keen "interest in the *Hodayot*"; see bibliography.

[30] É. Puech, *La croyance des Esséniens en la vie future: Immortalité, résurrection, vie éternelle? Histoire d'une croyance dans le judaïsme ancien* (2 Vols.; EBib 21–22; Paris, 1993) vol. 2, p. 335.

[31] Stegemann, "Methods for the Reconstruction of Scrolls from Scattered Fragments," in *AHDSS*, edited by L. H. Schiffman (JSPSup 8 and JSOT/ASOR Mon. 2; Sheffield, 1990) p. 200: "[O]ne can determine that in front of the first preserved column of 1QHodayotᵃ, which is column 17 of the Sukenik edition, exactly three columns, and not, for example, 7 or 11 columns, are lost. This calculation is secondarily confirmed by the existence and shape of the original handle-sheet from the beginning of the scroll. Being blank, this handle-sheet was never published, even though it is one of the best aids for the reconstruction of the 1QHodayotᵃ scroll." See the comments of

Steudel, "Basic Research, Methods and Approaches to the Qumran Scrolls in German-Speaking Countries," in *The Dead Sea Scrolls in Scholarly Perspective: A History of Research*, edited by D. Dimant (Leiden and Boston, 2002) p. 592.

[32] In Tov's magisterial "Conventions used at the beginnings and ends of scrolls," *Scribal Practices*, pp. 108–18, no mention is made of 1QHᵃ in "Table 21: Scrolls with Partially Preserved Beginnings," pp. 110–11.

[33] Stegemann, in *AHDSS*, p. 200.

[34] Stegemann, "The Material Reconstruction of 1QHodayot," p. 276. Stegemann adds that the handle-sheet at the end of the scroll seems to be lost. He is referring to 1QHᵃ.

[35] In 2006, Professors H. Rietz, L. Johns, and I traveled to Jerusalem to work in the Shrine of the Book to continue a search for the handle-sheet of 1QHᵃ. Schuller asked me what I knew about the handle-sheet. I informed her that our mission had not been successful and the images we took did not disclose the lost handle-sheet. On 8 March 2007, Emanuel Tov informed me that he could "not find SHR 4285 in our own DSS electronic library (Brill, 2006)," and when he wrote "Conventions used at the beginnings and ends of scrolls," in *Scribal Practices*, he "did not know about 1QHᵃ." M. Maggen of the Israel Museum helped me by providing infrared images.

[36] See my introduction to the *Self-Glorification Hymn* in the present volume.

[37] See Tov, "The Special Character of the Texts Found in Qumran Cave 11," in *Things Revealed: Studies in Early Jewish and Christian Literature in Honor of Michael E. Stone*, edited by E. G. Chazon, D. Satran and R. A. Clements (Leiden and Boston, 2004) p. 195.

sheets are often uninscribed.[38] Most of them were lost and some left only reinforcing tabs and thongs found on the floor of caves, notably in Cave IV and especially in Cave VIII.[39]

The handle-sheet to the *Rule of the Community* and following texts is known.[40] The title of the collection (1QS, 1QSa, and 1QSb) is preserved: "[the Rul]e of the Community and *mn*[." The Hebrew consonants were found on 1QS.[41] The handle-sheet of 4Q431 (4QH^e) may be discerned; the beginning, or right, margin (2.7 cm) is exceptionally broad and the piece had not been sewn onto a preceding column.[42] The handle-sheets of 4Q258 (4QS^d) and 4Q266 (4QD^a) have been recovered and published.[43] The handle-sheet of 4Q266 is impressive. It contains a large section of uninscribed leather, the reinforcing tab, and the thong that tied the scroll tight when it was rolled up. The handle-sheets of 4Q8^c (4QGen^h-title),[44]

4Q405 (*Words of the Lights*), and 4Q249 are extant; for each of them, the writing is on the *verso*. Presently, only one other published scroll preserves the tab and elements of the thong at the beginning; it is 4Q448 (*Prayer of King Jonathan*).[45]

Eventually, an image of SHR 4285 was found;[46] it shows a collection of miscellaneous, ostensibly unrelated, fragments.[47] The relation to the *Thanksgiving Hymns* becomes more evident when one notes that a small fragment on SHR 4285 preserves a portion of 1QH^a 8 (Sukenik 16 [see notes *ad loc.*]).

A large fragment of related pieces of leather on SHR 4285 looks like a handle-sheet. It is on the bottom and right half of SHR 4285. At least four fragments are related. Once they constituted one large sheet of leather. No lining can be detected, and no stitching is visible on the extensively preserved right margin.[48] I am thus led to conclude this sheet of leather is a handle-sheet.

The remains of a tab exist on the right edge of the leather near the middle. A tiny portion of the thong becomes visible under magnification. Only about 50% of the sheet is preserved, so the extant leather sheet is approximately the size of the columns in 1QH^a.[49] These observations suggest that the large portions of leather on the bottom of SHR 4285 is the handle-sheet of 1QH^a as Stegemann mentioned. However, subsequent to the time of the photograph the leather pieces have collapsed into many small and dark pieces.

[38] J. Carswell: "Amongst the enormous collection of fragments in the Palestine Archaeological Museum there are many uninscribed pieces of leather, often pierced and with the remains of thongs slotted through them; and in two cases there are the beginnings of scrolls with the fragments of fastenings still attached to them." See Carswell, "Appendix I: Fastenings on the Qumrân Manuscripts," in *Qumrân Grotte 4.II: Archéologie* (DJD 6; Oxford, 1977) pp. 23–28; see esp. p. 23. The scrolls are on skins without tanning; the fastenings are coarse leather (with tanning).

[39] J. Carswell, "Appendix I: Fastenings on the Qumrân Manuscripts," in *Qumrân Grotte 4.II: Archéologie*, DJD 6, pp. 23–28; Pls. 4 [the manuscripts with tabs] and 5 [dislocated tabs and thongs from Caves IV and VIII]. See p. 26 for an illustration showing scrolls with reconstructed tabs and fastenings.

[40] See the image of the handle-sheet to 1QS in DJD 1, Plate 22. It is unlined and the title is written on the inside *(recto)*, stitched on the left side to the following sheets of leather, with consonants written often too close, as in the handle-sheet to 1QH^a. I. Levitt in the Shrine of the Book has worked with me for over a decade, helping me obtain more information on the handle-sheet of 1QH^a. I am deeply grateful for her diligence and collegiality. She is the one who helped me find the data and images of the handle of 1QH^a.

[41] See E. Qimron and Charlesworth, PTSDDP 1.1, note 4. Also see DJD 1, Pl. 22.

[42] See Schuller in DJD 29, p. 200.

[43] I am grateful to Schuller for pointing this out to me. See, respectively, the following: P. S. Alexander and G. Vermes, *Qumran Cave 4.XIX: Serekh Ha-Yaḥad and Two Related Texts* (DJD 26; Oxford, 1998) Pl. 10 [the right margin is twice the normal and no stitching is visible (see also DJD 26.85)] and J. Baumgarten with J. T. Milik, *Qumran Cave 4.XIII: The Damascus Document* (DJD 18; Oxford, 1996) Pl. 1; also see pp. 23–24.

[44] See J. R. Davila's insights in *Qumran Cave 4.VII: Genesis to Numbers*, edited by E. Ulrich, *et al.* (DJD 12; Oxford, 1994) p. 63.

[45] See the color image in *Scrolls from the Dead Sea*, edited by A. Sussmann and R. Peled (Washington, D.C., 1993) p. 42. Also see the image of the handle-sheet at the end of a fragment from Masada (1043/A-D) published by S. Talmon and his discussion; the handle-sheet is stitched to the scroll perhaps "after the completion of the writing" (p. 152). It is blank and measures 9.7 x 11.0 cm. Talmon, "Fragments of a Deuteronomy Scroll from Masada: Deuteronomy 33.17-34.6," in *Boundaries of the Ancient Near Eastern World: A Tribute to Cyrus H. Gordon*, edited by M. Lubetski, C. Gottlieb, and S. Keller (JSOTSup 273; Sheffield, 1998) pp. 150–61 [see Figure 1]. Note also that 1QpHab does not need a concluding handle-sheet; the blank column is part of the last piece of leather.

[46] The photograph was taken about 1954 by the gifted photographer H. Bieberkraut. Her husband is the scholar who opened the *Genesis Apocryphon*; see him working with Y. Yadin in Miami Beach in *Jewish Floridian* (Sept 29, 1961). H. and J. Bieberkraut cleaned and photographed the Qumran Scrolls obtained by Hebrew University in Jerusalem. See W. W. Fields, *The Dead Sea Scrolls: A Short History* (Leiden and Boston, 2006) p. 100.

[47] The image (SHR 4285) can be found on microfiche in Tov, *The Dead Sea Scrolls on Microfiche* (1993).

[48] No stitching is evident on the right side of another fragment now separated from the largest fragment. Could it also be a portion of the handle-sheet of 1QH^a?

[49] It is no longer possible to obtain accurate measurements. SHR 4285 shows no scale and the leather has disintegrated into black pieces.

A study of the image in SHR 4285 reveals Hebrew consonants. The handle-sheet is not blank as Stegemann reported. Consonants are discernible on the upper right portion of this handle-sheet. Two are clear and more appear under magnification and enhancement (notably, by digitally changing the contrast and brightness). Upon initial inspection, the *beth* becomes clear. The next consonant looks at first like an *ʾaleph*, but the ink has run and the leather has shrunk and become dark. There are two consonants that look like one. Eventually, one can detect a *reš* and a *kaph*. On further study, one can discern a *waw* and the two feet of a *taw*. Months of study and self-criticism lead to the conclusion that these consonants may constitute "Blessings," בְּרָכוֹת (cf. Ps 21:4, 7 [6]).[50] The plural form, "Blessings," appears in 1QHᵃ 3.18 and the singular form in 4.32, 20.6, and 26.24.

Above בְּרָכוֹת is some form that may be a *lamedh*, and before it another *lamedh*. These consonants are large. Between them is a shadowy consonant; it seems to be an *ʾaleph*. After the putative לאל a *he* appears. Some ink is visible among the dirt on the left edge tear; it appears it may be the right portion of a *daleth*. Restore לאל הד]עות. This *terminus technicus* is a feature of Qumran thought and highlighted in the lore of the Community (and central to 1QS 3.13–4.26). It is a unique feature of 1QS (3.15) and of 1QHᵃ (9.28, 25.32, and esp. 22.34). Thus, we can detect and restore the title given in the first century BCE to 1QHᵃ:

For the God of Know[ledge]	לאל הד]עות
Blessings	בְּרָכוֹת

The letters are not clear and it has taken long hours of study and computer enhancement to discern them. The collapse of the fragment and the damage probably caused by humidity warrant caution about this speculative restoration; it has so far proved impossible to improve the early images.

The writing is on the right side (*recto*) of the manuscript. That is also the case with the handle-sheets of 1QS and 4Q8ᶜ [4QGenʰ⁻ᵗⁱᵗˡᵉ]. It is possible that the title appeared on both sides (*recto* and *verso*).[51]

The title, "Blessings," makes sense for the later Qumran perception of the *Hodayot* (the term we inherit from Sukenik). Some of the Qumranites shifted the *incipit* from "I thank you, O Lord" to "Blessed are you, O Lord;" this redaction occurred sometime in the first century BCE. The fact becomes clear not only by contrasting the "Teacher Hymns" (10.5–17.37) with the "Community Hymns" (the other columns) but also by the

late first-century BCE scribal correction from "I thank you" to "Blessed are you" in 1QHᵃ 13.22. The *incipit* "I bless you, O Lord (or God)" does not appear in the *Hodayot* between 8.25 and 18.15, except for the correction in 13.22. Clearly, the use of "to bless" is found most frequently in the "Community Hymns" (8.26, 17.38, 18.16; 19.30, 32, 35; 22.34) that are most likely the later compositions and close to the time when a handle-sheet would be added to 1QHᵃ. These observations suggest this collection was eventually known to the Qumranites as the *Scroll of Blessings*.

2. Original Language and Orthography

It is apparent that Hebrew is the original language of the *Thanksgiving Hymns*. The Hebrew shows development from Biblical Hebrew; it represents a rich vocabulary that has been mined from biblical symbolic language – probably from memory, since the author(s) were living and thinking within a community that knew Hebrew that was permeated with images from Scripture. M. Mansoor presented an admirable assessment: "The language is solidly based on Biblical Hebrew, but is strongly flavored with Palestinian Aramaic, late Hebrew and to some extent Samaritan."[52] I am not convinced, however, by influences from the Samaritan tradition and the influence from Aramaic is not strong.

Orthographically, the scribes who composed these documents frequently used *scriptio plena* writing, usually utilizing a *waw* to denote a *u, o,* or even an *a*. Many times, a scribe chose a *yodh* for a long *i* or *e*. The latter tendency is not as frequent as the former, as some cases exist where we would expect a *yodh* there is not one present (often when the root has a *yodh*; e.g., ותשימני = ותשמני and רבי = ריבי [in later Hebrew we might expect הריב שלי]).

A consonantal *waw* (מות for מוות and קו for קוו) and *yodh* (שבעתים for שבעתיים) are also sometimes surprisingly absent. Infrequently, the scribes insert a *yodh* when it is not expected (כאיב and גיזעו).[53] Other inconsistencies include the omission of a quiescent *ʾaleph* (e.g., כיא for כי), and the lengthening of suffixes (בראתה, לבכה, כבודכה, and עשיתה).

Sometimes an unexpected *he* is added at the end: עשיתה בראתה, לבכה, כבודכה.[54] This added *he* explains why a final *kaph* can appear within a word: בריתכה (10.24). The elision of laryngeals is most likely due to faulty pronunciation.[55]

Occasionally, some orthographic inconsistencies are subsequently corrected by another scribe, especially in 1QHᵃ. For example, in 1QHᵃ 6.35 a corrector took out a *waw* from an o-

---

[50] Better images are necessary (but now impossible); there are consonants on this handle-sheet. If SHR 4285 shows the handle-sheet of 1QHᵃ, one should imagine the writing to clarify the character of what we call the *Hodayot*.

[51] I. Levitt has seen writing on both sides of what appears to be the handle-sheet of 1QHᵃ. She is working with the pictures taken by Schlosser. I have not been able to see writing beneath the darkened leather of these images.

[52] M. Mansoor, *The Thanksgiving Hymns* (STDJ 3; Grand Rapids, 1961) pp. 9, 11–27.

[53] See the discussions in Reymond.

[54] These orthographic anomalies were early pointed out by Licht, מגילת ההודיות, p. 8. See now Reymond.

[55] See the superb discussion by Mansoor, *The Thanksgiving Hymns*, pp. 15–17. See esp. Reymond, p. 227.

riginal עוון. Since *yodh* and *waw* are orthographically difficult to differentiate at times, is it possible that a scribe has intended not עוון, "iniquity" but עין, "eye" or "spring?"

3. Paleography, Date, and Provenience

In 1956, Licht insightfully noted that the Qumran Scrolls illumine us "as in a flash of light" about "a whole sphere of religious and literary activity." In particular, the *Thanksgiving Hymns* "shows us the true essence of the sectarian life."[56]

Due to the fragmentary nature of all copies of the *Thanksgiving Hymns*, it is difficult to discern the date of individual compositions. Clearly, the lack of an entire copy of the document further complicates the process of dating the final collection. Many scholars have dated the individual copies of the *Thanksgiving Hymns* and such paleographical dates provide us with clues for dating the individual compositions and the final collection.

According to S. A. Birnbaum, the paleographic date of 1QH[a] is sometime "before the Herodian and Roman periods."[57] É. Puech rightly dates the script of 1QH[a] to the second half of the first-century BCE.[58] Radiocarbon dating of a sample from 1QH[a] also stipulated a time about 50 BCE or soon after it.[59] Recent spectroscopic investigation of the ink used on 1QH[a] indicates that the writing of this document occurred in the vicinity of the Dead Sea sometime during the first centuries BCE or CE.[60]

More than one scribe applied the ink to the leather of 1QH[a]. The work of the first scribe is clear in cols. 1–19. A second (less skilled) hand begins in 1QH[a] 19.22 and within a hymn.[61] It is possible, though not certain that three scribal hands are to be discerned;[62] they may also have worked in collaboration.[63] The second hand is most likely the corrector.[64] Sukenik's ob-

servations are perspicacious: "Two scribes were employed in copying the scroll. One was an expert and accurate calligrapher …. The second scribe wrote a crude and careless hand and was negligent in separating words."[65] In this edition, *inter alia*, we have followed those who noted the fragments that belong to Scribe A, Scribe B, and Scribe C; this method is clearer near the end of the text and translation.

The script of 1QH[a] consists of at least two different hands writing in a semi-formal Herodian script.[66] Manuscripts such as 1Q35 (1QH[b]) and 4Q432 (4QH[f]) are copied in a more formal, Herodian hand, whereas 4Q427 (4QH[a]), 4Q430 (4QH[c]), and 4Q431 (4QH[d]) are in a semi-formal Herodian hand. 4Q428 (4QH[b]) and 4Q429 (4QH[c]) are in a late Hasmonean or early Herodian semi-formal hand.

Some of the fragments from Cave IV (4Q428–4Q429) could be approximately dated somewhere between 100 and 50 BCE, whereas 1QH[a] and the other Cave IV fragments could be dated somewhere between 50 BCE and circa 36 CE. As a whole, all of the manuscripts in our possession seem to have been copied, at the latest, by the early first century CE. Some hymns were composed before the first century BCE.

It is now apparent that some of the compositions in the *Thanksgiving Hymns* antedate, and have a provenience other than, the settlement at Qumran and the creation of the Qumran Community.[67] Some works may have originated in Jerusalem and conceivably within the Temple; notably, the *Self-Glorification Hymn* antedates the *Thanksgiving Hymns* and shaped more than one Qumran creation, including at least two copies of the *Thanksgiving Hymns*.[68] Significant overlaps between the *Thanksgiving Hymns* and other documents (e.g., *Instruction*, the *Treatise of the Two Spirits*, *Mysteries*), as well as an overall

---

[56] Licht, "The Doctrine of the Thanksgiving Scroll," *IEJ* 6 (1956) 1–13, 89–101.

[57] S. A. Birnbaum, "How Old are the Cave Manuscripts? A Palaeographical Discussion," *VT* 1 (1951) 91–109; see p. 105.

[58] Puech, *La croyance des Esséniens en la vie future*, vol. 2, p. 336.

[59] G. Bonani, *et al.*, "Radiocarbon Dating of Fourteen Dead Sea Scrolls," *Radiocarbon* 34 (1992) 843–49; see esp. pp. 845 and 848. M. Broshi and J. Strugnell contributed to this report.

[60] I. Rabin, *et al.*, "On the Origin of the Ink of the Thanksgiving Scroll (1QHodayot[a])," *DSD* 16 (2009) 97–106.

[61] The two hands were observed early in research; see Sukenik, *The Dead Sea Scrolls of the Hebrew University*, p. 38 and Licht, מגילת ההודיות, p. 7.

[62] Puech doubts that there are three scribal hands evident in 1QH[a]; Puech, *La croyance des Esséniens en la vie future*, vol. 2, p. 336.

[63] See M. Martin, *Scribal Character*, vol. 2, p. 475.

[64] That point was also made by Lichtenberger, *Studien zum Menschenbild in Texten der Qumrangemeinde* (SUNT 15; Göttingen, 1980) p. 28 note 88.

[65] Sukenik, *The Dead Sea Scrolls of the Hebrew University*, p. 37.

[66] Lichtenberger also dates 1QH[a] to the Herodian period. See his excellent *Studien zum Menschenbild in Texten der Qumrangemeinde*; see esp. "Die Hodajot (H)," pp. 27–32; the citation is on p. 28.

[67] See esp. A. K. Harkins, "Observations on the Editorial Shaping of the So-called Community Hymns from 1QH[a] and 4QH[a] (4Q427)," *DSD* 12 (2005) 233–56; Harkins, "The Community Hymns Classification: A Proposal for Further Differentiation," *DSD* 15 (2008) 121–54. Harkins proposes that some of the hymns show significant connection to the *Yaḥad* while others do not. This conclusion is obvious from our work in editing and translating these eight witnesses to the *Thanksgiving Hymns*.

[68] See the introduction, text, and translation of the *Self-Glorification Hymn* in the present volume. Most likely, some at Qumran looked back at the sufferings of the Righteous Teacher and edited this *Hymn* by adding or altering some lines, eventually placing them in the *Thanksgiving Hymns*. Some Qumranites may have imagined that the glorification referred to the *postmortem* elevation of their beloved Teacher. Many reflections were allowed to germinate within the Community.

lack of particularly sectarian vocabulary and thought, supports such a pre-Qumran date for this "hymn."[69]

The corrections to the *Thanksgiving Hymns*, especially in 1QHᵃ, prove that Jews in a scribal school edited the script (see the notes to the text and translation). So-called defective spellings are shifted to *plene* forms (לא becomes לוא). A school of correcting scribes is clear since the corrections are often above the line. Most interesting among the corrections is the alteration of the Hodayot formula in 1QHᵃ 13.22. The first scribe wrote אודכה;[70] a different scribe added dots above and below each of the five consonants and wrote above the line ברוך אתה. It appears, as the notes indicate, that a scribe thought the reading of 4Q429 (4QHᶜ) was superior to 1QHᵃ and so corrected the latter manuscript.[71]

It follows, therefore, that these hymns as well as collections of hymns probably evolved over an extended period of time, beginning sometime in the second century BCE and continuing into the last decade of the first century BCE. Thus, some of the hymns were composed before the Qumranites settled into the Iron Age II ruins by the Dead Sea. Subsequently, devout Jews copied earlier hymns and related documents at Qumran; they or other Jews composed hymns and poetic works at Qumran.

4. Genre and Function

One of the difficulties in the analysis of the *Thanksgiving Hymns* has been discerning what genre(s) define this composition.[72] Terminologically,[73] many scholars prefer to call the individual compositions found in the *Thanksgiving Hymns* "psalms"[74] or "prayers"[75] as opposed to "hymns."[76] No one term sufficiently encompasses the complex and multifarious nature of the compositions collected within the *Thanksgiving Hymns*. As Licht made clear in 1957, even though the *Thanksgiving Hymns* bear many similarities to the Psalms of the Hebrew Bible, they simultaneously show considerable deviation from traditional biblical psalms.[77]

Attempts to discern the generic identity of the *Thanksgiving Hymns* have been further complicated by questions concerning how the compositions functioned in their sectarian *Sitz im Leben*.[78] On the one hand, some scholars have presumed that the *Thanksgiving Hymns* served as the cultic liturgy of the Qumran Community and were utilized in their worship services.[79] On the other hand, other scholars have presumed that the *Thanksgiving Hymns* were poetic rather than hymnic, and served as

[69] J. Murphy-O'Connor, "The Judaean Desert," in *Early Judaism and its Modern Interpreters*, edited by R. A. Kraft and G. W. E. Nickelsburg (The Bible and its Modern Interpreters; Atlanta, 1986) pp. 119–56; see esp. p. 132; Schuller, "Recent Scholarship on the Hodayot 1993–2010," 119–62 see esp. pp. 142–46. An insightful discussion of what constitutes "sectarianism" is found in Newsom, "'Sectually Explicit' Literature from Qumran," in *The Hebrew Bible and its Interpreters*, edited by W. H. Propp, B. Halpern, and D. N. Freedman (BJS 1; Winona Lake, 1990) pp. 167–87. Obviously, Schuller and almost all scholars recognize that the *Hodayot* is sectarian; that is, the work was composed and edited by the Qumranites. Also see A. Lange's helpful criteria for discerning sectarian compositions in *Weisheit und Prädestination: Weisheitliche Urordnung und Prädestination im den Textfunden von Qumran* (STDJ 18; Leiden and Boston, 1995) and H. W. Morisada Rietz, "Identifying Compositions and Traditions of the Qumran Community: *Songs of the Sabbath Sacrifice*, a Case Study," in *Qumran Studies: New Approaches and New Questions*, edited by M. T. Davis and B. A. Strawn (Grand Rapids, 2007) pp. 29–52.

[70] I have no doubt that two scribes (not necessarily three) are clear. Two ways of writing ʾaleph are apparent and the corrector places no foot on the *beth*. The corrector seems to have an earlier scribal hand; if so, he may have been older than the first scribe.

[71] Tov also observed this phenomenon and shares our judgment; Tov, *Scribal Practices*, p. 223.

[72] Newsom recognizes the lack of clarity in scholarly discussions of "genre," and calls for a descriptive catalogue of genres that will help us better categorize the *Hodayot*. See C. A. Newsom, "Pairing Research Questions and Theories of Genres: A Case Study of the Hodayot," *DSD* 17 (2010) 241–59.

[73] On a general discussion of genre in the *Hodayot*, see J. J. Collins, "Amazing Grace: The Transformation of the Thanksgiving Hymn at Qumran," in *Psalms in Community*, edited by H. Attridge and M. Fassler (SBL Symposium Series 25; Atlanta, 2003) pp. 75–86.

[74] For example, see B. P. Kittel, *The Hymns of Qumran: Translation and Commentary* (SBLDS 50; Chico, 1981); Schuller (e.g., DJD 29 and 40); and H. Stegemann, "The Number of Psalms in *1QHodayot*ᵃ and Some of their Sections," pp. 191–234.

[75] For example, see Newsom, *The Self as Symbolic Space: Constructing Identity and Community at Qumran* (STDJ 52; Leiden, 2004) p. 204; and A. K. Harkins, *Reading With an "I" to the Heavens: Looking at the Qumran Hodayot through the Lens of Visionary Traditions* (Ekstasis 3; Berlin, 2012).

[76] The most recent publication to use the term "hymn" to describe the individual compositions in *Thanksgiving Hymns* is E. Qimron, מגילות מדבר יהודה: החיבורים העבריים [The Dead Sea Scrolls: The Hebrew Writings, Volume One] (Between Bible and Mishnah; Jerusalem, 2010) p. xxvii.

[77] Licht, מגילות ההודיות, pp. 17–19.

[78] Notably, see Kittel, *Hymns of Qumran*, pp. 1–20; Schuller "Prayer, Hymnic, and Liturgical Texts from Qumran," pp. 166–69.

[79] Holm-Nielsen, *Hodayot*, p. 348. He describes them as "examples of the Qumran community's liturgical prayers and songs of praise."

expressions of personal reflection, private prayer, or instruction.[80]

Scholars are becoming more sensitive to the anachronisms and ambiguities that cloud this discussion. Scholars have too readily assumed a false dichotomy between a "psalm" and a "hymn." The ancients knew no such distinctions. There was probably also more fluidity than is commonly assumed between collective worship and private devotion; as is the case today, a psalm or prayer may be used in both settings.

Schuller is rightly cautious in the use of the term *liturgical* when describing the function of the *Thanksgiving Hymns*, stating that though there is evidence that the *Thanksgiving Hymns* may have served the *Yaḥad* liturgically at certain points in its history, it does not require that the *Thanksgiving Hymns* functioned *solely* as a liturgical composition.[81] Newsom astutely states that her working hypothesis concerning the function of the *Thanksgiving Hymns* is that they were recited communally, though "not necessarily in a liturgical context" such that a member might contribute their own personal prayer to the collection.[82] Harkins proposes that the *Thanksgiving Hymns* may have functioned as prayers which were ritualistically performed by those in the *Yaḥad* as a portal into visionary religious experiences.[83] E. Chazon claims that the liturgical function of the *Thanksgiving Hymns* is anchored in its unified theme: the worship of the Community together with the angels.[84] It is best to conclude that some of the compositions were probably used collectively as the Community worshipped, while others were reserved for individual meditation and reflection. A diversity of genre and function is obvious in the different compositions.

In 1956, H. Bardtke observed that the *Thanksgiving Hymns*, through the repetition of images, forms, and emotional patterns, shaped the beliefs of those who recited or meditated on them.[85] In 2004, Newsom developed this insight and suggested that the Qumranites (= Essenes) used the *Thanksgiving Hymns*

to develop a sectarian self-understanding (or subjectivity).[86] An intensive focus on the witnesses to this composition clarifies these scholarly perceptions; as Isaiah 40:3 defined the *raison d'être* for being "in the wilderness," so the *Thanksgiving Hymns* provided images and conceptions that helped the Qumranites live out their belief that the Community – ordained, chosen and protected by God – was a strong building with bolted gates through which no enemy in the endtime war might enter, for God was coming soon to judge all peoples (1QHᵃ 14.29–31 and 4Q429 frg. 4 2.11–12).

In summary, the question of genre and function is a difficult one that requires extensive knowledge of the poetry and hymnic material of the Second Temple period. As J. Kugel points out, poetry is evocative language and it connotes far more than it denotes.[87] What is found in the *Thanksgiving Hymns* cannot be confined to a particular existing genre (e.g., Hebrew Psalms, hymns, Jewish Prayers, benedictions, etc.). The full collection should be analyzed as individual poetic works without delimiting structure, and as an amalgamation of genres and writing styles that evolved into the literary traditions, sociohistorical context, and purposes of the Qumran Community.

5. Contents

Due to the frequent usage of first person pronouns and verbs, as well as a consistent mention of persecution and God's subsequent rescue, Sukenik initially proposed that the *Thanksgiving Hymns* were a compositional unity, initially written by the "Teacher of Righteousness." This compositional unity was challenged in 1960 by Holm-Nielson who observed that the "canticles" of the *Thanksgiving Hymns* could be divided into two large groups: "hymns" and "psalms of thanksgiving."[88] Holm-Nielson's theory was supported a year later by G. Morawe.[89] Both scholars noticed that the so-called "hymns" were concerned with the conditions of a community while the "psalms of thanksgiving" were dramatically introspective, seeking special deliverance from God in the face of adversity and oppression. These ideas were further developed by G. Jeremias,[90] J. Becker,[91] and H.-W. Kuhn,[92] who proposed that the

---

[80] E.g., H. Bardtke, "Considérations sur les cantiques de Qumrân," *RB* 63 (1956) 220–33. Schiffman, *Reclaiming the Dead Sea Scrolls* (Philadelphia and Jerusalem, 1994) p. 301; B. Nitzan, *Qumran Prayer and Religious Poetry* (STDJ 12; Leiden, 1994) pp. 321–24.

[81] See Schuller "Prayer, Hymnic, and Liturgical Texts," pp. 167–68; DJD 29, pp. 74–75.

[82] Newsom, *The Self as Symbolic Space*, pp. 196–204; the quotation is from p. 203. See also Newsom, "Pairing Research Questions and Theories of Genre: A Case Study of the Hodayot," 241–59; see esp. p. 250.

[83] Harkins, *Reading With an "I" to the Heavens.*

[84] E. Chazon, "Liturgical Function in the Cave 1 Hodayot Collection," in *Cave 1 Revisited: Sixty Years after Their Discovery, Proceedings of the Sixth Meeting of the IOQS in Ljubljana* (STDJ 91; Leiden, 2010) pp. 135–49.

[85] H. Bardtke, "Considérations sur les cantiques de Qumrân," 220–33; see esp. p. 231.

[86] Newsom, "What do Hodayot Do? Language and the Construction of the Self in Sectarian Prayer," in *The Self as Symbolic Space*, pp. 190–286.

[87] J. Kugel in *Harper's Bible Dictionary*, p. 804.

[88] Holm-Nielson, *Hodayot*, pp. 316–31.

[89] G. Morawe, *Aufbau und Abgrenzung der Loblieder von Qumrân: Studien zur gattungsgeschichtlichen Einordnung der Hodayôth* (Theologische Arbeiten 16; Berlin, 1961).

[90] G. Jeremias, *Der Lehrer der Gerechtigkeit* (SUNT 2; Göttingen, 1963).

[91] J. Becker, *Das Heil Gottes: Heils- und Sündenbegriffe in den Qumrantexten und im Neuen Testament* (SUNT 3; Göttingen, 1964).

[92] H.-W. Kuhn, *Enderwarung und gengenwärtiges Heil: Unter-*

voice behind the "psalms of thanksgiving" or *Lehrerlieder* was the "Teacher of Righteousness," whereas the voice behind the "hymns" or *Gemeindelieder* were the members of the Qumran Community. These scholars, often referred to as the "Heidelberg School," concluded that the *Thanksgiving Hymns* were the product of more than one author. For decades, their "Teacher Hymn" Hypothesis was considered the basis of historical-critical work on the *Thanksgiving Hymns* and has been supported by the recent work of M. Douglas and others.[93] Douglas's argument in particular utilizes historical and literary criticism of the "Teacher Hymns," making the claim that the "Teacher Hymns" originate from the earliest period of the Teacher's movement and were penned by the Teacher as a historical self-expression of the rejection which he was facing.[94]

In the past quarter of a century, a number of scholars have focused on the "Teacher Hymn" Hypothesis, reexamining both its authorial claims as well as its explanation for the distinctive attributes of the "Teacher Hymns." Some scholars have attempted to analyze the "Teacher Hymns" in light of their seeming lack of Hebrew wisdom language and themes, many of which are profuse in the "Community Hymns."[95] The dissertation of S. Berg analyzes the bipartite division of the *Thanksgiving Hymns* in light of the disparity of epistemology between the "Teacher Hymns" and "Community Hymns."[96] In 2004, Newsom published a monograph which focused on the rhetorical traits of the *Thanksgiving Hymns* rather than the form-critical methodology which has predominated the compositional question.[97] Puech's 1988 publication, rather than embracing the "Teacher Hymn" versus "Community Hymn" dichotomy, prescribes a five-fold division to the *Thanksgiving Hymns* mirroring the Hebrew Psalter.[98] In 2010, Harkins revised her 2008 proposal, embracing Puech's five-fold division, suggesting that the "Community Hymns" should be distinguished between the nonsectarian "Community Hymns" (cols. 1–8) and the particularly sectarian "Community Hymns" (cols. 19.6–end).[99]

The name "Thanksgiving Hymns" was coined by Sukenik since the *incipit* of many of the hymns consists of the phrase: "I thank you, O Lord." This "Hodayot formula" is often preceded by a *vacat*; a scribal mark is followed by a *vacat* in 4Q428 [4QH^b] fragment 10 line 11. Other common introductory phrases are ברוך אתה אדוני, "Blessed are you, O Lord" (e.g., 1QH^a 17.38; 18.16), אודכה אלי "I thank you, O my God" (1QH^a 19.6, 18), and ברוך אתה אל (1QH^a 19.32; 22.34). It is noteworthy that in 13.22 a scribe changed "I thank you, O Lord" (אודכה אדוני) to "Blessed are you" (ברוך אתה). Some of the transitions lack the standard *incipit* and rely solely on a *vacat*. Others begin with an *incipit* but are not preceded by a *vacat*.[100]

Note that the only preserved *vacat* in the minuscule fragment 1QH^b is precisely where it is in 1QH^a. The use of *vacat* in 4Q428 is where we would expect it according to 1QH^a. One *vacat* in 4Q427 is exactly where the *vacat* is in 1QH^a 20.6; the text of 1QH^a is lost where the *vacat* is in 4Q427 frg. 8 1.17.

The use of *incipit* is especially important for discerning the beginning or ending of a hymn. Here is a chart of the use of *vacat* in all the witnesses to the *Thanksgiving Hymns*:

suchungen zu den Gemeindeliedern von Qumran (SUNT 4; Göttingen, 1965).

[93] See M. C. Douglas, *Power and Praise in the Hodayot*, (Ph.D. diss., University of Chicago Divinity School, 1998); Douglas, "The Teacher Hymn Hypothesis Revisited: New Data for an Old Crux," *DSD* 6 (1999) 239–66. Other scholars holding the "Teacher Hymn" Hypothesis include M. O. Wise, *The First Messiah: Investigating the Savior Before Christ* (New York, 1999) and S. Hultgren, *From the Damascus Covenant to the Covenant of the Community: Literary, Historical, and Theological Studies in the Dead Sea Scrolls* (STDJ 66; Leiden, 2007) see esp. pp. 409–59.

[94] Douglas, "The Teacher Hymn Hypothesis Revisited," pp. 265–66.

[95] S. J. Tanzer, *The Sages at Qumran: Wisdom in the Hodayot* (Ph.D. diss., Harvard, 1987). See also M. J. Goff, "Reading Wisdom at Qumran: 4QInstruction and the Hodayot," *DSD* 11 (2004) 263–88.

[96] S. A. Berg, *Religious Epistemologies in the Dead Sea Scrolls: The Heritage and Transformation of the Wisdom Tradition* (Ph.D. diss., Yale, 2008).

[97] Newsom, *The Self as Symbolic Space*.

[98] Puech, "Quelques aspects de la restauration du Rouleau des Hymnes (1QH)," 38–55. Puech proposes that the five-fold division was anchored by the appearance of the expression למשכיל (1QH^a 5.12, 7.21, 20.7, 25.34), the first of which, Puech proposed, appeared at the lost beginning of 1QH^a. This division applies only to the non-Teacher Hymns.

[99] A. K. Harkins, "A New Proposal for Thinking about 1QH^a Sixty Years after its Discovery," in *Qumran Cave 1 Revisited, Texts from Cave 1 Sixty Years After Their Discovery: Proceedings of the Sixth Meeting of the IOQS in Ljubljana*, edited by D. K. Falk, *et al.* (STDJ 91; Leiden, 2010) pp. 101–34.

[100] See the notes to the text and also Stegemann, "The Number of Psalms in *1QHodayot*^a," pp. 220–23.

Chart 1: The Use of the Vacat

1QHa	1QHb	4Q427	4Q428	4Q429	4Q430	4Q431	4Q432
4.20	Frg. 1 line 8			N/A	N/A	N/A	N/A
4.28							
4.37			Frg. 12b 4 line 2				
4.41			Frg. 26 line 4				
6.18–19							
6.33							
7.20							
No extant text		Frg. 8 1.17					
10.21–22							
10.32							
11.19–20							
11.37–38							
12.6							
13.6							
13.21							
15.8–9							
15.28–29							
15.36							
16.4							
17.36–37			Frg. 10 line 11				
18.15							
19.5							
19.17							
No *vacat*[101]			Frg. 12a line 4				
20.6		Frgs. 2, 3 2.17	Frg. 12b line 2				
21.31							
25.33							
41.2							

[101] A *vacat* is necessitated in 19.30 of the Composite Text based on the extant *vacat* in the parallel text of 1QHᵃ 19.30 in 4Q428 frg. 12a line 4.

Chart 2: The Use of Incipit

1QHa	1QHb	4Q427	4Q428	4Q429	4Q430	4Q431	4Q432
4.21	N/A				N/A	N/A	
4.29							
4.38							
5.15							
6.19							
6.34							
7.21							
8.26							
10.5							Frg. 3 line 1
10.22							
10.33							
11.20							
11.38							
12.6							
13.7							
13.22							
15.9							
15.29							
15.37							
16.5			Frg. 10 line 11				
17.38							
18.16							
19.6							
19.18							
19.30			Frg. 12a line 4				
20.7		Frgs. 2, 3 2.18	Frg. 12b line 3				
22.34							
25.34							
41.3							
Not represented				Frg. 6 line 1?			

All extant uses of *incipit* in 4Q427 and 4Q428 are in line with 1QH^a. 4Q429 contains a possible *incipit* where the text is lost in 1QH^a. There are no extant examples of an *incipit* in 1QH^b.

6. The Thanksgiving Hymns: An Ordering for the Composite Text

Because we do not possess one full copy of the *Thanksgiving Hymns*, we cannot discern how many hymns were once in the full collection; and the extent of the work cannot be ascertained precisely. André Dupont-Sommer and Licht concluded that there were 32 hymns.[102] Holm-Nielsen and Puech estimated there were 31 hymns.[103] In 2003, Stegemann published an article in which he concluded that 28–34 psalms were contained within 1QH[a] columns 1–28. Of these, only 22 are represented by Sukenik's original publication.[104] I have ascertained that 1QH[a] contained at least 35 compositions.[105]

The order and estimate of the number of the hymns may be discerned by the presence of a *vacat* or an *incipit* with formula. However, the vast amount of lost text at times prohibits a clear identification of a *vacat* or an *incipit*. Only 1QH[a] columns 4 through 20 are preserved sufficiently; thus, the evidence of the beginning or ending of a hymn is virtually impossible in columns 1, 2, 3, and 21 to 28. Beginning with column 21, one may assume one hymn was preserved in the restored columns or attempt to discern the beginning of a hymn. We have chosen the latter option, basing our decisions on a shift in thought, and the one *vacat* that remains (in 1QH[a] 25.33).

Obviously, some hymns are rather short and others very long. This disparity in length reflects poetry generally, including the Hebrew Bible Psalter in particular.[106] Note that, for example, Psalm 23 is short but Psalm 119 is long. A study of the use of *vacat* and an *incipit* in all the witnesses to the *Thanksgiving Hymns* provides an estimation of the number of hymns and titles:[107]

Charts 4 and 5 clarify the autobiographical (or related) reflections in hymns presented in our Composite Text of cols. 10.5–17.37. Cumulatively, they strengthen the hypothesis that the author of almost all poems in this section of the *Thanksgiving Hymns* is the Righteous Teacher. Most likely they were transmitted with indiscernible variations (except for the clear alteration in 13.22).

7. Compositional Structure and Authorship

Licht did not speculate on the compositional history of the *Thanksgiving Hymns*. Many decades after his publication, we should conclude that the collection was not random but evolved within the Qumran Community so that hymns were added at the beginning and end with the "Teacher Hymns" in the middle; and the latter were probably edited. It is necessary to add that any attempt to recreate the compositional history must consider that the hymns that began the composition in all witnesses are lost. Moreover, the hymns often are very similar since an author (or authors) compose by repeating (or remembering) previous expressions.[108] Redactions and additions presuppose the traditions and symbolic language in earlier hymns now found in the collection we call the *Thanksgiving Hymns*.[109]

For Licht, who did not know about the massive number of Qumran scrolls, the *Thanksgiving Hymns* and the other Qumran sectarian scrolls represent one unified expression of an isolated sect.[110] Licht's position defines the beginning of Qumranology. It does not represent a present consensus. Clearly, Qum-ran was originally an isolated sect but it was connected to or virtually identical to the Essenes who lived eventually throughout Palestine. Some of the hymns are non-Qumranic; that is, some psalms are earlier compositions or composed outside of the Qumran *Yaḥad*.

Without any doubt, some of the *Thanksgiving Hymns* were composed by a powerful personality with an elevated ego. He was a dynamic leader who expressed the suffering he received from a dominant group that is probably the priests controlling the Temple. This composer is also a brilliant thinker with a marvelous vocabulary.[111] We should salute him as a literary and religious genius. Since the composition history of the *Thanksgiving Hymns* is shaped by a search for the identity and life of this person, probably the Righteous Teacher, a brief review of that focused research seems appropriate.

---

[102] For a chart depicting their numbering, see Mansoor, *The Thanksgiving Hymns*, pp. 33–34.

[103] Holm-Nielsen, *Hodayot*, p. 6; Puech, "Quelques aspects," p. 53.

[104] Stegemann, "The Number of Psalms in *1QHodayot*[a]," p. 209.

[105] The opening columns of 1QH[a] are lost.

[106] Note that the Psalter is witnessed as various collections by the Qumran manuscripts.

[107] The column numbers follow a reconstruction of 1QH[a].

[108] Licht, מגילת ההודיות, p. 16.

[109] J. J. M. Roberts wisely points out that additions to Isaiah, one unified composition according to early Jews, owe a great deal to earlier theological language in the book. See Roberts, "Isaiah in Old Testament Theology," *Interpretation* 36 (1982) 130–43; see p. 131. That is the case with the compositional history of the *Hodayot*; many apparently later hymns echo those that the author knew (some were in the Psalter, others in the evolving *Hodayot*).

[110] Licht, מגילת ההודיות, p. 5.

[111] See the notes to the texts and translations. The author also seems very fond of the permissive *hipʿil*; it signifies that God has allowed his servant to know secrets and truths. The servant is at least sometimes the Righteous Teacher.

Chart 3: The Number of Hymns and Titles

Number	Col. and Lines	Imagined Name
Lost	1	Unknown
1	2.1–4.20 *vacat*[112]	God's Mercies Upon the Poor Ones
2	4.21–28 *vacat*	Blessed is the God of Knowledge Who Cleanses Me
3	4.29–37 *vacat*	Blessed is the Lord, God of Mercies
4	4.38–41 *vacat*	Blessed is God for the Holy Spirit
5	5.1–14[113]	The Master Prostrates Himself Before God
6	5.15–6.18 *vacat*	Blessed is the Lord for His Power
7	6.19–33 *vacat*	I Thank the Lord for the Heart of Discernment
8	6.34–7.20 *vacat*	I Thank the Lord for the Multitude of His Wonders
9	7.21–8.25[114]	Bless God: A Psalm for the Master
10	8.26–10.5[115]	Blessed is the Lord for His Great Counsel
11	10.5–21 *vacat*	I Thank the Lord for Purification
12	10.22–32 *vacat*	I Thank the Lord for He Placed My Soul with the Living Ones
13	10.33–11.19 *vacat*	I Thank the Lord for Saving Me from Lying Interpreters
14	11.20–37 *vacat*	I Thank the Lord for Redeeming My Soul from the Pit
15	11.38–12.6 *vacat*	I Thank the Lord for Protection
16	12.6–13.6 *vacat*	I Thank the Lord for Enlightening Me for the Covenant
17	13.7–21 *vacat*	I Thank the Lord for Not Abandoning Me
18	13.22–15.8 *vacat*	Blessed is the Lord for His Righteousness to the Orphan
19	15.9–28 *vacat*	I Thank the Lord for Sustaining Me
20	15.29–36 *vacat*	I Thank the Lord for Instructing Me in Truth
21	15.37–16.4 *vacat*	I Thank the Lord for My Lot
22	16.5–17.37 *vacat*	I Thank the Lord for Making Me the Irrigator of the Garden
23	17.38–18.15 *vacat*	Blessed is the Lord for Making Me Mighty
24	18.16–19.5 *vacat*	Blessed is the Lord for His Loving-Kindness
25	19.6–17 *vacat*	I Thank God for Dealing Wonderfully with Dust
26	19.18–19.30 *vacat*[116]	I Thank My God for Allowing Me to Know Secret Truth[117]
27	19.30–20.6 *vacat*[118]	Blessed is the Lord for Insight

[112] The first preserved *vacat* is 1QHᵃ 4.20 but there was probably more than one hymn in the opening columns.

[113] The beginning of the line is lost.

[114] No *vacat* is evident; although there is no *vacat* in 1QHᵃ (perhaps in a previous manuscript), the *incipit* begins in line 26.

[115] A *vacat* may have been in the lost pieces of the leather.

[116] A *vacat* is found in 4Q428 frg. 12a line 4.

[117] In addition to the *incipit*, this hymn contains an additional blessing: "Blessed are you, O God of mercies and compassion, for" in 19.32.

[118] A *vacat* is evident in 4Q428 frg. 12b 49.2. Perhaps a *vacat* was not copied.

(Chart 3 continued)		
28	20.7–27[119]	For the Instructor: Concerning Night Prayers
29	20.27–22.34[120]	Confessions of a Creature of Dust, Clay, and Ashes[121]
30	22.34–23.19[122]	Blessed is the God of Knowledge Who Established His Servant
31	23.20–24.1[123]	Praise Be to God's Glorious Creation
32	24.2–25.33 *vacat*	Failure of the Cast-Down Heavenly Beings to Praise: Judgment
33	25.34–27.1[124]	For the Instructor: A Psalm to God, Our King[125]
34?	27.1–41.2 *vacat*	Fragments
35	41.3–?	I Thank the Lord Who Revealed

Many compositions in the *Thanksgiving Hymns* feature the frequent use of first person pronouns and verbs, as well as a consistent mention of persecution and God's subsequent rescue of one who imagines himself chosen by God who gave him special revelations, teachings, and eventual elevation. Thus, in the early decades of Qumran research, many scholars assumed that *all* the hymns in the *Thanksgiving Hymns* were composed by the Righteous Teacher. At the very beginning of Qumran research, Sukenik concluded that the *Thanksgiving Hymns* were composed by the Righteous Teacher. He pointed out that the author of the *Thanksgiving Hymns* and the Teacher, as we know from the *Damascus Document* and the *Pesharim*, were powerful leaders in the Community. Moreover, Sukenik claimed that in the early formative period there was probably only one master mind. He, thus, concluded that the importance of the *Thanksgiving Hymns* is increased by the following recognition:

> [T]he author refers to himself as a man who hoped for special revelations from the godhead and who, despite his opponents, had many followers flocking to him to listen to his teaching. A possible inference is that the author was

the Teacher of Righteousness often mentioned in these scrolls as well as in the 'Zadokite Document' of the Damascus Covenanters. His complaint over being compelled to leave his country – 'he thrust me out of my land like a bird from its nest' (col 4, 1.9)[126] – corresponds to the statement in the *Habbakuk Commentary* that the 'Wicked Priest' forced the Righteous Teacher into exile from the country (col. 11, 1.6).[127]

Other distinguished scholars in the 1950s, notably J. P. Hyatt and J. Carmignac, concluded that the Righteous Teacher is the sole author of the collection known as the *Thanksgiving Hymns*.[128]

Sukenik's proposal that the *Thanksgiving Hymns* were the product of the Righteous Teacher was disputed as early as 1957 by Licht who proposed that the author could have been any authoritative member within the Qumran Community, that is the "Examiner" (מבקר) or the "Master" (משכיל).[129] Both Sukenik and Licht assumed, incorrectly, that the *Thanksgiving Hymns* were the product of a single author.[130]

---

[119] No text is lost, but a new hymn probably begins in 20.27b.

[120] A blessing begins in 22.34b, but there is no *vacat*. Perhaps a *vacat* was not copied.

[121] With this hymn, one must not speculate unduly about the beginnings and endings of hymns. The fragmented manuscripts do not preserve a *vacat* or an *incipit*; there is only one *vacat* extant; it is in 25.33.

[122] 23.18–21a are lost. They may have contained evidence of the beginning or ending of a hymn.

[123] 23.17b–24.5 are lost. They may have contained a *vacat* or an *incipit*.

[124] 27.1–11a are lost; they may have contained evidence of the beginning of a new hymn.

[125] This hymn contains an excerpt from the *Self-Glorification Hymn*.

[126] An editor missed "col 4;" it should be col. 4. Note the next: "col. 11."

[127] Sukenik, *The Dead Sea Scrolls of the Hebrew University*, p. 39.

[128] J. P. Hyatt, "The View of Man in the Qumran 'Hodayot'," *NTS* 2 (1955–1956) 276–84; and J. Carmignac, "Les éléments historiques des 'hymnes' de Qumran," *RQ* 2 (1959–1960) 205–22. Note that this position defines early reflections in *Hodayot* research.

[129] Licht, מגילת ההודיות, pp. 24–26.

[130] See also H. Bardtke, "Considérations sur les cantiques de Qumrân," 227. Mansoor also seems to assume a single author, but admits that the question of authorship is "far from being settled;" *The Thanksgiving Hymns*, p. 45. Again, note the early date of the publication.

Chart 4: Autobiographical References in the Hodayot (Arranged According to Hymns)

10.5–21 (Sukenik 2.1–19)	10.33–11.19 (Sukenik 2.31–3.18)	12.6–13.6 (Sukenik 4.5–5.4)	13.7–21 (Sukenik 5.5–19)	13.22–15.8 (Sukenik 5.20–7.5)	15.9–28 (Sukenik 7.6–25)	16.5–17.37 (Sukenik 8.4–9.37)
I Thank the Lord for Purification	I Thank the Lord for Saving Me from Lying Interpreters	I Thank the Lord for Enlightening Me for the Covenant	I Thank the Lord for Not Abandoning Me	Blessed is the Lord for His Righteousness to the Orphan	I Thank the Lord for Sustaining Me	I Thank the Lord for Making Me the Irrigator of the Garden
You purified me 10.5	Your eye is on me during the humiliation of my soul 10.33	Like the dawn established for perfect lights, you have appeared to me 12.7	You did not abandon me when I lived among an alien people 13.7	All those bound to my council 13.26	You sustained me 15.9	You have placed me as the source of streams, pond of water, and Irrigator of the garden 16.5
I am a trap for transgressors, but a healing for all those who turn from transgression 10.10–11	You saved me from the zeal of the interpreters of the lie 10.33	They expelled me from my land 12.9	You hid me from the sons of Adam 13.13	Because you concealed the secret in me, they go slandering to the sons of disaster 13.27	You elevated the spirit of your holiness in me 15.9–10	Trees of life and trees of water 16.6–7
You set me as a disgrace and mockery to the unfaithful ones, a foundation of truth and discernment for the Upright Ones of the Way 10.11–12	Seekers of Smooth (Things) thought to consume the Poor One's blood to pour it upon your service 10.34–35	They are lying interpreters and treacherous seers 12.10–11	You concealed your Torah in me until the Endtime 13.13	They reached me in straits with no escape for me 13.31	You strengthened me in the face of the wars of wickedness 15.10	They will bring forth a shoot for an eternal planting 16.7
You set me ... the Interpreter of knowledge in the wonderful mysteries 10.15	You did not allow me to be afraid so that I would leave your service from fear of the threats of the wicked ones 10.37–38	They exchanged your Torah, which you reiterated in my heart, for smooth things 12.11	In order to show your might in me before the sons of Adam you set apart the Poor One 13.17–18	They sounded forth my dispute on musical instruments (Temple cult?) 13.31–32	You set me as a strong tower and as a high city wall 15.11	Its high branch is for all winged birds 16.10

I have become a man of strife for the interpreters of error, but the consummate debater for all the seers of correct things 10.16–17		They are not established in your truth 12.15		My tongue cleaves to my palate 13.33	You strengthened me in your covenant 15.13	You put into my mouth that which is like the early rain 16.17
		They do not regard me until you strengthen yourself in me 12.24		I was bound with ropes and chains 13.38–39	The opponents are speechless and have lying lips 15.14–15	If I withdraw my hand, it becomes like a juniper in the wilderness 16.25
		Assembled together for your covenant 12.25		All of your council is in my mouth 14.17	Those who attack me 15.15	The strength of my arm is bound in chains 16.36
		Through me, you enlightened the faces of many 12.28		Blossoming like the flowers until eternity to grow a shoot to become an eternal planting 14.18	You directed my footsteps in the paths of righteousness 15.17	The tongue you had strengthened in my mouth is no longer retrievable 16.36
		You allowed me to know the mysteries of your wonder, and the wonder is before the Many 12.28–29		They, the ones bound by my testimony, they were tempted by the erring interpreters 14.22	There are no righteous deeds to be delivered before you without forgiveness 15.20–21	
		To God Most High belongs all works of righteousness 12.32		I am speechless from their disasters 15.4	The greatness of your loving-kindness 15.21	
		The way of the human is not established except through the spirit God formed for him 12.32		Like an arm that is broken from the humerus 15.5	I leaned on your mercies to bring forth buds, as planting 15.21–22	
		You atone for iniquity and purify the human from guilt by your righteousness 12.38		My eyes are shut from seeing evil 15.5–6	The men of my war 15.25	

				My ears are shut from hearing blood that has been shed 15.6	You made me a father for the sons of loving-kindness and as a nursing father 15.23–25	
				My bones are dislocated 15.7	My dominion is over those who enter into your covenant 15.26	

Chart 5: Autobiographical References (Arranged According to Concept)

God's Continuing Help	Physical Mistreatment	Other Abuse	Other Historical Background	Endowment of Knowledge (as a Teacher)	Planting Metaphor	God's Salvation to the Teacher	The Followers' Temptation
To God Most High belongs all works of righteousness 12.32	My tongue cleaves to my palate 13.33	They reached me in straits with no escape for me 13.31	You strengthened me in the face of wars of wickedness 15.10	You set me as the Interpreter of knowledge in the wonderful mysteries 10.15	Blossoming like the flowers until eternity to grow a shoot to become an eternal planting 14.18	You purified me 10.5	Because you concealed the secret in me, they go slandering to the sons of disaster 13.27
The way of the human is not established except through the spirit God formed for him 12.32	I was bound with ropes and chains 13.38–39	They sounded forth my dispute on musical instruments (Temple cult?) 13.31–32	They are lying interpreters and treacherous seers 12.10–11	Like the dawn established for perfect lights, you have appeared to me 12.7	I leaned on your mercies to bring forth buds, a planting, 15.21–22	I am a trap for transgressors, but a healing for all those who turn from transgression 10.10–11	They, the ones bound by my testimony, they were tempted by the erring interpreters 14.22
You atone for iniquity and purify the human from guilt by your righteousness 12.38	I am speechless from their disasters 15.4	Your eye is on me during the humiliation of my soul 10.33	They exchanged your Torah, which you reiterated in my heart, for smooth things 12.11	Through me, you enlightened the faces of many 12.28	You have placed me as the source of streams, pond of water, and Irrigator of the garden 16.5	You set me as a disgrace and mockery to the unfaithful ones, a foundation of truth and discernment for the Upright Ones of the Way 10.11–12	You directed my footsteps in the paths of righteousness 15.17
There are no righteous deeds to be delivered before you without forgiveness 15.20–21	Like an arm that is broken from the humerus 15.5	Seekers of Smooth (Things) thought to consume the Poor One's blood to pour it upon your service 10.34–35	They are not established in your truth 12.15	You allowed me to know the mysteries of your wonder, and the wonder is before the Many 12.28–29	Trees of life and trees of water 16.6–7	I am a man of strife for interpreters of error, but the consummate debater for all seers of correct things 10.16–17	The greatness of your loving-kindness 15.21

	My bones are dislocated 15.7	They expelled me from my land 12.9	Assembled together for your covenant 12.25	You concealed your Torah in me until the Endtime 13.13	They will bring forth a shoot for an eternal planting 16.7	You saved me from the zeal of the interpreters of the lie 10.33	
	Those who attack me 15.15	My eyes are shut from seeing evil 15.5–6	In order to show your might in me before the sons of Adam you set apart the Poor One 13.17–18	All those bound to my council 13.26	Its high branch is for all winged birds 16.10	You did not allow me to be afraid so that I would leave your service from fear of the threats of the wicked ones 10.37–38	
	The strength of my arm is bound in chains 16.36	My ears are shut from hearing blood that has been shed 15.6	You made me a father for the sons of lovingkindness and as a nursing father 15.23–25	All of your council is in my mouth 14.17	You put into my mouth that which is like the early rain 16.17	They do not regard me until you strengthen yourself in me 12.24	
	The tongue you had strengthened in my mouth is no longer retrievable 16.36	The opponents are speechless and have lying lips 15.14–15	The men of my war 15.25	My dominion is over those who enter into your covenant 15.26	If I withdraw my hand, it becomes like a juniper in the wilderness 16.25	You did not abandon me when I lived among an alien people 13.7	
						You hid me from the sons of Adam 13.13	
						You sustained me 15.9	
						You elevated your spirit of holiness in me 15.9–10	
						You set me as a strong tower and a high city wall 15.11	
						You strengthened me in your covenant 15.13	

Licht argued that we should hesitate to equate the putative author of the *Thanksgiving Hymns* with the powerful mind behind the Community. 1QHª is only part of what "remains from the rich literature of the sect and is one unified composition."[131] Licht articulated the following conclusions:

The *Hymns* were composed by one person who had a very strong and dominant personality. He feels more loyalty to God than to the sect. He thanks God for allowing him to be the father of the sons of grace (cf. 1QHª 15.23).[132] The author is certain he was sent by God from heaven.[133]

According to Licht, the way the *Thanksgiving Hymns* are written leads to the conclusion that the sect is "the personal creation of the author of the *Thanksgiving Hymns*."[134] Licht thus concluded that while it is attractive to think that the author of the *Thanksgiving Hymns* is the Righteous Teacher, not even the *Pesher Habakkuk*, which reveals that the historical setting is Hasmonean, explains enough about the life of the Righteous Teacher to provide a convincing conclusion regarding the author of the *Thanksgiving Hymns*.

Licht pointed out that Community leaders and a Teacher are mentioned in the Qumran Scrolls. Thus, in the personal claims preserved in the *Thanksgiving Hymns*, we may be confronted with exaggeration, but the author's influence within the *Yaḥad* could be less than that of the Righteous Teacher. The functions of the author of the *Thanksgiving Hymns* are reminiscent of the functions of a leader in the *Yaḥad*, namely the "Examiner," the "Overseer" (פקיד), and especially the "Master" (the one who teaches). Licht was convinced that we should not consider the latter to be the leader of the Council as seems apparent for the Righteous Teacher, according to the *Rule of the Community* (col. 9).[135] Licht's comments should be judged within the continuum of conceivable-to-probable within scholarship; that is, scholars almost always do not say "always" and offer, at best, a probability. Thus, the earliest phase of research on the composition of the *Thanksgiving Hymns* led to two options: either the author of the *Thanksgiving Hymns* was the Righteous Teacher or was some other powerful person with a high sense of mission and election.

Contrary to Sukenik's claim that the *Thanksgiving Hymns* are a unified composition by the Righteous Teacher and Licht's argument that the collection is a unity, but by some unknown leader in the Community, most scholars now rightly observe the vast differences in the hymns, prayers, and psalms. More than one author produced these compositions.

Holm-Nielson observed,[136] and Morawe concurred,[137] that the hymns of the *Thanksgiving Hymns* could be divided into two large groups: "hymns" and "psalms of thanksgiving." Both scholars noticed that the so-called "hymns" were concerned with the conditions of a community while the "psalms of thanksgiving" were dramatically introspective, seeking special deliverance from God in the face of adversity and oppression. These ideas became a widely held consensus, and were further developed by Becker,[138] and H.-W. Kuhn,[139] P. Schulz,[140] P. von der Osten-Sacken,[141] and especially G. Jeremias.[142]

In 1963, G. Jeremias published a landmark monograph in which he pointed out two different uses of the first person pronoun in the *Thanksgiving Hymns*. Jeremias noted that the use of the first person pronoun can represent a specific individual or a collective unity, perceived as one. He went on to argue that some hymns mirrored the collective mind of the Community. Other hymnic compositions reflect the life, calling, and suffering of a specific individual and that person is most likely the Righteous Teacher who had, using Puech's words, a "forte personnalité."[143] Jeremias' research is fundamental; he provided criteria and specified what hymns were most likely composed by the Righteous Teacher.[144] Jeremias' foundational methodology and conclusion is universally received by many leading Qumranologists. Obviously, the Righteous Teacher

---

[136] Holm-Nielson, *Hodayot*, pp. 316–31.

[137] Morawe, *Aufbau und Abgrenzung.*

[138] J. Becker, *Das Heil Gottes.*

[139] H.-W. Kuhn, *Enderwartung und gegenwärtiges Heil.*

[140] P. Schulz, *Der Autoritätsanspruch des Lehrers der Gerechtigkeit in Qumran* (Meisenheim am Glan, 1974). Schulz states that some poems or hymns in the *Hodayot* were composed by the Righteous Teacher (see p. 1).

[141] P. von der Osten-Sacken, *Gott und Belial* (SUNT 6; Göttingen, 1969).

[142] G. Jeremias, *Der Lehrer der Gerechtigkeit.*

[143] Puech, *La croyance des Esséniens en la vie future*, vol. 2, p. 337.

[144] Jeremias concluded: "Wir haben damit die Psalmen, in denen wir mit Sicherheit den Lehrer der Gerechtigkeit als Verfasser erkannten, besprochen"; Jeremias, *Der Lehrer der Gerechtigkeit*, p. 264. Scholars who do not realize this certainty will continue to miss the obvious. The obvious appears when one comprehends the use of *beth* as a "*beth essentiae*" in col. 16. The author is the Righteous Teacher who perceives himself as the Irrigator of the Garden and that God placed the autumn rain in his mouth. See notes to the text and translation. Garnet rightly perceives that col. 16 indicates that the author is the Irrigator; see P. Garnet, *Salvation and Atonement in the Qumran Scrolls*, p. 27. Also see Garnet, "Atonement: Qumran and the New Testament," in *The Dead Sea Scrolls and the Bible*, pp. 357–80. P. Schulz rightly emphasized the poem's allegorical character; see P. Schulz, *Autoritätsanspruch des Lehrers der Gerechtigkeit in Qumran*, p. 27.

[131] Licht, מגילת ההודיות, p. 5.

[132] Licht, מגילת ההודיות, p. 23.

[133] Licht, מגילת ההודיות, p. 24.

[134] Licht, מגילת ההודיות, p. 24.

[135] Licht, מגילת ההודיות, p. 25.

composed more than the hymns we can, with assurance, attribute to him.

The distinct personality that defines the hymns composed by the Righteous Teacher has been observed by most editors of these hymns. He thanks the Lord for saving him from terrible persecution and refers to his opponents as men of my war (15.25). In contrast to the Psalter, these comments are specific and not generic. The references indicate not only the rejection of the Teacher's teaching but also terrible physical torture. The location of this suffering could be not only the Temple but also the Teacher's place of exile (see 1QpHab).

According to Jeremias, the Righteous Teacher composed the following hymns (converting the columns from Sukenik's to Stegemann's order):

Col. Number	Our Title
10.5–21	I Thank the Lord for Purification
10.33–41	I Thank the Lord for Saving Me from Lying Interpreters
12.6–13.6	I Thank the Lord for Enlightening Me for the Covenant
13.7–21	I Thank the Lord for Not Abandoning Me
13.22–15.8	Blessed is the Lord for His Righteousness to the Orphan
15.9–28	I Thank the Lord for Sustaining Me
16.5–41	I Thank the Lord for Making Me the Irrigator of the Garden

Notice that our titles highlight the use of the *Hodayot* formula: "I thank the Lord for ...." How can we explain the *incipit* that begins 13.22? Those who have studied these formulae and who have seen how 1QH^a was frequently edited and corrected could speculate that some scribe has most likely changed the *incipit* in 13.22. Is there any evidence that would support this assumption? Yes: A scribal corrector did change the *incipit* in 13.22. He first put dots over consonants to signify that they are incorrect. Then he added above the line a different formula: "Blessed is the Lord for ... ." It is imperative to comprehend that an editor changed "I thank the Lord for" to "Blessed is the Lord for" in 13.22. The author, indubitably the Righteous Teacher, chose to begin his compositions with "I thank the Lord for ... ." Unfortunately, this uniqueness was not honored much later in the Community when someone probably in the early decades of the first century CE altered 1QH^a 13.22.

The "Righteous Teacher" imagines himself sustained, purified, saved, and enlightened by God. He also looks back and believes that the God never abandoned him. He claims to be the Orphan and the Irrigator of the final Garden (16.5–17.37). He thus blesses God for his continuing righteousness, forgiveness, and acceptance.

While Jeremias' analysis of the *Thanksgiving Hymns* was both a turning point in research and a widely accepted conclusion, it also stimulated scholars for subsequent research. References to the Righteous Teacher were mined for a better com-

prehension of what passages in the *Thanksgiving Hymns* may with some assurance be attributed to the Righteous Teacher.

The widely accepted conclusion that portions of the *Thanksgiving Hymns* contain historically pertinent information concerning its author has been challenged in recent years, most notably by Harkins.[145] In particular, Harkins notes that this theory assumes that the "Teacher Hymns" and their "strong authorial voice" are autobiographical when they just as easily could be a rhetorical device that embraces lexemes of bodily experiences of suffering upon an "imaginal" body.[146] Similarly, Newsom imagines that these psalms articulate a "leadership myth" of the Community rather than the experiences of an individual,[147] though for her such a theory is, like the "Teacher Hymn" Hypothesis, mostly speculative.[148] Other scholars have begun to question whether the *Thanksgiving Hymns* provide any tangible information concerning the historical Teacher.[149]

As we have seen, a majority of early Qumran scholars concurred, at least partly, with Sukenik's proposition, concluding that at least some of the compositions in the *Thanksgiving Hymns* were composed by the Righteous Teacher. However, the work of Holm-Nielsen called into question both the number of authors involved in the composition of the *Thanksgiving Hymns* as well as the identities of those authors.[150] Following Holm-Nielsen's work, scholars developed the "Teacher Hymn" Hypothesis, which proposed the "Community Hymns" may have been the product of multiple authors situated in the Qumran Community, whereas at least some of the "Teacher Hymns" were most likely the product of the Righteous Teacher.[151] The "Community Hymns" reflect a community with clear rules, as explained in the *Rule of the Commnity*; thus, 5.20–31, 6.13–18, and 7.15–20 should be categorized as Community compositions. S. Tanzer suggests that these "Community Hymns" be subdivided into "Deuteronomic *Hodayot*" and "Niedrig-

[145] A. K. Harkins, "Who is the Teacher of the Teacher Hymns?" in *A Teacher for All Generations: Essays in Honor of James C. VanderKam*, edited by E. F. Mason, *et al.* (STDJ 153; Leiden, 2012) vol. 1, pp. 449–69.

[146] Harkins, "Who is the Teacher of the Teacher Hymns?" p. 464.

[147] Newsom, *The Self as Symbolic Space*, pp. 196–67, 287–300; see also Newsom, "Kenneth Burke Meets the Teacher of Righteousness," in *Of Scribes and Scrolls: Studies on the Hebrew Bible, Intertestamental Judaism, and Christian Origins*, edited by H. W. Attridge, J. J. Collins, and T. H. Tobin (Lanham, London, 1990) pp. 121–31.

[148] Newsom, *The Self as Symbolic Space*, p. 288.

[149] Kittel, *The Hymns of Qumran*, see esp. pp. 9–10; P. R. Davies, "What History Can We Get from the Scrolls, and How?" in *The Dead Sea Scrolls: Texts and Contexts*, edited by C. Hempel (STDJ 91; Leiden, 2010) pp. 31–46.

[150] Holm-Nielsen, *Hodayot*, p. 331.

[151] Notably, consult Jeremias, *Der Lehrer der Gerechtigkeit*, and Becker, *Das Heil Gottes*.

keitsdoxologie *Hodayot*."[152] That suggestion needs further exploration.

The "Teacher Hymn" Hypothesis, in which communal perceptions and regulations are noticeably absent, is widely considered the basis of historical-critical work on the *Thanksgiving Hymns*. Yadin referred, for example, to the "many biographical notes woven into the hymns."[153] This widely held consensus has been supported by the work of M. C. Douglas and others.[154] Douglas's argument in particular utilizes historical and literary criticism of the "Teacher Hymns," making the claim that these hymns originated from the earliest period of the Teacher's movement and were penned by the Righteous Teacher as a historical self-expression of the rejection which he was facing.[155] Douglas contends that the inspired individual who speaks in the "Teacher Hymns" "could not have been a later leader of the sect;" and so "it is difficult to avoid the logic" of Jeremias' conclusion that "the Teacher of Righteousness was the author of the 'Teacher Hymns.'"[156] Many of these arguments are dependent upon interpreting the first person singular statements of cols. 10.5–17.37 (our division) as being historically relevant, describing *mutatis mutandis* the unique, autobiographical experiences of their author, the Righteous Teacher.[157]

Due to the specificity and unusual references to physical torture, it is obvious that the Righteous Teacher suffered greatly from the Wicked Priest who may have cut his tongue (16.36)

so he could not talk or teach (16.36–37), bound him with ropes and chains (13.38–39 and 16.36) and dislocated his arm from the socket or humerus (15.5–7). The author seems to be the Righteous Teacher, since he is the quintessential Interpreter of "knowledge in the wonderful mysteries" (10.15).

Scholars have perceived that there is significant information about the life and career of the Righteous Teacher. According to the *Damascus Document*, the Righteous Teacher did not initiate or found the sect; he inherited it and defined and refined its thought and perspective. Scholars tend to agree that following the life of the Righteous Teacher, others performed his, or similar, leadership duties. Some of these leaders could also have composed hymns. Newsom contemplates, for example, "that the 'I' in this group of compositions [10–17] represents the persona of the current leader of the community, perhaps the *Mebaqqer*, rather than the historical Teacher."[158]

The *Pesharim* also preserve abundant evidence about the career of the Righteous Teacher, highlighting his suffering from the wicked priests who controlled the Temple.[159] The suffering he faced can be found mirrored in the *Thanksgiving Hymns*, as has been clarified and is found also in the notes to the following texts and translations. Exceptional is the autobiographical statement that "my arm is bound in chains" (16.36). The comment may indicate that the Righteous Teacher had been chained in the Temple precinct. It is not a generic statement or a well-known trope.

The author of Hymn 22 is most likely the Righteous Teacher. The author imagines himself involved in planting and, indeed is God's chosen Irrigator of the final Garden that restores Eden. As M. Daise astutely observes, 1QH^a 16.4–51a "carries the creation ideas embodied in Psalm 78 and Second Isaiah" so that "the overtones of chthonic creation in 1QH^a 16:4–51 remain strong and enhance the theological texture of the subsequent planting imagery."[160] The author imagines himself to be the Irrigator chosen by God to nourish the final Garden (Eden). The trees in it are the "Trees of Life." They have suffered and were rejected by the evil priests in the Temple, "the Trees of Water." Stunning proof that the Righteous Teacher composed this hymn is the claim that he is "the Irrigator of the garden" (16.5–6) in whose mouth God placed the early or spring rain (16.17). The Righteous Teacher is fond of elevated poetry and paronomasia; note that "early rain" (מורה) and "Teacher" (מורה) are identical in Qumran texts.

Our work supports the research of many Qumranologists, notably Jeremias and Douglas. Almost all of 10.5–17.37 may

[152] S. Tanzer, *The Sages at Qumran: Wisdom in the Hodayot*. See also H. -W. Kuhn, *Enderwartung und gegenwärtiges Heil*, pp. 26–33.

[153] Y. Yadin, *The Message of the Scrolls*, p. 111.

[154] See M. C. Douglas, *Power and Praise in the Hodayot: A Literary Critical Study of 1QH 9:1–18:14*; Douglas, "The Teacher Hymn Hypothesis Revisited" 239–66. Other scholars holding the "Teacher Hymn" Hypothesis include M. O. Wise, *The First Messiah* and S. Hultgren, *From the Damascus Covenant to the Covenant of the Community*, see esp. pp. 409–60.

[155] Douglas, *Power and Praise in the Hodayot: A Literary Critical Study of 1QH 9:1–18:14*; Douglas, "The Teacher Hymn Hypothesis Revisited," 265–66.

[156] Douglas, "The Teacher Hymn Hypothesis Revisited," 266. Douglas' conclusion is built on Jeremias' claims that 1) the "Teacher Hymns" have an earlier provenance than the "Community Hymns," which depend upon a fully instituted social organization (i.e., the *Yaḥad*); and 2) it is unlikely the Qumran Community would have embraced more than one revelatory leader. Both conclusions are tentatively supported by the present research (but the conclusions have not been a focus of concern as we prepared this edition).

[157] Jeremias, *Der Lehrer der Gerechtigkeit*, pp. 175–76; see also M. G. Abegg, Jr., "Who Ascended to Heaven? 4Q491, 4Q427, and the Teacher of Righteousness," in *Eschatology, Messianism, and the Dead Sea Scrolls*, edited by C. E. Evans and P. W. Flint (SDSSRL 1; Grand Rapids, 1997) pp. 61–73; see esp. pp. 70–73.

[158] C. A. Newsom, *The Self as Symbolic Space*, p. 288.

[159] See esp. Charlesworth, *The Pesharim and Qumran History: Chaos or Consensus?* (Grand Rapids, 2002). Also, see the contributions to M. Henze, ed., *Biblical Interpretation at Qumran* (Grand Rapids and Cambridge, 2005).

[160] M. Daise, "Creation Motifs in the Qumran Hodayot," in *Fifty Years*, edited by L. H. Schiffman, E. Tov, and J. C. VanderKam (Jerusalem, 2000) pp. 293–305; the quotations are on pp. 302 and 304.

well be the creation of one author, the Righteous Teacher, as long as we allow the caveat that not all lines, words, and even psalms must originate with him. The columns disclose one strong personality whose autobiographical asides often appear in poetry that is almost prose, are coherently united by themes and vocabulary, and represent an author who employs distinct literary affinities.[161] Among the latter, the most important linguistic evidence seems to be the repetitive use of the phrase "you manifest your might through me" (הגבירכה בי). The author uses the instrumental *beth* to signify "through me;" the Righteous Teacher seems to be the author since he claims to be the singular person through whom God has allowed (or chosen) to make monumental decisions.[162]

The autobiographical phrase "you manifest your might through me" appears only in cols. 10.5 through 13.28:

10.26–27 "and you manifest your might through me against the sons of Adam"

12.9 "and they do not regard me when you strengthened yourself in me."

12.24 "they do not regard [me un]til you strengthen yourself in me and appear to me with your power for perfect lights."

13.17–18 "And in order to show your might in me before the sons of Adam you set apart the Poor One."[163]

13.27–28 "And for the sake of showing [your] mig[ht] in me,[164] and because of their guilt you hid the fountain of discernment and the secret of truth."

These autobiographical reflections categorically reflect the sufferings of the Righteous Teacher. The passages above are within a section that seems to refer to the life and career of the incomparable Righteous Teacher.

In 10.22ff., the author thanks the Lord for guarding "me" from "the snares of the pit, be[cau]se ruthless ones sought my soul." His opponents are "the congregation of Belial" and "do not know that my position (is) because of you." That reflection makes best sense when one imagines that the Righteous Teacher composed the lines.

In 12.9–10, he adds: "For they expelled me from my land like a bird from its nest." That fits perfectly the expulsion of the Righteous Teacher from the Temple (cf. 1Mac 14:44–47).[165] He also laments that "all my companions and my acquaintances" regarded me "like a lost vessel" (12.10). They are certainly the wicked, illegitimate priests, in the Temple, because they are designated as "lying interpreters" who "plotted with Belial" against him, exchanging God's Torah for "smooth things" that are then presented to God's people (12.10–12).

In 12.23–24, the author refers to "my despisers" and those "who are scorning me" and "do not regard [me]." That makes sense of the suffering experienced by the Righteous Teacher, but these words may also be generic.

13.7–14 makes sense only when one perceives that the Righteous Teacher composed the poem. The author thanks God because he "did not abandon me when I lived among an alien people" (the Hasmoneans were not Aaronites), but "helped my life (out) from the pit," so that "the foundation of truth" was encouraged by God "in my heart," and "concealed your Torah in [me] until the Endtime when your salvation shall be revealed to me."

13.27ff. makes best sense when one recognizes that the author is the Righteous Teacher. He alone was allowed to know the secret, as is certain from 1QpHab 7. His opponents, again, are related to Belial (13.28), have "a deceitful tongue" (13.29), and "sounded forth my dispute on the lyre" (13.31–32) so that the author suffers pains "like pains of a woman giving birth" (13.32–33). These asides suggest the suffering of the Righteous Teacher may have occurred in the Temple, who may have served temporarily as high priest in the Temple (see 4Q171 [4QpPs^a] 3).[166] The passage does not so well fit other figures in

---

[161] See Douglas' Table 2: "Distinctive literary affinities among the compositions in 1QH cols 10–15," in *DSD* 6.3 (1999) 254.

[162] I am indebted to Douglas for this insight; *DSD* 6.3 (1999) 253–56. In contrast to him, I have perceived that cols. 16.5 to 17.37 is perhaps the clearest evidence of the Righteous Teacher's self-understanding. He imagines he was chosen by God to restore Eden and is "The Irrigator of the Garden." Douglas thinks that this poem is by the Righteous Teacher but places it in the second category.

[163] The בי is added above the line in 1QH^a and is found in 4Q429 frg. 1 2.1.

[164] The restoration is assured. It was first suggested by Sukenik and was supported by Licht and DJD. Qimron missed the formula; see the *apparatus criticus* to the text.

[165] The text demands that, now that the Jews have chosen Simon the Hasmonean as high priest, no priest may gather an assembly or he would be severely punished (ἔνοχος ἔσται. 1Mac 14:45). The Greek noun means "bound." All priests thus were bound by the new law. Could they also be literally bound or chained? The text does not permit us to imagine that one who deviates from the law will be put to death (that would require the noun "of death"). It is clear that if this law was followed, the Righteous Teacher could no longer have followers who would listen to him; he must leave Jerusalem.

[166] See Stegemann, *Die Entstehung der Qumrangemeinde* (Bonn, 1971) and Stegemann, *The Library of Qumran* (Grand Rapids and Cambridge, 1998) p. 147: "The Qumran Scrolls show that before he founded the Essene union, the Teacher of Righteousness must have been high priest at the Jerusalem Temple, and this as the immediate predecessor of Jonathan the Maccabee, who occupied the office of high priest in the year 152 B.C." Also see, H. Eshel, *The Dead Sea Scrolls and the Hasmonean State* (Grand Rapids and Cambridge, 2008) p. 55.

the Qumran Movement.[167]

It is now evident that, at least most of, the "Teacher Hymns" (*Lehrerlieder*) were probably composed by the Righteous Teacher. We cannot, however, be certain that only those poems or hymns highlighted by Jeremias may go back assuredly to the Righteous Teacher.

The authors behind the "Community Hymns" (*Gemeindelieder*) were members of the Qumran Community. Early hymns, notably the *Self-Glorification Hymn*, were edited and incorporated into the collection.[168] Thus, the *Thanksgiving Hymns* reveal the creativity of numerous authors.

Most scholars recognize a difference between the "Community Hymns" and the "Teacher Hymns" found in columns 10.5 through 17.37. The latter are distinct with vocabulary, theological perspective, and especially autobiographical details.

In summary, scholars have developed a methodology to discern which poems or hymns within the "Teacher Hymns" were the creation of the Righteous Teacher. The procedure was to isolate the passages most likely composed by the Righteous Teacher in the *Thanksgiving Hymns* beginning with the assumption that most leading scholars were correct to find in this scroll the Teacher's own compositions, since the Qumran Movement was a literary movement. The scholars who concur that the *Thanksgiving Hymns* contain, *inter alia*, the literary creativity of the Righteous Teacher constitute a "Who's Who Among Qumranologists," selectively and namely, Bardtke, Brownlee, Bruce, Carmignac, Delcor, Douglas, Dupont-Sommer, Flint,[169] Hogetherp, Howlett, Hyatt, Knibb,[170] Michaud, Milik, Molin, Paul,[171] Puech,[172] Ringgren, Stegemann,[173] Sutcliffe, Sukenik, Tournay, VanderKam,[174] and Ya-

din.[175] Thus, today it is wise to conclude that some poems in the *Thanksgiving Hymns* should be acknowledged to be the creation of the great mind of the Community, the Righteous Teacher. Other psalms of the hymns were composed by Qumranites who wrote in solidarity with the Righteous Teacher, continued his self-understanding, or created new poetic works that reflected their own piety and understanding as the Elect Ones in the Community. Thus, we have been led to perceive that 1QH^a 10.5–17.37 contains poetic compositions by the Righteous Teacher; yet we should allow that they also contain the editorial work of his followers. Moreover, the "Community Hymns" may preserve the Righteous Teacher's ideas, concepts, and expressions in a form that reflect the life of the *Yaḥad*.[176] Nevertheless, we should not read the poetic compositions as if they were intended to be autobiographies.[177] They are hymns of praise in which autobiographical reflections abound.

As we conclude a review of the advances made by experts on the *Thanksgiving Hymns*, additional studies should be cited. In 1988, Puech, who eventually embraced the "Teacher Hymn" and "Community Hymn" dichotomy, prescribed a five-fold division to the *Thanksgiving Hymns* mirroring the Hebrew Psalter.[178] This five-fold division is evident in the extant "Community Hymns" by the use of the *incipit* "for the Instructor" in 5.12, 7.21, 20.7, 25.34, and the same form in the lost columns at the beginning.

In 2010, Harkins revised her 2008 proposal, embracing Puech's five-fold division.[179] She concluded that the "Community Hymns" should be distinguished between the nonsectarian "Community Hymns" (cols. 1–8) and the particularly sectarian "Community Hymns" (cols. 19.6–end).

In 2004, Newsom published a monograph that focused on the rhetorical traits of the *Thanksgiving Hymns* rather than the form-critical methodology which had dominated the compositional question.[180] In 2011, S. Berg analyzed the bipartite divi-

---

[167] Perhaps 9.36 ("that you have strengthened in [me before the s]ons of Adam") may also reflect composition by the Righteous Teacher. With this line we have examined all instances of the phrase "have strengthened me."

[168] It is curious that the *More Psalms of David* (= Pss 151–155) were not incorporated into or edited for the *Thanksgiving Hymns*. Most likely, the Psalter included such psalms.

[169] In one of the most informed introductions to the Dead Sea Scrolls, P. W. Flint states: "In the Teacher Hymns (concentrated in cols. 10–17), the speaker is the movement's early charismatic leader, the Teacher of Righteousness;" Flint, *The Dead Sea Scrolls* (Core Biblical Studies; Nashville, 2013) p. 115.

[170] M. A. Knibb, *The Qumran Community* (Cambridge and New York, 1987) p. 158. Knibb admits that a distinct personality is found in some poems and it is possible the author could be the Righteous Teacher.

[171] A. Paul, *Les manuscrits de la Mer Morte* (Paris: 1997) p. 94.

[172] Puech, *La croyance des Esséniens en la vie future*; see esp. pp. 336–37.

[173] Stegemann, *The Library of Qumran*, p. 107. "The seventeen hymns of the middle part of this manuscript ... were composed by and large by the Teacher of Righteousness himself."

[174] J. C. VanderKam, *The Dead Sea Scrolls Today* (Grand Rapids

and Cambridge, 2010 [2nd ed.]) p. 87; VanderKam, *The Dead Sea Scrolls and the Bible*, p. 109 [with some reservations].

[175] See Y. Yadin, "The Thanksgiving Hymns," in *The Message of the Scrolls*, pp. 105–111. For bibliographical clarifications for the publications of scholars not mentioned in this introduction, see Douglas, *DJD* 6.3 (1999) 240.

[176] Although the use of the first person singular in some of the poems or hymns suggests, perhaps demands, that we imagine the life of the Righteous Teacher, it is also clear that the Community could use "I" as a collective voice, as we know from the principle of solidarity. See esp. J. A. Fitzmyer, *A Guide to the Dead Sea Scrolls* (Grand Rapids and Cambridge, 2008) p. 214.

[177] I appreciate the caution of P. Davies in *Behind the Essenes* (BJS 94; Atlanta, 1987) see esp. p. 97.

[178] É. Puech, "Quelques aspects de la restauration du Rouleau des Hymnes (1QH)," 38–55.

[179] A. K. Harkins, "A New Proposal for Thinking about 1QH^a Sixty Years after its Discovery," pp. 101–34.

[180] Newsom, *The Self as Symbolic Space*.

sion of the *Thanksgiving Hymns* in light of the disparity of epistemology between the "Teacher Hymns" and "Community Hymns."[181]

Scholars are beginning to celebrate the beauty of these poems or hymns. Their enchanting use of symbolic language is often lost until one sees them in poetic arrangement. Some of this poetic arrangement will be presented later in this introduction.

8. History, Qumran Sociology, and Theology

Licht erred in thinking that the *Thanksgiving Hymns* do not preserve history.[182] As with the book of Psalms, the *Thanksgiving Hymns* are examples of poetry that can mirror historical events. We know from studying the *Pesharim* that the Righteous Teacher was hated by the Wicked Priest and suffered from his persecution. The setting of this suffering is conceivably the Temple; it is also clearly in some places outside of Jerusalem, and probably at Qumran.[183] The Righteous Teacher's suffering may be reflected in numerous passages in the *Thanksgiving Hymns* (see the notes to the translation).

Strictly speaking, Jews did not write history as defined by the historiographies of Thucydides (460–? BCE), Herodotus (c. 484–425 BCE), Xenophon (?–355 BCE), and Polybius (c. 200–35 BCE). Not even 1 Maccabees and Josephus' works are "histories" in the classical sense; they contain *Tendenzen* that often reflect theological agendas and even apocalyptic eschatology. Jews were interested in writing histories not for secular purposes, but to explain God's actions in history. Thus, scholars must sift psalms with care in search of remnants of history sprinkled within the *Hodayot*.[184]

Since the psalms and poems in the *Thanksgiving Hymns* were used, most likely, both collectively and privately, this document helped define the Qumran Community and provided sociological and theological borders. Clearly many of the hymns guided reflection on how God has been present in Israel's history and especially in the lives of those who revered the *Thanksgiving Hymns*. As has become clear, this collection contains two types of hymns: Hymns of a Specific Person (originally by the Righteous Teacher) and Hymns of the Community. Among the Qumran compositions, the *Thanksgiving Hymns*, to use the words of D. K. Falk, offer us "the best insight into religious experience," and "open a window onto the emotional content of this way of life and the pull of its paradoxical tensions."[185]

Thus, the hymns were instrumental, as a sociology of knowledge, for developing historical perspectives and community oneness. H. Bardtke rightly noted that the *Thanksgiving Hymns*, shaped beliefs of those who recited them.[186] Newsom wisely perceived that the Qumranites (who were a strict type of the Essenes) used the *Thanksgiving Hymns* to develop a sectarian self-understanding (or subjectivity).[187]

While the *Thanksgiving Hymns* is an original and attractive artistic creation, its beauty is frequently marred by excessive exaggeration and complex metaphors.[188] Most likely, the Righteous Teacher was not interested in appealing to the masses. He intended his poetic creations for his own confessions and reflections or to help shape the Community that was being formed by God for his followers. Perhaps the opaqueness is caused by the secrecy demanded by the sect that is evident in almost all Qumran compositions and placarded by the cryptic texts.

The authors use language with skill; they are gifted linguistically, metaphorically, and symbolically. Some psalms are so convoluted that a literal translation often loses the complex meaning. In places, the images obtain sense only when we recognize paronomasia and the use of rhetoric by the gifted linguist and also imagine the personal history behind the poetry and the opposition between the Community and the priests in Jerusalem. Examples of this imperative are too literal translations; for example, note 1QHᵃ 16.5:

> I [praise Thee, O Lord, for] Thou placest me by a source of flowing streams in a dry ground, and a spring of water in a parched land, and a [d]rink for the garden …[189]

---

[181] S. A. Berg, *Religious Epistemologies in the Dead Sea Scrolls.*

[182] Licht, מגילת ההודיות, pp. 22–25.

[183] See Charlesworth, *The Pesharim and Qumran History: Chaos or Consensus?*

[184] While I do not share P. Davies' pessimism, I do appreciate his cautions. See Davies, "What History Can We Get from the Scrolls, and How?" in *The Dead Sea Scrolls: Texts and Context*, edited by C. Hempel (STDJ 90; Leiden, 2010) pp. 31–46.

[185] D. K. Falk in *Celebrating the Dead Sea Scrolls: A Canadian Collection*, edited by P. W. Flint, J. Duhaime, and K. S. Baek (SBL Early Judaism and Its Literature 30; Atlanta, 2011) p. 281.

[186] Bardtke, "Considérations sur les cantiques de Qumrân," 220–33; see esp. p. 231.

[187] Newsom, "What do Hodayot Do? Language and the Construction of the Self in Sectarian Prayer," pp. 190–286.

[188] See Licht, מגילת ההודיות, p. 10. In the past ten years, however, we have learned that ships plied the Dead Sea. Anchors and ports have been discovered near Qumran; thus, the references to "sailors" are not now so incongruous [see 11.15 ("like sailors in the depths") and 14.25 ("And [I,] I [was] like a sailor in a boat"). Do these images reflect life at Qumran? From there one could see sailors (but not in Jerusalem). Wooden anchors from ports on the western shores of the Dead Sea from the time of the Hasmoneans and Herodians are on display in the Israel Museum. The reference to a fishing net may be a well-known metaphor not related to an author's experience, or an author had been in Galilee or to the Mediterranean coast (11.27, 13.10).

[189] M. Mansoor, *The Thanksgiving Hymns*, p. 153. A similar

This translation misses the metaphorical language. The translator recognizes that the person claims to be a "[d]rink for the garden." If the composer imagines he is only "by a source of flowing streams" how does he provide water for the garden? Most likely, the *beth* of "by a source" is a *beth essentiae*. Thus, the author is the source of water for the "Trees of Life."[190] According to 16.17, the author thanks God for placing in his mouth something "like early rain (כיורה גשם)."[191] The author is thus the one who has been chosen by God to water the "eternal planting" and to nourish "the Trees of Life." Note this translation:

> I th[ank you, O Lo]rd, because you have placed me
> as the spring of streams in a dry land,
> and (as) the pond of water in an arid land,
> and (as) the Irrigator of the garden and of a poo[l of water],
> and (as) a field of planting of cypress and elm with cedar together FOR YOUR GLORY.[192]

Pondering the above translation of 16.5–6[193] one receives the impression that this hymn was composed by the Righteous Teacher. He is the one who has been chosen by God for the final Planting (= God's faithful from Israel). And "the Trees of Life" who suffer are his followers. They are oppressed by "the Trees of Water" who represent "the Wicked Priest" and "the Sons of Darkness."

The author provides a final clue, if any would be needed: The כיורה גשם, "as early rain (16.17),"[194] denotes המורה "the autumn rain." That is paronomasia for מורה הצדק, "the Righteous Teacher." For "autumn rain," the author probably had in mind Joel 2:23 ("And sons of Zion be pleased and rejoice in the LORD your God; for he gives to you the autumn rain moderate-

ly, and he will cause to come down for you the rain, the early rain and the latter rain in the first (month)."[195] Note the Hebrew of Joel 2:23 [citing the Aleppo Codex; underlining for emphasis]:

ובני ציון גילו ושמחו ביהוה אלהיכם כי נתן לכם
את המורה לצדקה ויורד לכם גשם מורה ומלקוש בראשון

Translation demands interpretation, and a translator of the *Thanksgiving Hymns* must imagine living within Qumran.

The relation between the *Rule of the Community*, the compilation that incorporates the laws and rules of the Qumranites, and the *Thanksgiving Hymns*, the collection of psalms and poems that defined their sectarian beliefs, is clarified by focusing on a *terminus technicus* that appears in the Hebrew Bible only in 1 Samuel 2:3 but is highlighted among the Qumran Scrolls. That is, "The God of knowledge" habitually replaced "the God of Israel" for the Qumranites (1QS 3.15).[196] A forged link with the *Rule of the Community* is obvious in the *Thanksgiving Hymns*, since both documents central to Qumran thought contain this exceptional expression. In Hymn 2, "Blessed is the God of Knowledge Who Cleanses Me," we hear the following (arranged poetically):

> [Blessed are you, the God of knowledge,
> for you cleanse me] from hidden (acts) of gu[ilt …]
> (4.21).

The phrase, "the God of knowledge," continues to appear in the *Thanksgiving Hymns*:
> To you, yourself, O God of knowledge,
> (belong) all the works of righteousness
> and the secret of truth.
> But to the sons of Adam
> (belong) the iniquitous deeds and the works of treachery.
> (9.28–29)

> And apart from it there has been nothing,
> and nothing else shall ever be.
> For the God of knowledge has established it,
> and there is not another except him. (20.13–14)

> And what (being) can strengthen itself before you?
> You (are) the God of knowledge, al[l …] (21.32)

---

translation with "beside a fountain of streams" was published by G. Vermes in *The Complete Dead Sea Scrolls in English* (London, 2004 [Revised Edition]) p. 284.

[190] See Charlesworth, "The *Beth Essentiae* and the Permissive Meaning of the Hiphil (Aphel)," in *Of Scribes and Scrolls*, pp. 67–78.

[191] See Charlesworth, "Autumnal Rain [המורה] for the Faithful Followers of the Moreh [המורה]: Joel and the Hodayot," in *Der Mensch vor Gott: Forschungen zum Menschenbild in Bible, antikem Judentum und Koran: Festschrift für Hermann Lichtenberger*, edited by U. Mittmann-Richert, F. Avemarie, and G. S. Oegema (Neukirchen-Vluyn, 2003) pp. 193–210.

[192] See Charlesworth, "An Allegorical and Autobiographical Poem by the Moreh haṣ-Ṣedeq (1QH 8:4-11)," in *ShaTalmon*, pp. 295–307.

[193] Puech translates 16.5 correctly; "tu as fait de moi une source de flots dans une terre aride" and rightly attributes it to the Righteous Teacher. Puech, *La croyance des Esséniens en la vie future*, vol. 2, pp. 339 and 346.

[194] The early rain usually is gentle and comes in late October and lasts until December.

[195] Note *God's Word Translation* of 1995: "People of Zion, be glad and find joy in the LORD your God. The LORD has given you the Teacher of Righteousness. He has sent the autumn rain and the spring rain as before".

[196] For discussion of "the God of knowledge" as a technical term, see H. W. Morisada Rietz, "Identifying Compositions and Traditions of the Qumran Community: The *Songs of the Sabbath Sacrifice* as a Test Case," pp. 27–52.

Blessed (are) you, O God of knowledge, that y[ou] established
[…] and thus you called upon your servant for your sake.
(22.34–35)

According to my knowledge,
I have announced in the assembly of your [Holy Ones:]
"Great and wonderful (is) God."
[For yo]u (are) the God of knowledge. (Composite Text of 25.31–33)

Cause to be heard and say:
[Blessed (be) the God of knowledge
who stretches out] the heavens by his power,
and all their thoughts [he] es[tablished by] his strength,
[creating] the earth by his migh[t]. (Composite Text of 26.42–43)

It is also fundamentally important to note, briefly, the deep connections between the *Thanksgiving Hymns* and the psalms in the concluding columns of the *Rule of the Community*. In these concluding psalms we confront, as in the *Thanksgiving Hymns,* many Qumranic terms, phrases, and concepts, including election, morning and evening prayers (1QS 10.10), the solar calendar, and God's chosen. The Holy Ones are joined with "the sons of heaven" (1QS 11.7–8). The Community is portrayed as "a House of Holiness" and "the eternal plant" (11.8). Anthropomorphic language defines both documents; note in particular the following: "the offering of the utterance of my lips" (1QS 10.14), "the light of my heart" (1QS 11.3), "a light (comes) into my heart from his wondrous mysteries" (1QS 11.5).[197] This Jewish Community has been given the secret of the mystery; note "the mystery of what shall occur and is occurring" (1QS 11.3–4). The psalms in the *Rule of the Community* share the same joyful attitude that defines the *Thanksgiving Hymns*. Constant joy is directed to God (1QS 10.14, 17).

Most importantly, the psalms in the *Rule of the Community* and the *Thanksgiving Hymns* emphasize the human need to confess iniquities and transgressions (1QS 10.11).[198] God's judgment is unearned and full of wonder (1QS 10.11, 18, 20; 11.2, 10–12). It is God who judges (1QS 10.13, 10.16);[199] and judgment is his alone. Authors stress continually that to God alone belongs salvation and judgment: "By his righteousness he shall blot out my transgression" (1QS 11.3; also see 11.6, 12). Note the seven-fold emphasis on human sin and unworthiness and upon God's gracious mercy and gift of unmerited sal-

vation in the *Rule of the Community* 11.9–22 (which constitute an *inclusio*):[200]

   (1) the human cannot establish his righteousness (11.10)
   (2) to God belongs judgment (11.10, 12, 14)
   (3) "the mercy of God (is) my salvation" (11.12)
   (4) God "rescues my soul from the pit" (11.13)
   (5) God "atones for all my iniquities" (11.14)
   (6) God "cleanses me of Adam's sin (11.14–15)
   (7) "Blessed are you, my God" (11.15)

Many leading experts in Christian Origins have recognized in these two fundamental scrolls that represent the main perspectives of the Qumranites – the *Rule of the Community* and the *Thanksgiving Hymns* – a foreshadowing of the concept of salvation by faith through grace, which from Luther to Käsemann was deemed to be the heart of Paul's theology.[201] This insight leads us to the theological ideas found in the *Thanksgiving Hymns.*

Much has been written about the numerous theological aspects of the *Thanksgiving Hymns* in the past 60 years.[202] This section will serve only as a basic overview of the more substantial theological themes represented in the *Thanksgiving Hymns.* Thus, we may now review the theological ideas and beliefs in the *Thanksgiving Hymns*. The thoughts, concepts, and beliefs are arranged in the following alphabetical order:

Alteration of God's Words
Angelology
Anthropology
Astounding Suffering
Astrology
Calendar
Cosmology
Creation and Wisdom
Determinism, Dualism, and Predestination
Determinism and Petition
God
Intermediary
Judgment
Knowledge
Messiah
Perception of the Endtime (Eschatology)
Resurrection
Revelation
Righteousness of God, Covenant, and Law

---

[197] Such anthropocentric language defines other early Jewish hymns; note the *Prayer of Manasseh*: "now I bend the knee of my heart."

[198] For text and translation of the *Rule of the Community*, see Qimron and Charlesworth in PTSDSSP 1.

[199] Contrast the *Parables of Enoch* in which the Son of Man, Enoch, is the eschatological Judge.

[200] In the *Rule of the Community*, the thought is shifted in 11.9 to Adam's sin (cf. *4Ezra*, according to which all humans inherit from Adam a *cor malignum*). Thus, 11.9 was created to share an *inclusio* with 11.20–22.

[201] The consensus on Paul's "central thought" has broken; see J. C. Beker, *Paul the Apostle: The Triumph of God in Life and Thought* (Philadelphia, 1980).

[202] See esp. H. Ringgren, *The Faith of Qumran: Theology of the Dead Sea Scrolls.*

Universalism

As we study the poetic reflections collected into these theological categories, let us perceive that they are paradigmatically related. They flow sometimes separately and often together to create a theological celebration of thankfulness. We all have learned through thought and experience that poetry should be appreciated and not analyzed; and we may harm the poetic imagination by seeking to find coherency or a system. In juxtaposing ostensibly contradictory ideas, the poets create a dynamic that invites us to engage life and history through challenging insights that seem to clash as they do in our own experiences.

Alteration of God's Words. The authors and editors of the *Thanksgiving Hymns* intermittently state that God's Word must not be altered; that polemic suggests that there are some who are altering the words of Scripture. Note these passages:

And all who know you do not *alter your words*,
because you are righteous,
and all your elect ones (are) truthful. (6.26)

But I know that in your hand (is) the inclination of every spirit [and all] its [activit]y you established before you created him. And how can anyone *alter your words*? (7.26–27)

The verb "to alter" when used with "words" demands changing some written work, most likely a manuscript that is determinative for thought and action. The possessive "your" in these lines refers to God; thus there should be no doubt that "your words" mean the words in Torah; they are being "altered." The words "all who know you do not alter your words" is a polemic against those who do not know God and God's Word and so alter God's words. These people are not God's "elect ones" and are not "truthful" (6.26).

The Qumran polemic against the Temple cult – and especially the copying scribes in the Temple *scriptorium* – becomes obvious. In 6.19–33, Hymn 7, "I Thank the Lord for the Heart of Discernment," the author castigates "the men of deceit" (6.25; probably the non-Aaronic priests in the Temple) who are not allowed to draw near to God and do not experience God's holy spirit, because they cannot distinguish between good and evil, "disobey" God's "edict," (6.25) and "alter" God's "words."

The Hasmoneans, the dreaded enemies of the Qumranites, were altering the texts of Scripture, as has become evident.[203] Now, we have found amazing evidence of a polemic against their changing of texts that all Jews deemed sacred.

What is remarkable is the fact that the Qumranites appreciated and used many text types of the books that became the Hebrew Scriptures. How then should we understand their attitude to the alteration of God's words? The *Pesharim* indicate that Qumranites also altered the words of Scripture; but they make it clear that they alone are guided by the Holy Spirit and were given secret knowledge.

Most likely, the Qumranies knew many versions of the biblical books, but they were ancient manuscripts they inherited. They appreciated that diversity even though at times they seem close to a fundamentalist understanding of Scripture. That they did not receive one text type cannot be a point of lamentation; rather, the secrets of God are revealed only to the Qumranites and they have a sophisticated method to prove their points. If they knew that a scribe in the Temple, especially a Hasmonean who is quintessentially one of the Sons of Darkness, altered the words of Scripture to support their own actions, then it would be soundly condemned.

Angelology. The Qumranites joined with the angels in praising God. That is the meaning of being a Qumranite and living in the *Yaḥad*. A member, one of the "Many," was born a "Son of Light" and joined in praise with angels in the *Yaḥad*. As Licht perceived, through membership in the *Yaḥad*, the Elect join a choir that joins "the choirs of heaven." That is, the *Yaḥad*, as a unity and a whole, defines itself as belonging with the lot of the Angels of the Presence.[204] For decades, the choice of words by M. Delcor has echoed in many lecture halls:

On peut parler d'une sorte de communion mystique entre les sectaires et les anges, dès ici-bas, ce qui se conçoit bien si la Communauté est une sorte de Paradis, une espèce d'antichambre du ciel.[205]

Anthropology.[206] As Lictenberger observed long ago, the *Thanksgiving Hymns* come into central focus when we explore the Qumran concept of the human.[207] The "Community Hymns" depict humans in an overwhelmingly pessimistic light, describing them with earth metaphors (עפר "dust," חמר "clay," מגבל מים "mixed water") and defining them as possessing nega-

---

[203] Perhaps the last condemnation refers to the deliberate alteration of Scripture to support Hasmonean policy (as most likely reflected in the fragment that preserves Deut 27:4).

[204] See Licht, "The Doctrine of the Thanksgiving Scroll," p. 101.

[205] M. Delcor, *Les Hymnes de Qumran*, p. 41.

[206] See the superb study by Newsom, "Flesh, Spirit, and the Indigenous Psychology of the *Hodayot*," in *Prayer and Poetry in the Dead Sea Scrolls*, pp. 339–54. Note esp.: "The *Hodayot* express the psychological anguish caused by the persistent presence of the perverted spirit and its attempt to 'rule over' the speaker" (p. 353).

[207] Lichtenberger: "Als zentral für die Frage nach dem Menschenbild ist die Liedersammlung der *Hodajot* heranzuziehend"; Lichtenberger, *Studien zum Menschenbild in Texten der Qumrangemeinde* (SUNT 15; Göttingen, 1980) p. 27.

tive attributes (עוון "iniquity," חטאה "sin").[208]3 For example, 1QH[a] 5.30–32 depicts the human as a "spirit of flesh" (רוח בשר; 5.30) who is "a form of dust and mixed water" (מבנה עפר ומגבל מים; 5.32) whose foundation is "g[uilt and si]n" (א[שמה וחט[אה) as well as "shameful nakedness" (ערות קלון; 5.32). Similar are the anthropological claims of 1QH[a] 18.5–8, which describes אדם as "(only) dirt." Adam,[209] the human, is "[from dust]" and "to dust he returns (18.5–6). This very well-known biblical theologoumenon is different from its deprecatory use in 1QH[a] 4.31–32 in which an author speaks of "[the transgress]ions of my works and the bewilderment of my heart" as well as the wallowing of the author in impurity (4.31).[210]

This deplorable and frail state of human nature appears in the "Community Hymns" to separate the human from the divine. For example, because of their earthly origins and sinful predication, humans cannot discern the divine will but must depend upon the graciousness and righteousness of God to provide knowledge of the mysteries and wonders (e.g., 1QH[a] 9.22–29, 18.3–7, 19.4–13).[211] This epistemological dependence upon God is often achieved by means of the intervention of spirits (e.g., 1QH[a] 4.29, 6.22, 8.20–21, 20.11–12) and being within the ברית (e.g., 1QH[a] 4.27, 6.13, 8.25, 18.30).[212]

Unlike the "Community Hymns," the "Teacher Hymns" depict the human as being wretched not due to his earthy origins or sinfulness. It is primarily due to his being oppressed by enemies (e.g., 1QH[a] 11.38–39, 13.7–14, 15.4–6) or suffering under the powers of Sheol and Belial (e.g., 1QH[a] 11.20–34, 15.6–8, 16.29–17.7). In the "Teacher Hymns," occasionally earth metaphors are chosen to describe the human (1QH[a] 11.25, 12.30), but in these hymns the perspective of the human condition does not reach the negative connotations seen in the "Community Hymns." Rather than being depicted as flawed and sinful, the human in the "Teacher Hymns" is depicted as the victim of persecution and terror (e.g., 1QH[a] 12.34, 15.6–9),

as a "disgrace and mockery" (1QH[a] 10.11–12), "in distress" (1QH[a] 11.8), and as one afflicted with suffering (1QH[a] 16.27–28). Through the work of God, the author is rescued from affliction and suffering (e.g., 1QH[a] 10.33–35, 13.7–15, 17.7–13), given unmediated insight (e.g., 1QH[a] 12.28–30, 15.29–30), and chosen by God to communicate and teach this knowledge (e.g., 1QH[a] 1QH[a] 10.15–17).

Astounding Suffering. Running through the "Teacher Hymns" is an expression of abject suffering that seems real and experiential, not metaphorical and imagined. Note especially the laments in 16.27–38:[213]

[And I] (am) a (temporary) abode with sicknesses.
And (my) heart is aff[licte]d with afflictions.

And I am as an abandoned man in agony [and sighin]g.
There is no shelter for me.

For my affl[ict]ion produces bitterness.
And a severe pain which (cannot) be contained in
    [my] b[ones.]

[And there was a tur]moil over me,
as those who descend into Sheol.

And with the dead it seeks my spirit.
For [my] life reached the pit.

[And in agony] my soul faints away day and night without rest.
And it shoots forth as a burning fire withheld in my bones.

For days, its flame consumes by consuming power for the endtimes,
And by destroying flesh until appointed times.

And the breakers fly over me;
And my soul is decaying within me to destruction,
Because my protection ceases from my body.

And my heart is poured out like water.
And my flesh melts like wax.
And the protection of my loins is turned to fear.

And my arm is broken from its socket.
[And it is impossib]le to lift (my) hand.

And my foot is caught in a chain.
And my knees wobble like water.
So it is impossible to put forth a footstep,
and there is no tread for the sound of my feet.

And the strength of my arm is bound in chains

---

[208] Borrowing the term from P. Berger, Newsom refers to the theological anthropology of the *Thanksgiving Hymns* as a "masochistic theodicy." See *The Self as Symbolic Space*, pp. 217–21. Licht calls humanity's sinfulness "an almost pathological abhorrence of human nature," Licht, *IEJ* 6 (1956). See Mansoor, *The Thanksgiving Hymns*, p. 59.

[209] The influence of "Adam" is lost by those who translate the noun as "human." For reflections on "Adam" in the *Hodayot*, see C. H. T. Fletcher-Louis, *All the Glory of Adam: Liturgical Anthropology in the Dead Sea Scrolls* (STDJ 42; Leiden, 2002).

[210] See esp. Lichtenberger's superb study of anthropology in the Hodayot: *Studien zum Menschenbild in Texten der Qumrangemeinde*, see esp. pp. 58–92.

[211] The contrast between the lowly sinfulness of the human and the righteousness of God in the "Community Hymns" was referred to by H.-W. Kuhn as "Niedrigkeitsdoxologiens." See his *Enderwartung und gegenwärtiges Heil*, pp. 26–33.

[212] For more on this, see Berg, *Religious Epistemologies in the Dead Sea Scrolls*, chapter 4.

[213] Poetic arrangement demands different punctuation.

That cause (me) to stumble.

And the tongue you had strengthened in my mouth is no
longer retrievable,
So it is impossible to raise (my) voice
to allow (my) disciples to h[e]ar,
to give life to the spirit of those who stumble,
and to sustain the weary one (through) speech.
The flow of my lips was silenced from horrors.

The authors of these compositions express their own self-
understanding by choosing three nouns that mean "poor." Each
noun must be translated with a different English word or the
links between translation and text are lost. אביון has been translated "the Poor One" in 10.34, 13.18, 13.20, and 26.27 [low-
ercase]. Likewise אביונים is rendered "the Poor Ones" in 2.27,
11.26, and 13.24. עני is represented by "the Needy One" in
9.38, 10.36, 13.15, and 13.16. רש is represented by "the Wretched One" in 10.36, 13.16, 13.22.

Obviously, these authors tend to refer to themselves as "the
Poor Ones" and identify with "the Poor One," "the Needy
One," and "the Wretched One." Following their spiritual ge-
nius, the Righteous Teacher, who may have served as High
Priest in the Temple and was certainly revered by his followers
as the only one to whom God had revealed all the mysteries of
God's Word (1QpHab 7), they have forsaken Jerusalem, the
Temple, sumptuous food, and luxurious homes for a life of po-
verty and wretchedness in the hot wilderness beside a foul-
smelling Dead Sea.

אביון, "the Poor One" appears, except for 26.27, only in the
"Teacher Hymns" (10.5–17.37). אביונים, "the Poor Ones" appear in the "Teacher Hymns" (see 13.24) and the "Community
Hymns" (the other sections; see 2.27). עני, "the Needy One" is
present only in the "Teacher Hymns," except for 9.38 in which
it mostly means "the Needy" Ones as it is parallel with "the
Perfect Ones of the Way." רש, "the Wretched One," appears
only in the "Teacher Hymns" (10.36; 13.16, 22). Apparently,
his followers were understandably comfortable with referring
to themselves as "the Poor" and "the Poor Ones," but not with
"the Wretched One."

Crucial for an understanding of the origin of the concept of
"the Poor One," "the Poor Ones," "the Needy One," and "the
Wretched One" are passages in column 13. All three words for
"poor" appear in it. אביון is noticeable in lines 18 and 20.
אביונים is present in line 24. עני is highlighted in lines 15 and
16. And רש is found in lines 16 and 22. No other column or
hymn has each noun. Thinking of Daniel, an author, most likely the Righteous Teacher, inscribed this autobiographical reflection:

And you saved the soul of the Needy One in the den of
lions, which sharpen their tongues as a sword. But you, O
my God, you shut tight their teeth lest they tear apart the
soul of the Needy One and the Wretched One. And you
withdrew their tongues like a sword into its sheath.
(13.15–17)

The use of the Hebrew nouns for "the Poor One" (13.18–24),
the "Needy One" (13.15–16), and "the Wretched One" (13.16–
22) is amassed in two hymns: Hymn 17 ("I Thank the Lord for
not Abandoning Me" in 13.7–21) and Hymn 18 ("Blessed is
the Lord for His Righteousness to the Orphan" in 13.22–15.8).
These Hymns appear among the "Teacher Hymns" (10.5–
17.37).

Most gifted Qumran specialists will find the conclusion
transparent: The Righteous Teacher imagined himself as "the
Poor One," "the Needy One," and "the Wretched One," and his
followers, applying the Semitic principle of solidarity, identified with him and continued this designation. Some Qumranites apparently referred to themselves as "the Poor One" and
most all his followers identified themselves, using their method
of interpreting history in light of living prophecy (emphasized
in the Pesharim), as "The Poor Ones."

Astrology. The interest of the Qumranites in the heavenly
bodies and their obedience to God's commands is evident
throughout the *Thanksgiving Hymns.* The best example is in
col. 20:

For the Instructor, thanksgivings and prayer to prostrate
oneself, and continually petition from the endtime (of the
day) to the endtime (of the night when) light comes out
from [its] domin[ion] at the periods of the day according
to its order, (and) according to the statutes of the great
light. When the evening turns and the light goes out at the
beginning of the dominion of darkness according to the
appointed time of night and its period at the turn of the
morning. And at the endtime (of the night) when it is
gathered to its domicile from before the light when the
night goes out and the day comes in. (And) continually in
all the births of time and the bases of endtime, and (during) the period of seasons in their courses with their signs
according to all their dominion (which is) faithfully established from the mouth of God and the fixed times of existence.

Obviously, any interest in astronomy results from theological
concerns and the need to pray and praise God and to provide
for festivals according to the solar calendar. The "great light" is
clearly the sun. What is missing is any reference to astrology.
One might have expected some asides to astrology in the poems or hymns, since horoscopes were found among the Qumran Scrolls (4Q561, 4Q186); and there is now abundant evi-

dence that before 70 CE some Jews turned to astrology to explain the seemingly inexplicable.[214]

Calendar. The following translations render the numerous Hebrew words for time consistently; the nouns are thus chosen: "appointed time, season, festival," "perpetual," "forever, everlasting," "eternity, eternal," "eternal acts," "Endtime, time, endtime," and "fixed times" (for the Hebrew nouns, see *Chart 6: The Consistency Chart for the Translations*). The solar calendar seems presupposed by the authors of the *Thanksgiving Hymns*. Column 9 is a passage that is important for the Community's concept of set times, periods of time, and festivals:

> Everything is engraved in your presence with the imprint of memory for all perpetual times, and the periods of the number of years of eternity in all their appointed times. (9.25–26)

Referring, *inter alia*, to this passage, S. Talmon shared this valid conclusion: "The proliferation of calendrical works and calendar-related statements attests to the dependence of the *Yaḥad's* messianic-millenarian expectations upon a foreordained sequence of 'divine(ly established) periods' in history."[215] The authors of these hymns or poems frequently refer to their own time as the "Endtime." The solar calendar also is demanded by the prayers that shaped Qumran thought and life.[216]

Cosmology. The *Thanksgiving Hymns* witnesses to a trifurcated universe: the heavens, the earth, and Sheol. Note this passage (arranged poetically):

> [The ho]st of the upper regions you shall judge in the upper regions,
> And the dwellers of earth (you shall judge) upon the earth.
> And also [in Sheo]l below you shall ju[d]ge. (25.13–14)

The location of "the upper regions" and the "earth" is clear. What is ambiguous is the place of Sheol; it is "below." Is Sheol beneath the "globe of the earth" or beneath the surface of the earth? Most likely, the deceased are placed beneath the ground of the earth in chambers; this is strikingly visible today when one enters, for example, the tombs of those from Adiabene, the chambers beneath the garden of the *École biblique*, and Herod's family tomb.[217]

Creation and Wisdom.[218] The identity of God as Creator of all things is a central theme within the *Thanksgiving Hymns*.[219] Creation imagery appears in 1QH^a 16.5–28 in which the author appears to draw upon biblical texts in order to describe how God has established him as a source of inspiration to his community.[220] In the "Community Hymns" in particular, God is depicted as the one who has created (ברא) and established (כון) all things in order to announce God's own glory (1QH^a 5.24–30). In column 9, the author explicitly describes creation, mentioning the spreading of the heavens (ואתה נטיתה שמים; 9.11), the establishing of spirits, angels, and luminaries (9.12–15), and the shaping of the earth and the seas (אתה בראתה ארץ בכוחכה; ימים; 9.15–16).

In the *Thanksgiving Hymns*, creation serves not only as a witness to God's glory and the greatness of his divine acts (e.g., 1QH^a 5.28),[221] but also acts as a witness to God's eternal will and ordering of the cosmos.[222] For example, the author of column 9 affirms that God created the cosmos according to the mysteries (לרזיהם; 9.13, 15) and established their fixed times before they came into being. As S. Thomas notes, the word פלא "wonder," is often employed to celebrate the order of God's creation (see 1QH^a 5.19; 9.23; 19.13).

Wisdom motifs are sparse in the "Teacher Hymns;" but they are prevalent in the "Community Hymns" as God's creative activity is explained using wisdom motifs.[223] God's mysteries are tied to the divine order of creation established by God and God's divine wisdom.[224] Thus, God's creative act is linked to the mysterious order which structures the cosmos.[225]

ploring Ancient Jewish Tombs Near Jerusalem's Walls (Grand Rapids and Cambridge, 2013).

[218] See Lange, *Weisheit und Prädestination*. Also see the contributions to *Wisdom and Apocalypticism in the Dead Sea Scrolls and in the Biblical Tradition*, edited by F. García Martínez (BETL 168; Leuven, 2003).

[219] See M. E. Gordley, "Creation Imagery in Qumran Hymns and Prayers," *JJS* 59 (2008) 252–72.

[220] See esp. M. A. Daise, "Creation Motifs in the Qumran Hodayot," pp. 293–305.

[221] Mansoor, *The Thanksgiving Hymns*, p. 54; see also M. E. Gordley, "Creation Imagery in Qumran Hymns and Prayers," 253–72, see esp. pp. 266–69.

[222] Mansoor, *The Thanksgiving Hymns*, p. 54–55; Qimron, *The Dead Sea Scrolls*, p. xxvii.

[223] J. Kampen makes numerous references to the use of Wisdom in the *Hodayot*, although his attention is on the specifically Qumran Wisdom Texts; see his *Wisdom Literature* (Grand Rapids and Cambridge, 2011).

[224] M. J. Goff, "Reading Wisdom at Qumran: 4QInstruction and the Hodayot," 263–88, see pp. 272–74.

[225] For further reflections see Tanzer, *The Sages at Qumran: Wisdom in the Hodayot*; M. J. Goff, "Reading Wisdom at Qumran"; H. Antonissen, "Die weisheitliche Terminologie in den 'Hodayot': Ein kontextbezogener Überblick," *Leqach* 7 (2007) 1–15.

[214] For a discussion, see Charlesworth, "Jewish Astrology in the Talmud, Pseudepigrapha, the Dead Sea Scrolls, and Early Palestinian Synagogues," *HTR* 70 (1977) 183–200; Charlesworth, "Jewish Interest in Astrology During the Hellenistic and Roman Period," in *Aufstieg und Niedergang der Römischen Welt*, edited by W. Haase (Berlin, New York, 1987) Band II.20.2, pp. 926–56, 6 Plates.

[215] S. Talmon in *BDSS*, vol. 2, p. 38.

[216] See D. Olson in *BDSS*, vol. 2, pp. 308–10.

[217] For a discussion of the architecture of such tombs, see Charlesworth, ed., *The Tomb of Jesus and His Family? Ex-*

Determinism, Dualism, and Predestination.[226] The dualism that is defined in the *Rule of the Community* 3.13–4.26 is only reflected, periodically, in the *Hodayot*. In 1QH[a] 5.20, an author refers to "the ways of truth and the works of evil." Light and darkness are often juxtaposed. More often, the usual biblical references to the wicked and the righteous define the poetic compositions. In 12.13–14, "every thought of Belial" is contrasted with "the thought of your heart" (God's heart). The former is to be despised, the latter "is established for perpetuity." Note these examples of dualism; they are arranged poetically and from the Composite Text (arranged poetically):

(With) *darkness* I am clothed,
And my tongue cleaves to (my) palate,
Since I am surrounded by the disasters of their heart,

And their inclination appeared to me as bitterness,
And the *light* of my face is *darkened* into *gloominess*,
And my majesty is turned into *blackness*. (13.33–34)

[... and] the fountain of *light* will become an eternal source. (14.20)

And (being) an (object of) scorn for my adversaries
(Becomes) to me a crown of glory,
And my stumbling (becomes) an eternal strength,
Because through [your] insight [you have allowed me to know],
And through your glory my *light* has appeared (or shined).

For *light* from *darkness*
You allowed to shine toward agony. (17.25–27)

When the evening turns
And the *light* goes out
At the beginning of the dominion of *darkness*
According to the appointed time of night
And its period at the turn of the morning.

And at the endtime (of the night)
When it is gathered to its domicile
From before the *light*
When the night goes out
And the day comes in. (20.8–10)

[And those perverted of heart ...]ˈ you lead back
(So as) to enter into covenant with you,
And to stand [before you in the judgments of witnesses]

In the establishment of eternity for the perfect *light*[227] unto perpetuity
And unto *darkness* [... withou]t end
And the endtimes of unfa[thomable ...] peace [...]. (21.14–16)

Even though, almost always, an author mentions "darkness" in proximity to the word "light," in many ways the light-darkness motif in the *Thanksgiving Hymns* seems closer to the Hebrew Scriptures than the dualistic paradigm developed in 1QS 3.13–4.26. We must allow, however, for the truncated manuscripts we possess; note, for example, the fragmentary column 23:

[...]
your *light*, and you caused to stand from of ol[d ...]
your *light* without ceasi[ng ...].
For with you (there is) *light* for [an eternal source ...] (23.1–4)

And there is no return of *darkness* because
[...] and *light* you have revealed and without returning [...]. (23.31–33)

No author of a psalm in the *Thanksgiving Hymns* mentions an "Angel of Light" or an "Angel of Darkness." There are no "Sons of Light" or "Sons of Darkness," and no one "walks in the light." These *termini technici* should not be expected. We should assume dualism would be only mirrored in a collection of psalms.

Because God established all of creation to be a divinely created order, it follows that all has been foreordained by God's divine will.[228] This determinism appears frequently throughout the *Thanksgiving Hymns*.[229] God as the Creator has established not only all times and things (1QH[a] 5.24–31, 7.16, 20.10–14); he has also created the righteous one: "and from the womb you have established him for the appointed time of (your) will" (ומרחם הכינותו למועד רצון; 7.28). The author of 1QH[a] 9.9–15 depicts God establishing eternity by God's wisdom, such that "before you created them, you knew all their works for everlasting eternity, and [without you not] any thing is done" ובטרם בראתם ידעתה כול מעשיהם לעולמי עד ו[מבלעדיכה לא] יעשה (9.9–10). This thought is continued in 9.22, where the author states that "according to your wi[l]l, everything [shall h]appen, and without you nothing is done."[230] A similar idea is found in 1QH[a] 18. In this column, the author declares that outside the will of God (ו[מ]בלעדיכה אל) nothing occurs (18.4, 11) and then attributes this to God's unequaled power (ואין עמכה בכוח ואין לנגד כבודכה; 18.12).

---

[227] Lit. "for light of lights."
[228] Holm-Nielsen, *Hodayot*, pp. 277–82.
[229] See M. Broshi, "Predestination in the Bible and the Dead Sea Scrolls," in *BDSS*, vol. 2, pp. 235–46.
[230] E. H. Merrill, *Qumran and Predestination: A Theological Study of the Thanksgiving Hymns*, pp. 24–32.

[226] See E. H. Merrill, *Qumran and Predestination: A Theological Study of the Thanksgiving Hymns* (Leiden, 1975) and Lange, *Weisheit und Prädestination: Weisheitliche Urordnung und Prädestination im den Textfunden von Qumran*.

This determinism acts not only as witness to God's eternal power but also as an explanation pertaining to the suffering of the author. B. Nitzan rightly notes that many of the psalms or poems seem to depict this suffering as a test that is the result of God's predetermined edict (e.g., 1QH^a 12.32–34, 17.23–25).[231] God is portrayed as the creator of "the righteous and the wicked" (כי אתה בראתה צדיק ורשע; 1QH^a 12.39) and, as such, has determined their activity such that the ones elected by God are given insight, while the doers of wickedness will be destroyed forever (1QH^a 6.19–27).[232] In 1QH^a column 7, the wicked ones are described as having been created by God "and from the womb you designated them for the day of killing" (ומרחם הקדשתם ליום הרגה; 7.30).[233] In this way, the paths of both the righteous and the wicked are determined by God's created order (e.g., 1QH^a 7.26–27); the righteous are destined for goodness in the Endtime (e.g., 1QH^a 20.24) while the wicked are destined for judgment (e.g., 1QH^a 7.38–39).[234] Ringgren rightly perceived that a "double predestination" appears in the *Thanksgiving Hymns*; the righteous are created for the covenant and blessings, but the wicked are created for God's wrath.[235]

Iranian influence on Palestinian Jewish language and thought is widely accepted and apparent in the Achaemenid Empire (c. 550 BCE to 330 BCE) and in the Parthian Empire (c. 250 BCE to 224 CE).[236] Iranian influence at Qumran was seen by R. E. Brown and M. Mansoor.[237] Evidence of Iranian influence appears in the *Thanksgiving Hymns*. The human is controlled by two cosmic spirits (cf. 1QS 3–4).[238]

More recently, J. M. Silverman has argued that a more refined methodology and a detailed study of Iranian thought (not just Zoroastrianism) are needed. He calls for "a new paradigm founded on the apocalyptic hermeneutic and complex oral-literate interactions situated within the Achaemenid and later

Parthian contexts."[239] The result is fundamentally important for a better perception of Iranian influence on "the so-called sectarian documents among the Dead Sea Scrolls." Additional studies are demanded. For example, we need a better understanding of "the gradual interiorization of literacy in the Persian (and Hellenistic) periods, how this related to the emergence of the apocalypse, and how this interacted with the Persian bureaucracy and its heirs."[240] Silverman seems optimistic that it will become much clearer how Iranian influences did impact Qumran language and thought. That possibility becomes increasingly apparent when one recognizes the growing evidence that Iranian influence began during the Exile and that Parthians did invade Palestine in 40 BCE, leaving their mark on the western littoral of the Dead Sea, near Qumran, and that Parthian infantry probably entered Jerusalem and may have reached the Upper City. This invasion is reflected in the *Parables of Enoch*.[241]

Determinism and Petition. How do the *Thanksgiving Hymns* reflect, or deal with, the tension between determinism and petitionary prayer? How can one who believes that they are born to be a Son of Light petition God for intercession and salvation? Schuller highlighted the issue;[242] actually, four years earlier, I. Knohl perceived the problem and argued that the Qumran doctrine of predestination "does not allow for petitional prayer in the usual sense of the word." The Elect one may only ask God "to deepen and complete the kindness which God has freely given." Thus, for Knohl, the petition in 1QH^a 8.29–30 is actually an author's request that God "fulfill that which God had destined and decreed for God's chosen one."[243] Perhaps a more refined question is "Did the author of a hymn in the *Thanksgiving Hymns* consider an inconsistency between determinism and petition?" Perhaps such concepts are more reflective of post-Enlightenment western desire for systematic coherency than of early Jewish thought that was apocalyptic.[244]

Clearly, the *Thanksgiving Hymns* are defined by praise and blessing, not petition. In many ways, the Community substitu-

[231] Nitzan, *Qumran Prayer and Poetry*, pp. 326–27.

[232] M. Philonenko, "Sur les expression 'élus de vérité,' 'élus de justice' et 'Elu de justice et de fidélité,'" in *The Words of a Wise Man's Mouth are Gracious (Qoh 10,12)*, edited by M. Perani (Berlin, 2005) pp. 73–76.

[233] For more on the determinism in col. 7, see J. A. Hughes, *Scriptural Allusions and Exegesis in the Hodayot* (STDJ 59; Leiden and Boston, 2006) pp. 63–95.

[234] Mansoor, *The Thanksgiving Hymns*, p. 56.

[235] See Ringgren, *Faith of Qumran*, pp. 106–07.

[236] See, e.g., S. Shaked, "The Myth of Zurvan: Cosmology and Eschatology," in *Messiah and Christos*, edited by I. Gruenwald, *et al.* (TSAJ 32; Tubingen, 1992) pp. 219–36.

[237] R. E. Brown, "The Qumran Scrolls and the Johannine Gospel and Epistles," in *SNT*, pp. 57–58. I emphasized Iranian influence in documents composed at Qumran in *John and Qumran*.

[238] See the chapters by J. R. Levison and E. Qimron in *BDSS*, pp. 169–94 [Levison] and 195–202 [Qimron].

[239] J. M. Silverman, *Persepolis and Jerusalem: Iranian Influence on the Apocalyptic Hermeneutic* (Library of Hebrew Bible 558; New York, 2012) p. 230.

[240] Silverman, *Persepolis and Jerusalem*, p. 229.

[241] See the discussions in *Parables of Enoch: A Paradigm Shift*, edited by Charlesworth and D. L. Bock (London, 2013).

[242] Schuller, "Petitionary Prayer and the Religion of Qumran," in *Religion in the Dead Sea Scrolls*, pp. 29–45; see esp. pp. 34–35.

[243] I. Knohl, "Between Voice and Silence: The Relationship Between Prayer and Temple Cult," *JBL* 115 (1996) 17–30; see esp. pp. 29–30.

[244] Penitential prayers are found in many apocalypses, especially Daniel, *4 Ezra*, and *2 Baruch*. See L. DiTommaso, "Penitential Prayer and Apocalyptic Eschatology in Second Temple Judaism" in *Prayer and Poetry in the Dead Sea Scrolls and Related Literature,* edited by J. Penner, K. Penner, and C. Wassen (STDJ 98; Leiden and Boston, 2012) pp. 115–33.

ted for the Temple in Jerusalem.[245] Yet, as Schuller noted, there are five passages that contain petition (19.33–34, 4.35, 8.29–36, 22.37, 23.10) and three others that refer to petition (19.36–37, 17.10–11, 20.7). None of these passages is in the "Teacher Hymns." In the beginning, virtually all the early members of the *Yaḥad* were priests who had worshipped in the Temple and knew the necessity of petition; hence, their need to continue a liturgy of petition is understandable.[246] Characteristically, the Qumran sectarian hymns praise God, almost constantly celebrating God's incomparable sovereignty, power, and dominion over all creation. The Qumranites habitually praised and thanked God, since they lived in a deterministic and scripted drama that was apocalyptically eschatological.[247] Theology was not a determinant for social action. Deterministic thought seems regnant at Qumran, but it did not negate possible petitions.[248] Ancient thought was not systematic; it was dialectical. Beliefs are held in tension that may be expressed but not comprehended.

God. Since the beliefs in and experience of "God," by the Qumranites pervade all categories – as is already evident – we have selected for discussion only a few additional comments focused on concepts of "God" that seem warranted. The reference for God and God's ineffable Oneness is placarded by the use of palaeo-Hebrew letters to designate "God" (אל; 1QHᵃ 7.38, 9.28, 10.36; 1QHᵇ frg. 1 line 6). Most likely, one was to substitute "Adonai" for אל that should not be pronounced. "Adonai" or "Lord" (אדוני) appears frequently in the *Hodayot* and supplies the *Hodayot* formula: "I thank you, O Lord, because ... ."

The *Tetragrammaton* does not appear in the *Hodayot* and is generally avoided by the Qumranites. Throughout the documents composed (or completed, not only edited) at Qumran, the *Tetragrammaton* appears customarily in Palaeo-Hebrew characters or with four dots; thus, the perpetual *Qere, Adonai*, defines laws, poems, and psalms. As Schiffman states: "Under-

lying these scribal and literary conventions is the desire to recognize the unique sanctity of God and God's name, which symbolized the essence of God in ancient Hebrew thought."[249]

The authors of the *Thanksgiving Hymns* claim to experience God as the Creator who continues to create and order the cosmos. God is not only transcendent but also witnessed within the history and lives of the Qumranites. God is ineffable and above all human comprehension.

The *Tetrapuncta* is clear in the *Rule of the Community* (1QS 8.14);[250] however, this scribal reverence for the *Tetragrammaton* does not occur in the *Thanksgiving Hymns*. Since almost all of the manuscripts (biblical and nonbiblical) that contain *Tetrapuncta* date from the Hasmonean period, one might not expect it to appear in the later edition of 1QHᵃ. The use of Palaeo-Hebrew would suffice. As Tov states, the use of special writing for the divine names indicates piety: "This practice undoubtedly reflects reverence for the divine name, considered so sacred that it was not to be written with regular characters lest an error be made or lest it be erased by mistake."[251] I would add, and perhaps more importantly, lest the ineffable name be pronounced when texts were read; and they were usually read out loud (see 1QS 6.27 [due to *lacunae* we are never told, not even in the fragments of the *Rule of the Community*, what would be the punishment for pronouncing God's name]). According to Leviticus, anyone who pronounces God's name (שם־יהוה) shall be killed (Lev 24:10–16). The Qumranites perspicaciously perceived that God can be experienced as present and manifest but remains fundamentally incomprehensible and veiled by wonder and mystery.[252]

Intermediary. According to the author of column 26, the Qumranites do not require an angel or high priest to serve as an intermediary. They have direct access to God and speak directly to God. They are priests; some of them imagined the *Yaḥad* replaced, until the Endtime, the Temple services and festivals.[253]

---

[245] See G. Klinzing, *Die Umdeutung des Kultus in der Qumrangemeinde und im Neuen Testament* (SUNT 7; Göttingen, 1971). See esp. "Die Gemeinde als Temple," pp. 50–93.

[246] See E. G. Chazon, "Liturgical Function in the Cave 1 Hodayot Collection," pp. 135–49.

[247] Similar thoughts are shared by Newsom in *The Self as Symbolic Space*, pp. 206–8. Petitionary prayer can be observed in texts that are clearly or implicitly deterministic. See E. Tukasi, *Determinism and Petitionary Prayer in John and the Dead Sea Scrolls* (LSTS 66; London, 2008).

[248] See the careful research on this issue by D. K. Falk in *Prayer and Poetry in the Dead Sea Scrolls and Related Literature*, pp. 135–59. Falk warns: "The important point is not whether their theology allowed real petition, but whether they really offered petition, and then to ask how their developing theology modulated that practice, and was in turn restrained by that practice" (p. 158). Two caveats are fundamental: our texts are very fragmentary and the Qumranites inherited and were influenced by Jewish texts that were not deterministic.

[249] L. H. Schiffman, *Reclaiming the Dead Sea Scrolls*, p. 146.

[250] See the photograph in Charlesworth, *et al.*, *Rule of the Community: Photographic Multi-Language Edition* (Philadelphia and New York, 1996) p. 46. The *Tetrapuncta* was inserted by a scribe who corrected the text of 1QIsaᵃ; the phenomenon appears also in 4Q53 [4QSamᶜ]. These four dots appear in 12 Qumran manuscripts (plus one from Ḥever or Seiyal). For a discussion of the use of *Tetrapuncta* in the Qumran Scrolls, see Tov, *Scribal Practices*, pp. 52, 218–19, 223, 239, 244, 252, 263–65, 278, and 331.

[251] Tov, *Scribal Practices*, p. 218.

[252] On the topic of experiencing that God is inextricably both manifest and hidden, see P. Schäfer, *The Hidden and Manifest God: Some Major Themes in Early Jewish Mysticism* (New York, 1992).

[253] The polemic against the Temple and the Hasmoneans defined Qumran history prior to Herod the Great, who like the followers of the Righteous Teacher, despised the Hasmoneans. During Herod's reign and up until 70 CE, it is conceivable that

According to the author of column 14, God's Holy Ones, the members of the *Yaḥad*, have no need of "an intermediate interpreter." The Holy Spirit and angels are believed to be present in the Community; but they do not serve as intermediators to help the Qumranites speak to God. The members of the *Yaḥad* do so directly as if they have the opportunity to be in the "presence" of God.

The author of column 14 seems to be the Righteous Teacher who probably imagined himself to be the legitimate high priest and officiated in the *Yaḥad* with unparalleled authority. Note these two passages:

> For you brought [the truth of] your secret to all men of your council, and together with the angels of the presence and without an intermediate interpreter for [your] H[oly Ones]. (14.15–16; this passage is echoed in 26.39–40)

The noun translated "interpreter" means "the official go-between."

Judgment. Connected to the determinism of the *Thanksgiving Hymns* is an underlying theme of judgment which offers comfort and justice for the righteous and punishment for the wicked. The word משפט ("judgment, ordnance, precept") appears over 50 times in the extant *Thanksgiving Hymns* and is used extensively in both the "Teacher" and "Community Hymns."[254] In the "Teacher Hymns," the judgment of God comes against the wicked who have persecuted the author. God's judgment of these wicked ones includes "the lot of anger on the forsaken ones, and the pouring of fury on the hidden ones, and the Endtime of fury for all of Belial" (11.28–29). In column 12, the judgment of God against the opponents of the author is directly tied to their allegiance to Belial (12.10–19). Because they plot with Belial, God is beseeched by the author to judge them "with your might [in accordance with] their idols and according to the multitude of their transgressions" (12.19–20). Similarly in column 15, God is said to condemn judgment upon the wicked ones "for you shall condemn to judgment any who attack me in order to distinguish through me between the righteous one and the wicked one" (כי כול גרי למשפט תרשיע להבדיל בי בין צדיק לרשע; 15.15). Those who abandon sin and walk in the way of God are judged in mercy "with the multitude of compassions and much forgiveness" (ובחסדיך תשפטם בהמון רחמים ורוב סליחה; 14.12). Despite this, the "Teacher Hymns" still note that, regardless of one's ethical activity, none can truly be justified in the presence of the eternal God (e.g.,

15.31–34; 17.14–15); it is only out of God's mercy that a human can be justified.

Similar ideas concerning God's judgment can be found in the "Community Hymns." Those who serve God in faithfulness will be freed of their iniquities and granted inheritance (4.26–27) while having their wanton works and impurities purified and forgiven (4.31–36). In column 6, those whom God justifies are given inheritance with the holy spirit and insight, while "all injustice and wickedness you will destroy forever" (וכול עולה ורשע תשמיד לעד; 6.26–27). In contrast to God's justification of the chosen, God's judgment of the wicked is rooted in God's anger (19.11) and leads to eternal destruction (21.36).[255] Again, it should be noted that judgment is intricately connected to God's created order. Humanity's earthen origins and sinful state in the "Community Hymns" means that none can stand before God, for "no one (is) righteous except you" (20.22; see also line 31). Righteousness belongs to God alone (4.32) and no human outside God's determination will be pronounced pure in God's judgment (e.g., 7.27–32; 22.28–29).

Knowledge. The emphasis on knowledge in the Qumran Scrolls has led some scholars in the 1950s to err in imagining that the Scrolls represented the earliest forms of Gnosticism.[256] This term is complex and cannot be defined neatly; it is a form of philosophical thinking that claims 'salvation' (if that term is appropriate) is only through knowledge of oneself and one's origins; it is not through faith. The Qumranites did not replace believing with knowing. Knowledge at Qumran was not only introspection; it was a knowledge of God and God's revelations and secrets. The Qumranites were biblically inspired men.[257]

The Qumran Scrolls do, however, share with many other pre-70 texts a preoccupation with "knowledge," and perhaps that is somehow related to a thought world that can be called proto-Gnosticism or "Gnosis," to use a non-Semitic noun. In both the "Teacher Hymns" and in the "Community Hymns," the verb "to know" (ידע) appears at least 75 times and the noun "knowledge" (דעת) no less than 24 times. In contrast, while in the Psalter ידע is found 93 times (in the *hipʿil* 11 times it denotes God as subject), דעת appears only four times. The contrast with the Psalter becomes even more obvious when one notes that in the Psalter the reference is often to the LORD knowing (e.g. 1:6; 37:18; 69:5, 19 [*bis*]) but at Qumran, it is the author who knows God's goodness (6.28). The devotee knows because of the spirit God put in him (5.35–36). The author, not the Righteous Teacher, knows "(things) … because" God "uncovered my ear to wonderful mysteries" (9.23). P. Sacchi emphasized that "knowledge" in the *Thanksgiving Hymns*

---

some members of the Community returned to Jerusalem and again worshipped in the Temple.

[254] 1QHᵃ 4.14, 16, 18, 22, 23, 25; 5.16, 23; 6.15, 17, 31, 38; 8.11, 17; 9.8, 11, 18, 25, 28, 32, 35, 39; 10.26, 41; 11.28 (4Q432 frg. 6 line 2); 12.21, 26, 27; 13.6, 10; 14.29, 32; 15.15, 38; 16.38; 17.9, 10, 15, 31; 18.36, 37, 38; 19.11; 21.11 (4Q427 frg. 10 line 5); 21.36; 22.28, 29, 30; 23.12; 24.8, 9, 25; 25.3, 12; 4Q427 frg. 10 line 8; 4Q427 frg. 7 2.15.

[255] Kittel notes that this equation of judgment with wrath is contrasted to the emphasized graciousness of God in 19.10–12. See *The Hymns of Qumran*, pp. 109–19.

[256] See, e.g., B. Reicke, "Traces of Gnosticism in the Dead Sea Scrolls," *NTS* 1 (1954–55) 138ff; K. Schubert, *The Dead Sea Community* (London, 1959).

[257] See W. D. Davies, "Knowledge in the DSS and Matthew 11:25–30," *HTR* 46 (1953) 113–39.

was so developed that it enabled the Essene to "see the entire cosmos in the light, that is the intelligence, of God himself."[258]

These Jews break with the usual reference to the "God of Israel," emphasizing the "God of knowledge" (9.28, 20.13, 21.32, 22.34, 25.32–33). Each of these occurrences is only in the "Community Hymns." Note the last of these:

> I have announced in the assembly of your [Holy
> Ones]: "Great and wonderful (is) God."
> [For yo]u are the God of knowledge. (25.32–33)

The Qumran leaders exhort those within the Community to learn, to know, and to study Torah (see esp. 1QS). The best way to honor God is by remaining true to the Covenant. The necessary power is provided by the continuing presence of the Holy Spirit, the focus on God's Word in Torah, and devotion to the divinely inspired creations of the Community.

One of the ongoing themes running through the *Thanksgiving Hymns* is the impartation of knowledge and insight from God to one person, the Righteous Teacher, and through him to those whom God has chosen. Those in the elect Community are convinced that they alone possess the means of interpreting Torah (see esp. *Some Works of the Torah*), have received the truth regarding God's Word and Will, and are defined by revealed knowledge because of the unparalleled importance of the Righteous Teacher in the economy of salvation (*viz.* 1QpHab 7).[259]

Both the "Community Hymns" and "Teacher Hymns" emphasize that only through God may the human receive knowledge and insight of the mysteries and secrets of God's created order (e.g., 18.5–6; 19.12–13, 27; 20.35–37). Throughout the *Thanksgiving Hymns*, the authors speak of God allowing them to have insight or knowledge (e.g., 6.19–25; 7.12, 34; 13.13–14; 17.26; 26.33). The authors refer to God uncovering (גלה) their ears (e.g., 6.13, 9.23, 14.7, 21.6, 22.31, 25.12), their eyes (21.5), and their heart (22.31), as well as receiving knowledge by means of spirits sent by God (e.g., 4.29, 6.36–37, 17.32, 20.15–16). Often, the knowledge that God imparts to the authors consists of understanding the "mysteries" (רזים; e.g., 5.19–21, 30; 9.26–29; 15.29–30; 20.15–16; 26.15).

In the "Teacher Hymns," the reception of knowledge on the part of the author also consists in the proclamation of that knowledge by the author. For example, in column 12, the author (the Righteous Teacher) says that through him, God has "enlightened the faces of many." He continues: "and with the secret of your wonder you have been mighty with me and the wonder is before the Many for the sake of your glory" (ובסוד פלאכה הגברתה עמדי והפלא לנגד רבים בעבור כבודכה; 12.29). In column 10, the same author proceeds to refer to himself as "a banner for the elect ones of righteousness, and the Interpreter of

knowledge in the wonderful mysteries" (נס לבחירי צדק ומליץ דעת ברזי פלא; 10.15).[260] In this way, the one who receives revealed knowledge in the "Teacher Hymns" functions as a transmitter of knowledge to those surrounding him; an idea that may lie behind the image of the author being placed "as the source of streams in a dry land" (16.5).[261]

Messiah. The term "the Messiahs" or "the Anointed Ones" appears in 1QS 9.11 (עד בוא נביא ומשיחי אהרון וישראל);[262] but the noun or title "the Messiah" does not occur in the *Thanksgiving Hymns*. Neither does the verb "to anoint" appear in these hymns. After 100 BCE when the concept of the Messiah is evident at Qumran, some at Qumran may have considered that the Righteous Teacher should be perceived as messianic (perhaps defined broadly). The *Pesharim* do elevate him in the history of salvation as singularly important; but they do not claim the Righteous Teacher is the Messiah. Some Qumranites conceivably imagined that the Righteous Teacher should be equated with the one whom the heavens and earth obey, namely "his Messiah" (4Q521). Perhaps such adoration occurred after his death (not martyrdom). Some of the Qumranties who revered the *Self Glorification Hymn* may have imagined the hymn mirrored the suffering and exaltation of their Teacher.

Perception of the Endtime (Eschatology).[263] Scholarly perspective concerning the "eschatology" of the *Thanksgiving Hymns* has been inconclusive. Some experts, such as H.-W. Kuhn,[264] have understood the *Thanksgiving Hymns* as portraying a predominantly realizing eschatology with a few state-

---

[258] P. Sacchi, *The History of the Second Temple Period* (JSOT Sup 285; Sheffield, 2000) p. 320.

[259] On the broad theme of salvation and atonement in the Qumran Scrolls, see P. Garnet, *Salvation and Atonement in the Qumran Scrolls* (WUNT 2.5; Tübingen, 1977).

[260] Note also the reference to the Righteous Teacher's opponents in 10.14, 31; 12.10, 19–20; 15.14.

[261] This translation identifies the preposition *beth* as a *beth essentiae*; see Charlesworth, "An Allegorical and Autobiographical Poem by the *Moreh haṣ-Ṣedeq* (1QH 8:4–11)," in *ShaTalmon*, pp. 295–307. For more on this psalm, see also J. R. Davila, "The Hodayot Hymnist and the Four who Entered Paradise," *RQ* 17 (1996) 457–78; Daise, "Biblical Creation Motifs in the Qumran Hodayot;" and Hughes, *Scriptural Allusions and Exegesis in the Hodayot*, pp. 135–83.

[262] See J. J. Collins, "What was Distinctive about Messianic Expectation at Qumran?" in *BDSS*, vol. 2, pp. 71–92; Collins, *The Scepter and the Star; The Messiahs of the Dead Sea Scrolls and Other Ancient Literature* (ABRL; New York and London, 1995); Charlesworth, *et al.*, eds., *The Messiah: Developments in Earliest Judaism and Christianity* (Minneapolis, 1992) and Charlesworth, with H. Lichtenberger, and G. S. Oegema, eds. *Qumran-Messianism: Studies on the Messianic Expectations in the Dead Sea Scrolls* (Tübingen, 1998); see the contributions to *Messiah and Christos*, edited by I. Gruenwald, *et al.* (TSAJ 32; Tubingen, 1992).

[263] See H. W. Morisada Rietz, "The Qumran Concept of Time," in *BDSS*, vol. 2, pp. 203–34.

[264] Kuhn, *Enderwartung und gegenwärtiges Heil*.

ments of future expectations. Others, like Puech,[265] have construed the *Thanksgiving Hymns* as having a predominantly futuristic eschatology, much like the *Rule of the Community* and the *War Scroll*. A. L. A. Hogeterp, in his "eschatological" analysis of the *Thanksgiving Hymns*, sees the "Teacher Hymns" as containing early sectarian eschatological traditions about a future and final judgment while other columns seem to contain later elaborations on this earlier eschatological tradition.[266]

One example of a "futuristic eschatology" can be found in 11.6–19, which speaks of the distress of the author and concludes by mentioning the opening of Sheol, the arrows of the pit, and "the gates of [eternity]"([עולם] שערי; 11.18). In this hymn, the rescue of the author from his personal suffering is recontextualized by the future judgment and deliverance of the world.[267] A similar eschatological picture can be seen in the following hymn (11.20–38) which describes the over pouring of "the rivers of Belial" (נחלי בליעל; 11.30) which follows the falling of the measuring line on the judgment (בנפול קו על משפט; 11.28) "and the Endtime of fury for all of Belial" (וקץ חרון לכול בליעל; 11.29).[268] In this column, however, aspects of both realizing eschatology (e.g., 11.20–24) and future eschatology (11.26–37) seem apparent. This complexity may arise from the contrast between the present sufferings of the author(s) and the deterministic perspective that underlies many of the compositions in the *Thanksgiving Hymns*. In this way, expectation of the future eschatological judgment of the chosen is held in tension with the sufferings of the present.

Other eschatological images include mentions of the Endtime (e.g., 4.22–23; 5.22, 26; 7.32–33; 13.13–14), the destruction of the wicked (e.g., 4.33; 6.27; 7.30–33; 14.20–22, 32–35), and future expectation of God's rescue and goodness (e.g., 20.24–25).

Resurrection. Some Qumran specialists concluded that many sectarian scrolls preserved a belief in the resurrection of the dead.[269] Puech is convinced that the resurrection of the individual is evident in some of the *Thanksgiving Hymns*.[270]

Many specialists on the development of the concept of resurrection in Second Temple Judaism do not find resurrection belief in the *Thanksgiving Hymns*.[271] Neither the Qumranite belief that the Sons of Light were predetermined for eternal life (1QS 3–4) nor the concept that the Community was an antechamber of heaven in which the Most Holy of Holy Ones in the Community become like angels (angelification),[272] and are ulti-

---

[269] Early in Qumran research, C. Rabin, K. Schubert, and M. Delcor concluded that a belief in resurrection can be found in the Qumran Scrolls. See Rabin, *Qumran Studies* (SJud 2; London, 1957) pp. 72–75; Schubert, "Das Problem der Auferstehungshoffnung in den Qumrantexten und in der frührabbinischen Literatur," *WZKM* 56 (1960) 158–61; Schubert, "Die Entwicklung der Auferstehungslehre von der nachexilischen bis zur frührabbinischen Zeit," *BZ* 6 (1962) 177–214; and Delcor, 'L'immortalité de l'âme dans le livre de la Sagesse et dans les documents de Qumrân," *NRT* 77 (1955) 614–30.

[270] Puech, "Les Hymnes (1QH)," in *La croyance des Esséniens en la vie future*, vol. 2, pp. 335–419. The resurrection of the righteous may be found, according to Puech, in cols. 14, 16, 19, and 5, and perhaps in 11; see esp. p. 362. Also, see Puech, "Resurrection: The Bible and Qumran," *BDSS*, vol. 2, pp. 247–81; see esp. pp. 272–74. In particular, note p. 274: "Very far from a realized eschatology, the *Thanksgiving Hymns* affirm the hope in a resurrection of the dead in order to participate with the living in the glory of Adam in an eternal life in the company of the angels in the presence of God and the eternal damnation of Belial and the wicked in infernal Sheol."

[271] See esp. the following: J. Carmignac, "Le retour de Docteur de Justice à la fin des jours?" *RQ* 2 (1958) 235–39. J. van der Ploeg, "The Belief in Immortality in the Writings of Qumran," *BO* 18 (1961) 118–24, see esp. H. Ringgren, *The Faith of Qumran*, p. 148: "There is nowhere any statement which can be taken as a substantiation of a belief in the resurrection of the dead." Ringgren focused on the Qumran sect's own creative compositions which included the *Hodayot* and he interprets 1QHᵃ 6.34 and 11.12, Sukenik's numbering, to "refer to weak insignificant men." See esp. G. W. E. Nickelsburg, *Resurrection, Immortality, and Eternal Life in Intertestamental Judaism* (HTS 26; Cambridge, MA, 1972) p. 144; A. F. Segal, *Life After Death: A History of the Afterlife in the Religions of the West* (ABRL; New York and London, 2010) p. 299 [in 1QHᵃ 6 and 11 "the poet's language may just be symbolic"]; Charlesworth in *Resurrection*, pp. 1–21, see esp. pp. 6–19.

[272] See esp. the *Self-Glorification Hymn* (in the present volume) as well as 1QSb 4:24–28 (in vol. 1) and the *Angelic Liturgy* (in vol. 4B). Some Qumranologists note that the Qumran elite imagined they would be transformed into angels (angelification). See esp. the following: Charlesworth, "The Portrayal of the Righteous as an Angel," in *Ideal Figures in Ancient Ju-*

---

[265] Puech, "Messianism, Resurrection, and Eschatology at Qumran and in the New Testament," in *The Community of the Renewed Covenant*, edited by E. Ulrich and J. C. VanderKam (Notre Dame, 1994) pp. 253–56; see esp. pp. 250–52; see also Puech, *La croyance des Esséniens en la vie future*.

[266] A. L. A. Hogeterp, *Expectations of the End: A Comparative Tradition-Historical Study of Eschatological, Apocalyptic and Messianic Ideas in the Dead Sea Scrolls and the New Testament* (STDJ 83; Leiden and Boston, 2009) pp. 55–59. Hogeterp's analysis obviously is dependent upon the conclusion that the "Teacher Hymns" antedate the "Community Hymns." That conclusion is supported by the present research.

[267] J. A. Hughes comes to a similar conclusion in *Scriptural Allusions and Exegesis in the Hodayot*, pp. 185–207; see esp. pp. 199–200.

[268] Kittel understands the thoughts in this psalm as "metaphorical rather than literal" (*The Hymns of Qumran*, p. 80) while Hughes denies that the scenarios are "merely metaphorical" (*Scriptural Allusion and Exegesis in the Hodayot*, pp. 228–30). For similar images of eschatological warfare in the *Thanksgiving Hymns*, see Composite Text 14.24–41.

mately considered among the Elim (the most elevated of Qumranites and angels), suggest a mind set in which resurrection is necessary or contemplated.[273] Nevertheless, the Qumranites certainly were familiar with resurrection beliefs as they knew *1 Enoch* (the early sections) and Daniel.

Puech may be correct to imagine that some Qumranites eventually believed, long after the death of the Righteous Teacher, that the righteous individual would be raised by God from the dead and found such beliefs in the *Thanksgiving Hymns*. Those buried in the cemetery are aligned north to south. Perhaps this habit masks the belief in a resurrection in which the deceased would rise and face the eternal resting place of the elect and righteous ones, which was imagined to be in the north (1En 70:1–4).[274] Likewise, the identification of 4Q521, *On Resurrection*, proves that some Jews at Qumran believed in resurrection. This scroll, like Daniel (which was found in the Qumran caves), clearly refers to the resurrection of the individual, and even if both documents originated outside Qumran they were known and studied at Qumran. Fortunately, we now have a taxonomy of resurrection beliefs,[275] so we can better discern among these diverse beliefs which one refers to a person who lived, died, and was raised to eternal life.[276] In summary, it is misleading to conclude that one of the authors of a poem or hymn in the *Thanksgiving Hymns* left a clear reference to the classical belief in the resurrection of an individual who had lived and has died but is raised from the dead to life eternal as in Daniel 12, *Jubilees, On Resurrection*, and *1 Enoch* (all were part of the Qumran Library).[277]

Revelation. If five compositions or collections can be singled out as most important for comprehending the thought and life of the Qumranites, they are *Some Works of the Torah* (focused on *halakot* and the right means to interpret Torah), the *Rule of the Community* (a collection of laws and rules, the origin of sin, the study of Torah, and hymns), the *War Scroll* (the final cosmic battle), the *Pesharim* (the Qumran hermeneutic), and the *Thanksgiving Hymns* (the poetic, introspective reflections of the Teacher and the members of the Community). Editing and translating the *Thanksgiving Hymns* enables one to see how poetry is a medium for revelation.[278] One must focus on the *Thanksgiving Hymns* with some knowledge of the Qumran mentality so as to be sensitive to echoes or mirror images that also originate from within the *Yaḥad*.[279]

The *Thanksgiving Hymns* reflect a Community that is certain of who they are. They claim unique and defining revelation. They believe they were created as the Holy Ones and are the only ones in history to whom God's Will was clearly disclosed; the pervasive *hipʿil* verbs often mean that God has "allowed" his chosen ones to know all the mysteries in his Word (see notes to the texts and translations). Note the paradigmatic importance of the *Pesher Habakkuk*:

(VACAT) And when it says, **so that he can run who reads it,** its interpretation concerns the Righteous Teacher (מורה הצדק), to whom God made known (or allowed to know) all the mysteries of the words of his servants the prophets. **For there is yet a vision concerning the appointed time. It testifies to the period, and it will not deceive.** Its interpretation is that the last period will be prolonged, and it will be greater than anything of which the prophets spoke, for the mysteries of God are awesome (להפלה). (1QpHab 7.3–8; Horgan in PTSDSSP 6B.172–173; bold designates Hab)

The Community claims to own this Knowledge because of the revelations to the Righteous Teacher and because all Scripture was directed to them and their time; thus, the Qumranites use a

daism, edited by J. J. Collins and G. W. E. Nickelsburg (SBLSCS 12; Chico, 1980) pp. 135–51; R. Elior, *The Paradoxical Ascent to God* (Albany, 1993); Elior, *The Three Temples* (Oxford, 2004); B. Nitzan, "Harmonic and Mystical Characteristics in Poetic and Liturgical Writings from Qumran," *JQR* 85 (1994) 163–83; C. H. T. Fletcher-Louis, *All the Glory of Adam: Liturgical Anthropology in the Dead Sea Scrolls* (Leiden, 2002). Segal wisely sees angelification in numerous Qumran texts; see his *Life After Death*, pp. 304–05.

[273] See Charlesworth: "The Qumranites thought of their 'House of Holiness' as an antechamber of heaven, in which angels dwell during ritual, and as a replacement of the Temple" (Charlesworth in *BDSS*, vol. 3, p. 29).

[274] The Qumran afterlife seems to be devoid of sexual pleasures. Contrast the Song of Songs; see F. W. Dobbs-Allsopp, "The Delight of Beauty and Song of Songs 4:1–7," *Interpretation* 59 (2005) 260–77.

[275] See Charlesworth, "Where Does the Concept of Resurrection Appear and How Do We Know That?" in *Resurrection*, pp. 1–21. Sixteen different, sometimes, interrelated concepts of resurrection should be observed and distinguished.

[276] The comments by Josephus and Hippolytus that the Essenes believed in the resurrection of the dead or immortality need to be separated from a study of such an idea in the *Hodayot*. They represent secondary sources edited for their own audiences. As Segal stated: "Josephus described the Essenes in terms completely appropriate to a Neo-Pythagorean sect, with their notion of the immortality of the soul;" Segal, *Life After Death*, p. 298.

[277] Resurrection belief is found, for example, in the *Psalms of Solomon* and the much later apocalypses, such as *4 Ezra* and *2 Baruch*. None of these were found at Qumran; that would be possible only for the *Psalms of Solomon*, as the others postdate 68 CE when Qumran was burned.

[278] M. P. Horgan and P. J. Kobelski perceive that there is "some special identification between prophecy and poetry as vehicles of revelation." See their "The Hodayot (1QH) and New Testament Poetry," in *To Touch the Text: Biblical and Related Studies in Honor of Joseph A. Fitzmyer* (New York, 1989) pp. 179–93; the quotation is on p. 180.

[279] Also, see the previous section on "Knowledge."

fulfillment hermeneutic.[280] The *Thanksgiving Hymns* witnesses to the Qumranite perception. These devout Jews not only devoted the day and night to studying Scripture, they were also convinced that they were living within Scripture or rather were indwelling the awesomeness of the Ineffable One.[281]

Divine revelation given by the Creator, the Lord, only to those in the *Yaḥad* may seem *prima facie* to emphasize dualism; however, absolute dualism tends to dissolve in some hymns or poems. The human, with the aid of the Holy Spirit, can be like the Elim;[282] thus, the division between humans and divine beings collapses. The future is breaking into the present; thus, a trifurcated time coalesces into one time: The Endtime. Finally, heaven can be experienced on earth so that the dualism between heaven and earth is collapsed; wisdom resides in the *Yaḥad*. Life in the Community is experienced as if it is part of heaven (cf. the *Angelic Liturgy*).

The Righteousness of God, Covenant, and Law. Repeatedly the authors of the poems or hymns celebrate the continuing righteousness of God. The "Covenant" is mentioned frequently.[283] One reference is to the "Covenant of Adam:" "to each covenant of Adam I will look" (4.39). Most often God's covenant appears as "your covenant"; that expression appears at least 21 times. An author, reflecting the rules of the Community, claims he will not bring into "the council of [your] tr[uth] those who turn [from] your [cov]enant" (6.32–33). A pertinent excerpt regarding "the covenant" is 7.27–31:

Only you, you have c[rea]ted the righteous one,
and from the womb you have established him
for the appointed time of (your) will
in order to guard (him) in *your covenant*
so as to walk continuously in everything
and to bring over him the abundance of your mercies,

and to open all the trouble of his soul to the eternal salvation and the everlasting peace with sufficiency. And you raise his honor from the flesh.

But the wicked ones you created for [the u]rge of your fury, and from the womb you designated them for the day of killing, because they walked in the way that is not good and rejected *your covenant*, [and] their soul abhorred your [truth].

Note the contrast between singular ("the righteous one") and plural ("the wicked ones") and the extension of parallel poetry to prose.

Hultgren demonstrates both that the *Thanksgiving Hymns* contain the covenant theology of the *Damascus Document* and that "the concept of the 'Righteousness of God' brings Qumran reflection on 'covenant' and the other major theological traditions to a pointed culmination."[284] Covenant and the "New Covenant" are Qumran concepts developed from Jeremiah, but הברית החדשה does not appear in the *Thanksgiving Hymns* (see CD MS A 6.19, 8.21; CD MS B 19.33, 20.12). In the compositions of the *Thanksgiving Hymns* the covenant is God's covenant, hence the repetitive בריתך and בריתכה.

Torah, "Law," appears only in 12.11, 13.13, and 14.13. Each of these poems seems to be composed by the Righteous Teacher:

They plotted with Belial against me,
to exchange your Torah which you reiterated in my heart,
for smooth things to your people. (12.11–12)

According to column 13, the author (probably the Righteous Teacher) refers to "the mouths of young lions" who sought to devour "me" but:

You, O my God, you hid me from the sons of Adam,
and concealed your Torah in [me] until the Endtime
when your salvation shall be revealed to me. (13.13–14)

In column 14, the author (probably the Righteous Teacher) explains that "in your council for your glory" you acted 'to magnify the Torah" (14.13).

There are inconsistencies and tensions in the *Thanksgiving Hymns*, but the authors present a complex world of thought that is almost always consistent.[285] In central focus is thanksgiving and praise that is based on a living covenantal relationship with a Creator within a dualistic and apocalyptic world

---

[280] I am most grateful to Strugnell for discussions, over decades, on Qumran Fulfillment Hermeneutic. See Charlesworth, *The Pesharim and History*.

[281] See the reflections by J. F. Elwolde in *The Scrolls and Biblical Traditions*, p. 83.

[282] See J. Davila, "The Hodayot Hymnist and the Four Who Entered Paradise," 457–78; D. Dimant, "Men as Angels: The Self-Image of the Qumran Community," in *Religion and Politics in the Ancient Near East*, edited by A. Berlin (Bethesda, MD, 1996) pp. 93–103; M. G. Abegg, "Who Ascended to Heaven? 4Q491, 4Q427, and the Teacher of Righteousness," pp. 61–73; J. J. Collins, "The Angelic Life," in *Metamorphoses*, edited by T. K. Seim and J. Økland (Berlin, 2009) pp. 291–310; J. Duhaime, "La prière d'action de grâce comme récit identitaire," in *Les Hymnes du Nouveau Testament et leurs Fonctions*, edited by D. Herber and P. Keith (Paris, 2009) pp. 463–85; J. L. Angel, *Otherworldly and Eschatological Priesthood in the Dead Sea Scrolls* (STDJ 86; Leiden, 2010).

[283] See M. Weinfeld, "The Covenant in Qumran," in *BDSS*, vol. 2, pp. 59–69.

[284] Hultgren, *From the Damascus Covenant to the Covenant of the Community*, p. 409.

[285] See A. Klęczar, "Do the *Hodayot* Psalms Display a Consistent Theology?" *The Qumran Chronicle* 11 (2003) 79–89.

view.[286] As Stegemann stated, the *Thanksgiving Hymns* "are the principal document of the Essenes' spiritual piety, their picture of human beings and of God, and their struggle for a deeper insight into God's unfathomable plan of salvation for the entire world."[287] The universalism in the *Thanksgiving Hymns* is not to be overlooked.

Universalism. The *Apocalypse of Abraham* contains a passage in which God announces the punishment of the Gentiles who will suffer through ten plagues (*ApAb* 29–30). Such early Jewish texts that contain polemics against Gentiles, the balustrade in the Temple beyond which no Gentile could pass, and the wars against the Greeks, Persians, and Romans, highlighted by the Jewish Revolts, have led many scholars to assume that all, or at least most, early Jews hated Gentiles. The assumption that all Jews denigrated Gentiles flows into research on the *Thanksgiving Hymns*. These compositions are often perceived within Qumran's hatred of all the Sons of Darkness; and that designation includes not only all Gentiles but even the priests officiating in the Temple.

It is quite surprising, therefore, to find a glimpse of universalism in these psalms: "And all peoples (גוים) shall know your truth and all nations (לאומים) your glory" (14.15). In the same psalm, the author had stated:

And I will be comforted over the multitude of people (עם) and over the uproar of ki[n]gdoms when they gather, [because] I [kn]ow that you raise the few who live among your people (עם) and a remnant among your inheritance. (14.10–11).

In line 11, the author states that he knows that God will raise only the few, a remnant within Israel; only three lines later, he shares a belief that all peoples will know God's truth and glory. Perhaps, he is imagining that non-Jews can know God and recognize his glory but not be raised (from some lower state). More likely, ancient traditions that are often antithetical in perspective flowed into one and the same hymn.

All passages that apparently are universalistic in perception need to be studied in light of the universalism in the soteriology of many early Jewish texts, especially the *Testament of Abraham*. New Testament scholars will recall Paul's optimistic apocalyptic eschatology: "And so all Israel will be saved" (Rom 11:26); yet, this is the same thinker who claimed, citing Isaiah, that though Israel be as numerous as the sands of the sea, "only a remnant of them will be saved" (Rom 9:27). Such divergent beliefs should be observed and the tension appreciated; no central logical thought should be assumed.

Admitting Conceivably Unattractive Tendencies in the Thought in the Thanksgiving Hymns. Before concluding a review of ideas and concepts in the *Thanksgiving Hymns*, it is best to be honest and observe possible flaws too often overlooked. We should admit that within the poetic beauty and elevated thought of the *Thanksgiving Hymns* are thoughts and concepts that are unattractive. Some of these theological blemishes help explain why the movement died out.

First, to claim that only those in the Community have knowledge given by God and that the "the sons of heaven" are primordially "your elect ones" (6.26) and far superior to all others, who are being damned, is offensive to all those outside the *Yaḥad*. Such thoughts are comprehensible, however, in light of sociology and anthropology; these priests, the legitimate sons of Aaron, were dethroned from their positions in the Temple and exiled from the Holy City. Sociology gave rise to denigrating dualism.

Second, the authors concur that the human "is but a form of dust and mixed water" (5.31–32), a "perverted s[p]irit" and an "inclination of dust" (8.18; see 18.5–8). To claim constantly that humanity is only dirt is to demean the human who biblically is perceived to be created in the image of God. Furthermore, portraying humans as worthless is a claim that clashes with the affirmation that angels worship within the Community as if it were an antechamber of heaven and that some in "the Many" can become divine or angelic and blend with the Elim. The balance between being part of God and a mortal is delicate, allowing neither abject denigration nor excessive glorification, as with the claim to be among the Elim in col. 26 and in the *Self-Glorification Hymn.*

Third, the perpetual emphasis and focus only on the Endtime and the perception that all previous acts of God were merely preliminary (and conceivably insignificant) does little justice to *Heilsgeschichte* (God's revelation of God's self in the past to those in previous history). The stress also diminishes the unparalleled honor so many Jews gave to the Lawgiver, Moses (with Adam the only name in the *Thanksgiving Hymns*). Stressing the paradigmatic and unparalleled importance of the Righteous Teacher tends to diminish the honor accorded by most Jews to Abraham, Joseph, Moses, Jacob, David, Solomon, and all the prophets, some of whom, unlike the Righteous Teacher, performed miracles, at least according to sacred traditions.

Fourth, the extreme emphasis on the unparalleled superiority of speech and lips, as in 18.9 and 26.3–6, demotes the importance of hearing and the ear. The former leads to praise; the latter to hearing and obedience as the Hebrew שמע indicates. According to biblical traditions, the human is defined not only by speech but also by deeds and obedience, and especially hearing God's Word, praise, and adoration. Speech without hearing is inarticulate. Praise is not only for God but also for all creatures, including those praising and hearing adulation.

Fifth, centripetal inwardness categorizes the supreme importance of a closed Community. That introspection leads to a failure to share wisdom, revealed knowledge, and a compassion for those outside the closed Community. If a group has received revealed truth the moral imperative should be to share it engagingly with enthusiasm and inclusion.

Sixth, the authors wish to stress that there is only one God. But, they too often slip into henotheism and praise God who is

---

[286] For a good discussion of "law," "grace," and "covenant" in the *Hodayot*, see E. P. Sanders, *Paul and Palestinian Judaism* (London, 1977) pp. 298–328.

[287] Stegemann, *The Library of Qumran*, p. 107.

merely one of the great ones. Note 18.10: God is "the Prince of the Elim and the king of the glorious ones." As with many passages in the Psalter, that affirmation falls short of absolute monotheism. In contrast, an author (most likely the Righteous Teacher) affirms absolute monotheism:

For you (are) an eternal God;
And all your ways are established for perpetuity (and) perpetuity.
And there is no one but you. (15.34–35)

Finally, the most egregious theological error in some of the hymns is to be so convinced of God's incomparable power that all, even evil, is attributed to God. Some authors miss the subtle sophistication of the Yahwist who composed Genesis 3. The *Naḥash* is not a demonic serpent; he is introduced as a creation of God and the wisest of the beasts of the field (cf. the LXX and Targumim). He asks a question. *Naḥash* cannot be the sole cause of the banishment from Eden.[288]

Many authors of the *Thanksgiving Hymns* learn from their humiliation and chastisement – and that is laudable – but they tend to cross a delicate line and incorrectly claim that all human suffering and hardships come from God. In texts that know about human sinfulness and the power of Belial (10.18), it is unfortunate the authors imply that apparently all human suffering originates with God. Note the following example of this subtle tendency (arranged poetically):

For through the mystery of your wisdom you chastised me;
And you concealed the truth until the
Endt[ime of your wrath until] its season.
And may your chastisement become joy and gladness to me,
And my afflictions became an e[ternal] healing [to all the endtimes of] perpetuity.
And (being) an (object of) scorn for my adversaries
(Becomes) to me a crown of glory. (17.23–25)

Previously, the author, probably the Righteous Teacher, laments that his "eyes (are) like a burning-fire in a furnace" and his "tears (are) like valleys of water" (17.5). Ironically, the perception that horrible suffering is a chastisement that purifies is lost in the claim that all suffering originates from the Creator.

Humans are incapable of perfect thought. Admitting some theological slips in the *Thanksgiving Hymns* only helps us perceive sublime poetic perceptions. An anonymous author imagined his heart was made of stone; but this stone did the incomprehensible; it quivered with a feeling of God's presence:

[How] can I look unless you uncover my eyes,
And hear [unless you uncover my ears]?

My heart was awestruck,
Because to an inattentive[289] ear a message was opened,
And the heart of [stone vibrated with mar]vels. (21.5–7)

The impossible happened: stone palpitated.[290] The poet imagines his heart was emotionally agitated as he felt God opening his eyes and ears and being "awestruck."

Final Theological Reflections. In continuing to comprehend, certainly not systematize, the thoughts found in the *Thanksgiving Hymns*, it might be helpful to mention briefly what ideas and concepts seem surprisingly absent. Four seem most important to report.

First, there is no mention of the Exodus from Egypt that is so central to many books in the Hebrew Scriptures. While, except for Adam, "Moses" is the only proper name mentioned in the collection, it appears only once and is used by some unknown poet to focus on forgiveness of iniquity and sin (4.24). As we shall see, there is an echo from the famous "Song of the Sea" in the *Thanksgiving Hymns*.

Second, despite the contemporaneous increased interest in angels, especially the archangels, and despite the intermittent preoccupation with the heavenly realm, it is stunning to note that no archangel is named; there is no mention of Gabriel, Uriel (despite over 12 cases of "light" in 1QHᵃ), Phanuel, Michael, or Sariel.[291]

How do we explain the absence of archangels' names when angelology is impressively developed in many apocalypses contemporaneous with the *Thanksgiving Hymns*? It may be because of the rhetoric of anonymity which may be a literary device in these poems.[292] That is clear, even though "Moses" is mentioned. The phenomenon should be assessed in light of the pervasive perspective that no mediator is needed, and the Elect Ones can have immediate access to God. "Mediator" or "Interpreter" (מליץ) appears at least nine times in 1QHᵃ. In some passages, the author (the Righteous Teacher most likely) claims he is "the interpreter of knowledge in the wonderful mysteries" (10.15). Thus, the Qumranites claim to speak directly to God and not to or through an intermediary or an archangel (26.39–40).

Third, David though so popular in the *Psalms Scroll* and in the *Non-Masoretic Psalms* (Psalms 151–55), is not mentioned. While a Davidic Messiah is mentioned in the *Rule of the Com-*

---

[288] See Charlesworth, *The Good and Evil Serpent* (New Haven and London, 2010).

[289] See Sir 25:9: "Blessed ... is the one who speaks to an attentive ear.

[290] The reference to a heart of stone and to palpitation is obtained from other lines in this and related poems. See the critical edition and notes for all the evidence.

[291] The authors do refer to God's "princes" (17.17) and declare: "you are the prince of the heavenly beings" (18.10).

[292] On the rhetorical use of anonymity in the Dead Sea Scrolls, see J. Roloff, "Der johanneische 'Lieblingsjünger' und der Lehrer der Gerechtigkeit," *NTS* 15 (1968-1969) 129–51; Charlesworth, *The Beloved Disciple* (Valley Forge, PA, 1995) pp. xiv–xvi, 16–17, 140–48, 205–10.

munity and in psalmic compilations like the *Psalms of Solomon*, there is no mention of "the Messiah" and apparently no interest in the Davidic Kingdom in the *Thanksgiving Hymns*. How do we explain this characteristic when an author mentions "dominion" (10 times in 1QHᵃ), "his kingdom" (3.27), and "kingdoms" (14.10); moreover, "king" appears five times in 1QHᵃ? Finally, those who composed these documents knew that the magnitude of the drama, especially in the Endtime, exceeds any word chosen.

Fourth, the authors do not mention some major nouns. Not only is the noun "Messiah" absent, but the Temple is never mentioned. More importantly, the authors use the verb "to love" 13 times but never mention the noun "love."

9. Relationship to the Hebrew Bible[293]

Text of Hebrew Scriptures. Those who composed works in the *Thanksgiving Hymns* were likely shaped not only by the biblical texts; rather, they poetically participated in shaping the fluid biblical texts within the Community.[294] That is, the Qumranites not only inherited a biblical text, they helped to shape it.[295]

Beside opening the door for better texts of the Hebrew Bible, the *Thanksgiving Hymns* often reflect evidence of more than one text type. It seems, *inter alia*, to witness to at least two text types, a "proto-Masoretic" text type and the Hebrew text behind the Septuagint. Mansoor stated: "For the first time we are able to see at first hand some of the types of pre-masoretic Biblical texts which were current in Palestine just before and after the turn of the Christian era."[296]

The Song of the Sea. In the Hebrew Bible, thinking about God's incomprehensibility, many authors ask rhetorically "Who is like you?" (Pss 35:10, 71:19; cf. 89:6–8, 113:5, 77:13, and Mic 7:18). The most influential passage is provided by the author of Exodus 15 who records the "Song of the Sea." It is purported to be a Song that was chanted by Moses and "the

children of Israel" when they saw the Egyptians who had pursued them out of Egypt, "lying dead on the seashore." The Song was memorized by many early Jews (and today by millions of Jews and Christians). It influenced the *Thanksgiving Hymns* in Hymn 20: "I Thank the Lord for Instructing Me in Truth." Note an echo of this famous Song:

For who is like you among the gods (אלים), O Lord?
And who is like your truth?
And who can be justified before you when he is judged?
(15.31)

כי מי כעוכה באלים אדוני
ומי כאמתכה
ומי יצדק לפניכה בהשפטו
(15.31)

מִי־כָמֹכָה בָּאֵלִם֙ יְהֹוָה
מִי כָּמֹכָה נֶאְדָּר בַּקֹּדֶשׁ
נוֹרָא תְהִלֹּת עֹשֵׂה פֶלֶא
(Exod 15:11; BHS)

Who is like you among the gods (אלים), O LORD?
Who is like you, majestic in holiness,
awesome in splendor, doing wonders?
(Ex 15:11; NRSV)

The words "Who is like you among the gods (or Elim), O LORD/Lord?" are identical in the *Thanksgiving Hymns* and in Exodus 15:11, except the *Tetragrammaton* is shifted to *Adonai*. It appears obvious that the author of Hymn 20 quoted from the "Song of the Sea," and likely had memorized it. He shifts "majestic in holiness" to "your truth," bringing out the emphasis in the Qumran Scrolls that the LORD is the God of Knowledge and the Community alone has God's truth. Then, the author (the Righteous Teacher) brings out his emphasis that only God can justify the human.

Creative Poetry. The new poetry flows as a river from many diverse streams. The origins of the words or symbols are not the key to interpretation; the key is the final complex collage of images. Thus the ideal forms of *parallelismus membrorum* so characteristic of the Psalter expand into complex poetic (even prose) passages.[297] At times the exegete who seeks understanding may imagine that the author is deliberately misleading the

---

[293] I am grateful to B. A. Beard for preparing notes for section 9. Also, see the numerous references to Scripture, notably the Hebrew Scriptures or Old Testament, in the preceding discussions and in the notes to the texts and translations.

[294] W. A. Tooman focused on 1QHᵃ 11.16–19 and illustrated how the author produced a new text, without implying any interpretation of the sources (namely, Jonah 2; Psalms 77, 107; Isaiah 66; Jeremiah 10, 51; and Job 36, 41). Most likely, the composer was a Hebraist who knew these texts by heart and let his memory dictate the creation of a new hymn evoked by Scriptures. See Tooman, "Between Imitation and Interpretation: Reuse of Scripture and Composition in *Hodayot* (1QHᵃ) 11.6–9," *DSD* 18 (2011) 54–73.

[295] See P. W. Flint, "The Dead Sea Scrolls and the Biblical Text," in *The Dead Sea Scrolls* (Nashville, 2013) pp. 73–81; on text types and theories, see esp. pp. 80–81.

[296] Mansoor, *The Thanksgiving Hymns*, p. 31.

[297] This distinction is not as clear as that which Lowth attempted to describe and biblical studies subsequently defended. See A. Berlin, *The Dynamics of Biblical Poetry* (Bloomington, 1985) p. 4. She notes that a proper reading of Lowth, *Lecture III: The First Part of the Hebrew Metre,* reveals that parallelism is also found in prose. Thus, it is reasonable to find the lines between poetry and prose beclouded in the *Hodayot*. Lowth's *Lectures on Sacred Poetry of the Hebrews* is available in its entirety on Princeton Theological Seminary's "Theological Commons."

reader by mixing so many different metaphors. This insight may help to explain the author's habit of ending abruptly a thought and shifting to another, often with a transition that alludes to a personal experience or to a confession of God's revelatory intervention into his life. Perhaps the complex imagery and deeply symbolic language was lucid to some in the *Yaḥad* (others may have needed helpful guidance). For later generations the meaning seems lost or confused.

The *Thanksgiving Hymns* appear frequently as a "mosaic of Old Testament Texts."[298] The vast allusions to Scriptural passages are clarified when one reads the hymns as poetry and with the imagination that one is within the Qumran Community.[299] This usage is unlike other common approaches in various Qumran texts, most notably, the *Pesharim*. That is, there is no *lemma* and the majority of the use of the Hebrew Bible in the *Thanksgiving Hymns* is not explicit. The *Thanksgiving Hymns* do not contain the introductory formulae found in other Qumran texts, notably, "as it is written," "as it is said."[300] The method of re-presenting Scripture clarifies that there is not one particular way in which the Hebrew Bible is utilized by the Qumran Community. The Qumranites were fond of biblical interpretation and developed a method identified as "Fulfillment Hermeneutics."[301]

Likewise, Scriptural allusions in the *Thanksgiving Hymns* are often "free"; that is, they not only change but also combine the biblical texts in ways that flow freely from the consciousness of the author and do not follow a prescribed ordering.[302] The authority of Scripture is by allusion or implicit quotation

but not by a formula.[303]

Prophets. The book of Isaiah is one of the most foundational texts for the *Thanksgiving Hymns*. Most of the Eden imagery comes from Isaiah. *Hymn 22: I Thank the Lord for Making Me the Irrigator of the Garden* (16.5–17.36) provides ample fodder for demonstrating the *Thanksgiving Hymns'* reliance on Isaiah. The main influence seems to come from Isaiah 40–66, with the references to specific trees and garden imagery. Hope in the Endtime is renewed by the vigor of the Community, meanwhile suffering remains necessary for purification and to maintain focus on the Creator.[304]

While Ezekiel is a source used by the composers of the *Thanksgiving Hymns*, Isaiah seems to be a more dominant influence on the collection. Perhaps this influence on the Qumranites is placarded by two copies of Isaiah in Cave I, six Pesharim on Isaiah, and the use of Isaiah 40:3 in the *Rule of the Community*. In contrast to Isaiah, there is no Pesher devoted to Ezekiel. The majority of the quotations from Ezekiel in Qumran compositions have been deemed nonexplicit. Those that are explicit are introduced by the formulae found in the *Pesharim*.[305] The noted absence of such formulae in the *Thanksgiving Hymns* complicates the relationship. While there is little doubt concerning the importance of Ezekiel to the Qumranites, further research devoted to uncovering the book's relationship to the *Thanksgiving Hymns*, the "Mystical gem of Qumran," would undoubtedly enrich studies regarding canon and *Rezeptionsgeschichte* in Early Judaism and Christian Origins. It has become clear that there were authoritative texts that many Jewish groups agreed contained Torah,[306] God's Will, but there was no set Hebrew text of the Hebrew Scriptures and no closed canon.[307]

The *Thanksgiving Hymns* reveal reliance upon the book of Jeremiah only through allusion and implicit quotation.[308] The allusions and quotations found seem to be based upon a reliance primarily on so-called proto-Masoretic manuscripts. Naturally these references to Jeremiah are used freely and loosely in keeping with the author's immersion in the Hebrew Scriptures and his unhampered reliance upon them as inspiration for the *Thanksgiving Hymns*. This is combined with the composer's

---

[298] Note the comments by Holm-Nielsen, *Hodayot*, p. 301.

[299] See the discussion by Hughes, *Scriptural Allusions and Exegesis in the Hodayot*.

[300] Fitzmyer, "The Use of Explicit Old Testament Quotations in Qumran and in the New Testament," in *The Semitic Background of the New Testament* (Grand Rapids, 1997) pp. 8–13.

[301] Bernstein wisely warned about limiting Qumran scriptural interpretation to the so-called commentaries; see his "Interpretation of Scriptures," *EDSS* 1.378–79. Also, see the important observations by S. J. Tanzer in "Biblical Interpretation in the *Hodayot*," in *A Companion to Biblical Interpretation in Early Judaism*, pp. 255–75. For an explanation of "Fulfillment Hermeneutics," see Charlesworth, *The Pesharim and Qumran History*.

[302] Tov, "The Biblical Texts from the Judaean Desert – An Overview and Analysis of the Published Texts" in *The Bible as Book: The Hebrew Bible and the Judaean Desert Discoveries*, edited by E. D. Herbert and Tov (New Castle, 2002) pp. 147–48. Also see, the discussion in Hughes, *Scriptural Allusions and Exegesis in the Hodayot*, pp. 42–46.

[303] Lange, "The Textual History of the Book of Jeremiah in Light of its Allusions and Implicit Quotations in the Qumran *Hodayot*" in *Prayers and Poetry in the Dead Sea Scrolls and Related Literature*, p. 254. Lange helpfully outlines his methodology for determining implicit allusions and explicit quotations.

[304] Hughes, *Scriptural Allusions and Exegesis in the Hodayot*, p. 168.

[305] Dimant, "The Apocalyptic Interpretation of Ezekiel at Qumran," in *Messiah and Christos*, p. 35.

[306] VanderKam, *The Dead Sea Scrolls and the Bible*, p. 71.

[307] The fluid canon before 70 CE is demonstrated in many of the books by L. M. McDonald; see esp. McDonald, *Formation of the Biblical Canon*, 2 vols. (London, New York, 2017).

[308] Lange, "Textual History of the Book of Jeremiah," p. 255.

reliance upon the "proto-Masoretic Text" and at times on the Septuagint.[309]

Davidic Psalter. The *Thanksgiving Hymns* are similar to the Psalms in their attribution, diverse lengths, shared symbolic language, and praise to God. The *Thanksgiving Hymns* offer, as do many of the Psalms, the texts that are "of" or "for" the משכיל; that is, the "Master." The Qumranites probably developed the concept of the משכיל from the Psalms and Daniel. The Masoretic Psalms (32, 42, 44, 45, 52, 53, 54, 55, 74, 78, 88, 89, 142) also designate למשכיל as an introduction to various psalms, the majority of which are found in the Second Book within the Psalter; but there are references in Books One, Two, Three, and Five.

The Psalms in the Psalter and the psalms in the *Thanksgiving Hymns* are of extravagantly diverse lengths. The psalm that begins in column 16 is very long. It has not been possible for scholars to agree where it might end.

The *Thanksgiving Hymns* share with the Psalter the same symbolic language and imagery, notably "rebelliousness" (2.25), God's "righteous deeds and patience" (4.29), "the works of your strong right hand" (4.30), "the multitude of your wonders" (6.34), "the wings of the spirit" (6.41), "the God of truth" (7.38), and "your holy spirit" (8.26). The imagery of "trees" in column 16 also echoes the Psalter.

As they had repeatedly done in the Temple, the Qumranites praise the Creator for goodness and faithfulness. They also mourn for the Community's suffering and yearn for the coming justice of God.

J. F. Elwolde suggests that the composers of the *Thanksgiving Hymns* are not simply alluding to or quoting the Psalms; instead they view themselves and the Community "within" the biblical text.[310] Thus, this usage demonstrates more than a simple cognitive knowledge of the biblical texts; it suggests that the authors perceived themselves living in the world shaped and defined by Hebrew Scriptures.[311] This suggestion is probable when one understands that before 70 CE no canon of Scripture has yet been solidified and closed. Therefore, the authors of the *Thanksgiving Hymns* continue to claim and seek revelation from God in the Community. Elwolde's "The Hodayot's Use of the Psalter," a series of articles, offers intensive study of

the Psalter in the *Thanksgiving Hymns* and provides insight for further study of the Psalms in the *Hodayot*.[312]

The *Thanksgiving Hymns* continue the traditions in the Psalter but also place more emphasis on personal thanksgiving.[313] The language of the *Thanksgiving Hymns* exaggerates emotion and compounds metaphors and images so that the precise meaning often recedes into opacity. The author of a hymn frequently imitates biblical Hebrew so that we find passages that are a complex mélange of biblical phrases and sentences.[314] See especially the complex character of the exceptionally long Hymn 22: "I Thank the Lord for Making Me the Irrigator of the Garden" (1QHᵃ 16.5–17.36). Thus, helpful is P. Flint's insight: "They [the *Thanksgiving Hymns*] do not share the same content as biblical psalms, but reflect the ideology of the Essene movement in forms that often flow free of biblical style."[315]

Job. C. L. Seow notes that among all the possible allusions to Job in the Dead Sea Scrolls some of the strongest allusions are those found in the witnesses to the *Thanksgiving Hymns*, especially in 1QHᵃ. The psalms and poems may provide insights into how the Righteous Teacher and the Community interpreted and understood Job. The passage in 17.14–15 appears to be a rebuttal of Job's claims that he will have an opportunity to justify himself in court with God. The author of 17.14–15, probably the Righteous Teacher, focuses on forensics: "and (no one) w[ins] your lawsuit" (17.15). He is convinced that no one is able to confront God to be justified (17.14). Forgiveness is possible only through God's "loving kindnesses," mercies, and power.

Numerous comments in the *Thanksgiving Hymns* seem reminiscent of the Book of Job and may perhaps form a response to it. Note the following: "in my troubles you have comforted me" (17.13), "a man can be more insightful than his companion" (17.15–16), "there is no power like your might" (17.16–17), "for your wisdom there is no measure" (17.17), and "[there is no hope!]" for those "in need" of "[your] truth" (17.17–18). Also the reception of Job may be found in the following: the reference to "my adversary" (17.21; cf. 17.25), the experience of being "a reproach to those who grumble against me" (17.22), so that "through the mystery of your wisdom you chastised me" (17.23) resulting in the perception that "your chastisement become joy and gladness to me" (17.24). The last exultation may be the Righteous Teacher's rejection of Job's failure to find an answer.

Simultaneously, allusions to Job in the *Thanksgiving Hymns* may in fact reveal the Righteous Teacher's theology of suffering. Seow states: "[T]he Teacher's interpretation suggests that patience is at issue after all, for suffering is not necessarily a consequence of human sin, but may in fact be a test for the suf-

---

[309] O. R. Sellers suggests לצדקה in some Hebrew texts of Joel 2:23 is a gloss added after המורה by a scribe who wanted to draw attention to the Righteous Teacher: "So when he saw the word מורה he automatically thought of the Teacher of Righteousness." Sellers, "A Possible Old Testament Reference to the Teacher of Righteousness," *IEJ* 5 (1955) 93–95; the quotation is on p. 95.

[310] Elwolde, "The Hodayot's Use of the Psalter: Text-Critical Contributions (Book 4: Pss 90–106)" in *The Scrolls and Biblical Traditions: Proceedings of the Seventh Meeting of the IOQS in Helsinki*, edited by G. J. Brooke, *et al.* (Leiden, 2012) p. 85.

[311] Elwolde, in *The Scrolls and Biblical Traditions*, p. 85.

[312] See the Selected Bibliography.

[313] See Licht, מגילת ההודיות, p. 19.

[314] See the comments by Licht, מגילת ההודיות, p. 11.

[315] Flint, *The Dead Sea Scrolls*, p. 115.

ferer and an opportunity for God to be glorified."[316] The authors of these psalms and poems perceive suffering as necessary, even desirable. It focuses the faithful one's perspective and is related to the Jewish systems of purification.

In a way reminiscent of the author of the *Testament of Job*, the author of the "Teacher Hymns" does not attribute suffering to sin; but unlike him, "patience" is attributed only to God (1QH[a] 4.29). Suffering seems to be necessary for a prophet and one chosen; it is necessary for chastisement. Further research should look to the interplay between the Teacher, the Community, and Job in relation to suffering and God's providence. Such studies should improve our understanding of theodicy during the Second Temple Period.[317]

Symbolism. The collection known as the *Thanksgiving Hymns* is replete with images inherited from Hebrew Scriptures. In many ways these psalms mirror the Psalter. The psalms and poems mix biblical symbols and imagery. Notably, Hymn 22, "I Thank the Lord for Making Me the Irrigator of the Garden," contains one of the most complex poems found in the collection. In these lines, the author uses "pool," "fountain," "spring," "garden," "pools of water," and "trees." The speaker identifies himself as the Irrigator of the Garden and in 16.21 he makes an explicit reference to "Eden." This imagery is certainly reliant upon Gen 2:8, 10, 15.

One notable difference is the description of the human. In Genesis 2:15 the human is charged to care for the garden by "tilling" it. In the *Thanksgiving Hymns*, the speaker, envisions himself as a cooling stream in the arid desert. He alters the expected imagery of "tiller" to "Irrigator." His task is no longer to simply till and care for the garden. Through God's election, he becomes the source of life and sustenance for the Community. This vision is unique to the speaker in the *Thanksgiving Hymns*; the prophets do not identify themselves as irrigators. Even Ezekiel, with copious Eden imagery, views the water as an impersonal force.

Throughout the *Thanksgiving Hymns* the image of sand-vipers represents the unrighteous enemies of the Community. In the Hebrew Bible, the word אפעה, translated by me as "sand-viper," is used three times, once in Job and twice in Isaiah.[318] In Isaiah 59, the sand-viper symbolizes those who "rely on emptiness and speak falsehood, conceiving wrong and begetting evil" (*TANAKH*, Isa 59:4). This polemical imagery represents those who, from birth, are diametrically opposed to the "wonderful counselor" and the "wise ones" of the Community.[319]

Biblical Allusions in the Thanksgiving Hymns. Building upon the publications of B. P. Kittel, D. Patte, and R. L.

Schulz,[320] J. A. Hughes examines the biblical allusions in the *Thanksgiving Hymns*. She concludes that the "most obvious poetic devise employed in the *Hodayot* is scriptural allusion."[321] She adds that the enduring power of the poems or psalms is the "multilayered quality" of the poetry.[322] G. J. Brooke summarizes the *status quaestionis* succinctly:

A combination of the insights of Newsom and Hughes permits the modern reader to appreciate the hypertextual character of the pastiche that makes up much of the *Hodayot* to be concerned with the construction of identity by the poet[323] through the carefully structured use of allusion – this is Scripture rewritten poetically, anthologically, hypertextually. [324]

In conclusion, the *Thanksgiving Hymns* are an important collection of psalms and poems that can shed light on the development of the canonical texts, the continuing influence of the Psalter, the desire for creatively new symbolic language, and a need to praise God. Most authors probably would want us to inculcate the truth that it is not so important how often we have read Scripture; it is more important how Scripture has been read in us.

10. Relationship to Early Jewish Literature

Within Second Temple Judaism, the *Thanksgiving Hymns* witness to the creation of many new poems, hymns, and psalms from 200 BCE to 70 CE. Among these hymn collections are *More Psalms of David*, the *Angelic Liturgy*, the *Pseudepigraphic Psalms*, the *Qumran Psalms Scroll* (which includes the Psalter and some non-Masoretic psalms), the *Psalms of Solomon*, and the *Odes of Solomon*.[325] To these collections must be

---

[316] C. L. Seow, *Job 1–21: Interpretation and Commentary* (Grand Rapids, 2013) pp. 116–18; the quotation is on p. 118.

[317] See Charlesworth, "Theodicy in Early Jewish Writings," in *Theodicy in the World of the Bible*, edited by A. Laato and J. C. de Moor (Leiden, 2003) pp. 470–508.

[318] See Charlesworth, *The Good and Evil Serpent*.

[319] Col. 11.1–19.

[320] Kittel, *The Hymns of Qumran*; D. Patte, *Early Jewish Hermeneutic in Palestine* (SBLDS 22; Missoula, 1975); and R. L. Schulz, *The Search for Quotation: Verbal Parallels in the Prophets* (JSOTSup 180; Sheffield, 1999).

[321] J. A. Hughes, *Scriptural Allusions and Exegesis in the Hodayot*, p. 231.

[322] Hughes, *Scriptural Allusions and Exegesis in the Hodayot*, p. 235.

[323] Brooke is not implying that the *Hodayot* are by one author.

[324] Brooke, *Reading the Dead Sea Scrolls: Essays in Method* (SBLEJL 39; Atlanta, 2013) p. 82. Brooke seeks to label "hypertextual" what was called "parabiblical" or "paratextual" (see p. 72).

[325] See, e.g., Charlesworth, "A Prolegomenon to a New Study of the Jewish Background of the Hymns and Prayers in the New Testament," in *Essays in Honour of Yigael Yadin*, edited by J. Neusner and G. Vermes (Oxford, 1982) pp. 265–85 and Charlesworth, "Jewish Hymns, Odes, and Prayers (ca. 167 B.C.E.–135 C.E.)," in *Early Judaism and its Modern Interpreters*, edited by R. A. Kraft and G. W. E. Nickelsburg (The

added the individual hymns such as, the *Hymn of Praise* (3Q6), the *Prayer for King Jonathan* (4Q448), the *Prayer of Nabonidus* (4Q242), the *Prayer of Enoch?* (4Q369) the *Prayer of Manasseh*, and the *Self-Glorification Hymn* (4Q471b; see col. 26).

One can perceive that while the Qumran hymns, psalms, and poems are composed by Jews who celebrated salvation within a Community that is both enjoying fellowship with God and still waiting for the conclusion of the Endtime, the Jews behind the *Psalms of Solomon* long for salvation.[326] While at least some of the Qumranites generally looked for the coming of a Messiah of Aaron and a Messiah of Judah (1QS), the group of Jews behind the *Psalms of Solomon* yearned for the coming of a Davidic Messiah (*PssSol* 17:21–34).

One of the remarkable characteristics of the *Thanksgiving Hymns*, notably the "Teacher Hymns," and the *Self-Glorification Hymn* is an elevated self-perception. As D. Flusser pointed out, this "exalted self-awareness" is not unusual in Second Temple Judaism and would include Hillel and Jesus.[327] Most likely, this high ego not only witnesses to the enthusiasm caused by a realizing apocalyptic eschatology but also to the pervasiveness of some continuing prophetic consciousness.

The apocalyptic "eschatology" found in the *Thanksgiving Hymns* is virtually identical to that preserved in the many Jewish apocalypses, namely Daniel, *1 Enoch* (a library of Enoch literature that covers c. 300 BCE to 4 BCE or 66 CE), and *4 Ezra* (80–100 CE). Investigations of the multifarious ways the *Thanksgiving Hymns* fit within Early Judaism during the "Axial Age"[328] illuminates how Jews claimed to experience the continuing presence of a loving, yet judgmental, God. Jews, especially under subjugation by Greece, Parthia, or Rome, affirmed God's continuing covenantal loyalty; such a phenomenon is evident in the preceding pages and is amplified in many monographs.

11. Relationship to the New Testament and Early Christian Literature

Focusing on how the *Thanksgiving Hymns* is important for the study of Christian Origins and the New Testament may elicit a reply: "*In all ways.*" That should be evident from the previous discussion of some major theological motifs in this massive collection of poems and hymns.

A tone of thanksgiving and gratefulness shapes both the *Thanksgiving Hymns* and the New Testament documents. The *Thanksgiving Hymns* help scholars understand the Jewish piety that shaped the lives of Jesus and his followers. A wide consensus is clear globally: the Dead Sea Scrolls provide much of the social, historical, and theological context for the poetic vision of the documents in the New Testament as well as many expressions, terms, concepts, and poetic passages preserved in them.

Due to the brevity required of a reference work, only three aspects will be chosen for reflection and further research as we focus on seeking to discern, how and in what ways, the *Thanksgiving Hymns* help us comprehend passages in the New Testament (initial focus will be on perceptions already published). At the outset, it is imperative to observe the contexts of words, sentences, and compositions, comprehend a taxonomy of how one text might influence another, apply the right use of "intertextuality,"[329] and perceive the need to use parallels with insight and reflection, as many luminaries have demanded, notably J. Barr and S. Sandmel.[330]

First, the Qumranites claimed to be living in a prophetic world they inherited notably from Isaiah, Jeremiah, and Ezekiel. As D. N. Freedman pointed out, the prophets were poets who absorbed and recreated Israel's poetic vision.[331] Thus, "the Many" at Qumran inherited not only the gift of prophecy but also its poetry and poetic vision.

The piety and theological erudition in the *Thanksgiving Hymns* is not only the background for but also the foreground

---

Bible and Its Modern Interpreters; Atlanta, 1986) pp. 411–36. Also see, *inter alia*, David Flusser, "Psalms, Hymns and Prayers," in *Jewish Writings of the Second Temple Period*, edited by M. E. Stone (CRINT 2.2; Assen and Philadelphia, 1984) pp. 551–77.

[326] See Holm-Nielsen, "Erwägungen zu dem Verhältnis zwischen den Hodayot und den Psalmen Salomos," in *Bibel und Qumran* [Hans Bardtke Festschrift], edited by S. Wagner (Leipzig, 1968) pp. 112–31.

[327] D. Flusser, *Judaism and the Origins of Christianity* (Jerusalem, 1988); see esp. p. 509.

[328] See the definition of Axial Age by R. Bellah in *Religion in Human Evolution* (Cambridge, 2011). "Axial Age" derives from the German Achsenzeit, "axis time." It was coined by Karl Jaspers (1883–1969) and refers to the period from 800 BCE to 200 BCE. During this time individual consciousness increases as a major factor in the philosophy and theology of the West (the Socratic School, the great Prophets of Judea) and East (Zoroaster, Upanishads, Confucius, Lao Tzu). The effects of the so-called Axial Age affected thought long after 200 BCE. Gradually, it defined Western Culture.

[329] A methodology may be found in Charlesworth, "Intertextuality: Isaiah 40:3 and the Serek Ha-Yaḥad," in *The Quest for Context and Meaning: Studies in Biblical Intertextuality*, edited by C. A. Evans and S. Talmon (Leiden, 1997) pp. 197–224.

[330] J. Barr, *The Semantics of Biblical Language* (London, 1961) and S. Sandmel, "Parallelomania," *JBL* 81 (1962) 1–13. Sandmel did not call for scholars to ignore parallels, as too many scholars imagine. Sandmel called for the restoration of "perspective and direction" (p. 13) and for the contextual use of parallels so as to "encourage" the study of parallels "especially in the case of the Qumran documents" (p. 1).

[331] D. N. Freedman, "Pottery, Poetry, and Prophecy: An Essay on Biblical Poetry," *JBL* 96 (1977) 5–26.

of Christian Origins. Prophecy is still alive but only for the Qumranites, it is revealed solely to those within the Community. Within Qumran, God is seen as continuing to create and control the cosmos through various means, including his created angels.

An apocalyptic "eschatology" (Endtime speculation and expectation) defines the authors of the *Thanksgiving Hymns*, Jesus, and the authors of most New Testament documents. The authors of the *Thanksgiving Hymns* and the poets found in the New Testament share a belief in God's goodness and God's steadfast covenant loyalty with God's elect people. The Jews represented by both compositions claim to experience a new day dawning. In both collections, intermittently, the Endtime or eschaton is experienced as a "realizing eschatology."[332] Thus, in the *Thanksgiving Hymns* and in the New Testament we have not only futuristic eschatology but a realizing-eschatology.

What was seen as a creation by Paul is now perceived to define not only the final columns of the *Rule of the Community* (hymns) but also many compositions in the *Thanksgiving Hymns*. Most importantly, the authors of the *Thanksgiving Hymns* stress that no righteous works can be presented to God as an offering for acceptance or salvation. The human is a creature who comes to God without any merit for acceptance. The human, including all the Elect Ones, stands before God with guilt and is accepted only because of confessed contrition and God's forgiveness.[333]

Second, an author of one psalm coined an expression to refer to the enemies of the Community: they were "works (= offspring)[334] of a sand-viper" (11.18).[335] This same unusual expression is attributed to John the Baptizer (Mt 3:7) who also used it to disparage those whom he despised.[336] Perhaps the Baptizer inherited the expression from Essenes in Jericho or even members of the Community at Qumran.[337] Jesus also uses the expression (Mt 23:33). Did Jesus learn this stunning imag-

ery and expression from the Baptizer or from Essenes?[338] No data or methodology is known that helps us adjudicate among these possibilities; nevertheless, the extreme importance of the *Hodayot* has become clearer.

Third, the *Thanksgiving Hymns* is full of data that is essential for an understanding of the language and poetic sections of the New Testament. Though the texts are extant in a Semitized Greek, they evolve from oral and written sources that were originally Semitic, Aramaic and Hebrew.[339] The *Thanksgiving Hymns'* symbolic language, sophisticated rhetoric, and poetic style (a development of *parallelismus membrorum*) has been seen, rightly, to have had an indirect, and perhaps direct, impact on many of the hymns and poetic sections of the New Testament documents.

Early hymns are quoted by Paul and his followers; most notably among them are the pre-Pauline Christological compositions in Philippians 2:6–11 and Colossians 1:15–20. The hymns found in Revelation, while very Jewish, do not seem to derive from early Jewish liturgical settings; they may have been composed by the author of Revelation.[340] Yet, the singing in heaven, found in Revelation, is reminiscent of the Qumran hymns and the *Angelic Liturgy.*

Obviously, the Logos hymn or poem that opens the Gospel of John comes first to mind when one contemplates Essene influences. R. Bultmann (whose publications usually antedate the discovery of the Dead Sea Scrolls) concluded that this "hymn" was added to John and is close to the *Odes of Solomon.* M. Testuz published the Greek text of *Ode* 11, and concluded that it is an Essene composition.[341] Many Johannine experts now assume that John 1:1–18 was originally a "hymn" chanted in

---

[332] E. P. Sanders notes "that some of the benefits of the new age had already been realized" in the Community; he then quotes 1QH 3.20–22. Sanders, *Judaism: Practice & Belief 63 BCE – 66 CE* (London and Philadelphia, 1992) p. 370.

[333] See esp. "Sünde und Vergebung in der Gemeinde von Qumran," in H. Thyen, *Studien zur Sündenvergebung* (FRLANT 96; Göttingen, 1970) pp. 77–98.

[334] Also, see *Mysteries* (4Q299 frg. 3a–b col. 2) in which "every [or all] work" means "every creature."

[335] For a discussion, see Charlesworth, *The Good and Evil Serpent* (ABRL; New Haven, 2010); see esp. pp. 359–60. See *Damascus Document* (4Q266 frg. 3 2.2) in which we find "[vip]ers." The term is used for those who lack understanding and so disobey the commandments of God.

[336] For the suggestion that the Baptizer had been at Qumran, knew some of the jargon, but never became one of "the Many," see Charlesworth in *BDSS*, vol. 3, pp. 1–35.

[337] O. Betz was the first to make this observation. Betz, "Die Proselytentaufe der Qumransekte und die Taufe im Neuen Testament," *RQ* 2 (1958) 213–34.

[338] For how Jesus may have been influenced by Essenes, see the contributions to *JDSS*, edited by Charlesworth (ABRL; New Haven, 1992); R. Horsley, "The Dead Sea Scrolls and the Historical Jesus," (pp. 37–60) and D. H. Juel, "The Future of a Religious Past: Qumran and the Palestinian Jesus Movement," (pp. 61–73) in *BDSS*, vol. 3, and P. W. Flint, "The Qumran Scrolls and the Historical Jesus," in *Jesus Research: New Methodologies and Perceptions*, edited by Charlesworth (Grand Rapids, 2014) pp. 261–82.

[339] Notably, see Fitzmyer, *The Semitic Background of the New Testament,* 2 vols., and the contributors to *Jesus Research: New Methodologies and Perceptions*, edited by Charlesworth, with B. Rhea and P. Pokorný (Grand Rapids, 2014).

[340] K.-P. Jörns, *Das hymnische Evangelium* (Gerd Mohn, 1971) see esp. p. 179: "Die Frage nach der Herkunft der Hymnen ist also wie folgt zu beantworten: sie sind Kompositionen des Verfassers der Apokalypse."

[341] R. Bultmann, *The Gospel of John,* translated by G. R. Beasley-Murray, R. W. Hoare and J. K. Riches (Oxford, 1971) and M. Testuz, *Papyrus Bodmer X–XII* (Cologny-Genève, 1959). Note Testuz's astute observation that the Odes and the *Hodayot* are astonishingly similar (p. 57) which leads to this valid conclusion: "Nous pensons donc que cette Ode est l'oeuvre d'un Essénien …" (p. 58).

early worship services.[342] Conceivably, Essenes were members of the Johannine Community and present during these times of worship.[343]

The discussion of the importance of the *Thanksgiving Hymns* for the origin of the New Testament should include the speculations regarding the origins of Luke's famous canticles. Thus, we conclude this section with a review of the importance of the *Thanksgiving Hymns* for the hymns that open Luke-Acts. Luke's birth narrative (1:4–2:52) is a literary unit with traditions that had independent origins. What were they?[344]

As has been pointed out repeatedly, the hymns found in Luke's infancy gospel, notably the *Magnificat* (1:46–55) and *Benedictus* (1:67–79) are fundamentally Jewish. The *Magnificat* has been singled out as the hymn most influenced by the *Hodayot*.[345] One may speak about the *Thanksgiving Hymns* being a "poetic bridge" from the Hebrew Scriptures to the Lucan hymns.[346]

The *Magnificat* is an individual song of praise like many poems or hymns in the *Thanksgiving Hymns*. Scholarly opinions on its origins may be arranged into three categories.[347] First, some experts concluded that Luke composed the *Magnificat*; these scholars include A. von Harnack, H. F. D. Sparks, and N. Turner. Second, other scholars contended that the poem or hymn was originally an early Jewish creation; among them would be K. B. Bornhäuser, H. Gunkel, E. Klostermann, S. O. P. Mowinckel, F. Spitta, P. Winter, and F. Bovon. Third, another group of scholars are convinced that these hymns were composed within the early community of those who believed in Jesus; that is the opinion of P. Benoit, J. Gnilka, and H. Schürmann.

Three distinguished and more recent scholarly publications are chosen for a perception of the source of Luke's canticles. R. E. Brown contended that both the *Magnificat* and *Benedictus* originated within the Jewish Christian circle of the *Anawim*, "the Poor Ones."[348] According to Psalm 149:4 "His [God's] people" is synonymous with "the Poor Ones." Fitzmyer pointed out that the words are more heavily Semitized than the contextual Semitized Greek. He concluded that the hymn originated in "the Jewish Christian early community."[349] Bovon judged that the *Magnificat* originates within Judaism. Most likely, it was originally "a poem of the Baptist's movement."[350]

All these suggestions are insightful. Scholars should not dismiss the possibility that the *Magnificat*, the *Benedictus*, and other poetic sections of Luke originated within Second Temple Judaism, possibly were translated from Hebrew to Greek (or composed in a Semitic Greek), and finally were redacted by Luke. Bovon represents succinctly the position of most scholars: "[T]he Magnificat can be compared not only with the Hebrew Bible but with more recent texts, such as the hymns from Qumran, the Psalms of Solomon, or isolated songs of praise."[351] It seems well established that Luke inserts these hymns within legends that have diverse origins. Almost all are within Second Temple Judaism (including the Palestinian Jesus Movement).

Five more reflections on the *Thanksgiving Hymns* provide data for a better comprehension of the origin of the *Magnificat*, allowing for the customary redaction of Jewish traditions by Luke. They are intended to provide the foundation for continued research.

First, an examination of the *Magnificat* reveals some interesting parallels with the *Thanksgiving Hymns*. Notably, the poetry begins with the *Hodayot* formula: the "Lord" is followed by "for": "My soul magnifies the Lord [*sic*]… for." Could the author of this poem have been influenced somehow by "the *Hodayot*"? The question leads us to the vast amount of hymns and psalms, as well as poems, composed by various types of Jews during the Second Temple period.

---

[342] For an insightful discussion, see C. S. Keener, "A Redacted Hymn?" in *The Gospel of John: A Commentary* (Peabody, MA, 2003) vol. 1, pp. 234–37.

[343] See the discussion in Charlesworth, "A Study in Shared Symbolism and Language: The Qumran Community and the Johannine Community," in *BDSS*, vol. 3, pp. 97–152.

[344] The Lucan canticles should not be attributed to the Therapeutae, even though Philo reported that these Jews were known for composing hymns (*De Vita Contemplativa* 10.79–80).

[345] See, e.g., N. Lohfink, *Lobgesänge der Armen: Studien zum Magnifikat, den Hodajot von Qumran und einigen späten Psalmen* (Stuttgarter Bibelstudien 143; Stuttgart, 1990).

[346] The term was coined by Horgan and Kobelski; "The Hodayot (1QH) and New Testament Poetry," in *To Touch the Text: Biblical and Related Studies in Honor of Joseph A. Fitzmyer* (New York, 1989) pp. 179–93.

[347] For bibliographical details, consult the publications by R. E. Brown, J. A. Fitzmyer, and F. Bovon [in the following notes]. Also see, H. Gunkel, "Die Lieder in der Kindheitsgeschichte Jesu bei Lukas," in *Festgabe von Fachgenossen und Freunden A. von Harnack* [Festschrift for A. von Harnack] (Tübingen, 1921) pp. 43–60; F. Gryglewicz, "Die Herkunft der Hymnen des Kindheitsevangeliums des Lukas," *NTS* 21 (1974–1975) 265–73; S. Muñoz Iglesias, *Los cánticos del Evangelio de la Infancia según San Lucas* (Madrid, 1983).

[348] Brown, *The Birth of the Messiah* (Garden City, New York, 1977) pp. 349–55. Recent research on Qumran and on pre-70 archaeological settings most likely would attract a positive response to Brown's comment that "the Qumran community" was "a sectarian group of Anawim" (p. 351) but not to the supposition that Luke's canticles come to us from a "community of Jewish Anawim who had been converted to Christianity, a group that unlike the sectarians at Qumran would have continued to reverence the Temple and whose messianism was Davidic" (p. 352). Further research is need on this group.

[349] J. A. Fitzmyer, *The Gospel According to Luke I–IX* (AB; Garden City, 1981) p. 361.

[350] F. Bovon, *Luke 1*, translated by C. M. Thomas (Hermeneia; Minneapolis, 2002) p. 68.

[351] F. Bovon, *Luke 1*, p. 55.

Second, before Luke's time it is not possible to distinguish between "Christian" and Jewish poetic compositions (if they are not defined by Christological affirmations); and the concept of "Jewish Christianity" is a confusing concept. Thus, we should not confuse reflections by seeking to discern if the author is a Jew, a Jew who composed this poem before he believed that Jesus was the Messiah, God's Son (or related perception), a converted Pharisee or Essene, or a so-called Jewish Christian.

Third, '*Anawim*' is a noun that may describe a group within Second Temple Judaism. Note this virtually unknown early Jewish hymn:

He [the Lord] magnified wisdom and understanding in
  his heart,
Great sanctity without measure:
Who is like him, who compares to him
Who has not forgotten the cry of *the poor*?
He recalled in his abundant mercies *the poor* and down
trodden.... (4.7–8)[352]

The noun "the poor," "the Poor," or "the Poor Ones" is also a term that is emphasized by the authors of the *Thanksgiving Hymns*. The authors use of the term "the Poor Ones" may involve reflections on a term that the Qumranites, or Essenes, used for themselves.[353] In the *War Scroll*, the Sons of Light are called "the Poor Ones" (1QM 11.9, 13; 13.13–14) and in *Psalm Pesher 1*, the Qumran Community is most likely "the congregation of the Poor Ones" (4Q471 frgs. 1–10 and 2.9–11). The Qumranites once had been wealthy priests. They became "the Poor Ones" to serve God and to follow the call of the Voice to prepare "the Way of the Lord." Note the use of "the Poor Ones" and "poor one" in the *Thanksgiving Hymns*:[354]

… his mercies upon *the Poor O*[*nes* ...] (2.27)

And from the assembly of the Seekers of Smooth (Things) you redeemed the soul of *the Poor One*, whose blood they thought to consume ... (10.34)

… and with the miserable ones in (one) lot. And the soul of *the Poor One* dwells with great turmoils. (11.26)

And in order to show your might in me before the sons of Adam you set apart *the Poor One*. And you brought him

to the smelting-pot like (fine) gold in the works of fire, and like silver refined in a furnace of the smiths, purifying sevenfold. (13.17–18)

But you, O my God, you turn storm into silence, and the soul of *the Poor One* you delivered like a bir[d from a trap and] like prey from the power of lions. (13.20–21)

for righteousness to rise from the tumult together (with) all the *Poor Ones* of mercy. (13.24)

And he raised up *the Poor One* from the dust to [eternal height] and unto the skies. (26.27)

I have chosen to capitalize, when apparently demanded by context, "the Poor One," and "the Poor Ones," as these seem to be technical terms at Qumran. Except for 26.27, a column that combines numerous separate fragments, "the Poor One" is found only in the "Teacher Hymns." Many Qumran specialists have concluded correctly that sometimes "the Poor One" is an autobiographical aside by the Righteous Teacher. In an extensive study, C. M. Murphy notes that the loss of wealth by the Qumran priests had a purifying effect and that the author of col. 18.22–30 and 33–35 "pits the wealth of outsiders against the knowledge of community members."[355]

Fourth, in Luke we find the expression "Bless the Lord, the God of Israel, for" (Εὐλογητὸς κύριος ὁ θεὸς τοῦ Ἰσραήλ, ὅτι; Lk 1:68). This formula appears in some early Jewish hymns; in particular note the following refrain that characterizes an early hymn:

Blessed is the name of his glory forever;
Blessed are you, O Lord God of Israel, for all eternity;
And the entire people said Amen ... (2.3–4)

Blessed is the Lord God of Israel for all eternity, and the people say: Amen. (4.15)

Blessed is the Lord God of Israel for all eternity,
And the people respond: Amen (3.9)[356]

These three doxological statements are borrowed from Psalm 106:48;

Blessed be the LORD, the God of Israel,
From everlasting to everlasting.
And let all the people say, "Amen."
Praise the LORD! (NRSV)

[352] S. Safrai and D. Flusser, "The Apocryphal Psalms of David," in *Judaism of the Second Temple Period*, translated by A. Yadin (Jerusalem and Grand Rapids, 2007) vol. 1, p. 163.
[353] See H. Bengtsson in *BDSS*, vol. 1, pp. 200–2; Charlesworth and J. D. McSpadden in *BDSS*, vol. 2, pp. 326, 330, 337, 339–40, 344. VanderKam states that "Poor Ones" may be "a sectarian designation" in the *Hodayot*; VanderKam, *The Dead Sea Scrolls and the Bible*, p. 103.
[354] All references are from the Composite Text.

[355] C. M. Murphy, *Wealth in the Dead Sea Scrolls and in the Qumran Community* (STDJ 40; Leiden and Boston, 2002) p. 343; see esp. "Poetic and Liturgical Texts" on pp. 242–50.
[356] Safrai and Flusser, "The Apocryphal Psalms of David," vol. 1, p. 163.

This verse ends the fourth book of the Masoretic Psalter; it was used by our anonymous author.

S. Safrai and D. Flusser speculated that the apocryphal psalm, written in the name of the prophet and king, David, was composed "during the Second Temple period." More importantly, these scholars were convinced that the psalm was a creation of "the same movement from which the Qumran community emerged."[357]

While the poem does not seem Qumranic, there are striking links to the Qumran *Psalms Scroll* (notably the elevation of David as prophet and the non-Masoretic text used) as well as the *Thanksgiving Hymns*;[358] these parallels require further research. The ancient Jewish psalm was found in the Cairo Geniza which preserved some Qumran compositions and may be related to the "more than 200 psalms of David" that were allegedly found in the ninth century CE near Jericho and Qumran during the time of the Nestorian Bishop Timotheos I.[359]

Fifth, some of the predictions in Luke's hymns are more appropriate for pre-70 Judaism – especially during the successes of the Hasmoneans and the Herodians – than Luke's time, since *the predictions did not come true* as claimed in Luke's canticles; note these hopes that characterize pre-70 Judaism and do not seem appropriate after the destruction of Jerusalem and the Temple:

The Lord scattered the proud in the imagination of their hearts (1:51).
He put down the mighty from their thrones (1:52).
He filled the hungry and sent the rich away empty (1:53).
He has helped Israel (1:54).
The God of Israel redeemed his people (1:68).
We are saved from our enemies (1:69–71, 74).
He performed the oath sworn to our father Abraham (1:72–73).

While the followers of Jesus after the Easter experience believed in salvation accomplished,[360] they looked for Jesus' return when these dreams would be actualities. They "knew" that God had redeemed his people, but he had not yet scattered the proud or put down those who were on the throne. He certainly had not saved Jews from their enemies or revitalized the promise to Abraham that his descendants would own the Land.[361]

Many Jews prior to the destruction of 70 CE expected the fulfillment of all these biblical promises and dreams. Such expectations were shared among Jews in Palestine from the time of the Maccabees to at least 66 CE when open revolt caused havoc in the Land promised to Abraham and his descendants.

Today, those who excavate in and around Jerusalem face shocking reminders of the horrors from the first Jewish revolt against Rome, the enemy of those who composed these poems. The proud and the mighty on thrones, the Romans, were not "scattered"; they took Jews as slaves to Italy. Starvation in Jerusalem before 70 seems to indicate a pre-66 date for the expectation that the Lord fed the hungry. The hope in the canticle is for God to redeem his people, a hope universal in Early Judaism; but, the verbs are in the aorists, the past tense; most likely they were Semitic verbs that are *perfectum profeticum* (a past tense that refers to a future act that is completed).[362]

If the hypothesis of Brown and Fitzmyer proves to be correct and these Lucan masterpieces were originally composed by followers of Jesus in Jerusalem, why would that exclude Essene influences upon them or composition of them by a convert from Essenism, like the Odist, as has become apparent?

Scholars are rightly amazed by how many poems, hymns, psalms, and prayers were composed by Qumranites or Essenes. Hymnic compositions dominate in the Qumran Scrolls. Were the Essenes not the great composers of poems and hymns in Second Temple Judaism? Has it not become likely that, after Herod's kingship was established in 37 BCE, many Essenes moved back into Jerusalem and into the area defined by "the Essene Gate," which is not far from where the Last Supper was held and where Jesus' family most likely moved after they believed he had been raised by God and would return near Jerusalem?

These questions will be debated, but almost all scholars will agree that the *Thanksgiving Hymns* and related hymnic collections and compositions within Second Temple Judaism ground the fact that the Palestinian Jesus Movement developed deep within Judaism.[363] As research continues, let it finally suffice to indicate that Lk 2:14, "men of good will" (a perplexing phrase for exegetes) or "men of his [God's] good will" (Coptic variant) is found in 1QHᵃ (= Composite Text) 12.33–34 (= Suk. 4.32–33). A similar judgment pertains to "And the multitude of his mercies is over all the sons [= men] of his will" as C. H.

---

[357] Safrai and Flusser, *Judaism of the Second Temple Period*, vol. 1, p. 269.

[358] In particular, both this non-Masoretic psalm and the *Hodayot* (and the *Self-Glorification Hymn*) share such unique images as the following: "the righteous and the evil," "You made him greater than all the angels," "the poor."

[359] O. Braun, "Ein Brief des Katholikos Timotheos I über biblische Studien des. 9. Jahrhunderts," *Oriens Christianus* 1 (1901) 300–13.

[360] Brown's words in *The Birth of the Messiah*, p. 350.

[361] The verbs do not seem to be examples of *perfectum futurum*, a past tense as viewed from the future.

[362] After Lk 1:50 are six aorists. This verb form usually denotes past completed action. It is not impossible that Luke perceived they were prophetic aorists; that is, they treated the future as present.

[363] Flusser also argued that Lk 2:14, the *Gloria*, reflects an exegetical tradition found also in the Aramaic Targum of Isaiah 6:3 and also on the *Kedusha*. See Flusser, "Sanktus und Gloria," in *Abraham Unser Vater: Festschrift für Otto Michel*, edited by O. Betz, *et al.* (Leiden, 1963) pp. 129–52.

Hunzinger[364] and Fitzmyer made clear long ago.[365] Fitzmyer rightly claims, we have found a "direct parallel for the expression 'men of God's good pleasure.' We have found in the Qumran texts a contemporary expression that provides the missing Hebrew equivalent."[366]

Studying the *Thanksgiving Hymns* helps reveal how deeply rooted "Christian" Origins are within Second Temple Judaism. Expressions of praise and joy in the New Testament are not something new within pre-70 Judaism (as some scholars imagined 100 years ago). The hymnic compositions in the New Testament reflect a continuity of praise from earliest times (perhaps before the tenth century BCE) to the period when "Christianity" was becoming distinct from other forms of Judaism.

During Second Temple Judaism, the Psalter was "the hymn-book" of the Temple which Jesus called "my Father's House," according to the Gospel of John (2:16; cf. 14:2),[367] but other "hymnbooks" defined the piety, memories, and hopes of many Jewish communities. Notably among such groups are two main collections. First, the *Psalms of Solomon* are the product of a Pharisaic-type of Jews living in Jerusalem. Second, the *Thanksgiving Hymns* are poems and hymns that are to be recited or studied by the Most Holy of Holy Ones and the Many at Qumran. Praising God and acknowledging God's continuing creativity, *mutatis mutandis*, expressed a commonality among pre-70 Jews. Behind all the discord and fratricidal tensions among various groups of Jews, one can find a shared love and devotion to the One God (exemplified in the *Shema* and perhaps in early forms of the *Amida* or *18 Benedictions*) and a need to express thanksgiving.

These wide sweeping glances at early Jewish piety may be supplemented by three new discoveries. First, after the conquest of Alexander the Great in the fourth century BCE, a few concepts became personified (and conceivably in some settings operated similarly to hyptostasis).[368] Wisdom is personified in the Wisdom of Solomon and the "hypostatic Voice" seems evident in some apocalypses. Now, it is apparent that some read-

ers may have imagined that "the earth" is personified in the *Thanksgiving Hymns*. Note 11.33–34 (arranged poetically):

> And the earth cries out about the disaster
> Which has happened in the world,
> And all its designs wail,
> And all who are upon it behave madly.

Such a personification, whether imagined by the author or supplied by some readers, is a fitting background to the personification of the earth in Revelation 12. In Revelation, the personification or hypostasis is clearer, perhaps due to its genre or the development over the previous century. In this chapter, the woman chased by the serpent or dragon is helped by the earth: "And the earth came to the help of the woman, and the earth opened its mouth and swallowed the river which the dragon had poured from his mouth" (Rev 12:16).

Second, it is likely that the *Thanksgiving Hymns* provides another source for the later idea of *descensus Christi ad inferos*. The concept is evident in Eph 4:8–10 and 1Pet 3:19–20 and may be reflected in other New Testament passages. The concept appears highly developed in the *Odes of Solomon*. The concept assumes that there are some in Sheol (or the underworld) who can hear Christ's call to be saved. The pre-Christological adumbration of this concept may be found in 25.13–15 (arranged poetically):[369]

> And (concerning) the Endtime of fixed times,
> You allowed fles[h] to have insight.
> [The ho]st of the upper regions you shall judge in the upper
>   regions,
> And the dwellers of earth (you shall judge) upon the earth.
> And also [in Sheo]l below you shall ju[d]ge.
>
> And (concerning) the dwellers of darkness,
> You shall contest a lawsuit,
> Declaring righte[ous] the righteous one
> And declaring w[icked the wicked one],
> For there is none ex[cept] you.

Third, a distinct person with a very high prophetic consciousness (most likely the Righteous Teacher) imagines that he is a "nursing-father:"[370]

> And you made me a father for the sons of loving kindness,
> And as a nursing-father to the men of a wondrous-sign.
>
> And they open (their) mouths like those suck[ing the breast]

[364] C. H. Hunzinger, "Neues Licht auf Lc 2:14 *anthrōpoi eudokias*," *ZNW* 44 (1952–1953) 85–90.

[365] Fitzmyer, "'Peace Upon Earth Among Men of His Good Will' (Lk 2:14)," in *The Semitic Background of the New Testament* (Grand Rapids and Cambridge, 1997) vol. 1, pp. 101–4. Fitzmyer's article was originally published in 1958.

[366] Fitzmyer, *The Semitic Background of the New Testament*, p. 101

[367] See the contributions by L. Ritmeyer, D. Bahat, L. H. Schiffman, G. A. Rendsburg, M. Aviam, J. H. Charlesworth, H. W. Attridge, and G. T. Zervos in *Jesus and Temple: Textual and Archaeological Explorations*, edited by Charlesworth (Minneapolis, 2014).

[368] The concept of hypostasis was not created in the fourth century CE, with the beginning of the Church Councils; yet, we must not read back the use of hypostasis by Greek Christians into earlier Jewish conceptions.

[369] See Charlesworth's contribution to the Bruce Chilton Festschrift, edited by J. Neusner and C. Evans, in press.

[370] See J. Cherian, "The Moses at Qumran: The מורה הצדק as the Nursing-Father of the יחד," in *BDSS*, vol. 2, pp. 351–61.

And like the babe who delights in the bosom of its nursing-father. (15.23–25)

This stunning image is unprecedented in biblical and parabiblical literature.[371] The author imagines that he, a "nursing-father" can nourish his followers like a mother nourishes her infant.

We probably have found the source of the belief that God has "breasts." In Isaiah 42:14, 45:10, 49:15, and 66:13 – and only in these passages – a biblical author explicitly compared the LORD (YHWH) to a mother.[372] This author (Second Isaiah) uses similes to describe God; the LORD is "like a woman in labor." A distinct development beyond that imagery is a poem in the *Thanksgiving Hymns* and an astonishing passage in the *Odes of Solomon*. The Odist explicitly states that God has "breasts." He is "the father" who "was milked." The metaphor is clear: the milk comes from the Father's two breasts. That is a significant development beyond the symbolic language in the Hebrew Bible. Note this excerpt from *Ode* 19:

The Son is the cup,
And the Father is He who was milked;
And the Holy Spirit is She who milked Him;
Because his breasts were full;
And it was undesirable that His milk should be
  ineffectually released.
The Holy Spirit opened Her bosom,
And mixed the milk of the two breasts of the Father.
(Ode 19:2–4)[373]

The book of Second Isaiah most likely influenced the author of the *Thanksgiving Hymns*, but the imagery in this poem is a creative advancement beyond the biblical imagery. The Teacher talks about being like a nursing father. What seems implicit in the *Thanksgiving Hymns* appears in the *Odes* in fully developed imagery that seems to be an exegetical hermeneutic on the Eucharist. The imagery of "the two breasts of the Father" is unique, even if we are closer to imagining that the *Thanksgiving Hymns* provided a catalyst for this unprecedented metaphor.

The "two breasts of the Father" is no longer without a background within Judaism. We may have found its origins in the *Thanksgiving Hymns*. This discovery adds weight to the argument by some influential scholars that the Odist knew the *Thanksgiving Hymns*.[374]

12. Text Edition

The present edition benefits from the work of many scholars. It inherits the order of columns devised by Stegemann and the numbering of lines by Puech. Placement of fragments, when possible, is according to insights by these two scholars and benefits from the work of Schuller and Newsom as well as from Strugnell (DJD 40)[375]. Thus, the columns and lines of DJD are assumed to be the universal standard.

For the first time, all fragments are read, thanks to better images, computer enhancement, and dedication.[376] In contrast to our usual practice, a *vacat* is often placed in the Hebrew text; this is necessary to ascertain the beginning or ending of a hymn.

Double brackets, ⟦⟧, signify the join between two fragments. Brackets, [], are inserted in the text to identify *lacunae* and clarify restorations.

Restorations of 1QHᵃ and of the other witnesses to the *Thanksgiving Hymns* are guided by "anchored consonants;" that is, letters before, above, after, or below a *lacuna* provide guidance for a restoration.[377] Magnification of a *lacuna* sometimes reveals the remains of a *lamed* above the line for hanging letters or a final consonant below the lower line of text. Such

---

[371] Reymond, *New Idioms Within Old: Poetry and Parallelism in the Non-Masoretic Poems of 11Q5 (=11QPsᵃ)* (Atlanta, 2011) p. 33.

[372] See M. I. Gruber, *The Motherhood of God and Other Studies* (South Florida Studies in the History of Judaism 57; Atlanta, 1992) see esp. pp. 3–15. I am grateful to G. Rendsburg for discussions devoted to the research of M. I. Gruber.

[373] Charlesworth, *The Odes of Solomon* (Oxford, 1973) p. 82.

[374] As previously noted, M. Testuz surmised that Ode 11 had been composed by an Essene. J. Carmignac concluded that the author of the *Odes of Solomon* was formerly a Qumranite. Charlesworth speculated that the Odist may have been a convert from Essenism. One of the major reasons is the observation that the Odist seems to have memorized the *Hodayot*. See Carmignac, "Un qumrânien converti au christianisme; L'auteur des Odes de Salomon," in *Qumran-Probleme*, edited by H. Bardtke (Deutsche Akademie der Wissenschaften zu Berlin 42; Berlin, 1963) pp. 75–108 and Charlesworth, "Les Odes de Salomon et les manuscrits de la mer morte," *RB* 77 (1970) 522–49.

[375] See Stegemann with Schuller, and Newsom, *et al.*, *1QHodayotᵃ with Incorporation of 1QHodayotᵇ and 4QHodayotᵃ⁻ᶠ* (DJD 40; Oxford, 2009). See A. Steudel's helpful review of the publication of the witnesses to the *Hodayot*; see her comment in *The Dead Sea Scrolls in Scholarly Perspective: A History of Research*, edited by D. Dimant (STDJ 99; Leiden and Boston, 2012) p. 592.

[376] I am most grateful to the indefatigable labors of L. Berkuz who worked with me for years trying to decipher images and went with me into the strong room at the Shrine of the Book to examine some fragments. Appreciations are also expressed to I. Levitt.

[377] See the methodology developed by Charlesworth, "Seven Rules for Restoring *Lacunae*," in *A Teacher for All Generations*, vol. 1, pp. 285–96.

examinations prove some earlier restorations to be inaccurate or misleading. Obviously, all restorations must be in accordance with the number of consonants and spaces determined by measuring a *lacuna*. In the past, some experts restored ten consonants where it is obvious that only four consonants or spaces remain to be filled. Sometimes, formulae (such as the determined introduction to a hymn) guide restorations.

Restorations in the Composite Text are not limited to such methodology. Often a line, expression, or word can be found in a witness. Thus, we have used the best preserved witness for restoring a line of text. This procedure dictates that we often do not need to use brackets since the chosen witness preserved a full text; the use of diacritics is governed by the text chosen for inclusion. Notes guide the reader to the source of the text; and that text may then be studied in this volume, as each witness to the *Thanksgiving Hymns* is presented individually.

Sukenik did not attempt to restore the *lacunae*. Licht's masterful commentary deserves more recognition than it has received. Licht labored to restore the text. I have endeavored to ensure that his restorations are reported. Abbreviations and Sigla in the notes to the text are as follows:

DJD   = DJD 40
DSSR = *The Dead Sea Scrolls Reader* vol. 5.
L   = Licht
S   = Sukenik (1954)
Q   = Qimron

The standard order in the notes is chronological: Sukenik, Licht, DJD, Qimron. I have decided not to list all the editors and others who have given us DJD 40, otherwise the notes would be impossibly cumbersome.

In the notes, "ctr." denotes that another reading is suggested but it is either improbable [due to better images] or unlikely due to orthography. In the notes, "ctr." is listed first (regardless of the author); that allows the reader to observe quickly how our readings are significantly different from those in previous editions. A notation "cf." indicates that another possible reading is provided. The use of "cf." will follow the standard order of listing editions. Our reflections will be placed last (unless there is a special reason to place the comment elsewhere). When we report that we agree with other editors that means we report identical consonants; we do not report different use of diacritics, as that would make the notes too long and complicated.

Scribal corrections appear frequently (see esp. cols. 13 and 20). For example, the *ʿayin* was not initially inscribed, but later added in 15.27, 19.31, 20.10, and 22.25. Perhaps the poets made a phonetic play between אנוש, "human," and "severe" pain. See 13.30 and 16.29. For additional comments see the notes to the text.

I appreciate the superb research published by Hartmut Stegemann (a friend with whom I shared many good times in the École Biblique and elsewhere), Eileen Schuller, and Carol Newsom (both of whom have contributed to the Princeton series). Their DJD volume is a monumental achievement. I profited

significantly from it. Discerning the original location of many fragments is daunting, but their placement of the fragments in the plates prepared by I. Kottsieper facilitated my examinations.

13. Translation

The translation has taken me over four years to polish, after more than fifty years of working on the *Thanksgiving Hymns*. The translation is linked to the Hebrew and is thus somewhat literal.[378] A more idiomatic translation occasionally appears in the notes.[379]

A good translation perceives and brings forward the poetic sophistication of an author or authors (or the lack of it). Thence, I have used 'have' in a verb form to denote continuous action (see 7.34). Sometimes I have not used 'have' when it denotes one-time action (see 8.32–36).

The text and translation, and the numerous notes about rhetoric, open the way for a concentrated study of the composition with attention to poetry,[380] acrostic construction, assonance, alliteration, rhyme, rhythm, metathesis,[381] onomatopoeia, polysemy, the use of interrogatives,[382] paronomasia,[383] and *double*

---

[378] Many previous editions omit the fragments. Mansoor, for example, did not translate the fragments; Mansoor, *The Thanksgiving Hymns*, p. 94. The fragments provide clarity and necessary insight, especially when we discern their original places.

[379] For a poetic arrangement of the translation and a more idiomatic rendering based on an earlier version of the present edition, see Charlesworth, *The Qumran Psalter* (Eugene, OR, 2014). I am grateful to Cascade Books for permission to re-publish some comments presented in that book; it serves to draw attention to this critical edition of the *Thanksgiving Hymns*.

[380] See the early work of C. F. Kraft, "Poetic Structure in the Qumran Thanksgiving Psalms," *BR* 2 (1957) 1–18 and the superb study by B. Nitzan, *Qumran Prayer and Religious Poetry*.

[381] M. Rand, "Metathesis as a Poetic Technique in Hodayot Poetry and its Relevance in the Development of Hebrew Rhyme," *DSD* 8 (2001) 51–66. Also, see Reymond, *Qumran Hebrew*, p. 25.

[382] See Elwolde, "Interrogatives in the Hodayot: Some Preliminary Observations," in *Hamlet on a Hill: Semitic and Greek Studies Presented to Professor T. Muraoka on the Occasion of his Sixty-Fifty Birthday*, edited by M. F. J. Baasten and W. T. van Peursen (Orientalia Lovaniensia Analecta 118; Leuven, 2003) pp. 129–51.

[383] For a study of paronomasia in Semitics, see I. Moses Casanowicz, *Paronomasia in the Old Testament* (Ph.D. diss., John Hopkins University, 1894); Casanowicz, "Paronomasia in the Old Testament," *JBL* 12 (1893) 105–67; M. Buber, "Leitwortstil in der Erzählung des Pentateuchs," in *Die Schrift und ihre Verdeutschung*, edited by M. Buber and F. Rosenzweig (Berlin, 1936) pp. 211–38 [now available in English: *Scripture and Translation*, translated by L. Rosenwald

entendre. The reflective translation also allows us to comprehend the rich symbolic language. Talmon suggested that chiastic parallelism is found in 1QH^a 20.10–12.[384] Such poetic features are usually not obvious until the words are arranged poetically and often according to *parallelismus membrorum*.[385]

In the past, too often one word in the text, and in the same context, was translated by three or more different English words. Also, sometimes three different nouns or verbs in Hebrew are rendered by the same English word. This practice breaks the link between text and translation. Allowing for the freedom of a poet, I have endeavored to translate all lines in all witnesses consistently. Obviously, with different authors and changing contexts it is misrepresentative to translate a word exactly the same; thus, poetic license demands that in different settings two words may be translated identically and two or more words should be translated with the same word. In one hymn or poem words must be translated with special attention to consistency and context. This method is time consuming but it allows us to see paronomasia and the relation between similar, or different, thoughts. Sometimes I place in a note how a word has usually been translated; an exceptional rendering may be needed due to a different context or author.

Careful and reflective translation brings out theological subtleties. Too often נושא in 1QH^a 8.34 is rendered "to forgive." It means "to forget;" that is, to remove from memory (see Gen 41:51). The author chose the verb נושא, "to forget" to indicate that *God has forgotten* all past transgressions and thus they

have been forgiven. This author knew that forgiveness entails forgetting past transgressions and misdeeds.

We have attempted to translate words consistently in this series. The consistency chart at the beginning of each volume helps the reader to discern the *termini technici* in the Qumran Scrolls and how we translate them. Occasionally for a major document, an additional consistency chart is provided. Here is the chart for the *Thanksgiving Hymns*:[386]

To Give Thanks to God

אודכה	I thank you
ברוך אתה	blessed are you
הודות	thanksgiving
הלל	to praise
זמר	to chant
רנן	to exalt (to glorify), to exult
רומם	to extol
שחה	(*hip̒il*) cause to bow down
שיר	to sing, written song
גילה	rejoicing
רנה	exaltation, exultation
שמחה	joy, joyful
ששון	happiness
תהלה	praise (only in 19.8, 26, 36)
תפילה	prayer

God's Attributes

אות	sign
אל הדעות	God of Knowledge
אמתכה	your truthfulness
ארוך פנים	patience
גבורתכה	your might
גדול העצה	great (in) council
גלה	to reveal
דין	to judge, judgment
חבא	to conceal
חנון	gracious
חסד	loving-kindness, mercy, grace
טוב	goodness
כבודך	your glory
מאור עולם	eternal light
מופת	portent, wondrous-sign
מנוס	escape
משגב	security
נשא	to forget (= to forgive)
נפלאותיכה	your wonderful acts, wonders
סלע עוזי	the rock of my strength
סליחה	forgiveness
פלא	wonder
רחום	compassion
רצון	will

with E. Fox (Bloomington, 1994)]; V. Kabergs and H. Ausloos, "Paronomasia or Wordplay? A Babel-like Confusion Towards a Definition of Hebrew Wordplay," *Biblica* 93 (2012) 1–20 [a major revision and better focus than in Casanowicz]; E. L. Greenstein, "Wordplay, Hebrew," *Anchor Bible Dictionary* (1992) 6.968–71 [also note his bibliography]; S. B. Noegel, ed., *Puns and Pundits: Word Play in the Hebrew Bible and Ancient Near Eastern Literature* (Bethesda, MD, 2000); S. B. Noegel, "Paronomasia," *Encyclopedia of Hebrew Language and Linguistics*, edited by G. Khan (Leiden and Boston, 2013) p. 24. Also see, E. Russell, *Paronomasia and Kindred Phenomena in the New Testament* (Leipzig, 1920). A monograph on rhetoric in the *Hodayot* is a desideratum.

[384] Talmon, *World*, pp. 220–21.

[385] J. F. Elwolde, "Some Lexical Structures in 1QH: Towards a Distinction of the Linguistic and the Literary," in *Sirach, Scrolls, and Sages*, edited by T. Muraoka and J. F. Elwolde (STDJ 33: Leiden, 1999) pp. 77–116. As in Sirach so in the *Hodayot*, with many authors, we find, in contrast to the MT, an increased emphasis on retribution, innovative expressions, occasional line-length in bicola (and narrative expansion of a bicola or tricola), and impressive aesthetic beauty. In the *Hodayot* we find new pairings such as God's covenant-loyalty with undeserved forgiveness. For Sirach, see E. D. Reymond, *Innovations in Hebrew Poetry* (Atlanta, 2004).

[386] Again, I am most grateful to Lea Berkuz who worked with me assiduously to compile and follow this chart for consistent translating.

The Human

אביון	poor one
איש	man, human
אנוש	human
גבר	man
דכא	oppress, crush
בוז	scorn
בני אור	Sons of Light
הוות	disasters, desires
זכר	male
זקק	(pu'al) refined
חבלים	tribulations
חלכאים	the miserable ones
חמר	clay
טהר	to purify
יצר	inclination, creature
מדהבה	disaster, oppressive
מצעדי	movement, tread
נוסרים	those warned
נפש	soul (= living self)
עני	needy, Needy One
עפר	dust
פעמי	my footsteps
פתאים/פתיים	simple ones
צוקה	distress, trouble, oppress
ציר	labor pain
צעדי	my steps
צרה	trouble
קורצתי	shaped clay
רום	haughtiness, haughty
רש(רוש)	wretched, the Wretched One

Human Knowledge

אזן	to be attentive to, to listen to,
בין	to understand, consider, examine closely, comprehend (hitpo'lel)
בינה	understanding, discernment
להבין	to understand
בדל	to discern, distinguish
דרש	to seek, interpret
הגה	to meditate
ידע	to know
דעה/ת	knowledge
הודיע	to cause, allow to know
זכר	to remember
זנח	to reject
חכמה	wisdom
חפש	to search
חקר	searching, searchable (always with אין = unfathomable)
ירא	to be in awe of
נכר	to acknowledge, to recognize
ספר	to recount, to tell
סתר	to hide
עזב	to forsake, abandon, leave

צפה	to watch
ראה	to see
שיח	to contemplate
שכל	to have insight; mind (human)
שמע	to hear, obey; (hip'il) cause to be heard, proclaim.

Community Language

אלים	Elim, gods, heavenly beings, divine beings (= fallen angels), or Most Holy Ones in the Yaḥad
אביונים	the Poor Ones
יחד	Community
ישרי דרך	the Upright Ones of the Way (10.12)
מלאכים	angels
סוד	council
עדה	congregation
קהל	assembly
תמימי דרך	the Perfect Ones of the Way (9.38)

Womb

כור	furnace, womb
משבר	breakers, the opening of the womb
רחם	womb

Sin and Wickedness

הולל	foolishness, act like a madman
חטאה	sin
זמם	infamies, plan (positive), plot (negative)
זמה	infamy
מדהבה	calamity, oppressive, terrible
מזמה	devise, devising, plot, design
מלכודת	snare
מעל	infidelity
מרמה	deceit
עוון	iniquity
עולה	deceit, injustice
פח	trap
פשע	transgression
רמיה	treachery, slackness
רע	evil
רעה	evilness
רשע	wicked
רשעה	wickedness
תעות	error

Furnishings

יצוע	bed
מטה	mat (portable bed)
ערש	couch

Metals

ברזל	iron
זהב	(fine) gold
יורים	precious stones
כסף	silver
כתם	gold

פז	(pure) gold	אמץ	to encourage, courage
		אנוש	severe (pain)
Musical Instruments		אף	anger
כנור	lyre	אסף	to be gathered, received again
חליל	flute	אשמה	guilt
נבל	harp	בלתי	lest
תוף	tambourine	גבור, גיבור	mighty one, hero, warrior
		גבורה	might
Nature		גבר	to make mighty, to prevail, to overcome
אפלה	gloominess	גדול	great
דלית	foliage, high branch	דורשי	the seekers of
חלמיש	flint	דין	to judge, to consider (to plead a cause)
חשך	darkness	דרך	way, Way
יבול	produce	הבל	nonsense
יובל	brook	היכל	shrine
מבוע	pond	הון	property, wealth
מעין	fountain	המה	to roar
מצולה	depth	המון	abundance, abundant, multitude, roar
מקוה	reservoir	המיה	noise
מקור	spring, source	חומה	city wall, wall
ענף	branch	חזק	strength
פארה	leafy branch	חיל	army
פלג	stream	חמדה	delight
פני מים	surface of the water	חמה	poison, wrath
צאצא	product, offspring	חמס	violence
רום	height, high	חרון	fury
רקיע	firmament	יגון	grief, agony
שחקים	skies	יצב	to present oneself, to stand
שמים	heaven, heavens	יצר	to fashion, pour out (created)
תהום	deep, depth	כוח	power
		כלה	ended, annihilate, fail
Trees		לענה	bitterness (a wormwood)
גזע	trunk, stem	מבצר	fortress
עץ	tree	מגבל מים	mixed water
ברוש	cypress, juniper	מדהבה	disaster
תדהר	elm, box tree, pine	מוט	to totter
תאשור	cedar, cypress, elm, box tree	מופת	portent, wonder (not sign)
		מוסר	discipline
Time		מורא	terror
מועד	appointed time, season, festival	מחסה	refuge
יעד	(niph.) assembled, to appoint	מליץ	interpreter, intermediate interpreter (14.16)
נצח	perpetuate, perpetual	מלוא	plentitude
עד	forever, everlasting, until, unto	ממלכה	kingdom (only in 1QH[a] 14.10), domicile
עולם	eternity, eternal, without end	ממשלה	dominion (see esp. 1QH[a] 20.8–26)
עולמי עד	forever and ever, everlasting eternity	מעוז	shelter, protection
עושי עולם	eternal acts	מעמד	guard, position, rank, stand firm
קדם	ancient-time	מעשה	creature, work
קדם עולם	eternal ages	מצודה	citadel, stronghold
קץ	Endtime (cosmic), time, endtime (for the individual)	מצודות	nets
		מצוה	commandment
תעודה	fixed times, testimony	מצרף	crucible, smelting pot
		משגב	hideout, shelter (or fortress), security
General		משרתים	ministers
אורתים	perfect lights, perfect light	מתנים	loins
אוש	foundation	נוף	(hip'il) to wave over, wave high, to elevate, to lift
אות	sign		

נטה	to turn aside
נמהרים	eager ones
נתיבות	paths
נתן	to place, put
סוד	secret, base, foundation, council
סמך	sustain (support)
עבודה	deed, service
עדנים	luxuries (possible: delights)
עושי מעשיהם	the acts of their works
עוז	strong, strength
עות	sustain (help)
עמד	to stand
עמל	to labor
עמל	trouble, misfortune
ערומים	clever ones
עשה	to do, to work
פה	edict, mouth
פחד	to fear, fear
פלט	to escape, deliverance, escape
פעולות	deeds
פקד	to deposit
צבא	host
קינה	lament
קיר	wall (like a wall of a house)
קו	measuring line
קול	sound, voice
קנאה	zeal, zealous
קיץ	to be extracted, shaped
רוב	many, much, multitude, multitudinous, abundant
רע	companion
רעד	tremble
רוש	poison
שוך	to hedge about
שביל	track
שבת	to cease
שוא	vanity, vain
שרת	to minister
תבל	world
תוכחה	chastisement
תורה	Torah (Law)
תם	to be completed, consumed, exhausted
תמך ב	adhere to
תשתוחח	dissolve

14. Composite Text

The Composite Text collects all the witnesses to the *Thanksgiving Hymns*. The base is provided by 1QHª, if extant. When a text is extant in one of the witnesses, brackets are not needed.

The insertions of single brackets, [], in the Composite Text are necessary; otherwise readers could not discern what consonants are extant in a column, as in column 26, and what is restored. The source of a reading is provided in a note.

The placement of brackets is according to the consonants on the leather; thus, for example, note the following:

a) בְּכֹול [מעשיכה in 8.23
b) ולְהֹתׄ[חנ]ן̊ [תמיד] in 8.25
c) כֹולׄ] תבל in 8.22

The first example reports a space visible on the leather after בכול. The second example reports a space visible on the leather after the final *nun*. The third example, however, indicates no leather visible after כול and thus the necessity of a space before תבל.

Brackets serve two different purposes. They may denote a *lacuna* (a hole in the leather or papyrus); or they may report leather that has no visible ink (but it was once inscribed).

Double brackets ⟦⟧ circumscribe joins of fragments: ⟦ denotes the beginning of a fragment (because one must denote the ending of the preceding text); ⟧ clarifies the end of a fragment (and usually the beginning of a continuing text). To keep the text uncluttered by notations, double brackets for joins also serve to indicate restorations. Here are examples (diacritics are not shown):

a) [ברוך אתה אל הדעות כי תנקני] in 4.21 (restoration based on formula and preceding VACAT)
b) ב[ל]וא[in 4.19 (restoration of one consonant, extant consonant, restoration of two consonants)
c) אוכל[ה in 4.25 (the *he* anchors the restoration)
d) רוח ב̊⟦שר in 5.15 (two fragments joined with a contiguous text)
e) בני אי⟦שׄ in 5.14 (בני אי restored before a join anchored with a שׁ)
f) הֹ̊דׄעׄ]תני בע⟦בׄור in 5.19 (restoration of the column and restoration within a join)
g) ובמעין ⟦בׄינתך ⟧ ̈ in 5.19 (a join at the end of a fragment with two preceding indiscernible consonants, space, single brackets circumcising a restoration, the join at the beginning of another fragment, and extant consonants)
h) ברוׄ]ה קודשך ו⟦בׄלׄכוׄה in 5.15 (three extant consonants, a join, restorations, a join, extant consonants)

Sometimes consonants within single brackets are provided that are not found in a witness to the *Thanksgiving Hymns*. The flow of the contiguous text and the appearance of words elsewhere in Qumran compositions guide these restorations and a note is provided to inform the reader of the source. Scholars who are not Qumran specialists may read the text oblivious of the single and double brackets.

15. Selected Bibliography

By Brady Alan Beard and Aaron Thomas Neff. Also see the articles appearing in *RQ, DSD, JSP, JBL, CBQ, NTS, ZNW, ZAW*, and the Orion Bibliography.)

Abegg, M. G., Jr. "Who Ascended to Heaven? 4Q491, 4Q427, and the Teacher of Righteousness." In *Eschatology, Messianism, and the Dead Sea Scrolls,* edited by C. A. Evans and P. W. Flint. SDSSRL; Grand Rapids, 1997, pp. 61–73.

Antonissen, H. "Die weisheitliche Terminologie in den 'Hodayot': Ein kontextbezogener Überblick." *Leqach* 7 (2007) 1–15.

Attridge, H. A. and M. E. Fassler, eds. *Psalms in Community: Jewish and Christian Textual, Liturgical, and Artistic Tradition.* Atlanta, 2003.

Berg, S. A. *Religious Epistemologies in The Dead Sea Scrolls: The Heritage and Transformation of the Wisdom Tradition,* Ph.D. diss., Yale, 2008.

Betz, O. "The Servant Tradition of Isaiah in the Dead Sea Scrolls." *JSS* 7 (1995) 40–56.

Brooke, G. J. "The Structure of 1QHa XII 5–XIII and the Meaning of Resurrection." In *From 4QMMT to Resurrection: Mélanges qumraniens en homage à Émile Puech,* edited by F. García Martínez *et al.* STDJ 61; Leiden, 2006, pp. 15–33.

Caquot, A. "Retour à la mère du Messie 1QH 3 (Sukenik), 6–18." *RHPR* 80 (2000) 5–12.

Carmignac, J. "Les citations de l'Ancien Testament, et spécialement des Poèmes du Serviteur, dans les Hymnes de Qumrân." *RQ* 2.3 (1960) 357–94.

Carmignac, J. "Localisation des fragments 15, 18 et 22 des Hymnes." *RQ* 1 (1958–59) 425–30.

Carmignac, J. "Remarques sur le texte des Hymnes de Qumran." *Bib* 39 (1958) 139–55.

Carmignac, J. "Review: Hodayot: Psalms from Qumran." *RQ* 3 (1960) 183–204.

Castaño Fonseca, A. M. "Algunos rasgos característicos del Maestro de Justicia en los Himnos de Qumrán: Un ejemplo en 1QH 5,5–19." *Qol* 39 (2005) 41–59.

Charlesworth, J. H. "An Allegorical and Autobiographical Poem by the Moreh haṣ-Ṣedeq (1QH 8:4–11)." In *Sha'arei Talmon: Studies in the Bible, Qumran, and the Ancient Near East Presented to Shemaryahu Talmon,* edited by M. Fishbane and E. Tov with W. W. Fields. Winona Lake, IN, 1991, pp. 295–307.

Charlesworth, J. H. "Autumnal Rain [המורה] for the Faithful Followers of the Moreh [המורה]: Joel and the Hodayot." In *Der Mensch vor Gott: Forschungen zum Menschenbild in Bible, antikem Judentum und Koran: Festschrift für Hermann Lichtenberger,* edited by U. Mittmann-Richert, F. Avemarie, and G. S. Oegema. Neukirchen-Vluyn, 2003, pp. 193–210.

Charlesworth, J. H. "The *Beth Essentiae* and the Permissive Meaning of the Hiphil (Aphel)." In *Of Scribes and Scrolls: Studies on the Hebrew Bible, Intertestamental Judaism, and Christian Origins,* edited by H. W. Attridge, J. J. Collins, and T. H. Tobin. CTSRIR 5; New York and London, 1990, pp. 67–78.

Charlesworth, J. H. "Jesus as 'Son' and the Righteous Teacher as 'Gardener'." In *Jesus and the Dead Sea Scrolls,* edited by J. H. Charlesworth. ABRL; New York, 1995, pp. 140–75.

Charlesworth, J. H. "Hymns and Odes in Early Judaism." In *Critical Reflections on the Odes of Solomon. Volume 1: Literary Settings, Textual Studies, Gnosticism, the Dead Sea Scrolls and the Gospel of John.* JSPSup 22; Sheffield, 1998, pp. 27–53.

Charlesworth, J. H. "Les Odes de Salomon et les manuscrits de la mer morte." *RB* 77 (1970) 522–49.

Charlesworth, J. H. *The Qumran Psalter: The Thanksgiving Hymns Among The Dead Sea Scrolls.* Eugene, 2014.

Charlesworth, J. H. "Prolegomenous Reflections Towards a Taxonomy of Resurrection Texts (1QHa, 1En, 4Q521, Paul, Luke, the Fourth Gospel, and Psalm 30)." In *The Changing Face of Judaism, Christianity, and Other Greco-Roman Religions in Antiquity: Presented to James Charlesworth on the Occasion of his 65th Birthday,* edited by I. H. Henderson and G. S. Oegema. JSHRZ 2; Gütersloh, Winona Lake, 2006, pp. 237–64.

Charlesworth, J. H. "The Righteous Teacher and the Historical Jesus." In *Earthing Christologies: From Jesus' Parables to Jesus the Parable,* edited by J. H. Charlesworth with W. P. Weaver. Faith and Scholarship Colloquies; Valley Forge, 1995, pp. 46–61.

Chazon, E. G. "Human and Angelic Prayer in Light of the Dead Sea Scrolls." In *Liturgical Perspectives: Prayer and Poetry in Light of the Dead Sea Scrolls. Proceedings of the Fifth International Symposium of the Orion Center for the Study of the Dead Sea Scrolls and Associated Literature, 19–23 January, 2000,* edited by E. G. Chazon with R. A. Clements and A. Pinnik. STDJ 48; Leiden, 2003, pp. 35–47.

Chazon, E. G. "Hymns and Prayers in the Dead Sea Scrolls." In *The Dead Sea Scrolls after Fifty Years: A Comprehensive Assessment,* edited by P. W. Flint and J. C. VanderKam. Leiden, 1998–1999, pp. 244–70.

Chazon, E. G. "Liturgical Function in the Cave 1 Hodayot Collection." In *Qumran Cave 1 Revisited: Texts from Cave 1 Sixty Years after Their Discovery. Proceedings of the Sixth Meeting of the IOQS in Ljubljana,* edited by D. K. Falk, *et al.* STDJ 91; Leiden, 2010, pp. 135–49.

Chazon, E. G. "Low to Lofty: The Hodayot's Use of Liturgical Traditions to Shape Sectarian Identity and Religious Experience." *RQ* 101 (2013) 3–19.

Chazon, E. G. "Tradition and Innovation in the Dead Sea Scrolls." In *Prayer and Poetry in the Dead Sea Scrolls and Related Literature: Essays in Honor of Eileen Schuller on the Occasion of Her 65th Birthday,* edited by J. Penner, K. M. Penner, C. Wassen. STDJ 98; Leiden, 2012, pp. 55–67.

Chazon, E. G. "The Use of the Bible as a Key to Meaning in Psalms from Qumran." In *Emanuel. Studies in Hebrew Bible, Septuagint and Dead Sea Scrolls in Honor of Emanuel*

Tov, edited by S.M. Paul et al. VTSup 94; Leiden, 2003, pp. 85–96.

Cherian, J. "The Moses at Qumran: The מורה הצדק as the Nursing Father of the יחד." In *The Bible and the Dead Sea Scrolls. Volume 2: The Dead Sea Scrolls and the Qumran Community*, edited by J. H. Charlesworth. Waco, 2006, pp. 351–61.

Collins, J. J., *The Scepter and the Star: Messianism in Light of the Dead Sea Scrolls.* Grand Rapids, 2010, pp. 136–53.

Collins, J. J. "Amazing Grace: The Transformation of the Thanksgiving Hymn at Qumran." In *Psalms in Community: Jewish and Christian Textual, Liturgical, and Artistic Traditions*, edited by H. W. Attridge and M. E. Fassler. SBLSS 25; Atlanta, 2003, pp. 75–86.

Daise, M. A. "Biblical Creation Motifs in the Qumran Hodayot." In *The Dead Sea Scrolls: Fifty Years after Their Discovery. Proceedings of the Jerusalem Congress, July 20–25, 1997*, edited by L. H. Schiffman, *et al*. Jerusalem, 2000, pp. 293–305.

Davila, J. R. "The Hodayot Hymnist and the Four Who Entered Paradise." *RQ* 17 (1996) 457–78.

Delcor, M. *Les Hymnes de Qumrân (Hodayot)*. Paris, 1962.

Dimant, D. "A Synoptic Comparison." *JQR* 85 (1994) 157–61.

Douglas, M. C. *Power and Praise in the Hodayot: A Literary Critical Study of 1QH 9:1–18:14*. Ph.D. diss., University of Chicago Divinity School, 1997.

Douglas, M. C. "The Teacher Hymn Hypothesis Revisited: New Data for an Old Crux." *DSD* 6 (1999) 239–66.

Elwolde, J. F. "The Hodayot's Use of the Psalter: Text-critical Contributions (Book 3: Pss 73–89)." *DSD* 17 (2010) 159–79.

Elwolde, J. F. "The Hodayot's Use of the Psalter: Text-Critical Contributions (Book 1)." In *Psalms and Prayers: Papers Read at the Joint Meeting of the Society for Old Testament Study and Het Oud Testamentisch Werkgezelschap in Nederland en België, Apeldoorn August 2006*, edited by B. Becking and E. Peels. OTS 55; Leiden, 2007, pp. 79–108.

Elwolde, J. F. "Interrogatives in the Hodayot: Some Preliminary Observations." In *Hamlet on a Hill: Semitic and Greek Studies Presented to Professor T. Muraoka on the Occasion of his Sixty-Fifth Birthday*, edited by M. F. J. Baasten, *et al*. Orientalia Lovaniensia Analecta 118; Leuven, 2003, pp. 129–51.

Elwolde, J. F. "Some Lexical Structures in 1QH: Towards a Distinction of the Linguistic and the Literary." In *Sirach, Scrolls, and Sages: Proceedings of a Second International Symposium on the Hebrew of the Dead Sea Scrolls, Ben Sira, and the Mishnah, Held at Leiden University, 15–17 December 1997*, edited by T. Muraoka and J. F. Elwolde. STDJ 33; Leiden, 1999, pp. 77–116.

Eshel, E. "The Identification of the 'Speaker' of the Self-Glorification Hymn." In *The Provo International Conference on the Dead Sea Scrolls: Technological Innovations, New Texts, and Reformulated Issues*, edited by D. W. Parry and E. C. Ulrich. STDJ 30; Leiden, 1999, pp. 619–35.

Falk, D. "The Contribution of the Qumran Scrolls to the Study of Ancient Jewish Liturgy." In *The Oxford Handbook of the Dead Sea Scrolls*, edited by T. H. Lim and J. J. Collins. Oxford, 2010, pp. 617–51.

Falk, D. "Psalms and Prayers." In *Justification and Variegated Nomism. Volume 1: The Complexities of Second Temple Judaism*, edited by D. A. Carson, *et al*. WUNT 2.140; Tübingen and Grand Rapids, 2001, pp. 7–56.

Fabry, H. J. "Der 'Lehrer des Rechts' – eine Gestalt zwischen Vollmacht und Ablehnung. Überlegungen zur frühjüdischen Rezeption der Leidensknechts-Thematik." In *Martyriumsvorstellungen in Antike und Mittelalter: Leben oder sterben für Gott?*, edited by S. Fuhrmann and R. Grundmann. Ancient Judaism and Early Christianity 80; Leiden, 2012, pp. 21–43.

Flint, P. W., ed. *The Bible at Qumran: Text, Shape, and Interpretation*. Grand Rapids, MI, 2001. [See esp. the second part of the book, pp. 129–236.]

Frechette, C. G. "Chiasm, Reversal and Biblical Reference in 1QH 11.3–18 (= Sukenik Column 3): A Structure Proposal." *JSP* 21 (2000) 71–102.

Goff, M. J. "Reading Wisdom at Qumran: 4QInstruction and the Hodayot." *DSD* 11 (2004) 263–88.

Harkins, A. K. "The Community Hymns Classification: A Proposal for Further Differentiation." *DSD* 15 (2008) 121–54.

Harkins, A. K. "A New Proposal for Thinking about 1QHᵃ Sixty Years after its Discovery." In *Qumran Cave 1 Revisited: Texts from Cave 1 Sixty Years after Their Discovery. Proceedings of the Sixth Meeting of the IOQS in Ljubljana*, edited by D. K. Falk, *et al*. STDJ 91; Leiden, 2010, pp 101–34.

Harkins, A. K. "Observation on the Editorial Shaping of the So-Called Hymns from 1QHᵃ and 4QHᵃ (4Q427)." *DSD* 12 (2005) 233–56.

Harkins, A. K. "The Performative Reading of the Hodayot: The Arousal of Emotions and the Exegetical Generation of Texts." *JSP* 21 (2011) 55–71.

Harkins, A. K. *Reading With an "I" to the Heavens: Looking at the Qumran Hodayot Through the Lens of Visionary Traditions.* Berlin, 2012.

Harkins, A. K. "Reading the Qumran Hodayot in Light of the Traditions Associated with Enoch." *Henoch* 32 (2010) 359–400.

Harkins, A. K. "Who is the Teacher of the Teacher Hymns? Re-examining the Teacher Hymns Hypothesis Fifty Years Later." In *A Teacher for All Generations: Essays in Honor of James C. VanderKam*, edited by E. F. Mason. JSJSup 153; Leiden, 2012, pp. 449–67.

Hawley, R. "On Maśkîl in the Judean Desert Texts." *Henoch* 28 (2006) 43–77.

Holm-Nielsen, S. *Hodayot: Psalms from Qumran*. ATDan 2; Aarhus, 1960.

Hughes, J. A. *Scriptural Allusions and Exegesis in the Hodayot*. STDJ 59; Leiden, 2006.

Jassen, A. P. *Mediating the Divine: Prophecy and Revelation in the Dead Sea Scrolls and Second Temple Judaism.* STDJ 68; Leiden, 2007.

Jeremias, G. *Der Lehrer der Gerechtigkeit.* Göttingen, 1963.

Kim, A. Y. "Signs of Editorial Shaping of the Hodayot Collection: A Redactional Analysis of 1QHa-b and 4QHa-f." Ph.D. diss., University of Notre Dame, 2003.

Kittel, B. P. *The Hymns of Qumran: Translation and Commentary.* SBLDS 50; Chico, CA, 1981.

Klęczar, A. "Do the Hodayot Psalms Display a Consistent Theology?" *The Qumran Chronicle* 11 (2003) 79–90.

Knohl, I. "The Suffering Servant: From Isaiah to the Dead Sea Scrolls." In *Scriptural Exegesis: The Shapes of Culture and the Religious Imagination. Essays in Honour of Michael Fishbane,* edited by D. A. Green and L. S. Lieber. Oxford, 2009, pp. 89–104.

Kuhn, H. W. *Enderwartung und gegenwärtiges Heil.* Göttingen, 1966.

Lange, A. "The Textual History of the Book of Jeremiah in Light of its Allusions and Implicit Quotations in the Qumran Hodayot." In *Prayer and Poetry in the Dead Sea Scrolls and Related Literature: Essays in Honor of Eileen Schuller on the Occasion of Her 65th Birthday,* edited by J. Penner, K. M. Penner, C. Wassen. STDJ 98; Leiden, 2012, pp. 251–84.

Levison, J. R. "The Two Spirits in Qumran Theology." In *The Bible and the Dead Sea Scrolls. Volume 2: The Dead Sea Scrolls and the Qumran Community,* edited by J. H. Charlesworth. Waco, TX, 2006, pp. 169–94.

Licht, J. "The Doctrine of the Thanksgiving Scroll." *IEJ* 6 (1956) 1–13, 89–101.

Licht, J. מגילת ההודיות ממגילות מדבר יהודה: *The Thanksgiving Scroll: A Scroll from the Wilderness of Judaea.* Jerusalem, 1957. [in Hebrew]

Lichtenberger, H. *Studien zum Menschenbild in Texten der Qumrangemeinde.* Göttingen, 1980.

Mansoor, M. *The Thanksgiving Hymns.* Grand Rapids, MI, 1961.

Mansoor, M. "Studies in the Hodayot – IV." *JBL* 76 (1957) 139–48.

Mędala, S. "The Alcimus of History and the Author of 1QH X–XVII." *The Qumran Chronicle* 12 (2004) 127–43.

Merrill, E. H. *Qumran and Predestination: A Theological Study of the Thanksgiving Hymns.* STDJ 8; Leiden, 1975.

Morawe, G. *Aufbau und Abgrenzung der Loblieder von Qumrân: Studien zur gattungsgeschichtlichen Einordnung der Hodajôth.* Theologische Arbeiten 16; Berlin, 1961.

Newsom, C. A. "Apocalyptic Subjects: Social Construction of the Self in the Qumran Hodayot." *JSP* 12 (2001) 3–35.

Newsom, C. A. *The Self as Symbolic Space: Constructing Identity and Community at Qumran.* STDJ 52; Leiden, 2004. [See especially chapter 6 on the *Hodayot*; pp. 287–346]

Nitzan, B. *Qumran Prayer and Religious Poetry.* STDJ 12; Leiden, 1994.

Puech, É. "Hodayot." Translated by R. E. Shillenn. In *The Encyclopedia of the Dead Sea Scrolls.* New York, 2000, pp. 365–69.

Puech, É. "Un hymne essénien en partie retrouvé et les Béatitudes: 1QH v 12–vi 18 (= col. xiii–xiv 7) et 4QBéat." *RQ* 13 (1988) 58–88.

Puech, É. *La croyance des Esséniens en la vie future: Immortalité, résurrection, vie éternelle? Histoire d'une croyance dans le judaïsme ancien.* 2 Vols.; EBib 21–22; Paris, 1993.

Puech, É. "Messianism, Resurrection, and Eschatology at Qumran and in the New Testament." In *The Community of the Renewed Covenant,* edited by E. Ulrich and J. C. VanderKam. Notre Dame, 1994. pp. 235–56.

Puech, É. "Quelques aspects de la restauration du Rouleau des Hymnes (1QH)." *JJS* 39 (1988) 38–55.

Puech, É. "Restauration d'un texte hymnique à partir de trois manuscrits framentaires: 1QHᵃ xv 37–xvi 4 (vii 34–viii 3), 1Q35 (Hᵇ) 1, 9–14, 4Q428 (Hᵇ) 7." *RQ* 16/64 (1995) 543–58.

Rand, M. "Metathesis as Poetic Technique in Hodayot Poetry and its Relevance in the Development of Hebrew Rhyme." *DSD* 8 (2001) 51–66.

Rietz, H. W. M. "Identifying Compositions and Traditions of the Qumran Community: The *Songs of the Sabbath Sacrifice* as a Test Case." In *Qumran Studies: New Approaches, New Questions,* edited by M. T. Davis and B. A. Strawn (Grand Rapids, 2007) pp. 27–52.

Rabin, Ira, *et al.* "On the Origin of the Ink of the Thanksgiving Scroll (1QHodayotᵃ)." *DSD* 16 (2009) 97–106.

Ringgren, H. "Two Biblical Words in the Qumran Hymns." *Yigael Yadin Memorial Volume. Erets-Yiśra'el* 20; Jerusalem, 1989, pp. 174–75.

Sanders, E. P. "Chiasmus and the Translation of 1QHodayot VII: 26–27." *RQ* 6 (1968) 427–31.

Schuller, E. M. "The Cave 4 Hodayot Manuscripts: A Preliminary Description." *JQR* 85 (1994–95) 137–50.

Schuller, E. M. "The Cave 4 Hodayot Manuscripts: A Preliminary Description." In *Qumranstudien: Vortäge und Beiträge der Teilnehmer des Qumranseminars auf dem internationalen Treffen der Society of Biblical Literature, Münster, 25.–26. Juli 1993,* edited by H.-J. Fabry, *et al.* Schriften des Institutum Judaicum Delitzschianum 4; Göttingen, 1996, pp. 87–100.

Schuller, E. M. "The Classification Hodayot and Hodayot-like (with Particular Attention to 4Q433, 4Q433a, and 4Q440)." In *Sapiential, Liturgical and Poetical Texts from Qumran: Proceedings of the Third Meeting of the International Organization for Qumran Studies, Oslo 1998, Published in Memory of Maurice Baillet,* edited by D. K. Falk, *et al.* STDJ 35; Leiden, 2000, pp. 182–93.

Schuller, E. M. "Hodayot," in *Qumran Cave 4.XX.* DJD 29; Oxford, 1999, pp. 69–254; Pls. IV–XVI.

Schuller, E. M. "Petitionary Prayer and the Religion of Qumran." In *Religion in the Dead Sea Scrolls,* edited by. J. J. Collins, *et al.* Grand Rapids, 2000, pp. 29–45.

Schuller, E.M. "Recent Scholarship on the *Hodayot* 1993–2010." *Currents in Biblical Research* 10 (2011) 119–62.

Schuller, E. M. "Some Contributions of the Cave Four Manuscripts (4Q427–32) to the Study of the Hodayot." *DSD* 8 (2001) 278–87.

Schuller, E. M. "A Thanksgiving Hymn from 4QHodayot b (4Q428 7)." *RQ* 16 (1995) 527–41.

Schuller, E. M. "Worship, Temple, and Prayer in the Dead Sea Scrolls." In *Judaism in Late Antiquity, Part 5: The Judaism of Qumran: A Systematic Reading of the Dead Sea Scrolls,* edited by A. J. Avery-Peck, *et al.* Handbook of Oriental Studies: Abt. 1, The Near and Middle East 56; Leiden, 2001, pp. 125–43.

Schuller, E. M. and C. A. Newsom, *The Hodayot (Thanksgiving Psalms): A Study Edition of 1QH*ᵃ. SBLEJL; Atlanta, 2012.

Schuller, E. M. and L. DiTommaso. "A Bibliography of the Hodayot, 1948–1996." *DSD* 4 (1997) 55–101.

Stegemann, H. *Rekonstruktion der Hodajot: Ursprüngliche Gestalt und kritisch bearbeiteter Text der Hymnenrolle aus Höhle 1 von Qumran.* Ph.D. diss., Heidelberg, 1963.

Stegemann, H., E. M. Schuller, and C. A. Newsom. *1QHodayot*ᵃ, with Incorporation of 1QHodayotᵇ 4QHodayotᵃ⁻ᶠ. DJD 40; Oxford, 2009.

Stegemann, H. "The Material Reconstruction of the Hodayot." In *The Dead Sea Scrolls: Fifty Years after Their Discovery*, edited by L. H. Schiffman, *et al.* Jerusalem, 2000, pp. 272–84.

Strugnell, J. and E. M. Schuller. "Further Hodayot Manuscripts from Qumran?" In *Antikes Judentum und frühes Christentum: Festschrift für Hartmut Stegemann zum 65. Geburtstag*, edited by B. Kollman, *et al.* BZNW 97; Berlin and New York, 1999, pp. 51–72.

Sukenik, E. L. *The Dead Sea Scrolls of the Hebrew University.* Jerusalem, 1955.

Sukenik, E. L. ‏מגילות גנוזות: מתוך גניזה קדומה שנמצאה במדבר יהודה.‏ ‏סקירה שנייה.‏ Jerusalem, 1950.

Talmon, S. *The World of Qumran from Within.* Jerusalem, 1989. [See especially, chapter 11, "The Emergence of Institutionalized Prayer in Israel in Light of Qumran Literature," pp. 200–43].

Tanzer, S. J. "Biblical Interpretation in the Hodayot." In *A Companion to Biblical Interpretation in Early Judaism*, edited by M. Henze. Grand Rapids, 2012; pp. 255–75.

Tanzer, S. J. "The Sages at Qumran: Wisdom in the Hodayot." Ph.D. diss., Harvard University, 1987.

Vegas Montaner, L. "Some Features of the Hebrew Verbal Syntax in the Qumran Hodayot." In *The Madrid Qumran Congress (2 vols.): Proceedings of the International Congress on Dead Sea Scrolls, Madrid 18–21 March, 1991* Vol. 1, edited by J. Trebolle Barrera and L. Vegas Montaner. STDJ 11; Leiden, 1993, pp. 273–86.

Weinfeld, M. "The Prayers for Knowledge, Repentance and Forgiveness in the 'Eighteen Benedictions' – Qumran Parallels, Biblical Antecedents, and Basic Characteristics." In *Early Jewish Liturgy: From Psalms to the Prayers in Qumran and Rabbinic Literature.* Jerusalem, 2004, pp. 179–97. [in Hebrew]

Williams, G. R. *Parallelism in the Hodayot from Qumran.* Ann Arbor, 2000.

Wise, M. O. "The Concept of a New Covenant in the Teacher Hymns from Qumran [1QHa X–XVII]." In *The Concept of the Covenant in the Second Temple Perio*d, edited by S. E. Porter, J. C. R. de Roo. JSJSup 71; Leiden, 2003, pp. 99–128.

Wise, M. O. "‏מי כמוני באלים‏: A Study of 4Q491c, 4Q471b, 4Q427 7 and 1QHa 25.35–26.10." *DSD* 7 (2000) 173–219.

Thanksgiving Hymns (*Hodayot*)
1QHª

Col. 2 [Frgs. 23 and 16]

]	**1**
]	**2**
]	**3**
]	**4**
]	**5**
]	**6**
]	**7**
]	**8**
]	**9**
]	**10**
]	**11**
נפל]וֹאתיכֹ[ה[1] אי]ןֿ פֹה[2]	**12**
ו]תׄוׄצׄא לֹעׄוׄלׄמׄיׄ[3]	**13**
ישמי]עׄוׄ בֹהמון רנה[4]	**14**
אר]נֿנֹהֿ [ ]°° [ ]לֿ[5]	**15**
]°°[	**16**
]	**17**

---

[1] Note the misspelling. See Reymond, p. 53.

[2] Frg. 23 provides lines 12–16. It is not, therefore, imperative to denote so-called "joins" because fragments are not joined. Sukenik: [ ]°כיׄ [ ]תׄיׄ. Licht and Qimron do not transcribe frg. 23.

[3] Sukenik:]אׄ°°° עׄולמי[.

[4] Sukenik:]בהמון רנה[.

[5] Sukenik:]לֿ[ ]נכה[.

Thanksgiving Hymns (*Hodayot*)
1QHᵃ

Col. 2 [Frgs. 23 and 16]

1   […]

2   […]

3   […]

4   […]

5   […]

6   […]

7   […]

8   […]

9   […]

10   […]

11   […]

12   […] yo[ur wonder]ful acts [there is n]o interpretation[1]

13   [… and] you brought forth[2] for the eternities of

14   [… th]ey [procla]im with abundant exultation[3]

15   [… I will re]joice °°[…]*l*[…]

16   […]°°[…]

17   […]

---

[1] Lit. "mouth" with the meaning of "declaration." Cf. Ps 106:2 and esp. *OdesSol* 26:11: "Who can interpret the wonders of the Lord?" (ܡܢܘ ܡܫܟܚ ܕܢܦܫܩ ܬܕܡܪܬܗ ܕܡܪܝܐ). For fuller notes to the translation, see the Composite Text, Hebrew and English.

[2] In these poems and hymns almost all verbs carry a present meaning.

[3] Or "a song;" not "a tumultuous cry." See the paronomasia in 2.15 and 2.16.

]   18

]   19

]   20

]   21

]   22

]   23

]ׄ[   ]   24

[מׄרות]ם   ]ׄ[⁶   25

ע[שׄוקים ⁷ וׄמׄיׄ ⁸   26

[רׄחמיו על אבׄיונׄ]יׄם ⁹   27

[ה ומי ¹⁰ מתכן ¹¹   28

[ומי מתכן גבורי]ם ¹²   29

ע[וׄד עולם מי חׄושׄבׄ ¹³   30

[ערומים ¹⁴ וׄמׄיׄ ¹⁵   31

גב[וׄרתכה ¹⁶]ׄׄ[ ]לׄ[¹⁷   32

Col. 3 [Frgs. 21 and 11]

]   1

---

⁶ Frg. 16 provides lines 24–32. Licht does not identify the *lacunae* in frg. 16. Qimron places frg. 16 by itself, after the columns.

⁷ Licht:]ׄ שוקים[. See עשוק CD MS A 13.10.

⁸ The consonants are barely detectable under magnification.

⁹ Sukenik and Licht:]חמיו על אביונׄ[. See אביוני חסד in 13.24 and אביון in 10.34, 11.26, 13.18 (cf. 13.16). No *yodh* is visible at the end of the line. Cf. DJD and Qimron: אביוני.

¹⁰ מי occurs four times in this column. For מי elsewhere in 1QHᵃ, see 11.25, 12.30, 15.31 [3 times], 18.12, 19.27, 21.12.

¹¹ See esp. 1QHᵃ 9.10, 15.

¹² Or with DJD: גבורהׄ. Sukenik, Licht, and Qimron:]ׄ גבור. Notice the plural in line 31.

¹³ Sukenik and Licht: עולם מי חושׄ [.

¹⁴ Sukenik: קׄדׄומים [. Licht:]ׄׄ קדומים [. DJD: עׄרומים [. Qimron: [ערומים. We are grateful to the Israel Museum for providing us improved images of frg. 16.

¹⁵ With DJD and Qimron: וׄמׄ[. Sukenik and Licht:]ׄׄ.

¹⁶ Sukenik and Licht:]רתכה[.

¹⁷ Ctr. DJD: []ׄ[]ׄׄ. Sukenik and Licht do not read]לׄ[ ]ׄׄ. Qimron: [ ]ׄׄ.

18   […]

19   […]

20   […]

21   […]

22   […]

23   […]

24   […]°[…]

25   [… their] rebelliousness […]°[…]

26   [… op]pressed ones and who

27   […] his mercies upon the Poor One[s]

28   […]*h* and who arranges[4]

29   […] and who arranges[5] the mighty one[s[6]]

30   [… un]to eternity, who thinks[7]

31   […] the clever ones.[8] And who

32   […] your [mi]ght °°[…]*l*[…]

Col. 3 [Frgs. 21 and 11]

1   […]

---

[4] Or "assesses," "measures."
[5] Or "assesses," "measures."
[6] Perhaps the author intends the celestial warriors; see 11.36.
[7] This word is translated here as a *qal* participle of חשב; DJD translates it as a *pi'el* participle: "who calculates."
[8] Sukenik text: "former ones." There is a small *vacat*; it does not introduce a hymn.

]	2
]	3
]	4
]	5
]	6
]	7
]	8
]	9
]	10
]	11
]	12
]	13
]	14
[°°°[18] מ̇	15
[כה ותׄעׄזׄוׄר נדיב[19]ׄי	16
[מׄנחם אבל [20]אתה כׄ[י	17
[°°ׄ נגע ובברכות [	18
אוד[כה אלֹיׄ °°° לׄ[21]	19
]	20
]	21
]	22

[18] Frg. 21 provides lines 15–19. Licht does not transcribe frg. 21. Qimron places it by itself after the columns. Qimron:] °°° [. He does not see the *mem*.

[19] Sukenik:].ׄוׄ ו °°°° ר נדי[.

[20] Sukenik:].אתה [.

[21] Sukenik:].כֹה אל[ ] לׄ לׄ[.

2   […]

3   […]

4   […]

5   […]

6   […]

7   […]

8   […]

9   […]

10   […]

11   […]

12   […]

13   […]

14   […]

15   […]*m* °°°[…]

16   […]° your […]. And you help those who are willi[ng…]

17   [… fo]r you are comforting the mourner […]

18   […] affliction[9] and with blessings °°[…]

19   […. I thank] you, O my God, °°°° *l*°[…]

20   […]

21   […]

22   […]

---

[9] Not "blow" as in DJD.

מ[עֹפֹר][22]   **23**

עֹ̇מדה[23] לכול שני עו]לם[24]   **24**

מֹ̇לבך[25] כול חותם ˚˚˚ ושלוֹ̇ם[26]   **25**

ם̇ ורוחם[27] בני[28] איש לפי שכלו ואי̇ן[29]   **26**

בה]יכל̇[30] מלכותו[31] כי[32] עשה כול אלה ˚]   **27**

ואתה יצ]רתם[33] ולך̇[34] חמר[35] ובצדק תשופטֹ[ם][36]   **28**

לפנכה[37] לֹ̇קֹ̇ץ[38] תהוֹ ויצר חֹמֹ̇ר̇[39]   **29**

[40˚˚ ואֹתה[41] נכבדתה מכול אֹ̇ל]ים[42]   **30**

[קוֹדשֹך̇[43] וכאשר בֹ̇נֹ̇פֹ̇שֹך̇][44]   **31**

ולהל]ל שמך̇[45] תביֹא̇[ני][46] בעדת קֹד]ושים[47]   **32**

[ל̇] [˚][48]   **33**

---

[22] Frg. 11 provides lines 23–33. Qimron combines frgs. 11 and 13 and places them by themselves after the column. Sukenik and Licht:[
]˚˚˚. Cf. DJD:]מֹעֹפֹר[. Qimron:]˚˚˚˚˚˚[.

[23] Qimron: בֹ̇מדה[.

[24] Ctr. DJD:]עולם. Sukenik and Licht:]מדה לכול שני עו[. The fragment is difficult to read because the ink is faded. For the formula שני עולם see 1QHᵃ 9.26.

[25] Sukenik and Licht: מֹ̇ר[. Qimron: מש]פֹט בֹך̇. Cf. DJD: כֹ̇לבך[. See Dan 11:4: מלבד.

[26] Ctr. DJD:]שֹ̇ם̇ וֹם̇ ˚˚˚˚˚ חיתם. Sukenik and Licht:]חותם נפֹ ˚ שֹ̇ ˚[. Qimron: חיתם כֹפֹ̇י ירשת[.

[27] Sukenik and Licht: רוחם ˚˚[.

[28] Ctr. DJD: ˚˚ וֹ. Qimron: כֹ̇י.

[29] Ctr. DJD:]˚ ו. Sukenik and Licht:]שכלו חֹ̇[. Qimron: וֹ̇דֹ̇עֹ̇תֹ̇ו.

[30] Ctr. DJD: פֹ̇ל̇[. Sukenik and Licht: ˚˚[. Qimron: בה]יֹ̇כֹ̇ל.

[31] Sukenik and Licht: מלכותו ˚˚[.

[32] See 1QHᵃ 8.27: כי. Cf. DJD: מֹ̇י.

[33] Ctr. DJD: תֹ̇ם̇[. Sukenik: תֹ̇ם[. With Qimron.

[34] With Sukenik, Licht, and Qimron. DJD: אֹ̇ל̇.

[35] Ctr. DJD: תֹ̇מֹ̇יד. Licht: וחמד. Ctr. Qimron: הֹ̇מֹ̇ה. See line 29: חֹמֹ̇ר. So also DJD and Qimron. Sukenik: חמד.

[36] Sukenik and Licht: תשים]מֹ. Cf. DJD: תשימני לֹ̇]. With Qimron.

[37] Ctr. Sukenik, DJD, and Qimron: לפניך [.

[38] Ctr. DJD: ם̇ ˚˚˚. Sukenik and Licht do not read קץ[ ]. Qimron: רֹ̇וֹ̇ח.

[39] Sukenik and Licht:]ח.

[40] Ctr. DJD: לֹ̇הֹ̇[.

[41] Sukenik and Licht: יענה[. Qimron: ˚˚˚˚[.

[42] Sukenik and Licht:]א. DJD: אלֹ̇]ים.

[43] Sukenik and Licht: קודש[.

[44] Ctr. DJD:]˚ ˚˚˚˚ בֹ̇. Sukenik and Licht have a final *kaph*, ending the word. With Qimron.

[45] Sukenik and Licht:]לשמך תבֹ. DJD:]ולהל]ל שמך̇. Qimron: ל שמך̇ ולהל]אלים. A space may be detected after לֹ[.

[46] Ctr. Qimron: תֹ̇מֹ̇יד.

[47] Sukenik and Licht:]˚.

[48] Sukenik and Licht do not report line 33.

23   [… from] dust […]

24   […] it stood for all the years of eter[nity…]

25   […] without you[10] each seal °°° and peace […]

26   […]*m* and their spirit, the sons of man according to his insight, and there is n[o …]

27   [… in the sh]rine of his kingdom, for he is working[11] all these things °[…]

28   [… and you,] you [creat]ed them and to you (they are) clay, and with righteousness you will judge [them …][12]

29   […] before you to the endtime of formlessness[13] and the creature[14] of cla[y …]

30   […]°°. And you, you are glorified above all god[s …]

31   […] your holiness and as in your soul[15] […]

32   [… and to prai]se your name, you will bring [me] into the congregation of the Hol[y Ones …]

33   […]*l*[…]° […]

---

[10] Or "besides you."

[11] Since this section emphasizes God's continuous action, the verb is a *qal* participle (not a *qal* perfect; "he has done," as in DJD). See the reference to God's "comforting" in 3.17. For "working," see Pss 115:15, 121:2, 124:8, and esp. Isa 44:24.

[12] Ctr. DJD: "I will walk continually, and in righteousness you set me."

[13] Or "chaos." See Gen 1:2.

[14] Heb. יצר.

[15] Heb. נפש. The noun that is translated "soul" does not denote the bifurcated Greek anthropology. It means the living principle in the human.

Col. 4 [= Sukenik Col. 17 + Frg. 14]
Parallels: 4Q428 Frg. 1

]	**1**
]	**2**
]	**3**
]	**4**
]	**5**
]	**6**
]	**7**
]	**8**
]	**9**
]	**10**
]	**11**

⁴⁹]ׄ ׄ[ ]ׄ[ ]ׄ [**12**

[ׄ וׄמשפלת מדה משׁׄ [[⁵⁰]] °°°⁵¹]]   **13**

[מגׄולה בלוא משׁפט]]⁵² כרוחׄ ⁵³ °°°]]   **14**

או]יׄבים ⁵⁴ אוכלת בשׂרׄ]]⁵⁵ מ]]שׁׄנׄאׄיׄה ⁵⁶ בלוא   **15**

[ת ביביישה ⁵⁷ ומכש]]לת ב]]לוא ⁵⁸ מׄשפט ⁵⁹   **16**

---

⁴⁹ The right side of col. 4 is lost. Qimron does not transcribe this line. A single bracket represents a column, a double bracket a fragment.

⁵⁰ Ctr. DJD and Qimron: [ ]°°מׄ. Sukenik:]°מׄ. Licht:]מכ.

⁵¹ Frg. 14 provides the left side and margin of lines 13–22. Licht does not include frg. 14. *DSSEL* places the image of frg. 14 in SHR 4329, not with col. 4.

⁵² Sukenik:]עׄוׄפןמׄ. Licht:]עופן[מׄ.

⁵³ Ctr. DJD: מרוח.

⁵⁴ Ctr. DJD: בׄים[. With Qimron.

⁵⁵ Sukenik:]שׄ°. Licht:]בש.

⁵⁶ Sukenik: תאוה[. DJD: שׁׄנׄאׄיה.

⁵⁷ DJD: ביביישה.

⁵⁸ Qimron: ומכש]ילות ב]לוא.

⁵⁹ Sukenik:]לוא משׁפ°[.

Col. 4 [= Sukenik Col. 17 + Frg. 14]
Parallels: 4Q428 Frg. 1

1   […]

2   […]

3   […]

4   […]

5   […]

6   […]

7   […]

8   […]

9   […]

10   […]

11   […]

12   […] °[…]°[…]° °[…]

13   […]° and from humiliation of measure *mš*°[…]°°°[…]

14   […] revealed without judgment as the spirit of °°°[…]

15   [… the ene]mies devouring[16] the flesh of its [h]aters without

16   […]*t* on dry land and the stumbli[ng wi]thout judgment

---

[16] Most likely the noun "fire" (אש) is lost in the *lacuna*; thus the fem. sing. "devouring" assumes "the fire is devouring the flesh."

פוגעות פתע פתאו[ם ⁶¹ בל[ו]א בֿרֿיתֿ⁶²   [כרוח⁶⁰   **17**

בלו[א]ֿ⁶³ מֿשפטֿ מרוח דורשתֿ[ם⁶⁴   ]ות ˚ שֿ ˚˚˚ מֿ⁶⁵   **18**

ב[ל]ֿ[וא]⁶⁶ מצוה עֿדֿ⁶⁷ מרוח כו[ן⁶⁸   ]ֿמוˇ˚˚˚[[מֿתרמה בֿ ˚[**19**

עֿ⁶⁹ ˚בנגיעי ב[שר   [[   ]]   [**20**

א[שֿ⁷² לא השיגום במ[⁷³]רֿדֿףֿ [⁷⁴   [ברוך אתה אל הדעות כי תנקני[⁷⁰ מנסתרות אש[מה⁷¹   **21**

מח[שֿבֿות⁷⁵ רשעה מֿנדתֿ[⁷⁶ [[˚˚ שֿ[[וממשפט קצ[ו   **22**

עֿ[וֿו]ן⁷⁷ וממשפט אחֿרֿי[ם⁷⁸ ותתהר את] עבדך מכול פשעיו בֿ[המון] רֿחמיֿ[ך⁷⁹   **23**

כאשר ד[ברתה ביד מושה עבֿדֿ[ך⁸⁰ לשא[ת⁸¹ עֿוֿוֿ]ן וחטאה ולכפר בעֿ[ד⁸² פשֿ[עֿ⁸³ ומעל   **24**

[⁸⁴ מוסדי הרים ואש[אוכל]ֿה⁸⁵ בשֿאול תחתיה ואת הנו[סרים⁸⁶ במשפטיך   **25**

---

⁶⁰ See 4.14: כרוח[[]]בלוא משֿפֿטֿ.

⁶¹ Sukenik: פתאו[.

⁶² Sukenik: [כדונ].

⁶³ Cf. DJD: בלו[א]ֿ.

⁶⁴ With DJD and Qimron.

⁶⁵ Sukenik: נֿ˚˚˚[. Cf. DJD:]ות ˚ שֿ ˚˚˚ [. Qimron: ˚ שֿ ˚ ות ˚[. Perhaps: ישֿיגֿום.

⁶⁶ Qimron does not see the *lamedh*.

⁶⁷ Not seen by previous editors.

⁶⁸ Qimron: [הלת]ֿמֿוˇ.

⁶⁹ Sukenik: ˚[. Licht does not transcribe. Qimron: תֿ[.

⁷⁰ For אל הדעות see 1QS 3.15 and 1QHᵃ 9.28; 20.13; 21.32; and 22.34. Cf. Licht: ותנקני[.

⁷¹ Ctr. DJD: אש[ר.

⁷² Licht: אש[ר תעו בם ומרזים א]. Cf. DJD: שֿ˚˚ר [. Puech (1993): כ[אשר.

⁷³ Sukenik: בֿמֿ[. Licht: במ[שובתם כול אנשי העול]. Cf. DJD: בֿמצֿ]רֿף. Qimron:]ֿ במ.

⁷⁴ Sukenik: רֿדֿףֿ[. Cf. DJD: ףֿ ˚˚[. Qimron: ˚˚ ˚[. Restore מרדף; see Prov 11:19, 12:11, 15:9, 28:19, and esp. 19:7. See 1QM 3.2 and 3.9.

⁷⁵ Licht: חרונכה ומהוות מח[שבות.

⁷⁶ Ctr. DJD: פֿˇˇמֿˇ˚ם; see 4.31 (בנדה). Sukenik: נער ˚[. Licht: נעוות [לב]. Qimron: מנֿדתֿ[.

⁷⁷ Sukenik: ין[. Licht: ותושיעני מאשמת עו[ן].

⁷⁸ Ctr. DJD: אחֿ[ר]. Sukenik: אחֿ[. Licht: אחֿ[רון. Qimron: אחֿרֿי[ת.

⁷⁹ Sukenik: חמיֿ[ך. Licht: רֿחמי[ך.

⁸⁰ Sukenik: מושה [ ]. Licht: מושה [לשאת פשע].

⁸¹ With DJD and Qimron. Sukenik: ˚[.

⁸² Cf. DJD: בעֿדֿ.

⁸³ Sukenik: ˚[ ]בעֿ. Licht: בעֿ[ד אשמה].

⁸⁴ Licht: [בהשרף].

⁸⁵ Ctr. DJD: ב[קֿ]לֿˇˇ˚ה. Licht: ה]אוכל[ה. Qimron: ה[ד]יק.

⁸⁶ With Qimron. Licht: הנו[עדים יחד].

17   [as the spirit of[17] …] striking all of a sudde[n wit]hout a covenant

18   [… witho]ut judgment from the spirit of seeking […]*wt* °°*š*°°° *m*

19   […] acting deceitfully *b*°[… with]o[ut] commandment until from the spirit *kw*[…]*mw*°°°

20   […]ᶜ in the afflictions of f[lesh ….] (VACAT) […] (VACAT)

21   [Blessed are you, the God of knowledge, for you cleanse me] from hidden (acts)[18] of gu[ilt[19]… wh]ich they did not reach them while pu[rs]uing[20] […]

22   […] and from the judgment of the Endtime of […] the [tho]ughts of wickedness, the impurity of […] °°°*š*[…]

23   [… in]iquity and from the judgment of the latter things. [And you purify][21] your servant from all his transgressions by [the abundance of] your mercies.

24   [… as] you have [sp]oken through Moses [your] servant [to forgi]ve[22] iniquity and sin and to atone fo[r transgress]ion and infidelity.

25   […] the foundations of the mountains, and fire [devou]rs in Sheol below and [those who are war]ned[23] by your judgments.

---

[17] See 4.14.

[18] The noun is plural.

[19] See the similar expression in Ps 19:13 [12], "Cleanse me from hidden guilt." Or "hidden acts."

[20] See 1QM 3.2 and 3.9.

[21] Restorations are according to the repetitive formulae and expressions in 1QHᵃ and the other known witnesses. Note "impurity" in the preceding line.

[22] Lit. "to take away."

[23] *Nipᶜal* plural participle of יסר. See 7.17.

26　בחר]תֹה⁸⁷ לעבדיך באמונה [ל]היות זרעם לפניך כול הימים ושמֹ[ותיהם⁸⁸]הֹקִימותה

27　מ]פֹשע⁸⁹ ולהשליך כול עוֹוֹנֹותֹם⁹⁰ ולהנחילם בכול כבוד אדם] [⁹¹לרוב⁹² ימים

28　[

29　[ברוך אתה אדוני אל הרחמי]ֹם⁹³ מרוחות אשר נתתה בי אמצֹאה⁹⁴ מענה לשון לספר צדקותיך וארוך אפים

30　[ֹרֹ⁹⁵ ומעשי ימין עוזך וֹלֹהֹודות⁹⁶ על פשעי ראשונים ולֹהֹ[תנפ]ֹל⁹⁷ ולהתחנן על

31　פש]עֹיֹ⁹⁸ מעשי ונעוות⁹⁹ לֹבֹבֹי¹⁰⁰ כי בנדה התגוללתי ומסוד עֹרֹ[וה נוצר]תי¹⁰¹ ולא נלֹאֹיתי¹⁰²

32　[ֹרֹשֹעֹ כי לך¹⁰³ אתה הצדקה ולשמך הברכה לעול]ם　　[כֹצֹדקתך¹⁰⁴]ופדה

---

⁸⁷ Ctr. DJD: תֹה[. Sukenik: ה ֹ[. Licht: [בחר]תה. Qimron: [יחד בחר]תֹה.
⁸⁸ With DJD. Sukenik:]ושם. Licht: [לטהרם. Cf. Qimron: וש]בֹ[ועתך ה]קימותה. ושבֹ]ועתך[. The horizontal foot typical of a *beth* is not extant in the images of this line, making Qimron's reading unlikely.
⁸⁹ Sukenik: שע ֹ[. Licht: מפ[שע. DJD: פֹשע].
⁹⁰ With DJD and Qimron. Sukenik: ע °°°°°ם. Licht: עונותיהם.
⁹¹ The small *lacuna* is the size of a word division.
⁹² Sukenik: לרוב[ ]. Licht and Qimron: [ו]רוב.
⁹³ The final *mem* can be discerned. See the formula in 18.16: ברוך אתה אדוני אל הרחמיֹם. Note restoration of ברוך is according to immediate context. Sukenik: מרוחות [ֹ. Licht: [אודך] מרוחות.
⁹⁴ Sukenik: אה °°°א. Licht: מצֹאֹ[א. Cf. DJD: וֹא[מֹ]צֹאה. Qimron: א[מֹצֹאה.
⁹⁵ Sukenik: [ֹ. Licht: [במשפטיכה.
⁹⁶ Sukenik: ות °°°°°. Licht: עוזך [וסלי]חות. Qimron: ולֹהֹודות.
⁹⁷ Sukenik: ל[ ]ולהֹ. Restoration follows Licht.
⁹⁸ With Qimron. Licht: [חטאותי ורוע]. Cf. DJD: °°[.
⁹⁹ With Licht. Cf. Sukenik and DJD: ונעוית.
¹⁰⁰ Sukenik: ל °°°°. Licht: לֹבֹ[בי.
¹⁰¹ Sukenik: תי[ ]. Licht: [ערוה נוצר]תי. Qimron: הֹעֹ[רוה נו]צֹרֹתי. Cf. DJD: רֹמֹ[ה י]צֹאֹתי.
¹⁰² Sukenik: נל ֹתי. Licht: נלאיתי. Cf. Qimron and DJD: נֹלֹויֹתי.
¹⁰³ Sukenik: לך[°°°. Licht: [ֹ. Qimron: ר]שֹעֹה כי לך. DJD: כי לך [ֹ. לבקש רחמיכה כיא]לך.
¹⁰⁴ Sukenik: צֹֹדֹקתך. Licht: צדקתך כ]עשה]לעול]ם. Qimron: בֹצֹדקתך[.

26 […] you [have chosen] those who serve you with faithfulness, that their seed [w]ill be before you all the days. And you established [their] reputation[s][24]

27 [… from] transgression and to discard all their iniquities, and (to grant) their inheritances in all the glory of Adam[25] for many days.

28 […] (VACAT)

29 [Blessed are you, O Lord, God of mercie]s, because of[26] the spirits that you granted me.[27] I will find an answer of the tongue to recount your righteous deeds and patience[28]

30 […]*k* and the works of your strong right hand, and to confess former transgressions, and to pr[ostra]te myself and to petition for mercy, concerning

31 [… the transgress]ions of my works and the bewilderment[29] of my heart. For in impurity I wallowed[30] and from the secret of naked[ness[31]] I was [created]; but I did not grow weary.

32 […] wicked, for to you (belongs) righteousness, and to your name (belongs) the blessing for eterni[ty …] according to your righteousness and redemption

---

[24] Lit. "[their] name[s]."
[25] Or "the human."
[26] Lit. "from."
[27] See 1QS 3.18; God gave to the human "two spirits."
[28] Heb. ‏וארוך אפים‎.
[29] See 21.14.
[30] Lit. "rolled."
[31] I.e., "the genitals (of a woman or a man)." See 5.32, 9.24, 20.28.

33   ‏וי[תמו¹⁰⁵ רשעים ואני הׄוׄבינותי¹⁰⁶ כי את אשר בחרתׄהׄ הׄ[כינותה]¹⁰⁷ דרכו ובשכל

34   ‏ותח[שכהו¹⁰⁸ מחטוא לך ול[ט]וׄב¹⁰⁹ לו¹¹⁰ עניתו¹¹¹ ביסוריך ובנס[וׄיׄיׄך חזק[תׄהׄ¹¹² לבו

35   ‏¹¹³]עבדך מחטוא לך ומכשול בכול דברי רצונך חזק מׄתׄנׄ[יו לעמו]דׄ¹¹⁴ על רוחות

36   ‏לה[תהלך¹¹⁵ בכול אשר אהבתה ולמאוס בכול אשר שנׄאׄתׄהׄ [ולעשות]¹¹⁶ הׄטׄוׄב¹¹⁷ בעיניך

37   ‏ממ[שׄלתם בתכמׄוׄ¹¹⁸ כי רוח בשׄׄרׄ¹¹⁹ עבדך   (VACAT)   [   ]   (VACAT)

38   ‏ברוך אתה אל כי¹²⁰] הניפותה רוח קודשׄךׄ¹²¹ על עבדׄךׄ [ותׄ]טׄהר מכׄ[ול]¹²²חזק[תׄהׄ לבׄוׄ

39   ‏א[נׄוׄש ואל¹²³ כול ברית¹²⁴ אדם אביט¹²⁵ [¹²⁶]הׄ ימצאוה

40   ‏שׄׄעׄ משיגיה¹²⁷ ואוהׄבׄיׄה¹²⁸[   ]לׄעׄולמי¹²⁹[עד

41   ‏¹³⁰[   ]   [

---

¹⁰⁵ Sukenik and DJD: ‏תמו[. Licht: ‏וי[תמו. ‏את עבדך].

¹⁰⁶ Sukenik and Qimron: ‏הׄבׄינותי.

¹⁰⁷ With Qimron and DJD. Sukenik: ‏בחרתה[   ]. Licht: ‏בחרתה [תתם].

¹⁰⁸ Sukenik: ‏שכהו[. Licht: ‏שכהו[תמ אמתכה]. Cf. DJD: ‏חׄשכהו[ת. Qimron: ‏שכהו[ותח וחנותו].

¹⁰⁹ Cf. DJD: ‏וׄלׄ ב.

¹¹⁰ Sukenik: ‏לׄוׄ. Licht: ‏לׄוׄ יב [הש]ולׄ.

¹¹¹ With Licht. Cf. Sukenik and DJD: ‏ענותו.

¹¹² See 4.38: ‏חזק[תׄהׄ. Sukenik: ‏]הׄ ‏תׄ[. Licht: ‏יסר]תׄה לבו. Qimron: ‏בחנתה וׄיׄ[וׄבׄנׄס]ובנס[תׄהׄ. Cf. DJD: ‏חזק[תׄהׄ וׄבׄנׄסׄ]תׄרׄוׄתׄיׄך.

¹¹³ Licht: ‏ותסוך בעד[.

¹¹⁴ With Sukenik. Licht: ‏מׄ[פלגותיך לע]ד. Qimron: ‏מׄוׄתׄניו לעמוד. Cf. DJD: ‏מׄתׄנׄ[יו לעמו]ד.

¹¹⁵ Sukenik: ‏תהלך[. Licht: ‏אנוש לה[תהלך]. Cf. DJD: ‏ולה[תׄהׄלׄך   ].

¹¹⁶ With Licht, DJD, and Qimron.

¹¹⁷ Sukenik: ‏שנא[ת הׄטׄוׄב]. Licht and Qimron: ‏שנא]תה ולעשות [הטוב   .

¹¹⁸ Sukenik: ‏לתם בתכמי. Licht: ‏וכול רוח עול[לתם בתכמי. Qimron: ‏ממ[שׄלתם בתכמׄי.

¹¹⁹ Sukenik: ‏בשׄׄ [   ]. Licht: ‏בשר [אין ל]עבדך.

¹²⁰ Cf. DJD: ‏ברוך אתה אל עליון אשר]. Licht: ‏אודכה[. Qimron: ‏אודך כי].

¹²¹ Sukenik: ‏קודש[. Licht: ‏קׄודׄ[שכה].

¹²² See 4.34: ‏חזק[תׄהׄ. Sukenik: ‏]הׄר מׄׄ [   ]תׄ[   ]תׄ. Licht: ‏עבדך [ותשמר]הו מ[חטוא לך ומנעוות]. Cf. DJD: ‏תׄ[   ]מׄ טהר[ות   ]שׄע[פׄ טהר[ות. Qimron: ‏חזק[תׄהׄ.

¹²³ Sukenik: ‏ש ואל[. Licht: ‏ש ואל ....(sic).

¹²⁴ Ctr. Qimron: ‏בׄיׄנׄת.

¹²⁵ Licht ends his reading here.

¹²⁶ Qimron: ‏הׄ[משחרי.

¹²⁷ Sukenik: ‏יׄגׄיה. Qimron: ‏יׄגׄוׄה [ישׄ]. Cf. DJD: ‏בׄ[וׄ. The waw and yodh do look distinct here. משיגיה

¹²⁸ Cf. DJD: ‏ואוהׄבׄיׄה‎[‎‎‎‎ˆˆˆ‎.

¹²⁹ Sukenik: ‏[עׄולמי. DJD: ‏לׄעׄולמי[.

¹³⁰ Lower margin is visible.

33 [… and] the wicked [will be] annihilated. And I understand that the one you have elected, his way is es-[tablished], and through the insight of

34 [… and you pre]vent him from sinning against you, and [go]od for him (is) his misery through your chas-tisements[32] and by [your] trial[s] you [strengthened][33] his heart

35 […] your servant from sinning against you, and from becoming an obstacle in all the matters of your will. Strengthening [his] loin[s to sta]nd[34] over spirits

36 [… to] walk continuously in everything that you love, and to reject[35] everything that you hate [and to do] the good in your eyes

37 […] their [dom]inion in his entrails,[36] for a spirit of flesh (is) your servant. (VACAT) […] (VACAT)

38 [Blessed are you, O God, for] you waved[37] your holy spirit over your servant [and you] purified (him) from a[ll …] you [strengthened][38] his heart

39 [… a h]uman, and to each covenant of Adam[39] I will look […]h they will find it

40 […]šᶜ those who reach it[40] and those who love it […] ˚ykh forever and ever

41 [….] (VACAT) […] (VACAT)

---

[32] See 7.17.
[33] See 4.38.
[34] See 10.9–10.
[35] Not תעב.
[36] Or "bones," "organs." The meaning of the word תכם is speculative and the root is not clear. See Composite Text, note 38. The context determines the meaning especially for this noun. See also 13.30, 15.7, 16.2, and 22.28. See also 1QS 4.29.
[37] *Hipˤil* perfect of נוף, "to move back and forth, to spread." Perhaps an allusion to the wave-offering in the Temple.
[38] See 4.34.
[39] Or "humankind."
[40] *Hipˤil* participle of נשג.

Col. 5 [= Sukenik Col. 13 + Frgs. 15a, 15b Col. 1, 31, 17, 20, and 33][131]
Parallels: 4Q428 Frg. 2

]	**1**
]	**2**
]	**3**
]	**4**
]	**5**
]	**6**
]	**7**
]	**8**
]	**9**
]	**10**
]	**11**

מֿעֿשֿׂיֿ אֿלֿ[134]   [מזמור למ]שֿׂכֿיֿל להתנפל[132] לֿפֿנֿי[133] אל **12**

או[שֿׂי[136] עולם   ]°°[[135]   ]°°[[ולהבין פתאים] **13**

בני אי[שֿׂ[140] התהלכו   בשר וסוד רוחי°[139]   [138]   [ת[137] ולהבין אנוש בֿ] **14**

[ברוך][141] אתה אדוני אשֿׁ[ר][142] יֿֿצֿר[143] רוח בֿ[[שר[144] ברו[ח][145] קודשך ו[בֿ]כֿוח גבורתך **15**

---

[131] Licht does not include frgs. 31, 17, 20, and 33.

[132] Sukenik and Licht:]הת°°°°[.

[133] Frg. 15a provides the right side of lines 12–17.

[134] Frg. 15b col. 1 begins with these letters and provides the far left portion of lines 12–20. The left margin is extant.

[135] Frg. 31 provides the left side of lines 13–15.

[136] Sukenik: שֿׂי[. Licht: שי[. Cf. DJD: יֿ[. With Qimron: או[שֿׂי. See 1QHᵃ 11.36: אושי עולם.

[137] Qimron: [ורוזי ד]עֿת.

[138] Qimron: [בֿ[יצר].

[139] Sukenik: רֿוֿחֿוֿ.Qimron reads: רוחי א]מֿת. Frg. 31 provides the middle of lines 14–15. For the term, בשר, frg. 31 provides the *šin*, and the *reš*, while frg. 17 provides the *beth*.

[140] Sukenik שֿׁ[. Licht: ש[. DJD: ֹ[. See 3.26: בני איש.

[141] Licht does not restore the *lacuna*.

[142] Sukenik, Licht, and Qimron:]א. DJD:]°°.

[143] Qimron: הודע[תֿֿה]. See 7.30.

[144] Sukenik: שֿׁ רוחב. The word is positioned on the edges of frgs. 31 and 17.

[145] DJD:] בֿבֿ. Qimron:]בד. Frg. 31 ends here.

Col. 5 [= Sukenik Col. 13 + Frgs 15a, 15b Col. 1, 31, 17, 20, and 33]
Parallels: 4Q428 Frg. 2

1   [...]

2   [...]

3   [...]

4   [...]

5   [...]

6   [...]

7   [...]

8   [...]

9   [...]

10 [...]

11 [...]

12 [A psalm[41] for the M]aster so he may prostrate himself befor[e God ...] the works of God

13 [...] and to be allowed to discern the simple ones [...]°°[...]°°[...] eternal [a]cts[42]

14 [...]°*t* and to be allowed to discern the human *b*[...] flesh and the secret of the spirits of [... the sons of ma]n to walk continuously.

15 [Blessed are] you, O Lord, wh[o] creates a fleshly[43] spirit by [your holy] spir[it and] by the power of your might

---

[41] See 7.21.
[42] This participle often refers to God's creative acts.
[43] A positive meaning is intended.

לאין ⟦חקר כול	⟦ה̇מ̇ת̇⟧148 וקנאת משפ̇⟦טי⟧ך	147⟦ך̇⟧עם רוב טוב	[ובגדול ח⟦ס̇ד̇⟧146	**16**
ה̊⟦כ̊ינותה152	⟦ורזי מחשבת וראש̊י̊ת̊⟧151	150כול בינה ומ̇⟦ו̇סר	בד⟦ע̊ת⟧149	**17**
⟦ק̊דושי̊ם	⟦תה155 ו̊ל̊ולמי עד אתה הוא̊⟧	154ו⟦לם	קודש מקדם ע̊ו̊⟧	153ה̊°°[	**18**
ובמעין ⟦ב̊ינתך159 לא	כבודך ובעומק °°⟧158	157בע̊⟦ב̊ור	⟦תני156 ⟦ה̊ו̊ד̊ע̊ן	] וברזי פלאך	**19**
⟦צ̊ד̊ק̊ 163	162חוכמה ואולת̊⟧	רע161 ⟦⟧	160ומעשי	[אתה גליתה דרכי א̊מ̊ת̊	**20**
	166כול̊ התהלכ̊ו̊⟧	165ו̊אן⟧ ⟦ל̊ת̊⟧	164מעשיהם אמת ו̊ב̊י̊נ̊ה̊ ע̊ו̊ל̊ה̊⟧	]	**21**
	169לשלום ושחת כו̇ל̇ °⟧	168ה̇ם̇⟧	וחסדי עולם לכ̊ו̊ל̊ ק̇צ̇⟦י̇	167ם̊[	**22**
ועו⟦ו̊שים לכ̊⟧ה173	172 עד למעשה⟧	171ו̊ה̊מ̊ד̊ה̊⟧ ו̊ש̊מחת	⟦פ̇טיהם170 כבוד עולם	[מש⟦	**23**

---

146 Sukenik and Licht: ד̊[.

147 Sukenik and Licht: טוב.

148 Frg. 17 provides the middle portion of text for lines 15–21. Licht does not include frg. 17. Sukenik: א̊ח̊[. Qimron: א̇פ̇י̇ך̇[.

149 Qimron: ⟦ד̊[ד̇]ע̊ת. Sukenik, Licht, and DJD: ת̊[.

150 Ctr. Qimron: ו̇ב̇⟦שכל].

151 Sukenik: [°°ורז.

152 Licht does not restore the *lacuna* here in frg. 15a.

153 Licht begins col. 13 here. Sukenik and Qimron: ה̊ °[. Licht: קודש ה[. DJD: °°[.

154 Col. 5 provides the right side and most of the left for lines 18–41. Sukenik:]ע̊. Licht: [ע̇ולם].

155 Sukenik and Qimron: הוא[.

156 Sukenik: [°°°. Licht: [הודעתם]. With DJD and Qimron.

157 Sukenik: ו̊ד̊[.

158 Qimron: [מ̇.

159 Sukenik and Licht: בינתך ו̇. With DJD and Qimron.

160 Qimron: ט̊ו̊ב̊.

161 Sukenik: [מעשי רע]. Licht: [מעשי] רזיכה גליתה. The terms רע חוכמה ואולת are part of frg. 17, which Licht does not include.

162 Sukenik: [חכמה ואול. With DJD and Qimron.

163 Frg. 15b col. 1 ends here.

164 Ctr. DJD: [ה̇] °[ ]° [ ]. With Qimron: ו̇ב̇י̇נ̇ה̇ ע̇ו̇ל̇ה̇.

165 Sukenik: [ל̊ת̊. Licht: [ה] ם ואול [ ]. The bottom of frg. 17 provides part of the *lamedh* and *taw* of ואולת.

166 The end of line 21 is seen on SHR 4277 [see DJD Pl. 3]. Part of the *lamedh* of כול is on frg. 17.

167 Sukenik: °[. Licht: [רוב נגיע]ם. Cf. DJD: [ ]° [. Qimron: [רחמי]ם̊.

168 Sukenik: לכול °°°°. Licht: [קצ]יהם. Qimron: ק̊צ̊יה̊ם.

169 With Sukenik. Licht: [ושחת. Cf. DJD: [° ושחת כו̇ל̇. Qimron: [מ̊ כול ושחת. The ו̇ל̇ can be seen on SHR 4277.

170 With DJD and Qimron. Sukenik: [שיה°°°°. Licht: [נועדו מן]עדיהם.

171 Qimron: ו̇°°°°.

172 Sukenik: [מחת]°. Licht: [מחת וש]עולם ורוב עדנים.

173 Frg. 20 provides the text for the far left portions of lines 23–27. Sukenik: [שים לכן. Cf. DJD: [°ל̊ שים. Qimron: [שים למ]עשה.

16 [and by] your [great[44] lovi]ng-kindness with the multitude of your goodness. [...][45] your wrath and the zeal of [your] judgme[nts ...] all [un]fathomable[46]

17 [.... In the k]nowledge of all discernment and dis[cipline][47] and the mysteries of thought and the beginnings of [...] you establish[ed].

18 [...]°°*h* holiness from ete[rnal] ages [and] to the everlasting eternity you, [you] were willing[48] [...] Holy Ones[49]

19 [...] and in the mysteries of your wonder [you] have allowed [me] to know.[50] [On ac]count of your glory and in the depth of °°[... and in the fountain of[51]] your discernment (will) not

20 [...] you, you revealed the ways of truth and the works of evil, wisdom, and foolishness [...] righteousness

21 [...] their works. (In) truth and discernment (or in) perversity and foolishness, all have walke[d] continuously [...]

22 [...]*m* and the eternal loving-kindnesses for all their endti[m]es of peace. But the pit[52] (is for) all °[...]

23 their [judg]ments, eternal glory, and delight, and everlasting joy. For the work [... and] they are [do]ing to yo[u]

---

[44] See 9.34; cf. 8.30.

[45] See 7.30.

[46] Heb. לאין חקר. See also Isa 40:28 and Ps 145:3. In the *Hodayot* see 11.21, 14.6 and 14.19–20, 16.18, and 4Q429 frg. 4 1.2.

[47] Or "tr[aining]." Not "instruction."

[48] Not "resolve." The *hip'il* perfect of this verb connotes God's politeness. See also 8.16, 26.

[49] The Holy Ones may refer to angels or the advanced spiritually in the *Yaḥad*.

[50] The permissive *hip'il*. In the *Thanksgiving Hymns*, the permissive *hip'il* is used far more often than in Biblical Hebrew. The authors intended to stress that God permits or allows the Righteous Teacher and his followers to know secrets and intervenes in human history by permitting events to move to his Endtime.

[51] See 13.28.

[52] DJD: "destruction."

24　מֺעֵֿשֵׁ֯י[¹⁷⁴　　　　　　] ואלה אשר הכ[ינותה¹⁷⁵ מקדם [[עֿוֺלֺם¹⁷⁶]] לשפוט בם

25　אֵת¹⁷⁷ כול מעשיך בטרם בראתם עם צבא רוחיך ועדת[¹⁷⁸　　ע]ֺֿם¹⁷⁹ רקיֿﬠ קֺוֺדשך וֺכֿוֺל

26　צבאותיו עם הארץ וכול צֿאֿצֿאֿיֺה¹⁸⁰ בימים ובתהומות[¹⁸¹ ו][כול מחשבותֿךֿ¹⁸² לכול קצי עֿוֺלֺם¹⁸³

27　ופקודת עד כי אתה הכינותמה מקדם עולם ומעשֿה[¹⁸⁴　　]ֺ [[　　]　　]ᵒᵒᵒᵒ[¹⁸⁵　　] בם בעבור¹⁸⁶

28　יספרו כבודך בֺכֺוֺל ממשלתך כי הראיתם את אשר לא יֺ[דעו¹⁸⁷　　אֿשֿר¹⁸⁸] קדם ולברוא

29　חדשות להפר קימי קדם ול[הק]ים נהיות עולם כי אֿתֿה הֺ[כינות]מֺֿה¹⁸⁹ ואתה תהיה

30　לעולמי עד וברזי שכלכה פלֿגֿ[תה]¹⁹⁰כול אלה להודיע כבֿוֺדֿך וֺמֺה[¹⁹¹　　ה]ֺיֿאֿ¹⁹² רוח בשר להבין

31　בכול אלה ולהשכיל בסבֿל[םֿ¹⁹³　ה]ֿגדול¹⁹⁴ ומה ילוד אשה בכוֺלֺ מֺﬠֵשׁיֿךֿ¹⁹⁵ הנוראים והוא

32　מבנה עפר ומגבל מים אֺ[שמה וחט]אֿה¹⁹⁶ סודו ערות קלוֺן וֺ[מקור ה]ֺנֺֿדֿה¹⁹⁷ ורוח נעוה משלה

---

¹⁷⁴ Qimron [רע]. DJD: ע[.
¹⁷⁵ Sukenik: הכ[. Licht: את ואתדע[עולם מקדם ינותה]הכ.
¹⁷⁶ See 5.18: עוֺ]לם מקדם.
¹⁷⁷ The right margin is clear.
¹⁷⁸ Licht: וכול הרקיע את ותכן [קדושיך ועדת.
¹⁷⁹ Sukenik: ֺ[.
¹⁸⁰ Sukenik: ה ᵒᵒᵒᵒצ. Licht, Qimron: צאֿצֿאֿיֺה.
¹⁸¹ Licht: עולמים לתעודת תכנתה ופעולתם[ובתהומות.
¹⁸² Sukenik: מחשבותֿךֿ[כול. Qimron: מחשביֺהֺם[כֿול[ו]. Cf. DJD: מחשבותֺם.
¹⁸³ Sukenik: עוֺ[ᵒᵒᵒ.
¹⁸⁴ Licht: והם אמתך לבני הודעתה גבורתך[ומעשה.
¹⁸⁵ Qimron: תֺֿהֺ[המשל עפר].
¹⁸⁶ Frg. 20 ends here. This fragment also preserves a portion of the *lamedh* of לברוא in the column below
¹⁸⁷ With Qimron. Sukenik: לֺא [. Licht: ב[כול ראה] לא. DJD: יֺ.
¹⁸⁸ Sukenik: שֺֿר[. Qimron: שֺר[.
¹⁸⁹ With DJD and Qimron. Sukenik: אֺ[ᵒᵒᵒᵒ]. Licht: מאז הכינותם אֿ]תה כי. For the formula, see line 27.
¹⁹⁰ With Qimron and DJD. Sukenik: פלֺ [. Licht: גתה]פל.
¹⁹¹ DJD misses ומֺֿהֺ. Qimron: וֺמֺה.
¹⁹² Sukenik: אֺ [. Licht: ולוֺא[ולמעשיך]כבודך. DJD: יֺאֿ ה]מה כי[. Qimron: הֺ[וֿא ה]אֿף אֺמֺהֺ.
¹⁹³ Sukenik and DJD: בסֺ [ ]. Licht: כוחך בסבוֺ]ר]גדול.
¹⁹⁴ Ctr. Qimron: הֺגדול] פלאך בסוֺד.
¹⁹⁵ Ctr. DJD: יֺ[ל]ֺדֿ[ג]. The letters, missed by some editors, are washed out. Sukenik: בלֿוֺל ᵒᵒᵒᵒ. Licht: פלאך] רזי [בכול. Qimron: בכול מֺﬠֵשׁיֿ֯ך.
¹⁹⁶ Sukenik:]ֺ [ה. Licht: וחטאה[עוון [אשר. DJD: וחטֺ]אֿה[שמה. Qimron: אֺֿמֺהֺ[וחט שמה. אֺ.
¹⁹⁷ One might expect קלון. With Licht. Sukenik: קלוֺן[ ]ᵒ ה. Cf. DJD and Qimron: הנ]דה וֺמֺ[קור קלוֺן.

24   works of [....] And these things which [you] est[ablished from] eternal [ages][53] to judge through them

25   all your creatures before you created them together with the host of your spirits, and the community of [... wi]th your holy firmament[54] and all

26   its hosts, together with the earth and all its offshoots in the seas and in the deeps. [And] all your thoughts (are) for the endtimes of eternity

27   and everlasting visitation. For you, you established them from eternal ages and the work [...]˚[...]°°° in them in order that

28   they will recount your glory within all your dominion for you have shown them that which [they] did not k[now ...] which (is from) ancient-time,[55] and to create

29   new (events), to annul the things that rise up (from) ancient-time, and to [establ]ish things that are of eternity. For you, [you] est[ablished] them and you will be

30   forever and ever.[56] And in the mysteries of your insight [you] assigned all these things to make known your glory. And how[57] c[an] the spirit of flesh (be able) to discern

31   in all these things and to have insight into [their] great suffering? And what (is) one born of a woman in all your terrifying works?[58] And he is

32   but a form of[59] dust and mixed[60] water. G[uilt and si]n (are) his foundation, shameful nakedness[61] and [the spring of] impurity, and a perverted spirit rule

---

[53] See 5.18.
[54] See Gen 1:6–8.
[55] Or "from old time."
[56] Or "everlasting eternity."
[57] "And how" has been missed by some previous editors.
[58] This noun has been missed by some previous editors.
[59] Lit. "a construction of," "a building of."
[60] Aramaic: "to knead;" Syriac: "to create."
[61] Or "genitals." See 9.24, 20.28.

33   בו   ואם ירשע והיהֿ[ע]וֿלם198 ומופת דורות רחוקֿ[יֿ]ֿם לבשר199 רק בטובך

34   יצדק איש ובֿרֿוֿב רֿחֿ[מיך תושיענו200 בהדרך תפארנו ותמשֿיֿלֿנֿ]ו בֿ[ֿ]רוב201 עדנים עם שלום

35   עולם ואורך ימים כי [מעשיך ו]דברך202 לא ישוב אחור   ואני עבדך ידעתי

36   ברוח אשר נתתה בי[כיא אמת]203 וצדק כול מעשיך ודֿבֿרֿך204 לֿאֿ ישוב אחור וֿכֿוֿלֿ[205

37   קציך מועדֿי עוֿ[ֿ]ֿלֿם206   סֿ[דורים207 לחפציהם ואדעֿהֿ [כי208   לֿ[209

38   ורשע שֿ]   ⟦ֿקֿ210⟧ להתבונן ⟦

39   ⟦°° ֿרוחיך ולֿ⟧211

40   ⟦ֿלֿהלֿ⟧212

41   ]

Col. 6 [= Sukenik Col. 14 + Frgs. 18, 22, 15b Col. 2, 44, and 19]213

1   ]

2   ]

3   ]

4   ]

---

198 With Sukenik. Licht: ע]וֿלם [לאות והיה. DJD: [ֿעוֿלם] עד לאות [והיה. יהיהֿ.
199 Ctr. Qimron: דורות כרוק מ°°° בשר [דריֿ[ ]. Licht: בשר[ ]. With DJD. Sukenik: דורות דֿרֿוֿןֿ [כוֿ]ל בשר.
200 With DJD and Qimron. Sukenik: [ ]רֿחֿ. Licht: תושיענו [מיך]רֿחֿ.
201 With DJD. Sukenik: [רֿוֿב] ותמ°]. Licht: ותמשֿיֿלהו על ר[וֿב. Qimron: ותמשֿיֿלהו]ן בֿ]רוב.
202 Sukenik: [דברך] כי[ ]. Licht: ו]דברך [אתה אל הדעות כי.
203 Licht: [כיא אמת כול פעלך].
204 Sukenik: ד°°°°. Licht: ודברך.
205 Sukenik:]°. Licht: [בכול]ו.
206 Sukenik:]לֿ[מוע°]. Licht: מועדֿי הכינותה מעשיך]. DJD: ל[מועֿדֿ]ים. Qimron: ל] מועֿדֿ[ם] עו[ל]ם. מועֿדֿי[ם].
207 With Qimron. Sukenik: דֿרורים [ב. Cf. DJD: סֿ[דורים]. Licht: סֿ[רורים].]רורים.
208 With DJD and Qimron. Sukenik:]ואדע. Licht ends his reading of the column with ואדעֿה.
209 Sukenik and Qimron do not transcribe the *lamedh*.
210 Sukenik: קֿ[. Frg. 33 begins here and provides the left side of lines 38–40.
211 Sukenik:]וֿחיך[.
212 Sukenink:]לֿ[. Frg. 33 ends here.
213 Licht does not include frgs. 19, 22, and 44. Note that fragments joins are indicated by ⟧ and ⟦; lacunae within a piece of leather are indicated by] and [.

33 in him.[62] And if he should be wicked, he shall be […] eternal and a portent[63] (for) dista[n]t generations of the flesh. Only by his goodness

34 can a man be justified; and in the multitude of [your] mer[cies you will save him]. With your splendor you glorify him, and you will let hi[m] rule [over] the multitude of delights with eternal

35 peace and length of days. For [your works and] your word shall not turn back. But I, your servant, know

36 through the spirit that you put in me [that true] and righteous (are) all your works, and your word shall not turn back and all […]

37 your endtimes (are) [ete]r[nal] appointed time[s[64] … o]rdered according to their purposes.[65] And I know [that …]*l*[…]

38 and wickedness *š*°[…]°*q* to comprehend […]

39 […]°° your spirits and *l*[…]

40 […]°*hl*[…]

41 […]

Col. 6 [= Sukenik Col. 14 + Frgs. 18, 22, 15b Col. 2, 44, and 19]

1 […]

2 […]

3 […]

4 […]

---

[62] The scribe leaves uninscribed space here, but it is not a *vacat* denoting a new hymn.
[63] Or "wonder," "sign." See 7.33 where the noun also means "portent." For "wonder" see 8:9, 15.24.
[64] Or "season[s]," "festival[s]."
[65] See 9.15.

5   ]

6   ]

7   ]

8   ]

9   ]

10   ]

11   ]

12   ‏[[תׄעׄוׄדׄוׄתׄמׄ]]214   ‏[[בעמך והׄיׄהׄ]]215°°°   ‏[°°°216

13   ‏וׄאׄ[[תה גליתה]]217 אׄוׄזננו לׄ[218   ‏[[אׄנשי אמת ובׄחׄיׄרׄiׄ219 צׄ]דק דורש[220°

14   ‏שׄכׄל221 ומבקשי בינה בׄ[[‏או[[הׄבׄיׄ222 רחמים ועוׄזׄiׄ223 רוח מזוקקי

15   ‏עׄוני וברורי מצרף °°° [‏מׄ[[תׄאפקים עד לעׄתׄ224 מׄשפטיכה

16   ‏וצופים לׄיׄשועתׄך[[‏[[אׄתׄהׄ]]225   ‏[[וחזקתה חוקיך בׄיׄדׄמׄ226 לעשות227

17   ‏מׄשפׄ[[ׄ]]ט228 תבל ולנחול[[ׄ]]229 [[בכול צׄ]דקותיכה230 ולהיות בס[[וׄ]דׄ231 קודש לדורות עולׄם232 וכול

---

214 With DJD and Qimron. Sukenik and Licht:]°°עׄׄ[. Frg. 18 begins here and provides the right margin of lines 13–16 and the middle right portion of lines 17–18.

215 Sukenik:]°חׄׄ. Licht: יׄחׄ]דיו. Qimron: יׄחׄׄיה.

216 Sukenik: °[. Qimron: כׄ]בׄוׄדׄ].

217 With DJD. Qimron: [גליתה]. Qimron does not read וׄאׄ.

218 Sukenik and Licht read only:] אׄוׄזננו[.

219 Sukenik and Licht: ובׄ. Qimron: ובׄחׄרׄיׄ.

220 I am indebted to DJD for this reading. Sukenik and Licht: אׄנשי אמת ובׄ [. Qimron: צׄ]דק שוחר[ׄיׄ.

221 The right margin is visible (see also lines 15–17 and 23–25).

222 With DJD and Qimron. Sukenik: בׄי[. Licht: רׄ]בׄי.

223 Sukenik: ועׄזׄי. Ctr. Licht, DJD, and Qimron: ועׄנׄׄוׄי.

224 Licht: [יום] עד. Qimron: עד קׄץׄ.

225 Frg. 22 (not in Licht) begins with the word וׄאׄתׄהׄ and provides part of the middle of lines 16–22. Ctr. Qimron: כׄׄי אתה.

226 I am here influenced by DJD. Sukenik: [ ]. Licht: [בהם]. Qimron: בׄׄידׄם.

227 Licht: [מעון] לעשות.

228 Frg. 15b col. 2 begins here and provides the right margin of lines 17–21. Sukenik and Licht: ט[. For the term מׄשפׄט: frg. 15b col. 2 provides the *mem*, *šin*, and the main portion of the *peh*. Frg. 18 provides a small portion of the *peh* and the *teth*.

229 The reading תבל ולנחול is provided by frg. 18.

230 The reading בכול צׄ is provided by frg. 22.

231 With DJD and Qimron.

232 Sukenik: °°°ע.

5 […]

6 […]

7 […]

8 […]

9 […]

10 […]

11 […]

12 […] their fixed times[…] among your people and it was °°[…]°°°

13 and yo[u, you uncovered⁶⁶] our ears for […] the men of truth and the elect ones of righ[teousness, the pursuers] of

14 insight and the seekers of discernment b[… the lov]ers of mercy and the strong ones of spirit⁶⁷ refined of

15 transgression, and those purged (in) the crucible⁶⁸ °°°[… thos]e who persevere until the time of your judgments,

16 and those waiting for your salvation […] you […] and you strengthened your statutes through their hand to do

17 judgment (in) the world,⁶⁹ and to inherit in all [your] rig[hteousness; and to be in the cou]ncil of holiness for eternal generations. And all

---

⁶⁶ *Piʿel* perfect of גלה; "you uncovered, revealed."
⁶⁷ Not the "humble of spirit" as in some renderings. The ones being praised are those who are strong, because God revealed insight to them. They may possibly be identified with the precursors of the Qumranites or the men of Qumran.
⁶⁸ Or "smelting-pot."
⁶⁹ Lit. "judgment of the world."

18 עֹ̇ושׁי233 מֹ̇[   ][עשׁי][   ]הֹם234 עם תענוֹ̇[ ]ג235   [   ][ואנשי חזונכה (VACAT)

19 אודכה]236 אדוני הנותן בלב עבדֹךְ237 בֹ̇ינֹ̇ה   [   ] (VACAT) [   ] [ ]

20 קדש238 לֹהֹ[   ][שכֹ̇][   ]ֹיל239 בכולֹ̇[ ] [אלה ולהתֹ̇][בונן240 [   ]241 ולהתאפק על עלילֹ̇ות242 רשע ולברך

21 בֹ̇[   ]צֹדק כוֹ[   ]ל בוחרֹ[   ][ ]י רצונֹ̇ך̇243 לבחור בכול א[   ]שׁ̇ר244 אהבתה ולתעב אֹת כוֹ̇ל אשר

22 [שנאתה [ ]ות][   ][שֹ̇]כל[   ][עֹבדֹך245 [   ][עֹבדֹך246 להפיל גור[   ]לֹ̇ות אנושׁ247 כי לפי רוחות תבֹ̇דֹ̇ילני248 בין

23 [אֹ̇יתם249 פעולתם ואני ידעתי ומבינתך250   [   ][תֹ̇כֹ̇ן] וֹ[ ]רשע] טוב

24 כי ברצונכה באֹ[   ]י[ ]שׁ̇ הֹ̇רֹ[   ][ביתה251 נחלתוֹ] בֹ̇רוחֹ[ ]252 קודשך וכן תגישני לבינתֹ̇ך ולפי

25 קֹ̇ורבי קנאתי253 על כול פועלי רשע ואנשי רמיה כי כול קרוביך לא ימרו פיך

26 וֹכֹ̇ולֹ̇ יודעיך לא ישנו דבריך כי אתה צדיק ואמת כול בחיריך וכול עולה

27 וֹ̇רשע254 תשמיד לעד ונגלתה צדקתך לעיני כול מעשיך

---

233 Ctr. Qimron: אֹ̇ושׁי. DJD: שׁי °°. Probably not אנשי. This word is provided by frg. 15b col. 2.

234 With DJD. Sukenik and Licht: [ ]עֹשׁי[ ] שׁומ. Frg. 15b col. 2 provides the main part of the *mem*, frg. 18, which ends here, provides a portion of the *mem*, the *ʿayin*, the *šin*, and the *yodh*, SHR 4284, which begins here, provides the *he* and the *mem*.

235 The reading עם תענוֹ[ ] is provided by frg. 22.

236 Licht: [אודכה]. Cf. DJD: [ברוך אתה]. Qimron: [אודך].

237 With DJD. Note the use of final *kaph* in lines 12, 16 [*bis*]; also see the use of כה- in line 15. Sukenik: עֹ̇בֹ̇. Licht: עבדכה.

238 קדש was missed by previous editors. It is visible on SHR 4281 and Sukenik Pl. 56.

239 Frg. 44 begins here. For the word להשׁכיל, frg. 15b col. 2 provides the *lamedh* and *he*, frg. 44 provides the *šin* and part of the *kaph*, and SHR 4284 provides part of the *kaph*, the *yodh*, and *lamedh*, as well as the term בכול.

240 Frg. 22 provides the letters אלה ולהתֹ̇[.

241 Sukenik: [אלה ולהֹ̇]. Licht: [להשכיל בכול רזיכה ולהתבונן בפלאיך] (*sic*). Qimron: ולהתֹ̇[חזק בבריתך]..

242 Sukenik: על°°°°.

243 For the words בֹ̇צֹדק כול בוחרי רצונֹ̇ך: frg. 15b col. 2, which ends here, provides the *beth*. Frg. 44 provides the *sade*, *daleth*, and *qoph* of בֹ̇צֹדק and the *kaph* and *waw* of כול. SHR 4284 provides the *lamedh* of כול and the *beth*, *waw*, *het*, and *reš* of בוחרי. Frg. 22 provides the *yodh* of בוחרי and the word רצונֹ̇ך.

244 Sukenik: ר°ֹ[. Licht: [תמיד את שמכה ולבחור בכול אשר].

245 SHR 4284 ends here. For the term ותֹ̇שׁכל, frg. 44 provides the *waw* and *taw*, SHR 4284 provides the *šin*, *kaph*, and the *lamedh*.

246 Sukenik: לֹ̇ ברך[. Frg. 22 ends here; part of the *ʿayin* is provided by SHR 4284.

247 Sukenik: תֹ̇ אנוש[. Licht: אנוש[ת אורחוֹ]ת. Ctr. Qimron: רוחֹ[ות אנוש. Our restoration follows DJD.

248 Sukenik: [ ]לֹ̇ם. Licht: גור[לם. Cf. DJD: תֹ̇פֹ̇ילם. Qimron: תֹ̇בֹ̇ולם. The leather is torn and creased at this point. See 13.31 and especially 15.15: להבדיל בי בין צדיק לרשע.

249 Sukenik: תם[°°. Licht: [תומם כא]ו וימלאו עבודתם פלגתה]. Cf. DJD: תֹ̇ם[°°. Qimron: [אֹ̇ותם למל[לבבם את]תֹ̇כן ת]וכן.

250 With Sukenik and Licht. Ctr. DJD and Qimron: מבינתך.

251 Frg. 44, which provides the *he* and *reš* in הֹ̇רֹ[ביתה, ends here. Part of the *he* and *reš* can be seen on the column.

252 With DJD and Qimron. Sukenik: ח[בא°°. Licht: בא[איש תטהרנו בר]וֹ̇ח.

253 With Sukenik, Licht, and Qimron. Ctr. DJD: קֹ̇ורבו קנאתו.

254 Sukenik: שׁע[. Licht and Qimron: ור[שע.

88

18   the acts of their works with pleasu[re ...] and men of your vision. (VACAT)

19   [...] (VACAT) [I thank you,][70] O Lord, who put in the heart of your servant holy

20   discernment to allow insight[71] into all these things and to allow to [discern ...], and to persevere[72] against the plots of wickedness. And to bless

21   in righteousness all the chosen ones of your will [and to choose all t]hat you love, and to abhor all that

22   [you hate].[73] And you allowed your servant to have insight [... to cast l]ots (for) a human. For in accordance with the spirits, you allow me to distinguish between

23   good and wicked.[74] [And] you established °[...] with them their activity.[75] And I, I know, through[76] your discernment,

24   that according to your will with the hu[m]an, [you] multipl[ied his inheritance] with your holy spirit. And thus you allow me to draw near to your insight, and (doing so) according to

25   my closeness. I am zealous against all the doers of wickedness and the men of slackness, because all those close[77] to you do not disobey your edict.[78]

26   And all who know you do not alter your words,[79] because you are righteous, and all your elect ones (are) truthful. Then all injustice

27   and wickedness you will destroy forever, and your righteousness will be revealed before the eyes of all your creatures.[80]

---

[70] Or with DJD: "[Blessed are you,] ..." as in 4.29, but see 4.38 (with Licht and Qimron). The author in 6.19 thanks the Lord for discernment.

[71] Note the string of *hip'il* permissives ("to allow," "to permit").

[72] Lit. "to preserve oneself."

[73] See 1QS 1.3–4: "and in order to love all that he [God] has chosen, and to hate all that he has rejected."

[74] See 13.31 and 15.15.

[75] See 1QS 3.15: "he [God] established all their designs."

[76] Lit. "and through."

[77] Note the emphasis on being "close" to God and God's edict.

[78] Lit. "your mouth."

[79] The author stands against "the men of deceit" (probably the non-Aaronic priests in the Temple) who are not allowed to draw near to God and do not experience God's holy spirit, because they cannot distinguish between good and evil, and they "disobey" God's "edict," and "alter" God's "words." Perhaps the last condemnation refers to the deliberate alteration of Scripture to support Hasmonean policy.

[80] Lit. "all your works." The line ends with a *vacat*, but it does not signal a new hymn. It highlights his affirmation.

28 וֹאֹנִי[255] ידעתי ברוב טובך ובשבועה הקימותי על נפשי לבלתי חטוא לך

29 [ו]לְבלתי[256] עשות מכול הרע בעיניך וכן הוגשתי ביחד כול אנשי סודי לפי

30 שֹׂכלוֹ[257] אגישנו וכרוב נחלתו אהבנו ולא אשא פני רֹע ושוֹחֹר ר[ש]עֹהֹ[258] לא אכיר

31 [ו]לֹ[א][259] אֹמיר[260] בהון אמתך ובשוחד כול משפטיך כי אם לפֹי קֹרֹבֹ[ך אי]ש[261]

32 [אה]בֹנו[262] וכרחקך אותו כן אתעבנו לֹעֹד[263] ולא אביא בסוד אֹ[מתך א]שבי[264]

33 [מב]רֹיתך[265]   ]

34 [או]דֹ[ך266] אדוני כגדול כוחך ורוב נפלאותיך מעולם ועד עֹוֹל[ם267] רב הרחמי[ם268] וגדול

35 [החס]דֹים[269] הסולח לשבי פשע ופוקד עו(ו)ן רשעים וֹמֹעֹל[ן   הֹ270] בנדבת

36 [צדקות]יֹ[ך271] ותשנא עולה לעד ואני עבדך חנותני ברוח דעה ל[בחור בא]מֹת[272]

37 [וצד]קֹ[273] ולתעֹב כול דרך עולה   ואהבכה נדבה ובכול לבֹ[י   לב274]

---

[255] Sukenik and Licht: נִי[וא].
[256] Sukenik: [בלתי.]ל. Licht: ול[בלתי.
[257] Sukenik: [כלו.]ש. Licht: ש[כלו.
[258] Sukenik: [וש. Licht: [וחד רשעים]ש[ו]ש. DJD: עֹה[ש]רֹ בֹ[וח]וֹ[ש]ור. Qimron: עֹה[ש]ר ר[וח]וֹש.
[259] Sukenik does not read the *lamedh*. Licht: [ולֹא].
[260] *Hipʿil* impf. of מור, "exchange."
[261] Sukenik: [פֹן.]ל [ש. Licht: אי]ש כל קרבך]קֹרֹ לפֹי. Qimron: אי]ש את בך]קֹרֹ לפֹי.
[262] Sukenik: [נו.]ל. Licht: [נו]אוהבֹ.
[263] Missed by previous editors.
[264] Sukenik: ֹ[ ]. Licht: לוא אשר אמתך]שבו. Cf. Qimron and DJD: אֹ[מתך כול].
[265] Sukenik: [יתך.]ל. Licht: [יתך]אל בר.
[266] With Qimron. Cf. Licht and DJD: [אודֹ]ך.
[267] Sukenik does not read these consonants.
[268] Sukenik: [ ]ם. Licht: [עולם קצי]ם. With DJD and Qimron. ועד כול.
[269] Sukenik: [ֹים.]
[270] Licht: [ורצית עליהם]. Qimron: [כי רצותה]עליהם. DJD: [ ]ֹ.
[271] Ctr. DJD: [לבבֹם]צֹ. Licht: [בחירך]. Qimron: [צדיֹ]ק.
[272] With DJD. Licht: [לבחור בא]מת. Qimron: [אהוב כול א]מֹת. לֹ.
[273] Licht: [וצדק].
[274] Licht: לבֹ[בי אברכ]ך. Qimron: אדרש]לבֹ[בי.

28 And I, I know through the multitude of your goodness and by a vow[81] I have bound[82] upon my soul[83] not to sin against you;

29 [and] not to do any evil before your eyes. And thus I was brought into the Community[84] (with) all the men of my council.[85] According to

30 his insight, I will bring him near; and according to the multitude of his inheritance, I will love him. But I will not accept evil.[86] And the one on the lookout (for) wic[ke]dness, I will not acknowledge.

31 [And] I will n[ot] exchange your truth for property,[87] nor any of your judgments for bribery. And as [you] bring close [...a m]an

32 [(so) I will lov]e him; and as you push him farther away, so I will abhor him forever.[88] And I will not bring into the council of [your] tr[uth] those who turn

33 [from] your [cov]enant. (VACAT) [...][89]

34 [I tha]nk you, O Lord according to your great power and the multitude of your wonders from eternity and unto eterni[ty, (and the) multitude of compass]ions and great

35 [mer]cies (because you are) the one who forgives those who turn (from) transgression, and the one who punishes the wicked ones (because of) iniquity and infidelity.[90] [...] through the generosity of[91]

36 your [righteousnesse]s; for you hate injustice forever. But (as for) me, your servant, you have benefited me with a spirit of knowledge to [choose tr]uth[92]

37 [and righteous]ness, and to abhor every way of injustice.[93] And I love you generously and with all [my] heart [...] heart

---

[81] Note 1QS 9.8: "The property of the men of holiness... must not be merged with the property of the men of deceit."

[82] Or "established."

[83] Heb. נפש; see the note to 6:3.

[84] Heb. יחד. Most likely, the author is the Righteous Teacher or a leading figure in the *Yaḥad*, "Community," who could refer to "*my* council."

[85] Or "the men of my secret." Cf. 4Q439 frgs. 1–2 1.2.

[86] Lit. "I will not lift the face of evil."

[87] Or "wealth."

[88] Note the emphasis on "love" and "hate;" it is found in 1QS 1–4. A *vacat* appears here, but it does not signal a new hymn.

[89] The brackets denote a *lacuna* that probably was uninscribed.

[90] Lit. "the one who visits the iniquity of the wicked ones and (their) infidelity."

[91] Lit. "through the voluntary offering of." Note the apparent emphasis on "freewill" in 6.35–37 and also on "determinism" in 6.29–41.

[92] The *beth* is a *nota accusativi*.

[93] A *vacat* separates two thoughts.

38   [בְּמִשְׁפָּטְךָ²⁷⁵ כי מידך היתה זאת ובלוא רֹצֹ[ונך] לֹ[וא יהיה כו]לֹ²⁷⁶

39   ⟦°°כה²⁷⁷ ימשׁוֹל בשׂר⟧   °°°⟦ ותרֹבֹהֹ⟧   [שב²⁷⁸

40   ⟦וֹ²⁷⁹ הוא ותבן בשׂר°²⁸⁰ את ותֹ⟧²⁸¹   °°°⟦

41   ⟦° רקיע עֹל כֹנֹפֹי רֹוח ויפֹל⟧²⁸²   ⟦°

Col. 7 [= Sukenik Col. 15 + Frgs. 10, 42, 34, SHR 4276, and Frg. 32]²⁸³
Parallels: 4Q427 Frg. 8 1.9–13

1   ]

2   ]

3   ]

4   ]

5   ]

6   ]

7   ]

8   ]

9   ]

10   ]

11   ⟦מֹ⟧²⁸⁴

---

²⁷⁵ Licht: שכליך [להביט ברזי]. Cf. DJD: [ ] °°°וֹבֹמֹשֹפֹטֹ. Qimron: בְּמִשְׁפָּטְךָ.
²⁷⁶ See 18.4: כֹ[וֹלֹ. Qimron and DJD: לֹ[וא יעשה כֹ]וֹל לֹ[ונך] רֹצֹ ובלוא. With Sukenik. Licht: ובלוא [רצונכה] לֹ[וא יהיה כו]לֹ.
²⁷⁷ Frg. 33 begins here and supplies the readings for right side of lines 39–41. Sukenik: כה[. Qimron: [רק בנֹפֹשׁכה]. The double brackets denote the beginning of a fragment. Note the beginning of a column in the previous lines. They are marked, as usual, with a [or a restoration within [ ].
²⁷⁸ This שב[is found after the large tear. DJD: שב ר[ק כי אנוש °°°°°[ ] וֹתֹ שֹׂיֹךֹ[ ]° בשׂ. Qimron: [שב] °° °°°°[ות] בשׂר.
²⁷⁹ Sukenik: °[. Qimron: אל ע[פֹ]ר°[. DJD: [לעפר]וֹן°.
²⁸⁰ Ctr. Qimron: ותכן ב°°°. Sukenik: [°°ות DJD: הוא ותבן בעזר את. °°הוא ותכן בשׂ.
²⁸¹ Ctr. DJD: °°[ ] °לֹ. Qimron: °.
²⁸² Frg. 33 ends here. The bottom margin is clear. Sukenik and Qimron: ויפֹ[°.
²⁸³ Licht does not include frgs. 34 and 42. Qimron places only frg. 32 in this column. He collects frgs. 10, 34, and 42 together after the numbered columns.
²⁸⁴ With DJD; the מֹ is not in Sukenik, Licht, and Qimron. Frg. 10 begins here and provides the middle of lines 11–21.

38   in your judgment. Because from your hand this happened, and without [your] wil[l al]l[will not occur].

39   […] your […]°° will rule flesh […]°°° and you will multiply […]šb

40   […]w (is) he; and you understood flesh the wt[…]°°°

41   […]° the firmament⁹⁴ upon the wings of the spirit⁹⁵ and ypl[…]°

Col. 7 [= Sukenik Col. 15 + Frgs. 10, 42, 34, SHR 4276, and Frg. 32]
Parallels: 4Q427 Frg. 8 1.9–13

1   […]

2   […]

3   […]

4   […]

5   […]

6   […]

7   […]

8   […]

9   […]

10   […]

11   […]m[…]

⁹⁴ See Gen 1:6–8.
⁹⁵ Or "wind."

[ ]°°[288]	הֹשׂכלתֹהֹ[287] גֹבֹוֹרֹתכה[286] במעין[285]	**12**
לֹ[ ]הֹפליא[290]	פֹ[ ]לֹאֹכה מה נשיב כי גמלתנו ו[ ]	חֹ[289] **13**
[ ]לֹא יעצרו כוח לדעת בֹכבודֹ[כה[292] ולס[ ]פֹר נפלֹא[ותיכה[293]	תֹ[291] **14**
[ל]עֹ[ו]לֹ[ם כֹיֹ יֹהֹלֹוֹכה[295] לֹפֹיֹ שכלם וכפי דעתֹם[296] בכֹ[בודכה[297] כֹן[298]	°°[294] **15**
שׁ להלל [מֹ]מכה לאין השֹבֹתֹ[300] מֹקֹץ לקץ[301] ישמיעו ומֹוֹעֹדֹ[ ]לֹמֹוֹעֹד[302] יברכוכה[303]	פֹתחתֹהֹ[299] **16**
לכה[304] [ ] ואנחנו ביחד נועדֹנֹוֹ[306] ועם ידעים נֹ[וס]רֹה[307] ונֹרֹ[ ]ננה ברוב[ ]	קדֹ[ו]שׁ[305] **17**
בכוֹ[ ]ח עם גבוריכה ובהפלא נספרה יחד בדעֹ[ ]תֹ[309] [ ]וֹעד[310]°[ ]ר[311]	רחמיכֹ[ ]ה[308] **18**

---

[285] DJD: בֹ[מֹעֹין אשר ב]אל עליון אתה ברוך. For במעין see 16.7, 13. Qimron does not report any consonants. See 9.7, 20.16.

[286] I am indebted to DJD for this reading. Qimron: גֹ[בֹוֹרֹתכה].

[287] Sukenik: [ ] שכלתי. Licht: [ה]שכלתי[נכה[ ]. DJD: ברצו]נכה[ ]. [ ]נֹוֹ[ ] הֹשכלתנֹוֹ. There is no trace of נֹוֹ[ ]. Qimron: נֹוֹ[ ]°°[ ] השכלתנוֹ.

[288] Frg. 42, which provides the left side of lines 12–16, starts here.

[289] Ctr. DJD: [...]. SHR 4309 shows the right portion of the column. A supralinear consonant may be seen above the *ḥet*, but the ink is indiscernible. After the *ḥet* a *šin* seems likely.

[290] The left margin is discernible. Cf. DJD: הֹמֹ[ון רחמים ל]הֹפליא.

[291] Ctr. DJD: ות[ ]. With Sukenik: תֹ[ ].

[292] Sukenik: לדעת בכבוד]כה. Licht: לדעת כבוד]כה.

[293] Sukenik: ר נפלֹא[.

[294] Sukenik: וֹ[ ].

[295] With DJD. Sukenik:]לליה[. Licht: לה]לליה. Qimron: הללוכה.

[296] Sukenik: דעת °[ ]. Qimron: דעתמֹהֹ.

[297] Ctr. Qimron: בכבודכֹה. With Sukenik.

[298] Qimron does not report the כֹן[יֹ.

[299] With DJD: פֹתחתֹהֹ. אתה פתחתה does not appear in 1QHᵃ.

[300] For לאין השבת see 14.15, 17.40, 23.3; cf. 15.18. See KB 1407. For a similar expression, see 19.27. The *šin* is supralinear, the *taw* is washed out. A study of Sukenik's photograph reveals the consonants. For להלל שמכה, see 3.32, 17.39; cf. 19.28, 20.6, 23.9.

[301] Sukenik: לקץ °°°[ ]מקץ לאין הש. Licht: לקץ[מקץ]בת[הש.

[302] Frg. 42 provides part of this line and ends here. Frg. 34 begins here and provides the left side of lines 16–20.

[303] Sukenik and Licht: ומי[ ]. DJD: יברכו]מֹוֹעֹד[ל ומועדֹ. Qimron: °יֹ מֹועד[ל]בֹוֹ[. See 4Q427 frg. 8 1.8.

[304] Sukenik: ונר[ ]דה לכה. Licht does not read ונר[ ]דה לכה. Cf. DJD: ננה ברוב]ונֹר[לכה]רֹה[ו]נֹ[וס]. The דה[is an attractive alternative, providing "we [thank] you and we shall si[ng]." The *daleth* is like the other two examples in frg. 34 and dissimilar to the examples of *reš* in line 18.

[305] Ctr. DJD: בֹקֹוֹל. Sukenik: ק[ ]. Qimron: קֹ[ ]. The alleged *lamedh* is not visible. Both 1QHᵃ and 4Q427 (restored) first word begins the line with this word. Was one of these manuscripts copied from the other?

[306] With Sukenik and Licht. DJD: נועדֹיֹם. Qimron: נועדה.

[307] There is room for the *nun* on frg. 10, but it is not clear. DJD: נֹ[וס]רֹה.

[308] Sukenik: רחמי[ן. Qimron: רחמי]כה.

[309] DJD: בדעֹ]תֹ אל]וֹעד. This restoration follows 4Q427 frg. 8 1.11. Cf. 4Q427: בעדת, "congregation". Apparently, the scribe of 1QHᵃ transposed the letters.

[310] Qimron: ועם.

[311] Qimron: נספרה בעדֹ]ת אל]רע[ם].

12   [… through the fountain of]^{96} your might, you have caused to have insight […]°°[…]

13   ḥ°[…] your [w]onder. What can we bring for what you have completed for us? And °[…to] act wondrously […]

14   t°[…]° they will not have the power to know^{97} [your] glory [and to re]count [your] wonder[s]

15   °°[…] for ete[rni]ty. For they will praise you according to their insight and according to their knowledge [in] your [g]lory. F[or…]

16   you opened [… to praise] your name^{98} without ceasing.^{99} From time to time they shall proclaim and from appointed time to appointed t[ime they shall bless you]

17   hol[y …].^{100} And we have gathered together^{101} and with those who have knowledge we ha[ve been warn]ed (through suffering) for you and [we] ex[ult in the multitude of]

18   yo[ur] compassions [… in pow]er with your mighty ones. And wondrously we shall recount together with knowledge [of…] and until °[…]

---

^{96} Restored in light of the expressions in 9.7 and 20.16.
^{97} Or "observe."
^{98} The first consonant in "your name" is written above the line, but no editor transcribed it. It can be seen on Sukenik's photographs. For "and to praise your name," see 3.32, 17.39; cf. 19.28, 20.6, 23.9.
^{99} For "without ceasing," see 14.15, 17.40, 23.3; cf. 15.18.
^{100} Not "with a voice of."
^{101} Heb. יחד; or "in community," "in the *Yaḥad*."

19   בעדת[   ]ה̇ וצאצאינו הודע̇[תה ע]ם̇[³¹² בני איש ב̇ת̇ו̇ך̇[³¹³ בני[אדם³¹⁴]

20   כי[ב][ה̇פלא³¹⁵ מאדה]   [   ]

      מזמור³¹⁶

21   בר̇ו̇[ך אתה אל³¹⁷   ב]ש̇י̇ר למש̇[כיל³¹⁸   [°°[   ]ד̇ ר̇נה³¹⁹]

22   י]א̇הבו³²⁰ אותך כול הימים וא̇נ̇י ° [³²¹

23   א̇מ̇[ת³²²   [   ] ואהבכה בנדבה ובכול לב ובכול נפש בררתי מ̇ע̇ו̇ו̇ן[נפ]ש̇י³²³

24   הק̇י̇[מותי לבלת]י̇ סור³²⁴ מכול אשר צויתה ואחזקה על רבים מ̇ו̇ע̇ד̇ים̇ ל̇[בלת]י̇³²⁵

25   עז̇וב³²⁶ מכול חוקיך   ואני ידעתי בבינתך כיאלא³²⁷ ביד בשר] להודיע [אדם³²⁸

26   דרכו ולא יוכל אנוש להכין צעדו ואדעה כי בידך י̇צ̇ר כול רוח [וכול פעול]ת̇ו̇³²⁹

27   הכינותה בטרם בראתו ואיכה יוכל כול להשנות את דבריכה רק אתה ב̇[רא]תה³³⁰

28   צדיק ומרחם הכינותו למועד רצון להשמר בבריתך ולתהלך³³¹ בכול ולה̇ג̇ו̇ש̇³³² עליו

29   בהמון רחמיך ולפתוח כול צרת נפשו לישועת עולם ושלום עד ואין מחסור ותרם

³¹² Sukenik: °[   ]הוד°. Licht: [ות]ה.

³¹³ Sukenik: [יר]ב̇. Licht: [ך]יברכו. DJD: [אדם בני]ת̇ו̇ך̇ב̇. Qimron: [אדם] בני]בתוך.

³¹⁴ With Sukenik, DJD, and Qimron. Frg. 34 ends here.

³¹⁵ Sukenik and Licht: [פלא. DJD: [ה̇פלא]ב.

³¹⁶ Perhaps, with Sukenik and Licht, מבין. The final consonant looks like a *reš*.

³¹⁷ Sukenik: [ב̇°]. DJD: [ש̇י̇ר]ב̇ הרחמים אל אתה ך̇ו̇ר̇ב.

³¹⁸ With DJD and Qimron: [כיל]למש̇°מ̇ו̇ר̇ש̇י̇ר̇]ב. Sukenik: °°[למש מבין ב̇°]. Licht: [למש מבין ב̇. SHR 4297, which constitutes a majority of this column, begins here and continues until the end.

³¹⁹ Frg. 10 ends here.

³²⁰ Sukenik: [הבו]. Licht begins the column with [הבו]יא. Qimron: [ל]אהבה. The column continues with this verb.

³²¹ Sukenik: [וא]. Licht: [אנשי כל ביחד הוגשתי]אני וא.

³²² Licht: ואברככה]אמ̇תך.

³²³ Sukenik: [   ]ש̇°° בררתי. Licht: [נפשי ועל]ביראתך בחרתי. Qimron: [נפ]ש̇ ועל   [ך̇ש̇ע̇מ̇ ברכתי. DJD: [נפ]ש̇ ועל [   ]מ̇ע̇ו̇ו̇ן. The left margin is apparent.

³²⁴ With DJD and Qimron. Sukenik: [   ]הק̇ [   ] סור. Licht: לבלתי]ימותי.

³²⁵ Sukenik: [   ] °[   ]°מ. Licht: [לבלתי ומשפטיכה]ראך[מן רבים. Cf. DJD: [לבלתי הרגה]ל̇[יום. Qimron: י̇[לבלת]כה̇ב̇ר̇ית̇[ה]מ̇ו̇א̇ד̇.

³²⁶ Qimron: ש̇ו̇ב.

³²⁷ Cf. DJD: כיאלא. The *lamedh* is very close to the ʾaleph in the manuscript. The ʾaleph may have been inserted later.

³²⁸ Licht: [אדם]ל ולא]אורחותיו[בשר. The left margin becomes clear.

³²⁹ With DJD and Qimron. Sukenik: [ו]. Licht: [ו פעולת]וכול.

³³⁰ Sukenik: [   ]תה אתה. Licht: [תה]ברא.

³³¹ Perhaps a mistake for ולהתהלך.

³³² With DJD: ש̇ו̇ג̇ה̇ל̇ו. Sukenik: °°°°ולה. Licht: [להגדיל]ו. Qimron: ולהג̇י̇ל̇.

19   in the congregation of [...]*h* and our offsprings [you] have allowed to know[102] [wi]th the sons of man in the midst of [the sons of] Adam [...]

20   for [... wo]ndrously exceedingly [....] (VACAT)

21   Bless[ed are you, O God of truth with] a song, a psalm[103] for the Mas[ter ...]°°[...]*d* exultation [...]

22   [...] they [will] love you all the days and I °[...]

23   tru[th ...] and I love you generously and with all (my) heart and with all (my) soul.[104] I have purged my-self from iniquity. [And a vow upon] my [so]ul[105]

24   [I ha]ve bound[106] n[ot] to depart from everything that you commanded; and I will hold to[107] all[108] ap-pointed times s[o as n]ot

25   to ab any of your ordinances.[109] And I, I know by your discernment that not through[110] flesh [can] Adam[111] [be allowed to know]

26   his way, and a human cannot establish his step. But I know that in your hand (is) the inclination of[112] every spirit [and all] its [activi]ty

27   you established before you created him. And how can anyone alter your words? Only you, you have c[r-ea]ted

28   the righteous one. And from the womb you have established him for the appointed time of (your) will in order to guard (him) in your covenant so as to walk continuously[113] in everything and to bring over him

29   the abundance of your mercies, and to open all the trouble of his soul[114] to the eternal salvation and the everlasting peace with sufficiency.[115] And you raise

---

[102] Permissive *hipʿil*.

[103] Perhaps: "a Psalm."

[104] Heb. נפש; see the note to 6:3.

[105] Heb. נפש; see the note to 6:3.

[106] See 6.28: "by a vow I have bound upon my soul."

[107] For חזק with על, see Neh 10:30. In the *hipʿil*, the verb can take the meaning of "to cleave, retain." See also Ex 9:2; Judg 7:8, 19:4.

[108] Lit. "many."

[109] A *vacat* highlights the next affirmation.

[110] Lit. "through the hand of." Note the paronomasia on "hand" in these lines.

[111] Or "humankind."

[112] Heb. יצר.

[113] The meaning is continuously to behave righteously.

[114] Heb. נפש; see the note to 6:3.

[115] Lit. "and without need."

30 מבשר כבודו ורשעים בראתה ל[י]צֹר חֹרֹונכה‏333 ומרחם הקדשתם ליום הרגה

31 כי הלכו בדרך לא טוב וימאסו בבריֹתֹכֹהֹ‏334 [ואמת]ךֹ‏335 תעבה נפשם ולא רצו בכול אשר

32 צויתה ויבחרו באשר שנאתה כיֹאֹ ל[קֹ]צֹי חרו[נ]ךֹ‏336 הכינותם לעשות בם שפטים גדולים

33 לעיני כול מעשיך ולהיות לאות וֹמֹוֹפֹ[ת‏337   ]עֹוֹלם לדעת כֹוֹל‏338 את כבודך ואת כוחך

34 הגדול ומה אף הוא בשר כי ישכיל[ויצ]רֹ‏339 עפר איך יוכל להכין צעדו

35 אתה יצרתה רוח ופעולתה הכינותֹ[ה‏340   ] ומאתך דרך כול חי ואני ידעתי כיא

36 לֹא ישוה כול הון באמתך ואין בֹֹתֹ[בל כמלאכי]‏341 קֹודשך‏342 ואדעה כי בם בחרתה מכול

37 ולעד הם ישרתוך ולא תקבל שֹוֹחֹד]‏343   [ולא‏344 תקח כופר לעלילות רשעהֹ כיא

38 ◀   345 אמת אתה וכול עולה תשמיד לֹ[עד וכול רֹ]שֹׁעֹהֹ‏346 לֹא‏347 תהיה לפניך וֹאני ידעתיֹ[ך‏348

39 כי לֹך‏349 דֹ[רך כ]וֹ[ו]ֹל חֹי וֹבֹרֹצֹוֹנֹך נֹהֹי[ה כול] מֹעֹשה ואֹדֹ[עה   לֹ]ן‏350

---

333 Sukenik:]ל [   ]ל. Licht:]ונכה[קצי חר]ל. Qimron: לֹקֹצֹי חֹרֹונכה. לֹ[קֹצֹי חר]ונכה.

334 Cf. DJD: בבֹרֹיֹתֹךֹ [ואמת]ךֹ. Qimron: בבריתכ]ה וחוקי[ך.

335 Sukenik:]ךֹ [   ]בבֹ. Licht:]בבריתכה ואמת[ך.

336 With DJD: כיֹאֹ ל[קֹצי חרו]נֹךֹ. Sukenik:]ךֹ [   ]כֹוֹלֹ. Licht: כיא ל[פי רזי שכל]ך. Qimron: כיא ל[קֹצי חרו]נֹךֹ.

337 Sukenik:] ֹ ֹֹ לֹאוֹתֹ. Licht: ומו]פת לקצי[. DJD: עֹוֹלם דורות]וֹמֹוֹפֹת.

338 Sukenik: ֹ ֹֹ.

339 Sukenik: [   ]. Licht:]ישכיל[ברזיך ויצר. DJD: ישכיל [באלה ויצ]רֹ.

340 Sukenik: הכינותֹ]תה. Licht:]הכינות[ה מקדם עולם. DJD: הכינ[ה מעולם.

341 With DJD. Sukenik:]ֹ ואיֹ ֹ. Licht:]ואוי[תי לבוא בעדת. Qimron: [בֹצֹ[ע לכוהני.

342 Sukenik:]ק[ודשך.

343 Sukenik:]תקֹ. Licht:]תק[בל שוחד עולה. DJD: שֹוֹחֹד [למעשי רע.

344 Sukenik: לֹא.

345 Sukenik: אֹל.

346 Sukenik:]ת עולה[. Licht: [תֹשמיד לעד וכול דרך רשעה. But the *lacuna* has room for only eight consonants and spaces. There is no room for דרך.

347 Sukenik: לֹא]ֹ ֹ[. Qimron: ורשעה לֹא.

348 Sukenik:]ידעתֹי. Qimron: ידעתיֹ.

349 Licht ends his reading of the column here.

350 Sukenik ends with this line; ctr. his reading:]ן[   ]ל[ואן עֹשה]ֹ ֹ[לֹ]ֹ ֹ[. Qimron:]   ]לן[   ]ֹ וֹאֹ מֹעשה]   [ֹ ֹֹ] וֹבֹ.

30 his honor from the flesh. But the wicked ones you created for [the u]rge of your fury,[116] and from the womb you designated them for the day of killing,

31 because they walked in the way that is not good and rejected your covenant, [and] their soul[117] abhorred your [truth]. And they did not want anything that

32 you commanded, and they chose that which you hated. For the end[times of] your [fur]y you established them in order to inflict[118] on them great judgments

33 before the eyes of all your creatures,[119] and that (they) may become a sign and a porte[nt[120] …] eternal, that all may know your glory and your power

34 (which is) great. But what is he of flesh that he will have insight?[121] [… And the inclina]tion of[122] dust, how can he establish his step?

35 You, you formed[123] the spirit, and its activity yo[u] established […] and from you is the way of every living being. And, I, I know that

36 all wealth is incomparable to your truth and nothing in the wo[rld (is) like the angels of] your holiness,[124] and I know that you chose them from among all (living beings),

37 and forever they will serve you. And you do not receive […] bribes […], and you do not take ransom for the plots of wickedness, for

38 you (are) the God of truth,[125] and all deceit you shall destroy for[ever. And all] wickedness shall not be before you. And I, I know you,

39 that to you (is) the w[ay of] e[ve]ry living being and by your will is do[ne …] work; and I kn[ow …] l[…]

---

[116] Lit. "for [the inc]lination of (יצר) your fury." Perhaps: "as a creature of your fury."
[117] Heb. נפש.
[118] Lit. "to do."
[119] Or "your works."
[120] Or "wond[er]," "sig[n]." See 5.33 for the same meaning; for "wonder" see 8.9 and 15.25.
[121] Or "may have insight."
[122] Heb. יצר.
[123] Heb. יצר.
[124] For the restoration, see 19.13.
[125] "God" is in paleo-Hebrew script.

40 קודשֿך בֿ[³⁵¹

41 כי ב[°°°°°°³⁵²

Col. 8 [= Sukenik Col. 16 + Frg. 13 (= SHR 4278, 4263) and Frg. 12 (= SHR 4287, 4263, 4298, 4297)]³⁵³

1]

2]

3]

4]

5]

6]

7]

8 [ו וֿ]³⁵⁶ [ ] °°וכולֿ °°°°מֿ³⁵⁵ [³⁵⁴

9 אנשי [[מֿוֿפֿת תֿבֿיא³⁵⁷ במספר

10 פ[[לֿאוֿ³⁵⁸ בשמֿים ובארץֿ

11 רו[[חֿוֿת³⁵⁹ ובידך משפט כולֿםֿ³⁶⁰

12 [[לֿנֿגֿדֿך³⁶³ ומה יחֿשֿבֿ וכולֿ³⁶⁴   [ד³⁶¹ [ ]°° שֿ °°°°[ ]³⁶²

13 [איש [[מֿתֿקֿדֿש³⁶⁵ בל יטה לאשֿמֿה לֿיֿשֿר לֿבֿבֿ[[וֿ³⁶⁶ [ֿיֿבֿיֿן³⁶⁷ ולא יעשה כול

---

³⁵¹ Frg. 32 begins here and provides lines 40–41.
³⁵² The bottom margin is visible. Qimron:] כיֿ.
³⁵³ SHR numbers are necessary for col. 8. Licht does not include frg. 12. Qimron places frg. 12 at the end of the column and by itself.
³⁵⁴ Frg. 13 begins here and provides the readings for the left side of the column for lines 8–16.
³⁵⁵ Sukenik and Licht: [ ] כֿוֿל[.
³⁵⁶ DJD: °°[ ]°°. Qimron places frg. 13 after the columns. Qimron: °°°°°°°°[.
³⁵⁷ Sukenik and Licht: שפת הביא[. DJD: אנשי מ[וֿפֿת תֿבֿיא. Qimron: תֿבֿיא[חֿוֿת רו].
³⁵⁸ Sukenik and Licht: תו[. DJD: ואין כרזי פ[לֿאוֿ.
³⁵⁹ DJD: וֿת[.
³⁶⁰ Sukenik: כולֿםֿ. Licht: כולם.
³⁶¹ Frg. 12 begins here and provides the readings for the right side of the column for lines 12–19.
³⁶² Qimron does not transcribe this line.
³⁶³ Sukenik and Licht: דך[. Qimron: יֿלֿוֿדֿ.
³⁶⁴ Sukenik and Licht: נֿחשבו ע.
³⁶⁵ Sukenik begins with: קדש[. Qimron: דֿשֿ°°°[ ]. DJD: [מֿתֿקֿדֿש[איש].
³⁶⁶ Sukenik: [ר לֿ ל[לאש[. Qimron: לֿבֿ לאשֿמֿתֿ יצֿר.
³⁶⁷ Sukenik and Licht: היו[. DJD: יֿבֿיֿן[איכה.

40   your holiness b °[…]

41   for b°°°°°°[…]

Col. 8 [= Sukenik Col. 16 + Frg. 13 (= SHR 4278, 4263) and Frg. 12 (= SHR 4287, 4263, 4298, 4297)]

1   […]

2   […]

3   […]

4   […]

5   […]

6   […]

7   […]

8   […]°°°°*m* and all °°[…]*w* and °[…]

9   [… men of] wondrous-sign[126] you shall bring by number

10   […] his [won]der within[127] the heavens and within the earth

11   [… sp]irits and within your hand is the judgment of all of them

12   […]°*k* °[…]°°°*š* °°[…] contrary to you. And how shall he think? And each

13   [man][128] who sanctifies himself will not turn aside to guilt to make straight his heart. […] discern? And nothing is done

---

[126] The same expression is found in 5.33, 7.33, and esp. 15.24 Also note Zech 3:8.
[127] Lit. "in" or "upon." Perhaps the meaning is within humans on earth. The preposition is the same for "heavens" and "earth."
[128] See line 22.

14 [מבלע[[דٰיך֞³⁶⁸ עַד עוֹלָם וֹמְקוֹר אוֹר פְּתֹחْתֹתْה[[³⁶⁹ וֹלְעֹצْתֹך֞ תֹקراֹنْٰي³⁷⁰[[

15 לְהֹלֵל קוֹדֹשֹך֞ בְּפִי³⁷¹ כֹּל מעשׂיך֞ [כִّ]א פעל[[תה³⁷² ולבוא יْ[[חֹד³⁷³ עֹם צֹבٰא³⁷⁴

16 [ג[[בֹוֹרֹיٰ³⁷⁵ עולם ורוח עורף קْשֹׁה³⁷⁶ לדממה[[³⁷⁷ [הֹוٰאלתֹהٰ[[לٰ]ן³⁷⁸

17 מ[[שׁفٰط³⁷⁹ ולֹهٰאזין קול נכבֹד לְמֹעֹשׁٰ]יך³⁸⁰

18 ור[[וח נֹעוה משׁל[[הٰ³⁸¹]בֹיٰצֹٰٰר עֹפֹٰٰر³⁸² °° [°°° [ו ٰٰ[³⁸³

19 מٰ°°[[³⁸⁴ °°°°°°°°°°³⁸⁵ שٰ °° [ ]°°°[[

20 [[אֹׁשٰ לٰ]ן³⁸⁶ [[יٰך֞ מֹעֹٰفٰر]³⁸⁷ צٰ]דיק וכֹ°]³⁸⁸

21 בֹٰروٰח³⁸⁹ קוٰ]דٰ]שֹׁך֞ [אשר נתٰ]ה בי °°°°°°° [[³⁹⁰] ولֹא יוכל אֹ[נוש³⁹¹

22 רٰוٰח קודٰ]שֹٰٰٰ]ך֞³⁹² °°] [מٰלֹוٰא השׁْמٰים³⁹³ וֹהٰאرٰץ]³⁹⁴ כ]בٰודך³⁹⁵ מלוא כֹלֹ]ن תבל³⁹⁶

---

³⁶⁸ Sukenik does not transcribe [דיך.

³⁶⁹ Sukenik: [ ]°°° קٰور אוֹן [[עַד עוֹלָם]. °°°

³⁷⁰ Sukenik and Licht: [פקד אٰ.

³⁷¹ Sukenik: בٰ בٰפٰי ٰ ٰ שֹׁ להٰקٰ]. DJD: מٰפֹי. Qimron: ٰ ٰ ٰ לٰ°°° שֹׁך֞ בֹפٰי ٰ. Elsewhere מפי appears 2 times in 1QHᵃ and בפי appears 10 times.

³⁷² The ink in this line is possible to read only with computer manipulated images. Sukenik: [ٰ ٰ מٰל°° מעשׂ]. DJD: מעשׂיך֞ כٰיٰא פעלٰתٰ]ה. Qimron: מעשׂ ٰ °° [כٰי]א ٰ לٰ.

³⁷³ DJD: ٰחٰ]ד להוٰ]. Qimron: יٰ]חٰد לברככה [.

³⁷⁴ Sukenik and Licht: עֹם °° אٰ [.

³⁷⁵ Sukenik and Qimron do not see these letters.

³⁷⁶ The dot over the *qoph* is scribal.

³⁷⁷ Sukenik: לٰדממ °° ק עורף ורוח לٰם [ٰ.

³⁷⁸ Sukenik and Licht: [אל ٰ]. DJD: [עשות]לٰ]הٰ הֹוٰאלٰתٰ]ה. Qimron: [עשות]ל[הٰ הٰוٰאלתٰ]ה [הנה]. Fragment 13 ends here.

³⁷⁹ DJD: בם מٰ]שׁفٰט.

³⁸⁰ Sukenik: נכבٰד קול להٰאזין [ٰ [שٰ]. Qimron: וٰמٰעשׂٰ]ي.

³⁸¹ Sukenik: [מֹעٰולٰ.

³⁸² With DJD, but the ink on frg. 12 has disappeared and the leather is split. See this well-known formula in 21.17, 34.

³⁸³ Sukenik does not report [ٰ ו ٰ [.

³⁸⁴ Qimron does not see מٰ.

³⁸⁵ Sukenik: [מ °°°°]. A *lamedh* and two consonants seem below.

³⁸⁶ Frg. 12 ends here.

³⁸⁷ The letters are on col. 8. DJD correctly reads line 19 as one line, but misses the letters at the beginning of the line. Qimron has line "19a," but numbers it "19"; he also missed the letters. He notes correctly that some lines before "19" are missing. With DJD, we relate frgs. 13 and 12, Qimron combines 13 with 11, and places 12 alone.

³⁸⁸ Sukenik: [ו יק]°°[. For line 19, Qimron only reads: [וכ דיק]צ. SHR 4263 preserves the letters.

³⁸⁹ Col. 8 begins here.

³⁹⁰ Sukenik: [ה °°] קון ברוח.

³⁹¹ Sukenik: [יוכ ולٰא. Licht begins the column here: [בלוא כול להבין ל/יוכ ולא. DJD: [לבקש]נוש אٰ. Qimron: [את לדעת]נוש אٰ.

³⁹² Sukenik: [קוٰ]דٰ. Licht: כיא דٰ]שׁך֞ קוٰ]. Qimron: [קודٰ]שׁ°°.

³⁹³ Sukenik: [ ]ים ה. Licht: מٰ]ים[ה]שׁ.

³⁹⁴ Sukenik: °°°ארץ. Ctr. Sukenik's partial reading of this line and column.

³⁹⁵ Licht: כٰ]בודך והדר גבורותיכה כוח].

³⁹⁶ Sukenik: כ. Licht: [תבל כٰ]ול. With DJD and Qimron.

14 [apart fr]om¹²⁹ you unto eternity. And a source of¹³⁰ light you opened [...] and for your council you called me

15 to praise your holiness through the mouth of all your works¹³¹ [tha]t [you] have done [.... And to come¹³² to]gether¹³³ with the host of¹³⁴

16 [the mi]ghty ones of eternity. And the obstinate spirit¹³⁵ to calmness¹³⁶ [...] you were willing¹³⁷ [...]*l*[...]

17 [... ju]dgment and to be attentive to¹³⁸ the glorious voice concerning [your] work[s of¹³⁹ ...]

18 [... and a] perverted [sp]irit has rul[ed] in the inclination of¹⁴⁰ dust °°[...]° and °[...]

19 [...]°° *m* °°°°°°°°° ° °*š*°[...]°°°[...]

20 [...]ʾ*š*°°*l*[...]°*yk*¹⁴¹ from dus[t ... rig]hteousness and *k*°[...]

21 by your ho[l]y spirit [that] yo[u placed] in me °°°°°°[...] and a hu[man] cannot [...]

22 your hol[y] spirit °°[...] the plenitude of the heavens and the earth [...] your [g]lory, the plenitude of all [the world....]

---

¹²⁹ Or "without."
¹³⁰ Or "a spring of."
¹³¹ Not "creatures" here. The author is moved to praise God's works.
¹³² See 11.23.
¹³³ Or "in co]mmunity."
¹³⁴ Or "the army of."
¹³⁵ See Deut 31:27.
¹³⁶ Or "silence."
¹³⁷ See 5.18 and 8.26.
¹³⁸ *Hipʿil* of אזן; "to listen to somebody."
¹³⁹ DJD: "by the creatures [of ...]."
¹⁴⁰ Heb. יצר.
¹⁴¹ Most likely the suffix *yk* denotes the possessive "your [...]."

23   ואדעה כי ברצוֹנ[ך]³⁹⁷ באיש הרביתה נחׄלתׄו בצׄדׄקׄותׄ[יך   [בׄסׄוד³⁹⁸ אמתך בכוׄלׄ [³⁹⁹

24   ומשׄמׄר⁴⁰⁰ צדק עׄלׄ דׄבׄרׄ[ך⁴⁰¹ אשר הפקדתה בו פֵׄן ישׄגׄה [ולׄ[בלתי⁴⁰² כשול בכׄוׄלׄ מעׄ[שׄין⁴⁰³

25   בדעתי⁴⁰⁴ בכול אלה אׄמצׄאׄה⁴⁰⁵ מענׄה⁴⁰⁶ לשון להתׄנׄפׄל ולׄהׄתׄ[חנ]ׄןׄ [⁴⁰⁷   עׄל פשעי⁴⁰⁸ ולבקש רוח בׄיׄנׄ[ה]⁴⁰⁹

26   ולהתחזק ברוח קוׄדׄשׄ[ך⁴¹⁰ ולדבוק באמת בריתך ולעבדך⁴¹¹ באמת ולב שלם ולׄאׄהׄוׄב אׄת דׄבׄרׄ פׄ[יך]⁴¹²

27   ברוך אתה אדוׄנׄי גׄדׄוׄלׄ העׄצׄהׄ⁴¹³ ורׄב העלילליה⁴¹⁴ אשר מעשיך הכול הנה הואלתה לעשׄוׄת עׄמׄדׄ[ין]⁴¹⁵

28   חסד ותחונני ברוחׄ⁴¹⁶ רחמיך ובעׄבׄור⁴¹⁷ כבודך לך אתה הצדקה כי אתה עשיתה את כול אׄלׄהׄ⁴¹⁸

29   ובדעתי כי אתה רשמתה רוח צדיק ואני בחרתי להבר כפי כרצונ[ב]ׄךׄ⁴¹⁹ ונפש עׄבׄדׄך תעׄבׄה⁴²⁰ כול

30   מעשה עולה ואדעה כי לׄא יצדק איש מבׄלעדיך ואחלה פניך ברוח אשר נתתה בׄיׄ⁴²¹ להשלים

---

³⁹⁷ Sukenik: ברצוֹ. Licht: [ונכה].
³⁹⁸ Sukenik: [   ]ׄדׄ[ ]°°°°ׄ הרביתה. Licht: נח[לתו בגודלך להתהלך במו]סר. Qimron: [תיכה]בׄמׄצׄוׄׄ. The leather is torn and worn.
³⁹⁹ Licht: [דרכין].
⁴⁰⁰ DJD: ומשׄׄמׄר and Qimron: ומשׄמׄר.
⁴⁰¹ Sukenik: °°°°°°°. Licht: ומעמד צדק א[מתכ]ה. ומעמד צדק א
⁴⁰² Sukenik: יׄ°[   ]°°ׄ פׄ. Licht: פן י[ש]גה [במצוותיך ותסרהו לב]לתי. DJD: ישׄגׄה [ממצוותיך ול]בׄלתי.
⁴⁰³ Sukenik: [מׄ. Licht and Qimron: [שפטיך. DJD: מע[שיו כי. מׄ[שׄין
⁴⁰⁴ Licht: בדעתו.
⁴⁰⁵ Sukenik: מענׄה°°. Licht does not read any consonants for אׄמצׄאׄה.
⁴⁰⁶ Sukenik: מענה. Licht: ובמענה.
⁴⁰⁷ Qimron: [לפני]ׄ ׄךׄ. DJD: תמיד.
⁴⁰⁸ Licht: ולהת[חנן על מע]ל פשעו.
⁴⁰⁹ Sukenik:]°. Licht does not read this word.
⁴¹⁰ Sukenik: [   ]ׄק. Licht: ק[ודשך].
⁴¹¹ Ctr. DJD and Qimron: ולעובדך. Sukenik: ול°°°°ׄ ׄ ר.
⁴¹² Sukenik:]°°°°ׄ את. Licht: את שמך.
⁴¹³ Licht: נוצר [חסד]כה ורב.
⁴¹⁴ Licht corrects to העליליה. Probably a scribal error; cf. Jer 32:19: גדול העצה ורב העליליה.
⁴¹⁵ Sukenik:]°°°°ׄ לעׄ. Licht: לעש[ות עם עבדך]. DJD: לעשׄוׄׄת בׄ[וב]ר. Qimron: עׄמׄדׄ[י. See 8.30–31.
⁴¹⁶ Ctr. Qimron: ברוׄב.
⁴¹⁷ Sukenik: ו]ׄ[   ]וׄ. Licht: וב[י]ס[ו]ד.
⁴¹⁸ Sukenik: את כׄו. Licht: כו[ל אלה].
⁴¹⁹ Sukenik: [   ]כרצונ. Licht: [ונך]כרצו.
⁴²⁰ Sukenik: ה°°ׄ ה.
⁴²¹ Sukenik: °°ׄ. Licht: [ה בין]נתת.

23   And I know that in [your] will towards[142] man, you multiplied his inheritance through [your] righteousnesses[143] and allowed (him) to discern the secret of your truth (that is) in all [....]

24   And the righteous one guards over your word[144] that you deposited in him, lest he would stray [... and so] he will not stumble in all [his] wor[ks].

25   By my knowledge in all these things, I will find the answer of the tongue, falling prostrate,[145] and petitioning (for) me[rc]y […], because of my transgression,[146] and seeking for a spirit of discern[ment],

26   and strengthening myself by your holy spirit, and adhering to the truth of your covenant, and serving you in truth and a perfect heart, and loving the word of [your] mou[th].

27   Blessed are you, O Lord, great of counsel, and multitudinous of action, because your works are everything. Indeed, you were willing[147] to manifest[148] with [me]

28   loving-kindness; and you benefited me with your spirit of mercies and for the sake of your glory. To you, you (alone), belongs righteousness,[149] because you, you made all these (things).

29   And (it is) for my knowledge that you, you recorded[150] the spirit of the righteous one, so I, I choose to cleanse[151] my hands according to your wil[l]; and the soul[152] of your servant abhors every

30   work of deceit. And I know that no man can be righteous apart from you. And I wait for you,[153] with the spirit that you put in me to complete

---

[142] See 19.7. The *beth* is a *nota accusativi*. Or "in."
[143] The noun is plural.
[144] Lit. "And the observance of righteousness over your word."
[145] Note the string of infinitives in Hebrew (participles in English).
[146] The noun could be a plural, since singular and plural consonantal forms are identical.
[147] See also 5.18 and 8.16.
[148] Lit. "to do."
[149] Lit. "To you, you, the righteousness."
[150] Or "guarded." רשם appears only here in 1QHᵃ. The author is recorded, perhaps, in the Book of Life. See Dan 10:21.
[151] *Hipʿil* of ברר.
[152] Heb. נפש.
[153] Heb. יחל in the *hipʿil* imperfect with פנים; lit. "to hope for your face (or presence)."

31   חֹסדיך[422] עם עבדֹךֹ[423] לֹ[עו]לֹם[424] לטהרני ברוח קודשך ולהגישני ברצונך כגדול חסדיך [א]שֹׁר עֹשיתהֹ[425]

32   עֹמדי וֹלֹ[ה]עֹמֹ[יד   [כֹל426] מֹעֹמד רצֹ[ו]נֹך[427] אשר בֹח[ר]תֹהֹ[428] לאוהביך ולשומרי מֹצֹוֹתֹ[יך[429]

33   לפניך לֹעֹולם וֹ[לכפר430] [וֹלֹהֹדש[ן [בֹרֹצֹוֹן ולהתערב[431] ברוח עבדך ובֹכֹול[432] מעשֹׁיֹ[ןֹ לֹ[עולם[433]

34   יֹעֹשֹׂה כֹֹל וֹֹ[ן   [וֹ[434] ואל יבֹ[וא]435] לפניו כול נֹגֹע מכשול מחוקי בריתך כי ̊ ̊ ̊[436]

35   פניך ואֹדֹעֹ]ה כי אתה [חֹנֹוֹן[437] ורחום אֹרֹוֹך אפֹים וֹרֹבֹ[438] חסד ואמת ונושא פשע וֹמֹעֹ]ל[439]

36   ונחם על כֹ[ול440]   אוהבֹ]יך ושומרי מצֹוֹ[ותֹ]תיך441] ה[שבים אליך באמונה ולב שלֹם]442]

37   לעוברך [לעשות הֹ[טוב443] בעינֹיךֹ אל תשב פני עבדך [וא]ל תֹזֹנֹחֹ444] בן אמתֹ[ך445]

38   [אֹה446] ואני על דבריך קרבֹתֹיֹ447] לֹ[448]

39   [̊ ̊ ̊] [לֹ449] [ ] ̊ ̊ ̊ [

[422] Sukenik: דיך[ ]. Licht: [חס]דיך.

[423] Sukenik: [עבֹ]. Licht: עבֹ]דֹך.

[424] Sukenik: [ ]לֹ. Licht: [עד]לֹ.

[425] Sukenik: בשות[ ]. Licht: חסדיך [ועד] עשות.

[426] Sukenik: ̊ ̊ ̊[   ]ֹ Licht: עמד. DJD: כֹל]וֹלֹ[ה]עֹמֹ[יד פעמי ב. עמדי [חסד כדבריך וככול.

[427] Sukenik: [רצֹ]. Licht: רצֹ]ונֹך. Qimron: ̊ ̊ ̊ מ ̊ מֹ כֹלֹ[ ]. With DJD.

[428] Sukenik: [ ]בֹח. Licht: בֹח[ורך.

[429] Sukenik: תֹ[ ]ֹ מ. Licht: מ[צוֹ]תֹ]יך להתיצב. DJD: מֹצֹוֹתֹ]ך להתיצב.

[430] Qimron: [ ].

[431] Ctr. Qimron: עֹדֹן ולהתערב. With DJD. Sukenik: [התערב]עֹ[ ]דֹ[ ]לֹם. Licht: [לע]ולם ו[עד אשר ח[דש]ה תבר[א התערב.

[432] Ctr. DJD: וֹֹשֹׁכיל. Sukenik, Licht, and Qimron: ובכול.

[433] Sukenik: לֹ[מעשֹׁ. Licht: ל[שומרו מהוות. Qimron: מעשֹׁיֹו לֹ]. וֹבֹכול מעשֹׁיֹו לֹ[.

[434] Sukenik: [ ]לֹ עיה ל[ ]ֹ. Licht: [ו]לֹ[ה. Qimron: [ו רשעים ולח]זק ובכול דרכיֹ[ו. לֹעֹולם ולֹ[ה.

[435] Sukenik: [ ]יֹ. Licht: [היה]יֹ. DJD: אֹ[וא]יבֹ.

[436] Licht: [בלב שלם בקש את] כי.

[437] Sukenik: [ ]ֹ וֹאֹ כֹֹ וד וֹאֹ. Licht: [חנון אדוני חנון]. Qimron: פנֹיך ואֹדֹעֹ]ה חנון רחום. DJD: פניך ואֹ[דֹעֹ]ה כי אתה אל [חֹנֹוֹן ורחום. ואֹדֹעֹ]ה כי אתה.

[438] Sukenik: ̊ ̊ ̊ ̊מֹ[ ] א[ ]ֹ[ ]אֹרֹֹך. Licht: [אר].

[439] Licht: וֹ[עוון לאוהביו. Cf. Qimron: [ומעל חטא]ו.

[440] Sukenik: [ ]. Licht: כֹֹ]ול עוון אוהבֹ]יך. DJD: [רעת אוהביך. Qimron: על [הרעה לאוהב.

[441] Sukenik: [מצוֹן]. Licht: מצוֹ]ותיך. DJD: מצֹוֹ[ותֹ]יך.

[442] Licht: [לאהבה את שמך].

[443] Licht: [ולדבקה בך ו]טוב.

[444] Sukenik: [ ]לֹ[ ]ֹ. Licht: [ות]לֹ[מד את. DJD: תֹזֹנֹחֹ[וא]. Qimron: [וא]ל תֹבֹשֹׁ.

[445] Sukenik: אמת[ה בן אמת. Licht: [כה בינה.

[446] Sukenik: [ה. Licht: ה... (sic).

[447] Sukenik: [קר קרֹ]. Licht: [קר]בתי. Licht ends his reading here.

[448] Qimron does not record the lamedh.

[449] Qimron ends the column with: [ ]ֹ ̊ ̊ ̊[ ].

31 your loving-kindnesses with your servant for [etern]ity, purifying me with your holy spirit and bringing me near by your will, according to your great loving-kindnesses [w]hich you have done

32 with me. And to cause to sta[nd]¹⁵⁴ [...] all the rank¹⁵⁵ of [your] wil[l] that you cho[se] for those who love you and for those who keep [your] commandments

33 before you for eternity; and [to atone¹⁵⁶ ...] and to enric[h]¹⁵⁷ with favor,¹⁵⁸ and to be involved in the spirit of your servant. And in all your work[s] for [ever]

34 he shall do everything. And *y*[...]°*w*. And it shall not en[ter] before him any affliction as a stumbling to the statutes of your covenant, because °°[...]

35 your face; and I kno[w that you are] gracious and compassionate, patient, and multitudinous (in) loving-kindness and truth, and one who forgets¹⁵⁹ transgression, and infidel[ity ...]

36 and one who comforts a[ll ... those loving] you, and those keeping [your] commandmen[ts], those returning to you with faithfulness and a perfect heart [...]

37 to serve you [... doing the] good in your eyes. Do not turn away the face of your servant [and do no]t reject the son of your handmaiden¹⁶⁰ [...]

38 [...]ʾ*h* and I, I draw near to your words to [...]

39 [...] °°°[...]*l*[...]°°°[...]

---

¹⁵⁴ See 20.38 and 10.10. The Heb. עמד appears three times in 8.31.
¹⁵⁵ The Heb. מעמד, "office," obtains a new meaning in Qumran Hebrew: "rank" or "position." Note the allusion to the Qumran concept of hierarchy, so clear in the *Rule of the Community* and in Josephus' reports about the Essenes.
¹⁵⁶ Note the string of infinitives.
¹⁵⁷ The *hipʿil* infinitive of דשן, "to become fat," does not appear in the Hebrew Bible; it (ולהדשן) seems to mean "enrich." See also 18.28.
¹⁵⁸ Or "will."
¹⁵⁹ Heb. נושה, "one who forgets (= forgives)."
¹⁶⁰ Possibly "the son of your truth," but note the context and parallelism.

		40
	]	40
	]	41
	]	42

Col. 9 [= Sukenik Col. 1 + Frg. 24]⁴⁵⁰
Parallels: 4Q432 Frgs. 1–2

	⁴⁵¹]	1
‖ בשובך מֹתֹוה[ו⁴⁵²	]ᵒᵒ	2
ע[[דת קדושיֹם⁴⁵⁴]ᵒ	⁴⁵³]ᵒᵒᵒ	3
יוד[[ᵒע בין טוֹב לֹרֹשֹ[ע⁴⁵⁵	]ᵒᵒᵒᵒ [	]וֹכֹוֹל[4
רֹשֹ[[עים וטֹ[ובים⁴⁵⁸	⁴⁵⁷]וֹם[ᵒᵒᵒᵒᵒᵒᵒ [	עולם⁴⁵⁶]ᵒא[5
שֹ[לום⁴⁵⁹ כיֹא [אתה מקור ד[ᵒֹעֹת⁴⁶⁰ ומקה המיֹם[⁴⁶¹		בם ומשֹ[פט 6
במֹֹשֹפטֹ[יכח⁴⁶²		
[גדול⁴⁶⁵ העצֹה] ⁴⁶⁶[אֹיֹן מספֹר⁴⁶⁷ וקנאֹתכֹה⁴⁶⁸		ומעין⁴⁶³ הגבֹ[ורה⁴⁶⁴ 7
[וארוך אפים במשפֹטֹ[יכ]ה⁴⁷⁰ צֹדקתה בכל מעשיכה		לפני חכמתֹכֹֹה[⁴⁶⁹ 8

---

⁴⁵⁰ Licht and Qimron do not include frg. 24.
⁴⁵¹ Ctr. Qimron: ᵒᵒ[ ]וֹכֹול. The column begins here.
⁴⁵² Frg. 24 begins here and provides the readings for the left side of lines 2–5. Sukenik:]ᵒᵒ בשובך[ב.
⁴⁵³ Conceivably: בֹֹיֹן. See 9.4.
⁴⁵⁴ Sukenik:]ֹדֹי קֹדֹושֹ[יֹ ם. Cf. DJD:]ֹם[דת קדוש.
⁴⁵⁵ Sukenik:]ᵒᵒ בין טוֹב לֹרֹשֹ[ע עד[. DJD:]ᵒ בין ט[ע.
⁴⁵⁶ Sukenik begins here (his line 3), but does not place frg. 24 in this column.
⁴⁵⁷ Sukenik:]ם ᵒᵒᵒᵒᵒᵒᵒ[. DJD: ים ᵒᵒᵒ ᵒᵒᵒ[.
⁴⁵⁸ Sukenik:]ᵒᵒ וᵒ[עים. DJD: [ ]ᵒᵒ וᵒ[עים. Frg. 24 ends here.
⁴⁵⁹ Sukenik: ם[ᵒ. Cf. DJD: ם ᵒ[. Qimron: ᵒ[ ]ומש.
⁴⁶⁰ DJD: כיא] אתה אלי מקור ד[ᵒֹעֹת.
⁴⁶¹ Sukenik:]ᵒ מ מקה[ᵒ מ. DJD:]ᵒᵒᵒ ומקֹה הם. Qimron: [ ]וֹמקֹוֹי הֹמ.
⁴⁶² Above line 7 appear five supralinear consonants not seen by previous editors.
⁴⁶³ Licht begins transcribing here (his line 5), but does not place frg. 24 in this column.
⁴⁶⁴ Sukenik:]הגב. DJD: ה[הגבֹוֹר.
⁴⁶⁵ Licht: הגב[ורה רב העלילה ו]גדול.
⁴⁶⁶ Licht: [ולרחמיכה].
⁴⁶⁷ For אין מספר see 12.28 and 17.38.
⁴⁶⁸ Licht: וקנאתכה. DJD: וקנֹאֹתֹכֹה. Qimron: וקנאתכ]ה עוברת.
⁴⁶⁹ Sukenik:] הֹמֹᵒᵒᵒ. Licht: [יקר חסדך אלי מה]ות[חנ. Qimron: [ ]ᵒ מ ᵒ ח.
⁴⁷⁰ Ctr. DJD: במשפֹטֹיֹך. Sukenik: במשפ[ט]. Licht: במשפֹ[ט כיא. Qimron: כי]א במשפט.

40   [...]

41   [...]

42   [...]

Col. 9 [= Sukenik Col. 1 + Frg. 24]
Parallels: 4Q432 Frgs. 1–2

1   [...]

2   °°[...] when you turn back from chao[s¹⁶¹ ...]

3   °°°[... the cong]regation of the Holy Ones °[...]

4   and all [...]°°°°[... kno]wing between good and evi[l. ...]

5   eternal ˒°[...]°°°°°°*wm*[... the wick]ed ones and the go[od ones ...]

6   in them and judg[ment ... pea]ce, for [you (are) the spring of kn]owledge and a reservoir of¹⁶²
        water¹⁶³[...]

7   and the fountain of mig[ht ...] great (in) counsel [...] without number, and your zeal in [your]
        judgment[s]¹⁶⁴ (are)

8   before your wisdom [...] and patient in [yo]ur judgment[s]. You are righteous in all your works.

---

¹⁶¹ See the first use of תהו in the Hebrew Bible, Gen 1:2.
¹⁶² Heb. מקוה. The noun denotes "reservoir" of water only here in the *Hodayot*. While the earliest portions of the *Hodayot* were being composed, מקוה obtained a technical meaning: "ritual bath."
¹⁶³ A possible echo of Gen 1:10: "a reservoir of water."
¹⁶⁴ Not transcribed by previous editors. Five superlinear consonants appear above this word; see the Heb. text of this line.

9   ובחכמתכﾞה ה[כינותה⁴⁷¹]עולם ובטרם בראתם ידעתה כﾞוﾞלﾞ⁴⁷² מעשיהם

10   לעולמי עﾞד וﾞ[מבלעדיכה לא]⁴⁷³ יעשה כו(ו)ל ולא יודע בלוא רﾞצﾞונכה אתה יצרתה

11   כול רוח ופﾞעולﾏﾞ[ם]⁴⁷⁴ הכינותﾞה ומשפט לכול מעשיהם   ואתה נטיתה שמים

12   לכבודכה וﾞכול [   ] הﾞכﾞיﾞנﾞוﾞﾞתﾞה⁴⁷⁵ לרצונכה ורוחות עוז לחוקיהם בטרם

13   היותם למלאכי ק[ודש⁴⁷⁶   ]ﾞﾏﾞ⁴⁷⁷ לרוחות עולם בממשלוﾞתﾞﾏﾞ מאורות לרזיהם

14   כוכביﾞﾏ לנﾞﾞתﾞיﾞבﾞותﾞﾞ[הם⁴⁷⁸   סער]ﾞה למשאם זקים וברקים לעבודתם ואוצרות

15   מחשבת לחפציﾞה[ם⁴⁷⁹   ]ﾏﾞ⁴⁸⁰ לרזיהם   אתה בראתה ארץ (ב)בכוחכה

16   ימים ותהומות עﾞשﾞיﾞ[תה   ויﾞ[שﾞביהם]⁴⁸¹ הכינותה בחוכמתכה וכל אשר בם

17   תכנﾞתה לרצונכ[ה]⁴⁸²   [   ] לﾞרוח אדם אשר יצרת בתבל לכל ימי עולם

18   ודורות נצח למ[שול בכול תב]ﾞל⁴⁸³ בקציהם פלגתה עבודתם בכול דוריהם ומש[פ]ט

19   במועדיה לממשלﾞ[תם   וד]ﾞרﾞﾞכﾞיהם הﾞכﾞיﾞנﾞוﾞﾞתﾞﾞﾏﾞ⁴⁸⁴ לדור ודור ופקודת שלומם עם

---

⁴⁷¹ Sukenik: [ ]ﾞה. Licht: [כינותה דורות]ﾞה. DJD: [ ]ﾞ. Qimron: [הכינותה].

⁴⁷² Licht does not note scribal dots.

⁴⁷³ Sukenik: [ ]. Licht: [ומבלעדיכה לוא]. DJD: מבלעדיך לא]ﾞוﾞ. With Qimron.

⁴⁷⁴ Sukenik: [ ]ﾞעﾞ ﾞוﾞ. Licht: ופעו[לתה הכינותה]. Qimron: ﾞה]ﾞﾞﾞﾞﾞﾞﾏﾞﾞ.

⁴⁷⁵ Sukenik: תה]ﾞ. Licht: [אשר בם תכנ]תה. Cf. DJD: ﾞה]ﾞכﾞיﾞנﾞוﾞﾞתﾞ. Qimron: ﾞה]ﾞ.

⁴⁷⁶ Sukenik: [ ]ﾞ. Licht: ק[ודש ידעתם והיו]ﾞ.

⁴⁷⁷ The *mem* is not in Qimron.

⁴⁷⁸ Sukenik: נתיבות]ﾞﾏﾞ. Licht: [נתיבות]ﾏ וכול רוחות סערה]. Qimron: [נתיבותﾞﾏ.

⁴⁷⁹ Licht: [חפציה]ﾏ ומפרש עבים.

⁴⁸⁰ Not seen by Qimron.

⁴⁸¹ Sukenik: [ ]ﾏﾞ ﾞ. Licht: עם [היבשה וכול יוש]ﾞביהם. DJD: ﾞ[תה בעוזכה ומﾞﾞ]ﾞﾞﾞ.

⁴⁸² Licht: [לרצונכ]ה ותתנם לממשלה.

⁴⁸³ With Qimron. Licht: [למ]ﾞﾞ לא פעולותיהמה. DJD: [ ]ﾞלﾞ למ].

⁴⁸⁴ Sukenik: ﾞﾞﾞﾞﾞﾞﾞﾞﾏ יהם°° [ ]ﾞﾞ למﾏﾞ. Licht: [לממשל]ﾏ תכנתה ודר]כיהם הכינותה.

9 And by your wisdom [you] es[tablished] eternity. And before you created them, you knew all[165] their works

10 for everlasting eternity, and [without you[166] not] any thing is done, and nothing is known without your will. You, you formed[167]

11 every spirit. And [yo]u [established] the[ir] deeds and the judgment for all their works.[168] And you, you spread out the heavens

12 for your glory.[169] And all [...] you established according to your will, and strong spirits according to their ordinances. Before

13 they became the angels of ho[liness ...]*m*, for eternal spirits in their dominions, luminaries according to their mysteries,

14 stars according to [their] paths [... stor]m according to their task; meteors and lightnings[170] according to their duty, and treasures

15 designed for the[ir] purposes [...]*m* according to their mysteries.[171] You, you created the earth by your power,

16 the seas and depths [you] made [.... And] their [inha]bitants you established by your wisdom, and all [which] (is) in them

17 you established according to yo[ur] will. [...] to the spirit of Adam[172] that you formed[173] in the world for all the days of eternity

18 and perpetual generations, to r[ule in all the wor]ld in their times. You assigned their duty in all their generations and judg[me]nt

19 in their appointed times[174] according to [their] dominion [... and] you established their [w]ays from generation to generation, and the visitation of their peace with[175]

---

[165] With dots above and below the consonant, a scribe deleted "all."

[166] Or "apart from you."

[167] Heb. יצר.

[168] A *vacat* highlights the next affirmation.

[169] Note the parallelism in these lines.

[170] The noun is in the plural.

[171] A *vacat* highlights, again, the affirmation of God's creation, first "the heavens" then "the earth" as in Genesis 1.

[172] Or "humankind."

[173] Heb. יצר.

[174] Or "festivals," "seasons."

[175] The preposition "with" is written at the end of line 19 and again at the beginning of line 20 [dittography due to *parablepsis*].

ה
20   עם⁴⁸⁵ כול נגיעיהם⁴⁸⁶[   ]ה⁴⁸⁷ ותפלג לכול צאצאיהם למספר דורות עולם

21   ולכול שני נצח ומ̊[עשיהם ידע]ת̊ה⁴⁸⁸ ובחכמת דעתכה הכ̇[י]נ̊ותה תע[ו]דתם בטרם

22   היותם ועל פי ר̊צ̊[ו]נ̊כ̊ה [נ]ה̊יה⁴⁸⁹ כול ומבלעדיך לא יעשה

23   אלה ידעתי מבינתכה כיא גליתה אוזני לרזי פלא ואנ̇י יצר החמר ומגבל המים

24   סוד הערוה ומקור הנדה כור העוון ומבנה החטאה רוח הת̇ועה ונעוה בלא

25   בינה ונבעתה ב̊מ̊שפטי צדק מה אדבר בלא נודע ואשמיעה בלא סופר הכול

26   חקוק לפניכה בחרת זכרון לכול קצי נצח ותקופות מספר שני עולם בכול מועדיהם

27   ולוא נסתרו ולא נעדרו מלפניכה ומה יספר אנוש חטאתו ומה יוכיח על עוונותיו

⁴⁹⁰ו
28   ומה ישיב על על⁴⁹¹ משפט הצדק לכה אתה 〵 הדעות כול מעשי הצדקה

29   וסוד⁴⁹² האמת ולבני האדם עבודת העוון ומעשי הרמיה   אתה בראתה

30   רוח בלשון ותדע דבריה ותכן פרי שפתים בטרם היותם ותשם דברים על קו

---

485 The second עם is an example of dittography due to *parablepsis*.
486 Note the parallel to נגֿעיהם in 1QS 3.23 (cf. 4.12): וכול נגֿעיהם. Qimron: נגועיהם.
487 Sukenik: ה[   ]°. Licht: ה[תכנת לקציהם]. Qimron: [לקציהם חקקת]ה.
488 Sukenik: ה[   ]°. Licht: ה[ידעת מעשיהם]ו. DJD: ה̊ [ ]°°°. Qimron: ה[עשיהם ידעת]מ̊ו.
489 Sukenik: יה[   ]°. Licht: ד[ברכה נה]יה.
490 Licht does not read the supralinear ו.
491 This is a scribal error for עול על. The text was probably corrected from כול על to על על to על על. See 15.39: ב̊ע̊ולה. Ctr. Qimron: כול על. Sukenik: על כול.
492 Sukenik: סוד.

20   all their afflictions […]*h*. And you assigned[176] it to all their offspring for the number of eternal generations,

21   and for all the perpetual years, and [their] w[orks] you [knew], and in the wisdom of your knowledge you est[ab]lished their fix[e]d times before

22   they came into being. And according to your wi[ll], everything [shall h]appen, and without you[177] nothing is done.[178]

23   These (things) I know from your discernment, because you uncovered my ear to wonderful mysteries. But I (am) an inclination of[179] clay and a mixture of water,[180]

24   a foundation of shame,[181] and a source of impurity, a furnace of iniquity, and a structure of sin, a spirit of error and (one) distorted without

25   discernment and horrified by the judgments of righteousness. What can I say that is not known, and (what) can I proclaim that has not been recounted? Everything

26   is engraved in your presence[182] with the imprint of[183] memory for all the perpetual times, and the periods of the number of years of eternity in all their appointed times.[184]

27   And they are neither hidden nor absent[185] from your presence. And how should a human recount his sin? And how shall he defend his iniquities?

28   And how can the deceitful reply to the righteous judgment? To you, yourself, O God of knowledge,[186] (belong) all the works of righteousness

29   and the secret of truth. But to the sons of Adam (belong) the iniquitous deeds and the works of treachery.[187] You, you created

30   the spirit in the tongue; and you know its words. And you established the fruit of the lips[188] before they existed. And you put words on a measuring-line,

---

[176] Lit. "to separate."
[177] Or "apart from you."
[178] A *vacat* allows a break in thought.
[179] Heb. יצר.
[180] See the similar expressions in 5.32.
[181] See 1QS 11.21–22.
[182] Or "before you."
[183] Aram. חרת or Heb. חרט means "stylus;" see Isa 8:1. See also 1QM 12.3.
[184] Or "festivals," "seasons."
[185] Lit. "they are not absent."
[186] "God" is in paleo-Hebrew.
[187] Again, a *vacat* highlights the celebration to creation.
[188] The expression "fruit of the lips" is a Qumranic expression; see esp. 1QS 9.28.

31   ומבע רוח שפתים במדה ותוצא קוים לרזיהם וֹמֹבֹעֹי רוחות לחשבונם להודיע

32   כבודכה ולספר נפלאותיכה בכול מעשי אמתכה ומֹ[ש]פֹ[ט]י צֹדקה[493] ולהלל שמכה

33   בפה כול יודעיכה לפי שכלם וֹבֹרכוכה[494] לעולמי [עד][495]   ואתה ברחמיכה

34   וגדול חסדיכה חזקתה רוח אנוש לפני נגע וֹנֹפֹשֹ[ ] טהֹרֹתֹהֹ[496] מרוב עוון

35   לספר נפלאֹוֹתֹיֹכֹהֹ לנגד כול מעשיכה   ואֹסֹפֹרֹ[ה בקהל] פֹתֹיֹם[497] משפטי נגיעי[498]

36   ולבני אנוש כול נפלאותיכה אשר הגברתה בֹ[י לנגד ב]נֹי אֹדֹ[ם][499]   שמעו

37   חכמים ושחי[500] דעת וֹנֹמֹהֹרים יהיו[501] ליצר סמוך [תמימי ד]רֹךֹ[502] הוסיפו ערמה

38   צדיקים השביתו עֹוֹלֹה וכול תמימי דרך החזיק[ו] נֹדֹכֹאֹ[503] עני האריכו

39   אפים ואל תמאסֹוֹ במֹשֹפטֹ[י צדק][504]   או[נ]יֹלֹיֹ[505] לב לא יבינו

40   אלה וֹבֹחֹסֹד אֹמֹ[תכה][506]

41   [ער]יצים יחרוקֹוֹ[507] שנים

---

[493] Sukenik: צ[ ]דקה ו[ ]°°]. Licht: ו.[פעלות צ]דקה.

[494] With Sukenik and Licht. Cf. DJD: יברכוכה.

[495] With Qimron. Ctr. DJD: לעולמי ע[ו]לֹמֹ[ם. Sukenik: לעולמי]. Licht: עד[לעולמי.

[496] Sukenik: °°°טה [ ]°. Licht: טה]רתה. DJD: ו.[רוח נעוה] אבוין. וֹנֹפֹשֹ.

[497] Sukenik: °°° [ ]. Licht: פ]תיים. DJD: ו.[אגידה בקהל]. Qimron: פֹתֹיֹם. See 5.13 and 10.11.]ובֹקֹרֹבֹם תמיד.

[498] Qimron: נגועי.

[499] Sukenik: °°° [ ]. Licht: בי לנגד ב]ני אדם. Cf. DJD: בֹ.[י לנגד ב]נֹי אֹדֹם.

[500] Qimron: וקחו.

[501] With Sukenik and Licht. Cf. DJD: יהיו. Qimron: היו.

[502] Sukenik: [ ]. Licht: ו]כול פתיים. Qimron:]ם וכול פותיֹ.

[503] Sukenik: א[ ]. Licht: נדכ]א[ו. החזיקו]. החזיק[ו מעמד וכול נדכ]א[ו.

[504] Cf. Qimron: בנֹגֹוֹעֹים.

[505] Sukenik: [ ]בכ. Licht: בכ]ול משפט הצדק כי אמת כל מעשי אל ואן. DJD:]ילי.

[506] Sukenik:]ד אמֹ. Licht: אלה ובחסד אמ]תכה הודעתם לאנשי עצתכה. Cf. DJD:]°°° ד אמֹ. Qimron:]לֹא ידעו וֹבֹסֹוֹד אֹמֹ[ת].

[507] For the restoration see 10.13. Sukenik:]יצים יחרו°°. Licht: [שנים]יחרוקֹו]יצים. Qimron: שנים]יחרוֹקֹו[ער.]וֹעֹרֹיצים יחרוֹקֹו.

31 and the expression of the breath of the lips (is) by measure. And you issued[189] measuring-lines according to their mysteries, and the expressions of breaths according to their design (so that they) might make known

32 your glory and recount your wonders in all the works of your truth, and your righteous ju[dg]me[nt]s, and praise your name

33 by the mouth of all who know you, according to their insight. And they bless you forever [and ever].[190] And you, in your compassions

34 and your great loving-kindnesses have strengthened the spirit of the human against affliction and the soul of[191] [...] you purified from a multitude of iniquity

35 to recount your wonders before all your creatures.[192] And I will recit[e in the assembly of] the simple ones[193] the judgments of my afflictions,

36 and to the sons of the humans all your wonders, that you have strengthened[194] in [me before the s]ons of Adam.[195] Hear,[196]

37 O wise ones and contemplators of knowledge, and ones eager (for righteousness),[197] be of firm inclination.[198] [O Perfect Ones of the W]ay, increase craftiness.

38 O righteous ones, cease injustice. And all the Perfect Ones of the Way,[199] strength[en ...]. O (you who are) oppressed, the needy,[200] be

39 patient, and do not reject the [righteous] judgment[s.... The foo]lish of heart will not discern

40   these (things). And in the mercy of [your] trut[h ...]

41 [the ruth]less ones grind [(their) teeth ...]

---

[189] Or "sent forth."
[190] Restoration follows Licht. For עד לעולמי, see 4.40; 5.18, 30; 9.10; 15.34; and 19.28.
[191] Heb. נפש.
[192] All God's creatures include "the simple" and not only "the wise ones." A *vacat* is in the text as a pause to shift the thought to a celebration.
[193] The "simple ones" seem to denote those needing instruction, and perhaps also those incapable of learning. See 5.13 and 10.11.
[194] Lit. "to make mighty."
[195] A *vacat* is used to introduce the exhortation.
[196] Note the following series of parallel thoughts.
[197] *Nipʿal* plural participle of מהר. Lit. "hasty ones;" but see 10.11 and esp. 13.23–24, those "eager for righteousness."
[198] Heb. יצר.
[199] For this technical phrase, see B. A. Strawn with H. W. Morisada Rietz, "(More) Sectarian Terminology in the *Songs of the Sabbath Sacrifice*: The Case of תמימי דרך," in *Qumran Studies: New Approaches, New Questions*, edited by M. T. Davis and B. A. Strawn (Grand Rapids, 2007) pp. 53–64.
[200] Lit. "the poor" or perhaps "the Poor."

Col. 10 [= Sukenik Col. 2]
Parallels: 4Q428 Frg. 3; 4Q432 Frgs. 3–4

1	[
2	[
3	[°°] [ ]דֿוֹ[
4	מע[שׂיו]508° ̊עׄ ̊[
5	אודכה אדוני כי ישרתה509 בלב[בֿיׄ כול מעשי עׄולֿהׄ ותֿתֿהׄ[רני]510
6	וׄ[תֿשם511 שׂ[ומרי אמת נגד עוני ומוכי]חׄי512 אׄמֿתֿ בכל513 חׄמֿ[סי]514 צדק
7	[לׄמחׄץ מכֿתֿוֹ]515 [ומשמיעי516 שמחה לאבל יג]וני517 מֿ[שפֿטֿ
8	[מבשר שׂ]לֿום518 לכול הווֿתֿ שמוע[תי]519 חזקים למוס לבבי ומאמצי כֿ[520
9	לפני521 [נ]גֿעׄ522 ותתן מענה לשון לׄעׄר[ול]523 שפתי ותסמוך נפשי בחזוק מותנים
10	ואמוץ כוח ותעמד פעמי בגבול רשעה ואהיה פח לפושעים ומרפא לכול
11	שבי פשע ערמה לפתיים ויצר סמוך לכול נמהרי לב ותשימני חרפה
12	וקלס לבוגדים סוד אמת ובינה לישרי דרך ואהיה על עוׄן רשעים

---

508 Ctr. DJD:]°°°°°[ ]°°° ̊יׄ°°°[. Sukenik:] ̊עׄ ̊עׄזי[. Qimron transcribes no consonants in lines 1–4.

509 With DJD.

510 I am indebted here to DJD. Sukenik:] ̊ ̊ כול מעשי עול [. Qimron: [ ]°°°וׄ.

511 Sukenik:]שֿמׄ[.

512 Cf. DJD: ומ[וֿכֿיׄחׄי. Sukenik: חׄי[. Qimron: ומוכ]יׄחׄי. The restoration is influenced by DJD. See 17.33.

513 Qimron: צדק בכל.

514 Sukenik: חֿ.

515 Cf. DJD: מכֿתֿיׄ. Sukenik:]°°מׄ מחׄץ[. See Isa 30.26: ומחץ מכתו.

516 Licht begins his reading here.

517 Sukenik:]יגׄ. Licht: יגׄ[ון]. Qimron: [יגׄ]וני. Cf. 4Q432 frg. 3 line 4: [יׄ]גׄוני.

518 Sukenik: ליׄם[. Licht: [ומתהול]ליׄם. Qimron: שׂ[לֿום]. DJD: [מבשר שׂ]לֿום. Cf. 4Q432 frg. 3 line 4: מבשר שלום.

519 Sukenik:] ̊שמוע. Licht: שמוע]ה ומשברים. Qimron: שמוע]תֿי.

520 Licht: [כוחיׄ. Cf. DJD: רׄ[וֹ]חׄ. Qimron: [כוחֿ.

521 The right margin is now preserved. The leather is lined both vertically and horizontally.

522 Sukenik: עׄ[ ]. Licht: [גׄ]עׄ. Qimron: נֿגֿעׄיׄ.

523 Sukenik: [לעׄ]. Licht: לעׄ[רול]. With DJD. See also 10.20.

Col. 10 [= Sukenik Col. 2]
Parallels: 4Q428 Frg. 3; 4Q432 Frgs. 3–4

1   […]

2   […]

3   […]°°[…]°*dw*[…]

4   […] his [wor]ks °[…]°°[….]²⁰¹

5   [(VACAT)   I thank you, O Lord, because you straighten in] my [hea]rt²⁰² all the works of deceit and you purif[ied] me

6   […. And] you placed gu[ardians²⁰³ of truth in the presence of my transgressor, and the chastis]ements of righteousness²⁰⁴ (were) with all [my] viole[nt ones]

7   […] for the wound of his blow.²⁰⁵ […] and the proclaimers of joyous ju[dgme]nt²⁰⁶ for [my] griev[ous] mourning,

8   [announcing pea]ce for all disasters [I] have heard, […] strong ones for the melting of my heart, and the courageous ones of *k*[…]

9   before [affl]iction. And you give an answer of the tongue to my unsk[illed] lips,²⁰⁷ and you sustained my soul²⁰⁸ with the strengthening of the loins

10   and the courage of power. And you set my footsteps within the border of wickedness, and I am a trap for transgressors, but a healing for all

11   those who turn from transgression, craftiness for the simple ones, and a firm inclination²⁰⁹ for all eager of heart.²¹⁰ And you set²¹¹ me (as) a disgrace

12   and mockery to the unfaithful ones, a foundation of²¹² truth and discernment for the Upright Ones of the Way.²¹³ And because of the iniquity of the wicked ones, I became

---

²⁰¹ A *vacat* may have been in the lost text.
²⁰² For the restoration, see 8.13.
²⁰³ The author thanks the Lord for his true guardians who insulated him from the violent ones (the wicked priests). The author of these lines seems to be the Righteous Teacher.
²⁰⁴ For the restoration, see 17.33. The word "truth" is marked to be ignored by scribal dots added above and below the word. The word "righteousness" is inscribed above the line.
²⁰⁵ See Isa 30:26. Most likely "his blow" denotes the blows delivered by the Wicked Priest on the Righteous Teacher.
²⁰⁶ Added above the line is "ju[dgme]nt."
²⁰⁷ Lit. "my uncirc[umcised] lips."
²⁰⁸ Heb. נפש.
²⁰⁹ Heb. יצר.
²¹⁰ See Isa 35:4.
²¹¹ Perhaps a *hip'il* permissive.
²¹² Or "a secret of."
²¹³ Or "the way."

13   דבה בשפת עריצים לצים יחרוקו שנים   ואני הייתי נגינה לפושעים

14   ועלי קהלת רשעים תתרגש ויהמו כנחשולי ימים בהרגש גליהם רפש

15   וטיט יגרישו[524] ותשימני נס לבחירי צדק ומליץ דעת ברזי פלא לבחון

16   [אנשי][525] אמת ולנסות אוהבי מוסר ואהיה איש ריב למליצי תעות וב̊ע̊ל̊[526]

17   [מד]נ̊י̊ם̊[527] לכול חוזי נכוחות ואהיה לרוח קנאה לנגד כל דורשי חל[קות][528]

18   [וכול][529] א̇נשי רמיה עלי יהמו כקול המון מים רבים ומזמות בליעל [כול][530]

19   מ̊ח̊שבותם[531] ויהפוכו לשוחה חיי גבר אשר הכינותה בפי[532] ותלמד(נ̊)ו[533] בינה

20   שמתה בלבבו לפתוח מקור דעת לכול מבינים וימירום בערול שפה

21   ולשון אחרת לעם לא בינות להלב̊ב במשגתם   (VACAT)

22   אודכה אד̊ונ̊י כי שמתה נפשי בצרור החיים

23   ותשוך בעדי מכול מוקשי שחת כ[י]א̊[534] עריצים בקשו נפשי בתומכי

---

[524] With Sukenik and Licht. Cf. DJD and Qimron: יגרישו.

[525] Licht: [דורשי].

[526] The leather is darkened. We follow DJD, Qimron, and the context here. Sukenik: ˚˚˚. Licht: [ובעל].

[527] Sukenik: וֹם[. Licht: שלֹ[ום].

[528] Sukenik: [חֹל. With Licht and Qimron: חל[קות]. DJD: חֹל[קית.

[529] With Licht, DJD, and Qimron. Possibly [עם].

[530] With Licht.

[531] With Sukenik. Licht: מחש[בותם. DJD: [מֹ]חֹשֹבותם. Qimron: מֹחֹשֹבותם.

[532] Read with Licht: בפיו.

[533] Licht does not report the scribal correction.

[534] Sukenik: [   ].

13   a slander on the lip of the ruthless ones. Scorners grind (their) teeth.[214] And I, I became a taunt[215] for transgressors;

14   and against me the assembly of the wicked roar, and they rumble as the gales of the seas in the roaring of their waves. Mud

15   and mire they roll up. But you set me[216] (as) a banner for the elect ones of righteousness, and the Interpreter of[217] knowledge in the wonderful mysteries,[218] to examine

16   [the men of] truth and to test the lovers of discipline. But I became a man of strife for the interpreters of the error, but the consummate

17   [deb]ater[219] for all the seers of correct things. And I became a zealous spirit against all seekers of sm[ooth things.][220]

18   [And all] the men of slackness roar against me as the sound of abundant waters. And from the devices of Belial[221] (are) [all]

19   their thoughts. And they cast into the pit the life of the man[222] in whose mouth[223] you established (instruction), and you taught him discernment;

20   you set in his heart to open a spring of[224] knowledge to all who have understandings; but they exchanged them for unskilled speech

21   and another language for a people of no discernment, so that they are ruined by their (own) error. (VACAT)

22   (VACAT) I thank you, O Lord, because you placed my soul[225] in the bundle of[226] the living ones,

23   and made a hedge about me (to protect) from all the snares of the pit, be[cau]se ruthless ones sought my soul,[227] while I adhered to

---

[214] See 9.41. A small *vacat* is used again to highlight a personal statement.

[215] Or "taunting-song." This word appears in Job 30:9.

[216] Perhaps a *hip‘il* permissive.

[217] See Job 33:23, the heavenly being.

[218] All these self-reflections most likely derive from the Righteous Teacher.

[219] Lit. "and the head of controversies (or contentions)." See Hab 1:3.

[220] The expression "seekers of smooth things" is a euphemism for liars; see 10.17. For the expression elsewhere in the extant Dead Sea Scrolls, see 4Q169 frgs. 3–4 2.2, 4; 4Q169 frgs. 3–4 3.3, 6.

[221] Or "devilry." The Heb. בליעל may not be a *nomen proprium* in the *Hodayot*.

[222] Heb. גבר.

[223] The text has "in my mouth."

[224] Or "a source of."

[225] Heb. נפש.

[226] See 1Sam 25:29. The noun means to be bound up as in a pouch.

[227] Heb. נפש.

24 בבריתכה[535] והמה סוד שוא ועדת בליעל לא ידעו כיא מאתכה מעמדי

25 ובחסדיכה תושיע נפשי כיא מאתכה מצעדי והמה מאתכה גרו

26 על נפשי בעבור הכבדכה במשפט רשעים והגבירכה בי נגד בני

27 אדם כיא בחסדכה עמדי ואני אמרתי חנו עלי גבורים סבבום[536] בכל

28 כלי מלחמותם ויפרו חצים לאין מרפא ולהוב חנית באש[537] אוכלת עצים

29 וכהמון מים רבים שאון קולם נפץ וזרם[538] להשחית רבים למזורות יבקעו

30 אפעה ושוא בהתרומם גליהם ואני במוס לבי כמים ותחזק נפשי בבריתך

31 והם רשת פרשו לי תלכוד רגלם ופחים טמנו לנפשי נפלו בם   ורגלי עמדה במישור

32 מקהלם אברכה שמכה

---

[535] Note final *kaph* in medial position. The correction seems immediate (see כה in lines 22 and 25). See also the ך in line 30.

[536] Licht correctly emmended the text to סבבוני.

[537] Sukenik: באש. Licht: כאש. Ctr. DJD: כאש, but the *beth* is square in contrast to the round *kaph* in the context. The contributors to DJD judge "that the incorrectly written באש was corrected to כאש" (p. 139). No scribal correction is obvious, though conceivable. Qimron: באש.

[538] Sukenik and Licht: זרם.

24 your covenant.[228] But they (are) the assembly of vanity, and the congregation of Belial.[229] They do not know that my position (is) because of you.

25 And through your mercies you save[230] my soul,[231] for my treads (are) because of you. And they, because of you, they were afraid[232] (to destroy)[233]

26 my soul[234] for you made heavy the judgment of the wicked ones,[235] but you may manifest[236] your might through me against the sons of

27 Adam,[237] for in your mercy (is) my standing. But I, I said, mighty ones encamped against me; they encircled me[238] with all

28 the instruments of their wars, and the arrows without cure (are) useless,[239] and the spear blazing with[240] fire devours trees.

29 And like the roar of many waters (is) the noise of their voice, a thunderclap and downpour[241] to destroy many. For healing purposes they cleave

30 the sand-viper, but in vain when their waves rise.[242] And me, when my heart melted like water, then my soul was strengthened by your covenant.

31 And they, they spread a net for me, but it entraps their (own) feet; and the traps which they set[243] my soul,[244] they fell into them. But my foot stood in firmness.[245]

32 Away from their assembly I shall bless your name. (VACAT)

---

[228] See the same expression in 12.2, 22.14; cf. 12.23 and 15.23.

[229] Or "devilry."

[230] Note the future tense that is an intensive present. In the hymns most likely composed by the Righteous Teacher the past tense ("you saved") is dominant.

[231] Heb. נפש.

[232] Heb. גור, "be afraid of." גור with על appears in Ps 59:4, but the meaning "attack" is not appropriate in the present context.

[233] The author suffers great physical harm, but is not killed. See 13.17. For the addition of a verb before על see 12.23

[234] Heb. נפש.

[235] The translation is very different from previous renderings and takes seriously the context and the repetitive "because of you." The author cannot be threatened because of God (as in many translations). See lines 37–38 and 12.19–21.

[236] An intensive present as a future tense.

[237] Or "the sons of humankind."

[238] The text has "them;" it is an error for "me."

[239] Hipʿil imperfect of פרר, lit. "shatter" or "make useless."

[240] Read כאש for באש.

[241] Heb. נפץ; see Isa 30:30 (זרם נפץ). Isaiah 30 has influenced the imagery and language in 10.9 and earlier.

[242] See Isa 30:6, 59:5. This sentence is one of the most difficult to understand, but not to translate in this scroll. The "mighty ones" cannot obtain healing from the venom of vipers.

[243] Lit. "they buried."

[244] Heb. נפש. A *vacat* separates two thoughts.

[245] Lit. "on level ground." The traps did not entrap the thinker.

33　אודכה אדוני כיא עינכה על]י [בֿשֿפֿוֿל[539] נפשי ותצילני מקנאת מליצי כזב

34　ומעדת דורשי חלקות פדיתהֿ[540] נפֿש אביון אשר חשבו להתם דמו

35　לשפוך על עבודתכה אפס כי]ֿ[541] [לוא] יֿדֿעֿוֿ[542] כי מאתך מצעדי וישימוני לבוז

36　וחרפה בפי כל דורשי רמיה　　　　ואתה ⟨אל⟩ עזרתה נפש עני וֿרֿש

37　מֿיד חזק ממנו ותפד נפשי מיד אֿדֿירים ובגדפותם לא החתותני[543]

38　לֿעֿזֿוב עבודתכה מפחד הוות רשֿעֿיֿם[544] ולֿהֿמיר (ב)בהולל[545] יצר סמוך אשר

39　נֿתֿתֿהֿ]　　　ות]לֿמֿדֿמוֿ[546] חוקֿיֿםֿ וֿבֿתעודות [כו]נֿנתני להֿחֿזֿיֿק[547]

40　[ב]שֿׄרֿ[548]　　　שֿׄחת לכול צאצאֿיֿ עֿדֿ[549]

41　לש]וֿןֿ[550] כלֿמֿוֿדֿיכה ובמֿשֿ[פט]י[551]

Col. 11 [= Sukenik Col. 3 + Frg. 25]
Parallels: 4Q428 Frgs. 4–5; 4Q432 Frgs. 5–7

1　　]

2　　[ֿםֿ בֿלֿי מ°°°[552]

---

[539] Sukenik: [עֿל[ ]°ֿע. Licht: על [ ]עֿ. The leather is torn and darkened. We follow DJD: בֿשֿׄפֿוֿל. Qimron: עלֿיֿ בשפול.
[540] Sukenik and Licht: פדית[ה].
[541] Ctr. Qimron: כיֿאֿ.
[542] Sukenik: [עו יד[. Licht: [לוא יד[עו.
[543] Sukenik and Licht: החתיתני.
[544] Sukenik: רֿ°°°מ. Licht: רשעים (no restoration).
[545] The scribe erroneously wrote בב and tried to erase the first ב.
[546] Sukenik: [מֿו[ ]ה. Licht: [מו[תלמד ואמתך בני לכל נת]תה :DJD. [ ] °°°° °°°°°°° מֿיֿ [ ] °°°° נֿתֿתֿה. Qimron: מֿיֿ°° [ ] נֿתֿתֿה.
[547] Licht: ובתעודות ננתנו לאזנים.
[548] Licht: [אשר גליתה]. Qimron: °°°.
[549] Sukenik: [צאצאיֿ]הם חֿת[. Licht: שחת לכול צאצאי]הם [ולא תראה].. Cf. DJD and Qimron: שחת לכול צאצאי עֿםֿ. The עֿדֿ is probably not עֿםֿ. The strong top of the *daleth* is evident and the *mem* by the present scribe is large.
[550] Qimron: °°[.
[551] Sukenik: [בלמודיכה וֿ]. Licht does not read any letters. The bottom margin appears visible.
[552] Sukenik: [ובֿיֿן]. DJD: [°°°מ בלי םֿ[. Qimron reports no consonants for line 1.

33 I thank you, O Lord, because your eye (is) on [me] during the humiliation of²⁴⁶ my soul,²⁴⁷ and you saved me from the zeal of²⁴⁸ the interpreters of the lie.²⁴⁹

34 And from the assembly of the seekers of smooth (things) you redeemed the soul of the Poor One, whose blood they thought to annihilate,²⁵⁰

35 in order to pour (it) upon your service. But they did [not] know that because of you²⁵¹ (are) my treads. And they placed me as (an object of) scorn

36 and disgrace in the mouth of all seekers of treachery.²⁵² But you, O my God,²⁵³ you rescued²⁵⁴ the soul of²⁵⁵ the Needy One and the Wretched One²⁵⁶

37 from the hand of one stronger than he.²⁵⁷ And you redeemed my soul from the hand of the powerful ones, and in their slanders you did not allow me to be afraid

38 (so that I would) leave your service from the fear of the threats of the wicked ones, and exchanging (for) foolishness a firm inclination²⁵⁸ that

39 you put [… and you] taught him statutes, and through the testimonies²⁵⁹ you [es]tablished me to hold

40 [f]lesh […] the pit for all everlasting descendants

41 [… the to]ngue according to your teachings and in the judg[ment]

Col. 11 [= Sukenik Col. 3 + Frg. 25]
Parallels: 4Q428 Frgs. 4–5; 4Q432 Frgs. 5–7

1 […]

2 […]*m* weeping *m*°°[…]

---

²⁴⁶ The *šapʿel* of נפל. See KB 1631. See 26:16.
²⁴⁷ Heb. נפש.
²⁴⁸ Or "from the jealousy of."
²⁴⁹ See "the man of (אדם or איש) the lie" in CD MS B 19.26, 20.15; 1QHab 2.2. A unique personality is reflected in these lines and a particular experience is shared. Most likely the words ultimately derive from the Righteous Teacher who may be thinking back on the problems he encountered within the Temple against his adversaries, the Hasmonean priests and the precursors of the Pharisees (the "Seekers of Smooth Things").
²⁵⁰ להתם.
²⁵¹ See 10.25.
²⁵² A *vacat* introduces the affirmation.
²⁵³ "O my God" (אלי) is written in Palaeo-Hebrew.
²⁵⁴ Lit. "you helped."
²⁵⁵ Heb. נפש.
²⁵⁶ See the same noun in 13.16, 22. Also see the discussion in the Introduction.
²⁵⁷ The first and third person speech refers to the speaker.
²⁵⁸ Heb. יצר.
²⁵⁹ Or "and through the fixed times."

3   [°°°°° °° לי הֹ֗בֹ וֹֹ הֹ [²⁵³

פֿנֿיֿ

4   [²⁵⁴הֹבֹרִיֹתֹכֹה[לֹ הֹ֗אֹוֹרוֹתה אֹלֹ֗יֹ [אתה

5   [²⁵⁶]°° °° [לכה בכבוד עולם עם כֹוֹלֹ [ ] הֹ[²⁵⁵

6   [²⁶⁰יֹֹ֗ם[[ומ [²⁵⁹ מֹ[סוד ²⁵⁸ותציליני ²⁵⁷אמ[ֹת פיכה

7   [הוש[ֹעֹתה²⁶¹ נפשֹ[י לחרפה ולקלֹ]סֹ²⁶² יחשיבוני²⁶³ וישימו נפשֹׁיֹ כֹאוניה²⁶⁴ במֹצֹ֗וֹלֹוֹת²⁶⁵ יֹם

8   וכעיר מבצר מלפֹנֹֹיֹ [אויב] ֹואהיֹהֹ²⁶⁶ בצוקה כמו אשת לדה מבכריה²⁶⁷ כיא נהפכו צירֹיֹֹם²⁶⁸

9   וחבל נמרץ על משבריה להחיל בכור הריה כיא באו בנים עד משברי מות

10   והרית גבר הצרה בחבליה כיא במשברי מות תמליט זכר ובחבלי שאול יגיח

11   מכור הריה פלא יועץ עם גבורתו ויפלט גבר ממשברים בהריתו החישו כול

12   משברים וחבלי מרץ במולדיהם ופלצות להורות²⁶⁹ ובמולדיו יהפכו כול צירים

---

²⁵³ Sukenik:]וֹלֹ הֹבֹ [. DJD:]°°°°° °° לֹ ֹ֗וֹהֹבֹ. Qimron: °°°°°°°לֹ °°°°°.
²⁵⁴ Sukenik does not see any consonants.
²⁵⁵ Sukenik: לכה[. Qimron: הֹלכה[ואת].
²⁵⁶ Ctr. Qimron: ש[קוֹדֹ בֹֹיֹ מלא].
²⁵⁷ See 1QHᵃ 22.14. Ctr. Qimron: כֹפיכה[.
²⁵⁸ Sukenik: פיכה ותצו לנו. Licht begins his reading with this line: לנו ותצו פיכה ח[כרו להתהלך]. The left margin is clear.
²⁵⁹ DJD: [סוד שוא מ].
²⁶⁰ Sukenik:]ומ [ ] מ. Licht: רשעים והות]ומ[צותיכה] מ.
²⁶¹ Licht: עתה[הוש.
²⁶² Sukenik: [ ] נפש °. Licht: לוא כי עבדכה] נפש. DJD: סֹ[וקל לחרפה כיא י]נפשֹׁ. Qimron does not see: סֹ[. See Jer 20:8: היִם כל ולקלס לחרפה.
²⁶³ DJD: יחשובוני.
²⁶⁴ With DJD and Qimron: כֹאוניה נֹפֹשֹׁ[י. See line 14. Sukenik: באוניה נפש. Licht: באוניה נפשֹ[י.
²⁶⁵ Sukenik: צֹ֗וֹלֹות °° ב[מֹ]ב. Licht: מצולות[ב.
²⁶⁶ Sukenik: אהיה[ ] מלפ.]אויב י[מלפנֹ. Licht: ואהיה[ו אויב י]מלפנֹ.
²⁶⁷ Licht corrects the text to מבכירה.
²⁶⁸ Sukenik: צירֹ°°. Licht and Qimron: ציר]יה.
²⁶⁹ Qimron: להוריתם.

3   […]$\mathring{}m$ and $hb\mathring{}\mathring{}ly$ $\mathring{}\mathring{}\mathring{}\mathring{}\mathring{}\mathring{}$[…]

4   [… you], O my God, you have made my face[260] to shine for your covenant […]

5   […]h to you in eternal glory with all […] $\mathring{}\mathring{}$ $\mathring{}\mathring{}$[…]

6   [… tru]th (is in) your mouth and you rescued me from [the assembly of …] and from […]ym

7   you [sav]ed [my] soul.[261] They consider me [a disgrace and a mocke]ry[262] and besiege[263] my soul[264] like a ship in the depths of the sea,

8   and like a fortified city before [the enemy]. And I am in distress like a woman laboring for the firstborn, for labor pains come upon (her),

9   and intensive tribulation (is) upon the opening of her womb[265] to cause anguish in the womb of[266] the pregnant one,[267] because sons reached the opening of the womb of death.

10   And she who is pregnant (with) a man[268] was troubled by her tribulations, for in the opening[269] of the womb of death she rescues[270] a male.[271] And in the tribulations of Sheol he shall burst forth

11   from the womb of[272] the pregnant one. (He shall be) a wonderful counselor[273] with his might; and a man[274] shall be delivered from the opening[275] of the womb of the one pregnant (with) him. All the

12   opening[276] of the womb[277] hastened, and intensive tribulations (occurred) when they[278] were born; and (they are) a shuddering to their parents. And at his birth all the labor pains turn

[260] The word "my face" is barely visible; it was added by a scribe as a superscript.

[261] Heb. נפש.

[262] See Jer 20:8.

[263] Lit. "put," "set," or "place." See 1Kgs 20:12.

[264] Heb. נפש.

[265] Not the Heb. word for "breakers," though it is identical in unpointed manuscripts to "opening of the womb." In this column the noun is plural in Hebrew.

[266] Lit. "furnace."

[267] Or "of the birth pangs (for her) firstborn of her pregnancy."

[268] Heb. גבר.

[269] The Hebrew is plural.

[270] *Hip̒il* of מלט: "to rescue," "give birth." See Isa 66:7.

[271] Heb. זכר. Many infants died during their birth.

[272] Lit. "from the furnace of."

[273] See Isa 9:5 which the author no doubt had memorized.

[274] Heb. גבר.

[275] The Hebrew is plural.

[276] The Hebrew is plural.

[277] The author is making paronomasia with two nouns: "the opening of the womb" and "breakers;" both are משבר. He will soon shift to "breakers." At birth the womb opens wide and vast amounts of liquid "break" forth. The author is simultaneously meaning sometimes a *double entendre*: both "the opening of the womb" and the "breakers" of water.

[278] This sentence is a generic interpolation between passages about the birth of a male.

13   בכור הריה והרית אפעה לחבל נמרץ ומשברי שחת לכול מעשי פלצות וירועו

14   אושי קיר כאוניה על פני מים ויהמו שחקים בקול המון וֹיושבי עפר

ם

15   כיורדי ימים נבעתים מהמון מים וחכמיה למוֹ[570] כמלחים במצולות כי תתבלע

16   כוֹל חכמתם בהמות ימים ברתוח תהומות על נבוכי מים וֹיתרגֹשו[571] לרום גלים

17   ומשברי מים בהמון קולם ובהתרגשם יפתחו שֹ[או]לֹ[   ]בֹּדֹ [ו]כֹוֹלֹ[572] חצי שחת

18   עם מצעדם לתהום ישמיעו קולם ויפתחו שערי [עולם   תח]תֹ[573] מעשי אפעה

19   ויסגרו דלתי שחת בעד הרית עול ובריחי עולם בעד כול רוחי אפעה   (VACAT)

20   אודכה אדוני כי פדיתה נפשי משחת ומשאול אבדון

21   העליתני לרום עולם ואתהלכה במישור לאין חקר ואדעה כיא יש מקוה לאשר

22   יצרתה מעפר לסוד עולם ורוח נעוה טהרתה מפשע רב להתיצב במעמד עם

---

[570] Sukenik: לֹמוֹ‏ֹ. Licht: כולמו.

[571] Sukenik: שֹ°°°°. Licht: [ויתרג]שו. DJD: וֹיֹתֹרֹגֹֹשו. Qimron: וֹיתרגֹשו.

[572] Sukenik: לֹ [ ]‏ֹ[ ] לֹ[ ]שׁ. Licht: לֹ[או]שֹ[או]לֹן ואבדון וכו]לֹ. DJD and Qimron: שֹ[או]לֹ[וא]בֹּדֹ[ון ו]כֹּוֹל.

[573] With DJD and Qimron. Licht: [שאול לכול].

13 in the womb of[279] the pregnant one. And she who is pregnant with a sand-viper[280] (suffers) intensive tribulation, and the breakers of the pit for all the works of shuddering. And the

14 foundations of the wall shall tremble like a ship on the surface of the water,[281] and the skies rumble with a roaring[282] sound.[283] And the dwellers of the dust (are)

15 like those who go down to the seas, terrified from the roar of the waters, and their wise ones for them[284] (are) like sailors in the depths, since all their

16 wisdom is swallowed up in the rumblings of the seas, when the depths boil over the sources of the water and are agitated to high waves,

17 and (to) the breakers of water with their roaring sound.[285] And through their agitation they will open Sh[eo]l [...]*bd*[... and] all the arrows of the pit

18 with their movement[286] into the depth, they will make loud their sound[287] and open the gates of [eternity, benea]th the works of[288] a sand-viper.[289]

19 And they shut the doors of the pit before the one pregnant (with) deceit, and the bars of eternity before[290] all the spirits of the sand-viper.[291] (VACAT)

20 (VACAT) I thank you, O Lord, because you redeemed my soul[292] from the pit; and from Sheol-Abaddon

21 you raised me to an eternal height. And I walk continuously in unfathomable[293] uprightness[294] so that I know that there exists hope for (him) whom

22 you fashioned[295] from dust for the eternal assembly. And a confused[296] spirit you purified from great transgression, to be present in rank with

---

[279] Lit. "in the furnace of."

[280] See Isa 30.6, and the discussion in J. H. Charlesworth, *The Good and Evil Serpent*, p. 446.

[281] Lit. "upon the faces of the water."

[282] Or "abundant." Note the paronomasia on "roaring" which can also mean "abundant."

[283] Lit. "voice."

[284] In this passage, למו ("for him") means להם ("for them") as in Isa 44:7.

[285] Or "voice."

[286] Lit. "their marching," "their treads."

[287] Or "voice."

[288] Or "offspring of."

[289] Or "the offspring of the sand-viper." See Isa 30.6, 59.5, and J. H. Charlesworth, *The Good and Evil Serpent,* p. 446.

[290] The deceitful ones and evil spirits are locked in Sheol. The gates are locked before them. They cannot get out of Sheol. The passage does not have the adverb "behind" (אחר).

[291] See notes to 10.30, 13.

[292] Heb. נפש.

[293] Heb. לאין חקר.

[294] Not "in a plain."

[295] The verb יצר. Note the *double entendre*; that is, the inclination of clay was inclined to dust.

[296] From the *nipʿal* of עוה.

23   צבא קדושים ולבוא ביחד עם עדת בני שמים ותפל לאיש גורל עולם עם רוחות

24   דעת להלל שמכה ביחד רנֹהֹ⁵⁷⁴ ולספר נפלאותיכה לנגד כול מעשיכה ואני יצר

25   החמר מה אני מגבל במיֹםֹ ולמי נחשבתי ומה כוח לי כיא התיצבתי בגבול רשעה

26   ועם חלכאים בגורל ותגור נפש אביון עם מהומות רבה והוות⁵⁷⁵ מדהבה עם מצעדי

27   בהפתח כל פחי שחת ויפרשו כול מצודות רשעה ומכמרת חלכאים על פני מים

28   בהתעופֿף כול חצי שחת לאין השב ויורו⁵⁷⁶ לאין תקוה בנפול קו על משפט וגורל אף

29   על נעזבים ומתך חמה ועל⁵⁷⁷ נעלמים וקץ חרון לכול בליעל וחבלי מות אפפו לאין פלט

עַל
30   וילכו נחלי בליעל כול אגפי רום בֿאש⁵⁷⁸ אוכלת בכול שנאביהם⁵⁷⁹ להתם כול עץ לח

31   ויבש מפלגיהם ותשוט בשביבי להוב עד אפס כול שותיהם באושי חמר תאוכל

32   וברקיע⁵⁸⁰ יבשה יסודי הרים לשרפה ושורשי חלמיש לנחלי זפת ותאוכל עד תהום

פ
33   רבה ויבקעו לאבדון נחלי בליעל ויהמו מחשבי תהום בהמון גורשי רש⁵⁸¹ וארץ

34   תצרח על ההווה הנֹהֹיה בתבל וכול מחשביה יריעו⁵⁸² ויתהוללו כול אשר עליה

---

⁵⁷⁴ Sukenik: רֹ ה. Licht: רֹ[נֹ]הֹ.
⁵⁷⁵ Qimron: והוית.
⁵⁷⁶ Ctr. Sukenik, Licht, and Qimron: ויפרו.
⁵⁷⁷ A scribal correction; see DJD 40, p. 151. But the manuscript still has the erroneous ועל. Read: על.
⁵⁷⁸ Sukenik: כֿאש. Licht: אש. Qimron: בֿאש. The square bottom of the *beth* is discernable.
⁵⁷⁹ *Hapex legomenon.* Sukenik in 1948 and 1950: שואביהם, "those who drew from them." See DJD 40, pp. 151–52.
⁵⁸⁰ Sukenik and Licht: וברקוע. Qimron: וברקיֹע
⁵⁸¹ Read: רפש.
⁵⁸² With DJD. Sukenik and Licht: ירועו. Qimron: יריעו.

23 the host of the Holy Ones, and to enter the Community[297] with the congregation of the sons of heaven. And to humankind you cast an eternal lot with the spirits of

24 knowledge to praise your name in common[298] exultation and to recount your wonders before all your creatures. But I am an inclination of[299]

25 the clay. What am I (but clay) mixed with water? And for whom was I considered and what power do I have? For I am present within the border of wickedness,

26 and with the miserable ones in (one) lot. And the soul of[300] the Poor One dwells with great turmoils. And oppressive disasters (are) with my treads,

27 when all the traps of the pit open, and all the nets of wickedness are spread, and a fishing net of the miserable ones (is) on the surface of the water,

28 when all the arrows of the pit fly without return, and are shot without hope, when the measuring-line is cast on the judgment and the lot of anger

29 on the forsaken ones, and the pouring of fury on the hidden ones, and the Endtime of fury for all of Belial, and the bonds of death[301] enclose with no deliverance.

30 And the rivers of Belial pour over[302] all the heightened banks with fire devouring all their growth[303] to annihilate[304] every tree, moist

31 and dry from their streams. And it sweeps with the sparks of[305] fire until[306] all their canals (are) no more.[307] It (the fire) consumes the foundations of clay

32 and the firmament[308] of the dry land, (and) the bases of mountains become a burning, and the sources of[309] flint (turn into) rivers of tar, and it (the fire) consumes as far as the great

33 depth. And the rivers of Belial break forth to destruction, and the designs of the depth roar with the abundance of those who roll up the mud. And the earth

34 cries out about the disaster which has happened in the world, and all its designs wail, and all who are upon it behave madly.

---

[297] Or "to enter together." Heb. יחד.

[298] Possibly a paronomasia on *Yaḥad.*

[299] Heb. יצר.

[300] Heb. נפש.

[301] Or "and the pains of death."

[302] Lit. "walk over."

[303] This noun is a *hapax legomenon*; it is perhaps the *šapʿel* form which denotes "causing growth." See Bardtke in *TLZ* 81 (1956) and 82 (1957).

[304] להתם.

[305] Lit. "with the flames of."

[306] Lit. "until utterly."

[307] Or "until all that drink of them are no more."

[308] See Gen 1:6–8.

[309] Lit. "and the roots of."

35   ויתמוגגו בהווֹה גֹּד[וֹ]לֹֹה[583] כיא ירעם אל בהמון כוחו ויהם זבול קודשו באמת

                   ב

36   כבודו וצבא השמים יתנו קולם וֹיֹתמוגגו[584] וירעדו אושי עולם ומלחמת גבורי

37   שֹמים תשוט בתבל ולֹא תשוֹב עֹד[585] כלה ונחרצה לעד ואפס כמֹוֹה (VACAT)

38   אודכה אדוני כיא הייתה לי לחומת עֹז

39   °°° [כוֹ[ן]לֹֹ[586]   משחיתים וכוֹל [כֹיֹ[587] תסתירני מהווֹת מֹהומהֹ אשֹֹר דֹ°°°[588]

40   דֹ[לֹתֹיֹ[589]   וברי[חֹיֹ][ ][ברזלֹ][590][בל יבוֹא גדוד[591] מֹשֹֹ[מר][592]

41   [[מֹֹ[593] בסביביה פן יוֹרֹה גֹבֹ[ור][594]

Col. 12 [= Sukenik Col. 4 + Frg. 43]
Parallels: 4Q430; 4Q432 Frgs. 7–10; 4Q428 Frg. 6

1   ]

2   [מֹ וֹאֹנֹיֹ בֹתוֹמֹכֹיֹ בֹבֹ[ריתכה[595]

3   [°°מֹוֹ °°°° וֹ מוֹ°°[596]

4   [וֹתֹכֹןֹ[597] עֹל סֹלֹעֹ רגלֹיֹ[598] ותֹסיר פֹֹעֹמֹיֹ מֹ[599]

                ב

5   [בֹֹדֹרֹ[ךֹ[600] עולם ונתיבות אשר בחרתה מֹצֹֹעֹדֹי °°°[601]

---

[583] Sukenik and Licht: גֹ[דו]לה.

[584] Sukenik and Licht: וֹ[ו]יתמוגגו. DJD: וֹיֹתמוגגו.

[585] Sukenik: תשוב עֹד. Licht, DJD, and Qimron: תשוב עד.

[586] Sukenik: לֹ[. Licht: [ותצילני מכו]לֹ. Cf. DJD: לֹ [ ] בֹֹ. Qimron: לֹ[.

[587] Sukenik: °°[וכוֹל. Licht: [שטן כי] וכוֹלֹ.

[588] Sukenik: °°°° ד א. Licht reads only]° א. Qimron: [דֹ אשֹר.

[589] Qimron: [דֹ]לֹ[תֹיֹ. Licht sees only the לֹ.

[590] Frg. 25 provides the word ברזל on this line and provides line 41.

[591] Sukenik: בֹ[יבוא בֹ]ל. Licht: גדוד [יבוא בל. Licht ends the col. here but states there are a few more lines.

[592] I am indebted for this line to DJD. A tear begins the line.

[593] Qimron:]° מֹ.

[594] The bottom of the column is clear on frg. 25, which ends here.

[595] With Sukenik. DJD: [בערמת]מֹ ואני בֹתוֹמכֹי [ב]בֹֹ[בֹ]ריתכה. Cf. 4Q432 frg. 7 line 4. Qimron: [.°° םֹ וֹאֹנֹיֹ בֹתוֹמי הֹ.

[596] With Sukenik. DJD:] °°°[ ] °°° יֹ מֹ קֹֹ[. Qimron: [.° תֹסֹכֹוֹרֹ.

[597] Licht: [ותקם]. Licht does not have lines 1–2. Qimron: ות[קם.

[598] Licht ends his transcription here.

[599] Licht does not read] פֹעֹמֹי. Qimron: [ע]רֹ°° פֹעמי מֹ]רֹ. DJD: פֹֹעֹמי מֹ[דֹרך.

[600] Sukenik: דרך]. Licht: ב]דֹֹרֹך[. Qimron: [להתהלך ב]דֹֹ[ךֹ. [ותעמד רגלי ב.

[601] Sukenik and Licht: °°°מֹ.

35   And they melt away in the gr[e]at disaster, because God thunders with his abundant power, and the habitation of his holiness roars through the truth of

36   his glory. And the host of heaven raised their voice,[310] and the eternal foundations melt away and shake. And the war of the mighty ones of[311]

37   heaven sweeps into the world and does not return until the completion and the extermination for ever. And nothing is like it. (VACAT)

38   (VACAT) I thank you, O Lord, because you became for me a strong city wall[312]

39   °°[... al]l the destroyers and all [...] for you hide me from disasters of turmoil which *d*°°°[...]

40   [... the d]oors of [... and the ba]rs of iron lest the guarding troop should enter

41   accompanied [...]*mm* in its surroundings lest a might[y man] should shoot [...]

Col. 12 [= Sukenik Col. 4 + Frg. 43]
Parallels: 4Q430; 4Q432 Frgs. 7–10; 4Q483 Frg. 6

1   [...]

2   [...]*m*. But I, when I hold fast to [your] co[venant[313] ...]

3   [...]°°°° *mw* °°°° *w mw* °°[...]

4   [...] and you established upon a rock my feet and you removed my footsteps from [...]

5   [...] on the eternal way and on the paths which you chose (for) my treads °°°[....]

[310] A Heb. idiom; see Ps 104:12.
[311] Or "warriors of."
[312] "City wall" is one word in Heb.
[313] See the same expression in 10.23 and 22.14; cf. 12.23 and 15.23.

אⁿ

6 [   ] אודכה אדוני כיֿ האירותה פני לבריתכה ומ[602

7 [603°[   ]ⁿ אדורשכה וכשחר נכון לאור[תיֿ]ⁿ604 הופעתה לי והמה עמכה]

8 בٰאٰ[מרים וב]דٰ̇בٰ̇רٰ̇ים605 החליקו606 למו ומליצי רמיה הٰתٰעٰוٰ̇ם607 וילבטו בלא בינה כיٰא

אⁿ

9 בהולל608 מעשיהם כי נמאסו609 למו ולא יחשבוני בהגבירכה בי כי ידיחני מארצי610

10 כצפٰור מקנה וכול רעי ומודעי נדחו ממני ויחשבוני לכלי אובד והמה מליצי

11 כזב וחוזי רמיה זממו עלי (בٰ̇יٰ)611 בליעל612 להמיר תורתכה אשר שננתה בלבבי בחלקות

12 לעמכה ויעצורו משקה דעת מצמאים ולצמאם ישקום חומץ למעٰ613 הבט אל

מٰ614

13 תעותם להתהולל במועדיה615 להתפש במצודותם כי אתה אל תנאץ כל מחשבת

14 בליעל ועצתכה היא תקום ומחשבת לבכה תכון לנצח והמה נעלמים זמות בליעל

15 יחשובו וידרשוכה בלב ולב ולא נכונו באמתכה שורש פורה רוש ולענה במחשבותם

16 ועם שרירות לבם יתורו וידרשוכה בגלולים ומכשול עוונם שמו לנגד פניהם ויבאו

---

602 Licht: [בוקר עד ערב ומ[עת. Qimron: [ומٰ°.
603 Qimron: [בٰ̇ לٰ בכול].
604 Sukenik: [לאו]רֿתוٰ̇ⁿ. Licht: [לאו]רٰתוⁿ. Qimron: [לٰאור]תוٰ̇ⁿ.
605 The leather is torn and darkened at the beginning of the line. Ctr. DJD: בٰאٰ̇[רים Sukenik: °°[ ]. Qimron: רים[. בٰ̇תٰעٰ̇[ותם ו]בٰ̇דٰ̇בٰ̇רים.
ו]בٰ̇דٰ̇בٰ̇רים.
606 Licht: [החליקו אמ]רים כיא יתעו].
607 Sukenik: °°°°ם. Licht: ם[התעו].
608 The right margin is now certain and continues to the end of this column.
609 Licht: נמאסתי.
610 The left margin is now obvious and continues to the end of the column.
611 The consonants were erased.
612 Two letters are erased at the beginning of the word, perhaps כז (with DJD) or, more likely, בליעל(בי), so that the scribe wrote בי, erased it, and began again, this time including the *lamedh*. The error is easily caused by copying from a text read aloud.
613 An error for למען. Licht: למען.
614 Note the supralinear medial *mem* in the final position.
615 Licht: במועדיהם.

6 [...] (VACAT) I thank you, O Lord, because you enlightened my face for your covenant, and *m*[...]

7 [...]° I seek you. And like the dawn established for per[fect li]ghts,[314] you appeared to me. And they (are) your people[315] [...]

8 in s[ayings and in] words they made smooth for themselves.[316] But the treacherous interpreters[317] led them to err, so that they are ruined[318] without discernment, because [...]

9 in foolishness (are) their works. For they were despised by them; and they do not regard[319] me when you strengthened[320] yourself in me. For they expelled me[321] from my land

10 like a bird from its nest.[322] And all my companions and my acquaintances were expelled from me, and regarded me like a lost vessel.[323] But they are

11 interpreters of the lie and seers of treachery. They plotted with[324] Belial against me, to exchange your Torah[325] which you reiterated in my heart, for smooth things

12 to your people. And they hold back the drink of knowledge from the thirsty; and for their thirst they give them vinegar to drink in order to look at

13 their error, behaving foolishly in their festivals,[326] (then) being caught in their nets. For you, O God, you despise every thought of

14 Belial, and your counsel perseveres;[327] and the thought of your heart is established for perpetuity. And they are hidden; (and) the infamies of Belial[328]

15 they think. And they seek you with a divided heart;[329] and they are not established in your truth. A root sprouting poison and bitterness (is) in their thoughts.[330]

16 And with the stubbornness of their heart, they wander around and seek you through idols. And the obstacle of their iniquity they put before their faces, and they come

---

[314] Cf. Ps 139:12. Or "for brigh[tnes]s."

[315] Or "with you."

[316] See the note to line 15.

[317] See 10.16 ("the interpreters of the error"), 10.33 ("the interpreters of the lie").

[318] *Nipʿal* imperfect. of לבט.

[319] Or "they shall not regard me."

[320] Or "you made mighty."

[321] Heb. ידיחני, which is from יחה, "to push." See Jer 23.12.

[322] Apparently "nest" is the Righteous Teacher's abode in Jerusalem.

[323] Not "broken pot." The author intimates that he alone was expelled from the Temple cult. Notice the contrast to *Some Works of the Torah*, which claims the Righteous Teacher and his group separated from the Temple cult.

[324] I assume an assimilated *beth*. See the scribal correction (בׄ).

[325] Or "Law."

[326] Or "appointed times," "seasons."

[327] Lit. "and your counsel rose up."

[328] Not "the hypocrites" as in DJD. See 10.18–19: "And from the devices of Belial (are) [all] their thoughts."

[329] Lit. "in heart and heart." See 1Chr 12:34 [12:33].

[330] Echoes of Deut 29:17: שרש פרה ראש ולענה.

17   לדורשכה מפי נביאי כזב מפותי תעות והם בל[ו]עٚגᵍ⁶¹⁶ שפה ולשון אחרת ידברו לעמך

18   להולל ברמיה כול מעשיהם כי לא⟧ ⟦בֿחרו בדٛر⟦ך⁶¹⁷ לבٚ⟧⟦כٛה⁶¹⁸ ולא האזינו לדברכה כי אמרו

19   לחזון דעת לא נכון ולדרך לבכה לא היאה כי אתה אל תענה להם⁶¹⁹ לשופטם

20   בגבורתכה [כ]גלוליהם וכרוב פשעיהם למען יתפשו במחשבותם אשר נזורו מבריתכה

21   ותכרת במٚ[שפ]ט כול אנשי מרמה וחוזי תעות לא ימצאו עוד כי אין הולל בכול מעשיך

22   ולא רמיה [ב]מזמת⁶²⁰ לבכה ואשר כנפשכה יעמודו לפניכה לעד והולכי בדרך לבכה

23   יכונו לנצֿח [וא]נٚי⁶²¹ בתומכי בכה אתעודדה ואקומה על מנאצי וידי על כול בוזי כٚיא

24   לא יחשבונٚ[י ע]ٚد⁶²² הגבירכה בי ותופע לי בכוחכה לאורתים⁶²³ ולא טחתה בבושת פני

יחד
25   כול הנדרש[י]ٚםٚ⁶²⁴ לי הנועדים לבריתכה וישומעוני ההולכים בדרך לבכה ויערוכו לכה

26   בסוד קדושים ותוצא לנצח משפטם ולמישרים אמת ולٕא תתעם ביד חלכאים

27   כזוממ למו ותתן מוראם על עמכה ומפץ לכול עמי הארצות להכרית במשפט כול

28   עוברי פיכה ובי האירותה פני רבים ותגבר עד לאין מספר כי הודעתני ברזי

---

⁶¹⁶ Sukenik and Licht: בל[ו]לٚ[ו]עٚגᵍ. DJD: [ב]לٚ[ו]עٚגᵍ. Qimron: בל[ו]עٚגᵍ.
⁶¹⁷ Frg. 43 provides בٚחרו בדרٛ.
⁶¹⁸ Sukenik: [כה]. Licht: שמעו בקול]כه. Qimron: בٛדٛרٛךٛ לב]כٛה . I am indebted here to DJD.
⁶¹⁹ Cf. 4Q430 frg. 1 line 7: בٚ[ה]םٚ.
⁶²⁰ Ctr. DJD and Qimron: בٚמזמת.
⁶²¹ Ctr. DJD: ו]אٚנٚي . Licht: [וא]נٚي.
⁶²² Sukenik: ד[ ] יٚחשבוٚ . Licht: יٚחשבונٚ[י ע]ד . DJD and Qimron: יٚחשבונٚ[י ע]ٚד. The ʿayin is not visible on the images.
⁶²³ Sukenik, Licht, and Qimron: לאורתום.
⁶²⁴ Sukenik and Licht: הנדרש[י]ٚם.

17   to seek you through the mouth of lying prophets tempted (by) error. And they, with a st[am]mering lip and another tongue,[331] speak to your people,

18   in order to turn all their works into treacherous foolishness, because they did not choose the wa[y of] your [heart], and do not listen to your word. For they say

19   concerning the vision of knowledge: "It is not true."[332] And concerning the way of your heart: "It is not this." For you, O God, you shall answer them, judging them

20   with your might [in accordance with] their idols and according to the multitude of their transgressions, in order that they be caught in their thoughts which turn aside from your covenant.

21   And with ju[dgme]nt you shall cut off all the men of deceit; and seers of error shall not be found any more. For there is no foolishness in all your works;

22   and no treachery [in] the devising of your heart. And (those) who are in accordance with you yourself[333] stand before you forever; and the ones who walk continuously in the way of your heart

23   are established for perpetuity. [But] I, when adhering to you, I will[334] be encouraged and I shall rise up against my despisers. And my hands (I shall raise) against all who are scorning me, because

24   they do[335] not regard [me un]til you strengthen[336] yourself in me and appear to me with your power for perfect lights.[337] And you have not smeared with shame the faces of[338]

25   all [those] who seek me, who are assembled together[339] for your covenant. And the ones who walk in the way of your heart listened to me and stand in array for you

26   in the council of the Holy Ones. And you bring forth their judgment for perpetuity and for the upright ones the truth. And you do not mislead them by the hand of the wretched ones,

27   as one who plotted against them. And you put their terror upon your people, and a crushing to all the peoples of the lands in order to destroy with judgment all

28   those who disobey[340] your edict.[341] But through me, you enlightened the faces of many, and you are infinitely[342] mighty, because you allowed me to know the mysteries of

---

[331] Meaning "other words."
[332] Lit. "It is not established."
[333] The Heb. כנפש with suffix has reflexive meaning.
[334] The future tense has a present meaning.
[335] Lit. "shall not." Note the use of the imperfect for continuous action.
[336] Lit. "make mighty."
[337] Note the use of tenses in these lines.
[338] Note the continuous use of "face" in these lines.
[339] Although not the *Yaḥad*; this meaning might have been heard by some Qumranites.
[340] Or "those who transgress." The *nomen regens* is clearly God; it is not the Wicked Priest.
[341] Lit. "your mouth." But this noun has many deep meanings in Qumran poetry.
[342] Or "everlasting," "beyond enumeration."

29 פלאכה ובׄסׄוד פלאכה הגברתה עמדי והפלא לנגד רבים בעבור כבודכה ולׄהודיע

30 לכול החייׄםׄ גׄבורותיכה מי בשר כזאת ומה יצר חמר להגדיל פלאות והוא בעוון

ו ו

31 מרחם ועד שבה באשמת מעל ואני ידעתי כי לא[625] לאנוש צדקה ולא לבן אדם תום

ו

32 דרך לאל עליון כול מעשי צדקה ודרך אנוש לא תכון כי אם ברוח יצר אל לו

33 להתם דרך לבני אדם למעןׄ ידעו כול מעשיו בכוח גבורתו ורוב רחמיו על כול בני

גרמי

34 רצונו ואניׄ רׄעׄד ורׄתׄת אחזוני וכול ירועו וימס לבבי כדונג מ(לׄ)פני אש וילכו ברכי

35 כמים מוגרים במׄורד כי זכרתי אשמותי עם מעל אבותי בקום רשעים על בריתך

36 וחלכאים על דׄברכה ואני אמרתי בפשעי נעזבתי מבריתכה ובזוכרי כוח ידכה עם

37 המון רחמׄיׄכׄהׄ התעודדתי ואקומה ורוחי החזיקה במעמד לפני נגע כי נשענתׄיׄ[626]

38 בחסדיכה וׄבׄהׄמׄון[627] רחמיכהׄ כי[628] תכפר עוון ולטהׄ[ר] אׄנׄוׄש[629] מאשמה בצדקתכה לׄכׄהׄ[א]לׄ[י][630]

39 ולא לאדם כׄוׄל אׄשׄר[631] עשיתה כי אתה בראתה צדיק ורשע ◦◦◦[

40 בׄמׄשׄפׄטׄיׄכׄהׄ בׄיׄחׄד[632] אתחזקה בבריתכה עד [[633]

[625] A different hand (most likely) later added a *matres lectiones* to three examples לא in lines 31 and 32. He probably also added יחד in line 25 and גרמי in line 34. His stylus is blunt and he lacks the skill of a gifted scribe.
[626] Sukenik and Licht: נשענ[תי].
[627] DJD: וׄכׄהמון.
[628] Ctr. DJD בי. Sukenik and Licht: כי. Qimron: כׄי. Note the use of כי in these lines.
[629] Sukenik: ש◦◦◦ [ ] ולט◦. Licht: ולט[הר אנו]ש.
[630] For the last two words I am indebted to DJD. Qimron: [ ]◦◦לׄ.
[631] Sukenik: ◦◦[ ]. Licht: לאדם [לכבוד]כה.
[632] Sukenik: ◦◦[. Licht: [ואני]. Qimron: ◦◦◦◦◦◦[ ].
[633] Licht: עד [מועד פקודתכה ואיחל לטובתכה ולחסד]יכה.

29   your wonder,[343] and with the secret of your wonder you have been mighty with me and the wonder is be-
     fore the Many[344] for the sake of your glory, and to announce

30   to all the living your mighty deeds. What flesh (is) like this? And how can an inclination of[345] clay in-
     crease wonders? For he is in iniquity

31   from the womb,[346] and until old age (he is) in the guilt of infidelity. But, I, I know that righteousness (is)
     neither for the human, nor for the son of Adam[347] (is) the perfection of

32   the way.[348] To God Most High (belongs) all works of righteousness. And the way of the human is not es-
     tablished except through the spirit God formed[349] for him,

33   to complete[350] the way for the sons of Adam,[351] so that they will know all his works through the power of
     his might. And the multitude of his mercies is over all the sons of

34   his will. But I, shuddering and terror grasp me, and all my bones break,[352] and my heart melts like wax
     before the fire, and my knees wobble[353]

35   like water tumbling down[354] a slope. For I remember my guilt[355] with the infidelity of my ancestors,
     when the wicked ones stand against your covenant,

36   and the wretched ones against your words. And I, I said: "In my transgression, I had been forsaken[356]
     from your covenant." But when I remembered the power of your hand with

37   the abundance of your compassions, I was encouraged and stood up, and my spirit was strengthened in
     rank against affliction because I leaned

38   on your mercies and on the abundance of your compassions. For you atone (for) iniquity and puri[fy] the
     human from guilt by your righteousness. For you, [O my G]od,

39   and not for Adam (is) all which you have done, for you, you created the righteous and the wicked °°°[....]

40   By your judgments in the Community, I will be strengthened in your covenant until [...]

---

[343] Note the claim in 1QpHab 7 that God allowed the Righteous Teacher to know "all thy mysteries of the words of his servants, the prophets."

[344] The "Many" is a *terminus technicus* among the followers of the Righteous Teacher.

[345] Heb. יצר. Or "creature of."

[346] The common word for "womb" (רחם) was used in 7.28 and 30; it has not been used since then.

[347] Or "humankind."

[348] Or "the Way."

[349] Heb. יצר. Note again the author's fondness for paronomasia.

[350] להתם; in other passages "annihilate."

[351] Or "humankind."

[352] It is possible that the Wicked Priest broke some of the bones of the Righteous Teacher.

[353] Lit. "walk;" see 16.35.

[354] Lit. "pouring down." See Ezek 7:17 and 21:12. Perhaps "urinating" from fear is implied. See also 16.35.

[355] The noun is a plural: "my guilts." The English is a collective; see "my transgression" in the next line.

[356] I.e., "was distant."

41   [מש]פֿטיכה⁶³⁴ כֹּי אמת אתה וצדֿק כוֹל מֿ[עשיכה⁶³⁵

Col. 13 [= Sukenik Col. 5 + Frg. 29]
Parallels: 4Q428 Frg. 7; 4Q429 Frgs. 1–3; 4Q432 Frg. 11

1   ]

2   ]

3   לֹיוֹם [ז]ֹעֹם חרוֹן]⁶³⁶

4   סליחותיכה והֿמוֹן רֹחֿמ[י]ֹכֿה]   [בֿ⁶³⁷

5   ובדֿעתי אלה נחמ[תי] בֹאֹמֿֿֿתֿכֹה ⁰⁰⁰]   [⁰,⁶³⁸

6   על פי רצונכה ובידֿכה⁶³⁹ מֿשפט כולם⁶⁴⁰ (VACAT)]   [(VACAT)

7   אודכה אדוני כי לא עזבתנֹי בגורי בעם נֹכֹרֿ]   [⁶⁴¹כאשמתי

8   שפטתני ולא עזבתני בזמות יצרי ותעזור משחת חיי ותתֿן לֹי מֿ[פ]לֿט בתוך⁶⁴²

9   לביאים מועדים לבני אשמה אריות שוברי עצם אדירים ושותי דֿם⁶⁴³ גבורים ותשמנֹֹי⁶⁴⁴

10   במגור עם דיגים רבים פורשי מכמרת על פני מים וצידים לבני עֹולה⁶⁴⁵ ושם למשפט

11   יסדתני וסוד אמת אמצתה בלבבי ומזה⁶⁴⁶ ברית לדורשיה ותסגור פי כפירים אשר

---

⁶³⁴ DJD: ⁰⁰⁰⁰⁰[ ]. Qimron: ⁰⁰⁰[ ].

⁶³⁵ With DJD. Sukenik:]ֿ. Licht: [מעשיכה]. The bottom margin is obvious.

⁶³⁶ Sukenik:] ⁰⁰לֹיום עם חד. Licht does not have this line but restores before the first word in the next line: [ובזוכרי רוב]. סליחותיכה. For some letters in the first three lines I am indebted to DJD. Note the scribal corrections in col. 13 (erasures, supralinears, dots).

⁶³⁷ Sukenik:]והֿמוֹן. Licht: רֿחֿמיכה התעודדתי ובהביטי בנפלאותיכה תשתעשע נפשֿי. Qimron: [רֿחמיכה].

⁶³⁸ Sukenik:] ⁰ [נֿחמ]. Licht: נֿחמ]תֿני כי אתה אלי תכלכל את כול מעשיכה ותכינם[על. Qimron: [נהיו] ⁰⁰ [ ]ֿֿ [נֿחמ]תי.

⁶³⁹ Sukenik and Licht: ובי[ד]כה.

⁶⁴⁰ It is probable that the rest of this line is a *vacat*.

⁶⁴¹ Sukenik:] ⁰⁰⁰ בעם. Licht: [כבד עוון וחטא ולוא כפשעי ו]כאשמתי. Qimron: כֿבֿד.

⁶⁴² Sukenik: ⁰[ ] ותתֿן. Licht: [את עבדכה לפליֿ]ֿט בתוך. DJD: פ]לֹֿט בתוך. Qimron: מ]עוז ומפ[לֿט.

⁶⁴³ Sukenik, Licht, and Qimron: [ם]ד.

⁶⁴⁴ DJD reports that four letters can be seen erased in the margin. The black spots in the margin are probably not inscribed letters – the margin, which was lined, was followed judiciously. Black spots also appear earlier in the margin above.

⁶⁴⁵ Qimron: צֹֿולה.

⁶⁴⁶ Sukenik and Licht: ומיה.

41   your [judg]ments, because you (are) truthful, and righteous (are) all [your] w[orks …]

Col. 13 [= Sukenik Col. 5 + Frg. 29]
Parallels: 4Q428 Frg. 7; 4Q429 Frgs. 1–3; 4Q432 Frg. 11

1   […]

2   […]

3   to the day of wrathful [fu]ry […]

4   your forgivenesses and the abundance of your compassion[s …]*b*°

5   and as I know these things, [I am] comforted by your truth °°°[…]°*y*,

6   according to your will; and in your hand (is) the judgment of them all. (VACAT) […] (VACAT)

7   I thank you, O Lord, because you did not abandon me when I lived among an alien[357] people […] according to my guilt

8   you judged me. And you did not abandon me in the infamy of my inclination,[358] but you helped my life (out) from the pit, and you put for me *m*[… del]ivered in the midst of

9   lionesses[359] appointed for the sons of guilt, lions[360] (which are) breakers of bones of the magnificent ones and drinkers of blood of mighty ones.[361] And you placed me

10   in a dwelling with many fishermen[362] who spread a net over the faces of the water, and (with) those who hunt for the sons of deceit. And there for judgment

11   you founded me, and the foundation of truth you encouraged in my heart,[363] and from it (is) a covenant for those who seek it. But you shut the mouths of young lions[364] whose

---

[357] Lit. "foreign." The people's actions have alienated them from God.
[358] Heb. יצר.
[359] Heb. לביאים.
[360] Heb. אריות.
[361] Lit. "warriors."
[362] See Jer 16:16.
[363] The author is fond of paronomasia. Or "you allocated me, and strengthened the secret (or assembly) of truth in my heart."
[364] The author's vocabulary is extensive. He knows many terms for a lion; but he did not use ליש, "lion," though it was known to the genius Isaiah who had an incredibly extensive vocabulary (see Isa 30:6).

12   כחרב שניהם ומתלעותם כחנית חדה חמת תנינים כול מזמותם לחת(ו)ף⁶⁴⁷ יורבו⁶⁴⁸ ולא

13   פצו עלי פיהם כי אתה אלי סתרתני נגד בני אדם ותורתכה חבתה ב[י] עֹֿד⁶⁴⁹ קץ

14   הגלֹות ישעכה לי כי בצרת נפשי לא עזבתני ושועתי שמעתה במרורי נפשי

15   ודנת⁶⁵⁰ יגוני הכרתה באנחתי ותצל נפש עני במעון אריות אשר שננו כחרב לשונם

16   ואתה אלי סגרתה בעד (לֹ)ש(ו)ניהם⁶⁵¹ פן יטרפו נפש(י)עני⁶⁵² ורש ותוסף לשונם

בֹ⁶⁵³

17   כחרב אל תערה בלואֹ⁶⁵⁴ נכר]תֹֿה⁶⁵⁵ נפש עבדכה ולמען הגבירכה לנגד בני אדם הפלתה

18   באביון ותביאהו במצר[ף] כֹֿזֹֿהֹֿב⁶⁵⁶ במעשי אש וככסף מזוקק בכור נופחים לטהֹר שבעתים

19   וימהרו עלי רשעי עמֹים⁶⁵⁷ במצוקותם וכול היום ידכאו נפשי

---

⁶⁴⁷ Sukenik: לחתוף. Either the ink of the *waw* faded or the letter was deliberately erased. See the three erasures in line 16. See Prov 23:28: כחתף; cf. Sir 50:4.

⁶⁴⁸ Sukenik and Licht: וירבו.

⁶⁴⁹ Sukenik: [ ]ֹ ֿז[י]. Licht: ב]י ע[ד.

⁶⁵⁰ One would expect ודנתה.

⁶⁵¹ First a scribe wrote לשונם, "their tongue." Second, he put dots above and below the *lamedh* and then erased them and the *lamedh*. Third, he erased the *waw*. Fourth, he erased part of the final *mem* and left what looks like a *yodh*. Fifth, he added a *he* and final *mem*: (לֹ)ש(ו)ניהם.

⁶⁵² An error for נפש עני. A scribe correctly erased the *yodh*. Sukenik and Licht: נפש.

⁶⁵³ The correction is the text of 4Q429 frg. 1 2.1.

⁶⁵⁴ Sukenik: בלי.

⁶⁵⁵ Sukenik: [תה]. Licht: בלי[א כר]תה. Qimron: בלוֹא [הכ]תֹה.

⁶⁵⁶ Sukenik:]בֹ [ ]ֹ במצֹ. Licht: במצר[ף כז]הֹב.

⁶⁵⁷ Sukenik and Licht: עֹזֹים.

12   teeth (are) like a sword and whose incisors (are) like a sharp spear (with) the poison of dragons;[365] all their devices for snatching are multiplied, but they have not

13   opened their mouth against me, because you, O my God, you hid me from the sons of Adam,[366] and concealed your Torah[367] in [me] until the Endtime

14   when your salvation shall be revealed to me. For in the anguish of my soul[368] you did not abandon me, and you heard my cry for help in the bitterness of my soul;[369]

15   and you adjudicated[370] my grief; (and) you acknowledged (me) when I sighed. And you saved the soul of[371] the Needy One in the den of lions,[372] which sharpen their tongues as a sword.

16   But you, O my God, you shut tight their teeth[373] lest they tear apart the soul of[374] the Needy One and the Wretched One. And you withdrew[375] their tongues

17   like a sword into its sheath,[376] without the soul of[377] your servant [being cut o]ff. And in order to show your might in me[378] before the sons of Adam[379] you set apart

18   the Poor One.[380] And you brought him to the smelting-pot[381] like (fine) gold in the works of fire, and like silver refined in a furnace of the smiths, purifying sevenfold.

19   But the wicked of the peoples hasten[382] against me with their oppressions, and the whole day they crush my soul.[383]

---

[365] The words may also be translated "wrath of crocodiles." The noun, תנינים, denotes the demonic; cf. Ps 91:13 in which "the young lion" and "the dragon (תנין)" are mentioned. See 13.29 "the venom of dragons."

[366] Or "humankind."

[367] Or "Law."

[368] Heb. נפש; this noun denotes the "living principle" in the human. Each time "soul" is translated it denotes *npš*.

[369] Heb. נפש.

[370] *Qal* perfect of דין which basically means "to plead a cause" or "help someone obtain results." The full meaning of the verb is supplied by Qumran Hebrew.

[371] Heb. נפש.

[372] The author may be imagining a situation similar to that portrayed in the book of Daniel.

[373] "Their tongue" appears at the end of lines 15 and 16. A scribe changed "their tongue" to "their teeth." First, he wrote לשונם, "their tongue." Second, he put dots above and below the *lamedh* and then erased them and the *lamedh*. Third, he erased *waw*. Fourth, he erased part of the final *mem* and left what looks like a *yodh*. Fifth, he added a *he* and final *mem*: (ל)ש(ו)ניהם.

[374] Heb. נפש.

[375] The Heb. root is אסף. In Qumran Hebrew the א elides.

[376] In antiquity, artists represented these thoughts by depicting in stone a lion with a sword protruding from his mouth. See the image in Charlesworth, ed., *The Messiah: Developments in Earliest Judaism and Christianity* (Minneapolis, 2009) p. 59, Fig. 5.

[377] Heb. נפש.

[378] Repeatedly the author adds after extreme suffering a confession that such trials reveal God's might in him. See esp. 10.26, 12.9, and 13.27.

[379] Or "humankind."

[380] Lit. "in the poor one." Perhaps the *beth* is a *nota accusativi*.

[381] Or "crucible," "refining-pot;" see Prov 17:3. See also 4.21; cf. 6.15 (a possible restoration).

[382] Notice the meaning of the "present tense" (*waw* consecutive imperfect) to indicate that the author is reliving the moment (if this is a biographical reflection).

[383] Heb. נפש. A *vacat* highlights the transition.

20   ואתה אלי תשיב נַֿפֿשִֿׁי‏⁶⁵⁸ סערה לדממה ונפש אביון פלטתה כצֿפֿוֿ‏[ר מפח‏⁶⁵⁹ ו]כֿטרף‏⁶⁶⁰ מכח‏⁶⁶¹

21   אריות   [   ]   (VACAT)

ברוך אתה‏⁶⁶²
22   אֿוֿדֿכֿהֿ אדוני כי לא עזבתה יתום ולא בזיתה רֿש כי גבורתכה לֿאֿ[ין קֿ]ֿץֿ‏⁶⁶³ וכבודכה

23   לאין מדה וגבורי פלא משר(י)תיכה‏⁶⁶⁴ ועם ענוים בטאטאיי רגליֿכֿ[ה‏⁶⁶⁵ יחד]‏⁶⁶⁶ עם נמהרי

24   צדק להעלות משאון יחד כול אביוני חסד ואני הייתי על עֿ[דני‏⁶⁶⁷ לריב

25   ומדנים לרעי קנאה ואף לבאי בריתי ורגן ותלונה לכול נועדי ו[כול אוֿ]ֿכֿלי‏⁶⁶⁸ לחמי

26   עלי הגדילו עקב ויליזו עלי בשפת עול כול נצמדי סודי ואנשי [ברי]תֿי‏⁶⁶⁹ סוררים

27   ומלינים סביב וברז חבתה בי ילכו רכיל לבני הוות ובעבור הגֿבֿ[ירכה]‏⁶⁷⁰ בֿי ולמען

28   אשמתם סתרת מעין בינה וסוד אמת והמה הוות לבם יחשובֿוֿ [ודברי בֿ]ליעל‏⁶⁷¹ פתחו

---

⁶⁵⁸ נפשי is clearly erased by a scribe. Cf. DJD. Licht does not read נפשי. The correction brings the text in line with 4Q429 frg. 1 2.5.
⁶⁵⁹ For פח, see 10.10, 10.31, and 11.27. See: בהפקה כל פחי שחת. Esp. see Ps 124:7: כצפור נמלטה מפח.
⁶⁶⁰ Sukenik: [   ]טֿרף. Licht: כֿ. Qimron: כצ]דקתכה ותצל נ[טרף. כצֿפֿוֿ]ר מפח ו]כֿטרף.
⁶⁶¹ Ctr. DJD and Qimron: מפי. With Sukenik: מכח. Licht: מבר.
⁶⁶² The scribal corrections should be studied in light of all corrections in this column. Note the significant redaction. The Hodayot formula is erased and replaced with ברוך אתה.
⁶⁶³ Sukenik: [   ]גבורתכה. Licht: לֿאֿ[ין מספר].
⁶⁶⁴ Licht: משרתיכה. With DJD.
⁶⁶⁵ The *yodh* is discernible. The full pronominal form (כה-) appears earlier in the line.
⁶⁶⁶ Sukenik: [   ]רגלי. Licht: רגלי[הם רצונכה].
⁶⁶⁷ Licht: עֿ[וון מת]דֿני. DJD: עֿ[דני. With Sukenik and Qimron.
⁶⁶⁸ DJD and Qimron: גֿם א]וֿכלי.
⁶⁶⁹ Sukenik: [   ]תֿי. Licht: בֿרי[תֿי. DJD: עֿצֿתֿי. Qimron: [עֿ]צֿתֿי.
⁶⁷⁰ With Sukenik. Licht: הגבֿ[ירכה בֿי. DJD: הגֿבֿ[רכה] בֿֿי. Qimron: הגֿי[לכה בֿי. See 9.36; 10.26; 12.9, 24.
⁶⁷¹ Sukenik: [   ]בֿליעל. Licht: [בזמות ב]ליעל. DJD and Qimron: בֿ]ליעל[דֿרֿי. יֿחֿשֿבֿוֿ. Restoration is from 4Q429 frg. 2 line 8.

20 But you, O my God, you turn a thunder-storm[384] into silence,[385] and the soul of[386] the Poor One you delivered like a bir[d from a trap and] like prey from the power of

21 lions. (VACAT) […] (VACAT)

22 Blessed are you,[387] O Lord, because you did not abandon the orphan and did not scorn the Wretched One. For your might (is) with[out en]d[388] and your glory

23 (is) without measure, and the wonderful mighty ones[389] (are) your ministers,[390] and a people (who are) suppressed ones[391] (are) among those who sweep away[392] yo[ur] footprints[393] [together][394] with those who are eager for

24 righteousness to rise from the tumult together (with) all the poor ones of mercy. And I, I on account of ʿ[…]dny for strife

25 and contention to my companions, jealousy and anger to those who enter into covenant (with) me,[395] and murmuring and complaint to all my assembled ones.[396] And [all those who a]te my bread

26 have lifted up the heel against me;[397] and all those bound to my council[398] have defamed me with deceitful lips.[399] And the men in [covena]nt (with) me[400] are rebellious

27 and complain round about. And because[401] you concealed the secret in me,[402] they go slandering to the sons of disaster. And for the sake of showing [your] mig[ht] in me, and because of

28 their guilt you hid the fountain of discernment and the secret of truth. But they think (only about) the desires[403] of their heart. [And the words of Be]lial have opened

---

[384] Lit. "storm."

[385] A scribe changed the text from "revived my soul (and) turned storm into silence." The author is obsessed with God's might revealed in his suffering.

[386] Heb. נפש.

[387] A scribe replaced "I thank you" with "blessed are you."

[388] Lit. "without endtime."

[389] Or "warriors," "heroes."

[390] Heb. משר(י)תיכה; the noun is not to be confused with the more familiar "your servants."

[391] Or "needy ones," "poor ones." The Righteous Teacher reflects on how he and his followers were "suppressed" by the illegitimate priests.

[392] See Isa 14:23.

[393] Lit. "yo[ur] feet."

[394] Heb. יחד.

[395] Lit. "those who enter into my covenant." The author's covenant is founded in God's covenant. Most likely a strong personality is indicated.

[396] Or "appointed ones." Note the paronomasia with line 24.

[397] See Ps 41:10 [41:9]. Also see Jn 13:18.

[398] Notice "my council." The author is most likely the Righteous Teacher.

[399] See Prov 4:24.

[400] Note the lit. "in my [covena]nt." That rendering would misrepresent the author's loyalty to God's covenant.

[401] Lit. "And by," or "And with."

[402] The author's adversaries could thus not know that God had given the author "the secret."

[403] In this line, the Hebrew הוות is from the first meaning of that noun, and denotes "desire" and "capriciousness." It is not to be confused with its use elsewhere, meaning "disaster."

29 לשון שקר כחמת תנינים פורחת לקצים וכזוחל עפר יורו לחתו[ף מבלגות]⁶⁷² פתנים

30 לאין חבר ותהי לכאיב⁶⁷³ אנוש ונגע נמאר בתכמי עבדכה להכשי̊ל [רו]ח̊⁶⁷⁴ ולהתם

31 כוח לבלתי החזק מעמד וישיגוני במצרים לאין מנוס ולא בהבדל[ ] מ̊מ̊[ ]ש̊פחות⁶⁷⁵ ויהמ̊ו

32 בכנור ריבי ובנגינות יחד תלונתם עם שאה⁶⁷⁶ ומשואה זלעופות [ ]א̊חזוני [ ]וחבלים כצירי⁶⁷⁷

33 יולדה ויהם עלי לבי קדרות לבשתי ולשוני לחך⁶⁷⁸ תדבק כ̊י̊ סבבוני [[בהוות⁶⁷⁹]] לבם ויצרם⁶⁸⁰

34 הופיע לי למרורים ויחשך מאור פני לאפלה והודי נהפך למשחי̊ר⁶⁸¹   ואת⁶⁸² אל̊י

35 מרחב פתחתה בלבבי ויוספוה⁶⁸³ לצוקה וישוכו בעדי בצלמות ואוכלה בלחם̊ אנחתי⁶⁸⁴

36 ושקוי בדמעות אין כלה כי עששו מכעס עיני ונפשי במרורי יום אׄנחה⁶⁸⁵ ויגון̊ ⁶⁸⁶

---

⁶⁷² Sukenik: [   ] לח̊°°. Licht: [לחתו̊ם ורואש. DJD: מ̊[בלגות] לחתו[ף. Qimron: לחתו[ף מבלגית. Cf. 4Q429 frg. 3 line 10: לחתוף מבלגות.

⁶⁷³ With Sukenik and Licht. Cf. DJD and Qimron: לכאוב.

⁶⁷⁴ Sukenik: [   ] להכשי̊ל. Licht: [להכש]יל רוח. DJD: ח̊[רו] להכשי̊ל. Qimron: [רוח] להכשיל.

⁶⁷⁵ Sukenik and Licht: [פחות ויהמו] מנוס ולא בהב. DJD: מ̊מ̊ש̊פחות בהבד̊ל ולא. Qimron: מ̊א̊נחות בהבדל ולא. The word מ̊מ̊ש̊פחות appears on frg. 29, which begins here, supplies the two mems and supplies the word א̊חזוני in line 32 and the word בהוות in line 33.

⁶⁷⁶ שואה = שאה.

⁶⁷⁷ Sukenik: וחבלים [   ] זלעופות. Licht: [אחזוני] וחבלים כצירי זלעופות. DJD and Qimron follow 4Q429.

⁶⁷⁸ Schuller astutely notes that the text seems to have been corrected from לחכי, the reading in 4Q429 frg. 3 line 4.

⁶⁷⁹ Frg. 29 ends here.

⁶⁸⁰ Sukenik: כ[יא] נב°°[   ] תדבק. Licht: לבם ויצרם מהוות נב]הלתי[כ[יא. תדבק

⁶⁸¹ Sukenik: למשחור. Licht and DJD: למשחית.

⁶⁸² An error for אתה.

⁶⁸³ Licht: ויוספיה.

⁶⁸⁴ Sukenik, Licht, and Qimron: אנחה. Cf. 4Q429 frg. 3 line 7: אנחה.

⁶⁸⁵ Sukenik: [   ]תח. Licht: [א][נחון]ת. Cf. 4Q429 frg. 3 line 8: אנחה.

⁶⁸⁶ An error; the scribe began to write יסובבוני that begins the next line. See 4Q429 frg. 3 line 8.

29   a deceitful tongue[404] like the venom of dragons,[405] shooting forth[406] to their borders.[407] And like the reptiles of dust[408] they spit, to lay ho[ld of the poison of] cobras

30   that cannot be charmed. And it becomes a severe pain and a festering affliction[409] in the entrails of your servant, making [the spir]it fail, and annihilating[410]

31   power so as not to stand firm. And they reached me in straits with no escape (for me),[411] and not distinguishing among the parts. And they sounded forth

32   my dispute on the lyre, and on musical instruments together their complaints. With storm[412] and raging destruction they seized me, and tribulations like pains of

33   a woman giving birth (overwhelmed me). And my heart grumbles against me. (With) darkness I am clothed, and my tongue cleaves to (my) palate,[413] since I am surrounded by the desires of their heart, and their inclination

34   appeared to me as bitterness, and the light of my face is darkened into gloominess,[414] and my majesty is turned into blackness.[415] But you, O my God,

35   you opened a spacious place in my heart. But they added distress (to) it and hedged me (with thorns)[416] in the shadow of death.[417] And I ate with the bread of my sighing,[418]

36   and (with) the drink of tears without end. For my eyes are dimmed from anger and my soul[419] by the bitterness of[420] the day. Sighing[421] and grief

---

[404] Lit. "a lying tongue," but see Prov 20:17. The snake is the consummate trickster in some biblical passages; see Gen 3:13.

[405] Heb. תנינים.

[406] This word is פרח in the *qal* participle (plural). The Hebrew verb means literally "blooming," "flourishing," "floating (in the air)."

[407] Lit. "for their endtimes."

[408] Lit. "crawling (in) the dust."

[409] See the note to the Composite Text.

[410] להתם.

[411] See the more familiar "without escape."

[412] Read: שואה.

[413] See 4Q429 frg. 3 line 4, "to my palate."

[414] Two different words are used for "darkness." Note the author's fondness for paronomasia. That skill allows him to resonate with meaning and echo previous or future reflections (when read repeatedly).

[415] These obscure comments make pellucid sense if the author is the Righteous Teacher who lost his powers in the Temple as the non-Aaronite Hasmonean priests received full authority when Simon was empowered by the Jewish people. They take on special meaning when one reflects that the Righteous Teacher may have served as High Priest during the period when no official priest was recognized even though a high priest was demanded by the Temple services, especially on the Day of Atonement. A small *vacat* appears here. It indicates a transition.

[416] See Hos 2:8 [2:6]. Contrast the use of שוד in 16.12.

[417] An echo of Ps 23:4.

[418] Cf. 4Q429 frg. 3 line 7: "sighing."

[419] Heb. נפש.

[420] A plural that cannot be represented in English, but one needs to observe that the author's bitterness is multiple.

[421] Cf. 4Q429 frg. 3 line 8: "sighing."

37   יסובבוני ובושת על פנים ויהפך לי לחׄמׄי[687] לריב ושקוי לבעל מדנים ויבוא בעצמׄי[688]

38   להכשיל רוח ולכלות כוח כרזי[689] פשע משנים מעשי אל באשמתם כי נאסׄרׄתׄי[690] בעבותים

39   לאין נתק וזקים ללוא ישוברו וחומת עׄוׄׄן[   ]וׄבריחי[691] ברזל ודלתי[692]

40   [כׄלׄאי[693] עם תהום נחשבתׄיׄ לאין [694]   ]ׄׄ[

41   [בׄלׄיׄעל[695] אפפו נפשי לאׄיׄן [פ]לׄ[ט[696]

Col. 14 [= Sukenik Col. 6 + Frg. 26]
Parallels: 4Q428 Frg. 8; 4Q429 Frg. 4

1   ]

2   ]

3   ]

4   עׄבׄדכה[697]ׄׄׄ

5   לבי בנאצות בׄפׄין[698]

6   ואתה אלי[700]   והווה[699] לאין חקר כלה לאׄיׄן[מספר

7   [702]ׄׄׄ[גליתה אוזני [למו]סׄר[701] מוכיחי צׄדק עם[

8   [אשׄמׄה[704]   מעדת שׄוׄא[703] ומסוד חמס ותביאני בעצת הקודש [

---

687 Sukenik: לׄׄי ל[. Licht: ל[חמי ל]ריב.
688 Sukenik: בעצׄׄ. Licht: בעצ[מי].
689 Licht: ברזי.
690 Sukenik: נאסׄׄר.
691 Sukenik: עׄ]ח בל תזוע ו[בעדי]בריחי[. Licht: עׄוׄן[ ]בריחי. DJD: וׄבריחי[ ]עון.
692 Licht: ודלתון[ת נחושת בל ישברו. DJD: ודלתי[נחושת לאין[.
693 Sukenik: לאי[. Licht: יא]לך.
694 Licht: [מנוס].
695 Sukenik: [לׄעל. Licht: לעׄיׄלׄב[. DJD: ונחלי ב]ליעל[ ]ילחנון.
696 Sukenik:]ל. Licht: ל[אין פלט. With DJD and Qimron; see 11.29: אפפו לאין פלט.
697 DJD and Qimron did not report these consonants.
698 Sukenik:]ׄׄׄ בנאצׄ. DJD: בנאצות בפׄי[. Qimron: בנאצות בפין[.
699 Licht begins with this word. Qimron: והויה.
700 Licht: [ואתה אלי כיא בהסדיכה עבדך נפש פדיתה אלי ואתה מ]ׄד[ה. DJD:]אלי ואתה. Qimron: אתה אלי מׄ]ד[ה.
701 Sukenik:]ׄסׄ[. Licht: [למו]סר. DJD: בׄמׄ[ון]סׄר. Qimron: בׄ[מון]סׄׄר.
702 Licht: [חזון מליצי דעת ותצילני].
703 Sukenik:]א[. Licht: [שו]א. With DJD.
704 Licht: מאשמה [ותטהרני מעוון ותזקקני אמתכה בני]. DJD:אשמה[ ]ׄ[ ]ׄׄׄ הׄקׄוׄדׄש. Qimron: אשמה ב]נׄׄׄׄ. הׄקׄׄודׄׄשׄׄ[.

146

37   surround me, and shame (is) over (my) face. And my bread is turned for me into a dispute, and my drink into an owner of confrontations.[422] And it enters my bones

38   to make the spirit fail and to annihilate power, as the mysteries of transgression are altering the works of God with their guilt. For I was bound with ropes

39   (that) cannot be cut off,[423] and (with) chains (that) cannot be broken, and a strong wall [....] And bars of iron and doors [...]

40   [...]. My prison with the depths is considered without [...]°° [....]

41   [...] Belial encompasses[424] my soul without [es]ca[pe ...]

Col. 14 [= Sukenik Col. 6 + Frg. 26]
Parallels: 4Q428 Frg. 8; 4Q429 Frg. 4

1   [...]

2   [...]

3   [...]

4   °°° your servant [...]

5   my heart (is) in disgrace in my mouth [...]

6   and unfathomable[425] disaster, destruction without [numbering.... But you, O my God,]

7   have uncovered[426] my ear [for the disci]pline of those reproved for righteousness with [...]°°°

8   from the congregation of vanity and the assembly of violence, and you brought me into the council of[427] holiness [...]° guilt.

---

[422] See Prov 23:29 and Jer 15:10: "a man of confrontation."

[423] The specificity and odd language may suggest that the author literally remembers being bound with ropes. He may not be speaking metaphorically. Biblical heroes do not lament that they are bound with ropes. Of course, Samson was bound with ropes but easily broke them (Judg 16:11–12, cf. 15:13–14).

[424] Notice the echo of previous references to being "surrounded."

[425] Heb. ‏לאין חקר‎.

[426] Or "you have revealed."

[427] Note the diverse terms for a gathering: "congregation," "assembly," and "council." See the consistency chart in the Introduction.

9 ואדעה כי יש מקוה לשבי פשע ועוזבי חטאה בה] ולהתהלֹךֹ[705

10 בדרך לבכה לאין עול ואנחמה על המון עם ועל שאוֹן מ[מל]כות706 בהאספם [כי יד]עתי707 אשר

11 תרים למצער מחיה בעמכה ושארית בנחלתכה ותזקקם להטהר מאשמה [ומח]טֹוא708 כול

12 מעשיהם באמתכה ובחסדיך709 תשפטם בהמון רחמים ורוב סליחה וכפיכה להורותם

13 וכישור710 אמֹתכה להכינם בעצתכה לכבודכה ולמענכה עשי[תה] לגֹֹדֹל תורה ו[אמת] להֹיֹחֹד711

14 אנשי עצתכה בתוך בני אדם לספר לדורות עולם נפלאותיכה ובגבורות[יכה יש]וֹחֹוֹ712

15 לאין השבת וידעו כול גוים אמתכה וכול לאומים כבודכה כי הביאותֹהֹ[   ]סֹודכה713

16 לכול אנשי עצתכה ובגורל יחד עם מלאכי פנים ואין מליץ בנים לק[דושיכה ות]שֹׁיֹֹב714

17 פריו715 כי כֹ[ו]ֹל [עֹ]צֹתכֹה בפיֹ716 והם ישובו בפי717 כבודכה718 ויהיו שריכה בגור[ל   ]719

18 פרח כצי[ץ השדה ע]ֹד720 עולם לגל721 נצר לעופי722 מטעת עולם ויצֹל צל על כול תבֹ[ל ודליותי]וֹ723

---

705 Sukenik: התהלך[.Licht: [. התהלך כי לאביון ותוחלה רחמיכה מון בה]. DJD: ולֹהתהלך[. Qimron: וֹבֹהתהלך[.

706 Sukenik: נות[מֹ. With Licht. DJD: מֹמֹלכות. Qimron: מֹמֹלכות.

707 Sukenik: עתי[   ]. Licht: [כי יד]עתי. DJD: [ליֹשֹ]ֹעֹתי. Qimron: [מד]עתי.

708 DJD: ומח[טֹוא]. Qimron: ולֹה[בֹיא].

709 Note the two different ways of representing the 2ms suffix in contiguity.

710 Sukenik and DJD: וכיֹשיר. Licht: וכיישור.

711 Sukenik: [ל]לֹ   . Licht: [ל תורה ו]ל. DJD: ל[גד]ל תורה ו[אמת ולסתר את]. Qimron: לגֹדֹל תורה ו[נח] כֹבֹוֹֹד   ֹלֹ . לגֹדֹל תורה ולֹ[נח]ֹ.

712 Sukenik: ֹֹֹחֹחו [יֹכֹה]ֹֹֹֹובגבורות.

713 Sukenik: [   ]ֹודכה. Licht: [בֹודכה כ]את. DJD: סֹודכה[   ]ֹ. Qimron: סֹודכה[   ].

714 See 13.20. Sukenik: שֹיב[לק] with Licht. DJD and Qimron: לֹהֹשיב[לק].

715 The leather is not abraded here; פריו is relatively clear. It fits the context which in 14.17–19 concerns "blossoming like the flo[wers]," "grow a shoot," "planting," and "clou[ds]." רוח does not appear in these lines. Sukenik: [תד ֹבֹה]ֹ לֹ[ ]כֹ ֹ ֹ ֹ]כרו. Licht: כי פריו ֹ ֹ תד[בֹה   ]. כֹרוֹחֹ כי לֹ[ן]ֹ תֹדֹ בם. DJD: ֹֹ תֹד ֹֹבֹ   ֹ[לֹ] [תֹד]ֹֹבֹ ֹ]ֹ כרוֹח פי. Qimron: כֹרוֹח בֹה[   ]תֹד[ ]לֹ[ ]ֹ תֹד בם.

716 בפי looks like בפב.

717 Probably a mistake for כפי. The פה does appear with כ. כ and ב are often confused paleographically.

718 Echoes of Isa 40:5: פי יהוה ... כבוד יהוה.

719 Sukenik: בגור[ל   ]ֹ. Licht: [בגור]ל עולם וירבו]. DJD: בגור]ל עולם וגזעֹֹם]. Qimron: ויעש[ל]ֹ.

720 Sukenik: [ד   ]ֹ כצֹ. Licht: [כצי]ץ השדה ע]ד. DJD: [כצי]ץ יציץ לֹ[ה]ֹֹֹד. Qimron: כצי]ץ השדה ע]ד. The thought echoes Isa 40:6: כציץ השדה.

721 Read: לגדל.

722 Licht: לעיפי.

723 With Sukenik. Licht: עד [לויותי]ו ֹֹ[בֹל ת]כול. DJD: [ליותי]ו זֹדֹ[בֹל תֹֹ כול. Qimron: וצמרת]ו [בֹל תֹ כול.

9   And I know that there is hope for those who return from transgression and (for) those who abandon sin *bh*[…] and walk continuously

10 in the way of your heart without deceit. And I will be comforted over the multitude of[428] people and over the uproar of ki[ngd]oms when they gather, [because] I [kn]ow that

11 you raise the few who live among your people and a remnant among your inheritance. And you refined them so they are purified from guilt [and s]in. All

12 their works (are) in your truth, and in your mercies you shall judge them with the multitude of compassions and much forgiveness. And according to your edict,[429] teaching them

13 and according to the straightness of your truth establishing them in your council for your glory. And for your sake [you have] acted to magnify the Torah[430] and [truth][431] to make one[432]

14 the men of your council among the sons of Adam,[433] to recount for the eternal generations your wonders. And about [your] mighty deeds they [con]template

15 without ceasing. And all peoples[434] shall know your truth and all nations your glory. For you brought […] your secret

16 to all men of your council, and together with[435] the angels of the presence and without an intermediate interpreter[436] for [your] Ho[ly Ones. And you shall] bring back[437]

17 his fruits,[438] for a[l]l of your [co]unsel (is) in my mouth.[439] And they, they shall come back according to your glory, and they shall become your princes[440] in the lo[t of …]

18 is blossoming like the flow[ers of[441] the field unt]il eternity to grow a shoot to (become) the thick-foliage[442] of the eternal planting. And it will cast a shadow over all the worl[d and] its [high-branches]

---

[428] Or "roar." Note paronomasia.

[429] Lit. "your mouth."

[430] Or "Law."

[431] There is space for three consonants and one space. See "your truth" at the beginning of the line.

[432] Not seen by previous editors. See 1QS 1.8.

[433] Or "humankind."

[434] גוים denotes Jews and non-Jews. Notice the surprising universalism.

[435] Note also the presence of angels in the *Yaḥad*.

[436] Lit. "the official go-between."

[437] *Hipʿil* imperfect of שוב. Lines 16–18 contain echoes of the well-known and influential images in Isa 40, which was the key passage for self-knowledge at Qumran (See 1QS 8.12–15).

[438] The word, "his fruits," was misread by some previous editors; it seems clear.

[439] The manuscript is torn and the ink difficult to read.

[440] For the *Hipʿil* of שוב with "princes" (נדיבים), see Ps 113:8.

[441] The Heb. ציץ is a collective noun.

[442] The noun is plural in the Hebrew; an Aramaism. See also 4Q302 frg. 2 2.7, 11.2.

19 עד שׁחֹקֹי[ם ו]שׁרשׁיו⁷²⁴ עד תהום וכול נהרות עדן [תלחלחנה⁷²⁵ ד]ל[י]ותיו⁷²⁶ והיה לי[מים לאין]⁷²⁷

20 חקר והֹתֹאֹזרו עֹל⁷²⁸ תבל לאין אפס ועֹד שאול [ו]היה⁷²⁹ מעין אור למקור

21 עולם לאין הסר⁷³⁰ בשביבי נוגהו יבערו כול בנֹ[י עולה והיו]⁷³¹ לאש בוערת בכול אנשי

22 אשמה עד כלה והמה נצמדי תעודתי פותו במלֹ[יצי תעות להב]ִֹיא זֹר⁷³² בעבודת צדק

23 ואתה אל צויתם להועיל מדרכיהם בדרך קֹ[ודש אשר ילכו]⁷³³ בה וערל וטמא ופריץ

24 בל יעוברנה ויתמוטטו מדרך לבכה ובהווֹת פֹ[שעם יכשלֹ]וֹ⁷³⁴ וכמואֹ⁷³⁵ יועִץ⁷³⁶ בליעל

25 עם לבבם[ויכֹ]נֹוֹ⁷³⁷ מחשבת רשעה יתגוללו באשמה וֹ[אני היֹ]תֹי⁷³⁸ כמלח באוניה בזעף

26 ימים גליהֹם וכול משבריהם עלי המו רוח עועיים[באין]⁷³⁹ דממה להשיב נפש ואין

27 נתיבת⁷⁴⁰ לישר דרך על פני מים ויהם תהום לאנחתי ונֹגֹשׁ[ו חיי]⁷⁴¹ עֹד⁷⁴² שערי מות ואהיה

ש
28 כבא בעיר מצור ונעוז בחומה נ(ס)(ס)גבה עד פלט ואשׁעֹ[נה]⁷⁴³ בֹאמתכה אלי כי אתה

⁷²⁴ Sukenik: [שרשיו]°°°ש. With Licht. DJD and Qimron (with different diacritics): שׁחֹקֹיֹם ושרשיו.

⁷²⁵ Cf. 4Q428 frg. 8 line 4: [ת.לחלחנה.

⁷²⁶ Sukenik: [ל[ ]ותיו. Licht: [ד]ל[י]ותיו. DJD: עדן [ישקו את ד]ל[י]ותיו. Qimron: [ת.ל]חלחנה ד]ל[י]ותיו. תשתינה ד]ל[י.

⁷²⁷ Ctr. DJD and Qimron: [לאין]. Licht: [ל והיה. Sukenik: [ל והיה. For the restoration, see 16.18: ולימים לאין חֹקֹר. והיה לימֹים ל[ואין. ולנהר ירום] על :Qimron. ולנהר ליֹ[ואבל לאין].

⁷²⁸ Sukenik: על°°°° חקר [ ]°°רו :Qimron. חקר והֹתֹאֹזרו על[ולנהר ירום. We follow DJD: חקר [ולנהר ירום] על. Licht: [חקר.

⁷²⁹ Licht: והיה ו[.

⁷³⁰ Ctr. DJD: חסר.

⁷³¹ Sukenik: [   ]בֹ. Licht: בנ[י עולה והיה]. See 4Q429 frg. 4 1.5.

⁷³² Ctr. DJD and Qimron: במלֹ[יצי תעות ל]הֹבֹיֹא זֹ. Sukenik: [ ]°° במ[. Licht: במח[שבתם לא להתאזר.

⁷³³ Ctr. DJD and Qimron: קֹ[וֹדֹש אשר ילכו]. With Licht.

⁷³⁴ Licht: [גדולה]ובהווה. With DJD. Qimron: ובהוֹוֹת. See 15.8.

⁷³⁵ Sukenik and Licht: יכמוא.

⁷³⁶ Sukenik and Licht: ויעץ.

⁷³⁷ Sukenik: °°[ ]°°. Licht: ם[וֹן]לֹ.

⁷³⁸ Sukenik: תֹי[. Licht and Qimron: [ואני היֹ]תֹי. See 4Q429 frg. 4 2.1.

⁷³⁹ Licht: [לאין].

⁷⁴⁰ An error for נתיבות. See Licht: נתיבות.

⁷⁴¹ With DJD.

⁷⁴² Ctr. Qimron: ונֹגֹאֹה [נפשי] עד. Sukenik: [ ]וֹ. Licht: עד ונ[פשי תגיע.

⁷⁴³ With DJD and Qimron: ואשׁעֹ[נה]בֹאמתכה. Ctr. Sukenik. Ctr. Licht: ואש[מחה ב]אמתכה.

19 (will be) unto the skie[s and] its roots unto the deep. And all the rivers of Eden[443] [will moisten] its [hig]h-br[an]ches, and will become w[aters that are un]fathomable[444]

20 and streaming over the world without end, and unto Sheol [… and] the fountain of light will become an eternal

21 source, (which) cannot be removed.[445] In the sparks of its flames will burn all the sons of dece[it, and they (the sparks) will become] a burning fire in all the men of

22 guilt until (their) annihilation. And they, the ones bound by my testimony, they were tempted by the [erring] interpret[ers to bri]ng a stranger into the service of righteousness.

23 But you, O God, you ordered[446] them to benefit from their ways in the way of holi[ness] in [which th]ey walk; but the uncircumcised and the impure and the brigand

24 will not pass over it. And they have fallen away from the way of your heart, and in the disasters of[447] [their] tran[sgression] they [stumble], and (are) like a counselor of[448] Belial

25 with their heart. [And] they [prep]ared a wicked thought; they will wallow constantly in guilt. And [I,] I [was] like a sailor in a boat (when) in raging

26 seas their waves and all their breakers roar over me (as) a twisting[449] wind [with no] silence to restore[450] the soul;[451] and there are no

27 paths[452] to straighten a way over the face of the waters. And the depth roars to my sighing, and [my life] approach[ed] unto the gates of death. And I am[453]

28 like one who enters a fortified city and finds shelter[454] behind[455] a high[456] city wall until delivered.[457] And I will lea[n on] your truth, O my God, because you,

---

[443] See the note to 16.21.

[444] Heb. לאין חקר. See 5.16, 11.21, 14.6. See Job 5:9, 9:10.

[445] See *OdesSol* 4.1: "No man can pervert Thy holy place, O my God; Nor can he change it, and put it in another place" (ܠܐ ܐܢܫ ܡܫܚܠܦ ܐܬܪܟ ܩܕܝܫܐ ܐܠܗܝ ܘܠܐ ܡܫܟܚ ܕܢܫܚܠܦܝܘܗܝ ܘܢܣܝܡܝܘܗܝ ܒܐܬܪ ܐܚܪܢܐ).

[446] Or "you commanded," "you gave an order."

[447] Or "in the desires of." Notice the paronomasia.

[448] See Isa 9:5. Note the paronomasia between "counselor" and "council" (e.g. in 14:8, 14, and 16).

[449] עועיים, from עוה, which in the *nip'al* means "to be agitated," and in the *pi'el* "to twist."

[450] Lit. "to bring back."

[451] Heb. נפש.

[452] From נתיבה, "path." See Prov. 8:2.

[453] This verb is another example of the imperfect tense used as a continuous present.

[454] *Nip'al* of עוז (not in biblical Hebrew).

[455] Heb. ב.

[456] *Nip'al* of שגב. Or "inaccessible."

[457] Or "escape."

29   תשים סוד[744] על סלע וכפיס על קו משפט ומשקלת אמ[ת ל]ל[ע]שׂות אבני בחן לב[נ]ית[745]

30   עוז ללוא תתזעזע וכול באיה בל ימוטו כי לא יבוא זר [בשע]ריה[746] דלתי מגן לאין

31   מבוא ובריחי עוז ללוא ישוברו בל יבוא גדוד בכלי מלחמתו עם[747] תום כול חצׄי[748]

32   מלחמות רשעה ואז תחיש חרב אל בקץ משפט וכול בני א[מ]תו יעורו לה[כ]ר[ית][749]

33   רשעה וכול בני אשמה לא יהיו עוד וידרוך גבור קשתו ויפתח מצׄורי השׁׄמיׁׄם[750]

34   למרחב אין קץ ושערי עולם להוציא כלי מלחמות ויעצׄו[מ]ו מקצׄה עד קצׄה[751]ו וחׄצים

35   יירו וא[י]ׄן[פׄלט[752] ליצר אשמה לכלה ירמוסו ואין שׄא[ר]י[ת ו[אין] תׄקׄוׄה ברוב פׄגׄרׄים[753]

36   ולׄכׄוׄל גבׄוׄרׄי מלחמת אין מנוס כי לאל עליון הכׄ[וח   ]ר[754]

37   וׄשׄוׄכׄבׄי עפר הרימו תרן ותולעת מׄתים נשאו נס להורות[מ][755] רשעים נ[תׄיבתׄם[756] רשׄעׄה[757]

38   במלחמות זדים ובעבור[758] שוט שוטף בל יבׄוא בׄמבצר[   ][759] ל[בׄ][760]

---

[744] Ctr. 4Q429 frg. 4 2.7: סודי.

[745] Sukenik: לֹ[נ]טׄות Qimron: אמ[ת ל]ל[ע]שׂות אבני בחן לבנית לֹבׄנׄיׄת. Licht: [חומת לבנית]א. DJD: אמ[ת לנט]ות אבני בחן לבנ[ת. א[ל]ל[ ]ות אבני בחן לב[י]ׄת[   ]. אבני בחן לפנית.

[746] Sukenik:]יה[   ]ׄ. Licht: [בדלת]יה. DJD: זר בׄשׄׄעׄׄריה. Qimron: זר בׄש[ע]ריה.

[747] Ctr. 4Q429 frg. 4 2.12: עד.

[748] Sukenik:]ׄח. Licht: ח[צׄי].

[749] Sukenik:]ׄל יעורו אׄ[מ]ׄתו[א]. Licht: יעורו ל[הכניע]א. DJD: א[מ]ׄתו יעורו לה[כׄר[ית]. Qimron: אמׄתו יעורו לה[כׄר[ית].

[750] Sukenik: [מצור]ׄמׄ. Licht: מצור [עולם]. DJD: מצור השׁׄמׄיׄם. Qimron:]ׄ מצׄׄוׄׄר[.

[751] Sukenik: עד מקצה]ׄ. ויעצון[ם] With Licht. DJD and Qimron: [ם]וׄחׄצׄי עד קצה וׄיעצׄומׄו מקצה עד קׄצׄה. ויׄעׄצׄׄוׄׄמׄׄוׄׄ.

[752] Sukenik: לׄטׄ[   ]ׄ. Licht: [פ]לט פׄ לאין מרץ וחבלי [קצה]. DJD: פׄלט וׄאׄ[ין יורו. Qimron: פלט וׄאׄ[ין יׄוׄרׄוׄ. For כוח, see line 36. For כוחכה, see 17.14: ותוחלה ברוב כוחכה, "and expectation in the abundance of your power."

[753] See 24.17. Sukenik: ברוב תקוה[   ]ׄ שׄ ואין[. Licht: [חסדיכה] תקוה ברוב ותׄי לׄדל[תקוה ואׄיׄן שׄאׄׄרׄׄית. DJD: פׄגׄׄרׄׄים ברוב תקוה ואׄׄיׄׄןׄ שׄרׄׄׄיׄׄׄת. Qimron: שׄׄׄׄׄרׄׄׄׄׄׄׄית. For כוה, see line 36. For כוחכה, see 17.14: ותוחלה ברוב כוחכה, "and expectation in the abundance of you power." גבׄורׄים ברׄוב תקוה ואׄׄׄיׄׄׄׄןׄ.

[754] Sukenik:]ׄה[   ]ר[ ]ׄ. Licht: מלפניו קמיו את להעביר והׄגבורה]ׄכׄוח[ה. DJD:]ׄה[ ]°°° °° °°°°. Qimron:]ׄה[   ]ר[°°°°°.

[755] The verb can mean "to instruct" or "to show." Perhaps, the meaning is to highlight the uplifted "standard" and "banner." See להורותם in line 12.

[756] The noun is an error for תׄיׄבתׄם[נ; which appears in 9.14. In line 27 נתיבת is an error for נתיבות. Also see 1QS 5.11: בדרך הרשעה.

[757] Sukenik:]ׄכרתו[   ]ׄׄלׄׄחׄׄ[. Licht: עולם ון[כרתו אויבים] לתׄ[חׄלת]ׄ. DJD:]ׄׄלׄׄחׄׄ[. Qimron: [ ]°° ׄׄׄׄלׄ[   ]ׄׄׄׄׄׄׄׄׄׄ. For רשעה, see lines 25, 32, and 33.

[758] Sukenik: ומעביר. Licht: ומעבור.

[759] Not in DJD. Cf. Qimron: [ׄ.

[760] Another possible reading: ם[לחׄיׄמׄׄתׄ.

29 you put the foundation on rock, and the beam according to[458] a measuring-line of judgment, and the weight of tru[th]in order to [m]ake tried stones[459] for a strong

30 bu[ildi]ng[460] (that) will not be shaken. And all those who enter it will not totter,[461] for no stranger will enter [into] its [gat]es. (It shall have) doors of defense[462] without

31 an entrance, and strong gate-bolts (that) cannot be broken, lest a troop[463] by means of[464] its weapons of war should enter exhausting[465] all the arrows of

32 the wars of wickedness. And then shall the sword of God hasten at the Endtime of judgment, and all the sons of his tr[u]th shall awaken to extermi[nate]

33 wickedness,[466] and all the sons of guilt shall be no more. And the mighty one shall stretch his bow, and he shall open the boundaries[467] of the heavens

34 to the endless expanse[468] and the eternal gates, to bring out the weapons of war.[469] And they shall be migh[ty] from end to end, and the arrows

35 will be shot with[ou]t deliverance for the guilty creature.[470] Unto destruction they will tread, and there is neither remn[a]nt n[or] hope in the abundance of the corpses.[471]

36 And for all the mighty ones of wars there is no escape, for the Most High God (has) the po[wer …] °°° r °°°°° .

37 And those lying (in) the dust raised[472] the standard, and the maggots of the dead ones lifted up the banner to instruct [them. (Concerning) the wicked ones], their [p]aths (were) wicked

38 in the wars of the insolent ones. And when an overflowing scourge[473] passes by, it will not enter into the fortress […] °°° ° °°°°°° l °°°°° b[…]

---

[458] This can mean also "upon," "with regard to."

[459] See Isa 28:16.

[460] Note the use of architectural images metaphorically.

[461] From מוט; could also be translated "be shaky."

[462] See 11.40. Lit. "doors of a shield."

[463] From גדוד; see also 11.40.

[464] Heb. ב.

[465] Heb. עם תום, lit. "with the completion of," "with perfection," or "entirely." The meaning seems to be that the quiver is empty. 4Q429 frg. 4 2.12 has "until (עד) the completion of." Either עם or עד may be original. עם תום is the more difficult reading. עד תום is well known and is found four times in the Qumran Scrolls (*GC* p. 517). עם תום is not found in biblical Hebrew and appears only here in 1QHª 14 and in 1Q28a (1QSa) 1.17, "along with the perfection of his way (עם תום דרכו). See *PTSDSSP* 1.112–13 (*Rule of the Congregation*). Most likely, עם תום was corrected in 4Q429 to עד תום (the difference is not caused by orthography, ם is not similar to ד). The passage presents a metaphor by which the *Yaḥad* perceives itself as the protected Community, "without an entrance," which is protected "at" (with the completion of the end of the cosmic wars [1QHª]) or "until" the Endtime (4Q429). See Licht, p. 117.

[466] See the same concept expressed in 1QM and 1QS 3–4.

[467] From מצור, denoting also "fortifications," "stronghold," or even "fortified city." In inscriptions, the noun specifies a "boundary."

[468] Lit. "to open space without end."

[469] Note the contrast between bolted gates and open gates.

[470] Heb. יצר, or "inclination."

[471] See 24.17.

[472] Note the shift from future to past tense. Perhaps we are to imagine a *perfectum futurum*.

[473] See the same words in Isa 28:15, 18.

39   [ל֯ל] [ ]   אמתך°°°°°[761]   [ל֯ל][762]   ]לתפל֯ וככפיס ל֯א °[763]

40   מ°°]֯[764]

41   אמת °°]֯[765]

Col. 15 [= Sukenik Col. 7][766]
Parallels: 1Q35 Frg. 1; 4Q428 Frg. 10 Lines 1–6; 4Q432 Frg. 12

1   ]

2   ]

3   ]

4   [֯ם֯ ו֯אני נאל֯מ֯תי מ֯ה֯ו֯]ם֯[767] °°° °° [מן[768] אל֯ה יג֯ד֯פ֯ו֯נ֯י[769]

5   כזרו]ע[770] נשברת מקניה ותטבע בבב֯ץ[771] רגלי שעו עיני מראו֯ת

6   רע[772] א֯ו֯ז֯ני משמוע דמים השם לבבי ממחשבת רוע כי בליעל עם הופע יצר

7   הוותם[773] וירו֯עו[774] כול אושי מבניתי֯ ו֯עצמי יתפ֯רדו ותכמי עלי כאוניה[775] בזעף

8   חרישית ויהם לבי לכלה ורוח עועיים תבלעני מהוות פשעם   (VACAT)

9   אודכה א֯דוני כי סמכתני בעוזכה ורוח

---

[761] Not transcribed by most editions, though DJD reports some supralinear letters. Puech (1993): נגע יאבד (also supralinear).

[762] Licht: ל[אבן ב]ל תפל.

[763] Licht: לא]יזדעזע.

[764] Frg. 26 begins here and provides the text for lines 40–41. Licht does not place frg. 26 in this column.

[765] Frg. 26, which ends here, reveals the bottom of the column.

[766] This column is lined horizontally and vertically.

[767] See line 8: מהוות.

[768] Ctr. Sukenik: ץ°°°[ ]֯. Ctr. DJD: ק°°°° °°[. Qimron: מ֯ן °°°°°°°°.

[769] Licht: ע[כזרו ידי והיתה גדפוני כי] אלה. DJD: ו֯ג֯ד֯פ֯ו֯נ֯י. Our reading here is influenced by Qimron.

[770] Sukenik: ע[. With Licht. Qimron: כזרו֯ע.

[771] An error for בבוץ.

[772] The right margin is visible.

[773] Sukenik and Licht: היותם.

[774] DJD: ויריעו.

[775] Sukenik and Licht: עלו כאוניה.

39   °°°°° your truth[474] [...]*l*[...]*l*[...]. For mortar[475] and as a beam not °[...]

40   *m*°°[...]

41   truth °°[...]

Col. 15 [= Sukenik Col. 7]
Parallels: 1Q35 Frg. 1; 4Q428 Frg. 10 Lines 1–6; 4Q432 Frg. 12

1   [...]

2   [...]

3   [...]

4   [...]°*m* and I, I am speechless from their disast[ers ...]°° °°°*mn* these (things); they shall curse me

5   [... like an ar]m that is broken from the humerus,[476] and my foot sunk in the mire.[477] My eyes are shut from seeing

6   evil, (and) my ears from hearing blood (that has been shed).[478] Terrified is my heart from evil thought, because Belial (is) with the appearing[479] inclination of[480]

7   their disaster. And all the foundations of my structure[481] tremble, and my bones are dislocated, and my entrails (are) within me like a ship in a raging

8   gale,[482] and my heart is turbulent unto destruction, and the twisting wind devours me from the disasters of their transgression. (VACAT)

9   (VACAT) I thank you, O Lord, because you have sustained me with your strength, and have elevated[483] the spirit

---

[474] The word is written above the line, perhaps not by a later correcting scribe since he usually changes the final *kaph* to כה.

[475] See Ezek 13:10, 11, 14, 15; 22:28.

[476] The words "broken from the humerus" (lit. "bone of the upper arm") are not typical of biblical metaphors; they may refer to an actual event. Did the Wicked Priest break the arm of the Righteous Teacher so he could not officiate as High Priest? See also 16.34.

[477] The translation corrects the scribal error. The author seems to know the poetry of Jer 38:22.

[478] See Gen 4:10.

[479] The *hipʿil* of יפע means "to appear." Cf. Akk. *(w)apu*, "to become visible."

[480] Heb. יצר.

[481] Note the repeated use of architectural terms to denote the physical and psychological experiences of the author.

[482] חרישית, from חרישי; cf. Jonah 4:8 (a "vehement wind").

[483] Heb. הניפותה, from נוף; the verb also denotes "to move back and forth," usually over one's head. Perhaps the author, remembering the ceremonies in the Temple, is making an allusion to the "wave-offering." See Ex 29:24–26.

10   קודֿשכה הניפותה בי בל אמוט ותחזקני לפני מלחמות רשעה ובכול הוותם

11   לֹא⁷⁷⁶ החתיתה⁷⁷⁷ מבריתכה ותשימני כמגדל עוז כֿחומה⁷⁷⁸ נשגבה ותכן על סלע

12   מבניתי ואושי עולם לסודי וכול קירותי לחֿומת בחן ללוא תד(י)עזֿע⁷⁷⁹

13   ואתה⁷⁸⁰ אלי נתתו⁷⁸¹ לעפים⁷⁸² לעצת קודש ות[חזק]נֿ[י] בֿבריתכה⁷⁸³ ולשוני כלמודיך

14   ואֿיֿן פֿה לרוח הוות ולא מענה לשון לכול בֿני⁷⁸⁴ אשמה כי תאלמנה שפתי

15   שפתי⁷⁸⁵ שקר כי כול גרי⁷⁸⁶ למשפט תרשיע להבדיל⁷⁸⁷ בי בין צדיק לרשע

16   כי אתה ידעתה כול יצר מעשה וכול מענה לשון הכרתה ותכן לבי

17   [כל]מודיכה⁷⁸⁸ וכאמתכה לישר פעמי לנתיבות צדקה להתהלך לפניך בגבול

18   [חי]יֿֿֿם⁷⁸⁹ לשביל⁷⁹⁰ כבוד (וחיים)⁷⁹¹ ושלום לאין הֿ[סר ולו]אֿ⁷⁹² להשבת⁷⁹³ לנצח

19   [מֿשֿענתו⁷⁹⁴ להרים לבֿ[ו]⁷⁹⁵   ] ואתה ידעתה יצר עבדכה כי לא צֿ

---

⁷⁷⁶ Sukenik and Licht: ל[א].

⁷⁷⁷ Ctr. DJD: ה החתֿ. Qimron: החתותה. Carmignac (1960): החתימה. There is no *yodh*.

⁷⁷⁸ A drop of ink is found after כֿחומה. It may have fallen from a stylus.

⁷⁷⁹ Cf. DJD: תֿדֿ(ז)עזע. The orthography suggests a י but a ז explains this scribal error.

⁷⁸⁰ Sukenik and Licht: [ו]אתה.

⁷⁸¹ Sukenik, Licht, and Qimron: נתתו.

⁷⁸² An error for לעיפים or ליעפים.

⁷⁸³ Sukenik: בריתכה [ ]וֿת[ ]. Licht: כֿבריתכה[ב לבי וֿת]כן פי. Our reading is influenced by DJD. Qimron: כֿבריתכה.

⁷⁸⁴ Sukenik and Licht: ב[ני.

⁷⁸⁵ The two instances of שפתי are not examples of dittography.

⁷⁸⁶ With Sukenik. Ctr. DJD: גדי.

⁷⁸⁷ Licht: [ל]הבדיל.

⁷⁸⁸ Ctr. DJD and Qimron: כֿ[ל]מודיכה. With Sukenik. Licht: [בל]מודיכה.

⁷⁸⁹ Sukenik: [ֿאֿ. Licht: [חיי]ם. DJD: [חי]יֿֿֿם. Qimron: [חי]יֿֿֿם.

⁷⁹⁰ Ctr. DJD: לֿשבולי. The final *yodh* is supplied by a supralinear.

⁷⁹¹ This word is marked with scribal dots and faded with erasure.

⁷⁹² For ולוא אין הסר see 14.21. Cf. DJD: א[ולֿ[ו]וֿ הֿ. Ctr. Qimron: [ולֿא]וֿ[י]. Sukenik: [ ]ֿ. Licht: הֿ[סר ולוא.

⁷⁹³ For להשבית להשבת.

⁷⁹⁴ Sukenik: [ ]ֿֿ[ ]אֿל. Licht: ש[ענתי ונש בצע והון על] לא. DJD: מֿשֿענתו [ ]ֿ צֿ. Qimron: מֿשֿענתי שֿ[מתי על הון].

⁷⁹⁵ Ctr. Qimron: לבֿ[בי. Sukenik: ל[. Licht: לֿ[מעלה קרני. With DJD: לבֿ[ו].

10   of your holiness in me, so that I do not totter. And you strengthened me in the face of the wars of wickedness, and in their disasters

11   you did not deviate[484] from your covenant. And you set me as a strong tower (and) as a high city wall.[485]
And you established my structure on

12   rock and the eternal foundations for my council, and (established)[486] all my walls[487] to a tried city wall
that cannot be shaken.

13   And you, O my God, you gave him to the weary ones for the holy council. And you [strengthened[488] m]e
in your covenant and my speech[489] according to your teachings.

14   And there is no mouth for the spirit of disaster, and no answer of the tongue for all the sons of guilt, because speechless[490] shall be the lips of

15   lying lips,[491] for you shall condemn to judgment any[492] who attack me in order to distinguish through
me[493] between the righteous one and the wicked one.

16   For you, you know each inclination of[494] (every) creature,[495] and you recognized every answer of the
tongue. And you established[496] my heart

17   [according to] your teachings;[497] and according to your truth, directing my footsteps to the paths of righteousness, to walk continuously before you within the border of

18   [li]fe in tracks of glory and peace that can neither be re[moved no]r cease[498] for perpetuity.

19   But you, you know the inclination[499] of your servant, because not ṣ[…] his support to raise [his] heart

---

[484] Lit. "to shatter."
[485] The Heb for "city wall" is one word.
[486] Heb. כון (which means lit. "to fix solidly") seems echoed in the present clause (see the previous "you established").
[487] The noun denotes the wall of a house.
[488] See line 10. Note how this verb, "strengthened," ties the thoughts together (*ein Stichwort*).
[489] Lit. "my tongue."
[490] I.e., without voice.
[491] Recall "the man of the lie (הכזב)" at Qumran. In 15.15 the noun is שקר. See 1QpHab 11.1, 5.11; 4Q171 frgs. 1–10 1.26– 2.1, 4.14. Cf. 1QS 6.24, 9.8.
[492] Or "each."
[493] Or "in me."
[494] Heb. יצר.
[495] Lit. "work." The Creator is in the mind of the poet.
[496] Note how frequently this verb is used within the *Thanksgiving Hymns* and within the scrolls composed at Qumran.
[497] See 15.13.
[498] Or "put an end to."
[499] Heb. יצר.

[797אין צדקות להנצל מפנ]יכה798	**20**	ולהעיז796 בכוח ומחסי בשר אין לי]
800[חסדכה אוחיל להציץ	**21**	בֿלֿוֿא799 סליחה ואני נשענתי ברוֹבֿ]
[צֿדקתכה802 העמדתני	**22**	כֿמֿטֿע801 ולגדל נצר להעיז בכוח ול]
803[ותשימני אב לבני חסד	**23**	לבריתכה ואתמוכה באמתכה ואת]ה
[וכשעשע804 עילול805 בחק806	**24**	וכאומן לאנשי מופת ויפצו פה כיונ]קי
ש]ארית אנשי807 מלחמתי ובעלי	**25**	אומניו ותרם קרני על כול מנאצי ויתפֿ]
	26	רבי כמוץ לפני רוח וממשלתי על באי בֿ]ריתכה א]לי808 עזרתה נפשי ותרם קרני
ה]כֿינותה810 לכבודכה	**27**	למעלה והופעתי באורֿ809 שבעתים בע]
811[(VACAT)	**28**	כי אתה לי למאור עוֹלם ותכן רגלי במֿ]ישור
	29	אוֹדֿכֿ]ה אדוני]כי812 השכלתני באמתכה
	30	וברזי פלאֿכֿה813 הודעתני ובחסדיכה לאיש [פשע]814 וֿברוב815 רחמיכה לנעוי816 לב

---

796 Sukenik and Licht: ו[להעיז.

797 Licht: לי] כיא ליצר חמר[.

798 Cf. Sukenik and DJD: מפ[. Licht: מפ]ניך. Qimron: מפ[שע]. For "before me" see Isa 63:19: מפניך and 1QHª 15.31: לפניכה.

799 Sukenik: וא[. Licht: בל]וא.

800 Sukenik: [ ]בֿ. Licht: ברו]ב רחמיכה ולגדול. DJD: ברו]ב רחמיכה ולהמון.

801 With DJD: כֿמֿטֿע. Sukenik: שע°°. Licht: בי]שע. Qimron: כמטע.

802 Sukenik: [ ]וֿ. Licht: ול]הפריח פרח כיא ב[צדקתך.

803 Licht: יסר בחוקיכה].

804 Licht: כיונ]קים וישמח]ו כשעשע.

805 With Sukenik. Ctr. DJD: עוליל. Ctr. Qimron: עילול.

806 Licht: עולול בחיק. The supralinear is by a different scribe.

807 Sukenik: א]רות אנשי. Licht: ויתפ]ורדו כפו]ארות אנשי.

808 Ctr. DJD: בלוזֿי כֿי] אתה א[. Ctr. Qimron: על בוזֿי א[לי. Sukenik: [לי]°°בֿ. Licht: א[לי על כי אתה א[. See line 23: לבריתכה. על בני]עול For בוא with ברית see 13.25, 21.10, and 21.14.

809 Sukenik: בא°°. Licht: בא]ור.

810 Sukenik: נותה]בֿ. Licht: ותה]כינותה. DJD: בא]ור אשר הכינ]ה. Qimron: ה]כֿינותה בֿ.

811 Sukenik: [ ]בֿ. Licht: במ]ישור נצח.

812 Sukenik: או]דכה אדוני. Licht: א]ודכה אדוני. DJD and Qimron: אוֹדֿכֿ]ה אדונֿ]יֿ.

813 Licht: פל]אכה.

814 With DJD.

815 Sukenik: ברוב. Licht: ו]ברוב[תהו.

816 1Q35 frg. 1 line 1: לֿנֿעוֹוֹ[.

20 and to cause shelter in power. And I have no refuge (in) the flesh; [...] there (are) no righteous (deeds) to be delivered[500] before [you][501]

21 without forgiveness. But I, I leaned on the multitude of [...] your loving-kindness I await, to bring forth buds[502]

22 as planting, and to grow a shoot to cause shelter in (your) power and *l*[...] your righteousness you allowed me to stand[503]

23 for your covenant. And I will adhere to[504] your truth and yo[u ...] and you made[505] me a father for the sons of loving-kindness,

24 and as a nursing-father[506] to the men of a wondrous-sign.[507] And they open (their) mouths[508] like those suck[ing ...] and like the babe who delights in the bosom of

25 its nursing-father. And you raised my horn against all who scorn me *wytp*[... the re]mnant of the men of my war, were dis[persed,] and those

26 who quarrel (with me are) as chaff before the wind. And my dominion (is) over those (who) enter into [your] co[venant, O] my G[od.] You have helped my soul,[509] and you have raised my horn

27 upwards, and I shone with a sevenfold light.[510] *bʿ*[...] you have [es]tablished your glory,[511]

28 because you are for me an eternal light, and you established my foot in upri[ghtness].[512] (VACAT)

29 (VACAT) I thank yo[u, O Lord,] because you allowed me to have insight into your truth

30 and allowed[513] me to know your wondrous mysteries[514] and your loving-kindnesses for a man of [transgression] and the multitude of your mercies to the perverted of heart.

---

[500] The *nipʿal* infinitive means "to be delivered."

[501] The Semitic idiom literally means, "from before [you]." See מפניך in Isa 63:19 and 1QHᵃ 15.31.

[502] *Hipʿil* infinitive of צִיץ; not a verb in biblical Hebrew.

[503] *Hipʿil* permissive.

[504] See also 10.23; 12.2, 23; 22.14.

[505] Lit. "set," "put," or "place."

[506] A stunning and unusual image that reappears in *OdesSol* 19:2–3. "His breasts" refer to "the father" who "was milked."

[507] The "wondrous sign" appears to refer to the Righteous Teacher who is also "a nursing-father." See the same expression in Zech 3:8.

[508] Singular in Hebrew.

[509] Heb. נפש.

[510] That is a "perfect light."

[511] The *lamedh* is a *nota accusativi*.

[512] Lit. "in the plain," signifying a settled and stable situation. See 10.31 and 11.21.

[513] Notice the repetitive use of the permissive *hipʿil*.

[514] See 1QpHab 7, according to which the Righteous Teacher alone was "allowed to know all the mysteries of the words of his servants, the prophets."

31 כ֯י֯ מ֯י֯ כ֯מ֯ו֯כ֯ה֯[817] באלים אדוני[818] ומי כאמתכה ומי יצ֯דק לפניכה בהשפטו[819] ואין

צב(ע)י[820]
32 להשיב על תוכחתכה כול רוח ולא יוכל כול להתיצב לפני[821] ח(כ)מתךה[822] וכול בני

תביא
33 אמתכה בסליחות לפניכה ל֯ט֯ה֯ר֯ם[823] מפשעיהם[824] ברוב טובכה ובהמון רח֯מיכה[825]

34 להעמידם לפניכה לעולמי עד כי [illegible] חצנל ונוכי הכיכרד לוכו התא מלוע[826]

35 נ֯צחי֯ם֯[827] ואין זולתכה ומה הוא איש תהו ובעל הבל להתבונן במעשי פלאך

36 ה֯ג֯ד֯ו֯ל֯י֯ם֯[828]

הפלתה[829] ע א[830]
37 א֯ו֯ד֯כ֯ה אדוני כ֯י֯ לוא ג֯ו֯ר֯ל֯י֯ ב(י)דת שו ובסוד נעלמים לא[831] שמתה חוקי

38 ו֯ת֯ק֯ר֯אני לחסדיכה ולסליחו֯[תיכה הביאות]נ֯י֯[832] ו֯ב֯ה֯מ֯ו֯ן֯ רחמיכה לכול משפטי[833]

39 [צדק ואני א]י֯ש ט֯מ֯[א[834]]ב֯ע֯ולה ובחי֯ק[835]

40 [°°°[836]

[817] Licht: [מי] כמוכה. Cf. Sukenik: מי כמוכה, but there is space for כי and the supralinear י is clear.
[818] An echo of Ex 15:11.
[819] 1Q35 frg. 1 line 2: לפני]כ֯ה בהשפטכה.
[820] The supralinear is written by a different (probably later) scribe. See 5.25 the צ is written with two strokes and thus resembles an ע. Sukenik: צב°. Licht does not report the supralinear letters. Qimron: צבי֯.
[821] 1Q35 frg. 1 line 3: לפני[.
[822] Licht: חמתכה. Note the final *kaph* in medial position (a scribe added ה).
[823] Sukenik: °°°°רם. Licht: ל[טהר]ם.
[824] 1Q35 frg. 1 line 4: מפשעי]הם.
[825] Sukenik: ר[ח]מיכה. Licht: רחמיכה.
[826] 1Q35 frg. 1 line 5: כי]א [illegible] .
[827] Sukenik: °צח°°. Licht: נצחים.
[828] Sukenik: °°°°°°ל֯ם֯. Licht: [הגדולים]. 1Q35 line 8: פל]אכה הגדולים.
[829] See 4Q432 frg. 12 line 4: הפלתה. Was 1QH[a] corrected to the reading in 4Q432?
[830] The supralinear was missed by previous editors. See 14.8. The correcting scribe erred and put the א above the ש.
[831] 1Q35 frg. 1 line 10: ובס]וד נעלמים לוא.
[832] Cf. DJD: ולסליחו֯[תיכה ה]ב֯י֯א֯[ות]נ֯י֯. Qimron: ולסליחו֯[תיכה ה]ב֯י֯[אות]נ֯י֯. Licht: ולסליח[ותיכה אקוה]. No formula in 1QH[a] assists in reading or restoring consonants. The consonants in line four are much more evident.
[833] Licht ends the column here.
[834] Sukenik:]שר[. See DJD and Qimron: אי]ש ט֯מ֯[א.
[835] Sukenik ends his transcription here: עולה ובחיק [.
[836] Cf. DJD:]ה֯ א֯ל֯י֯.

31   For who is like you among the gods, O Lord?[515] And who is like your truth? And who can be justified before you when he is judged? And no

32   hosts of[516] a spirit can reply to your chastisement. And none can stand before your wrath. And all the sons of

33   your truth you allow to come into forgiveness before you, purifying them from their transgressions with the multitude of your goodness, and with the abundance of your mercies,

34   allowing them to stand before you forever (and) ever.[517] For you (are) an eternal God, and all your ways are established for perpetuity

35   (and) perpetuity. And there is no one but you. And how may[518] a man of emptiness and the owner of nonsense comprehend[519] your wondrous works

36   which are great? (VACAT)

37   I thank you, O Lord, because you did not cast my lot in the congregation of the worthless; and in the council of the hidden ones you did not put my ordinances.

38   But you called me to your loving-kindnesses and [you brought] me to [your] forgivenesses and with the abundance of your mercies for all the judgments of

39   [righteousness. But I (am) a ma]n of impuri[ty …] in deceit, and in the bosom of

40   […]°°°

---

[515] An echo of Ex 15:11.

[516] Heb. צבא. See 5.25.

[517] As in the final columns of 1QS (the *Rule of the Community*) an emphasis is placed on God's forgiveness and covenant loyalty (loving-kindness) for acceptance (or salvation), rejecting any conception that a human can earn God's favor by doing good works.

[518] Lit. "what is."

[519] Lit. "to observe."

41   [בֵּאֲמִתֹּךְ‎837

Col. 16 [= Sukenik Col. 8]
Parallels: 1Q35 Frg. 2; 4Q428 Frg. 10 Lines 7–12; 4Q432 Frg. 13

1   [

2   [°°°]

3   [‎°לא כי לעד ‎838וצֹֽדֹקֹתכה תכוןֹ‎[ו

4   ‎839עֹ[שִֹׂיתֹה

5   ‎841ומֹשקי ציה בארץ מים ומבוע ביבשה נוזלים מקור ‎840נֹתתני בֹיֹ נֹ[דכה אדו]או

6   עצי   לכבודכה ‎844יחד תאשור עֹם ותדהר ברוש מטע ‎843ושֹדה‎[‎842גן ואֹגֹ[ם מים

7   עולם למטעת נצר להפריח והיו מים עצי כול בתוך מחובאים רז במעין חיים

8   ‎845יגזעו חיים למים ויפתח ישלחו ליוב[ל] ושורשיהם יפריחו טרם להשריש

9   עוברי לכל ‎847גיזעו ומרמס יער ‎846תֹ[חֹ]ין כול ירעו עליו ובנצר עולם למקור ויהי

---

837 With DJD.

838 Cf. Sukenik: צֹֽדֹקתכה תכוןֹ‎. Licht begins here: תכה תכוןֹ[צדק‎. Ctr. DJD: וצֹֽדֹקתכה תכיןֹ‎ [. Before צ there is only a drop of ink. Context indicates תכוןֹ‎. Qimron: וצֹֽדֹקתכה תכוןֹ‎.

839 Sukenik and Licht: תֹה[. With DJD and Qimron.

840 Sukenik and Licht also restore the formula but have כיא‎. Cf. נ]תתני כיא אדוני [דכה‎. DJD: נֹתתני בֹיֹ נֹ[דכה אד]או‎. Qimron: נֹ בֹיֹ‎[כה אד]או‎. נֹתתני‎.

841 Sukenik: ומ[שקי‎. Licht: ומשקי‎. Line 5 is parallel to 4Q428 frg. 10 lines 11–12.

842 There is room for four or five consonants in the *lacuna*.

843 Sukenik:] גן‎ [‎°°ה‎. Licht: מטע ב]ה נטעת[ה אשר רווה‎ [גן‎. DJD: השֹׂדה‎ °°°° ואֹגֹם גן‎. Qimron: ב]שֹׂדה[מים ואֹגֹ[ם גן‎.

844 These words are echoes of Isa 41:19.

845 With DJD. Ctr. Sukenik: ‎וגזעו‎. Licht: גזעו‎. A scribal error for גיזעו‎; see the next line. Also see lines 24 and 25 in which the word is written without *yodh*. Qimron: וגזעו‎.

846 Sukenik: ‎[‎°‎]. Licht: חית]‎.

847 Qimron: גוזעו‎.

41   […] your truth[520]

Col. 16 [= Sukenik Col. 8]
Parallels: 1Q35 Frg. 2; 4Q428 Frg. 10 Lines 7–12; 4Q432 Frg. 13

1   […]

2   […]°°°[…]

3   [… and] your righteousness shall be established forever, for not °[…]

4   […] you [d]id.(VACAT)

5   I tha[nk you, O Lo]rd, because you placed me as[521] the source of streams in a dry land, and (as) the gushing-pond[522] of water in an arid land, and (as) the Irrigator of[523]

6   the garden and of a poo[l of water], and (as) a field of planting of cypress and elm with cedar together[524] for your glory.[525] The trees

7   of life[526] (are) beside a mysterious fountain,[527] concealed among all the trees of water.[528] And they[529] will bring forth a shoot[530] for an eternal planting,

8   by taking root before they blossom. And their roots they send out to a broo[k],[531] and its stem is opened to the living water.

9   And it will become an eternal spring, for in the shoot of its leaves all the be[as]ts of the forest will graze, and its stem is trampled on by all who pass over

---

[520] The *beth* seems to be a *nota accusativi*. See the Composite Text and Translation for the reconstructed lines.

[521] The preposition functions as a *beth essentiae*. See *Of Scribes and Scrolls*, pp. 67–78. In 16.17, the author states that God put "the early rain" in him. See *Der Mensch vor Gott*, pp. 193–210. The poem is by the Righteous Teacher, as most scholars have concluded.

[522] From נבע, "to gush." A pond with gushing water; perhaps the author is thinking about Ain-Gedi.

[523] ומשקי can be ומשקה in Qumran Hebrew. The Irrigator is the Righteous Teacher.

[524] Heb. יחד which became a paronomasia for "Community," since the Righteous Teacher, the author, is imagining the planting of the eschatological Community. The words in the line are echoes from Isa 41:19.

[525] See Isa 35:7. Isa 41:18–21 has deeply influenced the mind of the poet who must have memorized Isaiah 41. Note the echo of the imagery from Isaiah 41 in these sentences: "a pool of water (לאגם מים)," "the dry land (ארץ ציה)," "the cypress (ברוש)," "the elm (תדהר)," and "the cedar (תאשור)." As is well-known from the *Rule of the Community*, the book of Isaiah also supplied the *raison d'être* for going into the wilderness, not only in Isa 40:3 but also in Isaiah 41: "I will make in the wilderness (במדבר)."

[526] Conceivably, the author is imagining the priests who are with the Righteous Teacher. See the notes to the Composite text.

[527] The Righteous Teacher is the mysterious fountain.

[528] Most likely, the poet with "trees of water" is representing the wicked priests who rejected the Righteous Teacher.

[529] I.e., "the trees of life."

[530] See Isa 11:21 and 60:21 (נצר מטעו).

[531] Perhaps a subterranean brook.

10   דרך ודליתו⁸⁴⁸ לכל עוף כנף וירמו עליו כול ע[צי] מים כי במטעתם יתשגשגו

11   ואל יובל לא ישלחו שורש ומפריח נצר ק[ו]דש למטעת אמת סותר בלוא

12   נחשב ובלא נודע חותם רזו   ואתֹה א[ל⁸⁴⁹ שכתה בעד פריו ברז גבורי כוח

13   ורוחות קודש ולהט אש מתהפכת בל י[בוא ז]ר⁸⁵⁰ בֹּמֹעין⁸⁵¹ חיים ועם עצי עולם

14   לא ישתה מי קודש בל ינובב פריו עם [מ]טֹע⁸⁵² שחקים כי ראה בלא הכיר

15   ויחשוב בלא האמין למקור חיים ויתן יבֹ[ול] פֹּרח עולם⁸⁵³ ואני הייתי ל[ב]זאי⁸⁵⁴ (נֹ)הרות

16   שוטפים כי גרשו עלי רפשם

17   ואתה אלי שמתה בפי כיורה גשם לכול [מטע]⁸⁵⁵ ומבוע מים חיים ולא יכזב לפתוח

18   הֹשמֹים לֹא⁸⁵⁶ ימושו⁸⁵⁷ ויהיו לנחל שוטף עֹ[ל כול עצי] מים⁸⁵⁸ ולימים לאין חֹקֹֹר⁸⁵⁹[

---

848   Qimron: ודלֹותו.

849   Licht: ואתֹה א[ל.

850   The restoration is from 1Q35 frg. 2 line 1. The image in DJD Pl. 14 is misleading. There is space for the restoration.

851   Sukenik: מֹּעין [   ]י. Licht: מעין ב]זר בוא[י.

852   Ctr. Sukenik: ע[. Licht: ט]מ[ע. Cf. DJD: מֹטֹע. The manuscript is torn from top to bottom. Photographs can be misleading. The right foot of one *mem* is visible on the right edge of the tear. Qimron: מֹטע.

853   Sukenik: עולם ח[   ]י. Licht: עולם פרח]בפ הזו[י. DJD: עולם פֹיח ל[ו]נֹבי. Qimron: עולם פֹּרח ה]פֹי.

854   Licht: לבזאי.

855   There is room for three letters and a space. Licht: [צמא]. Qimron: [בקשיו]מֹ.

856   Sukenik: השֹים. Licht: לא השדים. Qimron: השֹפים.

857   Ctr. Sukenik, Licht, DJD, and Qimron. ימישו. A *Qal* imperfect is required. In 1QH^a the *waw* and the *yodh* in this column are almost identical.

858   Licht: מים[גדות כול לֹע.

859   Sukenik: ח ֹ. Licht: [קר]ח.

10 the way,[532] and its high branch (is) for all winged birds, and all the tr[ees of] the water exalt over it,[533] for in their planting they flourish,

11 but they do not send a root to the brook. But the h[o]ly shoot shall grow to a planting of truth (which is) hidden, without

12 esteem, and its mysterious seal is unknown.[534] And you, [O Go]d, you hedged about[535] its fruits by means of the mystery of the powerful mighty ones,[536]

13 and the spirits of holiness, and the turning flame of fire,[537] lest [a stra]nger[538] should [enter] the fountain of life. And with the eternal trees

14 he must not drink the holy water, lest he will yield his fruits with the [pl]anting of skies, for he[539] sees without acknowledging,

15 and thinks without believing in the source of life. And it[540] gives forth prod[uce], the eternal blossom. And I, I became an (object of) [sc]orn (for) rivers (whose)

16 torrents expel their mud over me.[541]

17 But you, O my God, you put into my mouth (that which is) like the early rain[542] for all [plantings],[543] and (it becomes) the pond of living water.[544] And it will not fail to open.

18 (Moreover), the (rains from the) skies[545] will not subside[546] and will become a torrential ravine[547] up[on all the trees of] the water,[548] and to seas unfathomable.[549] [...]

---

[532] This reference eventually denoted "the Way," the Way of Qumran. The Qumranites referred to themselves as "the Perfect of the Way." See 1QS 8.10, 18, 21; 9.5, 9; 1QSa 1.28.

[533] Or "over him." The letters are the same for "leaves" as for "over it (him)." Did the author or those who read this text at Qumran imagine a paronomasia?

[534] Note the small *vacat*.

[535] See the note to the Composite Text.

[536] Or "powerful warriors," "heroes."

[537] Cf. Gen 3:24.

[538] The restoration is assured by the ample space and the reading in 1Q35.

[539] The pronoun refers back to "a stranger."

[540] A collective referring to "the eternal trees."

[541] A *vacat* is used for the transition.

[542] A paronomasia between "early rain" (מורה) and "teacher" (מורה); that is, the Righteous Teacher imagines himself to be like the early and gentle autumn rain that finally brings water and life to a parched Holy Land (for מורה see Ps 84:7 and Joel 2:23). See *Der Mensch vor Gott*, pp. 193–210. I will never forget driving into the Negev in early autumn and seeing the "desert" bloom with red flowers that covered the landscape. One week earlier, the area had not one flower.

[543] See the generic use of "planting" in 16.14.

[544] See the parallel thought in 16.6.

[545] Or "the heavens."

[546] The rain will not cease pouring from the heavens.

[547] Heb. לנחל שוטף.

[548] The torrent of heavenly water is from the Righteous Teacher; it will eventually wash away "the trees of the water," the evil and illegitimate priests under the control of the Wicked Priest. The links between the *Rule of the Community* and the *Thanksgiving Hymn* are well recognized.

[549] Heb. לאין חקר.

19   פיתאום⁸⁶⁰ יביעו מחובאים בסתר שׁ[   ]סׁ וׁיהיו למׁיׄ מ[ריבה⁸⁶¹

20   לחׄ ויבש וׄמׁצולה⁸⁶³ לכול חיה ועׄצׄי מים צללו⁸⁶⁴ כׄעופרת⁸⁶⁵ במים אדירי[ם]

21   בׁשׁבׁיׄבׁיׄ אש⁸⁶⁶ יבשו⁸⁶⁷ ומטע פרי יׄ[הי למ]קׄורׄ⁸⁶⁸ עולם לעדן כבוד ופאׄ[רת עד⁸⁶⁹

22   ובידי פתחתה מקורם עם פלגי[הם ומשברי]הׄם⁸⁷⁰ לפנות על קו נכון ומטע

23   עציהם על משקלת השמש לאׄו[ר עולם ויפריח]נׄו⁸⁷¹ לפארת כבוד בהניפי יד לׄעזוק

24   פלגיו יכו שרשיו בצור חלמיש ו[עד תהום י]כׄו⁸⁷² בארץ גזעם ובעת חום יעצור

25   מעוז⁸⁷³ ואם אשיב יד יהיה כערעׄׄר [במדבר]וׄגזעו⁸⁷⁴ כחרלים במלחה ופלגיו

26   יעל קוץ ודרדר לשמיר ושית וכׄ[ול עצי]⁸⁷⁵ שפתו יהפכו כעצי באושים לפני

27   חום יבול עליו ולא נפתח עם מעׄין גׄז[עו ואני]⁸⁷⁶ מגור עם חוליים ומׄ[נוג]ׄע לבׄ⁸⁷⁷

---

⁸⁶⁰ Qimron: פותאים.

⁸⁶¹ Sukenik:]ׄ ˚˚˚˚ לׄ. Licht: לח [בול לכול עץ] מׄ. DJD: [ריבה] מׄרׄ.

⁸⁶² The supralinear *yodh* was missed by previous editors. A scribe corrected חיה to חייה. The meaning is the same. There is no *dagesh forte* in Qumran Heb.

⁸⁶³ Sukenik: מצולה. Licht: מצולה[ו].

⁸⁶⁴ See Ex 15:10: צללו כעופרת במים אדירים.

⁸⁶⁵ Sukenik:]עׄ[ועׄ]ן. Licht:]עׄ[. Qimron: ועׄצׄי מים יצולי בו כ[עופרת. Licht:]ׄ עׄ[. וׄעׄצׄי מים יצולי בו כׄ]עופרת.

⁸⁶⁶ Sukenik: ˚˚˚˚˚. Licht: אש [ערה בם] ואם.

⁸⁶⁷ Ctr. Sukenik: וׄבשו.

⁸⁶⁸ Sukenik:]רׄ[. Licht: פרי] אמת סותר במק[ור. Qimron: קׄ[ודש יהיה למ]קׄור.

⁸⁶⁹ Cf. Sukenik and Qimron:]ופרׄ. Licht: ופר[ות הדר] See לפארת כבוד in line 23.

⁸⁷⁰ Sukenik:]ם[. Licht:]הׄם[לנטות קו. Qimron: מפלגי[הם מימי כול].

⁸⁷¹ Ctr. Sukenik: נׄו[. Licht: ו[דיר דלית]נׄו. DJD: ו]ׄנׄ[. The נׄו is clear. Qimron: לא[רוך דליו]נׄו.

⁸⁷² Sukenik:]˚[ונׄ. Licht: ו[בל ימי]תׄו. Qimron: נׄו[יזקי]ׄו.

⁸⁷³ Licht: מעין.

⁸⁷⁴ Sukenik:]גזעו[כער]ׄ. Licht: ו[גזעו כערו]ער במדבר. cf. Qimron: [בערבה].

⁸⁷⁵ Sukenik and DJD: [ ]ׄ. Licht:]עצי יׄ[היה י. Qimron: [ ]הׄ יׄהׄ.

⁸⁷⁶ Ctr. DJD: [ ]˚˚[מטׄ. Ctr. Qimron: מטׄ. Sukenik: [ ]ׄמ. Licht: ואני מעׄ[ין גזעו ואני] מעׄין. The *'ayin* in מעׄין seems to be written over the left edge of the *mem*.

⁸⁷⁷ Sukenik:]ׄ לׄ עׄ[ ]ומ. Licht: ע[נוג]ׄ לב ומׄ. Qimron: ומׄ[וג]עׄ לׄ יׄ. DJD: [ ]עׄׄ ומׄ.

19 sudden,[550] (the waters) concealed in secret will spring forth *š*[551][…]*m* and they will become waters of s[trife …]

20 wet and dry, and deep-water for every animal.[552] And the tree[s of the water sunk deep][553] like lead in migh[ty] waters,

21 in flames of fire they were dried out. But the planting of the fruit shall [be to] an eternal [s]ource for the Eden of[554] glory and the [everlasting] leafy b[ranches].[555]

22 And by my hand you opened their source with [their] streams [and] their [breakers] to turn on a correct measuring-line. And the planting of

23 their trees according to the sun's plumb line[556] for lig[ht eternal,[557] and he shall cause] them [to blossom] into leafy branches of glory. When I lift[558] my hand to dig about[559]

24 its streams, its roots strike through the flint stone. And [unto the depths] they will [st]rike into the earth their stem. So in times of heat it retains

25 (its) shelter. But if I withdraw (my) hand it becomes like a juniper [in the wilderness];[560] and its stem (is) like a stinging-weed[561] in a salty place.[562] And its streams

26 cause[563] thorns and thistles to grow into briars and brambles, and a[ll the trees of] its bank are changed into rotten trees. In the face of[564]

27 the heat, its leaves will wither;[565] for[566] [its] ste[m] was not opened to[567] the fountain. [And I] (am) a (temporary) abode with sicknesses, and (my) heart is aff[licte]d

---

[550] Or "suddenly."

[551] The ש is sometimes written with a curved right shoulder in this column.

[552] A scribe altered the text. Previous editors missed the correction.

[553] The restoration is influenced by the Song of the Sea in Ex 15:10; the rest of the line is identical to the text in Exodus. The author brings out paranomasia, since "deep-water" is echoed by "went deep."

[554] "Eden" here is a *nomen proprium*; it can also mean "luxury" and "luxuriant" (see 5.34; 18.26, 32). Only in the Teacher Hymns is "Eden" a proper noun; see 14.19.

[555] See 18.29.

[556] Or "balance."

[557] The "solar calendar" is confirmed.

[558] Lit. "in the waving of my hand." Most likely the Righteous Teacher lifted "the wave offering" in the Temple.

[559] Or "to hoe."

[560] The author intends to refer to a withering plant in semi-dry land.

[561] Lit. "stinging-weed." From חרול, "weed." See Prov 24:31 in which the noun is parallel to "thorns." The plant may be one of the thirty-nine "nettles" (of the genus *Urtica*). The author intends to denote the stinging nature of a plant. His vocabulary is extensive. All the plants mentioned in these lines have thorns or something which stings.

[562] The author alludes to brackish water; that is, water that is not healthy.

[563] The *hipʿil* imperfect of עלה means "cause to rise."

[564] Heb. לפני.

[565] The *qal* imperfect of נפל means "to weather," "to decay."

[566] Lit. "and."

[567] Lit. "with."

28   בנגיעים ואהיה כאיש נעזב ביגׄוׄןׄ [ואנח]הׄ[878] אין מעוז לי[879] כי פרח נגׄ[י]עׄי[880]

29   למרורים וכאוב אנוש לאין עצור בע[צמי ותהי מה]וׄמה[881] עלי כיורדי שׄאול ועם

30   מתים יחפש רוחי כי הגיעו לשחת חיׄ[ׄי   ][882] תתעטף נפשי יומם ולילה

31   לאין מנוח ויפרח כאש בוער עצור בעׄצמׄיׄ[883] עׄד ימימה תואכל שלבתה

32   להתם כוח לקצים ולכׄלות[884] בשר עד מׄועדים ויתעופפו עׄלׄיׄ[885] מׄשבׄרים

33   ונפשי עלי תשתוחח לכלה כי נשבת מעוזׄי מגויתי ויגר כמים לבי וימסׄ

34   כדונג בשרי ומעוז מותני היה לבהלה ותשבר זרועי מקׄנׄיׄהׄ] וא[ׄיׄ]ן[886] להניף יד

35   וׄרׄגׄלׄי[887] נלכׄדׄהׄ בכבל וילכו כמים ברכי ואין לשלוח פעם ולא מצעד לקול רגׄלׄי

36   וׄחׄזׄוׄק זׄרׄוׄעׄיׄ רׄוׄתקׄו[888] בזקי מכשול ולשון הגברתה בפׄי בלא נאספה[889] ואין להׄרׄים[890]

---

[878] Sukenik: ˚˚[   ]בׄ. Licht: בי]גון וכאבי]ון. With DJD. Qimron: אׄ[   ] בׄיׄגׄוׄןׄ [נפשי כי.
[879] Licht: לו.
[880] Sukenik: עׄ[   ]נׄ חׄ פׄ. Licht: נגׄ[גי]עׄי פרח. Qimron: פרח נגׄיׄעׄי.
[881] Sukenik: מה[   ]וׄמה. Licht: עצור] [נפשי תׄ]הׄמה. Qimron: עצור [בלבבי ויה]וׄמה. DJD: עצור כׄוׄ[ׄח ותהי מה]וׄמה. See 16.31 (עצור בעׄצׄמׄיׄ).
[882] Sukenik: [   ]חׄ. Licht: חׄ[י וגם].
[883] Sukenik: [   ]בׄ. Licht: בעׄ]צמותי. Cf. DJD: בעׄצׄמׄי. Qimron: בעׄצׄמׄיׄ.
[884] Ctr. DJD and Qimron: ולבלות. Sukenik: ולכלות. The *kaph* is evident by orthography (one stroke) and context.
[885] Sukenik: ˚˚˚. Licht: [פחי]. Qimron: מׄעׄלׄי.
[886] Sukenik:]ׄן[   ].
[887] Sukenik: [ׄ]לׄי[ורג]. Licht: ורגׄ]לׄי.
[888] Sukenik: תקׄו ˚˚עׄ˚˚˚˚. Licht: תׄ]תקׄו [נו]זׄרׄועׄי [וגידי. DJD and Qimron: וׄחׄזׄוׄק זׄרׄוׄעׄיׄ רׄוׄתקׄו. Our reading is evident under magnification. The reading also makes sense: "and the strength of my arm."
[889] Sukenik: בפׄ בלא נאספה. Licht: בפי לפלא נאספה.
[890] Sukenik: להׄׄׄים.

28   with afflictions;[568] and I am as an abandoned man in agony [and sighin]g. There is no shelter for me; for my affl[ic]tion produces

29   bitterness[569] and an severe pain which (cannot) be contained in [my] b[ones.[570] And there was a tur]moil over me, as those who descend (into) Sheol, and with

30   the dead it[571] seeks my spirit, for [my] life reached the pit. […] my soul[572] faints away day and night

31   without rest. And it shoots forth as a burning fire withheld in my bones. For days,[573] its flame consumes

32   by annihilating[574] power for the endtimes, and by destroying flesh until appointed times.[575] And the breakers[576] fly over me;

33   and my soul[577] is decaying[578] within me[579] to destruction, because my protection[580] ceases from my body. And my heart is poured out like water, and my

34   flesh melts like wax, and the protection of[581] my loins is turned to fear, and my arm is broken from its socket.[582] [And it is impossib]le to lift[583] (my) hand.

35   And my foot is caught in a chain; and my knees wobble[584] like water. So[585] it is impossible to put forth a footstep, and there is no tread for the sound of my feet.

36   And the strength of[586] my arm is bound in chains[587] that cause (me) to stumble, and the tongue you had strengthened[588] in my mouth is no longer retrievable,[589] so[590] it is impossible to raise

---

[568] Note the paranomasia.

[569] In the Hebrew, the noun is in the plural, "bitternesses."

[570] For the restoration, see line 31.

[571] The subject is "my affliction;" see line 28.

[572] Heb. נפש.

[573] See Ex 13:10.

[574] Note paranomosia on the same concept.

[575] Or "festivals."

[576] Note the use of this noun in 11.9–13 when an author talked about the opening womb of the pregnant one.

[577] Heb. נפש.

[578] *Ištapᶜal* imp. of שחח, not in Biblical Hebrew.

[579] Or "upon me."

[580] Heb. מעוזי; translated "shelter" in lines 25 and 28.

[581] Heb. ומעוז. Or "shelter."

[582] Or "from its bone of the upper arm (מקניה);" but one should seek to find one English noun (socket or humerus) to represent one Hebrew noun. קנה also denotes the familiar "measuring reed" which supplies the much later "canon." See 15.5 and its note.

[583] Lit. "the waving of my hand." The passage may mirror the wave-offering in the Temple.

[584] Lit. "to walk." See 12.34. See Ezek 21:12. Perhaps the expression denotes "water" (urine) pouring down the knees."

[585] Lit. "And."

[586] Heb. וחוזק. The author uses three nouns for "strength."

[587] See Nah 3:10.

[588] Lit. "you had made mighty."

[589] Or lit. "be taken away." The verb is the *nipᶜal* perfect of אסף which means literally "to be gathered," or "received again." The words here seem grounded in some real and horrible experience and are not simply metaphors. Was the tongue of the Righteous Teacher cut off so he could no longer speak or serve as High Priest? Recall that according to 1 Maccabees 14, after the ascension of Simon the Hasmonean, no priest could teach or gather a group of priests for instruction in the Temple. See 1Mac 14:41–45. See the notes to the Composite Text.

[590] Lit. "and."

37   קוֹל ולֹה[א]זֹין למֹודים‎891 לחיות רֹוח כֹושלים ולעות לעא֯ף‎892 דבר נאלם מֹזֹל‎893 שפתי

38   מפֹלֹצֹוֹת בֹקוֹ‎894 משפט לֹוח לבי פותֹח[ ]°°° [ ] בֹאוֹ‎895 במרורים לבב בֹאוֹ‎896 ברום‎897 ממשלת‎898

39   בֹלֹ[י]על לֹ[‎899   [ ]שֹלום‎900 וא]   נֹ[פ]ֹש התבלֹעֹה‎901

40   [‎902 °°   נאלמו כאין]

41   [°°°°   [אנוש לאי]ן‎903]

Col. 17 [= Sukenik Col. 9]

1   [°° אֹפֹלֹה °°]‎904 °

2   הוף[י]ֹע לֹמֹֹדֹנים בלילה ובֹי]ֹום‎905

3   [ ] °°°°[לֹאֹין רחמֹים‎906 באף יעורר קנאה ולכלה אֹ[ף]פוני‎907

4   משברי מות ושאול על יצועי ערשי בקינה תשא מֹט[תי‎908]בֹקול אנחה

5   עיני כעש‎909 בכבשֹן‎910 ודמעתי כנחלי מים כלו למנוח עיני [חסדכה]‎911 עמד לי

---

⁸⁹¹ Sukenik: °° ון לֹמודי [   ]. Licht: [פי]. Cf. DJD: וֹלֹהֹאֹזֹין ללמודי‎[להאזין]. Qimron: בֹל[ש]וֹן למודים.

⁸⁹² For לעי֯ף.

⁸⁹³ Sukenik: כֹול. Licht: מול.

⁸⁹⁴ Sukenik: בֹזקי [ ]מֹפ. Licht: בֹזקי [ות]מפלצֹ‎. Qimron: מֹנֹשֹֹא בֹקוֹ.

⁸⁹⁵ Sukenik: [או °°° [ ]. Licht: לֹ לבי פות[. Cf. DJD: [או]°°°]וֹת. Cf. Qimron: לבי בֹותֹר כֹיֹא בֹאו. ולבי פותֹ[ה בתוכי וידכ]או.

⁸⁹⁶ Ctr. Qimron: במרורים [חיֹי] לבבֹ שֹמֹ‎. Sukenik: במרורי] [לבב °°°. DJD: [לבב °°°‎ במרורֹ‎°°.

⁸⁹⁷ Ctr. DJD: כֹרים °°°. Sukenik: °רים °°°.

⁸⁹⁸ Sukenik: ממשל. Licht: במרור]ים נפשי [לבב [נמה]רים מכשל. Licht does not attempt to read the remainder of the column.

⁸⁹⁹ Cf. DJD: בֹיֹצֹ]רי. Qimron: [בֹלֹ]יעל. The last three lines are washed out and it can be misleading to speculate on the lost consonants.

⁹⁰⁰ Sukenik, Licht, and Qimron: לים. Cf. DJD: לֹים[.

⁹⁰¹ Sukenik: °°° ש התבל. DJD: נֹ[פֹש התבלֹעֹה‎]. Qimron: לֹ נֹ[פ]ֹש התבלֹעֹה].

⁹⁰² Cf. DJD: [מתם]תכֹל֯.

⁹⁰³ Sukenik ends the line with: [לֹא אנוש]. DJD and Qimron: [אנוש לאי]ן‎[.

⁹⁰⁴ Sukenik: [אֹף °‎].

⁹⁰⁵ Sukenik: °°° [[נום בלילה °°° יֹוף[י‎]ֹע לֹמֹֹדֹנים בלילה ובֹאֹ[פלה. Qimron:]ֹע[. Almost always לילה appears with יום in 1QH^a.

⁹⁰⁶ Licht begins the column with [לאין רחמים.

⁹⁰⁷ Licht: [כי אפפוני].

⁹⁰⁸ Ctr. DJD and Qimron: ֹמֹטֹ]תי. Sukenik: [ ]. Licht: [מטתי].

⁹⁰⁹ For כאש. א and ע are often confused in Qumran Hebrew. Conceivably a scribal error for כעש.

⁹¹⁰ Possibly: ככבשן.

⁹¹¹ There is room for five letters in the *lacuna*. Licht: [ישעי]. DJD: ֹ[מעוז]וֹ. Qimron: ֹ[צדק]וֹ. Dark edges of the leather should not be confused with imagined consonants.

37 (my) voice to allow (my) disciples to h[e]ar,[591] to give life to the spirit of those who stumble, and to sustain[592] the weary one (through) speaking.[593] The flow[594] of my lips was silenced

38 from horrors. In the measuring-line of judgment, the tablet of my heart opens [...] °°° [...] they enter with the bitterness of[595] heart. They enter in the height of the dominion of

39 Bel[ial ...]*l* (VACAT) [...] peace and ʾ[... s]oul[596] was swallowed up

40 °°[...] they were speechless as without

41 °°°[...] the human with[out]

Col. 17 [= Sukenik Col. 9]

1 [...]° gloominess[597] °°[...]

2 [... cause] controversies [to sh]ine[598] in the night and in the d[ay ...]

3 [...]°°°°[...] without mercies. He arouses jealousy with wrath. And for destruction, th[ey surround me ...]

4 the breakers of[599] death. And Sheol (is) on my bed. My couch resounds with lamentation, (and) [my] ma[t] with the sound of a sighing.

5 My eyes (are) like a burning-fire[600] in a furnace, and my tears (are) like valleys of water; my eyes fail for rest. [Your loving-kindness][601] remains (motionless)[602] to me

---

[591] *Hipʿil* permissive.

[592] This verb may be an Aramaism in the Hebrew text. עות in Aramaic equals עוש in Hebrew and means "to help." See the note to the Composite Text.

[593] Heb. דבר.

[594] *Piʿel* part. of נזל.

[595] In Heb. the noun is in the plural.

[596] Heb. נפש.

[597] Heb. אפלה. See Joel 2:2 in which "darkness"(חשך) and "gloominess" (אפלה) are present.

[598] Or "[to ap]pear."

[599] Here again "breakers" is not a metaphor as in col. 11 for the opening of the womb.

[600] The text has "like a moth." But the orthography is a Qumran way of writing "like a burning fire." The author intends to indicate "burning-red eyes." Conceivably the author intended to write כעשן, "as smoke."

[601] The suggested reconstruction of יש, "salvation," is unlikely since the noun appears only in 10.25 and 11.27, thus far from this context. The author longs for something. חסד, "loving-kindness," appears frequently in 1QHª; see esp. 17.7, 10, 14, and 31 (only in the plural, but that does not undermine the reconstruction of a singular noun which is demanded by the accompanying verb). In 17.10, the author expresses a longing for God's loving-kindness. In 17.14, he hopes for loving-kindness.

[602] Heb. עמד, lit. "stands."

6   מרחוק וחיי מצד ואני משאה אֶלמשוֹאה⁹¹² וממכאוב לנֹגע ומחבלים

7   למשברים תשוחח נפשי בנפלאותיכה ולא הזנחתני בחסדיכה מֹקץ⁹¹³

8   לקץ תשתֹשע⁹¹⁴ נפשי בהֹמון רחמיכה ואשיבה למבלעי דבר

9   ולֹמֹשתוֹחיחי בי תוכחת וארשיעה דינו ומשפטכה אצדיק כי ידעתי

10   באמתכה ואבחרה במשפטי ובנגיעי⁹¹⁵ רציתי כי יחלתי לחסדיכה ותֹתֶן

11   תחנה בפי עבדכה ולא גערתה חיי ושלומי לא הזנחתה ולֹא עזֹבֹתה

12   תקותי ולפני נגע העמדתה רוחי   כי אתה יסדתה רוחי ותדע מזמתי

13   ובצוקותי נחמתני ובסליֹחוֹתֹ אשתעשע ואנחמה על פשע ראשון

14   ואדֹעה כֹי⁹¹⁶ יש מקוה ב[ח]סדיכה⁹¹⁷ ותוחלה ברוב כוחכה כי לא יצדק

---

⁹¹² Licht and Qimron: למשאה. The first dots are by a scribe.
⁹¹³ Sukenik: קץ[מ]. Licht: קץ[מ]ה בחסדיכה. A hole is in the leather.
⁹¹⁴ Note the scribal dot (or perhaps, imperfection in the leather). There is room for an ʿayin, thus read תשתעשע (with Licht). Cf. DJD: תשתֹשע. See אשתעשע in line 13.
⁹¹⁵ Licht: ובנגיעי. Qimron: ובנגועי.
⁹¹⁶ Sukenik, Licht, and DJD: כֹֹי[ן].
⁹¹⁷ DJD: בֹחֹסדיכה. Qimron: בֹחסדיכה.

6   from a distance,[603] and my life (waits) from (the) side.[604] And as for me, from ruin to devastation, and from pain to affliction, and from tribulations

7   to breakers, my soul[605] contemplates your wonders,[606] and you have not rejected me[607] with your loving-kindnesses. From the endtime (of the day)

8   to the endtime (of the night)[608] my soul[609] delights in the abundance of your mercies.[610] And I will reply to those who wish to devour me (with) a speech,

9   and a chastisement to those who cast me down.[611] And I will renounce it,[612] his verdict,[613] but your judgment I will consider right.[614] Because I know

10 your truth, so I choose it as my judgment. And I accept[615] my affliction, for I long for your loving-kindnesses;[616] and you put

11 supplication in the mouth of your servant. And you have not rebuked my life, and my well-being you have not rejected.[617] And you have not forsaken

12 my hope; and before affliction you caused my spirit to stand (firm).[618] For you, you have founded my spirit and you know my design.

13 And in my troubles[619] you have comforted me, and in forgivenesses I take delight. And I find comfort concerning the first transgression.[620]

14 And I know that there is hope[621] in your [lov]ing-kindnesses[622] and expectation in the abundance of your power, because no one is justified

---

[603] The meaning is most likely "a distance" in time. The text is eschatological.

[604] The Hebrew is not clear. Perhaps the author intended to mean "I am (waiting) from the side."

[605] Heb. נפש.

[606] Again, the *beth* is a *nota accusativi*.

[607] The *hipʿil* of זנח means "to declare rejected." In 2Chr 11:14 this verb in the *hipʿil* connotes being rejected from serving as a priest.

[608] Or, "the end (of the day) to the end (of the night)."

[609] Heb. נפש.

[610] See 20.7. Also see 1QS 10.10–15 in which an author (perhaps the same one who wrote the present section of 1QHᵃ) explains how he constantly praises God at the beginning of the night and day. The day began in the evening (after sunset) at Qumran. There is a marvelous harmony between the endtime (קץ) of each day and the Endtime (קץ). Contrast "from time to time (עת בעת)," as in 1QS 8.15 and 9.13.

[611] The verb is apparently a *šapʿel* participle of שחח, probably denoting "those who throw down."

[612] Notice the anticipatory pronoun and the subsequent qualification.

[613] Heb. דין indicates a legal decision or judgment.

[614] Or "I will declare," even "I will justify."

[615] Lit. "And I am well disposed with." The author claims to appreciate his suffering because it has "fruits."

[616] Note that the author feels he is not now experiencing God's loving-kindness as he had earlier. See the reconstruction in 17.5.

[617] See the note to the verb form and meaning in line 7.

[618] See 17.5. There is a small *vacat* here.

[619] Or "And in distresses."

[620] The author is ambiguous. He may refer to his own transgression. He may also refer to the "first transgression" by Adam; thus, he lives in the eschatological hope that the "Eden of glory" (16.21) is now being planted through him, its Irrigator. The Irrigator is the Righteous Teacher.

[621] See the note to the Composite Text.

[622] The author hopes for what he remembers enjoying, the full presence of God's loving-kindnesses.

15   כול במ̇ש̇[פ]טכה ולא יז[כה ב]ר̊בכה אנוש⁹¹⁸ מאנוש יצדק וגבר מ̊ר̊ע̊ה̊ו⁹¹⁹

16   ישכיל ובשר מיצר מ̇[עשה]⁹²⁰ יכבד ורוח̊⁹²¹ מרוח תגבר וכגב̊ו̊ר̊ת̊כה⁹²² אין

17   בכוח ולכבודכה אין̊[ו]לחכמתכה אין מדה ו̊לאמ̊ת̊[כה אין] ח̊ש̊ה̊⁹²³

18   ולכול הנעזב ממנה [⁹²⁴] ואני בכה הצ̊[ב]תי מעמדי וחסדכ]ה̊⁹²⁵

19   עמדי ולא הפ̇[⁹²⁶   ב]א̊נ̊ש̊י ר̊י̊ב̊[ן⁹²⁷

20   וכזומם לי ת̇[   ] ואם⁹²⁸ לבושת פנים כו̇[ל   ]ו̊ב̊ו̊[⁹²⁹

21   לי ואתה בר̇[חמיכה   י]תגבר⁹³⁰ צרי עלי למכשול למ̇[⁹³¹

22   אנשי מלחמ[תי   בו]שת⁹³² פנים וכלמה לנרגני בי

23   כי אתה אלי מוע̇[דים⁹³³   ]תריב ריבי כי ברז חכמתכה הוכחתה בי

24   ותחבא א̊מת לק̇[ץ   מועדו⁹³⁴] ותהי תוכחתכה לי לשמחה וששון

25   ונגיעי⁹³⁵ למרפא ע̊[ולם   נצח⁹³⁶] ובוז צרי לי לכליל כבוד וכשלוני לגבורת

---

⁹¹⁸ Sukenik: אנוש]בכה{י}ר̊[   ] י̊ ולא [טכה יז]בר̊בכה..DJD: ב̊ר̊בכה] ̊ה̊ ולא יזכ]ה Qimron: במ̇שפטכה ולא יזכ̊ה. Licht: במ[שפ]טכה ולא י[זכה ב]ריבכה אנוש ..DJD: במ[שפ]טכה ולא י[זכה ב]ר̊בכה בר̊בכה. ולא יזכ]ה בר̊בכה.

⁹¹⁹ Sukenik: [   ]. Cf. Licht: [מעמיתו]; DJD: מ̊ר̊ע̊ה̊ו̊. Qimron: מ̊ר̊ע̊ה̊ו̊. The manuscript cannot be read as any ink is hidden now behind the cloth that was placed on the column.

⁹²⁰ Sukenik: [   ]̊. Licht: [עפר]. Qimron: מ̊[עשה]ה̊. The right shoulder of a *mem* is apparent. Cf. DJD: [   ]̊. For יצר מעשה see 15.16.

⁹²¹ Note the scribal dot.

⁹²² Sukenik: וכגב̊ כ̊ה̊. Licht: וכגבורותיכה.

⁹²³ Sukenik: ̊̊̊[   ]̊ ולא̊ מדה. Licht: מחיר ו]לחכמתכה אין מדה ולאמ[תכה אין כנגדה]. Cf. DJD: ̊̊̊[. Qimron: ̊̊̊̊.

⁹²⁴ Licht: [רוב נגיעים]. DJD: [   ]̊. Qimron: ר̊]וב נגיעים[.

⁹²⁵ Sukenik: הצ̊[. Licht: הצ[בתי ובחסדכה]. DJD: הצ[בתי ידי ובחסדכה]. Qimron: הצ[לותי אלי ובחסדכ]ה̊. הצ̊[בתי רגלי ובחסדכה]. See 11.22, 19.16, 26.36, and 4Q427 frg. 7 2.17.

⁹²⁶ See 10.27.

⁹²⁷ Sukenik: [ש̊י   ]̊. Licht: בי לא יכלו לי בגדפותם]. DJD: [   ]ב̊א̊נ̊ש̊י ר̊י̊ב̊ו̊. Qimron: הב̊[ישותה פני   ] ולא ה[חתיתני מפחד הוות רשעים וא]נ̊שי רי[. ה̊. Restored with the thought of this section; see line 23. עבדכה ב]א̊נ̊ש̊י ר̊י̊ב̊ו̊[   ]̊̊.

⁹²⁸ Sukenik: [   ]ת̊. Licht: ת[סתירני מהוותם]. Qimron: ת̊צ̊[ילני מכול מזמות]ה̊.

⁹²⁹ Sukenik: ̊̊[   ]כו̊. Licht: כו]ל מזמתם כי יארבו[. Cf. DJD: ̊ב̊ו̊[   ]כ̊ו̊ל̊. Qimron: כו̊ל̊[מזמותם כי יא]ר̊ו̊ב̊ו̊.

⁹³⁰ Sukenik: בר[חמיכה עזרתני פן י]תגבר. Licht: בר[חמיכה סמכתני ולא י]תגבר. DJD: י]תגבר. Qimron: י̊תגבר. בר̊[.

⁹³¹ Sukenik: [   ]ל̊. Licht: למ[בלעי הייתי ולכול]. Cf. DJD: לכ]ל̊ל̊[   ]מ̊. Qimron: למ[בלעי ולכ]ל̊ו̊ל̊.

⁹³² Licht: מלחמ[תי לפח לבעלי ריבי לבו]שת.

⁹³³ Sukenik: [   ]מ̊. Licht: מו̊ע̊[דיך הודעתני]. Cf. DJD: מוע̊]ד. Qimron: מ[קדם ועד עולם]. למ[ק]דם ועד עולם.

⁹³⁴ Licht: לק̊צ̊[ה וחסדכה ל]מועדו. DJD: מועדו[   ]לק̊ץ̊. Qimron: לק[ץ מועדו]. לק̊ץ̊ הגלותה ורזך ל]מועדו.

⁹³⁵ Qimron: ונגועי.

⁹³⁶ Sukenik: [   ]ע. Licht: נצח [עולם ושלום ע. DJD: נצח [ע]ולם וצרי ע. ע[ולם ושלום ע.

15   in your judg[me]nts; and (no one) w[ins] your lawsuit. A human can be more just than another, and a man[623] can be

16   more insightful than his companion, and flesh more honored than a cr[eature's] inclination,[624] and (one) spirit mightier than (another) spirit; but there is no power like

17   your might. And for your glory there is no [.... And] for your wisdom there is no measure. And for [your] truth [there is no] concealment.[625]

18   And to everyone who is left in need of it […]. And I, [I] plac[ed my rank] with you. [And] yo[ur loving-kindness]

19   (is) with me. And not *hp*[… with] the men of strife […]

20   and as they devised against me *t*°[…]° and if for the shame of the face (is) al[l …]°*wbw*

21   to me; and you in [your] me[rcies …] my adversary [ma]y be mightier[626] over me for stumbling[627] *lm*°[…]

22   men of [my] wa[r … sha]me of the face, and a reproach to those who grumble against me.[628]

23   For you, O my God, for seaso[ns[629]…], you will strive for my strife, for through the mystery of your wisdom you chastised me,

24   and you concealed the truth until the Endt[ime …] its season.[630] And may your chastisement become joy and gladness to me,

25   and my afflictions became an e[ternal] healing […] perpetuity. And (being) an (object of) scorn for my adversaries (becomes) to me a crown of glory, and my stumbling (becomes) an eternal

---

[623] Heb. גבר.

[624] Heb. יצר.

[625] The consonants are difficult to see on the leather; perhaps a *qal* participle of חשה, "to be silent," or "to conceal."

[626] Not "[ma]y prevail over me." The reigning high priest may be mightier than the Righteous Teacher, but he will not prevail in the Endtime.

[627] The adversary causes the poet to stumble.

[628] A *vacat* appears at the end of the line; it provides for the transition.

[629] Or "appointed ti[mes,]" "festiv[als.]"

[630] Or "appointed time," "festival."

26 עולם כי בשכֿלֿ[כה הודעתני]937 ובכבודכה הופיע אורי כי מאור מחושך

27 האירותה ליגׄוׄן [ומרפא למח]ץ938 מכתי ולמכשולי גבורת פלא ורחׄוׄב

28 עולם939 בצרת נפשֿיׄ[ן כיא אתה אלי]940מֿנוסי משגבי סלעׄ עוזי ומצודתי בכה

29 אחסיה מכול מכֿ[אוב]941   אתה]לי942 לפלט עד עולם   כי אתה מאבי

30 ידעתני ומרחם] אמי ומשדי[943 אֿמי גמלתה עלי ומשדי הריתי רחמיך

31 עלי944 ובחיק אומנתיׄ[   ]הֿ945 ומנעורי הופעתה לי בשכל משֿפטכהֿ

32 ובאמת נכון סמכתני וֿבֿרוח קודשכה תשעשעֿנֿי ועד היוׄם הוֿפֿעֿתֿה לי946

33 ותוכחת צדקכה עם נֿ[עׄ]וֿיתי947 ומשמר שלומכה לפלט נפשי ועמֿ מצעדי

34 רוב סליחות והמון רֿחֿמֿים בהשפטכה בי ועד שיבה אֿתה תכלכלני כיא

35 אבי לא ידעני ואמי עׄליכה עזבתני כי אתה אב לכׄוׄל בֿנֿי948 אמתכה ותגל

---

937 Sukenik: [   ] בשֿׄ. Licht: [כלכה הודעתני]בש. DJD: [ה הודעתני בש[כלכ. Qimron: ה ישמח לבי] בשמֿׄחֿתֿלֿ[. Restoration follows Licht.

938 Sukenik: ץ[   ] לֿ. Licht: ל]י ותתן מרפא למח[ץ. DJD: [למח]ץֿ [   ] לֿ°°°°°ׄ. Qimron: ל ותרפא למח[ץ . ליׄגׄוׄן אֿבֿ]לֿי.

939 Part of the ʿayin has faded.

940 Restoration is influenced by Licht. DJD and Qimron: [כֿי] אתה מפלטי. No consonants are visible after נפשֿיׄ

941 Sukenik: [   ]מֿ. Cf. DJD: מכֿאוֿבֿ. Qimron:]מֿ°°°.

942 Licht: לי[דהבה ויהי אדוני. DJD: [נפשי הושעתה]מֿ.

943 Licht: [תסוכני ומבטן]. DJD: [הקדשתני ומבטן]. ומרחם.

944 Licht: לי. The ink of the ʿayin has faded. See line 28. Ctr. Sukenik, DJD, and Qimron: לי*. Note the עלי in line 30. The context also requires עלי.

945 Ctr. DJD: יֿכֿֿֿה[חסד :רֿוֿב. Sukenik: [ ]°. Licht: [ה בחסדכ]ה חסד. Qimron: [תשעשעני. רֿוֿב [חסד]יֿכֿה.

946 See הופעתה לי in line 31. An examination of the different images reveals the consonants. Ctr. DJD: תֿנֿהֿלֿנֿי אֿתֿה[א]. Cf. Sukenik: [ ]°°° הל . היותֿ]י אֿ[תֿה תֿנֿהֿלֿנֿי. Qimron: [פתחתה ל[פ]יׄ. Licht: יׄ;

947 Sukenik: יתי°°°. Licht: [נעו]יתי. Qimron: נֿ[עׄ]וׄותי.

948 Sukenik: °°°. Licht: [בני].

26 strength, because through [your] insight [you have allowed me to know[631]], and through your glory my light has appeared.[632] For light from darkness

27 you allowed to shine[633] toward agony. [And a healing (is) for the blo]w of my wound. And my stumbling (gave) wonderful might, and an eternal

28 expansion for the trouble of my soul. [For you, O my God], (are) my escape,[634] my security, the rock of my strength,[635] and my fortress. In you

29 I find refuge from all su[ffering.[636] For you (are)] for me a deliverance[637] unto eternity. For you, from (the time of) my father

30 you have known me, and from the womb [of my mother. And from the breasts] of[638] my mother you weaned me.[639] And from the breasts of she that was pregnant with me, your mercies

31 (were) over me. And in the bosom of[640] my nursing-mother […]h, and from my youth you appeared to me with your insightful judgment.

32 And in established truth you supported me. And in the spirit of your holiness you delighted me, and unto today you appeared to me.

33 And your righteous chastisement (is) with[641] my pe[rv]ersity, and the guard of your peace (provides) a deliverance (for) my soul,[642] and with my treads (is)

34 an abundance of forgivenesses and a multitude of mercies when you enter into your judgment with me. And unto old age you, you will sustain me. For

35 my father did not know me, and my mother committed me to you,[643] because you are Father to all the sons of your truth and you rejoice

---

[631] *Hipʿil* permissive.

[632] Or "has shined."

[633] *Hipʿil* permissive.

[634] Or "my refuge."

[635] The noun also denotes "shelter."

[636] Lit. "p[ain."

[637] Or "savior."

[638] The suggested restoration בטן, "belly," is a noun that does not appear in 1QH^a and is thus not likely. The following verb, "wean," suggests the restoration "breasts." The noun appears soon after the restoration; the author is fond of repetitive concepts.

[639] See the note to the Composite Text.

[640] The noun denotes the upper part of the male or female human body. It signifies where loved ones, especially infants or little children, are held.

[641] I.e., "accompanies."

[642] Heb. נפש.

[643] The passage does not mean the mother of the author abandoned him (as in some translations). The statement seems to imply that the author's mother left him in God's house, the Temple, to be a priest. See Ps 10:14 in which the same expression is found (עליך יעזב); it means "commits to you (the Lord)." Our text echoes the famous story in 1Sam 1:23–28 in which Hannah, Samuel's mother, after "weaning" him, "commits" or places him on permanent loan in "the house of the Lord" (1Sam 1:24). Note also that the Hebrew verb for "weaning" appears in our text [see 17.3] and more than once in the biblical text.

36   עליהם כמרחמת על עולה וכאומן בחיק תכלכל לכול מעשׁיׄכה⁹⁴⁹   (VACAT)

37   (VACAT)

38   בׄ[רו]ךׄ אׄ[תה אדוני כיא]⁹⁵⁰ לׄ[ ] ˚˚˚ [ ]   ׄרׄ הגברתה⁹⁵¹ עד אין מספׄרׄ⁹⁵²

39   ולהל]ׄל שמכה⁹⁵³ בהפלא מאׄד[ה]⁹⁵⁴

40   לא[ין השבת לׄ]⁹⁵⁵

41   לפי [ ]שׄכלו יהלל[שמכה⁹⁵⁶

Col. 18 [= Sukenik Col. 10 + Frg. 30]
Parallels: 4Q428 Frg. 11

1   ]

2   ]

3   [ ]˚ [ב]ׄמׄחׄשׄבׄתׄכה נהׄיׄה כׄ[ול ו]בׄׄמׄזמת לבכה תוׄ[כן]⁹⁵⁷]

4   כׄ[ול⁹⁵⁸ ובלוא רצונכה לא יהיה ולא יתבונן כול בחוכׄ[מתכה]⁹⁵⁹

5   [ובסו]ׄד ׄרׄזׄיכה⁹⁶⁰ לא יביט כול ומה אפהו אדם ואדמה הוא [מעפר]⁹⁶¹

6   קורץ ולעפר תשובתו כי תשכילנו בנפלאות כאלה ובסוד אמׄ[תכה]⁹⁶²

7   תודיענו ואני עפר ואפר מה אזׄום בלוא חפצתה ומה אתחשב⁹⁶³

⁹⁴⁹ Sukenik: מעשׄ[י]כה.
⁹⁵⁰ Qimron: בׄ[רו]ךׄ אׄ[תה אדוני כי הפלתה עם עפר וביצר המׄ[רׄ.
⁹⁵¹ Licht: [אודכה אדוני כיא הגברתה.
⁹⁵² Sukenik: מסׄ[. Licht: מספׄ[רׄ. Licht does not attempt to read the remainder of the column.
⁹⁵³ With DJD and Qimron: ולהל]ׄל שמכה. For the restoration, see 17.39 and 11.24.
⁹⁵⁴ Sukenik: מׄ[.
⁹⁵⁵ Sukenik:]ׄן השבת]ׄ. Qimron: [ ] [.לא]ׄין השבת
⁹⁵⁶ Sukenik: כלו והלל]ׄ[. Perhaps this is the bottom of the column. See 3.26, 6.30.
⁹⁵⁷ Sukenik:]ׄ˚˚ [ ] ˚˚˚˚˚˚˚˚˚˚ [זׄמת לבכה]ׄ. Qimron: לבכה תכׄ[ין]ׄ ומבלעדיכה לא]. DJD: תׄו[כן].
⁹⁵⁸ Sukenik and Licht saw a *lamedh*. Ctr. DJD and Qimron: [יעשה. Licht began the column here.
⁹⁵⁹ Sukenik:]ׄ בחו. Licht: בחוׄ[קיד.
⁹⁶⁰ Sukenik: יכה]ׄ˚. Licht: [ובר]זׄיכה. Cf. DJD: ׄרׄ[סוד]ׄ וׄבׄ; few consonants are evident, as Sukenik and Licht report. Qimron: [סוד]ׄ וׄבׄ ׄרׄזיכה.
⁹⁶¹ Restoration is influenced by Licht; ctr. DJD: הׄ[מר. Ctr. Qimron: [מׄ[חמר.
⁹⁶² Sukenik:]ׄ א. Licht: [מתכה]א.
⁹⁶³ Licht: אחשב. Qimron: אחשב*.

36   over them like a compassionate one over her infant and like a nursing-father (over an infant) on (his) bosom you will sustain all⁶⁴⁴ your creatures.⁶⁴⁵ (VACAT)

37   (VACAT)

38   B[less]ed (are) y[ou, O Lord, for] *l*[...] °°°[...]*r* you made mighty without number

39   [... and to prai]se your name in doing wonders exceeding[ly]

40   [... with]out ceasing *l*[...]

41   [... according to] his insight he shall praise [your name ...]

Col. 18 [= Sukenik Col. 10 + Frg. 30]
Parallels: 4Q428 Frg. 11

1   [...]

2   [...]

3   [...]° [by] your thought a[ll] will occur, [and] by the design of your heart (all) is established [...]

4   [...] all and without your will nothing occurs, and all cannot have comprehension in [your] wisd[om.]

5   [And in the assem]bly of your mysteries⁶⁴⁶ no one can look.⁶⁴⁷ And what then (is) Adam?⁶⁴⁸ He is (only) dirt.⁶⁴⁹ [From dust]

6   he is extracted,⁶⁵⁰ and to dust he returns; however,⁶⁵¹ you allow him to have insight⁶⁵² into wonders like these. And in the assembly of [your] tru[th,]⁶⁵³

7   you allow him to know.⁶⁵⁴ But I am dust and ashes. What can I ponder without your desiring (it)? And what can I think about⁶⁵⁵

---

⁶⁴⁴ The *lamedh* is a *nota accusativi.*
⁶⁴⁵ Not "works."
⁶⁴⁶ See 18.6. Or "[And in secr]et of your mysteries."
⁶⁴⁷ Imperfect of נבט which means "to look with pleasure."
⁶⁴⁸ Or "humankind."
⁶⁴⁹ Or "earth."
⁶⁵⁰ Heb. קרץ denotes "to nip off" or "to break off." The idea seems influenced by Job 33:6. See 19.27.
⁶⁵¹ Heb. כי; this conjunction can mean "but" and "however." See esp. Gen 18:15.
⁶⁵² *Hipʿil* permissive.
⁶⁵³ See 18.5. Or "And in the secret of [your] tru[th]."
⁶⁵⁴ *Hipʿil* permissive.
⁶⁵⁵ *Hitpaʿel.*

8   באין רצונכה מה אתחזק בלא העמדתני ואיכה אֲשׂיל⁹⁶⁴ בלא יצרתה

9   לי   ומה⁹⁶⁵ אדבר בלא פתחתה פי ואיכה אשיב בלוא השכלתני

10   הנה אתה שר אלים ומלך נכבדים ואדון לכול רוח ומושל בכל מעשה

11   ומבלעדיכה לא יעשה כול ולא יודע בלוא רצונכה ואין זולתך

12   ואין עמכה בכוח ואין לנגד כבודכה⁹⁶⁶ ולגבורתכה אין מחיר   ומי

13   בכול מעשי פלאכה הגדולים יעצור כוח להתיצב לפני כבודכה

14   ומה אפהוא שב לעפרו⁹⁶⁷ כי יעצור כֺֿ[ו]ֺח רק⁹⁶⁸ לכבודכה עשיתה כול אלה

15   (VACAT)

16   ברוך אתה אדוני אל הרחמיֺם [ורב ה]ֺחֺסד⁹⁶⁹ כי הודעת[[ני⁹⁷⁰ אלה לֺסֺ[[ֺפֺֿר⁹⁷¹

17   נפלאותכה ולא להס יומם ול[י]ילה]ֺוֺלֺךֺ כֺֺוֺלֺ הֺחיל[[ֿוברב⁹⁷²[[ֺֺ[[⁹⁷³

18   לחסדכה בגדול טובכה ורֺ[וֺב⁹⁷⁴ ֺאֺשתעשעה בס[[ליחותיכה]⁹⁷⁵

19   כי נשענתי באמתכה] [˚˚ ˚˚˚˚]⁹⁷⁶

---

⁹⁶⁴ Sukenik: ˚אֲכֿשׂיל. The dashes (or "little strokes;" cf. Martin, p. 482) are distinguishable from the dots of a correcting scribe. Most likely a scribe intended the reader to invert the second and third letters. So read אשכיל (with Licht). See תשכילנו in line 6 and השכלתני in line 9. The scribe did not separate this word from the next.

⁹⁶⁵ A scribe may have erased some consonants after לי.

⁹⁶⁶ Sukenik: ככהבוד.

⁹⁶⁷ Ctr. DJD: שבלעפרו. These are two separate words. Sometimes the scribe (as here) did not separate words.

⁹⁶⁸ Licht: רק [כוח]. DJD: כֺֺוח. Qimron: כֺוֺח. See the exact same phrase in line 13.

⁹⁶⁹ Sukenik: [חסד]. Licht: [ורב ה]חסד. DJD: ה[רב ה]חסד. Qimron: ה[חסד ורב]ֺוֺ.

⁹⁷⁰ Frg. 30 begins with ני and supplies part of the left side of lines 16–18.

⁹⁷¹ Sukenik: [ל] [ל]. Licht: [ספר] ל[כה]ל[שכ]ני[הודעת. הודעת]ֺ [ל]ֺ [ל].

⁹⁷² An error for וברוב. See 19.6: וברוב טובכה.

⁹⁷³ Ctr. DJD: ˚˚ [ל]ל˚ [ל] [˚˚ ו]. Licht: ול]ילה ולתן. Sukenik: ˚[ל]ל [ל]. ול]ילה. Ctr. Qimron: ני[אֿ]בֿי[תבֿ בֿו רבֿ]ֺבֿ רֿבֿ בֿ הֿחֿיל בֿוֿל [ל]ל˚ ל˚[ ]ֺל [ל]ֺ אֿ. [יחלתי כיא ותוֿף] חול[מ] ל[בקו]ה[יל]תה.

⁹⁷⁴ Sukenik: [ורֿ].

⁹⁷⁵ Licht: [ורֺ]וב סליחותיכה ולרחמיך אצפה תמיֺד. With DJD and Qim-ron. Frg. 30 ends here.

⁹⁷⁶ Licht: [ ]ֺכֺֺֺה. Cf. DJD: [בלא] ˚˚˚˚[אֺֺ[ין [ו]ֺכֿ] [ ]ֺו. Qimron: [בֿאֺ]ֺין [ ]ֺֺֺ[כֺֺֺה [וֺב]ֺ. The leather is torn and only spots of ink are visible. [ומנוס אין כי מבינתכה ידעתי ואני].

8   apart from your will? How can I be strengthened without your allowing me to stand?[656] And how can I
gain insight[657] without your having fashioned (it)

9   for me? And how can I speak without your having opened my mouth? And (how) can I answer without
your having given me insight?

10   Behold, you are the Prince of the Elim[658] and the King of the glorious ones,[659] and Lord[660] to every spirit
and Ruler over every creature.

11   And apart from you nothing is done; and there is no knowledge without your will. And there is none but
you.[661]

12   And there is no one beside you[662] in power; and there is no one corresponding[663] to your glory. And for
your might there is no price. And who

13   among all your great wonderful creatures[664] can summon up the power to present (themselves) before
your glory?

14   And what then is he who returns to his dust that he can summon up po[w]er? Only for your glory you
have done all these things.

15   (VACAT)

16   Blessed are you, O Lord, God of mercies [and the multitude of] loving-kindness, because you allowed
me to know[665] these (things) so as to re[count]

17   your wonders, and not to keep silent day and n[ight ....] And to you (is) all the army[666] and in a multitude
of [...]°°[...]

18   to your loving-kindness in your great goodness and the multit[ude of ...] I shall delight in [your] for-
[givenesses]

19   because I leaned on your truth [...]°°° °°[...]

---

[656] *Hip'il* permissive.

[657] Reading אשכיל (*hip'il* imperfect), "to allow to have insight;" see 18.6 and 18.9. One scribe wrote אכשיל ("cause to stumble") and another correcting scribe provided our reading. The letters had been inadvertently transposed.

[658] Or "divine beings."

[659] Observe the henotheism.

[660] Heb. אדון.

[661] The author moves back and forth between henotheism (belief in One God among many gods) and monotheism (belief in One God
and the denial of other gods).

[662] Lit. "with." The author is imagining the celestial court.

[663] The preposition נגד means "corresponding" in Mishnaic Hebrew. In Biblical Hebrew, it means "before." The evidence of Mishnaic
Hebrew within the Qumran Scrolls is well-known. See the note to the Composite Text.

[664] Or "your great wonderful works."

[665] *Hip'il* permissive.

[666] The same noun for "army" appears in 18.17 and 18.26. Both times the reference is to God's army (not the Hasmonean army).

20   מצבֿוֹתכה⁹⁷⁷ ובלא °°°[⁹⁷⁸   ובלוא⁹⁷⁹ [גערתכה⁹⁸⁰ אין מכשׄוֹל] ואין]

21   נגע⁹⁸¹ בלוא ידעתה ול]א⁹⁸²   רצו]נֿכה⁹⁸³

22   ואני לפי דעתי באמֿת]כה⁹⁸⁴   [ובהביטי בכבודכה אספרה

23   נפלאותיכה ובהביני בס]וד⁹⁸⁵   בה]מון⁹⁸⁶ רחמיכה ולסליחותיכה

24   אקוה כי אתה יצרתה רו]ח⁹⁸⁷   וברצו]נכה⁹⁸⁷ הכינותני   ולא נתתה

25   משעני על בצע ובהו]ן⁹⁸⁸   ל]בֿי⁹⁸⁹ ויצר בשר לא שמתה לי מעוז

26   חיל גבורים על רוב עדנֿים]⁹⁹⁰   וב]רוב⁹⁹¹ דגן תירוש ויצהר

27   ויתרוממו במקנה⁹⁹² וקנין]⁹⁹³   כעץ ר]ענן⁹⁹⁴ על פלגי מים לשת עלה

28   ולהרבות ענף כי בחֿרֿתֿהֿ]⁹⁹⁵   בני]אדם ולהדשן כול מארץ

29   ולבני אמתכה נתתה שׄמֿ]חת⁹⁹⁶   ]רֿת⁹⁹⁷ עד ולפי דעתם יכבדו⁹⁹⁸

---

⁹⁷⁷ Licht: מצב]ות[כה. Cf. DJD and Sukenik: מצב°°כה. Qimron: מצבאֿכה.

⁹⁷⁸ Cf. DJD: ה]כֿלֿ[ה. Qimron:]°°°. The leather is torn and darkened; it is best not to speculate.

⁹⁷⁹ Licht: [מזמתך אין צרה ובלוא].

⁹⁸⁰ Ctr. DJD: מֿגערתכה]. Sukenik, Licht, and Qimron: גערתכה. Much dirt can be seen in the margin and on each side of the tear. The *mem* cannot be seen and seems inappropriate. See, however, 4Q511 frgs. 52–59 line 7: מגערתכה]. The context does not support a *mem* here.

⁹⁸¹ Licht: נגע [ולוא].

⁹⁸² See DJD and Qimron:]א[ול. Sukenik:]ֹ. See next note for Licht.

⁹⁸³ Sukenik: כה[. Licht: נכה[רצו. DJD:נכה[רצו ולא יעשה כל בלא רצו. ולא יעשה כול בלא רצו[נכה.

⁹⁸⁴ Sukenik:]בֿ. Licht:]באמֿת[כה אהללה שמכה. DJD: באמ]כה אזמרה בחסדכה[.

⁹⁸⁵ Ctr. Licht: ב]רזיכה[, but the curve of the *samekh* can be discerned. Sukenik:]בֿ [. DJD:]ל[ה]מון. בסֿ]וד פלאכה אוחיל [ה]ל

⁹⁸⁶ Ctr. DJD: [ה]מון], but a smear is read as a *lamedh*. Sukenik: ה]מון. Licht:]מון. בר]זיכה נשענתי וה[ה]מון.

⁹⁸⁷ Ctr. DJD: נכה[. Sukenik: רו]ח עבדכה וברצו[נכה. Licht: נכה[רוח עבדכה וברצו. Restoration follows Licht.

⁹⁸⁸ Sukenik:]ובה. DJD: חמס לא ובה]הון.

⁹⁸⁹ Licht: ל]בֿי [חמס לא יאוה.

⁹⁹⁰ DJD: עדנים [וישתעשעו ב]רוב.

⁹⁹¹ Sukenik:]ֹוב [ ]עד. Licht: עד]ני תבל וב]רוב.

⁹⁹² Sukenik and Licht: ויתרוממו אמקנה.

⁹⁹³ DJD: וקנין [ויפרחו כעץ ר]ענן.

⁹⁹⁴ Licht: וישגשגו כעץ ר]ענן[.

⁹⁹⁵ Sukenik:]בֿח [ ]. Licht: בחֿרֿתֿהֿ]רו בכל טוב בני. Qimron: בחֿרֿהֿ. DJD: בח]רו בם מכול בני]אדם.

⁹⁹⁶ Sukenik:]ש [ ]°°°. Licht: שמ]חת עולם וששון[. Cf. DJD:]°°°שכֿלֿ. Qimron: שכֿלֿ[ין בתעודוֿת. שכֿל לֿהֿבֿ]ין בתעודו.

⁹⁹⁷ Sukenik:]ש[ ]°.

⁹⁹⁸ Ctr. DJD: יכברו (a typographical error since the verb should be translated "they honor"). Sukenik: יכבדֿ.

20 from your outpost and without °°°[… and without] your rebuke. There is no stumbling [and there is no]

21 affliction without your knowing (it), and n[ot anything …] your [will].[667]

22 And I, according to my knowledge in [your] truth, [….] And when I look into your glory, I will recount

23 your wonders. And when I have insight into the se[cret of… the ab]undance of your mercies. And for your forgivenesses,

24 I hope. For you, you fashioned the spir[it of … and by] your [wil]l you established me.[668] And you have not given

25 me support through unjust gain, and for wealth […] my [hea]rt. And the creature of[669] flesh you have not set up for me (as) shelter.

26 The army of mighty men […] in a multitude of luxuries [and with] a multitude of grain, new wine, and oil.[670]

27 And they exalt themselves with possessions and acquisitions. [… like] a [ve]rdant[671] [tree] on streams of water producing leaves[672]

28 and multiplying branches. For you examined[673] [… the sons of] Adam, and made (them) thoroughly gluttonous[674] from the land.

29 But to the sons of your truth you have given jo[y…]rt everlasting, and according to their knowledge, they honor

---

[667] A *vacat* appears here; it allows for the transition.
[668] Note there is a small *vacat* in the text.
[669] Heb. יצר.
[670] The author polemically refers to the Hasmoneans, like John Hyrcanus, who gained wealth and led mercenary armies.
[671] Or "fresh," "luxuriant."
[672] The noun is singular in Hebrew.
[673] Heb. בחר.
[674] *Hipʿil* infinitive of דשן; see the note to 8.32.

30　אי֯ש מרעהו וכן לבן אד֯ם [　　　　] א[יש‎999 הרביתה נח֯לת֯ו‎1000

31　בדעת אמתכה ולפי דעתו יובא֯ן [נ֯פש‎1001 עבדכה תעבה ה֯ו֯ן‎1002

32　ובצע וברום עדנים לא יח֯פ֯ו֯ק‎1003 ש֯ש לבי בבריתכה ואמתכ֯ה‎1004

33　תשעשע נפשי ואפרחה כ֯ש֯ו֯ש֯נ֯ה֯‎1005 ולבי נפתח למקור עולם

34　ומשענתי במעוז מרום וי֯[ח]זק נ֯פ֯ש֯י֯ [ו]ת֯בין‎1006 עמל ויבול כנץ לפני רו֯ח֯‎1007

35　ויתהולל לבי בחלחלה ומותני ברעדה ונהמתי עד תהום תבוא

36　ובחדרי שאול תחפש יחד ואפחדה בשומעי משפטיכה עם גבורי

　　　　　　　　　　　　　　　　　　　　　　ה
37　כוח וריבכה עם צבא קדושיך ב֯מ֯שפ֯ט‎1008 [ש֯ה‎1009

38　ומשפט ב[כ]ול‎1010 מ֯עשיכ֯ה וצדק י֯[‎1011 　　　　　　[ל

39　　　　　　　　　　　　　　　　　　　　[

40　　　　　　　　　　　　　　　[ת֯י֯

41　　　　　　　　　　　　[ע֯ו֯נ,‎1012

Col. 19 [= Sukenik Col. 11 + Frg. 60 Col. 1]
Parallels: 4Q427 Frg. 1; 4Q428 Frg. 12a

1　　　　　　　　　　　　　　　　　　　　[

2　　　　　　　　　　　　　　　　　　　　[

---

999 Sukenik: ש[　　] א֯. Licht: מאי[ש. Qimron: איש בא[רצונכה כי אמת֯כה. א֯[דם כהבדלו מאי[ש.
1000 Sukenik: נ֯לתו.
1001 Sukenik: ש֯֯ [　　] ו֯֯ב֯. Licht: ו[נפש בסודך. DJD: י֯ב֯ב֯ [כ]י֯ נ֯פ֯ש יובא֯[ן. Qimron: נ֯פ֯ש [כיא] יכב֯ב֯.
1002 Sukenik:]֯֯֯. Licht: ה[ון].
1003 Ctr. DJD: כי ֯֯֯֯֯. Reading follows Licht's restoration. Ink is visible. Qimron: לא א֯ב֯ח֯ר כי.
1004 Sukenik and Licht: ואמתכ[ה.
1005 Sukenik: ש֯נ֯ ֯֯֯֯֯. Licht: כ[שו]שנה.
1006 Not seen previously. Licht: וי[בוא בשרי במצרף.
1007 Sukenik: [ ]֯. Licht: [רוח].
1008 Ctr. DJD: בש֯מ֯י֯ם ו֯. Qimron: ֯֯֯ ב֯. The last two consonants are washed out.
1009 Licht: ב[רוב כוחכה כי צדקה תע[שה.
1010 DJD: ב֯כ֯ו֯ל. Qimron: ב֯כ֯ו֯ל.
1011 Sukenik and Qimron: וצדק י֯[. Licht: וצדק ו[ ]. Licht ends his transcription here. DJD: וצדק י֯֯[.
1012 Sukenik and Qimron: עתי.

30   one more than the other.[675] And thus to the son of[676] Adam[677] [… m]an you enlarged his inheritance

31   through the knowledge of your truth, and according to his knowledge he will be brought into […] the soul of[678] your servant detests wealth

32   and unjust gain. And the pompous[679] luxuries he does not desire. My heart rejoices in your covenant and your truth

33   delights my soul.[680] And I blossomed like a lily, and my heart was opened to the eternal source,

34   and my support (lay) in shelter from on high. And he str[eng]thened my soul [so][681] it can understand[682] misfortune. But it crumbles[683] like a bud before the wind.

35   And my heart is mocked by anguish and my loins by trembling. And my moaning goes unto the depth,

36   and seeks oneness in the rooms of Sheol. And I am afraid when I hear your judgments with the powerful

37   heroes;[684] and your lawsuit[685] with the host of your Holy Ones in judgment […]*šh*.

38   And judgment over [a]ll your works and righteousness *y*[…]*l*

39   […]

40   […]*ty*

41   […]ʿ*wny*

Col. 19 [= Sukenik Col. 11 + Frg. 60 Col. 1]
Parallels: 4Q427 Frg. 1; 4Q428 Frg. 12a

1   […]

2   […]

---

[675] Lit. "a man from his companion."
[676] Note the singular.
[677] Or "humankind."
[678] Heb. נפש.
[679] Or "haughtiness."
[680] Heb. נפש.
[681] Lit. "and."
[682] These words are read for the first time.
[683] Or "it withers." The bud (or petal) separates from the flower. See Isa 34:4.
[684] Or "mighty ones."
[685] See 17.15.

3   [

4   בפחד מֹדֹהוֹבֹ[1013   עֹמל מעיני ויגו]ן   מֹגֹוֹיֹתֹי ˚˚˚˚˚˚˚˚]1014

5   בהגו לבי1015   [   ]   (VACAT)

מודה1016

6   אֹודכה אלי כי הפלתה עֹם עפר וביצר חמר הגברתה מודה ואני מה כיֹא

7   [הבי]נֹֹותני1017 בסוד אמתכה ותשכילני במעשי פלאכה ותתן בפי הודות ובלשוני

8   תֹהֹלֹהֹ ומזל1018 שפתי במכון רנה ואזמרה בחסדיכה ובגבורתכה אשוחחה כול

9   היום תמיד אברכה שמכה   ואספרה כבודכה בתוך בני אדם וברוב טובכה

10   תשתעשע נפשי ואני ידעתי כי אמת פיכה ובידכה צדקה ובמחשבתכה

11   כול דעה ובכוחכה כול גבורה וכול כבוד אתכה הוא באפכה כול משפטי נגע

12   ובטובכה רוב סליחות ורחמיכה לכול בני רצונכה כי הודעתם בסוד אמתכה

13   וברזי פלאכה השכלתם ולמען1019 כבודכה טהרתה אנוש מפשע להתקדש

14   לכה מכול תועבות נדה ואשמת מעל להיחד עֹם1020 בני אמתך ובגורל עֹם

15   קדושיכה להרים מעפר תולעת מתים לסוד עֹ[ולם]1021 ומרוח נעוה לבינתכֹהֹ1022

1013 Sukenik: []ֹהֹ ˚˚˚ בפח˚. Qimron: בפחֹ מֹדֹהוֹבֹ.

1014 Sukenik: [ ]˚˚˚˚˚˚˚ [ ]˚˚˚˚˚˚˚ ויגֹ[ ]ֹ. DJD: [ ]ֹ ˚˚ [ ]ֹ ˚˚˚˚˚˚˚ מֹל מעיני ויגֹ[ ]ֹ. Qimron: ˚˚˚ ˚˚˚˚ מֹ[ ]מ ˚ עמל מעיני ויגוֹ[ן מֹ]. ותעֹ[לֹם עמֹל מעיני ויגו]ן. The leather is torn and the ink washed out.

1015 Sukenik:]בהגו לבי. Licht begins the column with: בהגו לבי. Cf. DJD and Qimron: בֹהֹגו לבי.

1016 The supralinear word is probably by a different scribe; note the two forms for *daleth*. The double מודה (and correction) may be out of the desire to thank אל twice (cf. *mBerakot* 5.3). Sometimes in modern Hebrew, it is said: תודה תודה.

1017 Sukenik: תֹני[. Licht: [הודע]תֹני. DJD and Qimron: [ה]בֹיֹנֹותני. The triangular head of a *waw* or *yodh* (not an ʿayin) can be seen.

1018 See 16.37: שפתי נאלם מזל [תהיל]ֹהֹ ומֹול. Licht: [תהיל]הֹ ומול. Sukenik: הֹ ומול. DJD: תֹ[הֹ]לֹהֹ ומזל. Qimron: [תה]לֹה ומזל.

1019 An imperfection in the leather should not be judged a scribal dot (*pace* DJD).

1020 Ctr. DJD: עֹם להיחד (perhaps a typographical error). Sukenik: [ ] להיחד. Licht: [עם] להיחד. With Qimron. Perhaps this expression reflects paranomasia on היחד.

1021 Sukenik: [ ]. Licht: [עולם]. Ctr. DJD and Qimron: [מתכה]אֹ, but the first letter looks more like an ʿayin (see Sukenik's photographs).

1022 Sukenik: לבינת[. Licht: [לבינת]כה.

3 […]

4 in fear, disaster […] trouble from my eyes and grie[f …] from my body[686] °°°°°°°°[…]

5 through the meditation of my heart […]. (VACAT)

6 I thank you, O my God, because you dealt wonderfully with dust, and a creature of[687] clay you strengthened.[688] Thanks, thanks.[689] And what am I that

7 you [allowed] me [to dis]cern[690] the secret of your truth? And you allowed me to have insight[691] into your wonderful works, and you put in my mouth thanksgivings[692] and on my tongue

8 praise. And the flow[693] of my lips (is) in the establishment of[694] exultation. And I will chant of your loving-kindnesses. And about your might, I will contemplate all

9 the day. I will always bless your name; and I will recount your glory among the sons of Adam.[695] And in your multitudinous goodness

10 my soul[696] is delighted. And I, I know that truth (is in) your mouth, and righteousness (is) in your hand. And in your thought (is)

11 all knowledge. And in your power (is) all might. And all glory is with you. In your anger (are) all the judgments of affliction;

12 and in your goodness (is) a multitude of forgivenesses. And your mercies (are) with all the sons of your will, because you allowed them to know[697] the secret of your truth;

13 and into your wondrous mysteries you allowed them to have insight.[698] And for the sake of your glory, you purified the human from transgression that (he may) sanctify himself

14 for you from all the abominations of impurity and the guilt of infidelity, to be united with the sons of your truth. And in the lot together with

15 your Holy Ones to be raised from the dust (as) a worm of the dead ones to the e[ternal] council, and from a perverted spirit to your discernment.

---

[686] Or "my corpse."

[687] Heb. יצר. Most likely, again, the *beth* is a *nota accusativi*.

[688] Lit. "made mighty."

[689] The second "thanks" is penned above the line.

[690] *Hipʿil* permissive.

[691] *Hipʿil* permissive.

[692] The expression helped to name this scroll the *Thanksgiving Hymns*; but the main reason was the pervasive *incipit*: "I thank you, O Lord, because." The *incipit* has been labeled "the Hodayot formula."

[693] Perhaps a *piʿel* part. of נזל. The *piʿel* of this verb is not in Biblical Hebrew.

[694] Or "in the place of," "in the foundation of."

[695] Or "humankind."

[696] Heb. נפש.

[697] *Hipʿil* permissive.

[698] *Hipʿil* permissive.

16   ולהתיצב במעמד לפניכה עם צבא עד ורוחו[ת   ]¹⁰²³ להתחדש¹⁰²⁴ עם כול¹⁰²⁵

17   נהיה¹⁰²⁶ ועם ידעים ביחד רנה

18   [ואנ]י¹⁰²⁷ אודכה אלי ארוממכה צורי ובהפלא[ֿ]¹⁰²⁸

19   [כי הודעתני סוד אמת וֿבֿרֿזֿ]י¹⁰²⁹

20   [ונס]תֿרֿותֿיֿכֿה¹⁰³⁰ גליתה לי ואביֿט [   ]ֿי חסד¹⁰³¹ ואדעה

21   [כי]¹⁰³² לכה הצדק ובחסדיכה יש[ועת¹⁰³³   ]הֿ¹⁰³⁴ וכלה בלוא רחמיך

22   וֿאני נפתח לי מקור לאבל מרורים [   ]לא¹⁰³⁵ נסתר עמל מעיני

23   בדעתי יצרי גבר ותשובת אנוש אֿת[בוננה¹⁰³⁶ א]בֿל חטאה¹⁰³⁷ ויגון

24   אשמה ויבואו בלבבי ויגעו בעצמ[ֿי ל[   ]ֿים ולהגות הגי¹⁰³⁸
ואנחה בכנור קינה לכול אבל יֿגֿ[ון]¹⁰³⁹

25   יגון ומספד מרורים עד כלות עולה וא[י]ן¹⁰⁴⁰ מכאוב[¹⁰⁴¹ ואין נגע להחלות ואז

26   אזמרה בכנור ישועות ונבל שמֿחֿ[ות¹⁰⁴² ותוף גי]לֿה¹⁰⁴³ וחליל תהלה לאין

---

¹⁰²³ Sukenik:]ורוחי. Licht and Qimron: ורוחו[ת. DJD: [ורוחו]ת עלום.

¹⁰²⁴ Ctr. DJD and Qimron: וֿלהתחדש. There is no *waw* before the word. Lines do not always begin flush with the vertical lining.

¹⁰²⁵ DJD incorrectly imagines a final word: [כול הֿ[ויה. Qimron: [כול הֿ]ויה. כול is the last word in line 16; for a similar margin, see lines 20 and 24.

¹⁰²⁶ Ctr. DJD: וֿנהיה. Ctr. Qimron: [ו]נֿהֿיה. There is no *waw* to begin the word.

¹⁰²⁷ Sukenik and Licht do not see the ֿי[.

¹⁰²⁸ Licht: ובהפלא] תהלה אהללך בקול רנה.

¹⁰²⁹ DJD: וֿבֿרֿזֿ]י. Licht: וברזי] פלאכה השכלתני ואמתך למדתני ונפלא [ותי]כֿ[ה. Qimron: וֿבֿרֿזֿ]י אמת.

¹⁰³⁰ Sukenik: ה[כֿ]יתֿי. Restoration is influenced by Licht; cf. DJD and Qimron: [ונס]תֿרֿותֿיֿכֿה.

¹⁰³¹ Sukenik: ֿי חסד [   ]. Licht: וחסד[את. DJD: ֿ ֿי חסד [   ]בֿ. Qimron: מֿי חסד [   ]הֿ. בצדקותיכה ובכול רח[. בפלאיו ובנסתרות אמת

¹⁰³² Sukenik: לכה[. Licht: [כי]לכה. DJD and Qimron: [כ]ֿ לכה.

¹⁰³³ Restoration follows Licht; cf. DJD: ו]ישֿפֿטֿ. Sukenik and Qimron: יש[   ]ה. For ישועת see line 26.

¹⁰³⁴ Licht:]ה וע[ש]י. Qimron: הֿ חטא. ועת כול בני אמתכ[ה

¹⁰³⁵ Licht: [ומספד אנחה]וֿלא. DJD and Qimron: א]לֿא.

¹⁰³⁶ Licht: [לעפר ופקודתו]אֿ. Qimron: [תבוננה]אֿ. See 4Q427 frg. 1 line 3: אתבוננה.

¹⁰³⁷ Sukenik and Licht: לחטאה. Ctr. DJD and Qimron: א]בֿל חטאה. The leather is torn before this word; no consonants can be discerned.

¹⁰³⁸ Sukenik: בעצמי לֿ[הֿ]תם כוח לק[צֿים. Qimron: בעצמי לֿ[   ]ֿים ולהגות הגי. DJD: בעצמי ל[נגע ותחלוי]ֿים ולהגות הגו. Licht: בעצמ[י   ]ים ולהגות הגי ולהגות הגי.

¹⁰³⁹ Sukenik:]ֿגֿ. Licht: [ון]יג. Licht makes no mention of the supralinear correction and did not transcribe the second יגון. DJD: יֿגֿ[ו]ֿן[. Qimron: יגון. Scribe B wrote the interlinear letters which appear above lines 25 to 29.

¹⁰⁴⁰ Scribe A ended here and Scribe C begins.

¹⁰⁴¹ Sukenik: ֿ [   ] ואֿ. Licht: ה[רשע]ֿין וא.

¹⁰⁴² Sukenik:]שמ. Cf. DJD and Qimron: שמחֿ[ה.

¹⁰⁴³ Sukenik:]לה[. Licht: שמ[חות ותוף גי]לה.

16   And to be present in rank before you with an everlasting host and the spirits [of …], to be renewed together with all

17   that exists, and with those who have the knowledge (to be) in the common[699] exultation. (VACAT)

18   [And I,] I thank you, O my God. I exalt you, O my rock. And in the wondrous […]

19   […] that you allowed me to know[700] the secret of truth and in mysteri[es of ….]

20   [And] your [hidd]en things you revealed to me. And I look […]°*y* loving-kindness, and I know

21   [that] to you (is) righteousness and in your loving-kindnesses (is) salv[ation …]*h* and destruction (that is) without your mercies.

22   But (as) for me, there is opened to me a source of bitter mourning […]. Misfortune was not hidden from my eyes

23   in my knowing of the inclinations of[701] man.[702] And the return of the human, I will [examine closely[703] … mou]rning, sin, and the grief of

24   guilt. And they entered my heart and reached my bones *l*[…]°*ym* so as[704] to ponder meditatively

25   grief, and a sigh with a lyre, a lament to every mourning of gri[ef],[705] and the wailing of bitterness until the annihilation of injustice. And th[ere (is) no pain] and there is no affliction to cause illness. And then

26   I will chant with a lyre acts of salvation and (with) a harp joy[s, and (with) a tambourine[706] rejo]icing, and (with) a flute praise without

---

699 Heb. יחד.

700 *Hipʿil* permissive.

701 Heb. יצר.

702 Heb. גבר.

703 The *hitʿpol* of בין.

704 Lit. "and."

705 The words between the two nouns "grief" were missed by Scribe A. The error is an example of *parablepsis* probably facilitated by *homoiteleuton*. They were supplied by Scribe B who placed them above the line. He probably knew the reading in 4Q427 frg. 1 1.12.

706 See Jer 31:4. The Hebrew noun תוף means "tambourine," "hand-drum," or "timbrel." See the references in KB 1771. A conceivable restoration is מצלתים, "(two small) cymbals;" but there is not enough space for so many consonants. See Gen 31:27. See esp. Ps 81:1–3 which mentions "sing," "tambourine," "lyre," and "harp." Ps 150:3–5 notes "trumpet," flute," "harp," "tambourine," "dance," "strings," "pipe," and "cymbals."

27   השבת ומי בכול מעשיכה יוכל לספ֗ר [נפלאותי]כה¹⁰⁴⁵ בפֿי כולם יהולל

28   שמכה לעולמי עד יברכוכה כפי שכל[ם עד קצ]ים¹⁰⁴⁶ ישמיעו יחד

29   בקול רנה ואין יגון ואנחה ועולה ל[א תמצא ע]ו֗[וד]¹⁰⁴⁷ ואמתכה תופיע

30   לכבוד עד ושלום עולום¹⁰⁴⁸   ברוך את[ה   אדוני א]שֿר נתתה לעֿבֿד֗כֿה¹⁰⁴⁹

31   שכל דעה להבין בנפלאותיכה ומֿנֿה֗ן לשון ל[סֿפר¹⁰⁵⁰ ברוב חסדיכה

32   ברוך אתה אל הרחמים והנינה כגדו[ל]¹⁰⁵¹ כֿחֿכה¹⁰⁵² ורוב אמתכה והמו[ן]

33   חסדיכה בכול מעשיכה שמח נפש עבדכה באמתכה וטהרני

34   בצדקתכה כאשר יחלתי לטובכה ולחסדיכה אקוה ולסליחות[י]כֿה¹⁰⁵³

35   פתחתה משרי וביגוני¹⁰⁵⁵ נחמתני כיא נשנתי ברחמיכה ברוך את֗[ה]¹⁰⁵⁶

36   אדוני כי אתה פעלתה אלה ותשם בפי עבד֗כֿה הֿוֿד֗וֿת תֿ[הלה]¹⁰⁵⁷

37   ותחנה ומענה לשון והכינותה לי פֿעול[תכה¹⁰⁵⁸

38   ואעצו[ר כוח [ל֗]ל [   ] [   ]

39   ואתה]

---

¹⁰⁴⁴ Ctr. DJD: כֿו֗ל]ל.

¹⁰⁴⁵ Sukenik: כה[   ]. With Licht. Qimron: מֿ[עשי פלא]כה.

¹⁰⁴⁶ Sukenik: ים[   ]שֿפֿ. Licht: כפי ש[בי פשע וענו]ים.

¹⁰⁴⁷ Licht: [לא תהיה עוד]. DJD: לֿ[א֗] תמצא עוד. Qimron: לֿ[וא תמצא עו]ד֗. The restoration is provided by 4Q428 frg. 12a line 3.

¹⁰⁴⁸ A mistake for עולם. A *vacat* appears here in 4Q428 frg. 12a line 4.

¹⁰⁴⁹ Sukenik: °°°ל. Licht: [ל]עבדכה.

¹⁰⁵⁰ Sukenik: [{ע}]ֿ. Licht: ו֗[מ]ֿ[ע]נה לשון ל[ספר. DJD and Qimron: ו֗[מ]ֿ[ע]נה לשון ל[ספר.

¹⁰⁵¹ Sukenik: בגדו[ל]. Cf. Licht: [ל]בגדו. With DJD and Qimron, read *kaph* for context; the *kaph* and *beth* of Scribe C are often similar.

¹⁰⁵² Sukenik: וכה°[. Licht: טובכה. DJD: כֿ[ו֗]חֿכה. Perhaps כוחכה was misspelled, yet note the supralinears in lines 31, 32, 35, and 38.

¹⁰⁵³ Sukenik and Licht: [חות]יכה.

¹⁰⁵⁴ The *beth* looks like another hand.

¹⁰⁵⁵ Sukenik, DJD, and Qimron: וביגוני. Licht: ומיגוני. The *beth* looks like a *mem* in this hand.

¹⁰⁵⁶ Licht: [א]תה.

¹⁰⁵⁷ Licht: [ותהלה. DJD: עבדכה הודות. With DJD: הֿוֿד֗וֿת תֿ[ה]ל֗[ה. This is, indeed, speculative.

¹⁰⁵⁸ Sukenik: [עול]ֿ. Licht: הכינותה לפועל[כה. Licht did not transcribe the rest of the column. Qimron: וֿעול]ה. DJD: פֿעֿול]ת.

¹⁰⁵⁹ DJD: [   ]ֿ[   ]ל֗[   ]י֗[   ]ר כוח [ל֗]ל ואעצו.

27   ceasing. And who among all your creatures[707] can recount your [wonders]? In the mouth of all of them your name

28   is praised forever and ever. They will bless you according to [their] insight [unto the endti]mes. Together they make proclamation

29   with a voice of exultation, and there is neither grief nor sigh. And injustice (is) n[ot found] any[more]. And your truth will appear

30   for everlasting glory and the eternal peace. Blessed are yo[u, O Lord, t]hat you gave to your servant

31   insight (into) knowledge to discern your wonders, and the answer of [the tongue to] recount the multitude of your loving-kindnesses.

32   Blessed are you, O God of mercies and compassion, for your grea[t] power and the multitude of your truth and the abundan[ce of]

33   your loving-kindnesses. In all your works, the soul of[708] your servant (is) joyful in your truth. And purify me[709]

34   in your righteousness, when I await your goodness and hope for your loving-kindnesses. And to your forgiveness[es]

35   you released my breakers. And in my grief you consoled me, because I leaned on your mercies. Blessed are yo[u,]

36   O LORD, for you, you acted (in) these (things), and you put in the mouth of your servant thanksgivings, p[raise,]

37   and supplication and the answer of the tongue.[710] And you established for me [your] activiti[es ….]

38   And I will retai[n power …]l[…]b[…]

39   And you, […]

---

[707] Lit. "your works."
[708] Heb. נפש.
[709] A *piˁel* imperative of טהר ; or "O purify me."
[710] See 4.29; 8.24; 10.9; 15.14, 16; 19.37.

40   אמ]ת¹⁰⁶⁰

41   וא̊]¹⁰⁶¹

42   ו̊בֿעֿנֿהֿ]] לשון¹⁰⁶²   ]]°¹⁰⁶³

Col. 20 [= Sukenik Col. 12 + Frgs. 54 and 60 Col. 2]
Parallels: 4Q427 Frgs. 2–3, 8, 9; 4Q428 Frg. 12b

1   ]

2   ]

3   ]

4   ]ה̊[¹⁰⁶⁶   ]ח̊[   ]]° תרחב̊ נפשי]¹⁰⁶⁵   א̊]¹⁰⁶⁴   °]]

5   ]]בֿשמחה ו]ששון ואשב]ה̊ לבטח¹⁰⁶⁷ במעון קו]דש¹⁰⁶⁸   ב]שֿוֿקט¹⁰⁶⁹ ושלוה

6   [בשלו]ם̊ וברכה ב]]א̊הלי¹⁰⁷⁰ כבֿוֿד וישועה¹⁰⁷¹ ואהללה שמכה בתוך יראיכה

7   [למשכי]ל̊¹⁰⁷³ [ה]וֿדות¹⁰⁷⁴ ותפלה לתגל והתחנן תמיד מקצ¹⁰⁷⁵ לקץ עם מבוא אור¹⁰⁷⁶

8   ל̊ממשֿ]לתו]¹⁰⁷⁷ בתקופות יום לתכונו לחוקות מאור גדול בפנות ערב ומוצא

---

¹⁰⁶⁰ Sukenik:]אמ. DJD: אמת̊]כה. Qimron:]אמת̊.

¹⁰⁶¹ Qimron:]וא̊.

¹⁰⁶² Ctr. DJD and Qimron:]°°°. See 19.31, 37: ומענה לשון. Perhaps the bottom margin is visible.

¹⁰⁶³ Frg. 60 col. 1 supplies this unreadable consonant.

¹⁰⁶⁴ Frg. 54 begins here and provides part of the right side of lines 4–6.

¹⁰⁶⁵ Sukenik: [נפש ה̊תדה].

¹⁰⁶⁶ DJD: נפשי[°ר ל °]° [ ]° [ ].

¹⁰⁶⁷ Licht began the column with אשכנ]ה לבטח.

¹⁰⁶⁸ There may be ink before the קו[ן; see: DJD 29, pp. 92–93. It does look like: קו̊]דש.

¹⁰⁶⁹ With DJD. Ctr. Qimron: ש(ו)קט]. Sukenik: קט °° [ ]ק. Licht: קט]ודש בש]ק. Conceivably שקט°[.

¹⁰⁷⁰ Sukenik: אהלו]. Qimron: וברכה באהלי [שלום] (sic). Frg. 54 ends here providing the beth in the word באהלי.

¹⁰⁷¹ Sukenik: ב. וישועה °°°. Licht: בטח]וישועה לי ב]אהלי[ואנוחה].

¹⁰⁷² The interlinears are probably by the same scribe. Read: להתנפל (with Licht).

¹⁰⁷³ See 20.14. Restore with Puech and DJD; cf. 4Q427 frg. 8 2.10.

¹⁰⁷⁴ Sukenik: דור̊ [. Licht: ודור]ל̊[משכי]. DJD: ה]ודות̊. Qimron: ה]ודות [למשכיל. אודך לדור]ודור̊.

¹⁰⁷⁵ Note the medial ṣade in final position (bis).

¹⁰⁷⁶ No vacat is possible in 1QHᵃ, but it may be in the lost left margins of 4Q427 frgs. 2–3 2.17. A vacat must be presupposed in 4Q428 frg. 12b line 2. A new hymn begins with 1QHᵃ 20.8.

¹⁰⁷⁷ Sukenik:]°ממ. Licht: ממ[עונתו].

40   tru[th …]

41   and ᵓ[…]

42   and in the answer of [the tongue …]°

Col. 20 [= Sukenik Col. 12 + Frgs. 54 and 60 Col. 2]
Parallels: 4Q427 Frgs. 2–3, 8, 9; 4Q428 Frg. 12b

1   […]

2   […]

3   […]

4   […]° ᵓ[…]° my soul[711] broadens […]ḥ[…]ḥ

5   […] with joy and [happiness. And I si]t securely in the ho[ly] dwelling pea[cefully, and in] silence and tranquility,

6   [in pea]ce and blessing in the tents of glory and salvation. So I will praise your name among those who stand in awe of[712] you. (VACAT)

7   [For the Instruct]or, [th]anksgivings and prayer to prostrate oneself, and continually petition from the endtime (of the day) to the endtime (of the night[713] when) light comes out

8   for [its] domin[ion] at the periods of the day according to its order, (and) according to the statutes of the great light.[714] When the evening turns and the light

---

[711] Heb. נפש.
[712] Not "fear."
[713] See 17.7–8. Or "from the end (of the day) to the end (of the night)."
[714] The sun is "the great light." See Gen 1:6. The Qumranites celebrated time and festivals according to the "solar calendar." They opposed the use of the lunar calendar by the officiating priests in the Temple.

פ¹⁰⁷⁸

9   אור ברשית¹⁰⁷⁹ ממשלת חושך למועד לילה בתקופתו לנות בוקר ובקץ

א
ע
10   הֵאספו ל מונתו¹⁰⁸⁰ מפניתֹ¹⁰⁸¹ אור למוצא לילה ומבוא יומם תמיד בכול

11   מולדי עת יסודי¹⁰⁸² קצ¹⁰⁸³ ותקופת מועדים בתכונם באותותם לכול

12   ממשלתם בתכון נאמנה מפי אל ותעודת הווה¹⁰⁸⁴ והיאה תהיה

13   ואין אפס וזולתה לוא היה ולוא יהיה עוד כי אל ה(ו)ד(י)עות¹⁰⁸⁵

14   הכינה ואין אחר עמו   ואני משכיל¹⁰⁸⁶ ידעתיכה אלי ברוח

י
15   אשר נתתה בי ונאמנה שמעתי לסוד פלאכה ברוח קדשכה

16   [פ]תחתה לתוכי דעת ברז שכלכה ומעין גבורתֹ[כ]הֹ   ב]תֹוך¹⁰⁸⁷

17   [יראיכ]הֹ¹⁰⁸⁸ לרוב חסד וקנאת כלה והשב[ת]תה

18   [ל]¹⁰⁸⁹   ב]הדר¹⁰⁹⁰ כבודכה לאור עוֹל]ם¹⁰⁹¹

19   מ]פֹחד¹⁰⁹² רשעה ואין רמיה וֹ[ ] ול]

20   מֹועדי¹⁰⁹³ שממה כיא אין ע]וד¹⁰⁹⁴

---

¹⁰⁷⁸ The supralinear is probably by the same scribe. Read לפנות.
¹⁰⁷⁹ A scribal error for בראשית.
¹⁰⁸⁰ The text is two words: אל מעונתו. So also Sukenik and Licht. The supralinears are by the same scribe.
¹⁰⁸¹ The ת is erased. There is only one scribal dot. The scribe sometimes leaves excessive ink in the bottom of the right leg of the *taw*. Cf. DJD: מפני{תֹ}.
¹⁰⁸² Qimron: וסודי.
¹⁰⁸³ Note medial *ṣade* in final position.
¹⁰⁸⁴ Licht and Qimron: הויה.
¹⁰⁸⁵ Sukenik: אל ה/ד\עות. Licht and Qimron: אל *הדעות. The correction brings the thought in line with 1QS 3.15: מאל הדעות.
¹⁰⁸⁶ Sukenik: משֹכיֹל ל. Licht: משכלי.
¹⁰⁸⁷ Sukenik: יֹך[   ]גבור. Licht: גבורת]ך[דיך נפתח לי בחס]. Cf. DJD: גבורת]הֹ בֹתוך. Qimron: גבורת]כה בֹתוך]הֹ ואהי]כה.
¹⁰⁸⁸ Sukenik: הֹ[. Licht: והי]ה[.
¹⁰⁸⁹ Qimron: [ותאר]לֹ]יֹ.
¹⁰⁹⁰ Sukenik: הדר ˚[. Licht: ב]הדר. DJD: בֹ]הדר. Qimron: בֹהדר. והשב[ת רשעה לנצח ואמתכה תופיע ב]הדר.
¹⁰⁹¹ Sukenik:]עֹ[. Licht: עו]לם. DJD and Qimron: [   ]ם עוֹלֹ. The *lamedh* is not visible.
¹⁰⁹² Sukenik: חד ˚[. Licht: פ]חד. עו]לם וכול עולה תשמיד לעד ותכלה פ]חד.
¹⁰⁹³ Sukenik: עדי ˚[. Licht: מו]עדי רמיה. בכל מעשיך ובקץ פקודתכה יתמו כול מו]עדי.
¹⁰⁹⁴ See 12.21.

9 goes out at the beginning of the dominion of darkness according to the appointed time of night and its period at the turn of the morning. And at the endtime (of the night)

10 when it is gathered to its domicile from before the light when the night goes out and the day comes in.[715] (And) continually in all

11 the births of time and the bases of endtime,[716] and (during) the period of seasons[717] in their courses with their signs according to all

12 their dominion (which is) faithfully established from the mouth of God and the fixed times of existence. And this shall be,

13 and (continue) without end.[718] And apart from it there has been nothing, and nothing else shall ever be. For the God of knowledge[719]

14 has established it, and there is not another except him.[720] And I, the Instructor,[721] I know you, my God, with the spirit

15 that you put in me, and loyally I have listened to your wondrous secret.[722] Through the spirit of your holiness,

16 you [op]ened in the midst of me knowledge by the mystery of your insight, and (by) the fountain of [yo]ur might [in] the midst of[723]

17 [those who stand in awe of[724] yo]u for the multitude of loving-kindness and the zeal for annihilation. And [yo]u led back [...]

18 [...]l [... in] the splendor of your glory for an etern[al] light [...]

19 [... from] the fear of wickedness, and there is no treachery and [...]wl[...]

20 [...] the seasons of[725] desolation because there is no m[ore ...]

---

[715] See esp. 1QS 10.1–3 and the *Morning and Evening Prayers* found in the Qumran caves. See PTSDSSP vol. 4a.

[716] Or "Endtime."

[717] Or "appointed times," "festivals."

[718] It is apparent throughout this section that the author is criticizing the lunar calendar observed by those whom he deemed the wicked, ignorant, and illegitimate priests.

[719] See 1QS 3.15 for "the God of knowledge." There are many echoes of 1QS 3.13–4.26 in the *Thanksgiving Hymns*. Most likely the "treatise on two spirits" was part of the lore that those who entered the Community had to memorize.

[720] Lit. "with him," but there are many angels and archangels with God. The author is affirming monotheism, although in some lines he espouses henotheism.

[721] This is a technical term at Qumran; see 1QS 3.13.

[722] Or "council."

[723] Note the paronomasia with "midst of."

[724] Not "fear of."

[725] Or "appointed times of," "festivals of."

21　[ו]א֯ין¹⁰⁹⁵ עוד מדהבה כיא לפני אפכ֯[ה¹⁰⁹⁶

22　°° 　[　] יחפזו¹⁰⁹⁷ ואין צדיק עמכה [　]ה¹⁰⁹⁸

23　ו[ל]השכיל¹⁰⁹⁹ בכול רזיכה ולשיב דב֯ר[¹¹⁰⁰ 　כי֯[א¹¹⁰¹
　　　　　　　　　　　　　　　　א¹¹⁰²

24　ב֯תוכחתכה ולטובכה יצפו כי בחס֯ד[יכה¹¹⁰³ 　כו]ל֯

25　יודעיכה¹¹⁰⁴ ובקצ¹¹⁰⁵ כבודכה יגילו ולפי כ֯[　כי֯[א¹¹⁰⁶ כשכלם

26　הגשתם ולפי ממשלתם ישרתוכה למפלג[יהם לבלתי שו֯ב¹¹⁰⁷ ממכה

27　ולוא¹¹⁰⁸ לעבור על דברכה ואני מעפר לקח֯[תני 　ומחמר ק]ו֯ר֯צ֯ת֯י¹¹⁰⁹

28　למקור נדה וערות קלון מקוי עפר ומגבל֯[מים 　ומסוד ערו]ה֯¹¹¹⁰ ומדור

29　חושך ותשובת עפר ליצר חמר בקצ¹¹¹¹ אפ֯[כה מה יש]ו֯ב֯ ע֯פ֯ר֯¹¹¹²

30　אל אשר לקח משם ומה ישיב עפר וא֯פ֯ר֯[¹¹¹³ 　ומ]ה֯ יבין¹¹¹⁴

31　[במ]ע֯שיו¹¹¹⁵ ומה יתיצב לפני מוכיח בו ר֯[　]ק֯ו֯ד֯ש֯¹¹¹⁶

---

¹⁰⁹⁵ Sukenik:]ין. Licht: וא]ין. אין ע]ולה בממשלתכה וכול ישע לוא יהיה עוד וא]ין.

¹⁰⁹⁶ Sukenik: [אפ֯. Licht:]חפזו[י. אפ]כה ינוסו רוחות רשעה ומקול רעמכה י]חפזו.

¹⁰⁹⁷ Ctr. DJD: יחפזו ב֯. Sukenik:]חפזי. Licht: יחפזו[י. Qimron: כ֯ה֯ יחפזו מרוח]. But there are no traces of the *yodh* or *beth*.

¹⁰⁹⁸ Ctr. DJD and Qimron: כה]. Licht: ה[יכ]נפלאותי בניב יומי].

¹⁰⁹⁹ Sukenik:]השכיל. Licht: להשכיל.

¹¹⁰⁰ Licht:]דב֯ר על משפטיכה. DJD: להשיב דבר [על משפטיך ובני אמתך רצו]. Perhaps a mistake for דבר.

¹¹⁰¹ The א[has been missed by all others. כיא appears 6 other times in lines 23–37.

¹¹⁰² The correction is by the same scribe and brings the text into line with Qumran orthography. See the same correction in 7.20, 25, 35, 37; 12.9. Sometimes the correction is also supralinear.

¹¹⁰³ Sukenik:]בחס֯. Licht: [אוזנם גליתה סדיכה]בח.

¹¹⁰⁴ Sukenik and Licht: ויודעוכה. With DJD and Qimron: יודעיכה. Both readings are possible but the *waw* and *yodh* are sometimes distinguishable, as here. The *waw* consecutive is not to be preferred. If [כו]ל is restored, a participle is likely.

¹¹⁰⁵ Note the medial *sade* in final position.

¹¹⁰⁶ Sukenik: [　]ולפי֯. Licht: ו]כשכלם. ולפי[דעתם קרבתם ו]כשכלם.

¹¹⁰⁷ Ctr. DJD: [ל]שו֯ב. Licht: שו]ב. למפלג]יהם לבלתי שו]ב.

¹¹⁰⁸ Sukenik and Licht: לוא.

¹¹⁰⁹ Sukenik: [ר֯צ֯]י. Licht:]רצתי. לק[חתי ומחמר קו]רצתי (ואני מה כיא מעפר לוקחתי) See 23.24. ומחמר ק]ו֯ר֯צ֯ת֯י. DJD:

¹¹¹⁰ See 4.31 and 9.24. Sukenik: [ה. Licht:]ה[משמ אשם מגולל המים]ומגבל. DJD: סוד רמ]ה. ומגבל[המים מגולל אשם מ]ה.

¹¹¹¹ Note the medial *sade* in the final position.

¹¹¹² Sukenik: [　]ב֯עפר. Licht: עפר]ב בקץ. ב בקץ]יעוד לו וסופ[ו. DJD: י]שו֯ב עפר. Qimron: וי]שו֯ב עפר.

¹¹¹³ Qimron: וא֯פ֯ר֯. These consonants are evident. DJD: על משפטכה וא֯פ֯ר֯.

¹¹¹⁴ Licht: יבין]ה. ו]אפר לתוכחתכה ומה יבין.

¹¹¹⁵ Sukenik:]שיו. Licht: [מע]שיו[ב. Qimron:]ע֯שיו.

¹¹¹⁶ Sukenik: [ודש. Licht: [בו]ק֯ו֯ד֯ש. DJD: ק֯ו֯ד֯ש[　] ו֯°° . Qimron: [קודש]ה֯כ֯מ֯ל֯א֯. ו]יעמוד לפני מעין ק[ודש.

196

21   [and] there is no more disaster because before yo[ur] anger […]

22   °°[…] they will hurry, and no one (is) righteous except you[726] […]h

23   and [to] allow to gain insight[727] into all your mysteries, and to answer a word [… f]or

24   in your chastisement and in your goodness they will wait. For in [your] loving-kindness[es … al]l

25   who know you, so in the Endtime of your glory they shall rejoice. And according to k[… f]or as according to their insight

26   you brought them near, and according to their dominion they shall serve you in line with [their] division[s without] turning from you

27   so as[728] not to transgress your word. And I, from dust [you] took [me and from clay] I [was s]haped

28   into a source of impurity and nakedness of shame. A reservoir of dust and mixed [water and a foundation of nakedne]ss,[729] and a habitation of

29   darkness, and a return (to) dust for the creature of[730] clay at the Endtime of [your] anger. [How can] dust [ret]urn

30   to the place where it was taken from? And how can dust and ashes answer […? And ho]w can he discern

31   [in] his [w]orks? And how can he stand before the one who chastises him? r°°°[…] holiness.

---

[726] Lit. "with."
[727] *Hipʿil* permissive.
[728] Lit. "and."
[729] Or "genitals."
[730] Heb. יצר.

32 ‏[ורום]1117 עולם ומקוי כבוד ומקור דעת וגבורֹתֹ [פל]א̊1118 והמה לֹוא1119

‏ה

33 ‏[יוכ]לֹו לספר כול כבודכה ולתיצב̊1120 לפני אפכה ואין להשיב דבֹ̊ר̊1121

34 ‏על תֹוכחתכה1122 כיא צדקתה ואין לנגֹ̊דכה ומה אפהו שב אל עפרו

‏דברתי1123

35 ‏ואני נאלמתי ומה אֹדבר על זות כדעתי מצירוק1124 יצר חמר ומה

36 ‏אדבר כיא אם פתחתה פי ואיכה אבין כיא אם השכלתני ומה אֹ̊[בר]1125

37 ‏בלוא גליתה לבי ואיכה אישר דרך כיא אם הכינֹ̊[תה1126 פ]ע̊מֹ̊[י]1127

38 ‏תעמוד פעמֹ̊[י כיא אם1128 ת]ח̊זק1129 בכוח ואיכה אתקומם [1130

39 ‏וכולֹ °°° [   ] פֹ̊עֹמֹ̊י בא̊[ין]1131

40 ‏ה̊[1132

41 ‏כֹ̊[

42 ‏ו̊[1133

1117 Licht and Qimron: [ורום]. DJD: ̊[ ].

1118 Sukenik: ̊א̊[   ]וגבן. Licht: וגבן̊[רי פל]א.

1119 Sukenik: א[ ]ל. Licht: לֹ[ו]א.

1120 The correction is by the same scribe. Read ולהתיצב.

1121 Sukenik and Licht did not see more consonants on the line. The alignment of the tears is misleading. Cf. DJD: דֹ̊בֹ̊ר̊. There appears faintly three consonants, perhaps דבֹ̊ר̊. See ולשיב דבֹ̊ר̊ in 20.23.

1122 Ctr. DJD: בוכחתכה. See Sukenik, Licht, and Qimron: תוכחתכה. What looks like a *beth* is a *taw*; the feet are separate.

1123 The correction is by the same scribe.

1124 Or מצידוק. See 1QS 11.21: מצירוק (or מצי רוק). See 1QHª 23:28, 36. Sukenik and Licht: מצידוק; cf. DJD: מצורוק. Qimron: מצירוק. A *daleth* is possible (*pace* Carmignac and DJD); it has a "crown;" see דרך in line 37. The issue is complex, see PTSDSSP 1 pp. 50–51 and DJD 40 pp. 258–59. Two meanings are conceivable: 1) "a mixture, a creature of clay…." The influence of 1QS on 1QH should not be overlooked. 2) "According to my knowledge, I spoke from rightness, a creature of clay…." That is, God's gift of rightness allows the human to praise God (see Licht's note 32 on p. 178).

1125 Sukenik: אֹ̊[ר. Licht: מֹר[או.

1126 Sukenik: [ ]°°[הכי. See Licht: הכינ]ותני. Cf. DJD and Qimron (different diacritics): הכינֹ̊תֹ]ה.

1127 Sukenik:]°°[. Licht: הכינ]ותני ורגלי איך. Qimron: מצֹ̊צֹ̊]די. DJD: [עֹ̊מֹ̊]י ומה. פ.

1128 Sukenik: ̊פ. Licht: ב]גבול. DJD: פֹ̊עֹמֹ̊]י. Qimron: פֹ̊עֹמֹ̊]י. For כיא אם see line 37.

1129 Ctr. DJD: מת]חֹ̊זק. Licht: ב]גבול רשעה ואין את]חֹ̊זק. With Qimron.

1130 Licht: לפני נגע]. Licht does not attempt to read the rest of the column. DJD: אתקומם [כיא אם.

1131 Sukenik:]ו במי ב[. DJD: פֹ̊עֹמֹ̊י בא̊[ין]. Qimron: פֹ̊עֹמֹ̊י בא̊[ן].

1132 Frg. 60 col. 2 begins here and provides the readings for lines 40–42.

1133 Frg. 60 ends here. The bottom margin may be visible.

32   [And (as for)] the eternal [height] and the reservoirs of glory, and the source of knowledge and of [wonder]ful might, and they are not

33   [able] to recount all your glory, and to be present before your anger. And it is impossible to return a word[731]

34   against your chastisement, for you are righteous and nothing (is) against you. And what is that which returns to its dust?

35   But I, I am dumb, and what can I say concerning this? According to my knowledge, I spoke from a mixture, a creature of[732] clay. And what

36   can I say unless you open my mouth? And how can I discern unless you allow me to have insight?[733] And what ca[n I say]

37   if you do not reveal (it to) my heart? And how can I straighten the way unless [you] establish [my foo]tstep?

38   [My] footstep stands [only when you] make (it) strong with power. And how can I raise […]

39   and all °°°[…] my footstep with[out …]

40   h[…]

41   k°[…]

42   and °[…]

---

[731] Lit. "and (it is) not (possible) to return a word." Note the paronomasia on "return" in lines 26–34.

[732] Heb. יצר. See 23.28, 36 and 21.11–12.

[733] *Hipʿil* permissive.

Col. 21 [= Sukenik Col. 18 + Frg. 3][1134]
Parallels: 4Q427 Frgs. 10, 11, 12; 4Q428 Frg. 13

[**1**

פ[שׁ֯ע[1135] ילוד א֯[שׁה][1136]   **2**

[י֯כה[1137] וצדקתכה[1138]   **3**

ו[א֯י֯]כ֯[ה] א֯כ֯י֯ר[בל][וא[1139] ראיתי זות   **4**

איכ]ה֯[1140] אביט בלוא גליתה֯ עיני ואשמעה   **5**

[בלוא גליתה אוזני[1141] השׁ֯ם֯ לבבי[1142] כיא לערל אוזן נפתח דבר ולב   **6**

[האבן   בנפ]לאות֯[1143] ואדעה כיא לכה עשיתה אלה אלי ומה בשר   **7**

ל]ה֯פליא[1144] ובמחשבתכה להגביר ולהכין כול לכבודכה   **8**

ו
להבי]ן֯[1145] בצבא[1146] דעת לספר לשׁר[1147] גבורת וחוקי נכונות לילוד   **9**

      ב

[אשה ואת עבדכה ה]ב֯יאותה[1148] בברית עמכה ותגלה֯[1149] לב עפר להשמר   **10**

[1150] מפחי משפט לעומת רחמיכה ואני יצר   **11**

[החמר מגבל מים מקוי עפ]ר֯[1151] ולב האבן למי נחשבתי עד זות כיא   **12**

[1134] Col. 21 is from many pieces. The readings from Sukenik's col. 18 now appear in cols. 21, 22, 23, and 24.

[1135] Sukenik: שׁ֯ע[. Licht: ל[פ]שע[. Licht has lines 2–3 in 18.16–18.

[1136] Licht: א]שה.

[1137] Sukenik: כה֯[. Licht: יכה[. The scribe inscribed the consonants smaller.

[1138] The left margin is preserved. With DJD and Qimron: וצדקתכה.

[1139] Sukenik: א֯[. Licht: [כי]א. Photographs sometimes show joins that are wrong. Cf. DJD and Qimron: ו֯א֯י֯כ֯ה א֯כ֯י֯ר ב֯ל[וא. Only the bottom portions of some consonants remain.

[1140] Sukenik: ֯[. DJD: ה֯[ואיכ בלוא השכלתני ואבין באלה].

[1141] Licht's restoration. Sukenik: ֯[. DJD: °°°°[. Qimron: ה֯ת֯ה֯ב[.

[1142] Licht: ל[בבי.

[1143] Sukenik: ֯[. Licht: חות[האבן יבין נשכ]בנ. DJD: בנ[פ]לאות֯. Qimron: בנ[פ]לאות֯ יתבונן האבן.

[1144] Sukenik: פליא ֯[. Licht: פליא[לה עמו תעשה כי]ה֯כ. DJD and Qimron: ל֯ה֯פליא.

[1145] Licht: [עם אנוש להיחד].

[1146] Sukenik and Licht: צבא[. Cf. DJD: בצבא ֯נ֯[. Qimron: בצבא ֯נ֯[תביא.

[1147] Read: לבשר. The correction is probably by the same scribe.

[1148] Sukenik: אותה[. Licht: אותה[הבי עבדך ואת אשה].

[1149] Sukenik and Licht do not report the dots. The leather shows many dots that are not scribal; cf. DJD: ה֯תגל.

[1150] Licht: [ותצילנו רע מדבר].

[1151] Ctr. DJD and Qimron: ר֯[ע]מבנה מים ומגבל חמר[. Sukenik: ר֯[. Licht: עפ]ר[מקוי מים מגבל החמר]. The *peh* is not visible. For the restoration, see 20.28 and line 26.

Col. 21 [= Sukenik Col. 18 + Frg. 3]
Parallels: 4Q427 Frgs. 10, 11, 12; 4Q428 Frg. 13

1   […]

2   [… trans]gression, one born of a wo[man]

3   […] your […] and your righteousness.

4   [… and] ho[w] can I recognize [unl]ess I see it?

5   [.… How] can I look unless you uncover my eyes, and hear

6   [unless you uncover[734] my ears]? My heart was awestruck,[735] because to an inattentive[736] ear a message[737] was opened, and the heart of

7   [stone[738] … with ma]rvels. And I know that for yourself, you did these (things), O my God. And how can flesh

8   [… to] act wonderfully,[739] and in your plan[740] to prevail,[741] and to establish everything for your glory,

9   […to disce]rn the host of knowledge, to recount to the flesh mighty deeds and the established statutes to one born of

10 [a woman? And] you [br]ought [your servant] into covenant with you, and you revealed (to) the heart of dust (how) to guard itself

11 [from …] from the traps of judgment corresponding (to)[742] your mercies. And I am a creature of[743]

12 [clay, and a mixture of water, a reservoir of dus]t, and a heart of stone. For whom was I considered until this (Endtime)?[744] For

---

[734] See 9.23 and 14.7.
[735] See Jer 4:9. From שמם, *Hipʿal* ("to be dumbfounded").
[736] Lit. "uncircumcised."
[737] Or "a word."
[738] For לב האבן see Ezek 11:19 and 36:26. The book of Ezekiel was exceptionally influential upon the Qumranites.
[739] Or "wonderful acts."
[740] Or "in your thoughts."
[741] Lit. "to make mighty."
[742] Apparently the judgments of the wicked are compared to God's mercies.
[743] Heb. יצר.
[744] See 21.16.

13   נ[תתה¹¹⁵² באוזן עפר ונהיות עולם חקותה בלב

14   [האבן ונעוי לב¹¹⁵³   ]   ֯השבתה להביא בברית עמכה ולעמוד

15   במשפטי עדים[¹¹⁵⁴ ב֯מכון עולם לאור אורתים¹¹⁵⁵ עד נצח וע֯ד֯¹¹⁵⁶ חושך

16   לאי[ן¹¹⁵⁷ סוף וקצי שלום לאין ח֯[קר¹¹⁵⁸

17   [ואני יצר העפר¹¹⁵⁹ °°°]

18   ולבר]ך֯ ש֯מ֯כה¹¹⁶⁰ אפתח פ֯[י¹¹⁶¹

19   [י֯צ֯ר֯¹¹⁶²]אל[°° °]

20   ]

21   נפ[רשה¹¹⁶³ ר֯ש֯ת֯[¹¹⁶⁴

22   °°[ ] ו֯ה֯י֯א֯¹¹⁶⁵[ ]ח֯ה¹¹⁶⁶[נפתחה ד֯ר֯ך֯ ל֯[

23   ב֯נ֯תיבות¹¹⁶⁷ שלום ועם בשר להפליא֯[

24   [ת י֯הלכו¹¹⁶⁸ פעמי על מטוני¹¹⁶⁹ פחיה ומפרשי֯ ר֯[שת   איכה[¹¹⁷⁰

25   א֯ש֯מ֯ר ביצר עפר מהתפרר¹¹⁷¹ ומתוך¹¹⁷² דונג ב֯ה֯[מס לפני אש¹¹⁷³

---

¹¹⁵² Sukenik: תתה[֯. Licht: נ[תתה]. DJD: ת[֯.]ק֯נתה והשכלתני וקימי קדם.

¹¹⁵³ Licht's restoration.

¹¹⁵⁴ Licht: במ[שפטי עדים לפניך לעד ולהתיצב]. 4Q427 frg. 10 line 8 reads: .

¹¹⁵⁵ Sukenik, Licht, and Qimron: אורתום.

¹¹⁵⁶ Sukenik: ו֯°°°. Licht: ו[אבד]. Qimron: ונ֯ח֯. Cf. DJD: ונ֯ס֯.

¹¹⁵⁷ Sukenik: סוף °[. Licht: סוף [לעד ותשמד עולה עד אין].

¹¹⁵⁸ Sukenik:]ח.

¹¹⁵⁹ Licht ended his col. 18 with העפר.

¹¹⁶⁰ Sukenik: ה[. Cf. DJD and Qimron: ולבר]ך֯ ש֯מ֯כה   ]. It is too speculative to imagine letters from the remaining dots of ink.

¹¹⁶¹ Sukenik: אפתה[.

¹¹⁶² Col. 21 ends here. Sukenik:]צ֯°[.

¹¹⁶³ Frg. 3 begins here, providing consonants for the completion of the column. Licht included frg. 3 as a "floating" fragment. Most of frg. 3 is in *scriptio continua*.

¹¹⁶⁴ Cf. 4Q428 frg. 13 52.4: ה נפרשה רשת שוחה[.

¹¹⁶⁵ Sukenik and Licht:]הוא[. DJD:]ו ֯ה֯°°[ ]°°. Qimron:]ו֯ ֯ה֯°°[ ]°°.

¹¹⁶⁶ Sukenik: ה֯°[. Licht: ה[. DJD and Qimron: ה֯°°[.

¹¹⁶⁷ The right border of the column is preserved. Sukenik and Licht: נ֯ת֯יבות[(Sukenik's diacritics).

¹¹⁶⁸ Licht: ו[עמד. Cf. DJD: ת֯ה֯ל֯כ֯ו. Qimron: י֯הלכו.

¹¹⁶⁹ See DJD 40, p. 266. An error for מטמוני. See יטמוני in line 28.

¹¹⁷⁰ With DJD. Licht: אשמר [רשתה].

¹¹⁷¹ Ctr. DJD: מהתפרד. Sukenik, Licht, and Qimron: מהתפרר. Each *reš* is clear in 1QHª.

¹¹⁷² Ctr. DJD and Qimron: ומת(ו)ך. The ink is only faded.

¹¹⁷³ With DJD. See 12.34.

13   [...] you [p]ut in the ear of dust. That which will be for eternity, you engraved on the heart of

14   [stone.[745] And those perverted[746] of heart ...]° you lead back (so as) to enter into covenant with you, and to stand

15   [... in the judgments of witnesses] in the establishment of eternity for the perfect light[747] unto perpetuity and unto darkness

16   [... withou]t end and the endtimes of unfa[thomable[748] ...] peace [...]

17   [...] and I am a creature of[749] dust °°°[...]

18   [.... And to ble]ss your name I shall open [my] m[outh]

19   [...] a creature of[750] [...] *ʾl*°° °[...]

20   [...]

21   [... it is sp]read out, a net of [...]

22   °°[...]°° and it [...]*ḥh* a way was opened to °[...]

23   in the paths of peace, and with flesh to act wonderfully [...]

24   [...]*t* my footsteps proceed[751] on the hidden parts of[752] traps and the spread out (places of) a n[et .... How]

25   can a creature[753] of dust be guarded from being crumbled and from the midst of wax mel[ting before fire ...]

---

[745] Lit. "the stone."
[746] *Nipʿal* participle of עוה, "be bewildered," "be disconcerted." See 4.31.
[747] Lit. "for light of lights."
[748] Heb. לאין חקר.
[749] Heb. יצר.
[750] Heb. יצר.
[751] Lit. "walk."
[752] Or "on the buried parts of."
[753] Heb. יצר.

26   וֹמקוי אפֹר איכה אעמוד לפני רוח סוע]רת1174

27   וישמורהו לרזי חפצו כיא הוא ידע למֹ]1175

28   ר]1176 כלה ופח לפח יטמונו צמי רשֹעֹה̇ [ ]

29   וֹ בעול יתמו כול יצר רמיה כיא לאֹף]1177

30   לאין ואפס1178 יצר עולה ומעשי רמיה]1179

31   עֹ[(VACAT)   ואני צֹר ה]חמר

32   וֹמה יתחזק לכה אתה אֹל הֹדֹעֹוֹת̇1180 כֹו]ל

33   עשיתם ומבלעדיכה לוֹא ידֹעֹתֹי דֹבֹר]1181

34   ואני י]צֹר1182 העפר ידעתי ברוח נתתה בי בידֹ]1183

35   לֹמה כֹוֹל1184 עולה ורמיה יגורו יחד לזדון]1185

36   כול מ]עֹשֹי1186 נדה לתחלויים ומשפטי נגע וכלת [עולם1187

37   הֹ]1188[יֹ̇שֹ̇בֹ̇ לכֹה1189 חמה וקנאה נוק]מת1190

38   ואני1191 יצר חֹמֹר וֹר]וח 1192

39   ]

40   ]

41   ]

1174 Ctr. DJD and Qimron: סוע]רה. Licht: סוע]רת.

1175 Licht: [זמתו]למ.

1176 Qimron: זֹ]לפקו[.

1177 Sukenik: [לאֹ. Licht: לאין [כול רשעה תהיה]לֹא.

1178 Ctr. DJD: מגב]לֹ און[. Licht: לאין ואפס]. See 14.17: לאין אפס.

1179 Licht: יֹואבד[רמיה.

1180 Sukenik: [˚˚˚˚˚אל. Licht: אל ה]דעות. The leather is torn and the ink was exposed and now faded.

1181 Sukenik: [˚˚˚˚ לוא. DJD: [˚˚˚˚. Licht: לוֹא י]היה כול ואני יצר]העפר.

1182 With DJD and Qimron: ואני י]צֹר[.

1183 Ctr. DJD: בי כֹיֹאֹ. Sukenik: [˚בֹיֹ. Licht: בי כיא]בֹי.

1184 Sukenik: [ל [ ]מה[. Licht: לעולה[ ] מה[.

1185 Licht: יגורו יחד לזדון. Sukenik and Qimron: וחדל זדון. With DJD: יחד לזדון].

1186 Sukenik [עֹשֹי˚.

1187 Licht does not reconstruct עולם].

1188 Qimron: ˚˚˚˚˚˚ת [ ].

1189 Sukenik: לכה[ ]שֹ[ ]חֹ[. DJD: לכה [ ]ˇשˇ ˇ ˇ ˇחˇ ˇ˚˚[. Qimron:]ˇ˚ˇˇˇˇˇˇˇ ˇתˇ ˇשˇ לכה[.

1190 Sukenik: נֹ]ן וקנאה. Licht: נו]קמת.

1191 See the formula in 21.17 and 34.

1192 DJD and Qimron:]יצר החֹמֹר[. Sukenik:]˚יֹצֹר[. Licht: ה]חמר יצר. Frg. 3 ends here. See 21.34.

26 and reservoirs of ash. How can I stand before the sto[rmy] wind? [....]

27 And he guards him according to the mysteries of his wish,⁷⁵⁴ because he knows *lm*°[...]

28 [...]*r* destruction. And those thirsting⁷⁵⁵ after wickedness hide⁷⁵⁶ trap after trap °°[...]

29 [...]°*w* in iniquity, all the creatures of⁷⁵⁷ treachery will be annihilated⁷⁵⁸ for to anger [...]

30 [...] for nothing an inclination of⁷⁵⁹ injustice and the works of treachery [...]

31 [...]°ᶜ·⁷⁶⁰ And I (am) a creature of⁷⁶¹ [clay ...]

32 [...]. And what (being) can strengthen itself before you? You (are) the God of knowledge,⁷⁶² al[l ...]

33 [...] you created them, and apart from you, I cannot know a thing [....]⁷⁶³

34 [And I (am) a cre]ature of⁷⁶⁴ dust. I know by the spirit which you put in me through [...]

35 [....] For what (is) all injustice and treachery? They will dwell together with insolence [....]

36 [All the w]orks of impurity fall ill, and the judgments of affliction and [eternal] destruction [...]

37 [...]°°*ḥ* [...]°*š*°*b*°°° to you (is) wrath and aven[ging] jealousy [...]

38 [.... And I (am)] a creature of⁷⁶⁵ clay and a sp[irit of ...]

39 [...]

40 [...]

41 [...]

---

⁷⁵⁴ Or "his desire."

⁷⁵⁵ Cf. DJD: "they hide snares of wickedness." For "thirsting after" (צמי), see Ps 42:1–3 esp. צמאה נפשי לאלהים, "my soul thirsts for God." In Heb. "to thirst" means to "long for" or "be passionate for," as a deer yearns for water brooks. It is possible that Job 18:9 (צמים), the only verse in the Hebrew Bible in which צמים may be a noun ("snare"), has influenced the string of synonyms ("nets," "traps," "noose"). The term "thirsting" denotes "those who passionately" seek to "grasp him." Either צמים is a noun from צמא "to thirst," or it is a separate lexeme unattested.

⁷⁵⁶ See paranomasia with line 24.

⁷⁵⁷ Heb. יצר.

⁷⁵⁸ Heb. יתמו.

⁷⁵⁹ Heb. יצר.

⁷⁶⁰ A space allows for a shift in thought.

⁷⁶¹ Heb. יצר.

⁷⁶² See the notes to this expression in previous columns.

⁷⁶³ See 20.33–36. Note the *inclusio* in lines 31 and 34.

⁷⁶⁴ Heb. יצר.

⁷⁶⁵ Heb. יצר.

42   [

Col. 22 [= Sukenik Frgs. 1 Col. 1, 52, 4, and 47]

1   [

2   [

3   [

4   [[°°°°]¹¹⁹³

5   קו[דש¹¹⁹⁴ אשר בשמים

6   ג[דול¹¹⁹⁵ והואה פלא¹¹⁹⁶ והם לוא יוכלו

7   ל[°¹¹⁹⁷   בנפלאו[תיכה¹¹⁹⁸ ולוא יעצורו לדעת בכול

8   ש[ב¹¹⁹⁹ אל עפרו ואני איש פשע ומגולל

9   [[א̇שמת¹²⁰⁰ רשעה ואני בקצי חרון

10   לה[[תקומם¹²⁰¹ לפני נ̇געי ולהשמר¹²⁰²

11   [[°   תוד[[י̇עני¹²⁰³ אלי¹²⁰⁴ כיא יש מקוה לאיש

12   [[מ̇על¹²⁰⁵ ואני יצר החמר נשענתי

13   ע̇ל ה[[סדיכה¹²⁰⁶   [[א̇לי¹²⁰⁷ ואדעה כיא אמת

14   פיכה [[¹²⁰⁸   [[אחור ואני בקצי אתמוכה

---

¹¹⁹³ No consonants are visible from lines 1–3. Frg. 1 col. 1 begins here and provides the text for lines 4–16 and the first extant word of line 17. It also preserves the left margin.

¹¹⁹⁴ Licht: [מלאכי קו]דש.

¹¹⁹⁵ Licht: [ג]דול [הג]דול שמך את ידעו לא. DJD: ג̇דו̇ל. Qimron: ה[ג̇דול.

¹¹⁹⁶ With Sukenik, Licht, and Qimron. Cf. DJD: הפלא והוא.

¹¹⁹⁷ The *lamedh* is faintly visible to the left of col. 21; see image SHR 4302.

¹¹⁹⁸ Licht: [תיכה]בנפלאו בנ[להבין. DJD: [תיכה]נפלא ולספר באלה ל̇[הבין.

¹¹⁹⁹ Licht: [ש]ב אפהוא ומה [רזיכה.

¹²⁰⁰ Licht: [אשמת]ב וטמא נדה בדרכי.

¹²⁰¹ Licht: [תקומם]לה אוכל איכה כשלתי.

¹²⁰² With Sukenik and Licht. Cf. DJD: ולהשמר נגע. Qimron: ולהשמר נגע. The scribe wrote above two indiscernible consonants.

¹²⁰³ Sukenik: [ענו̇. Licht: [שמ]ומבינתך הווה מפחד. Licht: [ענו.

¹²⁰⁴ Sukenik and Licht: אלה. Both readings provide good meaning. The left part of the ה may be visible, with ink cracked off.

¹²⁰⁵ Sukenik: [גע]מ תטהרנו כיא מפשע [שב. Licht: [גע̇ל.

¹²⁰⁶ With Qimron: ה[סדכה] ע̇ל. Cf. DJD: וב[עכה] זר̇ו̇ע̇. זרוע never denotes God's arm in the *Thanksgiving Hymns*. Sukenik: ז̇°. The right column can be seen to the left of col. 21; see SHR 4302.

¹²⁰⁷ Sukenik: [אלי. Licht: [א רחמיכה ובהמון בחסדיכה. Licht: א[לי̇. DJD: ר̇ג̇לי̇[. Qimron: לי [°. The orthography and context suggest א̇לי̇.

¹²⁰⁸ DJD: [ישוב לוא ודברכה] פיכה. Licht: [ישוב לוא דברכה וכול].

42   [...]

Col. 22 [= Sukenik Frgs. 1 Col. 1, 52, 4, and 47]

1   [...]

2   [...]

3   [...]

4   [...]°°°°[...]

5   [... holi]ness which (is) in the heavens[766]

6   [... g]reat, and he is a wonder; but they are not able

7   *l*[... in] your [wonderful deed]s, and they are not capable to know in all

8   [... ret]urns to his dust? And I (am) a man of transgression and am rolling

9   [...] the guilt of wickedness. And I, in the endtimes of fury,

10   [... to] arise in the face of my afflictions, and to guard myself

11   °[... you shall allow] me to [k]now,[767] O my God, because there is hope for the human

12   [...] infidelity. And I (am) a creature of[768] clay; I leaned

13   upon [your] lo[ving-kindnesses ...,] O my God. And I know that truth

14   (is in) your mouth [...] backwards. And I, in my endtime, I shall adhere

---

[766] Or "in heaven."
[767] *Hip'il* permissive.
[768] Heb. יצר.

15	ואתקו[מ]מה^{1209} במעמד העמדתני כיא בבריֿת[כה
16	[אֿיש^{1210} ותשיבהו ובמה יתֿ°°[^{1211}]°̊
17	הֿשבֿ[תה^{1212}][וֿאתה^{1213} עצמתֿה וֿמֿפחֿ[ד]^{1214} [[
18	בושהֿ°°^{1215} ללוא מקו[ה]ה [[
19	ואני יצֿרֿ^{1216}][החמר [[
20	פ[]לגתהֿ]^{1217}
21	אֿ[אשר הֿ]^{1218}
22	עֿ[]רֿבֿ^{1219} ובוקר עם מֿ[בוא]^{1220}
23	נג[]עֿי^{1221} גבר וממכאֿ[ ]בות איש[]^{1222}
24	]הֿ^{1223} נשמחהֿ[^{1224}][וֿאל זרתו צפו^{1225} ועל משמרתֿםֿ]°^{1226}
25	וֿנדיבים לוא כֿ[לו כיא א[]תה^{1227} תגר בכול שטן משחית ומרעֿ[ים]^{1228}
26	ליֿ^{1229} מאז כוננתי ל[]ֿ^{1230}][כה ואתה גליתה אוזני כיֿ[א]^{1231}

---

^{1209} Sukenik: [ ]°̊בבר [מֿה :Licht:]ממה ואתקו[מ]מה. DJD:]מֿה° כה]בבריֿת. Qimron: מֿ[מ]ה ועֿ[תכה בבריֿ]כה. [בגודל אמתכה ואתקו[מ]מה.

^{1210} Licht: ב[איש רצֿיתה רחֿמיכה [בהמון].

^{1211} Licht: יֿתֿ[גבר]. Qimron: יֿתֿצֿב.

^{1212} Frg. 1 col. 1 ends here and provides the upper part. Part of the *beth* is on frg. 52 the *he* and *šin* are on frg. 1.

^{1213} Frg. 52 begins here and provides the text for lines 17–19. Licht does not include frg. 52. DJD restores this as just one word: הֿשֿ°°°תה.

^{1214} Sukenik:]הֿפֿ וי עצמתה[°. Cf. DJD: [ ]פֿ° עצמתה תה°°°הֿשֿ. Qimron: [ ]הֿפֿ וי עצמתה תה°°הֿשֿ[ואֿתה]. Sukenik and Licht:]בֿיֿש°.

^{1215} Sukenik: °°בֿיֿש[. DJD: בֿ יש°[. Qimron: [ושבֿֿר שֿ[אֿין ל].

^{1216} Frg. 52 ends here.

^{1217} Frg. 4 begins here and provides the text for lines 20–23, the left side of lines 24–28, and the text for lines 29–39. Sukenik:]גֿתֿ[. Licht:]גֿתֿ[.

^{1218} Sukenik:]אשר °א[. Licht:]אשֿר[. DJD:]° אֿשֿר °[. Qimron:]°̊ אשר [ ]°̊[.

^{1219} Sukenik:]בֿ[. Licht:]עֿר[ב.

^{1220} Sukenik: עם °̊[. Licht: עם מֿ[ואֿצֿא].

^{1221} Sukenik:]עֿי[. Licht:]עֿי[מֿנֿגֿי. DJD:]נֿגֿ[°̊עֿי. Qimron:]וֿעֿי[מֿנֿגֿ.

^{1222} Sukenik:]וממכ[. Licht: [ומכאֿ]וֿב. The *waw* and *yodh* in frg. 4 are identical.

^{1223} Frg. 47 begins here and provides the readings on the right side for lines 24–28. Qimron places frg. 47 at the right bottom of col. 25.

^{1224} Ctr. DJD: [וֿא בֿשֿמחה[תוצ]. Sukenik and Licht: [הֿ נשמחֿ]°. Qimron: נשמחֿ[ ]בֿיֿחֿדֿ°°°.

^{1225} Ctr. DJD: [וֿרֿת יצפו חֿוֿת לסליֿ]°°° כיא יצפו. Sukenik and Licht:]וֿרֿת יצֿפֿו. Qimron:]וֿרֿתֿ יצֿפֿוֿ°°°[ᵛ. The letters are now clear.]חֿוֿת looks improbable. Those in the יחד are watching for God's help and salvation; see 6:16: וצופים לֿיֿשֿוֿעֿתֿך; cf. 1QS 9.25.

^{1226} Licht:]יֿתֿיצֿבֿו. DJD:]יֿ[תיצבו°.

^{1227} Ctr. DJD and Qimron:]°̊כֿלֿא[ᵛ. The תה is clear.

^{1228} Sukenik:]וֿמרֿ.

^{1229} Right side of the column is preserved.

^{1230} Qimron:]לֿכֿ[°.

^{1231} Ctr. DJD:]°כֿ°. See כיא in 22.11, 35. cf. 22.26: [א]כיֿ.

15 to [your] covenant[769] [.... And I shall ari]se in the position where you allowed me to stand[770] because

16 °[…] human, and you allowed him to come back.[771] And in what *yt*°°[…]

17 [… you] brought back. And you, you are powerful; and from fea[r]

18 […] shame without hop[e …]

19 [….] And I (am) a creature of[772] [clay …]

20 […] you [di]vided […]

21 […]ʾ which *h*[…]

22 [… ev]ening and morning with the co[ming of …]

23 [… the afflic]tions of a man[773] and from the miser[ies of a human]

24 […]*h* we will have joy [….] And unto his (God's) help[774] they look out, and upon their watchtower °[….]

25 And the noblemen[775] [were] not exte[rminated, for y]ou rebuke every ruinous adversary[776] and [those] who do evil

26 to me, from when I was established *l*°[…]*kh*. And you, you uncovered my ear fo[r …]

---

[769] The *beth* is not a *nota accusativi*; in Hebrew, one writes "I shall adhere to your covenant."
[770] *Hipʿil* permissive.
[771] *Hipʿil* permissive.
[772] Heb. יצר.
[773] Heb. גבר.
[774] Those in the *Yaḥad* are eagerly looking for God's help.
[775] The noun denotes those who are willing or "volunteers."
[776] Hebrew שטן. See 24.23.

27   לוא יבוא כיא[1232]‬ ‬ [‫א]וֹ̇ ואנושי ברית[1233] פותו בם ויבוא]

28   במבניתי[1234] ותכמ[‫י[1235] בתו]כ̇חות[1236] לפניכה ואני פחדתי ממשפטכה̇[1237]

29   לפ]נ̇יכה[1238] ומי יזכה במשפטכה ומה אפה]ו̇[1239] אדם]

30   [‫א̇ אני[1240] במשפט ושב אל עפרו מה י̇ב̇י̇ן]ו[1241]

31   כי אתה א[‫ל̇י̇[1242] פתחתה לבבי לבינתכה ותגל אוֹז]ני[1243]

32   [‫להשען על טובכה ויהם לב̇י̇[1244] ש̇ °°°[1245]

33   [‫°ו ‬ ולבבי כדונג ימס על פשע וח̇ט̇א̇ה̇

34   עד [‫ת̇ומה[1246] ברוך אתה אל הדעות אשר הכינות̇ה̇]ה[1247]

35   [‫ותפגע בעבדכה זות למענכה כיא ידעתי

36   ולחסד]כ̇ה̇[1248] אחל[1249] בכול היותי ושמכה אברכה תמיד

37   [‫מ̇ק̇ו̇ה̇ ל̇ע̇ב̇ד̇כ̇ה̇[1250] ואל תעזובנו בקצי

38   [‫ה וכבודכה וטו]בכה[1251]

39   [‫על ב̇]ן[1252]

40   [‫]

[1232] Qimron: ‫בי א]ני ישבתי.

[1233] Sukenik: ‫ו̇ אנוש וברית [. Licht: ‫אנוש וברית [. Qimron: ‫ו̇ ואנושי ברית [.

[1234] With DJD and Qimron: ‫במבניתי.

[1235] Licht does not restore. Frg. 47 ends here.

[1236] Licht: ‫ותו]כחות.

[1237] Licht: ‫מי יצדק]°°.

[1238] Sukenik: ‫יכה [. Licht: ‫לפנ]יכה [.

[1239] Licht: ‫ו]אדם. See 18.5.

[1240] Licht: ‫תבי]אנו [. DJD: ‫אני א̇°[. Qimron: ‫ב̇י̇אנו °ת.

[1241] Sukenik: ‫מה °°[.

[1242] Sukenik: ‫ל̇°[. Licht: ‫א[‫ל̇י̇[. Licht does not restore the lacunae at the beginning of lines 26–29 and 32–33. With DJD.

[1243] Sukenik: ‫או̇[. Licht: ‫ני]אזן.

[1244] Contrast the spelling in lines 31 and 33.

[1245] DJD: ‫לב̇י̇ כ °°°°[ ].

[1246] Read with DJD; cf. Sukenik and Licht: ‫תימה[. The *waw* and *yodh* are very similar in 1QHᵃ. DJD (p. 274) refers to עד תום in 14.31, but this is a mistake for עם תום. See עד תום in 1QM frg. 16 line 1, 4Q260 frg. 3 line 1, 4Q266 frg. 1 line 2, 4Q416 frg. 3 line 3, 4Q444 frgs. 1–4 line 7; cf. ועד תום in 4Q511 frg. 121 line 2. For עד תומה see 1QM frg. 1 line 12.

[1247] Sukenik and Licht: ‫הכינו]תה.

[1248] Licht's restoration.

[1249] Licht: ‫אוחיל. The *matres lectionis* are added by another scribe, bringing the script closer to Qumran orthography.

[1250] Sukenik: ‫ל[ ]דכה. DJD: ‫דברכה לה]קים ל[עב]דכה. Licht: ‫ק̇י̇ה̇ ל[.

[1251] Licht: ‫וט]ובכה.

[1252] Frg. 4 ends here. Sukenik and Qimron: ‫על̇[. Licht: ‫על]°.

27 it⁷⁷⁷ will not enter for […]°*w*°. But the men of the covenant were misled⁷⁷⁸ by them.⁷⁷⁹ And it⁷⁸⁰ entered […]

28 in my frame and [my] entrails [in chasti]sements before you. And I, I was afraid of your judgment […]

29 [… be]fore you. And who will be (pronounced) pure in your judgment? And what then [(is) Adam]?⁷⁸¹

30 […]° I (am) in judgment. And he (Adam) returns to his dust. What can he discer[n]

31 [… ? For you, O] my [G]od, opened my heart to your discernment, and you uncovered [my] ear

32 […] to lean upon your goodness. But my heart was agitated⁷⁸² *š*°°°[…]

33 […]° and my heart (was) like wax melting on account of transgression and sin

34 [… until] it⁷⁸³ is annihilated.⁷⁸⁴ Blessed (are) you, O God of knowledge,⁷⁸⁵ that y[ou] established

35 […] and thus you called upon⁷⁸⁶ your servant for your sake. For I know

36 [… and for] your [loving-kindness] I long with all my being, and your name I bless continuously

37 […] hope for your servant. And do not abandon him in the endtimes of

38 […]*h* and your glory and [your] goodne[ss …]

39 […] upon *b*[…]

40 […]

---

⁷⁷⁷ The *nomen regens* is "adversary" in line 25.
⁷⁷⁸ The form is the *puʿal* perfect of פתה. The verb often denotes "to be seduced (or misled)."
⁷⁷⁹ I.e., "those who do evil."
⁷⁸⁰ I.e., the "adversary."
⁷⁸¹ Or "humankind." See 18.5: "But what then (is) Adam?"
⁷⁸² The verb is not a conjugation of המה, "to moan," because the *qal* imperfect has a final *he*. The verb is the *qal* imperfect of המם, "to bring into motion," "to disturb." See 13.33.
⁷⁸³ A reference to "sin?"
⁷⁸⁴ תומה.
⁷⁸⁵ This expression was probably memorized from 1QS 3.15.
⁷⁸⁶ Or "you entreated." Heb. verb פגע with *beth* could also mean "to fall upon," or "assault."

] **41**

] **42**

Col. 23 [= Sukenik Col. 18 + Frgs. 57 Col. 1, 2 Col. 1]
Parallels: 4Q428 Frg. 14

1 [

2 אורכה[^1253] ותעמד מא[ז]

3 אורכה[^1254] לאין השב[ת]

4 כיא אתכה אור ל[^1255]

5 ותגל אוזן עפר[^1256] [ו]ת ולהֿבֿ[י]ן

6 מזמה אשר הו[דעתני ברזי פלאכה[^1257]] אלו עמֿדי[^1258] ותאמנה בֿאֿ[וזני][^1259]

7 עבדכה עד עולם ̊[ש[מֿ]עות[^1260] פלאכה להופֿיֿע

8 לעיני כול שמעי[כה][^1261] [בימין עוזכה לנהֿל כֿלֿם[^1262]

9 בכוח גבורתכה [יהל[ל] שמכה[^1263] ויתגבר בכבודֿכֿהֿ[^1264]

10 אל תשב ידכה [^1265] ל[היות[^1266] לו מתחזק בבריתכה

11 ועומד לפניכה בֿ[כיא מק[ור[^1267] פתחתה בפי עבדכה ובלשונו[^1268]

[^1253]: Frg. 57 begins here and provides the right side of lines 2–16.
[^1254]: Licht: אודכה.
[^1255]: Licht: אור [עולם].
[^1256]: Licht: [עפ]ר.
[^1257]: Licht: [הו]דעתה לבחיריך. See 5.19, 15.30, and 18.16.
[^1258]: Sukenik: [אפוֹ עֹ]דֿ. DJD: עֹ ̊ ̊עֹ אֿ. Possibly Qimron: עוֹדֿ אֿיֿןֿ. Licht: אפו עֿ.
[^1259]: Sukenik:]בֿאֿ. Licht: באו[זני]. DJD and Qimron: [ז]ןֿאֿוֿבֿ. Frg. 57 col. 1 provides the left side of this line.
[^1260]: Licht: [כי נאמנה הודעתה ש]מועות.
[^1261]: Licht: [דברך לעשית נפלאות].
[^1262]: DJD: כֿלֿם. Sukenik: [ל] לֿ לנהל. Qimron: לנהל דֿלֿם.
[^1263]: Licht: [למען עבדך המהלל] לשמכה.
[^1264]: Sukenik: [בכבו]ן. Licht: בכב[דכה].
[^1265]: No ink is visible; cf. DJD: מֿ.
[^1266]: Licht: [מבן אמתכה ל]היות.
[^1267]: Licht: [לעד ואתה אלי מק]ור. DJD: בֿ[תמים כיא מק]ור.
[^1268]: Ctr. DJD: ובלשוני. Sukenik: ובלשונו. "His tongue" refers to עבדכה and ובלשונו is paralleled by מבינתו in line 12. Also note לו in line 10. The theme is focused on God's servant rather than the author here.

41 […]

42 […]

Col. 23 [= Sukenik Col. 18 + Frgs. 57 Col. 1, 2 Col. 1]
Parallels: 4Q428 Frg. 14

1 […]

2 your light, and you caused to stand from of o[ld …]

3 your light without ceasi[ng …].

4 For with you (there is) light for [….]

5 And you uncovered the ear of dust […]*wt* and to […]

6 the design[787] which [you] allowed [me] to [know[788] in wondrous mysteries.] They are with me and confirmed in the e[ar of]

7 your servant unto eternity °[… the re]ports of your wonder, (and) to appear

8 before the eyes of all who listen [to you …] in your strong right hand to guide all of them

9 through the power of your might [… to prai]se your name and become mighty through your glory.

10 Do not withdraw your hand [… to] be for him one who is strengthened in your covenant,

11 and (one who) stands before you with [.… For a sou]rce you opened in the mouth of your servant, and by his tongue

---

[787] The eternal plan of God.
[788] *Hipʿil* permissive.

12 חקקֿתה על קו מֿ[שפט]¹²⁶⁹ למ[שמיע¹²⁷⁰ ליצר מבינתו ולמליץ¹²⁷¹ באלה¹²⁷²

13 לעפר¹²⁷³ כמוני ותפתח מֿק[ור¹²⁷⁴]להוכיח ליצר חמר דרכו ואשמות¹²⁷⁵ ילוד

14 אשה כמעשיו ולפתֿחֿ מ[קו]רֿ¹²⁷⁶ אמתכה ליצר אשר סמכתה בעוזכה

15 לֿ[הרים] כאמתכה¹²⁷⁷ מבשר] ולספ[רֿ¹²⁷⁸ טובכה לבשר עניים¹²⁷⁹ לרוב רחמיכה

16 [ולהֿ]שֿבֿיֿע¹²⁸⁰ ממקור דֿ[עת¹²⁸¹   לֿנ[כֿאי¹²⁸²   רוח ואבלים לשמחת עולם

17 [   ]ֿתים לֿ[ֿ   ]לֿ[   ]לֿ[

18 [

19 [

20 [

21 [ישֿמיעוֿ]¹²⁸³לֿ

22 [עוֿלם ולהֿלֿלֿכה]¹²⁸⁴°°°[

---

¹²⁶⁹ With DJD and Qimron: קו מֿ[שפט. The *mem* is an attractive restoration, and its right vertical stroke is evident. See 14:29; cf. 11.28, 16.38.

¹²⁷⁰ Licht: קו [משפטיכה לה]שמיע. A participle is required because of the following ולמליץ. Cf. לה]שמיע, which S. Holm-Nielsen reported "one must read" (p. 255).

¹²⁷¹ Qimron: ולמלוצ. Note the medial *ṣade* in final position.

¹²⁷² The *beth* seems to be a *nota accusativi*.

¹²⁷³ Under the *peh* is a drop of ink.

¹²⁷⁴ Licht: מק[ורי].

¹²⁷⁵ Ctr. DJD. The *waw* is not erased; the ink is faded.

¹²⁷⁶ Sukenik: °[   ]מֿ. Licht: מֿ[קור].

¹²⁷⁷ Sukenik: אמתכה [   ]מֿ. Licht: [באמתכה. DJD: לֿ[הרימו כֿאֿמתכה לֿ[הרי. Qimron: כאמתכה לֿ[הקיֿ]מֿ.

¹²⁷⁸ Sukenik: [   ]°. Licht: [לספר].

¹²⁷⁹ Ctr. DJD: ענוים.

¹²⁸⁰ Sukenik: °[ע. Licht: וסליחה להשמ]יע. Cf. DJD:]שֿבֿיֿע[ולה. Qimron: [ולהש]מֿיֿע.

¹²⁸¹ For ממקור דעת see 10.20, 20.32.

¹²⁸² Licht: [עולם לנד]כאי.

¹²⁸³ Licht does not read these consonants. Sukenik: °[הוֿ]. DJD:]יֿשֿמֿיֿעֿ[. Qimron: [יֿכֿיֿנֿוֿ]לֿ°°[. Frg. 2 col. 1 begins with this line and provides the text for lines 21–38.

¹²⁸⁴ Sukenik: [ם ושללכה]°. See 23.24. Cf. DJD: [עוֿלֿם]שֿלֿלֿהֿ[ ]. Qimron: קֿדושים ולֿה°°°כה. Licht does not report the consonants. A *lamedh* follows another *lamedh*.

12 you engraved on the measuring-line of [jud]gment [for the one who] proclaims to a creature[789] his discernment. And for the one who interprets these (things)

13 to dust like me. And you opened a sou[rce] to reprove a creature of[790] clay (concerning) his way and the guilts of one born of

14 a woman according to his works, and to open the s[our]ce of your truth to the creature[791] whom you supported with your strength,

15 to [raise up] according to your truth from the flesh [and to recou]nt your goodness, announcing[792] to the Poor Ones[793] according to the multitude of your mercies.

16 [And to sa]tisfy from the source of kno[wledge … to the mi]serable ones of spirit and mourners to an eternal joy.

17 […]°*tym l*°[…]*l*[…]*l*[…]

18 […]

19 […]

20 […]

21 […]*l* they shall proclaim […]

22 […] eternal […]°°° and to praise you […]

---

[789] Heb. יצר.
[790] Heb. יצר.
[791] Heb. יצר.
[792] The *pïel* infinitive of בשר means "to bring good news" or "to announce."
[793] Not "humble ones."

[וֹם¹²⁸⁵ ובארצכה¹²⁸⁶ ובבני אלים יֹכֹבֹדֹ¹²⁸⁷ קֹ[[אֹשֹׁר יעמֹ[ודו]¹²⁸⁸	**23**
[לֹהֹללכה¹²⁸⁹ ולספר כול כבודכה ואֹנֹי מה כיא מעפר לוקחתי וא[תה]¹²⁹⁰	**24**
[א]לֹי לכֹבֹודכה¹²⁹¹ עשיתה כול אלה כרוב חסדיכה תן משמר צדקכה	**25**
[לעבדכ]ה¹²⁹² תמיד עד פלט ומליצי דעֹת עם כול צעודי¹²⁹³ ומוכיחי אמת	**26**
[בכ]וֹל פֹעֹמֹי כיא מה עפר בכוֹל¹²⁹⁴ [יצר מע]שה אפר¹²⁹⁵ בידם לוא הנה ואתה	**27**
יצר] הֹחֹמֹר ומֹצוֹרוֹק[¹²⁹⁶ [לרצונכה¹²⁹⁷ על הבנים תבחננני¹²⁹⁸	**28**
[כֹגֹוֹדֹלֹכה] א]לֹ עֹפֹרו ועל¹²⁹⁹ עפר הניפותה רוח	**29**
[קודשכה [בֹטיֹטֹ¹³⁰⁰ בנֹ]י אלים¹³⁰¹ להחיד¹³⁰² עם בני שמים	**30**
ע]וֹלם¹³⁰³ ואין תשבת חושך כיא	**31**
[ומאור גליתה ולוא להשיב	**32**
ורוח קוֹ[דֹשכה הניפותה לכפור¹³⁰⁴ אשמה	**33**

¹²⁸⁵ Sukenik: °°[. Licht does not have ם[. DJD: בֹה°[. Qimron: כֹה°[.

¹²⁸⁶ Licht: ארצכה. Licht begins reading frg. 2 here.

¹²⁸⁷ Sukenik: ובבנ. Licht: [....י]אֹיש. We concur with DJD.

¹²⁸⁸ Sukenik:]רוֹע°[. Licht: רוֹע°°°[. DJD:]קֹ[ ] [אֹשֹׁר יעמֹ[ודו]. Qimron: אֹשֹׁר]יעצֹ[ורו].

¹²⁸⁹ DJD and Qimron: לֹהֹללכה.

¹²⁹⁰ Licht: לוקחתי וא[תה] אלי רק.

¹²⁹¹ DJD and Qimron: [אלי]לכֹבֹודכה.

¹²⁹² Licht: צדקכה [עם עבדכ]ה. Cf. DJD: [לפניכ]ה.

¹²⁹³ Licht: צעודו.

¹²⁹⁴ Ctr. DJD and Qimron:]בכול עפר ומה פֹעֹמֹי[בלכֹפֹיֹהֹםֹ]. Sukenik:]כֹ°°בכ עפר מה כיא[. See 15.16: כול יצר מעשה. The text became clear only with SHR 4304 and the Revised Edition of *DSSEL*. These consonants can be discerned. Also see the formula in line 24.

¹²⁹⁵ The self-same scribe first wrote עפר thinking about the preceding עפר. For עפר with אפר see 18.7. Licht: בכוֹל[בכוֹן עפר מה כיא]ו[דרכי בכול. המע]שה אפר.

¹²⁹⁶ Sukenik and Licht: חמר ומצון[. Cf. DJD:] עשיתה ומֹצוֹרוֹק[הֹחֹמֹר יֹצֹר. Qimron: ומצידֹוֹק הֹחֹמֹר יֹצֹר תכנתה[. [בראתה יֹצֹר (*sic*). The root of צרק seems to be the Aramaic טרק, "to mix." See DJD 40, pp. 258–59.

¹²⁹⁷ Licht: לרצונכה]. DJD: [ב צויתו ומצון]תכה חמר ביצר בחרת עשיתה[.

¹²⁹⁸ A scribal error for תבחנני. Licht: תבחננו.

¹²⁹⁹ Sukenik: [להביאו בגורלכה [ולחבוש לש]בֹרי ועל. Licht: [גֹו ולֹכֹה] [לֹבֹרי ועל.

¹³⁰⁰ Licht: [קודשכה וי]צֹֹֹר טיֹטֹ. Qimron: [קודשך ובינתך].

¹³⁰¹ Sukenik: אלים °[. Licht: [להביאו בסוד] אלים. DJD: אלים °[. Qimron: [הביאותה בס]דֹֹֹם.

¹³⁰² Ctr. DJD: להחיד but translated "to unite" (without a note). Ctr. Licht: להיחד. Licht emends the text. We also think the scribe erred. See להיחד in 19.14.

¹³⁰³ With Licht and Qimron. Sukenik:]ולם. DJD: עֹוֹלם[.

¹³⁰⁴ The *waw* is not erased (*pace* DJD). It was added by a scribe probably different than the one who added the *waw* in line 31. The correction shifts the meaning from "to cover."

23 […]*m* and in your land and among the sons of Elim[794] he shall honor[795] *q*[…] who shall st[and]

24 […] to praise you and to recount all your glory. And what (am) I? For from the dust I was taken. And y[ou,]

25 [O] my [G]od, for your glory you made all these (things) in accordance with the multitude of your loving-kindnesses. Guard[796] your righteousness

26 [for yo]ur [servant] always until deliverance, and the interpreters of knowledge (who are) with all my steps, and the mediators of[797] truth (who are)

27 [with a]ll my footsteps. For what is dust? In each [inclination[798] (is) a crea]ture of ashes.[799] In their[800] hands, they[801] are insignificant. But you

28 [… a creature of][802] clay and a mixture of […] for your will, and before[803] the members[804] you reprove me

29 […] as your greatness. [… t]o its dust. And over the dust you waved high[805] a spirit of

30 [your holiness …] in the mud [… the son]s of Elim[806] unite with the sons of heaven

31 [… e]ternity, and there is no return of darkness because

32 […] and light you have revealed and without returning

33 [… and the spirit of] your [holi]ness you have waved high (as an offering)[807] to atone for guilt

---

[794] Or "divine beings."

[795] A *pi'el* imperfect of כבד (not a *pu'al* which would probably have a ו). The Elim are "in your land."

[796] Lit. "Give a guard."

[797] The *hip'il* participle of יכח, which means "to reproach," "to avenge," and "to mediate."

[798] Heb. יצר.

[799] The noun literally means "ashes," but it has metaphorical meaning in the Bible and Qumran. The noun connotes insignificance, especially when combined with "dust." See Abraham's words, according to Gen 18:27.

[800] The pronoun "their" apparently refers back to "interpreters" and "mediators." Many translators found it impossible to obtain meaning from these lines. Our translation, benefited by improved images, is not elegant but it is tied to Hebrew orthography and grammar. The author seems to say that in the hands of the true interpreters of God's Word, ostensible ashes are not really ashes.

[801] The pronoun "they" refers to "ashes."

[802] Heb. יצר.

[803] Heb. על which means "upon," "against," "in front of," "on account," and "before."

[804] The Heb. noun means "sons," "individuals," and "members" (probably here of the administering priests in the Temple). See also "[the son]s of Elim" and "the sons of heaven" in 23.30. See also "the sons of Elim" in line 23.

[805] The *hip'il* perfect of נוף means "to move back and forth high." Perhaps a reference to the wave-offering.

[806] Or "divine beings."

[807] Heb. perfect of נוף, "to move back and forth high." The allusion may be to Exodus 29 in which one reads about the "sin offering." The terms "to wave high" and "atone" are present in this chapter.

מ[שׁרתים¹³⁰⁵ עם צבאכה ומתהלכים　　　**34**

בנת[יׄבות¹³⁰⁶ מלפניכה כיא נכונו באמתכה　　　**35**

הׄפׄלתה¹³⁰⁷ אלה לכבודכה ומצורוק¹³⁰⁸[　　　**36**

לגׄוׄרׄל¹³⁰⁹ עול יצׄר נׄתׄעב[　　　**37**

יׄצׄרׄ¹³¹⁰ נתעב¹³¹¹[　　　**38**

]　　　**39**

]　　　**40**

]　　　**41**

]　　　**42**

Col. 24 [= Sukenik Col. 18 Col. 2 + Frgs. 9, 50, 57 Col. 2, 45, 6, 2 Col. 2; and SHR 4301]¹³¹²
Parallels: 4Q428 Frgs. 15–16

]　　　**1**

]　　　**2**

]　　　**3**

¹³¹³°⟦⟦　　　**4**

°°⟦⟦　　　　　　　¹³¹⁴]°°⟦⟦　　　**5**

⟦⟦יׄצר ב⟦⟧⟦שר¹³¹⁶　　　　　בׄאׄשמ[ה¹³¹⁵　　　**6**

---

¹³⁰⁵ Licht: רתים[מש להיותם אמתכה בני את ולטהר] אשמה.
¹³⁰⁶ Licht: בות[להר חקר לאין במישור]. Qimron: שׁבות[יׄ לוא ואיש]. See 21.22–23: בנתיבות להתהלך.
¹³⁰⁷ Licht: הפלתה אלי ואתה רציתה באשר ויבחרו.
¹³⁰⁸ With DJD; see p. 280, note to line 36. Sukenik and Licht: ומצידוק, "and from righteousness." Qimron: ומצירוק. The *reš* seems clear, but perhaps the scribe again erred.
¹³⁰⁹ Sukenik: ל[°°°ל. Licht does not read °°°ל[.
¹³¹⁰ Sukenik: ר°[. Licht: ר[יצ.
¹³¹¹ Frg. 2 col. 1 ends here.
¹³¹² For frgs. 9, 50, 57, 45, 6, and 2, see the images arranged on Pl. 22 in DJD 40.
¹³¹³ Frg. 9 begins here and supplies the margin and far left side of lines 4–8.
¹³¹⁴ Frg. 57 col. 2 provides the margin and the text for the right side of lines 5–10.
¹³¹⁵ Sukenik and DJD: שׁמ°°°[]. Qimron: בׁאשמ[ה.
¹³¹⁶ Sukenik and Licht read שר[in frg. 9 and ב יצר [in frg. 50 but they do not place them together. Frg. 50 begins here and provide the text for the left side of lines 6–17. The left margin is certain.

34 [… those s]erving with your army and those who are walking

35 [… in the pa]ths before you, because they are established in your truth

36 […] you caused to fall[808] these (things) for your glory, and from a mixture of

37 […] to the lot of iniquity, the abhorred creature[809]

38 […] abhorred [cr]eature[810] […]

39 […]

40 […]

41 […]

42 […]

Col. 24 [= Sukenik Col. 18 Col. 2 + Frgs. 9, 50, 57 Col. 2, 45, 6, 2 Col. 2; and SHR 4301]
Parallels: 4Q428 Frgs. 15–16

1 […]

2 […]

3 […]

4 […]°

5 […]°°[…]°°

6 in guil[t …] a creature of[811] flesh

---

[808] *Hip'il* of נפל; see 15.37.
[809] Heb. יצר.
[810] Heb. יצר.
[811] Heb. יצר.

7	ו̇[מ̇]י̊̇[1318] יו̊ע̇[ ]דכה[1319] עַד קֹצֿ[1317]
8	[ ]ה למל[ ]אכי̇[1321] בֿמשפטי[1320]
9	[ ]ורזי פשע[ ][להשנות[1323] נֿגע במשפֿ[ ]ט[1322]
10	אר[צ̊[1325] ויע[ ]ופפו[1326] בה כול בשר בא̊[ ]שמתם[1324]
11	מק[ ]ום[1328] בעבותי[1329] רוח ותכנע מלאכי שמֿ[ ]ים[1327]
12	אלים ממכון[ ] קודשכה כיא לוא יהלל[ ]וכה[1330] במעון כבודכה ואתה
13	[ ]אסור[1332] עד קץ רצונכה אדם על ה̊[ ][1331]
14	[ ]רמות כוח ורוב בשר להרשיע ולשלחם̊[ ][1333]
15	[ ]ל̊א̊[1335] להכין בסוד עמכה בקצֿ[ ]י[1334]
16	[ ] ממזרים כי ל[ ]וא[1336]
17	[ ] פֿגרי̊ם לל[ ]וא[1337]

[1317] Sukenik:]ד קצֿ[.

[1318] Sukenik and Licht:]מו[.

[1319] Sukenik and Licht: ויעדכה. We combine the reading of the 2 fragments: frg. 50 provides the *yodh*, *waw*, and *ʿayin* and frg. 9 provides the *daleth*, *kaph*, and *he*.

[1320] Or with Sukenik: במשפטו. We agree with DJD. Qimron: בֿמ̇שפט ומ̇י.

[1321] Sukenik and Licht have למל on frg. 50 and אבי on frg. 9. We combine the 2 fragments: frg. 50 provides the *lamedh*, *mem*, and *lamedh* and frg. 9 provides the *ʾaleph*, *kaph*, and *yodh*.

[1322] Sukenik:]כבש̈[. DJD: עד̇ במשפ̇ט. Qimron: נֿגע בבשר̇. Line 8 helps discern this line. SHR 4301 supplies the right side and margin of lines 9–15. Licht does not transcribe frg. 57.

[1323] Sukenik and Licht reads להשנות in their frg. 9 and]ורזי פשע̊ in their frg. 50, but do not place them together.

[1324] Sukenik:]בשר בן.

[1325] Sukenik and Licht:]לֿ[   ]ע צוי̇ צ. The medial *ṣade* is similar to a final *ṣade*. For medial *ṣade* in final position, see 20.25, 29; 26.29.

[1326] Sukenik and Licht:]ופפו[. Frg. 50 ends here providing the *waw*, *yodh*, and *ʿayin*. Frg. 9 begins and provides the *waw*, *peh*, *peh*, and *waw* of the word ויעופפו.

[1327] Sukenik:]ש̊[. Qimron: שח̇ת.

[1328] DJD: מקו̇[רם.

[1329] Qimron: בֿעבותי.

[1330] Ctr. DJD: ישר[תֿוכה. Sukenik and Licht: יכה. Qimron: שר[תֿוכה. No *taw* is visible. The photographs in Sukenik often reveal the consonants best. Note DJD's insightful restoration: ממכון [קודשכה והמה לוא ישר[תֿוכה.

[1331] Ctr. DJD: הכֿ̊ל. See SHR 4301; the torn leather shows no other consonants. Sukenik:]̊. Qimron:]̊ה.

[1332] Sukenik and Licht: אסיר.

[1333] Ctr. DJD:]ידו בֿל שלח̇[. Sukenik:]לשל̊[ ]̊. Qimron:]ולֿשל̊[ ]̊.

[1334] Sukenik:]בק[. DJD: בקצֿ̊י חרונכה.

[1335] Sukenik and Licht: א[.

[1336] Sukenik and Licht:]כול[. DJD: הֿמ̊מזרים כי ל[וא]̊̊[.

[1337] Sukenik and Licht:]גדו[   ]לל[. Frg. 9 ends here.

7   unto the Endtime of [.... And] who can arraign[812] you

8   in the judgments of [...]*h* to the angels of

9   punishment[813] in judgme[nt ...] and the mysteries of transgression cause to alter[814] (those of the)

10   flesh in [their] gu[ilt ... a la]nd; and on it[815] fly all

11   the (evil)[816] angels of heav[en ... a pla]ce with spiritual ropes.[817] And you cast down

12   the heavenly beings[818] from the establishment [of your holiness, for they did not praise][819] you in the dwelling of your glory.[820] But you,

13   Adam[821] upon the °[...] confined until the Endtime of your will,[822]

14   and to dismiss them [...] the heights of power, and the multitude of flesh causing to be condemned[823]

15   in the endtime[s of ...]*l*, to establish in council[824] with you

16   [...] the illegitimate ones[825] for n[ot]

17   [...] corpses witho[ut]

---

[812] The *hipʿil* imperfect of יעד means "to make an appointment," or "to summon (or arraign)" in a court of law. See Jer 49:19 and 50:44. For the forensic meaning, see Job 9:19.

[813] The Hebrew noun denotes "affliction," and "blow." It can also mean punishment (see line 25). See esp. Deut 17:8. The meaning of 24.1–32 [and further] becomes clear only if one imagines the myth of the fallen angels found in Genesis 6 and especially in *1 Enoch* 1–36. Both texts were known to those at Qumran, as many copies of *1 Enoch* 1–36 and Genesis were found in the Qumran caves. Translating the present lines of text is guided by the helpful images found in 13.38: "as *the mysteries of transgression are altering the works of God with their guilt. For I was bound with ropes....*" Italics indicate verbal and metaphorical connections.

[814] See 13.38: "the mysteries of transgression are altering." The concept seems to refer to the origin of transgression. It occurred when the Watchers fell from heaven to copulate with the beautiful human women, mentioned in Genesis 6 and developed in *1 Enoch* 1–36.

[815] Or "and in it."

[816] There should be no doubt that evil angels are intended.

[817] The translator confronts a major decision: Does בעבותי derive from עב (the feminine plural עבות, "clouds") or from עבות ("rope" [fem. construct plural: "the ropes of"]). 1QH[a] 13.38 provides a key for unlocking the mystery: "bound with ropes." The author may denote how the fallen angels were bound "with spiritual ropes." God did not need to fashion a rope of cords to bind them. As he created with a word, so God could bind the Watchers with spiritual ropes. Thus, the rendering "clouds of the wind" not only lacks clarity but does not fit the context.

[818] Heb. אלים. According to a well-known Jewish myth, the fallen angels, the Watchers, leave the heights (or heaven) and descend to earth to mate with human women. The author probably imagined that God cast them out of heaven (that they could not return is clear). The Watchers were punished by God. See *1En* 10:4 according to which Azazel is bound hand and foot and cast into darkness by God. In *1En* 10:14, we are told the evil angels are "bound together" until the Endtime.

[819] The evil angels did not praise, or honor, God's infinite authority. They rebelled against God's will and plan.

[820] Note also the attractive restoration in DJD: "[and they could no longer ser]ve you in your glorious dwelling."

[821] The transition is abrupt, but we have only a portion of the text. "Adam" is mentioned. Could the *Books of Adam* or the Adam compositions (known at Qumran, but again only in fragments) have influenced the poet? Is it conceivable that Adam is being addressed?

[822] The author refers to God's will. See *1En* 10:6, according to which Azazel is confined and cast into the desert until "the great day of judgment."

[823] The *hipʿil* of רשע means "to pronounce guilty," or "cause to be condemned."

[824] Or "in secret."

[825] See *1En* 10:9 and the reference to "the illegitimate" offspring of the Watchers.

]	**18**
]	**19**
]	**20**
⟦ צדקה דעֺתֺ⟧¹³³⁸	**21**
⟦עֺב ¹³³⁹ לחת בעת עוונותֺ⟧ינו¹³⁴⁰	**22**
⟦ֺם¹³⁴¹ כול שטן ומשחית ⟧	**23**
⟦בֺרשתם ולשלחם גוי בֺ⟧גוי¹³⁴² ⟦יֺכֺה רשע¹³⁴³	**24**
⟦איש זֺידן¹³⁴⁴ במרבי מעל ועֺ⟧ ֺ בֺנֺגֺיֺעֺיֺם¹³⁴⁵ ובמשפטים	**25**
לֺ⟧¹³⁴⁶ ֺבים בבסר¹³⁴⁷ כי כול רוחותֺ ⟧⟦מֺזרים להרשיע בבשר	**26**
וֺמֺ⟧¹³⁴⁸ הרשיעו בחייהֺם ⟧ ⟦לֺו⟧אֺ כן¹³⁴⁹ רוחם להרשיע¹³⁵⁰	**27**
עֺלֺ⟧¹³⁵¹ לֺ⟧¹³⁵² ולֺ⟧פֺלֺא¹³⁵³ רזיכה גליתה	**28**
לבֺ⟧¹³⁵⁴ ⟦אֺני לבשר ידעתי	**29**
כיאֺ⟧ ⟦ם עולה בקץ	**30**
כלֺ⟧ות¹³⁵⁵ ⟦ה ולכול מביט	**31**
⟦ ולו יכחד	**32**

¹³³⁸ Ctr. DJD:]ֺועֺ[. Frg. 45 begins with this line and provides the text for the center of lines 21–28. Sukenik and Licht: צדקה וע].

¹³³⁹ DJD and Qimron: בֺ[.

¹³⁴⁰ Sukenik and Licht:]ֺעוונו.

¹³⁴¹ Qimron: הם[מ.

¹³⁴² Cf. Sukenik and Licht: בֺ]גוי. DJD:]ֺ גוי. Qimron: גוי בֺ].

¹³⁴³ Sukenik and Licht: רשע ˚˚˚[. DJD: יֺכֺה[ ]ֺ גוי. Qimron:]ֺ בֺח רשע ז[מֺ]. Frg. 6 begins here and provides the margin and left side of lines 24–37.

¹³⁴⁴ Sukenik and Licht: זודן.

¹³⁴⁵ Sukenik and Licht: ם˚˚˚[ ]ֺ ועֺ. DJD: בֺנֺגֺיֺעֺיֺם [ ]ֺ ר. Qimron: עֺ בֺנֺגֺיֺעֺיֺם[נוג]ומֺ.

¹³⁴⁶ Frg. 2 col. 2 provides the right margin and text of lines 26–39. Sukenik does not transcribe the *lamedh*. Licht does not transcribe this fragment.

¹³⁴⁷ Read: בשר. The orthography may indicates an Aramaism.

¹³⁴⁸ Sukenik:]ֺ.

¹³⁴⁹ DJD: כן לֺ[ ]וכ. Qimron: לֺו]אֺ.

¹³⁵⁰ The *reš* may have been a *waw*: להושיע, "to save."

¹³⁵¹ Sukenik:]ֺעֺ. DJD: עֺלֺ]. Qimron: עֺלֺ].

¹³⁵² Frg. 45 ends here.

¹³⁵³ Sukenik and Licht: לא[.

¹³⁵⁴ Sukenik:]לב.

¹³⁵⁵ DJD: כל]ות רשעה.

18   [...]

19   [...]

20   [...]

21   [...] righteousness. Knowledge [...]

22   [...]ᶜ*b* to the pit at the time of [our] iniquities [...]

23   [...]°*m* each adversary[826] and destroyer [...]

24   [...] in their net and dismissing them, nation by [nation[827] ...]your [...]wickedness.

25   [...] an arrogant man with much infidelity and ᶜ[...]° with punishments and in judgments

26   *l*[...]°*bym* with flesh[828] for all the spirits of the illegitimate ones[829] to cause wickedness with flesh[830]

27   and *m*[...] to cause wickedness during their lives [...] n[o]t like their spirits to cause wickedness

28   ᶜ*l*[...]*l*[... and for] the wonder of your mysteries you revealed

29   to my heart [...] I for flesh. I know

30   that [...]*m* injustice at the Endtime of

31   annih[ilation ...]*yh* and to each who looks upon[831]

32   [...] and it will not be concealed

---

[826] Heb. שטן; see 22.25.
[827] Or "people by [people ...]."
[828] The orthography may indicate an Aramaism.
[829] The myth of the Watchers clearly refers to their offspring as "illegitimate."
[830] The author seems influenced by the myth of the Watchers, best known today by its development in *1 Enoch* 1–36.
[831] The *hipᶜil* participle of נבט means "to look" or "to watch."

כׄ]וׄבדתה1357 מבני	מֶׄלׄפֶׄנֶׄיׄ]1356	33
גׄ]בׄוׄלות עמים	אל שׄוׄ]מעׄיׄ1358	34
לׄ]הׄׄרבות1359 אשמה	לחזקם]]	35
עׄוׄזׄבׄתׄםׄ] ביד	בנחלתו]ׄ	36
אׄ]ׄׄ ׄדׄ1361	כול מבל]עׄי דבר1360	37
	תׄבׄאׄ]1362	38
	עׄל]	39
	[	40
	[	41
	[	42

Col. 25 [Frgs. 5, 56 Col. 1, 46 Col. 1, 51, 55 Col. 1, 63, 8, and 7 Col. 1]
Parallels: 4Q428 Frgs. 17–20

[	1
[	2
מש]פֶׄטׄ צדק בׄ]כול1363	3
ול]הׄפרידם ממעמד קׄדׄ]וׄשים1364	4
]וׄת עם עׄדׄת קדושיכה בהפלא]]	5
]עׄ]דׄ עׄוׄלם1365 ורוחות רשעה תבית1366 מא]]	6

1356 The speculative nature of the reading is caused by a tear and lost leather. Sukenik:]ׄׄׄ.
1357 Sukenik and Licht: בדתה[. Qimron: וׄ]כׄבדתה.
1358 Sukenik:]ש אל.
1359 Sukenik and Licht: רבות[.
1360 Sukenik:]כול מכ. Qimron: כול מבק]שי. DJD:]כול מב. See 17.8.
1361 Licht: א־ד [. Frg. 6 ends here.
1362 Sukenik:]תב. Qimron: תביׄאׄ]נו.
1363 Sukenik:]ׄ ׄ ט צדק [. Licht: משפ]ט. DJD: צדק בׄ]. For צדק בכול, see 10.6. Perhaps צדקה. For צדקה with משפט see 9.32. Frg. 5 begins here and provides the margin and right side of lines 3–17.
1364 Sukenik:]ׄ. Licht does not read קׄ.
1365 Licht: ע]ד ענ]ו[לם. DJD: עׄדׄ עׄוׄלם. Qimron: עׄד עולם.
1366 Licht: תבות.

33   from before [...] you are [ho]nored above the sons of

34   God, those who h[ear of ... the bo]undaries of the peoples

35   to strengthen them [... to] multiply guilt

36   in his inheritance °[...] you abandon them into the hand of

37   all the destroy[ers of the word ...]ᵒ°°d

38   *tbʾ*[...]

39   upon [...]

40   [...]

41   [...]

42   [...]

Col. 25 [Frgs. 5, 56 Col. 1, 46 Col. 1, 51, 55 Col. 1, 63, 8, and 7 Col. 1]
Parallels: 4Q428 Frgs. 17–20

1   [...]

2   [...]

3   [...] righteous [judg]ment in[all ...]

4   [... and to] separate⁸³² them from the rank of the Ho[ly Ones ...]

5   [...]*wt* with the congregation of your Holy Ones in doing wondrously [...]

6   [un]to eternity. And the wicked spirits⁸³³ you shall cause to be housed⁸³⁴ *mʾ*[...]

---

⁸³² The *hipʿil* inf. of פרד denotes "to separate," "to segregate," or "to keep apart from." The condemnation of the Watchers seems to be in the mind of the author. God "segregated" them from "the Ho[ly Ones]," most likely the Holy Angels in heaven. A *double enten-dre* is also possible since "the Holy Ones" at Qumran can mean angels and the advanced members of the Community (the *Yaḥad*).

⁸³³ These wicked spirits should be recognized as the fallen angels, the Watchers, who brought evil and wickedness to the earth, as is well known from Genesis 6 and the *Books of Enoch*.

⁸³⁴ The noun בית, "house," is well-known in Biblical and related texts, but the verb בית is not familiar. The *qal* imperfect of the verb בית is unique. The verb continues into modern Hebrew to denote housing something like a dog.

‏[[כול‎1369	‏רֹע‎1367 לוא יהיו עוד ותשם מקום רשׁ[[עה‎1368	7
‏[[הֹ‎1370	‏רוחות עולה אשר יושדו לאבל[[	8
	‏יעֹגֹן‎1371 לדורי נצח וברום רשעה למ[עשה רע	9
‏[[°°	‏יֹרבה‎1372 אנינם לכלה ונגד כול מעשכׄ[[ה	10
‏מ[[ׄוֹעד הֹ[[וׄ[[דׄעתה‎1374	‏חסדיכה ולדעת כול בכבודכה ולפׄ[[ן‎1373	11
‏[[לאׄ[[ׄ[[נוש‎1375 בֹמזמת	‏משפט אמתכה ואוזן בשר גליתה ו[[	12
‏בצ[[בֹא המרֹום ת[[שֹׁפוט‎1378 במרום	‏לבכה וקצ‎1376 תעודה השכלתה לבשֹׁ[[ר‎1377	13
‏תחתיה תשפׄ[[וׄ[[טׄ‎1380 וֹבׄיושבי‎1381	‏וביושבי הֹאֹדֹמֹה על האדמה וגמ[בשאו[[לׄ‎1379	14
‏רשע [[כׄיא אין מבׄ[[לעדי[[כֹהֹ‎1385	‏חושך תריב להצדׄ[[יק‎1382 צׄדיק‎1383 ולהרׄ[[שׄׄיע‎1384	15
‏[[ת אׄ[[‎1388	‏ולוא להפרד מ[אמת‎1386 [דׄברכה]‎1387	16

‎1367 Sukenik: לוא ֗°°. DJD: רֹעׄ [מעשׂי. The participle was restored at the end of line 6.

‎1368 Sukenik: ר]. Licht: ר[שעה]. DJD: רשׁ[עה להפיל גורלות.

‎1369 The word כול is supplied by frg. 56 col. 1, which provides the margin and left side of line 7. Licht does not transcribe this fragment.

‎1370 Frg. 46 col. 1 begins here and provides the margin and far left side of lines 8–14. Sukenik does not transcribe the *he*. Licht does not transcribe this fragment.

‎1371 Sukenik and Licht read: ועדן. Cf. DJD: יעֹגֹן. Qimron: וׄמֹגֹן. The *gimel* is strikingly similar to the form in line 10: ונגד.

‎1372 Sukenik and Licht: רבה. Qimron: תֹרבה.

‎1373 Sukenik: ולפׄ[. Licht: ולפר].

‎1374 Frg. 51 begins here and provides part of the left side for lines 11–16. Licht does not transcribe this fragment. Sukenik: [. עד ֗[דעתה. For the term הֹ[וׄ]דׄעתה: frg. 51 provides the *he* and frg. 46 col. 1 provides the *daleth*, *'ayin*, *taw*, and *he*.

‎1375 Sukenik: [. לא [יֹשׁ. For the word לאׄנוׄשׁ: frg. 51 provides the *lamedh* and *'aleph*. Frg. 56 col. 1 provides the *nun*, *waw*, and *šin*.

‎1376 Licht: וקץ. Note the use of the medial form in the final position. It is clearly a medial *ṣade* contra Licht's reading. The manuscript's reading is an example of ancient orthography, indicating an earlier exemplar.

‎1377 Sukenik: [. לבֹׄ[. Licht: לב]שר.

‎1378 Sukenik: [. שׁׄפוט [ת]ים[שֹׁ[אהֹ]. DJD: בצ[בֹא המרׄום תשׁפוט. For the word תשׁפוט, frg. 51 provides the *taw* and frg. 46 col. 1 provides the *šin*, *peh*, *waw*, and *teth*.

‎1379 See 4Q428 frg. 18 line 4: בשאוֹלׄ.

‎1380 Sukenik: [. שׂׄ[. The reading is improved thanks to images made by Charlesworth, Johns, and Rietz.

‎1381 Frg. 46 col. 1 ends here. Sukenik: [. ביושבי.

‎1382 Sukenik and Licht: [. לאצו. DJD: להצדׄ[י]קׄ. Qimron: להצדׄ[י]קׄ.

‎1383 Sukenik: [. דוקׄ. Licht: דׄיק. Qimron: צׄדיק.

‎1384 Sukenik and Licht: ולהר]. Qimron: ולהרשׁׄ[יע].

‎1385 These letters are difficult to read. I am influenced by DJD. Frg. 55 col. 1 supplies [כׄהֹ for this column. Sukenik: [מן אין. Licht does not transcribe this portion of frg. 55.

‎1386 Sukenik and Licht do not read the מ.

‎1387 Sukenik: [. בֹרכה]. Licht: [דׄ]ברכה. Frg. 55 ends here.

‎1388 Frg. 51 ends here. Sukenik: [. ֗תׄ]ֹ.

7 evil will not continue anymore.[835] And you shall make desolate[836] the place of wicked[ness …] all

8 the spirits of injustice that shall be devastated[837] for sorrow […]*h*,

9 he shall be locked up[838] for eternal generations. And when wickedness rises up to d[o evil…][839]

10 their lament shall increase unto annihilation. But before all yo[ur] creatures[840] […]°°

11 your loving-kindnesses, and to know all in your glory. And according to [… the app]ointed time you allowed to be [kn]own[841]

12 your true judgment.[842] And you uncovered the ear of flesh and […] to humans in the design of

13 your heart. And (concerning) the Endtime of fixed times, you allowed fles[h] to have insight.[843] [The ho]st of the upper regions[844] you shall judge in the upper regions,

14 and the dwellers of earth (you shall judge) upon the earth. And also [in Sheo]l below you shall ju[d]ge.[845] And (concerning) the dwellers of

15 darkness, you shall contest a lawsuit, declaring righte[ous] the righteous one and declaring w[icked the wicked one] for there is none ex[cept] you.

16 And not to separate from the [truth…] your word […]°*t* ʾ[…]

---

[835] Lit. "it will not be again."

[836] The *hipʿil* imperfect of שׁמם (the י is not shown, as is often the case in Qumran Hebrew) means "cause to be deserted."

[837] The *hopʿil* imperfect of שׁדד means "to be devastated."

[838] The verb עגן means "to lock up" in late Hebrew. The *qal* or *piʿel* imp. appears here in Qumran Hebrew but not in Biblical Hebrew. Most likely, Aramaic has influenced the language (as is obvious elsewhere in the *Thanksgiving Hymns*). It seems obvious that the leader of the fallen angels is the one who is "locked up for eternal generations." Jewish reflections on human suffering are complex. While we should not try to harmonize conflicting traditions or ideas, we should observe that many Jews probably imagined that the leader of the fallen angels had been imprisoned deep in the desert, but not yet those influenced by him (the demons who populate this earth and world).

[839] The Wicked Spirit is locked up, but will rise from his confinement to do evil.

[840] Or "works." See Ps 145:9.

[841] *Hipʿil* permissive.

[842] The Jews who read these lines believed that the Watchers had already been condemned by God. While evil angels continued to cause wickedness on the earth and were the source for sickness, their fate was sealed, as explained in *1 Enoch* 1–36.

[843] *Hipʿil* permissive.

[844] The authors of the *Thanksgiving Hymns* use another noun for "heaven."

[845] Perhaps this belief influenced the *descensus ad inferos* passages in the *Odes of Solomon*. See esp. *OdesSol* 42:11–20.

17	לʾ[ן¹³⁸⁹	
18	]̇	
19	]̇	
20	]̇	
21	]̇	
22	]̇	
23	]̇	
24	]̇	
25	לֹבֹלֹ[תי¹³⁹⁰	]̊ה ולוֹא יֹכֹירוֹ[ן¹³⁹¹
26	מעשׁ̊י[ן	שׁ[מֹ]ים ובסוד קד[ושים[]
27	יתרומ[]ם¹³⁹²	[]יֹב̊°°°[]¹³⁹³
28	עצה ו[]̊	
29	משרתים[]	[]̊ו¹³⁹⁴
30	ו̊הכירום[]	[]ל[]ז[]מֹר̊¹³⁹⁵
31	ולהלל לֹ[]	[]כֹדעתי¹³⁹⁶
32	ספרתי בֹ̊ע̊[ד]ת¹³⁹⁷	כיא את[]ה̊ אל¹³⁹⁸
33	הדעות ובֹפֹ̊י[ן¹³⁹⁹	
34	למשכיל מזמ̊[]ור	[]̊כה¹⁴⁰⁰

---

¹³⁸⁹ Sukenik and Licht do not transcribe the *lamedh*. Frg. 5 ends here.

¹³⁹⁰ Frg. 8 begins here and provides the right side of lines 25–36. Sukenik:]ל̊. Licht does not transcribe this fragment. Qimron:]ל̊.

¹³⁹¹ Frg. 63 begins here and provides the left side for lines 25–27. We are influenced by DJD. Sukenik:]°°[ ]ו ול[. Licht does not transcribe this column. Qimron: [ה ולוֹא יֹכיר]ן.

¹³⁹² DJD and Qimron: יתרומ[]ו.

¹³⁹³ Frg. 63 ends here.

¹³⁹⁴ Frg. 7 col. 1 begins here and provides the left side of lines 29–37. Sukenik and Licht: °[. Licht does not read this consonant.

¹³⁹⁵ Sukenik and Licht: °[.

¹³⁹⁶ With Sukenik and Licht. DJD: כֹדעתי ר[החמ. Qimron: החמֹר כֹדעתי.

¹³⁹⁷ DJD and Qimron: בֹע[ד]ת.

¹³⁹⁸ Sukenik and Licht: אל[. DJD and Qimron: את[]ה̊ אל.

¹³⁹⁹ DJD and Qimron: בֹפֹֹ[.

¹⁴⁰⁰ Licht: ה̊[. DJD: כֹה°°°[. Qimron: כה°°°[.

17 *l*[…]

18 […]

19 […]

20 […]

21 […]

22 […]

23 […]

24 […]

25 with[out …]*h* and they will not recognize […]

26 works of [… he]aven, but in the council of the Hol[y Ones]

27 th[ey] will be pompous[846] […]*yb*°°°[…]

28 the council and °[…]

29 those who serve […]*n*.

30 And they recognize them […] to ch[ant]

31 and praise *l*[…] According to my knowledge,

32 I have announced in the ass[embly of …. For yo]u are the God of

33 knowledge.[847] And with a [strong] voice[848] [….]

34 For the Instructor, a psa[lm of …] your […]°.

---

[846] The *hithpoʿlel* imp. of רום means "to lift oneself up proudly." The author seems to be imagining the angels in heaven who acted with self-importance at the beginning of their refusal to obey fully God in the heavenly council. "Satan" ("adversary" in Hebrew) appears in Job as God's antagonist; in later texts he is a fallen angel who leads evil against good.

[847] See 1QS 3.15: "the God of knowledge."

[848] Or "at the command of." Lit. "at the mouth of." The meaning is to a loud voice. See Ps 68:34: קול עז, "a strong voice."

[̊ מֹלֹכֹי קדם[1402] ‖[	35 כיא[1401]
‖[וחמתו[1404]	36 [̊‖[1403]
[ורומם[1405] דֹעֹתֹי[1406]	37
]	38
]	39
]	40
]	41
]	42

Col. 26 [Frgs. 56 Col. 2, 46 Col. 2, 55 Col. 2, and 7 Col. 2]
Parallels: 4Q427 Frg. 7; 4Q428 Frg. 21; 4Q431

]	1
]	2
]	3
]	4
]	5
יעדני[1407]	6
יבוא [1408]	7
וכבוד]	8
בי וה ̊[1409]	9

[1401] Sukenik, Licht, and DJD rightly transcribe כיא. It is missed by Qimron. Qimron places frg. 47 on the right portions of lines 35–39.
[1402] Sukenik and Licht: מלכי ̊דם [. DJD: ̊[. מלכי קדם
[1403] Frg. 8 ends here.
[1404] Licht: מתו °°[. Ctr. DJD: נֹהֹמתי[. Cf. Qimron: [ברזי ̊עֹוֹרמתו]. Cf. 5.16, 21.37.
[1405] Ctr. DJD: תֹרוממֹהֹ[א. Sukenik and Licht: רומם[. Qimron: מֹרומם[. Frg. 7 col. 1 ends here.
[1406] For דעתי see 18.22, 25.31.
[1407] Cf. 4Q427 frg. 7 1.9: יעידני. Frg. 56 col. 2 provides the right side of lines 6–10. The right margin is clear. Sukenik: [ו. Licht does not transcribe this fragment.
[1408] Qimron: יבא (*sic*) at the end of the preceding line.
[1409] Qimron: בי זהֹב. See 4Q427 frg. 7 1.12: ביורים. The script continues in 1QHᵃ: ביוה ̊[. Perhaps a ור was miscopied as וה.

35   For [...]° kings of the east

36   [...]°[...] and his wrath.

37   [...] and he exalted my knowledge[849]

38   [...]

39   [...]

40   [...]

41   [...]

42   [...]

Col. 26 [Frgs. 56 Col. 2, 46 Col. 2, 55 Col. 2, and 7 Col. 2]
Parallels: 4Q427 Frg. 7; 4Q428 Frg. 21; 4Q431

1   [...]

2   [...]

3   [...]

4   [...]

5   [...]

6   can appoint me[850] [...]

7   can go [...]

8   and glory [...]

9   with me and *h*°[...]

[849] The author uses the *po'lel* of רום. Here he wants to praise God who exalts his knowledge.
[850] *Hip'il* impf. of יעד. See 26.16.

10   שׂ֯מֹח[ו]¹⁴¹⁰

11   רוממ[ו]¹⁴¹¹

12   [ו]°¹⁴¹²

13   הֿשׁמ֯[י]עו¹⁴¹³

14   בֿיֿחֿד[ו]¹⁴¹⁴

15   רֿזים¹⁴¹⁵ ולגלות נסֿתרות וֹהֿ[ן¹⁴¹⁶

16   [ולהש]פיל נועדת¹⁴¹⁷ רום גאים֯[¹⁴¹⁸

17   [   ] ל[   ]לֹ[¹⁴¹⁹

18   ]

19   ]

20   ]

21   ]

22   ]

23   ]

24   ]

25   ]

26   עוד¹⁴²⁰ [הש]מ֯[י]עו¹⁴²¹ וֹאֿמֿרֿ[ו¹⁴²²   גבהות[¹⁴²³

---

¹⁴¹⁰ Sukenik:]מח [. Cf. DJD: שׂ֯מֹח[ו]. Qimron: שׂמֹח[ו]. Frg. 56 col. 2 ends here and is placed with frg. 46 col. 2 which begins here and provides the right side of lines 10–14. The right margin is clear. Licht does not transcribe frg. 46 col. 2.

¹⁴¹¹ Sukenik:]°רומם.

¹⁴¹² Cf. DJD: שׁ֯[מו]. Only a tiny piece of ink remains. Sukenik also does not discern a consonant.

¹⁴¹³ Cf. DJD: הֿשׁמ֯[י]עו.

¹⁴¹⁴ DJD:]ביחֿד. Sukenik: ביח. Qimron: בֿיֿחֿד. The ʾaleph seems unmistakable and erased; the consonant is not a daleth. Frg. 46 col. 2 ends here.

¹⁴¹⁵ Sukenik and Licht: ים[   ]°°[. Frg. 55 col. 2 begins here and provides the right side of lines 15–18. The right margin is clear.

¹⁴¹⁶ Sukenik and Licht:]°°.

¹⁴¹⁷ Sukenik and Licht: עדת פילנו[. Qimron: ולהשפיל נועדות. This section of the leather is lost.

¹⁴¹⁸ Sukenik:]גא° רום עדת פילנו[. Licht:]גא°. Qimron: רום גאים.

¹⁴¹⁹ DJD:]לֹ[ה]ל[כ. Qimron: השופט באף כלה. Frg. 55 col. 2 ends here.

¹⁴²⁰ Frg. 7 col. 2 begins here and provides the right side of lines 26–38. The right margin is clear. Qimron's multicolored composite text should be studied for further divergent readings in lines 26–42.

¹⁴²¹ Sukenik and Licht do not read the מ.

¹⁴²² Sukenik and Licht:]חמ [. 4Q431 frg. 2 2.6: עוד השמיעו ואמרו.

¹⁴²³ See 4Q427 frg. 7 2.8: גבהות רוח.

10   be joyf[ul ...]

11   extol [...]

12   ˚[...]

13   cause to be he[ard ...]

14   in the common [...]

15   mysteries, and to reveal hidden things *wh*[...]

16   [and to bring d]own the pompous gatherings of[851] the proud ones [...]

17   [...]*l*[...]*l*[...]

18   [...]

19   [...]

20   [...]

21   [...]

22   [...]

23   [...]

24   [...]

25   [...]

26   more. Cause to [be] heard and say: [the pompous]

---

[851] The noun is from the *nipʿal* of יעד which means "to meet at" or "to gather together."

27   רום[1424] לאין שֵׁרית ויר[ם][1425]

28   יגביה[1426] בקומה ועם]

29   עולם וכשלי ארצ[1427] יר[ם][1428]

30   ושמחת עולם במכוניהֵֹם[1429]

31   לֵהֹוֹדִיֹע גֵּבֹוֹרֵֹהֹ[1430] ומֵצֹדֵֹיֹ[ק][1431]

32   בדעתם ברוב[1432] חסדיֹ[ו][1433]

33   אל הצדק והשכלֵֹנֹוֹ[1434] בֵֹאֹ[מתכה[1435]

34   בֹכֹוח גבורה והכֹרֹ[נו[1436]

35   מה בשר לאלה וֹמֹ[ה][1437]

36   ולהתיצב בֹמעמד[1438]

37   להשיב דבר כֹפֵֹֹיֹכֹהֹ וֹ[ן][1439]

38   לֹרֹצֹ[ונכ]הֹ בֵֹֹ[1440]

39   ]

40   ]

41   ]

42   ]

[1424] An error for רוח; see 4Q427 frg. 7 2.8. In Hasmonean Script a *mem* can be confused with a *ḥet*.

[1425] Sukenik and Licht: שֵׁרית ֹֹ[. See 4Q431 frg. 2 2.7: וירם.

[1426] Sukenik and Licht: וגבוה.

[1427] Sukenik and Licht: וכושלי ֹ ארצ. Note the medial *ṣade* in the final position. See 4Q431 frg. 2 2.9: וכושלי ארץ.

[1428] Licht: [ו.

[1429] Sukenik and Licht: במכונוֹ [.

[1430] Note the scribal dots. Licht does not reference the scribal dots. Licht: גבורהֹ. Before line 31 DJD speculates a line 31a. See 4Q427 frg. 7 2.12: להופיע גבורה.

[1431] Sukenik and Licht: [וֹֹֹ.

[1432] Sukenik and Licht: ברית.

[1433] Sukenik and Licht: חסד [.

[1434] Sukenik and Licht: והשכל [.

[1435] Sukenik and Licht do not see בֹאֹ. Restore with DJD.

[1436] Sukenik and Licht: וה[.

[1437] Sukenik and Licht do not see וֹמֹ.

[1438] Sukenik and Licht: מעמ[ֹ.

[1439] Sukenik and Licht: דבר בן[. For lines 37 and 38 we are indebted to DJD. As the diacritics warn, all readings are speculative. Qimron also follows DJD.

[1440] Sukenik and Licht: ו ף[ל[. Frg. 7 col. 2 ends here.

27 spirit,[852] so there is no remnant.[853] And he raise[d up …]

28 he will elevate[854] on high, and with […]

29 eternal. And those who stumble earthward,[855] he shall raise [up ….]

30 And eternal joy (is) in their establishments, […]

31 to make known (his) might, and acts righteou[sly …]

32 with their knowledge in the multitude of his loving-kindnesses […]

33 O God of righteousness, and we were allowed to have insight[856] into [your] tr[uth …]

34 with your mighty power, and we recognized […]

35 What (is) flesh (compared) to these (things)? And wh[at shall …]

36 and to present in rank […]

37 to cause to return a word according to your edict[857] and […]

38 for [yo]ur wi[ll] in °°[…]

39 […]

40 […]

41 […]

42 […]

---

[852] See 4Q427 frg. 7 2.8: גבהות רוח.
[853] The spelling of "remnant" without the א. For the noun with אין, see Ezek 9:14.
[854] The *hipꜥil* imp. of גבה means "to make (something) high;" the direct object is often a wall or an entrance.
[855] Or "who stumble (to the) earth."
[856] *Hipꜥil* permissive.
[857] Or "mouth."

Col. 27 [Frgs. 62 and 61]

] **1**

] **2**

] **3**

] **4**

] **5**

] **6**

] **7**

] **8**

] **9**

] **10**

] **11**

[1443]⟧ל̊ ⟦[ ]⟧[1442]ש̊ם̊⟦[1441]   **12**

[1444]רצי⟦[ ]⟧תה ב̇⟦[**13**

[1445]בל⟦[ ]⟧ו̊א יד⟦[ ]⟧עתה   **14**

Col. 28 [Frg. 48]

] **1**

] **2**

] **3**

[1441] Frgs. 61 and 62, which were joined by Carmignac, provide the text for lines 12–14. The placement in this column is tentative. Licht and Qimron do not transcribe either of these fragments. Frg. 62 provides the right side of this column and frg. 61 provides the left side.

[1442] Sukenik:]שד[. Carmignac: ̊ש̊ח[. Cf. DJD: ̊י̊ם[   ].

[1443] Sukenik:]̊ ̊[.

[1444] The margin is evident on frg. 62. Sukenik:]תהמ̊[רצו]. For the term רציתה: frg. 62 provides the *reš*, *ṣade*, and *yodh* and frg. 61 provides the *taw* and *he*.

[1445] Sukenik:]̊ות[בל]. DJD:]̊ ̊. See 18.21: רצו]נ̊כה   א[ו̇ל ידעתה בלוא. For the word, בלוא, frg. 62 provides the *beth* and *lamedh* and frg. 61 provides the *waw* and *'aleph*.

Col. 27 [Frgs. 62 and 61]

1   […]

2   […]

3   […]

4   […]

5   […]

6   […]

7   […]

8   […]

9   […]

10   […]

11   […]

12   […]*šm l*[…]

13   you were pleased *b*°[…]

14   without [.… You] kne[w…]

Col. 28 [Frg. 48]

1   […]

2   […]

3   […]

]   **4**

]   **5**

]   **6**

]   **7**

]   **8**

]   **9**

]   **10**

ע[פֹּר‎1446 כמוני בֹּ]‎1447   **11**

[כֹּבודכֹה ל]אור עולם‎1448   **12**

ולהלל]מכה‎1449 בהלא‎1450 ואיֹןֹ]‎1451   **13**

ברוח ק]וֹדש‎1452 על ידי גבורתֹ]כה‎1453   **14**

[בֹפֹיֹן]‎1454   לֹ]‎   **15**

Unplaced Fragments [Probably by Scribe A]

‎1455*Frg. 39* (= A1)

]א[**1**

[רֹוֹח לֹמֹשפטכהֹ]‎1456   **2**

‎1457]וֹֹ[**3**

‎1446 Sukenik: רֹ[.

‎1447 Frg. 48 begins with this line and provides the text for lines 11–15. The placement of this fragment is conceivably indicated by the shape at the top. See DJD, p. 41 and p. 311. Licht does not transcribe this fragment. DJD:]ֹ כמוני. Qimron: כמונו בֹ]כה.

‎1448 Sukenik:]ֹבודכֹהֹ[. DJD:]ֹכֹבודכֹה[. The *lamedh* has been overlooked. For the restoration see 20.18 and the notes to the translation.

‎1449 The supralinear was missed by previous editors.

‎1450 For the restoration see 17.39: ולהל]לֹ שמכה בהפלא.

‎1451 Sukenik:]בהֹלל או. Qimron: יֹחֹ. All editors missed וֹאֹיֹן; but it is visible in the photographs published by Sukenik.

‎1452 Sukenik:]דש. See 4.38: רוח קודשך על. 1QHᵃ has only "*your* holy spirit."

‎1453 Qimron: גבורה.

‎1454 Sukenik:]ֹבפ[.

‎1455 Licht and Qimron do not include frg. 39.

‎1456 Sukenik:]שפט[. DJD:]מ[שפטכ]ה (*sic*).

‎1457 Sukenik does not report a partial consonant. Cf. DJD:]ֹ[.

4   […]

5   […]

6   […]

7   […]

8   […]

9   […]

10   […]

11   [… d]ust like me *b*[…]

12   […] your glory for [eternal light …]⁸⁵⁸

13   [… and to praise] your name in doing wonders and without […]

14   [… by the H]oly [Spirit] upon⁸⁵⁹ [your] mighty hands […]

15   […] in the mouth of⁸⁶⁰ […]*l*[…]

Unplaced Fragments [Probably by Scribe A]

Frg. 39 (= A1)

1   […]ᵖ[…]

2   […] a spirit for your judgment […]

3   […]*w*[…]

---

⁸⁵⁸ For the restoration, see 20.18 and contiguous lines, which have similar expressions, notably "name," "light," "praise," "Holy Spirit," and "mighty."

⁸⁵⁹ Or "according to."

⁸⁶⁰ Or "at the edict (or command) of."

[1458]*Frg. 40* (= A2)

1   בסוד אמת]ךֿ[1459] אתֿחנן[1460]

2   [מענֿהֿ [לשון[1461]

3   [לֿ לֿ ˚[1462]

[1463]*Frg. 28* (= A3)

1   [˚˚˚˚ ˚˚˚[1464]

2   [˚ נהיה בתבל[1465]

3   [˚˚ לאנֿשֿי בֿרֿיתֿךֿ[1466]

[1467]*Frg. 35* (= A4)

1   [עֿוון וֿאֿשֿ]מה[1468]

2   [אֿ כי אין פֿ]ה[1469]

3   [˚˚˚ ותודיֿ]עני[1470]

[1471]*Frg. 37* (= A5)

1   קד]ושיכה ובפק]וד[1472]

[1458] Licht and Qimron do not include frg. 40.

[1459] See 1QHᵃ 6.23; 18.6; 19.7, 12; cf. 19.19.

[1460] DJD:]ךֿ אֿתֿחֿנֿ[. Sukenik:]נֿ ˚ א ˚ תֿןֿ[. Conceivably]בסוֿ]ךֿ אֿמֿתֿ; see 6.32; 18.6; 19.7, 12.

[1461] Sukenik:]מֿעֿנֿהֿ[.

[1462] Cf. DJD:] ˚˚[.

[1463] Licht and Qimron do not include frg. 28.

[1464] Sukenik:] ˚˚[.

[1465] Conceivably the left margin may be speculative because of the space after בתבל.

[1466] Sukenik:] ˚ חֿ ˚ לאנֿשֿי ˚[. The last word is speculative but (with DJD) some consonants appear above the tears and the context helps. See ואנושי ברית in 22.27. See also אנשי בריתם in 1QS 5.9 and 6.19; cf. 1QSa 1.2. Cf. 1Q36 frg. 7 line 2.

[1467] Licht and Qimron do not include frg. 35. Frg. 35 is now unfortunately covered with a transparent "gauze."

[1468] This is the speculation of DJD, but no consonant seems discernible. Sukenik reads only] ˚˚ עֿוון[.

[1469] See 12.21, 20.20, 25.15.

[1470] Cf. DJD: ותודיֿעֿ]ני. Sukenik:]ותודֿ ˚[.

[1471] Licht and Qimron do not include frg. 37.

[1472] With Sukenik and DJD.

Frg. 40 (= A2)

1   [… in the secret of] your [truth.]⁸⁶¹ I petition […]

2   […] the answer of [the tongue …]

3   […]*l*ᵒ*l*ᵒ[…]

Frg. 28 (= A3)

1   […]ᵒᵒᵒᵒ ᵒᵒᵒ

2   […]ᵒ it will be⁸⁶² in the world

3   […]ᵒᵒ for the men of your covenant

Frg. 35 (= A4)

1   […] iniquity and gui[lt …]

2   […]ᵖ for there is no ed[ict⁸⁶³ …]

3   […]ᵒᵒᵒ and you allowe[d me] to kn[ow …]⁸⁶⁴ […]

Frg. 37 (= A5)

1   […] your [Hol]y Ones and in the visit[ation of …]

---

⁸⁶¹ See 6.23; 18.6; 19.7, 12; cf. 19.19.
⁸⁶² Or "it will occur."
⁸⁶³ Lit. "there is no mo[uth …]."
⁸⁶⁴ *Hipʿil* permissive.

2   [לֹ]1473 [כה בני אֹ]דם1474

1475*Frg. 38* (= A6)

1   [קְדוֹשִׁיֹם]1476

2   [יברכו שמכֹהֹ בֹֹן]1477

1478*Frg. 36* (= A7)

1   [בֹיֹנֹה בֹלֹן]ב1479

2   [°°בֹנך ולספר °°]1480

1481*Frg. 27* (= A8)

1   [וֹעֹד °°]1482

2   כ[וֹל אלה תֹראה]1483

3   [°° ואֹדֹעֹה כי בש]כלכה1484

4   [לֹ °° לֹן] [לֹ]1485

1473 Sukenik does not report the *lamedh*.
1474 Sukenik:]°בני כה[. For the restoration, בני אֹ]דם, see 4.8; 10.24; 12.32; 13.11, 15; 14.11; 19.6.
1475 Licht and Qimron do not include frg. 38.
1476 Following DJD, but speculative. Sukenik:]דושים[.
1477 Sukenik:]°°שמ ובברכו[.
1478 Licht and Qimron do not include frg. 36.
1479 With DJD, but speculative. Sukenik:]°נֹה[.
1480 Ctr. DJD:]°°ל]ספֹר°° כֹבודך ולספר גֹבֹוֹ]רותיך[. Cf. Sukenik:]ולספר בנך[.
1481 Licht and Qimron do not include frg. 27.
1482 Ctr. DJD:]°°ל]ספֹר, but the *ʿayin* is unmistakable and the *daleth* likely. The *waw* is also likely. Sukenik:]עד[.
1483 Ctr. DJD:]בֹ כֹי ואדֹעֹה אלה וֹל[כ. Sukenik:]ה וֹאֹ וֹל אלה ל[.
1484 Sukenik:]בש °°°°ץ[. DJD: בש]°°°°°°[. See 17.26: כי בשכל]כה הודעתני.
1485 Sukenik does not transcribe this line.

2   […]*l*[…]*kh* the sons of A[dam …]

Frg. 38 (= A6)

1   […] the Holy Ones […]

2   […]they will bless your name in […]

Frg. 36 (= A7)

1   […] discernment in the hea[rt of …]

2   […]°°*bnk* and to recount °°[…]

Frg. 27 (= A8)

1   […] and ever[865] °°[…]

2   […a]ll these (things) you will allow to see[866] […]

3   […]°°. And I know that in [your] in[sight …]

4   […]*l*° °*l*[…]*l*[…]

---

[865] Or "until," or "unto."
[866] *Hipʿil* permissive.

Unplaced Fragments [Probably by Scribe C]

[1486]*Frg. 49* (= C1)

]°°[	**1**
גד[ו]ֹֿל רחמי[כה[1487]	**2**
הו[ד]ֿעתה[1488] א[לה	**3**
ת[ֹעות מרֹמֹ[ה[1489]	**4**
]°[מענֹֿה[1490]	**5**

[1491]*Frg. 53* (= C2)

[בֹֿשלֹ]וה[1492]	**1**
יא[י]רו כֹשֹמֹשֹ[1493]	**2**
במ[עֹוֹן הקודֹ[ש[1494]	**3**

[1495]*Frg. 58* (= C3)

[אבֹי]ֿן	**1**
ו[להביֹ]ן[1496]	**2**
[עֹולה תֿ[1497]	**3**
[°°ה ולהביֹ]ן[1498]	**4**

[1486] Licht and Qimron do not transcribe frg. 49.
[1487] Sukenik:]ולרחמ[.
[1488] Sukenik:]עֿתה א[.
[1489] Sukenik:]°ֿעותמד.
[1490] Sukenik:]מעֿ[. Only the first two consonants are visible.
[1491] Licht and Qimron do not include frg. 53.
[1492] Sukenik:]שֿל[. See 20.5 and frg. 58 line 6.
[1493] Sukenik:]°ירו בשמֿ[.
[1494] Sukenik:]°ֿן הקוֿ[. See 20.5 ([דש קוֹ]עון במ). The bottom margin may be visible.
[1495] Qimron does not include frg. 58.
[1496] Sukenik and Licht:]להֿפֿ[. DJD:]להב[.
[1497] Sukenik and Licht:]°°ֿר[. DJD:]°°°°[. See 7.38: [עד]לֿ תשמיד עולה וכול.
[1498] Sukenik and Licht:]ה ולהבי[. DJD:]°°ולהבי[.

Unplaced fragments [Probably by Scribe C]

Frg. 49 (= C1)

1   […]°°[…]

2   […gr]eat. [Your] mercies […]

3   […] you [allowed to] know[867] t[hese (things) …]

4   […e]rror, dece[it …]

5   […]° answer[…]

Frg. 53 (= C2)

1   […] in tranqui[lity[868]…]

2   […th]ey [shall s]hine like the sun […]

3   [… in] the hol[y dw]elling […]

Frg. 58 (= C3)

1   […] I will discer[n[869] …]

2   [… and] to discer[n …]

3   […] iniquity *t*[…]

4   […]°*h* and to disce[rn …]

---

[867] *Hipʿil* permissive.
[868] See 20.5 and frg. 58 line 6.
[869] Not "my father" as in 17.29 and 17.35.

5   ע[ו]֯ד קצ¹⁴⁹⁹ משפטכ֯ה]

6   [לרוות בש֯ל֯ו]ה¹⁵⁰⁰

¹⁵⁰¹*Frg. 59* (= C4)¹⁵⁰²

1   להב[י]ן֯ בת֯ש֯וב֯ת]¹⁵⁰³

2   מע[ו]מ֯ד֯י֯ ב֯ל֯וא תן]¹⁵⁰⁴

3   [ע֯ד קצ¹⁵⁰⁵ תשוב]ה¹⁵⁰⁶

4   [ר֯בים¹⁵⁰⁷ למת]¹⁵⁰⁸

5   [ול֯ק֯צ]¹⁵⁰⁹

¹⁵¹⁰*Frg. 66* (= C5)

1   [°°°°]¹⁵¹¹

2   [ע֯ ומ֯]¹⁵¹²

3   [ש֯לבת]ה¹⁵¹³

4   [מ֯°°°]¹⁵¹⁴

5   [מ֯ע֯°°°]¹⁵¹⁵

---

¹⁴⁹⁹ Note medial *ṣade* in final position.

¹⁵⁰⁰ Or בש֯ל֯ום. Ctr. DJD:]°°°°ב. Sukenik and Licht:]בשמ. See col. 20.5: ב[ש֯וקט ושלוה.

¹⁵⁰¹ Licht and Qimron do not include frg. 59.

¹⁵⁰² Frg. 59 is nearly impossible to read according to many images. Our transcription is our best guess and is similar to DJD.

¹⁵⁰³ Sukenik:]°°°°°[. Puech saw מע֯שה. Puech's letter to Stegemann in August 1997.

¹⁵⁰⁴ Sukenik began to transcribe here:]את°°°[.

¹⁵⁰⁵ Note medial *ṣade* in final position

¹⁵⁰⁶ Sukenik:]קצ תע֯°[.

¹⁵⁰⁷ Sukenik: ים°[. DJD:]י֯֯רים[. Cf. 11Q10 [11QTJob] 33.9: ירים. But with magnification one can see בים and perhaps a *reš*. Cf. רבים with 10.18. 10.29 [*bis*], 12.28, 12.29, 13.10.

¹⁵⁰⁸ Sukenik:]°למ°[. Ctr. Puech: לבב. DJD:]ל֯מ. The *taw* can be seen under magnification; cf. למת. Cf. 11Q19 [11QT] 48.9.

¹⁵⁰⁹ Sukenik does not observe this line.

¹⁵¹⁰ Licht and Qimron do not include frg. 66.

¹⁵¹¹ Sukenik:]°°[.

¹⁵¹² Sukenik:]ע ומ[. DJD:]מ°°[.

¹⁵¹³ Sukenik:]של ע[. DJD:]ש֯ל ע֯[. The *beth* is clear. See 16.31: שלבתה.

¹⁵¹⁴ Sukenik:]מ֯ל°[.

¹⁵¹⁵ Sukenik:]נע [. DJD:]ע֯°°°[.

5   […un]til the Endtime of your judgment[…]

6   […]to water thoroughly⁸⁷⁰ in tranquili[ty⁸⁷¹…]

Frg. 59 (= C4)

1   [… to disce]rn the return of[…]

2   […] my [stan]ding⁸⁷² without *tw*[…]

3   […] until the Endtime of returni[ng …]

4   […] the many⁸⁷³ *lmt*[…]

5   […] and to the Endtime […]

Frg. 66 (= C5)

1   […]°°°[…]

2   […]ᶜ and *m*[…]

3   [… its] flame⁸⁷⁴ […]

4   […] °°*m*°°[…]

5   […]°°*m*ᶜ°[…]

---

⁸⁷⁰ Most likely not "to saturate" since too much watering kills vegetation.
⁸⁷¹ Or with a different restoration: "in peac[e …]." But see 20.5 and frg. 53 line 1.
⁸⁷² Or "my rank."
⁸⁷³ Or perhaps, "the Many," a technical term at Qumran.
⁸⁷⁴ See 16.31.

¹⁵¹⁶*Frg. 65* (= C6)

1   [°°°°°[¹⁵¹⁷

2   כֹ֯יֿא מאו]ר¹⁵¹⁸

3   וֹלטהֹר פשֹ֯ע[֯יהם¹⁵¹⁹

4   ברצונכהֿ]¹⁵²⁰

¹⁵²¹*Frg. 64* (= C7)

1   [כֹ֯ע°°°]°°°¹⁵²²

2   ת[פֿתח לוֹחות °]¹⁵²³

3   [°בעו]לֹם¹⁵²⁴

¹⁵²⁵*Frg. 41* (= C8)

1   [° °]°¹⁵²⁶

2   ](VACAT)[

3   אודכה אדוני כיא] אֿתה גלִי[תה¹⁵²⁷

4   [°°]°¹⁵²⁸

---

¹⁵¹⁶ Licht and Qimron do not include frg. 65.
¹⁵¹⁷ Sukenik:]°°°°[.
¹⁵¹⁸ Sukenik:]כיא מאו[. The right margin can be seen.
¹⁵¹⁹ Ctr. DJD:]וֹלטחר נֿמֿהֿ[רי. Sukenik:]ולטהר פשֹ֯. Cf. 11.22, 15.33: לֿטֿהֿרם מפשעיהם, 19.13.
¹⁵²⁰ Sukenik:]ברצונכ..
¹⁵²¹ Licht and Qimron do not include frg. 64.
¹⁵²² Sukenik:]°°°°[. DJD:]°°°°°°[.
¹⁵²³ Ctr. DJD:]°ת[פתח לוחות. Sukenik: פתח לֿ֯חות [. The consonants חות are clear. Cf. 11Q19 [11QTª] 7.3: לוחות.
¹⁵²⁴ Ctr. DJD:]°מע °[. Sukenik:] °בֿע °[. The *beth* is clear.
¹⁵²⁵ Licht and Qimron do not include frg. 41.
¹⁵²⁶ Cf. DJD:]° יֿ °[. No consonants can be discerned.
¹⁵²⁷ Sukenik:]תה בל[. DJD: בלו]א. The *gimel* seems obvious. For אתה גליתה see 5.20 and 22.26. Perhaps the *Hodayot* formula preceded these words: "I thank you, O Lord, for you revealed (uncovered)...." See 14.7. The *Hodayot* formula often follows a *vacat*.
¹⁵²⁸ Sukenik:]וֿת[בל[. DJD:]°°. See 18.21: רצו]א נֿכה בלוא ידעתה ולֿ[א. For the word, בלוֹא, frg. 62 provides the *beth* and *lamedh* and frg. 61 provides the *waw* and *’aleph*.

Frg. 65 (= C6)

1   […]^{ooooo}[…]

2   because ligh[t …]

3   and to purify [their] transgression[s…]

4   in your will[875] […]

Frg. 64 (= C7)

1   […]^{oo}k^{c} ^{ooo}[…]

2   [… you] opened the tablets of ^{o}[…]

3   […]^{o} in eter[nity …]

Frg. 41 (= C8)

1   […]^{o} ^{o}[…]

2   […] (VACAT) […]

3   […I thank you, O Lord, because][876] you, [you] revealed […]

4   […]^{oo}[…]

---

[875] Or "favor."

[876] The *Hodayot* formula was most likely in the lost pieces of leather; note the preceding *vacat*.

Thanksgiving Hymns (*Hodayot*)
1Q35 (1QHᵇ)

JAMES H. CHARLESWORTH with LEA BERKUZ and BLAKE A. JURGENS[1]

Introduction

First published by J. T. Milik in 1955 as "Recueil de cantiques d'action de grâces (1QH),"[2] these two fragments overlap portions of two columns of the *Thanksgiving Hymns* preserved on 1QHᵃ.

1. Paleography and Orthography

The scribe composed this manuscript in an early Herodian formal bookhand, similar to the one used in the *War Scroll* (1QM), suggesting a date sometime around the end of the first century BCE. The leather is carefully lined, and the consonants are consistent and written with broad strokes, indicating an experienced scribe.

This manuscript deviates from 1QHᵃ several times. First, a second person singular suffix is added to the verb שפט in 1QHᵇ fragment 1 line 2 (בהשפטכה), contrasting the third person singular suffix found in 1QHᵃ 15.31 (בהשפטו). Second, in 1QHᵇ fragment 1 line 5 the word אל "God" appears in Palaeo-Hebrew, unlike in 1QHᵃ 15.36. Third, in 1QHᵇ fragment 1 line 6, the second person singular suffix on the verb פלא is written with the final *he* (see also frg. 1 line 2, 11), whereas the suffix is written defectively in 1QHᵃ 15.35 (פלאך). Fourth, in 1QHᵇ the word לא is written *scriptio plene* (לוא) twice (frg. 1 line 9; frg. 2 line 2) as opposed to the defective spelling found in 1QHᵃ 15.37 and 16.14. Thus, 1QHᵇ was written *scriptio plene* and with full second-person suffixes. The second-person suffix in fragment 1 line 2 appears to have been a scribal error, perhaps resulting from the large number of second person suffixes in the surrounding context.

2. History and Relationship to Other Manuscripts

When first discovered, these two fragments were originally thought to belong to the large 1QH scroll purchased by E. Sukenik. In 1962, when H. Stegemann began his work restructuring Sukenik's initial organization of the fragments, he realized that these fragments were not part of the larger collection of fragments (1QHᵃ) but were a second copy of the same document.[3] This discovery was affirmed by É. Puech, who was the first to analyze extensively the relationship of 1QHᵇ to the other copies of the *Thanksgiving Hymns*.[4] Puech also proposed that the first fragment consisted of fourteen lines, rather than the twelve lines initially proposed by Milik.[5]

1Q35 (1QHᵇ) overlaps 1QHᵃ, 4QHᵇ (4Q428), and 4QHᶠ (4Q432) in the following places:

1QHᵇ frg. 1 line 1	4QHᵇ (4Q428) frg. 9 line 2
1QHᵇ frg. 1 lines 1–9	1QHᵃ 15.30–38
1QHᵇ frg. 1 lines 5–7	4QHᶠ (4Q432) frg. 12 lines 1–3
1QHᵇ frg. 1 lines 9–12	4QHᵇ (4Q428) frg. 10 lines 1–5
1QHᵇ frg. 2 lines 1–2	1QHᵃ frg. 16 lines 13–14

Of particular interest is the estimated size of the columns from which these fragments originated. While fragment 1 suggests a

---

[1] The introduction is by J. H. Charlesworth. The text and translation is by J. H. Charlesworth with L. Berkuz and B. Jurgens.

[2] J. T. Milik, "Recueil de cantiques d'action de grâces (1QH)" in *Qumran Cave I* (DJD 1; Oxford, 1955) pp. 136–38.

[3] Stegemann's personal recollection of this work can be found in his "The Material Reconstruction of 1QHodayot," in *The Dead Sea Scrolls: Fifty Years After Their Discovery. Proceedings of the Jerusalem Congress, July 20–25, 1997*, edited by L. H. Schiffman, E. Tov, and J. C. VanderKam (Jerusalem, 2000) p. 279.

[4] "Quelques aspects de la restauration du Rouleau des Hymnes (1QH)," *JJS* 39 (1988) 38–55; see pp. 39–40. See also *idem.* "Restauration d'un texte hymnique à partir de trois manuscrits fragmentaires: 1QHᵃ xv 37–xvi 4 (vii 37–viii 3), 1Q35 (1QHᵇ) 1, 9–14, 4Q428 (4QHᵇ) 7," *RQ* 16 (1995) 543–48.

[5] See the diagram in Puech, "Restauration d'un texte hymnique," *RQ* 16 547.

scroll slightly wider than 1QH^a, with a minimum of 27–28 lines per column,[6] fragment 2 is quite different. Only two lines of writing are extant on fragment 2, with empty leather visible both above and below these lines. Moreover, the line length of fragment 2 appears to span only between twenty-three and twenty-four consonants, less than half the length of most of the lines in 1QH^a and fragment 1 of 1QH^b. Recently, A. K. Harkins has suggested that 1QH^b may have been an excerpted text rather than part of larger collection of psalms.[7] This theory is supported by the appearance of a final handle sheet following the left uninscribed margin of fragment 2.[8] If correct, the theory may suggest that small collections containing some of the *Thanksgiving Hymns* may have been circulated between various Jewish (Essene?) groups.

3. Selected Bibliography

See bibliography to introduction and to 1QH^a.

Harkins, A. K. "A New Proposal for Thinking about 1QH^a Sixty Years After its Discovery." In *Qumran Cave 1 Revisited: Texts from Cave 1 Sixty Years After their Discovery. Proceedings of the Sixth Meeting of the 1QOS in Ljubljana*, edited by D. K. Falk, *et al.* STDJ 91; Leiden and Boston, 2010, pp. 101–34.

Milik, J. T. "Recueil de cantiques d'action de grâces (1QH)." In *Qumran Cave I*. DJD 1; Oxford, 1955, pp. 136–138.

Puech, É. "Restauration d'un texte hymnique à partir de trois manuscrits fragmentaires: 1QH^a xv 37–xvi 4 (vii 37–viii 3), 1Q35 (1QH^b) 1, 9–14, 4Q428 (4QH^b)7." *RQ* 16 (1995) 543–48.

Stegemann, H. "The Material Reconstruction of 1QHodayot." In *The Dead Sea Scrolls: Fifty Years After Their Discovery. Proceedings of the Jerusalem Congress, July 20–25, 1997*, edited by L. H. Schiffman, E. Tov, and J. C. VanderKam. Jerusalem, 2000, pp. 272–84.

---

[6] É. Puech, "Restauration d'un texte hymnique," *RQ* 16 544. Frg. 1 of 1QH^b is extant in three pieces. See fig. 2.

[7] A. K. Harkins, "A New Proposal for Thinking about 1QH^a Sixty Years After its Discovery," in *Qumran Cave 1 Revisited: Texts from Cave 1 Sixty Years After their Discovery. Proceedings of the Sixth Meeting of the IOQS in Ljubljana*, edited by D. K. Falk, *et al.* (STDJ 91; Leiden, 2010) p. 129.

[8] This was noted by Milik (DJD 1, p. 137); see also E. Tov, *Scribal Practices and Approaches Reflected in the Texts from the Judean Desert* (STDJ 54; Leiden and Boston, 2004) p. 117.

Thanksgiving Hymns (*Hodayot*)
1Q35 (1QH^b)

Frg. 1[1]

]	**1**
וברוב רחמיכה [לנֿעוֿיֿ[2]	**2**
[לֿב[3] ומי יצדק לפני[כֿה[4] בהשפטכה[5]	**3**
ולוא יוכל כול להתיצב [לפני[6]	**4**
לפניכה לטהרם מפשעי]הם[7]	**5**
כי]אֿ[8] 𐤀𐤋[9]	**6**
ומה הו]אֿ[10]	**7**
במעשי פל]אֿכה[11] הגדולים	**8**
(VACAT) [	**9**
ובס]וֿד[12] נעלמים לוא[13]	**10**
ולסליחותיכה הביאות]נֿי ובֿ[המון[14]	**11**
ומרחם [הוריתי בא]שמת[15]	**12**

---

[1] Parallels to this fragment include the following: 1QH^a 15.30–37; 4Q428 frgs. 9–10; 4Q432 frg. 12. The left margin is clear. We follow E. Puech's restoration and numeration. The Brill images reflect Milik's earlier work.

[2] Ctr. Milik: לֿמֿעֿנֿוֿ. The *lamedh* is relatively clear; the *nun* is obvious. See 1QH^a 15.30: וֿברוב רחמיכה לנעוי לב; see also 4Q428 frg. 9 line 2: [לֿנעו]יֿ.

[3] The left margin is extant, so לב is restored here. See note 2.

[4] The foot of the *kaph* is visible.

[5] Restoration follows 1QH^a 15.31: ומי יצדֿק לפניכה בהשפטו.

[6] See 1QH^a 15.32: ולוא יוכל כול להתיצב לפני ח(כ)מתה.

[7] Restoration follows 1QH^a 15.33: לפניכה לֿטֿהֿרם מפשעיהם.

[8] Cf. 1QH^a 15.34: כי אל עולם אתה.

[9] In 1QH^a 15.34 the אל is not in Palaeo-Hebrew.

[10] Restoration follows 1QH^a 15.35: ומה הוא איש תהו.

[11] Restoration follows 1QH^a 15.35–36: במעשי פלאך הֿגֿדֿולֿים.

[12] Restoration follows 1QH^a 15.37: ובסוד נעלמים לא שמתה חוקי. The image is not clear.

[13] 1QH^a 15.36 does not use *plene* spelling for לוא.

[14] Restoration follows 1QH^a 15.38: ולסליחותֿ]נֿי וֿבֿהֿמֿוֿן [.

[15] 4Q428 frg. 10 line 3: הוריתי באשמת מעל[.

Thanksgiving Hymns (*Hodayot*)
1Q35 (1QH^b)

Frg. 1

1   […]

2   […and the multitude of your mercies] to the perverted of[1]

3   [heart…. And who can be justified before] you when you are judged?[2]

4   […and none can stand] before

5   […before you, purifying them from] their [transgressions][3]

6   […fo]r God

7   […. And how m]ay

8   […at the works of] your great [wond]ers

9   [….] (VACAT)

10   […and in the cou]ncil of the hidden ones not[4]

11   […and to your forgivenesses you brought] me and with the [abundance of]

12   […and from the womb of] her who conceived me in gu[ilt]

---

[1] 1QH^a 15.30: "and the multitude of your mercies to the perverted of heart."

[2] The verb שפט in the *nipʿal* can also be translated "to enter into controversy, plead." The second person sg. suffix deviates from 1QH^a 15.31: "And who can be justified before you when he is judged?"

[3] The word "transgression" appears at least 36 times in the Dead Sea Scrolls, including in 1QH^a (e.g., 4.23; 12.20, 36; 14.24; 15.8).

[4] See 1QH^a 15.37: "and in the council of the hidden ones you did not put my ordinances."

13   לרוב נדה ו[מ֯נעורי בדמים¹⁶ ועד

14   כוננתה רגלי בדר[ך֯¹⁷ לבכה ולשמועו֯ת

15   ולוא [א֯טומם֯¹⁸

Frg. 2¹⁹

1   [אש²⁰ מתהפכת בל יבוא [ז֯ר²¹ במעין חיים

2   ועם] ע֯צי ע[ו]לם לוא²² ישתה²³ מ֯י֯ קוד[ש]²⁴

---

¹⁶ Cf. 4Q428 frg. 10 line 4: לרוב נדה ומנעורי בד֯]מים.

¹⁷ Cf. 4Q428 frg. 10 line 5: אלי כוננתה רגלי בדרכ֯]י.

¹⁸ Ctr. Milik:] ת֯ טובה[. The *mem* is clear and the top of the *ʾaleph* is apparent. From the verb טמם "to stop up, lock" (e.g., Sir 10:16; Job 18:3). The Hebrew verb אטם "to stop, close" (Syr. ܐܛܡ "to be deaf") often describes the closing of one's ear (e.g., Isa 33:15; Prov 21:13) or one's lips (e.g., Prov 17:28).

¹⁹ This fragment seems to belong to another hymn. For a parallel text, see 1QHᵃ 16.13–14. The left margin and bottom are evident.

²⁰ The right margin can be ascertained.

²¹ Puech does not report this noun; it is required by the context and partly visible in 1QHᵃ. Someone must "drink the holy water." The top of the *reš* is clear; however, the ink of the horizontal stroke is lost, and the *lamedh* below intrudes into the *zayin*. See 1QHᵃ 16.13: ר[ז.

²² 1QHᵃ 16.13–14 does not use *plene* spelling for לוא.

²³ Cf. 1QHᵃ 16.13–14: ועם עצי עולם לא ישתה.

²⁴ Milik suggested that this reading was in line 3. Puech saw some consonants. We discerned these consonants with computer enhancement. See 1QHᵃ 16.14: מי קודש.

13   […for multitudinous impurity. And] from my youth in bloodshed and until

14   […you established my foot in the wa]y of your heart. And to reports of

15   […and] I will [not] close

Frg. 2

1   [turning fire, lest] a stranger [should enter] in the fountain of life.[5]

2   […. And with] the et[e]rnal trees he must not drink[6] the hol[y] water

---

[5] See 1QHᵃ 16:13: "lest [a stra]nger should [enter] the fountain of life."
[6] See 1QHᵃ 16:13–14: "And with the eternal trees he must not drink the holy water."

Thanksgiving Hymns (Hodayot)
4Q427 (4QHᵃ)

J AMES H. C HARLESWORTH and C ASEY D. E LLEDGE

Introduction

The fragments of 4Q427 preserve portions of the *Hodayot* that intermittently overlap with the same hymns preserved in 1QHᵃ columns 19–20, 26, 7, and 20–21.

1. Script and Date

The script of 4Q427 attest a late Hasmonean or early Herodian semi-cursive hand,[1] placing the manuscript within the first century BCE. An earlier or later date within the range 75–1 BCE, however, is more difficult to specify. Select features of the hand may be most favorably compared with those of 4Q114 [4QDanᶜ] and 4Q212.[2] The scroll has been described as the work of "a careful scribal hand" that "contains traces of very few corrections."[3] Where they are visible, scribal deletion dots are occasionally utilized to mark corrections, and small interspaces are only inconsistently employed to mark textual or syntactic divisions.[4]

2. Contents

Several features of 4Q427 seem to suggest that it was originally a shorter and more specialized witness to the *Hodayot* than 1QHᵃ, one that also presented a different ordering of materials. If indeed the original scroll measured approximately 3.7 meters in length,[5] then 4Q427 could not have provided a version of all the content found in 1QHᵃ. Moreover, among the coinciding passages between the two manuscripts, the preserved portions of 4Q427 feature only materials that have been traditionally classified as the "Community Hymns." It is likely impossible that all the so-called "Community Hymns" known from 1QHᵃ could have been presented within the estimated length of 4Q427.

Regarding the sequence of materials in 4Q427, fragment 1 preserves portions of the hymn found in 1QHᵃ 19.19–30. Fragment 3 then presents the same materials found in 1QHᵃ 20.4–6, yet they are immediately followed by a new directive "To the Maskil" (4Q427 frg. 3 line 4) that introduces a different hymn than is found in 1QHᵃ, possibly the same hymn introduced in 1QHᵃ 25.34. Portions of 4Q427 again coincide with passages of 1QHᵃ in fragment 7, where 4Q427 preserves a distinctive version of the so-called "Self-Glorification Hymn" attested in very fragmentary form in 1QHᵃ 26.6–17, 26–38, as well as in 4Q428 (frg. 21 lines 1–5) and in 4Q431 (frgs. 1–2).[6] Columns 1–2 of fragment 8 once again diverge from the sequence found in 1QHᵃ. After preserving the same hymn found in 1QHᵃ 7.12–20 (frg. 8 1.6–12), 4Q427 presents material found nowhere else in the entire surviving corpus of *Hodayot* witnesses (frg. 8 1.13–2.9), material followed in turn by the same hymn that is introduced in 1QHᵃ 20.7. The unidentified hymn of fragment 8 1.13–2.9 may conceivably preserve otherwise missing portions of the *Hodayot* (1QHᵃ cols. 1–3, 17–18) or hymnic materials that were unattested elsewhere among ancient witnesses. The remaining fragments of 4Q427 that can be compared to other witnesses (frgs. 9–12) remain consistent with the ordering attested in 1QHᵃ 20–21.

Much remains unknown regarding the original purpose and function of this particular selection and ordering of hymns. Three factors converge to form a strong argument that 4Q427 represented a concise collection of communal hymns that were "more liturgically oriented" than the other surviving witnesses.[7] These factors may include the abundance of first-person plural

---

[1] See also E. Schuller, DJD 29, p. 83; on the basis of F. M. Cross, "The Development of the Jewish Scripts," in *The Bible and the Ancient Near East*, edited by G. Wright (Garden City, NY, 1961).

[2] E. Schuller, DJD 29, pp. 83–85.

[3] A. K. Harkins, "Observations on the Editorial Shaping of the So-Called Community Hymns from 1QHᵃ and 4QHᵃ (4Q427)," *DSD* 12 (2005) 250.

[4] See further the notes on the Hebrew Text.

[5] E. Schuller, DJD 29, p. 79.

[6] Cf. 4Q491, 4Q471b.

[7] E. Schuller, DJD 29, p. 87.

formulations,[8] the frequency of doxologies,[9] and the inclusion of the list of hours appointed for praise.[10] Whether 4Q427 represents an excerption from the larger collection represented by 1QH[a] or a specimen of the kinds of earlier sources that contributed to the larger arrangement of 1QH[a] itself remains an unresolved issue in current research. Even so, select features of 4Q427 may reveal more fully a number of tendencies in 1QH[a]. 4Q427, for example, reveals how a number of scribal corrections in 1QH[a] revise the text make it reflect the same readings found in 4Q427.[11] Other comparisons have called attention to a more sapiential rendering of variants in 1QH[a] (26.31, 7.18) than may be found in the corresponding portions of 4Q427 (frg. 7 2.12; frg. 8 1.10).[12] Thus, 4Q427 does more than present a distinctive version of hymns worthy of study in its own right; it also contributes a number of valuable comparative insights that enhance scholarly understandings of the more extensively preserved 1QH[a] scroll.

3. Selected Bibliography

Harkins, A. K. "Observations on the Editorial Shaping of the So-Called Community Hymns from 1QH[a] and 4QH[a] (4Q427)." *DSD* 12 (2005) 233–56.

Schuller, E. M. "Hodayot." In *Qumran Cave 4.XX: Poetical and Liturgical Texts, Part 2*, edited by E. Chazon, *et al.*, in consultation with J. VanderKam and M. Brady. DJD 29; Oxford, 1999, pp. 69–254, Pls. 4–6.

Schuller, E. M. "Recent Scholarship on the *Hodayot* 1993–2010." *CBR* 10 (2011) 119–62.

---

[8] 4Q427 frg. 7 1.13–18; 2.7, 12, 14–22; frg. 8 1.9–12.

[9] 4Q427 frg. 7 1.7–14, 2.22–23.

[10] 4Q427 frg. 8 2.10–15.

[11] See, for example, 1QH[a] 19.25, 26; 20.10, 13; 7.17; 26.29; see also DJD 29, p. 88.

[12] A. K. Harkins, "Editorial Shaping of the So-Called Community Hymns," p. 251.

Thanksgiving Hymns (Hodayot)
4Q427 (4QHᵃ)

Frg. 1 (Col. 1 lines 9–15)
Parallels: 1QHᵃ 19.20–29 [= Sukenik Col. 11.16–27]
4Q428 frg. 12a 1–4

9   גלי]תֿה לֿ]יֿ [וֿאביטֿ]¹

10   [וֿכלה בלוא רֿחמיכה ואנֿי]²

11   גֿ]בֿֿר ותֿ]שובת [אֿנושׁ אתבוננה³ ואכירה אֿ]⁴

12   ולהגוֿ]תֿ הגי יגֿ]וֿן וֿ]אנחה בכנוֿר קֿ]יֿנה [לכול אבֿ]ל יגון⁵

13   [ישועות ונבלֿ]⁶

14   בפֿ]יֿ כולֿמֿֿהֿ⁷ [יהוֿ]לל שֿמֿכֿ]הֿ⁸

15   [לֿֿ]⁹

Frgs. 2–3 (Col. 2 lines 11–18)¹⁰
Parallels: 1QHᵃ 20.5–7 [= Sukenik Col. 12], 25.34
4Q428 frg. 12b 1–2

11   התוע]ֿה ונעוה בדעת לֿבֿֿיֿ]ן

12   [ואשכחה נגע מכאובֿיֿ]

13   ומוסר אֿ]כֿזרי לא אזכור עוד ולוא יֿ]

14   [לֿ]]ה לפניכה כֿשֿ]

---

¹ The text and translation are by Charlesworth with Berkuz. 1QHᵃ 19.20: [ואביטֿ גליתה לי ונסֿ]תֿֿרֿותֿיֿכֿֿהֿ.
² 1QHᵃ 19.21–22: [ה וכלה בלוא רחמיך וֿאני.
³ 1QHᵃ 19.23: גבר ותשובת אנוש אֿתֿ]בוננה.
⁴ Conceivably: אֿ]בל.
⁵ 1QHᵃ 19.24–25: [וֿן]\ יֿם ולהגות הגי יגון /ואנחה בכנור קינה לכול אבל יֿגֿ]וֿן. In a supralinear correction to 1QHᵃ, a scribe has inserted the same reading preserved here in 4Q427 frg. 1 line 12. Thus 4Q427 is the older text.
⁶ 1QHᵃ 19.25–26:]ות ואין נגע להחלות ואז אזמרה בכנור ישועות ונבל שמחֿ.
⁷ A scribe corrected כולהמֿהֿ to כולֿמֿה. See 1QHᵃ 19.27: בפֿי כולם יהולל.
⁸ 1QHᵃ 19.27–28: נפלאותי]כה בפֿי כולם יהולל שמכה.
⁹ 1QHᵃ 19.29: בקול רנה ואין יגון ואנחה ועולה לֿ]א.
¹⁰ Frg. 2 preserves lines 11–14 of col. 2; frg. 3 preserves the remaining lines. While the remains of frg. 2 (lines 11–14) are not paralleled in 1QHᵃ, frg. 3 seems to preserve materials attested in 1QHᵃ 20.4–6 (lines 15–17) and 25.34 (line 18).

Thanksgiving Hymns (Hodayot)
4Q427 (4QHª)

Frg. 1 (Col. 1 lines 9–15)
Parallels: 1QHª 19.20–29 [= Sukenik Col. 11.16–27]
4Q428 frg. 12a 1–4

9   […] you [revealed] to [me]. And I look […][1]

10   […] and destruction without your mercies. But (as) for me […]

11   [… m]an. And the re[turn of] the human I will examine closely.[2] And I acknowledge ʾ[…]

12   [… and to ponde]r meditatively gr[ief and] a sigh with a lyre, a la[ment] to every mourni[ng of grief …]

13   […] salvation and (with) a harp […]

14   […. In the mouth] of all of them yo[ur] name [will be pr]aised […]

15   […]*l*[…]

Frgs. 2–3 (Col. 2 lines 11–18)
Parallels: 1QHª 20.5–7 [= Sukenik Col. 12], 25.34
4Q428 frg. 12b 1–2

11   [… erro]r and perverted. In the knowledge of my heart […]

12   […] and I forgot my painful affliction […]

13   [… and the cr]uel [discipline][3] I will no longer remember and not *y*[…]

14   […]*l*[…]*h* before you *kš*[…]

---

[1] The 4Q fragments are translated to match the PTSDSSP translation of the fuller manuscript; 4Q427 preserves some material that cannot be identified in 1QHª.

[2] Or "comprehend."

[3] Ctr. DJD, "[and the chastisement of the on]e who is cruel." The context, however, refers to the author's experience.

15   ר̊ר̇[   ]ל[   ]ה̊ ב̊[11

16   לב[ט̊ח במעון שק̊]ט ושלוה ב[ש̊לום וברכה̊]12

17   ] VACAT   13כבוד ויש[ועה וא̊[ה]̊ללה שמכ]ה בתוך יר[איכה

18   למשכיל [ש̊י̊ר [מזמור [ש̊]י̊]ר̊ ל[14

Frg. 4 (Col. 3 lines 1–4)[15]

1   ]°°° [

2   [°°°°ב̊ת̊ עלי16 בכב̊ו̊]דכה

3   ש[מים כי̊א̊]

4   [ש̊]

Frg. 5 (Col. 3 lines 1–4)

1   ]° [

2   [י̊ם̊ מי̊]

3   [ה̊קיד̊]17 [°° [

4   [נ̊ה̊]

Frg. 6 (Col. 3 lines 1–2)

1   [°°°ת̊י וישב̊]18

---

11 Portions of this line may be preserved in 1QH^a 20.1–4. 1QH^a seems to represent a longer text.

12 1QH^a 20.5–6: לבטח במ̊[עון קודש. 4Q428 frg. 12b line 1: ואשב]ה̊ לבטח במעון קו̊[דש ושלוה ב]ש̊וקט ושלוה [בשלו]̊ם וברכה

13 1QH^a 20.6: בתוך ירא]יכה. 4Q428 frg. 12b line 2: בן[[[א]הלי כבו̊ד̊ וישועה ואהללה שמכה בתוך יראיכה.

14 Ctr. 1QH^a 20.7: [למשכי]ל̊ [ה]̊ודות ותפלה ל/ה\תנ/פ\ל. The line may preserve the directive, "To the Maskil," or "Instructor."

15 An uninscribed space at the top of the fragment may indicate the upper margin of a column or perhaps the remains of a *vacat* in earlier lines.

16 Ctr. DJD: ר̊ע לי[, but see the note to this reading.

17 The reading of ד̊ is uncertain; *waw* may also be possible.

18 Ctr. DJD:]לו̊א̊.

15   [...]˚*r*[...]*l*[...]*h b*[...]

16   [... saf]ely in the dwelling[4] of sile[nce and tranquility in] peace and blessing [...]

17   [... glory and salv]ation. So[5] I will [p]raise yo[ur] name [among those who stand] in awe of you. (VACAT)[6] [...]

18   [.... For the Instructor,] a song, [a psalm,][7] a s[o]ng for [...]

Frg. 4 (Col. 3 lines 1–4)

1   [...] °°° [...]

2   [...]°°°*bt* upon me in [your] glor[y...]

3   [... he]aven because [...]

4   [...]*š*[...]

Frg. 5 (Col. 3 lines 1–4)

1   [...] ˚[...]

2   [...]*ym my*˚[...]

3   [...] your statutes[8] [...]°°[...]

4   [...] *nh*[...]

Frg. 6 (Col. 3 lines 1–2)

1   [...]°°°*ty* and it returned[9] [...]

---

[4] Cf. 1QH^a 20.5: "in the ho[ly] dwelling."
[5] Lit. "And."
[6] See 1QH^a 20.6 and 4Q428 frg. 12b line 2.
[7] For "a song, a psalm" see Pss 48:1, 66:1, 83:1, 88:1, 108:1.
[8] Or "his statutes."
[9] Ctr DJD: "not."

4Q427   Thanksgiving Hymns

2   ו[אֹני ישבת]י[19]

Frg. 7 Cols. 1 and 2 (Cols. 3.6–23, 4.3–23)[20]
Parallels: 1QHᵃ 26.3[?][21]–17, 26–38
4Q471b frgs. 1a–d, lines 3–10

Frg. 7 Col. 1 (Col. 3.6–23)

1   ]

2   ]

3   ]

4   ]

5   ]

6   [הֹרע

7   בהר[וֹתי

8   [באלים

9   מ[י] בלשון יעידני[22] [

10   המ[לֹכ רע לקדשים ולוא יבא[23]

11   ולכבו[דֹי לוא ידמה כֹ[י]אֹ אני עם אלים מעמֹדֹ[י][24]

12   [25]ֹר לא בפז אכתי[ר][26] לי וכתם[27] או ביורימ[28] לוא[29]

---

[19] Material resemblance may associate this line somehow with 4Q427 frg. 7 col. 1. The phrase does, in fact, appear in the version of the psalm found in 4Q491 frg. 11 col. 1 line 13 (DJD 29).

[20] Frg. 7 preserves the bottom margin of both columns, the left hand margin of col. 1, and the right hand margin of col. 2.

[21] 1QHᵃ 26.1–5 are lost. 4Q427 frg. 7 1.9 aligns with 1QHᵃ 26.6

[22] 1QHᵃ 26.6:]יעדני.

[23] 1QHᵃ 26.7:] יבוא. Note the *plene* spelling. 4Q471b frgs. 1a–d line 7: ידיד המלך רע לק[דושים ולוא יבוא.

[24] 4Q471b frgs. 1a–d line 8: לוא ידמה כֹי אֹ[ני עם אלים מעמדי.

[25] Perhaps restore וכבוד near the beginning of this line, in light of the reading preserved in 1QHᵃ 26.8:] וכבוד.

[26] 4Q471b frgs. 1a–d line 9: בפז /אֹ\וכֹתֹ]יר. Ctr. DJD: ᵒᵒᵒאכ. The consonant is a *taw*. See line 16.

[27] Hebrew has three nouns denoting "gold:" זהב, פז, and כתם, "gold," "(fine) gold," and "(pure) gold."

[28] The phrase וכתם או ביורימ does not represent a scribal error for כתם אופירים (cf. Isa 13:12, Ps 45:10, Job 28:16, 4Q491 frg. 11 1.18). The present reading seems correct: the words seem to represent two synonyms. יורים may represent some precious metal. The Aramaic יוהרים seems to mean "precious (or gleaming) stones."

[29] Note *plene* spelling and לא earlier in line 12.

2   [… and] I, [I] sat […]

Frg. 7 Col. 1 and 2 (Col. 3.6–23, Col.4.3–23)
Parallels: 1QH^a 26.4[?]–17, 26–38
4Q471b frgs. 1a–d, lines 3–10

Frg. 7 Col. 1 (Col. 3.6–23)

1   […]

2   […]

3   […]

4   […]

5   […]

6   […] the evil[10]

7   [… with] my [teach]ing

8   […] among the Elim[11]

9   [….] Wh[o] with language[12] can appoint me?[13]

10   [… the K]ing, a companion to the Holy Ones, and no one can enter[14]

11   […. And to] my [glor]y no one can be compared, f[o]r I (am) with the Elim.[15] [My] rank

12   […]°*r*. Not with (pure) gold will I cro[wn] myself, and (neither with) gold or with precious stones. Not[16]

---

[10] The left margin is visible.
[11] Or "divine beings."
[12] Or "speech." Lit. "tongue."
[13] Ctr. DJD: "is similar to me." See 1QH^a 26.6.
[14] Or "it will not come."
[15] Or "divine beings."
[16] Ctr. DJD: "and the gold of Ophirim not."

13 [עם בני עו]לֿה[30 י]תֿחשב בי זמרו[31 ידידיֿם שירו למלכ

14 [הכבוד שמחו[32 בע]דֿת אל הרנינו באהֿלֿי ישועה הללו במעון

15 [קודש ר]וֿממו[33 יחד בצבא עֿולם הבו גדול לאלנו וכבוד למלכֿנֿו

16 [הקדי]שֿו שמו[34 בשפתי עוז ולשון נצח הרימו לבד קולכמה

17 [בכ]ול קצים הֿשֿמֿיֿעו[35 הגידנה[36 הביעו בשמחות עולמים ואין

18 [ה]שֿבת השתֿחֿוֿו[37 בֿיֿחֿד[38 קהל ברכו המפלי גאות ומודיע עוז ידו

19 [ל]חֿתום רזים ולגלות נסתרות להריֿם[39 כושלים ונופליהמה

20 [לש]ב לכת קוי דעות ולהשפיל נועדות רומ[40 גאים[41 עולם

21 [להת]מֿ רזי ה[ו]וד [ולהקֿ]ים פל[אֿוֿת כבוד השופט באף כלה[42

22 [בחסד צדקה וברוב רחמים תֿחֿנה

23 [רחמים למפרי טוֿב גודלו ומקור[43

Frg. 7 Col. 2 (Col. 4.3–23)

1 [

2 [

3 מ[זֿדֿהבֿה]

[30] See 1QHᵃ 13.10: לבני עֿולֿה; also see 4Q429 frg. 4 1.5: בֿנֿי עֿולֿה].

[31] 4Q471b frgs. 1a-d line 10: [זמרו].

[32] 1QHᵃ 26.10: שֿמחו[ו.

[33] 1QHᵃ 26.11: [רוממוֿו.

[34] 1QHᵃ 26.12: [ˁ. In this poorly preserved line of 1QHᵃ, DJD reads שֿ[מו.

[35] 1QHᵃ 26.13: הֿשֿמֿ]יעו; DJD: הֿשֿמֿ]יעו.

[36] The *daleth* is certain; yet read הגי רנה (cf. 4Q491 frg. 11 1.21).

[37] Read: השתחוו. See 1QHᵃ 16.33 and 17.9.

[38] Or read כוחא. 1QHᵃ 26.14: בֿיֿחֿד]; DJD: בֿיחד.

[39] 1QHᵃ 26.15: רֿזֿים ולגלות נסֿתרות וֿה]. Perhaps read the final word of the phrase in 1QHᵃ: לֿה]רים (DJD).

[40] Notice medial *mem* is in final position.

[41] 1QHᵃ 26.16: [ולהש]פֿיל נועדת רום גֿאֿיֿם].

[42] 1QHᵃ 26.17: לֿל[לֿל[. The reading of 1QHᵃ suggests that a *lamedh* may originally have been preserved near the beginning of line 22.

[43] The bottom margin is visible.

13 [with the sons of de]ceit [shall] he reckon me. Chant, O beloved ones, sing to the King of[17]

14 [glory,[18] be joyful in the cong]regation of God, exult in the tents of salvation, give praise in the habitation of

15 [holiness, e]xtol together with the eternal hosts, give greatness to our God and glory to our King.[19]

16 [Declare h]oly his name with strong lips and (with) a perpetual tongue, raise up alone[20] your voice

17 [at a]ll Endtimes, cause to be heard[21] meditations of exultation,[22] express[23] with everlasting joy without

18 [ce]asing, cause to bow down in the common[24] assembly. Bless the one who does majestic wonders, and causes to make known his strong hand

19 [to] seal mysteries and to reveal hidden things, raising up those who stumble and those who fell

20 [to res]tore walking (to) those who await knowledge and bring down the pompous gatherings of the perpetually proud ones,

21 [to confir]m the mysteries of sp[lendor] and to establi[sh ma]rvels of glory. The one who judges with destructive wrath

22 […] with loving kindness, righteousness, and with abundant mercies, beseeching

23 […] mercies for those who violate[25] his great goodness, and a source of

Frg. 7 Col. 2 (Col. 4.3–23)

1 […]

2 […]

3 [… d]isaster […]

---

[17] The king is God. See 4Q471b frgs. 1a–d line 7.

[18] The *Self-Glorification Hymn* is expanded, most likely. It is unlikely that all other witnesses abbreviated the *Hymn* similarly. See esp. *vacat* in 4Q491 frg. 11 line 19. A *vacat* is often used to denote the end of a hymn.

[19] This exhortation must antedate the claim of kingship by Aristobulus I in circa 102 BCE

[20] Ctr. DJD: "raise up together your voice." לבד means "alone."

[21] Ctr. DJD: "sound aloud." The *hipʿil* impv. of שמע means "to cause to be heard."

[22] Reading the corrected text. The text has "a saying."

[23] The *hipʿil* of נבע literally means "to gush forth."

[24] Heb. בְּיֹחַד.

[25] *Hipʿil* of פרר.

4　　　[כלת]הֿ רֿמֿיֿהֿ וֿאֿיֿן נעוות בלוא דעת הופיע אור ושֿ[מחה תביע אבד][44]

5　　　אבל ונס יגון הופיע שלום שבת פחד נפתח מקור לב[רכת עד][45]

6　　　ומרפא בכול קצי עולם כלה עוון שבת נגע לאין מחל[ה נאספה עולה][46]

7　　　[ואשמ]הֿ לוֿאֿ תהיה עֿ[וֿ]ד הֿ[שֿמֿיֿעֿו ואמ[ו]רו[47] גדול אֿלֿ עֿ[וֿשה פלא][48]

8　　　כיא השפיל גבהות רוח[49] לאין שרית וירם[50] מעפר אביון ל[רום עולם]

9　　　ועד שחקים יגבירהו בקומה ועמ[51] אלים בעדת יחד ורפֿ[]

10　　　אֿכֿ[52] לכלת עולם וכושלי ארץ ירים[53] לאין מחיֿר וגב[ורת עד עם]

11　　　מצֿעדם ושמחת עוֿלֿם במכוניֿהֿמה[54] כבוד נצח ואין השבת[לעולמי עד]

12　　　יומרו[55] ברוכ אל הֿ[מפ]לֿי [פ]לֿאֿוֿת גֿאֿות ומגדיל להופיע גבורהֿ[ומצדיק][56]

13　　　בדעתֿ לכול מעשיו וטֿוֿבֿ על פניהמה בדעתמה ברוב חס[דיו[57] והמון]

14　　　רחמיו לכול בני אמתו ידענוכה אל הצדק והשכלנוֿ[באמתכה[58] מלך]

---

[44] See 4Q431 frg. 1 2.3: אור ושמחה תֿבֿיֿעֿ.

[45] See 4Q431 frg. 1 2.4: לברכת עד.

[46] See 4Q431 frg. 1 2.5: מחלה נאספֿ[ה].

[47] 1QHᵃ 26.26: עוד [הש]מֿ[יעו]וֿאֿמֿרֿו. A small interspace precedes the following phrase, one that is not attested in the parallel passages of 1QHᵃ or 4Q430.

[48] See 4Q431 frg. 7 2.6.

[49] This reading is accurate; other parallel passages are miscopies of the exemplar. Ctr. DJD 40 for 1QHᵃ 26.27: רום (correct in DJD 29: רוח). See 4Q431 frg. 2 2.7: [רום.

[50] 1QHᵃ 26.27: רום לאין שֿרית ויר[ם.

[51] 1QHᵃ 26.28:] יגביה בקומה ועם, and 4Q431 line 8: יגביה.

[52] DJD: אֿלֿ. For medial *kaph* in final position, see line 12. Medial forms frequently appear in final position in this manuscript. See frg. 7 1.21: באף כלה.

[53] 1QHᵃ 26.29: עולם וכ/ו\שלי ארץ ירֿ]ים.

[54] 1QHᵃ 26.30:] ושמחת עולם במכוניהֿם.

[55] Perhaps the scribe wrote originally ידברו.

[56] 1QHᵃ 26.31: ק[להוֿדֿיֿעֿ גֿבֿוֿרֿה ומצֿדֿיֿ]. 1QHᵃ apparently did not contain the phrase יומרו ברוכ אל הֿ[מפ]לֿי [פ]לֿאֿוֿת גֿאֿות, found here in 4Q427.

[57] 1QHᵃ 26.32:] בדעתם ברוב חסדיו[ן.

[58] 1QHᵃ 26.33: אל הצדק והשכלנוֿ בֿאֿ[מתכה.

4 treachery [ende]d, and there are no perversions without knowledge. Light shines forth,[26] and j[oy pours forth.][27]

5 Mourning and the standard of grief [perished]. Peace shines forth, fear ceased. A source was opened for [eternal] bl[essing],

6 and healing for all everlasting times. Iniquity ended, affliction ceased, so there is no sickne[ss. Injustice was taken away,][28]

7 [and guil]t [is] no [m]or[e.] [Ca]use to be heard and s[a]y: Great (is) God who ac[ts wonderfully,]

8 because he brought low the pompous spirit[29] so there is no remnant. And he raised up the poor one from the dust to [eternal height],

9 and unto the skies he will elevate him on high,[30] and with the Elim[31] and in the congregation of the Community.[32] And *rp*°[…]

10 even to eternal annihilation. And those who stumble earthward, he shall raise up without cost, and [everlasting] mig[ht (is) with]

11 their tread. And eternal joy (is) in their establishments, everlasting glory without ceasing [forever and ever].

12 They will say: Blessed (is) God who [wonderfully does m]ajestic [wo]nders,[33] and acts greatly to make his might appear,[34] [and acts righteously]

13 with knowledge toward all his creatures and (with) goodness upon their faces, so they will know the multitude of [his] loving kind[ness and the abundance of]

14 his mercies to all sons of his truth. We have known you, O God of righteousness, and we have obtained insight [in your truth, O King of]

[26] Or "appears."
[27] *Hipʿil* impf. of נבע.
[28] See 1QHᵃ 16.36.
[29] See 1QHᵃ 26.27. Perhaps "the pompous spirit" is the "Wicked Priest."
[30] Not in physical stature. Ctr. DJD: "he magnifies him in stature."
[31] Or "divine begins."
[32] Or "*Yaḥad.*"
[33] See 4Q427 frg. 7 1.18.
[34] Ctr. 1QHᵃ 26.31: "to make known." Or "shine forth."

15   הכבוד כיא ראינו קנאתכה בכוח גבורתכה והכרנו⁵⁹ מֿ[שפטיכה בהמון]⁶⁰

16   רחמיכֿהֿם והפלא סליחות מה בשר לאלה ומה⁶¹ יחשֿ[ב עפר ואפר]

17   לספר אלה מקץ לקץ ולהתיצב במעמֿדֿ]⁶² לפניכה ולבוא ביחד עם]

18   בני שמים ואין מליץ להשיב] דבר כפיכה ו⁶³

19   לכה כיא העמדתנו לרצ]ונכה⁶⁴
                    שמע נפלאותיֿכֿה
20   כוח לֿהֿשֿיֿבֿ לֿכֿה⁶⁵ כֿ]אלה

21   דברנו לכה ולוֿאֿ לאיש בֿיֿ]נים   ופתחתה]⁶⁶

22   אוֿזֿ]ן]למוצא שפתינו⁶⁷ השמֿיֿ]עו ואמורו ברוך אל הדעות הנוטה]⁶⁸

23   שמים בכוחו וכול מחשביהמה מֿ[כין ב]עֿוֿזֿוֿ ארץ בגבורֿ[תו בורא]⁶⁹

Frg. 8⁷⁰ Cols. 1–2 (Cols. 5.6–21, 6.8–21)
Parallels: 1QHª 7.14–20 [= Sukenik Col.15], 20.7–21 [= Sukenik Col.12]
4Q428 frg. 12a line 2

Fgr. 8 Col. 1 (Col. 5.6–21)

1   ]

2   ]

3   ]

⁵⁹ 1QHª 26.34: בֿכֿוֿח גבורה והכֿר]נו.
⁶⁰ The reading is speculative.
⁶¹ 1QHª 26.35: מה בשר לאלה וֿמֿ]ה.
⁶² 1QHª 26.36: ולהתיצב במעמד].
⁶³ 1QHª 26.37: להשיב דבר כֿפֿיֿכֿה וֿ].
⁶⁴ 1QHª 26.38: לֿרֿצֿ]וֿנֿכֿ]הֿ בֿ]ˌˌ.
⁶⁵ The dots above all the letters of the phrase לֿהֿשֿיֿבֿ לֿכֿה indicate probable readings. Read also the supralinear phrase שמע נפלאותיֿכֿה.
⁶⁶ The verb פתח refers to God in 1QHª 7.16; 8.14; 13.35; 16.22; 19.35; 20.16, 36; 22.31; and 23.11.
⁶⁷ The scribe may have mistakenly written שעתינו.
⁶⁸ Restoration from line 7 and from 1QHª 9.11, 28. The usual formula is ברוך אתה אל.
⁶⁹ For the restoration of ברא, see 1QHª 9.15. The bottom margin is visible.
⁷⁰ Frg. 8 preserves the bottom margin of both columns, the left hand margin of col. 1, and the right hand margin of col. 2.

15 glory, because we have seen your zeal with your[35] mighty power, and we have recognized [your] ju[dgments with the abundance of]

16 your[36] mercies and wondrous forgiveness. What (is) flesh (compared) to these (things)? And what shall [dust and ashes] devi[se][37]

17 to recount these (things) from end time to end time;[38] and to present in rank [before you and to come together with][39]

18 the sons of heaven? And there is no interpreter to cause to return [a word according to your edict and[40] ...]

19 to you, because you established us for [your] wi[ll ...]

20 power to answer you. Hearing (about) your wonderful acts[41] like [these ....]

21 We spoke to you and not to an intermed[iary[42].... And you opened]

22 an ea[r] to the utterance of our lips. Cause to be hea[rd and say: Blessed (be) the God of knowledge who stretches out][43]

23 (the) heavens by his power, and all their thoughts [he] es[tablished by] his strength, [creating] the earth by [his] might

Frg. 8 Col. 1 and 2 (Col. 5.6–21, Col. 6.8–21)
Parallels: 1QHᵃ 7.14–20 [= Sukenik Col.15], 20.7–21 [= Sukenik Col.12];
4Q428 frg. 12a line 2

Frg. 8 Col. 1 (Col. 5.6–12)

1 [...]

2 [...]

3 [...]

---

[35] 1QHᵃ 26.34 does not have "your."
[36] A scribe erroneously added a *mem* at the end.
[37] *Pi'el* impf. of חשב.
[38] Ctr. DJD: "How is [dust and clay] to be recko[ned] that he should recount these things continually ...."
[39] ביחד, or "into Community."
[40] For this section, see 1QHᵃ 26.37.
[41] The words "hearing (about) your wonderful acts" are sup-ralinear.
[42] Lit. "to a man (who is) an intermediate."
[43] See: 4Q428 frg. 21 line 4.

]	4
]	5
לא יעצרו כוח לדעת בכבוד[כֹה ול[ספ]ר נֹפֹל]אותיכה[⁷¹	6
כי יהללוכה לפי שכלם ⁷² [וכפי דעתֹמֹ בכֹבודכֹהֹ ⁷³ [כי] ⁷⁴	7
מקץ לקץ י]שֹׁמיעו ומועד למועד יֹ[בר]כֹוֹ ⁷⁵ פֹתחתֹהֹ]	8
ואנחנו ביחד נועדנו ו]עֹם ידעים נוסרה לכה ונרננה ⁷⁶ קדוש]	9
בכוח עם גבוריכה ו]בֹהפלא נספרה יחד בעדת אל ועם ⁷⁷ ברוב רחמיכה]	10
וצאצאינו [הודעתה עם בני איש בתוך בני אדם ⁷⁸]°	11
⁷⁹[	12
בי]חֹד רנה גדול אל הֹמֹפלי	13
בֹדֹו[ ]לֹ[	14
תֹה איש[	15
שֹׁכו[ ]בֹל אור ממשל[	16
כיא זוקקה ⁸⁰[	17
לֹעולם ומ[ק]ֹור ברכה[	18
כי]א [אין יג]ון ואנחה	19

---

⁷¹ 1QHᵃ 7.14: ⟦°⟧ לֹא יעצרו כוח לדעת בֿכבוד[כה ולס[פֹר נפלֹא[ותיכה. 1QHᵃ preserves two more illegible consonants after this reading, but they shed no further light on this line of 4Q427.

⁷² Restored from 1QHᵃ col. 7 line 15.

⁷³ 1QHᵃ 7.15: וכפי דעתֹמֹ[בכֹ[בודכה כֹ]ֹי.

⁷⁴ Perhaps restore כי here in light of 1QHᵃ 7.15.

⁷⁵ 1QHᵃ 7.1: . פתחתֹה] ולהלל[ ]שֹׁ\מֹכה לאין השֹׁבֹת מֹקֹץ לקץ ישמיעו ומוֹעֹד[ ]למֹוֹ[עֹ]ד יברכוכה.

⁷⁶ 1QHᵃ 7.17: קדֹוֹ[ש] ואנחנו ביחד נועדנֹוֹ ועם ידעים נֹ[וס]ֹרה /לכה\ ונרֹ[נ]נה ברוב. The text in 1QHᵃ appears to have been corrected to the reading also found here in 4Q427.

⁷⁷ Cf. 1QHᵃ 7.18:]°עֹד[ ]° רחמיכֹה. בכוֹ[ח עם גבוריכה ובהפלא נספרה יחד בדעֹ[ת.

⁷⁸ 1QHᵃ 7.19:]° וצאצאינו הודֹעֹ[תה ע]ֹם בני איש עֹ[בני אדם.

⁷⁹ The corresponding remains from this line in 1QHᵃ 7.20 read:] בֹ[הֹפלא מאדה כי]א\וֹ[.

⁸⁰ A brief interspace precedes the following words.

4   […]

5   […]

6   [… they will not have the power to know] your [glory] and to [recou]nt [your] wonde[rs]

7   [… for they will praise you according to their insight], and according to their knowledge in your glory [for]

8   you opened[…. From time to time t]hey shall cause to hear and from appointed time to appointed time they [will ble]ss you

9   [holy …. And we have gathered together[44] and] with those who have knowledge we have been warned (through suffering) for you and we exult

10   [in the multitude of your compassions … in power with your mighty ones. And] wondrously we shall recount together in the congregation of[45] God, and with

11   °[… and our offsprings] you have allowed to know[46] with the sons of men in the midst of the sons of Adam

12   [….] (VACAT)

13   [… tog]ether an exultation, great is God who does wonders

14   […]*l*[…]*bdw*

15   […]*th* a man

16   […]*škw* […]*bl* light, dominion

17   [….] Because it is refined.[47]

18   […] forever and a so[u]rce of blessing

19   [… becau]se [there is no sig]hing and grieving[48]

---

[44] Or "in the Community," or *Yaḥad*.
[45] Ctr. 1QHᵃ 7.18: "with knowle[dge of] and until."
[46] Note the string of *hipʿil* forms.
[47] Not "purified" which is טהר.
[48] Or "groaning."

20　　　　　　　　　　　　　　　　 נ]חמתה

21　　　　　　　　　　　　　　　　א̇ל[‎81

Frg. 8 Col. 2 (Col. 6.8–12)[82]

1　　　　[

2　　　　[

3　　　　[

4　　　　[

5　　　　[

6　　　　[

7　　　　[

8　　בׄסׄ°[　　[ם　[

9　　עם רוחות עו]לם

10　　למשכיל הודותׄ[ן ותפלה[83]

11　　מבא אור לממשל[תו[84]

12　　אור ברשית ממשלות חׄ]ושך[85]

13　　אל מעונתו מפני אור למׄ]וצא לילה[86]

14　　ותקופות מועדים[87]

15　　הווה והיא̇]ה[88]　　　　　　כי אל[

---

[81] Ctr. DJD: ל °[. The ink is faded. The bottom margin is visible.

[82] Frg. 8 preserves the right-hand and lower margins of col. 2.

[83] 1QHᵃ 20.7: ל[ה̇]דות ותפלה ל/ה\תנ/פ\ל והתחנן תמיד מקץ לקץ עם . למשכי[ל . Compared with 1QHᵃ, 4Q427 preserves room for approximately fifteen to twenty additional spaces, which may have been filled with additional content or a *vacat*.

[84] 1QHᵃ 20.7–8: מבוא אור למˊמש̇]לת[בתקופות יום לתכונו לחזוקות מאור גדול בפנות ערב ומוצא.

[85] 1QHᵃ 20.9–10: אור ברשית ממשלת חושך למועד לילה בתקופתו .ל/פ\נות בוקר ובקץ הˊאספו

[86] 1QHᵃ 20.10–11: /א\ל מ/ע\ונתו מפנית אור למוצא לילה ומבוא יומם .תמיד בכול מולדי עת יסודי קץ

[87] 1QHᵃ 20.11–12: ותקופת מועדים בתכונם באותותם לכול ממשלתם .בתכון נאמנה מפי אל ותעודת

[88] 1QHᵃ 20.12–13: הווה והיאה תהיה ואין אפס זולתה לוא היה ולוא יהיה עוד כי אל . As compared with 1QHᵃ, 4Q427 leaves room for additional letter spaces, which may have been occupied by an interspace before כי.

20   […] you have [com]forted

21   […] God

Frg. 8 Col. 2 (Col. 6.8–21)

1   […]

2   […]

3   […]

4   […]

5   […]

6   […]

7   […]

8   *bs*°[…]*m* […]

9   with the ete[rnal] spirits [….]

10   For the Instructor, thanksgiving [and prayer …]

11   light comes out to [its] domini[on …]

12   light at the beginning of the dominions[49] of da[rkness …]

13   to its domicile from before the light when [the night] go[es out …]

14   and (during) the period of seasons […]

15   existence. And thi[s …. For the God of]

---

[49] Ctr. 1QHª 20.9: "dominion."

16   הדעות[^89] הכ[ו]ינה[^90]

17   ואני מש[כיל[^91]

18   ברוח[^92]

19   לרו[ב חסד[^93]

20   עו[ולם[^94]

21   ול[^95]

Frg. 9 (Col. 7.9–10)
Parallels: 1QH[^a] 20.31–34 [= Sukenik Col. 12]

9   עול[ם ומק[ו]וי[^96]

10   [לפני אפכ[ה[^97]

Frg. 10 (Col. 8.5–9)
Parallels: 1QH[^a] 21.11–16 [= Sukenik Col. 18]

5   מש[פט לערמת ר[חמיכה[^98]

6   [למי נחשב[תי[^99]

7   עול[ם חקותה בלב[^100]

8   במ[שפטי עדים במ[כון[^101]

---

[^89]: See 1QS 3.15 מאל הדעות נול הויה ונהייה

[^90]: 1QH[^a] 20.13–14: ה(ו)ד(י)עות הכינה ואין אחר עמו. As the very next words in 1QH[^a] correspond with ואני מש[כיל in 4Q427 (line 17), the remaining portions of line 16 probably ended with an extended *vacat*, perhaps anticipating the start of a new hymn at the beginning of line 17.

[^91]: 1QH[^a] 20.14–15: ואני משכיל ידעתיכה אלי ברוח אשר נתתה בי ונאמנה. שמעתי לסוד פלאכה

[^92]: 1QH[^a] 20.15–17: ברוח ק/ו\ודשכה [פ]תחתה לתוכי דעת ברז שכלכה. ומעין גבורת[כ]ה[ב]תוך [יראיכ]ה

[^93]: 1QH[^a] 20.17–18: לרוב חסד וקנאת כלה והשב[תה] [ל] ב]הדר .כבודכה לאור

[^94]: Portions of 1QH[^a] may attest to the content of this line; however, no direct connection with the first consonants of 4Q427 (line 21) is attested; 1QH[^a] 20.18–19: עול[ם] [מ]פחד רשעה ואין רמיה ו]. [

[^95]: Ctr. 1QH[^a] 20.20–21: מ[ועדי שממה כיא אין ע[וד ו]אין עוד ו[ ]וד.

[^96]: 1QH[^a] 20.31–32: קודש [ורום] עולם ומקוי כבוד דעת וגבורת [פל]א והמה ל[וא.

[^97]: 1QH[^a] 20.33: יוכ]לו לספר כול כבודכה ול/ה\תיצב לפני אפכה.

[^98]: 1QH[^a] 21.11–12: מפחי משפט לעומת רחמיכה ואני יצר [החמר מגבל מים מקוי עפ]ר[.

[^99]: 1QH[^a] 21.12–13: ולב האבן למי נחשבתי עד זות כיא [נ]תתה באוזן עפר.

[^100]: 1QH[^a] 21.13–14: ונהיות עולם חקותה בלב [האבן ונעוי לב] השבתה להביא בברית עמכה.

[^101]: 1QH[^a] 21.14–15: ב]מכון .Ctr. DJD: ולעמוד] במשפטי עדים] במכון עולם לאור אורתים עד נצח ועד חושך.

16 knowledge[50] has establ[ished it....]

17 And I, the Inst[ructor ...]

18 with the spirit [...]

19 for the multit[ude of loving-kindness ...]

20 ete[rnal ...]

21   and *l*[...]

Frg. 9 (Col. 7.9–10)
Parallels: 1QHᵃ 20.31–34 [= Sukenik Col. 12]

9 [... the etern]al and the reservo[irs of ...]

10 [...] before yo[ur] anger. [...]

Frg. 10 (Col. 8.5–9)
Parallels: 1QHᵃ 21.11–16 [= Sukenik Col. 18]

5 [... judg]ment according to the heap of [your] m[ercies[51] ...]

6 [....] For whom was [I] considered [...]

7 [... etern]ity, you engraved on the heart [...]

8 [... in the ju]dgments of witnesses in the est[ablishment of ...]

[50] See 1QS 3.15 "from the God of knowledge comes all that is occurring and shall occur."
[51] Ctr. 1QHᵃ 21.11: "judgment corresponding (to) your mercies."

9　　　ותח֯ל֯ לֿ]אין[102

Frg. 11 (Col. 8.15–19)
Parallels: 1QHª 21.23–27
4Q428 frg. 13 lines 6–8

15　　　וע]ם֯ בשר[103

16　　　ומ]פ֯רשי רשת וערמ֯]ת[104

17　　　דונ]ג֯ בהמס לפני אש[105

18　　　ואת106 יכינֿנ֯י בֿ]ן[107

19　　　]לֿ[108

Frg. 12 (Col. 9.7)
Parallels: 1QHª 21.36

7　　　נ]ג֯ע וכל]֯ת[109

*Frg. 13 Col. 1*110

1　　　]

2　　　]לוא֯111

3　　　]

---

102 Ctr. DJD:]ות֯°°לֿ לֿ]אין[. The skin is darkened; there is no second *lamedh*. 1QHª 21.16: קר]חֿ לאין שלום וקצי סוף ולא]ן. 4Q427 preserves the *lamedh* in the first appearance of לאי]ן, preserved in 1QHª.

103 1QHª 21.23–24: ת יהלכו[　　　　בֿנֿתֿיבות שלום ועם בשר להפליא[. 4Q428 frg. 13 line 6:]ועם בשר[. Ctr. DJD:]בשר[.

104 1QHª 21.24–25: איכה[אֿשֿמ֯ר ביצר]שת ומפרשֿי֯ ר[. 4Q428 frg. 13 line 7: פע]מי על מטוני פחים ומפרשי ר]שת. פע]מי על מטוני פחיה.

105 1QHª 21.25–26:]מס לפני אש ו֯מקוי אפר֯ איכה[עפר מהתפרר ומתוך דונג בֿ]הֿ.

106 Ctr. DJD:]ואנֿ֯י.

107 1QHª 21.26–27 does not directly preserve the remaining words of 4Q427; yet it may attest to what originally appeared before and after: אעמוד לפני רוח סוע]רת[　　וישמורהו לרזי חפצו.

108 For line 4 there is no parallel. 1QHª 21.27–28 does not preserve the remaining consonants of 4Q427; yet it may attest to what originally appeared before and after: כיא הוא ידע למֿ°]　　]ר כלה ופח לפח יטמונו צמי רֿשֿעֿהֿ°[.

109 1QHª 21.36–37: שֿ֯ב֯° לכה חמה[חֿ]°°[עולם]ומשפטי נגע וכלת.

110 Frg. 13 preserves portions of the left hand margin of col. 1 and the right hand margin of col. 2.

111 Perhaps: לונו[.

9   […]*wtḥ°l* wi[thout …]

Frg. 11 (Col. 8.15–19)
Parallels: 1QHª 21.23–27
4Q428 frg. 13 lines 6–8

15   [… and wi]th flesh […]

16   [… and the s]pread out (places of) a net and the heap [of …]

17   [… wa]x melting before fire […]

18   […]*w'ṭ*, he will establish me in […]

19   […]*l*[…]

Frg. 12 (Col. 9.7)
Parallels: 1QHª 21.36

7   [… aff]liction and the destruction [of …]

Frg. 13 Col. 1

1   […]

2   […] not

3   […]

Frg. 13 Col. 2

1 בֹּרכ]ה[^112

2 [עֹֹ[ל

3 א[

Frg. 14

1 א[ו]לל]ו[

2 ט[פל עד י]

3 [ל]

Frg. 15

1 [ ]°°[

2 מעש]יכה[^113]

3 [ ]°°[

Frg. 16[^114]

1 [ ]°[ ]צֹדֹק]

2 [ ]אֹל בֹקשו[

3 [הכושלים[^115]°°[

4 [מות]° [ ]°[ ]

---

[^112] The reading derives from Strugnell.
[^113] Ctr. DJD: מוש] [. In 1QH^a 17 to 25 מעשיכה appears frequently.
[^114] The formation of ש, מ, and ה may call into question whether this fragment belongs to 4Q427, but the association remains possible. The image for this fragment has been misnumbered "20" in both the DJD and the PAM images.
[^115] The first consonant was corrected from ה (so also DJD 29).

Frg. 13 Col. 2

1   blessi[ng …]

2   upon […]

3   '[…]

Frg. 14

1   […] with[ou]t […]

2   […]*y* unto esca[pe …]

3   […]*l*[…]

Frg. 15

1   […]°°[…]

2   [… your] work[s …]

3   […]°°[…]

Frg. 16

1   […] righteousness […] °[…]

2   […] they searched for God °[…]

3   […]°° those who stumble […]

4   […] °[…]° *mwt*°[…]

Other Fragments Assigned to 4Q427

Frg. 17[116]

1   ]ֹת אֵין[ ]ֹ[ ]

Frg. 18[117]

1   [ד ⁰⁰⁰⁰ כִֹים][118]

2   ]ֹלֹ[ ]

Frg. 19[119]

1   [פִים]ֹֹ[

2   ]לֹ[

Frg. 20[120]

1   [ֹֹ]ֹנֹו[121]

2   [ֹ נֹו]ֹ[

3   [ ]ֹ[ ]לֹ[

Frg. 21[122]

1   [וֹעֹתה]

2   [תֹיֹראוֹ[123]

---

[116] The image for this fragment has been misnumbered "16" in both the DJD and PAM images.
[117] The image for this fragment has been misnumbered "17" in both the DJD and PAM images.
[118] Ctr.]ֹ יֹכִֹים[.
[119] The image for this fragment has been misnumbered "18" in both the DJD and PAM images.
[120] The image for this fragment has been misnumbered "19" in both the DJD and PAM images.
[121] Perhaps:]ֹ מֹ[.
[122] The image for this fragment has been misnumbered "20" in both the DJD and PAM images.
[123] Ctr. DJD:]ֹאֹ[.

Other Fragments Assigned to 4Q427

Frg. 17

1   […]°[…] there is not *t*°[…]

Frg. 18

1   […]*kym d*°°°°[…]

2   […]*l* °[…]

Frg. 19

1   […]°°*pym* […]

2   […]*l*[…]

Frg. 20

1   […]*nw* °[…]

2   […]°*nw* °[…]

3   […]°[…]*l*[…]

Frg. 21

1   […] and now

2   […] you will see

Frg. 22[124]

]°°°מׄ[ ]ׄ[**1**

]ׄ[**2**

---

[124] The image for this fragment has been misnumbered "21" in both the DJD and PAM images.

Frg. 22

1   […]˚[…]*m*˚˚˚[…]

2   […]˚[…]

Thanksgiving Hymns (Hodayot)
4Q428 (4QHᵇ)

JAMES H. CHARLESWORTH and CASEY D. ELLEDGE

Introduction

Fragments 1–21 of 4Q428 preserve portions of the *Hodayot* that intermittently overlap with the same hymns preserved in 1QHᵃ 4–5, 10–16, 18–21, and 23–26. Fragments 22–69, however, preserve no conclusive intersections with other known portions of the *Hodayot*, but they frequently utilize familiar language and themes attested elsewhere in the hymns.

1. Scribal Practices and Date

4Q428 was penned in a Hasmonean semi-formal script whose characteristics associate it with the "the first half of the first century BCE, 100–50 BCE."[1] This suggests that 4Q428 is an earlier copy than the large 1QHᵃ scroll of Cave 1. Corrections are seldom, once indicated by a strike-through (4Q428 frg. 4 line 1) and once by supralinear addition (frg. 12a line 3). A scribal mark accentuates the end of the hymn in fragment 10 line 11. In contrast to overlapping passages in 1QHᵃ, 4Q428 preserves regular square script for אלי and אל consistently throughout.[2]

2. Contents

The original scroll has been estimated as having measured 9.5 meters in length. If so, then 4Q428 would have been capable of presenting a version of the hymns comparable in length to 1QHᵃ. Shorter line lengths in 4Q428 (40–50 scribal units per line in frgs. 3–10, 40–45 in frgs. 12a, 12b, 21) are estimated to have required some 68 columns to include the same collection found in 1QHᵃ (28 cols.). Among the preserved portions of the scroll, there are no deviations from the order and content of the same hymns found in 1QHᵃ. The reconstruction originally proposed in DJD 29 views 4Q428 as having preserved an earlier and probably complete version of the same collection found in 1QHᵃ. While fragments 1–2 preserve only very limited remains

of the materials found in 1QHᵃ 4–5, the surviving portions of fragments 3–21 preserve the majority of hymns found in 1QHᵃ columns 10–26.[3] This includes ample presentation of hymns from both the "Teacher Hymns" and the "Community Hymns" units of the *Hodayot*. Where clear evidence of structural transition between hymns is preserved (frg. 10 line 11), the sequence attests the same order found in 1QHᵃ. There is otherwise no evidence among the preserved remains for a different sequence than 1QHᵃ or for additional hymns not found in 1QHᵃ. These factors suggest the conclusion that 4Q428 originally presented the same collection of hymns found in 1QHᵃ. Unfortunately, the other fragments of 4Q428 that have no convincing overlap with 1QHᵃ are too indistinct to indicate whether the manuscript might offer previously unknown contents of the *Hodayot*. Nevertheless, 4Q428 poses an important early witness to the *Hodayot*. Since it is an earlier copy than the 1QHᵃ manuscript, it demonstrates that the same collection of hymns attested in 1QHᵃ was already in existence earlier in the first century BCE. Moreover, 4Q428 demonstrates that this relatively more complete version co-existed side-by-side with the more selective version of "Community Hymns" found in 4Q427. This reconstruction of the scroll has occasionally been challenged in subsequent research. A. K. Harkins, for example, disputes whether fragments 1–2 truly preserve portions of the materials found in 1QHᵃ columns 4–5, associating fragment 1, instead, with 1QHᵃ 15.33–34 and regarding fragment 2 as too indistinct to determine. Such a reading of fragments 1–2 would suggest that 4Q428 may originally have comprised only the "Teacher Hymns" and not the second unit of "Community Hymns" found in 1QHᵃ.[4] Thus, scholarship on the *Hodayot* continues to consider other possibilities for defining the extent of the origi-

---

[1] E. M. Schuller, DJD 29, p. 129. The hand is perhaps most comparable to that of 4Q499, 4Q500, 4Q503, 4Q505, 4Q509.

[2] 4Q428 frg. 10 line 5.

[3] Exceptions include the psalms found in 1QHᵃ 12.6–13.6, 13.7–21, 15.9–28, 17.38–18.14, 15.16–29.5, 19.6–17; see DJD 29, p. 130.

[4] A. K. Harkins, "A New Proposal for Thinking about 1QHa Sixty Years After its Discovery," in *Qumran Cave 1 Revisited, Texts from Cave 1 Sixty Years After their Discovery: Proceedings of the Sixth Meeting of the IOQS in Ljubljana*, edited by D. Falk, *et al.* (STDJ 91; Leiden, 2010) pp. 101–134.

nal collections preserved in the 4QH witnesses.[5]

3. Selected Bibliography

Harkins, A. K. "A New Proposal for Thinking about 1QHa Sixty Years after its Discovery." In *Qumran Cave 1 Revisited, Texts from Cave 1 Sixty Years after their Discovery: Proceedings of the Sixth Meeting of the IOQS in Ljubljana*, edited by D. Falk, *et al.* STDJ 91; Leiden, 2010, pp. 101–34.

Puech, É. "Hodayot." In *EncyDSS*, edited by L. Schiffman and J. VanderKam. 2 vols. Oxford, 2000, vol. 1 pp. 365–69.

Puech, É. "Restauration d'un texte hymnique à partir de trois manuscrits fragmentaires: 1QH$^{(a)}$ xv 37–xvi 4 (vii 34–viii 3), 1Q35 (H^b) 1, 9–14, 4Q428 (H^b) 7." *RQ* 16.4 (1995) 543–58.

Schuller, E. M. "Hodayot." In *Qumran Cave 4.XX: Poetical and Liturgical Texts, Part 2*, edited by E. Chazon, *et al.*, in consultation with J. VanderKam and M. Brady. DJD 29; Oxford, 1999, pp. 69–254, Pls. 7–11.

Schuller, E. M. "Recent Scholarship on the *Hodayot* 1993–201." *CBR* 10 (2011) 119–62.

---

[5] E. M. Schuller, "Recent Scholarship on the *Hodayot* 1993–2010," *CBR* 10 (2011) 119–62.

Thanksgiving Hymns (*Hodayot*)
4Q428 (4QH^b)

Frg. 1[1] (Col. 11)
Parallels: 1QH^a 4.39–40 (= Sukenik 17.27–28)[2]

1]א֯ד֯[ם[3]

2]וב [

3]◦יכה לעולמׄ[י עד[4]

Frg. 2 (Col. 13)
Parallels: 1QH^a 5.19–20 (= Sukenik 13.2–3, frg. 17 lines 5–6, frg. 15)[5]

1]ו֯

2 ומעש]י֯ רע[6]

Frg. 3 (Col. 27)[7]
Parallels: 1QH^a 10.35–41 (= Sukenik 2.32–39)

1 עב]ו֯ד֯ת֯כׄה֯ [

2 וישימונ]י לבוז וחׄר֯[פה

3] נפש ע֯נ֯י֯[[8]

4 ו֯[תפד נפשי מיד אדירים ובגדפו]ת֯ם לוא[החתותני לעזוב][9]

5 עבו֯[דתכה מפחד הוות רשעים ו]ל֯[המיר בהולל יצר סמוך אשר][10]

[1] Frg. 1 preserves the bottom margin of a column.
[2] Identification uncertain.
[3] 1QH^a 4.39: אדם.
[4] 1QH^a 4.40:]ל֯עׄולמי עד.
[5] Identification uncertain.
[6] 1QH^a 5.20: ומעשי֯[[ ]]רע.
[7] Frg. 3 is preserved in 5 frgs.
[8] 1QH^a 10.36: נפש עני.
[9] Restored according to the text in 1QH^a 10.37–38: ותפד נפשי מיד אׄדירים ובגדפותם לא החתותני לעׄזוב.
[10] Restored according to the text in 1QH^a 10.38: עבודתכה מפחד הוות רש֯ע֯ים ולׄה֯מיר (ב)בהולל (ב)ב יצר סמוך אשר.

Thanksgiving Hymns (Hodayot)
4Q428 (4QH[b])

Frg. 1 (Col. 11)[1]
Parallels: 1QH[a] 4.39–40 (= Sukenik 17.27–28)

1   […] Ada[m …]

2   […]*wb* […]

3   […]°*ykh* foreve[r and ever…]

Frg. 2 (Col. 13)
Parallels: 1QH[a] 5.19–20 (= Sukenik 13.2–3, frg. 17 lines 5–6, frg. 15)

1   […]*n*

2   [… and work]s of evil

Frg. 3 (Col. 27)
Parallels: 1QH[a] 10.35–41 (= Sukenik 2.32–39)

1   […] your [serv]ice […]

2   [… . And they placed] me (as an object of) scorn and disg[race …]

3   […] the soul of the Needy One[2] [….]

4   And [you redeemed my soul from the hand of the powerful ones, and in] their [slanders you did] not [allow me to be afraid (so that I would) leave]

5   [your] servi[ce from the fear of the threats of the wicked ones, and] ex[changing for foolishness a firm inclination that]

---

[1] For the parallels in 1QH[a] and other copies of the *Hodayot,* see the Hebrew texts.
[2] See 1QH[a] 10.36.

6 נת[ן]תה[^11]

7 ב[ש̇ר̇][^12]

8 [לכול צאצאי̇ן̇] עד[^13]

9 [ל̇ש̇ו̇ן̇ כלמוד[י̇כה[^14] ובמשפט

Frg. 4 (Col. 28.4–5)
Parallels: 1QHª 11.13 (= Sukenik 3.11–13)

1 [ ] ב̇כ̇ו̇ר̇ ה̇ר̇י̇ה[^15]

2 ומש[ב̇ר̇י שחת לכול][^16]

Frg. 5 (Col. 29)
Parallels: 1QHª 11.28–32 (= Sukenik 3.26–31); 4Q432 Frg. 6

1 ח[צ̇י̇ שחת ל[^17]אין]

2 וג[ו̇רל א̇[ף ע[^18]ל̇]

3 וח[ב̇ל̇י̇[^19]] מות

4 כול]א̇גפי רום ב̇[אש אוכל]ת בכ̇[ול שנאביהם][^20]

5 [לה]ת̇ם̇ [כול עץ] לח̇[^21] ויב[ש̇ מפלגיהם] ותשוט [בשבי̇[ב]י להוב][^22]

6 [עד אפס כו]ל̇[^23] שותיהם באושי]ח̇מר [תאוכל] וברקיע יב[שה][^24]

---

[^11] 1QHª 10.39: נ̇ת̇ת̇ה].

[^12] 1QHª 10.40: ב[ש̇ר̇].

[^13] The separation may indicate frg. 3d and 3e should not be joined. 1QHª 10.40: ש̇חת לכול צאצא̇י̇ עד].

[^14] 1QHª 10.41: לש[ו̇ן̇ כלמודיכה ובמ[ש]פט].

[^15] 1QHª 11.13: בכור הריה. A scribe has struck through the preceding word with a horizontal line, perhaps to correct a dittography error due to the many repetitions of this phrase within the hymn.

[^16] 1QHª 11.13: ומשברי שחת לכול.

[^17] 1QHª 11.28: חצי שחת לאין.

[^18] 1QHª 11.28–29: וגורל אף על.

[^19] 1QHª 11.29: וחבלי מות.

[^20] 1QHª 11.30: כול אגפי רום ב̇אש אוכלת בכול שנאיהם. 4Q432 frg. 6 line 4: כול]ש̇ אוכלת ב̇[א. The *beth* of בכ̇[ול is a *nota accusitivi*.

[^21] 4Q432 frg. 6 line 5: להתם̇] כול עץ ל̇[ח.

[^22] 1QHª 11.30–31: להתם כול עץ לח ויבש מפלגיהם ותשוט בשביבי להוב. 4Q432 frg. 6 line 5: וחשו]ט̇ בש̇[ביבי.

[^23] 4Q432 frg. 6 line 6: עד אפס כ̇ו̇ל̇].

[^24] 1QHª 11.31–32: עד אפס כול שותיהם באושי חמר תאוכל וברקיע יבשה.

6 [you] put […]

7 [… f]lesh […]

8 […] for all [everlasting] descendants […]

9 […] the tongue, according to [your] teaching[s and in the judgment of …]

Frg. 4 (Col. 28.4–5)
Parallels: 1QHᵃ 11.13 (= Sukenik 3.11–13)

1 […] the womb of the pregnant one[3] […]

2 [… and the bre]akers of the pit for all […]

Frg. 5 (Col. 29)
Parallels: 1QHᵃ 11.28–32 (= Sukenik 3.26–31); 4Q432 Frg. 6

1 [… the a]rrows of the pit wi[thout …]

2 [… and the l]ot of an[ger o]n […]

3 [… and the b]onds of [death …]

4 [… all] the heightened banks with [fire devouri]ng a[ll their growth]

5 [to an]nihilate[4] [every tree,] moist [and dr]y from their streams. [And it sweeps] with the spa[rks[5] of fire][6]

6 [until al]l [their canals (are) no more. It (the fire) consumes the foundations] of clay and the firmament of the dr[y land,]

---

[3] A scribe deleted this phrase with a horizontal line. See the note in the Hebrew.
[4] Heb. להתם.
[5] Not "flames," (ctr. DJD). שביב means "sparks."
[6] Different nouns in Hebrew are used for "fire." English has only one word for "fire."

7   ושורשי ח[ל]מיש לנח[לי ז֯פֿת֯] ותאוכל[²⁵

*Frg. 6*²⁶ (Col. 30.1–2)
Parallels: 1QHᵃ 12.2 (= Sukenik 4.[0]–1); 4Q432 Frg. 7

1   גבור[ת]ם ויפולו²⁷ מגבור[תם

2   ח֯כמֿים בערמתם ו֗[אני בתומכי בבריתכה²⁸

Frg. 7 (Col. 34)
Parallels: 1QHᵃ 13.26 (= Sukenik 5.24)?

1   [בֿשפת] עול²⁹

*Frg. 8*³⁰ (Col. 36)
Parallels: 1QHᵃ 14.17–20 (= Sukenik 6.14–17); 4Q429 Frg. 4

1   כ[בֿ֗ודכה והיו³¹

2   ע[ד֗ עולם³²

3   [תֿבֿל]³³

4   [עד ש[חקים ושורשי֗]ו³⁴ עד תהום וכול נהרות] עדן ת[לחלחנה]³⁵

5   [דליו]תיו והיה לימים³⁶ ל[אין חקר והתאזרו [עֿל תבל לֿאֿי֗[ן]³⁷

---

²⁵ 1QHᵃ 11.32: ושורשי חלמיש לנחלי זפת ותאוכל.
²⁶ Frg. 6 preserves the upper and right-hand margins of a column.
²⁷ 4Q432 frg. 7 line 3: [לֿ֗ גבורתם ויפולו].
²⁸ 1QHᵃ 12.2: בערמ[תם ואני. 4Q432 frg. 7 line 4: [ם וֿא֗נֿי֗ בֿתֿוֿמֿכֿי֗ בֿב[ֿריתכה].
²⁹ 1QHᵃ 13.26: בשפת עול.
³⁰ Frg. 8 preserves the bottom and left-hand margins of a column.
³¹ Ctr. 1QHᵃ 14.17: כבודכה ויהיו.
³² 1QHᵃ 14.17–18: שריכה בגור[ל   [פרח כצ֗יֿ[ץ השדה.
³³ 1QHᵃ 14.18: ע[ד֗ עולם לג/ד\ל נצר מטעת עולם ויצל צל על כול תב]ל ודליותי[ו.
³⁴ 1QHᵃ 14.19: עד שחקֿ֗[ים ו]שרשיו.
³⁵ 1QHᵃ 14.19: עד תהום וכול נהרית עדן [תלחלחנה.
³⁶ 1QHᵃ 14.19: ד[לֿ]יֿ[ו֗]תיו והיה ל[ֿמים.
³⁷ 1QHᵃ 14.20: והתתֿאֿזֿרו עֿל תבל לאין.

7   [… and the sources of[7] f]l[int (turn into) rive]rs of tar, [and it (the fire) consumes]

Frg. 6[8] (Col. 30.1–2)
Parallels: 1QH[a] 12.2 (= Sukenik 4.[0]–1); 4Q432 Frg. 7

1   the[ir] might. And they will fall from [their] might […]

2   the wise ones in their craftiness. But [I, when I hold fast to your covenant …]

Frg. 7 (Col. 34)
Parallels: 1QH[a] 13.26 (= Sukenik 5.24)?

1   […] with [deceitful] lips […]

Frg. 8 (Col. 36)
Parallels: 1QH[a] 14.17–20 (= Sukenik 6.14–17); 4Q429 Frg. 4

1   […] your [g]lory, and they will become

2   [… unt]il eternity

3   […] world […]

4   [unto the s]kies, and [its] roots [unto the deep. And all of the rivers of] Eden will [moisten]

5   its [high-branch]es, and will become waters th[at are unfathomable and streaming] over the world withou[t]

---

[7] Lit. "roots of."
[8] This passage supplies the first three lines of 1QH[a] 12.

Frg. 9[38] (Col. 40.1–3)
Parallels: 1QH[a] 15.30–31 (= Sukenik 7.26–28); 1Q35 Frg. 1

פלא[כֹ]ה[39]	**1**
[לֹ]נעו[ן]י[40]	**2**
ומי י]צֹדק[41]	**3**

Frg. 10[42] (Col. 40.13–24)
Parallels: 1QH[a] 15.37–16.5 (= Sukenik 7.34–8.5); 1Q35 Frg. 1

חוקי ותקֹראני[43]	**1**
ובהמון רחמיכה לכֹ[ו]ל[44]	**2**
הוריתי באשמת מעל[ן[45]	**3**
לרוב נדה ומנעורי בדֹ[מים[46]	**4**
אלי כוננתה רגלי בדרכֹ[י[47]	**5**
אוזני ולבי להבין באמתכֹ[ה[48]	**6**
אוזן בלמודיכה עד אשֹר[	**7**
דעת הכֹאֹתֹה מתכמי וכבֹו[ד לב[49]	**8**
לי עוד למכשול עוון כי תגֹל[ה	**9**
לעד כיא לוא[לאד[מֹ דרכו כ]ול	**10**
א]וד[כֹה אדוני כי]א[51] (VACAT) [50]➐	**11**

---

[38] Frg. 9 seems to preserve the left-hand portions of a column.
[39] 1QH[a] 15.30: פלאֹכֹה. Puech agrees with these readings. The restoration in line 3 is not in Puech (*RQ* 16 [1993–95]).
[40] 1QH[a] 15.30: לנעוי. 1QH[b] frg. 1 line 2: לֹנֹעוֹי[.
[41] 1QH[a] 15.31: יצֹדק.
[42] Frg. 10 preserves the right-hand and bottom margins of a column.
[43] 1QH[a] 15.37–38: חוקי ותֹקֹראני.
[44] 1QH[a] 15.38: ובֹהֹמוֹן רחמיכה לכול.
[45] 1Q35 frg. 1 line 12: הֹוריתי בא]שמת[.
[46] 1Q35 frg. 1 line 13: ו]מֹנעורי בדמים[.
[47] Ctr. DJD: בדרך]. The medial *kaph* is obvious and a plural is demanded by the context. See 1Q35 frg. 1 line 14.
[48] בֹאֹמֹתֹך [is the last word in 1QH[a] 15.41.
[49] Restore with Puech.
[50] Line 11 has a marginal scribal mark, followed by a *vacat*.
[51] 1QH[a] 16.5: או]דכה אדו[ני] כֹֹי.

Frg. 9 (Col. 40.1–3)
Parallels: 1QH^a 15.30–31 (= Sukenik 7.26–28); 1Q35 Frg. 1

1   [...] yo[ur wonders]

2   [...] to the perverted [of]

3   [... and who can] be justified

Frg. 10 (Col. 40.13–24)
Parallels: 1QH^a 15.37–16.5 (= Sukenik 7.34–8.5); 1Q35 Frg. 1

1   my ordinances. But you called me [...]

2   and with the abundance of your mercies for a[ll ...]

3   her who conceived me (I have remained) in the guilt of infidelity [...]

4   for much impurity, and from my youth in bl[ood ...]

5   my God, you established my foot in the way[s of ...]

6   my ears and allowed my heart to understand yo[ur] truth [...][9]

7   ear to your teachings until which [....]

8   Knowledge of (perversities)[10] you removed[11] from my entrails and heavine[ss of[12] heart ...]

9   for me again a stumbling block of iniquity because you shall reve[al ...]

10   forever. For not [to Ada]m is not his way. A[ll....]

11   (VACAT) I [thank] you, O Lord, be[cause ...]

---

[9] The *beth* is a *nota accusativi*. Lit. "in your truth."
[10] Some negative phrase or term defined this noun. Perhaps בלוא was on the preceding line.
[11] From Aramaic נכא; see A. Even-Shoshan: המלון החדש, vol. 4, p. 1669.
[12] Not "glory of." The author is praising God for errors and problems removed.

12   ביבשה ומב[וע] מים בארץׄ [ציה⁵²

Frg. 11 (Col. 45.11–12)
Parallels: 1QHᵃ 18.4–5 (= Sukenik 10.2–3)⁵³

1   רצונכ[ה לוא]⁵⁴

2   ובסו[ד]ׄ⁵⁵ רזי[כה⁵⁶

*Frg. 12a*⁵⁷ (Col. 48.20–24)
Parallels: 1QHᵃ 19.28–31 (= Sukenik 25–28); 4Q427 Frg. 1

1   שמכׄ[ה⁵⁸ לעולמי עד יברכוכה כפי שכלם עד [קׄצים⁵⁹

2   ישמיעו [י]חׄד[בׄ]קׄ[ו]לׄ רנה ואין⁶⁰ [יגון ואנחה ועול]ׄה לוא⁶¹

עד

3   תמצא עׄ[וד⁶² ואמת]כׄׄה תופיע לכבוד ושלׄום עׄ[ולם⁶³

4   [(VACAT)   ברוך אתה א[דׄוני אשר נתתׄה⁶⁴ לעבדכה]

5   [לׄשׄו]ׄן]

*Frg. 12b*⁶⁵ (Col. 49)
Parallels: 1QHᵃ 20.5–7 (= Sukenik 12.2–4, frg. 54, line 3); 4Q427 Frg. 3; 4Q427 Frg. 8

1   לבטח במׄ[עון⁶⁶ קודש

2   בתוך יראׄ[יכה⁶⁷   (VACAT)   [

---

⁵² 1QHᵃ 16.5: ביבשה ומבוע מים בארץ. Only lines 11 and 12 are parallel to 1QHᵃ 16.5.
⁵³ The association is tentative.
⁵⁴ The scribe wrote:]לוא, but his *yodh* looks like a *pe*. 1QHᵃ 18. 4: רצונכה לא.
⁵⁵ Ctr. DJD: [ובסוד].
⁵⁶ 1QHᵃ 18.5: ובסו[ד]ׄ רזיכה.
⁵⁷ Frg. 12a preserves portions of the right- and left-hand margins of a column.
⁵⁸ 1QHᵃ 19.28: שמכה.
⁵⁹ 1QHᵃ 19.28: קצ]ים.
⁶⁰ 1QHᵃ 19.28–29: ישמיעו יחד בקול רנה ואין.
⁶¹ 1QHᵃ 19.29: ל]אׄ.
⁶² 1QHᵃ 19.29: עׄ[וד].
⁶³ 1QHᵃ 19.29–30: עׄׄ[לם] ואמתכה תופיע לכבוד עד ושלום עולם. Ctr. DJD: עׄׄ[ולם].
⁶⁴ 1QHᵃ 19.30: א[שׄר נתתה.
⁶⁵ Frg. 12b preserves portions of the right-hand margin of a column.
⁶⁶ 1QHᵃ 20.5: לבטח במעון.
⁶⁷ 1QHᵃ 20.6: בתוך יראיכה. 4Q427 frg. 2–3 line 17: יר[א]יכה.

12   in a dry land, and (as) the gushing-po[nd of][13] water in an [arid] land [...]

Frg. 11 (Col. 45.11–12)
Parallels: 1QH[a] 18.4–5 (= Sukenik 10.2–3)

1   [...] yo[ur] will (is) not [...]

2   [... and in the sec]ret of [your] mysteries [...]

Frg. 12a (Col. 48.20–24)
Parallels: 1QH[a] 19.28–31 (= Sukenik 25–28); 4Q427 Frg. 1

1   yo[ur] name [forever and ever. They will bless you according to their insight unto the] endtimes.

2   [Tog]ether they make proclamation [with] a vo[ic]e of exultation, and there is neither [grief nor sigh. And injusti]ce (is) not

3   found any [more]. And your [truth] will appear for everlasting[14] glory and the e[ternal] peace.

4   [(VACAT) Blessed are you, O L]ord, that you gave [to your servant]

5   [...] the tongu[e ...]

Frg. 12b (Col. 49)
Parallels: 1QH[a] 20.5–7 (= Sukenik 12.2–4, frg. 54, line 3); 4Q427 Frg. 3; 4Q427 Frg. 8

1   securely in the [holy] dw[elling ...]

2   among those who stand in awe [of you. (VACAT)]

[13] See 1QH[a] 16.5. A pond of gushing water. Perhaps the author was thinking about Ain-Gedi.
[14] עד supplied above the line.

3   למשכיל[⁶⁸ ⁶⁹]

Frg. 13[⁷⁰] (Col 52)
Parallels: 1QHᵃ 21.18–25 (= Sukenik 18.32–33, frg. 3); 4Q427 Frg. 11

1   [א̊]

2   [ ]̊ י̊צֿ̊ר̊[⁷¹]   ד אל°°]

3   ומלכ]ֺדת נסתרה   [נפ]תֿחה נה]   עפר[ ]

4   [ה נפרשֿה רשת⁷² שוחֿהֿ] ובד]ֺר̊כֿ̊יֺה צמי א̊[בדון]

5   [ים להתהלך   נפ]תֿחה דרך[⁷³]

6   ועם בשר⁷⁴ [להפלי]א̊[⁷⁵ כאלה כיא

7   יהלכו פע]מי על מטמוני⁷⁶ פחים⁷⁷ ומפרשי⁷⁸

8   [רשת   אי]כה אשמר ביצר עפר מה[ת]פרד⁷⁹

Frg. 14 (Col. 56)
Parallels: 1QHᵃ 23.12–17 (= Sukenik 18.11–16)

1   ולמליץ בא[ל]ֿה לעפֿ̊ר] כמוני⁸⁰

2   ד]רכו ואשמֿ̊]ות⁸¹ ילוד אשה

3   א[מֿתכה ליצֿ]ר⁸²

4   מב]שר ול]ֿספר⁸³

---

⁶⁸ 1QHᵃ 20.7: ל̊[משכיל]. 4Q427 frg. 8 2.10: למשכיל.
⁶⁹ The bottom of the column seems preserved. Ctr. DJD and their reading of lines 3 and 4, each with a *vacat*.
⁷⁰ Frg. 13 preserves the bottom and left-hand margins of a column.
⁷¹ 1QHᵃ 21.19: י̊צֿ̊ר̊[.
⁷² 1QHᵃ 21.21: נפ]ר̊שה רשֿתֿ].
⁷³ 1QHᵃ 21.22: נפתחה דֿרֿך.
⁷⁴ 4Q427 frg. 11 line 15: וע]ם̊ בשר].
⁷⁵ 1QHᵃ 21.23: ועם בשר להפליא̊].
⁷⁶ Contrast the error in 1QHᵃ 21.24 (מטוני).
⁷⁷ Ctr. 1QHᵃ 21.24: פחיה.
⁷⁸ 1QHᵃ 21.24: ומ]פֿרשי̊. 4Q427 frg. 11 line 16: פעמי על מטוני פחיה ומפרשי.
⁷⁹ 1QHᵃ 21.25: א̊שֿמֿר ביצר עפר מהתפרר.
⁸⁰ 1QHᵃ 23.12–13: ולמליץ באלה לעפר.
⁸¹ 1QHᵃ 23.13: דרכו ואשמות.
⁸² 1QHᵃ 23.14: אמתכה ליצר.
⁸³ 1QHᵃ 23.15: מבשר] ולספ]ֿר.

3   For the Instructor [...]

Frg. 13 (Col. 52)
Parallels: 1QHᵃ 21.18–25 (= Sukenik 18.32–33, frg. 3); 4Q427 Frg. 11

1   [...]ʾ [...]

2   [...]° [a cre]ature of [...]*d* ʾ*l*°°

3   [...] dust it was [ope]ned *nh*[... and a] hidden [sna]re[15]

4   [...]*h* it is spread out, a net of the pit [and in] its [w]ays (are) those thirsting[16] after A[baddon][17]

5   [...] a way [was op]ened [...]*ym* to walk continuously

6   [...] and with flesh [to act wonderfu]lly like these. Because

7   [...] my [footste]ps [will proceed] on the hidden parts of traps and the spread out (places of)

8   [a net .... H]ow can a creature of dust be guarded from be[ing] crumbled

Frg. 14 (Col. 56)
Parallels: 1QHᵃ 23.12–17 (= Sukenik 18.11–16)

1   [.... And for the one who interprets th]ese (things) to dust [like me ...]

2   [...] his [w]ay and the guilt[s of one born of a woman ...]

3   [...] your [t]ruth to the creatu[re ...]

4   [... from the f]lesh and to [recount ...]

---

[15] The noun "snare" only appears here in the witnesses to *The Thanksgiving Hymns.*

[16] Not "the snares of A[baddon]." See 1QHᵃ 21.28: צמי רִשׁעָה "those thirsting after wickedness." It is tempting to be misled by the parallelism and imagine a noun "snares of." See the note to the translation of 1QHᵃ 21.28.

[17] "Abaddon" means "destruction." The metaphor has many meanings, esp. "those passionately rushing to destruction."

5   דעת [84ר[ממקו]

6   ותפת[חֿ פי עבֿ]דכה

Frg. 15 (Col. 58)
Parallels: 1QHᵃ 24.10–15 (= Sukenik 19.2–7, frg. 9, frg. 50)

1   87[ויֿ[וֿ]פֿֿפֿוֿ 85 בה86 [כול]

2   מלאכי שמים]

3   מ[מֿכון88 קוֿד[שכה]

4   כ[בודכה ו[אתה]89

5   אדם]   כעו[ף אסו[ר90 עד]

6   קץ רצונכה]

7   ור[וב בשֿר]91

8   [כֿה לֿ[הפלא

Frg. 16 (Col. 60)
Parallels: 1QHᵃ 24.36–37 (= Sukenik frg. 2, col. 2; frg. 6)

1   ולוא עזבת[ם ביד [כול92

2   [מֿ]

Frg. 17 (Col. 60.17–19)
Parallels: 1QHᵃ 25.7–9 (= Sukenik frg. 5, frg. 56 col. 1, frg. 46 col. 1)

1   רשע[ה]הֿ93 להפ[יל

---

84 1QHᵃ 23.16: ממקור.
85 This word is now on two frgs. (15a and 15b). The reading is possible only because of the text in 1QHᵃ.
86 1QHᵃ 24.10: ויען[[]]ופפו בה כול.
87 The left-hand margin can be discerned.
88 1QHᵃ 24.12: ממכון[[].
89 1QHᵃ 24.12: כבודכה ואתה.
90 1QHᵃ 24.13: אסור.
91 1QHᵃ 24.14: ו[]רוב בשר. Ctr. DJD:]ורוב בשר.
92 1QHᵃ 24.36: [עֿזֿבֿתֿםֿ ביד כול.
93 1QHᵃ 25.7: רֿשֿ[[]]עה.

5   […] from the sour[ce of knowledge …]

6   [.… And you ope]ned the mouth of [your] serva[nt …]

Frg. 15 (Col. 58)
Parallels: 1QHᵃ 24.10–15 (= Sukenik 19.2–7, frg. 9, frg. 50)

1   […] and on it f[l]y [all]

2   [the (evil)[18] angels of heaven …]

3   [… from] the establishment of [your] holine[ss]

4   […] your [g]lory. But [you,]

5   [Adam … like a bir]d confine[d until]

6   [the Endtime of your will …]

7   [… and the multi]tude of flesh […]

8   […]°*kh* for [wonders …]

Frg. 16 (Col. 60)
Parallels: 1QHᵃ 24.36–37 (= Sukenik frg. 2, col. 2; frg. 6)

1   […you did not abandon th]em into the hand of [all …]

2   […]*m* […]

Frg. 17 (Col. 60.17–19)
Parallels: 1QHᵃ 25.7–9 (= Sukenik frg. 5, frg. 56 col. 1, frg. 46 col. 1)

1   […wickedne]ss in order to ca[st …]

---

[18] See the note to the translation of 1QHᵃ 24.11.

2   יוש]דו לאב]ל[^94](#)

3   ו]בֿ]רום[^95](#) רשעה

Frg. 18[^96](#) (Col. 61.1–5)
Parallels: 1QHᵃ 25.12–15 (= Sukenik frg. 5, frg. 46 col. 1, frg. 51)

1   ואוזן בשר גליתה ו]ן[^97](#)

2   לבכה וקץ תעודה השכלתהֿ]ן[^98](#)

3   תשפוט במרום וביושבי]ן האדמה[^99](#)

4   בשאוֹל תחתי]ה[תֿשֿפֿוֿן]ט[^100](#)

5   [צדיק] ולהֿ]רֿ]שֿ]יע[^101](#)

Frg. 19 (Col. 61.12–18)
Parallels: 1QHᵃ 25.26 (= Sukenik frg. 8, frg. 63)

1   [לבֿני °°]

2   [˚ וגם רוחו]ת

3   [מחושך וי ˚]

4   [מֿ ונמארים[^102](#)]

5   [רשעתם בחכמֿ]ת

6   [צ]דקכה לעוו]ן

7   ובסו]ד קדוש]ים[^103](#)

[^94]: 1QHᵃ 25.8: יושדו לאבל‖.
[^95]: 1QHᵃ 25.9: וברום.
[^96]: Frg. 18 preserves the upper and right-hand margins of a column.
[^97]: 1QHᵃ 25.12: ואוזן בשר גליתה ו‖.
[^98]: 1QHᵃ 25.13: לבכה וקץ תעודה השכלתה.
[^99]: 1QHᵃ 25.13–14: ‖שֿפֿוט במרום וביושבי האֿדֿמֿה ‖תֿ.
[^100]: בֿשֿאוֿל‖ appears on two fragments. The line can be read only in light of the text in 1QHᵃ. 1QHᵃ 25.14: בשאו]ל‖ תחתיה תשפֿ]וֿ[טֿ.
[^101]: 1QHᵃ 25.15: ולהֿ‖שיע.
[^102]: The root is מאר. The form is a *nipʿal* part. pl. Only the *hipʿil* of this verb appears in biblical Hebrew.
[^103]: 1QHᵃ 25.26: ובסוד קד]ושים.

2   [...] they [will be devast]ed for sorro[w ...]

3   [... and] when [wickedness rises up ...]

Frg. 18 (Col. 61.1–5)
Parallels: 1QH[a] 25.12–15 (= Sukenik frg. 5, frg. 46 col. 1, frg. 51)

1   And the ear of flesh you uncovered and [...]

2   your heart. And (concerning) the Endtime of[19] fixed times, you allowed to have insight [...]

3   you shall judge in the upper regions, and the dwellers [(on) earth] (you shall judge)[20] [...]

4   in Sheol belo[w] you shall judg[e ...]

5   [the righteous one] and decla[r]ing wic[ked ...]

Frg. 19 (Col. 61.12–18)
Parallels: 1QH[a] 25.26 (= Sukenik frg. 8, frg. 63)

1   [...] for the sons of °°[...]

2   [...]° and also the spirit[s of ...]

3   [...] from darkness and y°[...]

4   [...]*m* and those festering[21] [...]

5   [...] their wickedness in the wisdom[of ...]

6   [...] your [righ]teousness for iniquity [...]

7   [... and in the counc]il of the Holy One[s ...]

---

[19] Or, "Endtime of."
[20] See the text and translation of 1QH[a] 25.13–14.
[21] Or "graved."

Frg. 20[104] (Col. 62.1–4)
Parallels: 1QHᵃ 25.30–33 (= Sukenik frg. 8, frg. 7 col. 1)

‏[ ]ֹם ירננו לזמר ולהלל ל[‏[105]	**1**
‏לאין הש]בֹֿת ואני יצר החמר] כדעתי[‏	**2**
‏[ספרתי בעדת קדושי]כֹה בהגדל והפלא לאֹל [כיא‏	**3**
‏[אתה אל הדעות וב]פֿי[‏[106] ‏[עוז [מֹנֹשף ל]ערב‏	**4**

Frg. 21[107] (Col. 64)
Parallels: 4Q427 frg. 7 2.19–23

‏[כוח לשמוע‏[108]	**1**
‏[נפלאותיכה כאלה‏[109] דבר]נו לכה ולוא‏[110]	**2**
‏[לאי]ש בינים‏[111] ‏[‏	**3**
‏[ל]מוצא שפתינו‏[112] ‏[השמיעו ואמורו ברוך אל הדעות הנ]וטה‏[113]	**4**
‏[שמים בכו]חו וכול מֹח]שביהם‏[114] עו]שֹה‏	**5**

Frg. 22[115]

‏]ֹ[‏	**1**
‏[מו בֹ]‏	**2**
‏[ֹרתי לוא]‏	**3**

---

[104] Frg. 20 preserves the upper and left margin of a column.
[105] 1QHᵃ 25.30–31: ‏[ל [ז]מֹֹר ולהלל ל]ֹ[.‏
[106] 1QHᵃ 25.33: ‏ובֹפֹֿי].‏
[107] Frg. 21 preserves the left-hand margin of a column.
[108] No parallel exists to 1QHᵃ 26.38 (*pace* DJD).
[109] 4Q427 frg. 7 2.20.
[110] 4Q427 frg. 7 2.21: ‏דברנו לכה ולֹוֹא.‏
[111] 4Q427 frg. 7 2.21: ‏לאיש בֹֿ]נים.‏
[112] 4Q427 frg. 7.22: ‏[למו]צא שפתינו.‏
[113] See 1QHᵃ 9.11, 28 and 4Q427 frg. 7 2.22.
[114] 4Q427 frg. 7 2.23: ‏שמים בכוחו וכול מחשביהמה.‏
[115] Frgs. 22–24 bear material resemblances to each other, as well as to frgs. 15–21. This may suggest that they, too, belong to the latter part of the scroll. It has not been possible, however, to ensure a certain identification.

Frg. 20 (Col. 62.1–4)
Parallels: 1QH^a 25.30–33 (= Sukenik frg. 8, frg. 7 col. 1)

1 […]*m* they will exult, chant, and praise *l*[…]

2 [… without ce]asing. But I (am) a creature of clay. [According to my knowledge,]

3 [I have announced in the assembly of] your [Holy Ones:] "Great and wonderful (is) God." [For]

4 [you (are) the God of knowledge. And with a strong] voice[22] from dawn[23] to [dusk…]

Frg. 21 (Col. 64)
Parallels: 4Q427 frg. 7 2.19–23

1 […] strength to hear

2 [your wonderful acts like (these) …] we [spoke] to you and not

3 [to an in]termediary[24] […]

4 [to] the utterance of our lips. [Cause to be heard and say: "Blessed (be) the God of knowledge who stretc]hes out

5 [the heavens by] his [pow]er, and all [their] thou[ghts … ma]king"

Frg. 22

1 […]˚[…]

2 […]*mw b*˚[…]

3 […]*rty* not […]

---

[22] Lit. "mouth." The metaphor denotes a loud voice. See Ps 68:34, "a strong voice."
[23] The noun "dawn" indicates the twilight before sunrise.
[24] Lit. "to a man (who is) an intermediator."

4   א֯ בֿ֯ר֯[

Frg. 23

1   [ר֯ו לוא י֯]

2   [דו עם לֿ]

3   [לֿ]

Frg. 24

1   ח[ו]שך להי֯[

2   [ישמחֿו[ן]¹¹⁶

Frg. 25

1   [א֯פֿ֯]

2   [מֿר אסור]

3   [וֿעֿבוד]ת

*Frg. 26*¹¹⁷

1   יופ]יע [

2   [הו]פיע לה[ן]

3   מלאכי שלום¹¹⁸ ותי֯[

4   עֿד [¹¹⁹

---

¹¹⁶ While an exact identification does not seem possible, the phraseology of the fragment may be compared with 1QHᵃ 25.15.

¹¹⁷ Frg. 26 preserves portions of the right-hand and bottom margins of a column. It strongly resembles the material features of frg. 27, yet a join does not seem possible.

¹¹⁸ On this phrase, see 1QHᵃ 24.11: מלאכי שמֿ[ים.

¹¹⁹ An uninscribed space seems to suggest that the word עד represents the last word of a psalm; cf. לעולמי עד in 1QHᵃ 4.40, 9.20, 15.34, 19.28, 5.30, 5.18.

4   […]ʾ *br*°[…]

Frg. 23

1   […]°*rw* not *y*[…]

2   […]*dw* with[25] *l*[…]

3   […]*l*[…]

Frg. 24

1   [da]rkness *lhy*°[…]

2   […] they will be joyful […]

Frg. 25

1   […] ʾ*p*°[…]

2   […]*mr* confined […]

3   […] and deed[s of …]

Frg. 26

1   […] it will app[ear …]

2   [it app]eared *lh*[...]

3   the angels of peace, and *ty*°[…]

4   everlasting. (VACAT) [...]

[25] Or "people."

Frg. 27

1   ]°°°

2   [לוא

3   ]°[

Frg. 28

1   ]°[]°[

2   כ]יֹא בזות רֹ[איתי[120]

3   [בֹֹ[

Frg. 29

1   [וֹעֹמֹ][121]

2   [לֹ[

Frg. 30

1   ]°°[

2   [לֹחֹ[122]

3   [לֹ[

Frg. 31

1   [לאֹוֹ][123]

---

[120] Ctr. DJD:]°א בזות °[. Cf. 1QHᵃ 21.4 ראיתי זות.
[121] Ctr. DJD: [וֹעֹמֹ[.
[122] Ctr. DJD:]לֹ °[.
[123] Ctr. DJD:]°א לֹא[.

Frg. 27

1   °°°[…]

2   not […]

3   […]°[…]

Frg. 28

1   […]°[…]°[…]

2   […be]cause in this [I] s[aw…][26]

3   [...]*b*[...]

Frg. 29

1   […] and with […]

2   […]*l*[…]

Frg. 30

1   […]°°[…]

2   […] *lḥ*[…]

3   […]*l*[…]

Frg. 31

1   […] *lʿw*[…]

---

[26] Cf. 1QHᵃ 21.4: "[…h]o[w] may I recognize [un]less I saw it."

Frg. 32

1 [בֿו בֿ]

Frg. 33

1 [ ]ֿ[

2 [ם בֿא] ם

Frg. 34

1 [מליכה]124

2 [ל]

Frg. 35

1 [שֿ כיא]

2 [אֿת]

Frg. 36

1 [ ]ֿהֿתיסר[

Frg. 37

1 [אֿנֿ]125

Frg. 38

1 [בֿתוֿכ]י

---

124 See Prov 23:9: לשכל מליך, "the insight of your words." Or perhaps מלוכה, "kinship." See 1QM 6.6 and similar texts.
125 Perhaps: אֿנֿ[ן.

Frg. 32

1   [...]*bw b*[...]

Frg. 33

1   [...]°[...]

2   [...]*m bʾ*[...]

Frg. 34

1   [...] your words[27] [...]

2   [...]*l*[...]

Frg. 35

1   [...]*š* because [...]

2   [...]ʾ*t*[...]

Frg. 36

1   [...] he was instructed[28] °[...]

Frg. 37

1   [...]ʾ*n* °[29][...]

Frg. 38

1   [...] in the midst [of [30]...]

---

[27] See Prov 23:9: "the insight of your words." Or "kinship"; see 1QM 6.6.

[28] The form התיסר, from יסר, does not appear in biblical Hebrew. See 1QS 3.6: התיסר ביחד, "he cannot be instructed within the Community."

[29] Perhaps "I."

[30] For בתוך see 1QHᵃ 7.19, 13.8, 14.14, 15.7, 19.9, 20.6 and 20.16.

Frg. 39

1   [כיא]֯‎126

Frg. 40

1   [֯ ל]

Frg. 41

1   [ים]

Frg. 42

1   [ביצ]ר‎127

Frg. 43

1   [קד֯]

*Frg. 44*128

1   [ח֯ד֯

2   [

3   [ת

Frg. 45

1   [מיצר]

---

126 Ctr. DJD: [כיא֯. The third consonant does not look like an *aleph*.
127 Ctr. DJD: [ב֯ו֯ב̇. The first *beth* seems clear. The right of the *ṣade* is evident. ביצר עפר appears frequently in 1QHᵃ and in 4Q428 frg. 13 line 8.
128 Frg. 44 seems to preserve portions of the left-hand margin of a column and the beginning of another sheet of leather.

Frg. 39

1   […] because […]

Frg. 40

1   […]° *l*[…]

Frg. 41

1   […]*ym*[…]

Frg. 42

1   […] in the creatu[re of[31] …]

Frg. 43

1   […]*qd*[…]

Frg. 44

1   […]*ḥd*

2   […]

3   […]*t*

Frg. 45

1   […] from the creature of[32] […]

---

[31] Or "in the inclinat[ion of …]."
[32] Or "from the inclination of."

2   [גֿליתה א]וזני[129](#)

Frg. 46

1   [בכולֿ]

Frg. 47

1   [דֿ בֿ]

2   [ֿ]

Frg. 48

1   [ֿ באֿֿ [דב]רכה וֿֿ [130](#)

2   [ה כיא]

3   [יֿה ולֿ]

Frg. 49[131](#)

1   וֿ]

2   בהֿ]

Frg. 50

1   [דיֿ]

---

[129](#) The restored phrase is familiar in the *Hodayot*, yet מיצר cannot be identified in the comparable passages where the phrase is used; 1QHᵃ 9.23, 14.7, 22.26, 25.12.

[130](#) Ctr. DJD:] ֿבאֿ ֿ[. The Hebrew word דברכה appears frequently in 1QHᵃ, see especially 12.18, 12.36, 20.27, and 25.16.

[131](#) The legible remains seem to preserve a right-hand margin.

2   […] you opened [my] e[ars …]

Frg. 46

1   […] in all […]

Frg. 47

1   […]*d b*°[…]

2   […]°[…]

Frg. 48

1   […]° *b*'°° your [wor]d and °°

2   […]*h* because […]

3   […]*yh* and *l*[…]

Frg. 49

1   and °[…]

2   *bh*°[…]

Frg. 50

1   […]*dy*° […]

Frg. 51[132]

1 [בכוח]בְּכוח[133]

Frg. 52

1 כי לא[יבו]אָ זר[134]

2 ללוא [יש]וֹ[ברו]ישׁוֹ[135]

Frg. 53[136]

1 [תה°ׁ

2 [אבדהׁ

3 [חׁהׁ

Frg. 54

1 [השׁׁ

Frg. 55[137]

1 [היאׁ]

Frg. 56

1 [כי אמ]רו כׁיׁ[138]

2 [°°°]

---

[132] Frgs. 51–52 bear material resemblances that are also shared with frgs. 8 and 12.

[133] Ctr. DJD: בְּכיהׁ[. For בכוח, see 1QHᵃ 5.15, 12.33, 15.20, 17.17, 18.12, 20.38, 23.9, 26.34. Also see 4Q427 frg. 7 2.15: בכוח גבורתכה.

[134] Ctr. DJD: אָ ידׁ[. See 1QHᵃ 14.30: כי לא יבוא זר.

[135] Ctr. DJD: [°°°. See 1QHᵃ 14.31: ללוא ישוברו.

[136] Frg. 53 preserves the remains of a left-hand margin.

[137] Frg. 55 seems to preserve the bottom margin of a column. Frgs. 55–56 bear material resemblance to frg. 6. If, indeed, frgs. 55–56 derived from the same original column as frg. 6 (col. 30), then one might identify their content with the text of 1QHᵃ 12.18–19. One problem with this possible reconstruction is that the preserved remains of frgs. 6, 55–56 in 4Q428 would require a text significantly longer than the comparable passage of 1QHᵃ 12. For this reason, the possibility remains conjectural.

[138] Ctr. DJD: אמ °°[. DJD missed line 2 and 3. Cf. 1QHᵃ 12.18: כי אמרו.

Frg. 51

1   […] in the power of […]

Frg. 52

1   […] for no stranger [will ent]er[33] […]

2   [… (that) cannot] be brok[en …]

Frg. 53

1   […]°*th*

2   […] it perished

3   […]*ḥh*

Frg. 54

1   […]*ḥš*[…]

Frg. 55

1   […] it[34] […]

Frg. 56

1   […]*ky* [they] sai[d …]

2   […]°°°[…]

[33] See 1QH[a] 14.30: "for no stranger will enter."
[34] Or "she."

3   [‏‏י֯‎֯]

Frg. 57

1   [‏כֹה֯‎]

2   [‏ומ֯‎ ֯]

Frg. 58

1   [‏ל֯‎]‏‎[139] ֯ל

Frg. 59

1   [‏ו֯‎]

2   [‏ממכֹה֯‎]‏[140]

Frg. 60[141]

1   [֯]

2   [‏בֹח֯‎]

3   [‏א֯‎]

Frg. 61

1   [‏כֹ‎]‏[142]

Frg. 62

1   ‏פן י[‏ורה֯‎] גבור

---

[139] The *lamedh* is problematic.
[140] Cf. the only extant attestation of ‏ממכה in 1QHᵃ 20.26.
[141] Frgs. 60–67 bear only a tentative relationship to the other fragments of 4Q428.
[142] The *kaph* could be a *mem* or simply a *kaph* followed by a *ṣade*.

3   […]°y[…]

Frg. 57

1   […]ykh[…]

2   […]° and m°[…]

Frg. 58

1   […]l °[…]

Frg. 59

1   […]n[…]

2   […] from you […]

Frg. 60

1   […]°[…]

2   […] bḥ°[…]

3   […]ʾ°[…]

Frg. 61

1   […]k[…]

Frg. 62

1   [… lest a mighty man should] shoot […]

Frg. 63

1   ]° °[143]

2   [שׁ°ו]ן[144]

Frg. 64

1   [טׁוב]145]

Frgs. 65–68[146]

Frg. 69[147]

1   [בׁן]

2   [ר ונהיוׁ]ת עולם[148]

3   [אׁ בׁ°°]

4   [°]

---

[143] Ctr. DJD:]°°[.
[144] Ctr. DJD:]°שׁ[.
[145] This image is not in the *DSSEL*. It is in DJD 29, Pl. 11.
[146] Frgs. 65–68 preserve no legible remains, only the trace of an indiscernible consonant on each fragment.
[147] The right portion is washed out. See DJD 29, Pl. 11 and the *DSSEL*. It is conceivable that frg. 69 reflects the same content found in 1QH^a 21.11–15 and 4Q427 frg. 10 lines 2–4. Yet this identification remains problematic. If such an identification were possible, frg. 69 would then have to derive from the middle portions of 4Q428 frg. 13, whose line length is sufficiently shorter to preclude certainty. Therefore, it seems that frg. 69 either provides a separate manuscript witness to the same hymn found in 1QH^a 21.11–15 and 4Q427 frg. 10 lines 2–4, or it presents the remains of an otherwise unidentified wisdom or hymnic writing. In DJD 19, it was reported that frg. 69 was "lost already in the 1960s."
[148] See 1QH^a 5.29 and 1QH^a 21.13: נהיות עולם.

Frg. 63

1   […]° °[…]

2   […]*šw*[…]

Frg. 64

1   […] good […]

Frgs. 65–68[35]

Frg. 69

1   […]*bn* […]

2   […]*r* and [things] that are [of eternity ….]³⁶

3   […]°̕ *b*°° […]

4   […]° […]

---

³⁵ No discernible consonant appears.
³⁶ See 1QH^a 5.29: "and to r[aise u]p things that are of eternity." Also see 1QH^a 21.13: "That which will be for eternity…."

Thanksgiving Hymns (*Hodayot*)
4Q429 (4QHᶜ)

JAMES H. CHARLESWORTH and CASEY D. ELLEDGE

Introduction

Fragments 1–4 of 4Q429 preserve portions of the "Teacher Hymns" found in 1QHᵃ columns 13–14. Fragments 5–6 indicate no certain relationship to the other fragments within this manuscript or to portions preserved in other manuscripts of the *Thanksgiving Hymns*.

1. Script and Date

The semiformal hand of 4Q429 represents the transitional phase between the "late Hasmonean–early Herodian period."[1] The scribe's practices are cautious and uniform, insofar as can be determined by the remains of fragments 1–4. Corrective practices are not apparent; the scribe does not separate individual units with uninscribed spaces in the preserved fragments.

2. Contents

The small height of approximately ten centimeters for 4Q429 virtually precludes the possibility that it originally contained a full collection of the hymns found in 1QHᵃ. Instead, it is more plausible that fragments 1–4 are a collection of "Teacher Hymns" (1QHᵃ cols. 10–17), perhaps prefaced by the "Creation Psalm" of 1QHᵃ 9.1–10.4. The sequence of the hymns found in 4Q429 preserves the same order of 1QHᵃ, even if the remains offer only a very limited vantage for comparison. If indeed 4Q429 contained a collection mainly composed of "Teacher Hymns," it would provide yet another instance of a *Hodayot* witness whose contents were more limited in comparison with 1QHᵃ. É. Puech, on the other hand, is more cautious regarding the question of whether 4Q429 contained only the "Teacher Hymns."[2]

3. Selected Bibliography

Puech, É. "Hodayot." In *EncyDSS*, edited by L. Schiffman and J. VanderKam. 2 vols. Oxford, 2000, vol. 1, pp. 365–69.

Schuller, E. M. "429. 4QHodayotᶜ." In *Qumran Cave 4.XX: Poetical and Liturgical Texts, Part 2*, edited by E. Chazon, *et al.*, in consultation with J. VanderKam and M. Brady. DJD 29; Oxford, 1999, pp. 177–194, Pls. 11–12.

Schuller, E. M. "Recent Scholarship on the *Hodayot* 1993–2010." *CBR* 10 (2011) 119–62.

---

[1] E. M. Schuller, DJD 29, p. 180.

[2] É. Puech, "Hodayot," in *EncyDSS*, edited by L. Schiffman and J. VanderKam, 2 vols., (Oxford, 2000) vol. 1, pp. 365–69.

Thanksgiving Hymns (*Hodayot*)
4Q429 (4QH^c)

Frg. 1 Col. 1 (Col. 1)¹
Parallels: 1QH^a 13.9–11 (= Sukenik 5.7–9)

ושותי דם גב]וֹרים ותשימני במגורי²	**1**
ע[ל] פני] מים וצידים³	**2**
א]מת אמצתה⁴	**3**
]	**4**
]	**5**
]	**6**
]	**7**
]	**8**
]	**9**
]	**10**
]	**11**
]	**12**
]	**13**

Frg. 1⁵ Col. 2 (Col. 2)
Parallels: 1QH^a 13.17–21 (= Sukenik 5.15–19)

בֹי]⁶	**1**

---

¹ Frg. 1 preserves the upper and left–hand margins of col. 1.
² 1QH^a 13.9–10: ושותי דֹם גבורים ותשמנֹי במגור.
³ 1QH^a 13.10: על פני מים וצידים.
⁴ 1QH^a 13.11: אמת אמצתה.
⁵ Frg. 1 preserves the upper and right–hand margins of col. 2.
⁶ In 1QH^a 13.17 בי is a supralinear correction.

Thanksgiving Hymns (*Hodayot*)
4Q429 (4QHᶜ)

Frg. 1 Col. 1 (Col. 1)[1]
Parallels: 1QHᵃ 13.9–11 (= Sukenik 5.7–9)

1   [… and drinkers of blood of mi]ghty ones. And you placed me in a dwelling

2   [… ov]er [the faces of] the water, and (with) those who hunt

3   [… t]ruth you encouraged

4   […]

5   […]

6   […]

7   […]

8   […]

9   […]

10   […]

11   […]

12   […]

13   […]

Frg. 1 Col. 2 (Col. 2)
Parallels: 1QHᵃ 13.17–21 (= Sukenik 5.15–19)

1   in me[2] […]

---

[1] See the Hebrew text for parallels.
[2] Note that בי is a supralinear correction in 1QHᵃ 13.17.

2   במצרף כֹּ[זהב[^7]   בכור]

3   נופחים לטוֹהֹר] שבעתים וימהרו עלי רשעי[^8]

4   עמים במצוקותיהמה[^9]   ואתה]

5   [א]לֹי ת]שב סעֹרֹה ל]דממה[^10]

6   וכט]רֹ]ף[^11]

7   ]

8   ]

9   ]

10   ]

11   ]

12   ]

Frg. 2[^12] (Col. 3)
Parallels: 1QH[a] 13.28–30 (= Sukenik 5.26–28)

1   ]

2   ]

3   ]

4   ]

5   ]

6   ]

7   [מעי]וֹ] בינה ו]סֹ]וד אמת[^13]

[^7]: 1QH[a] 13.18: במצֹר]ף] כֹזֹהֹב.

[^8]: The scribe seems to have penned לטוהר. 1QH[a] 13.18–19: נופחים לתהֹר שבעתים וימהרו עלי רשעי.

[^9]: 1QH[a] 13.19: עמֹים במצוקותם.

[^10]: 1QH[a] 13.20: אלי תשיב נֹפֹשֹׁי סערה לדממה.

[^11]: The reading is speculative. 1QH[a] 13.20: וֹכֹטרף.

[^12]: Frg. 2 preserves portions of the right and bottom margins of col. 3. The bottom margin is clear.

[^13]: 1QH[a] 13.28: מעין בינה וסוד אמת.

2   to the smelting-pot like [(fine) gold … in a furnace of]

3   the smiths, purifying [sevenfold. But they hasten against me, the wicked of]

4   the peoples with their oppressions [.… But you,]

5   [O my G]od, [t]urn a thunder storm[3] into [silence …]

6   [… and like p]re[y …]

7   […]

8   […]

9   […]

10   […]

11   […]

12   […]

Frg. 2 (Col. 3)
Parallels: 1QH[a] 13.28–30 (= Sukenik 5.26–28)

1   […]

2   […]

3   […]

4   […]

5   […]

6   […]

7   [… the founta]in of [discernment and] the se[cret of truth …]

---

[3] Lit. "storm."

8   יחשבו ודברי ב[ליעל[14]

9   כחמת תנינים פורחת לק̇צ̇ים ו̇כ̇[זוחלי[15]

10   עפר יורו לחתוף מבלגות פתנים לאין̇[16]

11   [חב]ר̇ ותהי לכאוב אנוש ונגע נמאר[17]

12   [בתכמי]עבדכה להכשיל רוח ולהתם[18]

Frg. 3[19] (Col. 4)
Parallels: 1QH^a 13.31–41 (= Sukenik 5.29–38 + Frg. 29 lines 1–4)
4Q432 Frg. 11 lines 1–2

1   [כוח ל]ב̇לתי החזק מ̇[עמד[20]

2   [ממשפחו]ת ויהמו בכנור ריב̇י̇[21]

3   [זל]ע̇ו̇פ̇ות אחזוני וחבלים [כצי]ר̇י[22] [

4   [ו]ל̇ש̇ו̇נ̇י לחכי דבקה[23] כי סבבוני בה̇[וות[24] לבם

5   [ויחשך]מאור פני לאפלה והוד̇י̇[25]

6   [פ]ת̇חתה בלבבי ויוספוהו לצו̇[קה[26]

7   [ב]ל̇חם אנחה ושקוי בדמעות̇[27]

8   [במרו]ר̇י יום אנחה ויגון י̇[סובבוני[28]

9   ו[שק]ו̇י̇ לבעל מ̇[דנים[29]

---

[14] 1QH^a 13.28: יחשובו̇ [ודברי ב]ליעל.
[15] 1QH^a 13.29: כחמת תנינים פורחת לקצים וכזוחל/י\.
[16] 1QH^a 13.29–30: עפר יורו לחתו̇[ף מבלגות] פתנים לאין.
[17] 1QH^a 13.30: חבר ותהי לכאיב אנוש ונגע נמאר.
[18] 1QH^a 13.30: בתכמי עבדכה להכשי̇ל [רו]ח̇ ולהתם.
[19] Frg. 3 preserves the bottom margin of col. 4.
[20] 1QH^a 13.31: כוח לבלתי החזק מעמד.
[21] 1QH^a 13.31–32: ממ[[ש̇ף̇חות ויהמ̇ו בכנור ריבי.
[22] 1QH^a 13.32: זלעופות [[א̇חזוני [וחבלים כצירי.
[23] Cf. 1QH^a 13.33: ולשוני לחך תדבק.
[24] 1QH^a 13.33: ולשוני לחך תדבק כ̇[[סבבו̇נ̇י]] בהוות.
[25] 1QH^a 13.34: מאור פני לאפלה והודי.
[26] 1QH^a 13.35: פתחתה בלבבי ויוספה לצוקה.
[27] 1QH^a 13.35–36: אנח]ת̇י וש̇[קוי. 4Q432 frg. 11 line 1:]בל̇חם אנחתי ושקוי בדמעות.
[28] 1QH^a 13.36–37: במרו]ר̇י]ום. 4Q432 frg. 11 line 2: במרורי יום א̇נחה ויגון י̇ סובבוני.
[29] 1QH^a 13.37: ושקוי לבעל מדנים.

8   they think [….] And the words of B[elial …]

9   like the venom of dragons, shooting forth to their boarders. And like [the reptiles of]

10   dust they spit to lay hold of the poison of cobras that cannot

11   [be char]med.[4] And it becomes a severe pain of humankind and a festering affliction

12   [in the entrails of][5] your servant, making the spirit fail, and annihilating

Frg. 3 (Col. 4)
Parallels: 1QH[a] 13.31–41 (= Sukenik 5.29–38 + Frg. 29 lines 1–4)
4Q432 Frg. 11 lines 1–2

1   [power so as] not to st[and] firm […]

2   [among the part]s. And they sounded forth my dispute on the lyre […]

3   [ra]ging they seized me, and tribulations [like pai]ns of […]

4   [and] my tongue cleaves to my palate, since I am surrounded by the des[ires of their heart …]

5   [and] the light of my face [is darkened] into gloominess, and my majesty […]

6   you [op]ened in my heart. And they added dist[ress] to it […]

7   [with] the bread of sighing,[6] and (with) the drink of tears […]

8   [by the bitter]ness of the day. Sighing[7] and grief s[urround me[8] …]

9   [… and] dr[in]k into an owner of con[frontations,[9] …]

---

[4] For the charming of serpents, see Ps 58:6.
[5] Lit. "[in the midst of]."
[6] Ctr. 1QH[a] 13.35: "my sighing."
[7] Ctr. 1QH[a] 13.36: "my sighing."
[8] Or "will surround me."
[9] The author refers to one who confronts him.

10   כרזי פש[ע]עֹ[30] משֹׁנֹיֹם][31]

11   [לֹאין נ]תֹק וזקים ללוֹ[32] [ישוברו

12   לאין]וֹ[33] פתוח]

Frg. 4 Col. 1[34] (Col. 7)
Parallels: 1QH^a 14.19–25

1   ]

2   לאין חק]רֹ[35]

3   ]

4   למק]וֹר עולם לֹ[אין][36]

5   כל] בֹנֹיֹ[37] עֹולֹ[ה והיה]

6   ]

7   ]

8   ואתה אל [צֹ[ו]יֹתם] להועיל מדר[כֹיֹהֹ[מֹ]הֹ[38]

9   אשר י]לכוֹ] בה ו[עֹרל וטמֹ]א[39] ופריץ][40]

10   ] ויתמוטטו] מֹדרך לבכהֹ] ובהוות][41]

11   [פשעם יכש]לו וכמו[42] יועֹץ] בליע]לֹ עם לבבֹ[ם][43]

12   מחשבת [רשעה וית[גול]לֹ[ו] באשמתם[44]

---

[30] The reading is speculation.
[31] This reading is speculative. 1QH^a 13.38: פשע משנים.
[32] 1QH^a 13.39: נתק וזקים ללוא.
[33] 1QH^a 13.40: לאין.
[34] Frg. 4 preserves the bottom margin of col. 1, as well as the left–hand margin of lines 2, 8, and 12.
[35] The spot of ink for the *reš* is on the leather for frg. 4 col. 2. 1QH^a 14.20: חקר.
[36] 1QH^a 14.20–21: למקור עולם לאין.
[37] 1QH^a 14.21: בנ]י. Ctr. DJD: כל ב]ני.
[38] 1QH^a 14.23: צויתם להועיל מדרכיהם.
[39] 1QH^a 14.23: וערל וטמא.
[40] Restored from 1QH^a 14.23.
[41] 1QH^a 14.24: ויתמוטטו מדרך לבכה ובהוות.
[42] Cf. 1QH^a 14.24: וכמוא.
[43] 1QH^a 14.24–25: יכשל]י וכמוא יועץ בליעל עם לבבם.
[44] Ctr. 1QH^a 14.25: רשעה יתגוללו באשמה.

10   [… as the mysteries of transgress]ion are altering […]

11   [(that) cannot be c]ut off, and (with) chains (that) cannot [be broken[10] …]

12   [… (which) cann]ot be opened […]

Frg. 4 Col. 1 (Col. 7)
Parallels: 1QH[a] 14.19–25

1   […]

2   [… without lim]it

3   […]

4   [… to an] eternal [sou]rce (which) ca[nnot]

5   [… all] the sons of decei[t, and they are]

6   […]

7   […]

8   [.… But you, O God,] or[de]red them [to benefit from] th[ei]r [wa]ys

9   [… in which] they [wa]lk, [but] the uncircumcised and the impu[re and the brigand][11]

10   [.…] And th[ey] have fallen away from the way of your heart, [and in the disasters of]

11   [their transgression][12] they [stumb]le, and (be) like the counselor of [Belia]l with [their] heart.

12   […] wicked [thought]. And th[ey] will [wall]ow constantly in their guilt.[13]

---

[10] The author may refer to being chained.
[11] See 1QH[a] 14.23.
[12] See 1QH[a] 14.24.
[13] Cf. 1QH[a] 14.25: "they will wallow constantly in guilt."

Frg. 4 Col. 2[45] (Col. 8)
Parallels: 1QHᵃ 14.25–31 (= Sukenik 6.22–29)

1 וֹ[אני[46] הייתי

2 וכל מֹ[שבריהם[47]

3 להשיבֹ[ן נפש[48]

4 ויהם תֹ[הום[49]

5 וֹא[היה[50]

6]

7 סודי[51]]

8 ומשקֹלֹת[52]]

9 לבֹ[ני]תֹ עוז ללוֹ[53]]

10 ימוטו כי לֹ[וא[54]

11 [מבוא] ובֹרֹ[י]חֹ עֹוֹז[ללוא ישוברו בל יבוא גדוד][55]

12 בכֹלי מֹ[לֹ]חֹמתו עד תום כל חֹ[צי[56] מלחמות רשעה]

Frg. 5[57]

1 [וֹ]רֹ אין[

2 [עֹלֹ]ֹ

---

[45] Frg. 4 preserves the upper, lower, and right-hand margins of col. 2.
[46] 1QHᵃ 14.25: וֹ[אני היי]תי.
[47] 1QHᵃ 14.26: וכול משבריהם.
[48] 1QHᵃ 14.26: להשיב נפש.
[49] 1QHᵃ 14.27: ויהם תהום.
[50] 1QHᵃ 14.27: ואהיה.
[51] Ctr. 1QHᵃ 14.29: סוד. The first word of this line in 4Q429 is followed by an unusually long uninscribed space. Lines 7–9 also seem to have been at least two words shorter than the corresponding passage in 1QHᵃ.
[52] 1QHᵃ 14.29: ומשקלת.
[53] An error. See 1QHᵃ 14.29–30: לבֹ[נית] עוז ללוא.
[54] 1QHᵃ 14.30: ימוטו כי לא.
[55] 1QHᵃ 14.31: ובריחי עוז ללוא ישוברו בל יבוא גדוד.
[56] 1QHᵃ 14.31–32: בכלי מלחמתו עם תום כול חצי מלחמות רשעה.
[57] The identification of frg. 5 with 4Q429 is uncertain.

Frg. 4 Col. 2 (Col. 8)
Parallels: 1QH[a] 14.25–31 (= Sukenik 6.22–29)

1   And [I , I was …]

2   And all [their] br[eakers …]

3   to restore [the soul …]

4   And the de[pth] roars [….]

5   And I [am …]

6   […]

7   my foundation[14] […]

8   and the weight […]

9   for a strong bui[ldi]ng (that) will not […]

10   they will (not) totter, for n[o …]

11   [an entrance,] and strong gate-[bo]lts [(that) cannot be broken lest a troop should enter]

12   by means of its weapons of w[a]r, until[15] exhausting of all the ar[rows[16] of the wars of wickedness][17]

Frg. 5

1   […]*yr* there is no […]

2   […]° *l* °[…]

---

[14] Ctr. 1QH[a] 14.29: "foundation."
[15] Ctr. 1QH[a] 14.31: "with."
[16] I.e., until the quiver is empty.
[17] As Licht (p. 117) pointed out, the Qumranites imagined the *Yaḥad* was a strong edifice bolted from those presently winning "the wars of wickedness" until the Endtime of God's judgment.

Frg. 6[58]

[הֹודֹו] [	**1**
̊ [ליֹהֹוה]	**2**
[ה וֹיש] ̊	**3**
[59] ̊וֹ[	**4**

---

[58] The identification of frg. 6 with 4Q429 is based upon its appearance in PAM 42.836 and 43.531. Its association is otherwise uncertain; and if, indeed, line 2 preserves the letters of the *Tetragrammaton*, it would seem not to have been a fragment of the *Hodayot* at all.

[59] Ctr. DJD:] ̊ן̊[.

Frg. 6

1   […] give thanks […]

2   […]° to the LORD[18] […]

3   […]°*h* and *yš*[…]

4   […]*wy* […]

[18] Hebrew: יהוה.

Thanksgiving Hymns (*Hodayot*)
4Q430 (4QHᵈ)

JAMES H. CHARLESWORTH and CASEY D. ELLEDGE

Introduction

Within a larger grouping of nonbiblical, Herodian rustic semi-formal fragments assorted by J. Strugnell was a single fragment whose content overlapped with 1QHᵃ 12.14–20.

1. Script and Date

The hand of 4Q430 places it early in the Herodian era.[1] It is very similar in character to 4Q431.

2. Contents

Because of its hand and content, 4Q430 might possibly be considered as part of the same manuscript found in 4Q431. Indeed, it is unusual to find the remains of only a single *Hodayot* fragment. Since 1QHᵃ attests two different scribal hands at work in copying the manuscript, one might consider the possibility that 4Q430 represents the work of one copyist, while 4Q431 preserves another section of the same scroll penned by a different scribe. In spite of such conjecture, however, there is no direct evidence to confirm this possibility. Instead, these two groups of fragments may simply represent two separate witnesses to the *Hodayot*.

Since 4Q430 preserves a selection from among the "Teacher Hymns," one might consider the possibility that the original scroll may have contained only this collection or possibly even a select number of "Teacher Hymns."[2] This possibility, however, remains impossible to confirm, given the limited remains.

3. Selected Bibliography

Schuller, E. M. "430. 4QHodayotᵈ." In *Qumran Cave 4.XX: Poetical and Liturgical Texts, Part 2*, edited by E. Chazon, *et al.* in consultation with J. VanderKam and M. Brady. DJD 29; Oxford, 1999, pp. 195–98, Pl. 12.

Schuller, E. M. "Recent Scholarship on the *Hodayot* 1993–2010." *CBR* 10 (2011) 119–62.

---

[1] See also E. M. Schuller, DJD 29, p. 196.

[2] Note the reflections by E. M. Schuller, "Recent Scholarship on the *Hodayot*," p. 130.

Thanksgiving Hymns (*Hodayot*)
4Q430 (4QHᵈ)

Frg. 1
Parallels: 1QHᵃ 12.15–20 (= Sukenik 4.13–19 + frg. 43)

יחשו[בו] ו[י]ׄדׄר[שוכה]	**1**
רו[ש] ולעׄנׄה [ב]מׄחשׄבׄ[ו]תׄׄמׄ[	**2**
]ומכשול עוונם שמׄו לׄ[נׄ]גׄד פניׄ[הם]	**3**
מפי נביאי] כזב מפותי תעות והם בל[ועג שפה	**4**
כו[ל] מעׄשׄיהם כי[	**5**
כׄ[יׄ]⁶ אמׄר[ו ל]חׄזׄוׄן דעׄתׄ]	**6**
] תעׄנׄה בׄ[ה]מׄ[	**7**

---

¹ 1QHᵃ 12.15: יחשובו וידרשוכה.
² 1QHᵃ 12.15: רוש ולענה במחשבותם.
³ 1QHᵃ 12.16: ומכשול עוונם שמו לנגד פניהם.
⁴ 1QHᵃ 12.17: כזב מפותי תעות והם בל[ו]עׄג שפה.
⁵ 1QHᵃ 12.18: כול מעשיהם כי.
⁶ Ctr. DJD: כׄיׄ[.
⁷ 1QHᵃ 12.18–19: כי אמרו לחזון דעת.
⁸ 1QHᵃ 12.19: תענה להם.

Thanksgiving Hymns (*Hodayot*)
4Q430 (4QH^d)

Frg. 1
Parallels: 1QH^a 12.15–20 [= Sukenik 4.13–19 + frg. 43]

1   […] they [thin]k. [And they] see[k you …]

2   [… pois]on and bitterness (is) [in] their though[t]s […]

3   […]. And the obstacle of their iniquity they put be[f]ore [their] faces

4   [… through the mouth of] lying [prophets] tempted (by) error. And they with a stam[mering lip …]

5   [… al]l their works because […]

6   [… f]or [they] say [concerning] the vision of knowledge […]

7   […] you shall answer t[h]em […]

Thanksgiving Hymns (*Hodayot*)
4Q431 (4QH[e])

JAMES H. CHARLESWORTH and CASEY D. ELLEDGE

Introduction

4Q431 offers the remains of two fragments. Fragment 1 had previously been classified among Cave IV fragments of the *War Scroll* (4Q171), yet was determined to represent a different composition under the designation 4Q471b. On the basis of content and select material features, it was then added to 4Q431.

Fragment 1 contains a witness to the "Self-Glorification Hymn" (*olim* "Prayer of Michael"), versions of which also appear in 1QH[a] 26.6–10 (frg. 56 2.1–5, frg. 46 2.1), 4Q427 fragment 7 1.6–13, and 4Q491 fragment 11 1.13–19. It is comprised of four smaller fragments (a–d). Fragment "a" preserves the right-hand margin of a column, offering lines 2–9 of the extant remains. Fragment "c" offers the remains of line 1. Fragment "b" preserves portions of lines 2–4, and fragment "d," the remains of line 10.

Fragment 2, then, attests to content that is shared with 1QH[a] 26.20–29 (frg. 7 2.1–4) and 4Q427 fragment 7 2.3–10. It preserves the lower and left-hand margins of a column.

While the scribal and material features of fragments 1 and 2 are not identical, the similarities allow the possibility that they originally belonged to the same manuscript. The spacing of words in fragment 2 is somewhat inconsistent, with occasionally larger spacing (4–5 mm) between particular words and phrases (frg. 2 lines 2 and 4). The differences in skin texture, line ruling, and letter size between the two fragments could be explained as a sewing together of columns from two different sheets, representing two different animal skins.[1] The placement of fragment 1 rests with the sequence of these materials in 1QH[a] and the unusually extended right-hand margin (2.7 cm), before which there are no visible remains from a previous column. One possible interpretation of this feature is that it represents a small handle margin for the larger scroll.[2] If so, then fragment 1, containing portions of the "Self-Glorification Hymn," would represent the first column of the original manuscript.

1. Script and Date

The script of the two fragments of 4Q431 places the manuscript in the early Herodian era; the hand is very similar to that of 4Q430.[3]

2. Contents

Calculations based upon the circumvolutions of 4Q431 indicate an original length of approximately 4.25 meters or 24 more columns after column 2.[4] If, indeed, fragment 1 preserves the first column of the original scroll, several different possibilities emerge for imagining its original contents. It is possible that 4Q431 preserved a selection of the "Community Hymns" that differed in order from the collection found in 1QH[a] (17.38–col. 28) by placing this particular psalm first. If so, perhaps its ordering was more approximate to that of 4Q427, which placed this psalm closer to the beginning of the scroll. However, it is also conceivable that 4Q431 was not an originally complete *Hodayot* collection of any kind, but rather a more diverse collection of materials.

3. Selected Bibliography

Abegg, M.G. "4Q471: A Case of Mistaken Identity?" In *Pursuing the Text: Studies in Honor of B.Z. Wacholder on the Occasion of his Seventieth Birthday*, edited by J. Reeves and J. Kampen. Journal for the Study of the Old Testament Supplement 184; Sheffield, 1994, pp. 136–47.

Eshel, E. "4Q471b: A Self-Glorification Hymn." *RQ* 18 (1996) 175–203.

Eshel, E. "4Q471b: 4QSelf-Glorification Hymn (= 4QH[e] frg. 1?)." In *Qumran Cave 4.XX: Poetical and Liturgical Texts, Part 2*, edited by E. Chazon, *et al.* in consultation with J.

---

[1] E. M. Schuller, DJD 29, p. 201.
[2] Schuller, DJD 29, p. 201.

[3] Schuller, DJD 29, pp. 201–202.
[4] Schuller, DJD 29, p. 201.

VanderKam and M. Brady. DJD 29; Oxford, 1999, pp. 69–254, Pls. 12, 28.

Schuller, E. M. "Hodayot." In *Qumran Cave 4.XX: Poetical and Liturgical Texts, Part 2*, edited by E. Chazon, *et al.* in consultation with J. VanderKam and M. Brady. DJD 29; Oxford, 1999.

Schuller, E. M. "Recent Scholarship on the *Hodayot* 1993–2010." *Currents in Biblical Research* 10 (2011) 119–162.

Wise, M. O. "מי כמוני באלים: A Study of 4Q491c, 4Q471b, 4Q427 7 and 1QH^a 25:35–26:10." *DSD* 7 (2000) 173–219.

Thanksgiving Hymns (*Hodayot*)
4Q431 (4QH^c)

Frg. 1 (Col. 1 lines 12–20)[1]
Parallels: 4Q471b

1   קֹודש ֯]   [נֹבֹזה כמונֹ]י

2   כמוני ֹוחדל [ה]רע ודמה בֹ]י

3   תדמה בהריתי [ו]מֹֹי ישוֹ]ה

4   מֹֹי כמוני בֹאלים לֹ]

5   שפֹתי מי יכיל מֹי]

6   ידיד המלכֹ[2] רעֹ[3] לקֹד]ושים

7   לוא ידמה כֹֹי אֹ]ני

8   בפז כ ֹֹ]

9   יֹ]חשב [זמרו]

Frg. 2 (Col. 2 lines 11–19)
Parallels: 1QH^a 26; 4Q427 frg. 7 2.3–10

1   [ותמה רשעה]

2   [מדה]בה שבת נוגש בזעֹם]

3   [ואין נ]עֹוות בלוא דעת הופיע אור ושמחה תֹבֹֹיעֹ [אבד] אֹבֹל

4   [ונס יגון ה]ופיע שלום[4] שבת פחד נפתח מקור לברכת עד

---

[1] The right margin is extant. The leather is lined horizontally and vertically.
[2] Note the medial *kaph* in final position.
[3] Note the paronomasia with רע in line 2.
[4] 4Q427 frg.7 2.5.

Thanksgiving Hymns (*Hodayot*)
4Q431 (4QH^e)

Frg. 1 (Col. 1 lines 12–20)
Parallels: 4Q471b

1   holiness °[… has been despised] like m[e] […]

2   like me. And [the] evil ceases and it compares to [me …]

3   it is comparable to my teaching[1] [and] who is equa[l …]?

4   who is like me among the Elim? *l*[…]

5   my speech,[2] who can measure (it)[3]? Who […]

6   the beloved of the king, a companion of the Ho[ly Ones …]

7   he does not compare, for I [(am) …]

8   with pure gold *k*°°[…]

9   he is [considered …] they sing […]

Frg. 2 (Col. 2 lines 11–19)
Parallels: 1QH^a 26; 4Q427 frg. 7 2.3–10

1   […] and wickedness is annihilated […]

2   [disas]ter, the oppressor ceased with fury.[4] […]

3   [and there are no pe]rversions without knowledge. Light shines forth;[5] and joy pours forth.[6] Mourning

4   [and the standard of grief perished]. Peace [sh]ines forth,[7] fear ceased. A source was opened for eternal blessing,

---

[1] Or "with my teaching."
[2] Lit. "my lips."
[3] Lit. "Who is able?"
[4] See 1QH^a 13.3: "to the day of wrathful [fu]ry."
[5] The *hip'il* perfect perhaps signifies God's actions. God causes light to shine forth.
[6] *Hip'il* imperfect.
[7] Again, the *hip'il* perfect.

5   בכו]לֹ [קצי]⁵ עולם כלה עוון שבת נגע לאין מחלה נאספֿ[ה

6   ת]הֿיה עוד השמיעו אמורו גדול אל עושה

7   גבהות]רום⁶ לאין שרית וירם מעפר אביון

8   ועד ש]חֿקים יגביה בקומה ועם אלים בעדת

9   [יחד   לֹ]כ[לֹ]וֹ]ת עולם וכושלי ארץ

---

⁵ 4Q427 frg. 7 2.6.
⁶ A mistake for רוח. Restored from 4Q427 frg. 7 2.8.

5   [… for al]l everlasting [times]. Iniquity ended, affliction ceased, so there is no sickness. Taken away was

6   [… wi]ll be [no] more.[8] Cause to be heard[9] and say: Great (is) God who acts

7   [… the pompous] spirit[10] so there is no remnant. And he raised up[11] the Poor One from the dust

8   [… and unto the skie]s he will elevate (him)[12] on high and with the Elim in the congregation of

9   [the Community[13] …] to eternal an[ni]hi[la]tion. And those who stumble earthward

---

[8] See 4Q427 2.6–7.

[9] The *hipʿil* plural.

[10] See 1QH^a 26.27 and 4Q427 frg. 7 2.8. The scribe miscopied his exemplar, confusing a *mem* for a *ḥet* (the error is also in 1QH^a). See note to the translation of 4Q427.

[11] *Hipʿil* imperfect of רום, "to lift high."

[12] *Hipʿil* imperfect of גבה, "to make high."

[13] Heb. יחד.

Thanksgiving Hymns (*Hodayot*)
4Q432 (4QH^f)

JAMES H. CHARLESWORTH and CASEY D. ELLEDGE

Introduction

In twenty four papyrus fragments, 4Q432 presents an additional witness to portions of the *Hodayot*. While fragments 14–24 present no conclusive intersections with text found elsewhere in the *Hodayot*, fragments 1–13 preserve materials that are also found in 1QH^a columns 9–13, 15–16.

1. Script and Date

4Q432 preserves an early Herodian hand that tends toward more formal characteristics.[1] The scribe utilizes the practice of supralinear correction (frg. 7 line 1); frequently, the spacing between individual words is inconsistent. Fragment 23 appears to have been penned by a different scribe and is unlikely to have preserved a text of the *Hodayot*.

2. Contents

The identifiable fragments of 4Q432 preserve upper margins of a scroll, whose original length is difficult to determine. Given its spacing and line length, 4Q432 would have had to extend some 10 meters in length, if indeed it contained all the materials found in 1QH^a columns 9–28. As this length is considerable, it remains uncertain as to whether 4Q432 did, in fact, contain a full version of these materials. Calculations based upon the turns preserved in the remaining fragments suggest that fragment 1 was originally very close to the beginning of the scroll, with space allowable only for a column and perhaps a handle sheet prior to fragment 1.[2]

Since the text preserved in fragment 1 is very close to the beginning of the original scroll, the collection appears to have begun with the "Creation Psalm" (1QH^a cols. 9–10.4), immediately followed by portions corresponding to the "Teacher Hymns" (1QH^a 10.5–17.36). If so, then the specific contents of the scroll might be compared with those of 4Q429, which may also have preserved a collection of the materials found in 1QH^a columns 9–17. Puech, however, disputes the certainty of this possibility.[3] The ordering of 4Q432 presents the same sequence attested in 1QH^a and 4Q428. Fragments 14–24 do not preserve sufficient remains for a confident identification with materials found elsewhere in the *Hodayot*. Fragment 14 may preserve portions of the same materials found in 1QH^a 15.13–15; and fragment 15 has been compared with the same passage found in 1QH^a 9.24. It remains equally difficult to demonstrate that the remaining fragments preserved any previously unknown psalms.

3. Selected Bibliography

Puech, É. "Hodayot." In *EncyDSS*, edited by L. Schiffman and J. VanderKam. 2 vols. Oxford, 2000, vol. 1, pp. 365–69.
Schuller, E. M. "4QpapHodayot^f." In *Qumran Cave 4.XX: Poetical and Liturgical Texts, Part 2*, edited by E. Chazon, *et al*. in consultation with J. VanderKam and M. Brady. DJD 29; Oxford, 1999, pp. 209–32, Pls. 13–14.
Schuller, E. M. "Recent Scholarship on the *Hodayot* 1993–2010." *CBR* 10 (2011) 119–62.

---

[1] E. M. Schuller, DJD 29, p. 211.
[2] Schuller, "Recent Scholarship on the *Hodayot* 1993–2010," *CBR* 10 (2011) 119–62.

[3] É. Puech, "Hodayot," in *EncyDSS*, edited by L. Schiffman and J. VanderKam, 2 vols. (Oxford, 2000) vol. 1, p. 366.

Thanksgiving Hymns
4Q432 (4QH^f)

Frg. 1 (Col. 2)[1]
Parallels: 1QH^a 9.13–15 (= Sukenik 1.11–13)

1   [לרזיהֿ]ם[2]

2   למ[שֿ]אם[3]

3   [לחפציהֿ]ם[4]

Frg. 2 (Col. 4)
Parallels: 1QH^a 9.35–37 (= Sukenik 1.33–35)

1   א[שֿ]ר הגברתה[5]

2   [דֿעתֿ[6] ונמהֿר[ים][7]

Frg. 3[8] (Col. 5)
Parallels: 1QH^a 10.5–9 (= Sukenik 2.3–7)

1   [אודכה אד]וֿנֿיֿ כֿיֿ[9] ישרתה בלבבי[10] כול][11]

2   ות[שם שומ]רֿי[12] אמת נגד עוני[13] ומוכיחֿי צדק] בכול חמסי[14]

---

[1] The top margin of the papyrus is preserved.

[2] 1QH^a 9.13: לרזיהם. For this expression elsewhere, also see 1QH^a 9.15, 31.

[3] 1QH^a 9.14: למשאם.

[4] 1QH^a 9.15: לחפציה]ם. For this expression elsewhere, also see 1QH^a 5.37. The reading is supported by the parallel text in 1QH^a. The consonant after ṣade seems connected at the top, suggesting a *he*.

[5] 1QH^a 9.36: אשר הגברתה. The left margin seems visible.

[6] The scribe has left a space after this word that is longer than usual.

[7] 1QH^a 9.37: דעת ונמהרים.

[8] Frg. 3 preserves the upper margin of a column. Line 2 seems to present the right-hand margin. Frg. 3 is composed of frgs. 3a, 3b, and 3c. Their association is likely, yet not conclusive.

[9] Ctr. DJD [יֿ]כֿ.

[10] 1QH^a 10.5: בלב]בֿיֿ.

[11] It is possible that this line of 4Q432 preserves a shorter text than the comparable passages in 1QH^a. Perhaps the scribe has omitted words due to homoioarcton with ות]שם at the beginning of line 2.

[12] 1QH^a 10.6: ות[שם שֿ]ומרי.

[13] Probably not עיני, "my eyes," because of the parallelism with the next line.

[14] 1QH^a 10.6: ומוכי]חֿי אֿמֿת /צדק\.

Thanksgiving Hymns (Hodayot)
4Q432 (4QH^f)

Frg. 1 (Col. 2)
Parallels: 1QH^a 9.13–15 (= Sukenik 1.11–13)

1   [… to their] mysteries […]

2   [… according to their ta]s[ks…]

3   […] for th[eir] purposes […]

Frg. 2 (Col. 4)
Parallels: 1QH^a 9.35–37 (= Sukenik 1.33–35)

1   [… t]hat you have strengthened[1]

2   […] knowledge and eager [ones]

Frg. 3 (Col. 5)
Parallels: 1QH^a 10.5–9 (= Sukenik 2.3–7)

1   [I thank you, O L]ord, because you straighten in my heart all [….]

2   And you [placed guard]ians of truth in the presence of my transgressor, and the chastisements of righteousness [(were) with all my violent ones]

---

[1] The left margin is preserved.

3   [לׄמחץ מכתי¹⁵ מנחמי כוׄ]ח

4   [שמחה לאב]לׄ¹⁶ [י]גוני מבשר שלום¹⁷

5   [לׄהׄ]מׄ[ס]ׄ לבבי ומׄ[אמצי¹⁸

Frg. 4 (Col. 6)¹⁹
Parallels: 1QHᵃ 10.19 (= Sukenik 2.16–17)

1   [ ]ויהׄוׄפכו²⁰

Frg. 5 (Col. 9)²¹
Parallels: 1QHᵃ 11.14–19 (= Sukenik 3.13–18)

1   [ויושבי עפ]ר כיוׄ[רדי י]מים נבעתים מהׄמׄון מים וׄחׄ[כמיהם²² למו]

2   [כמלחים במ]צׄולוׄ[ת כי] תתבלע כול חוכמתׄמה בה[מות²³ ימים]

3   [בר]תׄוׄח תהו[מות על נבו]כׄיׄ [מי]ׄסׄ יׄ[ת]ׄרׄגשׄו לרו[ם²⁴ גלים ומשברי]

4   [מים] בהמון קׄוׄל[ם²⁵   שאו]ל[²⁶   וכול הצי]

5   [ש]ׄחׄת עם מצעדמׄ[²⁷   ויפתׄחׄ]וׄ²⁸ שערי]

6   [עו]לׄ[ם תח]ׄת מׄעשׄ[י²⁹ אפעה   ב]ׄעׄד הׄרׄ[ית³⁰ עול]

7   [ובריחי עו]לׄׄם בׄעׄ[ד³¹

---

¹⁵ 1QHᵃ 10.7: לׄמחץ מכׄתׄוׄ].

¹⁶ See 1QHᵃ 10.7: שמחה לאבל יג]וני.

¹⁷ 1QHᵃ 10.7–8: לאבל יג]וני מבשר שׄלׄום].

¹⁸ 1QHᵃ 10.8: למוס לבבי ומאמצי.

¹⁹ Frg. 4 preserves the left-hand margin of a column.

²⁰ 1QHᵃ 10.19: ויהפוכו.

²¹ The top margin of the papryus is preserved. The fragment is separated into eight small fragments.

²² 1QHᵃ 11.14–15: עפר כיורדי ימים נבעתים מהמון מים וחכמיה/ם\.

²³ 1QHᵃ 10.15–16: במצולות כי תתבלע כול חכמתם בהמות.

²⁴ 1QHᵃ 11.16: ברתוח תהומות על נבוכי מים ויתרגׄשו לרום.

²⁵ 1QHᵃ 11.17: בהמון קולם.

²⁶ 1QHᵃ 11.17: שׄ[או]ל[ן.

²⁷ The *mem* is on a small fragment seen in some images. It is evident in DJD 29, Pl. 13. 1QHᵃ 11.17–18: שחת עם מצעדם.

²⁸ 1QHᵃ 11.18: ויפתחו.

²⁹ 1QHᵃ 11.18: תח]ׄת מעשי.

³⁰ 1QHᵃ 11.19: בעד הרית.

³¹ 1QHᵃ 11.19: עולם בעד.

3   […] for the wound of my blow.[2] The powe[rful] comforters […]

4   [joyous for] my [gr]ievous [mourn]ing, announcing peace […]

5   […] for the mel[ti]ng of my heart, and the cou[rageous ones of …]

Frg. 4 (Col. 6)
Parallels: 1QH[a] 10.19 (= Sukenik 2.16–17)

1   [….] And they cast […]

Frg. 5 (Col. 9)
Parallels: 1QH[a] 11.14–19 (= Sukenik 3.13–18)

1   [And the dwellers of the dus]t[3] (are) like [those] who go [down to the s]eas, terrified from the roar of the waters, and [their] wi[se ones for them]

2   [(are) like sailors[4] in the de]pth[s, since] all their wisdom is swallowed up in the rum[blings of the seas,]

3   [when] the dep[ths bo]il [over the sourc]es of [the wa]ter (and)[5] are a[gi]tated to hi[gh waves, and (to) the breakers of]

4   [water] with [their] roaring sound. [… Sheo]l [… and all the arrows of]

5   [the p]it with their movement […] and ope[n the gates of]

6   [et]er[nity, benea]th the work[s[6] of a sand-viper …. be]fore the one pre[gnant (with) deceit,]

7   [and the bars of eter]nity bef[ore …]

---

[2] Ctr. 1QH[a] 10.7: "his blow." It is clear in both versions that the speaker received the blow.
[3] See 1QH[a] 11.14.
[4] See 1QH[a] 11.15.
[5] 1QH[a] 10.16 has the "and."
[6] Or "offspring."

Frg. 6 (Col. 10)[32]
Parallels: 1QH[a] 11.27–32 (= Sukenik 3.26–31); 4Q428 Frg. 5

1   חֹלכאֹם [על] פני מים בהתֹ[עופף כול חצי שחת לאין השב ויורו לאין][33]

2   תֹקוה בנפול קו על משפֹ[ט][34]

3   נֹעלמים וקץ חרון לכולֹ[ן][35]

4   [וי]לֹ[כו נח]לֹֹי [בֹּליעל על כֹּוֹ]לֹ[36] אגפי רום בא[ש אוכלת בֹ[כול][37]

5   להתֹם[38] כול עץ לֹ[ֹ]ח[39]   ותשוֹ[ט בשֹ[ביבי[40] להוב עד אפס[

6   כֹולֹ[ן] שותיהם באוֹ[שֹי[41] [חמר

Frg. 7 (Col. 11)[42]
Parallels: 1QH[a] 11.40–12.2; 4Q428 Frg. 6

             ה

1   [גדוד [משמר[43] גבורים בלוות[

2   [בס[בֹיבי   פן יורה גבֹ[ו]רֹ[44]

3   [לֹֹיֹ[45] גבורתם ויפולֹ[ן] מגבורתם[46]

4   [חכמים בערמ]תֹם ואני בתומ[כי ברבריתכה[47]

5   ] ֹ[   ]קֹ[

---

32 The top margin of the papyrus is preserved.

33 1QH[a] 11.27–28: חלכאים על פני מים בהתעופף כול חצי שחת לאין השב ויורו.

34 1QH[a] 11.28: תקוה בנפול קו על משפט.

35 1QH[a] 11.29: נעלמים וקץ חרון לכול.

36 1QH[a] 11.30: וילכו נחלי בליעל /על\ כול.

37 1QH[a] 11.30: באש אוכלת בכול.

38 1QH[a] 11.30: להתם.

39 1QH[a] 11.30: לח.

40 1QH[a] 11.31: ותשוט בשביבי.

41 1QH[a] 11.31: כול שותיהם באושי.

42 The top margin of the papyrus is preserved.

43 1QH[a] 11.40: גדוד מֹשֹ[מר.

44 1QH[a] 11.41: בסביביה פן יֹוֹרֹהֹ גֹבֹ[ו]ר. Note the spelling difference of בס[בֹיבי between 4Q432 and 1QH[a].

45 Possible restorations may include גמו]לֹי.

46 4Q428 frg. 6 line 1: חכמֹים בערמתם ו]אני בתומכי בבריתכה. 4Q428 frg. 6 line 2: גבור[ת]ם ויפולו מגבור[תם.

47 1QH[a] 12.2: [ֹם]ֹאֹנֹי בֹתֹוֹמֹלֹי בֹבֹ]ריתכה.

Frg. 6 (Col. 10)
Parallels: 1QH^a 11.27–32 (= Sukenik 3.26–31); 4Q428 Frg. 5

1   the miserable ones (is)[7] [on] the surface of the water, when [all the arrows of the pit] fl[y without return and are shot without]

2   hope, (and) when the measuring-line falls on the judgme[nt …]

3   the hidden ones, and the end time of fury for all [….]

4   [And the rive]r[s of] Belial [p]o[ur] over al[l the heightened banks with f]ire devouring [all …]

5   to consume [every tree,] moi[st …. And it swee]ps with sp[arks of fire[8] until][9]

6   all [their canals (are) no more. [… the found]ations of [clay …]

Frg. 7 (Col. 11)
Parallels: 1QH^a 11.40–12.2; 4Q428 Frg. 6

1   the guarding [troop] of the mighty ones accompanied […]

2   [in] its [su]rroundings lest a mighty m[an] should shoot […]

3   […]*ly* their might. And they will fall [from their might …]

4   [the wise ones in] their [craftiness]. But I, when [I] hold fa[st to your covenant …]

5   […]° […]*q*[…]

---

[7] The *nomen regens* is "a fishing net." See 1QH^a 11.27.

[8] Lit. "flame," (להוב) but not "flame of fire."

[9] Lit. "until utterly."

Frg. 8 (Col. 12)[48]
Parallels: 1QH[a] 12.11 (= Sukenik 4.10)?

1   לה[מ̇יר[49]]

Frg. 9 (Col. 13)
Parallels: 1QH[a] 12.23 (= Sukenik 4.22)

1   וי[ד̇י ע̇[ל[50]

Frg. 10 (Col. 14)[51]
Parallels: 1QH[a] 12.36–37 (= Sukenik 4.35–36)

1   אמרת[י̇ בפש[עי[52]

2   רחמיכ[ה̇[53]

Frg. 11 (Col. 17)
Parallels: 1QH[a] 13.35–37 (= Sukenik 5.33–35)
4Q429 (4QH[c]) 3.7–9

1   בלחם אנח[ת̇י וש̇[קוי[54] בדמעות

2   עש[שו[55]]   במרו[ר̇י י̇[ום[56]

3   ל̇[ר]ריב[57]

Frg. 12 (Col. 24)[58]
Parallels: 1QH[a] 15.33–37; 1Q35 frg. 1

1   ר[ח̇מיכה ל[ה̇עמידם[59]

---

[48] The top margin is visible.
[49] 1QH[a] 12.11: להמיר.
[50] 1QH[a] 12.23: וידי על.
[51] A top margin may be preserved.
[52] 1QH[a] 12.36: אמרתי בפשעי.
[53] 1QH[a] 12.37: רחמיכה.
[54] 1QH[a] 13.35–36: אנחה ושקוי. 4Q429 frg. 3 line 7: בלחם אנחתי ושקוי בדמעות.
[55] 1QH[a] 13.36: עששו.
[56] 1QH[a] 13.36: במרורי יום. 4Q429 frg. 3 line 8: במרו[ר̇י יום].
[57] 1QH[a] 13.37: לריב.
[58] Top margin is possibly visible.
[59] 1QH[a] 15.33–34: רח̇מיכה להעמידם.

Frg. 8 (Col. 12)
Parallels: 1QHᵃ 12.11 (= Sukenik 4.10)?

1   [… to ex]change […]

Frg. 9 (Col. 13)
Parallels: 1QHᵃ 12.23 (= Sukenik 4.22)

1   […. And] my [ha]nds aga[inst …]

Frg. 10 (Col. 14)
Parallels: 1QHᵃ 12.36–37 (= Sukenik 4.35–36)

1   […] I [said:] "In [my] transgress[ion …]

2   [… yo]ur [compassions …]

Frg. 11 (Col. 17)
Parallels: 1QHᵃ 13.35–37 (= Sukenik 5.33–35)
4Q429 (4QHᶜ) 3.7–9

1   [… with the bread of] my [sighing,] and (with) the dr[ink of tears …]

2   […] they [are dimm]ed [… by the bittern]ess of the d[ay …]

3   […] into [a dispute …]

Frg. 12 (Col. 24)
Parallels: 1QHᵃ 15.33–37; 1Q35 frg. 1

1   […] your [com]passions, al[lowing them to stand …]

2   [דרכיכה[^60]]

3   [וֹבֹעֹלֹ[^61] [הבל להתב]וֹנֹ בֹ[מעשי[^62] פלאך]

4   הפ[לֹ]תה[^63]

Frg. 13 (Col. 25)
Parallels: 1QH[a] 16.9–10

1   לכל עו]ברי[^64]

2   [דרך   מ]יֹם כֹיֹ[^65]

Frg. 14[^66]

1   [ם וֹאֹ]

2   [עֹנֹי]

3   תר[שֹׁיע]

Frg. 15[^67]

1   נ]תֹתה[

2   מש]פֹט צדֹ]ק[^68]

3   [˚]

Frg. 16

1   [˚˚]

[^60]: 1QH[a] 15.34: דרכיכה.
[^61]: 1QH[a] 15.35: ובעל.
[^62]: 1QH[a] 15.35: להתבונן במעשי פלאך. 1Q35 frg. 1 line 8: אכה[פל במעשי].
[^63]: 1QH[a] 15.37: הפלתה/.
[^64]: 1QH[a] 16.9: עוברי.
[^65]: 1QH[a] 16.10: מים כי.
[^66]: Frg. 14 preserves the upper margin of a column. These lines may preserve the same portions of the same materials found in 1QH[a] 15.13–15 (= Sukenik 7.10).
[^67]: The top margin seems visible.
[^68]: Perhaps too speculative.

2   [...] your ways [...]

3   [...] and the owner of [nonsense compre]hends [your wondrous works ...]

4   [... you c]as[t ...]

Frg. 13 (Col. 25)
Parallels: 1QH^a 16.9–10

1   [... by all who p]ass over

2   [the Way ... wa]ter, for

Frg. 14

1   [...]*m* and ᵓ[...]

2   [...] needy [...]

3   [... you ac]cuse[...]

Frg. 15

1   [...] you [g]ave [...]

2   [...] righte[ous judg]ment[10] [...]

3   [...]°[...]

Frg. 16

1   [...]°°[...]

---

[10] Perhaps too speculative.

2 [ ]לֹ[

Frg. 17

1 [ ]מֺ[69] [

Frg. 18

1 [ ]תֺ [ ]

2 [ ]לֺתֺהֺ[

Frg. 19

1 [ ]תֺ הֺ[

Frg. 20

1 [ ]נֺהֺ[

Frg. 21[70]

1 [ ]והֺ[

Frg. 22

1 [ ] תה [71]

Frg. 23[72]

1 [ ]וֺדֺ[ ]

[69] The consonant is not a *daleth*; note the vertical stroke of a final *mem* and the horizontal stroke that continues to the right.
[70] See DJD 29, Pl. 14.
[71] The ink cracked off the papyrus.
[72] The remains of frg. 23 were penned by other hands than those who copied the rest of 4Q432. There is no evidence that they preserve portions of the *Hodayot*.

2   […]*l*[…]

Frg. 17

1   […]*m* […]

Frg. 18

1   […]*t* […]

2   […] ° *lth*[…]

Frg. 19

1   […]° *t h*[…]

Frg. 20

1   […]*nh*[…]

Frg. 21

1   […]*wh*[…]

Frg. 22

1   […] *th* […]

Frg. 23

1   […]*wd* °[…]

2   ]לׄ[

Frg. 24

1   ל]אׄלׄ עליון[73

---

73 Ctr. DJD:]גׄלׄ עליהׄ[. See 1QHª 13.22 and 14.36.

2   […]*l*[…]

Frg. 24

1   [… to] God Most High […]¹¹

---

¹¹ See "to God Most High" in 1QH^a 13.32 and 14.36.

Composite Text of the Thanksgiving Hymns (*Hodayot*)[1]

JAMES H. CHARLESWORTH with LEA BERKUZ

Col. 2 [Frgs. 23 and 16]
Hymn 1
God's Mercies Upon the Poor Ones

]	**1**
]	**2**
]	**3**
]	**4**
]	**5**
]	**6**
]	**7**
]	**8**
]	**9**
]	**10**
]	**11**
נפל]וֹאֵתיכֹ]ה[2] אי]ןֹ פֹה	**12**
ו]תּוֹצֹא לֹעֹוֹלֹמֹיֹ	**13**
ישמי]עֹוֹ בֹהֹמון רנה	**14**
אר]נֹנֹהֵ ֺֺ] [לֹ]	**15**

---

[1] Texts and translations of each witness to the *Thanksgiving Hymns* are sensitive to variants and *lacunae* in each witness. Then, the composite text is prepared in light of all witnesses. At each step we have followed our consistency chart to be precise and represent in English words what is in the Hebrew text. The flow is from witnesses to the composite text; hence, the readings in the composite text are informed by decisions made to prepare the composite text and yet preserve the unique text and translation of each witness.

[2] Note the misspelling; see Reymond, p. 53.

Composite Text of the Thanksgiving Hymns (*Hodayot*)

JAMES H. CHARLESWORTH with LEA BERKUZ

Col. 2 [Frgs. 23 and 16]
Hymn 1
God's Mercies Upon the Poor Ones[1]

1   […]

2   […]

3   […]

4   […]

5   […]

6   […]

7   […]

8   […]

9   […]

10   […]

11   […]

12   […] yo[ur wonder]ful acts [there is n]o interpretation[2]

13   [… and] you brought forth[3] for the eternities of

14   [… th]ey [procla]im with abundant exultation[4]

15   [… I will re]joice °°[…]*l*[…]

---

[1] At least one hymn must be assumed before "Hymn 2" that begins at 4.21. The Qumranites imagined themselves to be "the Poor Ones."

[2] Lit. "mouth" with the meaning of "declaration." Cf. Ps 106:2 and esp. *OdesSol* 26:11: "Who can interpret the wonders of the Lord?" (ܡܢܘ ܡܫܟܚ ܕܢܦܫܩ ܬܕܡܖ̈ܬܗ ܕܡܪܝܐ).

[3] In this poetic document, verbs tend to have a present meaning, but the tense in Hebrew is represented in this Composite Text.

[4] Or "a song;" not "a tumultuous cry." See the paronomasia in 2.15 and 2.16.

]°°[16

] 17

] 18

] 19

] 20

] 21

] 22

] 23

]°[ ] 24

[מ֯רות]ם [ ]֯[25

ע[שׁוקים ו֯מ֯י 26

[ר֯חמיו על אב֯יונ֯]ים 27

[ה ומי מתכן 28

[ומי מתכן גבורי]ם 29

ע[ד֯ עולם מי חושב֯ 30

[ערומים ו֯מ֯י 31

גב[ו֯רתכה °° [ ] ל֯] 32

Col. 3 [Frgs. 21 and 11]

] 1

] 2

16   […]°°[…]

17   […]

18   […]

19   […]

20   […]

21   […]

22   […]

23   […]

24   […]°[…]

25   [… their] rebelliousness […]°[…]

26   [… op]pressed ones and who

27   […] his mercies upon the Poor One[s][5]

28   […]*h* and who arranges[6]

29   […] and who arranges[7] the mighty one[s][8]

30   [… un]to eternity, who thinks[9]

31   […] the clever ones.[10] And who

32   […] your [mi]ght °°[…]*l*[…]

Col. 3 [Frgs. 21 and 11]

1   […]

2   […]

[5] See 11.26; cf. 13.24. For "the Poor One," see 10.34; 13.18, 20; and 26.27.
[6] Or "assesses," "measures."
[7] Or "assesses," "measures."
[8] Perhaps the author intends the celestial warriors; see 11.36.
[9] This word is translated here as a *qal* part. of חשׁב; DJD translates it as a *piʿel* part.: "who calculates."
[10] Sukenik text: "former ones." There is a small *vacat* here; it does not introduce a hymn.

]	3
]	4
]	5
]	6
]	7
]	8
]	9
]	10
]	11
]	12
]	13
]	14
[ׄ°°° םׄ]	15
[יׄנדיב ותׄעׄזׄור כהׄ]	16
[אבל מׄנחם אתה יׄ]כ	17
[°°ובברכות נגע]	18
[לׄ °°°° ³יׄאלׄ]כה[אוד	19
]	20
]	21
]	22
[רׄעפׄ]מ	23
[לׄם עוׄ]שני ⁴לכולׄ עׄמדה]	24
[ושלׄוׄם °°° חותם כול מׄלבך]	25

---

³ See אודכה אלי in 19.6 and 19.18.
⁴ In 1QHᵃ both כול (circa 208 instances) and כל (circa 13 times) are found. See Qimron, p. 18 and Reymond, p. 35.

3 […]

4 […]

5 […]

6 […]

7 […]

8 […]

9 […]

10 […]

11 […]

12 […]

13 […]

14 […]

15 […]*m* °°°[…]

16 […]° your […]. And you help those who are willi[ng …]

17 [… fo]r you are comforting the mourner […]

18 […] affliction[11] and with blessings °°[…]

19 [.... I thank] you, O my God, °°°° *l*°[…]

20 […]

21 […]

22 […]

23 [… from] dust […]

24 […] it stood for all the years of eter[nity …]

25 […] without you[12] each seal °°° and peace […]

---

[11] Not "blow" as in DJD.
[12] Or "besides you."

26 [ם ורוחם בֹני איש לפי שכלו ואיֹ]ן

27 בה]יכֹל מלכותו כי עשה כול אלה ֹ[

28 ואתה יצ]רתם וֹלֹך חמר ובצדק תשופֹט]ם

29 [לֹפֹנכה לֹקֹץ תהוֹ ויצר חֹמֹ]ר

30 [ֹֹ ואֹתה נכבֹדתה מכול אֹלֹ]ים

31 [קוֹדֹשֹך וכאשר בֹנֹפֹשֹך]

32 ולהֹל]ל שמך תבֹיאֹ]ני] בעדת קֹד]ושים

33 [ֹ [לֹ]]

Col. 4 [= Sukenik Col. 17 + Frg. 14]
Parallels: 4Q428 Frg. 1

1 [

2 [

3 [

4 [

5 [

6 [

7 [

8 [

9 [

10 [

26 […]*m* and their spirit, the sons of man according to his insight, and there is n[o …]

27 [… in the sh]rine of his kingdom, for he is working[13] all things ˚[…]

28 [… and you,] you [creat]ed them and to you (they are) clay, and with righteousness you will judge [them …][14]

29 […] before you to the endtime of formlessness[15] and the creature of[16] cla[y …]

30 […]˚˚. And you, you are glorified above all god[s …]

31 […] your holiness and as in your soul[17] […]

32 [… and to prai]se your name, you will bring [me] into the congregation of the Hol[y Ones …]

33 […]*l* […]˚ […]

Col. 4 [= Sukenik Col. 17 + Frg. 14]
Parallels: 4Q428 Frg. 1

1 […]

2 […]

3 […]

4 […]

5 […]

6 […]

7 […]

8 […]

9 […]

10 […]

[13] Since this section emphasizes God's continuous action, the verb is a *qal* part. (not a *qal* pf.; "he has done," as in DJD). See the reference to God's "comforting" in 3.17. For "working," see Pss 115:15, 121:2, 124:8, and esp. Isa 44:24.

[14] Ctr. DJD: "I will walk continually, and in righteousness you set me […]."

[15] Or "chaos." See Gen 1:2.

[16] Heb. יצר.

[17] Heb. נפש. The noun that is translated "soul" does not denote the bifurcated Greek anthropology. It means the living principle in the human.

] **11**

] ̊ [ ] ̊ [ ] ̊ [**12**

[̊ ו֯מׁשפלת מדה משׁ ̊ [] °°°] **13**

[מגׁולה בלוא משׁפט[] כרוח °°°] **14**

או]֯בים אוכלת בשר֯] מ[]שׁנׄאיה בלוא **15**

ת ביבישה ומכש[]לת ב[]לׄוא מׁשפט **16**

פוגעות פתע פתאו[]ם בל[]וֹֽא בׁׄרׁׄית **17** [כרוח⁵

בלו[]ֹֽא מׁשפטׁ מרוח דורשתֹ֯] ̊ [ ]ות ̊ שׁ °°° ̊ ם **18**

ב[]ל[]וא מצוה עׄד֯ ⁶ מרוח כו[] ̊ [ ]מו ̊ °°°] ... מׁתרמה ב ̊] **19**

(VACAT) [ ] [... עׁ ̊ בנגיעי ב[]שר **20**

Hymn 2
Blessed is the God of Knowledge Who Cleanses Me

א]שׁ֯ר לא השיגום במ[]ר[]דׁׄף֯ ⁷] ... [ברוך אתה אל הדעות כי תנקני] מנסתרות אש[]מה **21**

מח[]שׁבות רשעה מׁ֯נדתׁ] ̊ [ ]שׁ] ... [וממשפט קצׁ] **22**

עׁ[]וׄן וממשפט אחֹרֹים֯] ותטהר את] עבדך מכול פשעיו ב[]המו[]ן רׁחמיך **23**

כאשר ד]ברתה ביד מושה עבֹ֯ד[]ך לשא[]תׁ עֹ֯וֹ֯ו֯ן וחטאה ולכפר בע[]ד פשׁ[]עׁ ומעל **24**

[מוסדי הרים ואש] אוכל[]ה בׁשׁאול תחתיה ואת הנו[]סרים] במשפטיך **25**

---

⁵ See 4.14: כרוח []] בלוא משׁפט.
⁶ Not seen by previous editors.
⁷ See המרדף in 1QM 3.2 and 3.9.

11 […]

12 […] °[…]°[…]° °[…]

13 […]° and from humiliation of measure *mš*°[…]°°°[…]

14 […] revealed without judgment as the spirit of °°°[…]

15 [… the ene]mies devouring[18] the flesh of its [h]aters without

16 […]*t* on dry land and the stumbli[ng wi]thout judgment

17 [as the spirit of[19]…] striking all of a sudde[n wit]hout a covenant

18 [… witho]ut judgment from the spirit of seeking […]*wt*°° *š*°°° *m*

19 […] acting deceitfully *b*°[… with]o[ut] commandment until from the spirit *kw*[…]*mw*°°°[…]

20 […]ᶜ in the afflictions of f[lesh ….] (VACAT) […] (VACAT)

Hymn 2
Blessed is the God of Knowledge Who Cleanses Me

21 [Blessed are you, the God of knowledge, for you cleanse me] from hidden (acts)[20] of gu[ilt[21] … wh]ich they did not reach them while pu[rs]uing[22] […]

22 […] and from the judgment of the Endtime of […] the [tho]ughts of wickedness, the impurity of […]°°° *š*[…]

23 [… in]iquity and from the judgment of the latter things. [And you purify][23] your servant from all his transgressions by [the abundance of] your mercies.

24 [… as] you have [sp]oken through Moses [your] servant [to forgi]ve[24] iniquity and sin and to atone fo[r transgress]ion and infidelity.

25 […] the foundations of the mountains, and fire [devou]rs in Sheol below and [those who are war]ned[25] by your judgments.

---

[18] Most likely the noun "fire" (אש) is lost in the *lacuna*; thus the fem. sing. "devouring" assumes "the fire is devouring the flesh."

[19] See 4.14.

[20] The noun is plural.

[21] See the similar expression in Ps 19:13 [12]: "Cleanse me from hidden guilt." Or "hidden acts."

[22] See 1QM 3.2 and 3.9.

[23] Restorations are according to the repetitive formulae and expressions in 1QHª and the other seven witnesses. Note "impurity" in the preceding sentence.

[24] Lit. "to take away."

[25] *Nipʿal* pl. part. of יסר. See 7.17.

26 בחר]תֿה לעבדיך באמונה [ל]היות זרעם לפניך כול הימים ושמֿ[ותיהם]הֿקימותה

27 מ]פֿשע ולהשליך כול עוֹוֹנֹתֿם ולהנחילם בכול כבוד אדם] [8לרוב ימים

28 [

Hymn 3
Blessed is the Lord, God of Mercies

29 [ברוך אתה אדוני אל הרחמי]ֿםֿ מרוחות אשר נתתה בי אמצֿאה מענה לשון לספר צדקותיך וארוך אפים

30 בכוח גבורת]ֿך9 ומעשי ימין עוזך וֿלֿהֿוֿדוֹת על פשעי ראשונים ולה[תנפ]ֿל ולהתחנן על

31 פשע]ֿי מעשי ונעוות לֿבֿֿבֿי כי בנדה התגוללתי ומסוד עֿ[וה נוצר]ֿתי ולא נלֿאֿיתי

32 [רֿשֿֿעֿ כי לך אתה הצדקה ולשמך הברכה לעול[ם   כֿצֿֿדֿקתך ופדה]

33 וי]ֿתמו רשעים ואני הֿוֿבינותי כי את אשר בחרתֿהֿ הֿ[כינותה] דרכו ובשכל

34 ותח]שכהו מחטוא לך ול[ט]ֿוב לו עניתו ביסוריך ובנס[וייך חזק]ֿתֿה10 לבו

35 [עבדך מחטוא לך ומכשול בכול דברי רצונך חזק מתֿנֿ[יו לעמו[ד11 על רוחות

36 לה]ֿתהלך בכול אשר אהבתה ולמאוס בכול אשר שנֿאֿתֿהֿ [ולעשות] הטֿוב בעיניך

---

8 The small *lacuna* is the size of a word division.
9 See 23.9: בכוח גבורתכֿהֿ.
10 See 4.35: מֿתֿנֿ[ין לעמו[ד.
11 See 10.9–10.

26 [...] you [have chosen] those who serve you with faithfulness, that their seed [w]ill be before you all the days. And you established [their] reputation[s]²⁶

27 [... from] transgression and to discard all their iniquities, and (to grant) their inheritances in all the glory of Adam²⁷ for many days.

28 [...] (VACAT) [...]

Hymn 3
Blessed is the Lord, God of Mercies

29 [Blessed are you, O Lord, God of mercie]s, because of the spirits that you granted me.²⁸ I will find an answer of the tongue to recount²⁹ your righteous deeds and (your) patience³⁰

30 [... in the power of] your [might], and the works of your strong right hand, and to confess former transgressions, and to pr[ostra]te myself, and to petition for mercy, concerning

31 [... the transgress]ions of my works and the bewilderment³¹ of my heart. For in impurity I wallowed³² and from the secret of naked[ness³³] I was [created]; but I did not grow weary.

32 [...] wicked, for to you (belongs) righteousness, and to your name (belongs) the blessing for eterni[ty ...] according to your righteousness and redemption

33 [... and] the wicked [will be] annihilated. And I understand that the one you have elected, his way is es-[tablished], and through the insight of

34 [... and you pre]vent him from sinning against you, and [go]od for him (is) his misery through your chastisements³⁴ and by [your] trial[s] you [strengthened]³⁵ his heart

35 [...] your servant from sinning against you, and from becoming an obstacle in all the matters of your will. Strengthening [his] loin[s to sta]nd³⁶ over spirits

36 [... to] walk continuously in everything that you love, and to reject³⁷ everything that you hate, [and to do] the good in your eyes

---

²⁶ Lit. "their names."
²⁷ Or "the human."
²⁸ See 1QS 3.18: God created "two spirits."
²⁹ Note the string of infinitives.
³⁰ Heb. ‏וארוך אפים‎.
³¹ See 21.14.
³² Lit. "rolled."
³³ I.e., "the genitals (of a woman or a man)." See 5.32, 9.24, 20.28.
³⁴ See 7.17.
³⁵ See 4.38.
³⁶ See 10.9–10.
³⁷ Not ‏תעב‎.

37 ממ[שׁ]לתם בתכמ֯ז כי רוח בשׂ֯ר עבדך (VACAT) [   ] (VACAT)

Hymn 4
Blessed is God for the Holy Spirit

38 [ברוך אתה אל כי] הניפותה רוח קודשׁ֯ך על עבדך֯ [ות]ט֯הר מכ֯[ול] פשעיו[12] חזק[תה֯֯[13] לבו

39 א[נ֯ו֯ש ואל כול ברית אדם[14] אביט [   ] ֯ה ימצאוה

40 [ש֯֯ע מ֯שׁיגיה ואה֯ב֯יה[15]] ֯יכה לֿעֿולמי עד[16]

41 [   ] [   ] [   ] (VACAT)

Col. 5 [= Sukenik Col. 13 + Frgs. 15a, 15b Col. 1, 31, 17, 20, and 33]
Parallels: 4Q428 Frg. 2
Hymn 5
The Master Prostrates Himself Before God

1]

2]

3]

---

[12] See 4.23: מכול פשעיו.
[13] See 4.34: חזק[תה לבו.
[14] 4Q428 frg. 1 line 1: א]ד֯ם[.
[15] 4Q428 frg. 1 line 2:]וב[.
[16] 4Q428 frg. 1 line 3:]י עולמ֯[י ֯יכה לעולמ.

37 [...] their [dom]inion in his entrails,[38] for a spirit of flesh (is) your servant. (VACAT) [...] (VACAT)

Hymn 4
Blessed is God for the Holy Spirit

38 [Blessed are you, O God, for] you waved[39] your holy spirit over your servant [and you] purified (him) from a[ll his transgressions].[40] You [strengthened][41] his heart.

39 [... a h]uman, and to each covenant of Adam[42] I will look [...]*h* they will find it

40 [...]*š*^c those who reach it[43] and those who love it [...]°*ykh* forever and ever

41 [....] (VACAT) [...] (VACAT)

Col. 5 [= Sukenik Col. 13 + Frgs 15a, 51b Col. 1, 31, 17, 20, and 33]
Parallels: 4Q428 Frg. 2
Hymn 5
The Master Prostrates Himself Before God[44]

1 [...][45]

2 [...]

3 [...]

---

[38] The root תכם does not appear in biblical Hebrew; hence, its appearance in the Qumran Scrolls is a lexeme previously unattested in documents. It appears in 1QS 4.20–21 (מתכמי בשרו). תכם can be plural or singular in the *Thanksgiving Hymns* (DJD lists the root under תכמים); the noun denotes "entrails" or "body." In 1QH^a 4.37, the noun is in context with "heart" and "[loins]." In 13.30, the noun may be plural denoting "the entrails of" or singular "the body of"; the metaphorical context supports both understandings. In 15.7, it appears with "my bones" so the moving of the ship metaphor can be like "entrails" or "a body." In 16.2, it is linked with "heart." In 22.28, it is after "my frame." The form מתכמי also appears in 4Q428 frg. 10 line 8 and בתכמי in 4Q511 frgs. 28–29 line 4 and 48–51 2.3 as well as 4Q444 frgs. 1–4 1.3 (the *beth* is restored) and 1Q36 frg. 14 line 2 and ובתכמיה in 4Q525 frg. 13 line 4 and תכמי in 4Q525 frg. 23 line 1. Hence, the root תכם can be synonymous with גוף, "body" or with קרב that denotes "bowels," or "entrails." Some influence from Aramaic seems likely. If so, then Ps 103:1 is pertinent; in this verse the psalmist praises God with his "soul" and "entrails." The first two instances of תכם in the *Thanksgiving Hymns* are with a preformative *beth*; for example, 4.37 "in his (or my) entrails" or "in his (or my) body." It is possible that the root תכם originates with תוך that denotes what is "within" or "in the midst." Most translators chose "entrails" (Yadin and DJD) or "bowels" (Vermes, Abegg and Harkins in *OTB*) but note the forthcoming publication by N. Mizrahi who argues for an Aramaism meaning "shoulder" and then "body parts" that is a metonymy for "body" (conference presentation in Strasbourg in June 2014). It is certain that the lexeme denotes body parts or body. I express appreciations to G. Rendsburg for discussions on this philology. See also Y. Yadin in *JBL* 74 (1955) 40–43 and J. Baumgarten and M. Mansoor in *JBL* 75 (1956) 107–13.

[39] *Hip'il* pf. of נוף, "to move back and forth, to spread." Perhaps an allusion to the wave-offering in the Temple.

[40] See 4.23.

[41] See 4.34.

[42] Or "humankind." Note the reference to many covenants: "each covenant." Some Jews probably perceived God's commandments (or covenants) with Adam.

[43] *Hip'il* part. of נשג.

[44] It is impossible to discern if a new hymn begins here or in 5.12.

[45] An *incipit* was most likely here.

]	**4**
]	**5**
]	**6**
]	**7**
]	**8**
]	**9**
]	**10**
]	**11**

12 [מזמור למ[שׁכּ֯י֯ל]17 להתנפל לפֿנ[ֹן]י אל   [מֹ֯עֹ֯שֹ֯י֯ אֹל

13 [ו]להבין פתאים18][֯[֯]֯[ ][֯[֯]֯[או[שֹ֯י עולם

14][֯ת ולהבין אנוש בֹ֯][בשר וסוד רֹ֯וחי[ן][בני אי[שֹ֯]19 התהלכו

Hymn 6
Blessed is the Lord for His Power

15 [ברוך][אתה אדוני אֹֹשֹ֯][ר][יֹ֯צֹ֯ר רוח בֹֹ][[ֹ]שר ברֹו[][ח קודשך ו][בֹ֯כֹוח גבורתך

16 [ובגדול ח][ֹסֹֹדֹ֯ך]20 עם רוב טובֹֹכֹ֯[ ][יצר21][חֹ֯מֹ֯תֹך וקנאת משפֹֹ][טיך   לֹֹאין][חֹ֯קר כול

17 בד][עֹ֯ת כול בינה וֹ[מֹֹ֯]וסר][ורזי מחשבת וראשֹֹ֯֯יֹֹתֹ֯][הֹ[כֹ֯ינותה

18 [֯֯]ה קודש מקדם עו[ל]ם ו[ל]עולמי עד אתה הואֹֹ֯[ֹ]תה   [קֹ֯דושיֹֹ֯ם

---

17 See 7.21: מזמור למשֹׁ[כיל].
18 Cf. פתיים in 10.11.
19 See 3.26: בני איש.
20 See וגדול חסדיכה in line 9.34; cf. 8.30.
21 Cf. 7.30.

4   [...]

5   [...]

6   [...]

7   [...]

8   [...]

9   [...]

10 [...]

11 [...]

12 [A psalm[46] for the M]aster so he may prostrate himself befor[e God ...] the works of God

13 [...] and to be allowed to discern the simple ones [...]°°[...]°°[...] eternal [a]cts[47]

14 [...]°t and to be allowed to discern the human b[...] flesh and the secret of the spirits of [... the sons of ma]n to walk continuously.

Hymn 6
Blessed is the Lord for His Power

15 [Blessed are] you, O Lord, wh[o] creates a fleshly[48] spirit by [your holy] spir[it and] by the power of your might

16 [and by] your [great[49] lovi]ng-kindness with the multitude of your goodness. [The urge of][50] your wrath and the zeal of [your] judgme[nts ...] all [un]fathomable[51]

17 [.... In the k]nowledge of all discernment and dis[cipline][52] and the mysteries of thought and the beginnings of [...] you establish[ed].

18 [...]°°h holiness from ete[rnal] ages [and] to the everlasting eternity you, [you] were willing[53] [...] Holy Ones[54]

---

[46] See 7.21. A new psalm does not begin here.
[47] This participle often refers to God's creative acts.
[48] A positive meaning is intended.
[49] See 9.34; cf. 8.30.
[50] See 7.30.
[51] Heb. לאין חקר. See also, Isa 40:28 and Ps 145:3. In the *Hodayot* see 1QHᵃ 11.21; 14.6, 19–20; 16.18.
[52] Or "training." Not "instruction."
[53] Not "resolve." The *hipʿil* pf. of this verb connotes God's politeness. See also 8.16, 26.
[54] The Holy Ones may refer to angels or the advanced spiritually in the *Yaḥad.*

19] וברזי פלאך הֹוֹדֹעֹ[תני בע[[בֹור כבודך ובעומק ׳׳[ובמעי׳[[²²[ ]בֹינתך לא

20 [אתה גליתה דרכֹי אֹמֹת ומעשי[[ ]רע²³ [חוכמה²⁴ ואולֹתֹ[[   ]] צֹדֹק

21] מעשיהם אמת וֹבֹיֹנֹה עֹוֹלֹה ואו[[]לֹת כולֹ התהלכֹ[]ו

22 [ֹם וחסדי עולם לֹכֹולֹ קֹצֹ[י]הֹם לשלום ושחת כֹֹל ׳ [

23 [מש]פֹטיהם כבוד עולם וֹחֹמֹדֹה וֹשֹמחת עד למעשה[[וע[[וֹשים לכֹ]ה

24 מֹעֹשֹׂי [רע²⁵   ] ואלה אשר הכֹ[[ינותה מקדם [[עֹוֹלֹםֹ ²⁶ לשפוט בם

25 אֹת כול מעשיך בטרם בראתם עם צבא רוחיך ועדתֹ[[בני שמים²⁷ עֹ[[ֹם רקיֹעֹ קֹוֹדשך²⁸ וֹכֹוֹל

26 צבאותיו עם הארץ וכול צאֹצֹאֹיֹה בימים ובתהומות[[ו[[כול מחשבותֹךֹ לכול קצי עֹוֹלֹם

27 ופקודת עד כי אתה הכינותמה²⁹ מקדם עולם ומעֹשֹׂה[[   ]][[   ]׳׳׳[בם בעבור

28 יֹספרו כבודך בֹכֹוֹל ממשלתך כי הראיתם את אשר לא יֹ[דעו ואת כול³⁰ [אֹשֹר קדם ולברוא

29 חדשות להפר קימי קדם ול[הק]ים נהיות עולם כי אֹתֹהֹ הֹ[כינות[מֹהֹ ואתה תהיה

30 לעולמי עד וברזי עד שכלכה פלֹגֹ[תה] כול אלה להודיע כֹבֹוֹדֹך וֹמֹהֹ הֹ[]אֹ רוח בשר להבין

---

²² 4Q428 frg. 2 line 1: ן[. See מעין בינה in 13.28.

²³ 4Q428 frg. 2 line 2: ומעש[י רע.

²⁴ For חוכמה see 9.16, 18.4; for חכמה see 9.8, 9, 21; 11.16; 15.32; 17.17, 23; 25.25.

²⁵ See line 20.

²⁶ See 5.18: מקדם עוֹ[לם.

²⁷ See 11.23: בני שמים.

²⁸ The *plene* is used consistently in 1QHᵃ.

²⁹ The long form of the 3mp suffix appears in 5.27, 29; see Reymond's reflections (p. 161).

³⁰ There is room in the *lacuna* for twelve spaces or consonants.

19 […] and in the mysteries of your wonder [you] have allowed [me] to know.[55] [On ac]count of your glory and in the depth of °°[… and in the fount]ain of[56] your discernment (will) not

20 […] you, you revealed the ways of truth and the works of evil, wisdom, and foolishness […] righteousness

21 […] their works. (In) truth and discernment (or in) perversity and foolishness, all have walke[d] continuously […]

22 […]*m* and the eternal loving-kindnesses for all their endti[m]es of peace. But the pit[57] (is for) all °[…]

23 their [judg]ments, eternal glory, and delight, and everlasting joy. For the work [… and] they are [do]ing to yo[u]

24 works of [evil….] And these things which [you] est[ablished from] eternal [ages],[58] to judge through them

25 all your creatures before you created them together with the host of your spirits, and the community of [the sons of heaven[59] wi]th your holy firmament[60] and all

26 its hosts, together with the earth and all its offshoots in the seas and in the deeps. [And] all your thoughts (are) for all the endtimes of eternity

27 and everlasting visitation. For you, you established them from eternal ages and the work […]°[…]°°° in them in order that

28 they will recount your glory within all your dominion for you have shown them that which [they] did not k[now and all] which (is from) ancient-time,[61] and to create

29 new (events), to annul the things that rise up (from) ancient-time, and to [establ]ish things that are of eternity. For you, [you] est[ablished] them and you will be

30 forever and ever.[62] And in the mysteries of your insight [you] assigned all these things to make known your glory. And how[63] c[an] the spirit of flesh (be able) to discern

---

[55] The permissive *hipʿil*. In the *Thanksgiving Hymns*, the permissive *hipʿil* is used far more often than in Biblical Hebrew. The authors intended to stress that God permits or allows the Righteous Teacher and his followers to know secrets and intervenes in human history by permitting events to move to his Endtime.

[56] See 13.28.

[57] DJD: "destruction."

[58] See 5.18.

[59] See 11.23.

[60] See Gen 1:6–8.

[61] Or "from old time."

[62] Or "everlasting eternity."

[63] "And how" has been missed by some editors.

31   בכול אלה ולהשכיל בסבל[ם]הֿגדול ומה ילוד אשה בכוֿל מֿעֿשיֿך הנוראים והוא

32   מבנה עפר ומגבל מים אֿ[שמה וחט]אֿה סודו ערות קלֿןֿ וֿ[מקור הֿ]נֿֿדה ורוח נעוה משלה

33   בו   ואם ירשע והיהֿ[לאות][31] [עֿולם ומופת דורות][32] רחוקֿ[י]ֿם̇ לֿבשר רק בטובך

34   יצדק איש ובֿרֿוֿב רחֿ[מיֿך תושיענו] בהדרך תפארנו ותמשֿׁיֿלֿןֿו בֿ[רֿוב עדנים עם שלום

35   עולם ואורך ימים כי [מעשיך ו]דברך לא ישוב אחור ואני עבדך ידעתי

36   ברוח אשר נתתה בי[כיא אמת] וצדק כול מעשיך ודֿבֿרֿ֗ך לֿאֿ ישוב אחוֿר וֿכֿוֿל[ן

37   קציך מועד[י עו]לֿ[ם   והם ס]דורים לחפציהם ואדעֿה [כי   ]לֿ[

38   [ֻ קֿ להתבונן]]   ורשע שֿׁ]]

39   [] ֺ֗ רֿוחיך ולֿ]]

40   []ֺ֗הלֿ]]

41   ]

Col. 6 [= Sukenik Col. 14 + Frgs. 18, 22, 15b Col. 2, 44, and 19]

1   ]

2   ]

3   ]

4   ]

---

[31] See 7.33.
[32] See 7.33: עֿולם] דורות וֿמֿוֿפֿת לאות ולהיות.

31 in all these things and to have insight into [their] great suffering?[64] And what (is) one born of a woman in all your terrifying works?[65] And he is

32 but a form of[66] dust and mixed[67] water. G[uilt and si]n (are) his foundation, shameful nakedness[68] and [the spring of] impurity, and a perverted spirit rule

33 in him.[69] And if he should be wicked, he shall be an eternal [sign][70] and a portent[71] (for) dista[n]t generations of the flesh. Only by your goodness

34 can a man be justified; and in the multitude of [your] mer[cies you will save him]. With your splendor you glorify him, and you will let hi[m] rule [over] the multitude of delights with eternal

35 peace and length of days. For [your works and] your word shall not turn back. But I, your servant, know

36 through the spirit that you put in me, [that true] and righteous (are) all your works, and your word shall not turn back and all […]

37 your endtimes (are) [ete]r[nal] appointed time[s,[72] … and they are o]rdered according to their purposes.[73] And I know [that …]*l*[…]

38 and wickedness *š*̊[…]̊*q* to comprehend […]

39 […]̊̊ your spirits and *l*[…]

40 […]̊*hl*[…]

41 […]

Col. 6 [= Sukenik Col. 14 + Frgs. 18, 22, 15b Col. 2, 44, and 19]

1 […]

2 […]

3 […]

4 […]

---

[64] Lit. "burden."
[65] This noun is missed by some previous editors.
[66] Lit. "construction of," "building of."
[67] Aramaic: "to knead," Syriac: "to create."
[68] Or "genitals." See 9.24, 20.28.
[69] The scribe leaves an uninscribed space here. It does not denote a new hymn.
[70] See 7.33.
[71] Or "wonder," "sign." See 7.33 where the noun also means "portent." For "wonder" see 8:9 and 15.24.
[72] Or "seasons," "festivals."
[73] See 9.15.

5 [

6 [

7 [

8 [

9 [

10 [

11 [

12 [תׄעׄוׄדׄוׄתׄם]] [בעמך והיׄהׄ] [°°

13 וׄאׄ[תה גליתה]] אוזננו ל[מוסר³³ [אׄנשי אמת ובׄחׄיׄרׄיׄ צ[דק דורש]יׄ

14 [שׄכׄל ומבקשי בינה ב]] או[הׄבי רחמים ועוזי רוח מזוקקי

15 עׄוני וברורי מצרף °°°]] מ[תׄאפקים עד לׄעׄתׄ מׄשׄפׄטיכה

16 וצופים ליׄשועתךׄ]] [אתׄהׄ]] וחזקתה חוקיך בׄיׄדׄם לעשות

17 מׄשׄפׄ[]ׄט תבל ולנחול]]בכול צׄ[דקותיכה³⁴ ולהיות בס[]ׄׄׄוׄד קודש לדורות עולׄם וכול

18 עׄׄושי מׄ[]]עשי[]]הׄם עם תענׄ[]]ג [ואנשי חזונכה (VACAT)

Hymn 7
I Thank the Lord for the Heart of Discernment

19 [[(VACAT) []] (VACAT) [[אודכה]] אדוני הנותן בלב עבדךׄ בׄיׄנׄה

---

³³ See 14.7.
³⁴ This hymn has כה... and ך....

5   […]

6   […]

7   […]

8   […]

9   […]

10 […]

11 […]

12 […]their fixed times[…] among your people and it was °°[…]°°°

13 and yo[u, you uncovered[74]] our ears for [the discipline of …] the men of truth and the elect ones of righ[teousness, the pursuers] of

14 insight and the seekers of discernment *b*[… the lov]ers of mercy and the strong ones of spirit[75] refined of

15 transgression[76] and those purged (in) the crucible[77] °°°[… thos]e who persevere until the time of your judgments,

16 and those waiting for your salvation […] you […] and you strengthened your statutes through their hand to do

17 judgment (in) the world,[78] and to inherit in all [your] rig[hteousness; and to be in the cou]ncil of holiness for eternal generations. And all

18 the acts of their works with pleasu[re …] and men of your vision. (VACAT)

Hymn 7
I Thank the Lord for the Heart of Discernment

19 […] (VACAT) [I thank you,][79] O Lord, who put in the heart of your servant holy

---

[74] *Pi'el* pf. of גלה; "you uncovered, revealed."

[75] Not the "humble of spirit" as in some renderings. The ones being praised are those who are strong, because God revealed insight to them. They may possibly be identified with the precursors of the Qumranites or the men of Qumran.

[76] עוני, not עני.

[77] Or "smelting-pot."

[78] Lit. "of the world."

[79] Or with DJD: "[Blessed are you,] …" as in 4.29, but see 4.38 (with Licht and Qimron). The author in 6.19 thanks the Lord for discernment.

20 קדש לה֯[[ ]]שכ֯[[ ]]יל בכו֯ל֯[[ ]][[א]לה ולהת֯[[בונן]] ולהתאפק על עלי֯ל֯ות֯ רשע ולברך

21 ב֯[[ ]]צ֯דק כו֯[[ ]]ל בוחר[[ ]][י רצו֯נ֯֯[ך]י ולבחור בכול א[[ ]]ש֯ר אהבתה ולתעב א֯ת֯ כו֯ל֯ אשר

22 [שנאתה[35] [[ ]]ות֯[[ ]]ש֯כ֯ל[[ ]][[ע]֯ב֯דך[[ ]][להפיל גור[[ ]]ל֯֯ות אנוש כי לפי רוחות תב֯ד֯֯[י]לני בין

23 [[ ]][א֯יתם פעולתם ואני ידעתי ומבינתך   טוב לרשע֯[[ ]] ו֯[[ ]]ת֯כן ֯[[ ]]

24 כי ברצונכה בא֯[[י]֯ש֯ ה֯ר֯[ ]ביתה נחלתו[[ ]] ב֯ר֯וח קודשך וכן תגישני לבינת֯ך ולפי

25 ק֯ורבי קנאתי על כול פועלי רשע ואנשי רמיה כי כול קרוביך לא ימרו פיך

26 ו֯כ֯ו֯ל יודעיך לא ישנו דבריך כי אתה צדיק ואמת כול בחיריך וכול עולה

27 ו֯רשע תשמיד לעד ונגלתה צדקתך לעיני כול מעשיך

28 ו֯א֯֯ני ידעתי ברוב טובך ובשבועה הקימותי על נפ֯שי לבלתי חטוא לך

29 [ו]֯לבלתי עשות מכול הרע בעיניך וכן הוגשתי בי֯חד כול אנשי סודי[36] לפי

30 ש֯כלו֯ אגישנו וכרוב נחלתו אהבנו ולא אשא פני ר֯ע֯ ושו֯ח֯ר֯ ר֯[ש]֯ע֯ה לא אכיר

---

[35] See 4.36; 1QS 1.3–4; and CD MS A 2.13, 15.
[36] Cf. 4Q439 frgs. 1–2 1.2: אנשי סודי.

20 discernment to allow insight[80] into all these things and to allow to [discern …], and to persevere[81] against the plots of wickedness. And to bless

21 in righteousness all the chosen ones of your will [and to choose all t]hat you love, and to abhor all that

22 [you hate].[82] And you allowed your servant to have insight [in order to cast l]ots (for) a human, because in accordance with the spirits, you allow me to distinguish between

23 good and wicked.[83] [And] you established °[…] with them their activity.[84] And I, I know, through[85] your discernment,

24 that according to your will with the hu[m]an, [you] multipl[ied his inheritance] with your holy spirit. And thus you allow me to draw near to your insight, and (doing so) according to

25 my closeness. I am zealous against all the doers of wickedness and the men of slackness, because all those close[86] to you do not disobey your edict.[87]

26 And all who know you do not alter your words,[88] because you are righteous, and all your elect ones (are) truthful. Then all injustice

27 and wickedness you will destroy forever, and your righteousness will be revealed before the eyes of all your creatures.[89]

28 And I, I know through the multitude of your goodness and by a vow[90] I have bound[91] upon my soul[92] not to sin against you;

29 [and] not to do any evil before your eyes. And thus I was brought into the Community[93] (with) all the men of my council.[94] According to

30 his insight, I will bring him near; and according to the multitude of his inheritance, I will love him. But I will not accept evil.[95] And the one on the lookout (for) wic[ke]dness, I will not acknowledge.

---

[80] Note the string of *hip'il* permissives ("to allow," "to permit").

[81] Lit. "to preserve oneself."

[82] See 1QS 1.3–4: "and in order to love all that he (God) has chosen, and to hate all that he has rejected."

[83] See 13.31 and 15.15.

[84] See 1QS 3.15: "he (God) established all their designs."

[85] Lit. "and through."

[86] Note the emphasis on being "close" to God and God's edict.

[87] Lit. "mouth."

[88] The author stands against "the men of deceit" (probably the non-Aaronic priests in the Temple) who are not allowed to draw near to God and do not experience God's holy spirit, because they cannot distinguish between good and evil, "disobey" God's "edict," and "alter" God's "words." Perhaps the last condemnation refers to the deliberate alteration of Scripture to support Hasmonean policy.

[89] Lit. "all your works." The line ends with a *vacat*, but it does not signal a new hymn. It highlights his affirmation.

[90] Note 1QS 9.8: "The property of the men of holiness... must not be merged with the property of the men of deceit."

[91] Or "I have established."

[92] Heb. נפש; see the note to 6:3.

[93] Heb. יחד. Most likely, the author is the Righteous Teacher or a leading figure in the *Yaḥad*, "Community," who could refer to "*my* council."

[94] Or "the men of my secret." Cf 4Q439 frgs. 1–2 1.2.

[95] Lit. "I will not lift the face of evil."

31 [ו][ל]א [א]ׁמיר בהון אמתך ובשוחד כול משפטיך כי אם לפׂי קׂרׂבׂ[ך אי]ש

32 [אה]ׁבׂנו וכרחקך אותו כן אתעבנו לעׂד[37] ולא אביא בסוד אׁ[מתך] [שבי

33 [מב]ׁרׂיתך   ]

Hymn 8
I Thank the Lord for the Multitude of His Wonders

34 [או]ׁדך אדוני כגדול[38] כוחך ורוב נפלאותיך מעולם ועד עׂוׂלׂ[ם רב הרחמי]ם וגדול

35 [החס]ׁדׁים הסולח לשבי פשע ופוקד עו(ו)ן רשעים וׂמׁעׂלׁ[ן39] ואהבכ]הׁ[40] בנדבת

36 [צדקות]יׂךׂ[41] ותשנא עולה לעד ואני עבדך חנותני ברוח דעה לׂ[בחור בא]ׁמׂת

37 [וצד]ׁק ולתעׁב כול דרך עולה   ואהבכה נדבה ובכול לׂבׁ[י] ולעובדך ב[כ]לב

38 [שלם]ׁ[42] בׂמׁשפטׁך כי מידך היתה זאת ובלוא רׂצׂ[ונך] לׂו[א יהיה כו]ׁל

39 ⟦ׂ̊כה ימשׁוׂל בשׂר⟧   ⟦̊̊̊ותרׂבׂהׁ⟧ ⟦   [שב

40 ⟦ׂו הוא ותבׁן בשר את וׂתׁ⟧   ̊̊⟦

41 ⟦ׂ̊ רקיע עׁל כׂנׂפׂי רׂוח ויפלׂ⟧   ⟦

---

[37] Not seen previously.
[38] The form is an adjective; see Reymond, pp. 182–83.
[39] Not seen previously.
[40] See line 37 and 7.23: ואהבכה בנדבה.
[41] See 7.22. The thought echoes lines 26 and 27.
[42] See 8.26: ולב שלם.

31 [And] I will n[ot] exchange your truth for property,[96] nor any of your judgments for bribery. But as [you] bring [a ma]n close

32 [(so) I will lov]e him; and as you push him farther away, so I will abhor him forever.[97] And I will not bring into the council of [your] tr[uth] those who turn

33 [from] your [cov]enant. (VACAT) [...][98]

Hymn 8
I Thank the Lord for the Multitude of His Wonders

34 [I tha]nk you, O Lord, according to your great power and the multitude of your wonders from eternity and unto eterni[ty, (and a) multitude of compass]ions, and great

35 [mer]cies, (because you are) the one who forgives those who turn (from) transgression, and the one who punishes the wicked ones (because of) iniquity and infidelity.[99] [And I love yo]u through the generosity of[100]

36 your [righteousnesse]s;[101] for[102] you hate injustice forever. But (as for) me, your servant, you have benefited me with a spirit of knowledge to [choose tr]uth

37 [and righteous]ness, and to abhor every way of injustice.[103] And I love you generously and with all [my] heart [so as to serve you with] a [perfect]

38 heart[104] in your judgment. Because from your hand this happened, and without [your] wil[l al]l [will not occur].

39 [...] your [...]°° will rule flesh [...]°°° and you will multiply[...]*šb*

40 [...]*w* (is) he; and you understood flesh the *wt*[...]°°°

41 [...]° the firmament[105] upon the wings of the spirit[106] and *ypl*[...]°

---

[96] Or "wealth."
[97] Note the emphasis on "love" and "hate;" it is found in 1QS 1–4. A *vacat* appears here, but it does not signal a new hymn.
[98] The brackets denote a *lacuna* that probably was uninscribed.
[99] Lit. "the one who visits the iniquity of the wicked ones and (their) infidelity."
[100] Lit. "voluntary offering." Note the apparent emphasis on "freewill" in 6.35–37 and also on "determinism" in 6.29–41.
[101] See line 37 and also 7.23.
[102] Lit. "and."
[103] A *vacat* separates the thought.
[104] See 8.25.
[105] See Gen 1:6–8.
[106] Or "wind."

Col. 7 [= Sukenik Col. 15 + Frgs. 10, 42, 34, SHR 4276, and Frg. 32]
Parallels: 4Q427 Frg. 8 1.9–3

1	]
2	]
3	]
4	]
5	]
6	]
7	]
8	]
9	]
10	]
11	⟦מ̊⟧
12	⟦ ⟧ ̊ ̊] גֿב̊ו̊רתֿכה הֿשכלתֿה̊⟧ במעין⟦[43](#43)
13	ה̊ ⟦] ל̊⟧הֿפליא ⟦ וֿ גמלתנו כי נשיב מה ⟧לֿא̊כֿה פֿ[44](#44)שמועות
14	תֿ ⟦] [45](#45)ל̊⟧פֿר נפֿלא̊⟧ולֿ⟧ס̊⟧בֿכבודכה ולדעת כוח יעצרו לֿא ⟧
15	⟧ ̊ ̊ [46](#46) י⟧בכבודכה דעתֿם̊ שכלם וכפי לפֿי̊ יֿהֿללוֿכה כֿ̊י̊ מ̊⟧ולֿ⟧לֿעֿ⟦
16	[48](#48)יברכו⟧כה ל̊מ̊ו̊עֿד⟧ ומ̊ו̊עֿד⟧ ישמיעו לקץ מ̊ק̊ץ הש̊ב̊ת̊ לאין [47](#47)מֿכה⟧ להלל ⟦פיהם⟧ פ̊תחתה̊

---

43 See 9.7 and 20.16: ומעין.
44 See 23.7. Col. 23 contains similar thoughts.
45 4Q427 frg. 8 1.6: ⟦אותיכה⟧נֿ פֿל̊⟧ר⟧ וֿל̊⟧סף⟧כֿ⟧בכבוד.
46 4Q427 frg. 8 1.7: ⟦כי⟧ בכֿבודכה דעתֿמ̊ה וֿכֿפי.
47 For להלל שמכה, see 3.32, 17.39; cf. 19.28, 20.6, 23.9.
48 4Q427 frg. 8 1.8: ⟦בר⟧כֿו למועד למועד ומועד ישמיעו̊⟧י. אתה פתחתה never appears in 1QHᵃ.

Col. 7 [= Sukenik Col. 15 + Frgs. 10, 42, 34, SHR 4276, and Frg. 32]
Parallels: 4Q427 Frg. 8 1.9–3

1   […]

2   […]

3   […]

4   […]

5   […]

6   […]

7   […]

8   […]

9   […]

10   […]

11   […]*m*[…]

12   [… through the fountain of][107] your might, you have caused to have insight […]°°[…]

13   *ḥ*°[… the reports of] your [w]onder. What can we bring for what you have completed for us? And °[… to] act wondrously

14   *t*°[…]° they will not have the power to know[108] your glory and to [re]count [your] wonder[s][109]

15   °°[…] for ete[rni]ty. For they will praise you according to their insight and according to their knowledge in your glory. F[or …][110]

16   you opened [their mouths to praise] your name[111] without ceasing.[112] From time to time they shall proclaim and from appointed time to appointed time they shall bless [you][113]

---

[107] Restored in light of the expression in 9.7 and 20.16.
[108] Or "observe."
[109] See 4Q427 frg. 8 1.6.
[110] See 4Q427 frg. 8 1.7.
[111] The first consonant in "your name" is written above the line, but no editor transcribed it. It can be seen on Sukenik's photographs. For "and to praise your name," see 3.32; 17.39; cf. 19.28; 20.6; 23.9.
[112] For "without ceasing," see 14.15; 17.40; 23.3; cf. 15.18.
[113] See 4Q427 frg. 8 1.8.

לכה

17 קדו[ש]   [[ ]] ואנחנו ביחד נועדנֿוֿ ועם ידעים נֿוסרה ונֿרננה [ברוב]⁴⁹

18 רחמיכֿ[ה]   בכו[[ח עם גבוריכה ובהפלֿא נספרה יחד בדעֿ[[ת אל [[וֿעד]ֿ⁵⁰

19 בעדתֿ[[קדושיכֿ[[הֿ⁵¹ וצאצאינו הודֿעֿתה עמֿ בני איש בֿתֿוֿך בני אדם]⁵²

א

20 כי[[ב[[הֿפלֿא מאדה]   [VACAT]

Hymn 9
Bless God: A Psalm for the Master

מזמור

21 ברו[[ך אתה אל האמת⁵³ ב[[שֿיֿר למשֿ[כיל   [ ]°°   [[רֿנה]]ד°

22 יֿ]אהֿבו אותך כול הימים ואֿנֿי [°

23 אמֿ[ת   [ ] ואהבכה בנדבה ובכול לב ובכול נפש בררתי מֿעֿוֿוֿן[ושבועה על נפ]שֿיֿ

24 הקֿיֿ[מותי לבלתֿ]יֿ סור מכול אשר צויתה ואחזקה על רבים מֿעֿדֿיֿם מֿ[ל]בלתֿ[י°

25 עזוב מכולֿ חוקיך   ואני ידעתי בבינתך כיאלֿא ביד בשר[להודיע]אדם

26 דרכו ולא יוכל אנוש להכין צעדו ואדעה כי בידך יֿצֿר כול רוח [וכול פעול]תֿוֿ

⁴⁹ 4Q427 frg. 8 1.9: עֿם ידעים נוסרה לכה ונרננה וֿ.

⁵⁰ 4Q427 frg. 8 1.10: בֿהפלא נספרה יחד בעדת אל ועם וֿ].

⁵¹ See: 25.5, 32.

⁵² 4Q427 frg. 8 1.11: הֿ]ודעתה עם בני איש בתוך בני אדם וצאצאינו.

⁵³ See 9.38.

17   hol[y …].[114] And we have gathered together[115] and with those who have knowledge we ha[ve been warn]ed (through suffering) for you and we exult [in the multitude of][116]

18   yo[ur] compassions […] in pow]er with your mighty ones. And wondrously we shall recount together with knowledge [of God][117] and until °[…]

19   in the congregation of [yo]ur [holy ones][118] and our offsprings you have allowed to know[119] with the sons of man in the midst of the sons of Adam[120] […]

20   for [… wo]ndrously exceedingly [….] (VACAT) […]

Hymn 9
Bless God: A Psalm for the Master

21   Bless[ed are you, O God of truth,[121] with] a song, a psalm[122] for the Mas[ter …]°°[…]d exultation […]

22   […] they [will] love you all the days and I °[…]

23   tru[th …] and I love you generously and with all (my) heart and with all (my) soul.[123] I have purged myself from iniquity. [And a vow upon] my [so]ul[124]

24   [I ha]ve bound[125] n[ot] to depart from everything that you commanded; and I will hold to[126] all[127] appointed times s[o as n]ot

25   to abandon any of your ordinances.[128]   And I, I know by your discernment that not through[129] flesh [can] Adam[130] [be allowed to know]

26   his way, and a human cannot establish his step. But I know that in your hand (is) the inclination of[131] every spirit [and all] its [activi]ty

---

[114] Not "with a voice of."
[115] Heb. יחד; or "in community," "*Yaḥad*."
[116] See 4Q427 frg. 8 1.9.
[117] See 4Q427 frg. 8 1.10.
[118] See 3.32; cf. 25.5, 32.
[119] Permissive *hipʿil*.
[120] See 4Q427 frg. 8 1.11.
[121] See line 38 esp. and also 31.
[122] Perhaps: "a Psalm."
[123] Heb. נפש; see the note to 6:3.
[124] Heb. נפש; see the note to 6:3.
[125] See 6.28: "a vow I have bound upon my soul."
[126] For חזק with על, see Neh 10:30. In the *hipʿil*, the verb can take the meaning of "to cleave, retain." See also Ex 9:2; Judg 7:8, 19:4.
[127] Lit. "many."
[128] The scribe adds a *vacat* to highlight his next affirmation.
[129] Lit. "through the hand of." Note the paronomasia on "hand" in these lines.
[130] Or "humankind."
[131] Heb. יצר.

27   הכינותה בטרם בראתו ואיכה יוכל כול להשנות את דבריכה רק אתה בֹּ[רא]תה

28   צדיק ומרחם הכינותו למועד רצון להשמר בבריתך ולתהלך בכול ולהֹגֹּישֹ עליו

29   בהמון רחמיך ולפתוח כול צרת נפשו לישועת עולם ושלום עד ואין מחסור ותרם

30   מבשר כבודו ורשעים בראתה לֹ[י]צֹּר הֹרֹונכה ומרחם הקדשתם ליום הרגה

31   כי הלכו בדרך לא טוב[54] וימאסו בברֹיֹתֹכֹה [ואמת]ך תעבה נפשם ולא רצו בכול אשר

32   צויתה ויבחרו באשר שנאתה כיֹא לֹק[צי חרו]ֹנֹך הכינותם לעשות בם שפטים גדולים

33   לעיני כול מעשיך ולהיות לאות וֹמֹופֹ[ת דורות]עֹולם[55] לדעת כֹוֹל את כבודך ואת כוחך

34   הגדול ומה הוא אף הוא בשר כי ישכיל[בכול אלה[56] ויצ]ֹר עפר איך יוכל להכין צעדו

35   אתה יצרתה רוח ופעולתה הכינותֹ[ה מקדם עולם][57] ומאתך דרך כול חי ואני ידעתי כיא

36   לא ישוה כול הון באמתך ואי[ן בֹת]בל כמלאכי] קֹודשך[58] ואדעה כי בם בחרתה מכול

37   ולעד הם ישרתוך ולא תקֹבֹּל שֹֹוֹחֹד] רשעה[59] [ולא תקח כופר לעלילות רשעֹה כיא

---

[54] דרך appears to be a masculine noun here; ctr. 12.19 and 12.32 in which דרך seems to be a feminine noun.
[55] See 5.33: והיהֹ] לאות]עֹולם ומופת דורות.
[56] See 6.20.
[57] See 5.27.
[58] For the restoration, see 9.13.
[59] See 6.30 and the repetitive use of רשעה in lines 37–38.

27 you established before you created him. And how can anyone alter your words? Only you, you have c[r-ea]ted

28 the righteous one, and from the womb you have established him for the appointed time of (your) will in order to guard (him) in your covenant so as to walk continuously[132] in everything and to bring over him

29 the abundance of your mercies, and to open all the trouble of his soul[133] to the eternal salvation and the everlasting peace with sufficiency.[134] And you raise

30 his honor from the flesh. But the wicked ones you created for [the u]rge of[135] your fury, and from the womb you designated them for the day of killing,

31 because they walked in the way that is not good and rejected your covenant, [and] their soul[136] abhorred your [truth]. And they did not want anything that

32 you commanded, and they chose that which you hated. For the end[times of] your [fur]y you established them in order to inflict[137] on them great judgments

33 before the eyes of all your creatures,[138] and that they may become a sign and a porte[nt][139] (for) eternal [generations],[140] that all may know your glory and your power

34 (which is) great. But what is he of flesh that he will have insight[141] [into all these (things)?[142] And the inclina]tion of[143] dust, how can he establish his step?

35 You, you formed[144] the spirit, and its activity yo[u] established [from eternal ages][145] and from you is the way of every living being. And, I, I know that

36 all wealth is incomparable to your truth and nothing in the wo[rld (is) like the angels of] your holiness,[146] and I know that you have chosen them from among all (living beings),

37 and forever they will serve you. And you do not receive [wicked] bribes, and you do not take ransom for the plots of wickedness, for

---

[132] The meaning is continuously to behave righteously.
[133] Heb. נפש; see the note to 6:3.
[134] Lit. "and without need."
[135] Lit. "for [the in]clination of (יצר)." Perhaps: "as a creature of your fury."
[136] Heb. נפש.
[137] Lit. "to do."
[138] Or "your works."
[139] Or "wonder," "sign." See 5.33 for the same meaning; for "wonder" see 8.9 and 15.25.
[140] See 5.33.
[141] Or "may have insight."
[142] See 6.20.
[143] Heb. יצר.
[144] Heb. יצר.
[145] See 5.27.
[146] For the restoration, see 19.13.

38   אל אמת אתה וכול עולה תשמיד לֿ[עד וכול]רֿשֿעֿהֿ לא תהיה לפניך וֿאני ידעתיֿךֿ

39   כי לֿךֿ דֿ[רך]כֿ[וֿ]ֿל חֿיֿ וֿבֿרֿצֿוֿנֿךֿ נֿהֿיֿ[ה כול] מֿעשה ואֿ[ֿעה כי יֿ]לֿ[כו ברוח

40   ⟦קודשֿךֿ בֿֿ⟧

41   ⟦כי בֿ°°°°°°°⟧

Col. 8 [= Sukenik Col. 16 + Frg. 13 (= SHR 4278, 4263) and Frg. 12 (= SHR 4287, 4263, 4298, 4297)]

1   ]

2   ]

3   ]

4   ]

5   ]

6   ]

7   ]

8   ⟦°°°°°מֿ וכֿוֿלֿ °°] [וֿ]

9   אנשי⟧מֿוֿפֿֿת תֿבֿיא במספר

10   וברזיף⟧לֿאֿוֿ[60] בֿשֿמֿים ובארֿץֿ

11   רו⟧חֿוֿת ובידך משפט כולֿם

12   ⟦°°דֿ [ ] שֿ °°° ⟧   ואין⟧לֿנֿגֿדֿך[61] ומה יֿחֿשֿבֿ וכוֿלֿ

13   [איש]מֿתֿקדש בל יטה לאשֿמֿהֿ ליֿשֿר לבבוֿ⟧ ומה ⟦יֿבֿין ולא יעשה כול

---

[60] See 12.28, 15.30, 19.13.
[61] See 20.34.

38   you (are) the God of truth,[147] and all deceit you shall destroy for[ever. And all] wickedness shall not be before you. And I, I know you,

39   that to you (is) the w[ay of] e[ve]ry living being and by your will is do[ne all] work; and I kn[ow that they will w]al[k by the spirit of]

40   your holiness *b*˚[…]

41   for *b*˚°°°°°°[…]

Col. 8 [= Sukenik Col. 16 + Frg. 13 (= SHR 4278, 4263) and Frg. 12 (= SHR 4287, 4263, 4298, 4297)]

1   […]

2   […]

3   […]

4   […]

5   […]

6   […]

7   […]

8   […]°°°°*m* and all °°[…]*w* and ˚[…]

9   [… men of] wondrous-sign[148] you shall bring by number

10   [… and in the mysteries of][149] his [won]der within[150] the heavens and within the earth

11   [… sp]irits and within your hand is the judgment of all of them

12   […]˚*k* ˚[…]°°°*š* °°[… and nothing (is)][151] contrary to you. And how shall he think? And each

13   [man][152] who sanctifies himself will not turn aside to guilt to make straight his heart. [And how[153] shall he] discern? And nothing is done

---

[147] "God" is in Palaeo-Hebrew script in 1QHᵃ.
[148] See 5.33, 7.33, and esp. 15.24. Also note Zech 3:8.
[149] See 12.28, 15.30, 19.13.
[150] Lit. "in" or "upon." Perhaps the meaning is within humans on earth. The preposition is the same for "heavens" and "earth."
[151] See 20.34.
[152] See line 22.
[153] See מה in line 12 and 20.30.

14 [מבלע]ֹדֹיֹךְ עֹד עֹוֹלֹם וֹמֹקֹוֹר אוֹר פֹתֹחֹתֹהֹ]]   [[וֹלֹעֹצֹתֹךְ תֹקראֹנֹי

15 לֹהֹלֹל קֹוֹדֹשֹךְ בֹּפֹי כֹֹל מֹעֹשֹיֹךְ [כֹי]ֹא פֹעֹל[[תֹה ולבוֹאבֹי]]חֹֹדֹ[[עֹם צֹֹבֹֹא

16 [גֹ][בֹֹוֹֹרֹי עֹולם ורֹוח עורף קֹשֹֹה לֹדממהֹ]]   [[הֹֹוֹאלתֹֹהֹֹ לֹ]עֹשות

17 מֹ][שֹֹפֹֹט וֹלהאזין קול נכבֹדֹ לֹמֹֹעֹֹשֹֹ]יֹך

18 ורֹ][וֹח נֹעֹֹוה משֹלֹ]ה [בֹֹיֹֹצֹֹר עֹֹפֹֹֹֹר ֹֹ] [ֹֹ וֹ]

19 [[ֹֹ מֹ ֹֹ ֹֹ ֹֹֹֹֹֹֹֹֹֹֹֹ ֹֹ שֹֹ ֹֹ] [ֹֹ]]

20 [[אֹֹשֹֹ לֹֹ]   [ ]ֹֹיֹֹךְ מֹֹעֹֹפֹֹֹר   צֹ]דֹיק וֹֹכֹ]

21 בֹֹרֹוֹח קֹוֹֹ[דֹ]שֹֹךְ [אשר נתתֹ]ה בֹֹי ֹֹֹֹֹֹֹֹֹ   [וֹֹלֹא יוכל אֹֹ]נוש [

22 רֹוֹֹח קֹוֹדֹ[שֹֹ]ךֹֹ ֹֹ [ ] מֹֹלֹוֹֹא השֹֹמֹֹֹים וֹֹהארֹֹץ]   כ]בֹֹודך מלוֹא כֹוֹֹל]ֹֹ תבל

23 ואדעה כי ברצֹוֹֹנֹ[ךֹֹ] באֹיש הרביתה נחֹֹלֹֹתֹֹוֹֹ בֹֹצֹֹדֹקֹותֹֹ[יֹֹך ולהתבוֹנֹֹן] בֹֹסֹֹוֹֹד אמתֹֹך בכֹוֹֹל [מעשיֹכֹה]

24 ומשֹֹמֹֹר צדק עֹֹל דֹֹבֹֹרֹֹךְ אשר הפקֹדֹֹתֹֹה בֹו פֹן ישֹֹגֹֹה [ממצוֹוֹתֹיךֹֹ וֹֹל]בֹֹלֹתֹֹי כשול בכֹוֹֹל מֹֹעֹֹ[שֹֹיֹו]

25 בדעתי בכוֹל אלה אֹֹמֹצֹֹאֹֹה מֹעֹֹנֹֹה לֹשֹֹון להֹֹתֹֹנֹֹפֹֹל וֹֹלֹהֹֹֹֹתֹֹ[חֹֹנֹֹ]ֹֹן [תֹֹמיד] עֹֹל פֹֹשֹׁעֹי ולבקש רוֹח בֹֹיֹֹנֹ[ֹֹהֹֹ]

---

[62] See 11.23.
[63] See line 26.
[64] An image of the left side of lines 19–25 are also evident in SHR 4285.
[65] See 19.7.
[66] See line 31.
[67] See 20.7.

14 [apart fr]om[154] you unto eternity. And a source of[155] light you opened [...] and for your council you called me

15 to praise your holiness through the mouth of all your works[156] [tha]t [you] have done. [And to come[157] to]gether[158] with the host of[159]

16 [the mi]ghty ones of eternity. And the obstinate spirit[160] to calmness[161] [...] you were willing to [do][162]

17 [... ju]dgment and to be attentive to[163] the glorious voice concerning [your] work[s of[164] ...]

18 [... and a] perverted [sp]irit has rul[ed] in the inclination of[165] dust °°[...]° and °[...]

19 [...]°° *m* °°°°°°°°°° °°*š*[...]°°[...]°°°[...]

20 [...]ʾ*š*°°*l*[...]°*yk*[166] from dus[t ... rig]hteousness and *k*°[...]

21 by your ho[l]y spirit [that] yo[u placed] in me °°°°°°[...] and a hu[man] cannot [...]

22 your hol[y] spirit °°[...] the plenitude of the heavens and the earth [...] your [g]lory, the plenitude of all [the world ....]

23 And I know that in [your] will towards[167] man, you multiplied his inheritance through [your] righteousnesses[168] and allowed (him) to discern the secret of your truth[169] (that is) in all [your works.]

24 And the righteous one guards over your word[170] that you deposited in him, lest he should stray [from your commandments, and so] he will not stumble in all [his] wor[ks].

25 By my knowledge in all these things, I will find the answer of the tongue, falling prostrate,[171] and petitioning (for) me[rc]y [always],[172] because of my transgression,[173] and seeking for a spirit of discern-[ment],

---

[154] Or "without."

[155] Or "spring of."

[156] Not "creatures" here. The author is moved to praise God's works.

[157] See 11.23.

[158] Or "in co]mmunity."

[159] Or "army of."

[160] See Deut 31:27.

[161] Or "silence."

[162] See 5.18 and 8.26.

[163] *Hipʿil* of אזן; "to listen to somebody."

[164] Cf. DJD: "by the creatures [of ...]."

[165] Heb. יצר.

[166] Most likely *yk* denotes "your."

[167] Or "in."

[168] The noun is plural.

[169] See 19.7. The *beth* is a *nota accusativi*.

[170] Lit. "And the observance of righteousness over your word."

[171] Note the string of infinitives in Hebrew (participles in English).

[172] See 20.7.

[173] The noun could be a plural, since singular and plural consonantal forms are identical.

26 ‍ולהתחזק ברוח קודשֹׁךָ ולדבוק באמת בריתך ולעבדך באמת ולב שלם ולֹאֹהֹוֹב אֹת דֹּבֹּר פֹ[ֹיד]

Hymn 10
Blessed is the Lord for His Great Counsel

27 ברוך אתה אדוֹנֹי גֹּדֹוֹל העֹצֹה ורֹב העלילליה אשר מעשיך הכול הנה הואלתה לעֹשֹׁוֹֹת עֹמֹד[ֹי]

28 חסד ותחוננני ברוח רחמיך ובעֹבֹּור כבודך לך אתה הצדקה כי אתה עשיתה את כול אֹלֹה

29 ובדעתי כי אתה רשמתה רוח צדיק ואני בחרתי להבר כפי כרצוֹ[נֹ]ךֹ ונפש עֹבֹֹדֹךֹ תֹעֹבֹה תֹעֹבֹה כול

30 מעשה עולה ואדעה כי לֹא יצדק איש מֹבֹלעדיך ואחלה פניך ברוח אשר נתֹתֹה בֹֹי להשלים

31 חֹסֹדיך עם עבדֹךֹ לֹ[עֹו]לֹֹם לטהרני ברוח קודשך ולהגישני ברצונך כגדול חסדיך [אֹ]שֹׁר עֹשיתֹה

32 עֹמדי ולֹ[הֹ]עֹמֹ[יד פעמי ב]כֹֹול מֹעֹמד רצֹוֹ[נך] אשר בח[ר]תֹֹה לאוהביך ולשֹׁומרי מֹצֹוֹות[ֹיך]

33 לפניך לֹעֹוֹלם ֹו[לכפר עוון ‍[68] ֹ]ֹולֹהֹחדש[ן]בֹֹרֹצֹוֹן ֹולֹהתערב ברוח עבדך ובכול מעשֹׁ[י]ֹךֹ לֹ[עולם]

34 יֹעֹשֹׁה כֹֹול וֹןֹ ‍ [ֹו ואל יבֹ[וא] לפניו כול נֹֹגע מכשול מחוקי בריתך כי ֹֹ]

35 פנֹיך ואֹדֹעֹ[ה] כי אתה]חֹֹנֹֹון ‍[69] ורחום אֹרֹֹוֹך אפֹֹים ורֹֹב חסד ואמת ונושא פשע וֹמֹֹעֹ[ל]

---

[68] See 12.38.

[69] The leather is creased and stained. The noun חנון appears only here in 1QHᵃ. The restoration fits the loss of eight letters or spaces and the address to God in the second person.

26   and strengthening myself by your holy spirit, and adhering to the truth of your covenant, and serving you in truth and a perfect heart, and loving the word of [your] mou[th].[174]

Hymn 10
Blessed is the Lord for His Great Counsel

27   Blessed are you, O Lord, great of counsel, and multitudinous of action, because your works are everything. Indeed, you were willing[175] to manifest[176] with [me]

28   loving-kindness; and you benefited me with your spirit of mercies and for the sake of your glory. To you, you (alone), belongs righteousness,[177] because you, you made all these (things).

29   And (it is) for my knowledge that you, you recorded[178] the spirit of the righteous one, so I, I choose to cleanse[179] my hands according to your wil[l]; and the soul[180] of your servant abhors every

30   work of deceit. And I know that no man can be righteous apart from you. And I wait for you,[181] with the spirit that you put in me to complete

31   your loving-kindnesses with your servant for [etern]ity, purifying me with your holy spirit and bringing me near by your will, according to your great loving-kindnesses [w]hich you have done

32   with me. And to cause to sta[nd][182] [my steps in] all the rank[183] of [your] wil[l] that you have cho[sen] for those who love you and for those who keep [your] commandments

33   before you for eternity; and [to atone[184] for iniquity] and to enric[h][185] with favor,[186] and to be involved in the spirit of your servant. And in all your work[s] for[ever]

34   he shall do everything. And *y*[…]°*w*. And it shall not en[ter] before him any affliction as a stumbling to the statutes of your covenant, because °°[…]

35   your face; and I kno[w that you are] gracious, and compassionate, patient, and multitudinous (in) loving-kindness and truth, and one who forgets[187] transgression, and infidel[ity …]

---

[174] No *vacat* can be discerned as expected before another psalm.
[175] See also 5.18 and 8.16.
[176] Lit. "to do."
[177] Lit. "to you, you, the righteousness."
[178] Or "guarded." רשם appears only here in 1QHᵃ. The author is recorded, perhaps, in the Book of Life. See Dan 10:21.
[179] *Hipʿil* of ברר.
[180] Heb. נפש.
[181] Heb. יחל in the *hipʿil* impf. with פנים; lit. "to hope for your face (or presence)."
[182] The Heb. עמד appears three times in 8.31.
[183] See 20.38 and 10.10. The Heb. מעמד, "office," obtains a new meaning in Qumran Hebrew: "rank" or "position." Note the allusion to the Qumran concept of hierarchy, so clear in the *Rule of the Community* and in Josephus' reports about the Essenes.
[184] Note the string of infinitives.
[185] The *hipʿil* infinitive of דשן, "to become fat," does not appear in the Hebrew Bible; it (ולהדשן) seems to mean "enrich." See also 18.28.
[186] Or "will."
[187] Heb. נושה, "one who forgets (= forgives)."

36 ונחם על כ[ול צוקות[70] אוהב]יך ושומרי מצֺוֺ[תיך ה]שבים אליך באמונה ולב שלֺם]

37 לעובדך [באמת[71] לעשות ה]טוב בעיניֿך אל תשב פני עבדך [וא]ל תֺזֺנֺח בן אמתֿך]

38 א̇ה ואני על דבריך קרֺבֺתֺיֿ ל[ן

39 [°°° [ ] ל]ל [ ] °°°]

40]

41]

42]

Col. 9 [= Sukenik Col. 1 + Frg. 24]
Parallels: 4Q432 Frgs. 1–2

1]

2 [בשובך מֺתֺוה]ו °°]

3 ע[[דֺת קדושיֺם °] °°°]

4 יוד]][ע̇ בין טוֺב לֺרֿשֺ[ע [°°°°] וֺכֺוֺל]

5 רש[[עים וטֿ[ובים [ ] וֺם]][°°°°°°° עולם אֿ]

6 ש]ֺלום כיֺא [אתה מקור ד]ֺעֺת ומקה המיֺם] בם ומש[פט

---

36 and one who comforts a[ll who are in distress,[188] those loving] you, and those keeping [your] commandmen[ts], those returning to you with faithfulness and a perfect heart […]

37 to serve you [in truth, doing the] good in your eyes. Do not turn away the face of your servant [and do no]t reject the son of your handmaiden[189] […]

38 [...]ʾh and I, I draw near to your words to […]

39 [...] °°°[...]l[...] °°°[...]

40 [...]

41 [...]

42 [...]

Col. 9 [= Sukenik Col. 1+ Frg. 24]
Parallels: 4Q432 Frgs. 1–2

1 [...][190]

2 °°[...] when you turn back from chao[s[191] …]

3 °°°[… the cong]regation of the Holy Ones °[…]

4 and all [...] °°°°[… kno]wing between good and evi[l. …]

5 eternal ʾ[...] °°°°°°wm[… the wick]ed ones and the go[od ones …]

6 in them and judg[ment … pea]ce, for [you (are) the spring of kn]owledge and a reservoir of[192] water[193] […]

---

[188] See 11.8, 13.35, 17.13.

[189] Possibly "the son of your truth," but note the context and parallelism.

[190] A. K. Harkins notes that 9.1–10.4 may have served to introduce the "Teacher Hymns" section; and 4Q432 may be a scroll that was devoted only to the "Teacher Hymns." See Harkins, *OTB* 2.2037. Harkins points out that 9.1–10.4 consists of seven units that are indicated by six blanks within the line consecutively at 9.11, 15, 23, 29, 33, and 36. Perhaps, these *vacats* were used liturgically.

[191] See the first use of תהו in the Hebrew Bible, Gen 1:2.

[192] Heb. מקוה. The noun denotes "reservoir of" water only here in the *Thanksgiving Hymns*. It obtained a technical meaning: "ritual bath."

[193] A possible echo of Gen 1:10: "a reservoir of water." The noun מקוה, *mikveh*, means "hope" elsewhere in the *Thanksgiving Hymns*. Only in 9.6 does the noun mean reservoir of water. About the time the *Thanksgiving Hymns* began to appear, *mikveh* denoted a Jewish bath for ritual purification. *Mikvaot* first appear in Hasmonean strata in Jericho, Jerusalem, Modein, Zippori, Gamla, and Qeren Naftali.

בּמֹשֹׁפֹּטֹ[יכה]⁷²

7   וֹמעין הגבֹוֹ[רה כיא אתה [גֹדול העצֹהֹ⁷³ [ומעשיך] אֹיֹן מספר וקנֹאתכֹהֹ

8   לפני חכֹמֹתֹכֹהֹ] אתה חנון ורחום]⁷⁴ וארוך אפים במשפטֹ[יכ]ה צֹדֹקֹתה בכל מעשיכה

9   ובחכמתכֹהֹ ה[כ]ינותה]עולם ובטרם בראתם ידעתה כֹוֹלֹ מעשיהם

10   לעולמי עֹד וֹ[מבלעדיכה לא] יעשה כו(ו)לֹ⁷⁵ ולא יודע בלוֹא רֹצוֹנכה אתה יצרתה

11   כול רוח ופֹעולֹתֹ[ם הכינות]הֹ ומשפט לכול מעשיהם   ואתה נטיתה שמים

12   לכבודכה וֹכול [צבאם]⁷⁶ הֹכֹיֹנֹוֹתה לרצוֹנכה ורוחות עוז לחוקיהם בטרם

13   היותם למלאכי קֹ[ודש הניפות]מֹ⁷⁷ לרוחות עולם בממשלוֹתֹמֹ מאורות לרזיהם

14   כוכביֹמֹ לֹנֹתיבותֹיֹ[הם רוחות סער]הֹ⁷⁸ למשאם זקים וברקים לעבודתם ואוצרות

15   מחשבת לחפציהֹ[ם ותוצא קוֹיֹ]מֹ⁷⁹ לרזיהם   אתה בראתה ארץ (ב)בכוחכה

16   ימים ותהומות עֹשֹׂיֹ[תה בעוזכה]⁸⁰ ויֹ[ם]שֹׁביהם הכינותה בחוכמתכה וכל אשר בם

---

⁷² Not transcribed by previous editors.
⁷³ See ברוך אתה אדוֹנֹי גֹדוֹל העֹצֹהֹ in 8.27.
⁷⁴ See 8.34. The lacuna shows space for 12–14 consonants or spaces.
⁷⁵ For a discussion of two *maters*, see Reymond, pp. 27–28.
⁷⁶ See 11.36, 18.37, 26.11.
⁷⁷ See 4.38; 23.29, 33.
⁷⁸ See 21.6.
⁷⁹ See 9.31.
⁸⁰ See 23.14.

7   and the fountain of mig[ht. For you (are)][194] great (in) counsel [and your works (are)][195] without number, and your zeal[196] in [your] judgment[s][197] (are)

8   before your wisdom. [You are gracious, and compassionate,][198] and patient in [yo]ur judgment[s]. You are righteous in all your works.

9   And by your wisdom [you] es[tablished] eternity. And before you created them, you knew all[199] their works

10 for everlasting eternity, and [without you[200] not] any thing is done, and nothing is known without your will. You, you formed[201]

11 every spirit. And [yo]u [established] the[ir] deeds and the judgment for all their works.[202] And you, you spread out the heavens

12 for your glory.[203] And all [their hosts][204] you established according to your will, and strong spirits according to their ordinances. Before

13 they became the angels of ho[liness, you spread] them [out][205] to (be) eternal spirits in their dominions, luminaries according to their mysteries,

14 stars according to [their] paths, [storm]y [winds][206] according to their task, meteors and lightnings[207] according to their duty, and treasures

15 designed for the[ir] purposes, and you issued[208] [measuring-lin]es[209] according to their mysteries.[210] You, you created the earth by your power,

16 the seas and depths [you] made [by your strength. And] their [inha]bitants you established by your wisdom, and all which (is) in them

---

[194] See 8.27.

[195] See 8.27.

[196] Five supralinear consonants appear above this word; see the Hebrew text of this line.

[197] Not transcribed by previous editors.

[198] See 8.34.

[199] With dots above and below the consonants, a scribe has deleted "all."

[200] Or "apart from you."

[201] Heb. יצר.

[202] A *vacat* highlights the next affirmation.

[203] Note the parallelism in these lines.

[204] See 11.36, 18.37, 26.11.

[205] See 4.38; 23.29, 33.

[206] See 21.26.

[207] The noun is in the plural.

[208] Or "sent forth." See 9.31.

[209] See 9.31.

[210] See line 31. A *vacat* highlights, again, the affirmation of God's creation, first "the heavens" then "the earth" as in Genesis 1.

17   תכנّתה לרצונכ[ה ונתתמ] ל[רוח אדם אשר יצרת[^81] בתבל לכל ימי עולם

18   ודורות נצח למ[שול בכול תב]לֹ בקציהם פלגתה עבודתם בכול דוריהם ומש[פ]ט

19   במועדיה לממשْלֹ[תם פעמיהם[^82] וד]רֹכّיהם הֹכّיֹנוֹתֹהֹ לדור ודור ופקודת שלומם עם[^83]

20   עם כול נגיעיהם   [ה ותפלג   לכול צֹאצֹאיהם למספר דורות עולם

21   ולכול שני נצח ומֹ[עשיהם ידע]תֹה ובחכמת דעתכה הכّ[י]נّותה תע[ו]דתם בטרם

22   היותם ועל פי רّצّ[ונ]כֹّהֹ [נ]הֹّיה כול ומבלעדיך לֹא יעשה

23   אלה ידעתי מבינתכה כיא גליתה אוזני לרזי פלא ואנֹי יצר החמר ומגבל המים

24   סוד הערוה ומקור הנדה כור העוון ומבנה החטאה רוח התّוֹעה ונעוה בלא

25   בינה ונבעתה בّمֹّשפטי צדק מה אדבר בלא נודע ואשמיעה בלא סופר הכוّל

26   חקוק לפניכה בחרת זכרון לכול קצי נצח ותקופות מספר שני עולם בכול מועדיהם

27   ולוא נסתרו ולא נעדרו מלפניכה ומה יספר אנוש חטאתו ומה יוכיח על עוונתיו

---

[^81]: Note defective spelling; ctr. line 8 (צֹדֹקתה).
[^82]: See 20.37.
[^83]: The preposition "with" is written at the end of line 19 and again at the beginning of line 20 (dittography due to *parablepsis*).

17   you established according to yo[ur] will. [And you gave them] to the spirit of Adam[211] that you formed[212] in the world for all the days of eternity

18   and perpetual generations, to r[ule in all the wor]ld in their times. You assigned their duty in all their generations and judg[me]nt

19   in their appointed times[213] according to [their] dominion. [Their steps and] their [w]ays[214] you established from generation to generation, and the visitation of their peace with[215]

20   all their afflictions […]*h*. And you assigned[216] it to all their offspring for the number of eternal generations,

21   and for all the perpetual years, and [their] w[orks] you [knew], and in the wisdom of your knowledge you est[ab]lished their fix[e]d times before

22   they came into being. And according to your wi[ll], everything [shall h]appen, and without you[217] nothing is done.[218]

23   These (things) I know from your discernment, because you uncovered my ear to wonderful mysteries.[219] But I (am) an inclination of[220] clay and a mixture of water,[221]

24   a foundation of shame,[222] and a source of impurity, a furnace of iniquity, and a structure of sin, a spirit of error and (one) distorted without

25   discernment and horrified by the judgments of righteousness. What can I say that is not known, and (what) can I proclaim that has not been recounted? Everything

26   is engraved in your presence[223] with the imprint[224] of memory for all the perpetual times and the periods of the number of years of eternity in all their appointed times.[225]

27   And they are neither hidden nor absent[226] from your presence. And how should a human recount his sin? And how shall he defend his iniquities?

---

[211] Or "humankind."

[212] Heb. יצר.

[213] Or "festivals," "seasons."

[214] See 20.37: "And how can I straighten the way unless [you] establish [my s]tep."

[215] The preposition "with" is written at the end of line 19 and again at the beginning of line 20 (dittography due to *parablepsis*).

[216] Lit. "to separate."

[217] Or "apart from you."

[218] A *vacat* allows a break in thought.

[219] There may be a small *vacat* in the text. The ink has run with the next word and the leather is torn.

[220] Heb. יצר.

[221] See the similar expressions in 5.32.

[222] See 1QS 11.21–22.

[223] Or "before you."

[224] Aram. חרת or Heb. חרט means "stylus." See Isa 8:1, and also 1QM 12.3.

[225] Or "seasons," "festivals."

[226] Lit. "they are not absent."

ו

28 ומה ישיב על על משפט הצדק לכה אתה אל הדעות כול מעשי הצדקה

29 וסוד האמת ולבני האדם עבודת העוון ומעשי הרמיה   אתה בראתה

30 רוח בלשון ותדע דבריה ותכן פרי שפתים בטרם היותם ותשם[84] דברים על קו

31 ומבע רוח שפתים במדה ותוצא קוים לרזיהם וֹמֹבֹעֹ רוחות לחשבונם להודיע

32 כבודכה ולספר נפלאותיכה בכול מעשי אמתכה ומ[ש]פֹ[ט]וֹ צֹדֹקכה ולהלל שמכה

33 בפה כול יודעיכה לפי שכלם וֹבֹרכוכה לעולמי [עד][85]   ואתה ברחמיכה

34 וגדול חסדיכה חזקתה רוח אנוש לפני נגע וֹנֹפֹשֹ[עבדכה][86] טהֹרֹתֹה מרוב עוון

35 לספר נפֹלֹאֹוֹתֹיֹכֹה לנגד כול מעשיכה   וֹאֹסֹפֹרֹ[ה בקה]ה פֹתֹיֹם משפטי נגיעי

36 ולבני אנוש כול נפלאותיכה אשר הגברתה בֹ[ֹ]י לנגד ב]נֹי אֹדֹם   שמעו

37 חכמים ושחי דעת וֹנֹמֹהֹרים יהיו ליצר סמוך [תמימי][87] ד]רֹך הוסיפו ערמה

---

[84] Note defective spelling; see also 13.15.
[85] Restoration follows Licht. For לעולמי עד, see 4.40; 5.18, 30; 9.10; 15.34; and 19.28. A *vacat* appears in the text.
[86] There is space for about six consonants or spaces. See 13.17 and 19.33.
[87] See 9.38.

28 And how can the deceitful reply to the righteous judgment? To you, yourself, O God of knowledge,[227] (belong) all the works of righteousness

29 and the secret of truth. But to the sons of Adam (belong) the iniquitous deeds and the works of treachery.[228] You, you created

30 the spirit in the tongue; and you know its words. And you established the fruit of the lips[229] before they existed. And you put words on a measuring-line,

31 and the expression of the breath of the lips (is) by measure. And you issued[230] measuring-lines according to their mysteries, and the expressions of breaths according to their design (so that they) might make known

32 your glory and recount your wonders in all the works of your truth, and your righteous ju[dg]me[nt]s, and praise your name

33 by the mouth of all who know you, according to their insight. And they bless you forever [and ever].[231] And you, in your compassions

34 and your great loving-kindnesses have strengthened the spirit of the human against affliction and the soul of[232] [your servant][233] you purified from a multitude of iniquity

35 to recount your wonders before all your creatures.[234] And I will recit[e in the assembly of] the simple ones[235] the judgments of my afflictions,

36 and to the sons of the humans all your wonders, that you have strengthened[236] in [me before the s]ons of Adam.[237] Hear,[238]

37 O wise ones and contemplators of knowledge, and ones eager (for righteousness),[239] be of firm inclination.[240] [O Perfect Ones of the W]ay, increase prudence.

---

[227] "God" is in Palaeo-Hebrew in 1QHᵃ.

[228] Again, a *vacat* is used to highlight the transition to creation.

[229] The expression "fruit of the lips" is a Qumranic expression; see esp. 1QS 9.28.

[230] Or "sent forth."

[231] Restoration follows Licht. For עד לעולמי, see 4.40; 5.18, 30; 9.10; 15.34; and 19.28. A *vacat* appears in the text.

[232] Heb. נפש.

[233] There is space for about six consonants or spaces. See 13.17 and 19.33.

[234] All God's creatures include "the simple" and not only "the wise ones." A *vacat* is in the text as a pause to shift the thought to a celebration.

[235] The "simple ones" seem to denote those needing instruction, and perhaps also those incapable of learning. See 5.13 and 10.11.

[236] Lit. "to make mighty."

[237] A *vacat* is used to introduce the exhortation.

[238] Note the following series of parallel exhortations.

[239] *Nipʿil* pl. part. of מהר. Lit. "hasty ones;" but see 10.11 and esp. 13.23–24, those "eager for righteousness."

[240] Heb. יצר.

38 צדיקים השביתו עׄוׄלׄה וכוׄל תמימי דרך הׄחׄזיק[ו מתנים]נׄׄדׄכׄאׄ[88](עני האריכו

39 אפים ואל תמאסׄו במׄשׄפט[י צדק   או]יׄלׄי לב לא יבינו

40 אלה וׄבׄחׄסׄד אׄמׄ[תכה

41 [ער]יצים יחרוׄקׄוׄ[ן שנים

Col. 10 [= Sukenik Col. 2]
Parallels: 4Q428 Frg. 3; 4Q432 Frg. 3

1   ]

2   ]

3   ]ׄׄ דׄוׄן[   ] ׄׄ[

4   מעׄ[שיו ׄ[   ] ׄעׄ[

Hymn 11
I Thank the Lord for Purification

5   ] (VACAT)[89]   אודכה אד[וׄנׄיׄ כׄי ישרתה בלבבי כול מעשי עׄוׄלׄה וׄתׄטׄהׄ[רני]

צדק
6   [בצדקתכה[90] מפשעי] וׄתשם שׄ[וׄמ]רׄי אמת נגד עוני ומוכיחי אׄמׄׄתׄ בכל חׄמׄ[סי]

מׄ[שפ]טׄ
7   [   ] לׄמחץׄ מכׄתׄׄוׄ] ותשם [מנחמי כוח[91] ומשמיעי שמחה לאבל יגׄ[וני][92]

---

[88] See 10.9.
[89] Probably restore a *vacat*.
[90] See 12.38 and 19.33.
[91] See 4Q432 frg. 3 line 3: למכתי מנחמי כׄוׄ]ח.
[92] See 4Q432 frg. 3 line 4:]גוני[י.

38   O righteous ones, cease injustice. And all the Perfect Ones of the Way,[241] strength[en the loins].[242] O (you who are) oppressed, the Needy,[243] be

39   patient, and do not reject the [righteous] judgment[s.... The foo]lish of heart will not discern

40   these (things). And in the mercy of [your] trut[h ...]

41   [the ruth]less ones grind [(their) teeth ...]

Col. 10 [= Sukenik Col. 2]
Parallels: 4Q428 Frg. 3; 4Q432 Frg. 3

1   [...]

2   [...]

3   [...]°°[...] °*dw*[...]

4   [...] his [wo]rks °[...]°ͨ°[....][244]

Hymn 11
I Thank the Lord for Purification

5   [(VACAT) I thank you, O L]ord, because you straighten in my heart all the works of deceit and you purif[ied] me

6   [by your righteousness[245] from my transgression.] And you placed gu[ardi]ans[246] of truth in the presence of my transgressor, and the chastisements of righteousness[247] (was) with all [my] viole[nt ones][248]

7   [...] for the wound of his blow.[249] [And you placed] the powerful comforters[250] and the proclaimers of joyous ju[dgme]nt[251] for [my] griev[ous] mourning,

---

[241] For this technical phrase, see B. A. Strawn with H. W. Morisada Rietz, "(More) Sectarian Terminology in the *Song of the Sabbath Sacrifice:* The Case of תמימי דרך" in *Qumran Studies: New Approaches, New Questions,* edited by M. T. Davis and B. A. Strawn (Grand Rapids, 2007) pp. 53–64.

[242] See 10.9.

[243] In this context, a plural is probably intended: "the Needy" Ones. It is parallel to "the Perfect Ones of the Way."

[244] A *vacat* may have been in the lost text.

[245] See 12.38 and 19.33.

[246] The author thanks the Lord for his true guardians who insulated him from the violent ones (the wicked priests). The author of these lines seems to be the Righteous Teacher.

[247] For the restoration, see 17.33. The word "truth" is marked to be ignored by scribal dots added above and below the word. The word "righteousness" is inscribed above the line.

[248] See 4Q432 frg. 3 line 2.

[249] See Isa 30:26. Most likely "his blow" denotes the blows delivered by the Wicked Priest on the Righteous Teacher.

[250] See 4Q432 frg. 3 line 3.

[251] Added above the line is [judgmen]t."

8 [מבשר ש]ֹלֹום לכול הווֹת שמוע[תי   חזקים למוס לבבי ומאמצי כֹ]וחי[93]

9 לפני [נ]ֹגֹע ותתן מענה לשון לער[ול] שפתי ותסמוך נפשי בחזוק מותנים

10 ואמוץ כוח ותעמד פעמי בגבול רשעה ואהיה פח לפושעים ומרפא לכול

11 שבי פשע ערמה לפתיים[94] ויצר סמוך לכול נמהרי לב ותשימני חרפה

12 וקלס לבוגדים סוד אמת ובינה לישרי דרך ואהיה על עוֹן רשעים

13 דבה בשפת עריצים לצים יחרוקו שנים   ואני הייתי נגינה לפושעים

14 ועלי קהלת רשעים תתרגש ויהמו כנחשולי ימים בהרגש גליהם רפש

15 וטיט יגרישו ותשימני נס לבחירי צדק ומליץ דעת ברזי פלא לבחון

16 [אנשי] אמת ולנסות אוהבי מוסר ואהיה איש ריב למליצי תעות וֹבֹעֹלֹ

17 [מד]נֹיֹם לכול חוזי נכוחות ואהיה לרוח קנאה לנגד כל דורשי חל[קות]

18 [וכול] אֹנשי רמיה עלי יהמו כקול המון מים רבים ומזמות בליעל [כול]

---

[93] See line 10.
[94] For the form see 5.13.

8   [announcing] peace for all disasters [I] have heard, […] strong ones for the melting of my heart, and the courageous ones of [my] p[ower][252]

9   before [affl]iction. And you give an answer of the tongue to my unsk[illed] lips,[253] and you sustained my soul[254] with the strengthening of the loins

10   and the courage of power. And you set my footsteps within the border of wickedness, and I am a trap for transgressors, but a healing for all

11   those who turn from transgression, prudence for the simple ones, and a firm inclination[255] for all eager of heart.[256] And you set[257] me (as) a disgrace

12   and mockery to the unfaithful ones, a foundation of[258] truth and discernment for the Upright Ones of the Way. And because of the iniquity of the wicked ones, I have become

13   a slander on the lip of the ruthless ones. Scorners grind (their) teeth.[259] And I, I have become a taunt[260] for transgressors;

14   and against me the assembly of the wicked roar, and they rumble as the gales of the seas in the roaring of their waves. Mud

15   and mire they roll up. But you set me[261] (as) a banner for the elect ones of righteousness, and the Interpreter of[262] knowledge in the wonderful mysteries,[263] to examine

16   [the men of] truth and to test the lovers of discipline. But I have become a man of strife for the interpreters of error, but the consummate

17   [deb]ater[264] for all the seers of correct things. And I have become a zealous spirit against all seekers of sm[ooth things.][265]

18   [And all] the men of slackness roar against me as the sound of abundant waters. And from the devices of Belial[266] (are) [all]

---

[252] See line 10. The expression denotes those who have "adopted" or "espoused" "my power." The text brings up a connection with the Righteous Teacher.

[253] Lit. "my uncirc[umcised] lips."

[254] Heb. נפש.

[255] Heb. יצר.

[256] See Isa 35:4. See 13.23–24.

[257] Perhaps a *hipʿil* permissive.

[258] Or "secret of."

[259] See 9.41. A small *vacat* is used again to highlight a personal statement.

[260] Or "taunting-song." This word appears in Job 30:9.

[261] Perhaps a *hipʿil* permissive.

[262] See Job 33:23, the heavenly being.

[263] All these self-reflections most likely derive from the Righteous Teacher.

[264] Lit. "and the head of controversies (or contentions)." See Hab 1:3.

[265] The expression "seekers of smooth things" is a euphemism for liars; see 10.17. For the expression elsewhere in the Dead Sea Scrolls, see 4Q169 frgs. 3–4 2.2, 4; 4Q169 frgs. 3–4 3.3, 6–7.

[266] Or "devilry." The Heb. בליעל may not be a *nomen proprium* in the *Thanksgiving Hymns*.

19 מֵחֹשְׁבוֹתם ויהפוכו לשוחה חיי גבר אשר הכינותה בפיו[95] ותלמד(ֹנ)ו בינה

20 שמתה בלבבו לפתוח מקור דעת לכול מבינים וימירום בערול שפה

21 ולשון אחרת לעם לא בינות להלֹבֹט במשגתם (VACAT)

Hymn 12
I Thank the Lord for He Placed My Soul with the Living Ones

22 אודכה אֹדוֹני כי שמתה נפשי בצרור החיים (VACAT)

23 ותשוך בעדי מכול מוקשי שחת כֹ[י]אֹ עריצים בקשו נפשי בתומכי

24 בבריתֹכֹה[96] והמה סוד שוא ועדת בֹליעל לא ידעו כיא מאתכה מעמדי

25 ובחסדיכה תושיע נפשי כיא מאתכה מצעדי והמה מאתכה גרו

26 על נפשי בעבור הכבדכה במשפט רשעים והגבירכה בי נגד בני

27 אדם כיא בחסדכה עמדי ואני אמרתי חנו עלי גבורים סבבום בכל

---

[95] 1QHᵃ: בפי; read with Licht: בפיו.
[96] Note the final *kaph* in medial position in 1QHᵃ.

19 their thoughts. And they cast into the pit the life of the man[267] in whose mouth[268] you established (instruction), and you taught him discernment;

20 you set in his heart to open a spring of[269] knowledge to all who have understandings; but they exchanged them for unkilled speech[270]

21 and another language for a people of no discernment,[271] so that they are ruined by their (own) error. (VACAT)

Hymn 12
I Thank the Lord for He Placed My Soul with the Living Ones

22 (VACAT) I thank you, O Lord, because you placed my soul[272] in the bundle of[273] the living ones,

23 and made a hedge about me (to protect) from all the snares of the pit, be[cau]se ruthless ones sought my soul,[274] while I adhered to

24 your covenant.[275] But they (are) the assembly of vanity, and the congregation of Belial.[276] They do not know that my position (is) because of you.

25 And through your mercies you save[277] my soul,[278] for my treads (are) because of you. And they, because of you, they were afraid[279] (to destroy)[280]

26 my soul[281] for you made heavy the judgment of the wicked ones,[282] and you manifest your might through me against the sons of

27 Adam;[283] for in your mercy (is) my standing. But I, I said, mighty ones encamped against me; they encircled me[284] with all

---

[267] Heb. גבר.
[268] The text has "my mouth." It is a scribal error.
[269] Or "source of."
[270] Lit. "uncircumcised lips."
[271] Note the dualism between those who have discernment and those who have no discernment.
[272] Heb. נפש.
[273] See 1Sam 25:29. The noun means to be bound up as in a pouch.
[274] Heb. נפש.
[275] See the same expression in 12.2, 22.14; cf. 12.23 and 15.23.
[276] Or "devilry."
[277] Note the future tense that is an intensive present. In this section of hymns most likely composed by the Righteous Teacher the past tense ("you saved") is dominant. Did a Qumran scribal editor change the verbal tense?
[278] Heb. נפש.
[279] גור, "be afraid of." גור with על appears in Ps 59:4, but the meaning "attack" is not appropriate in the present context.
[280] The author suffers great physical harm, but is not killed.
[281] Heb. נפש.
[282] The author cannot be threatened because of God (as in some translations). See lines 37–38 and 12.19–21.
[283] Or "sons of humankind."
[284] The text has "them;" it is an error for "me."

28 כלי מלחמותם ויפרו חצים לאין מרפא ולהוב[97] חנית באש אוכלת עצים

29 וֹבֹהמון מים רבים שאון קולם נפץ וֹזרם להשחית רבים למזורות יבקעו

30 אפעה ושוא בהתרומם גליהם ואני במוס לבי כמים ותחזק נפשי בבריתך

31 וֹהֹם רשת פרשו לי תלכוד רגלם ופחים טמנו לנפשי נפלו בם   ורגלי עמדה במישור

32 מקהלם אברכה שמכה   (VACAT)

Hymn 13
I Thank the Lord for Saving Me from Lying Interpreters

33 אודכה אדוני כיא עינכה על[י]בֹשֹׁפֹוֹל נפשי ותצילני מקנאת מליצי כזב

34 ומעדת דורשי חלקות פדיתֹ נֹפֹש אביון אשר חשבו להתם דמו

35 לשפוך על עבודתכה[98] אפס כי [לוא] יֹדֹעֹו כי מאתך מצעדי וישימוני לבוז[99]

---

[97] Note the *mater*. See 11.37.
[98] 4Q428 frg. 3 line 1: עב]וֹֹדֹתֹכֹה[ ].
[99] 4Q428 frg. 3 line 2: וישימונ]י לבוז וחֹֹרֹ[פה.

28 the instruments of their wars, and the arrows without cure (are) useless,[285] and the spear blazing with fire devours trees.

29 And like the roar of many waters (is) the noise of their voice, a thunderclap and downpour[286] to destroy many. For healing purposes they cleave

30 the sand-viper, but in vain when their waves rise.[287] And me, when my heart melted like water, then my soul[288] was strengthened[289] by your covenant.

31 And they, they spread a net for me, but it entraps their (own) feet; and the traps which they set[290] for my soul,[291] they fell into them. But my foot stood in firmness.[292]

32 Away from their assembly I shall bless your name. (VACAT)

Hymn 13
I Thank the Lord for Saving Me from Lying Interpreters

33 I thank you, O Lord, because your eye (is) on [me] during the humiliation of[293] my soul,[294] and you saved me from the zeal of[295] the interpreters of the lie.[296]

34 And from the assembly of the Seekers of Smooth (Things) you redeemed the soul of the Poor One,[297] whose blood they thought to annihilate,

35 in order to pour (it) upon your service. But they did [not] know that because of you[298] (are) my treads. And they placed me as (an object of) scorn

---

[285] *Hipʿil* imperfect of פרר , lit. "shatter" or "make useless."

[286] Heb. נפץ; see Isa 30:30 (נפץ וזרם). Isaiah 30 has influenced the imagery and language in 10.29 and earlier.

[287] See Isa 30:6, 59:5. This sentence is one of the most difficult to understand, but not to translate in this scroll. The "mighty ones" cannot obtain healing from the venom of vipers.

[288] Heb. נפש.

[289] Or "was restored." *Piʿel* impf. of חזק.

[290] Lit. "buried."

[291] Heb. נפש. A *vacat* separates two thoughts.

[292] Lit. "on level ground." The traps did not entrap the thinker.

[293] The *šapʿel* of נפל. See KB 1631. See 26:16.

[294] Heb. נפש.

[295] Or "jealousy."

[296] See "the man (אדם or איש) of lie" in CD MS B 19.26, 20.15; 1QHab 2.2, 5.11; and 4Q471. A unique personality is reflected in these lines and a particular experience is shared. Most likely the words ultimately derive from the Righteous Teacher who may be thinking back on the problems he encountered within the Temple against his adversaries, the Hasmonean priests and the precursors of the Pharisees (the Seekers of Smooth Things).

[297] The Poor One (the Righteous Teacher) and the Poor (the Many at Qumran) are *termini technici*.

[298] See 10.25.

36   ואתה אלי עזרתה נפש עני וֹרשׁ[101   וחרפה[100 בפי כל דורשי רמיה

37   מ̇יד חזק ממנו ותפד נפשי מיד אֹדירים ובגדפותם לא החתותני[102

38   לעֹזוב עבודתכה מפחד הוות רשׁעֹים ולֹהֹמיר (ב)בהולל יצר סמוך אשר[103

39   נֹתֹתה[104   ות[למֹדמו חוקֹים וֹבתעודות [כו]ננתני להֹחזֹיק

40   [ב]שֹׁר[105   ]שֹׁחת לכול צאצאֹי עֹד[106

41   [לֹשֹוֹן כלמֹודיכה ובמֹשֹ[פט][107

Col. 11 [= Sukenik Col. 3 + Frg. 25]
Parallels: 4Q428 4.1–2; 5.1–7; 4Q432 5–7

1   ]

2   ]מֹ בֹכֹי מֹ°°[

3   ]מֹ וֹהֹבֹ °לֹיֹ° ° °°°°[

4   אתה] אֹלֹי האֹירֹותה לֹבֹרֹיֹתֹכֹה[

5   ]הֹ לכה בכבוד עולם עם כוֹלֹ [ ] °° ° [

6   ואדעה כי אמ[ת] פיכה ותצילֹיני מֹ[סוד שוא][108 ומ[עון רשע]יֹם[109

---

100 4Q428 frg. 3 line 2: וישׁימונֹ]י לבוז ובֹוֹ[זֹ ומחֹ]פֹה.

101 4Q428 frg. 3 line 3: [. נפש עֹנֹי].

102 4Q428 frg. 3 line 4: וֹ[תֹפד נפשי מיד אדירים ובגדפו]תֹם לוא[החתותני לעזוב].

103 4Q428 frg. 3 line 5: עבוֹ]דתכה מפחד הוות רשעים וֹל[ֹהֹמיר בהולל יצר סמוך אשר].

104 4Q428 frg. 3 line 6: נֹתֹ[תה].

105 4Q428 frg. 3 line 7: [ב]שֹׁר[.

106 4Q428 frg. 3 line 8:]לכול[צאצאֹי עד].

107 4Q428 frg. 3 line 9: [לֹשֹוֹן כלמוֹד]יכה ובמשפט [.

108 See 10.24.

109 See 10.12.

36 and disgrace in the mouth of all seekers of treachery.[299] But you, O my God,[300] you have rescued[301] the soul of[302] the Needy One[303] and the Wretched One[304]

37 from the hand of one stronger than he.[305] And you redeemed my soul[306] from the hand of the powerful ones, and in their slanders you did not allow me to be afraid

38 (so that I would) leave your service from the fear of the threats of the wicked ones, and exchanging for foolishness a firm inclination[307] that

39 you put [… and you] taught him[308] statutes, and through the testimonies you[309] [es]tablished me to hold

40 [f]lesh […] the pit for all everlasting descendants

41 […] the tongue according to your teachings and in the judg[ment][310]

Col. 11 [= Sukenik Col. 3 + Frg. 25]
Parallels: 4Q428 4.1–2; 5.1–7; 4Q432 5–7

1 […]

2 […]*m* weeping *m*°°[…]

3 […]°*m* and *hb*°°*ly*° °° °°°°[…]

4 [… you], O my God, you have made my face[311] to shine for your covenant […]

5 […]*h* to you in eternal glory with all […] °° °°[…]

6 [… . And I know that tru]th[312] (is in) your mouth and you rescued me from [the assembly of vanity][313] and from [the iniquity of the wicked] ones[314]

---

[299] A *vacat* introduces the affirmation.
[300] "O my God" (אלי) is written in Palaeo-Hebrew in 1QHª.
[301] Lit. "helped."
[302] Heb. נפש.
[303] See the same term in 13.15, 16; cf. 9.38.
[304] See the same noun in 13.16, 22. Also see the discussions in the Introduction.
[305] The first and second person speech refers to the same person.
[306] Heb. נפש.
[307] Heb. יצר.
[308] The author refers to himself using "him" and "me."
[309] Or "fixed times."
[310] See 4Q428 frg. 3 line 9.
[311] The word "my face" is barely visible; it was added by a scribe as a superscript.
[312] No *vacat* is discernible; the flow of one hymn continues.
[313] See 10.24.
[314] See 10.12.

7 [הוש]ֿעתה נפשֿ[י] לחרפה ולקל[ֿסֿ יחשיבוני[110] וישימו נפשֿי כֿאוניה במֿצֿולות יֿם

8 וכעיר מבצר מלפֿנֿיֿ [אויב] וֿאהיֿה בצוקה כמו אשת לדה מבכריה[111] כיא נהפכו צירֿיֿם

9 וחבל נמרץ על משבריה להחיל בכור הריה כיא באו בנים עד משברי מות

10 והרית גבר הצרה בחבליה כיא במשברי מות תמליט זכר ובחבלי שאול יגיח

11 מכור הריה פלא יועץ עם גבורתו ויפלט גבר ממשברים בהריתו החישו כול

12 משברים וחבלי מרץ במולדיהם ופלצות להורותם ובמולדיו יהפכו כול צירים

13 בכור הריה[112] והרית אפעה לחבל נמרץ ומשברי שחת לכול[113] מעשי פלצות ויריעו

14 אושי קיר כאוניה על פני מים ויהמו שחקים בקול המון וֿיֿושבי עפר

15 כיורדי ימים נבעתים מהמון מים וחכמיה למו כמלחים במצולות כי תתבלע ֿם[114]

[110] Note the *waw mater* after the second root consonant.
[111] A metathesis for מבכירה.
[112] 4Q428 frg. 4 line 1: [בְּכוֹר הֵרִיהֿ .
[113] 4Q428 frg. 4 line 2: ומשֿ[בֿ]רי שחת לכול].
[114] See 12.13.

7   you [sav]ed [my] soul.[315] They consider me [a disgrace and a mocke]ry[316] and besiege[317] my soul[318] like a ship in the depths of the sea,

8   and like a fortified city before [the enemy]. And I am in distress like a woman laboring for the firstborn, for labor pains come upon (her),

9   and intensive tribulation (is) upon the opening of her womb[319] to cause anguish in the womb of[320] the pregnant one,[321] because sons[322] have reached the opening of the womb of death.[323]

10   And she who is pregnant (with) a man[324] was troubled by her tribulations, for in the opening of the womb of death she rescues[325] a male.[326] And in the tribulations of Sheol he shall burst forth

11   from the womb of[327] the pregnant one. (He shall be) a wonderful counselor[328] with his might; and a man[329] shall be delivered from the opening of the womb of the one pregnant (with) him. All the

12   opening of the womb[330] hastened, and intensive tribulations (occurred) when they were born; and (they are) a shuddering to their parents. And at his birth all the labor pains turn

13   in the womb of[331] the pregnant one. And she who is pregnant with a sand-viper[332] (suffers) intensive tribulation, and the breakers of the pit for all the works of shuddering. And the

14   foundations of the wall shall tremble like a ship on the surface of the water,[333] and the skies rumble with a roaring[334] sound.[335] And the dwellers of the dust (are)

15   like those who go down to the seas, terrified from the roar of the waters, and their wise ones for them[336] (are) like sailors in the depths, since all their

---

[315] Heb. נפש.

[316] See Jer 20:8.

[317] Lit. "put," "set," or "place." See 1Kgs 20:12.

[318] Heb. נפש.

[319] Not the Heb. word for "breakers," though it is identical in unpointed manuscripts to "mouth of the womb." In this column the noun is plural in Hebrew.

[320] Lit. "furnace."

[321] Or "of the birthpangs (for her) firstborn of her pregnancy."

[322] The author mixes two thoughts: the birth of sons and the birth of one male.

[323] Is the poet expressing the thought that those who are born will die?

[324] Heb. גבר.

[325] *Hipʿil* מלט: "to rescue," "give birth." See Isa 66:7.

[326] Heb. זכר. Many infants died during their birth.

[327] Lit. "furnace."

[328] See Isa 9:5 which the author no doubt had memorized.

[329] Heb. גבר.

[330] The author is making paronomasia with two nouns: "the opening of the womb" and "breakers;" both are משבר. He will soon shift to "breakers." At birth the womb opens wide and vast amounts of liquid "break" forth. The author utilizes a *double entendre*: "the opening of the womb" and the "breakers" of water.

[331] Lit. "furnace of."

[332] See Isa 30:6, and J. H. Charlesworth, *The Good and Evil Serpent* (New Haven, 2010) p. 446.

[333] Lit. "upon the faces of the water."

[334] Or "abundant." Note the paronomasia on "roaring" which can also mean "abundant."

[335] Lit. "voice."

[336] In this passage, למו ("for him") means להם ("for them") as in Isa 44:7.

16 כול חכמתם בהמות ימים ברתוח תהומות על נבוכי מים וֹיתרגֹשו לרום גלים

17 ומשברי מים בהמון קולם ובהתרגשם יפתחו שֹ[או]לֹ[ן וא]בֹֹדֹ[ון ו]כֹוֹל[115](https://) חצי שחת

18 עם מצעדם לתהום ישמיעו קולם ויפתחו שערי [עו]לֹ[ם   תח]תֹ מעשי אפעה

19 ויסגרו דלתי שחת בעד הרית עול ובריחי עולם בעד כול רוחי אפעה   (VACAT)

Hymn 14
I Thank the Lord for Redeeming My Soul from the Pit

20 אודכה אדוני כי פדיתה נפשי משחת ומשאול אבדון

21 העליתני לרום עולם ואתהלכה במישור לאין חקר ואדעה כיא יש מקוה לאשר

22 יצרתה מעפר לסוד עולם ורוח נעוה טהרתה מפשע רב להתיצב במעמד עם

23 צבא קדושים ולבוא ביחד עם עדת בני שמים ותפל לאיש גורל עולם עם רוחות

24 דעת להלל שמכה ביחד רנֹהֹ ולספר נפלאותיכה לנגד כול מעשיכה ואני יצר

25 החמר מה אני מגבל במיםֹ ולמי נחשבתי ומה כוח לי כיא התיצבתי בגבול רשעה

---

[115] See line 20.

16   wisdom is swallowed up in the rumblings of the seas, when the depths boil over the sources of the water and are agitated to high waves,

17   and (to) the breakers of water with their roaring sound.[337] And through their agitation they will open Sh[eo]l [and A]badd[on and] all the arrows of the pit

18   with their movement[338] into the depth, they will make loud their sound[339] and open the gates of [et]er[nity, benea]th the works of a sand-viper.[340]

19   And they shut the doors of the pit before the one pregnant (with) deceit, and the bars of eternity before[341] all the spirits of the sand-viper.[342] (VACAT)

Hymn 14
I Thank the Lord for Redeeming My Soul from the Pit

20   (VACAT) I thank you, O Lord, because you redeemed my soul[343] from the pit; and from Sheol-Abaddon

21   you raised me to an eternal height. And I walk continuously in unfathomable[344] uprightness[345] so that I know that there exists hope for (him) whom

22   you fashioned[346] from dust for the eternal assembly. And a confused[347] spirit you have purified from great transgression, to be present in rank with

23   the host of the Holy Ones, and to enter the Community[348] with the congregation of the sons of heaven.[349] And to humankind you cast an eternal lot with the spirits of

24   knowledge to praise your name in common[350] exultation and to recount your wonders before all your creatures. But I am an inclination of[351]

25   the clay. What am I (but clay) mixed with water? And for whom was I considered and what power do I have? For I am present within the border of wickedness,

---

[337] Or "voice."

[338] Lit. "marching," "treads."

[339] Or "voice."

[340] Or "the offspring of a sand-viper." See Isa 30.6; 59.5, and J. H. Charlesworth, *The Good and Evil Serpent,* p. 446.

[341] The deceitful ones and evil spirits are locked in Sheol. The gates are locked before them. They cannot get out of Sheol. The passage does not have the adverb "behind" (אחר).

[342] See the note to 10.36.

[343] Heb. נפש.

[344] Heb. לאין חקר.

[345] Not "in a plain."

[346] The verb יצר. Note the *double entendre*; that is, the inclination of clay was inclined to dust.

[347] From the *nip'al* of עוה.

[348] Or "to enter together." Heb. יחד.

[349] "The Holy Ones" and "the sons of heaven" can mean both the enlightened in the *Yaḥad* and the angels. The Community (the *Yaḥad*) is an antechamber of heaven. Angels worship on earth with the humans who are now "the Holy Ones," because God purified them of darkness or the evil inclination.

[350] Possibly a paronomasia on *Yaḥad.*

[351] Heb. יצר.

26   ועם חלכאים בגורל ותגור נפש אביון עם מהומות רבה והוות מדהבה עם מצעדי

27   בהפתח כל פחי שחת ויפרשו כול מצודות רשעה ומכמרת חלכאים על פני מים

28   בהתעופף כול חצי שחת לאין[116] השב ויורו לאין תקוה בנפול קו על משפט וגורל אף

29   על[117] נעזבים ומתך חמה על[118] נעלמים וקץ חרון לכול בליעל וחבלי מות[119] אפפו לאין פלט

על[120]

30   וילכו נחלי בליעל כול אגפי רום בֿאש אוכלת בכול[121] שנאביהם להתם כול עץ לח

31   ויבש מפלגיהם ותשוט בשביבי להוב[122] עד אפס כול שותיהם באושי חמר תאוכל

32   וברקיע יבשה[123] יסודי הרים לשרפה ושורשי חלמיש לנחלי זפת[124] ותאוכל עד תהום

פ

33   רבה ויבקעו לאבדון נחלי בליעל ויהמו מחשבי תהום בהמון גורשי רש[125] וארץ

34   תצרח על ההווה הנהֿיה בתבל וכול מחשביה יריעו ויתהוללו כול אשר עליה

35   ויתמוגגו בהווֿה גדֿ[ו]לֿהֿ כיא ירעם אל בהמון כוחו ויהם זבול קודשו באמת

ב

36   כבודו וצבא השמים יתנו קולם וֿיֿתמוגגו וירעדו אושי עולם ומלחמת גבורי

37   שֿמים תשוט בתבל ולֿא תשוֿבֿ עֿד כלה ונחרצה לעד ואפס כמֿוֿהֿ   (VACAT)

---

[116] 4Q428 frg. 5 line 1: ח[צֿיֿ שחת לֿ]אין.
[117] 4Q428 frg. 5 line 2: וג[ֿוֿרל אֿ]ף עֿ[לֿ].
[118] 1QH[a]: ועל.
[119] 4Q428 frg. 5 line 3: וח[בֿלֿיֿ] מות.
[120] Haplography.
[121] 4Q428 frg. 5 line 4: כול [אֿגפי רום בֿ]אש אוכל]ת בכֿ]ול שנאביהם].
[122] 4Q428 frg. 5 line 5: לה[תֿםֿ] לֿחֿ] כול עץ] ויב]שֿ מפלגיהם] ותשוט [בֿשביֿ]בי להוב]. See 10.28.
[123] 4Q428 frg. 5 line 6: [עד אפס כו]לֿ] שותיהם באושי]חֿמר [תאוכל] וברקיע יב]שה].
[124] 4Q428 frg. 5 line 7: ושורשי ח[לֿ]מיש לנח]לֿי זֿפֿת] ותאוכל].
[125] Read: פרש.

26 and with the miserable ones in (one) lot. And the soul of[352] the Poor One dwells with great turmoils. And oppressive disasters (are) with my treads,

27 when all the traps of the pit open, and all the nets of wickedness are spread, and a fishing net of the miserable ones (is) on the surface of the water,

28 when all the arrows of the pit fly without return, and are shot without hope, when the measuring-line falls on the judgment and the lot of anger

29 on the forsaken ones, and the pouring of fury on the hidden ones, and the Endtime of fury for all of Belial, and the bonds of death[353] enclose with no deliverance.

30 And the rivers of Belial pour over[354] all the heightened banks with fire devouring all their growth[355] to annihilate every tree, moist

31 and dry from their streams. And it sweeps with the sparks of[356] fire until[357] all their canals (are) no more.[358] It (the fire) consumes the foundations of clay

32 and the firmament[359] of the dry land, (and) the bases of mountains become a burning, and the sources of[360] flint (turn into) rivers of tar, and it (the fire) consumes as far as the great

33 depth. And the rivers of Belial break forth to destruction, and the designs of the depth roar with the abundance of those who roll up the mud. And the earth

34 cries out about the disaster which has happened in the world,[361] and all its designs wail, and all who are upon it behave madly.

35 And they melt away in the gr[e]at disaster, because God thunders with his abundant power, and the habitation of his holiness roars through the truth of

36 his glory. And the host of heaven raised their voice,[362] and the eternal foundations melt away and shake. And the war of the mighty ones of[363]

37 heaven sweeps into the world and does not return until the completion and the extermination for ever. And nothing is like it. (VACAT)

---

[352] Heb. ‬נפש‬.

[353] Or "pains of death."

[354] Lit. "walk over."

[355] This noun is a *hapax legomenon*; it is perhaps the *šap'el* form which denotes, "causing growth." See Bardtke in *TLZ* 81 (1956) and 82 (1957).

[356] Lit. "flames of."

[357] Lit. "until utterly."

[358] Or "until all that drink of them are no more."

[359] See Gen 1:6–8.

[360] Lit. "roots of."

[361] See the personification of the earth in Rev 12:16.

[362] A Heb. idiom; see Ps 104:12.

[363] Or "warriors of."

Hymn 15
I Thank the Lord for Protection

38 אודכה אדוני כיא הייתה לי לחׄומת עׄוז

39] °° כוׄ]ׄל משחיתים וכוׄל[   ]כי תסתירני מהׄוות126 מהׄומה אשׄׄר דׄ°°°[

40 דׄ]לׄתׄיׄן מגן127 ובריׄ]ׄחׄיׄן[ ][ברזל][ ]בל יבואׄ גדוד משמר

41 גבורים בהלוות]128   ]מׄׄם בסביביה פן יורׄה גׄבׄוׄ]ׄר

Col. 12 [= Sukenik Col. 4 + Frg. 43]
Parallels: 4Q428 Frg. 6; 4Q430;129 4Q432 Frgs. 7–10

1 גמו]לי גבורתם ויפולו מגבור]תם[130

2 חׄכמיׄם בערמתם ואׄנׄיׄ131 בׄתׄוׄמׄכׄׄיׄ132 בׄבׄ]ׄריתכה

3] °°°מׄׄו °°°°° ו מוׄ°°[

4]וׄתׄכׄׄן עׄל סׄלׄׄע רגלׄי ותׄסיר פׄעמׄי מׄׄ]דרך עולה133

ב
5 [להתהלך]134 בׄׄדׄרׄך עולם ונתיבות אשר בחרתה מׄצׄׄעׄׄדׄׄי °°°[

Hymn 16
I Thank the Lord for Enlightening Me for the Covenant

א
6 [אודכה אדוני כׄי האירותה פני לבריתכה ומ]

7 [° אדורשכה135 וכשחר נכון לאור]ׄתׄי[ׄׄם הופעתה לי והׄמה עמכׄ]ׄה

---

126 Perhaps read: מהיות or מהוות.
127 See 14.30: דלתי מגן.
128 See 4Q432 frg. 7 line 1: גבורים בהלוות.
129 4Q430 provides no lost consonants.
130 Restored from 4Q432 frg. 7 line 3: לׄי גבורתם ויפולו מגבורתם[; and 4Q428 frg. 6 line 1: גבור]תׄ]ׄם ויפולו מגבור]תם[.
131 4Q428 frg. 6 line 2: חׄכמיׄם בערמתם וׄ]אני בתומכי בבריתכה.
132 Restored from 4Q432 frg. 7 line 4: תם ואני בתומ]ׄ.
133 See 6.37.
134 See 15.17.
135 Note the *mater* after the first root consonant.

Hymn 15
I Thank the Lord for Protection

38   (VACAT) I thank you, O Lord, because you became for me a strong city wall[364]

39   °°[… al]l the destroyers and all […] for you hide me from disasters of turmoil which *d*°°°[…]

40   [… the d]oors of [defense[365] and the ba]rs of iron lest the guarding troop of the mighty ones[366] should enter

41   accompanied […]*mm* in its surroundings lest a mighty m[an] should shoot […]

Col.12 [= *Sukenik Col. 4 + Frg. 43*]
Parallels: 4Q428 Frg. 6; 4Q430; 4Q432 Frgs. 7–10

1   [… the retaliation]s of their might. And they will fall from [their] might,[367]

2   wise ones[368] in their craftiness.[369] But I, when I hold fast to [your] co[venant[370] …]

3   […]°°°°*mw* °°°°*w mw*°°[…]

4   […] and you established upon a rock my feet and you removed my footsteps from [the way of injustice …][371]

5   [to walk continuously][372] on the eternal way and on the paths which you have chosen (for) my treads °°° [….]

Hymn 16
I Thank the Lord for Enlightening Me for the Covenant

6   […] (VACAT) I thank you, O Lord, because you enlightened my face for your covenant, and *m*[…]

7   […]° I seek you. And like the dawn established for per[fect li]ghts,[373] you have appeared to me. And they (are) your people[374] […]

---

[364] "City wall" is one word in Heb.
[365] See 14.30. Lit. "d]oors of [a shield;" i.e., shielding doors.
[366] See 4Q432 frg. 7 line 1.
[367] Restored from 4Q432 frg. 7 line 3 and 4Q428 frg. 6 line 1.
[368] See 4Q432 frg. 7 lines 3–4.
[369] See 4Q432 frg. 7 line 4. The text means that "wise men [in] their [craftiness] fell from their might (or mighty office)."
[370] See the same expression in 10.33 and 22.14; cf. 12.23 and 15.23.
[371] See 6.37.
[372] See 15.17.
[373] Cf. Ps 139:12. Or "for bright[ness]."
[374] Or "with you."

8 בֹּא[מרים וב]דֹּבֹרים החליקו למו ומליצי רמיה הֹתֹעֹוֹם וילבטו בלא בינה כיֹא

א

9 בהולל מעשיהם כי נמאסו למו ולא יחשבוני בהגבירכה בי כי ידיחני מארצי

10 כצפֹור מקנה וכול רעי ומודעי נדחו ממני ויחשבוני לכלי אובד והמה מליצי

11 כזב וחוזי רמיה זממו עלי בליעל[136] להמיר תורתכה אשר שננתה בלבבי בחלקות

12 לעמכה ויעצורו משקה דעת מצמאים ולצמאם ישקום חומץ למע[137] הבט אל

מ[138]

13 תעותם להתהולל במועדיה להתפש במצודותם כי אתה אל תנאץ כל מחשבת

14 בליעל ועצתכה היא תקום ומחשבת לבכה לנצח תכון והמה נעלמים זמות בליעל

15 יחשובו וידרשוכה בלב ולב ולא נכונו באמתכה שורש פורה רוש ולענה במחשבותם

16 ועם שרירות לבם יתורו וידרשוכה בגלולים ומכשול עוונם שמו לנגד פניהם ויבאו

17 לדורשכה מפי נביאי כזב מפותי תעות והם בלֹ[ו]ֹעֹג שפה ולשון אחרת ידברו לעמך

18 להולל ברמיה כול מעשיהם כי לא[ ][בֹחרו בדרֹ]ך לבכֹ[ה ולא האזינו לדברכה כי אמרו

---

[136] See the note in the text of 1QH[a].

[137] Read למען; a scribal error.

[138] A medial *mem* for a final *mem* added above the line. See 11.15.

8   in s[ayings and in] words they made smooth for themselves. But the treacherous interpreters[375] led them to err, so that they are ruined[376] without discernment, because […]

9   in foolishness (are) their works. For they were despised by them; and they do not regard[377] me when you strengthened[378] yourself in me. For they expelled me[379] from my land

10   like a bird from its nest.[380] And all my companions and my acquaintances were expelled from me, and regarded me like a lost vessel.[381] But they are lying

11   interpreters and treacherous seers. They plotted with[382] Belial against me, to exchange your Torah[383] which you reiterated in my heart, for smooth things

12   to your people. And they hold back the drink of knowledge from the thirsty; and for their thirst they give them vinegar to drink in order to look at

13   their error, behaving foolishly in their festivals,[384] (then) being caught in their nets. For you, O God, you despise every thought of

14   Belial, and your counsel perseveres;[385] and the thought of your heart is established for perpetuity. And they are hidden; (and) the infamies of Belial[386]

15   they think. And they seek you with a divided heart;[387] and they are not established in your truth. A root sprouting poison and bitterness (is) in their thoughts.[388]

16   And with the stubbornness of their heart, they wander around and seek you through idols. And the obstacle of their iniquity they put before their faces, and they come

17   to seek you through the mouth of lying prophets tempted (by) error. And they, with a st[am]mering lip and another tongue,[389] speak to your people,

18   in order to turn all their works into treacherous foolishness, because they did not choose the wa[y of] your [heart], and do not listen to your word. For they say

---

[375] See 10.16, "erring interpreters," and 10.33, 12.10, "lying interpreters."
[376] *Nipʿal* impf. of לבט.
[377] Or "they shall not regard me."
[378] Or "made mighty."
[379] Heb. ידיחני, which is from יחה, "to push." See Jer 23:12.
[380] Apparently, "nest" is the Righteous Teacher's abode in Jerusalem.
[381] Not "broken pot." The author intimates that he alone was expelled from the Temple cult. Notice the contrast to *More Works of the Torah*, which claims the Righteous Teacher and his group separated from the Temple cult.
[382] I assume an assimilated *beth*.
[383] Or "Law."
[384] Or "appointed times," "seasons."
[385] Lit. "it rose up."
[386] Not "the hypocrites" as in DJD. See 10.18–19: "And from the devices of Belial (are) [all] their thoughts."
[387] Lit. "in heart and heart." See 1Chr 12:33.
[388] Echoes of Deut 29:17: שרש פרה ראש ולענה.
[389] Meaning "other words."

19   לחזון דעת לא נכון ולדרך לבכה לא היאה[139] כי אתה אל תענה להם לשופטם

20   בגבורתכה [כ]גלוליהם וכרוב פשעיהם למען יתפשו במחשבותם אשר נזורו מבריתכה

21   ותכרת במֿ[שפ]ט כול אנשי מרמה וחוזי תעות לא ימצאו עוד כי אין הולל בכול מעשיך

22   ולא רמיה [ב]מזמת לבכה ואשר כנפשכה יעמודו לפניכה לעד והולכי בדרך לבכה

23   יכונו לנצֿח [וא]נֿי בתומכי בכה אתעודדה ואקומה על מנאצי וידי על כול בוזי כֿיֿאֿ

24   לא יחשבונֿ[י ע]דֿ הגבירכה בי ותופע לי בכוחכה לאורתים ולא טחתה בבושת פני

יחד
25   כול הנדרשֿ[י]ֿםֿ לי הנועדים לבריתכה וישומעוני[140] ההולכים בדרך לבכה ויערוכו לכה

26   בסוד קדושים ותוצא לנצח משפטם ולמישרים אמת ולא תתעם ביד חלכאים

27   כזומם למו ותתן מוראם על עמכה ומפץ לכול עמי הארצות להכרית במשפט כול

28   עוברי פיכה ובי האירותה פני רבים ותגבר עד לאין מספר כי הודעתני ברזי

29   פלאכה וֿבֿסֿוֿד פלאכה הגברתה עמדי והפלא לנגד רבים בעבור כבודכה ולֿהֿודיע

---

[139] The long form appears only here and in 20.12. Cf. היא in 5.30 and 12.14.
[140] See the conclusions by Reymond, pp. 217–18. Read: וישמעוני. Note the *waw mater* after the first root consonant.

19 concerning the vision of knowledge: "It is not true."[390] And concerning the way of your heart: "It is not this." For you, O God, you shall answer them, judging them

20 with your might [in accordance with] their idols and according to the multitude of their transgressions, in order that they be caught in their thoughts which turn aside from your covenant.

21 And with ju[dgme]nt you shall cut off all the men of deceit; and seers of error shall not be found any more. For there is no foolishness in all your works;

22 and no treachery [in] the devising of your heart. And (those) who are in accordance with you yourself[391] stand before you forever; and the ones who walk continuously in the way of your heart

23 are established for perpetuity. [But] I, when adhering to you, I will[392] be encouraged and I shall rise up against my despisers. And my hands (I shall raise) against all who are scorning me, because

24 they do[393] not regard [me un]til you strengthen[394] yourself in me and appear to me with your power for perfect lights.[395] And you have not smeared with shame the faces of[396]

25 all [those] who seek me, who are assembled together[397] for your covenant. And the ones who walk in the way of your heart listened to me and stand in array for you

26 in the council of the Holy Ones. And you bring forth their judgment for perpetuity and for the upright ones the truth. And you do not mislead them by the hand of the wretched ones,

27 as one who plotted against them. And you put their terror upon your people, and a crushing to all the peoples of the lands in order to destroy with judgment all

28 those who disobey[398] your edict.[399] But through me, you enlightened the faces of many, and you are infinitely[400] mighty, because you allowed me to know the mysteries of

29 your wonder,[401] and with the secret of your wonder you have been mighty with me and the wonder is before the Many[402] for the sake of your glory, and to announce

---

[390] Lit. "It is not established."

[391] The Heb. כנפש with suffix has reflexive meaning.

[392] The future tense has a present meaning.

[393] Lit. "shall not." Note the use of the imperfect for continuous action.

[394] Lit. "make mighty."

[395] Note the use of tenses in these lines.

[396] Note the continuous use of "face" in these lines.

[397] Although not the *Yaḥad*; this meaning might have been heard by some Qumranites.

[398] Or "those who transgress." The *nomen regens* is clearly God; it is not the Wicked Priest.

[399] Lit. "your mouth." But this noun has many deep meanings in Qumran poetry.

[400] Or "everlasting," "beyond enumeration."

[401] Note the claim in 1QpHab 7 that God allowed the Righteous Teacher to know "all the mysteries of the words of his servants, the prophets."

[402] The "Many" is a *terminus technicus* among the followers of the Righteous Teacher.

30 לכול החיׄיׄם גבורותיכה מי בשר כזאת[141] ומה יצר חמר להגדיל פלאות והוא בעוון

31 מרחם ועד שבה באשמת מעל ואני ידעתי כי לא לאנוש צדקה ולא לבן אדם תום

32 דרך לאל עליון כול מעשי צדקה ודרך אנוש לא תכון[142] כי אם ברוח יצר אל לו

33 להתם דרך לבני אדם למעׄן ידעו כול מעשיו בכוח גבורתו ורוב רחמיו על כול בני

34 רצונו ואנׄׄי רׄעׄד וׄרׄתׄת אחזוני וכול ירועו וימס לבבי כדונג מׄ(ל)פני אש וילכו ברכי

35 כמים מוגרים בׄמורד כי זכרתי אשמותי עם מעל אבותי בקום רשעים על בריתך

36 וחלכאים על דברכה ואני אמרתי בפשעי נעזבתי מבריתכה ובזוכרי כוח ידכה עם

37 המון רחמׄיׄכׄה התעודדתי ואקומה ורוחי החזיקה במעמד לפני נגע כי נשענתׄי

38 בחסדיכה וׄבׄהׄמׄוׄן רחמיכה כי תכפר עוון ולטה[ר] אׄנׄוׄש מאשמה בצדקתכה לׄכׄׄה אׄ[לׄ]ׄי

39 ולא לאדם כׄׄול אׄשׄׄר עשיתה כי אתה בראתה צדיק ורשע ׄׄׄ]

40 בׄמׄשׄׄפׄטׄׄיׄכׄה בׄיׄׄחׄד[143] אתחזוקה בבריתכה עד]

41 [מש]פׄטיכה כׄׄי אמת אתה וצדק כׄול מׄ[עשיכה

---

[141] Cf. זות in 20.35; different spellings are used by different poets and even the same author.
[142] The feminine verb form discloses that דרך in this instance is feminine. Ctr. 7.31.
[143] According to 13.7–8, an author has already been "judged." Judgment has already begun, see 6.31. For judgment "[in the assembly of] the simple ones," see 9.35. For similar expressions, see 15.38–39 and 17.10.

30 to all the living your mighty deeds. What flesh (is) like this? And how can an inclination of[403] clay increase wonders? For he is in iniquity

31 from the womb,[404] and until old age (he is) in the guilt of infidelity. But I, I know that righteousness (is) neither for the human, nor for the son of Adam[405] (is) the perfection of

32 the way.[406] To God Most High (belongs) all works of righteousness. And the way of the human is not established except through the spirit God formed[407] for him,

33 to complete the way for the sons of Adam,[408] so that they will know all his works through the power of his might. And the multitude of his mercies is over all the sons of

34 his will. But I, shuddering and terror grasp me, and all my bones break,[409] and my heart melts like wax before the fire, and my knees wobble[410]

35 like water tumbling down[411] a slope. For I remember my guilt[412] with the infidelity of my ancestors, when the wicked ones stand against your covenant,

36 and the wretched ones against your words. And I, I said: "In my transgression, I had been forsaken[413] from your covenant." But when I remembered the power of your hand with

37 the abundance of your compassions, I was encouraged and stood up, and my spirit was strengthened in rank against affliction because I leaned

38 on your mercies and on the abundance of your compassions. For you atone (for) iniquity and puri[fy] the human from guilt by your righteousness. For you, [O my G]od,

39 and not for Adam (is) all which you have done, for you, you created the righteous and the wicked °°°[…].

40 By your judgments in the Community,[414] I will be strengthened in your covenant until […]

41 your [judg]ments, because you (are) truthful, and righteous (is) all [your] w[orks …]

---

[403] Heb. יצר. Or "creature."
[404] The common word for "womb" (רחם) was used in 7.28 and 30; it has not been used since then.
[405] Or "humankind."
[406] Or "the Way."
[407] Heb. יצר. Note again the author's fondness for paronomasia.
[408] Or "humankind."
[409] It is possible that the Wicked Priest broke some of the bones of the Righteous Teacher.
[410] Lit. "walk," see 16.35.
[411] Lit. "pouring down." See Ezek 7:17 and 21:12. Perhaps "urinating" from fear is implied. See also 16.35.
[412] The noun is a plural: "guilts." The English is a collective.
[413] I.e., "was distant."
[414] *Yahad* is a *terminus technicus* in the *Thanksgiving Hymns* only in 12.40, 26.28, and 26.38. Contrast 14.16.

Col. 13 [= Sukenik Col. 5 + Frg. 29]
Parallels: 4Q428 Frg. 7; 4Q429 Frgs. 1–3; 4Q432 Frg. 11

1   [

2   [

3   לֿיֿוֹםֿ [ז]עֿםֿ חרוֹ[ן]

4   סליחותיכה והֿמוֹן רֿחֿמ[י]כֿהֿ]   [בֿ°[144]

5   ובדעתי אלה נחמ[תי] בֿאֿמֿתֿכֿהֿ °°°]   [°לֿ[145]

6   על פי רצונכה ובידֿכה מֿשפט כולם   [(VACAT) [

Hymn 17
I Thank the Lord for Not Abandoning Me

7   אודכה אדוני כי לא עזבתנֿי בגורי בעם נֿכֿר]   [כֿאשמתי

8   שפטתני ולא עזבתני בזמות יצרי ותעזור משחת חיי ותתֿן לֿי מֿ[עוז עד פ]לֿט[146] בתוך

9   לביאים מועדים לבני אשמה אריות שוברי עצם אדירים ושותי דֿם גבורים ותשמנֿי

10   במגור[147] עם דיגים רבים פורשי מכמרת על פני מים וציֿדים[148] לבני עֿולה ושם למשפט

11   יסדתני וסוד אמת אמצתה[149] בלבבי ומזה ברית לדורשיה ותסגור פי כפירים אשר

---

[144] Perhaps בֿ[.
[145] Perhaps לֿ[.
[146] See 14.28.
[147] 4Q429 frg. 1 1.1: ושותי דם גב[ורֿ]ים ותשימני במגורי.
[148] 4Q429 frg. 1 1.2: ע[ל] פֿני מים וצידים.
[149] 4Q429 frg. 1 1.3: א[מת אמצתה.

Col. 13 [= Sukenik Col. 5 + Frg. 29]
Parallels: 4Q428 Frg. 7; 4Q429 Frgs. 1–3; 4Q432 Frg. 11

1   […]

2   […]

3   to the day of wrathful [fu]ry […]

4   your forgivenesses and the abundance of your compassion[s …]b°[415]

5   and as I know these things, [I am] comforted by your truth °°°[…]°y,[416]

6   according to your will; and in your hand (is) the judgment of them all. (VACAT) […] (VACAT)

Hymn 17
I Thank the Lord for Not Abandoning Me

7   I thank you, O Lord, because you did not abandon me when I lived among an alien[417] people […] according to my guilt

8   you judged me. And you did not abandon me in the infamy of my inclination,[418] but you helped my life (out) from the pit, and you put for me pro[tection[419] until del]ivered in the midst of

9   lionesses[420] appointed for the sons of guilt, lions[421] (which are) breakers of bones of the magnificent ones and drinkers of blood of mighty ones.[422] And you placed me

10   in a dwelling with many fishermen[423] who spread a net over the faces of the water, and (with) those who hunt for the sons of deceit. And there for judgment

11   you founded me, and the foundation of truth you encouraged in my heart,[424] and from it (is) a covenant for those who seek it. But you shut the mouths of young lions[425] whose

---

[415] Perhaps "in me."

[416] Perhaps "to me."

[417] Lit. "foreign." The people's actions have alienated them from God.

[418] Heb. יצר.

[419] Or "sh[elter." See 14.28.

[420] Heb. לביאים.

[421] Heb. אריות.

[422] Lit. "warriors."

[423] See Jer 16:16.

[424] The author is fond of paronomasia. Or "you allocated me, and strengthened the secret (or assembly) of truth in my heart."

[425] The author's vocabulary is extensive. He knows many terms for a lion; but he did not use ליש, "lion," though it was known to the genius Isaiah who had an incredibly extensive vocabulary (see Isa 30:6).

12 כחרב שניהם ומתלעותם כחנית חדה חמת תנינים כול מזמותם לחת(ו)ף¹⁵⁰ יורבו¹⁵¹ ולא

13 פצו עלי פיהם כי אתה אלי סתרתני נגד בני אדם ותורתכה חבתה ב[י] עֿד קץ

14 הגלוֿת ישעכה לי כי בצרת נפשי לא עזבתני ושועתי שמעתה במרורי נפשי

15 ודנת יגוני הכרתה באנחתי ותצל¹⁵² נפש עני במעון אריות אשר שננו כחרב לשונם

16 ואתה אלי סגרתה בעד (לֿ)ש(ו)ניהם¹⁵³ פן יטרפו נפש(י)עני¹⁵⁴ ורש ותוסף¹⁵⁵ לשונם

ב¹⁵⁶

17 כחרב אל תערה בלוֿאֿ[נכר]תֿה נפש עבדכה ולמען הגבירכה לנגד בני אדם הפלתה

18 באביון ותביאהו במצרף כֿזֿהֿב במעשי אש וככסף מזוקק בכור¹⁵⁷ נופחים לטהֿרֿ שבעתים

19 וימהרו עלי רשעי¹⁵⁸ עמֿים במצוקותם וכול היום ידכאו נפשי

---

¹⁵⁰ Note the numerous errors in this column. The form may indicate spirantization.
¹⁵¹ Probably not from ארב; ctr. Reymond, pp. 71, 200, and DJD, p. 179. From רוב. The reference to 1Sam 15:5 is erroneous.
¹⁵² Note defective spelling.
¹⁵³ First a scribe wrote לשונם, "their tongue." Second, he put dots above and below the *lamedh* and then erased them and the *lamedh*. Third, he erased the *waw*. Fourth, he erased part of the final *mem* and left what looks like a *yodh*. Fifth, he added a *he* and final *mem*: (לֿ)ש(ו)ניהם.
¹⁵⁴ In this line a scribe twice corrects metathesis.
¹⁵⁵ Notice the loss of the glottal stop.
¹⁵⁶ 4Q429 frg. 1 2.1: בֿ[.
¹⁵⁷ 4Q429 frg. 1 2.2: במצרף כֿ[זהב   בכור].
¹⁵⁸ 4Q429 frg. 1 2.3: נופחים לטוֿהֿרֿ] שבעתים וימהרו עלי רשעיֿ.

12   teeth (are) like a sword and whose incisors (are) like a sharp spear (with) the poison of dragons;[426] all their devices for snatching are multiplied, but they have not

13   opened their mouth against me, because you, O my God, you hid me from the sons of Adam,[427] and concealed your Torah[428] in [me] until the Endtime

14   when your salvation shall be revealed to me. For in the anguish of my soul[429] you did not abandon me, and you heard my cry for help in the bitterness of my soul;[430]

15   and you adjudicated[431] my grief; (and) you acknowledged (me) when I sighed. And you saved the soul of[432] the Needy One in the den of lions,[433] which sharpen their tongues as a sword.

16   But you, O my God, you shut tight their teeth[434] lest they tear apart the soul of[435] the Needy One and the Wretched One. And you withdrew[436] their tongues

17   like a sword into its sheath,[437] without the soul of[438] your servant [being cut o]ff. And in order to show your might in me[439] before the sons of Adam[440] you set apart

18   the Poor One.[441] And you brought him to the smelting-pot[442] like (fine) gold in the works of fire, and like silver refined in a furnace of the smiths, purifying sevenfold.

19   But the wicked of the peoples hasten[443] against me with their oppressions, and the whole day they crush[444] my soul.[445]

---

[426] The words may also be translated "wrath of crocodiles." Heb. תנינים. The noun denotes the demonic; cf. Ps 91:13 in which "the young lion" and "the dragon (תנין)" are mentioned. See 13.29 "the venom of dragons."

[427] Or "humankind."

[428] Or "Law."

[429] Heb. נפש; this noun denotes the "living principle" in the human. Each time "soul" is translated it denotes *npš*.

[430] Heb. נפש.

[431] *Qal* perfect of דין which basically means "to plead a cause," or "help someone obtain results." The full meaning of the verb is supplied by Qumran Hebrew.

[432] Heb. נפש.

[433] The author may be imagining a situation similar to that portrayed in the book of Daniel.

[434] A scribe changed "their tongue" to "their teeth." First, he wrote לשונם, "their tongue." Second, he put dots above and below the *lamedh* and then erased them and the *lamedh*. Third, he erased *waw*. Fourth, he erased part of the final *mem* and left what looks like a *yodh*. Fifth, he added a *he* and final *mem*: (ל)ש(ו)ניהם.

[435] Heb. נפש.

[436] The Heb. root is אסף. In Qumran Hebrew the א elides.

[437] In antiquity, artists represented these thoughts by depicting in stone a lion with a sword protruding from his mouth. See the image in J. H. Charlesworth, ed., *The Messiah: Developments in Earliest Judaism and Christianity* (Minneapolis, 2009) p. 59, Fig. 5.

[438] Heb. נפש.

[439] See the note to 1QH^a.

[440] Or "humankind."

[441] Lit. "in the poor one." Perhaps the *beth* is a *nota accusativi*.

[442] Or "crucible," "refining-pot;" see Prov 17:3. See also 4.21; cf. 6.15 (a possible restoration).

[443] Notice the meaning of the "present tense" (*waw* consecutive imperfect) to indicate that the author is reliving the moment (if this is an autobiographical reflection).

[444] Or "oppress."

[445] Heb. נפש. A *vacat* highlights the transition.

20   ואתה[159] אלי תשיב נָֿפְשִֿׁי סערה לדממה[160] ונפש אביון פלטתה כצֿפֿוֿ[ר מפח[161] ו]כֿטרף[162] מכח

21   אריות   (VACAT)   [   ]

Hymn 18
Blessed is the Lord for His Righteousness to the Orphan

ברוך אתה[163]

22   אֿוֿדֿכָֿהֿ אדוני כי לא עזבתה יתום ולא בזיתה רֿש כי גבורתכה לֿאֿ[י]ן קֿ[ץ] וכבודכה

23   לאין מדה וגבורי פלא משר(י)(ת)יכה[164] ועם ענוים בטאטאיי[165] רגלֿיֿכֿ[ה יחד] עם נמהרי

24   צדק להעלות משאון יחד כול אביוני חסד ואני הייתי על ע[נוים ויוע]דני לריב

25   ומדנים לרעי קנאה ואף לבאי בריתי ורגן ותלונה לכול נועדי ו[כול או]כלי לחמי

26   עלי הגדילו עקב ויליזו עלי בשפת עול[166] כול נצמדי סודי ואנשי [ברי]תֿי סוררים

---

[159] 4Q429 frg. 1 2.4: [עמים במצוקותיהמה]   ואתה].

[160] 4Q429 frg. 1 2.5: .[א]לֿי ת[שב סעֿרֿהֿ ל]דממה.

[161] See 12.10: כצפור מקנה; and Ps 124:7: כצפור נמלטה מפה.

[162] 4Q429 frg. 1 2.6: וכט]רֿ[ף.

[163] This scribal correction is exceptionally significant; see the introduction.

[164] A correction of a metathesis.

[165] For a discussion of double *yodhs*, see Reymond, pp. 61–62.

[166] 4Q428 frg. 7 line 1: [בשפת] עול.

20   But you, O my God, you turn a thunderstorm[446] to silence,[447] and the soul of[448] the Poor One you delivered like a bir[d from a trap and][449] like prey from the power of

21   lions. (VACAT) [...] (VACAT)

Hymn 18
Blessed is the Lord for His Righteousness to the Orphan

22   Blessed are you,[450] O Lord, because you did not abandon the orphan and did not scorn the Wretched One. For your might (is) with[out en]d[451] and your glory

23   (is) without measure, and the wonderful mighty ones[452] (are) your ministers,[453] and a people (who are) suppressed ones[454] (are) among those who sweep away[455] yo[ur] footprints[456] [together][457] with those who are eager for

24   righteousness to rise from the tumult together (with) all the poor ones of[458] mercy. And I, I, on account of the s[uppressed ones and] I [was appoin]ted for strife

25   and contention to my companions, jealousy and anger to those who enter into covenant (with) me,[459] and murmuring and complaint to all my assembled ones.[460] And [all those who a]te my bread

26   have lifted up the heel against me;[461] and all those bound to my council[462] have defamed me with deceitful lips.[463] And the men in [covena]nt (with) me[464] are rebellious

---

[446] Lit. "storm."

[447] A scribe changed the text from "revived my soul (and) turned storm into silence."

[448] Heb. נפש.

[449] Cf. 12.10.

[450] A scribe replaced "I thank you" with "blessed are you."

[451] Lit. "without endtime."

[452] Or "warriors," "heroes."

[453] Heb. משרת(י)תיכה; the noun is not to be confused with the more familiar "your servants."

[454] Or "needy ones," "poor ones." The Righteous Teacher reflects on how he and his followers were "suppressed" by the illegitimate priests.

[455] See Isa 14:23.

[456] Lit. "yo[ur] feet."

[457] Heb. יחד.

[458] Or, "the Poor Ones."

[459] Lit. "those who enter into my covenant." See line 26. The author's covenant is founded in God's covenant. Most likely a strong personality is indicated. In line 13, the author claims God's Torah is hidden in him. Also, see line 27.

[460] Or "appointed ones." Note the paronomasia with line 24.

[461] See Ps 41:10 [41:9 in ET]. Also see Jn 13:18.

[462] Notice "my council." The author is most likely the Righteous Teacher.

[463] See Prov 4:24.

[464] Note the lit. "in my [covena]nt." That rendering would misrepresent the author's loyalty to God's covenant.

27 ומלינים סביב וברז חבתה בי ילכו רכיל לבני הוות ובעבור הגْבֹ[ירכה] בי ולמען

28 אשמתם סתרת[167] מעין בינה וסוד אמת[168] והמה הוות לבם יחשובֹו ודברי בליעל[169] פתחו

29 לשון שקר כחמת תנינים פורחת לקצים וכזוחל[170] עפר יורו לחתוף מבלגות פתנים

30 לאין[171] חבר ותהי לכאיב אנוש ונגע נמאר[172] בתכמי עבדכה להכשיל רוח ולהתם[173]

31 כוח לבלתי החזק מעמד[174] וישיגוני במצרים לאין מנוס ולא בהבדל[[]] ממْ[[]]שֹׁפחות ויהמْו

32 בכנור ריבי[175] ובנגינות יחד תלונתם עם שאה ומשואה זלעופות[[]][[]]אֹחזוני[[]] וחבלים כצירי[177]

33 יולדה ויהם עלי לבי קדרות לבשתי ולשוני לחך תדבק כֹי סבבונֹי [[]] בהוות[[]] לבם ויצרם[178]

34 הופיע לי למרורים ויחשך מאור פני לאפלה והודْי[179] נהפך למשחْיֹר   ואת[180] אלْי

---

[167] For the use or loss of the *he* marker, see Tov, *Scribal Practices*, pp. 339–43 and Reymond, p. 35. Also see עזבתה in line 22.
[168] 4Q429 frg. 2 line 7: [מעי]וْ[ן] בינה וסֹ[וד אמת].
[169] 4Q429 frg. 2 line 8: יחשבו ודברי ב[ליעל].
[170] 4Q429 frg. 2 line 9: כחמת תנינים פורחת לקْצْים וכْ[זוחל].
[171] 4Q429 frg. 2 line 10: עפר יורו לחתוף מבלגות פתנים לאין.
[172] 4Q429 frg. 2 line 11: [חב]וْר ותהי לכאוב אנוש ונגע נמאר.
[173] 4Q429 frg. 2 line 12: בתכמי [עבדכה להכשיל רוח ולהתם].
[174] 4Q429 frg. 3 line 1: [כוח ל]בْלתי החזק מْ[עמד].
[175] 4Q429 frg. 3 line 2: [ממשפחו]ת ויהמו בכנור ריבْיֹ.
[176] The bilabial פ causes a shift in the vowel; see Reymond, p. 175.
[177] 4Q429 frg. 3 line 3: [זל]עْוֹפֹות אחזוני וחבלים [כצי]רֹי.
[178] 4Q429 frg. 3 line 4: [ו]לْשֹׁוֹנֹי לחכי דבקה כי סבבוני בה[וות לבם].
[179] 4Q429 frg. 3 line 5: [ויחשך] מאור פני לאפלה והודْ[ן].
[180] An error for אתה.

27 and complain round about. And because[465] you concealed the secret in me,[466] they go slandering to the sons of disaster. And for the sake of showing [your] mig[ht] in me, and because of

28 their guilt you hid the fountain of discernment and the secret of truth. But they think (only about) the desires[467] of their heart. And the words of Belial have opened

29 a deceitful tongue[468] like the venom of dragons,[469] shooting forth[470] to their borders.[471] And like the reptiles of dust[472] they spit, to lay hold of the poison of cobras

30 that cannot be charmed. And it becomes a severe pain[473] and a festering[474] affliction in the entrails of your servant, making the spirit fail, and annihilating

31 power so as not to stand firm. And they reached me in straits with no escape (for me),[475] and not distinguishing among the parts. And they sounded forth

32 my dispute on the lyre, and on musical instruments together their complaints. With storm[476] and raging destruction they seized me, and tribulations like pains of

33 a woman giving birth (overwhelmed me). And my heart grumbles against me. (With) darkness I am clothed, and my tongue cleaves to (my) palate,[477] since I am surrounded by the desires of their heart, and their inclination[478]

34 appeared to me as bitterness, and the light of my face is darkened into gloominess,[479] and my majesty is turned into blackness.[480] But you, O my God,

---

[465] Lit. "And by," or "And with."

[466] The author's adversaries could thus not know that God had given the author "the secret."

[467] In this line, the Hebrew הווה is from the first meaning of that noun, and denotes "desire" and "capriciousness." It is not to be confused with its use elsewhere, meaning "disaster."

[468] Lit. "lying tongue," but see Prov 20:17. The snake is the consummate trickster in some biblical passages; see Gen 3:13.

[469] תנינים, "dragons."

[470] This word is פרח in the *qal* pl. part. The Hebrew verb means literally "blooming," "flourishing," "floating (in the air)."

[471] Lit. "for their endtimes."

[472] Lit. "crawling (in) the dust."

[473] Or "the pain of human." אנוש can be pointed to support either translation. Note the paronomasia between "pain" and "human." Also see Reymond, p. 180 n. 96.

[474] The *nipʿal* of מאר is not extant in BH. The affliction festers like an open wound. A wound festers and becomes rotten, as when organs putrefy from a cobra's bite. נמאר evolves from the verb מאר, "to break open" (a wound). See KB. Also see 25.24. In 13.27, "the sons of disaster" are the wicked priests who control the Temple cult. They spit "the poison of cobras" so the Righteous Teacher has "incurable pain" and "a festering affliction."

[475] See the more familiar "without escape."

[476] Read: שואה.

[477] See 4Q429 frg. 3 line 4, "to my palate."

[478] Heb. יצר.

[479] Two different words are used for "darkness." Note the author's fondness for paronomasia. That skill allows him to resonate with meaning and echo previous or future reflections (when read repeatedly).

[480] These obscure comments make pellucid sense if the author is the Righteous Teacher who lost his powers in the Temple as the non-Aaronite Hasmonean priests received full authority when Simon was empowered by the Jewish people. They take on special meaning when one reflects that the Righteous Teacher may have served as High Priest during the period when no official priest was recognized even though a high priest was demanded by the Temple services, especially on the Day of Atonement. A small *vacat* appears here. It indicates a transition.

35 מרחב פתחתה בלבבי ויוספוה לצוקה[181] וישׁוכו בעדי בצלמות ואוכלה בלֹחֹם אנחתי

36 ושקוי בדמעות[182] אין כלה כי עששו מכעס עיני ונפשי במרורי יום אֹנחה ויגון

37 יסובבוני[183] ובושת על פנים ויהפך לי לֹחֹמֹי לריב ושקוי לבעל מדנים[184] ויבוא בעצמֹי

38 להכשיל רוח ולכלות כוח כרזי פשע משנים[185] מעשי אל באשמתם כי נאסרֹתֹי בעבותים

39 לאין נתק וזקים ללוא ישוברו[186] וחומת עֹוֹז[עלי]וֹבריחי ברזל ודלתי[מגן[187] לאי[ן

40 פתוח[188] בֹלֹאי עם תהום נחשבתֹיֹ לאין]   [°°]

41 [ומזמות]בֹלֹיֹעל אפפו נפשי לאֹיֹן [פ]לֹ[ט

Col. 14 [= Sukenik Col. 6 + Frg. 26]
Parallels: 4Q428 Frg. 8; 4Q429 Frg. 4

1   [

2   [

3   [

4 עֹבֹדכה[°°°

5 לבי בנאצוֹת בֹפֹי[

---

[181] 4Q429 frg. 3 line 6: פ]תֹחתה בלבבי ויוספוהו לצֹו[קה.

[182] 4Q429 frg. 3 line 7: ב]לֹחֹם אנחה ושקוי בדמעוֹת[.

[183] 4Q429 frg. 3 line 8: במרו]רֹי יום אנחה ויגון יֹ[סובבוני.

[184] 4Q429 frg. 3 line 9: ושקֹ]וֹיֹ לבעל מֹ[דנים.

[185] 4Q429 frg. 3 line 10: כרזי פשֹ]עֹ משֹנֹיֹם[.

[186] 4Q429 frg. 3 line 11: לאין נ]תֹק זקים ללו]ישוברו[.

[187] See 14.30.

[188] Cf. 4Q429 frg. 3 line 12:] פתוח [לאי]ן.

35   you opened a spacious place in my heart. But they added distress (to) it and hedged me (with thorns)[481] in the shadow of death.[482] And I ate with the bread of my sighing,[483]

36   and (with) the drink of tears without end. For my eyes are dimmed from anger and my soul[484] by the bitterness of[485] the day. Sighing[486] and grief

37   surround me, and shame (is) over (my) face. And my bread is turned for me into a dispute, and my drink into an owner of confrontations.[487] And it enters my bones

38   to make the spirit fail and to annihilate power, as the mysteries of transgression are altering the works of God with their guilt. For I was bound with ropes

39   (that) cannot be cut off,[488] and (with) chains (that) cannot be broken, and a strong wall[489] [(was) higher[490] than me]. And bars of iron and [shielding][491] doors [that cann]ot

40   be opened.[492] My prison with the depths is considered[493] without [...]°°[....]

41   [And the devices of][494] Belial encompass my soul without [es]ca[pe ...]

Col. 14 [= *Sukenik Col. 6 + Frg. 26*]
Parallels: 4Q428 Frg. 8; 4Q429 Frg. 4

1   [...]

2   [...]

3   [...]

4   °°° your servant [...]

5   my heart (is) in disgrace in my mouth [...]

---

481 See Hos 2:8 [2:6]. Contrast the use of שׁוך in 16.12.
482 An echo of Ps 23:4.
483 Cf. 4Q429 frg. 3 line 7, "sighing."
484 Heb. נפשׁ.
485 A plural that cannot be represented in English, but one needs to observe that the author's bitterness is multiple.
486 Cf. 4Q429 frg. 3 line 8, "sighing."
487 See Prov 23:29 and Jer 15:10, "a man of confrontation."
488 The specificity and odd language may suggest that the author literally remembers being bound with ropes. He may not be speaking metaphorically. Biblical heroes do not lament that they are bound with ropes. Of course, Samson was bound with ropes but easily broke them (Judg 16:11–12; cf. 15:13–14).
489 In 11.38 the same expression is used in a different context to denote a "city wall" under attack.
490 See 14.28.
491 See 14.30–31, "protecting doors without an entrance."
492 See 4Q429 frg. 3 line 12.
493 Corrected by a scribe from "I was considered" (which may be original and better).
494 See 10.18. Notice the echo of previous references to being "surrounded."

6 והווה לאין חקר כלה לאׄיׄן[מספר ואתה אלי[189]

7 גליתה אוזני [למו]סׄר מוכיחי צׄדק עם[ ]°°

8 מעדת שׁוׄא ומסוד חמס ותביאני בעצת הׄקׄוׄדׄשׁ[190] [ ]° אשׁמׄה

9 ואדעה כי יש מקוה לשבי פשע ועוזבי חטאה בה[ ]ולׄהתהלׄך

10 בדרך לבכה לאין עול ואנחמה על המון עם ועל שאוׄן מ[מל]כות בהאספם [כי יד]עתי אשר

11 תרים למצער מחיה בעמכה ושארית[191] בנחלתכה ותזקקם להטהר מאשמה [ומח]טׄוא כול

12 מעשיהם באמתכה ובחסדיך תשפטם בהמון רחמים ורוב סליחה וכפיכה להורותם

ו

13 וכישור[192] אמׄתׄכה להכינם בעצתכה לכבודכה ולמענכה עשׄי[תה] לגׄדׄל תורה ו[אמת] להׄיׄחׄד

14 אנשי עצתכה בתוך בני אדם לספר לדורות עולם נפלאותיכה ובגבורות[יכה יש]וחׄחׄו

15 לאין השבת וידעו כול גוים אמתכה וכול לאומים כבודכה כי הביאותׄהׄ[193] אמת]סׄודכה

16 לכול אנשי עצתכה ובגורל יחד עם מלאכי פנים ואין מליץ בנים לק[דושיכה ות]שׁׄיׄבׄ

17 פריו כי כׄ[ו]לׄ [ע]צתכׄהׄ בפׄי והם ישובו בפי כבודכה ויהיו[194] שריכה בגור[ל יחד וגזעו]

[189] See 13.34 and 14.23. Cf. DJD and Licht.
[190] See 1QH[a] 15.13: לעצת קודש.
[191] See 26.27: שרית.
[192] A recognized but only partially corrected error.
[193] Note full spelling.
[194] 4Q428 frg. 8 line 1: כ[בׄודכה והיו.

6   and unfathomable[495] disaster, destruction without [numbering…. But you, O my God,]

7   have uncovered[496] my ear [for the disci]pline of those reproved for righteousness with […]°°°

8   from the congregation of vanity and the assembly of violence, and you brought me into the council of[497] holiness […]° guilt.

9   And I know that there is hope for those who return from transgression and (for) those who abandon sin *bh*[…] and walk continuously

10   in the way of your heart without deceit. And I will be comforted over the multitude of[498] people and over the uproar of ki[ngd]oms when they gather, [because] I [kn]ow that

11   you raise the few who live among your people and a remnant among your inheritance. And you refined them so they are purified from guilt [and s]in. All

12   their works (are) in your truth, and in your mercies you shall judge them with the multitude of compassions and much forgiveness. And according to your edict,[499] teaching them

13   and according to the straightness of your truth establishing them in your council for your glory. And for your sake [you have] acted to magnify the Torah[500] and [truth] to make one[501]

14   the men of your council among the sons of Adam,[502] to recount for the eternal generations your wonders. And about [your] mighty deeds they [con]template

15   without ceasing. And all peoples[503] shall know your truth and all nations your glory. For you brought [the truth of] your secret

16   to all men of your council, and together with[504] the angels of the presence and without an intermediate interpreter[505] for [your] Ho[ly Ones. And you shall] bring back[506]

17   his fruits,[507] for a[l]l of your [co]unsel (is) in my mouth.[508] And they, they shall come back according to your glory, and they shall become your princes[509] in the lo[t of the Community.[510] And its stem]

---

[495] Heb. לאין חקר.

[496] Or "you have revealed."

[497] Note the diverse terms for a gathering: "congregation," "assembly," and "council." See the consistency chart in the Introduction.

[498] Or "roar." Note paronomasia.

[499] Lit. "your mouth."

[500] Or "Law."

[501] Not seen previously. See the same form in 1QS 1.8.

[502] Or "humankind."

[503] In this passage גוים denotes Jews and non-Jews. Notice the surprising universalism.

[504] Note also the presence of angels in the *Yaḥad*.

[505] Lit. "the official go-between."

[506] *Hipʿil* impf. of שוב. Lines 16–18 contain echoes of the well-known and influential images in Isaiah 40 which was the passage for self-knowledge at Qumran (See 1QS 8.12–15).

[507] The word, "his fruits," was misread by previous editors; it seems clear.

[508] The manuscript is torn and the ink difficult to read.

[509] For the *hipʿil* of שוב with "princes" (נדיבים), see Ps 113:8.

[510] Heb. יחד.

ד

18 פרח כצי[ץ] השדה ע[ז] עולם[195] לגל[196] נצר לעופי[197] מטעת עולם ויצל צל על כול תבל [ודליותי]ו[198]

19 עד שחקים ושרשיו עד תהום וכול נהרות עדן ת[לחלחנה[199] ד]ל[י]ותיו והיה לימים ל[אין]

20 חקר[200] וה֯ת֯א֯זרו על תבל לאין[201] אפס ועד שאול[תחתיה[202] ו]היה מעין אור למקור

21 עולם לאין[203] הסר בשביבי נוגהו יבערו כול בנ֯י עו֯ל[ה והיו[204] לאש בוערת בכול אנשי

22 אשמה עד כל֯ה והמה נצמדי תעודתי פותו במלי[צי תעות להב]י֯א ז֯ר בעבודת צדק

23 ואתה אל צויתם להועיל מדרכיהם[205] בדרך קו[דש אשר י]לכו בה וערל וטמא ופריץ[206]

24 בל יעוברנה[207] ו֯יתמוטטו מדרך לבכה ובהוות[208] פ[שעם יכש]לו וכמוא[209] יועץ בליעל

25 עם לבבם[210] ויכי[נו]נ֯ו מחשבת רשעה יתגוללו באשמה[211] ו[אני הי]ת֯י[212] כמלח באוניה בזעף

26 ימים גליהם וכול משבריהם[213] עלי המו רוח עועיים[214] ב[אין] דממה להשיב נפש[215] ואין

[195] 4Q428 frg. 8 line 2: ע[ז] עולם. The following passage has many echoes from Ezekiel 31.

[196] Read: לגדל.

[197] Scribe A corrected the second letter, a *mem*, to an *ʿayin*. The noun עפי is an Aramaism for "thick foliage." See A. Even-Shoshan, vol. 5, p. 1965.

[198] 4Q428 frg. 8 line 3: [תֹבֹל].

[199] 4Q428 frg. 8 line 4: [עד ש]חקים ושורשי]ו עד תהום וכול נהרות] עדן ת[לחלחנה.

[200] 4Q429 frg. 4 1.2: [אין חק]ר.

[201] 4Q428 frg. 8 line 5: [דליו]תיו והיה לימים ל[אין חקר והתאזרו]על תבל לא[ין].

[202] See 4.25, 15.4.

[203] 4Q429 frg. 4 1.4: [למק]ור עולם ל[אין.

[204] 4Q429 frg. 4 1.5: כל] בני עו֯ל[ה והיה.

[205] 4Q429 frg. 4 1.8: .ואתה אל [צוי]תם להועיל מדר[כיה]מ[ה.

[206] 4Q429 frg. 4 1.9: .אשר י]לכו בה ו[ע֯ר֯ל וטמ[א ופריץ.

[207] Note the *waw mater* after the first root consonant and energic *nun*.

[208] 4Q429 frg. 4 1.10: [.ויתמוטטו] מ֯דרך לבכֹה ובהווֹת.

[209] Note the supplementation of a final long vowel.

[210] 4Q429 frg. 4 1.11: .[פשעם יכש]לו וכמו יועץ בליע]ל֯ עם לבב[ם.

[211] 4Q429 frg. 4 1.12: .מחשבת [רשעה ית]גול[ל]ו[ן] באשמתם.

[212] 4Q429 frg. 4 2.1: .ו[אני הייתי.

[213] 4Q429 frg. 4 2.2: .וכל מ[שבריהם.

[214] See the same spelling in 15.8.

[215] 4Q429 frg. 4 2.3: להשיב֯ן נפש.

18 is blossoming[511] like the flow[ers of[512] the field unt]il eternity to grow a shoot to (become) the thick-foliage[513] of the eternal planting. And it will cast a shadow over all the world [and] its [high-branches]

19 (will be) unto the skies and its roots unto the deep. And all the rivers of Eden[514] wi[ll moisten] its [hig]h-br[an]ches, and will become waters that are [un]fathomable,[515]

20 and streaming over the world without end, and unto Sheol [beneath and] the fountain of light will become an eternal

21 source, (which) cannot be removed.[516] In the sparks of its flames will burn all the sons of dece[it, and they (the sparks) will become] a burning fire in all the men of

22 guilt until (their) annihilation.[517] And they, the ones bound by my testimony, they were tempted by the [erring] interpret[ers to bri]ng a stranger into the service of righteousness.

23 But you, O God, you ordered[518] them to benefit from their ways in the way of holi[ness] in [which th]ey walk; but the uncircumcised and the impure and the brigand

24 will not pass over it. And they have fallen away from the way of your heart, and in the disasters of [their] tran[sgression] they [stumb]le, and (are) like a counselor of[519] Belial

25 with their heart. [And] they [prep]ared a wicked thought; they will wallow constantly in guilt. And [I,] I [was] like a sailor in a boat (when) in raging

26 seas their waves and all their breakers roar over me (as) a twisting[520] wind [with no] silence to restore[521] the soul;[522] and there are no

---

[511] A participle that demands a singular subject.

[512] The Heb. ציץ is a collective noun.

[513] The noun is plural in the Hebrew. See also 4Q302 frg. 2 2.7.

[514] See the note to 16.21.

[515] Heb. לאין חקר. See Job 5:9; 9:10. See 5.16, 11.21, 14.6.

[516] See *OdesSol* 4.1: "No man can pervert your holy place, O my God; nor can he change it, and put it in another place" (ܐܠܐ ܐܢܫ .(ܠܐ ܐܢܫ ܡܫܚܠܦ ܠܗ ܘܣܡ ܠܗ ܒܐܬܪܐ ܐܚܪܢܐ, ܕܘܟܬܟ ܩܕܝܫܬܐ ܐܠܗܝ, ܡܫܚܠܦ ܠܗ ܐܢܫ).

[517] See 1QS 3.13–4.26. The Sons of Darkness will eventually be annihilated.

[518] Or "commanded," "gave an order."

[519] See Isa 9:5. Note the paronomasia between "counselor" and "council" (e.g. in 14:8, 14, and 16).

[520] עועיים, from עוה, which in the *nip'al* means "to be agitated," and in the *pi'el* "to twist."

[521] Lit. "bring back."

[522] Heb. נפש.

27   נתיבת לישר דרך על פני מים ויהם תהום²¹⁶ לאנחתי ונג̇ש[ו חי]ן עד שערי מות ואהיה²¹⁷

                             ש

28   כבא בעיר מצור ונעוז בחומה נ(ס)(ס)גבה עד פלט ואשע̇[נה]²¹⁸ ב̇אמתכה אלי כי אתה

29   תשים סוד²¹⁹ על סלע וכפיס על קו משפט ומשקלת²²⁰ אמ̇[ת]ל̇[ע]ש̇ות אבני בחן לב̇[נ]ת̇

30   עוז ללוא²²¹ תתזעזע וכול באיה בל ימוטו כי לא²²² יבוא זר [בשע]ריה דלתי מגן לאין

31   מבוא ובריחי עוז ללוא ישוברו בל יבוא²²³ גדוד בכלי מלחמתו עם תום כול חצ̇י

32   מלחמות רשעה ואז תחיש חרב אל בקץ משפט וכול בני א[מ]תו יעורו לה̇כ̇ר̇[ית]

33   רשעה²²⁴ וכול בני אשמה לא̇ יהיו עוד וידרוך גבור קשתו ויפתח מצו̇רי ה̇ש̇מ̇ו̇ם̇

34   למ̇רחב אין קץ ושערי עולם להוציא כלי מלחמות ויעצ̇ו̇[מ]ו מקצ̇ה עד קצ̇ה̇ ו̇ח̇צ̇ים

---

²¹⁶ 4Q429 frg. 4 2.4: ויהם ת̇[הום.

²¹⁷ 4Q429 frg. 4 2.5: ו̇א̇[היה.

²¹⁸ See 18.19.

²¹⁹ 4Q429 frg. 4 2.7:] סודי.

²²⁰ 4Q429 frg. 4 2.8:] ומשק̇לת.

²²¹ 4Q429 frg. 4 2.9:] לב̇[נ]ת̇ עוז ללו.

²²² 4Q429 frg. 4 2.10: [וא ימוטו כי לא.

²²³ 4Q429 frg. 4 2.11: [מבוא] ובר̇[י]ח̇י ע̇ו̇ז̇] ללוא ישוברו בל יבוא גדוד.

²²⁴ 4Q429 frg. 4 2.12: [בכלי מ̇[ל]ח̇מתו עד תום כל ח̇[צי מלחמות רשעה.

27 paths[523] to straighten a way over the face of the waters. And the depth roars to my sighing, and [my life] approach[ed] unto the gates of death. And I am[524]

28 like one who enters a fortified city and finds shelter[525] behind[526] a high[527] city wall[528] until delivered.[529] And I will lea[n] on your truth, O my God, because you,

29 you put the foundation on rock, and the beam according to[530] a measuring-line of judgment, and the weight of tru[th] in order to [m]ake tried stones[531] for a strong

30 bu[ildi]ng[532] (that) will not be shaken. And all those who enter it will not totter,[533] for no stranger will enter [into] its [gat]es. (It shall have) doors of defense[534] without

31 an entrance, and strong gate-bolts (that) cannot be broken, lest a troop[535] by means of[536] its weapons of war should enter exhausting[537] all the arrows of

32 the wars of wickedness. And then shall the sword of God hasten at the Endtime of judgment, and all the sons of his tr[u]th shall awaken to extermi[nate]

33 wickedness,[538] and all the sons of guilt shall be no more. And the mighty one shall stretch his bow, and he shall open the boundaries[539] of the heavens

34 to the endless expanse[540] and the eternal gates, to bring out the weapons of war.[541] And they shall be migh[ty] from end to end, and the arrows

---

[523] From נתיבה, "path." See Prov. 8:2.

[524] This verb is another example of the imperfect tense used as a continuous present.

[525] *Nipʿal* of עוז (not in Biblical Hebrew). See 13.8.

[526] Or "by." Heb. ב.

[527] *Nipʿal* of שגב . Or "inaccessible." See 13.39.

[528] The words "city wall" are one word in Hebrew.

[529] Or "escape."

[530] This can mean also "upon," "with regard to."

[531] See Isa 28:16.

[532] Note the use of architectural images metaphorically.

[533] From מוט; could also be translated "be shaky."

[534] See 11.40. Lit. "doors of a shield."

[535] From גדוד; see also 11.40.

[536] Heb. ב.

[537] Heb. עם תום, lit. "with the completion of," "with perfection," or "entirely." The meaning seems to be the quiver is empty. 4Q429 frg. 4 2.12 has "until (עד) the completion of." Either עם or עד may be original. עם תום is the more difficult reading. עד תום is well known and is found four times in the Qumran Scrolls (*GC* p. 517). עם תום is not found in biblical Hebrew and appears only here in 1QHᵃ 14 and in 1Q28 (1QSᵃ) 1.17, "along with the perfection of his way (עם תום דרכו). See PTSDSSP 1.112–13 (*Rule of the Congregation*). Most likely, עם תום was corrected in 4Q429 to עד תום (the difference is not caused by orthography, ם is not similar to ד). The passage presents a metaphor by which the *Yaḥad* perceives itself as the protected Community, "without an entrance," which is protected "at" (with the completion of the end of the cosmic wars [1QHᵃ]) or "until" the Endtime (4Q429). See Licht, p. 117.

[538] See the same concept expressed in 1QM and 1QS 3–4.

[539] From מצור, denoting also "fortifications," "stronghold," or even "fortified city." In inscriptions, the noun specifies a "boundary."

[540] Lit. "to open space without end."

[541] Note the contrast between bolted gates and open gates.

35 יْ‍ירו וא[‍י][‍ו]ן פלט ליצר אשמה לכלה ירמוסו ואין שא‍ר[‍י]ת‍ ו[אין] ת‍‍קוה ברוב פْ‍גْ‍רْים²²⁵

36 ו‍לْ‍כْ‍ו‍לْ גב‍ו‍רי מלחמת אין מנוס כי לאל עליון ה‍כْ[‍ו]ח   [°°°°° ‍ر

37 וْ‍שْ‍ו‍כْ‍ב‍ي עפר הרימו תרן ותולעת מْ‍תים נשאו נס לה‍ו‍ר‍ות[‍ם רשעים נ]תْ‍יבת‍ם‍ רש‍ע‍ה

38 במלחמות זדים ובעבור שוט שוטף בל יבוא ב‍מבצ‍ר] [°°°°°°° ° ل °°° ب‍ن

39 א‍מْ‍ת‍ך‍   °°] [ل‍ן   [‍ל‍ן   [לתפ‍ל‍ וככפיס לא °[   ]

40 מ°°]]

41 אמת]]°° ²²⁶

Col. 15 [= Sukenik Col. 7]
Parallels: 1Q35 (1QHᵇ); 4Q428 Frgs. 9–10; 4Q432 Frg. 12

1 [

2 [

3 [

4 [°م وאני נאלْ‍מתי מْ‍הْ‍ו]ת[‍מْ] [°°°° °° מן אלْ‍ה יגדפו‍נْ‍י

5 כזרו]ע נשברת מקניה ותטבע בבבץ²²⁷ רגלי שעו עיני מראוْ‍ת

6 רע אْ‍וْ‍זْ‍נْ‍י משמוע דמים השם לבבי ממחשבת רוע כי בליעל עם הופע יצר

---

²²⁵ See 24.17.
²²⁶ The right margin and bottom of the column is clear.
²²⁷ Dittography for בבוץ.

35 will be shot with[ou]t deliverance for the guilty creature.[542] Unto destruction they will tread, and there is neither remn[a]nt n[or] hope in the abundance of the corpses.[543]

36 And for all the mighty ones of wars there is no escape, for the Most High God (has) the po[wer …] °°° °°°°° *r* .

37 And those lying (in) the dust raised[544] the standard, and the maggots of the dead ones lifted up the banner to instruct [them. (Concerning) the wicked ones], their [p]aths (were) wicked

38 in the wars of the insolent ones. And when an overflowing scourge[545] passes by, it will not enter into the fortress […] °°° ° *l* °°°°°° *b*[…]

39 °°°°° your truth[546] […]*l*[…]*l*[…]. For mortar[547] and as a beam not °[…]

40 *m* °°[…]

41 truth °°[…]

Col. 15 [= Sukenik Col. 7]
Parallels: 1Q35 (1QH^b); 4Q428 Frgs. 9–10; 4Q432 Frg. 12

1 […]

2 […]

3 […]

4 […]° *m* and I, I am speechless from their disast[ers …]°° °°° *mn* these (things); they shall curse me

5 [… like an ar]m that is broken from the humerus,[548] and my foot sunk in the mire.[549] My eyes are shut from seeing

6 evil, (and) my ears from hearing blood (that has been shed).[550] Terrified is my heart from evil thought, because Belial (is) with the appearing[551] inclination of[552]

---

[542] Heb. יצר, or "inclination."
[543] See 24.17.
[544] Note the shift from future to past tense. Perhaps we are to imagine a *perfectum futurum*.
[545] See the same words in Isa 28:15, 18.
[546] The word is written above the line, perhaps not by a later correcting scribe since he usually changes the final *kaph* to כה.
[547] See Ezek 13:10, 11, 14, 15; 22:28.
[548] The words "broken from the humerus" (lit. "bone of the upper arm") are not typical of biblical metaphors; they may refer to an actual event. Did the Wicked Priest or his followers break the arm of the Righteous Teacher so he could not officiate as High Priest? See also 16.34.
[549] The translation corrects the scribal error. The author seems to know the poetry of Jer 38:22.
[550] See Gen 4:10.
[551] The *hip'il* of יפע means "to appear." Cf. Akkadian *(w)apū*, "to become visible."
[552] Heb. יצר.

7 הוותם וירזֹעו כול אושי מבניתֹ֞י וֹ֞עצמי יתפֹרדו ותכמי עלי כאוניה בזעף

8 חרישית ויהם לבי לכלה ורוח עועיים[228] תבלעני מהוות פשעם (VACAT)

Hymn 19
I Thank the Lord for Sustaining Me

9 אודכה אֹדוני כי סמכתני בעוזכה ורוח

10 קוֹדשכה הניפותה בי בל אמוט ותחזקני לפני מלחמות רשעה ובכול הוותם

11 לֹ֞א החתיתה מבריתכה ותשימני כמגדל עוז כֹחומה נשגבה ותכן על סלע

12 מבניתי ואושי עולם לסודי וכול קירותי לחֹומת בחן ללוא תד(י)עזע

13 וֹאתה אלי נתתו לעפים לעצת קודש ות֞[חזק]נֹ[י] בֹבריתכה ולשוני כלמודיך

14 וֹאֹיֹן פֹה לרוח הוות ולא מענה לשון לכול בֹני אשמה כי תאלמנה שפתי

15 שפתי[229] שקר כי כול גרי למשפט תרשיע להבדיל בי בין צדיק לרשע

---

[228] See the same spelling in 14.26.
[229] Not dittography but poetry. Ctr. Reymond, p. 24.

7   their disaster. And all the foundations of my structure[553] tremble, and my bones are dislocated, and my entrails (are) within me like a ship in a raging

8   gale,[554] and my heart is turbulent unto destruction, and the twisting wind devours me from the disasters of their transgression. (VACAT)

Hymn 19
I Thank the Lord for Sustaining Me

9   (VACAT) I thank you, O Lord, because you have sustained me with your strength, and have elevated[555] the spirit

10   of your holiness in me, so that I do not totter. And you strengthened me in the face of the wars of wickedness, and in their disasters

11   you did not deviate[556] from your covenant. And you set me as a strong tower (and) as a high city wall.[557] And you established my structure on

12   rock and the eternal foundations for my council, and (established)[558] all my walls[559] to a tried city wall that cannot be shaken.

13   And you, O my God, you gave him to the weary ones for the holy council. And you [strengthened[560] m]e in your covenant and my speech[561] according to your teachings.

14   And there is no mouth for the spirit of disaster, and no answer of the tongue for all the sons of guilt, because speechless[562] shall be the lips of

15   lying lips,[563] for you shall condemn to judgment any[564] who attack me in order to distinguish through me[565] between the righteous one and the wicked one.

---

[553] Note the repeated use of architectural terms to denote the physical and psychological experiences of the author.

[554] חרישית, from חרישי; cf. Jonah 4:8 (a "vehement wind").

[555] Heb. הניפותה, from נוף; the verb also denotes "to move back and forth," usually over one's head. Perhaps the author, remembering the ceremonies in the Temple, is making an allusion to the "wave-offering." See Ex 29:24–26.

[556] Lit. "to shatter."

[557] The Heb. for "city wall" is one word.

[558] Heb. כון (which means lit. "to fix solidly") seems echoed in the present clause (see the previous "you established").

[559] The noun denotes a wall of a house.

[560] See line 10. Note how this verb, "strengthened," ties the thoughts together (*ein Stichwort*).

[561] Lit. "tongue."

[562] Or "dumb," without voice.

[563] Recall "the man of the lie (הכזב)" at Qumran. In 15.15 the noun is שקר. See 1QpHab 11.1, 5.11; 4Q171 frgs. 1–10 1.26, 4.14. Cf. 1QS 6.24, 9.8.

[564] Or "each."

[565] Or "in me."

16 כי אתה ידעתה כול יצר מעשה וכול מענה לשון הכרתה ותכן לבי

17 [כל]מודיכה וכאמתכה לישר פעמי לנתיבות צדקה להתהלך לפניך בגבול

18 [חי]ֹ֯ם לשביל כבוד (וחיים) ושלום לאין ה֯[סר ולו]א֯ להשבת לנצח

19 ואתה ידעתה יצר עבדכה כי לא צ֯[מ֯]ש֯ענתו להרים לב֯[ו]

20 ולהעיז בכוח ומחסי בשר אין לי[אין צדקות להנצל מפנ֯]יכה[

21 בלֹ֯וֹא סליחה ואֹני נֹשענתי ברוֹ֯ב[רחמיכה230 ולגדול] חסדכה231 אוחיל להציץ

22 כֹ֯מֹטֹע ולגדל נצר להעיז בכוח ול֯[כי ב]צֹדקתכה העמדתני

23 לבריתכה ואתמוכה באמתכה ואת֯[ה השכלתני]ותשימני אב לבני חסד

24 וכאומן לאנשי מופת ויפצו פה כיונ[קי שדים232]וכשעשע עילול233 בחק

25 אומניו ותרם קרני על כול מנאצֹ֯י ויתפ֯[רדו כול ש]ארית אנשי מלחמתי ובעלי

---

230 See 15.30.
231 See 8.30 and 9.34.
232 See Joel 2:16: אספר־עם קדשו קהל קבצו זקנים אספו עוללים וינקי שדים יצא חתן מחדרו וכלה מחפתה.
233 A spelling for עולל. In Qumran Hebrew "babe" or "child" is regularly spelled עילול. See Joel 2:16: אספר־עם קדשו קהל קבצו זקנים אספו עוללים וינקי שדים יצא חתן מחדרו וכלה מחפתה.

16 For you, you know each inclination of[566] (every) creature,[567] and you recognized every answer of the tongue. And you established[568] my heart

17 [according to] your teachings;[569] and according to your truth, directing my footsteps to the paths of righteousness, to walk continuously before you within the border of

18 [li]fe in tracks of glory[570] and peace that can neither be re[moved no]r cease[571] for perpetuity.

19 But you, you know the inclination[572] of your servant, because not ṣ[…] his support to raise [his] heart

20 and to cause shelter in power. And I have no refuge (in) the flesh; […] there (are) no righteous (deeds) to be delivered[573] before [you][574]

21 without forgiveness. But I, I leaned on the multitude of [your mercies, and for the greatness of] your loving-kindness I await, to bring forth buds[575]

22 as planting, and to grow a shoot to cause shelter in (your) power and l[…. For by] your righteousness you allowed me to stand[576]

23 for your covenant. And I will adhere to[577] your truth and yo[u, you allowed me to have insight,][578] and you made[579] me a father for the sons of loving-kindness,

24 and as a nursing-father[580] to the men of a wondrous-sign.[581] And they open (their) mouths[582] like those suck[ing the breast[583]] and like the babe[584] who delights in the bosom of

25 its[585] nursing-father. And you raised my horn against all who scorn me, and [all the re]mnant of the men of my war were dis[persed,] and those

---

[566] Heb. יצר.

[567] Lit. "work." The Creator is in the mind of the poet.

[568] Note how frequently this verb is used within the *Thanksgiving Hymns* and within the scrolls composed at Qumran.

[569] See 15.13.

[570] A scribe has erased "and life."

[571] Or "put an end to."

[572] Heb. יצר.

[573] The *nipʿal* infinitive means "to deliver oneself." The author cannot bring anything to deliver (or save) him (himself).

[574] In Semitics, literally "from before [you]." See 15.31 and Isa 63:19.

[575] Infinitive of ציץ; not a verb in Biblical Hebrew.

[576] *Hipʿil* permissive.

[577] See also 10.23; 12.2, 23; 22.14.

[578] See line 29.

[579] Lit. "set," "put," or "place."

[580] A stunning and unusual image that reappears in *OdesSol* 19:2–3, "His breasts" refer to "the father" who "was milked." The "wondrous sign" appears to refer to the Righteous Teacher who is also "a nursing father." See the notes in the *Qumran Psalter*, and 15.25, 17.31, and 17.36 (in which we are told about God being compassionate "like a nursing-father").

[581] See the same expression in Zech 3:8.

[582] Singular in Hebrew.

[583] See Joel 2:16.

[584] See Joel 2:16.

[585] Plural in Hebrew.

26 רבי כמוץ לפני רוח וממשלתי על באי ב̇[ריתכה א]לי עזרתה נפשי ותרם קרני

27 למעלה והופעתי באור̇ שבעתים בע̊[בור זה[234] ה]כ̇ינותה לכבודכה

28 כי אתה לי למאור עו̊לם ותכן רגלי במ̊י̇[שור   [(VACAT)

Hymn 20
I Thank the Lord for Instructing Me in Truth

29 או̊ד̊כ̇[ה אדוני]כי השכלתני באמתכה

30 וברזי פלאכ̊ה̊[235] הודעתני ובחסדיכה לאיש [פשע] ו̇ברוב רחמיכה לב לנעוי[236]

צב(ע)י
31 כ̊י̊   מ̊י̊ כמ̊ו̊כ̇ה באלים אדוני[237] ומי כאמתכה ומי יצד̊ק[238] לפניכה בהשפטו[239] ואין

תבי̇א
32 להשיב על תוכחתכה כול רוח ולא יוכל כול להתיצב לפני[240] ח(כ)מתרה[241] וכול בני

33 אמתכה בסליחות לפניכה לט̊ה̊ר̊ם מפשעיהם[242] ברוב טובכה ובהמון רח̊מיכה

34 להעמידם לפניכה לעולמי עד   כי אל[243] עולם אתה וכול דרכיכה יכונו לנצח

35 נ̊צחי̊ם ואין זולתכה ומה הוא איש תהו ובעל הבל להתבונן במעשי פלאך

36 הגדולים[244]

[234] There is space for 6–7 consonants or spaces.
[235] 4Q428 frg. 9 line 1: פלא[כ̊]ה̇.
[236] 4Q428 frg. 9 line 2: [ו]ל̊נעו[י.
[237] An echo of Ex 15:11: מי־כמכה באלים יהוה מי כמכה נאדר בקדש נורא תהלת עשה פלא.
[238] 4Q428 frg. 9 frg. 3: ומי י̊[צדק.
[239] 1Q35 frg. 1 line 3: לפני[כ̊ה בהשפטכה.
[240] 1Q35 frg. 1 line 4: [לפני̇.
[241] A scribe corrected "your wisdom" to "your wrath."
[242] 1Q35 frg. 1 line 5: מפשעי[הם.
[243] 1Q35 frg. 1 line 6: כי[א ◄ ◄.
[244] 1Q35 frg. 1 line 8: פל[א]כה הגדולים.

26 who quarrel (with me are) as chaff before the wind. And my dominion (is) over those (who) enter into [your] co[venant, O] my G[od.] You have helped my soul,[586] and you have raised my horn

27 upwards, and I shone with a sevenfold light.[587] On ac[count of this] you have [es]tablished your glory,[588]

28 because you are for me an eternal light, and you established my foot in upri[ghtness].[589] (VACAT)

Hymn 20
I Thank the Lord for Instructing Me in Truth

29 (VACAT) I thank yo[u, O Lord,] because you allowed me to have insight into your truth

30 and allowed[590] me to know your wondrous mysteries[591] and your loving-kindnesses for a man of [transgression] and the multitude of your mercies to the perverted of heart.

31 For who is like you among the gods, O Lord?[592] And who is like your truth? And who can be justified before you when he is judged? And no

32 hosts[593] of a spirit can reply to your chastisement. And none can stand before your wrath. And all the sons of

33 your truth you allow to come into forgiveness before you, purifying them from their transgressions with the multitude of your goodness, and with the abundance of your mercies,

34 allowing them to stand before you forever (and) ever.[594] For you (are) an eternal God, and all your ways are established for perpetuity

35 (and) perpetuity. And there is no one but you. And how may[595] a man of emptiness and the owner of nonsense comprehend[596] your wondrous works

36 which are great? (VACAT)

---

[586] Heb. נפשׁ.
[587] That is a "perfect light."
[588] The *lamedh* is a *nota accusativi*.
[589] Lit. "in the plain," signifying a settled and stable situation. See 10.31 and 11.21.
[590] Notice the repetitive use of the permissive *hipʿil*.
[591] See 1QpHab 7, according to which the Righteous Teacher alone was "allowed to know all the mysteries of the words of his servants, the prophets."
[592] An echo of Ex 15:11.
[593] Heb. צבא. See 5.25.
[594] As in the final columns of 1QS (the *Rule of the Community*) an emphasis is placed on God's forgiveness and covenant loyalty (loving-kindness) for acceptance (or salvation), rejecting any conception that a human can earn God's favor by doing good works.
[595] Lit. "what is a."
[596] Lit. "observe."

Hymn 21
I Thank the Lord for My Lot

הפלתה ע א[245]

37 א֗ו֗ד֗כה אדוני כ֗י לוא גו֗ר֗ל֗י ב(י)דת שו ובסוד נעלמים לא[246] שמתה חוקי

38 ו֗ת֗ק֗ר֗אני[247] לחסדיכה ולסליחה֗ו[תיכה הביאות]ני ו֗ב֗ה֗מו֗ן[248] רחמיכה לכול[249] משפטי

39 [צדק ואני א]י֗ש טמ֗[א ומרחם] הוריתי באשמת[250] מעל[251] [ומשדי אמי ב]ע֗ולה ובחי֗ק

40 אומנתי[252] לרוב נדה ומנעורי בדמים[253] ועד[254] שיבה אתה תכלכלני[255] [ואתה] אלי

41 כוננתה רגלי בדרכי[256] לבכה ולשמועות֗[257] פלאכה גליתה אוזני ולבי להבין בא֗מ֗ת֗כ֗[258]

Col. 16 [= Sukenik Col. 8]
Parallels: 1Q35 2; 4Q428 10.7–12; 4Q432 13

1 [ולוא א֗ט֗ומם[259] אוזן בלמודיכה עד אשר֗[260]] כלת]ה֗ ר֗מ֗י֗ה֗ ו֗א֗י֗ן נעוות[261]

2 בלוא דעת דעת הכא֗ת֗ה מתכמי וכבו֗[ד לב[262] ‵‵‵ [ואין] לי עוד

3 למכשול עוון כי תג֗ל֗[ה[263]] ישעכה ו֗צ֗ד֗קתכה תכון לעד כי לא ל֗[אד]ם דרכו

---

245 See ישוא in 10.30.
246 1Q35 frg. 1 line 10: ובס[ו]ד נעלמים לוא.
247 4Q428 frg. 10 line 1: חוקי ותק֗ר֗אנ֗י.
248 1Q35 frg. 1 line 11: הביאות]נ֗י וב֗[המון.
249 4Q428 frg. 10 line 2: ובהמון רחמיכה לכ֗[ו]ל.
250 1Q35 frg. 1 line 12: ה֗וריתי בא[שמת].
251 4Q428 frg. 10 line 3: ומרחם ה֗וריתי באשמת מעל֗[; also 1Q35 frg. 1 line 12: ה֗וריתי בא[שמת.
252 See 17.31: ובחיק אומנתי.
253 4Q428 frg. 10 line 4: לרוב נדה ומנעורי בד֗[מים.
254 1Q35 frg. 1 line 13: מ֗נעורי בדמים ועד.
255 See 17.34.
256 4Q428 frg. 10 line 5: אלי כוננתה רגלי בדרכ֗[י.
257 1Q35 frg. 1 line 14: בדר]ך֗ לבכה ולשמועות֗.
258 4Q428 frg. 10 line 6: אוזני ולבי להבין באמתכ֗[ה.
259 See 1Q35 frg. 1 line 15: א֗ט֗ומם֗.
260 From 4Q428 frg. 10 line 7: אוזן בלמודיכה עד אשר֗.
261 4Q427 frg. 7 2.4: כלת]ה֗ ר֗מ֗י֗ה֗ ו֗א֗י֗ן נעוות בלוא דעת הופיע אור וש[מחה תביע אבד].
262 4Q428 frg. 10 line 8: דעת הכא֗ת֗ה מתכמי וכבו֗[ד לב.
263 4Q428 frg. 10 line 9: לי עוד למכשול עוון כי תג֗ל֗[ה.

Hymn 21
I Thank the Lord for My Lot

37   I thank you, O Lord, because you did not cast my lot in the congregation of the worthless; and in the council of the hidden ones you did not put my ordinances.

38   But you called me to your loving-kindnesses and [you brought] me to [your] forgivenesses and with the abundance of your mercies for all the judgments of

39   [righteousness. But I (am) a m]an of impuri[ty and from the womb of] her who conceived me (I have re-mained) in guilt of infidelity.[597] [And from the breasts of my mother][598] in deceit, and in the bosom of

40   my nurse[599] for much impurity. And from my youth in blood[600] (that has been shed)[601] and until old age you will sustain me.[602] [And you], O my God,

41   you established my foot in the ways of your heart.[603] And to reports of[604] your wonder you opened my ears and allowed[605] my heart to understand your truth.[606]

Col 16 [= Sukenik Col. 8]
Parallels: 1Q35 2; 4Q428 10.7–12; 4Q432 13

1   [And] I will [not] close an ear[607] to your teachings until[608] [...] deceit [ende]d; and there are no perversi-ties[609]

2   without knowledge. Knowledge of (perversities) you removed from my entrails and heavine[ss of heart][610] °°° [there is not] for me again

3   a stumbling block of iniquity because you shall reve[al[611] your salvation[612] and] your righteousness shall be established forever. For not to [Ad]am (is) his way.

---

[597] Restored from 4Q428 frg. 10 line 3. See 21.31; cf. 12.35 and 19.14.
[598] See 17.29–31 and also 15.24–25.
[599] See 17.31.
[600] From 1Q35 frg. 1 line 13.
[601] The noun is in the plural. See 15.6.
[602] See 17.34.
[603] From 4Q428 frg. 10 line 5.
[604] From 1Q35 frg. 1 line 14.
[605] A permissive *hipʿil*.
[606] The *beth* serves as a *nota accusativi*. From 4Q428 frg. 10 line 6.
[607] From 1Q35 1.15.
[608] From 4Q428 frg. 10 line 7.
[609] From 4Q427 frg. 7 2.4.
[610] From 4Q428 frg. 10 line 8.
[611] From 4Q428 frg. 10 line 9.
[612] From 13.14.

4   כ[ול] אלה לכבודכה עשיתה[264]

Hymn 22
I Thank the Lord for Making Me the Irrigator of the Garden

5   או[ד]כֿה אדוני כי[265] נֿתתני במקור נוזלים ביבשה ומבוע מים בארץ ציה ומֿשקי

6   גן ואֿגֿ[ם מים] וֿשֿדֿה מטע ברוש ותדהר עֿם תאשור יחד[266] לכבודכה   עצי

7   חיים במעין רז מחובאים בתוך כול עצי מים[267] והיו להפריח נצר למטעת עולם

8   להשריש טרם יפריחו ושורשיהם ליובֿ[ל] ישלחו ויפתח למים חיים יגזעו[268]

9   ויהי[269] למקור עולם ובנצר עליו ירעו כול חֿ[יו]תֿ יער ומרמס גזעו לכל עוברי

10   דרך ודליתו לכל עוף כנף וירמו עליו כול ע[צי] מים כי[270] במטעתם יתשגשגו

11   ואל יובל לא ישלחו שורש ומפריח נצר קֿ[ו]דש למטעת אמת סותר בלוא

---

[264] 18.14: לכבודכה עשיתה כול אלה. Also see 23.25.
[265] See 4Q428 frg. 10 line 11: אֿ[וד]כֿה אדוני כי[א.
[266] The passage echoes Isa 41:19: אתן במדבר ארז שטה והדס ועץ שמן אשים בערבה ברוש תדהר ותאשור יחדו.
[267] See Ezek 31:14: כָּל־עֲצֵי־מָיִם.
[268] A metathesis for גיזעו. See line 9.
[269] See 4Q432 frg. 13 line 1: לכל עו[ברי.
[270] See 4Q432 frg. 13 line 2: מ[יֿם כֿיֿ.

4   A[ll][613] these (things) you did for your glory.[614] (VACAT)

Hymn 22
I Thank the Lord for Making Me the Irrigator of the Garden

5   I tha[nk] you, O Lord, because you have placed me as[615] the source of streams in a dry land, and (as) the gush-pond of water in an arid land, and (as) the Irrigator of[616]

6   the garden and of a poo[l of water],[617] and (as) a field of planting of cypress and elm with cedar together[618] for your glory.[619] The trees

7   of life[620] (are) beside a mysterious fountain,[621] concealed among all the trees of water.[622] And they will bring forth a shoot[623] for an eternal planting,

8   by taking root before they blossom. And their roots they send out to a broo[k],[624] and its trunk opened to the living water.

9   And it will become an eternal spring, for in the shoot of its leaves all the be[as]ts of the forest will graze, and its stem is trampled on by all who pass over

10   the way,[625] and its high branch (is) for all winged birds, and all the tr[ees of] the water exalt over it,[626] for in their planting they flourish,

11   but they do not send a root to the brook. But the h[o]ly shoot shall grow to a planting of truth (which is) hidden, without

---

[613] From 4Q428 frg. 10 line 10.

[614] See 18.14 and 23.25.

[615] The preposition functions as a *beth essentiae*. See Charlesworth's reflections in *Of Scribes and Scrolls*, pp. 67–78. In 16.17, the author states that God put "the early rain" in him. See Charlesworth's comments in *Der Mensch vor Gott*, pp. 193–210. The poem is by the Righteous Teacher, as most scholars have concluded.

[616] ומשקי can be ומשקה in Qumran Hebrew. The Irrigator is the Righteous Teacher.

[617] The author seems to echo many passages in the Hebrew Bible, notably Isa 14:23; 41:18; Pss 107:35 and 114:8.

[618] Heb. יחד which is perhaps a paronomasia for "Community," since the Righteous Teacher, the author, is imagining the planting of the eschatological Community. The words in the line are echoes from Isa 41:19.

[619] See Isa 35:7. Isa 41:18–21 has deeply influenced the mind of the poet who must have memorized Isaiah 41. Note the echo of the imagery from Isaiah 41 in these sentences: "a pool of water (לאגם מים)," "the dry land (ארץ ציה)," "the cypress (ברוש)," "the elm (תדהר)," and "the cedar (תאשור)." As is well-known from the *Rule of the Community*, the book of Isaiah also supplied the *raison d'être* for going into the wilderness, not only in Isa 40:3 but also in Isaiah 41: "I will make in the wilderness (במדבר)."

[620] Conceivably, the author is imagining the priests who are with the Righteous Teacher. According to Proverbs, Wisdom is "a tree of life" (3:18), and the fruit of the righteous is "a tree of life" (11:30). Also see Prov 13:12 and 15:4.

[621] The Righteous Teacher is the mysterious fountain.

[622] Most likely, the poet with "trees of water" is representing the wicked priests who rejected the Righteous Teacher.

[623] See Isa 11:21 and 60:21: נצר מטעו.

[624] The Hebrew noun is rare; see Jer 17:8. See line 11.

[625] This seems to be a reference to "the Way," the Way of Qumran. The Qumranites referred to themselves as "the Perfect of the Way." See 1QS 8.10, 21; 9.5, 9; 1QSa 1.28.

[626] Or "over him." The letters are the same for "leaves" as for "over it (him)." Did the author or those who read this text at Qumran imagine a paronomasia?

12   ואתּהֿ א]ל שכתה בעד פריו ברז גבורי כוח   נחשב ובלא נודע חותם רזו

13   ורוחות קודש ולהט אש מתהפכת בל י]בוא [זֹר בֿמֿעין חיים ועם עצי עולם

14   לא ישתה[271] מי קודש בל ינובב פריו עם [מֿ]טֿע[272] שחקים כי ראה בלא הכיר

15   ויחשוב בלא האמין למקור חיים ויתן יבֿ]ול] פֿרח עולם ואני הייתי ל]ב[זֹאי (נֿ)הרות

16   שוטפים כי גרשו עלי רפשם

17   ואתה אלי שמתה בפי כיורה גשם לכול [מטע] ומבוע מים חיים ולא יכזב לפתוח

18   הֿשמֿים לא ימושו ויהיו לנחל שוטף עֿ]ל כול עצי] מים ולימים לאין חקֿר [פתע]

19   פיתאום[273] יביעו מחובאים בסתר שֿ]וטפים עם מפלגיה]מֿ וֹיהיו למֿי מ]ריבה לכול עץ]

271 1Q35 frg. 2 line 1: זֹר במעין חיים [and 2.2 ועם] עֹצי עֹ]ו]לם לוא ישתה.
272 The *mem* is lost in the *lacuna*.
273 The superfluous *yodh* may denote a short "i."

12   esteem, and its mysterious seal is unknown.[627] And you, [O Go]d, you hedged about[628] its fruits by means of the mystery of the powerful mighty ones,[629]

13   and the spirits of holiness, and the turning flame of fire,[630] lest a stranger should [enter] the fountain of life. And with the eternal trees

14   he must not drink the holy water, lest he will yield his fruits with the [pl]anting of skies,[631] for he[632] sees without acknowledging,

15   and thinks without believing in the source of life.[633] And it[634] gives forth prod[uce], the eternal blossom. And I, I have become an (object of) [sc]orn (for) rivers (whose)

16   torrents expel mud over me.[635]

17   But you, O my God, you put into my mouth (that which is) like the early rain[636] for all [plantings],[637] and (it becomes) the pond of living water.[638] And it will not fail to open.

18   (Moreover), the (rains from the) skies[639] will not subside[640] and will become a torrential ravine[641] up[on all the trees of] the water,[642] and to seas unfathomable.[643] [All of a][644]

19   sudden,[645] (the waters) concealed in secret will spring forth t[orrents with th]eir [streams.] And they will become waters of s[trife[646] for every tree]

---

[627] Note the small *vacat*.

[628] The root can be the *qal* perfect of שוך, "he hedged about" or the *qal* perfect of שכך, "he covered" and also "he shaded." See Ps 139:13 (spelled סכך). שוך (סור) is the source of סֻכָה, "booths which provide shade."

[629] Or "powerful warriors," "heroes."

[630] Cf. Gen 3:24.

[631] Heb. שחקים.

[632] The pronoun refers back to "a stranger."

[633] See Ps 36:10; Prov 10:11, 13:14, 14:27, and 16:22.

[634] A collective referring to the "eternal trees." See line 13.

[635] A *vacat* is used for transition.

[636] A paronomasia between "early rain" (יורה) and "teacher" (מורה); that is, the Righteous Teacher imagines himself to be like the early and gentle Autumn rain that finally brings water and life to a parched Holy Land (for מורה, see Ps 84:7 and Joel 2:23). See *Der Mensch vor Gott*, pp. 193–210. I will never forget driving into the Negev in early Autumn and seeing the "desert" bloom with red flowers that covered the landscape. One week earlier, the area had not one flower.

[637] See the generic use of "planting" in 16.14.

[638] See the parallel thought in 16.6.

[639] Or "the heavens."

[640] The rain will not cease pouring from the heavens.

[641] Heb. נחל שוטף.

[642] The torrent of heavenly water is from the Righteous Teacher; it will eventually wash away "the trees of the water," the evil and illegitimate priests under the control of the Wicked Priest. The links between the *Rule of the Community* and the *Thanksgiving Hymns* are internationally affirmed.

[643] Heb. לאין חקר.

[644] See 4.17. Heb. פתע.

[645] Heb. פיתאום.

[646] See Num 20:13, 20:24; Deut 33:8; Ps 106:32.

20 לֹה ויבש וֹמֹצולֹה לכול חיה ועֹצֹ]י מים צללוֹ] כֹעופרת במים אדירי]ם[

21 בֹּשֹׁבֹּיֹבֹּיֹ אש יבשו ומטע פרי יֹ]הי למ]קֹוֹר עולם לעדן כבוד ופאֹ]רת עד[

22 ובידי פתחתה מקורם עם פלגי]הם ומשברי]הֹם לפנות על קו נכון ומטע

23 עציהם על משקלת השמש לאוֹ]ר עולם ויפריח]נו לפארת כבוד בהניפי יד לֹעזוֹק

24 פלגיו יכו שרשיו בצור חלמיש ו]עד תהום יֹ]כֹו בארץ גזעם ובעת חום יעצור

25 מעוז ואם אשיב יד יהיה כערעֹר]במדבר]וֹגזעו כחרלים במלחה ופלגיו

26 יעֹל קוץ ודרדר לשמיר ושית וכֹ]ול עצי] שפתו יהפכו כעצי באושים לפני

27 חום יבול עליו ולא נפתח עם מעֹין גֹזֹ]עו ואני] מגור עם חוליים ומ]נוג]ע לֹב

28 בנגיעים ואהיה כאיש נעזב ביגוֹן]ואנח]הֹֹ[274] אין מעוז לי כי פרֹח נגֹ]י]עֹי

---

[274] See 13.36.

20   wet and dry, and deep-water for every animal.[647] And the tree[s of the water sunk deep][648] like lead in migh[ty] waters,

21   in flames of fire they were dried out. But the planting of the fruit shall [be to] an eternal [s]ource for the Eden of[649] glory and the [everlasting] leafy b[ranches].

22   And by my hand you opened their source with [their] streams [and] their [breakers][650] to turn on a correct measuring-line. And the planting of

23   their trees according to the sun's[651] plumb line[652] for lig[ht eternal, and he shall cause] them [to blossom] into[653] leafy branches of glory. When I lift[654] my hand to dig about[655]

24   its streams, its roots strike[656] through the flint stone. And [unto the depths] they will [st]rike into the earth their stem. So in times of heat it retains

25   (its) shelter. But if I withdraw (my) hand it becomes like a juniper [in the wilderness];[657] and its stem (is) like a stinging-weed[658] in a salty place.[659] And its[660] streams

26   cause[661] thorns and thistles to grow into briars and brambles, and a[ll the trees of] its bank are changed into rotten trees. In the face of[662]

27   the heat, its leaves will wither;[663] for[664] [its] ste[m] was not opened to[665] the fountain. [And I] (am) a (temporary) abode with sicknesses, and (my) heart is aff[licte]d

28   with afflictions; and I am as an abandoned man in agony [and sighin]g. There is no shelter for me; for my affl[ic]tion produces

---

[647] A scribe corrected the text. Previous editors missed the correction.

[648] The restoration is influenced by the Song of the Sea in Ex 15:10; the rest of the line is identical to the text in Exodus.

[649] "Eden" here is a *nomen proprium*; it can also mean "luxury" and "luxuriant" (see 5.34; 18.26, 32). Only in the "Teacher Hymns" is "Eden" a proper noun; see 14.19.

[650] See 14.26. There is room for 11 consonants (the number restored).

[651] A possible allusion to the solar calendar.

[652] Or "balance."

[653] There is sufficient space for this restoration.

[654] Lit. "in the waving of my hand." Most likely the Righteous Teacher lifted "the wave offering" in the Temple.

[655] Or "to hoe."

[656] See Ex 7:20.

[657] The author intends to refer to a withering plant in semidry land.

[658] From חרול, "weed." See Prov 24:31 in which the noun is parallel to "thorns." The plant may be one of the 39 "nettles" (of the genus *Urtica*). The author intends to denote the stinging nature of a plant. His vocabulary is extensive. All the plants mentioned in these lines have thorns or something which stings.

[659] The author alludes to brackish water; that is, water that is not healthy.

[660] It is "a salty place."

[661] The *hipᶜil* impf. of עלה means "cause to rise."

[662] Heb. לפני.

[663] The *qal* imperfect of נפל means "to weather," "to decay."

[664] Lit. "and."

[665] Lit. "with."

29   למרורים וכאוב אנוש לאין עצור בֹּ[צמי ותהי מה]ֹומה עלי כיורדי שֹאול ועם

30   מתים יחפש רוחי כי הגיעו לשחת חֹ[י וביגון] תֹתעטף נפשי יומֹם ולילה

31   לאין מנוח ויפרח כאש בוער עצור בעֹצֹמֹי עֹד ימימה תואכֹל שלבתה[275]

32   להתם כוח לקצים ולכלות בשר עד מֹועדים ויתעופפו עֹלֹי מֹשבֹרֹים

33   ונפשי עלי תשתוחח לכלה כי נשבת מעוזֹי מגויתי וינגר כמים לבי וימֹס

34   כדונג בשרי ומעוז מותני מותני היה לבהלה ותשבר זרועי מֹקֹנֹיֹהֹ וא]ֹֹין להניף יד

35   וֹֹרגֹלי נלכֹדֹה בכבל וילכו כמים ברכי ואין לשלוח פעם ולא מצעד לקול רגֹלי

36   וֹחֹוזֹק זֹרֹועֹי רֹותקו בזקי מכשול ולשון הגברתה בפֹ בלא נאספה ואין להֹרֹים

---

[275] Note the quiescent *he*; read שלהבתה.

29 bitterness[666] and a severe pain which (cannot) be contained in [my] b[ones.[667] And there was a tur]moil over me, as those who descend (into) Sheol, and with

30 the dead it[668] seeks my spirit, for [my] life reached the pit. [And in agony][669] my soul[670] faints away day and night

31 without rest. And it shoots forth as a burning fire withheld in my bones. For days,[671] its flame consumes

32 by annihilating power for the endtimes, and by destroying flesh until appointed times.[672] And the break-ers[673] fly over me;

33 and my soul[674] is decaying within me[675] to destruction, because my protection[676] ceases from my body. And my heart is poured out like water, and my

34 flesh melts like wax, and the protection of[677] my loins is turned to fear, and my arm is broken from its socket.[678] [And it is impossib]le to lift[679] (my) hand.

35 And my foot is caught in a chain; and my knees wobble[680] like water. So[681] it is impossible to put forth a footstep, and there is no tread for the sound of my feet.

36 And the strength[682] of my arm is bound in chains[683] that cause (me) to stumble, and the tongue you had strengthened[684] in my mouth is no longer retrievable,[685] so[686] it is impossible to raise

---

[666] In the Hebrew, the noun is in the plural ("bitternesses").

[667] For the restoration, see line 31.

[668] The subject continues to be "my affliction" (see line 28).

[669] See line 28.

[670] Heb. נפש.

[671] Or "years." See Ex 13:10.

[672] Or "festivals."

[673] Note the use of this noun in 11.9–13 when an author (probably the same one) talked about the opening womb of the pregnant one.

[674] Heb. נפש.

[675] Or "upon me."

[676] Heb. מעוזי; translated "shelter" in lines 25, 28, 33, and 34.

[677] Heb. ומעוז.

[678] Or "from its bone of the upper arm (מקניה);" but one should seek to find one English noun (socket or humerus) to represent one He-brew noun: קנה (that also denotes the familiar "measuring reed" which supplies the much later "canon"). See 15.5 and its note.

[679] Lit. "the waving of my hand." The passage may mirror the wave-offering in the Temple.

[680] Lit. "to walk." See 12.34. See Ezek 21:12. Perhaps the expression denotes "water (urine) pouring down the knees."

[681] Lit. "And."

[682] Heb. וחוזק. The author uses three nouns for "strength" and "protection."

[683] See Nah 3:10.

[684] Lit. "made mighty."

[685] Lit. "be collected." Not "be taken away." The verb is the *nip'al* pf. of אסף which means literally "to be gathered," or "received a-gain." The words here seem grounded in some real and horrible experience and are not simply metaphors. Was the tongue of the Righteous Teacher cut off so he could no longer speak? Recall that according to 1 Maccabees 14, after the ascension of Simon the Hasmonean, no priest could teach or gather a group of priests for instruction in the Temple. See 1Mac 14:41–45. The ears of John Hycanus II were cut off so he could not serve as High Priest (*War* 1.8–13 and *Ant* 14.5–13).

[686] Lit. "and."

37 קוֹל וּלֹה[א]זֹין למֹודים לחיות רֹוח כֹושלים ולעות לעאף‎[276] דבר נאלם מֹזל‎[277] שפתי

38 מפֹלצֹוֹת בֹקו משפט לֹוח לבי פֹותֹחֹ[ ]°°°[ ]בֹאו במרֹורים לבב בֹאוֹ ברום ממשֹלת

39 בֹל[י]על [ל   ]   [שֹלום וא]   נ[פֹש התבלֹעֹהֹ

40 °°[   ]   נאלמו כאין [

41 °°°°[   ]   אנוש לאֹי[ן]‎[

Col. 17 [= Sukenik Col. 9]

1 [   ]°° אֹפֹלֹהֹ °[

2 הוף]יֹע לֹמֹֹדֹנֹים בלילה ובֹי[ֹ]ום

3 [   ]°°°°[ ]לֹאֹין רחמֹים באף יעורר קֹנאה ולכלה אֹ[פפוני

4 משברי מות ושאול על יצועי ערשי בקינה תשא מֹטֹ[תי]בֹקול אנחה

5 עיני כעש בכבשן ודמעתי כנחלי מים כלו למנוח עיני [חסדכה]‎[278] עמד לי

[276] Read לעיף; an allusion to Isa 50:4.
[277] See 19.8. ומזל שפתי.
[278] See 17.7, 10, 14, and 31.

37 (my) voice to allow (my) disciples to h[e]ar,[687] to give life to the spirit of those who stumble, and to sustain[688] the weary one (through) speaking. The flow of my lips[689] was silenced

38 from horrors. In the measuring-line of judgment, the tablet of my heart opens [...]°°° [...] they enter with the bitterness of[690] heart. They enter in the height of the dominion of

39 Bel[ial ...]*l.* (VACAT) [...] peace and ʾ[... s]oul[691] was swallowed up

40 °°[...] they were speechless as without

41 °°°[...] the human with[out]

Col. 17 [= Sukenik Col. 9]

1 [...]° gloominess[692] °°[...]

2 [... cause] controversies [to sh]ine[693] in the night and in the d[ay ...]

3 [...]°°°° [...] without mercies. He arouses jealousy with wrath. And for destruction, th[ey surround me, ...]

4 the breakers of[694] death. And Sheol[695] (is) on my bed. My couch resounds with lamentation, (and) [my] ma[t] with the sound of a sighing.

5 My eyes (are) like a burning-fire[696] in a furnace, and my tears (are) like valleys of[697] water; my eyes fail for rest. [Your loving-kindness][698] remains (motionless)[699] to me

---

[687] *Hiʿpil* permissive.

[688] This verb may be an Aramaism in the Hebrew text. עות in Aramaic equals עוש in Hebrew and means "to help" and "to restore" (only in Joel 4:11). עות appears in BH only in Isa 50:4. This verse is evoked by the poet: "the tongue of the learned ones (disciples) that I may know how to sustain the weary with a word" (cf. NRSV).

[689] See 19.8.

[690] In Hebrew, the noun is in the plural.

[691] Heb. נפש.

[692] Heb. אפלה. See Joel 2:2 in which "darkness" (חשך) and "gloominess" (אפלה) are present.

[693] Or "to appear."

[694] Here again "breakers" is not a metaphor as in col. 11 for the opening of the womb.

[695] Sheol designates the "pit" of suffering. See 11.20–37.

[696] The author intends to indicate "burning-red eyes." The text has "like a moth (כעש)." But the orthography is a Qumran way of writing "like a burning fire (כאש)." At Qumran the gutterals were weakened and ע sounded like א. See the scribal correction in 1QS 7.14 (see Charlesworth, *Rule* (Photog. Ed.) and Reymond.) Conceivably the author intended to write כעשן, "as smoke."

[697] I.e. like *wadiyot*.

[698] The suggested reconstruction of ישע, "salvation," is unlikely since the noun appears only in 10.25 and 11.27, thus far from this context. The author longs for something. חסד, "loving-kindness," appears frequently in 1QHᵃ; see esp. 17.7, 10, 14, and 31 (only in the plural, but that does not undermine the reconstruction of a singular noun which is demanded by the accompanying verb). In 17.10, the author expresses a longing for God's loving-kindness. In 17.14, he hopes for loving-kindness.

[699] Heb. עמד, lit. "to stand for."

6   מרחוק וחיי מצד ואני משאה אֱלְמשׁוֹאה[279] וממכאוב לֹנֹגע ומחבלים

7   למשברים תשוחח נפשי בנפלאותיכה ולא הזנחתני בחסדיכהֹ מֹקץ

8   לקץ תשתֹשעֹ[280] נפשי בהֹמון רחמיכה ואשיבה למבלעי דבר

9   ולֹמֹשתוחיחי בי תוכחת וארשיעה דינו ומשפטכה אצדיק כי ידעתי

10   באמתכה ואבחרה במשפטי ובנגיעי רציתי כי יחלתי לחסדיכה ותֹתן

11   תחנה בפי עבדכה ולא גערתה חיי ושלומי לא הזנחתה ולא עזבֹתה

12   תקוותי ולפני נגע העמדתה רוחי   כי אתה יסדתה רוחי וֹתדע מזמתי

13   ובצוקותי נחמתני ובסליחֹותֹ אשתעשע ואנחמה על פשע ראשון

---

[279] Note a scribe deleted the initial ʾaleph by placing dots above and below it.
[280] Read: תשתעשע.

6   from a distance,[700] and my life (waits) from (the) side.[701] And as for me, from ruin to devastation, and from pain to affliction, and from tribulations

7   to breakers, my soul[702] contemplates your wonders,[703] and you have not rejected me[704] with your loving-kindnesses. From the endtime (of the day)

8   to the endtime (of the night)[705] my soul[706] delights in the abundance of your mercies.[707] And I will reply to those who wish to devour me (with) a speech,[708]

9   and a chastisement to those who cast me down.[709] And I will renounce it,[710] his verdict,[711] but your judgment I will consider right.[712] Because I know

10   your truth,[713] so I choose it as my judgment. And I accept[714] my affliction, for I long for your loving-kindnesses;[715] and you put

11   supplication in the mouth of your servant. And you have not rebuked my life, and my well-being you have not rejected.[716] And you have not forsaken

12   my hope; and before affliction you caused my spirit to stand (firm).[717] For you, you have founded my spirit and you know my design.

13   And in my troubles[718] you have comforted me, and in forgivenesses I take delight. And I find comfort concerning the first transgression.[719]

---

[700] The meaning is most likely "a distance" in time. The text is eschatological.

[701] The Hebrew is not clear. Perhaps the author intended to mean "I am (waiting) from the side."

[702] Heb. נפש.

[703] Again, the *beth* is a *nota accusativi*.

[704] The *hipʿil* of זנח means "to declare rejected." In 2Chr 11:14 this verb in the *hipʿil* connotes being rejected from serving as a priest.

[705] Or, "the end (of the day) to the end (of the night when)."

[706] Heb. נפש.

[707] See 20.7. Also see 1QS 10.10–15 in which an author (perhaps the same one who wrote the present section of the *Thanksgiving Hymns*) explains how he constantly praises God at the beginning of the night and day. The day began in the evening (at sunset) at Qumran. There is a marvelous harmony between the endtime (קץ) of each day and the Endtime (קץ). Contrast "from time to time (עת בעת)," as in 1QS 8.15 and 9.13.

[708] Contrast 16.36–37.

[709] The verb is apparently a *šapʿel* part. of שחח, probably denoting "those who throw down."

[710] Notice the anticipatory pronoun and the subsequent qualification.

[711] Heb. דין indicates a legal decision or judgment.

[712] Or "declare just," even "I will justify."

[713] The *beth* serves as a *nota accusativi*.

[714] Lit. "be well disposed with." The author claims to appreciate his suffering because it has "fruits."

[715] Note that the author feels he is not now experiencing God's loving-kindness as he had earlier. See the reconstruction in 17.5.

[716] See the note to the verb form and meaning in line 7.

[717] See 17.5. There is a small *vacat*.

[718] Or "distresses."

[719] The author is ambiguous. He may refer to his own transgression. He may also refer to the "first transgression" by Adam; thus, he lives in the eschatological hope that the "Eden of glory" (16.21) is now being planted through him, its Irrigator. The Irrigator is the Righteous Teacher.

14 ואדעה כֿיֿ יש מקוה ב[ח]סדיכה ותוחלה ברוב כוחכה כי לא יצדק

15 כול במֿשֿ[פ]טכה ולא יזֿ[כה ב]רֿבכה אנוש מאנוש יצדק וגֿבר מֿרֿעֿהֿוֿ

16 ישכיל ובשר מיצר מֿ[עשה] יכבד ורוחֿ מרוח תגבר וכשגֿבֿוֿרֿתֿכֿה אין

17 בכוח ולכבודכה אינֿ[ן] מחיר[281] וֿ[ל]חכמתכה אין מדה וֿלֿאמֿתֿ[כה אין] חֿשֿהֿ

18 ולכול הנעזב ממנה [אין מקוה][282] ואני בכה הצֿ[בתי מעמדי][283] וחסדכ[ה]

19 עמדי[284] ולא הפֿ[לתה גורלי ב]אֿנֿשֿיֿ ריֿבֿ[ין]

20 וכזוממ לי ת[ ] [ ] ואם לבושת פנים כו[ל] [ ]וֿבֿו

21 לי ואתה בֿ[ר]חמיכה י]תגבר צרי עלי למכשול לֿמֿ[ ]

22 אנשי מלחמ[תי בו]שת פנים וכלמה לנרגני בי

23 כי אתה אלי מועֿ[דים תריב ריבי כי ברז חכמתכה הוכחתה בי

24 ותחבא אֿמת לק[ץ חרונך עד]מועדו ותהי תוכחתכה לי לשמחה ושֿשֿון

25 ונגיעי למרפא עֿ[ולם לכול קצי]נצח ובוז צרי לי לכליל כבוד וכשלוני לגבורת

[281] See 18.12: ואין עמכה בכוח ואין לנגד כבודכה ולגבורתכה אין מחיר.
[282] Cf. 22.18.
[283] See 11.22; 19.16; 26.36 and 4Q427 frg. 7 2.17.
[284] See 10.27.

14 And I know that there is hope[720] in your [lov]ing-kindnesses[721] and expectation in the abundance of your power, because no one is justified

15 in your judg[me]nts; and (no one) w[ins] your lawsuit. A human can be more just than another, and a man[722] can be

16 more insightful than his companion, and flesh more honored than a cr[eature's] inclination,[723] and (one) spirit mightier than (another) spirit; but there is no power like

17 your might. And for your glory there is no [price.[724] And] for your wisdom there is no measure. And for [your] truth [there is no] concealment.[725]

18 And to everyone who is left in need of it [there is no hope].[726] And I, [I] plac[ed my rank] with you. [And] yo[ur loving-kindness]

19 (is) with me. And [you] did not c[ast my lot with] the men of strife […]

20 and as they devised against me *t*°[…]° and if for the shame of the face (is) al[l …]°*wbw*

21 to me; and you in [your] me[rcies…] my adversary [m]ay be mightier[727] over me for stumbling[728] *lm*°[…]

22 men of [my] wa[r … sha]me of the face, and a reproach to those who grumble against me.[729]

23 For you, O my God, for seaso[ns[730]…], you will strive for my strife, for through the mystery of your wisdom you chastised me,

24 and you concealed the truth for the Endt[ime of your wrath[731] until] its season.[732] And may your chastisement become joy and gladness to me,

25 and my afflictions became an e[ternal] healing [to all the endtimes of] perpetuity.[733] And (being) an (object of) scorn for my adversaries (becomes) to me a crown of glory, and my stumbling (becomes) an eternal

---

[720] The Heb. *miqweh*, "hope," resonates with the homonym, *miqweh*, "reservoir," and the water imagery at the beginning of Hymn 22. See 14.9 and 22.11, 18, 37.

[721] The author hopes for what he remembers enjoying, the full presence of God's loving-kindnesses.

[722] Heb. גבר.

[723] Heb. יצר.

[724] See 18.12 for a similar thought.

[725] The consonants are difficult to see on the leather; perhaps a *qal* part. of חשה, "to be silent," or "to conceal."

[726] Cf. 22.18.

[727] Not "[ma]y prevail over me." The reigning high priest may be mightier than the Righteous Teacher, but he will not prevail in the Endtime.

[728] The adversary causes the poet to stumble.

[729] A *vacat* at the end of the line provides for the transition.

[730] Or "appointed times," "festivals."

[731] See 7.32, 11.21, 22.9, and 24.15.

[732] Or "appointed time," "festival."

[733] Cf. 9.26.

26 עולם כי בשכֿלֿ[כה הודעתני] ובכבודכה הופיע אורי כי מאור מחושך

27 האירותה ליגון [ומרפא למח]ץ מכתי ולמכשולי גבורת פלא ורחֿוֹב

28 עולם בצרת נפשֿיֿ[כיא אתה אלי]מֿנוסי משגבי סלעֿ עוזי ומצודתי בכה

29 אחסיה מכול מכֿ[אוב כי אתה]לי לפלט עד עולם   כי אתה מאבי

30 ידעתני ומרחם[אמי ומשדי]285 אֹמי גמלתה עלי ומשדי הריתי רחמיך

31 עֿלי ובחיק אומנתיֿ[אשתעשע]הֿ286 ומנעורי הופעתה לי בשכל משֿפטכֿה

32 ובאמת נכון סמכתני וֹבֿרוח קוֹדשכה תשעשעניֿ ועד היוֹם הופֿעֿתֿה לי

33 ותוכחת צדקכה עם נֿ[עֿ]וֿיתי ומשמר שלומכה לפלט נפשי ועֿם מצעדי

34 רוב סליחות והמון רֿחֿמֿים בהשפטכה בי ועד שיבה אֿתה תכלכלני כיא

35 אבי לֹא ידעני ואמי עֿלֿיכה עזבתני כי אתה אב לכֿוֹֹל בֿנֿי אמתכה ותגל

---

285 Not בטן; see note to the English.
286 See 15.24; 17.8, 13, 32; and esp. 18.18.

26 strength, because through [your] insight [you have allowed me to know],[734] and through your glory my light has appeared.[735] For light from darkness

27 you allowed to shine[736] toward agony. [And a healing (is) for the blo]w of my wound. And my stumbling (gave) wonderful might, and an eternal

28 expansion for the trouble of my soul.[737] [For you, O my God], (are) my escape,[738] my security, the rock of my strength,[739] and my fortress. In you

29 I find refuge from all su[ffering.[740] For you (are)] for me a deliverance[741] unto eternity. For you, from (the time of) my father

30 you have known me, and from the womb [of my mother. And from the breasts of][742] my mother you weaned me.[743] And from the breasts of her that was pregnant with me, your mercies

31 (were) over me. And in the bosom of[744] my nursing-mother [I deligh]t,[745] and from my youth you appeared to me with your insightful judgment.

32 And in established truth you supported me. And in the spirit of your holiness you delighted me, and unto today you appeared to me.

33 And your righteous chastisement (is) with[746] my pe[rv]ersity, and the guard of your peace (provides) a deliverance (for) my soul,[747] and with my treads (is)

34 an abundance of forgivenesses and a multitude of mercies when you enter into your judgment with me. And unto old age you, you will sustain me. For

35 my father did not know me, and my mother committed me to you,[748] because you are Father to all the sons of your truth and you rejoice

---

[734] *Hipʿil* permissive.

[735] Or "shined."

[736] *Hipʿil* permissive.

[737] Heb. נפש.

[738] Or "refuge."

[739] The noun also denotes "shelter."

[740] Lit. "pain."

[741] Or "savior."

[742] The suggested restoration בטן, "belly," is a noun that does not appear in 1QHᵃ and is thus not likely. The following verb, "wean," suggests the restoration "breasts." The noun appears soon after the restoration; the author is fond of repetitive concepts.

[743] See the similar use of symbolic language in 15.39–40. The author, the Righteous Teacher, develops the imagery in Jer 1:5–6 to express his prophetic self-understanding.

[744] The noun denotes the upper part of the male or female human body. It signifies where loved ones, especially infants or little children, are held.

[745] See 15.24; 17.8, 13, 32; and esp. 18.18.

[746] I.e., "accompanies."

[747] Heb. נפש.

[748] The passage does not mean the mother of the author abandoned him (as in some translations). The statement seems to imply that the author's mother left him in God's house, the Temple, to be a priest. See Ps 10:14 in which the same expression is found (עליך יעזב); it means "commits to you, (the Lord)." Our text echoes the famous story in 1Sam 1:23–28 in which Hannah, Samuel's mother, after "weaning" him, "commits" or places him on permanent loan in "the house of the LORD" (1Sam 1:24). Note also that the Hebrew verb for "weaning" appears in our text [see 17.3] and more than once in the biblical text.

36   (VACAT) עליהם כמרחמת על עולה וכאומן בחיק תכלכל לכול מעשׂיׄכה

37   (VACAT)

Hymn 23
Blessed is the Lord for Making Me Mighty

38   בׄ[רו]ךׄ אׄ[תה אדוני כיא] לׄ[ ] ˚˚[ ]   ]רׄ הגברתה עד אין מספׄרׄ

39   ולהלׄ[לׄ שמכה בהפלא מאׄד[ה]

40   לא]ין השבת לׄ[

41   לפי]שׄכלו יהללׄ[שמכה

Col. 18 [= Sukenik Col. 10 + Frg. 30]
Parallels: 4Q428 Frg. 11

1   [

2   [

3   [ ]˚ [ב]מׄחׄשׄבׄתכה נהׄיׄה כׄ[ול ו]בׄמׄזמת לבכה תוׄ[כ]ןׄ ומבלעדיכה לא

4   [יעשה כ]וׄלׄ[287] ובלוא רצונכה[288] לא יהיה ולא[289] יתבונן כול בחוכ[מתכה]

5   [ובסו]דׄ רׄזיכה[290] לא יביט כול ומה אפהו אדם ואדמה הוא [מעפר]

6   קורץ ולעפר תשובתו כי תשכילנו בנפלאות כאלה ובסוד אמׄ[תכה]

---

[287] See 9.22: כול ומבלעדיך לא יעשה.
[288] See 18.24.
[289] See 4Q428 frg. 11 line 1: רצונכ]ה לוא.
[290] See 4Q428 frg. 11 line 2: ובסו]ד רזי]כה.

36   over them like a compassionate one over her infant and like a nursing-father (over an infant) on (his) bosom you will sustain all[749] your creatures.[750] (VACAT)

37   (VACAT)

Hymn 23
Blessed is the Lord for Making Me Mighty

38   B[less]ed (are) y[ou, O Lord, for] *l*[…] °°°[…]*r* you made mighty without number

39   [… and to prai]se your name in doing wonders exceeding[ly]

40   [… with]out ceasing *l*[…]

41   [… according to] his insight he shall praise [your name …]

Col. 18 [= *Sukenik Col. 10 + Frg. 30*]
Parallels: 4Q428 Frg. 11

1   […]

2   […]

3   […]° [by] your thought (all) will occur, [and] by the design of your heart (all) is established. And without you no[th]ing

4   [will be done].[751] And without your will[752] nothing occurs, and all cannot have comprehension in [your] wisd[om.]

5   [And in the assem]bly of your mysteries[753] all cannot look.[754] And what then (is) Adam?[755] He is (only) dirt.[756] [From dust]

6   he is extracted,[757] and to dust he returns; however,[758] you allow him to have insight[759] into wonders like these. And in the assembly of [your] tru[th,][760]

---

[749] The *lamedh* is a *nota accusativi*.
[750] Not "works."
[751] See 9.22.
[752] See 18.24.
[753] See 18.6. Or "[And in the secr]et of your mysteries."
[754] Imperfect of נבט which means "to look with pleasure."
[755] Or "humankind."
[756] Or "earth."
[757] Heb. קרץ denotes "to nip off" or "to break off." The idea seems influenced by Job 33:6. See 19.27.
[758] Heb. כי; this conjunction can mean "but" and "however." See esp. Gen 18:15.
[759] *Hipʿil* permissive.
[760] See 18.5. Or "And in the secret of [your] tru[th]."

7   תודיענו ואני עפר ואפר מה אזום בלוא חפצתה ומה אתחשב

8   באין רצונכה מה אתחזק בלא העמדתני ואיכה אַבַּשׂיל²⁹¹ בלא יצרתה

9   לי ומה אדבר בלא פתחתה פי ואיכה אשיב בלוא השכלתני

10   הנה אתה שר אלים ומלך נכבדים ואדון לכול רוח ומושל בכל מעשה

11   ומבלעדיכה לא יעשה כול ולא יודע בלוא רצונכה ואין זולתך

12   ואין עמכה בכוח ואין לנגד כבודכה ולגבורתכה אין מחיר ומי

13   בכול מעשי פלאכה הגדולים יעצור כוח להתיצב לפני כבודכה

14   ומה אפהוא שב לעפרו כי יעצור כֹ[ו]חֿ רק לכבודכה עשיתה כול אלה

15   (VACAT)

Hymn 24
Blessed is the Lord for His Loving-Kindness

16   ברוך אתה אדוני אל הרחמיֹם [ורב ה]חֿסד כי הודעת₪₪ני אלה לסֹ₪₪פֹֿֿר

---

²⁹¹ Note the two scribal lines that indicate an error. Metathesis for אשכיל.

7   you allow him to know.[761] But I am dust and ashes. What can I ponder without your desiring (it)? And what can I think about[762]

8   apart from your will? How can I be strengthened without your allowing me to stand?[763] And how can I gain insight[764] without your having fashioned (it)

9   for me? And how can I speak without your having opened my mouth? And (how) can I answer without your having given me insight?[765]

10   Behold, you are the Prince of the Elim[766] and the King of the Glorious Ones, and Lord[767] to every spirit and ruler over every creature.

11   And apart from you nothing is done; and there is no knowledge without your will. And there is none but you.[768]

12   And there is no one beside you[769] in power; and there is no one corresponding[770] to your glory. And for your might there is no price. And who

13   among all your great wonderful creatures[771] can summon up the power to present (themselves) before your glory?

14   And what then is he who returns to his dust that he can summon up po[w]er? Only for your glory you have done all these things.

15   (VACAT)

Hymn 24
Blessed is the Lord for His Loving-Kindness

16   Blessed are you, O Lord, God of mercies [and the multitude of] loving-kindness, because you allowed me to know[772] these (things) so as to re[count]

---

[761] *Hipʿil* permissive.

[762] *Hitpaʿlel.*

[763] *Hipʿil* permissive.

[764] Reading אשכיל (*hipʿil* impf.), "to allow to have insight;" see 18.6 and 18.9. One scribe wrote אכשיל ("cause to stumble") and another correcting scribe provided our reading. The letters had been inadvertently transposed.

[765] *Hipʿil.*

[766] Or, "divine beings."

[767] Heb. אדון.

[768] The author moves back and forth between henotheism (belief in One God among many gods) and monotheism (belief in One God and the denial of other gods).

[769] Lit. "with you." The author is imagining the celestial court.

[770] The preposition נגד means "corresponding" in Mishnaic Hebrew. In Biblical Hebrew, it means "before." See the odd expression in Gen 2:18 and 2:20 (עזר כנגדו) which is often mistranslated. The evidence of Mishnaic Hebrew within the Qumran Scrolls is well-known.

[771] Or "great wonderful works."

[772] *Hipʿil* permissive.

17 נפלאותכה ולא להס יומם ול[י]לה ול[ן]ילה]ולך כֹּל הֹחיל[̊] [וברוב]292 [ ]° [°°°

18 לחסדכה בגדול טובכה ורֹו[ב רחמיכה293 ואני [אשתעשעה בסֹ[[ליחותיכה]

19 כי נשענתי באמתכה] [° °°° °

20 מצבֹֹתֹכה ובלא °°° ובלוא [גערתכה אין מכשֹֹול] ואין]

21 נגע בלוא ידעתה וֹלֹ[א יעשה כול בלא294 רצו]נֹֹכה

22 ואני לפי דעתי באמֹתֹ[כה אזמרה בחסדיכה295 הגדולים]ובהביטי בכבודכה אספרה

23 נפלאותיכה ובהביני בס[וד פלאכה296 אוחיל297 לה]מון רחמיכה ולסליחותיכה

24 אקוה כי אתה יצרתה רֹו[ח עבדכה298 וברצו]נֹכה הכינותני   ולא נתתה

25 משעני על בצע ובהֹוֹ[ן לוא אמיר299 אמתכה בל[בי ויצר בשר לא שמתה לי מעוז

26 חיל גבורים על רוב עדנֹֹי[ם ישתעשעו וב]רוב דגן תירוש ויצהר

27 ויתרוממו בֹמקנה וקנין] ויתחשבו300 כעץ ר]ענן על פלגי מים לשת עלֹה

292 Read: וברוב.
293 See 5.34, 15.21, 18.18, 23.15; cf. 12.33.
294 See 18.3–4.
295 See 19.8: ואזמרה בחסדיכה.
296 See 12.29, 20.15.
297 See 15.21 and 22.36.
298 See 5.35, 8.32; cf. 8.31.
299 See 6.31. *Hipʿil* impf. of מור, "exchange."
300 For the verbal root see 18.7.

17 your wonders, and not to keep silent day and n[ight ....] And to you (is) all the army[773] and in a multi-tude of [...]°°[...]

18 to your loving-kindness in your great goodness and the multit[ude of your mercies.[774] And I], I shall de-light in [your] for[givenesses],

19 because I leaned on your truth [...]°°° °°[...]

20 from your outpost[775] and without °°[... and without] your rebuke. There is no stumbling [and there is no]

21 affliction without your knowing (it), and n[ot anything will be done without][776] your [wil]l.[777]

22 And I, according to my knowledge in [your] truth, [I will chant about your great loving-kindness.][778] And when I look into your glory, I will recount

23 your wonders. And when I have insight into the se[cret of your wonder,[779] I will await[780] the ab]undance of your mercies. And for your forgivenesses

24 I hope. For you, you fashioned the spir[it of your servant;[781] and by] your [wil]l you established me.[782] And you have not given

25 me support through unjust gain, and for wealth [I will not exchange your truth in][783] my [hea]rt. And the creature of[784] flesh you have not set up for me (as) shelter.[785]

26 The army of mighty men [(are) those who delight] in a multitude of luxuries [and with] a multitude of grain, new wine, and oil.[786]

27 And they exalt themselves with possessions and acquisitions. [And they imagine themselves[787] (to be) like] a [ve]rdant[788] [tree] on streams of water producing leaves[789]

---

[773] The same noun for "army" appears in 18.17 and 18.26. Both times the reference is to God's army (not the Hasmonean army).

[774] See 5.35; 15.21; 18.18; 23.15; cf. 12.33.

[775] Or "guard." מַצָּבָה ("watch") not מַצֵּבָה ("stone pillar"). The noun מצבה (a military "garrison" or "outpost") appears in BH only in 1Sam 14:12. See line 17. Ctr. DJD: "your *mṣb*, ..."

[776] See 18.3–4.

[777] A *vacat* appears here; it allows for the transition.

[778] See 19.8.

[779] See 12.29, 20.15.

[780] See 15.21 and 22.36.

[781] See 5.35, 8.32; cf. 8.31.

[782] Note that there is a small *vacat* in the text.

[783] In the *Hodayot* "wealth" appears with "truth;" see 6.31 and 7.36. See lines 19, 22, 29, 31, and 32 for "your truth."

[784] Heb. יצר.

[785] The author has repeatedly intimated that the harms to his flesh have harmed the shelter for his soul. The author here affirms that flesh is not a permanent shelter. See 18.34; "shelter is from above."

[786] The author polemically refers to the Hasmoneans, like John Hyrcanus, who gained wealth and led mercenary armies.

[787] The verb appears in 18.7.

[788] Or "f]resh." See 16.25–26. The alleged luxuriant tree is a rotten tree.

[789] The noun is singular in Hebrew.

28 ולהרבות ענף כי בחֹרתֹהֹ[בם מכול[301] בני]אדם ולהֹדשן כול מארץ

29 ולבני אמתכה נתתה שמֹ[חת עולם[302] ופא]רֹת עד ולפי דעתם יכבדו

30 איש מרעהו וכן לבן אדֹם [כי ברצונכה בא]יֹש הרביתה נחֹלֹתֹוֹ

31 בדעת אמתכה ולפי[303] דעתו יובֹאֹ[304] בֹ[בריתכה[305] נפֹש עבדכה תעבה הֹוֹןֹ

32 ובצע וברום עדנים לא יֹחֹפֹוֹץ שש לבי בבריתכה ואמתכה

33 תשעשע נפשי ואפרחה כֹשֹוֹשֹנֹהֹ ולבי נפתח למקור עולם

34 ומשענתי במעוז מרום וי[ח]זֹק נֹפֹשֹיֹ [ו]תֹבין עמל ויבול כנץ לפני רוֹחֹ

35 ויתהולל לבי בחלחלה ומותני ברעדה ונהמתי עד תהום תבוא

36 ובחדרי שאול תחפש יחד ואפחדה בשומעי משפטיכה עם גבורי

ה
37 כוח וריבכה עם צבא קדושיכ בֹמֹשפֹטֹ[צדקכה יע]שֹה

38 ומשפט בֹ[כ]ול מֹעֹשיכֹה וצדק יֹ[   ]לֹ

---

[301] See 7.36.

[302] See 23.16; 26.30; cf. 4Q427 frg. 7 1.17: מצֹעדם ושמחת עוֹלם במכוניֹהֹמה כבוד 2.11: and ,[בכ]ול קצים הֹשֹמֹיֹע הגידנה הביעו בשמחות עולמים ואין נצח ואין השבת] לעולמי עד].

[303] Drops of ink are visible in this line and the following ones.

[304] Hopʿil of בוא, "be brought."

[305] See 21.10, 14 and line 32.

28 and multiplying branches. For you examined[790] [them from all[791] the sons of] Adam,[792] and made (them) thoroughly gluttonous[793] from the land.

29 But to the sons of your truth you have given jo[y eternal[794] and] everlasting [leafy b]ranches,[795] and according to their knowledge, they honor

30 one more than the other.[796] And thus to the son of[797] Adam[798] [according to your will for a m]an[799] you enlarged his inheritance

31 through the knowledge of your truth, and according to his knowledge he will be brought into [your covenant].[800] The soul of[801] your servant detests wealth

32 and unjust gain. And the pompous[802] luxuries he does not desire. My heart rejoices in your covenant and your truth

33 delights my soul.[803] And I blossomed like a lily, and my heart was opened to the eternal source,

34 and my support (lay) in shelter from on high. And he str[eng]thened my soul[804] [so] it can understand misfortune.[805] But it crumbles[806] like a bud before the wind.

35 And my heart is mocked by anguish and my loins by trembling. And my moaning goes unto the depth,

36 and seeks oneness[807] in the rooms of Sheol. And I am afraid when I hear your judgments with the powerful

37 heroes;[808] and your lawsuit[809] with the host of your Holy Ones in [your righteous] judgment [will b]e done.[810]

38 And judgment over [a]ll your works and righteousness *y*[…]*l*

---

[790] Heb. בחר. Lit. "choose."

[791] See 7.36.

[792] Or "humankind."

[793] *Hipʿil* infinitive of דשׁן; see the note to 8.32.

[794] See 23.16; 26.30; cf. 4Q427 frg. 7 1.17 and 2.11.

[795] Lit. "everlasting [gl]ory." See 16.21 and 23. In all cases the noun derives from a verb that denotes glory. The "sons of truth" refer to the members of the Community who are "the trees of life." See col. 16.

[796] Lit. "a man from his companion."

[797] Note the singular.

[798] Or "humankind."

[799] See 8.22.

[800] See the next line and 21.10, 14.

[801] Heb. נפשׁ.

[802] Or "haughtiness."

[803] Heb. נפשׁ.

[804] Heb. נפשׁ.

[805] Or "trouble."

[806] Or "to wither." The bud (or petal) separates from the flower. See Isa 34:4.

[807] Heb. יחד.

[808] Or "mighty ones."

[809] See 17.15.

[810] See the grammar in 9.22.

] **39**

תֹֿ[**40**

עֹֿוֹני[**41**

Col. 19 [= Sukenik Col. 11 + Frg. 60 Col. 1]
Parallels: 4Q427 1 Frg. 1; 4Q428 Frg. 12

] **1**

] **2**

] **3**

בפחד מֿדֿהוֹבֿ[‏]עֹֿמל מעיני ויגו[ן ‏]מֿגֿוֹיֿתֿי °°°°°°°°°[**4**

בהגו לבי] [(VACAT) **5**

Hymn 25
I Thank God for Dealing Wonderfully with Dust

מודה
אֹודכה אלי כי הפלתה עֹם עפר וביצר חמר הגברתה מודה ואני מה כיֿאֿ **6**

[הבי]נֿוֹתני בסוד אמתכה ותשכילֿני במעשי פלאכה ותתן בפי הודות ובלשוני **7**

תֿהֿלֿה ומזל שפתי במכון רנה ואזמרה בחסדיכה ובגבורתכה אשוחחה כול **8**

היום תמיד אברכה שמכה ואספרה כבודכה בתוך בני אדם וברוב טובכה **9**

39   […]

40   […]*ty*

41   […]*'wny*

Col. 19 [= Sukenik Col. 11 + Frg. 60 Col. 1]
Parallels: 4Q427 1 Frg. 1; 4Q428 Frg. 12

1   […]

2   […]

3   […]

4   in fear, disaster […] trouble from my eyes and grie[f …] from my body[811] °°°°°°° […]

5   through the meditation of my heart […]. (VACAT)

Hymn 25
I Thank God for Dealing Wonderfully with Dust

6   I thank you, O my God, because you dealt wonderfully with dust; and a creature of[812] clay you strength-ened.[813] Thanks, thanks.[814] And what am I that

7   you [allowed] me [to dis]cern[815] the secret of your truth? And you allowed me to have insight[816] into your wonderful works, and you put in my mouth thanksgivings[817] and on my tongue

8   praise. And the flow[818] of my lips (is) in the establishment of[819] exultation. And I will chant about your loving-kindnesses. And about your might, I will contemplate all

9   the day. I will always bless your name; and I will recount your glory among the sons of Adam.[820] And in your multitudinous goodness

---

[811] Or "corpse."
[812] Heb. יצר. Most likely, again, the *beth* is a *nota accusativi*.
[813] Lit. "made mighty."
[814] The second "thanks" is penned above the line.
[815] *Hip'il* permissive.
[816] *Hip'il* permissive.
[817] The expression helped to name this scroll: *The Thanksgiving Hymns*; but the main reason was the pervasive *incipit*: "I thank you, O Lord, because." It has been labeled "the Hodayot formula."
[818] Perhaps a *pi'el* part. of נזל. The *pi'el* of this verb is not in BH.
[819] Or "place," "foundation."
[820] Or "humankind."

10 תשתעשע נפשי ואני ידעתי כי אמת פיכה ובידכה צדקה ובמחשבתכה

11 כול דעה ובכוחכה כול גבורה וכול כבוד אתכה הוא באפכה כול משפטי נגע

12 ובטובכה רוב סליחות ורחמיכה לכול בני רצונכה כי הודעתם בסוד אמתכה

13 וברזי פלאכה השכלתם ולמען כבודכה טהרתה אנוש מפשע להתקדש

14 לכה מכול תועבות נדה ואשמת מעל להיחד עֹם בני אמתך ובגורל עֹם

15 קדושיכה להרים מעפֿר תולעת מתים לסוד עֹ[ולם] ומרוח נעוה לבינתֹכֿה

16 ולהתיצב במעמד לפניכה עם צבא עד ורוחו[ת דעת]³⁰⁶ להתחדש עם כול

17 נהיה ועם ידעים ביחד רנה

Hymn 26
I Thank My God for Allowing Me to Know Secret Truth

18 [ואנ]ֹי אודכה אלי ארוממכה צורי ובהפלֹא[א] סליחותיכה³⁰⁷

19 [כי הודעתני סוד אמת וֹבֹרֹזֹ]י פלאכה השכלתני]³⁰⁸

20 [ונס]תֹרֹותֹכֿה גליתה לי ואביֿט³⁰⁹ בֿ[כבודכה וברוב מע]שֹי³¹⁰ חסד ואדעה

---

³⁰⁶ See 11.23–24; cf. 6.36.
³⁰⁷ See 26.34.
³⁰⁸ See 15.29; 18.9.
³⁰⁹ 4Q427 frg. 1 line 9: גלי[תה ל]ֹי וֹ[אביֿט].
³¹⁰ See 8.30, 18.22, 20.17. About 16 spaces or consonants are lost.

10   my soul[821] is delighted. And I, I know that truth (is in) your mouth; and righteousness (is) in your hand. And in your thought (is)

11   all knowledge. And in your power (is) all might. And all glory is with you. In your anger (are) all the judgments of affliction;

12   and in your goodness (is) a multitude of forgivenesses. And your mercies (are) with all the sons of your will, because you allowed them to know[822] the secret of your truth;

13   and into your wondrous mysteries you allowed them to have insight.[823] And for the sake of your glory, you purified the human from transgression that (he may) sanctify himself

14   for you from all the abominations of impurity and the guilt of infidelity, to be united[824] with the sons of your truth. And in the lot together with

15   your Holy Ones to be raised from the dust (as) a worm of the dead ones to the e[ternal] council, and from a perverted spirit to your discernment.

16   And to be present in rank before you with an everlasting host and the spirits [of knowledge],[825] to be renewed together with all

17   that exists, and with those who have the knowledge (to be) in the common[826] exultation. (VACAT)

Hymn 26
I Thank My God for Allowing Me to Know Secret Truth

18   [And I,] I thank you, O my God. I exalt you, O my rock. And in [your] wondrous [forgivenesses[827] …]

19   […] that you allowed me to know[828] the secret of truth and in [your wondrous] mysteri[es[829] you allowed me to have insight.][830]

20   [And] your [hidd]en things[831] you revealed to me. And I look at [your glory and at the multitude of the wor]ks of loving-kindness, and I know

---

[821] Heb. נפש.
[822] *Hip'il* permissive.
[823] *Hip'il* permissive.
[824] The verb alludes to יחד. See line 17 for the noun. It gives the name to the Qumran Community.
[825] See 11.23–24; cf. 6.36.
[826] Heb. יחד.
[827] See 26.34.
[828] *Hip'il* permissive.
[829] See 5.19, 15.30, 19.13.
[830] *Hip'il* permissive. See 15.29, 18.9.
[831] See 26.15.

21 [כי] לכה הצדק ובחסדיכה יש[ועת אשמ]ה[311] וכלה בלוא רחמיך

22 וֹאֹני[312] נפתח לי מקור לאבל מרורים [וכאוב אנוש[313] לא נסתר עמל מעיני

23 בדעתי יצרי גבר ותשובת אנוש אתבוננה ואכירה אֹבֹל חטאה ויגון[314]

24 אשמה ויבואו בלבבי ויגעו בעצמי לֹאֹ[ין עצור עד ק]צֹים ולהגות הגי

ואנחה בכנור קינה לכול אבל יֹגֹ[ון][315]

25 יגון ומספד מרורים עד כלות עולה וא[ין מכאוב] ואין נגע להחלות ואז

26 אזמרה בכנור ישועות ונבל[316] שמחֹ[ות ותוף גי]לה וחליל תהלה לאין

27 השבת ומי בכול מעשיכה יוכל לספֹר [נפלאותי]כה בפֹי כולם יהולל

28 שמכה[317] לעולמי עד יברכוכה כפי שכלֹ[ם עד] קֹצים[318] ישמיעו יחד

29 בקול רנה ואין יגון ואנחה ועולה לֹאֹ[319] תמצא עֹ[וד] ואמתכה תופיע

30 לכבוד עד ושלום עולום[320]

---

[311] Perhaps restore קנאה; see 20.17. A drop of ink appears next on the leather.
[312] 4Q427 frg. 1 line 10: [.וֹכלה בלוא רֹחמיכה ואנֹי].
[313] See 16.29; cf. 13.30.
[314] 4Q427 frg. 1 line 11: [ג]בֹרֹ ות[שובת]אֹנוש אתבוננה ואכירה אֹ[.
[315] 4Q427 frg. 1 line 12: ולהגו]תֹ הגי יֹגֹון ו[אנחה בכנור קֹ]ינה [לכול אבן]ל.
[316] 4Q427 frg. 1 line 13: [. ישועות ונבלֹ].
[317] 4Q427 frg. 1 line 14: בפֹ]יֹ כולֹמֹה [יהו]לֹל שֹמֹכֹ]ה.
[318] 4Q428 frg. 12a line 1: שמכֹ]ה לעולמי עד יברכוכה כפי שכלם עד [קֹצים.
[319] 4Q428 frg. 12a line 2: ישמיעו [יֹ]חֹדֹ[ב]קֹ[ו]לֹ רנה ואין [יגון ואנחה ועול]ה לוא.
[320] A mistake for עולם. 4Q427 frg. 1 line 15: [ולֹ]. 4Q428 frg. 12a line 2: לֹ רנה ואין [יגון ואנחה ועול]ה לוא ישמיעו [יֹ]חֹדֹ[ב]קֹ[ו]לֹ .4Q428 frg. 12a line 3: [תמצא עֹ]וד ואמת]כֹה תופיע לכבוד /עד\ ושלום עֹ]ולם.

492

21   [that] to you (is) righteousness and in your loving-kindnesses (is) salv[ation (from) guil]t,[832] and destruction (that is) without your mercies.

22   But (as) for me, there is opened to me a source of bitter mourning [and human pain].[833] Misfortune was not hidden from my eyes

23   in my knowing of the inclinations of[834] man.[835] And the return of the human, I will examine closely.[836] And I acknowledge mourning, sin, and the grief of

24   guilt. And they entered my heart and reached my bones un[ceasingly unto the en]dtimes;[837] so as[838] to ponder meditatively

25   grief, and a sigh with a lyre, a lament to every mourning of gri[ef],[839] and the wailing of bitterness[840] until the annihilation of injustice. And th[ere (is) no pain] and there is no affliction to cause illness. And then

26   I will chant with a lyre acts of salvation and (with) a harp joy[s, and (with) a tambourine[841] rejo]icing, and (with) a flute praise without

27   ceasing. And who among all your creatures[842] can recount your [wonders]? In the mouth of all of them your name

28   is praised forever and ever. They will bless you according to [their] insight [unto] the endtimes. Together[843] they make proclamation

29   with a voice of exultation,[844] and there is neither grief nor sigh. And injustice (is) not found any[more.] And your truth will appear

30   for everlasting glory and the eternal peace. (VACAT)[845]

---

[832] Perhaps restore "zeal." See 20.17.

[833] See 16.29; cf. 13.30.

[834] Heb. יצר.

[835] Heb. גבר.

[836] The *hithpoʿel* of בין.

[837] See 16.29 and 19.28.

[838] Lit. "and."

[839] The words between the two nouns "grief" were missed by Scribe A. The error is an example of *parablepsis* perhaps facilitated by *homoioteleuton*. They were supplied by Scribe B who placed them above the line. He probably knew the reading in 4Q427 frg. 1 line 4.

[840] In the Hebrew, the noun is in the plural ("bitternesses").

[841] See Jer 31:4. The Hebrew noun תוף means "tambourine," "hand-drum," or "timbrel." See the references in KB 1771. A conceivable restoration is מצלתים, "(two small) cymbals;" but there is not enough space for so many consonants. See Gen 31:27. See esp. Ps 81:1–3 which mentions "sing," "tambourine," "lyre," and "harp." Ps 150:3–5 notes "trumpet," flute," "harp," "tambourine," "dance," "strings," "pipe," and "cymbals."

[842] Lit. "works."

[843] יחד evokes the group's name.

[844] The expression appears in Pss 42:5, 47:2, 118:15; cf. Isa 48:20.

[845] The *vacat* is found in 4Q428 frg. 12a line 4.

Hymn 27
Blessed is the Lord for Insight

30 ברוך את[ה   א]דֹוני אשֹר נתתה לעֹבֹדֹכֹהֹ[321](321)

31 שכל דעה להבין בנפלאותיכה ומֹנֹהֹ[322](322) לֹשֹוֹן[323](323) ל]סֹפר ברוב חסדיכה

32 ברוך אתה אל הרחמים והנינה כגדו[ל] כֹחֹכה[324](324) ורוב אמתכה והמו[ן]

33 חסדיכה בכול מעשיכה שמח נפש עבדכה באמתכה וטהרני

34 בצדקתכה כאשר יחלתי לטובכה ולחסדיכה אקוה ולסליחות[י]כֹהֹ

35 פתחתה משרי וביגוני נחמתני כיא נשנתי[325](325) ברחמיכה ברוך את[ה]

36 אדוני כי אתה פעלתה אלֹה ותשם בפי עבדֹכֹהֹ הֹוֹדֹוֹת תֹ[הלה]

37 ותחנה ומענה לשון והכינותה לי פֹעול[תכה]

38 ואעצו[ר כוח ל[ֹל[ֹ[דעת]   [כבודכה ולספר נפלאותיכה[326](326)

39 ואתה] אל[327](327)

40 אמ[תכה

41 וֹא[ֹתה

42 וֹבעֹנֹהֹ[לשון

Col. 20 [= Sukenik Col. 12 + Frgs. 54 and 60 Col. 2]
Parallels: 4Q427 3 Frgs. 2–3; Frgs. 8–9; 4Q428 Frg. 12

1]

---

[321](321) 4Q428 frg. 12a line 4: ברוך אתה א[דֹוני אשר נתתֹה] לעבדכה.
[322](322) Ctr. DJD: ֹוֹ[מ]ֹנֹה.
[323](323) 4Q428 frg. 12a line 5: לֹשֹוֹן].
[324](324) See כוח in line 38.
[325](325) An error for נשענתי. Perhaps elision of an ע due to pronunciation.
[326](326) See 7.14; cf. 18.13.
[327](327) See 19.32: ברוך אתה אל.

Hymn 27
Blessed is the Lord for Insight

30 Blessed are yo[u, O L]ord, that you gave to your servant

31 insight (into) knowledge to discern your wonders, and the answer of the tong[ue to] recount the multitude of your loving-kindnesses.

32 Blessed are you, O God of mercies and compassion, for your grea[t] power and the multitude of your truth and the abundan[ce of]

33 your loving-kindnesses. In all your works, the soul of[846] your servant (is) joyful in your truth. And purify me[847]

34 in your righteousness, when I await your goodness and hope for your loving-kindnesses. And to your forgiveness[es]

35 you released my breakers. And in my grief you consoled me, because I leaned on your mercies. Blessed are yo[u,]

36 O Lord, for you, you acted (in) these (things), and you put in the mouth of your servant thanksgivings, p[raise,]

37 and supplication and the answer of the tongue.[848] And you established for me [your] activiti[es....]

38 And I will retai[n[849] power] to [have knowledge] in [your glory and to recount your wonders....][850]

39 And you, [God ...]

40 [your] tru[th ...]

41 and y[ou...]

42 and in the answer of [the tongue ...]°

Col. 20 [= Sukenik Col. 12 + Frgs. 54 and 60 Col. 2]
Parallels: 4Q427 3 Frgs. 2–3; Frgs. 8–9; 4Q428 Frg. 12

1 [...]

---

[846] Heb. נפש.
[847] A *pi'el* impv. of טהר ; or "O purify me."
[848] See 4.29; 8.24; 10.9; 15.14, 16; 19.37.
[849] Or "summon up."
[850] See 7.14; cf. 18.13.

2 [

3 [

4 ‏ה] [ח] ‏ה[[‏תרחב נפשי] ‏ ° [‏א ° [

‏שׁ]לום
5 ‏[בשמחה ו]שׁשון ואשב]ה לבטח במעון קו]דש‏328 ‏ב[שׁ]וֹקט‏329 ‏ושלוה

6 ‏[ב]שׁלום וברכה‏330 ‏ב[]]אהלי כֹּבֹוֹד וישועה ואהללה שמכה בתוך יראיכה‏331 (VACAT)

Hymn 28
For the Instructor: Concerning Night Prayers

‏ה פ
7 ‏למשכיל הׄוׄדות ותפלה‏332 ‏לתנל והתחנן תמיד מקץ לקץ עם מבוא אור

8 ‏לממשׁל]תו]‏333 ‏בתקופות יום לתכונו לחוקות מאור גדול בפנות ערב ומוצא

‏פ
9 ‏אור ברשית ממשלת חושך]‏334 ‏למועד לילה בתקופתו לנות בוקר ובקץ

‏א ע
10 ‏הׄאספו ל מונתו מפנית אור למוצא לילה‏335 ‏ומבוא יומם תמיד בכול

11 ‏מולדי עת יסודי קץ ותקופת מועדים‏336 ‏בתכונם באותותם לכול

12 ‏ממשלתם בתכון נאמנה מפי אל ותעודת הווה והיאה תהיה‏337

---

328 4Q427 frgs. 2–3 line 15: ‏ה] בֹּ] [‏ל] [‏ר] [. 4Q428 frg. 12b line 1: ‏לבטח במֹ]עון קודש.

329 Note a scribe has deleted a *waw* by putting a dot above and a dot below it.

330 4Q427 frgs. 2–3 line 16: ‏לבֹ]טֹח במעון שקֹ]ט ושלוה ב]שׁ]לום וברכֹה].

331 4Q427 frgs. 2–3 line 17: ‏בתוך יראֹ]יכה [. 4Q428 frg. 12b line 2: ‏כבד ויש]ועה ואֹ]ה]ללה שמכֹ]ה בתוך יר]איכה.

332 4Q427 frg. 8 2.10: ‏למשכיל הודותֹ] ותפלה. 4Q428 frg. 12b line 3: ‏למשכיל. Ctr. 4Q427 frgs. 2–3 line 18.

333 4Q427 frg. 8 2.11: ‏מבא אור לממשלֹ]תו.

334 4Q427 frg. 8 2.12: ‏אור ברשית ממשלות חֹ]ושך.

335 4Q427 frg. 8 2.13: ‏אל מעונתו מפני אור למֹ]וצא לילה.

336 4Q427 frg. 8 2.14: ‏ותקופות מועדים.

337 4Q427 frg. 8 2.15: ‏כי אל] ‏הווה והיֹאֹ]ה.

2   […]

3   […]

4   […]° ʾ[…]° my soul[851] broadens […]ḥ[…]ḥ

5   […] with joy and [happiness. And I si]t securely in the ho[ly] dwelling pea[cefully, and in] silence and tranquility,

6   [in] peace and blessing in the tents of glory and salvation.[852] So[853] I will praise your name among those who stand in awe of you.[854] (VACAT)[855]

Hymn 28
For the Instructor: Concerning Night Prayers

7   For the Instructor,[856] thanksgivings and prayer to prostrate oneself, and continually petition from the endtime (of the day) to the endtime (of the night[857] when) light comes out

8   to [its] dominion at the periods of the day according to its order, (and) according to the statutes of the great light.[858] When the evening turns and the light

9   goes out at the beginning of the dominion of darkness according to the appointed time of night and its period at the turn of the morning. And at the endtime (of the night)

10   when it is gathered to its domicile[859] from before the light when the night goes out and the day comes in.[860] (And) continually in all

11   the births of time and the bases of endtime,[861] and (during) the period of seasons[862] in their courses with their signs according to all

12   their dominion (which is) faithfully established from the mouth of God and the fixed times of existence. And this shall be,

---

[851] Heb. נפש.

[852] Conceivably, the author is a Qumranite who abides safely in the holy dwelling. The author imagines himself sharing the *spiritus* of the Righteous Teacher (as the author of the *Odes of Solomon* writes *ex ore Christi*).

[853] Lit. "and."

[854] Not "fear."

[855] A *vacat* is demanded by 4Q427 frgs. 2–3 line 17 and 4Q428 frg. 12b lines 2–3.

[856] משכיל is a well-known superscription in the Davidic Psalter. At Qumran, the noun signifies that *Yaḥad*'s Instructor.

[857] See 17.7–8. Or, "the end (of the day) to the end (of the night when)."

[858] The sun is "the great light." See Gen 1:6. The Qumranites celebrated time and festivals according to the "solar calendar." They opposed the use of the lunar calendar by the officiating priests in the Temple. Most likely, at Qumran a new calendrical day began at sunset (cf. CD MS A 10.14–16), as in rabbinic Judaism.

[859] מעון. See Deut 33:27.

[860] See esp. 1QS 10.1–3 and the *Morning and Evening Prayers* found in the Qumran caves.

[861] Or "Endtime."

[862] Or "appointed times," "festivals."

13 ואין אפס וזולתה לוא היה ולוא יהיה עוד כי אל ה(ו)ד(י)עות

14 הכינה[338] ואין אחר עמו   ואני משֹׁכיל[339] ידעתיכה אלי ברוח

15 אשר נתתה בי ונאמנה שמעתי לסוֹד פלאכה ברוח קדשכה[340]

16 [פ]תחתֿה לתוכי דעת ברז שכלכה ומעין גבורתֿ[כ]הֿ ב]תֿוך

17 [יראיכ]הֿ לרוב חסד[341] וקנאת כלה והשב[תה[342]

18 [ותאר]לֿ[י ב]הדר כבודכה לאור עוֹלֿ[ם[343]

19 מ]פֿחד רשעה ואין רמיה וֹ[ ]ולֿ[344]

20 [מֿוֿעדי שממה כיא אין ע]וד

21 [ו]אֿין עוד מדהבה כיא לפני אפכֿ[ה

22 [   ]°° [ ] יחפזו ואין צדיק עמכה [   ]ה

23 וֹ[לֿ]השכיל בכול רזיכה ולשיב דבֿרֿ] על צדקתכה[345] כי[אֿ

24 בֿתוכחתכה ולטובכה יצפו כי בחסֿדֿ]יכה חזקתֿה[346] כו[ן]לֿ

25 יודעיכה ובקץ כבודכה יגילו ולפי בֿ]וחכה ירננו כי]אֿ כשכלם

---

[338] 4Q427 frg. 8 2.16: הדעות הכֿ]ינה.
[339] 4Q427 frg. 8 2.17: ואני משֿׁ]כיל.
[340] The numerous mistakes are not due to pronunciation; the scribe may suffer from poor eyesight. 4Q427 frg. 8 2.18: ברוֿחֿ].
[341] 4Q427 frg. 8 2.19: לרוֹ]ב חסד.
[342] See 1QH[a] 21.14.
[343] 4Q427 frg. 8 2.20: עוֹ]לם.
[344] 4Q427 frg. 8 2.21: ול].
[345] See 20.33–34: להשיב דֿבֿר על תוכחתכה כיא צדקתה.
[346] See 7.34; cf. 20.38.

13 and (continue) without end.[863] And apart from it there has been nothing, and nothing else shall ever be. For the God of knowledge[864]

14 has established it, and there is not another except him.[865] And I, the Instructor,[866] I know you, my God, with the spirit

15 that you put in me, and loyally I have listened to your wondrous secret.[867] Through the spirit of your holiness,

16 you [op]ened in the midst of me knowledge by the mystery of your insight, and (by) the fountain of [yo]ur might [in] the midst of[868]

17 [those who stand in awe[869] of yo]u for the multitude of loving-kindness and the zeal for annihilation. And [yo]u led back[870] [....]

18 [And you enlightened] m[e in] the splendor of your glory for an etern[al] light [...]

19 [... from] the fear of wickedness, and there is no treachery and [...]wl[...]

20 [...] the seasons of[871] desolation because there is no m[ore ...]

21 [and] there is no more disaster because before yo[ur] anger [...]

22 °°[...] they will hurry, and no one (is) righteous except you[872] [...]h

23 and [to] allow to gain insight[873] into all your mysteries, and to answer a word [on behalf of your righteousness.[874] F]or

24 in your chastisement and in your goodness they will wait. For in [your] loving-kindness[es you have strengthened[875] al]l

25 who know you, so[876] in the Endtime of your glory they shall rejoice. And according to [your] p[ower they shall exult. F]or as according to their insight

---

[863] It is apparent throughout this section that the author is criticizing the lunar calendar observed by those whom he deemed the wicked, ignorant, and illegitimate priests.

[864] See 1QS 3.15 for "the God of knowledge." There are many echoes of 1QS 3.13–4.26 in the *Thanksgiving Hymns*. Most likely the "treatise on two spirits" was part of the instruction that those who entered the Community had to memorize.

[865] Lit. "with him," but there are many angels and archangels with God. The author is affirming monotheism, although in some lines he espouses henotheism. Notice the small *vacat.*

[866] This is a technical term at Qumran; see 1QS 3.13.

[867] Or "council."

[868] Note the paronomasia with "midst of."

[869] Not "fear."

[870] Or "bring back." *Hipʿil* pf.

[871] Or "appointed times," "festivals."

[872] Lit. "with you."

[873] *Hipʿil* permissive.

[874] See 20.33.

[875] See 7.34; cf. 20.38.

[876] Lit. "and."

26   הגשתם ולפי ממשלתם ישרתוכה למפלג[יהם לבלתי] שֹׁוֹב מֹמכה

27   וֹלוא לעבור על דברכה[347]

Hymn 29
Confessions of a Creature of Dust, Clay, and Ashes

27   ואני מעפר לקחֹ[תני ומחמר ק]וֹֹרֹצֹתֹיֹ

28   למקור נדה וערות קלון מקוי עפר ומגבל[מים ומסוד ערו]ֹה ומדור

29   חושך ותשובת עפר ליצר חמר בקץ אפ[כה מה יש]וֹב עֹֹפֹֹר

30   אל אשר לקח משם ומה ישיב עפר ואֹפֹֹר[אל האדמה ומ]ֹה יבין

31   [במ]ֹעֹשיו ומה יתיצב לפני מוכיח בו רֹ°°°[ ]   קֹֹוֹֹדֹֹש[ ]

32   [ורום] עולם ומקוי[348] כבוד ומקור דעת וגבורֹֹת [פל]ֹא וֹהמה לֹֹוא

ה
33   [יוכ]ֹלֹוֹ לספר כול כבודכה ולתיצֹב לפני אפכה[349] ואין להשיב דֹֹבֹֹר

34   על תֹוכחתכה כיא צדקתה ואין לנגֹֹדֹכה ומה אפהו שב אל עפרו

דברתי
35   ואני נאלמתי ומה אֹדבר על זות[350] כדעתי מצירורק יצר חמר ומה

36   אדבר כיא אם פתחתה פי ואיכה אבין כיא אם השכלתני ומה אֹד[בר]

---

[347] There is no *vacat*, yet it seems another hymn begins here.
[348] 4Q427 frg. 9 line 9: וֹי[עול]ֹם ומקֹ.
[349] 4Q427 frg. 9 line 10: ה]לֹפֹני אפכֹ[.
[350] See זאת in 12.30.

26 you brought them near, and according to their dominion they shall serve you in line with [their] division[s[877] without] turning from you

27 so as[878] not to transgress your word.

Hymn 29
Confessions of a Creature of Dust, Clay, and Ashes[879]

27 And I, from dust [you] took [me and from clay] I [was s]haped[880]

28 into a source of impurity and a nakedness of shame. A reservoir of dust and mixed [water and a foundation of nakedne]ss,[881] and a habitation of

29 darkness, and a return (to) dust for the creature of[882] clay at the Endtime of [your] anger. [How can] dust [ret]urn

30 to the place where it was taken from? And how can dust and ashes answer [the ground? And ho]w can he discern[883]

31 [in] his [w]orks? And how can he stand before the one who chastises him? r°°°[...] holiness.

32 [And (as for)] the eternal [height] and the reservoirs of glory, and the source of knowledge and of [wonder]ful might, and they are not

33 [abl]e to recount all your glory, and to be present before your anger. And it is impossible to return a word[884]

34 against your chastisement, for you are righteous and nothing (is) against you. And what is that which returns to its dust?

35 But I, I am dumb, and what can I say concerning this? According to my knowledge, I spoke from a mixture, a creature of[885] clay. And what

36 can I say unless you open my mouth? And how can I discern unless you allow me to have insight?[886] And what ca[n I say]

---

[877] Not "springs" as in 11.31 and 16.22.

[878] Lit. "and."

[879] Although there is no *vacat* in 1QH[a] and no liturgical formula, a new hymn seems to begin here. The previous lines celebrated God's obedient creation, are about night prayers, and concern the Instuctor. None of these appear in Hymn 29. 4Q427, the only parallel text, often has divergent readings. The next hymn begins in 22.34.

[880] Or "I [was ex]tracted." See 18.6 and note.

[881] Or "genit]als."

[882] Heb. יצר.

[883] Or "it discern." See 22.30.

[884] Lit. "and (it is) not (possible) to return a word." Note the paronomasia on "return" in lines 26–34.

[885] Heb. יצר. See 23.28, 36 and 21.11–12.

[886] *Hip'il* permissive.

37   בלוא גליתה לְבִי ואיכה אישר דרך כיא אם הכינוֹ[תה פ]עֹמֹ[י

38   תעמוד פעֹמֹי כיא אם ת[חֹזק בכוח ואיכה אתקומם]

39   וכול °°°]   [פֹעֹמֹי באֹ]ין

40   הֹ[

41   כֹֹ[

42   וֹֹ[

Col. 21 [= Sukenik Col. 18 + Frg. 3]
Parallels: 4Q427 Frgs. 10–12; 4Q428 Frg. 13

1   ]

2   פ[שֹׁע ילוד אֹ[שה]

3   ]ֹיכה וצדקתכה

4   ו[אֹ]יֹ[כֹ]ה אֹכֹיֹר[בל]ֹוא ראיתי זות

5   איכֹ]ה אביט בלוא גליתהֹ עיני ואשמעה

6   [בלוא גליתה[351] אוזני] השֹׁמֹ לֹבבי כיא לערל אוזן נפתח דבר ולב

7   [האבן[352] יהם[353] בנפ]לֹאֹוֹת ואדעה כיא לכה עשיתה אלה אלי ומה בשר

8   [להבין בכול אלה ל]הֹפֹליא ובמחשבתכה להגביר ולהכין כול לכבודכה

9   להבי]ֹן בֹצבא דעת לספר לשר גבורת וחוקי נכונות לילוד

---

[351] See 9.23 and 14.7.
[352] See lines 12–14; cf. Ezek 11:19 and 36:26.
[353] See 22.32.

37   if you do not reveal (it to) my heart? And how can I straighten the way unless [you] establish [my foo]tstep?

38   [My] footstep stands [only when you] make (it) strong with power. And how can I raise […]

39   and all °°°[…] my footstep with[out …]

40   *h*[…]

41   *k*°[…]

42   and °[…]

Col. 21 [= Sukenik Col. 18 + Frg. 3]
Parallels: 4Q427 Frgs. 10–12; 4Q428 Frg. 13

1   […]

2   [… trans]gression, one born of a wo[man]

3   […] your […] and your righteousness.

4   [… and] ho[w] can I recognize [unl]ess I see it?

5   […. How] can I look unless you uncover my eyes, and hear

6   [unless you uncover[887] my ears]? My heart was awestruck,[888] because to an inattentive[889] ear a message[890] was opened,[891] and the heart of

7   [stone[892] vibrated[893] with marv]els. And I know that for yourself, you did these (things), O my God. And how can flesh

8   [discern among all these things] wonderful acts, and in your plan[894] to prevail,[895] and to establish everything for your glory,

9   […to disce]rn the host of knowledge, to recount to the flesh mighty deeds and the established statutes to one born of

---

[887] See 9.23 and 14.7.
[888] From שמם, *hipʿil* ("to be dumbfounded"). See Jer 4:9.
[889] Lit. "uncircumcised."
[890] Or "a word."
[891] From פתח, *nipʿal*.
[892] See lines 12–14. For לב האבן see Ezek 11:19 and 36:26. The book of Ezekiel was exceptionally influential upon the Qumranites.
[893] From המם; lit. "bring into commotion." See 22.32.
[894] Or "in your thoughts."
[895] Lit. "to make mighty." *Hipʿil*.

10   [אשה ואת עבדכה ה]בֿיֿאותה בברית עמכה ותגלהֿ לב עפר להשמר

11   [מכול פשעיו[354   ] מפחי משפט לעומת רחמיכה[355 ואני יצר

12   [החמר ומגבל מים מקוי עפ]ר ולב האבן למי נחשבתי[356 עד זות כיא

13   [סוד פלאכה[357 נ]תתה באוזן עפר ונהיות עולם חקותה בלב[358

14   [האבן ונעוי לב   ]ׄ השבתה להביא בברית עמכה ולעמוד

15   לפניכה במ]שפטי עדים בֿמכון[359 עולם לאור אורתים עד נצח ועֿדֿ חושך

16   לאיֿ]ן[360 סוף וקצי שלום לאין חֿ]קר

17   [ואני יצר העפר °°°]

18   ולבר]ךֿ שֿׄמֿכֿה אפתח פֿ]יֿ[361

19   [יֿצֿר] עפר   [אל°° °[362

20   יצר [עפר] נפ]תֿחה נה]   ומלכ]דֿת נסתרה[363

21   [ה נפרשה רשת שוחֿהֿ] ובד]רֿכֿיֿה צמי אֿ]בדון[364

22   [°°°]ׄ וֿהֿיֿאֿ [ ]חֿה נפתחה דֿרֿךֿ לֿ]ׄ [ ] להתהלך[365

23   בֿנֿתֿיבות שלום ועם בשר להפליאֿ כאלה כיא[366

---

[354] See 4.23: מכול פשעיו בֿ]המון[רחמיךֿ.

[355] 4Q427 frg. 10 line 5: מש]פֿט לערמת ר]חמיכה.

[356] 4Q427 frg. 10 line 6: למי נחשב]תי.

[357] See 19.19 and esp. 20.15.

[358] 4Q427 frg. 10 line 7: עול]ם̊ חקותה בלב.

[359] 4Q427 frg. 10 line 8: במ]שפטי עדים במֿ]כון.

[360] 4Q427 frg. 10 line 9: ותחֿ ל֯ ל]אין.

[361] 4Q428 frg. 13 line 1:] א̊[.

[362] 4Q428 frg. 13 line 2: ד אל °[ ]°[ ]°[יֿצֿר].

[363] From 4Q428 frg. 13 line 3: עפר [ ] נפ]תֿחה נה[ ] ומלכ]דֿת נסתרה.

[364] 4Q428 frg. 13 line 4: ה נפרשה רשת שוחֿהֿ[ ]ובד]רֿכֿיֿה צמי אֿ]בדון.

[365] 4Q428 frg. 13 line 5: נפ]תֿחה דרךֿ[ ]ים להתהלך.

[366] 4Q427 frg. 11 line 15:]ועם בשר [להפלי]א כאלה כיא. 4Q428 frg. 13 line 6: ועם̊ בשר[.

10 [a woman? And] you [br]ought [your servant] into covenant with you, and you revealed (to) the heart of dust (how) to guard itself

11 [from all his transgressions, …] from the traps of judgment corresponding (to)[896] your mercies. And I am a creature of[897]

12 [clay, and a mixture of water, a reservoir of dus]t, and a heart of stone. For whom was I considered until this (Endtime)?[898] For

13 [your wondrous secret][899] you [p]ut in the ear of dust. That which will be for eternity, you engraved on the heart of

14 [stone. And those perverted[900] of heart …]° you lead back (so as) to enter into covenant with you, and to stand

15 [before you in the ju]dgments of witnesses in the establishment of eternity for the perfect light[901] unto perpetuity and unto darkness

16 [… withou]t end and the endtimes of unfa[thomable[902] …] peace […]

17 […] and I am a creature of[903] dust °°°[…]

18 […. And to ble]ss your name I shall open [my] m[outh]

19 […] a creature of[904] [dust …] ʾl°° °[905]

20 [… a creature of] dust it was [ope]ned nh[… and a] hidden [sna]re[906]

21 […]h it is spread out, a net of the pit [and in] its [w]ays (are) those thirsting after A[baddon][907]

22 °°[…]° and it […]hh a way was opened to °[…] to walk continuously[908]

23 in the paths of peace, and with flesh to act wonderfully like these. Because

---

[896] Apparently the judgments of the wicked are compared to God's mercies.

[897] Heb. יצר.

[898] See 21.16.

[899] See 19.19, and esp. 20.15.

[900] *Nipʿal* part. of עוה, "be bewildered," "be disconcerted." See 4.31.

[901] Lit. "for light of lights."

[902] Heb. לאין חקר.

[903] Heb. יצר.

[904] Heb. יצר.

[905] From 4Q428 frg. 13 line 2.

[906] From 4Q428 frg. 13 line 3.

[907] From 4Q428 frg. 13 line 4.

[908] From 4Q428 frg. 13 line 5.

24 ‏אי[כה368 רשת וערמ[ת ומפרשי367 פחיה מטוני על פעמי יֿהלכו ת[

25 ‏אשמר ביצר עפר מהתפרר369 ומתוך370 דונג בהמס לפני אש[ן371

26 ‏וֿמקוי אפֿר איכה אעמוד לפני רוח סוע[רת   ‏ואת יכיֿנֿו בֿ[ן372

27 ‏וישמורהו373 לרזי חפצו כיא הוא ידע למֿ[‏לֿו[ן374

28 ‏ר כלה ופח לפח יטמונו צמי רֿשֿעֿהֿ °°[

29 ‏ו בעול יתמו כול יצר רמיה כיא לאֿף[

30 ‏לֿאין ואפס יצר עולה ומעשי רמיה[

31 ‏ואני צֿר ה[חמר   (VACAT)   עֿ[375

32 ‏וֿמה יתחזק לכה אתה אֿל הֿדֿעֿוֿֿת כֿוֿ[ל

33 ‏עשיתם ומבלעדיכה לוֿא ידֿעֿתֿי דֿבֿר[376

34 ‏ואני יֿ]צֿר העפר ידעתי ברוח אשר נתתה בי בי[ד[ן בשר377

35 ‏לֿמה כֿוֿל עולה ורמיה יגורו יחד לֿזדוֿ[ן

36 ‏כול מ]עֿשֿי נדה לתחלוייֿם ומשפטי נגע וכֿלת [עולם378

37 ‏[°ֿ°ֿ חֿ[ן]°ֿ°ֿשֿ°ֿבֿ [לכֿה חמה וקנאה נוק[מת

367 4Q428 frg. 13 line 7: ‏יהלכו פע[מי על מטמוני פחים ומפרשי.

368 4Q427 frg. 11 line 16: ‏ומ[פֿרשי רשת וערמֿ[ת.

369 4Q428 frg. 13 line 8: ‏אי[כה אשמר ביצר עפר מה[ת]פֿרד.

370 Possible metathesis for ‏ומותך.

371 4Q427 frg. 11 line 17: ‏דונ[גֿ בהמס לפני אש.

372 From 4Q427 frg. 11 line 18: ‏וֿאת יכיֿנֿו בֿ[.

373 Note the *mater* after the second root consonant.

374 From 4Q427 frg. 11 line 19: ‏לֿו[.

375 A space allows for a shift in thought.

376 The scribe pens *daleth* in various ways. For the thought, see 20.33–36.

377 Three drops of ink can be seen between lines 33 and 34. For the imagery, see 7.25–26.

378 4Q427 frg. 12 line 7: ‏נ[גֿע וכלֿ[ת.

24 [...]*t* my footsteps proceed[909] on the hidden[910] parts of traps and the spread out (places of) a net and the heap [of .... H]ow

25 can a creature of[911] dust be guarded from being crumbled and from the midst of wax melting before fire [...]

26 and reservoirs of ash. How can I stand before the stor[my] wind? [...]*wʾt* he will establish me in [....]

27 And he guards him according to the mysteries of his wish,[912] because he knows *lmˆ*[...]*l*[...]

28 [...]*r* destruction. And those thirsting[913] after wickedness hide[914] trap after trap ˚˚[...]

29 [...]ˆ*w* in iniquity, all the creatures of[915] treachery will be annihilated, for to anger [...]

30 [...] for nothing an inclination of[916] injustice and the works of treachery [...]

31 [...]ˆ.[917] And I (am) a creature of[918] [clay ...]

32 [...]. And what (being) can strengthen itself before you? You (are) the God of knowledge,[919] al[l ...]

33 [...] you created them, and apart from you, I cannot know a thing[920] [....]

34 [And I (am) a cre]ature of[921] dust. I know by the spirit which you put in me through [the flesh ....][922]

35 [....] For what (is) all injustice and treachery? They will dwell together with insolence [....]

36 [All the w]orks of impurity fall ill, and the judgments of affliction and [eternal] destruction [...]

37 [...]˚˚*ḥ*[...]ˆ*š̊ b*˚˚˚ to you (is) wrath and aven[ging] jealousy [...]

---

[909] Lit. "walk."

[910] Or "buried."

[911] Heb. יצר.

[912] Or "desire."

[913] Cf. DJD: "they hide snares of wickedness." For "thirsting after" (צמי), see Ps 42:1–3 esp. צמאה נפשי לאלהים, "my soul thirsts for God." In Heb. "to thirst" means to "long for" or "be passionate for," as a deer yearns for water brooks. It is possible that Job 18:9 (צמים), the only verse in the Hebrew Bible in which צמים may be a noun ("snare"), has influenced the string of synonyms ("nets," "traps," "noose"). The term "thirsting" denotes "those who passionately" seek to "grasp him." Either צמים is a noun from צמא, "to thirst," or it is a separate lexeme previously unattested.

[914] See the paronomasia with line 24.

[915] Heb. יצר.

[916] Heb. יצר.

[917] A space allows for a shift in thought.

[918] Heb. יצר.

[919] See the notes to this expression in previous columns, notably 20.13 and 1QS 3.15.

[920] See 20.33–36. Note the *inclusio* in lines 31 and 34.

[921] Heb. יצר.

[922] See 7.25–26.

38	ואני] יׄצר חמׂׄר וׁרׄ[וח נעוה[379]
39	]
40	]
41	]
42	]

Col. 22 [= Sukenik Frgs. 1 Col. 1, 52, 4, 47]

1	]
2	]
3	]
4	°°°⟧
5	קו[ו]דש אשר בשמים
6	ג[ד]ולׄ והואה פלׄא זׄהם לוא יוכלו
7	לׄ[ה]בין בכול אלה ולספר בנפלאו[ת]יכה[380] ולוא יעצורו לדעת בכול
8	[מ]עשי אמתכה ומה אפהוא[381] ש[ב] אל עפרו ואני איש פשע ומגולׄלׄ
9	[ב]אשמה [א]ׁשמת רשעה ואני בקצי חרון
10	לה[ת]קומם לפני נׄגעי ולהשמר
11	°⟧ תוד[ע]ׁעני אלי כיא יש מקוה לאיש

379 See 5.32 and 8.18.
380 See 5.30–31; 19.31; 7.14; 9.32, 35; 18.16–17, 22–23.
381 See lines 29–30.

38   [.... And I (am)] a creature of[923] clay and a [perverted] s[pirit[924] ...]

39   [...]

40   [...]

41   [...]

42   [...]

Col. 22 [= Sukenik Frgs. 1 Col. 1, 52, 4, and 47]

1   [...]

2   [...]

3   [...]

4   [...]°°°°
5   [... holi]ness which (is) in the heavens[925]

6   [... g]reat, and he is a wonder. But they are not able

7   to [discern in all these (things) and to recount[926] in] your [wonderful deed]s, and they are not capable[927] to know in all

8   [the works of your truth.[928] And what (is) he who ret]urns to his dust?[929] And I (am) a man of transgression and am rolling

9   [in guilt ...] the guilt of wickedness. And I, in the endtimes of fury,

10   [... to] arise in the face of my afflictions, and to guard myself

11   °[... you shall allow] me to [k]now,[930] O my God, because there is hope for the human

---

[923] Heb. יצר.
[924] See 5.32 and 8.18.
[925] Or "heaven."
[926] See 5.30–31; 7.14; 9.32, 35; 18.16–17, 22–23; 19.31.
[927] Lit. "cannot retain."
[928] See 9.32.
[929] See 20.34.
[930] *Hipʿil* permissive.

12 ⟦אשר יצרתה מעפר וטהרת מאשמת ⟦מֹעל[382] ואני יצר החמר נשענתי

13 עֹל ח⟧סדיכה אשר עשיתה עמדי[383] וברוב רחמיך[384] ⟦אֹלי ואדעה כיא אמת

14 פיכה ⟦ ⟧ ודברכה לוא ישוב[385] ⟦אחור ואני בקצי אתמוכה

15 בבריֹתֹ⟧כה   ואתקו⟧מֹמה במעמד העמדתני כיא

16 ⟦   ⟧ ⟦אֹיש ותשיבהו ובמה יתֹֹ ⟧

17 ⟦ הֹשבֹ⟧תֹה⟧ ואתה עצמתֹה וֹמֹפח⟧ד[ ]

18 ⟦ בושהֹ ללוא מקו⟧הֹלאיֹש[386]

19 ⟦ ואני יצֹר ⟧החמר

20 פ⟧לֹגתהֹ⟧

21 אֹ אשר הֹ⟧

22 עֹֹרֹבֹ ובוקר עם מֹ⟧בואאור

23 נג⟧יֹעי גבר וממכאֹ⟧ובות אנוש[ ]

24 ⟦הֹ נשמחהֹ⟧   ⟦וֹאל זרתו צפו ועל משמרתֹם ֹ[ ]

25 ֹונדיבים לוא כֹ⟧לֹו כיא אֹ⟧תה תגר בכול שטן משחית ומרעֹ[ים][387]

---

[382] See 12.38.
[383] See 8.31–32: חסדיך [א]שֹֹר עֹשיתֹה עֹמֹדי.
[384] See 5.34, 15.21.
[385] See 5.35: ו[דברך לא ישוב אחור. See also 5.36.
[386] See line 11.
[387] See 4Q171 [4QPsᵃ] frgs. 1–10 2.2: כיא מרעים.

12 [whom you fashioned from dust[931] and purified from the guilt of] infidelity.[932] And I (am) a creature of[933] clay; I leaned

13 upon [your] lo[ving-kindnesses[934] which you did with me in your multitudinous mercies,][935] O my God. And I know that truth

14 (is in) your mouth [and your word shall not turn][936] backwards. And I, in my endtime, I shall adhere

15 to [your] covenant[937] [.... And I shall ari]se in the position where you allowed me to stand[938] because

16 °[…] human, and you allowed him to come back.[939] And in what *yt*°°[…]

17 [… you] brought back. And you, you are powerful; and from fea[r]

18 […] shame without hop[e for the human[940] …]

19 [….] And I (am) a creature of[941] [clay …]

20 […] you [di]vided […]

21 […]ʾ which *h*[…]

22 [… ev]ening and morning with the co[ming of light …]

23 [… the afflic]tions of a man[942] and from the miser[ies of a human]

24 […]*h* we will have joy [….] And unto his (God's) help[943] they look out, and upon their watchtower °[….]

25 And the noblemen[944] [were] not exte[rminated;[945] for y]ou rebuke every ruinous adversary[946] and [those] who do evil[947]

---

[931] See 11.21–22.
[932] See 12.38 and also 4.38, 14.11.
[933] Heb. יצר.
[934] Or "covenant loyalty."
[935] See 5.34 and esp. 15.21.
[936] See 5.35–56.
[937] The *beth* is not a *nota accusativi*; in Hebrew, one writes "I shall adhere to your covenant." See the same expression in 10.23 and 12.2.
[938] *Hipʿil* permissive.
[939] *Hipʿil* permissive.
[940] See line 11.
[941] Heb. יצר.
[942] Heb. גבר.
[943] Those in the *Yaḥad* are eagerly looking for God's help.
[944] The noun denotes those who are willing or "volunteers."
[945] *Piʿel* כלה.
[946] Heb. שטן. See 24.23.
[947] See 4Q171 [4QPsᵃ] frgs. 1–10 2.2.

לי מאז כוננתי לב֗ב֗[רית]כה ואתה גליתה אוזני כי[א] למוסר   **26**

[[א֗ו֗ ֗ ואנושי ברית³⁸⁸ פותו בם ויבוא]]   לוא יבוא כיא֗]]   **27**

במבניתי ותכמ[יבתו]כ֗חות לפניכה ואני פחדתי ממשפטכה֗]   **28**

לפ[נ]יכה ומי יזכה במשפטכה ומה אפה֗[ו אדם]   **29**

[[֗ אני במשפט ושב אל עפרו מה יב֗ב֗[ן]   **30**

כי אתה א[ל֗ל֗ פתחתה לבבי לבינתכה ותגל אוז֗[נ]ני]   **31**

[[להשען על טובכה ויהם לב֗בי ש֗ ֗ ֗]   **32**

[[ולבבי כדונג ימס על פשע וח֗ט֗אה֗   **33**

עד [[תומה   **34**

Hymn 30
Blessed is the God of Knowledge Who Established His Servant

ברוך אתה אל הדעות אשר הכינות֗[ה]   **34**

[[ותפגע בעבדכה זות³⁸⁹ למענכה כיא ידעתי   **35**

ולחסד[[כ֗ה אחל³⁹⁰ בכול היותי ושמכה אברכה תמיד   **36**

כי יש [[מ֗ק֗ו֗ה לע֗ב֗ד֗כה ו֗אל תעזובנו³⁹¹ בקצי   **37**

[[ה֗ וכבודכה וטו֗[בכה]   **38**

[[על ב֗ן]   **39**

---

³⁸⁸ Read: אנשי ברית.
³⁸⁹ See זות in 20.35 and זאת in 12.30.
³⁹⁰ The *matres lectionis* are added perhaps by an another scribe.
³⁹¹ Note the *waw mater* and energic *nun*.

26   to me, from when I was established for your co[venant]. And you, you uncovered my ear fo[r instruction[948] …]

27   it[949] will not enter for […]˚ʾw˚. But the men of the covenant were misled[950] by them.[951] And it[952] entered […]

28   in my frame and [my] entrails [in chasti]sements before you. And I, I was afraid of your judgment […]

29   [… be]fore you. And who will be (pronounced) pure in your judgment? And what then [(is) Adam]?[953]

30   […]˚ I (am) in judgment. And he (Adam) returns to his dust. What can he discer[n]

31   [...?] For you, O] my [G]od, opened my heart to your discernment, and you have uncovered [my] ear

32   […] to lean upon your goodness. But my heart was agitated[954] šˊˊˊˊ[…]

33   […]˚ and my heart (was) like wax melting on account of transgression and sin

34   [… until] it[955] is completed.

Hymn 30
Blessed is the God of Knowledge Who Established His Servant[956]

34   Blessed (are) you, O God of knowledge,[957] that y[ou] established

35   […] and thus you called upon[958] your servant for your sake.[959] For I know

36   [… and for] your [loving-kindness] I long with all my being, and your name I bless continuously

37   [… for there is] hope for your servant. And do not abandon him in the endtimes of

38   […]*h* and your glory and [your] goodne[ss …]

39   […] upon *b*[…]

[948] See 14.17.

[949] The *nomen regens* is "adversary;" see line 25.

[950] The form is the *puˈal* pf. of פתה. The verb often denotes "to be seduced (or misled)."

[951] That is "those who do evil" in line 25.

[952] That is, the "adversary."

[953] Or "humankind." See 18.5; or "And what then (is) Adam?"

[954] The verb is not a conjugation of המה, "to moan," because the *qal* impf. has a final *he*. The verb is the *qal* impf. of המם, "to bring into motion," "to disturb." See 13.33.

[955] A reference to "sin."

[956] There is no *vacat* in 1QHᵃ.

[957] This expression was probably memorized from 1QS 3.15.

[958] Or "entreated." Heb. verb פגע with *beth* could also mean "to fall upon," or "assault."

[959] Lit. "and thus you called upon your servant, this for your own sake."

] **40**

] **41**

] **42**

Col. 23 [= Sukenik Col. 18 + Frgs. 57 Col. 1 and 2 Col. 1]
Parallels: 4Q428 Frg. 14

] **1**

2 אורכה ותעמד מא[ז

3 אורכה לאין השב[ת

4 כיא אתכה אור ל[מקור עולם[392]

5 ותגל אוזן עפר[לרזי פלאכה לגלות נסתר]ות ולהֹבֹ[י]ןֹ

6 מזמה אשר הו[דעתני ברזי פלאכה] אלו עמֹדי ותאמנה בֹא[וזני]

7 עבדכה עד עולם ֯[להשמיע ש[מֹועות פלאכה להופֹיֹע

8 לעיני כול שמעִי[כהובכול מעשיכה][393] בימין עוזכה לנהֹל כֹלֹמֹ

9 בכוח גבורתכהֹ [ובגדול חסדך יהל]ל שמכה ויתגבר בכבודֹכֹהֹ

10 אל תשב ידכה [מיד עבדכה ל]הֹיות לו מתחזק בבריתכה

11 ועומד לפניכה בֹ[תמים[394] כיא מק]ור פתחתה בפי עבדכה ובלשונו

[392] See 14.20.
[393] See 11.24 and 19.27.
[394] See 9.38.

40   […]

41   […]

42   […]

Col. 23 [= Sukenik Col. 18 + Frgs. 57 Col. 1, and 2 Col. 1]
Parallels: 4Q428 Frg. 14

1   […]

2   your light, and you caused to stand[960] from of o[ld …]

3   your light without ceasi[ng ….]

4   For with you (there is) light for [an eternal source[961] ….]

5   And you uncovered the ear of dust [to your wondrous mysteries to reveal hidden thing]s, and to compre-[he]nd

6   the design[962] which [you] allowed [me] to [know[963] in your wondrous mysteries.] They are with me and confirmed in the e[ar of]

7   your servant unto eternity °[… to announce the re]ports of your wonder, (and) to appear

8   before the eyes of all who listen [to you. And with all your works][964] in your strong right hand to guide all of them

9   through the power of your might; [and with your great loving-kindness[965] to prai]se your name and become mighty through your glory.

10   Do not withdraw your hand [from the hand of your servant, but rather to] be for him one who is strengthened in your covenant,

11   and (one who) stands before you with [the perfect ones.[966] For a sou]rce you opened in the mouth of your servant, and by his tongue

---

[960] Taken as a *hiʿpil*, also possible is *qal*, "stand."
[961] See 14.20.
[962] The author is referring to the eternal plan of God.
[963] *Hipʿil* permissive.
[964] See 11.24 and 19.27.
[965] See 5.16.
[966] See 9.38.

12 חקקתה על קו מ֯[שפט למ֯[שמיע ליצר מבינתו ולמליץ באלה

13 לעפר כמוני³⁹⁵ ותפתח מ֯ק[ור]להוכיח ליצר חמר דרכו ואשמות ילוד

14 אשה³⁹⁶ כמעשיו ולפתֹח מ֯[קו]ר֯ אמתכה ליצר³⁹⁷ אשר סמכתה בעוזכה

15 לֹ[הרים] כאמתכה מבשר ולֹ[ספ]ר֯³⁹⁸ טובכה לבשר עניים³⁹⁹ לרוב רחמיכה

16 [ולה]ש֯ב֯֯יֹע ממקור דֹ[עת]⁴⁰⁰   לנ֯[כֹאי רוח ואבלים לשמחת עולם

17 [ותפת]ֹח פי עב֯[דכה]⁴⁰¹ [֯תים לֹ[[לֹ[[לֹ[

18   ]

19   ]

Hymn 31
Praise Be to God's Glorious Creation

20   ]

21 [לֹ יֹש֯מיעֹו]

22 [˚˚˚ עוֹלֹם ולֹהֹללכה]

23 [ֹם ובארצכה ובבני אלים יֹכֹבֹד קֹ[ודשכה והם⁴⁰² [אֹשֹר יעמֹ[ודו]

24 [לעד]לֹהֹללכה ולספר כול כבודכה ואֹנֹי מה כיא מעפר לוקחתי ואֹ[תה]

³⁹⁵ 4Q428 frg. 14 line 1: ולמליץ בא[לֹה לעפֹר] כמוני.
³⁹⁶ 4Q428 frg. 14 line 2: ד]רכו ואשמֹ[ות ילוד אשה.
³⁹⁷ 4Q428 frg. 14 line 3: א]ֹמתכה ליצֹ[ר.
³⁹⁸ 4Q428 frg. 14 line 4: מב]שר ול[ספר.
³⁹⁹ Ctr. DJD: ענוים.
⁴⁰⁰ 4Q428 frg. 14 line 5: ממקֹ[ור דעת.
⁴⁰¹ From 4Q428 frg. 14 line 6: ותפת]ֹח פי עב֯[דכה.
⁴⁰² There is room for 10–11 consonants or spaces.

12 you engraved on the measuring-line of [jud]gment [for the one who] proclaims to a creature[967] his discernment.[968] And for the one who interprets these (things)

13 to dust like me. And you opened a sou[rce] to reprove a creature of[969] clay (concerning) his way and the guilts of one born of

14 a woman[970] according to his works, and to open the s[our]ce of your truth to the creature[971] whom you supported with your strength,

15 to [raise up] according to your truth from the flesh and to [recou]nt your goodness, announcing[972] to the Poor Ones[973] according to the multitude of your mercies.

16 [And to sa]tisfy from the source of kno[wledge … to the mi]serable ones of spirit and mourners to an eternal joy.

17 [And you open]ed the mouth of [your] serva[nt[974]…]°*tym l*°[…]*l*[…]*l*[…]

18 […]

19 […]

Hymn 31
Praise Be to God's Glorious Creation[975]

20 […]

21 […]*l* they shall proclaim […]

22 […] eternal […]°°° and to praise you […]

23 […]*m* and in your land and among the sons of Elim[976] he shall honor[977] [your] ho[liness, and they] who shall st[and]

24 [forever] to praise you and to recount all your glory. And what (am) I? For from the dust I was taken. And y[ou,]

---

[967] Heb. יצר.
[968] The form does not mean "from his discernment;" see Reymond, p. 168 n. 56.
[969] Heb. יצר.
[970] See Job 14:1, 15:14, and 25:4.
[971] Heb. יצר.
[972] The *pi'el* infinitive of בשר means "to bring good news" or "to announce."
[973] Or "the Needy Ones." Not "the humble ones."
[974] See 4Q428 frg. 14 line 6.
[975] 23.18–21a may have contained indications of the beginning or ending of a hymn.
[976] Or "divine beings."
[977] A *pi'el* impf. of כבד (not a *pu'al* which would probably have a ו). The Elim are "in your land."

25 [א]לֹי לכֹֿבֹודכה עשיתה כול אלה כרוב חסדיכה תן משמר צדקכה

26 [לעבדכ]ה תמיד עד פלט ומליצי דעת עם כול צעודי ומוכיחי אמת

27 [בכ]וֹל פֹּעֹמֹי כיא מה עפר בכוֹל [יצר מע]שה אפר בידם לוא הנה ואתה

28 [יצרתה⁴⁰³ יצר] הֹחֹמֹר וֹמֹצוֹרֹוֹק] עפר [לֹרצונכה על הבנים תבחננני⁴⁰⁴

29 [כֹֿגֹודֹלֹכה] ומה אפהו שב א[ל עפרו⁴⁰⁵ ועל עפר הניפותה רוח

30 [קודשכה [בֹטיֹטֹ] בנ[י אלים להחיד עם בני שמים

31 ע[ולם ואין תשבת חושך כיא

32 [ומאור גליתה ולוא להשיב

33 ורוח קו[דשכה הניפותה לכפור אשמה

34 מ[שרתים עם צבאכה ומתהלכים

35 בנת[יֹבות מלפניכה כיא נכונו באמתכה

36 [הֹפֹלתה אלה לכבודכה ומצורוק

---

⁴⁰³ See 7.35; 9.10; 18.24.
⁴⁰⁴ Read: תבחנני. A scribal error.
⁴⁰⁵ See 20.34: ומה אפהו שב אל עפרו.

25 [O] my [G]od, for your glory you made all these (things) in accordance with the multitude of your loving-kindnesses. Guard[978] your righteousness

26 [for yo]ur [servant] always until deliverance, and the interpreters of knowledge (who are) with all my steps, and the mediators of[979] truth (who are)

27 [with a]ll my footsteps. For what (is) dust? In each [inclination[980] (is) a crea]ture of ashes.[981] In their[982] hands, they[983] are insignificant. But you,

28 [you made[984] a creature of][985] clay and a mixture of [dust] for your will, and before[986] the members[987] you reprove me

29 [...] as your greatness. And what is that which returns to its dust?[988] And over the dust you waved high[989] a spirit of

30 [your holiness ...] in the mud [... the son]s of Elim[990] unite with the sons of heaven

31 [... et]ernity, and there is no return of darkness because

32 [...] and light you have revealed and without returning

33 [... and the spirit of] your [holi]ness you have waved high (as an offering)[991] to atone for guilt

34 [... those s]erving with your army and those who are walking

35 [... in the pa]ths before you, because they are established in your truth

36 [...] you caused to fall[992] these (things) for your glory, and from a mixture of

---

[978] Lit. "give a guard."

[979] The *hipʿil* part. of יכח, which means "to reproach," "to avenge," and "to mediate."

[980] Heb. יצר.

[981] The noun literally means "ashes," but it has metaphorical meaning in the Bible and Qumran. The noun connotes insignificance, especially when combined with "dust." See Abraham's words, according to Gen 18:27.

[982] The pronoun "their" apparently refers back to those from whom the author needs "guarding;" see line 25. Many translators found it impossible to obtain meaning from these lines. Our translation, benefited by improved images, is not elegant, but it is tied to Hebrew orthography and grammar. The author seems to say that in the hands of the true interpreters of God's Word, ostensible ashes are not really ashes.

[983] The pronoun "they" refers to "their hands;" that is, the hands of the author's opponents.

[984] See 7.35, 9.10, 18.24.

[985] Heb. יצר.

[986] Heb. על which means "upon," "against," "in front of," "on account," and "before."

[987] The Heb. noun means "sons," "individuals," and "members" (probably here of the administering priests in the Temple). See also "[the so]ns of gods" and "the sons of heaven" in 23.30. See also "the sons of Elim" in line 23.

[988] See 20.34.

[989] The *hipʿil* pf. of נוף means "to move back and forth high." Perhaps there is a reference to the "wave offering."

[990] Or "divine beings."

[991] *Hipʿil* pf. of נוף, "to move back and forth high." The allusion may be to Exodus 29 in which one reads about the "sin offering." The terms "to wave high" and "atone" are present in this chapter.

[992] *Hipʿil* of נפל; see 15.37. The meaning is the casting of the lot; see the next line.

37 [עפר] [לגֹ֯ו֯רל עול יצֹ֯ר נֹתעב

38 יֹ]צֹ֯ר נתעב

39]

40]

41]

42]

Col. 24 [= Sukenik Col. 18 Col. 2 + Frgs. 9, 50, 57 Col. 2, 45, 6, 2 Col. 2; and SR 4301]
Parallels: 4Q428 Frgs. 15–16

1]

Hymn 32
Failure of the Cast-Down Heavenly Beings to Praise: Judgment

2]

3]

4 [

5]°°[⟦

6 ⟦י֯צר ב⟦ ⟧שר   בֹ֯אשמ⟦ ⟧ה

7 ו⟦מֹ֯י יוע֯⟦ ⟧דכה   עֹ֯ד קֹצֹ֯⟦ ⟧ משפטכה

8 ⟦ה למל⟦ ⟧אכי   בֹ֯משפטי ⟦עדים

37   [dust ...] to the lot of iniquity, the abhorred creature[993]

38   [...] abhorred [cr]eature[994] [...]

39   [...]

40   [...]

41   [...]

42   [...]

Col. 24 [= Sukenik Col. 18 Col. 2 + Frgs. 9, 50, 57 Col. 2, 45, 6, 2 Col. 2; and SHR 4301]
Parallels: 4Q428 Frgs. 15–16

1   [...]

Hymn 32
Failure of the Cast-Down Heavenly Beings to Praise: Judgment[995]

2   [...]

3   [...]

4   [...]°

5   [...]°°[...]°°

6   in guil[t ...] a creature of[996] flesh

7   unto the Endtime of [your judgment.... And] who can arraign[997] you

8   in the judgments of [witnesses[998] ...]*h* to the angels of

---

[993] Heb. יצר.

[994] Heb. יצר.

[995] A new hymn is indicated by a shift in the subject. The *lacunae* may have contained a *vacat* and an *incipit*.

[996] Heb. יצר.

[997] The *hipʻil* impf. of יעד means "to make an appointment," or "to summon (or arraign)" in a court of law. See Jer 49:19 and 50:44. For the forensic meaning, see Job 9:19.

[998] See 21.14–15.

9   נֹגע במשפֿ⟧ט   ⟦ ורזי פשע⟧ ⟦לֹהשנות

10   בשר בֿא⟦שמתם   אר⟦ץ ויע⟧⟦ופפו בה כול[406]

11   מלאכי שמֿ⟦ים   מק⟦ום בעבותי רוח ותכנע

12   אלים ממכון קודֿ⟦שכה[407] כיא לוא יהלל⟧וכה במעון כבודכה ואתה[408]

13   אדם על הֿ⟦   כעו⟧ף אסור עד קץ רצונכה[409]

14   וֹלשלֿחֿמֿ⟧   ⟦רמות כוח ורוב בשר[410] להרשיע

15   בקצֿ⟦י חרונכה וברזי פֿ⟦לֿא[411] להכין בסוד עמכה

16   כול רוחות[412]⟧ ממזרים כי לֿ⟦וא[

17   ⟦ פֿגריֿם לֿל⟦וא[

18   ]

---

[406] 4Q428 frg. 15 line 1: [כול] בה ⟦פֹפֿﬡ⟧וֹ⟦ויﬠֹ].

[407] 4Q428 frg. 15 line 3: [שכה]קודֿ ﬦ⟦מכון ﬦ.

[408] 4Q428 frg. 15 line 4: [ואתה ו⟦בודכה]כ.

[409] 4Q428 frg. 15 line 5: [עד ר]אסוֹ⟦ף כעו אדם].

[410] 4Q428 frg. 15 line 7: [בשֹרֹ וֹב]ור.

[411] See line 28.

[412] See line 26.

9   punishment[999] in judgme[nt …] and the mysteries of transgression cause to alter[1000] (those of the)

10   flesh in [their] gu[ilt … a lan]d; and on it[1001] fly all

11   the (evil)[1002] angels of heav[en … a pla]ce with spiritual ropes.[1003] And you cast down

12   the heavenly beings[1004] from the establishment of [your] holine[ss, for they did not praise][1005] you in the dwelling of your glory.[1006] But you,

13   Adam[1007] upon the °[… like a bir]d confined until the Endtime of your will,[1008]

14   and to dismiss them […] the heights of power, and the multitude of flesh causing to be condemned[1009]

15   in the endtime[s of your anger. And in the mysteries of wo]nder,[1010] to establish in council[1011] with you

16   [… all the spirits of][1012] the illegitimate ones[1013] for n[ot]

17   […] corpses with[out]

18   […]

[999] The Hebrew noun denotes "affliction," and "blow." It can also mean punishment (see line 25). See esp. Deut 17:8, and cf. 4Q525 frgs. 2–3 2.4. The meaning of 24.1–32 [and further] becomes clear only if one imagines the myth of the fallen angels found in Genesis 6 and especially in *1 Enoch* 1–36. Both texts were known to those at Qumran, as many copies of *1 Enoch* 1–36 and Genesis were found in the Qumran caves. Translating the present lines of text is guided by the helpful images found in 13.38: "as *the mysteries of transgression are altering* the works of God with *their guilt. For I was bound with ropes* …." Italics indicate verbal and metaphorical connections.

[1000] See 13.38, "the mysteries of transgression are altering." The concept seems to refer to the origin of transgression. It occurred when the Watchers fell from heaven to copulate with the beautiful human women, mentioned in Genesis 6 and developed in *1 Enoch* 1–36.

[1001] Or "in it."

[1002] There should be no doubt that evil angels are intended.

[1003] The translator confronts a major decision: Does בעבותי derive from עב (the feminine plural עבות, "clouds") or from עבות ("rope" [fem. construct plural: "the ropes of"]). 13.38 provides a key for unlocking the mystery: "bound with ropes." The author may denote how the fallen angels were bound "with spiritual ropes." God did not need to fashion a rope of cords to bind them. As he created with a word, so God could bind the Watchers with spiritual ropes. Thus, the rendering "clouds of the wind" not only lacks clarity but does not fit the context.

[1004] Heb. אלים. According to a well-known Jewish myth that first appears in Genesis 6, the fallen angels, the Watchers, leave the heights (or heaven) and descend to earth to mate with human women. The author probably imagined that God cast them out of heaven (that they could not return is clear). The Watchers were punished by God. See *1En* 10:4 according to which Azazel is bound hand and foot and cast into darkness by God. In *1En* 10:14, we are told the evil angels are "bound together" until the Endtime.

[1005] For praising without ceasing, see 25.31 at the conclusion of this hymn. Also possible: "[and they will now serve you in the abode of] your [gl]ory." The evil angels did not praise, or honor, God's infinite authority. They rebelled against God's will and plan.

[1006] Note also the attractive restoration in DJD: "[and they could no longer ser]ve you in your glorious dwelling."

[1007] The transition is abrupt, but we have only a portion of the text. "Adam" is mentioned. Could the *Books of Adam* or the Adam compositions (known at Qumran, but again only in fragments) have influenced the poet? Is it conceivable that Adam is being addressed?

[1008] The author refers to God's will. See *1En* 10:6, according to which Azazel is confined and cast into the desert until "the great day of judgment."

[1009] The *hip'il* of רשע means "to pronounce guilty," or "cause to be condemned."

[1010] See line 28.

[1011] Or "in secret."

[1012] See line 26.

[1013] See *1En* 10:9 and the reference to "the illegitimate" offspring of the Watchers.

]	**19**
]	**20**
⟦צדקה דע֯ת֯⟧[413]	**21**
⟦ע֯ב לחת בעת עוונות֯⟧ינו	**22**
⟦֯ם כול שטן ומשחית ⟧	**23**
⟦ב֯ר֯שתם ולשלחם גוי ב⟧גוי ⟦֯כ֯ה֯ רשע	**24**
⟦איש ז֯ידן במרבי מעל וע⟧֯ ⟦ ֯ ב֯נ֯ג֯י֯ע֯י֯֯ם ובמשפטים	**25**
ל֯⟧ **26**   ⟦ ֯בים בבסר[414] כי כול רוחות֯⟧ ⟦מ֯מזרים להרשיע בבשר
ומ֯⟧ **27** ⟦הרש֯יעו בחייהם ⟧   ⟦ל֯⟧ו֯א כן רוחם להרשיע
ע֯ל֯⟧ **28**   ⟦ל֯⟧   ול⟧פ֯לא רזיכה גליתה
לב֯י֯⟧ **29**   ⟦א֯ני לבשר ידעתי
כיא֯⟧ ברצונכה באיש[415] **30**   ⟦ם עולה בקץ
כ֯ל֯⟧ות רשעה[416] **31**   ⟦י֯ה ולכול מביט
32   ⟦ ולו יכחד
מ֯ל֯פ֯נ֯י֯⟧ **33**   כ⟧ו֯בדתה מבני
אל ש֯ו֯⟧מעי דבריכה **34**   ג⟧ב֯ולות עמים
לחזקם ⟧ **35**   ל⟧ה֯רבות אשמה
בנחלתו ֯⟧ **36**   ולוא ⟦ע֯ו֯ז֯ב֯ם֯ ⟧ ביד

---

[413] Ctr. DJD:]ע֯[.
[414] בסר for בשר.
[415] See 6.24 and 8.22.
[416] For the restoration, see lines 24, 26, and 27.

19   [...]

20   [...]

21   [...] righteousness. Knowledge [...]

22   [...]ʿb to the pit[1014] at the time of [our] iniquities [...]

23   [...]°m each adversary[1015] and destroyer [...]

24   [...] in their net and dismissing them, nation by [nation[1016] ...] your [...] wickedness.

25   [...] an arrogant man with much infidelity and ʿ[...]° with punishments and in judgments

26   l[...]°bym with flesh[1017] for all the spirits of the illegitimate ones[1018] to cause wickedness with flesh[1019]

27   and m[...] to cause wickedness during their lives [...] n[o]t like their spirits to cause wickedness

28   ʿl[...]l[... and for] the wonder of your mysteries you revealed

29   to my heart [...] I for flesh. I know[1020]

30   that [in your will towards man[1021] ...]m injustice at the Endtime of

31   annih[ilation of wickedness[1022] ...]yh and to each who looks upon[1023]

32   [...] and it will not be concealed

33   from before [...] you are [ho]nored above the sons of

34   God,[1024] those who h[ear of your words ... the bo]undaries of the peoples

35   to strengthen them [... to] multiply guilt

36   in his inheritance °[... and] you did [not] abandon them into the hand of

---

[1014] The supralinear ש gives us לשחת, "to the pit."
[1015] Heb. שטן; see 22.25.
[1016] Or "people by [people."
[1017] The orthography may indicate an Aramaism, since the word is spelled with ס instead of ש, as occurs more frequently in Aramaic (and not Hebrew) Qumran texts.
[1018] The myth of the Watchers clearly refers to their offspring as "illegitimate."
[1019] The author seems influenced by the myth of the Watchers, best known today by its development in *1 Enoch* 1–36.
[1020] Sometime the Hebrew perfect can denote the present or the past.
[1021] See 6.24, 8.22.
[1022] For "wickedness," see lines 24, 26, and 27.
[1023] The *hipʿil* part. of נבט means "to look" or "to watch." Perhaps some Jewish readers at this point in the poem may have thought about the Watchers of Genesis 6 and *1 Enoch* 1–36.
[1024] The "sons of God" often means "angels" in post-biblical Hebrew compositions.

37 כול[417] מבל[עי דבר[418] א̊ ̊̊ד[

38 ת̊ב̊א̊[

39 על[

40 [

41 [

42 [

Col. 25 [Frgs. 5, 56 Col. 1, 46 Col. 1, 51, 55 Col. 1, 63, 8, and 7 Col. 1]
Parallels: 4Q428 Frgs. 17–20

1 [

2 [

3 מש[פ̊ט̊ צדק ב[כול מעשיכה[419]

4 ול[הפרידם ממעמד ק̊ד̊[ושים

5 [רוח[ות[420] עם ע̊ד̊ת קדושיכה בהפלא[

6 [ע[ד̊ עולם ורוחות רשעה תבית מא[

7 ר̊ע̊ לוא יהיו עוד ותשם מקום רש̊[ע[ה להפ[יל גורלות[כול[421]

8 רוחות עולה אשר יושדו לאבל[422] ה[

---

[417] 4Q428 frg. 16 line 1: כול] עזבת[ם ביד.
[418] See 17.8: למבלעי דבר.
[419] See 9.8: במשפט[יכ]ה צדקתה בכל מעשיכה.
[420] See the next line.
[421] 4Q428 frg. 17 line 1: רשע]ה להפ[יל. See 6.22.
[422] 4Q428 frg. 17 line 2: יוש]דו לאב[ל.

37 all the destroy[ers of[1025] the word …]ᵒᵒᵒd

38 *tbʾ*[…]

39 upon […]

40 […]

41 […]

42 […]

Col. 25 [Frgs. 5, 56 Col. 1, 46 Col. 1, 51, 55 Col. 1, 63, 8, and 7 Col. 1]
Parallels: 4Q428 Frgs. 17–20

1 […]

2 […]

3 […] righteous [judg]ment in[all your works[1026]…]

4 [… and to] separate[1027] them from the rank of the Ho[ly Ones …]

5 [spirit]s with the congregation of your Holy Ones in doing wondrously […]

6 [un]to eternity. And the wicked spirits[1028] you shall cause to be housed[1029] *mʾ*[…]

7 evil will not continue anymore.[1030] And you shall make desolate[1031] the place of wicked[ne]ss in order to ca[st lots] (for) all

8 the spirits of injustice that shall be devastated[1032] for sorrow […]*h*,

---

[1025] See Isa 25:7–8.

[1026] See 9.8.

[1027] The *hipʿil* infinitive of פרד denotes "to separate," "to segregate," or "to keep apart from." The condemnation of the Watchers seems to be in the mind of the author. God "segregated" them from "the Ho[ly Ones]," most likely the Holy Angels in heaven. A *double entendre* is also possible since "the Holy Ones" at Qumran can mean angels and the advanced members of the Community (the *Yaḥad*).

[1028] These wicked spirits should be recognized as the fallen angels, the Watchers, who brought evil and wickedness to the earth, as is well known from Genesis 6 and the *Books of Enoch*.

[1029] The noun בית, "house," is well-known in biblical and related texts, but the verb בית is not familiar in biblical texts. The *qal* impf. of the verb בית is unique. The verb "to house" or "to lodge" is an Aramaism; see Dan 6:9 (ובת) and 11Q10 [11QTgJob] 36.7. The verb continues into modern Hebrew; e.g., "to house" something like a dog.

[1030] Lit. "it will not be again."

[1031] The *hipʿil* impf. of שמם (the י is not shown, as is often the case in Qumran Hebrew) means "cause to be deserted."

[1032] Either the *hopʿil* impf. of שדד, "to be devastated," or a *qal* passive.

9   יעׄגׄ לדורי נצח וברום רשעה[423] למׄ[[עשה רע

10   יׄרבה אנינם לכלה ונגד כול מעשכׄ[[ה   °°[[

11   חסדיכה ולדעת כול בכבודכה ולפׄ[[שכלם יברכוכה[424] ולמׄ[[ועד הׄ[[וׄ]]דׄעתה

12   משפט אמתכה ואוזן בשר גליתה וׄ[[425]   [[לא[[נוש בׄמזמתׄ

13   לבכה וקץ תעודה השכלתהׄ[426] לבׄשׄ[[רבצ[[בׄא המרום תׄ[[שׄפוט במרום

14   וביושבי הׄאׄדׄמׄה[427] על האדמה וגם בשאוׄל תחתיה תשׄפׄוׄטׄ[428] וׄבׄיושבי

15   חושך תריב להׄצׄדׄ[[יק] צׄדיק ולהׄרׄשׄ[[יע[429] רשע [[כׄיא אין מבׄ[[לעדיׄ[[כׄה

16   ולוא להפרד מׄ[אׄמת   [דׄברכה[[[[ׄת אׄ[[

17   לׄ[

18   ]

19   ]

20   ]

21   ]

22   [לׄבׄני °°[430]

23   ׄ[וגם רוחו[ת[431]   [מחושך ויׄ[432]

---

[423] 4Q428 frg. 17 line 3: ו.[בׄ]רום רשעה.

[424] See 9.32–34.

[425] 4Q428 frg. 18 line 1: [ואוזן בשר גליתה ו.

[426] 4Q428 frg. 18 line 2: [לבכה וקץ תעודה השכלתהׄ.

[427] 4Q428 frg. 18 line 3: האדמה [וביושבׄ תשפוט במרום.

[428] 4Q428 frg. 18 line 4: בשאוׄל תחתי[ה] תׄשׄפׄוׄ[ט. The reading is improved by images taken in 2006 by Charlesworth, Johns, and Rietz.

[429] 4Q428 frg. 18 line 5: [צדיק] ולהׄ[רׄ]שׄ[י]ע.

[430] From 4Q428 frg. 19 line 1:] °° לׄבׄני[.

[431] From 4Q428 frg. 19 line 2: [וגם רוחוׄ[ת.

[432] From 4Q428 frg. 19 line 3:] ׄ וי[מחושך.

9   he shall be locked up[1033] for eternal generations. And when wickedness rises up to d[o evil...][1034]

10   their lament shall increase unto annihilation. But before all yo[ur] creatures[1035] [...]°°

11   your loving-kindnesses, and to know all in your glory. And according to [their insight they will bless you,[1036] and for the app]ointed time you allowed to be [kn]own[1037]

12   your true judgment.[1038] And you uncovered the ear of flesh and [...] to humans in the design of

13   your heart. And (concerning) the Endtime of fixed times, you allowed fles[h] to have insight.[1039] [The ho]st of the upper regions[1040] you shall judge in the upper regions,

14   and the dwellers of earth (you shall judge) upon the earth. And also in Sheol below you shall judge.[1041] And (concerning) the dwellers of

15   darkness, you shall contest a lawsuit, declaring righte[ous] the righteous one and declaring wic[ked the wicked one] for there is none ex[cept] you.[1042]

16   And not to separate from the [truth...] your word [...]°*t* ʾ[...]

17   *l*[...]

18   [...]

19   [...]

20   [...]

21   [...]

22   [...] for the sons of °°[...][1043]

23   [...]° and also the spirit[s] from darkness and *y*°[...]

[1033] The verb עגן means "to lock up" in late Hebrew. The *qal* or *piʿel* impf. appears here in Qumran Hebrew but not in biblical Hebrew. Most likely, Aramaic has influenced the language (as is obvious elsewhere in the *Thanksgiving Hymns*). It seems probable that the leader of the fallen angels is the one who shall be "locked up for eternal generations." Jewish reflections on human suffering, sin, and demonology are complex.

[1034] The Wicked Spirit is locked up, but will rise from his confinement to do evil.

[1035] Or "works." See Ps 145:9.

[1036] For the restoration, see 9.32–34. In line 10, the poet shifts to God's "loving-kindnesses."

[1037] *Hipʿil* permissive.

[1038] The Jews who read these lines believed that the demons (the Watchers) had already been condemned by God. While demons continued to cause wickedness on the earth and were the source for sickness, their fate was sealed, as explained in *1 Enoch* 1–36.

[1039] *Hipʿil* permissive.

[1040] The authors of the *Thanksgiving Hymns* use another noun for "heaven." The author of this hymn uses מרום, "upper regions" or "elevated" region of heaven. See Isa 24:21.

[1041] Perhaps this belief influenced the *descensus ad inferos* passages in the *Odes of Solomon*. See esp. *OdesSol* 42:11–20.

[1042] See the similar expression of monotheism in Isa 43:11; 44:6, 8, and 45:6, 21.

[1043] For the readings in the next three lines see 4Q428 frg. 19 lines 1–4.

24 [ונמארים433]ͦם

25 לͦבͦלתי רשעתם בחכמת[433 כבודכ]ͤה ולוͦא יͦכͦͦͦͦιͦרͦן

26 מͦעשͦͦי[צͦ]דͦקכה435 לעווͦן436 [ולבוא ביחד עם עדת בני ש]מͦים437 ובסוד קדוש[ים]438

27 יתרומ[ם] [ͦͦιͦב]

28 עצה ו[ͦ]

29 משרתים[[ͦι

30 וͦהͦכירום[[ͦם ירננו לͦזמר

31 ולהלל439 ל[ͦ]אין הש[ͦ]בͦת ואני יצר החמר440[[כͦדעתי

32 ספרתי בͦעͦ[ͦ]דת קדושי[כͦ]ה441 בהגדל והפלא לאͦל442[כיא את[ͦ]ה אל

33 הדעות ובͦפͦͦιͦ[עוז[מͦנͦשף ל[ͦ]ערב443 (VACAT)

Hymn 33
For the Instructor: A Psalm to God, Our King

34 למשכיל מזͦמ[ͦ]ור [ͦͦͦ כה

---

433 From 4Q428 frg. 19 line 4: [ונמארים]ͦם.
434 From 4Q428 frg. 19 line 5: רשעתם בחכמ[ͦ]ת [.
435 From 4Q428 frg. 19 line 6: [צ]דͦקכה לעווͦן[.
436 See 9.28; 12.33.
437 See 11.23.
438 4Q428 frg. 19 line 7: ובסו[ͦ]ד קדוש[ים.
439 4Q428 frg. 20 line 1: [ͦ]ם ירננו לזמר ולהלל לͦ[ן.
440 From 4Q428 frg. 20 line 2: [ͦ]אין הש[ͦ]בͦת ואני יצר החמר] כדעתי.
441 For קדושכה, see 25.5.
442 From 4Q428 frg. 20 line 3: [ספרתי בעדת קדושי]כͦה בהגדל והפלא לאͦל [כיא.
443 4Q428 frg. 20 line 4: [אתה אל הדעות וב]פͦי [עוז]מͦנͦשף ל[ͦ]ערב.

24 [...]*m* and those festering[1044] [...]

25 without their wickedness in the wisdom of[1045] [yo]ur [glory] and they will not recognize [...]

26 works of your [righ]teousness[1046] for iniquity.[1047] [And to enter together[1048] with the congregation of the sons of he]aven,[1049] but in the council of the Holy One[s][1050]

27 th[ey] will be pompous[1051] [...]*yb*°°°[...]

28 the council and °[...]

29 those who serve [...]*n*.

30 And they recognize them [...]*m* they will exhult, chant,[1052]

31 and praise with[out cea]sing. But I (am) a creature of[1053] clay [....] According to my knowledge,

32 I have announced in the assembly of your [Holy Ones:] "Great and wonderful (is) God."[1054] [For yo]u are the God of

33 knowledge.[1055] And with a [strong] voice[1056] from dawn[1057] to [dusk[1058] ....]

Hymn 33
For the Instructor: A Psalm to God, Our King

34 For the Instructor, a psa[lm of ...] your [...]

[1044] DJD: "malignant," which makes little sense in this context. At Qumran the *nip'al* pt. of מאר appears. In BH only the *hip'il* pt. is preserved. The translation is apposite in context: those who exhibit "wickedness" (line 25), exchange righteousness "for iniquity" (25), and are the "pompous" (27). The wicked priests polluting the Temple were "festering" like rotting flesh due to a cobra's bite. See 13.30.

[1045] From 4Q428 frg. 19 line 5.

[1046] From 4Q428 frg. 19 line 6.

[1047] See 9.28 and 12.33.

[1048] ביחד.

[1049] See 11.23 and 26.36.

[1050] From 4Q428 frg. 19 line 7.

[1051] The *hithpo'lel* impf. of רום means "to lift oneself up proudly." The author seems to be imagining the angels in heaven who acted with self-importance at the beginning of their refusal to obey fully God in the heavenly council. "Satan" (adversary in Hebrew) appears in Job as God's antagonist; in later texts he is a fallen angel who leads evil against good.

[1052] For the readings in the next three lines see 4Q428 frg. 20 lines 1–3.

[1053] Heb. יצר.

[1054] The Hebrew is unusual.

[1055] See 1QS 3.15: "the God of knowledge."

[1056] Or "at the command of a [strong] voice." Lit. "at the mouth of." The meaning is to a loud voice. See Ps 68:34, קול עז, "a strong voice."

[1057] נשף is extant only here in the *Thanksgiving Hymns*. It denotes both the twilight of the evening and the twilight before sunrise. I agree with DJD; hence, the day at Qumran began in the evening (with most scholars, esp. Baumgarten) and not at sunrise (as Talmon concluded). See esp. 1QS 9.26–10.10.

[1058] From 4Q428 frg. 20 line 4.

35 ⟦כֿיֿא⟧   מֿלֿכֿי קדם ⟦ ⟧

36 ⟦ ⟧   ⟦וֿחמתו⟧

37]   ⟦ורוממֿדֿעֿתֿיֿ⟧

38]

39]

40]

41]

42]

Excerpted from the *Self-Glorification Hymn*

Col. 26 [Frgs. 56 Col. 2, 46 Col. 2, 55 Col. 2, and 7 Col. 2]
Parallels: 4Q427 Frg. 7; 4Q428 Frg. 21; 4Q431 Frg. 2; 4Q471b Frgs. 1a–d

1   [אני עם אלים אתחשב ומכוני בעדת[444]

2   קֿודש מֿיֿא לבוז נחשב ביא ומיֿא[445] נֿבזה כמונֿי ומי[446]

3   כמוני חדל] אישים[447] ומי יסבול [רע ידמה בֿ[יֿ] והוריה לוא[448]

4   תדמה בהריתי כי אנֿיֿ יֿשֿבֿתיֿ[449] לבטח במעון קו[דש][450]

5   מֿי כמוני בֿאלים[451] וֿמזל שפתי מיא יכיל מיֿא[452] בלשון[453]

---

[444] From 4Q471b frgs. 1a–d line 1: [אני עם אלים א[תחשֿ]ב ומכוני בעדת]. Col. 26 begins in line 6.
[445] From 4Q491 frg. 11 1.15: [מע]וֿן הקודש מֿיֿא לבוז נחשב ביא ומיֿא בכבודי ידמה ליֿא מיא הֿואֿכֿבֿבֿאֿיֿ ים ישוב וסֿפֿר.
[446] From 4Q471b frgs. 1a–d line 2: [נֿבֿזה כמונֿיֿ ומי   קֿודש יֿ]   ומי.
[447] See Isa 53:3.
[448] From 4Q471b frgs. 1a–d line 3: [רע ידמה בֿ[יֿ] והוריה לוא] ומי יסבול כמוני חדל] אישים.
[449] From 4Q471b frgs. 1a–d line 4: תדמה בהריתי כֿ[י א]נֿיֿ יֿשֿבֿ[תי.
[450] From 1QHᵃ 20.5 and 4Q428 frg. 12b line 1: לבטח במֿ[עון קודש.
[451] From 4Q471b frgs. 1a–d line 5: [מֿי כמוני בֿאלים וֿ]מזל   יגודני בפתחי פי ומזל. Note the omission of: [ני בפת]ני יאדֿניא ומיא from the composite text of the *Self-Glorification Hymn*.
[452] From 4Q491 frg. 11 1.17: [וֿמזל שפתי מיֿא יכיל ומיא יועדני וידמה במשפתי ומיא יגֿ'דֿנֿיֿא בפת]חֿי פיא.
[453] From 4Q427 frg. 7 1.9: [מֿ[יֿ] בלשון יעידני.

35 For […]° kings of the east

36 […]°[…] and his wrath.

37 […] and he exalted my knowledge[1059]

38 […]

39 […]

40 […]

41 […]

42 […]

Excerpted from the *Self-Glorification Hymn*[1060]

Col. 26 [Frgs. 56 Col. 2, 46 Col. 2, 55 Col. 2, and 7 Col. 2]
Parallels: 4Q427 Frg. 7; 4Q428 Frg. 21; 4Q431 Frg. 2; 4Q471b Frgs. 1a–d

1 […] I, I reckon myself with the Elim;[1061] and my established-place (is) in the congregation of[1062]

2 holiness. Who was reckoned contemptible with me? And who has been despised like [me? And who][1063]

3 like me was rejected [(by) men?[1064] And who bears] evil compared with [me?] And no teaching[1065]

4 is comparable with my teaching. For I, I sat[1066] safely in the dwelling of holi[ness.][1067]

5 Who is like me among the Elim?[1068] And the flow of my speech,[1069] who can measure (it)? Who with language[1070]

[1059] The author chooses the *po'lel* of רום. Here he wants to praise God who exalts his knowledge. In this poetry almost all verbs carry a present meaning.

[1060] See the longer text and translation of the *Self-Glorification Hymn* in this volume.

[1061] Or "divine beings."

[1062] From 4Q471b frgs. 1a–d line 1.

[1063] From 4Q471b frgs. 1a–d line 2.

[1064] See Isa 53:3.

[1065] From 4Q471b frgs. 1a–d line 3.

[1066] From 4Q471b frgs. 1a–d line 4.

[1067] From 1QHª 20.5 and 4Q428 frg. 12b line 1.

[1068] From 4Q471 frgs. 1a–d line 5.

[1069] Lit. "lips."

[1070] Lit. "tongue." From 4Q427 frg. 7 1.9.

6 יעדני[454] וידמה במשפטי[455] [כ]י אני ידיד המלך רע[456] לקדשים ולוא[457]

7 יבוא[458] בי [ולכבו]ד̇י לוא ידמיה כ̇י̇א אני עם אלים מעמד̇[י][459]

א

8 וכבודי עם בני המלך̇ לא בפז אכתי[ר] לי וכתם או ביורים לוא[461]

9 ב̇י וה̊[462]   י[ת̇חשב בי זמרו ידידים[463] שירו למלך [הכבוד][464]

10 ש̊מ̊ח[ו בע[ד̇ת אל הרנינו באה̊ל̊י ישועה הללו במעון [קודש][465]

11 רוממו יחד בצבא ע̊ולם הבו גדול לאלנו וכבוד למלכנ̊ו̊[466] ה̊[קדי]ש̊ו

12 שמו[467] בשפתי עוז ולשון נצח הרימו לבד קולכמה[468] [בכ]ול קצים

13 ה̊ש̊מ̊יעו הגי רנה הביעו בשמחות עולמים ואין[469] [ה]ש̊בת השתח̊ו̊ו̊

14 ב̊י̊ח̊ד̊[470] קהל ברכו המפלי גאות ומודיע עוז ידו [ל]ח̊תום[471]

15 רזים ולגלות נסתרות להרים כושלים ונופליהמה [לש]ב לכת קוי דעות[472]

[454] See 1QH^a 26.6: יעדני; 4Q427 frg. 7 1.9: יעידני.

[455] Cf. 1QH^a 24.8.

[456] From 4Q471b frgs. 1a–d line 7: ידיד המלך רע לק[דושים.

[457] From 4Q427 frg. 7 1.10: המ[לך רע לקדשים ולוא יבא.

[458] 1QH^a 26.7: יבוא.

[459] From 4Q427 frg. 7 1.11: לוא ידמה כ̇י א̇[ני; ולכבו]ד̇י לוא ידמה כ̇[י]א̇ אני עם אלים מעמד̇[י]; and 4Q471b frgs. 1a–d line 8: נ̇י.

[460] See 4Q491 frg. 11 1.18: [כ]י̇א אניא עם אלים אח̊ש̊ב̇ ו]כ̇ב̇ודי̊ עם בני המלך לוא [פ]ז̇ ולוא כתם אופירים.

[461] From 4Q427 frg. 7 1.12: ר̇ לא בפז אכתי[ר] לי וכתם או ביורים לוא; see 4Q471b frgs. 1a–d line 9: בפז /א\כת̇יר.

[462] 4Q427 frg. 7 1.12: ביורים.

[463] 4Q471b frgs. 1a–d line 10: זמרו] ידידים.

[464] From 4Q427 frg. 7 1.13–14: [עם בני עו]ל̇ה [י]ת̇חשב בי זמר ידידים̇ שירו למלך [הכבוד שמחו בע]ד̇ת אל הרנינו באה̊ל̊י ישועה הללו במעון.

[465] From 4Q427 frg. 7 1.14: [הכבוד שמחו בע]ד̇ת אל הרנינו באה̊ל̊י ישועה הללו במעון.

[466] From 4Q427 frg. 7 1.15: [קודש ר]ו̇ממו יחד בצבא ע̇ולם הבו גדול לאלנו וכבוד למלכנ̊ו̊.

[467] 1QH^a 26.12:]°; Ctr. DJD: ש̊מו.

[468] 4Q427 frg. 7 1.16: [הקדי]ש̊ו שמו בשפתי עוז ולשון נצה הרימו לבד קולכמה.

[469] 4Q427 frg. 7 1.17: [בכ]ול קצים ה̊ש̊מ̊יעו הגידנה הביעו בשמחות עולמים ואין.

[470] A scribe wrote כוחא, erased the ʾaleph, but did not correct the kaph to a beth and replace the ʾaleph with a daleth. Read ביחד and see 4Q427 frg. 7 1.18: [ה]ש̊בת השתח̊ו̊ו̊ ב̊י̊ח̊ד̊ קהל ברכו המפלי גאות ומודיע עוז ידו.

[471] From 4Q427 frg. 7 1.18–19: [ה]ש̊בת השתח̊ו̊ו̊ ב̊י̊ח̊ד̊ קהל ברכו המפלי גאות ומודיע עוז ידו [ל]ח̊תום רזים ולגלות נסתרות להרים כושלים ונופליהם.

[472] From 4Q427 frg. 7 1.19–20: רזים ולגלות נסתרות להרים כושלים ונופליהמה [לש]ב לכת קוי דעות.

6   can appoint me[1071] and can be compared with my ruling?[1072] [F]or I (am) the beloved of the King, a companion of the Holy Ones. And no one

7   can go[1073] [with me. And to my glo]ry no one can be compared; for I (am) with the Elim.[1074] [My] rank

8   and my glory[1075] (are) with the sons of the King.[1076] Not with (pure) gold will I cro[wn] myself, and (neither with) gold nor with precious stones. Not[1077]

9   with me and *h*°[...[1078] shall] he reckon me. Chant, O beloved ones, sing to the King of [glory,][1079]

10   be joyf[ul[1080] in the cong]regation of God, exult in the tents of salvation,[1081] give praise in the habitation of [holiness,][1082]

11   extol[1083] together with the eternal hosts, give greatness to our God, and glory to our King.[1084] D[eclare h]oly

12   his name with strong lips and (with) a perpetual tongue, raise up alone your voice [at a]ll endtimes,[1085]

13   cause to be he[ard][1086] meditations of exultation, express with everlasting joy without [ce]asing, cause to bow down[1087]

14   in the common[1088] assembly. Bless the one who does majestic wonders, and causes to make known his strong hand [to] seal[1089]

15   mysteries, and to reveal hidden things,[1090] to raise up those who stumble and those who fell, [to res]tore walking (to) those who await knowledge[1091]

[1071] Partly preserved at the beginning of col. 26 line 6.
[1072] Or "judgment," "decision." Heb. משפט.
[1073] From 1QHᵃ col. 26.
[1074] From 4Q427 frg. 7 1.11.
[1075] From 1QHᵃ col. 26.
[1076] See 4Q491 frg. 11 1.18.
[1077] From 4Q427 frg. 7 1.12.
[1078] From 1QHᵃ col. 26.
[1079] From 4Q427 frg. 7 1.13–14.
[1080] From 1QHᵃ col. 26.
[1081] The lexemes appear in Ps 118:15: רנה וישועה באהלי.
[1082] From 4Q427 frg. 7 1.14–15.
[1083] From 1QHᵃ col. 26.
[1084] From 4Q427 frg. 7 1.15.
[1085] From 4Q427 frg. 7 1.16–17.
[1086] From 1QHᵃ col. 26.
[1087] From 4Q427 frg. 7 1.17–18.
[1088] Heb. יחד. From 1QHᵃ col. 26.
[1089] From 4Q427 frg. 7 1.18–19.
[1090] From 1QHᵃ col. 26.
[1091] From 4Q427 frg. 7 1.19–20.

16 ולהשפיל נועדת רום גאים עולם [להת]ם̊ רזי ה[ו]ד [ו]להק̊[ים פל]א̊ו̊ת כבוד[473]

17 השופט באף כלה[474] [ל]ל̇[ ] [בחסד צדקה וברוב

18 רחמים תח̊נה[475] [ ] [רחמים למפרי טוב̇ גודלו

19 ומקור[476]

20 ותמה רש̇ע̊ה[477] [ ]

21 ו[א̊ין עוד[478] [מ]ד̊הבה שבת נוגש[479]

22 בזע̊ם̊[480] [ ] כלת]ה̊ ר̊מ̊י̊ה̊ ו̊א̊י̊ן̊ נעוות בלוא דעת[481]

23 הופיע אור ושמחה תב̇י̊ע̊ [אבד][482] אבל[ ] ונס יגון הופיע שלום[483]

24 שבת פחד נפתח מקור לברכת עד[484] ומרפא בכול קצי עולם כלה[485]

25 עוון שבת נגע לאין מחלה נאספ̊[ה[486] עולה ואשמ[ה̊ לו̊א̊ [ת]היה[487]

26 עוד השמיעו אמרו גדול אל עושה[ה[488] [פלא] כיא השפיל גבהות[489]

27 רוח לאין שרית[490] וירם[491] מעפר אביון ל[רום עולם][492] ועד שחקים[493]

[473] From 4Q427 frg. 7 1.20–21: ולהשפיל נועדות רום גאים עולם [להת]ם̊ רזי ה[ו]ד [ו]להק̊[ים פל]א̊ו̊ת כבוד.

[474] From 4Q427 frg. 7 1.21: השופט באף כלה.

[475] From 4Q427 frg. 7 1.22: בחסד צדקה וברוב רחמים תח̊נה [.

[476] From 4Q427 frg. 7 1.23: רחמים למפרי טוב̇ גודלו ומקור [.

[477] From 4Q431 frg. 2 line 1:] ותמה רשעה [.

[478] From 1QH[a] 20.21: א̊ין עוד[.

[479] From 4Q431 frg. 2 line 2: מדה[בה שבת נוגש.

[480] From 4Q431 frg. 2 line 2: בזע̊ם̊.

[481] From 4Q427 frg. 7 2.4: כלת]ה̊ ר̊מ̊י̊ה̊ ו̊א̊י̊ן̊ נעוות בלוא דעת [.

[482] From 4Q431 frg. 2 line 3: הופיע אור ושמחה תב̇י̊ע̊ [אבד] א̊ב̊ל̊ [.

[483] From 4Q427 frg. 7 2.5: אבל ונס יגון הופיע שלום.

[484] From 4Q431 frg. 2 line 4: שבת פחד נפתח מקור לברכת עד.

[485] From 4Q427 frg. 7 2.6: ומרפא בכול קצי עולם כלה.

[486] From 4Q431 frg. 2 line 5: עוון שבת נגע לאין מחלה נאספ̊[ה.

[487] From 4Q431 frg. 2 line 6: ת]היה.

[488] The first three words are from 1QH[a] 26; the rest is from 4Q431 line 6 and 4Q427 frg. 7 2.7.

[489] From 4Q427 frg. 7 2.7–8: פלא] כיא השפיל גבהות. See 4Q431 lines 6–7.

[490] See 14.11: ושארית.

[491] From 1QH[a] 26.27 and from 4Q427 frg. 7 2.8. See also 4Q431 line 7.

[492] From 4Q427 frg. 7 2.8: מעפר אביון ל[רום עולם.

[493] From 4Q427 frg. 7 2.9: ועד שחקים.

16   and to bring down the pompous gatherings of the perpetually[1092] proud ones,[1093] [to comple]te the mysteries of spl[endor] and to establi[sh ma]rvels of glory.[1094]

17   The one who judges with destructive wrath[1095] […]l/[…] with loving-kindness, righteousness, and with abundant[1096]

18   mercies, beseeching[1097] […] mercies for those who violate his great goodness,

19   and a source of[1098] […]

20   […] and wickedness is annihilated,[1099]

21   [… and] there is no more [di]saster,[1100] the oppressor ceased

22   with fury.[1101] […] treachery [ende]d; and there are no perversions without knowledge.[1102]

23   Light shines forth, and joy pours forth.[1103] Mourning and the standard of grief [perished.] Peace shines forth,[1104]

24   fear ceased. A source was opened for eternal blessing, and healing for all everlasting times. Iniquity

25   ended, affliction ceased, so there is no sickness. [Injustice] was taken aw[ay,[1105] and gui]lt [will] be no

26   more.[1106] Cause to be heard and say: "Great (is) God who acts [wonderfully,] because he brought low the pompous

27   spirit, so there is no remnant."[1107] And he raised up the Poor One from the dust to [eternal height] and unto the skies

---

[1092] Lit. "eternally," but the proud ones are to be destroyed.
[1093] From 1QHᵃ col. 26 (except "perpetually").
[1094] From 4Q427 frg. 7 1.20–21.
[1095] From 4Q427 frg. 7 1.21.
[1096] From 4Q427 frg. 7 1.22.
[1097] From 4Q427 frg. 7 1.22.
[1098] From 4Q427 frg. 7. 1.23.
[1099] From 4Q431 frg. 2 line 1.
[1100] From 1QHᵃ 20.21.
[1101] From 4Q431 frg. 2 line 2.
[1102] From 4Q427 frg. 7 2.4.
[1103] From 4Q427 frg. 7 2.4.
[1104] From 4Q427 frg. 7. 2.4–5.
[1105] From 4Q431 frg. 2 lines 4–5.
[1106] From 4Q431 frg. 2 line 6.
[1107] From 1QHᵃ col. 26. See also 4Q427 frg. 7 2.7–8.

28 יגביה בקומה ועם[494] אלים בעדת יחד ורפֹ[   ]אﬞפ[לכלת[495]

29 עולם וכושלי ארץ ירים לאין מחיֿר וגב[ורת עד עם[496] מצﬞעדם

30 ושמחת עולם במכוניהֹﬞם[497] כבוד נצח ואין השבת[לעולמי עד][498]

31 [ו]יומרו ברוכ אל הֹ[מפ]לֹיﬞ [פ]לֹאﬞוﬞתﬞ גﬞאﬞות ומגדיל[499]

32 להודיע גבורﬞה ומצﬞדﬞיֿ[ק][500] בדעﬞתﬞ לכול מעשיו וטֹוֿבﬞ על פניהמה[501]

33 בדעתם ברוב חסדיﬞוﬞﬞ[502][והמון] רחמיו לכול בני אמתו ידענוכה[503]

34 אל הצדק והשכלנֹוﬞﬞ בֹאﬞ[מתכה[504] מלך] הכבוד כיא ראינו קנאתכה[505]

35 בכוח גבורה והכרנו[506] מﬞ[שפטיכה בהמון] רחמיכֹהﬞם והפלא סליחות[507]

36 מה בשר לאלה[508] ומה יחשﬞ[ב עפר ואפר] לספר אלה מקץ לקצﬞ[509]

[494] From 1QHᵃ 26.28.
[495] From 4Q427 frg. 7 2.9–10: אלים בעדת יחד ורפﬞ[   ] אﬞפ[לכלת.
[496] From 4Q427 frg. 7 2.10: אﬞלֹ לכלת עולם וכושלי ארץ ירים לאין מחיֿר וגב[ורת עד עם.
[497] From 1QHᵃ 26.30.
[498] From 4Q427 frg. 7 2.11: כבוד נצח ואין השבת].
[499] From 4Q427 frg. 7 2.12. Scribal errors are apparent, causing the loss of this line. See DJD 40 p. 306.
[500] From 1QHᵃ 26.31 and from 4Q427 frg. 7 2.12: להופיע גבורﬞהﬞ[ומצדיק].
[501] From 1QHᵃ 26.31 and from 4Q427 frg. 7 2.13: בדעﬞתﬞ לכול מעשיו וטֹוﬞבﬞ על פניהמה.
[502] From 1QHᵃ 26.32.
[503] From 4Q427 frg. 7 2.13–14: והמון] רחמיו לכול בני אמתו ידענוכה.
[504] From 1QHᵃ 26.33 and 4Q427 frg. 7 2.14: אל הצדק והשכלנֹוﬞﬞ באמתכה.
[505] From 4Q427 frg. 7 2.15: הﬞכבוד כיא ראינו קנאתכה].
[506] From 1QHᵃ 26.34 and from 4Q427 frg. 7 2.15: בכוח גבורתכה והכרנו.
[507] From 4Q427 frg. 7 2.15–16: מﬞ[שפטיכה בהמון] רחמיכֹהﬞם והפלא סליחות.
[508] From 1QHᵃ 26.35.
[509] From 4Q427 frg. 7 2.16–17: וﬞמﬞה יחשﬞ[בפר ואפר] לספר אלה מקץ לקצ.

28 he will elevate (him)[1108] on high,[1109] and with[1110] the Elim[1111] and in the congregation of the Community.[1112] And *rp*˚[...] even to eternal

29 annihilation.[1113] And those who stumble earthward, he shall raise up[1114] without cost, and [everlasting] mi[ght (is) with] their treads.[1115]

30 And eternal joy (is) in their establishments,[1116] everlasting glory without ceasing [forever and ever.][1117]

31 [And] they will say: "Blessed (is) God who [wonderfu]lly does majestic [wo]nders, and acts greatly[1118]

32 to make known (his) might, and acts righteou[sly][1119] with knowledge toward all his creatures and (with) goodness upon their faces,[1120]

33 with their knowledge[1121] in the multitude of his loving-kindnesses[1122] [and the abundance of] his mercies to all sons of his truth. We have known you,[1123]

34 O God of righteousness, and we were allowed to have insight[1124] into [your] tr[uth,[1125] O King of] glory, because we have seen your zeal[1126]

35 with your mighty power, and we recognized[1127] [your] ju[dgments with the abundance of] your mercies and wondrous forgivenesses."[1128]

36 What (is) flesh (compared) to these (things)?[1129] And what shall dust and ashes[1130] devis[e] to recount these (things) from endtime to endtime;[1131]

[1108] Note that 4Q427 frg. 7 2.9 has "him."
[1109] From 4Q427 frg. 7 2.8–9. See also 4Q431 lines 7–8.
[1110] The opening of this line is found in 1QHᵃ col. 26.
[1111] Or "divine beings."
[1112] Heb. יחד. In light of the claims in the *Self-Glorification Hymn*, it is evident that some at Qumran would have imagined this passage meant the elevation of the Righteous Teacher. See 4Q471b, "Self-Glorification Hymn," frgs. 1a–d lines 1–2: "[I, I] reck[on myself with the Elim; and my established-place (is) in the congregation of] holiness ˚[..."
[1113] From 1QHᵃ col. 26 and from 4Q427 frg. 7 2.9–10. See also 4Q431 frg. 2 lines 8–9. The adjective "eternal" (עולם) is the first word of line 29.
[1114] From 1QHᵃ col. 26.
[1115] From 4Q427 frg. 7 2.10–11. See also 4Q431 frg. 2 line 9.
[1116] From 1QHᵃ col. 26.
[1117] From 4Q427 frg. 7 2.11.
[1118] From 4Q427 frg. 7 2.12. The line was omitted in 1QHᵃ due to a copyist error.
[1119] From 1QHᵃ col. 26.
[1120] From 4Q427 frg. 7 2.13.
[1121] See 4Q427 frg. 7 2.13: "so they will know the multitude of [his] loving-kind[ness ...."
[1122] From 1QHᵃ col. 26.
[1123] From 4Q427 frg. 7 2.13–14.
[1124] *Hipʿil* permissive.
[1125] From 1QHᵃ col. 26.
[1126] From 4Q427 frg. 7 2.14–15.
[1127] From 1QHᵃ col. 26 and from 4Q427 frg. 7 2.15.
[1128] From 4Q427 frg. 7 2.15–16.
[1129] From 1QHᵃ col. 26.
[1130] The noun is singular in Hebrew.
[1131] From 4Q427 frg. 7 2.16–17.

37 ולהתיצב בֹמעמֹדֹ[510] [לפניכה ולבוא ביחד עם] בני שמים ואין מליצ[511]

38 להשיב דבר כֹפֹיֹכֹה וֹ[512] [לכה כיא העמדתנו[513]

39 לרֹצֹ[ונכ]הֹ[514] בֹ[עדת יחד ומי בכול מעשי פלאכה הגדולים יעצור[515]

40 כוח להֹשֹיֹבֹ לֹכֹה[516] שמע נפלאותיֹכֹה כֹ[אלה[517]   [דברנו לכה ולוֹֹאֹ[518]

41 לאיש בֹֹ[י]נים   ופתחתה] אוֹֹזֹ[ן] למוצא שפתינו[519]

42 השמיעו אמורו[520] [ברוך אל הדעות הנוטה][521]

43 שמים בכוחו וכול מחשביהמה מֹ[כין ב]עֹֹוֹֹזֹֹוֹ ארץ בגבור[תו בורא][522]

Col. 27 [Frgs. 62 and 61]

] 1

] 2

] 3

] 4

] 5

---

[510] From 1QHᵃ 26.36 and from 4Q427 frg. 7 2.17:]ולהתיצב במעמֹדֹ.

[511] From 4Q427 frg. 7 2.18: בני שמים ואין מליצ.

[512] From 1QHᵃ 26.37:]להשיב דבר כֹפֹיֹכֹה וֹ; and from 4Q427 frg. 7 2.18:]להשיבֹ.

[513] From 4Q427 frg. 7 2.19: לכה כיא העמדתנו.

[514] From 1QHᵃ 26.38, which ends here. 4Q427 frg. 7 2.19 also has the same lacuna:]לרצ. One of the scribes probably copied from a manuscript that was defective. It is difficult to determine which was earlier.

[515] From 1QHᵃ 18.12–13.

[516] From 4Q427 frg. 7 2.20: כוח להֹשֹיֹבֹ לֹכֹה.

[517] Reading the supralinear correction in 4Q427 frg. 7 2.20 and the restoration in line 20.

[518] From 4Q427 frg. 7 2.21: דברנו לכה ולוֹאֹ לאיש בֹֹ[י]נים.

[519] From 4Q427 frg. 7 2.22: אוֹֹזֹ[ן] למוצא שפתינו.

[520] See 4Q431 line 6.

[521] From 4Q427 frg. 7 2.22. See also, 1QHᵃ 9.11, 28.

[522] From 4Q427 frg. 7 2.23.

37   and to present in rank[1132] [before you and to come together with] the sons of heaven? And there is no interpreter[1133]

38   to cause to return a word according to your edict[1134] and[1135] [...] to you, because you established us[1136]

39   for [yo]ur wi[ll] in[1137] [the congregation of the Community.[1138] And who among all your great wonderful creatures can summon][1139]

40   power to answer you[1140] (while) hearing (about) your marvelous acts[1141] like [these?][1142] We spoke to you and not[1143]

41   to an intermed[iary[1144] .... And you opened] an ea[r] to the utterance of our lips.[1145]

42   Cause to be heard and say:[1146] "[Blessed (be) the God of knowledge who stretches out][1147]

43   (the) heavens by his power, and all their thoughts [he] es[tablished by] his strength, [creating][1148] the earth by [his] migh[t]."[1149]

Col. 27 [Frgs. 62 and 61]

1   [...]

2   [...]

3   [...]

4   [...]

5   [...]

[1132] From 1QHᵃ col. 26 and from 4Q427 frg. 7 2.17.
[1133] From 4Q427 frg. 7 2.17–18.
[1134] Lit. "mouth."
[1135] From 1QHᵃ col. 26 and from 4Q427 frg. 7 2.18.
[1136] From 4Q427 frg. 7 2.19.
[1137] From 1QHᵃ col. 26. See 4Q427 frg. 7 2.19.
[1138] Heb. יחד. See 26.28.
[1139] See 18.14.
[1140] From 4Q427 frg. 7 2.20.
[1141] Not "creatures." Note the paronomasia: "wonderful" creatures celebrate "marvelous" (or wonderful) acts. Both words are from פלא.
[1142] Reading the supralinear correction in 4Q427 frg. 7 2.20 and the restoration in line 20.
[1143] From 4Q427 frg. 7 2.21.
[1144] Varieties of thought enrich this collection of hymns and poems. In 10.15 the speaker, the Righteous Teacher, praises God for making him "the Interpreter" (מליץ). Ctr. line 36. See also 23.12.
[1145] From 4Q427 frg. 7 2.22.
[1146] From 4Q431 line 6. See 4Q427 frg. 7 2.22.
[1147] From 4Q427 frg. 7 2.22.
[1148] See 9.15.
[1149] From 4Q427 frg. 7 2.23.

] **6**

] **7**

] **8**

] **9**

] **10**

] **11**

12 [שׂ֯מֹ֯]]]ל֯]

13 רציׄ][תה בׄ֯]

14 בל][]ו֯א יׄד]עתה

Col. 28 [Frg. 48]

] **1**

] **2**

] **3**

] **4**

] **5**

] **6**

] **7**

] **8**

] **9**

] **10**

11 ע]פֹ֯ר כמוני בֹ֯]

12]כֹבודכֹה ל]אור עולם[523]

---

[523] For the restoration, see 20.18.

6 […]

7 […]

8 […]

9 […]

10 […]

11 […]

12 […]*šm l*[…]

13 you were pleased *b*°[…]

14 without [.… You] kne[w…]

Col. 28 [Frg. 48]

1 […]

2 […]

3 […]

4 […]

5 […]

6 […]

7 […]

8 […]

9 […]

10 […]

11 [… d]ust like me *b*[…]

12 […] your glory for [eternal light …][1150]

[1150] For the restoration, see 20.18 and contiguous lines, which have similar expressions, notably "name," "light," "praise," "Holy Spirit," and "mighty."

שֿ
פֿ
13 ולהלל [מכה בהלא ואיֿן]

14 ברוח ק[וֿדש על ידי גבורתֿ]כה

15 [בֿפֿיֿן] [לֿן]

Unplaced Fragments [Probably by Scribe A]

Frg. 39 (= A1)

1 [א]

2 [רֿוחֿ לֿמֿשפטכהֿ]

3 [וֿ]

Frg. 40 (= A2)

1 בסוד אמת[גֿ524 אתֿחננ]

2 [מענהֿ [לשון

3 [לֿ לֿ]

Frg. 28 (= A3)

1 [°° °°°°°

2 [°נהיה בתבל

3 [°° לאֿנֿשי בֿרֿיֿתֿך

Frg. 35 (= A4)

1 [עֿוון וֿאֿשֿ]מה

___

524 See 6.32; 18.6; 19.7, 12; cf. 19.19.

13   [… and to praise] your name in doing wonders and without […]

14   [… by the H]oly [Spirit] upon[1151] [your] mighty hands […]

15   […] in the mouth of[1152] […]*l*[…]

Unplaced Fragments [Probably by Scribe A]

Frg. 39 (= A1)

1   […]ʾ[…]

2   […] a spirit for your judgment […]

3   […]*w*[…]

Frg. 40 (= A2)

1   [… in the secret of] your [truth.][1153] I petition […]

2   […] the answer of [the tongue …]

3   […]*l̊l* ˚[…]

Frg. 28 (= A3)

1   […]˚˚˚˚ ˚˚˚

2   […]˚ it will be[1154] in the world

3   […]˚˚ for the men of your covenant

Frg. 35 (= A4)

1   […] iniquity and gui[lt …]

[1151] Or "according to."
[1152] Or "at the edict (or command) of."
[1153] See 6.32; 18.6; 19.7, 12; cf. 19.19.
[1154] Or "it will occur."

2   א̊ כי אין פ̊]ה

3   ̊°°[ותודי]עני

Frg. 37 (= A5)

1   קד]ושיכה ובפק[ודת

2   ל̊] [כה בני א̊]דם

Frg. 38 (= A6)

1   קֿד̊ושׁי̊ם̊]

2   יברכו שמכֿה̊ בֿ]פה[525]

Frg. 36 (= A7)

1   בֿי̊נ̊ה בֿל̊]ב

2   °°[בנך ולספר °°]

Frg. 27 (= A8)

1   ו̊עֿד °°[ ]

2   כ]ו̊ל אלה תֿר̊אה]

3   °°[ואֿד̊עֿה̊ כי בש]כלכה

4   ל̊ °ל̊ן] [ל̊ן]

---

[525] See 9.32–33.

2 [...]ᵓ for there is no ed[ict¹¹⁵⁵ ...]

3 [...]°°° and you allowe[d me] to kn[ow¹¹⁵⁶ ...]

Frg. 37 (= A5)

1 [...] your [Hol]y Ones and in the visit[ation of ...]

2 [...]*l*[...]*kh* the sons of A[dam ...]

Frg. 38 (= A6)

1 [...] the Holy Ones [...]

2 [...] they will bless your name in [the mouth of ...]¹¹⁵⁷

Frg. 36 (= A7)

1 [...] discernment in the hea[rt of ...]

2 [...]°° *bnk* and to recount °°[...]

Frg. 27 (= A8)

1 [...] and ever¹¹⁵⁸ °°[...]

2 [...a]ll these (things) you will allow to see¹¹⁵⁹ [...]

3 [...]°°. And I know that in [your] in[sight ...]

4 [...]*l*° °*l*[...]*l*[...]

---

¹¹⁵⁵ Lit. "no mo[uth ...].
¹¹⁵⁶ *Hipʿil* permissive.
¹¹⁵⁷ See 9.32–33.
¹¹⁵⁸ Or "until," "unto."
¹¹⁵⁹ *Hipʿil* permissive.

Unplaced Fragments [Probably by Scribe C]

Frg. 49 (= C1)

]°[	**1**
גד]ול רחמי[ךה	**2**
הו]דעתה א[לה	**3**
ת]עֹות מרֹמֹ[ה	**4**
]° מענֹהֹ[	**5**

Frg. 53 (= C2)

בֹשלֹ]וה[526	**1**
יא]ירו כשמֹשֹ[	**2**
במ]עֹוֹן הקודֹ[ש527	**3**

Frg. 58 (= C3)

אביֹ]ן[	**1**
ו]להביֹ]ן[	**2**
עֹולֹהֹ ת]ן[	**3**
]הֹ ולהביֹ]ן[	**4**
עֹ]וד קץ משפטכהֹ[	**5**
לרוות בשֹלֹוֹ]ה[	**6**

---

526 See frg. 58 line 6 and 20.5.
527 See 20.5.

Unplaced fragments [*Perhaps by Scribe C*]

Frg. 49 (= C1)

1   […]°°[…]

2   […gr]eat. [Your] mercies […]

3   […] you [allowed to] know[1160] t[hese (things) …]

4   [… e]rror, dece[it …]

5   […]° answer […]

Frg. 53 (= C2)

1   […] in tranqui[lity[1161]…]

2   [… th]ey [shall s]hine like the sun […]

3   [… in] the hol[y dw]elling […]

Frg. 58 (= C3)

1   […] I will discer[n[1162] …]

2   [… and] to discer[n …]

3   […] iniquity *t*[…]

4   […]°*h* and to disce[rn …]

5   […un]til the Endtime of your judgment […]

6   […] to water thoroughly[1163] in tranquili[ty[1164] …]

[1160] *Hipᶜil* permissive.
[1161] See 20.5 and frg. 58 line 6.
[1162] Heb.]יֹבא[. Not "my father" as in 17.29 and 17.35.
[1163] Most likely not "to saturate" since too much watering kills vegetation.
[1164] Or with a different restoration: "in peac[e …]." But see 20.5 and frg. 53 line 1.

Frg. 59 (= *C4*)

1   לֹהב]וּן בֹּתֹשֹֹוֹבֹתֹ[

2   מע]מֹֹדֹי בֹֹלֹוֹא תוֹ[ן

3   עֹֹד קץ תשוֹבֹ]ה

4   רֹבֹים למֹתֹ[

5   וֹלֹֹקֹצֹ[

Frg. 66 (= *C5*)

1   ]°°°[

2   עֹ ומֹ]

3   שֹֹלֹבֹתֹ]ה

4   [°°°מ°°°]

5   [°°°עֹֹמֹ]

Frg. 65 (= *C6*)

1   ]°°°°°[

2   כֹֹיֹֹא מאו]ר

3   וֹלטהר פשֹֹעֹ]יהם

4   ברצונכֹֹה]

Frg. 64 (= *C7*)

1   [°°°עֹֹ כֹֹ°°°]

2   תֹ]פֹֹתח לֹוחות °[

Frg. 59 (= C4)

1   [… to disce]rn the return of […]

2   […] my [stan]ding[1165] without *tw*[…]

3   […] until the Endtime of returni[ng …]

4   […] the many[1166] *lmt*[…]

5   […] and to the Endtime […]

Frg. 66 (= C5)

1   […]°°°[…]

2   […]ʿ and *m*[…]

3   [… its] flame[1167]

4   […] °° *m* °°[…]

5   […] °° *m*ᶜ[…]

Frg. 65 (= C6)

1   […]°°°°°[…]

2   because ligh[t …]

3   and to purify [their] transgression[s …]

4   in your will[1168] […]

Frg. 64 (= C7)

1   […] °° *k*ᶜ °°°[…]

2   [… you op]ened the tablets of °[…]

[1165] Or "my rank."
[1166] Or perhaps, "the Many," a *terminus technicus* at Qumran.
[1167] See 16.31.
[1168] Or "favor."

3   בעֹו]לם ̊[

Frg. 41 (= C8)

1   ]̊ ̊[

2   ] (VACAT) [

Hymn 35
I Thank the Lord Who Revealed

3   אודכה אדוני כיא] אֿתה גלֹי]תה

4   ]̊ ̊[

3   […]° in etern[ity …]

Frg. 41 (= C8)

1   […]° °[…]

2   […] (VACAT) […]

Hymn 35
I Thank the Lord Who Revealed

3   [I thank you, O Lord, because]¹¹⁶⁹ you, [you] revealed […]

4   […]°°[…]

---

¹¹⁶⁹ The "*Hodayot* formula" was most likely in the lost pieces of leather; note the preceding *vacat*.

Self-Glorification Hymn
4Q427 (4QH^a) Frg. 7 1.6–13, 4Q491 Frg. 11 1.13–19, 1QH^a 26.6–9, 4Q471b Frgs. 1a–d Lines 1–10

JAMES H. CHARLESWORTH with LEA BERKUZ[1]

Introduction

1. Texts and Relationships Between Manuscript Fragments

The primary source for reconstructing the *Self-Glorification Hymn* is 4Q471b. The manuscript is unlined and in a late Herodian script with characteristic *ʾaleph, daleth, he, mem,* and *reš.*

4Q471b and 4Q431 (4QH^e) apparently belong to the same manuscript, since the handwriting and skin are identical. The arrangement of this manuscript seems to be in the following order: a handle, 4Q471b, and then 4Q431. Most likely, two hymns (4Q471b and 4Q431) eventually evolved individually and then together, becoming sections of one manuscript.[2] It is now in fragments.[3]

Each version of the *Self-Glorification Hymn* is presented separately for perception and discussion, as is the method in this series. All versions are then constructed as a composite text. The *Thanksgiving Hymns* most likely absorbed, *inter alia,* some earlier hymns and perhaps a portion of an earlier collection of hymns; among them appears to be more than one copy of the *Self-Glorification Hymn.* This insight is suggested by the texts of 4Q427 and 1QH^a 26.6–9.[4]

The *Self-Glorification Hymn* can be understood only through a composite text that is based on 4Q471b. The composite text and translation evolves from four sources. They may be arranged in the following chronological order according to paleographical dates:

> 4Q427 frg. 7.1.6–13 (4QH^a) [late Hasmonean script]
> 4Q491 frg. 11 1.13–19 (4QM1) [early Herodian script][5]
> 1QH^a 26.6–9 [Herodian script][6]
> 4Q471b Frgs. 1a–d lines 1–10 (*olim* 4QM^g) [late Herodian script]

Each of these sources is presented with text and translation after this introduction. 1QH^a 26.6–9 is unfortunately fragmentary. Only four words begin from the right margin which is preserved. Obviously, one cannot discern to what extent 1QH^a 26 preserves this text. The *Self-Glorification Hymn* seems to be known to more than one person who composed hymns within the collection known as the *Thanksgiving Hymns* (*Hodayot*).

There are different forms or editions of the *Self-Glorification Hymn.* E. Eshel discerns two recensions. Recension A is represented by 4Q427 (4QH^a), 4Q471b, and 1QH^a. Recension B is

---

[1] Charlesworth provided the introduction; Berkuz assisted with the texts and translations. I am indebted to Blake A. Jurgens for his improvements on the final draft.

[2] In contrast to previous editors, É. Puech assumed that the *Self-Glorification Hymn* can be created by combining the following:1QH^a 25.34–27.3 (?), 4Q227 [an error for 4Q427], 4Q431, and 4Q428 [a section of the *Hodayot* but not part of the SGH]. See Puech, "L'Hymne de la Glorification du Maître de 4Q431," in *Prayer and Poetry in the Dead Sea Scrolls and Related Literature: Essays in Honor of Eileen Schuller,* edited by J. Penner, *et al.* (Leiden and Boston, 2012) pp. 377–407.

[3] See the discussion in DJD 29, p. 202 (Schuller) and p. 421 (Eshel). Schuller claims that the texts in 4Q471b and 4Q431 "are from a single psalm" (p. 202). Eshel judges that these are "two hymns." Also see Eshel, "The Identification of the 'Speaker' of the Self-Glorification Hymn," in *The Provo International Conference on the Dead Sea Scrolls,* edited by D. W. Parry and E. Ulrich (STDJ 30; Leiden, Boston, 1999) pp. 619–35. They are similar, at times, in thought, but are not the same psalm. The arrangement on "Foldout Plate III" placed in the slip at the back of DJD 29 is misleading. There is an indiscernible distance from 4Q471b (it is not 4Q431) and 4Q431; clearly more than one hymn can be imagined on these disjointed pieces of leather. The best procedure seems to be to present each hymn separately.

[4] See the discussions of the *Self-Glorification Hymn* in the "Introduction" to the *Thanksgiving Hymns.* Themes in the *Self-Glorification Hymn* reverberate through the texts of some Qumran Scrolls, especially the *Thanksgiving Hymns* (Hodayot).

[5] See J. Duhaime in PTSDSSP vol. 2, pp. 152–53.

[6] In contrast to Eshel in DJD 29, p. 428, we do not find evidence of the *Self-Glorification Hymn* in 1QH^a 25; Eshel based her reconstruction of the *Self-Glorification Hymn* line 1 on restorations of 1QH^a 25.26, which seems too speculative.

found only in 4Q491; thus, it is possible to explain its many differences with Recension A.[7]

It is certain that the text of 4Q491 (= 4QM1) is noticeably different from the other copies;[8] but it may be due to the editing of the *Self-Glorification Hymn* so that it was suitably incorporated within the *War Scroll*. First, the redactor omitted "I, I reckon myself among the Elim," because he had earlier inscribed a poem in line 13:

[And to] my glory it cannot be compared.
And none will be exalted except me;
And no one may come with me.

For I, I sat in [tranquili]ty in the heavens;
And there is no [st]rife

Perhaps, this line shows the redactor had memorized, knew, or was looking at the *Hymn* and felt subsequently it was judicious to add it to his composition, as other scribes had added it to the *Hodayot*.

Second, the compiler or redactor created a new thought: "Who like sea travelers will come back and recount his [migh]t?" This sentence breaks the flow of the poetry; it may have been added because of the mention of the *Kittim* (כתיאים), the Greeks and then Romans, who come from the sea to the West (frg. 11 2.1, 5, 7, 8, 19, 20).

Third, in the preceding lines of his composition, he had written that the Sons of Light in the War were to sing about God's mighty works, and to exult at the beginning of the day and night "[all the thanks]giving hymns of the battle (frgs. 8–10 1.17)." The so-called Recension B may thus be due to *Redaktionsgeschichte* (the editing of the *Hymn* for a later composition).

The composite text depends on the flow of words and meaning in 4Q471b (the fundamental source) and the flow within 4Q491 (which provides numerous parallels and restorations). Due to other lost words of the *Self-Glorification Hymn*, 4Q427 fragment 7 column 1 is helpful in completing some restorations. The witnesses to the document may be reflected in extant fragments that have the following characteristics:

4Q427 frg. 7 col. 1 is an early first-century BCE copy of the *Thanksgiving Hymns* (4QH[a])[9]

4Q491 frg. 11 col. 1 is the *Hymn* that was probably interpolated into the *War Scroll*.[10]

1QH[a] 26 seems to be copied from 4Q427 (or a document organically like it but earlier), or corrected from it, in places.

4Q471b is not excerpted.[11] It is the *Self-Glorification Hymn*; it also begins a scroll that has collapsed into fragments.[12]

2. Qumran Relationship

In 1957, C. H. Hunzinger judged that the fragments in 4Q491 represented a copy of the *War Scroll* (4QM1 or 4QM[a]).[13] In 1958, J. L. Teicher, who was in Cambridge and had been working on the Hebrew manuscripts in the Cairo Geniza, judged that the fragments Hunzinger had studied exhibited different scribal hands, even though the deteriorated leather may have altered the appearance of consonants on some fragments. Teicher focused on the scribal hand: "Different appearance of the script denotes as a rule a different hand" (p. 257). Teicher reported that a "spurious" work had been produced by overlooking different scribal hands in 4Q491.[14] Contrary to what some recent scholars have suggested, Teicher concluded that the fragments are genuine copies of the *War Scroll*: "They are genuine in the sense that the fragments are derived from different genuine copies of the War Scroll, not in the sense, as claimed by Dr. Hunzinger, that the fragments derive from the same scribe" (p. 258). In the same year, 1958,[15] Teicher added: "A most disturbing feature of the Oxford edition is that fragments of scrolls written in distinctly different hands are put together by the editors and printed as a continuous text" (p. 63). He concluded: "If these criticisms are well founded, what can be done to stop the flood of spurious texts from the Palestine Archaeological Museum?" (p. 64).

What should be clear for work on the *Hymn* is that Teicher made no comment about the *Self-Glorification Hymn* and that M. Baillet published Hunzinger's texts in DJD 7, pp. 12–44. Recently, Abegg challenges Hunzinger's identification and contends that 4Q491 represents three manuscripts because of different scribal hands. He concludes that none is clearly a portion of the *War Scroll*.[16]

---

[7] Eshel in DJD 29, p. 422.

[8] See the texts and translations provided after this introduction.

[9] As Schuller, J. Collins, and D. Dimant state, 4Q427 is a copy of the *Hodayot* but the text represents a document that differs from it in style and subject matter. See Collins and Dimant, "A Thrice-Told Hymn: A Response to Eileen Schuller," *JQR* 85 (1994) 151–55; see esp. p. 151.

[10] Morton Smith rightly pointed out that 4Q491 frg. 11 col. 1 differs from the style of the *War Scroll*. See his "Ascent to the

Heavens and Deification in 4QM[a]," in *Archaeology and History in the Dead Sea Scrolls: The New York University Conference in Memory of Yigael Yadin*, edited by L. H. Schiffman (Sheffield, 1990) pp. 181–88.

[11] M. Baillet thought the work could be a "Cantique de Michel (?)." See DJD 7, p. 29.

[12] See the arrangement in the insert placed in the back of DJD 29.

[13] C. H. Hunzinger, "Fragmente einer älteren Fassung des Buches Milhama aus Höhle 4 von Qumran," *ZAW* 69 (1957) 131–51.

[14] J. L. Teicher, "A Spurious Version of the War Scroll," *ZAW* 70 (1958) 257–58.

[15] Teicher, "Spurious Texts from Qumran?" *PEQ* 90 (1958) 61–64.

[16] See M. G. Abegg, "4Q491 (*4QMilhama[a]*) – An 'Ensemble' of Manuscripts?" in *Abstracts: AAR/SBL* (1990) 378. Also see, Abegg, "Who Ascended to Heaven? 4Q491, 4Q427, and the Teacher of Righteousness," in *Eschatology, Messianism, and*

What is obvious is the judgment that not all the pieces that are now labeled fragment "11" in 4Q491 can be assigned to the *Self-Glorification Hymn*. Line 14 in 4Q491 fragment 11 column 1 begins with [...]; line 19 (according to more than one fragment) ends with *vacat*; thus, the intervening text is free from the context of the column.

PAM 42.474 (= 4Q491) clearly shows the words "For I, I sat" (כיא אני ישבתי) in line 13. The consonants that begin the *Self-Glorification Hymn* appear with line 13. In PAM 42.474, many fragments are numbered "11." The "fragment 11" (on the top right of the image) consists of many little pieces joined together. The correctness of the joins is confirmed by the portions of letters that appear on both sides of the joined pieces. Thus, line 13 is part of the *War Scroll* with three words from the *Self-Glorification Hymn*, and line 14 which is on the same original fragment of leather begins the excerpted *Self-Glorification Hymn*.

It must follow, therefore, that the *Hymn* was most likely chosen by the composer of the *War Scroll* to indicate the source and incomparable power of the "perfect ones" (4Q491 frg. 11 1.11). Knowing the *Hymn*, this compiler or author could have excerpted it to illustrate a point; he had previously contemplated "a powerful throne in the congregation of the *Elim* (or divine beings)" (4Q491 frg. 11 1.12). The copyist of 4Q491 inscribed the words "For I, I sat" (כיא אני ישבתי), which is part of the *War Scroll*, and then, perhaps having memorized the *Self-Glorification Hymn*, excerpted it and knew it also contained the words כי א]נֹ֯ני יֹֹשֹֹבֹֹ]תי (see 4Q471b frg. 1b line 3). He left out these words when he redacted the *Hymn* for inclusion in the *War Scroll*. He may have known the *Hymn* directly from a copy before him or learned it while chanting the *Hodayot*.

Abegg rightly pointed out that there are numerous fragments numbered "11" and that they are not by the same scribe; but the "fragment 11" that is now in focus is by one scribe and contains portions of the *War Scroll* and the *Self-Glorification Hymn*. As is obvious, at least two hands are certain in the script of 1QHᵃ; however, two scribal hands do not prove the existence of two manuscripts. Thus, while Eshel bases her reconstruction of the *Self-Glorification Hymn* on 4Q491, she incorrectly concludes that 4Q491 fragment 11 column 1 "is no longer classified as a copy of the *War Scroll*" (DJD 29, p. 422).

What is clear? Scholars rightly have judged that 4Q491 fragment 11 1.13–19 witnesses to the *Self-Glorification Hymn*. Other fragments in 4Q491 fragment 11 belong to other compositions.

The importance of the *Self-Glorification Hymn* at Qumran is evident. It helps to shape at least two Qumran documents, not

only, probably the *War Scroll* (4Q491),[17] but also, clearly two copies of the *Thanksgiving Hymns* (4Q427 and 1QHᵃ). The *Hymn* itself, 4Q471b, also was known at Qumran (and may contain redactions).

I. Knohl suggests that the *Self-Glorification Hymn* does refer to a great teacher of the Essenes. He imagines that the one intended could be Menahem the Essene.[18] M. Wise imagined that the one glorified should be identified with a certain Judah.[19] Morton Smith did not identify the author who expresses some self-glorification. He thought that the author, in an ecstatic vision, imagined an ascent into heaven, reminiscent of Enoch (according to the authors of the *Books of Enoch*).[20] Certainly, there are striking images shared between the *Self-Glorification Hymn* and the *Parables of Enoch*; only two must suffice for the present: the "Chosen One" is seated on "the throne of glory" (*1En* 45:3) and "all the secrets of wisdom" (cf. 1QpHab 7) issue from the one seated on the throne (*1En* 51:3).[21] E. Miller suggests that we contemplate that the one who composed the *Self-Glorification Hymn* was imagining what Enoch might have said after he was identified as that Son of Man in the *Parables of Enoch*.[22]

Two more options should be shared regarding the identity of the one seated "among the Elim." First, the exalted one may be a collective for Israel.[23] Note these points: 1) such an interpretation may be harmonious with the Book of Daniel in which Daniel sees a powerful figure on "his throne" (7:9) among myriads of angels. Then Daniel sees coming on the clouds, "one like a human being (or son of man)" (7:13). The reference can be either to an archangel like Michael or to Israel, the chosen of God. 2) Both compositions are dated to the mid-second century BCE. 3) Those living in Palestine believed that Israel's "established-place" is certainly "in the congregation of holiness." 4) Looking on the long history of suffering, especially from Jo-

---

[17] Note the insight of Collins and Dimant (*JQR* 85 [1994] 155): "While the ascription of 4Q491 11 and 4Q471b to the War Rule has been questioned, the War Rule certainly contains liturgical material that could also be used in other settings, and our hymn stands apart from the rest of the *Hodayot*. There was some fluidity between the literary corpora and genres found in the Scrolls."

[18] I. Knohl, *The Messiah Before Jesus: The Suffering Servant of the Dead Sea Scrolls* (Berkeley, 2000) see esp. pp. 58–68.

[19] M. O. Wise, *The First Messiah: Investigating the Savior Before Jesus* (San Francisco, 1999).

[20] M. Smith, "Two Ascended to Heaven – Jesus and the Author of 4Q491," in *JDSS*, edited by Charlesworth (New York, 1992) pp. 290–301; see esp. pp. 297–99.

[21] Note that "the Chosen One," not Enoch is seated on the throne. See the chapters in *Parables of Enoch: A Paradigm Shift*, edited by Charlesworth and D. Bock (London, 2013).

[22] E. Miller, "The Self-Glorification Hymn Reexamined," *Henoch* 31 (2009) 322.

[23] H. Stegemann and A. Steudel suggested that the speaker in the *Hymn* is a collective for Israel. See Stegemannn in *RQ* 17 (1996) 502 and Steudel in *RQ* 17 (1996) 525.

---

the Dead Sea Scrolls, edited by C. A. Evans and P. W. Flint (Grand Rapids, 1997) pp. 61–73. Puech in *Prayer and Poetry in the Dead Sea Scrolls*, p. 406, n. 89, rightly rejects Abegg's claims.

seph to the Righteous Teacher, it is apparent that Israel can be intended by references to being "reckoned contemptible," "despised," and "rejected." 5) Collectively, Israel can claim that only they had been forced to bear "evil" so long and so painfully. 6) Israel can assert that their teaching, through Wisdom, is incomparable. 7) Israel can be the one who is "the beloved of the King."

Against this interpretation are references that seem to point to an individual, as most commentators have concluded.[24] The speaker is one who will not be reckoned with the sons of deceit. He is one who turns to others to "Chant, O beloved ones, sing to the King of [glory]." A collective rendering seems excluded by the claim: "And no one can come with me." The expectation of the Sons of Israel is to be with Israel.

Second,[25] it is possible that the Righteous Teacher is the one who composed the *Self-Glorification Hymn*.[26] In favor of this interpretation are the following observations. 1) The date of composition fits the career of the Righteous Teacher. 2) The *Hymn* was exceptionally important for the Qumranites and most likely many of them thought of their Teacher when they read it. 3) The *Hymn* does seem to refer to some important person in the history of the Community. 4) The numerous references to suffering and torture, now found in the new edition of the *Thanksgiving Hymns* (see the Introduction) most likely indicate that the Righteous Teacher suffered great tortures, conceivably in the Temple, including insults, beatings, perhaps a broken arm, and a tongue that was severed so he could no longer withdraw it to teach his followers. These new insights help link the Righteous Teacher with references to being "reckoned contemptible," "despised," "rejected" by humanity, and one who bears incomparable "evil."[27] 5) In light of passages such as 1QpHab 7 that God allowed only the Righteous Teacher to know all the secrets of God's Word, a new meaning is given to "no teaching is comparable with my teaching." 6) *Hymn* 22 (6.5–17.37) in the *Thanksgiving Hymns* is similar to the *Self-Glorification Hymn* with a shared emphasis on election along with rejection and lament of being scorned (16.15).

The arguments against composition by the Righteous Teacher should also come before us for reflection. 1) The *Self-Glorification Hymn* does not appear within the section of the *Thanksgiving Hymns* that contain the compositions of the Righteous Teacher. 2) A distinction must be made between what this anonymous Teacher claimed about himself and what others claimed about him; that is *Habakkuk Pesher* (1QpHab) 7 is a declaration by his later admirers and defenders. 3) In the history of Israel, deification and angelification of Adam, Abel, Enoch, Moses, and Jacob is something attributed to them by later generations. 4) The self-understanding of the speaker in the *Hymn* is one of self-aggrandizement and self-glorification; *Hymn* 22 in the *Thanksgiving Hymns* praises God for making him the Irrigator of the final "Eden of glory" (16:21). As we search for the identity of the speaker in the *Self-Glorification Hymn*, we should recall the repeated consensus that nothing else in the *Thanksgiving Hymns* echoes such elevated self-adoration.[28]

All these possibilities most likely were imagined by early Jews. The central fact is that the person remains unidentified.[29] That is the beauty of leaving a spectacular person anonymous. Anonymity allows for human speculation and protects God's spontaneity. Only God knows the identity of the "Perfect One." Similarly, only God, as so clear in Jewish thoughts on the Messiah, can reveal the identity of the Anointed One, or Messiah. Since the *Self-Glorification Hymn* does not intimate the identity of the speaker, it seems best to leave all suggestions open for contemplation.

By the middle of the first century BCE, some Qumranites probably would have imagined the *Hymn* mirrored the remembered life of their favored Teacher. For them, perhaps in a Qumran expansion, the suffering and rejection of the Righteous Teacher was apparent in lines 2–4 of the *Hymn*. They would most likely have also assumed that his elevation would be prophesied or acknowledged in the subsequent lines.[30] Conceivably, some at Qumran might conclude that the Righteous Teacher had been or would soon be resurrected.

P. Alexander contends that the *Self-Glorification Hymn* helps us understand mystical phenomena within the *Yaḥad*.[31] Open for discussion are the extent of mystical traditions at

---

[24] See esp. J. R. Davila who contends the speaker is "a human speaker," and "clearly not angelic or heavenly by nature." Davila in *The Oxford Handbook of the Dead Sea Scrolls*, p. 438.

[25] Also, after the review of the adoration of Moses, see the suggestion that the *Self-Glorification Hymn* could be from a lost Moses pseudepigraphon.

[26] M. G. Abegg concluded that the speaker in the *Hymn* is the Righteous Teacher; see Abegg in *Eschatology, Messianism, and the Dead Sea Scrolls*, pp. 61–73. There should be no doubt that the *Hymn* was later seen as autobiographical. If the Qumranites imagined it referred to the Righteous Teacher, then I must agree with Allison that this *Hymn* becomes exceptionally important for understanding the claim of Jesus' followers and perhaps Jesus himself. See Allison, *Constructing Jesus*, pp. 262–63.

[27] References to suffering do not appear in 4Q471b frgs. 1 a,c; they are only in frg. 1b. But, this fragment is part of 4Q471b and joined to it. Nevertheless, one has to be open to the possibility that 4Q471b, because of its date (late Herodian period) may itself bear Qumran editing. The anonymous ones' suffering appears in both recensions of this text.

[28] In *The Scepter and the Star*, Collins presents additional reasons why the speaker in the Hymn is not the Righteous Teacher (see esp. p. 148).

[29] Notably, see Collins, *Apocalypticism in the Dead Sea Scrolls*, p. 147, and D. C. Allison in *Constructing Jesus*, p. 262.

[30] Eshel rightly points out "that some followers of the Teacher of Righteousness identified him with" the person imagined in the *Self-Glorification Hymn*. See her chapter in *The Provo International Conference on the Dead Sea Scrolls*, p. 635.

[31] P. Alexander, *Mystical Texts* (LSTS 61; London, 2006) see esp. pp. 85–92.

Qumran (generally accepted) and the evidence of an active practice of ascent within the Community (debated).[32]

3. Composition and Date

In interpreting the *Self-Glorification Hymn*, it is imperative to be cautious. We may be able to guess where the *Hymn* ends, because of the *vacat* in line 11 of the Composite Text that follows the exhortation to chant and to sing; but we cannot be certain where it begins. The right margin of 4Q471b is evident and a scroll begins here because the handle can be seen to the right of the right margin; but, the top, left portion and bottom of the manuscript are lost. We have only portions of the text and the beginnings and ends of lines are sometimes lost; yet, by comparing all the witnesses to this *Hymn* we may comprehend its purpose and meaning. Then, we should imagine how it was interpreted within the *Yaḥad* and within Second Temple Judaism.

The Composite Text indicates that the author is rejected by a group. They are the ones who do not acknowledge the speaker's "teaching" and "speech;" they are those who are rejecting, not regarding, and despising him. This group did not recognize the heavenly rank of the exalted one. God, the King, is the one who appoints him; that is why he is "the beloved of the King (= God)." With this perception, the reader is exhorted to chant and sing to "the King of glory."

The *Hymn* probably antedates the establishment of the *Yaḥad* at Qumran. It appears in 4Q471b. It was clearly excerpted into two copies of the *Thanksgiving Hymns* and was most likely redacted and interpolated by the compiler and composer of the *War Scroll*.

The *Hymn* was included within the *Thanksgiving Hymns* when Qumranites collected psalms, hymns, and poems composed by the Righteous Teacher along with other poems and hymns, most of which were composed (and being composed) by the Community or *Yaḥad*. While the *Self-Glorification Hymn* was composed before 125 BCE, eventually it was seen to depict both the suffering of the Righteous Teacher and his elevation among the divine beings and angels. In this *Hymn* and in the Hebrew Bible "Elim" (אלים) denotes the divine beings or angels. Within the Qumran corpus of compositions, however, Elim denotes not only divine beings and angels but also humans who are the Most Holy of Holy Ones (*Angelic Liturgy*) within the Community that have been elevated to the status of

the Elim.[33] The present form of the *Hymn* reflects Qumran expansion and editing.

Thus, the composition history of the *Hymn* is apparent. The work was apparently created first and was later excerpted by the composer(s) of the *War Scroll* and clearly the complier(s) of the *Thanksgiving Hymns*. The *Unterscript* antedates 125 BCE and was composed sometime in the second century BCE.[34] Redactions by the followers of the Righteous Teacher are apparent, and particularly in the opening lines that mirror his sufferings, especially in the Temple. Thus, evident redactions impede any clarification of the pre-Qumranic history of this amazing composition.

4. Theology and Commentary

The consensus today, widely held, is that the *Self-Glorification Hymn* is a self-congratulatory hymn about the ascent and enthronement of an eschatological high priest.[35] The improved text and translation challenges this opinion.

First, although it may be implied, there is no ascent described in the text.[36] The speaker does not only laud his exalted rank but considers himself one of the most exalted among the Elim, the divine beings or angels.

Second, the "self-congratulatory" dimension of this *Hymn* should be muted. The new Composite Text indicates that the person knows his status ("rank"), and affirms that wisdom derives only from God. He has been given an "established-place," and God is the one who shall regard or reckon him (in 1QS 3.1 and in Num 23:9 the passive meaning is clear).[37] The *Hymn* is thus not only a "self-glorification" composition but a glorification of God. The *Hymn* concludes not with self-glorification

---

[32] E. R. Wolfson rejects Alexander's claims; see Wolfson, "Mysticism and the Poetic-Liturgical Compositions from Qumran: A Response to B. Nitzan," *JQR* 85 (1994) 187. For a different definition of mysticism, see P. Schaefer, *The Hidden and Manifest God* [see discussions in the introduction to the *Hodayot*]. Also, see the judicious review of the discussion in E. Miller, "The Self-Glorification Hymn Reexamined," *Henoch* 31 (2009) 307–24.

[33] See the reflections by Charlesworth, "The Portrayal of the Righteous as an Angel," in *Ideal Figures in Ancient Judaism: Profiles and Paradigms*, edited by J. J. Collins and G. W. E. Nickelsburg (SCS 12; Chico, 1980) pp. 135–51.

[34] In *Prayer and Poetry in the Dead Sea Scrolls*, É. Puech concludes that the *Self-Glorification Hymn* was composed no later than 100 BCE (p. 397) and belongs among the "Community Hymns" section of the *Thanksgiving Hymns* (p. 406). This claim explains why Puech's version of the *Hymn* is considerably longer and includes 4Q431 and 4Q428. Puech also contends that the *Hymn* provides "irrefutable" proof that the Essene Community at Qumran believed in the resurrection from the dead (pp. 406–7).

[35] Eshel has written that the *Self-Glorification Hymn* "was composed in the name of the Eschatological High Priest." See her chapter in *The Provo International Conference on the Dead Sea Scrolls*, p. 635. Also see Eshel in DJD 29, pp. 424–27.

[36] For a general discussion of heavenly ascents in the Dead Sea Scrolls, see J. R. Davila, "Heavenly Ascents in the Dead Sea Scrolls," in *DSSAFY*, pp. 461–85.

[37] Note Num 23:9, "not to be reckoned (יִתְחַשָּׁב) with the nations" and 1QS 3.1, "and he is not to be accounted (יתחשב) with the upright ones."

but with the exhortation: "Chant, O beloved ones, sing to the King of [glory]" which is a restoration anchored by 4Q427 fragment 7 1.13–14.

Third, the composition may be a hymn to be chanted or a poem to be read privately. Perhaps the concluding exhortation to chant and to sing implies that the composition is a hymn; but were these words added at Qumran? The work could be a poem since the characteristics of Semitic poetry, especially the apparent *parallelismus membrorum*, are not only typical of the Psalter, but appear in the poetic speeches of prophets, including Jesus. It also is a hallmark of Wisdom literature.

Fourth, the claim that the *Self-Glorification Hymn* is eschatological appears frequently in secondary literature.[38] We should distinguish between apocalyptic eschatology, which is focused on the end of times,[39] and apocalyptic vision, which is directed to another time or world.[40] The two concepts are often, but not always related; they may appear separately. There is no emphasis on, or mention of, the Endtime or coming denouement in the *Self-Glorification Hymn*, although it is prominent in the *Thanksgiving Hymns*.[41] The work is apocalyptic with a focus on the heavenly realm; it fits aptly within Jewish apocalyptic literature devoted to otherworldly journeys.[42]

Fifth, the author does not mention that he is a priest. Passages that suggest he is seated are preserved in 4Q471b fragment 1b line 3 and in 4Q491 fragment 11 1.13.[43] The elevated one may be depicted standing; the passage in 4Q427 fragment 7 1.11 is translated "rank;" it literally means "position" or "standing."

Eshel's effort to prove that the *Self-Glorification Hymn* describes "the eschatological high priest" seems unconvincing; less forced is her following perception:

The *Self-Glorification Hymn* describes a figure sitting in the company of the angels in the 'holy dwelling.' This figure does not seem to be of angelic origin, but rather a human being who has been elevated to share the lot of the angels.[44]

Almost every line of the *Hymn* indicates a human; there are references to human activities, like "teaching," and an angel would not need to claim that he reckons himself among the "angels," "divine beings," or "Elim."[45] That would be unnecessary and tautological. As extant, the *Hymn* contains the laments of a human who teaches but who is scorned, not regarded, "despised," "rejected," and who grieves, but whose instruction is incomparable.

Obviously, the reception history of this *Hymn* allows for alterations in meaning. Some Jews may have eventually imagined the person exalted is a priest. At Qumran, the exalted figure may have been interpreted in light of the blessing found in 1QSb:

And (may) you (be) like an Angel of the Presence in the
Abode of Holiness, for the glory of the God
of [H]ost[s.... May] you be round about serving in the
temple of the kingdom and may you cast lot
with the Angels of the Presence, and (be) a common
council [... for] eternal time, and for all glorious Endtime.
(1QSb 4.24–26)[46]

As with the exalted figure in the *Self-Glorification Hymn*, this blessed priest is among the Elim or divine beings (1QSb 4.25).

---

[38] See, notably, Eshel in DJD 29, pp. 423–27 and Puech, in *Prayer and Poetry in the Dead Sea Scrolls*, pp. 402–3.

[39] Note the warning by J. Carmignac about the misuse of "eschatology;" see his *Le mirage de l'eschatologie: Royauté, règne et royaume de Dieu – sans eschatologie* (Paris, 1979).

[40] Note the insights by C. Rowland in *The Open Heaven: A Study of Apocalyptic in Judaism and Early Christianity* (New York, 1982).

[41] C. H. T. Fletcher-Louis, in *All the Glory of Adam: Liturgical Anthropology in the Dead Sea Scrolls* (STDJ 42; Leiden and Boston, 2002, pp. 204–16) rightly points out that there is nothing eschatological in the *Self-Glorification Hymn*. Eschatology denotes a reference to the Endtime. The *Hymn* provides a vision that is apocalyptic.

[42] See the discussion of an apocalypse by J. J. Collins in *The Oxford Handbook of Apocalyptic Literature*, edited by J. J. Collins (Oxford, 2014) p. 2.

[43] See esp. the reflections of J. J. Collins, *The Scepter and the Star*, pp. 138–39, 150. Collins rightly points out that ישבתי appears in 4Q491. In DJD 29, p. 422, Eshel responds that the words are to be "reconstructed" in the text. The word, "I sat," is found in 4Q491 frg. 11 1.13 and in 4Q471b frg. b line 3.

[44] Eshel in DJD 29, p. 423.

[45] Eshel adds that "[My] desire (is) not according to the flesh," (4Q491 frg. 11 1.14) "was not spoken by an angel but by a human being who took part in the angelic ceremonies" (DJD 29, p. 423). *Prima facie* this judgment seems valid; but the myth of the Fallen Angels (Gen 6; *1En* 1–36) is a tradition, well known at Qumran and in other groups within Second Temple Judaism, that depicts "heavenly beings," or fallen angels, desiring "the flesh." This myth has shaped 1QH^a; see *Hymn* 32 (24.2–25.33) that is entitled "The Failure of the Cast-Down Heavenly Beings to Praise: Judgment." This Hymn refers to "the mysteries of transgression," "(those of the) flesh," "the (evil) angels," and notably: "And you cast down the heavenly beings from the establishment of [your holiness, for they did not praise] you in the dwelling of your glory." In the *Hodayot*, "heavenly beings" always denotes the fallen angels (see the Consistency Chart under אלים). Thus, early Jews believed that fallen angels had a desire "according to the flesh;" hence, a divine being, a holy angel, could be imagined to state that his desire was "not according to the flesh." This note does not erode the conclusion, shared with Eshel, that the *Self-Glorification Hymn* depicts a human that is exalted "among the Elim." In this *Hymn*, "Elim" denotes the divine beings within "the holy congregation."

[46] The translation is by Charlesworth and L. Stuckenbruck, PTSDSSP vol. 2, pp. 127–29.

A. Segal focuses on 1QSb 4 and suggests that the author was contemplating "angelification" or "angelomorphism."[47] Segal wisely pointed to the ambiguity of "like." What does it mean to be "like an Angel of the Presence?" He noted that *Visions of Amram* (4Q543–548) states that Aaron is "an angel of God." We have seen that Elim can mean not only angels but also the Most Holy of Holy Ones within Qumran; that is, the most elevated of the Sons of Light.

Within the Qumran Scrolls, "Prince" (שר) is in places ambiguous; it could mean "prince" as an angelic being or as a member of the Community. Note especially the two passages in which the noun appears in the *Hodayot*. In 14.17, we read: "And they, they shall come back according to your glory, and they shall become your princes in the lo[t of the *Yaḥad*]." In 18.10, we learn: "Behold, you are the Prince of the Elim and the King of the glorious ones, and Lord to every spirit and Ruler over every creature." The next line, "And apart from you nothing is done," indicates that the author imagined this adoration referred to God.

E. Eshel concludes: "One may assume that a scribe, coping with the death of the Teacher of Righteousness, composed the *Self-Glorification Hymn* thinking of the Teacher of Righteousness while describing the eschatological high priest" (DJD 29, p. 426). In light of the present research and reflections, "composed" should be changed to "redacted," and the reference to "the eschatological high priest" muted. The *Hymn* is not a Qumran composition. It antedates Qumran, does not contain the Qumran *termini technici*, apparently uses Elim only for divine beings, and was eventually excerpted in at least one Qumran composition.

In conclusion, the *Self-Glorification Hymn* provides ideas that are important for an improved perception of charismatic figures in Early Judaism. The *Hymn* echoes the so-called Suffering Servant poem in Isaiah 53 (see the notes to text and translation).[48] Most likely, some Qumranites eventually imagined the text aptly described the life and postmortem existence of their incomparable Righteous Teacher.

5. Relation to Hebrew Bible and Early Judaism

The *Self-Glorification Hymn* is a development and an elevation of the self-esteem found in the Hebrew Scriptures. While tradi-

tions related to David, Solomon, Isaiah, Jeremiah, Ezekiel, and Daniel reflect high self-esteem, the boundaries between divinity and the human were never crossed, as they seem to be in the preserved lines of this *Hymn*

At least two passages in the Hebrew Bible probably influenced those who have given us the *Self-Glorification Hymn*. Eshel notes that דמה, which appears seven times in 4Q491 frg. 11 and 4Q471b, "seems to link this *Hymn* to two biblical passages."[49] The first is Psalm 89:5–8 [MT 89:6–9]. The verses are an exhortation for the holy ones, the divine beings, to praise the LORD God.

> Let the heavens praise your wonders, O LORD,
> your faithfulness in the assembly of the
> Holy Ones (בקהל קדשים).
> For who (כי מי) in the skies can resemble the
> LORD (ליהוה)?
> Who among the sons of the gods (בבני אלים)
> is like the LORD (ידמה ליהשה),
> a God feared in the council of the
> Holy Ones (בסוד־קדשים),
> great and awesome above all that are around him?
> O LORD God of hosts,
> who is as mighty as you (מי כמוך), O LORD?
> Your faithfulness surrounds you.

Surely the author of the *Self-Glorification Hymn* knew this psalm; there are many echoes in the *Hymn* to the images and words highlighted by the Hebrew in Psalm 89:5–8 [89:6–9].

The second passage in the Hebrew Bible that should be brought into focus is Isaiah 14:13–14.[50] In a proverb against the king of Babylon, the king is made to declare:

NRSV	BHS
I will ascend (to) heaven;	הַשָּׁמַיִם אֶעֱלֶה
Above the stars of God	מִמַּעַל לְכוֹכְבֵי־אֵל
I will raise my throne.	אָרִים כִּסְאִי
And I will sit on the mount of assembly	וְאֵשֵׁב בְּהַר־מוֹעֵד
on the heights of Zaphon.	בְּיַרְכְּתֵי צָפוֹן׃
I will ascend unto the tops of the cloud,	אֶעֱלֶה עַל־בָּמֳתֵי עָב

---

[47] See A. Segal, *Life after Death*, pp. 304–5.

[48] Focusing on the use of Isaiah 53 in Judaism, D. Flusser suggested that we should be cautious in claiming that no Jew before 70 CE imagined that a messianic figure, or the Messiah, would suffer and perhaps die. Clearly Isaiah 53 was used by the Rabbis to refer to the Messiah's suffering (in 4 Ezra, the Messiah dies, but his death is not efficacious). See Flusser, "Hystaspes and John Patmos," in *Judaism and the Origins of Christianity* (Jerusalem, 1988) p. 423. Also, see M. D. Hooker, *Jesus and the Servant: The Influence of the Servant Concept of Deutero-Isaiah in the New Testament* (London, 1959).

[49] Eshel in DJD 29, p. 423.

[50] M. Hengel (with D. P. Bailey) suggested numerous ways that the *Self-Glorification Hymn* reveals an indebtedness to the Suffering Servant language of Isaiah 53, including readings in 1QIs[a] and the Septuagint of Isaiah that took shape in the late second century BCE. Hengel and Bailey conclude, however, that the "motif of vicarious atoning death" found in Isaiah 53 "is not visible at all in the *Self-Glorification Hymn*" (p. 146). See our texts and translations, for echoes of Isaiah 52–53 in the *Hymn*. See M. Hengel (with D. P. Bailey), "The Effective History of Isaiah 53 in the Pre-Christian Period," in *The Suffering Servant: Isaiah 53 in Jewish and Christian Sources*, edited by B. Janowski and P. Stuhlmacher, translated by D. P. Bailey (Grand Rapids, 2004) pp. 75–146.

I will resemble the Most High.　　　　　אֲדַמֶּה לְעֶלְיוֹן:

Centuries later, some Jews imagined that these verses concerned Satan's pride and refusal to honor Adam; that was the cause of the Fall according to the author of the *Vita Adae et Evae*.[51]

A third text in the Hebrew Scriptures probably influenced the author (and editors) of the *Self-Glorification Hymn*. Contemplating God's incomprehensibility, many biblical authors ask rhetorically "Who is like you?" (Pss 35:10, 71:19; cf. 89:6–8, 113:5, 77:13; and Micah 7:18). For our purposes, the most significant text for this expression is the "Song of the Sea." In the narrative of Exodus, this psalm was chanted by Moses and "the children of Israel" when they saw the once pursuing Egyptians "lying dead on the seashore." The "Song of the Sea" provided the sentence, "Who is like you among the gods, O Lord?" in 1QH^a 15.31 (with the *Tetragrammaton* shifted to "Adonai"). Here is the famous "Song of the Sea" excerpted from Ex 15:11:

Who is like you among the gods,	מִי־כָמֹכָה בָּאֵלִם
O LORD?	יְהוָה
Who is like you,	מִי כָּמֹכָה
majestic in holiness,	נֶאְדָּר בַּקֹּדֶשׁ
awesome in splendor	נוֹרָא תְהִלֹּת
doing wonders?	עֹשֵׂה פֶלֶא:
(NRSV)	[BHS]

The *Self-Glorification Hymn* preserves faint echoes from the "Song of the Sea." Shifting the focus from the "LORD" to himself; the author offers in lines one and five the following:

> […] I, I reckon myself together with the Elim;
> Who is like me among the Elim?

The phrase "together with the Elim" is found in Exodus 15:11. The expression "Who is like me" may also echo the selfsame words in Isaiah and Jeremiah (Isa 44:7; Jer 49:19, 50:44).

When the author of this *Hymn* refers to "the congregation of holiness" and "the dwelling of holi[ness]," he may be remembering Exodus 15:13: "the habitation of your holiness" (נוה קדשך). His words, "[And to] my glory it cannot be compared" may also echo "Who is like you, majestic in holiness" (Ex 15:11). The emphasis throughout is upon incomparability.

The *Self-Glorification Hymn* should also be understood in light of the late Jewish texts already cited and the heavenly worship, or association with angels, found in the *Angelic Liturgy* (*Songs of the Sabbath Sacrifice*), *Berakot* (4Q286–290), some sections of the *War Scroll*, and the *Hodayot*. In the *Hodayot*, we hear about the Holy Ones, the most advanced Sons

of Light, worshipping with angels. While we knew this already from the *Rule of the Community* (1QS 2.5–10), the level of exaltation in the *Self-Glorification Hymn* is unparalleled in these Qumran Scrolls,[52] and is closer to the exaltation of "Christ" found in the book of Revelation which contains many early Jewish traditions that should also be included for reflection.[53]

Other texts should also be mentioned; these indicate that Jews developed the concepts of deification and angelification before the compilation of the Mishnah, and even during the time that the *Self-Glorification Hymn* was composed.[54] Moses is perceived as deified or angelificated in four early Jewish texts that were often considered sacred or very important.

First, according to Sirach,[55] the distinguished scribe and sage who headed an academy (*bêth midhrâš*) in Jerusalem about 180 BCE,[56] Moses is highly esteemed and equal in glory to "the holy ones" or "the Holy Ones," which probably originally meant the biblical saints but could within a decade be interpreted to denote the angels; note 45:1–5:

> From his [Jacob's] descendants the Lord brought forth a
> godly man,
> who found favor in the sight of all
> and was beloved by God and people,
> Moses, whose memory is blessed.
> He made him equal in glory to the holy ones,
> and made him great, to the terror of his enemies.
> By his words he performed swift miracles;
> the Lord glorified him in the presence of kings.
> He gave him commandments for his people,

---

51 See *Vita Adae et Evae* 15:3, in which Satan (= the Devil) is depicted telling Michael: "And I said, 'If he be wrathful with me, I will set my throne above the stars of heaven and will be like the Most High;'" see M. D. Johnson in *OTP* 2.262.

52 See Collins and Dimant in *JQR* 85 (1994) 154. Collins rightly notes that the "level of exaltation" in the *Self-Glorification Hymn* is "unparalleled in the Hodayot." Collins, *The Scepter and the Star: The Messiahs of the Dead Sea Scrolls and other Ancient Literature* (New York, 1995) see esp. pp. 136–39; the quotation is on p. 138.

53 See the helpful reflections by P. A. de Souza Nogueira in "Ecstatic Worship in the Self-Glorification Hymn (4Q471B, 4Q427, 4Q491C): Implications for the Understanding of an Ancient Jewish and Early Christian Phenomenon," in *Wisdom and Apocalypticism in the Dead Sea Scrolls and in the Biblical Tradition*, edited by F. García-Martínez (BETL 168; Leuven, 2003) pp. 385–93.

54 See J. J. Collins, "A Throne in the Heavens. Apotheosis in pre-Christian Judaism," in *Death, Ecstasy and Otherworldly Journeys*, edited by J. J. Collins and M. Fishbane (Albany, NY, 1995).

55 R. Egger-Wenzel notes the differences in the Hebrew text and Greek translation of Sirach and urges a distinction between the intentions of Sirach and his grandson, the translator of the document. See Egger-Wenzel, "The Change of the Sacrifice Terminology from Hebrew into Greek in the Book of Ben Sira. Did the Grandson Understand his Grandfather's Text Correctly?" *BN* 140 (2009) 89–93.

56 See the discussion by E. Nodet, "Alexandrie, Ben Sira, Prophètes, Écrits," *RB* 119 (2012) 110–18.

and revealed to him his glory. (NRSV)

The claim that God ὡμοίωσεν αὐτὸν δόξῃ ἁγίων ("he made him like unto the glory of the holy ones") is arresting and of importance for understanding the composition of the *Self-Glorification Hymn*.[57] Note a similar concept in Sirach 45:

Beloved of God and men
Was Moses of happy memory.
And <He made him glorious as> God,[58]
And mighty in awe-inspiring deeds.
(Sir 45:1–2)

This reading may have been earlier and edited by scribes;[59] the Hebrew is defective.[60] The claim that Moses was "glorious as" God would seem blasphemous to later scribes who did not know the complex world of Second Temple Judaism. Sirach is contemporaneous or perhaps a little earlier than the *Self-Glorification Hymn*. The term "the holy ones" is known at Qumran. Within the Community, "the Holy Ones," like the E-lim, may denote not only the Most Holy of Holy Ones among the Qumranites but also divine beings or angels (who are not only in heaven but also on earth). We may conclude with Sirach by quoting W. Horbury: "[T]he book attests the 'inclusive' tendency in Old Testament monotheism, with room for a quickly restrained bow in the direction of pantheism (43:27–8), for the divine assembly and the heavenly host (17:17), for the divine wisdom (1:1–4, etc.), word (43:26), glory (17:13) and name (47:13), and for humanity 'made like to the glory of the holy ones' (42:5)."[61] Sirach seems to adumbrate a type of deifi-

cation or oneness with the Holy Ones that appears in the *Self-Glorification Hymn* and in the *Hodayot*.[62]

Second, according to the skilled poet who composed the document known as *Ezekiel the Tragedian* (2nd cent. BCE), which is extant in iambic trimeter, Moses is imagined as seated on God's throne.[63] Moses is not only the leader of the angels, he is also above them. They are represented as stars (= angels [cf. Job 38:7; cf. also Dan 12:3]) who bow down to Moses. Departing from the account in Exodus and being influenced by the famous Greek tragedians, this Jewish author reports a dream in which Moses sits on God's throne and God withdraws. Notice the first-person discourse and claims as in the *Self-Glorification Hymn*:

He [God] handed o'er the scepter and he bade
me mount the throne, and gave to me the crown;
then he himself withdrew from off the throne....
Then at my feet a multitude of stars
Fell down, and I their number reckoned up.
They passed by me like armed ranks of men.
Then I in terror wakened from the dream.
(70–82; *OTP* 2.812)

The author of *Ezekiel the Tragedian* most likely imagined that Moses is seated on God's throne and among the angels who worship him. He is thus seated among the Elim but far superior to all of them, including any archangel. After the section quoted, Jethro interprets Moses' dream so that he is to "rule and govern men," and be able to see all time inclusively (82–89). Moses, within this dream, can be imagined to reckon himself among the Elim.

Third, the thought of Philo of Alexandria (c. 20 BCE–c. 50 CE) should be included, if only briefly. At the outset, it seems that any deification of Moses by Philo should be unthinkable. Had Philo not emphasized God's ineffability? He perceives that "God" is not a category, but supra-categorical, invisible, and incomprehensible.[64] Philo depicts God telling Moses that "no name at all can properly be used of Me, to Whom existence

---

[57] The transmission of this verse is complex; see G. H. Box in Charles, *APOT* 1.484–85. Perhaps the original may have implied that Moses was made equal to God's glory. Scribes would likely alter such a claim as it seems blasphemous in later contexts.

[58] See G. H. Box in Charles, *APOT* 1.484–85. The Hebrew in this verse seems corrupt. Peters restored: ויכבדהו כאלהים; two Greek manuscripts, G and S, seem to rephrase the lost Hebrew (so Box, *APOT* 1.485). Most likely each scribe imagined the claim was offensive to monotheism. There are great divergences among the Greek manuscripts of Sirach. In *APOT* 1.281, W. O. E. Oesterley offered this insight: "It seems clear that there existed at a very early period, probably as early as the last century B.C., two types of the Greek text."

[59] A. Linder, "Ricerche sul linguaggio di Ben Sera," *RivB* 54 (2006) 385–411.

[60] See E. Tov, *The Parallel Aligned Hebrew-Aramaic and Greek Texts of Scripture*. [only on LOGOS]

[61] W. Horbury, "Deity in Ecclesiasticus," in *The God of Israel*, edited by R. P. Gordon (Cambridge, 2007) pp. 267–92; the quotation is from p. 267.

[62] In the explicit monotheism of 1QS and 1QM, scribes avoided the absolute use of the Tetragrammaton and Elohim. In the documents now under examination, is there a tendency to portray both God and some divine humans as "exalted" or transcendent?

[63] Lucius Cornelius Alexander Polyhistor (c. 105–c. 35 BCE) preserved portions of *Ezekiel the Tragedian* and some other Jewish writings, otherwise lost (see *OTP* 2), and interpreted Pythagorean doctrine in the early 1st cent. BCE. He was known as Polyhistor because of his many works on "history." Sections of his writings are preserved only by Eusebius and other scholars in the Early Church. See the judicious discussion of the date of *Ezekiel the Tragedian* by R. G. Robertson in *OTP* 2.803–804. Based on the polemic in *LetAris* 312–16, which may refer to *EzekTrag*, and the excerpts in Alexander Polyhistor, Robertson suggests the work was composed in "perhaps the first part of the second century B.C."

[64] Note, in particular, Philo, *Special Laws*, 36–50.

belongs" (*Moses I*, 75 LCL). Philo stresses that Moses was "a man," even "a created and mortal being" (*Moses II*, 6). Philo contended in *Special Laws* (36–50), that Moses is incapable of comprehending God and God's essence.

Philo is emphatically monotheistic; yet, he does intermittently portray Moses as more than human, and almost divine in some passages. Combining what he had read with what he had heard, and being knowledgeable about Jewish legends (and perhaps lost works), Philo shares the reflections of some Jews that Moses was the greatest and most perfect human that ever lived. In *Moses I*, Philo contemplates: "Has he [Moses] not also enjoyed an even greater communion with the Father and Creator of the universe …?" Philo ponders if Moses was not also called god and king of the whole nation (θεὸς καὶ βασιλεύς; *Moses I*, 158). Philo explains that Moses not only had kingly power, but was high priest, lawgiver, and prophet (*Moses I*, 334; *Moses II*, 3 and 292). Moses had the genius of the philosopher and king (τὴν τε βασιλικὴν καὶ φιλόσοφον; *Moses II*, 2).[65] In describing Moses' unparalleled gifts and accomplishments, Philo probably gave some readers the impression that he was a demigod, like Alexander the Great (see *Moses II*, 10–11). Moses can be acknowledged to be "most holy Moses" (ὁ ἱερώτατος Μωυσῆς; *Special Laws*, 59).

Moses is none other than the perfect mediator and reconciler (*Moses II*, 166). He is "the all-great Moses" (ὁ πάντα μέγας Μωυσῆς; *Moses II*, 211). Moses may approach the invisible judgment seat (*Moses II*, 217). Moses can apparently command the earth to open and swallow sinful men, because they had not obeyed "my truthfulness" (*Moses II*, 280–81). And before his death, Moses, filled with a supernatural spirit, can explain his death and burial perfectly in Deuteronomy (*Moses II*, 291). Philo is capable of creative exegetical moves; yet, we should avoid a systematic presentation of Philo. It is at Moses' death that he is transformed and becomes immortal (*Moses II*, 288).

Fourth, the author of the *Testament of Moses* (1st cent. CE) also raises Moses above his portrayal in the Hebrew Scriptures. In this pseudepigraphon, which like the *Self-Glorification Hymn* was most likely composed within Palestine, an author imagines the farewell by Moses to Joshua. Convinced that God's covenantal promises are inviolate (1, 3, 4, 12) and any deliverance, past or future, is solely by God's power, the author has Moses announce to Joshua: "He did design and devise me, who (was) prepared from the beginning of the world, to be the mediator of his covenant" (1:14; Priest in *OTP* 1.927). Commentators have rightly debated whether this passage means Moses or his role as mediator was pre-existent before creation. In any case, Moses is clearly elevated as "the mediator" (3:12). God, the "heavenly Lord," is the "king on the lofty throne" (4:2), but Joshua, falling at Moses' feet proclaims that Moses is "the divine prophet for the whole world," and "the perfect teacher in the world" (11:16). Obviously, in the air are many images and conceptions that relate this document to the *Self-Glorification Hymn* and Qumran thought; given the date of the

Testament of Moses, it is possible the author knew some of these earlier traditions.

Reviewing the Jewish texts that reveal adoration, even deification or angelification, of Moses, leads me to offer a hypothesis that is surprisingly absent among scholars.[66] Acknowledging that many Jewish compositions have been lost due to the two Jewish Revolts (66–74 and 132–36) as well as the ravages of time and climate, it is possible that the *Self-Glorification Hymn* may be an ode that was part of a Moses pseudepigraphon or apocryphon.

Moses may be the speaker in the Hymn and depicted as seated among the Elim. In Jewish compositions, Moses was portrayed as one who was enthroned in the heavens. As we have seen from the preceding review of texts like Sirach, *Ezekiel the Tragedian*, Philo, and the *Testament of Moses*, Moses is depicted in ways reminiscent of the speaker in the *Self-Glorification Hymn*. The author of *Ezekiel the Tragedian* imagines Moses seated on God's throne in heaven and adored by angels (= stars). Furthermore, note that Philo, in the *Sacrifices of Abel and Cain*, presents Moses, among others, as one who did "soar above" and was allowed by God to be "seated beside himself" (ἵδρυσε δὲ πλησίον ἑαυτοῦ; *De Sacrif.* 8, LCL 227, p. 98).

Other biblical luminaries are also perceived as elevated above humanity and perhaps depicted as divine; notably, Adam, Abel, Enoch, and Jacob (Israel).[67]

Adam and Abel. According to the Jewish author of the *Testament of Abraham* (circa 100 CE), some biblical luminaries are exalted.[68] When Adam, "this most wondrous man" who is "adorned in such glory" (11:8), sees the souls being saved, he "sits on his throne rejoicing and exulting cheerfully" (11:10). Abel is also glorified and elevated as the eschatological judge. He is "seated on the throne" (13:2); he will "judge the entire creation, examining both righteous and sinners" (13:3).

The author (or compiler) of *2 Enoch* (circa 100 CE?)[69] hails Adam as angelic. Contemplating how God created man in his "image," the author continues to claim that Adam had been assigned "to be a second angel, honored and great and glorious" (30:10–11 [J]).[70] Though Adam "does not know his own na-

---

[65] The influence from Plato is obvious.

[66] In suggesting this new hypothesis, I wish to express indebtedness to many conversations with my colleague, Dale C. Allison, who asked me why no scholar had suggested that the Hymn might come from a lost Moses pseudepigraphon.

[67] In *Aramaic Levi*, preserved in 7 Qumran Aramaic fragments and a better preserved Aramaic manuscript in the Cairo Geniza, Levi, in a vision, reaches heaven and is with divine beings. Melchizedek, according to *Melchizedek* (11Q13), becomes an exalted angel and eschatological judge.

[68] See E. P. Sanders in *OTP* 1.871–902. The quotations are from Recension A.

[69] See the discussion by F. I. Andersen in *OTP* 1.91–97.

[70] Many ancient Jewish sources record that some Jews believed in angelification; see the superb review of most of these by A. Segal, *Paul the Convert* (New Haven, 1990) pp. 43–44.

ture" (30:16) and sins, God finally hands over paradise to Adam, and gives him a command to perceive the heavens, and "look upon the angels, singing the triumphal song" (30:1–2 [J]). This allows Adam to fulfill God's first commandment (30:1 [J]).

Enoch. According to the author or compiler of the *Parables of Enoch* (c. 37 BCE–c. 66 CE), "that Son of Man" is not only the heavenly and cosmic Judge but also eventually revealed to be none other than Enoch.[71] The Antecedent of Time with the archangels and innumerable angels come to Enoch who is then transformed; subsequently, an angel announces that Enoch is "that Son of Man" (*1 Enoch* 71). Henceforth, all who come into existence will not be separated from Enoch, the Son of Man, and the righteous ones will have peace. The elevation and relation with angels brings to mind many passages in the *Self-Glorification Hymn*.

Jacob (Israel). According to the author of the *Prayer of Joseph* (1st cent. CE),[72] Jacob makes an announcement that is helpful in comprehending the *Self-Glorification Hymn*: "I, Jacob, who is speaking to you, am also Israel, an angel of God and a ruling spirit" (Frg. A 1). Uriel announces that Jacob "had descended to earth." Strikingly similar and important for contextualizing and comprehending the *Self-Glorification Hymn* is the following excerpt from the *Prayer of Joseph*:

I told him his name and what rank he held among the sons of God. "Are you not Uriel, the eighth after me, and I, Israel, the archangel of the power of the Lord and the chief captain among the sons of God? Am I not Israel, the first minister before the face of God?" And I called upon my God by the inextinguishable name. (Frg. A 6–9)

According to Genesis, Jacob is the son of Isaac, the son of Abraham; but according to the *Prayer of Joseph*, Jacob is "the firstborn of every living thing to whom God gives life" (Frg. A 3). He is even superior to Uriel who was created eighth after Jacob. Jacob is also "the first minister before the face of God." He clearly sits among the Elim, "the sons of God," and is superior to them. Pre-existence is transferred to the patriarch and Exodus 4:22 ("Israel my first-born son") is interpreted literally and midrashically.[73] Thus, the glorification of Jacob is central to perceiving the importance of the *Self-Glorification Hymn*. In addition, in both compositions the elevated person receives an exalted "rank." Could the author of the *Prayer of Joseph* have known this *Hymn*?[74]

According to the author of the *Prayer of Jacob*, which dates from the first to the fourth century CE,[75] God is the "Father of (the) Patria[rch]s," the Creator, the Father to whom the cheru-

bim are subject, the God of the powers, and the one who sits upon Mount Sinai (1–8). The one who utters the prayer asks God to hear him: "I summon you" (10). He asks to be filled with wisdom and to be empowered; most importantly he asks to be filled with good things because he has become:[76]

As an ear[th]ly angel,
as [hav]ing become immortal,
as having recei[ved] the gift which (is) from [yo]u
[a]men, amen. (19)

As these diverse texts disclose, angelification is clearly well attested in Early Judaism. It is, therefore, not unique to Qumran.

The so-called pagan world deeply influenced many dimensions of early Jewish thought.[77] For example, Jews and Christians attributed to the pagan Sibyl characteristics that the Hebrew Scriptures usually reserved for God. This prophetess is a seer who has the "most perfectly wise song" (2.1). Most importantly, the Sibyl prophesies "unfailing truth" (3.3, 4.2), and can extol the "woeful history" of the Greeks, Egyptians, and Romans (Book 5). These claims about the Sibyl are in sections of Book 3, possibly having been composed sometime before the non-battle at Actium in 31 BCE, in earlier passages in Book 3 that were composed about 300 BCE and later redacted by a Jew about 80 CE. Book 5 was composed shortly before 100 CE.[78]

Such adoration seems congruent with the monotheism of the *Sibylline Oracles*, with the celebration of God as the one who has "the cherubim as a throne" (3.2), "who alone rules," the "exceedingly great unbegotten" (Prologue 94), the "one God, sole ruler, ineffable, who lives in the sky" (3.11), the "imperishable God," "the begetter who is eternal," "the king," and "the great eternal God" (5.497–500). The one God "sees all at once but is seen by no one himself" (4.12); he is the source of the Sibyl's words, as he drove a whip through her heart "to narrate accurately to men what now is, and what will yet be" (4.18–20). Thus, the apparent deification of the Sibyl seems to be reduced by Jewish monotheism.

There are vestiges of her divinity that apparently remain: "my honey-voiced mouth from our shrine" (4.3) and "listen to the Sibyl in all things" because "she pours forth true speech from her holy mouth" (4.22–23). In these excerpts, the Sibyl is central; the emphasis is not that she is allowed to speak because of the biblical God. Adoration of the Sibyl helps us understand the context and claims within the *Self-Glorification Hymn*.

---

[71] See the discussions in Charlesworth and Bock, eds., *The Parables of Enoch*.

[72] See the discussion by J. Z. Smith in *OTP* 1.699–700.

[73] See the brilliant reflections by J. Z. Smith in *OTP* 1.699–714.

[74] Also see frg. B and esp. frg. C.

[75] See Charlesworth in *OTP* 2.715–23.

[76] See Charlesworth's note in *OTP* 2.723 no i2; the author believes he has already become an angel. See the additional references to angelification in the *Cologne Mani Codex*, 1QH[a], *JosAsen, HistRech, TSol* 22, and the *Book of Adam and Eve* (ed. C. S. Malan; Bk. 1, ch. 10).

[77] As M. Hengel demonstrated in many publications, notably in *JudHell*.

[78] See Collins' discussion in *OTP* 1.317–472.

When does metaphor become personification? And when does personification become hypostasis?

It is clear that the early Jewish imagination was creative and had few restrictions. The "voice" was a metaphor in Isaiah 40:3; at Qumran it became personified. Later we are shown the hypostatic Voice, conceivably in Revelation 4, and with pellucid clarity (and with wings) in the *Apocalypse of Sedrach*.[79] Philo knows about a "visible voice" that can be more clarifying than a mere voice because it may not only be heard but seen (διὰ φωνῆς - τὸ παραδοξότατον ὁρατῆς; *Moses II*, 213; cf. *Decalogue* 46–48).[80] Long after Sirach and close to the time of Judah the Prince, Rabbis could assume the concept of בת קול ("Bath Qol;" lit. "the daughter of the voice" = *vox dei* in the West).[81]

The earliest reference to an ascent to heaven is apparently in Mesopotamia. Etana, a shepherd, is reported to have ascended into heaven. Ascents appear in Greek sources beginning in the fifth century and in Hebrew traditions with Ezekiel.[82]

Ascensions of holy men into the heavens are described or mentioned in many early texts; some of them also, as in the *Self-Glorification Hymn*, mention some glorification. These texts date during the period of Second Temple Judaism and long after it. The list of such texts would include at the least the following: *1 Enoch* and *2 Enoch* (Enoch ascends and is eventually identified and glorified as "that Son of Man," and eventually Metraton [*3 Enoch*]); *Testament of Levi* (Levi ascends into the heavens to the "Holy Ones," "the Great Glory," and to "many thrones"); *Testament of Job* (after their death, Job's children and then Job are described as ascending into heaven [and glorified]; and Job refers to his own throne in heaven which is among "the Holy Ones;" *Testament of Job* 33:2); 2 Corinthians 12:2–14 (Paul ascends into the third heaven and paradise);[83] Acts 1:6–11 (Jesus ascends into heaven [see also Lk 24:5–53]); *4 Ezra* 14:9 (Ezra is told he "shall be taken up from among men"); *Joseph and Aseneth* 17 (a "god" from heaven visits Aseneth and then ascends to heaven on a chariot before her); *Apocalypse of Abraham* 15–18 (Abraham ascends into heaven and sees "a throne of fire"); *3 Baruch* (Baruch ascends into the fifth heaven where he supposedly sees "the glory of God"); b. *Ḥagigah* 11b–16a (esp. 14b, the well-known reference to the ascent of four rabbis into what may be Paradise[84] [but the rabbis taught that to claim a throne in heaven disrespects God]);[85] *3 Enoch* (this late apocalypse has Rabbi Ishmael ascend to heaven and he sees God's throne).

Within the Second Temple period, and especially in the Jewish apocalypses, we also see the appearances of the names of archangels; notably, Gabriel, Michael, Phanuel, Sariel, and Uriel. Angels and archangels help connect the human on earth with God and his retinue in a far-off heaven.[86] The House of God in Jerusalem only mirrors imperfectly the Heavenly Temple. Contemplating the origins and meaning of the *Self-Glorification Hymn*, we glimpse the adumbrations of concepts that will inspire Jewish and Christian imagination for the future.

This review makes it clear that long before and shortly after the destruction of the Temple in 70 CE, Jews contemplated biblical luminaries who were perceived to have crossed the boundary between the human and the divine; yet, other Jews, perhaps the same ones, recognized the incomprehensibility of the incomparable One, using the *Tetrapuncta* and Palaeo-Hebrew consonants to represent the ineffable *Tetragrammaton*. To pronounce God's ineffable name resulted in a death sentence (Lev 24:16) or exclusion from the World to Come (b. *Sanhedrin* 10:1).[87]

Until one studies the deep and complex meaning in the texts cited, reflects on deification and angelification in Early Judaism, and ponders the amazing imagination of the early Jews, one assumes that only deviant Jews could have concocted such an alteration of what is often assumed to be "the theology of the Old Testament;" yet, that term and concept is seldom used today, as many scholars perceive there is no one central theology in the Old Testament or Hebrew Scriptures. The creative diversity within Early Judaism must never be systematized or reduced to one orthodox standard. The incredible breadth and depth of Early Judaism was lost; it was not approximated by

---

[79] See Charlesworth, "The Jewish Roots of Christology: The Discovery of the Hypostatic Voice," *SJT* 39 (1986) 19–41. Note Rev 1:12.

[80] According to Ex 20:18 [v. 15 in the MT], all the people saw the voice (Καὶ πᾶς ὁ λαὸς ἑώρα τὴν φωνὴν in LXX) or thundering (הקולת in MT).

[81] Note the commentaries on Mk 1:11; cf. also Jn 1:1–2.

[82] See the succinct and authoritative review by J. N. Bremmer, "Descents to Hell and Ascents to Heaven in Apocalyptic Literature," in *The Oxford Handbook of Apocalyptic Literature*, edited by J. J. Collins (Oxford, 2014) pp. 340–57.

[83] For an impressive attempt to explain the complexities within Pauline thought and divination, see C. Tilling, *Paul's Divine Christology* (Tübingen, 2012). For a scholarly examination of messianic language in Paul, see M. V. Novenson, *Christ Among the Messiahs: Christ Language in Paul and Messiah Language in Ancient Judaism* (Oxford, 2012).

[84] In *OTP* 1.231, P. Alexander speculates: "[I]t would seem that in talmudic times Ma'aśeh Merkabah contained a doctrine of mystical ascent to heaven."

[85] See also *Hekalot Rabbati* and *Sepher haRazim*.

[86] A previous generation of scholars, not so well informed by early Jewish literature, contended that angels separated the human from the totally transcendent God. It is not easy for me to find a Jewish text that portrays God as totally transcendent and inaccessible; if one were found, it would be an aberration and not representative of Qumran thought (as latitudinous as it is). The recognition of God's ineffableness does not mean God's absence; the authors of the *Hodayot* perceived God to be ineffable but real and near to the human who is faithful to the Covenant. In many passages authors of the *Hodayot* perceive that they are the Poor who became rich because of God's presence and forgiveness.

[87] Unfortunately, the penalty for this infraction is lost in the *lacunae* in the manuscripts of 1QS and 4QS.

Rabbinic Judaism and Christianity combined (without including Gnosticism and other speculative systems [indeed, these systems or developments are sometimes strikingly influenced by early Jewish traditions]).

6. Relation to the New Testament and Early Christianity

We cannot ascertain whether any of Jesus' followers knew the *Self-Glorification Hymn*, but they certainly portrayed Jesus in similar terms, declaring him to be the Son of God to whom God had given unparalleled revelations and supernatural wisdom; and some of Jesus' followers hailed him as divine and perhaps even to be equal to "God."[88] The exaltation of the anonymous person in the *Self-Glorification Hymn* is reminiscent of the exaltation of "Christ" found in the book of Revelation, whose author in describing the heavenly court employed many early Jewish traditions that should also be included for reflection as we study the possible reception history of the *Self-Glorification Hymn*.[89] Christ, as the Lamb, is seen seated on the throne and promises those who conquer that they will sit on his throne with him and the Father: Ὁ νικῶν δώσω αὐτῷ καθίσαι μετ' ἐμοῦ ἐν τῷ θρόνῳ μου, ὡς κἀγὼ ἐνίκησα καὶ ἐκάθισα μετὰ τοῦ πατρός μου ἐν τῷ θρόνῳ αὐτοῦ (Rev 3:21).[90] The author of Hebrews imagined Jesus in similar terms, portraying him as the enthroned high priest who is in heaven: Κεφάλαιον δὲ ἐπὶ τοῖς λεγομένοις, τοιοῦτον ἔχομεν ἀρχιερέα, ὃς ἐκάθισεν ἐν δεξιᾷ τοῦ θρόνου τῆς μεγαλωσύνης ἐν τοῖς οὐρανοῖς, (Heb 8:1; cf. Ps 110:4).[91]

Glorification and deification are found in two other noteworthy sacred texts. In Psalm 82:6 we are told: "I, I announce (to you), 'You are gods,[92] and sons of the Most High, all of you.'"

ἐγὼ εἶπα Θεοί ἐστε	אֲנִי־אָמַרְתִּי אֱלֹהִים אַתֶּם
καὶ υἱοὶ ὑψίστου πάντες	וּבְנֵי עֶלְיוֹן כֻּלְּכֶם
(LXX)	(BHS)

According to the Gospel of John, Jesus knew and presented an exposition (or midrash) on this Psalm (Jn 10:34–38):

Jesus answered, "Is it not written in your law,[93] 'I said, you are gods' (οὐκ ἔστιν γεγραμμένον ἐν τῷ νόμῳ ὑμῶν ὅτι ἐγὼ εἶπα· θεοί ἐστε)? If those to whom the word of God came were called 'gods' – and the scripture cannot be annulled – can you say that the one whom the Father has sanctified and sent into the world is blaspheming because I said, 'I am God's Son'? If I am not doing the works of my Father, then do not believe me. But if I do them, even though you do not believe me, believe the works, so that you may know and understand that the Father is in me and I am in the Father." (NRSV)[94]

Psalm 82 is extremely important for the perception of the *Self-Glorification Hymn*, because of its beginning:

God stands[95]	אֱלֹהִים נִצָּב
in the divine congregation.[96]	בַּעֲדַת־אֵל
Among the gods he shall judge.	בְּקֶרֶב אֱלֹהִים יִשְׁפֹּט׃

We have perused many early Jewish documents that preserve the claim that Israelites and Jews are the ones "to whom God

---

[88] See, notably, L. W. Hurtado, *How on Earth Did Jesus Become God? Historical Questions About Earliest Devotion to Jesus* (Grand Rapids, 2005); A. H. I. Lee, *From Messiah to Preexistent Son* (Eugene, OR, 2009); J. D. G. Dunn, *Did the First Christians Worship Jesus?: The New Testament Evidence* (Louisville, 2010); G. A. Cole, *God Who Became Human: A Biblical Theology of Incarnation* (Downers Grove, IL, 2013); B. D. Ehrman, *How Jesus Became God: From Good Teacher to Divine Savior* (San Francisco, 2014); and C. B. Kaiser, *Seeing the Lord's Glory: Kyriocentric Visions and the Dilemma of Early Christology* (Minneapolis, 2014).

[89] See the helpful reflections by P. A. de Souza Nogueira in "Ecstatic Worship in the Self-Glorification Hymn (4Q471B, 4Q427, 4Q491C): Implications for the Understanding of an Ancient Jewish and Early Christian Phenomenon," in *Wisdom and Apocalypticism in the Dead Sea Scrolls and in the Biblical Tradition*, edited by F. García-Martínez (BETL 168; Leuven, 2003) pp. 385–93.

[90] Reading this verse an attentive reader becomes confused by mixed metaphors and contemplates how many are possibly depicted on one throne. A chariot may provide for two thrones in heaven, since a chariot may have two seats.

[91] Recall Ps 110:4: "The Lord has sworn and will not change his mind, 'You are a priest forever according to the order of Melchizedek.'" There are, of course, parallels between *Melchizedek* (11Q13) and the *Self-Glorification Hymn*.

[92] This noun in Pss 82:1 and 82:6 has been translated as "angels" or "heavenly beings" (Bl Hup; Calvin; cf. Ps 8:6 [5]). The noun may denote "divine ones,""superhuman beings," a "mighty" (Gen 23:6) and "majestic human of high social status" (Ps 36:8 [7]), even a "ghost" (1Sam 28:13) or "majestic and awesome things" (Ps 68:16[15]). In the *Hodayot*, "Elim" can mean "gods," "divine beings," "heavenly beings," and the Qumranites that are the Most Holy of Holy Ones. For a defense of "gods," see Charlesworth, "The Classical Protestant View of Human Nature," in *On Human Nature: The Jerusalem Center Symposium*, edited by T. G. Madsen, D. N. Freedman, and P. F. Kuhlken (Ann Arbor, 2004) pp. 69–84; and esp. "The Dignity of the Human: *Imago Dei*," *Inaugural Truman G. Madsen Lecture on Eternal Man* (Provo, UT, 2008).

[93] Jesus, who was a devoted Jew, would have been inclusive, referring to "our" Torah.

[94] For discussions, see especially the commentaries by R. E. Brown, C. S. Keener, F. J. Maloney, and U. C. Von Wahlde.

[95] *Nipʿal* part.; sometimes translated incorrectly as "has taken his place." God is not shown seated.

[96] Lit. "in the congregation of god." אל and its plural has many meanings in this verse.

came" and these humans could also be compared to gods, Elim, divine beings, or angels.

John's Christology is not pure literary creativity; through expansion and redaction, it evolves from early Jewish exaltation and messianic language.[97] As is well known, passages in John often mirror debates within Early Judaism; perhaps 10:34–38 also indicates the search of early Jews for meaning in Psalm 82.[98]

It has been customary to assume that the elevated language of Jesus in the Gospel of John cannot be found in Second Temple Judaism and so should be attributed to Greek thought. Particularly in focus is the "I am" (ἐγώ εἰμί) sayings in John. Note especially the following passage memorized by many Christians: "Jesus said to him, 'I am the way, and the truth, and the life'" (ἐγώ εἰμί ἡ ὁδὸς καὶ ἡ ἀλήθεια καὶ ἡ ζωή; Jn 14:6).

In the *Self-Glorification Hymn* and in the Gospel of John we have poetry that contains an emphasis on "glory," heavenly abode, and the claim that no one can go, or enter, where the luminary is going. Note this impressive shared emphasis:

And no one can come[99] with me. (SGH Composite 7)

Εἶπεν οὖν πάλιν αὐτοῖς· ἐγὼ ὑπάγω καὶ ζητήσετέ με,
καὶ ἐν τῇ ἁμαρτίᾳ ὑμῶν ἀποθανεῖσθε·
ὅπου ἐγὼ ὑπάγω ὑμεῖς οὐ δύνασθε ἐλθεῖν
(Jn 8:21)

He said, therefore, again to them:
"I, I go and you will seek me.
And die in your sin.
Where I, I go, you cannot come."

In the Gospel of John we find these words attributed to Jesus: "Where I am going you cannot come." This concept needs further exegesis in light of the *Hymn*. The following verses also stress the heavenly origin of Jesus: He is from above; he is not of this world (Jn 8:23). Also see John 16:5–6:

νῦν δὲ ὑπάγω πρὸς τὸν πέμψαντά με,
καὶ οὐδεὶς ἐξ ὑμῶν ἐρωτᾷ με·
ποῦ ὑπάγεις;
ἀλλ' ὅτι ταῦτα λελάληκα ὑμῖν

ἡ λύπη πεπλήρωκεν ὑμῶν τὴν καρδίαν.

But, now, I go to the one who sent me,
And none of you ask me:
"Where are you going?"
But because these things I have spoken to you,
Sorrow has filled your hearts.

Jesus' comment that he is going to the one who sent him has Christological overtones, a "Sending Motif," and a narrative that are unique to John; but the language, metaphors, and symbolism is known widely within Second Temple Judaism.

The "Logos Hymn" or "Logos Poem" in John 1:1–18 shares, and conceivably reflects, many of the ideas emphasized in the *Self-Glorification Hymn*. As the glorified one in the *Hymn* is portrayed in the heavenly court with the divine beings, so the Logos is also in the same setting "before God" ("and the Word was with (or before) God, and the Word was God (or divine);" 1:1). Notably, the unique "glory" of the Word is highlighted:

Καὶ ὁ λόγος σὰρξ ἐγένετο
καὶ ἐσκήνωσεν ἐν ἡμῖν,
καὶ ἐθεασάμεθα τὴν δόξαν αὐτοῦ,
δόξαν ὡς μονογενοῦς παρὰ πατρός,
πλήρης χάριτος καὶ ἀληθείας.
(1:14)

And the Word flesh became
And dwelt among us.
And we have beheld his glory,
The glory as the only Son from the Father,
Full of grace and truth.

The step parallelism from τὴν δόξαν αὐτοῦ to δόξαν ὡς emphasizes "glory" in this tricolon; the celestial "glory" of the Logos is seen on earth; because he has been transformed into flesh (an idea unique to the Logos Hymn or Logos Poem). Many scholars have rightly concluded that this Logos Hymn of Poem was prefixed to the Gospel by later editors in the Johannine Circle or School.

Similar elevated claims are now found within Second Temple Judaism. Scholars should not assume the author of John knew the *Self-Glorification Hymn*, but scholars also should not resist contemplating the possibility that some Jews within the Johannine Circle or School may well have been influenced by it.[100] We have seen that the claims found in the *Hymn* are also reflected in "Teacher Hymns" in the *Thanksgiving Hymns*. Before the Exile, prophets, priests, and kings claimed a special

---

[97] For reflections, see J. Verheyden, *et al.*, eds., *Studies in the Gospel of John and its Christology: Festschrift Gilbert Van Belle* (Leuven, 2014).

[98] The tradition within and behind Jn 10:34–38 knows about the Jewish debates over the Hebrew text of Gen 2:2: Did God work on the seventh day, finishing his creating, or did he finish his work on the sixth day (as the LXX states)? Jesus, according to John, knows the debates and sides with the literal meaning of Gen 2:2 in Hebrew. Jesus works on Shabbat because God had also worked to create on Shabbat.

[99] Cf. Ps 66:13 (אבוא ביתך): "I will enter into your house [= the Temple]." See 4Q427 frg. 7 1.10.

[100] For the argument that Jews in the Johannine Circle or School were influenced by Essenes who joined the Palestinian Jesus Movement, see Charlesworth, "The Dead Sea Scrolls and the Gospel According to John," in *Exploring the Gospel of John: In Honor of D. Moody Smith*, edited by R. A. Culpepper and C. C. Black (Louisville, 1996) pp. 65–97.

connection with divinity; some Israelites would have imagined these inspired and chosen individuals were seen to be among the Elim. Later, in light of the extant literature of Early Judaism, the adoration of select chosen ones and elevated egos evolved into angelification and deification. The beginning of this process may be foreshadowed in Genesis 18:1–19:1;[101] in this narrative "three men" (שלשה אנשים) appear to Abraham "by the terebinth trees of Mamre;" these mysterious visitors are eventually disclosed to be YHWH and "two angels" (שני המלאכים).

Many scholars have rightly seen enthronement in New Testament passages as political and eschatological, not apocalyptic; that is, the enthronement is contemplated within time and on earth. Now, we might question that exegesis and be permitted to entertain additional meanings.[102] According to Mark,[103] James and John, the sons of Zebedee, asked Jesus to sit (presumably on thrones) on either side of Jesus.

> James and John, the sons of Zebedee, came forward to him and said to him, "Teacher, we want you to do for us whatever we ask of you." [36] And he said to them, "What is it you want me to do for you?" [37] And they said to him, "Permit us to sit in your glory, one at your right and one at your left (δὸς ἡμῖν ἵνα εἷς σου ἐκ δεξιῶν καὶ εἷς ἐξ ἀριστερῶν καθίσωμεν ἐν τῇ δόξῃ σου)."[104]
> (Mk 10:35–37)

Is the reference to "in your glory" (ἐν τῇ δόξῃ σου) to be associated with an earthly kingdom or is it an apocalyptic perspective of another world, as in the *Self-Glorification Hymn*?

According to Matthew, Jesus tells the Twelve that they will sit on thrones:

> But Jesus said to them, "Truly I say to you who have been following me, in the new age (ἐν τῇ παλιγγενεσίᾳ), when the Son of Man shall sit (καθίσῃ) on his glorious throne (ἐπὶ θρόνου δόξης αὐτοῦ), you will also sit (καθήσεσθε) on twelve thrones (ἐπὶ δώδεκα θρόνους), judging Israel's twelve tribes." (Mt 19:28)

Does ἐν τῇ παλιγγενεσίᾳ denote another world or the new messianic age[105] (and is it at the Endtime of the present age or after the present age)? In what ways, if at all, do the images and thoughts in the *Self-Glorification Hymn* initiate better interpretations of Matthew 19:28? Where is the place in which the Twelve will sit on thrones; is it in Jerusalem or among the Elim, the divine beings, in heaven?

Jesus proclaimed that God's Kingdom is not of this world,[106] hence, he probably entertained a sense of some apocalyptic end to his life. The Evangelists are convinced Jesus' confidence was always in God's continuing involvement in his life and proclamations. Some of his later followers most likely imagined that a cosmic shift in time and space had occurred, especially with their conviction that God had raised Jesus to new life. The members in the post-Easter community clearly believed, as we know from Stephen's vision (Acts 7:56),[107] that Jesus was now elevated on high among the Elim. Jesus' earliest followers probably entertained not only eschatological hopes but apocalyptic visions of enthronement in the fast approaching Kingdom of God. Did not some of Jesus' Twelve contemplate that they would be sitting among the Elim (as Mt 19:28 reveals)?

Studying the *Self-Glorification Hymn* helps us in the long process of entering the apocalyptic culture that shaped the transmission of Jesus traditions, notably the Transfiguration that is highlighted in three Gospels (Mt 17:1–13, Mk 9:2–13, Lk 9:28–36; cf. 2Pet 1:16–18):

> Now about eight days after these sayings Jesus took with him Peter and John and James, and went up on the mountain to pray. And while he was praying, the appearance of his face changed, and his clothes became dazzling white. Suddenly they saw two men, Moses and Elijah, talking to him. They appeared in glory (οἳ ὀφθέντες ἐν δόξῃ) and were speaking of his departure, which he was about to accomplish at Jerusalem. Now Peter and his companions

---

[101] Portions of Gen 18:20–25 have been detected in 8Q1, but no help is provided in reading this section.

[102] God is depicted as sitting on a throne in many Hebrew Bible passages; note, for example, Lam 5:19; 1Kgs 22:19; Isa 37:1, 66:1; Ezek 1:26; Ps 47:8; 2Chr 18:18; cf. esp. Rev 1–4. Of earthly kings, Solomon's throne is most emphasized; see, e.g., 1Kgs 1:46, 10:18. According the author of Ps 122:5, there are many thrones in heaven.

[103] Out of embarrassment for the sons of Zebedee, Matthew shifts the request to their mother. See Mt 20:20–28.

[104] In the Greek "one at your right hand and one at your left" is placed within the sentence for emphasis. James and John want the right and left thrones, with Jesus sitting in the center. Is there any intended irony with the crucifixion when Jesus is in the center between two thieves? Note Jesus' charge that they do not know that they are asking for martyrdom. Allison, I now note, argues that the two images (the expectation of the sons of Zebedee and Jesus' crucifixion) "engenders irony, for while the two sons have the first scene in mind, Jesus is contemplating the second." See Allison, *Studies in Matthew* (Grand Rapids, 2005) pp. 230–33.

[105] The term παλιγγενεσίᾳ is well-known from Gnosticism and the Hermetica; it is used of the κόσμος, and its renewal, by the Stoics and seems to have originated with the Pythagoreans (*M. Ant.* 11, 1, 3).

[106] Scholars concur that the numerous traditions about an apocalyptic inbreaking of God's Rule (the Kingdom of God) may be confidently traced back to the historical Jesus; see Charlesworth, *The Historical Jesus: An Essential Guide* (Nashville, 2008).

[107] Stephen, according to Luke, states: "I see the heavens opened and the Son of Man standing at the right hand of God!" (Acts 7:56; NRSV).

were weighed down with sleep; but since they had stayed awake, they saw his glory (εἶδον τὴν δόξαν αὐτοῦ) and the two men who stood with him. (Lk 9:28–32)

In the *Hymn* and in the Transfiguration account we are shown divine men[108] standing and radiating God's glory and light (καὶ μετεμορφώθη ἔμπροσθεν αὐτῶν, καὶ ἔλαμψεν τὸ πρόσωπον αὐτοῦ ὡς ὁ ἥλιος, τὰ δὲ ἱμάτια αὐτοῦ ἐγένετο λευκὰ ὡς τὸ φῶς; Mt 17:2).

Both documents also reveal to us beliefs in a cosmos defined by divine beings, Moses, Elijah, and Jesus. Moses was deified by some Jews, as we have noted. Elijah was taken up to heaven in a chariot, as described in the Hebrew Scriptures (2Kgs 2:9–12); he was expected to return as the forerunner of the coming Day of Yahweh (Mal 4:5–6; MT 3:23–24). He is celebrated in the *Apocalypse of Elijah* (1st–4th cent CE)[109] in which he promises crowns and thrones in heaven for those who have obeyed God (*ApEl* 1:8). Jesus was thought to be Elijah by some of his followers (Mt 16:14). He was also hailed as angelic (*GosThom* 13) and full of divine glory (e.g., the Logos Hymn in John).[110]

The ideas and beliefs found in the *Self-Glorification Hymn* influenced many compositions and permeated more than one group within Second Temple Judaism. We have seen evidence that Qumranites within the *Yaḥad* revered the composition; one can appreciate that the imagined meaning of the *Hymn* became part of secret lore, as it portrayed the life of the Righteous Teacher. Most likely, the *War Scroll* (which contains an excerpt from the *Hymn*) and the *Thanksgiving Hymns* (which represents an expanded version of the *Hymn*) were known to Essenes living throughout the Holy Land. Thus, the *Self-Glorification Hymn*, indirectly and directly, would stimulate reflections about the cosmos and God's eternal promises to be with his chosen Holy Ones, proved by the elevation of the one who sits among the Elim.

7. Text and Translation

Within the texts, double brackets indicating joins, [[]], are possible with individual witnesses; but in the composite text, the use of single brackets and double brackets would make the text difficult to read. Thus, double brackets (to denote joins as in the *Hodayot*) are not introduced into the Composite Text of the *Self-Glorification Hymn*, because it is a collage of witnesses guided by the main witness, the text of 4Q471b. Notes are provided to clarify the source of words in the lines and also the consonants with diacritics. The few single brackets inserted in

the text signify necessary restorations not based on the manuscript witnesses to the *Hymn*; these bracketed restorations are guided by the flow of the *Hymn* and the vocabulary found in the *Thanksgiving Hymns*. Within brackets no diacritics are used; these appear in each witness.

For a guide to our methodology for the translation of words, terms, and concepts in precise ways and consistently when context demands, see the "Consistency Chart" in the introduction to the *Thanksgiving Hymns* (notably 1QHᵃ).

8. Selected Bibliography

Abegg, M. G., Jr. "4Q491 (*4QMilhamaᵃ*) – An 'Ensemble' of Manuscripts?" *Abstracts: AAR/SBL* (1990) 378. [This is only an abstract of a lecture.]

Abegg, M. G., Jr. "4Q471: A Case of Mistaken Identity?" In *Pursuing the Text: Studies in Honor of Ben Zion Wacholder on the Occasion of his Seventieth Birthday*, edited by J. C. Reeves and J. Kampen. JSOTSup 184; Sheffield, 1994, pp. 136–47.

Abegg, M. G., Jr. "Who Ascended to Heaven? 4Q491, 4Q427, and the Teacher of Righteousness." In *Eschatology, Messianism, and the Dead Sea Scrolls*, edited by C. A. Evans and P. W. Flint. Studies in the Dead Sea Scrolls and Related Literature; Grand Rapids, 1997, pp. 61–73.

Alexander, P. *Mystical Texts: Songs of the Sabbath Sacrifice and Related Manuscripts*. London, 2006.

Allison, D. C. *Constructing Jesus*. London, 2010; see pp. 261–63.

Baillet, M. *Qumrân Grotte 4.III*. DJD 7; Oxford, 1982.

Betz, O. "The Servant Tradition of Isaiah in the Dead Sea Scrolls." *JSS* 7 (1995) 40–56.

Charlesworth, J. H. "Hymns and Odes in Early Judaism." In *Critical Reflections on the Odes of Solomon. Volume 1: Literary Settings, Textual Studies, Gnosticism, the Dead Sea Scrolls and the Gospel of John*. JSPS 22; Sheffield, 1998, pp. 27–53.

Charlesworth, J. H. "Prolegomenous Reflections Towards a Taxonomy of Resurrection Texts (1QHᵃ, 1En, 4Q521, Paul, Luke, the Fourth Gospel, and Psalm 30)." In *The Changing Face of Judaism, Christianity, and Other Greco-Roman Religions in Antiquity: Presented to James Charlesworth on the Occasion of his 65th Birthday*, edited by I. H. Henderson and G. S. Oegema with the assistance of S. Parks Richter. JSHRZ 2; Gütersloh, 2006, pp. 237–64.

Collins, J. J. *Apocalypticism in the Dead Sea Scrolls*. London, 1997.

Collins, J. J. *The Scepter and the Star: The Messiahs of the Dead Sea Scrolls and other Ancient Literature*. New York, 1995; see esp. pp. 136–39.

Collins, J. J. "A Throne in the Heavens: Apotheosis in Pre-Christian Judaism." In *Death, Ecstasy, and Otherworldly Journeys*, edited by J. J. Collins and M. Fishbane. Albany, N.Y., 1995, pp. 41–56.

---

[108] Luke calls Moses and Elijah "two men" (9:30).

[109] The Jewish stratum most likely antedates the problems in Egypt in 117 CE.

[110] In the Gospel of Thomas, Peter claims Jesus is like an angel. For a discussion of angelic Christology, see C. A. Gieschen, *Angelomorphic Christology: Antecedents and Early Evidence* (AGAJU 42; Leiden and Boston, 1998).

Collins, J. J. and D. Dimant, "A Thrice-Told Hymn: A Response to Eileen Schuller." *JQR* 85 (1994) 151–55.

Davila, J. R. "Exploring the Mystical Background of the Dead Sea Scrolls." In *The Oxford Handbook of the Dead Sea Scrolls*, edited by T. H. Lim and J. J. Collins. Oxford, 2010, pp. 433–54.

Davila, J. R. "The Hodayot Hymnist and the Four Who Entered Paradise." *RQ* 17 (1996) 457–78.

de Souza Nogueira, P. A. "Ecstatic Worship in the Self-Glorification Hymn (4Q471B, 4Q427, 4Q491C): Implications for the Understanding of an Ancient Jewish and Early Christian Phenomenon." In *Wisdom and Apocalypticism in the Dead Sea Scrolls and in the Biblical Tradition*, edited by F. García-Martínez. BETL 168; Leuven, 2003, pp. 385–93.

Dean-Otting, M. *Heavenly Journeys: A Study of the Motif in Hellenistic Jewish Literature*. Frankfurt am Main and New York, 1984.

Dimant, D. "A Synoptic Comparison of Parallel Sections in 4Q427 7, 4Q491 11 and 4Q471B." *JQR* 85 (1994) 157–61.

Eshel, E. "4Q471b: A Self-Glorification Hymn." *RQ* 17 (1996) 176–203.

Eshel, E. "471b. 4QSelf-Glorification Hymn (= 4QHᵉ frg. 1?)." In *Qumran Cave 4.XX: Poetical and Liturgical Texts, Part 2*. DJD 29; Oxford, 1999, pp. 421–32, Pl. 28.

Eshel, E. "The Identification of the 'Speaker' of the Self-Glorification Hymn." In *The Provo International Conference on the Dead Sea Scrolls: Technological Innovations, New Texts, and Reformulated Issues*, edited by D. W. Perry and E. Ulrich. STDJ 30; Leiden and Boston, 1999, pp. 619–35.

Eshel, E. "Self-Glorification Hymn." In *Outside the Bible: Ancient Jewish Writings Related to Scripture*, edited by L. H. Feldman, J. L. Kugel, and L. H. Schiffman. Philadelphia, 2013, pp. 1924–26.

Eshel, E. and M. Kister. "A Polemical Qumran Fragment." *JJS* 43 (1993) 277–81.

Fletcher-Louis, C. H. T. *All the Glory of Adam: Liturgical Anthropology in the Dead Sea Scrolls*. STDJ 42; Leiden and Boston, 2002, pp. 204–16.

Gallusz, L. "Self-Glorification Hymn (4Q491)." In *The Throne Motif in the Book of Revelation*. London and New York, 2014, pp. 73–74.

Himmelfarb, M. *Ascent to Heaven in Jewish and Christian Apocalypses*. New York, 1993.

Knohl, I. *The Messiah Before Jesus: The Suffering Servant of the Dead Sea Scrolls*. Berkeley, 2000, see esp. pp. 58–68.

Knohl, I. "The Suffering Servant: From Isaiah to the Dead Sea Scrolls." In *Scriptural Exegesis: The Shapes of Culture and the Religious Imagination: Essays in Honour of Michael Fishbane*, edited by D. A. Green and L. S. Lieber. Oxford, 2009, pp. 89–104.

Miller, E. "The Self-Glorification Hymn Reexamined." *Henoch* 31 (2009) 307–24.

Morray-Jones, C. R. A. "Paradise Revisited (2 Cor 12:1–12): The Jewish Mystical Background of Paul's Apostolate, Part 1: The Jewish Sources." *HTR* 86 (1993) 177–217. "Part 2: Paul's Heavenly Ascent and Its Significance." *HTR* 86 (1993) 265–92.

Puech, É. "L'Hymne de la Glorification du Maître de 4Q431." In *Prayer and Poetry in the Dead Sea Scrolls and Related Literature: Essays in Honor of Eileen Schuller*, edited by J. Penner, *et al*. Leiden and Boston, 2012, pp. 377–407.

Segal, A. F. "The Risen Christ and the Angelic Mediator Figures in Light of Qumran." In *JDSS*, edited by J. H. Charlesworth. ABRL; New York, 1992, pp. 302–28.

Schuller, E. "A Hymn from a Cave Four Hodayot Manuscript: 4Q417 7 I + ii." *JBL* 112 (1993) 605–28.

Schuller, E. "The Cave 4 Hodayot Manuscripts: A Preliminary Description." *JQR* 85 (1994) 137–50.

Smith, M. "Two Ascended to Heaven – Jesus and the Author of 4Q491." In *JDSS*, edited by J. H. Charlesworth. ABRL; New York, 1992, pp. 290–301.

Stegemann, H. "Some Remarks to *1QSa*, to *1QSb*, and to Qumran Messianism." *RQ* 17 (1996) 479–505.

Steudel, A. "The Eternal Reign of the People of God – Collective Expectations in Qumran Texts (4Q246 and 1QM)." *RQ* 17 (1996) 507–25.

Tabor, J. D. *Things Unutterable: Paul's Ascent to Paradise in Its Greco-Roman, Judaic, and Early Christian Contexts*. Lanham, MD, 1986.

Wise, M. O. "מי כמוני באלים: A Study of 4Q491c, 4Q471b, 4Q427 7 and 1QHᵃ 25:35–26:10." *DSD* 7 (2000) 173–219.

Wise, M. O. *The First Messiah: Investigating the Savior Before Jesus*. San Francisco, 1999.

Wolfson, E. R. "Mysticism and the Poetic-Liturgical Compositions from Qumran: A Response to Bilhah Nitzan." *JQR* 85 (1994) 185–202.

Self-Glorification Hymn
4Q427 (4QHª) Frg. 7 1.6–13
4Q491 Frg. 11 1.13–19
1QHª 26.6–9
4Q471b Frgs. 1a–d Lines 1–10
(1QHª 25–26.5 has no parallels to this text)

Composite Text

4Q427 [4QHª] *Frg. 7 1.6–13*[1]

6	[הֿרע
7	בהר]וֿתי
8	באלים]
9	מ[ֿי] בלשון יעידני [
10	המ[ֿלֿכֿ[2] רע לקדשים ולוא יבא
11	ולכבו]ֿדי לוא ידמה כֿ[ֿי]אֿ אני עמ[3] אלים מעמֿדֿ[ֿי]
12	ֿר לא בפֿז אכתי[ֿר] לֿי וכתם או ביורימ[4] לוא [
13	עם בני עו]ֿלֿהֿ [ֿי]ֿתֿחשב בי זמרו ידידיֿם שירו למלכֿ[5]
14	הכבוד שמחו בע]ֿדֿת אל הרנינו באהֿלֿי ישועה הללו במעון

---

[1] Frg. 7 preserves both the bottom margin and the left margin of col. 1.

[2] Note medial *kaph* in final position.

[3] Note medial *mem* in final position.

[4] Note medial *mem* in final position. Schuller also reads: ביורימ but translates it as "Ophirim." That translation follows Eshel's reading of וכתם אופירים in 4Q471b which is rendered "with refined gold."

[5] Note medial *kaph* in final position.

572

Self-Glorification Hymn
4Q427 (4QHᵃ) Frg. 7 1.6–13
4Q491 Frg. 11 1.13–19
1QHᵃ 26.6–9
4Q471b Frgs. 1a–d Lines 1–10
(1QHᵃ 25–26.5 has no parallels to this text)

Composite Text

4Q427 [4QHᵃ] *Frg. 7 Col. 1.6–13*

6   […] the evil

7   [… with] my [teach]ing[1]

8   […] among the Elim[2]

9   [….] Wh[o] with language[3] can appoint me?

10   [… the K]ing, a companion to the Holy Ones, and no one can come[4]

11   […. And to] my [glor]y it cannot be compared, f[o]r I am with the Elim.[5] [My] rank

12   […]°r. Not with (pure) gold will I cro[wn] myself, and (not with) gold or with precious stones. Not

13   [with the sons of dec]eit [shall he] reckon me. Chant, O beloved ones, sing to the King of[6]

14   [glory, be joyful in the cong]regation of God, exult[7] in the tents of salvation, give praise in the habitation of

---

[1] The reference seems to be to the Righteous Teacher.
[2] Or "divine beings."
[3] Or "speech."
[4] Or "it will not come."
[5] Or "divine beings."
[6] The king is God. See 4Q471b frgs. 1a–d line 7.
[7] See Isa 12:6.

4Q491 Frg. 11 1.13–19[6]

13 [ול]כֿבודי[7] לוא יֿדֿמֿהֿ[8] ולוא ירומם זולתי ולֿוֿ[ ]אֿ יבוא ביא כיא אני ישבתי בֿ[ ]שלוֿ[ ]הֿ בשמֿים ואין

14 [ר]יבים[9] אני עם אלים אתחשב[10] ומכוניֿ[ ]בעדת קודש לוֿא כבשר תאוֿ[ ]תי[ת] [כול יקרֿ[ ]לי בכבוד[11]

15 [מע]וֿן הקודש מֿיֿא לבוז נחשב ביא ומֿיֿ[ ]א בכבודי ידמה לֿיֿא מיא הֿוֿ[ ]א כֿבֿאֿ[ ]יֿם[ ] ישובֿ[ ] וסֿפֿר[13]

16 [גבור]תֿוֿ[14] מיא יֿשֿ[א]15 [צערים כמוני ומיאֿ[ ] יסבוֿ[ ]לֿ[16] רֿע הדמה ביא ואין נשֿ[ ]ניתי והוריהֿ[ ] לוא תדמה

17 [בהריתי]17 ומיא יגדֿוֿֿנֿיֿא[18] בפתֿ[ ]חי פיא [ ]וֿמזל שפתי מיא יכיל ומֿיֿאֿ[ ]וֿ[יוע]דֿני[ ][19] וֿידמֿ[ ]ה במשפטי

18 [כ]יֿא אניא עם אלים אֿהֿשֿ[ ]ב וֿ[כֿ]בֿודי וֿ[א] עם בני המלך לוֿאֿ[ ] פֿ[ ]זֿ ולוֿא כתם אֿ[ ]וֿפירים[20]

19 (VACAT)[   ]   (VACAT) [   ] (VACAT) [

1QHᵃ 25.26[21]

26 מֿעשֿיֿ[ ]   שֿ[ ]מֿים ובסוד קד[ושים]

1QHᵃ 26.6–9 [Frgs. 56 Col. 2, 46 Col. 2, 55 Col. 2, and 7 Col. 2]
Parallels: 4Q427 Frg. 7; 4Q428 Frg. 21; 4Q431

6 יועדני[22]

---

[6] The text is found on six fragments. See PAM 42.473 and 42.474.

[7] See 4Q427 frg. 7 1.11.

[8] Scribal dots.

[9] See 1QHᵃ 17.23.

[10] The scribal dots on the superlinear *taw* indicates it should be ignored.

[11] The left margin is visible.

[12] These letters are now almost completely lost.

[13] Read: ישוב וספר. The scribe wrote the *pe* in a cursive form.

[14] See 4Q491 frg. 11 1.9: גבורותו.

[15] See 1QHᵃ 4.24, 5.30, 8.34.

[16] See 4Q471b frgs. 1a–d line 3.

[17] From 4Q471b frg. 1a line 4.

[18] Read: יגודניא.

[19] Qal. impf. of יעד. 4Q427 frg. 7 1.9: יעידני.

[20] The scribe made a long, vertical stroke here that may signal the end of the hymn.

[21] This fragment is included to show that it does not preserve part of the *Self-Glorification Hymn*.

[22] See 4Q491 frg. 11 1.17.

4Q491 Frg. 11 1.13–19[8]

13 [and to] my glory nothing can be compared. And none will[9] be exalted except me; and no one can come with me. For I, I sat in [tranquili]ty in the heavens; and there is no

14 [st]rife. I, I reckon myself with the Elim;[10] and my established-place (is) in the congregation of holiness. [My] desire (is) not according to the flesh. All that is precious to me (is) in the glory of

15 the [dwel]ling of holiness. Who was reckoned contemptible with me,[11] and who is comparable to me in my glory? Who (is) he? Like (one of) [the sea] travellers, can he come back and recount

16 his [migh]t? Who can suf[fer] sorrows as I do, and who can [bear] evil compared with me? And there is none. I have been taught, and no teaching is comparable

17 [with my teaching]. And who can cut me off when [I] ope[n my mouth,] and the flow of my speech,[12] who can measure (it)? And who can appoint me and be compared with my utterance?[13]

18 [F]or I, I (am) recko[ned] with the Elim,[14] [and] my glory (is) with the sons of the King. Not [(pure) g]old and not gold (of) Ophir[15]

19 [….] (VACAT) […] (VACAT) […] (VACAT)

1QH^a 25.26

26 works of [… he]aven, and in the council of the Ho[ly Ones][16]

1QH^a 26.6–9 [Frgs. 56 Col. 2, 46 Col. 2, 55 Col. 2, and 7 Col. 2]
Parallels: 4Q427 Frg. 7; 4Q428 Frg. 21; 4Q431

6 can appoint[17] [me …]

---

[8] For the notes see *PTSDSSP* vol. 2. The translation is by Charlesworth.

[9] Or "can."

[10] Or "divine beings."

[11] An echo of Isa. 53.

[12] Heb: שפתי.

[13] Heb: במשפתי. Perhaps a mistake for במשפטי. Note the paronomasia. Three synonymous nouns (לשון, שפת, משפת) are used for "language," "speech," and "utterance."

[14] Or "divine beings."

[15] Ctr. our composite text. The alteration seems to be caused by the editor of the *War Scroll*.

[16] This fragment does not preserve portions of the *Self-Glorification Hymn*. Puech (2012) claims that the *Hymn* begins in 1QH^a 25.34.

[17] *Nipʿal* imperfect of יעד.

7   יבוא[23]

8   וכבוד[24]

9   בִֿי והֿ[25]

4Q471b Frgs. 1a d
Self-Glorification Hymn
(*olim* Prayer of Michael)[26]

Frgs. 1 a,c[27]

1   [א]תֿחשֿ[ב28]

2   קֿוֹדש ֿ[ ]

3   כמוני חדל[ן]

4   תדמה בהריתי כֿ[ני]

5   מֿיֿ כמוני בֿאלים[29]וֿ[ן]

6   שפֿתי מי יכיל מֿ[ן]

7   ידיד המלכֿ[30]רע לק[ן]דשים

8   לוא ידמה כֿיֿ אֿ[נ]י
                 אֿ

9   בפז כֿתֿ[נ]יר[31]לי

Frg. 1b

1   מי]נֿבֿזה כמונֿ[י]

2   [רע ידמה בֿ[ני]

---

[23] See 4Q427 frg. 7 1.10.

[24] Cf. 4Q491 frg. 11 1.18.

[25] Cf. 4Q427 frg. 7 1.13.

[26] M. Baillet offered the opinion that 4Q471b could be a "Cantique de Michel (?)."

[27] The right margin and bottom margin are visible.

[28] On frg. 1c.

[29] באלים with 4Q427 frg. 7 1.8; see עם אלים in 4Q427 frg. 7 1.11 and 4Q491 frg. 11 1.14, 18. See Ex 15:11: מִי־כָמֹכָה בָּאֵלִם [the Song of the Sea].

[30] Note medial *kaph* at the end of the word.

[31] See 4Q427 frg. 7 1.12: [בפז אכתי]ר. Puech: בפז דמ]ה.

7   can come […]

8   and glory […]

9   with me and h°[…]

4Q471b Frgs. 1a–d
Self-Glorification Hymn
(olim Prayer of Michael)

Frgs. 1 a,c

1   [I] reck[on myself …][18]

2   holiness $^{\circ}$[…]

3   like me was rejected […]

4   is comparable with my teaching. F[or…]

5   Who is like me among[19] the Elim? And […]

6   my speech,[20] who can measure (it)? Who […]

7   the beloved of the King, a companion of the Ho[ly Ones …]

8   it cannot be compared, for I [(am) …]

9   with (pure) gold will I cro[wn myself …]

Frg. 1b

1   [… who] has been despised like m[e? …]

2   […] evil compared with [me …]

---

[18] On frg. c.
[19] Lit. "with." ב and עם are often synonymous.
[20] Lit. "my lips."

3   כי א[נֹ֯י יֹשֹׁבֹ֯תי]֯[

Frg. 1d

1   [זמרו]

Frgs. 1a-d

1   אני עם אלים א[תֹחֹשֹׁ]ב[32] ומכוני בעדת]

2   קֹודש ֯[[ומי [[נֹ֯בֹזה כמונֹ֯י ומי]

3   כמוני[33] חדל[[אישים[34] ומי יסבול[35] [[רע ידמה בֹ֯י והוריה לוא]

4   תדמה בהריתי כֹ[[י א[[נֹ֯י יֹשֹׁבֹ֯תי[36]

5   מֹ֯י כמוני בֹאלים וֹ[מי[37]   יגודני בפתחי פי ומזל]

6   שפתי מי יכיל מֹ[ין בלשון יעודני[38]   כי אני]

7   ידיד המלכֹ[39] רע לק[דושים ולוא יבוא בי   ולכבודי]

8   לוא ידמה כֹ֯י אֹ[נֹי עם אלים מעמדי וכבודי עם בני המלך לוא]

֯א
9   בפז כֹתֹ[ר]יר[40] לי

10   [[זמרו[[[41] ידידים

---

[32] With Eshel (DJD 29).
[33] Puech (2012): יחדל.
[34] See Isa 53:3: נבזה וחדל אישים.
[35] Puech (2012) restores: בכול.
[36] Puech (2012): תדמה בהריתי א[י]ן ושוה בהן כין.
[37] Puech (2012): ע[מ בני המלך מי.
[38] Or with Puech (2012): יעידני.
[39] Note the medial *kaph* in final position.
[40] Read as אכתיר. Puech: בפז דם]ה, but see 4Q427 frg. 7 1.12.
[41] Puech (2012): בני.

3   […]°[…. For] I, [I] sat […]

Frg. 1d

1   [….] Chant […]

Frgs. 1a–d

1   […. I, I] reck[on myself with the Elim; and my established-place (is) in the congregation of]

2   holiness °[…. And who] has been despised like m[e?²¹ And who]

3   like me was rejected [(by) men?²² And who bears] evil compared with [me? And no teaching]

4   is comparable with my teaching. F[or I, I] sat […]

5   Who is like me among²³ the Elim? And [who can cut me off when I open my mouth? … And the flow of]

6   my speech, who can measure (it)? Who [with language can appoint me? … For I (am)]

7   the beloved of the King, a companion of the Ho[ly Ones. And no one can come with me …. And to my glory]

8   nothing can be compared, for I [(am) with the Elim. My rank and glory (are) with the sons of the King. Not]

9   with (pure) gold will I cro[wn myself …]

10   […]. Chant, [O beloved ones, …]

---

²¹ The following references to suffering seem to refer to the Righteous Teacher as in 1QHᵃ 16.
²² An echo of Isa. 53:3.
²³ Lit. "with."

Self-Glorification Hymn Composite Text[42]

1   ] אני עם אלים אתחשב[43] ומכוני בעדת[44]

2   קודש[45] מיא לבוז נחשב ביא ומיא[46] נבזה כמונ[י ומי][47]

3   כמוני חדל [אישים[48] ומי יסבול [רע ידמה בֿ]יֿ[49] והוריה לוא

4   תדמה[50] בהריתי[51] כיא אני ישבתי[52] לבטח במעון קו[ן]דש][53]

5   מֿי כמוני בֿאלים ומיא יגדניא בפת[חי פיא]וֿמזל

6   שפֿתי[54] מיא יכיל מֿי בלשון יעידני[55] וידמה במשפֿתֿי [כ]יֿ[א אני

7   ידיד המלך רעֿ[56] לקדשים ולוא יבוא[57] ביא[58] [ול]כבודי[59]

8   לוא ידמה[60] כיֿא אֿני עם אלים מעמֿדֿ[י][61] וכבודי[62] עם בני המלך לוא[63]

---

[42] The composite text is based on 4Q471b. Frg. 1 of 4Q471b preserves the right margin. The bottom margin of the leather is also preserved. Final forms and spellings are according to each manuscript that provides consonants for this column.

[43] The scribal dot on the superlinear *taw* indicates it should be ignored.

[44] The image of 4Q471b is on Plate 28 and in the fold-out of DJD 29. The handle can be seen to the right of this column. Eshel (DJD 29): [תֿחשֿ]ב ומעוני בעדת] [אני עם אלים א. See 4Q491 frg. 11 1.14: אני עם אלים אתחֿשב ומכוני בעדת קודש.

[45] See 1QHa 20.5: במעון קו[דש]. Also see Ps 89:6.

[46] The space between the two pieces of leather should be filled with about 19 consonants; see 1QHa 12.23–24 (not part of the hymn): כול בוזי כיֿא לא יחשבונֿי.

[47] From 4Q471b frg. 1a–d line 2.

[48] This is an echo and a quotation from Isa 53:3: נבזה וחדל אישים. "He is despised and rejected (by) men." Lit. "incompetent men." Does this phrase reflect the Righteous Teacher's loss of followers?

[49] See 4Q471b frg. 1 a–d line 3.

[50] See 4Q491 frg. 11 1.16: והוריה לוא תדמה.

[51] From 4Q471b frg. 1 a–d line 4.

[52] From 4Q491 frg. 11 1.13: כיא אני ישבתי.

[53] See 1QHa 20.5 and 4Q428 frg. 12b 49.1.

[54] See 4Q491 frg. 11 1.17: וֿמזל שפתי [ומיא יגֿדוניא בפת[חי פיא]. Also see the helpful notes by Eshel in DJD 29, pp. 429–30.

[55] See 4Q427 frg. 7 1.9: מֿ[י] בלשון יעודני. See also, 1QHa 26.6: יֿוֿ[עֿ]דֿ[ני].

[56] Note the paronomasia with רע in line 3. From 4Q471b frg. 1c line 7.

[57] See 1QHa 26.7: יבוא and 4Q427 frg. 7 1.10: רע לקדשים ולוא יבא.

[58] Cf. 4Q491 frg. 11 1.13.

[59] See 4Q427 frg. 7 1.11: ולכבו[ד]יֿ and 4Q491 frg. 1 11.13: ול[כבודי.

[60] From 4Q471b frg. 1 a–d line 8.

[61] From 4Q427 frg. 7 1.11.

[62] See 4Q491 frg. 11 1.18: וֿכֿבודיﬡ.

[63] See 4Q427 frg. 7 1.11: כֿ[י]ﬡ אני עם אלים מעמֿדֿ[י].

Self-Glorification Hymn Composite Text

1   […] I, I reckon myself[24] together with the Elim;[25] and my established-place (is) in the congregation of[26]

2   holiness.[27] Who was reckoned contemptible with me? And who has been despised like [me? And who]

3   like me was rejected [(by) men?[28] And who bears][29] evil compared with m[e?] And no teaching

4   is comparable with my teaching.[30] For I, I sat safely in the dwelling of holi[ness].[31]

5   Who is like me among[32] the Elim? And who can cut me off[33] when [I] ope[n my mouth?] And the flow of[34]

6   my speech,[35] who can measure[36] (it)? Who with language[37] can appoint me and can be compared with my utterance?[38] [F]or I (am)

7   the beloved of the King,[39] a companion of the Holy Ones. And no one can come with me. [And to] my glory

8   it cannot be compared;[40] for I (am) with the Elim. [My] rank and my glory (are) with the sons of the King. Not

---

[24] *Hithpaʿel* of חשב, "to reckon oneself." The verb "reckon" denotes a conclusion based upon reflection. "To resemble" and "to be compared" denotes "to be like." The author uses words carefully. Note the restoration. It is conceivable that the passage once read: "He reckoned me." See the same verb in line 10.

[25] Or "divine beings."

[26] Eshel (DJD 29): "[I am] recko[ned with the angels, my dwelling is in] the holy [council." See Ps 89:6–9.

[27] See 1QHᵃ 20.5: "in the ho[ly] dwelling." Or better, 4Q491 frg. 11 1.14. Note the cosmic perspective in 1QHᵃ 20 and 4Q491.

[28] This is an echo and a quotation from Isa 53:3: נבזה וחדל אישים; "He is despised and rejected by men." Lit. "incompetent men." Echoes from Isaiah 53, "the servant song," are obvious throughout this hymn.

[29] See Isa 53:4: "And he bears (סבלם) our sorrows." The same verb is restored in our text.

[30] According to the *Pesher Habakkuk* col. 7, God permitted the Righteous Teacher alone to know all his mysteries.

[31] Cf. 4Q491 frg. 11 1.13: "for I, I sat in [tranquili]ty in the heavens."

[32] Lit. "with."

[33] The root seems to be גדד. It appears in Ps 94:21 to denote "to gather together" (יגודו) and in Jer 5:7 to mean "to assemble themselves" (יתגדדו). In Rabbinics, in Aramaic, and in Arabic *gdd* means "to cut off." In Akkadian *gadādo* means "to detach" or "to separate." See DJD 29, p. 430 and Even-Shoshan (1975) vol. 1, p. 158.

[34] See נזל, "to trickle," "to flow" (Qal). The noun מזל derives from the verb. In Rabbinics we find מזיל and מזל (see Even-Shoshan (1975) vol. 2, p. 840). See Deut 32:2: "Let my teaching drop as the rain. My speech distill (תזל) as the dew."

[35] Lit "lips." שפה denotes the means of speaking, tongue, or vocabulary. See Gen 11:1, 6–7 (the famous account of Babel).

[36] The *hipʿil* impf. of כול, "to contain," "to hold in." Conceivably, the root is the Aramaic כיל, "to measure."

[37] Lit. "tongue." See Neh 13:24, Isa 66:18. For שפת with לשון see Ps 34:14 and Isa 28:11. The noun "tongue" indicates "language." The author contends that no human can appoint him to proclaim and to interpret Torah. He claims that God appointed him. See Job 9:19.

[38] Or "judgment," "decision." Perhaps a mistake for "ruling;" Heb.: משפט.

[39] "King" denotes God.

[40] I.e. "and no one may resemble my glory." Note the line division and the various verbs that denote "to compare," "to resemble," and "to be considered," and the words "like me."

9 בפז אכתי[ר]⁶⁴ לי וכתם או ביורים⁶⁵ לוא⁶⁶ [עם בני עו]לֹה⁶⁷

10 [י]תֹחשב בי⁶⁸ זמרו ידידיֹם שירו למלך [הכבוד]⁶⁹

11 (VACAT)

---

⁶⁴ Ctr. Schuller in DJD 29, p. 203: [֯כֹ֯ ; cf. Eshel in 4Q471b: כֹת[א)יר.

⁶⁵ See 1QHᵃ 26.9: [בי וה֯ (perhaps a copying error for ביורים).

⁶⁶ Cf. 4Q427 frg. 7 1.12: לֹא בפז אכתי[ר] לי וכתם או ביורים לוא.

⁶⁷ See 1QHᵃ 13.10: לבני עֹ֗ולה and 4Q429 frg. 4 1.5: בֹני֗ עֹ֗ול]ה; cf. 1QHᵃ 14.21.

⁶⁸ See 4Q427 frg. 7 1.13: [י]תֹחשב בי.

⁶⁹ 4Q427 frg. 7 1.13: זמרו ידידיֹם שירו למלכ. An addition is found in 4QHᵃ (4Q427): שמחו בע[דֹת אל הרנינו באהֹלֹי ישועה הללו במעון.

9   with (pure) gold will I cro[wn] myself, and (not with) gold or with precious stones. Not [with the sons of de]ceit

10   [shall] he reckon me.[41] Chant, O beloved ones, sing to the King of [glory].[42]

11   (VACAT)[43]

---

[41] Or "regard me." See 4Q427 frg. 7 1.13: תֹחשׁב בי[י]. In Num 23:9 and 1QS 3.1 יתחשב has a passive meaning: "to be reckoned."

[42] See 4Q427 frg. 7 1.13–14: "Chant, O beloved ones, sing to the King of [glory]." Also see line 15: "e]xtol together with the eternal hosts, give greatness to our God and glory to our King." In 4Q427 col. 1 the following may be and addition: "be joyful in the cong]regation of God, exult in the tents of salvation, give praise in the habitation of...."

[43] See 4Q491 11 1.19. The *Self-Glorification Hymn* ends here; ctr. Puech (2012).

Hodayot-Like Texts A–D
4Q433, 4Q433a, 4Q440, 4Q440a

JAMES H. CHARLESWORTH

with LEA BERKUZ and BLAKE A. JURGENS[1]

Introduction

During the initial analysis of the Cave 4 *Hodayot* manuscripts (4Q427–4Q432 [4QH^{a-f}]), scholars observed that some miscellaneous fragments bore particular resemblances to the *Thanksgiving Hymns*, but ultimately contained no material which overlapped any substantial section of text from the official *Hodayot* manuscripts.[2] Three of these "*Hodayot-Like*" fragments (4Q433, 4Q433a, 4Q440) were first published in a preliminary assessment by J. Strugnell and E. Schuller,[3] and eventually were published in *Discoveries of the Judaean Desert* by Schuller.[4] A fourth *Hodayot-Like* fragment, 4Q440a (*olim* 4Q427 [4QH^{a}] frg. 14), was subsequently published by A. Lange in 2000, along with a fragment formerly considered part of 4Q440, now known as 4Q440b.[5]

1. Provenience and Categorization

4Q433, 4Q433a, 4Q440, and 4Q440a were preserved but not necessarily composed at Qumran. Since they are related to the *Thanksgiving Hymns* (*Hodayot*), they were clearly known at

Qumran and may have been edited there. A "*Hodayot-Like*" text can be defined as a composition that potentially could be a witness to the collection of psalms found in the *Thanksgiving Hymns* (Hodayot), but lacks sufficient documentary evidence to solidify that claim. These texts contain considerable linguistic similarities to the *Thanksgiving Hymns* (e.g., incipits such as ברוך אתה אדוני or אודכה אדוני, frequent use of first person singular pronouns, verbal parallels, etc.)[6] but do not parallel any of the known psalms found in the *Thanksgiving Hymns*.

One problem with this categorization is that many scholars have concluded that the *Thanksgiving Hymns* was not a static corpus of psalms, but instead was transmitted through various manifestations.[7] If this is the case, it becomes increasingly difficult to delineate what qualifies a text as "*Hodayot*-like" as opposed to being a liturgical text which bears similarities to the *Thanksgiving Hymns*. Moreover, further analysis of these *Hodayot-Like Texts* has suggested that the similarities shared between these manuscripts and the *Thanksgiving Hymns* are not as conclusive as originally had been presumed.[8] It cannot be denied that particular motifs and linguistic patterns are

---

[1] Berkuz helped with the text and translation. Jurgens helped with the introduction.

[2] See J. Strugnell, "Le travail d'édition des fragments manuscrits de Qumrân," *RB* 63 (1956) 49–67.

[3] J. Strugnell and E. Schuller, "Further *Hodayot* Manuscripts from Qumran?" in *Antikes Judentum und Frühes Christentum: Festschrift für Harmut Stegemann zum 65. Geburtstag*, edited by B. Kollmann, W. Rienbold, and A. Steudel (BZNW 97; Berlin, 1999) pp. 51–72.

[4] See the contributions by E. Schuller in *Qumran Cave 4.XX: Poetical and Liturgical Texts, Part 2* (DJD 29; Oxford, 1999) pp. 233–54, Pls. 15–16.

[5] A. Lange, "4Q440a. 4QHodayot-like Text D," and "4Q440b. 4QFragment Mentioning a Court," in *Qumran Cave 4.XXVI: Cryptic Texts and Miscellanea, Part 1* (DJD 36; Oxford, 2000) pp. 347–50, Pls. 24, 26. Though 4Q440b is not considered a *Hodayot*-like fragment, and paleographically differs from 4Q440, nevertheless the editors of the present volume have decided to publish it after the other 4Q440 material.

[6] Strugnell and Schuller, "Further *Hodayot* Manuscripts from Qumran?" pp. 53–55; E. Schuller, "The Classification Hodayot and Hodayot-like (with Particular Attention to 4Q433, 4Q433a and 4Q440)," in *Sapiential, Liturgical and Poetical Texts from Qumran: Proceedings of the Third Meeting of the International Organization for Qumran Studies*, edited by D. K. Falk, F. García-Martínez, and E. Schuller (STDJ 35; Leiden, 2000) pp. 182–97.

[7] For example, see A. K. Harkins, "Observations on the Editorial Shaping of the So-Called Community Hymns from 1QH^{a} and 4QH^{a} (4Q427)," *DSD* 12 (2005) 233–56. The Cave IV manuscripts, especially 4Q427 [4QH^{a}], 4Q429 [4QH^{c}], and 4Q431 [4QH^{e}], deviate from the order found in 1QH^{a}, suggesting that the psalms which constitute 1QH^{a} most likely were transmitted in different collections which may have omitted or moved certain psalms, and perhaps adding others.

[8] E.g., Schuller, "The Classification Hodayot and Hodayot-like," p. 193.

shared between the *Hodayot-Like Texts* and the *Hodayot*; yet, many parallels remain for exploration.

2. Contents

4Q433 (*Hodayot-Like Text A*): This manuscript, written on horizontally-lined skin in an Early Herodian bookhand, dates to the latter half of the first century BCE. Consisting of three fragments, this manuscript appears to depict the author's humiliation (frg. 1 lines 1–4a) and subsequent rescue at the hands of God (frg. 1 lines 4b–10). Certain features, such as the usage of rhetorical questions (מֹי אני: frg. 1 line 2), God being spoken of in the second-person singular (אתה משפיל וא[ת]ה[: frg. 1 line 4; תשפיל מֹו]שלי כול [תבל: frg. 1 line 5), and the first-person singular psalmist (ואנֹי: frg. 1 line 2; ואהיה: frg. 1 line 3), are typical of the *Thanksgiving Hymns*, though nothing else in this text suggests any particular relationship to them. These fragments also mention the "Most High" (עֹליון: frg. 1 line 7) and "the hi]dden things of your Torah" (נ]סֹתרי תורתך: frg. 2 line 2), as well as utilizes the imagery of chaff being cast from the threshing floor (כעור כמגרן: frg. 1 line 3). This text may depict the self-effacement of an individual, followed by the casting down of worldly power (frg. 1 lines 4–5) and a section praising God and Torah (frg. 1 line 7 to frg. 2 line 2), though the fragmentary nature of the text makes any assessment purely speculative.

4Q433a (*Hodayot-Like Text B*): Preserved on the reverse side of the papyrus manuscript 4Q255 (4QSª), these four fragments are extant in a Hasmonean semi-formal hand, dating the manuscript to the early half of the first century BCE.[9] In light of the restoration of 4Q255, it appears that fragment 1 was in the bottom left corner of the first column, while fragment 2 would have followed two columns later. Fragments 3 and 4 are difficult to place, though it is possible that they followed shortly after fragment 2.[10]

The first fragment of 4Q433a seems to provide a liturgical introduction to the body of the text. It mentions God giving songs to sing (נ]תֹן ושירתו קודש לֹא[ל: frg. 1 line 4) and "praises according to [his] plan" (ותשבוחות כפי עצה]ֹו: frg. 1 line 5).

Fragment 2 is divided into two sections. The first section (lines 1–2a) consists of only two extant words and an extended *vacat* which serves as a section marker. The second section (lines 2b–9) depicts a parable "For the Instructor" (לֹמֹשֹכיל לֹ[ש]מֹל: frg. 2 line 2). This parable portrays a "planting of delights" (נטע שעשועים: frg. 2 line 3) which, much like similar biblical arboreal parables (e.g., Isa 5:1–7, Ezek 17, 19:10–14,

Job 14:7–9, etc.), is described in extensive detail, including its branches (lines 4, 5, 6) and fruit (lines 4, 6–7).

4Q440 (*Hodayot-Like Text C*): Preserved on horizontally and vertically-lined skin, 4Q440 was written in an early Herodian formal hand, though some letters have features typical of a late Hasmonean hand, suggesting a *terminus ante quem* sometime during the latter half of the first century BCE. Three fragments constitute this manuscript. The first fragment describes what appears to be the fourth day of creation and the creation of light (frg. 1 lines 1–7).

4Q440a (*Hodayot-Like Text D*): Originally identified as fragment 14 of 4Q427 (4QHª), this shrunken fragment is extant in a late Hasmonean semi-formal hand. The appearances of first-person singular suffixes (lines 2–5) and a verb in second-person singular (שננתה: line 5) caused Lange to suggest that this was a composition "somewhat related" to the *Thanksgiving Hymns*.[11] The image of the author's speech being sharpened by God "like a swor[d" (דֹברי שננתה כחֹ[ב: line 5) appears not only in 1QHª but also in the Psalms and in *Barki Nafshi* (Pss 64:4, 140:4; 4Q436 frg. 1 1.7). The fragment seems to depict the author as one who is being oppressed (line 3) due to his divinely-imparted words, though the lack of surrounding context restricts any further analysis of the fragment.

3. Selected Bibliography

Harkins, A. K. "Observations on the Editorial Shaping of the So-Called Community Hymns from 1QHª and 4Qª (4Q427)." *DSD* 12 (2005) 233–56.

Lange, A. "4Q440a. 4QHodayot-like Text D." In *Qumran Cave 4.XXVI: Cryptic Texts and Miscellanea, Part 1*, edited by S. J. Pfann, *et al.* DJD 36; Oxford, 2000, pp. 347–48, Pl. 26.

Lange, A. "4Q440b. 4QFragment Mentioning a Court." In *Qumran Cave 4.XXVI: Cryptic Texts and Miscellanea, Part 1*, edited by S. J. Pfann, *et al.* DJD 36; Oxford, 2000, pp. 349–50, Pl. 24.

Metso, S. *The Textual Development of the Qumran Community Rule.* STDJ 21; Leiden, 1997, pp. 18–21.

Qimron, E. and J. H. Charlesworth. "Cave IV Fragments Related to the Rule of the Community." PTSDSSP vol. 1, pp. 53–57.

Schuller, E. M. "433. 4QHodayot-like Text A." In *Qumran Cave 4.XX: Poetical and Liturgical Texts, Part 2*, edited by G. Brooke, *et al.* DJD 29; Oxford, 1999, pp. 233–36, Pl. 15.

Schuller, E. M. "433a. 4QpapHodayot-like Text B." In *Qumran Cave 4.XX: Poetical and Liturgical Texts, Part 2*, edited by G. Brooke, *et al.* DJD 29; Oxford, 1999, pp. 237–45, Pl. 15.

Schuller, E. M. "440. 4QHodayot-Like Text C." In *Qumran Cave 4.XX: Poetical and Liturgical Texts, Part 2*, edited by G. Brooke, *et al.* DJD 29; Oxford, 1999, pp. 247–54, Pl. 16.

---

[9] For an early rendition of the text, see S. Metso, *The Textual Development of the Qumran Community Rule* (STDJ 21; Leiden, 1997) pp. 18–21. For more on 4Q255, see the work of E. Qimron and J. H. Charlesworth in PTSDSSP vol. 1, pp. 53ff.

[10] Schuller notes that frgs. 3 and 4 may have followed frg. 2 at the lower half of the sheet, though the bottom margin is not visible (DJD 29, p. 238).

[11] See DJD 36, p. 357.

Schuller, E. M. "The Classification Hodayot and Hodayot-like (with Particular Attention to 4Q433, 4Q433a and 4Q440)." In *Sapiential, Liturgical and Poetical Texts from Qumran: Proceedings of the Third Meeting of the International Organization for Qumran Studies*, edited by D. K. Falk, F. García-Martínez, and E. M. Schuller. STDJ 35; Leiden, 2000, pp. 182–97.

Strugnell, J. "Le travail d'édition des fragments manuscrits de Qumrân." *RB* 63 (1956) 49–67.

Strugnell, J. and E. M. Schuller. "Further *Hodayot* Manuscripts from Qumran?" In *Antikes Judentum und Frühess Christentum: Festschrift für Harmut Stegemann zum 65. Geburtstag*, edited by B. Kollmann, W. Rienbold, and A. Steudel. BZNW 97; Berlin, 1999, pp. 51–72.

Hodayot-Like Text A
4Q433

Frg. 1[1]

1	וארומ֯[מכה אלי]ֿ[2]
2	[מ֯י֯[3] אני ומי[4] כמ֯[וני ו]֯מֿה[5] כאין ואני֯[
3	[רוחך כעור כמגרן[6] ואהיה כמו אין וכֿ[
4	[לנצח והמלכ֯[ים [א֯תה משפיל ואֿ[ת]֯הֿ[
5	[תשפיל מ֯ו֯[שלי כול]תבל[8] תהשחֿ[9]
6	[֯ העמדתני כזאת לעֿצתֿ[א֯[ל]ֿ[10]
7	[֯אֿל[11] עֿליון יהללֿ[
8	א[נ֯י בע֯ו֯רֿ[12]
9	[דה על]
10	[תד]

---

[1] No margins are visible; the leather is lined.

[2] Ctr. Schuller: ֯[ואריכֿ. The *daleth* is distinguishable from the *reš* in this manuscript (cf. כעיר in כמגרן in line 3). The *waw* and *yodh* in this manuscript are difficult to distinguish. For דכא, see Isa 53:5, 10; Jer 44:10; 1QHᵃ 13.19: וכול היום ידכאו נפשי. This restoration also fits the context of lines 1–3. Another plausible restoration is ֯[ואדונֿי.

[3] This reading is speculative but suggested by context. Some ink can be seen.

[4] For a similar construction, see 1Chr 29:14: וְכִי מִי אֲנִי וּמִי עַמִּי. The utilization of מי with rhetorical questions appears in the *Thanksgiving Hymns* (e.g., 1QHᵃ 12.30, 19.27), as well as in the *Self-Glorification Hymn* (e.g., 4Q491 frg. 11 1.15–17; 4Q431 [4QHᵉ] frg. 1 lines 3–5).

[5] From כ to ה is space for nine consonants or spaces. See 4Q491 frg. 11 1.16: כמוני ומיא. See also line 3 below: כמו אין.

[6] This line is exceptionally confusing; כעור may be translated "as a blind one" (cf. Isa 59:10: נְגַשְׁשָׁה כַעְוְרִים קִיר) or as a form of the root ערה/ערר "to lay bare, strip, empty." In biblical literature, the threshing floor often is a symbolic location of judgment (e.g., Jer 51:33, Isa 21:10, Hos 13:3, Mt 3:12, Lk 3:17). García-Martínez and Tigchelaar read רוחך כעור כמגבן, "your spirit like a blind person, like a hump-backed;" see *DSSSE*, pp. 2.908–09.

[7] For the casting down or humbling of kings, see Jer 13:18, Dan 7:24. In the *Thanksgiving Hymns* the verb שפל is used to describe the casting down of "haughty of spirit" (גבהות רוח; 4Q427 [4QHᵃ] frg. 7 2.8).

[8] A similar phrase appears in the *Prayer of Enosh* (4Q369) frg. 1 2.7: ומושל בכול תבל ארצכה.

[9] See Isa 25:12 and 26:5.

[10] Ctr. Schuller: לעֿצ֯רֿ[ת א֯[לֿ. What Schuller reads as a *reš* is distorted by the tear and could plausibly be a *he* or a *taw*. The phrase may read לעֿצה֯[א]֯לֿ[, לעצ֯תֿ[ע]ֿ[ל]ֿ[, or לעצה֯[ע]֯[ל]֯ם.

[11] The top of the *lamedh* is above the tear.

[12] Conceivably: כעז֯ר֯[or כעו֯ד֯[. See 1QHᵃ 16.37.

Hodayot-Like Text A
4Q433

Frg. 1

1   […] and I will exal[t you, O my God,[1] …]

2   […] who (am) I; and who resemb[les me and] what is like nothing. And I […]

3   […] your spirit (is) like chaff[2] as from the threshing floor; and I will be like nothing and like […]

4   […] for perpetuity. And the king[s] you are casting down, and y[o]u […]

5   […] you shall cast down. The rul[ers of all] the world you shall humble[3] […]

6   […]° you allowed me to stand like this for the counsel of [G]od[4] […]

7   […] God Most High, he will praise […]

8   […] I with the faint […]

9   […]*dh* upon […]

10   […]*tk* […]

---

[1] See 1QHª 19.18.
[2] Or "as stripped." The word may be a participle from the root ערר, but it seems more likely that it is an Aramaism (Syriac: ܓܠܝܐ).
[3] See Isa 25:12 and 26:5; שפל appears with שחה which is a *hipʿil* here.
[4] Or "for the [ete]rn[al] counsel" or "for the counsel [of ete]rn[ity."

Frg. 2

1   ממך יצ[או ¹³בֿתֿוֹמֿ[

2   ¹⁴[סֿתרי תורתך וֹבֿי]נ

3   [לֹ]

Frg. 3

1   [רֹמֿ]

2   [ ] ואניֿ

3   [ ] אֹרֹהֿ ֿ

4   [כֿ]יֿ

---

¹³ The top of this word is obscured by the tear in the fragment. The bottom of the *beth* is visible, as is the left foot of the *taw*.

¹⁴ Ctr. Schuller: [ֿ ֿ ֿ]וֿ תורתך סֿתרי[נ. The top of the second to last letter in the line may also indicate a *kaph*. All the words in this line appear together in 1QH^a 13.13: כי אתה אלי סתרתני נגד בני אדם ותורתכה חבתה בֿ[י.

Frg. 2

1   […] in their innocence[5] they will g[o out] from you […]

2   [… the hi]dden things[6] of your Torah[7] and *by*[…]

3   […]*l*[…]

Frg. 3

1   […]*rm*[…]

2   […] and I ˚[…]

3   […]ʾ*rh* ˚[…]

4   […]*yk*[…]

---

[5] Or "integrity," "honesty." The Hebrew noun is in the plural.
[6] Cf. 4Q417 frg. 2 1.11 (נס[תֹרי). Cf. הנסתרות in 1QS 5.11; 1QHᵃ 4.21, 26.15; CD MS A 3.14
[7] Or "Law."

Hodayot-Like Text B
4Q433a

Frg. 1

1 [°°°]

2 הו]דות[[1]

3]בשיבׄת֯[ו וי]ו֯צׄי֯א֯ °[

4 נ]תׄן֯[2] ושירתו קודש לא֯[ל

5]°ק ותשבוחות כפי[3] עצתׄ[ו

6 יש]ת֯ו[4] תירוש אז ישמח אל[5] [

Frg. 2

1 ל֯מט֯[עת[6]]ע֯ולמים (VACAT)

2 [7] ל֯מ֯ש֯כיל מ֯[ש]ל ע֯ל כבוד ו֯[[8]

3 נטע שעשועים[9] נט֯ע בע֯[רוגתו]°[10] ו֯ב֯כׄ֯רמו °[

4 ש֯ׄריג֯י֯ו֯ ותפרינה ותר֯ב֯י֯נה[11] דליותיו בא֯[[12]

[1] With Schuller (DJD 29, p. 241). See 1QH[a] 19.7, 36.
[2] Schuller: תׄן֯[. This restoration is based on Ps 40:4[3]: וַיִּתֵּן בְּפִי שִׁיר חָדָשׁ.
[3] See 2Chr 31:2.
[4] Ctr. Schuller: נ֯י[. What Schuller reads as a *nun* looks more like the left side of a *taw* (see the examples on line 5 on PAM 43.255).
[5] Cf. Judg 9:13, Isa 24:7. See also Ps 104:15: וְיַיִן יְשַׂמַּח לְבַב־אֱנוֹשׁ.
[6] Schuller: ל֯מו֯[עדי; García Martínez and Tigchelaar: למל[ך כול. Numerous potential restorations exist, including למא֯[ורי]ע֯ולמים (cf. 1QH[a] 15.28) and esp. למט֯[עת]ע֯ולמים (cf. 1QH[a] 16.7).
[7] Perhaps the scribe erred and began with the next line: נטע.
[8] For the word למשכיל followed by a word (e.g., משל) indicating the type of composition which follows, see 1QS 3.13, 9.12; 1QSb 5.20; 4Q403 frg. 1 1.30, 2.18; 4Q405 frgs. 8–9 line 1; 4Q406 frg. 1 line 4; 4Q427 frg. 8 2.10; 4Q511 frg. 2 1.1. See also Ezek 17:2.
[9] Cf. Isa 5:7: וְאִישׁ יְהוּדָה נְטַע שַׁעֲשׁוּעָיו. See also 4Q500 frg. 1 line 6.
[10] Schuller: בע֯ד֯[נ]ו֯. Due to a tear in the fragment, it is difficult to ascertain a reading. What Schuller restores as the bottom stroke of a *daleth* is most likely the bottom of the *ʿayin*. Not בג֯נ֯[ת]ו֯ (cf. Milik). See Ezek 17:7, 10.
[11] The verbs פרה and רבה often appear together as a divine blessing (e.g., Gen 1:22, 28; Jer 3:16; Ezek 36:11). The Greek translation of the phrase (αὐξάνω, πληθύνω) appears in *1En* 89:49, as well as in Acts 6:7, 12:24. However, this is the only known instance of this phrase being applied to a particularly agricultural context.
[12] Perhaps restore בא֯[רץ.

Hodayot-Like Text B
4Q433a

Frg. 1

1   […] °°° […]

2   [… thank]sgiving […]

3   […] in [his] returning,[1] [and he wi]ll bring forth °[…]

4   [… he ga]ve and his songs (were) holy to G[od …]

5   […]°*q* and praises according to [his] counsel[2] […]

6   […th]ey [will dr]ink new wine; then God shall rejoice […]

Frg. 2

1   for an everlasting plan[ting.…] (VACAT)

2   *n*[3] (VACAT) For the Master, a pa[ra]ble concerning the glory and [.…]

3   He planted a planting[4] of delights in [his] te[rrace][5] and in his vineyard °[…]

4   its vines,[6] and its high branches will bear fruit and multiply *bʾ*[…]

---

[1] Or "restoration." See the translation of fragment 2 line 9.
[2] I.e. "[his] plan."
[3] See the Hebrew text.
[4] See Isa 5.
[5] See Ezek 17:7, 10. See line 9. A "te[rrace]" denotes fertile ground for luxurious plants.
[6] Or "twigs." From the root שׂרג "to be interwoven, entangled." See Gen 40:10, 12; Joel 1:7.

5   וכפותיו עלמשענת¹³ רום השׁמים וׁיׁתנדבׁ[ן

6   פארה¹⁴ לדורות עולמים¹⁵ ולעשות פר[ ]י

7   לכול טועמיו ובפריו לוא יראה באוש[י]ם¹⁶

8   עׁפׁיו ועליו ואבו¹⁷ יהיו בו וׁ[ן   כ]בׁוׁד¹⁸ בׁ[ן

9   משורשיו לוא ינתקו מערוגׁת מׁשׁ[י]בׁו[ ] כין¹⁹

Frg. 3

1   [בׁוער ל]ׁ   [ ]תׁ[   ]

2   [על וי]שׁמט²⁰   [ ]בׁ נתך[י   ]

3   [אׁ מפץ לׁתת]   [ ]נׁ[ופחים²¹   ]
                                   [וזעמוׁ²²

4   בׁר²⁴]עׁ לכול חׁרונו[לח²³]יׁשׁ כן זׁה[

5   להבה²⁵ באש וׁ[ן   ותבער]ׁ[   ]ׁ

6   צאון²⁷בטירות]שׁ אׁ להבת ²⁶לׁ[וׁ]לאכ

---

¹³ Read as על משענת. The merging of the preposition על with the proceeding word is not uncommon in the Qumran texts. See Tov, *Scribal Practices*, p. 133.

¹⁴ Cf. 1QH^a 16.21: כבוד ופא[ר]ת עד; cf. 1QH^a 16.23.

¹⁵ The phrase דורות עולם is extant four times in the *Thanksgiving Hymns* (1QH^a 6.17, 7.33, 9.20, 14.14) and twice in the Hebrew Bible (Gen 9:12, Isa 51:9). See also Sir 24.33 (LXX).

¹⁶ Cf. Isa 5:2, 4. From the root באש "to stink, smell." This word also appears in 1QH^a 16.26: שפתו יהפכו כעצי באושים.

¹⁷ From the root אבב "to make ripe, green." Cf. Job 8:12.

¹⁸ Cf. line 2.

¹⁹ Ctr. Schuller: בׁשׁמו. Though Schuller's restoration does replicate a biblical parallel (Song 5:13, 6:2), she admits that her reading is orthographically difficult. The first consonant is very similar to the medial *mem* in line 6. The *beth* is clearly visible to the right of the *waw*. From the root שוב.

²⁰ Perhaps restore a form of the root שמט "to be thrown down," or "to slide." Cf. Jer 17:4: וְשָׁמַטְתָּה וּבְךָ מִנַּחֲלָתְךָ אֲשֶׁר נָתַתִּי לָךְ וְהַעֲבַדְתִּיךָ אֶת־אֹיְבֶיךָ בָּאָרֶץ אֲשֶׁר לֹא־יָדָעְתָּ כִּי־אֵשׁ קְדַחְתֶּם בְּאַפִּי עַד־עוֹלָם תּוּקָד.

²¹ Cf. 1QH^a 13.18: נופחים לטהר שבעתים.

²² Ctr. Schuller: וזעם[עו. The medial *mem* is clear. The tops of each *lamed* extends into the supralinear line. The same scribe noted he had omitted a word due to similar meanings. Schuller considers these words to be part of line 4a. It appears that וזעמו is meant to be inserted following חׁרונו[.

²³ It is also possible to restore יׁש]פך. For this verb with חרון, see Lam 4.11: כִּלָּה יְהוָה אֶת־חֲמָתוֹ שָׁפַךְ חֲרוֹן אַפּוֹ. For the verb with זעם, see Ezek 21:36, 22:31; Zeph 3:8; Ps 69:2. For the restoration חׁרונו[כן יׁשׁ]לח, cf. Ex 15:7, Ps 78:49, Job 20:23, 11Q11 3.5.

²⁴ Cf. 1QH^a 11.29: וקץ חרון לכול בליעל.

²⁵ Cf. Isa 4:5, Hos 7:6, Ps 105:32, Lam 2:3.

²⁶ Schuller: ל ׁ[. The consonant to the right of the *lamedh* looks quite similar to the one in לאכול in line 9.

²⁷ A similar idea appears in 2Chr 14:14: וְגַם־אָהֳלֵי מִקְנֶה הִכּוּ.

5 and its fronds[7] (are) over the high supports of the heavens.[8] And it freely offers[9] […]

6 a leafy branch[10] for eternal generations, and to produce[11] the fru[it of …]

7 for all who taste it. And in its fruits there is not seen sour grape[s[12] …]

8 its foliage,[13] and its leaves and its ripeness will be in it. And [… gl]ory *b*[…]

9 from its roots; they will not tear it out from the terrace of his resto[rat]ion,[14] because […]

Frg. 3

1 […]*t* […] burning *l*̊[…]

2 [… it will] be[15] melted[16] in ̊[… and will] slide down upon […]

3 [… b]lowers[17] […] to give a pulverizing of ʾ[…]

4 […]*zh* thus he shall s[end] his wrath and his indignation[18] to every s[ide …]

5 […]̊ and it will burn […]*w* with flaming fire […]

6 [… devou]ring (with) flames of fi[re] in the encampments of[19] the flo[ck …]

---

[7] Or "shoots." The literal translation "palm fronds" does not fit the type of plant which is being described here.

[8] Lit. "the high leaning-staffs of the heavens." The word משענה figuratively takes the meaning "supports." From the root שען "to lean upon, support oneself upon."

[9] From נדב "to impel, freely offer." The "plant of delights" offers its fruits to the people of the eternal generations.

[10] Or "shoots." The word פארה appears in Ezek 17 in the allegory of the vine (17:6: וַתְּשַׁלַּח פֹּארֹות). See also Ezek (וַתְּהִי לְגֶפֶן וַתַּעַשׂ בַּדִּים וַתְּשַׁלַּח פֹּארֹות). See also Ezek 31:5, 6, 8, 12, 13; Isa 10:33). See also 1QHᵃ 16.21: ופֹּא̇רת עד and 16.23: לפארת כבוד.

[11] Lit. "to make."

[12] Cf. Isa 5:2, 4. The root of this word (באש "to stink, smell") suggests that these wild grapes are sour with a pungent odor, as opposed to good grapes (עֲנָבִים). See 1QHᵃ 16.26.

[13] The word עפי is an Aramaic loanword; possibly a synonym of עלה "foliage, leaves." Cf. Ps 104:12; Dan 4:9, 11, 18; 4Q302 frg. 2 2.7, 10.2; 1QHᵃ 14.18; 1Q20 frg. 13 line 13.

[14] Lit. "from the terrace of his bringi[ng b]ack." A translation of the *hipʿil* participle of שוב, which can insinuate conversion from evil (e.g., Mal 2:6, Isa 58:13), restoration (e.g., Dan 9:25; Ps 80:4, 8, 20; Isa 1:26), or renewal of one's vitality (e.g., Ps 19:8, Ruth 4:15, Lam 1:11). This may also be a possible reference to Jer 6:9, which uses the verb שוב to describe the activity of the grape-gatherer among the vine: כֹּה אָמַר יְהוָה צְבָאֹות עֹולֵל יְעֹולְלוּ כַגֶּפֶן שְׁאֵרִית יִשְׂרָאֵל הָשֵׁב יָדְךָ כְּבֹוצֵר עַל־סַלְסִלֹּות.

[15] Some kind of metal is intended.

[16] Or "poured out." The verb נתך can have either meaning. For "melting," see Ezek 22:20–22, 24:11; CD MS B 20.3; 1QHᵃ 21.25; 4Q424 frg. 1 line 5.

[17] The one who is working on the melted metal by blowing on the fire.

[18] The words "and indignation" are supplied by a supralinear mark. The same scribe added what he missed in his exemplar due to similar meanings.

[19] The preposition ב with the verb אכל can indicate the object which is being devoured (e.g., 1QHᵃ 13.35, 4Q251 frg. 16 line 2).

‫[ב֯ שואפי לצון²⁸ שא[פו	7
‫[ב֯פ֯חם²⁹ ומאזרי להב[ת אש³⁰	8
‫[נחלי זפת³¹ לאכול מ[³²	9
‫[לדור]ות³³	10

Frg. 4

‫]°°°[	1
‫בליעל בעל[°³⁴	2
‫גדופים[³⁵	3
‫אשמת[³⁶	4
‫תבער[³⁷	5
‫ובה[ו]ל[ל³⁸	6

---

²⁸ Schuller understands לצון to be an alternate spelling of צאון, which appears in line 6.

²⁹ See Isa 44:12, 54:16; Prov 26:21; 4Q162 2.6, 10.

³⁰ Cf. Isa 50:11.

³¹ Cf. Isa 34:9: ‫יסודי הרים לשרפה ושורשי חלמיש לנחלי זפת ;1QHᵃ 11.32: ‫וְנֶהֶפְכוּ נְחָלֶיהָ לְזֶפֶת וַעֲפָרָהּ לְגָפְרִית.

³² Perhaps restore ‫לאכול מ[ן. This line shares many elements with 1QHᵃ 11.30–32.

³³ This word is extant seven times in the *Thanksgiving Hymns* (1QHᵃ 5.33; 6.17; 9.18, 19, 20; 16.14; 25.9). The phrase ‫[לדור] ודור is also a possible restoration here (cf. 1QHᵃ 9.19; Isa 34:17; Joel 4:20; Pss 33:11, 49:12, 77:9, 79:13, 85:6, 89:2, 102:13, 106:31, 119:90, 135:13, 146:10; Lam 5:19).

³⁴ Perhaps restore ‫בליעל בעל[ות רשע; cf. 1QHᵃ 6.20; 7.37. This phrase also appears in 1QS 4.21, as does the similar phrase ‫עלילות עולה in 1QS 4.17.

³⁵ This word appears in 1QHᵃ 15.4, which is followed by mention of Belial in line 6: ‫כי בליעל עם הופע יצר הוותם.

³⁶ This word appears over 25 times in the *Thanksgiving Hymns* (e.g., 1QHᵃ 12.31, 35, 38; 14.22, 25, 33, 35). In the *Berakot* אשמה is connected to the cursed lot of Belial (4Q286 frg. 7 2.1–2; 4Q287 6.2). See also 1QM 13.4.

³⁷ Cf. 1QHᵃ 14.21: ‫בוערת בכול אנשי ;16.31: ‫בוער עצור בעצמ֯י֯.

³⁸ Cf. 1QHᵃ 10.38: ‫בהולל יצר סמוך ;12.9: ‫בהולל מעשיהם ;12.21: ‫כי אין הולל בכול מעשיך.

7   […]*b* those who pant after arrogance[20] pan[t after[21] …]

8   […] with coals[22] and gird themselves (with) a flam[e of fire[23] …]

9   […] rivers of tar to devour[24] *m*[…]

10   […] for generation[s …]

Frg. 4

1   […]°°°[…]

2   Belial *bˀl*°[…]

3   cursing[25] […]

4   the guilt of […]

5   it will burn […]

6   and in foo[lis]hn[ess …]

---

[20] Schuller translates לצון as an alternative spelling of צאן "flock" (see line 6). However, it seems more likely that this is from the root ליץ "to scoff, scorn." For לצון, see Prov 1:22, 29:8; Isa 28:14; CD MS A 1:14; CD MS B 20:11; 4Q162 2.6, 10.

[21] The Hebrew root שאף bears two meanings. The first, as rendered by Schuller's translation of this line, is "to trample." The second, more common meaning is "to pant, gasp for" (e.g., Isa 42:14; Jer 2:24, 14:6; Ps 119:131; Job 5:5, 7:2, 36:20). Figuratively, it often comes to mean "to long after, desire."

[22] The word פחם appears three times in the Hebrew Bible and is translated with three different words in the LXX (Isa 44:12: τερέτρῳ "a borer, an awl"; 54:16: ἄνθρακας "charcoal"; Prov 26:21: ἐσχάρα "hearth"). The word ἄνθραξ in particular describes the appearance of divine beings (e.g., Ezek 1:13, 10:9; *TSol* 5.9) and sacred places (e.g., Ezek 28:13). At times, ἄνθραξ is better translated "ruby, carbuncle" (e.g., Gen 2:12; Ex 28:18; *Ant* 3.168, 12.71; Philo, *Legum Allegoriarum*, 1.66, 67, 81).

[23] Schuller rightly suggests that this line may be describing the appearance of an angelic figure (DJD 29, p. 244). The LXX often uses the verb περιζώννυμι to translate אזר "to gird" (e.g., Pss 18:33, 40; 30:12; 1Sam 2:4; Jer 1:17) the Greek verb is used in the description of the Son of Man in Rev 1 and the seven angels in Rev 15.

[24] Or "to consume."

[25] Or "reviling."

Hodayot-Like Text C
4Q440

Frg. 1

1   ביום ה[רביעי¹ פתחתה² מאור גדול³ בממש֯[לת היום

2   ת[ש֯עה וארבעים גורלות אור⁴ שבע֯[תים⁵

3   [רי֯◦ ⁶ לשלושת עולמי חושך⁷ שבי֯[עים

4   [◦◦ בכול ימי ממשלתו֯⁸]

5   [עולמים להאיר שב֯[עתים⁹

6   [ה֯] ר[ ] ר֯[

7   ברוך א[תה אל֯י֯]¹⁰

Frg. 2

1   מו[עדי כב]וד¹¹

---

¹ Cf. Gen 1:19. See also *Jub* 2:8 (4Q216 [4QJubᵃ] 6.5–7).

² Though the verbs ברא or עשה are more common in similar creation description, the verb פתח is not without precedent (e.g., Ps 119:130; 1QS 11.3; 4Q418 frg. 81 line 9).

³ For מאור גדול, see 1Q34ᵇⁱˢ frg. 3 2.1, 1QHᵃ 20.8, 1QSb 4.27.

⁴ גורל אור also appear in 1QM 13.9, 4Q177 frgs. 1–4 line 8, and 4Q503 frgs. 51–55 line 14.

⁵ See note to חושך in line 3.

⁶ Schuller: רי֯ם[. The final letter is not clear.

⁷ The author of *TLevi* 17:6–7, mentions three Jubilees which shall be overtaken by darkness (ὁ πέμπτος ἐν σκότει παραληφθήσεται. ὡσαύτως καὶ ὁ ἕκτος καὶ ὁ ἕβδομος). Schuller (DJD 29, p. 250) insightfully notes that line 3 may suggest a Jubilee system in which the three periods of darkness would be equated with three weeks, equaling twenty–one lots of darkness (3 x 7). This, added to the lots of light mentioned in line 2, would insinuate a total system of seventy lots (forty–nine of light, twenty–one of darkness). Systems of seventy are not uncommon in Jewish literature (cf. Dan 9:24–27, *TLevi* 16–17).

⁸ The antecedent of the possessive pronoun could be the sun (cf. Gen 1:16, Ps 136:8, *1En* 82:15, *Jub* 2:9), as seen in line 1 above, or Belial (cf. 1QS 2.19, 4Q177 frgs. 1–4 line 8, 4Q390 frg. 2 1.4). Light may also be the subject here, as the dominion of light is prominent in 1QHᵃ 20.7–8: עם מבוא אור לממש֯[לת] בתקופות יום.

⁹ Cf. Schuller: שב֯[עתים. The *beth* could plausibly be a small *mem*, suggesting the restoration: להאיר שמ֯[ים. However, note 1QHᵃ 15.27: והופעתי באור שבעתים.

¹⁰ The restoration ברוך א[תה אל֯י֯] is not out of the question (ctr. Schuller), as the tear of the leather obscures most of the right side of the *taw*. Another possibility is אוד[כה אל֯י֯] (cf. 1QHᵃ 19.6, 18). See frg. 2 line 2 and frg. 3 line 20.

¹¹ For מועדי כבוד, see CD MS A 3.14–15; 4Q286 frg. 1 2.10; 4Q503 frgs. 1–6 3.13, 15; 4Q508 13.2. The word עדי is also a possibility (cf. 1QM 12.15; 19.7).

Hodayot-Like Text C
4Q440

Frg. 1

1   [… on the] fourth [day] you opened a great light[1] for the domini[on of the day …]

2   […] forty-[n]ine lots of[2] light, seven[fold …]

3   […]*ry*° for three epochs of[3] darkness, seve[nty …]

4   […]°° in all the days of its[4] dominion […]

5   […] eternal[5] […] to give light sev[enfold …]

6   […]*h* […]*r* […]*y*[…]

7   […. Blessed (are) y]ou, O my God[6] […]

Frg. 2

1   […] glor[ious fest]ivals […]

---

[1] Or "luminary." The author refers to the creation of the sun. See Gen 1.

[2] Or "portions of."

[3] The word עולמי here connotes an extended period of time rather than the usual "forever, eternal." A similar appropriation of the concept appears in *4Ezra* (e.g., 6:7). ܪܚܡ̈ܐ ܕܥܠܡܐ ܗܘ ܝܗܒ ܐܢ.

[4] Or "his."

[5] Or "epochs" (see line 3). Both translations are equally plausible given the limited context.

[6] Or "I thank y]ou, O my God [." See frg. 2 line 2 and frg. 3 1.20.

2   מן[עׄדׄיׄ   ברוך אׄלׄ]¹²

3   [°° וׄמשׄפטי צדקׄ]¹³

4   לׄאישוני [לילה ¹⁴

5   [לׄהׄ]

Frg. 3 Col. 1

1   [

2   [

3   [

4   [

5   [

6   [

7   [

8   [

9   [

10   [

11   [

12   [

13   [

14   [°לׄ[ ]°°°]

15   [ׄרים[ ] בכו[ל] נצביׄ[ם]¹⁵

---

¹² The consonants are no longer visible.

¹³ For משׁפט צדק, see 1QS 3.1; 4.4; 9.17; 1QSb 2.26; 1QHᵃ 9.25, 32; 25.3; 4Q299 frg. 80 line 3. See also Ps 119:7, 62, 106, 160, 164.

¹⁴ Perhaps restore לׄאישוני [חושך (cf. Prov 20:20: בְּאִישׁוֹן חֹשֶׁךְ) or more likely לׄאישוני [לילה (cf. Prov 7:9: בְּאִישׁוֹן לָיְלָה; 4Q184 frg.1 line 6: ובאישׁני ליל[ה ממ[שׁלותיה).

¹⁵ The top, left, and bottom margins are visible. The end of a scroll (the handle) is clear. The bottom of the *yodh* intersects the base of the *beth*. נצבו is also possible, though less likely.

2   [… fest]ivals. Blessed (be) God […]

3   […]°° and judgments of righteousness […]

4   […] for the dark midsts of[7] [night]

5   […]*lh*[…]

Frg. 3 Col. 1

1   […]

2   […]

3   […]

4   […]

5   […]

6   […]

7   […]

8   […]

9   […]

10   […]

11   […]

12   […]

13   […]

14   […] °*l*[…]°°°[…]

15   […]*rym* […] in al[l] those standin[g][8]

---

[7] Lit. "the middle of the eye, the pupil." Figuratively, this word can be understood as a dark place (e.g., Prov 7:9, 20:20).
[8] The top, side, and bottom margins are visible.

16 [ ] ולבבשר[16] שלום[17] ע]ול[ם

17 [לֹבִֹי[18]   (VACAT)

18 לכול לכו]ל רוח ומבינתכה[19]

19 כ]בֹודכה לכול הויה

20 בכול ברוך]אתה אלי הזכי[20]

21 כולנו להעשותנו כיא

22 א]לה ובֹטובכה[21] הכינותה[22]

23 עומ]ק[23] רזיכה הנוראים[24]

24 מח]שבת[25] כבודכה ברוך

25]הֹ ועד אחרונות[26] לוא

Frg. 3 Col. 2

1 [ ]נו[27] [ ]בֹֹ ֹ

---

[16] Read ולבשר. A scribe erred and wrote ולבבשר.

[17] Cf. 4Q432 frg. 3 line 4: מבשר שלום. See also the parallel text 1QH[a] 10.8, as well as Isa 52:7; Nah 2:1.

[18] These letters were not seen before.

[19] In the *Thanksgiving Hymns*, the word בינה is extant 19 times and is often depicted as God's gift which allows the hymn's author to acquire knowledge (e.g., 1QH[a] 9.23: אלה ידעתי מבינתכה כיא גליתה אוזני לרזי פלא; see also 10.19, 13.28, 22.31).

[20] Cf. Ps 51:6. The purity of God in relation to humanity is mentioned in 1QH[a] 22.29. Similar ideas are also present in Job 15:14, 25:4; Prov 20:9.

[21] Note the scribal mark appearing over the preposition, perhaps suggesting the deletion of the consonant.

[22] Cf. Ps 68:11: תָּכִין בְּטוֹבָתְךָ לֶעָנִי אֱלֹהִים.

[23] Restoration follows 1QS 11.19: ולהביט בעומק רזיכה.

[24] For הנוראים, see 1QH[a] 5.31.

[25] Cf. 1QS 11.18–19: ולהשכיל בכול מחשבת קודשכה. Schuller notes that the restoration of line 23 influences the restoration of line 24, as the two lines present parallel phrases (cf. 1QS 11.18–19). שבת כבודכה] is also possible (cf. Jub 2.32).

[26] Cf. 4Q268 frg. 1 line 1; *Angelic Liturgy* [Mas1k 1.3–4].

[27] Plausibly the final word of the scroll, as the lines below are empty. Possibly restore תע]זֹבֹנו.

16 […] and to announce news of et[ern]al peace.

17 […] my heart. (VACAT)

18 [… to eve]ry spirit, and from your discernment to every

19 […] your [gl]ory to all that is[9]

20 [… . Blessed are] you, O my God, (who is) pure[10] in all

21 […] all of us, that we were made because

22 [… th]ese and by your goodness you established

23 [… the dep]th of your awesome mysteries

24 […] your glorious [tho]ughts. Blessed

25 […]*h* and until the last things, not

Frg. 3 Col. 2

1 […]°*b*[…]*nw*[11]

<hr />

[9] Or "to all which exists."
[10] Or "victorious." See 1QH^a 17.15.
[11] Or "us." The scroll seems to end with those consonants.

Hodayot-Like Text D
4Q440a

Frg. 1

1   [ ]ْ[ ] ֯עֹ דב]רי¹

2   [שפתי לוא מ֯וֹ]

3   [אל רב² עלי מיד ח֯]זק³

4   [בשפתי ולשונֵ]י⁴

5   [דֹברי⁵ שננתה כחרֹ]ב⁶

6   [שֹתה לוא יתחגו]ן⁷

7   [לֹ]   [תֹנֹיֹ]⁸

---

¹ See line 5.

² This word is not visible on PAM 41.389.

³ Lange:]ח֯. A similar *ḥet* appears below on line 6. Both consonants have their right leg curved slightly to the left. For the phrase מיד חזק, see 1QHᵃ 10.37, Jer 31:11, Job 5:15.

⁴ Cf. 4Q427 [4QHᵃ] frg. 7 1.16: הקדי]שֹו שמו בשפתי עוז ולשון נצח.

⁵ This word is most clearly seen on PAM 43.532.

⁶ The final consonants of כחרֹ]ב are only visible on PAM 41.389. Strugnell suggested the reading כחו]ק. But see 1QHᵃ 13.15: אריות אשר שֹגֹנֹוֹ לֹשֹוֹנֹם כְּמוֹ־נָחָשׁ; Ps 140:4: שָׁנֲנוּ לְשׁוֹנָם כְּמוֹ־נָחָשׁ; Ps 64:4: וְתֹשׁם פִּי כחרב חדה; 4Q436 (*Barki Nafshiᶜ*) frg. 1 1.7: שננו כחרב לשונם.

⁷ Most likely from the root חגג, though in biblical Hebrew there are no other instances of this verb in the *hithpaʿel*. The word at times serves as a description of storms or waves that cause sailors to act like drunken men (cf. Ps 107:27, 4Q418 frg. 115 line 3), a prominent theme in the *Thanksgiving Hymns* (e.g., 1QHᵃ 11, 14.23–29).

⁸ Line 7 is not visible in any of the photographs of this fragment. This line is supplied through the early reading of Strugnell (see DJD 36, p. 348). Portions of fragments have disappeared since they were first seen by scholars.

Hodayot-Like Text D
4Q440a

Frg. 1

1   […]°[…]ᶜ [my] wor[ds[1] …]

2   […] my lips not *m*°[…]

3   […]ʾl much over me from the hand of one str[onger[2]…]

4   […] with my lips and my tongue […]

5   […] my words you sharpened like a swor[d …]

6   […]*šth*[3] they will not stagger[4] […]

7   […]*l*[…]*tny* […]

---

[1] See line 5.

[2] The translation of this phrase is dependent upon the following word which is lost. Two possibilities include "from the hand of one str[onger than me" (Jer 31:11; מִיַּד חָזָק מִמֶּנּוּ) and "from the hand of the m[ighty" (Job 5:15; וּמִיַּד חָזָק אֶבְיוֹן).

[3] It is likely that this is the final consonant and second-person singular suffix of a verb. Lange translates: "]you have[."

[4] See Ps 107:27.

Court of the Righteous [Ones]
4Q440b

JAMES H. CHARLESWORTH

with LEA BERKUZ and BLAKE A. JURGENS

This fragment was initially associated with fragments of 4Q440. A. Lange correctly identified it as a different manuscript from 4Q440 and 4Q440a. It is in a semi-formal Hasmonean or early Herodian script.[1] Since "courtyard" (חצר), is not extant in any of the *Thanksgiving Hymns* or *Hodayot-Like Texts*, there is no evidence to indicate 4Q440b is related to the *Thanksgiving Hymns*.[2]

Selected Bibliography

Lange, A. "4Q440b. 4QFragment Mentioning a Court." In *Qumran Cave 4.XXVI: Cryptic Texts and Miscellanea, Part 1*. DJD 36; Oxford, 2000, pp. 349–50, Pl. 24.

---

[1] A. Lange, "4Q440b. 4QFragment Mentioning a Court," in *Qumran Cave 4.XXVI: Cryptic Texts and Miscellanea, Part 1* (DJD 36; Oxford, 2000) pp. 349–50, Pl. 24.

[2] Though 4Q440b is not considered a *Hodayot-Like* fragment, and paleographically differs from 4Q440, nevertheless the editors of this volume have decided to publish it after the other 4Q440 material.

Court of the Righteous [Ones]
4Q440b

Frg. 1[1]

1 [שִׁ֯י ֯ [2ק]מֹזֹר]

2 [שֻׁ֯ן[3]]מֹ֯ולכי[5] רבִים֯]4

3 [נֹ֯בֹט[6] לוחצר[7] צדיֹק]ים[8]

4 [שֹׁ ֯ לכֹֹל ֯ [9]

---

[1] The leather is not lined.

[2] The scribe is gifted, but his *reš* sometimes looks like a *daleth*. Due to the loss of some ink, this line is difficult to discern. Lange's reading is influenced by the appearance of the word חצר in line 3.

[3] Ctr. Lange:]קֹ[.

[4] The ink is lost with the upper level of the leather.

[5] Ctr. Lange:]וֹילכו.

[6] Ctr. Lange: בֹּט[. The bottom stroke of the *beth* appears beneath the *tet*. To the right appears a second bottom stroke, which could be either a *beth*, a *kaph*, a *nun*, or a *ṣade*. Lange suggests]נֹבֹט and]צֹבֹט as possible reconstructions. נבט seems more likely, as צבט appears only once in the Hebrew Bible (Ruth 2:14) and is not in the extant Dead Sea Scrolls.

[7] Read as לו חצר.

[8] Cf. Lange: צֹ]קים. The front portion of the *qoph* is visible.

[9] Cf. Lange:]שׁ.

Court of the Righteous [Ones]
4Q440b

Frg. 1

1   […] bow[l[1] …]° *šy*[…]

2   […]*šn*[…] those ruling the Many[2] […]

3   […] he looked across to a court of the Righteous [Ones[3] …]

4   […]° for all *š*°[…]

---

[1] This noun denotes the bowl in the Temple for wine or for collecting sacrificed blood that would be thrown on the altar. See Amos 6:6, Ex 27:3. Lange reads ‏מזרק[‏, which he translates as "a sprinkling bowl."

[2] Ctr. Lange: "and many walked." The *mem* is discernible. The text seems to refer to "the many;" see 1QS 6.25 and 1QS *et passim*.

[3] See esp. 1QH[a] 9.38 and 15.15.

A Poem Similar to the Thanksgiving Hymns (*Hodayot*)
4Q439

JAMES H. CHARLESWORTH with LEA BERKUZ and JOLYON G. R. PRUSZINSKI[1]

Introduction

Initially grouped with the *Barkhi Nafshi* texts in the early days of Qumran research,[2] 4Q439 has since been recognized as a document variously entitled "a work similar to Barkhi Nafshi,"[3] "4QLament by a Leader,"[4] and "A Poem Similar to the Thanksgiving Hymns."[5] 4Q439 is comprised of two leather fragments that were discovered in Cave 4.[6] The Herodian script is an early rustic semi-formal hand.[7] The terminology and perspective share similarities to those of the "Teacher Hymns," but the text is too fragmentary to allow definitive connection to any particular individual or larger work. It may have been part of a lament psalm used at Qumran, but there is no conclusive evidence that it was part of the collection known as the *Thanksgiving Hymns*.[8]

Selected Bibliography

Kister, M. "שלוש מילים מצפוני מגילות מדבר יהודה, Three Unknown Hebrew Words in Newly-Published Text from Qumran." *Leshonenu* 63/1–2 (2001) 35–40.

Qimron, E. "פתרון טקסט סתום ממגילות מדבר יהודה, An Interpretation of an Enigmatic Scroll." *Tarbiz* 70/3–4 (2001) 627–30.

Seely, *D. R. "The Barki Nafshi Texts (4Q434–439)." In Current Research and Technological Developments on the Dead Sea Scrolls: Conference on the Texts from the Judean Desert, Jerusalem, 30 April 1995,* edited by D. W. Parry and S. D. Ricks. STDJ 20; Leiden, 1996, pp. 194–214.

Tigchelaar, E. "More Identifications of Scraps and Overlaps." *RQ* 73/19 (1999) 61–67.

Wacholder, B. Z. and M. G. Abegg. "4QWork Similar to Bar^ekhi Nafshi." In *A Preliminary Edition of the Unpublished Dead Sea Scrolls: The Hebrew and Aramaic Texts from Cave Four, Fascicle Three*, edited by B. Z. Wacholder and M. G. Abegg. Washington, D. C., 1995, pp. 327–28.

Weinfeld, M. and D. R. Seely. "439. 4QLament by a Leader." In *Qumran Cave 4.XX: Poetical and Liturgical Texts, Part 2*, edited by E. G. Chazon, *et al.* DJD 29; Oxford, 1999, pp. 335–41, Pl. 24.

---

[1] J. G. R. Pruszinski assisted with the introduction and L. Berkuz assisted with the text and translation.

[2] This original categorization was made by J. Strugnell. See the introduction by J. H. Charlesworth with J. G. R. Pruszinski to "*Barkhi Nafshi* (4Q434–438)" in PTSDSSP, forthcoming.

[3] See B. Z. Wacholder and M. G. Abegg, "4QWork Similar to Bar^ekhi Nafshi," in *A Preliminary Edition of the Unpublished Dead Sea Scrolls: The Hebrew and Aramaic Texts from Cave Four, Fascicle Three* (Washington, D. C., 1995) pp. 327–28.

[4] DJD 29, pp. 335–41.

[5] The present volume.

[6] See DJD 29, Pl. 24.

[7] DJD 29, pp. 336–337. The usage of this script allows likely dating of the manuscript to between 50 BCE and 6 CE.

[8] Tigchelaar suggests a connection based on a parallel text between 4Q439 and 4Q469 (4QNarrative Work I, also known as 4QApocryphon?). See E. Tigchelaar, "More Identifications of Scraps and Overlaps," in *RQ* 73/19 (1999) 61–67.

A Poem Similar to the Thanksgiving Hymns
4Q439

Frgs. 1 and 2 Col. 1[1]

1		ל[אֹסף צדֹּי[קי]עֹמי ולהקים דרך
2	חיים]]	ולהעבי]ֹר בברית אנשי סודי[2] וכול מלוש[3]
3	[וֹ]	וי]ֹ[ורש לנחלתי על כן עיני מקור מים
4		ב[מֹוסר והעומדים אחריהם אשר
5		]וֹהֹנֹה כול עירי נהפכה לסירִיֹם[
6		ה[נֹה כול שופטי נמצאו אוֹיֹל[י]ם
7		]וֹ צדיקי פותיים אשֹ[ר
8		]ֹבוגדיֹם[

Frg. 1 Col. 2[4]

1	נאמנֹ[ות[5]
2	והתנק]ם
3	גורלם וֹ]ם[6]

---

[1] The top margin is visible in frg. 1. The horizontal and vertical lining of the manuscript is notable in both fragments. Frg. 2 provides the beginning of lines 2–3.

[2] See Ps 25:14: "the secret of the LORD is for those who fear him (or are in awe of him)." 4Q439 is related to the *Thanksgiving Hymns*. See 1QH^a 6.29: וכן הוגשתי ביֹחד כול אנשי סודי. Qumran expressions are apparent in noting those who cross over into the covenant. E. Qimron rightly states that lines 1–3 refer to God's great people to whom God had revealed his mysteries (Qimron, *Tarbiz* 70 [2001] 627–30).

[3] Kister, in *Leshonenu* 63 (2001) 35–40, and Qimron, in *Tarbiz* 70 (2001) 627–30, note the difficulty of understanding the meaning of this noun מלוש. Kister suggests the noun is a metaphor for "fate" and judges it to refer to one of the signs of the zodiac. For horoscopes at Qumran, see 4Q186 and 4Q561.

[4] The right margin is clear.

[5] Cf. Weinfeld and Seely: נאמנֹ[ות.

[6] Cf. Weinfeld and Seely: גורלם]ֹם.

A Poem Similar to the Thanksgiving Hymns
4Q439

Frgs. 1 and 2 Col. 1

1   [… to] gather in the righte[ous ones of] my people, and to raise up the way of

2   life [… and to cause to cross ov]er into the covenant the men of my council.[1] And every kneading bowl[2]

3   and °[… and the one pos]sessing my inheritance. Thus my eyes (are) a well of water

4   [… in] instruction, and the ones standing after them who

5   […] and behold all of my city has been turned into thorns[3] […]

6   [… be]hold all my judges have been found to be fool[s …]

7   […]°w my righteous ones (to be) ignorant ones wh[o …]

8   […]° traitors […]

Frg. 1 Col. 2

1   faithfuln[ess …]

2   and he will avenge th[em …]

3   their lot and […]

---

[1] Or "my secret." The self-understanding mirrors that of the Righteous Teacher. See also Qimron in *Tarbiz* 70 (2001) 627–30.

[2] See Gitt 8.49ᵇ. The noun מלוש represents a bowl for kneading dough. Cf. משארת in Deut 28:5. See ܡܠܐܐ, "a bronze vessel." The noun seems to denote the fate of an individual according to the sign of the zodiac in which one is born. See the *Treatise of Shem* and Kister, in *Leshonenu* 63 (2001) 35–40. For early Jewish interest in astrology, see Charlesworth in *HTR* 70 (1977) 183–200; reprinted with additions and images in *ANRW* Band II.20.2, pp. 926–56 and Plates.

[3] The noun is known in Jewish Aramaic. E. Tigchelaar, in *RQ* 73 (1999) 61–67, and Qimron, in *Tarbiz* 70 (2001) 627–30, suggest that this line may echo Jer 2:21.

Hymn of Praise
3Q6

JOSEPH L. TRAFTON

Introduction

The *Hymn of Praise* (3Q6) is a fragmentary text which was designated by its first editor, M. Baillet, as "Hymne de louange."[1] Portions of only six lines of the text have been preserved.

1. Text

The *Hymn of Praise* consists of two small Hebrew fragments of a leather manuscript written in Herodian script.[2]

2. Original Language, Date, and Provenience

The fragmentary nature of the *Hymn of Praise* precludes certainty concerning introductory matters. It was probably composed in Hebrew. On paleographical grounds it can be dated no later than the first century CE. A Palestinian provenience seems relatively certain.

3. Language, History, and Theology

Because it is so fragmentary, the *Hymn of Praise* adds little to our knowledge of Hebrew. Similarly, it provides no historical insights. The language of the *Hymn of Praise* is reminiscent of the Psalms. The *Hymn of Praise* exhibits a concern for worship: God is worthy of everlasting praise. Whether or not the *Hymn of Praise* was composed by someone in the Qumran Community cannot be determined,[3] but its presence among the manuscripts found in the Qumran Caves is consistent with the Community's rich hymnody and, in turn, its strong focus on worship (cf., e.g., *Hodayot*, 11Q5 [11QPsᵃ], *Angelic Liturgy* [4Q400–407, Mas1k]).

4. Relation to the Hebrew Bible, other Jewish Writings, and the New Testament

The *Hymn of Praise* stands in the general tradition of Jewish hymnody, from the Pslams, through the *Psalms of Solomon* and other apocryphal psalms, to the hymns in Luke 1 and in Revelation.

5. Selected Bibliography

Baillet, M. *Les 'Petite Grottes' De Qumrân: Exploration de la falaise, Les grottes 2Q, 3Q, 5Q, 6Q, 7Q, à 10Q, Le rouleau de cuivre*. DJD 3; Oxford, 1962, p. 98, Pl. 18.

---

[1] The *editio princeps* was published by M. Baillet, DJD 3 (Oxford, 1962) p. 98, Pl. 18.

[2] Baillet, DJD 3, p. 98.

[3] J. A. Fitzmyer classifies 3Q6 simply as an apocryphal text; see *The Dead Sea Scrolls: Major Publications and Tools for Study* (Missoula, 1977) p. 1.

Hymn of Praise
3Q6[1]

Frg. 1

1 [כ֯ו֯ל֯[2] אשר ישמחו֯][3]

2 [ ]֯ ושירם יערב על[יכה][4]

3 ל[עולם יהללוכ]ה[5]

Frg. 2[6]

1]֯

2 ע֯][7]

3]֯

---

[1] An early Herodian semi-formal hand; the fragments are lined.

[2] A plausible reading. Only the bottom of these consonants are visible.

[3] Perhaps restore בכה with Baillet. Qoh 3:22: כִּי אֵין טוֹב מֵאֲשֶׁר יִשְׂמַח הָאָדָם בְּמַעֲשָׂיו. For שמח אשר, see 1Q34[bis] frgs. 2+1 line 4; 4Q502 frg. 33 line 2; 4Q509 frg. 3 line 9.

[4] Baillet notes ערב with the preposition על appears in Ezek 16:37 and Ps 104:34.

[5] Ps 115:8: וְאַתָּה כִּמְקוֹר עוֹלָם הלל. See also 4Q418 frgs. 81+81a line 1: וַאֲנַחְנוּ נְבָרֵךְ יָהּ מֵעַתָּה וְעַד־עוֹלָם הַלְלוּ־יָהּ ;117:2: וֶאֱמֶת־יְהוָה לְעוֹלָם הַלְלוּ־יָהּ. Similar phrases with the verb ידה can be found in Pss 30:13, 44:9, 52:11. The bottom margin may be visible.

[6] The right margin is visible.

[7] Possibly restore עוֹ]לם.

Hymn of Praise
3Q6

Frg. 1

1   […] all who will rejoice […]

2   […]°. And their song may be pleasing[1] to [you …]

3   [… for]ever they will praise y[ou …]

Frg. 2

1   °[…]

2   ͨ°[…]

3   °[…]

---

[1] Lit. "may be sweet."

Hymnic Fragment 1: "Like My Soul"
4Q498 (4QpapSap/Hymn)

JAMES H. CHARLESWORTH with LEA BERKUZ and BRADY A. BEARD[1]

Introduction

1. Contents

4Q498 was originally published by M. Baillet in 1982 in DJD 7.[2] The text is preserved on 15 pieces of papyrus. It is impossible to discern the provenience of the respective fragments and the nature of the text. Baillet rightly noted that it is difficult to ascertain which fragments belong together despite the early work of the experts who collected the fragments. It is doubtful that the fragments all belong to the same manuscript. Some are hymnic in nature, but others may possibly be related to Deuteronomy or Sapiential traditions.

2. Text

The script is early Herodian and dates between 30–1 BCE. In places the ink is faded and the consonants difficult to read. The fragments are written on a thick papyrus with irregular fibers. The *recto* is gray while the *verso* is yellowed.[3]

3. Selected Bibliography

Baillet, M. "498. Fragments hymniques ou sapientiels(?)." In *Qumrân Grotte 4.III (4Q482–4Q520)*. DJD 7; Oxford, 1982, pp. 73–74, Pl. 27.

---

[1] Brady A. Beard assisted with the introduction. Lea Berkuz helped with the transcription and translation.

[2] M. Baillet, "498. Fragments hymniques ou sapientiels(?)," in *Qumrân Grotte 4.III (4Q482–4Q520)* (DJD 7; Oxford, 1982) pp. 73–74, Pl. 27.

[3] Baillet, DJD 7, p. 73.

Hymnic Fragment 1: "Like My Soul"
4Q498 (4QpapSap/Hymn)

Frg. 1 Col. 1

לֹ֯בֹב[^1] כנפשי[^2]	**1**
יֹ֯ם֯[^3]	**2**

Frg. 1 Col. 2

]°[	**1**

Frg. 2

[מבקק]עים[^4]	**1**
[ו]נחלֹי מֹ]ים	**2**
[יוצר כֹ]	**3**
[מֹה כול]	**4**
[הֹוות לֹר]זֹי[^5]	**5**

Frg. 3 Col. 1

[ו֯ח[^6]	**1**
[זֹה כול	**2**
[מֹחשבֹ[^7]	**3**

[^1]: Ctr. Baillet: חו]רֹבֹב. See 1QHᵃ 7.23 for לב with נפש.
[^2]: The top and left margins of the papyrus are clear.
[^3]: Baillet: ת֯[.
[^4]: *Puʿal* part. of בקע.
[^5]: Baillet:]°יֹות לֹ[.
[^6]: Baillet: וֹה[.
[^7]: Read: מֹחשבֹת.

Hymnic Fragment 1: "Like My Soul"
4Q498 (4QpapSap/Hymn)

Frg. 1 Col. 1

1 […] heart like my soul[1]

2 […]*ym*

Frg. 1 Col. 2

1 °[…]

Frg. 2

1 […] burs[ting[2] …]

2 […] and rivers of w[ater …]

3 […] forming *k*[…]

4 […] what (is) all […]

5 […] it is for the myst[eries of …]

Frg. 3 Col. 1

1 […]*wḥ*[3]

2 […] this all

3 […] thought

---

[1] Heb. נפש. The margin of the papyrus is preserved. Or "his soul."

[2] See 1QHᵃ 11.33.

[3] The margin is preserved.

Frgs. 1–3 Col. 1[8]

1   ‏[לֹבב כנפשי‏]

2   ‏מֹֹ[ע]ֹ[קבמ‏]

3   ‏[מ]ים‏ ‏וֹנחלֹי‏[

4   ‏וֹ[]ֹ[]כ יוצר‏]

5   ‏כול זֹה]‏[[] כול מֹֹ[‏

6   ‏מֹחשבֹֹ[זי]ר[לֹ הוות‏]

Frg. 3 Col. 2[10]

1   ‏[

2   ‏[כֹֹ

3   ‏[ֹ

Frg. 4

1   ‏[11]‏[ו רֹ צֹֹילֹ]מ

2   ‏[הֹֹ [

Frg. 5

1   ‏[12]‏[רֹ הֹלֹ[

Frg. 6

1   ‏[בכול לבבכהֹ]

---

[8] As shown in *DSSEL*.
[9] See 1QH[a] 5.17: ‏ורזי מחשבת‏.
[10] The right margin is preserved.
[11] Baillet: ‏[הֹ צֹֹילֹ]‏.
[12] Ctr. Baillet: ‏[ֹ רֹ ה‏.

Frgs. 1–3 Col. 1

1   […] heart like my soul[4]

2   […] burs[t]ing

3   […] and rivers of w[ater]

4   […] forming power

5   […] what (is) all this? All

6   […] it is for the myst[eries of] thought

Frg. 3 Col. 2[5]

1   […]

2   *k*°[…]

3   °[…]

Frg. 4

1   [… he who] saves and °[…]

2   […] *hy*[…]

Frg. 5

1   […]*lh r*°[…]

Frg. 6

1   […] with all your heart […]

---

[4] Heb. נפש. Or "his soul." The right margin can be discerned.
[5] The right margin is preserved.

2   [ ]ֹ[ ] [דֹּ֯בֹּ֯ר] [לֹ]

Frg. 7

1   [ה לגור]

2   [ ]ֹי֯[ ]

Frg. 8

1   במצֹ֯רֹ]ים [ ] [13]

Frg. 9

1   [ֹ]

2   [כול ובתע]ודות [14]

Frg. 10

1   [ליֹ°°]

Frg. 11

1   [שֹמעוֹ לי]

2   בֹחֹוֹ]קים °° [ ] [15]

Frg. 12

1   [בֹוֹ ש]

---

[13] The lower margin seems extant.
[14] See 1QHᵃ 10.39 חוקֹיֹם ֹוֹבתעודות for the restoration of ובתע]ודות.
[15] See 1QHᵃ 10.39 חוקֹיֹם ֹוֹבתעודות for the restoration of בֹחֹוֹ]קים.

2   […]°[…] a word […]*l*[…]

Frg. 7

1   […]*h* to dwell […]

2   […]*y*°[…]

Frg. 8

1   […] in Egy[pt …]

Frg. 9

1   […]°[…]

2   […] all. And the testim[onies …]

Frg. 10

1   […]°°*ly*°°[…]

Frg. 11

1   […] listen to me […]

2   […]°° in the statu[tes …]

Frg. 12

1   […]*bw s*[…]

Frg. 13

1   [עבר]

Frg. 14

1   [וֹב]

2   [יֹ̊צ]

Frg. 15

1   [אותו ➚]16

---

16 A scribal mark.

Frg. 13

1 […] moved […]

Frg. 14

1 […]°*wb* […]

2 […]*ys*° […]

Frg. 15

1 […] him[6] […]

---

[6] A scribal mark follows "him."

Hymnic Fragment 2: Mentioning Nebo
4Q499 (4QpapHymns)

JAMES H. CHARLESWORTH with LEA BERKUZ[1]

Introduction

1. Contents

Hymnic Fragment 2 is inscribed on the *recto* of 4Q497,[2] which is published in PTSDSSP vol. 2. In DJD 7, Baillet published a description of the fragment for both 4Q497 and 4Q499.[3] 4Q499 contains a hymn or poem. The second person singular verb forms and pronominal suffixes refer to God and suggest that the author is addressing God. Thus, it is likely that 4Q499 preserves a hymn.

2. Text

The papyrus, broken into 54 fragments, is in poor condition, darkened. Much of the ink is lost or smudged. Many of the consonants are faded or obscured, making it difficult to read the text.[4] Baillet records, "*Papyrus d'épaisseur variable*...."[5] The script is Hasmonean which dates between 100–50 BCE. The dating is based on the exceptional forms of the final *mem*, elongated *lamedh*, *beth*, and *qoph*.[6]

3. Relation to Other Jewish Texts

E. J. C. Tigchelaar correctly notes that fragments 47 and 48 of 4Q499 contain an "almost complete overlap with 4Q369 (*4QPrayer of Enosh*)."[7] Tigchelaar observes that this reading seems to have been forgotten or lost, since it was recorded by one of de Vaux's early researchers but not subsequently published in DJD. Further, Baillet was unsure of whether or not the fragments of 4Q497 and 4Q499 should be grouped together. If fragments 47 and 48 do preserve 4Q369, they may represent the *Prayer of Enosh*.[8] They are included in the present volume, but our reading of fragments 47 to 54 restores Moses' expectation of being glorified and looking down on Israel from Mount Nebo. The mention of "Nebo" in fragment 47 may indicate the Hymn is about Moses' glorification on Mount Nebo.

4. Selected Bibliography

Baillet, M. "499. Hymnes ou prières." In *Qumrân Grotte 4.III (4Q482–4Q520)*. DJD 7; Oxford, 1982, pp. 74–77, Pl. 25.
Tigchelaar, E. J. C. "*4Q499* 48+47 (PAR *4Q369* 1 II): A Forgotten Identification." *RQ* 18/2 (1997) 303–06.

---

[1] Berkuz helped with the text and translation.

[2] M. Baillet, "499. Hymnes ou prières," in *Qumrân Grotte 4.III (4Q482–4Q520)* (DJD 7; Oxford, 1982) p. 74, Pl. 25.

[3] Baillet, DJD 7, p. 69, Pl. 26.

[4] Many fragments are not numbered or identified with 4Q499. See the final note to the text.

[5] Baillet, DJD 7, p. 69.

[6] Baillet reaches the same conclusion. See DJD 7, p. 74.

[7] E. J. C. Tigchelaar, "*4Q499* 48+47 (PAR 4Q369 1 II): A Forgotten Identification," *RQ* 18/2 (1997) 303.

[8] For more on this issue see, Tigchelaar, "*4Q499* 48+47 (PAR *4Q369* 1 II)," 303–06. See the notes to our text and translation.

Hymnic Fragment 2: Mentioning Nebo
4Q499 (4QpapHymns)

Frg. 1[1]

]°°°[	**1**
[ל°ר ²דם]	**2**
[לשׁלמוֹן³	
⁵ל]וּ כגמ[⁴ור°°°°[	**3**
[ן בֹ עֹיֹנֹינוּ⁶]	**4**
[פתחתה]	**5**
[הֹכריתה⁷]	**6**

Frg. 2[8]

[עֹ]	**1**
[מע[שֹׁיכהֹ]	**2**
[אֹיֹרֹ°]	**3**
[ם זֹ]	**4**
[רֹשׁעֹהֹ]	**5**
[וֹרֹ °וֹ]	**6**
[°]	**7**

---

[1] The lower margin is preserved. The fragment is upside down in the DSSEL image.
[2] Perhaps restore: א[דם.
[3] Baillet:]°מלשׁל[. This supralinear line seems to be written in a different scribal hand.
[4] The *waw* and *reš* are difficult to distinguish. The consonant may be a *he*.
[5] Baillet:]גֹב[כ. See 1Q36 frg. 15 line 3.
[6] Baillet:]ינֹינוֹ[.
[7] *Hipʿil* pf. Ctr. Baillet: כרתה.
[8] The fragment is shown upside down in the DSSEL image.

Hymnic Fragment 2: Mentioning Nebo
4Q499 (4QpapHymns)

Frg. 1

1   [...]°° °[...]

2   [...]*dm*[1] and °*l*[...]

3   [...]°*wr* as retributi[on[2] ...] to pay him [[3]...]

4   [...] our eyes *b*[...]

5   [...] you opened [...]

6   [...] you cut [...]

Frg. 2

1   [...]ᶜ[...]

2   [...] your [wo]rks [...]

3   [...]ʾ*yr*°[...]

4   [...]*m z*°[...]

5   [...] wickedness [...]

6   [...]°*w* and *r*[...]

7   [...]°[...]

---

[1] Perhaps "A]dam."
[2] See Isa 66:6: משלם גמול.
[3] The phrase "] to pay him [" is supplied by an interlinear.

Frg. 3[9]

1   אׄ מׄבׄ]

2   [הגידׄ]וּ ׄ

3   [לׄידעיםׄ]

4   רשׄ]עה[10] ׄ[

Frg. 4

1   [ׄ ׄ]

2   [ל בל יראׄוׄ]

3   פ]יׄהם ודב]ר

4   [ל]

Frg. 5[11]

1   [דיר אמׄ]

2   [ל דרכיׄם]

3   [חנׄוׄן אבׄ]

Frg. 6[12]

1   [ׄתׄ]

2   [מאן] ׄ

3   [ׄרׄל רוחׄ]ן[13]

---

[9] In some images, frg. 3 is upside down.
[10] Cf. Baillet:]רׄשׄ. See frg. 2 line 5.
[11] The image is upside down.
[12] The image is upside down.
[13] Ctr. Baillet:]ריׄחׄ. Or: כוח.

Frg. 3

1   […]ʾ *mb*[…]

2   […]° tell [him …]

3   […] to those who know […]

4   […]° wicke[dness[4] …]

Frg. 4

1   […]°°[…]

2   […]*l* lest they see […]

3   […] their [mo]uth and he spo[ke …]

4   […]*l*[…]

Frg. 5

1   […]*dyr* ʾ*m*[…]

2   […]*l* ways […]

3   […] gracious ʾ*b*[…]

Frg. 6

1   […] *t* ° […]

2   […]° refuse […]

3   […]° *rl* spirit […]

[4] See frg. 2 line 5.

Frg. 7

1   [ע ¹⁴תֹ̊ו̊ע¹⁵]

2   ] (VACAT) [

3   בֹ̊ו אם לשֹ̊מ̊[ו]ע בקולכֹ̊]ה[

4   ]לֹ[

Frg. 8

1   ] ֹמ̊ ֹ[

2   בחֹוצֹותֹ]¹⁶[

3   מן¹⁷] מֹועד למֹוֹעֹדֹ[

4   ]לֹ[¹⁸

5   הם]ֹ[

6   מֹקֹ][

Frg. 9

1   ]ֹ[ ]ֹ[

2   ]לֹ ֹ[

3   ]לֹכה [

4   ]וי כג[

5   ]כֹהֹ[

---

¹⁴ This ‘*ayin* is considerably larger than the following ‘*ayin* and the preceding characters. Could is be an example of a final ‘*ayin*?

¹⁵ Perhaps: עֹרכ].

¹⁶ See Jer 33:10: ובחצות ירושלם; cf. Jer 7:34.

¹⁷ Restore מן as suggested by Baillet. See 1QHᵃ 7.16.

¹⁸ The papyrus is deteriorated at this point in the fragment. Images from *DSSEL* make it clear that whatever ink that may have existed has broken off. This image in DJD is contrasted against a darker background that may be mistaken for a character.

Frg. 7

1   [...]°*tw*ᶜ ᶜ°°[...]

2   [....] (VACAT) [...]

3   [...]*bw* if to ob[e]y yo[ur] voice [...]

4   [...]*l*[...]

Frg. 8

1   [...]°°*m* [...]

2   [...] in the streets [...]

3   [... from] appointed time to appointed time [...]

4   [...]*l*[...]

5   [...]*hm* °[...]

6   [...]*mq*[...]

Frg. 9

1   [...]°[...]°[...]

2   [...]° *l*[...]

3   [...]*lkh* [...]

4   [...]*wy kg*[...]

5   [...]*kh*[...]

Frg. 10

1   ]°[

2   ] ° מק[ץ לק̊ץ]

3   [19]° ק[ד]שים

4   [מ̊ס̊פ̊ר̊ כו̊ל]

Frg. 11

1   [מ̊][20]

2   [מ̊ה]

3   ]ו̊[

4   ]ש[

5   ]°[

Frg. 12[21]

1   ]°[

2   ]מ̊°[

3   ]כפ̊ °°[

Frg. 13

1   ]°[[22]

2   ]°°[

3   ]י̊° °[

[19] Baillet did not transcribe the final trace of ink.
[20] This appears to be a typical late Hasmonean final *mem*.
[21] The bottom margin is visible.
[22] The papyrus fragment has lost the left side and top. We thus follow Baillet's early transcriptions.

Frg. 10

1   […]°[…]

2   [… from End]time to Endtime °[…]

3   [… H]oly Ones °[…]

4   […] recount all […]

Frg. 11

1   […]*m*[…]

2   […]*mh*[…]

3   […]*w* […]

4   […]*š*[…]

5   […]° […]

Frg. 12

1   […]°[…]

2   […]°*m*[…]

3   […]°° *kp*[…]

Frg. 13

1   […]°[…]

2   […]°°[…]

3   […]° *y*°[…]

]°°קׄ [23]מ[**4**

Frg. 14

]°° [**1**

]° °° [**2**

]° [24]בוׄ° י]חד   **3**

]כׄ°ׄ[**4**

Frg. 15

]° [**1**

]מׄי[**2**

] דׄת [**3**

Frg. 16

]ים ו[25]
]הׄוׄ[26]   **1**

] שׄיׄו[**2**

]°°° [**3**

Frg. 17

] בׄ [**1**

]ומולׄ [**2**

---

[23] The form looks like a medial *mem*.

[24] Or בי.

[25] Cf. Baillet:]°מׄ°[. This scribal emendation contains a final *mem* immediately followed by some ink. It is unclear if this could have been a Hebrew character or is simply due to dropped ink. Baillet also notes the final *mem* but in an apparent (and unacceptable) medial position. See DJD 7, p. 74.

[26] Baillet:]הׄיׄ[.

4   […]*m q*°°[…]

Frg. 14

1   […]°°[…]

2   […]°° °[…]

3   […tog]ether with him °[…]

4   […]°*k*°[…]

Frg. 15

1   […] °[…]

2   […]*my*[…]

3   […]*dt* […]

Frg. 16

1   […]*ḥy*[…]*ym* and [⁵…]

2   […]*šyw* […]

3   […]°°°[…]

Frg. 17

1   […] *b*°[…]

2   […] and *mwl*[…]

⁵ Baillet notes a superscript above the line, supplying "]*ym* and [."

3	]א̊ל̊[
4	]ל̊[

Frg. 18

1	[כ̊ ב̊][27]
2	]ת̊[

Frg. 19

1	]כ̊צ̊[
2	תם][28]

Frg. 20

1	]°°°[
2	]שׂו̊[
3	]°°°[

Frg. 21

1	]מ̊ט̊[
2	ד[ע̊ת]
3	]שׂ°°[

Frg. 22

1	דב[רי[29] פיכה]

[27] Ctr. Baillet:]כ̊ב̊[ ].
[28] The bottom margin is visible.
[29] See frg. 4 line 3.

3 […]°ʾ[…]

4 […]*l*[…]

Frg. 18

1 […]°*k b*[…]

2 […]°*ṭ*°[…]

Frg. 19

1 […]*kṣ*[…]

2 […]*tm* […]

Frg. 20

1 […]°°°[…]

2 […]*šw*°[…]

3 […]°°°[…]

Frg. 21

1 […]°*mṭ*[…]

2 [… kno]wledge […]

3 […]°°*š*[…]

Frg. 22

1 [… the wor]ds of[6] your mouth […]

---

[6] See frg. 4 line 3.

2   [ל֯ל]³⁰

Frg. 23

1   כ[בודכ֯]ה³¹

2   [מ֯ועד]

Frg. 24

1   [֗]

2   [ם וכ֯]

3   [א֯֯]

Frg. 25

1   [כ֯ו֯]

2   [ד ֗]

3   [֗֗]

Frg. 26

1   [֗ עמ֯]

2   [לת֯ ק֯]³²

Frg. 27

1   [֗֗֗]

2   [ו֯ן ימ]

³⁰ Baillet:] ֗ל[.
³¹ Baillet:] ֗בו֗ד[. See *GC* p. 63. See also 1QH^a 9.32, 12.29, 13.22, 14.15, etc.
³² Baillet:] ֗ת ק֯[.

2   […]*l*˚[…]

Frg. 23

1[…] yo[ur g]lory […]

2[…] appointed time […]

Frg. 24

1   […]˚[…]

2   […]*m* and *k*[…]

3   […]ʾ˚[…]

Frg. 25

1   […]*kw*˚[…]

2   […]˚*d* […]

3   […]˚˚[…]

Frg. 26

1   […]˚ᶜ*m* […]

2   […]*lt q*˚[…]

Frg. 27

1   […]˚˚˚[…]

2   […]*yn ym*[…]

Frg. 28

1   [וּבִֿיֿ]

2   [רֿשעהֿ]33

Frg. 29

1   ]ֿ[

2   [הֿכינוֿ]תה34

3   [לֿ ֿ]

Frg. 30

1   ]מֿֿ[

2   [בניֿ]

Frg. 31

1   [ֿֿֿ] [ֿֿ לֿב]35

2   [לֿ36   ]

Frg. 32

1   קֿ[צֿים37]

Frg. 33

1   ]ֿ הֿ ֿ[

2   ]ֿ[ ]ֿ[

---

33 See frg. 2 line 5 and frg. 3 line 4.
34 See *GC* p. 137. 1QHa 7.27; 9.12, 16, 19; 10.19; 19.37.
35 Ctr. Baillet:]לֿמֿ. There is a drop of ink at the end of the *beth*.
36 The mast of the *lamedh* in this scribal hand are exceptionally high.
37 Perhaps *scriptio continua*, so]ים זֿ[. Note the final *nun*.

Frg. 28

1   […] and *by*°[…]

2   […] wickedness […][7]

Frg. 29

1   […]°[…]

2   [… you] established […]

3   […]*l*° °[…]

Frg. 30

1   […]°*m*[…]

2   […] sons of […]

Frg. 31

1   […]°°°[…]°° *lm*°[…]

2   […]*l*   […]

Frg. 32

1   [… end]times […]

Frg. 33

1   […]°*h* °[…]

2   […]°[…]°[…]

---

[7] See frg. 2 line 5 and frg. 3 line 4.

Frg. 34

]°°°[**1**

³⁸]עׄתׄיׄד[ע   **2**

Frg. 35

]°°[**1**

]גׄד[**2**

]לׄ[**3**

Frg. 36

]°[**1**

³⁹]לׄ[]°[**2**

Frg. 37[40]

]°[**1**

]כׄ°°°[   ] (VACAT) [**2**
]מׄ[

] וׄ°[   ] (VACAT) [**3**

Frg. 38[41]

⁴²]°שׄ°[**1**

⁴³]שׄוׄעׄ[**2**

---

³⁸ Baillet:]תׄיׄ[. See Job 15:24: תתקפהו כמלך עתיד לכידור.

³⁹ The mast of the *lamedh* is especially lengthy.

⁴⁰ This fragment is not in PAM 43.659 as recorded in *DSSEL*.

⁴¹ The image on *DSSEL* is fragmented. DJD 7, Pl. 25 offers a better, fuller image.

⁴² Ctr. Baillet:]°מׄשׄ[.

⁴³ Today only]°שׄ[is visible. The papyrus has continued to deteriorate.

Frg. 34

1   [...]°°°[...]

2   [... fu]ture [...]

Frg. 35

1   [...]°°[...]

2   [...]*gd*[...]

3   [...]*l*[...]

Frg. 36

1   [...]°[...]

2   [...]°[...]*l*[...]

Frg. 37

1   [...]°[...]

2   [...] (VACAT) [...]°°°*k*[...]

3   [...]°*m*[8] (VACAT) [...] and °[...]

Frg. 38

1   [...]°*š*°[...]

2   [...]*šw*ᶜ°[...]

---

[8] The "]°*m*" is supplied by an interlinear.

Frg. 39

1   [המבֿ]

2   [לֹהֿ]

Frg. 40

1   [וֿ]

2   [וֿזֿכֿ]רתי

Frg. 41

1   [֯]

2   ב]רֿיֿתֿ[44

Frg. 42[45]

1   [הֿ ֯]

2   [עֿדֿ]

Frg. 43

1   [֯]

2   [שֿ רֿ]

Frg. 44

1   [֯]

2   [דֿ]

---

[44] With Baillet:]רֿיֿתֿ[; restore ב]רית. Frg. 40 line 2 was probably linked to frg. 41 line 2:]וֿזֿכֿרתי ב]רֿיֿתֿ[. See 1QHᵃ 12.35, 36. For ברית see 1QHᵃ 4.17, 39, etc.

[45] *DSSEL* does not record this fragment and Baillet only states, "traces insignifantes de 2 lignes." (DJD 7, p. 77). See also DJD 7, Pl. 25.

Frg. 39

1   […] *hmb*[…]

2   […]*lh* […]

Frg. 40

1   […] and […]

2   […] and [I] remem[bered …]

Frg. 41

1   […]˚[…]

2   [… co]venant […]

Frg. 42

1   […]*h* ˚[…]

2   […] until […]

Frg. 43

1   […]˚[…]

2   […]*š r*[…]

Frg. 44

1   […]˚[…]

2   […]*d* […]

Frg. 45[46]

1   ]°°°[

2   ]°°[

Frg. 46

1   ]°תׄ°[

Frg. 47[47]

1   ת[דׄבק נפשׁ]יׄ[48]

2   [°°ם נׄבו וקׄ][49]

3   מ[שנתׄו תמׄ]יד[50]

Frg. 48

1   ]°ׄ ותשימ[ני]לכׄ[בידכה[51]

2   ]°ׄ בכול תבל אׄר][52]

3   ]°ׄ וׄכׄ[בו]ד שׄחקׄ[ים[53]

Frg. 49

1   ]°ׄ ש°°[

2   [ולׄמׄוׄעׄ]ד[54]

---

[46] *DSSEL* does not record frg. 45. Baillet only reports, "traces insignifiantes de 2 lignes." (DJD 7, p. 77). See also DJD 7, Pl. 25.

[47] 4Q369 indicates that frg. 47 follows frg. 48. Hence, the fragments of 4Q499 are not in order.

[48] See 4Q369 frg. 1 2.11: תדבק נפשכה.

[49] Cf. Baillet:]°ׄ נׄבׄוׄ °°ם[.

[50] For תמיד with כבוד see 1QH^a 9.9. 4Q369 frg. 1 col. 2 breaks off before line 3.

[51] Ctr. Baillet: °°תשים. *DSSEL* does not record any ink that may represent consonants after the medial *mem*. However, DJD 7, Pl. 25 may. Cf. 4Q369 frg. 1 2.6: ותשימהו לכה.

[52] The *lamedh* is atypical and written with an artistic top swirl. For the restoration, see 4Q369 frg. 1 2.7: [בכול תבל ארצ/כ\ה. See 1QH^a 14.18; תבל is extant eight times in 1QH^a. See also 1QS 3.17–18.

[53] For the restoration, see 4Q369 frg. 1 2.8: שׄמים וכבוד שחקים[.

[54] Baillet:]°ׄלׄמׄוׄ[. Either *qal* impf. of לין or more likely *nipʿal* impf. of לון, "murmur against." See Ps 59:16: וילינו. See frg. 8 line 3 and frg. 3 line 2.

Frg. 45

1   […]°°°[…]

2   […]°°[…]

Frg. 46

1   […]°ť°[…]

Frg. 47

1   [… my] soul [will] adhere […]

2   […]°°*m* Nebo[9] and *q*[…]

3   […] his [te]aching alw[ays …]

Frg. 48

1   […] and you shall set [me] for [your] g[lory …]

2   […]° in all the world ʾ*r*[…]

3   […]° and the g[lor]y of the ski[es …]

Frg. 49

1   […]°°*š*°[…]

2   […] and for the appointed ti[me …]

---

[9] The hymn seems to celebrate Moses' glorification.

Frg. 50

1   יש[רא]לֹ ֯[

2   ]ֹ[

Frg. 51[55]

1   ] ֯אל [

2   ]כֹֹ[וֹ
        כי

3   [

Frg. 52

1   ]בֹ[

2   [56]] ֯ ֯ [

3   ]ֹ[

Frg. 53

1   ]ֹֹֹ[

2   ]אֹ [

3   ]ֹמֹ[

4   ]ֹ[

Frg. 54

1   ]ֹ[]ֹ[

2   אֹ[ר]ֹ [57]

---

[55] Frgs. 51–54 are not identified in *DSSEL*. See DJD 7, Pl. 25.

[56] Although this image is not identified in *DSSEL* there does seem to be ink on this fragment in DJD 7, Pl. 25. Ctr. Baillet:] *vacat* [.

[57] Baillet:]רֹ֯[. Many additional fragments never edited may be related to 4Q499. For example, on PAM 43.657, to the right of 4Q499 frg. 46 are the following: 80, 79, 78, 171, 77, 76, 170, 87, 86, 85, 84, 83, 96, 82, and 81.

Frg. 50

1   […]° Isr[ael[10] …]

2   […]°[…]

Frg. 51

1   […] unto °[…]

2   […] and as°[…]

3   […] for[11] […]

Frg. 52

1   […]*b* […]

2   […]° °[…]

3   […]°[…]

Frg. 53

1   […]°°°[…]

2   […] ᵓ°[…]

3   […]*m* °[…]

4   […]°[…]

Frg. 54

1   […]°[…]°[…]

2   […l]and […]

[10] See frg. 54 line 2.
[11] The word "for" is supplied by an interlinear.

Hymnic Work?
4Q579

JAMES H. CHARLESWORTH with LEA BERKUZ[1]

Introduction

1. Contents

4Q579 was published by É. Puech in DJD 25.[2] Initially assigned to J. Starcky, 4Q579 contains three small fragments totalling eight lines.[3] The texts seem to be hymnic in nature; there are similarities to the Psalms.

2. Text

The script is late Hasmonean, dating the fragments sometime between 50–25 BCE. The scribe does not distinguish between a *waw* and a *yodh*.

3. Language, History, and Theology

The only distinguishing language throughout the fragments is in fragment 1 line 2. Here the author mentions "all the angels and E[lim ...]." The author also alludes to the תהום (frg. 1 line 4), "the deep."[4] This word is used in the creation narrative of Genesis 1 and refers to the "subterranean waters." It is also used multiple times throughout the Psalter and in other poetic and prophetic literature, often to describe God's greatness over creation and ability to control the depths of the waters.[5] This language supports the hymnic designation.

4. Selected Bibliography

Puech, É. "579. 4QOuvrage hymnique?" In *Qumrân Grotte 4.XVII. Textes Hébreux (4Q521–4Q528, 4Q576–4Q579)*. DJD 25; Oxford, 1998; pp. 209–11, Pl. 15.

---

[1] Berkuz helped with the text and translation.

[2] É. Puech, "579. 4QOuvrage hymnique?," in *Qumrân Grotte 4.XVII. Textes Hébreux (4Q521–4Q528, 4Q576-4Q579)* (DJD 25; Oxford, 1998) pp. 209–11, Pl. 15.

[3] See PAM 43.676 and 43.675. On PAM 43.675, sixteen additional fragments with consonants are pictured directly above and to the right of frgs. 2 and 3, and seven unidentified fragments are pictured below them. The script is similar. The fragments to the left of frg. 1 are also unidentified but the script is different (if we may trust the old photographs).

[4] For תהום in the *Hodayot*, see 1QH[a] 5.26; 9.16; 11.16, 18, 32, 33; 13.40; 14.19, 27; 18.35; 4Q432 frg. 5 line 3; 4Q429 frg. 4 2.4.

[5] See esp. Isa 51:10; Pss 33:7, 71:20, 77:17, 78:15, 135:6.

Hymnic Work?
4Q579

Frg. 1

1 [בֹּכֹל] מ[עֹשֹׂ]יֿ[1](#fn1)

2 [כל מלאכים וֹא]לים[2](#fn2)

3 [היות ליֿדֹוֹעֹים מש]פֿט

4 [תֹהום ממשֹׁפֿטֹ]יֿכה[3](#fn3)

5 [ ]לֹֿ[ ]לֹֿ[4](#fn4)

Frg. 2

1 [ ]°°מ ואתם[ ]מֹֿ

Frg. 3

1 [ ]מֹֿ[ ]

2 [ ]לֹיֿמֹ[ ]

Frg. a[5](#fn5)

1 [ ] יֿנֹטֹעֹ[

---

[1] Or perhaps: מ[עֹשֹׂ]ה, "wo]rkin[g."
[2] The leather is lost above the ʾaleph.
[3] Puech: ממ{שׁ}<יטֹ>הֿ °[.
[4] Each *lamedh* is highly speculative.
[5] There are additional unidentified fragments of the same script as frgs. 1–3 directly to the right of frg. 2 and alone at the bottom of PAM 43.675.

Hymnic Work?
4Q579

Frg. 1

1   […] in all the [wo]rkin[gs of …]

2   […] all the angels and E[lim …]

3   […] it will be for those knowing[1] judg[ment …]

4   […] the deep.[2] From [your] judgment[s[3] …]

5   […]*l*[…]*l*[…]

Frg. 2

1   […]*m* and you[4] °°[…]

Frg. 3

1   […]*m* […]

2   […]*lym*°[…]

Frg. a[5]

1   […] he shall plant […]

---

[1] *Hipᶜil* infinitive construct. Puech: "…] *devenant connus* de . . [."
[2] See Gen 1:2; Ps 104:6; Job 38:16; Prov 8:27, 28. The word is also found in 1Q27 frg. 13 line 3.
[3] According to Puech, ה̊‹יט›{ש}ממ is a *hipᶜil* part. from מוט.
[4] The pronoun is plural.
[5] There are additional fragments that are unidentified to the right of frg. 2 and of the same script as frgs. 1–3 and isolated on PAM 43.675.

Frg. b

1   [ה̊ס̊]⁶

Frg. c

1   [   ]˚[

2   [יום תע̊]⁷

Frg. d

1   [ריב]⁸

2   [   ]˚˚[

Frg. e

1   [ח̊]

Frg. f

1   [   ]˚[

2   [   ]˚˚ נג̊לו̊ ˚˚[

---

⁶ The margin is visible.

⁷ Cf. 4Q418 frg. 137 line 5: יום תע̊[. Perhaps restore: תע̊[נית, "the day of humi[liation."

⁸ Not רוב as the scribe does not use the *matres lectionis* in frg. 1 lines 1–2; cf. 4Q300 frg. 9 line 2: יום הריב.

Frg. b

1   [...]˚*h*

Frg. c

1   [...]˚[...]

2   [...] day of *t*[⁶...]

Frg. d

1   [...] strife⁷ [...]

2   [...]˚˚[...]

Frg. e

1   [...]*ḥ*˚[...]

Frg. f

1   [...]˚[...]

2   [...]˚˚ they were revealed ˚˚[...]

---

⁶ Conceivably restore "day of humi[liation"; cf. 4Q418 frg. 137 line 5.
⁷ This noun has forensic dimensions denoting a legal case. Cf. 4Q300 frg. 9 line 2: יום הריב, "day of strife."

Benediction 2
6Q16

JOSEPH L. TRAFTON

Introduction

Benediction 2 (6Q16) is a fragmentary text which was categorized by its editor, M. Baillet, as a series of benedictions.[1] Portions of only thirteen lines of the text have been preserved.

1. Text

Benediction 2 consists of five small Hebrew fragments of a thin papyrus manuscript written in a script from the first century CE.[2]

2. Original Language, Date, and Provenience

The fragmentary nature of *Benediction 2* precludes certainty concerning introductory matters. The hymn was probably composed in Hebrew. On paleographical grounds it can be dated no later than the first century CE. A Palestinian provenience seems obvious.

3. Language, History, and Theology

Because it is so fragmentary, *Benediction 2* adds little to our knowledge of Hebrew beyond the use of *waw* as a vowel letter (frg. 1 line 2), which is characteristic of the Scrolls.[3] Similarly, it provides no historical insights. The document may have combined blessings and curses in the manner of the *Rule of the*

Community (1QS 2). If so, then the document would have been consistent with the spirit of, and may even have been composed within, the Qumran Community.[4]

4. Relation to the Hebrew Bible, Other Jewish Writings, and the New Testament

The formal combination of blessings with curses is a standard element in Ancient Near Eastern treaties. Such is the setting for the blessings and curses in the Mosaic covenant (Deuteronomy 27–28). Similarly, in the Qumran *Rule of the Community*, the covenantal theology of column 1 provides the context for the blessings and curses in column 2. In some Jewish and Christian writings lists of woes stand by themselves (e.g., Isa 5:8–23; *1En* 94–100; Mt 23); the same is true for blessings (e.g., Mt 5:3–12). In the New Testament blessings and woes are combined in Jesus' "Sermon on the Plain" (Lk 6:20–26)[5] and are scattered throughout Revelation.

5. Selected Bibliography

Baillet, M. "16. Bénédictions." In *Les 'Petite Grottes' De Qumrân: Exploration de la falaise. Les grottes 2Q, 3Q, 5Q, 6Q, 7Q, à 10Q. Le rouleau de cuivre.* DJD 3; Oxford, 1962, pp. 131–32, Pl. 27.

---

[1] The *editio princeps* was published by M. Baillet, "16. Bénédictions," in *Les 'Petite Grottes' de Qumrân: Exploration de la falaise. Les grottes 2Q, 3Q, 5Q, 6Q, 7Q, à 10Q. Le rouleau de cuivre* (DJD 3; Oxford, 1962) pp. 131–32, Pl. 27.

[2] Baillet, DJD 3, pp. 131–32, Pl. 27.

[3] Cf. E. Qimron, *The Hebrew of the Dead Sea Scrolls* (HSS 29; Atlanta, 1986) p. 17.

[4] Baillet (DJD 3, p. ix) placed it among "*textes juridiques et liturgiques.*"

[5] The Sermon on the Mount contains blessings only; see Mt 5:3–12.

Benediction 2
6Q16

Frg. 1

1 [̊ כניחוח ̊]

2 ק[לכול אנשי חל]

3 ל[גמולים לכו]

4 [ל]כו[ל ב̇ן]

Frg. 2

1 [ ] ̊ה[ ] ̊[ ]

2 [רשע פו]̊עלי רשע[^1]

3 [ממשלת]

Frg. 3

1 [ב̊רית̊]

2 [מ̊צ̊ות̊]

3 ק[מצד]

4 [ברכות]

Frg. 4

1 ג[רפת̊]²

[1] See 1QHᵃ 6.25; also see Ps 28:3.
[2] See 4Q511 and 4Q152 and *GC*.

Benediction 2
6Q16

Frg. 1

1   […]° like a pleasant fragrance ° […]

2   […] to all the men of the porti[on …]

3   […] rewards to al[l …]

4   […] to [al]l *b*[…]

Frg. 2

1   […]°[…]*ḥ* […]

2   [… doe]rs of wickedness[1] […]

3   […] dominion of […]

Frg. 3

1   […] covenant […]

2   […] commandment […]

3   […] declaring j[ust[2] …]

4   […] blessings […]

Frg. 4

1   […] you [was]hed away […]

---

[1] See 1QH[a] 6.25.
[2] Or "from justi[ce."

Frg. 5

1   ]מ ה[

Frg. 5

1   […]*h m*[…]

Hymns
6Q18 (6QpapHymn)

JOSEPH L. TRAFTON

Introduction

6Q18, *Hymns* (6QpapHymn), is a fragmentary text which was designated by its first editor, M. Baillet, as "Composition hymnique."[1]

1. Text

6Q18 consists of 27 small Hebrew fragments of a single papyrus manuscript written in Herodian script.[2]

2. Original Language, Date, and Provenience

The document was composed in Hebrew. On paleographical grounds it can be dated no later than the first century CE. 6Q18 attests to several orthographic features which are characteristic of the Qumran Scrolls, including the use of *waw* as a vowel letter (frg. 2 line 3, frg. 2 line 8, frg. 4 line 2, frg 5 line 4, frg. 6 line 3, frg. 23 line 1),[3] the writing of כי with an ʾ*aleph* (כיא: frg. 16 line 2, frg. 20 line 2),[4] and the writing of the second person masculine singular pronominal suffix as כה, rather than ך (frg. 14 line 3, frg. 20 line 2).[5] 6Q18 also attests to the use of the orthographical variant ישחק for יצחק (frg. 2 line 7; cf. CD MS A 3.3; Ps 105:9; Jer 33:26; Amos 7:9, 16). It contains one word which is not found in the Hebrew Bible (תשבוחות: frg. 2 line 8; cf. 1QM 4.8, Sir 51:12)[6] and two which take on new meanings (בליעל: frg. 3 line 3 and מֹשטמה: frg. 9 line 1).[7] Finally, 6Q18

consistently uses Palaeo-Hebrew script in writing אל (frg. 6 line 5, frg. 8 line 1, frg. 10 line 3).[8]

3. History and Theology

6Q18 provides no historical insights. The tone of the extant text seems to be oriented towards warfare; certain phrases are reminiscent of the *War Scroll* (see notes to the Translation). Perhaps the *Hymns* are an expression of trust in God in the face of enemies (perhaps at the time of the eschatological war; cf. frg. 2 line 3). Other concepts (e.g. Belial [frg. 3 line 3; cf. 1QS 1.18, 24; 2.5, 19; 10.21; 1QM 1.1, 5, 13; 4.2; 11.8; 13.2, 4, 11; 14.9; 15.3; 18.1, 3; 1QHᵃ 10.18, 24; 11.29, 30, 33; 12.11, 14; 13.41; 14.24; 15.6; 4Q175 line 23; 4Q174 1.8, 9; 2.2; CD MS A 4.13, 15; 5.18; 8.2; 12.2; 19.14; 4Q171 [4QPsᵃ] frgs. 1–10 2.11; 1Q40 frg. 9 line 3], "our assembly" [frg. 14 line 2; cf. 1QM 4.10; 11.16; 14.5; 15.10; 18.1; 1QSa 1.25; 2.4; CD MS A 7.17; 11.22; 12.6; 14.18; 4Q169 [4QpNah] 3.5, 7]) are found frequently at Qumran as well. Thus, 6Q18 is consistent with the thought of, and may well have been composed within, the Qumran Community.[9]

---

[1] The *editio princeps* was published by M. Baillet, "18. Composition Hymnique," in *Les 'Petite Grottes' De Qumrân: Exploration de la falaise. Les grottes 2Q, 3Q, 5Q, 6Q, 7Q, à 10Q. Le rouleau de cuivre* (DJD 3; Oxford, 1962) p. 133–36, Pl. 27.

[2] Baillet, DJD 3, pp. 133–36.

[3] Cf. E. Qimron, *The Hebrew of the Dead Sea Scrolls* (HSS 29; Atlanta, 1986) p. 17.

[4] Qimron, *The Hebrew of the Dead Sea Scrolls*, p. 21.

[5] Qimron, *The Hebrew of the Dead Sea Scrolls*, p. 58.

[6] Qimron, *The Hebrew of the Dead Sea Scrolls*, p. 106.

[7] Qimron, *The Hebrew of the Dead Sea Scrolls*, p. 106.

[8] On Palaeo-Hebrew characters at Qumran, see E. Tov, *Scribal Practice and Approaches Reflected in the Texts Found in the Judean Desert* (STDJ 54; Leiden, 2004) pp. 238–46; see F. M. Cross, *The Ancient Library of Qumran and Modern Biblical Studies* (Garden City, 1961 [2nd ed.]) p. 34n. On the use of Palaeo-Hebrew for the Tetragrammaton, see J. P. Siegal, "The Employment of Palaeo-Hebrew Characters for the Divine Names at Qumran in the Light of Tannaitic Sources," *HUCA* 42 (1971) 159–72 and P. W. Skehan, "The Divine Name at Qumran, in the Masada Scroll, and in the Septuagint," *BIOSCS* 13 (1980) 14–44.

[9] J. A. Fitzmyer classifies 6Q18 as a sectarian text. See his *The Dead Sea Scrolls: Major Publications and Tools for Study* (Missoula, 1977) p. 21.

4. Relation to the Hebrew Bible, Other Jewish Writings, and the New Testament

6Q18 stands in the general tradition of early Jewish hymnody. In particular it seems to have affinities with national lament psalms (e.g., Psalms 44, 60, 74, 79, 80, 85, 90, 123, 125, 129; *Psalms of Solomon* 1, 7, 8, 17). The mention of Belial (frg. 3 line 3) apparently situates the *Hymns*, along with *Jubilees* (1:20, 15:33), the *Testaments of the Twelve Patriarchs* (TReu 4:7, 11; 6:3; TSim 5:3; TLevi 3:3; 18:12; 19:1; TJud 25:3; TIss 6:1; 7:7; TZeb 9:8; TDan 1:7; 4:7; 5:1, 10, 11; TNaph 2:6; 3:1; TAsh 1:8; 3:2; 6:4; TJos 7:4; 20:2; TBenj 3:3, 4, 8; 6:1, 7; 7:1, 2), the *Sibylline Oracles* (3:63, 73), the *Martyrdom of Isaiah* (1:8, 9; 2:4; 3:11; 5:1, 15), and the *Lives of the Prophets* (4:6, 20; 17:2), within a Jewish tradition which gave the name to Satan, a tradition which continues into the Christian Scriptures (cf. 2Cor 6:15) and early Christianity (cf. GBart 1:10–20, 4:12–60). Similarly, if Mastemah is a proper name for Satan in fragment 9 line 1, there is an even stronger connection with *Jubilees*, which alone of the pre-70 Jewish writings makes such an identification (10:8; 11:5, 11; 17:16; 18:9, 12; 19:28; 48:2, 9, 12, 15; 49:2).

5. Selected Bibliography

Baillet, M. "18. Composition hymnique." In *Les 'Petite Grottes' De Qumrân: Exploration de la falaise. Les grottes 2Q, 3Q, 5Q, 6Q, 7Q, à 10Q. Le rouleau de cuivre.* DJD 3; Oxford, 1962, pp. 133–36, Pl. 27.

Hymns
6Q18 (6QpapHymn)

Frg. 1[1]

1	מֹ]
2	וה][2]
3	אב]
4	יד̊]
5	תרוע̊]ה
6	להכנ̊י]ע
7	ה̊וי][3]

Frg. 2

1	]̊[
2	[ח̊י̊י̊[4] נצח וכב]וד[5]
3	כ]ֹל̊ חושך וֹאֹפ]לה[6]
4	אל ח]ושך תשוקתנ̊ו̊[7]
5	[לֹחי עולמים[8] ויהי̊]
6	[̊[ ] [עד שמח̊]ה[9]

---

[1] The right margin is preserved.

[2] Ctr. Baillet:]וא.

[3] Baillet takes this as a complete word "malheur" ("woe"). Most likely a form of הוה in the *pi̇̆el*.

[4] Baillet notes that the deterioration of this part of the fragment occurred prior to the taking of the image, causing this word,]ֹל̊ below, and the *waw* of ח]ושך in line 4 to be absent from the PAM images.

[5] See Ps 49:10; CD MS A 3.20: לחיי נצח וכל כבוד אדם להם הוא; 1QS 4.7: ולכליל כבוד; 4Q511 frg. 2 1.4. ;ושמחת עולמים בחיי נצח

[6] A scribe added a dot over and below the *waw* and a dot over the ʾ*aleph*. Joel 2:2: יום חֹשֶׁךְ וַאֲפֵלָה; Zeph 1:15: יום חֹשֶׁךְ וַאֲפֵלָה. See also Amos 5:20 and Isa 29:18.

[7] See Gen 3:16 and 4:7.

[8] Cf. Gen 3:22, Zech 1:5, Neh 2:3, 4Q442 frg. 1 line 1.

[9] Ctr. Baillet:]עד שמח [. See 2Chr 29:30: וַיְהַלְלוּ עַד־לְשִׂמְחָה וַיִּקְּדוּ וַיִּשְׁתַּחֲווּ; 1QHᵃ 5.23.

Hymns
6Q18 (6QpapHymn)

Frg. 1[1]

1   *m*[…]

2   and *h*[…]

3   *ʾb*[…]

4   *yd*°[…]

5   a war cr[y[2] …]

6   to subdu[e[3] …]

7   *hwy*[[4]…]

Frg. 2

1   […]°[…]

2   […] eternal life and glo[ry …]

3   [… a]ll darkness and glo[ominess …]

4   [… unto da]rkness (is) o[ur] penchant[5] […]

5   […]*lḥy* forever. And may be […]

6   […]°[…] until jo[y…]

---

[1] The right margin of the Hebrew is preserved.

[2] This word appears frequently in the *War Scroll* (1QM 1.11, 17; 2.16; 3.1; 7.13; 8.7, 10, 15; 9.1; 16.5, 6, 8, 9; 17.11, 13, 14; 18.2). Cf. Josh 6:5, 6:20; 1Sam 4:5; Amos 1:1, 1:14, 2:2; Num 10:5, 10:6. Or "a shou[t" as in a "shout (of joy) to God" (see Ps 27:6, 33:3, 47:6, 89:16; Ezra 3:11–13).

[3] See 1QM 1.6, 14; 6.5; 11.3; 12.5; 17.5. The verb does not appear with the *lamedh* prefix in the Hebrew Bible.

[4] Probably a *piʿel* from היה "to be."

[5] See Gen 3:16 and 4:7. Or "longing." The noun denotes the human natural propensity.

7   [א[מֹר¹⁰ בן ישחק¹¹]

8   [בֹתשבחות¹² ע[ולמים¹³

9   [לֹ]

Frg. 3

1   [ ]ֹ[

2   [ת עולמיֹם]¹⁴

3   [בבליעל וֹ]

Frg. 4

1   [אילים אֹ]

2   [בֹלי¹⁵ לוא]

3   [לֹ] [יֹפלוֹ לֹ]

Frg. 5

1   [ֹ[ ] [ ]ֹל וֹמֹ]

2   מל[אכי צדק¹⁶ במעֹ]¹⁷

3   יֹ[חֹזקו¹⁸ ברוח דעתֹ]¹⁹

---

¹⁰ Restoration by Charlesworth and Berkuz.

¹¹ This unique spelling of the name יצחק can also be found in Jer 33:26; Amos 7:9, 16; Ps 105:9; and CD MS A 3.3.

¹² From the root שבח "to grow in value, to praise." The word is extant over 25 times in the Dead Sea Scrolls (e.g., 1QM 4.8, 4Q286 frg. 1 2.5, 11Q5 22.11, 11Q17 10.5) but never in the Hebrew Bible.

¹³ For עולמים, see line 5 and frg. 3 line 2.

¹⁴ Possible restorations include בתשבחוֹ[ת עולמיֹם (frg. 2.8); שמח[ת עולמיֹם (Isa 35:10, 51:11, 61:7; 1QS 4.7; 1QHᵃ 23.16); לשמח[ת עולמיֹם (4Q491 frg. 11 1.21: (בשמח[ת עולמיֹם; דורו[ת עולמים (Isa 51:9, 4Q219 2.33, 4Q433a 2.6); or ברי[ת עולמיֹם (1QS 4.22; cf. Gen 9:6, 17:7; Ex 31:16; Isa 24:5; Ps 105:10).

¹⁵ Baillet: רֹלי].

¹⁶ 4Q287 frg. 2 line 13: מ[לאכי צדקכה.

¹⁷ Perhaps restore: במעֹ[מדם.

¹⁸ This verb, from חזק "to be strong, make firm, seize hold of," may either be a *qal* impf. or a *hitpaʿel* impf. with the preposition ב.

¹⁹ See 1QSb 5.25, 1QS 4.4, 1QHᵃ 6.36, Isa 11:2.

7 [...] he [s]aid, the son of Isaac [...]

8 [...] with et[ernal] praises [...]

9 [...]*l*[...]

Frg. 3

1 [...]°[...]

2 [...]*t* eternities [...]

3 [...] with Belial and [...]

Frg. 4

1 [...] rams ᵓ[...]

2 [...]*bly* not [...]

3 [...]*l*[...] they will fall *l*[...]

Frg. 5

1 [...]°[...]*l* and *m*°[...]

2 [... the ang]els of righteousness *bmʿ*[⁶...]

3 [... th]ey [will] be strengthened through the spirit of knowledge⁷ [...]

---

⁶ Perhaps "in their ranks" (במעמדם) or "in their arrangements" (במערכיתם). Both appear frequently in the *War Scroll*.
⁷ For "the spirit of knowledge," cf. 1QS 4.4, 1QHᵃ 6.36, 1QSb 5.25.

4   לעו[למים לוא יֹכֹלוֹ]²⁰

Frg. 6

1   [עליוֹן] ̊[ ] [

2   ל[פני הד]²¹

3   [מֹושלים]²²

4   [אֹמתו לֹ]

5   ל[הלל ⸌⸍]²³

Frg. 7

1   ]̊[

2   [אֹת]

3   [ם לֹ]

4   [דֹל]²⁴

5   [לֹ]

Frg. 8

1   [ל⸌⸍ ²⁵ ישר]אֹל²⁶

2   [̊ם ביום]

---

[20] The bottom margin is preserved.

[21] The *daleth* could conceivably be a *reš*.

[22] The *mem* is barely visible; its left arm can be seen intersecting the stroke of the *waw*.

[23] See 4Q417 frg. 1 2.9.

[24] Baillet:] כֹל[. This reading is in tension with the use of *matres lectionis*; cf. כֹול[in frg. 3 line 3 and frg. 8 line 4, and לוא in frg. 4 line 2, frg. 5 line 4, and frg. 23 line 1. Also see כיא in frg. 16 line 2 and frg. 20 line 2.

[25] Ctr. Baillet: ב⸌⸍. The left shoulder of the *lamedh* is visible and the bottom is too angled to be a *beth*. See 1QM 6.6.

[26] This phrase appears in Ps 68:16 and frequently occurs in the Dead Sea Scrolls (e.g., 1QS 3.24; 1QM 6.6, 10.8, 14.4; 4Q502 frg. 24 line 2; 4Q503 frg. 14 line 2) and the Pseudepigrapha (e.g., *JosAsen* 7.5; *PrJos* 1.2; *PssSol* 4.1, 9.8).

4   [… for eter]nities they will not be destroyed […]

Frg. 6

1   […]°[…] upon him […]

2   [… be]fore *hd*[…]

3   […] they are ruling […]

4   […] his truth *l*[…]

5   [… to] praise God […]

Frg. 7

1   […]°[…]

2   […]ʾ*t*[…]

3   […]*m l*[…]

4   […]*dl* […]

5   […]*l*[…]

Frg. 8

1   […] to the God of Isra[el …]

2   […]°*m* in the day […]

3 נ]ט̊ל עלינו[[27]

4 כ]ול מו[

5 [° °]

Frg. 9[28]

1]מ̊שטמה[29] בז[את[30]

Frg. 10

1]ם̊ מצ°[

2]עד וא[

3 [illegible][[illegible] לה̇[

Frg. 11

1]הזה[

2]בחרב̇[[31]

Frg. 12[32]

1 נד]ע̊ כבו[דכה

2 מ]ע̊שכה[[33]

3]ל̊[

[27] Ctr. Baillet:]°ל עלינו[. For נטל with על, see Lam 3:18, 2Sam 24:12. The left-side of the letter is visible and curves to the right, suggesting either an ʾ*aleph*, a *ṭet*, a *samekh*, or possibly a *mem* or *qoph*. The phrase: ג]מ̊ל עלינו[(Ps 13:6, 103:10, 116:7, 131:2, 142:8) is possible, though paleographically less likely.

[28] The top margin appears extant.

[29] This word appears in Hos 9:7, 8; CD MS A 16.5; 1QS 3.23; 1QM 13.4, 11; 4Q390 frg. 1 line 11; 4Q525 frg. 19 line 4; *Jub* 10:8; 11:5, 11; 17:16; 18:9, 12; 19:28; 48:2, 9, 12, 15; 49:2.

[30] Baillet: ב°[. See the *zayin* in frg. 11 line 1.

[31] For בחרב, see 1QpHab 6.10; 1QM 11.2, 11; 4Q418 frg. 172 line 14.

[32] Restorations are by Charlesworth and Berkuz.

[33] Baillet:]°שכה[.

3   [...he l]aid upon us [...]

4   [...a]ll *mw*[...]

5   [...]° °[...]

Frg. 9

1   [...] hatred[8] in the[se things ...]

Frg. 10

1   [...]*m ms*°[...]

2   [...] until and ᵓ[...]

3   [... G]od to *h*[...]

Frg. 11

1   [...] this (VACAT) [...]

2   [...] with the sword [...]

Frg. 12

1   [... may we[9] kn]ow [your] glo[ry ...]

2   [...] your [w]orks [...]

3   [...]*l*[...]

---

[8] The Heb. משטמה ("hatred") came to denote a proper name, "Mastema," in Palestine before 70 CE. See *Jubilees* and the Introduction to 6Q18. In some Jewish circles, "Mastema" was identified with "Satan." Both names may derive from the same verbal form, שטן ("he hated"). Satan early appears associated with "the sons of God." See Job 1:1–12. Cf. Belial in frg. 3 line 3.

[9] For the first person plural rhetoric, see frg. 2 line 4, frg. 8 line 3, and frg. 14 line 2.

Frg. 13

1　‏א[ֹו]

2　‏[לֹע]תֹ[

3　‏ל[א וֹרני‏][34]

Frg. 14

1　‏[　　]מ ֹ ֹ ֹ[

2　‏[ב ֹקהלנו]

3　‏[ֹעֹליֹכֹה][35]

Frg. 15

1　‏[בֹוֹ]

2　‏[חיֹ　]

3　‏[　ֹה]

Frg. 16

1　‏[　ֹ　ֹז]

2　‏[אֹיכ　ֹ　]

Frg. 17

1　‏[　ֹיֹע　ֹ]

2　‏[ֹוֹֹכֹל]

---

[34] See Ps 84:3: ‏לבי ובשר ירננו אל אל חי.

[35] Perhaps: ‏[ֹעֹליֹכֹם].

Frg. 13

1 […]*w* ʾ[…]

2 […]*t lʿ*[…]

3 […] and exult t[o …]

Frg. 14

1 […]°°°*m* […]

2 […] our assembly *b*[…]

3 […] upon you […]

Frg. 15

1 […]*wb*[…]

2 […]°*yḥ*[…]

3 […]*ḥ* °[…]

Frg. 16

1 […]*d* °[…]

2 […]° for […]

Frg. 17

1 […]° ʿ*y*[…]

2 […]*lkw*[…]

Frg. 18

1   ב[טח]^{36}

2   ]ל[

Frg. 19

1   ]חֹבלֹוֹ[

Frg. 20

1   ]ה ותפאֹרת [

2   ]כיא לכה חכֹ[מה]^{37}

3   ]ׄתׄ [ ]הׄוׄ לׄ[ ]

Frg. 21

1   ]°°°°° [

2   ]ׄדׄ^{38} ורוחֹ[

Frg. 22

1   ]ׄעגׄ[^{39}

Frg. 23

1   ]לוא [

---

^{36} Restoration by Charlesworth and Berkuz.

^{37} Cf. Baillet:]המ. For the *kaph* see frg. 12 line 1. Reading by Charlesworth and Berkuz.

^{38} Cf. Baillet: ׄיׄ[.

^{39} Baillet:]ׄלגׄ[. In the other fragments, *'ayin*'s extend lower than the *lamedh*'s in relation to other letters. See frg. 8 line 3 where the *lamedh* stops higher than the *'ayin* and the *'ayin* (with a slightly curved bottom stroke – see also frg. 22) drops below the other letters. The same is true in frg. 13. Note also how in frgs. 22 and 23, which are side-by-side on the plate, the first letter in frg. 22 drops below the other letters while the first letter (a *lamedh*) in frg. 23 stops midway down. Most of the *lamedh*'s in these fragments stop in the middle of the other letters, while a few go to the bottom of other letters, but none drop below the other letters. The *'ayin*'s do.

Frg. 18

1   [… t]rust […]

2   […]*l*[…]

Frg. 19

1   […] they destroyed […]

Frg. 20

1   […]*h* and the beauty […]

2   […] for to you (is) wis[dom …]

3   […]˚*t*˚[…]*hn l*˚[…]

Frg. 21

1   […]°°°°°[…]

2   […]˚*d* and the spirit […]

Frg. 22

1   […] ʿ*g*˚[…]

Frg. 23

1   […] not […]

Frg. 24

1 ‏[נֹות]

Frg. 25

1 ‏[ ]ׄ

2 ‏[כֹהׄ]

Frg. 26

1 ‏[ ]ׄחׄ[

Frg. 27

1 ‏[ ]ׄז

Frg. 24

1 […]*nwt* […]

Frg. 25

1 […]˚[…]

2 […]*kh*˚[…]

Frg. 26

1 […]˚*ḥ*[…]

Frg. 27

1 […]*d*[…]

A Hymn Concerning the "Mighty One"
8Q5

JAMES H. CHARLESWORTH with LEA BERKUZ[1]

Introduction

1. Contents

The two fragments of 8Q5 are in poor condition, obscured by streaks across the right side, containing an ink blot above the middle of fragment 1 line 1, and multiple words with possible reconstructions. Nevertheless, the appearance of the *Tetragrammaton* in fragment 2 line 3 (יהוה) and hymnic syntactical features suggest that this is a liturgical text. The appearance of the first person singular pronoun in the first line draws significant and immediate attention because of its frequent use in the *Hodayot* and Psalms. It also seems to indicate this fragment's hymnic quality.

2. Text

The text consists of ten lines and is hymnic in nature. The script is Herodian and dates between 30 BCE to 50 CE. The leather is lined, and the consonants are neat and straight with even spacing. The upper margin is visible on fragment 1. *Plene* spelling is used.

3. Language and Theology

The reconstruction of the term "Mighty One" sets a framework for some of the other key themes in the two fragments preserved. In fragment 1 line 2, there is a possible reference to the בני חו[שך] "the sons of dark[ness]," an expression similar to one found frequently in the Qumran Community's compositions. The mention of destruction, judgment, and persecution in the remaining lines also fits as conflict terminology consistent with ג]בּ[ור, "[Mi]ghty One" (see the note to the text, frg. 1 line 1). Taken as a whole, fragment 1 line 1, fragment 1 lines 3–4, and fragment 2 lines 5–6 offer a picture of one who is powerfully aligned as the warrior of YHWH, one who stands in the sha-dow of the divine warrior whose light is invincible and whose judgment is sure.

Fragment 1 line 3 declares rhetorically the inviolability of the divine light.[2] Often the intentional withholding of light by God is equated with divine punishment or destructive judgment (cf. 1QM 13.9–16, Isa 13:9–13).

The verb in fragment 2 line 2 can be reconstructed on the basis of fragment 1 line 3: ו]תשבית being read as ותשביׁתן with the second person plural determined by the preformative.

The use of יהוה in fragment 2 line 3 is distinct and stands in direct contrast to those scrolls which substitute four dots or palaeo-Hebrew letters for the divine name.

4. Relation to Other Jewish Writings

If the reconstruction ג]בּׁור, "[Mi]ghty One" or "[wa]rrior," is correct in fragment 1 line 1, it establishes a distinct metaphorical context for this brief hymn. Possibly these words of praise are on the lips of a non-human being or form a self-congratulatory hymn put into the mouth of a super-human hero, similar to the angelic *Songs of the Sabbath Sacrifice* or the words of a mythological figure, as in the *War Scroll*. The close association of God's name and "might," and those who are God's chosen "Mighty Ones," is well established (cf. 4Q404 frg. 21 line 2, 4Q405 frg. 13 1.4, 1QM 11.2, Ps 54:4, Jer 16:21, Ps 20:7ff.) The "Mighty One" exhibits extraordinary strength precisely because he manifests divine power.[3]

The phrase "to the con[ste]llations of the heaven[s" may suggest a context of worship for this hymn, or even an apocalyptic backdrop as the cosmic arena of the divine battle. In Isaiah 13:10 the synonym for מזלות, במזלים, meaning constella-

---

[1] Berkuz helped with the text and translation.

[2] Note: מה + causative verb, *hipʿil* impf. second person pl. of שנת; cp. Song 8:4, Job 31:1 (BDB 553b.2.a. [b]; R. J. Williams, *Hebrew Syntax: An Outline* [Toronto, 1984, 2nd ed.] p. 128).

[3] See R. G. Marks, "Dangerous Hero: Rabbinic Attitudes Toward Legendary Warriors," *HUCA* 54 (1983) 181–94; *TDOT* 11, pp. 373–82.

tions, is used in parallel with the more common כוכבי השמים "stars of heaven." This context of divine judgment where all the sources of light will be made dark as an expression of the dreaded day of the LORD seems to match that of 8Q5.

5. Selected Bibliography

Baillet, M. "5. Passage Hymnique." In *Les 'Petites Grottes' De* *Qumrân: Exploration de la falaise. Les grottes 2Q, 3Q, 5Q, 6Q, à 10Q. Le rouleau de cuivre*. DJD 3; Oxford, 1962, pp. 161–62, Pl. 35.

A Hymn Concerning the "Mighty One"
8Q5 (8QHymn)

Frg. 1[1]

1   [בשמכה] ג[בּ]וֹר[2] אני מירא[3] ומשֹ[4] [

2   [רֹבִני[5] האישׁ הזה אשר הוא מבני חוֹ[שך[6]

3   [הֹנֹה[7] ומה תשביתו אורוֹ לֹהֹ[ ] °° לֹ[ ]

4   [למֹ[ז]לֹוֹת[8] השֹמֹ]ים

Frg. 2

1   [וֹבֹ]

2   [ ]ֹר וֹתֹשביתֹ]וֹ[9]

3   [ ]ֹ   לֹת יהוה[10]   ]ֹ

4   [כֹה רבה למעלה מכוֹלֹ[11]

5   [וֹמרדפֹוֹת והמשפטים[12]

6   [וֹכול הרוחות לפניכה ע[ומדות[13]

---

[1] The top margin is visible.

[2] The "Mighty Ones" are prominent in the *War Scroll* (e.g., 1QM 10.6; 11.1, 13; 12.8–10, 17; 19.1–2) as well as in the *Thanksgiving Hymn* (e.g., 1QHᵃ 7.18; 10.27; 11.36, 41; 13.9, 23; 14.33, 36; 18.26). See also *Songs of the Sabbath Sacrifice* (4Q404 frg. 2 line 2: יבֹרך בשם גבורו[ן]; 4Q403 frg. 1 1.21; 4Q405 frg. 13 line 5).

[3] 4Q511 frg. 35 line 6: ואני מירא אל בקצי דורותי לרומם שם. A *piʿel* participle from ירא.

[4] Ctr. Baillet (DJD 3): ומעֹ[. The bottom of the consonant is visible and is too long to be an ʿayin. It is more akin to the *šin* in אשר in line 2. Possibly restore ומשלתי.

[5] Baillet: נֹיׄ[. The top of the *reš* is visible; could also be a *daleth*.

[6] Ctr. Baillet: מבני הׄ[. The first consonant is distinguishable from the *he* in הוא and הזה in the same line. For examples of בני חושך, see 1QS 1.10; 1QM 1.1, 7, 10, 16; 3.6, 9; 13.16; 14.17; 16.11.

[7] Baillet: הזה[. The bottom of the *nun* is faintly visible on PAM 42.594.

[8] Cf. 2Kgs 23:5.

[9] See frg. 1 line 3.

[10] The scribe distinguishes between the *yodh* and *waw*.

[11] The bottom margin is conceivably preserved.

[12] Ps 119:84: כַּמָּה יְמֵי־עַבְדֶּךָ מָתַי תַּעֲשֶׂה בְרֹדְפַי מִשְׁפָּט. See also 4Q424 frg. 3 line 2.

[13] Baillet's restoration. For the expression "stand before," see 1QHᵃ 12.22, 15.34, 23.11.

A Hymn Concerning the "Mighty One"
8Q5 (8QHymn)

Frg. 1

1   [….] In your name, [O Mi]ghty One,[1] I became afraid and *mš*[…]

2   […]*rny* this man who is from the sons of dark[ness …]

3   […] here. And why do you[2] cause his light to cease[3] *lh*[…]°°*l*[…]

4   […] to the con[ste]llations of the heaven[s …]

Frg. 2

1   […]*wb*[…]

2   […]°*r* and yo[u] shall cause to cease […]

3   […]°*lt* of YHWH.[4] (VACAT) °[…]

4   […]*kh* has become great above from all […]

5   […] and from the persecutions and the judgments […]

6   […] and all the spirits s[tanding] before you […]

---

[1] The one imagined seems to be one of "the Mighty Ones" who are highlighted in the *Hodayot, War Scroll,* and *Songs of the Sabbath Sacrifice.*

[2] *Hipʿil* impf. of שבת. The pronoun is anticipatory: "you caused it to cease."

[3] A *hipʿil* first person impf. Lit. "to bring to a finish, to end."

[4] Or LORD.

Blessings of the High Priest 1
11Q14 (11QBer; Sefer ha-Milḥamah, cf. 4Q285)

JAMES H. CHARLESWORTH with LEA BERKUZ[1]

Introduction

1. Contents

11Q14 is a fragmentary text which was designated by its editor, A. S. van der Woude, as a "Segensspruch" or "Benediction."[2] It is probably a liturgical document. The extant portion includes a blessing spoken over the people, followed by a benediction characterized by the repeated use of the second person plural pronoun.

2. Text

11Q14 consists of four Hebrew fragments of a single leather manuscript containing portions of five columns.[3] The largest fragment (frg. 1 col. 2) contains nine virtually complete lines as well as over half of four more lines. Additionally, fragment e was once joined to column 2. To the right of column 2, there are three additional lines of consonants and words. The manuscript is written in a Herodian script with horizontal and vertical lining.

3. Original Language, Date, and Provenience

11Q14 was probably composed in Hebrew. On paleographical grounds, the manuscript can be dated to the early first century CE or perhaps a little earlier. Some conceptual factors, such as "congregation," (cf. 1QSa), Endtime speculation, and God's holy angels suggest a possible Qumran provenience. Other thoughts indicate a provenience elsewhere in Palestine; among

these factors are a reference to the God of Israel (and not the God of Knowledge as in 1QS), the admiration of the High Priest who ostensibly serves in the Temple, and the present blessed state of the land (or Land). A suitable setting for the document would be Hanukkah in Jerusalem.

11Q14 attests to several orthographic features which are found within Qumran Scrolls composed at Qumran and elsewhere, including the use of *waw* as a vowel letter (frg. 1 2.5, 9, 11, 14),[4] the writing of כי with an *aleph* (frg. 1 2.14),[5] and the use of כם (frg. 1 2.2, 7, 11, 13, 14, 15) for the third person masculine plural pronominal suffix.[6] The presence in fragment 1 2.7 of את with the pronominal direct object following a finite verb runs contrary to the tendency in the Qumran scrolls to attach the pronominal suffix directly to the verb.[7]

The author imagines liturgically the mighty acts of God during the Exodus and envisions the Promised Land as the Perfect Land. The setting may be a blessing by the High Priest in the Temple. The presence of apparently pro-Hasmonean documents in the Qumran caves is surprising within the anti-Hasmonean Qumran Community. The document, 11Q14, may be early and represent the time when the Hasmoneans were tolerated by those in the pre-Qumran sect and should be contemplated in light of the ideas found in other documents, especially in the *Prayer of King Jonathan* (4Q448).

4. History and Theology

11Q14 contains no historical insights. As a blessing, its concerns are primarily theological and pietistic. God is identified as "God Most High" and as "the God of Israel." God's "name" is central. It is eternally blessed and deemed holy. God's people are called by it and blessed in it. God is the source of natu-

---

[1] J. H. Charlesworth is responsible for the introduction. He is grateful to Joseph L. Trafton for an early draft of this introduction. The transcription and translation are by Charlesworth and Berkuz.

[2] A. S. van der Woude, "Ein neuer Segensspruch aus Qumran (11QBer)," *Bibel und Qumran*, edited by S. Wagner (Berlin, 1986) pp. 253–58.

[3] According to J. Strugnell, "Recueils et Mélanges," *RB* 77 (1970) 268, a fragment from Cave 4 of another manuscript of this document awaits publication. Perhaps he was referring to 4Q285.

[4] Cf. E. Qimron, *HDSS*, p. 17.

[5] Qimron, *HDSS*, p. 21.

[6] Qimron, *HDSS*, p. 62.

[7] Qimron, *HDSS*, pp. 75–76. Perhaps the explanation here is that the writer wanted to avoid a double *kaph* – i.e. יברככם.

ral blessings and is present with those who are called the "congregation." Alongside of God stand the holy angels, who like God, are blessed and present within the congregation.

There are insignificant connections between 11Q14 and the sectarian compositions like 1QS, 1QSa, CD, 1QM, and the *Pesharim*. 11Q14 is similar in form to 1Sb; both are community blessings to be recited by an individual; however, in 1QSb he is identified as the Maskil. Although the opening of 11Q14 is lost, no Maskil is mentioned. Along with other Jews, the Community that created the Qumran Scrolls emphasized the presence of holy angels (1QSa 2.8–9; 4Q400–4Q407 [4QShirShabb]; cf. 1QSb 3.6). The Qumranites perceived themselves as "the Congregation" (see esp. 1QS 5.20, 1QM 2.1, 1QH^a 3.22, 1QSa 1.1, 1QSb 3.3, CD MS A 10.4, 1QpHab 5.12, 4Q173 [4QpPs^a] 1.5). The lack of historical references precludes any certainty concerning where 11Q14 fits into the history of the Qumran sect, although 4Q285 seems to be a later copy edited at Qumran.

5. Relation to the Hebrew Bible, Other Jewish Writings, and the New Testament

The overall theology of 11Q14 is consistent with the general portrait of God in the Hebrew Bible (see notes to the Translation). Indeed, the language of the document is based primarily upon certain blessings in the Hebrew Bible, especially Isaiah 10:34–11:1 and Jeremiah 33:15 (see notes). Prayers for God's blessings on the people remained important in Judaism both within the Qumran Community (1QSb) and as a part of the ongoing Temple cult in Jerusalem. Similar prayers in the New Testament tended to be brought under the general concept of "the grace of the Lord Jesus Christ" (Phil 4:23; cf. 1Cor 16:23, 2Cor 13:14, Gal 6:18, 1Thess 5:28, Philemon 25).

Connecting 11Q14's relation to 4Q285, W. J. Lyons has argued that the claim the two texts overlap has been greatly exaggerated since the reconstruction is based upon five characters.[8] Despite F. García Martínez and van der Woude's suggestion

that a variant may exist between the two texts, Lyons contends their work is problematic.[9] Only when the character counts and variants are accounted for can the relation between the two documents be affirmed.[10] However, E. Tigchelaar, argues that "[I]t is beyond doubt that 11Q14 Frg. 1 Col. 1 and 4Q285 Frg. 1… preserve a virtually identical text."[11] The evidence suggests that the overlap is too strong to simply be coincidental; most likely these works are two copies of the same composition.[12] Our speculation is that 4Q285 is a later Qumran redaction of a Hasmonean celebration (perhaps Hanukkah). See the introduction to 4Q285 for a discussion of "the Sprout of Da]vid" in fragment 1 1.7–15.

6. Selected Bibliography

García Martínez, F. and A. S. van der Woude. "14. 11QSefer ha-Milḥmah." In *Qumran 11.II: 11Q2–18, 11Q20–31*. DJD 23; Oxford, 1998, pp. 243–51, Pl. 28.

Lyons, W. J. "Clarifications Concerning 4Q285 and 11Q14 Arising from *Discoveries in the Judean Desert* 23." *DSD* 6/1 (1999) 37–43.

Qimron, E. *The Hebrew of the Dead Sea Scrolls*. Harvard Semitic Studies 29; Atlanta, 1986.

Schultz, B. "Re-Imagining the Eschatological War – 4Q285/11Q14." In *'Go Out and Study the Land' (Judges 18:2): Archaeological, Historical and Textual Studies in Honor of Hanan Eshel*, edited by A. M. Maeir, J. Magness, and L. H. Schiffman. JSJSup 148; Leiden, 2012, pp. 197–212.

Strugnell, J. "Recueils et Mélanges." *RB* 77 (1970) 267–70.

Tigchelaar, E. J. C. "Working with Few Data: The Relation Between 4Q285 and 11Q14." *DSD* 7/1 (2000) 49–56.

Van der Woude, A. S. "Ein neuer Segensspruch aus Qumran (11QBer)." In *Bibel und Qumran*, edited by S. Wagner. Berlin, 1968, pp. 253–58.

---

[9] García Martínez and van der Woude suggest this overlap using a reconstruction based on Isa 10:34–11:1. See DJD 23, p. 246.

[10] Lyons, "Clarifications Concerning 4Q285 and 11Q14," 43.

[11] E. J. C. Tigchelaar, "Working with Few Data: The Relation Between 4Q285 and 11Q14," *DSD* 7/1 (2000) 49.

[12] Tigchelaar, "Working with Few Data," 53. See also, B. Schultz, "Re-Imagining the Eschatological War – 4Q285/11Q14," in *'Go Out and Study the Land' (Judges 18:2): Archaeological, Historical and Textual Studies in Honor of Hanan Eshel*, edited by A. M. Maeir, J. Magness, and L. H. Schiffman (JSJSup 148; Leiden, 2012) p. 197.

[8] W. J. Lyons, "Clarifications Concerning 4Q285 and 11Q14 Arising from *Discoveries in the Judean Desert* 23," *DSD* 6/1 (1999) 39.

Blessings of the High Priest 1
11Q14 (11QBer; Sefer ha-Milḥamah, cf. 4Q285)[1]

Frg. 1 Col. 1

בום[2]	**5**
לו[	**6**
צמח ד[ויד[3]	**7**
[	**8**
כאשר כתוב בספר ישעיהו הנביא ונוקפו[4]	**9**
[סבכי היער בברזל והלבנון באדיר יפול ויצא חו[טר	**10**
צמ[ח [מגזע ישי ונצר משורשיו יפרה[5]	**11**
[[דויד ונשפטו את[6]	**12**
לה[8] והמיתו צמח דויד[7]	**13**
בנגעים ובמחוללות וצוה כוהן הרואש[9]	**14**
[ ]פֿ[ ] חֿלֿלֿי[10]	**15**

---

[1] 4Q285 is most likely a redaction of 11Q14.

[2] See PAM 43.977, frg. 1a, for lines 5 and 6. For the numbering of lines, see frg. 1 col. 2. The left margin is visible. The Leon Levy images, available online, are clear and helpful.

[3] See lines 11 to 13, but restored from 4Q285. See PAM 43.977, frg. 1b for lines 7 and 10. See Jer 33:15: לדוד צמח צדקה. For צמח דויד, see 4Q174 frgs. 1–3 1.11, 4Q252 5.3–4.

[4] From 4Q285 frg. 1 line 1. These restorations can be misleading, given the difference between 11Q14 and 4Q285.

[5] See 4Q285 frg. 7 lines 2–3 and Isa 10:34–11:1.

[6] From 4Q285 frg. 7 line 3.

[7] Restored according to the preceding lines and from 4Q285 frg. 7 lines 4 and 5 but without the redaction נשיא העדה.

[8] See PAM 42.176, frg. 1c.

[9] From 4Q285 frg. 7 lines 5 and 6.

[10] Cf. 4Q285 frg. 7 line 6: ח[ללי[י]כתיֿיֿם]. The bottom and left margin are preserved. See PAM 43.977.

Blessings of the High Priest 1
11Q14 (11QBer; Sefer ha-Milḥamah, cf. 4Q285)

Frg. 1 Col. 1

5 […]*bwm*

6 […]*lw*

7 [… the Sprout[1] of Da]vid

8 […]

9 [… as it is written in the Book of Isaiah, the Prophet:[2] "And they will be cut down]

10 [the most massive of the forest with iron. And Lebanon, with its magnificence, will fall.[3] And a sh]oot [will emerge]

11 [from the Stump of Jesse, and an offshoot from his roots will bear fruit." … the Spr]out of

12 [David. And they will enter into judgment with …]

13 [… and the Sprout of David will cause him to die …]*lh*

14 [… by afflictions and by wounds. And the High Priest will command]

15 […]°*p*[…] the slain of

---

[1] Or "Branch."

[2] From Isa 10:34–11:1.

[3] The fall of "Lebanon" may have been understood by the Qumranitess as celebrating the defeat of the Seleucids centered there.

Frg. 1 Col. 2[11]

1	[12]]°[
2	]°°[ ] [וברכם בשׁם [אל]
3	[י]שראל[13] וענה[ואמר לפני כול בני[14] [ישראל[15] ברוכים א[תם]
4	בשם אל עליון ° [וברוך שם קודש[ו]
5	לעולמי עד[16] וברוכים° [תו וברוכים כול
6	מלאכי קודשו (VACAT)
7	יברך אתכם אל עליון[17] ויאר פניו אליכם[18] ויפתח לכם את
8	אוצרו הטוב אשר בשמים[19] להוריד על ארצכמה[20]
9	גשמי ברכה טל ומטר יורה ומלקוש בעתו ולתת[21] לכם פר[י]
10	תנובות דגן תירוש ויצהר לרוב והארץ תנובב לכם[22] פרי
11	[ע]דנים ואכלתם והדשנתם[23] ואין משכלה[24] בארצכם
12	[ו]לוא[25] מוחלה שדפון וירקון לוא יראה בתבואתיה[26]
13	[ואין [כ]ול] נגע ומ[כ]שול[27] בעדתכם וחיה רעה שבתה[28] מן
14	[הארץ ואין דב]ר בארצכם כיא אל עמכם ומלאכי

---

[11] The beginning and end of the column and the bottom margin are clear. See PAM 43.977.

[12] See PAM 43.977, frg. 1e, for lines 1–5, left portion of the column.

[13] See PAM 43.977, frg. 1a, for lines 3–15. For אל ישראל, see 1Q33 [1QM] 10.8.

[14] Our restoration is based on 4Q285 frg. 8 line 2.

[15] Also in 4Q285 frg. 8 line 2: שרא[ל]י. The *lacuna* would contain 17 to 18 consonants or spaces.

[16] Cf. 4Q285 frg. 8 line 3: ל[ע]ו[ר]לׁמי עד.

[17] Cf. 4Q285 frg. 8 line 4: אתכׁם אל עׁ [.

[18] An echo from Num 6:24–25, the Aaronic Blessing.

[19] Cf. 4Q285 frg. 8 line 5: ה[טוׁב [אש[ר בׁשמים לׁ].

[20] The scribe added a *he*, but did not change the final *mem*. For ארצכם see lines 11 and 14.

[21] Cf. 4Q285 frg. 8 line 6: ו[מׁטר יו[ר]ׁה ומלקו[ש] בעתו ולתׁת.

[22] Cf. 4Q285 frg. 8 line 7: וי[צׁהר לרוב והאר[ץ [תנו]בׁב ל[כם.

[23] In 11Q14 there is space for four consonants. In 4Q285 there is no space to indicate a *vacat*.

[24] The word מְשַׁכֵּלָה denotes "miscarriage;" cf. 4Q285 frg. 8 line 8. The base text is Ex 23:36. See Even-Shoshan, *loc. cit.* The root is שכל, "loss of children."

[25] Cf. 4Q285 frg. 8 line 8: ׁם [ואין משכלה [ב]אׁ[ר]צׁכׁם] ולׁוא.

[26] Cf. 4Q285 frg. 8 line 9: לוא יראׁה בתבואׁ]תיה.

[27] Cf. 4Q285 frg. 8 line 9: ואׁ[ין כׁוׁל נגעׁ].

[28] A *perfectum propheticum*; see GKC, pp. 312–13.

Frg. 1 Col. 2

1   […]˚[…]

2   […]°°[…] and he[4] will bless them in the name of [the God of]

3   [I]srael, and he will answer [and say before all the sons of][5] Israel: "Blessed be y[ou]

4   in the name of God Most High[6] ˚[…] and blessed be [his] holy name[7]

5   for everlasting eternity.[8] And blessed be […]*tw*. And blessed be all

6   the angels of his holiness. (VACAT)

7   May God Most High bless you, and may he shine his face toward you,[9] and may he open for you

8   his good treasure which is in the heavens, to cause to fall down on your land

9   showers of blessing, dew, and rain, early and late rain in its season, and to give to you fru[it],

10   the produce of wheat, new wine, and oil in plenty. And may the land produce for you [de]licious

11   fruits. And may you eat and may you be full.[10] And may there not be miscarriage in your land,

12   [nor] sickness. May drought and blight not be seen in its harvests.

13   [And may there not be] any [affliction nor stum]bling obstacle in your congregation, so injurious[11] beast(s)[12] ceased[13] from

14   [the land. And may there not be pestilen]ce[14] in your land. For God (is) with you and the angels of

---

[4] "He" refers to the High Priest (see preceding). See also van der Woude, p. 255.

[5] The *lacuna* would contain 17–18 consonants or spaces.

[6] For this appellation for God, cf. 1QH[a] 12.32; Gen 14:18, 19; Ps 78:35.

[7] For the concept of blessing the name of God, see Ps 96:2; 100:4; 145:1, 21.

[8] See 1QH[a] 5.18.

[9] An echo from Num 6:24–25, the Aaronic Blessing.

[10] Lit. "juicy" or "fat."

[11] Heb. רע, or "bad," "wicked," "evil."

[12] Hebrew is singular but plural intended.

[13] As Alexander and Vermes judge, the past tense may indicate the author imagines the High Priest offering the blessing at the Endtime (DJD 36, p. 243). The Hebrew verbal tense is a *perfectum propheticum* (a future event perceived as accomplished), see GKC, pp. 312–13.

[14] Heb. דבר.

15   קודשו מתיצבי]ם[^29](ׄ בעדתכם ושם קודשו נׄקרא עליכם[^30]

Frg. 2

1   משפ]טי[^31] הגוי הנב]ל

2   קומה גב]ור שבה פל[שׄתים

3   הנ]בׄונים[^32]

Frg. 3

1   [בוזׄ[^33] ׄ]

2   [קׄח וׄ]

3   [ׄ]

Frg. 4[^34]

1   [כׄי כוׄ]

2   [ה]

---

[^29]: Cf. 4Q285 frg. 8 line 10.
[^30]: The bottom of the column is clear. Thanks to the Leon Levy image, it is now obvious that the ostensible two consonants are dirt and the periodization between lines for a possible *vacat* is too large (see line 6).
[^31]: Cf. DJD 23:]טי. See the Leon Levy image. Cf. 1QpHab 5.4: וביד בחירו יתן אל את משפט כול הגוים.
[^32]: See נבונים in CD MS A 6.2 and והנבונים in 1QSa 1.28.
[^33]: The *zayin* has a turned foot like the *ḥet* and *waw* below it; it has a curve to the left as a belly. Also conceivable is בור.
[^34]: We follow DJD 23 Pl. 28. The fragment is mislabeled in PAM 44.007. The fragment is not included in the Leon Levy images.

15 [his holiness are presen]t[15] in your congregation. And may his holy name be invoked over you.

Frg. 2

1 [… judgme]nts of the godle[ss][16] nations[17] […]

2 [… rise up he]ro, imprison the Phili[stines …]

3 [… those of d]iscernment[18] […]

Frg. 3

1 […] scorn[19] °[…]

2 […]*qḥ* and […]

3 […]°[…]

Frg. 4

1 […] for "yes" […]

2 […]*ḥ* […]

---

[15] Lit. "standing."

[16] Heb. נבל, or "unbelieving."

[17] See 1QpHab 5.4, "but into the hand of his chosen God will give the judgment of all the nations."

[18] The root בין is well known at Qumran. See esp. נבונים in CD MS A 6.2, "men of discernment," and והנבונים in 1QSa 1.28.

[19] See "godle[ss]" in frg. 2 line 1. Or "pit" as a prison. See Gen 37:20–29, 40:15, 41:14; Isa 24:22; Jer 28:6–7, 9–13; 37:16; Zech 9:11; Ex 12:29.

Blessings of the High Priest 2
4Q285 (4QSefer ha-Milḥamah; cf. 11Q14)

JAMES H. CHARLESWORTH with LEA BERKUZ[1]

Introduction[2]

1. Text and Original Language

4Q285 is now assembled into ten fragments. Some fragments are now joined; fragment 8 consists of seven pieces and fragment 10 has four pieces. The spelling is *scriptio plena*; for example "David" is דויד (frg. 7 line 3). Final forms are given for ץ ם, ף,, and ך (in order of their appearance). There are no rulings. The consonants are about 2.5 millimeters high. The distance between lines and characters varies, and the space between words is unusually wide. All evidence suggests that Hebrew is the original language.

2. Date and Provenience

4Q285 is a version of 11Q14, with significant variants, and is in an early Herodian formal script that dates to the end of the first century BCE.[3] 4Q285 may be a Qumran redaction of the document represented by 11Q14, adding references to "the Prince of the Congregation," the "Kittim," and a quotation from Ezekiel. It is important to observe that 4Q285, and not 11Q14, preserves a quotation and echoes from Ezekiel 39 and 47. Qumran's dependence on Ezekiel is well attested and acknowledged. Likewise, "Kittim" in 4Q285 replaces the enemy of Israel or "the Philistine" in 11Q14 fragment 2 line 2 (if the restoration is sound).

3. History, Theology, and Relation to the Hebrew Bible and Other Jewish Writings

The work is a "Blessing of the High Priest," and is thus another liturgical text (as 11Q14 which seems to represent a much older document). The opening announces that the blessing is also a prayer "for the sake of your name" (frg.1 line 2).

The archangels, "Michael, G[abrie]l, [Sariel, and Raphael] are apparently named in fragment 1 line 3 (most editors have restored what is missing due to anchored consonants). The "Levites" are mentioned in fragment 3 line 2; they are probably given the task to blow the trumpet in the battles against the Kittim.

Using quotations from Ezekiel and then Isaiah, the author prophesies how the Prince of the Congregation will cause the bow and arrows to fall from the king of the Kittim. He and all his troops will fall upon the mountains of Israel. The Prince of the Congregation will "bring" the king of the Kittim before him for judgment and condemn him to death. The images seem also to be shaped by the account of the Exodus from Egypt.

Subsequently, basing his prophecy on Isaiah 10:34–11:1, the author announces the coming of "the Sprout of David" (frg. 7 line 3). Most likely, the Prince of the Congregation is identified as a Warrior-Messiah[4] and with "the Sprout of David" (frg. 7 lines 4–5)[5] who will cause the king of the Kittim to die (frg. 7 line 4).[6] In line with Qumran's two messiahs, one of Aaron and one of Israel (in 1QS 9.10), the Prince of the Congregation

---

[1] The transcription and translation are by Charlesworth with Berkuz.

[2] See the Introduction to 11Q14.

[3] See also P. S. Alexander and G. Vermes, "285. 4QSefer ha-Milḥamah," in *Qumran Cave 4.XXVI: Cryptic Texts and Miscellanea, Part 1* (DJD 36; Oxford, 2000) p. 232.

[4] See G. S. Oegema in *Qumran-Messianism*, p. 71. As Abegg and Evans point out, "the Prince of the Congregation" occurs ten times in the Qumran Scrolls and "all are messianic." See their contribution in *Qumran-Messianism*, pp. 194–97.

[5] The term "the Sprout of David" occurs five times in the Qumran Scrolls. See Abegg and Evans in *Qumran-Messianism*, pp. 197–98.

[6] Probably not "and they killed the Prince of the Congregation." See J. Tabor, "A Pierced or Piercing Messiah? – The Verdict is Still Out," *BAR* 18/6 (1992) 58–59. As J. J. Collins reports, the context of 4Q285 and the text preserved prove that the initial claims that the work reported the death of a messianic figure or the Messiah, "have been shown to be unwarranted." See Collins, *The Scepter and the Star* (Anchor Bible Reference Library; New York and London, 1995) p. 58.

seems to be a Davidic messiah-figure who leads with the Priest. The High Priest is given a command and offers the end-time blessing (frg. 8). His words are shaped by Sacred Scripture, especially the Aaronic Blessing (Num 6:24–25). 4Q285 also reflects the fulfillment hermeneutic dominant in the *Pesharim*.[7]

Alexander and Vermes cogently summarize the messianic endtime thought:

> The situation envisaged is after the final victory of Israel, when the Prince of the Congregation and the High Priest will try the King of the Kittim for war-crimes and sentence him to death. The High Priest will then give orders for the disposal of the corpses of the dead Kittim which threaten to pollute the land.[8]

The scenario is also reflected in *2 Baruch* in which we are given a vision and explanation of how the last ruler will be convicted, and killed:

> The last ruler who is left alive at that time will be bound, whereas the entire host will be destroyed. And they will carry him on Mount Zion, and my Anointed One (or "and my Messiah:" ܡܫܝܚܝ) will convict him of all his wicked deeds and will assemble and set before him all the works of his hosts. And after these things he will kill him and protect the rest of my people who will be found in the place that I have chosen. And his dominion will last forever until the world of corruption has ended and until the times which have been mentioned before have been fulfilled. This is your vision and this is its explanation.[9]

The passage in both 4Q285 and *2 Baruch* depicts a militant Messiah who will bind, convict, and kill the "last ruler." While it is conceivable the earlier text has influenced the author of *2 Baruch* who may have composed his work near Jerusalem around 100 CE, it is more probable we have a well-known tradition that continues from First Isaiah to the *Psalms of Solomon* and into the *Targumim* (esp. TPseudo-Jonathan on Gen 49:11).

The blessing to "God Mo[st Hi]gh" concludes with a vision of the purified Holy Land: it will witness "no miscarriage," "sickness," "drought," "blight," "affliction," "pestilence," or "injurious beast(s)." At that Endtime, God and "the angels of his holiness" are to be "present in your congregation." As at Qumran, those in the congregation are "[those who r]eturn (from) iniquity" (frg. 10 line 7 [see the note to the text]). Trumpets in the battle between the Sons of Light against the Sons of Darkness are mentioned 18 times in 1QM 3.

4Q285 is related to the *War Scroll* either as part of that document or as a similar edited tradition. Still conceivable is the possibility it alone preserves the end of the *War Scroll*, a

thought advanced by J. T. Milik in 1972.[10] 4Q285 and 1QM share references to "Michael" (1QM 9.15, 16; 17.6, 7),[11] "the Prince of the Congregation" (cf. 1QM 5.1), and "the king of the Kittim" (1QM 15.2). 4Q285 could be the ending of 1QM,[12] as the script in both 1QM and 4Q285 is an early Herodian formal script,[13] and the present concluding refrain suits 4Q285's high priest's blessing at the Endtime: "Zion rejoice greatly! Be glad all you, cities of Ju[dah!...] the wealth of the nations! Their kings shall serve you and [al]l [your oppressors] shall bow down before you [... .] Daughters of my people, burst into a voice of jubilation!" (1QM 19.5–7). 4Q285 may, then, supply the ending to the third and final section of the *War Scroll*: "The War Against the Kittim."

4Q285, however, may represent speculations about the final battle among the Essenes but may not be part of the *War Scroll*. It is also possible that the traditions are related to the concept of the final endtime war shared by many Jews during Second Temple Judaism. The list of such documents extends from the Hebrew Bible to the *Psalms of Solomon, 4 Ezra, 2 Baruch*, the Revelation of John, Akiba, *Pseudo-Jerome*, to *Targum Pseudo-Jonathan*.[14]

If 4Q285 is the ending of 1QM, the script must be not only a Herodian early formal script but the manuscript must be copied by the same scribe; that is unlikely, if not impossible.[15] Certainly, 4Q285 could be from another manuscript of the *War Scroll* or a virtually identical document, but the scholar who makes this argument would have to consider the existence of another manuscript of the *War Scroll* and not a similar text and present a cogent argument why Duhaime did not include the work in his critical edition of the *War Scroll*.

---

[7] See Charlesworth, *The Pesharim and Qumran History: Chaos or Consensus?* (Grand Rapids and Cambridge, 2002).

[8] DJD 36, p. 239.

[9] 2Bar 40:1–2; A. F. J. Klijn in *OTP*.

[10] J. T. Milik, "Milkî-ṣedeq et Milkî-reša' dans les anciens écrits juifs et chrétiens," *JJS* (1972) 142–43. Vermes concluded, with Milik, that 4Q285 preserves "probably" the "missing end section" of the *War Scroll*. See Vermes, *The Complete Dead Sea Scrolls in English* (London, 2004 [rev. ed.]) p. 188.

[11] It is also impressive that "Michael" is not found in 1QS, CD, 1QH, and other Qumran compositions.

[12] *Prima facie*, some fragments of 4Q285 could be from the bottom of 1QM, since it is lost; but the orthography is by another scribe. There are also seven other fragmentary manuscripts of the *War Scroll* and 1Q33 seems to prove that there was at least one more column to the *War Scroll*. See J. Duhaime in PTSDSSP vol. 2, p. 81.

[13] However, see the arguments below.

[14] See J. Duhaime, "Relation to Later Literature," in PTSDSSP 2.91. Also see, H. Avenary, "Pseudo-Jerome Writings and Qumran Tradition," *RQ* 4 (1963) 1–10.

[15] Comparing 1QM (Sukenik's images or those available electronically) with 4Q285 (PAM 43.325 = Pls. 12 and 13 in DJD 36) reveals major scribal differences. The scribe of 4Q285 leaves unusually long spaces between words but the scribe of 1QM col. 19 often does not separate words (*scriptio continua*). The forms of *lamedh*, final *mem*, and most consonants are markedly different in the two manuscripts.

In contrast to 1QM that does not mention messianic figures,[16] 4Q285 contains reflections on a messianic figure related to David.[17] There are 20 columns (and fragments numbered 3 and 7)[18] in 1QM but the parallels with 4Q285 are usually to 1QM 15 and not the final columns (1QM 19–20?). The final column ends with a *vacat* (1QM 19.8 which parallels 12.7–16, "Prayers on the Battlefield;" cf. perhaps 4Q491 [4QM1] frgs. 5–6) and is preceded by an exhortation: "Daughters of my people, burst into a voice of jubilation," and a declaration: "and Israel shall reign forever. (VACAT)." But the beginning of 4Q285 with its *vacat* does not seem to follow the *vacat* of 1QM. Redactions of 1QM and of 4Q285 are obvious and each indicates how traditions are developing.

4Q285 is probably not the ending of the *War Scroll* even though that possibility remains for contemplation. Thus, to be preferred to Milik's hypothesis are the following similar options: the view of Alexander that 4Q285 is a slightly different work,[19] J. Norton's insight that 4Q285 is a reworking of the *War Scroll* that highlights a messianic figure (and, for us, that includes the redaction of 11Q14),[20] and Duhaime's reluctance to include 4Q285 as a fragment of the *War Scroll* (probably not the ending), a similar recension of it, or another recension.[21]

Research on 4Q285 has led in different and exciting directions and now turns to an impressive consensus. What has appeared with relative certainty is that, unlike 11Q14, 4Q285 reflects editing and shaping at Qumran.

4. Selected Bibliography

Abegg, M. G. "Messianic Hope in 4Q285: A Reassessment." *JBL* 113 (1994) 81–91.

Alexander, P. S. "A Reconstruction and Reading of 4Q285 (*4QSefer ha-Milḥamah*)." *RQ* 19 (1999–2000) 333–48.

Alexander, P. S. and G. Vermes. "285. 4QSefer ha-Milḥamah." In *Qumran Cave 4.XXVI: Cryptic Texts and Miscellanea, Part 1.* DJD 36. Oxford, 2000, pp. 228–46.

Brockmuehl, M. "A 'Slain Messiah' in 4QSerekh Milḥamah (4Q285)?" *Tyndale Bulletin* 43 (1992) 155–69.

Charlesworth, J. H., H. Lichtenberger, and G. S. Oegema, eds. *Qumran-Messianism: Studies on the Messianic Expectations in the Dead Sea Scrolls.* Tübingen, 1998.

Collins, J. J. *The Scepter and the Star.* Anchor Bible Reference Library; New York and London, 1995.

Duhaime, J. *The War Texts: 1QM and Related Manuscripts.* Companion to the Qumran Scrolls 6; London and New York, 2004.

Eisenmann, R. H. and M. O. Wise. *Dead Sea Scrolls Uncovered.* Shaftesbury and Rockport, 1992.

Gordon, R. P. "The Interpretation of Lebanon and 4Q285." *JJS* 43 (1992) 92–94.

Lyons, W. J. "Clarifications Concerning 4Q285 and 11Q14 Arising from *Discoveries in the Judaean Desert 23.*" *DSD* 6 (1999) 37–43.

Lyons, W. J. "Possessing the Land: The Qumran Sect and the Eschatological Victory." *DSD* 3 (1996) 130–51.

Milik, J. T. "Milkî-ṣedeq et Milkî-rešaʿ dans les anciens écrits juifs et chrétiens." *JJS* 23 (1972) 142–43.

Nitzan, B. "Benedictions and Instructions for the Eschatological Community (11QBer; 4Q285)." *RQ* 16 (1993) 77–90.

Nitzan, B. *Qumran Prayer and Religious Poetry.* Leiden, 1994. See esp. pp. 139–43, 167–70.

Norton, J. "Observations on the Official Material Reconstruction of *Sefer ha-Milḥamah* (11Q14 and 4Q285)." *RQ* 21 (2003) 546–48.

Schiffman, L. *Reclaiming the Dead Sea Scrolls.* Philadelphia and Jerusalem, 1994.

Sussman, A. and R. Peled, eds. *Scrolls from the Dead Sea.* Washington, D.C., 1993.

Tabor, J. "A Pierced or Piercing Messiah? – The Verdict is Still Out." *BAR* 18 (1992) 58–59.

---

[16] In 1QM, the "messiah" or "anointed one" is a prophet. Also, there is no allusion to two Messiahs, and David's defeat of Goliath has "absolutely no messianic overtones" (p. 123). See L. H. Schiffman in *The Messiah*, edited by Charlesworth, *et al.* (Minneapolis, 1992) p. 123.

[17] See J. Duhaime, *The War Texts: 1QM and Related Manuscripts* (Companion to the Qumran Scrolls 6; London and New York, 2004).

[18] See Duhaime in PTSDSSP 2.140–41.

[19] P. S. Alexander, "A Reconstruction and Reading of 4Q285 (*Sefer ha-Milḥamah*)," *RQ* 19 (1999–2000) 333–48.

[20] J. Norton, "Observations on the Official Material Reconstruction of *Sefer ha-Milḥamah* (11Q14 and 4Q285)," *RQ* 21 (2003) 546–48.

[21] J. Duhaime, "The Manuscripts of the War Texts and Their Contents," in *The War Texts: 1QM and Related Manuscripts*, pp. 12–35.

Blessings of the High Priest 2
4Q285 (4QSefer ha-Milḥamah; cf. 11Q14)[1]

Frg. 1

1   [(VACAT) ועל̊ ם[

2   [ם למען שמכה ומ̊]

3   [את מיכאל ג[בריא]ל̊] שריאל ורפאל

4   [עם בחיר̊י̊]

Frg. 2

1   [ש̊ם ̊ם]

2   [עמו א[שר]

3   [מ̊]

Frg. 3

1   [ ]̊

2   [הלויא̊]י̊[]ם̊ וחצ[וצרות

3   יו[בל לריע[2] בהם̊]

4   [י̊ כתיים יבזם̊]

5   [ע̊]

---

[1] 4Q285 is most likely a redaction of 11Q14.
[2] Read להריע.

Blessings of the High Priest 2
4Q285 (4QSefer ha-Milḥamah; cf. 11Q14)

Frg. 1

1   […]*m* and upon (VACAT) […]

2   […]*m* for the sake of your name and *m*°[…]

3   […] Michael, G[abrie]l [Sariel and Raphael …]

4   […] with the chosen ones of […]

Frg. 2

1   […]°*m š*[…]

2   [… w]hich (is) with him […]

3   […]*m*[…]

Frg. 3

1   […]°[…]

2   […] the Levit[e]s and (metal) tru[mpets[1] …]

3   [… the ra]m (horns)[2] to blow[3] with them […]

4   […]*y* the Kittim[4] will despise them […]

5   […]ʿ[…]

---

[1] The author contrasts metal trumpets with ram's horns.
[2] The shofar.
[3] To blow an alarm; see Num 10:9.
[4] Not in 11Q14.

Frg. 4

1   היאה ע[ת֯[3] תנגף רש֯ע֯ה֯]

2   נשׁי[א֯ העדה וכול ישר֯[אל

3   כאשר הי[ה כתוב֯] בספר יחזקאל הנביא והכיתי קשתכה מיד שמאולכה[[4]

4   [וחציכה מיד ימינכה אפיל[5] [על הר֯י י֯[שראל תפול אתה וכול אגפיכה[6]

5   נגד מלך ה[כ֯תיים[7] ו֯[

6   ורדף אחריהם[8] נש[יא העדה עד הים ה[גדול[9]

7   וינוס[ו֯ מפני ישראל בעת ההיא֯ה[

8   ו[יעמוד עליהם ונעכרו[10] עליהם[

9   [ו֯ ושבו אל היבשה בעת הה֯י֯א[ה

10   [ו֯י֯ביאוהו לפ֯נ֯י֯ נ֯שׁיא[העדה[11]

Frg. 5

1   [ל֯ו֯א֯]

2   [ל֯]

Frg. 6

1   [י֯ר֯א֯ו֯]

---

[3] We follow Nitzan's restoration, "Benedictions and Instructions for the Eschatological Community (11QBer; 4Q285)," *RQ* 16 (1993) 87. עת is a foundational word and concept at Qumran; see esp. 1QM 1.5.

[4] From Ezek 39:3.

[5] From Ezek 39:3.

[6] From Ezek 39:4.

[7] See 1QM 15.2: נגד מלך הכתיים.

[8] From Ex 14:4.

[9] From Ezek 47:10, 15, 19, and 20; cf. Num 34:7.

[10] Not a scribal error for ונערכו, ctr. Alexander and Vermes.

[11] See line 6.

Frg. 4

1   [... this is the ti]me (when) wickedness will be defeated [...]

2   [... the Prin]ce of the Congregation[5] and all Isra[el ...]

3   [... as it i]s written [in the Book of Ezekiel, the Prophet: "And I[6] shall strike your bow from your left hand]

4   [and shall make your arrows drop out of your right hand].[7] Upon the mountains of I[srael you will fall, you and all your troops ...]"[8]

5   [... against the king of the] Kittim.[9] And [...]

6   [... and he will pursue after them, the Pri]nce of the Congregation[10] until the [great] sea[11] [...]

7   [... and] they [will flee] before Israel at that time [...]

8   [... and] he will stand against them, and the (waters) were stirred up[12] upon them [...]

9   [...]w and they[13] will return to the dry land in th[at] time [...]

10   [...] and they will bring him[14] before the Prince of [the Congregation[15] ...]

Frg. 5

1   [...] *not* [...]

2   [...]*l*[...]

Frg. 6

1   [...] they will see [...][16]

---

[5] Not in 11Q14; see 1QM 15.1 and 1QSa *Rule of the Congregation*.
[6] The LORD God is speaking. See Ezek 39:3–4 (not in 11Q14).
[7] From Ezek 39:3.
[8] From Ezek 39:4.
[9] Not in 11Q14. See 1QM 15.2: "against the king of the Kittim."
[10] Not in 11Q14.
[11] An allusion to Ezek 47:10, 15, 19, and 20. Not in 11Q14.
[12] *Nip'al* of עכר; also "be ruined."
[13] "They" refers to all Israel. See frg. 2 line 4.
[14] "Him" refers to the king of the Kittim.
[15] Not in 11Q14.
[16] Restorations are too speculative.

2   [תֹו באו]

3   לֹ[ל אֹ יסעו]לֹ

4   [לליֹלֹה[12]]

5   [עליון]

Frg. 7

1   כאשר כתוב בספר [ישעיהו הנביא[13] וֹנֹקֹפֹ[ו][14]

2   [סבכי היער בברזל ולבנון באדיר י]פֹול ויצא חוטר מגזע ישי

3   [ונצר משורשיו יפרה[15]   ] צמח דויד ונשפטו[16] את

4   [ ]ׄ והמיתו נשיא העדה צמֹ[ח][17]

5   [דויד   בנגעי]ם ובמחוללות[18] וצוה כוהן

6   [הרואש[19]   ח]לֹלֹ[י]ן כתיֹיֹמֹ[ ] לֹ[ ]

Frg. 8[20]

1   וברכם בשם אל ישראל וענה[21]

2   [ואמר]לפֹני [כול בני י]שראל[22] [ברוכים אתם בשם אל עליון][23]

---

[12] Read לילה.

[13] A well-known formula.

[14] Isa 10:34 ונקף. From the end of line 1 to line 3a is a text restored from Isa 10:34–11:1. Lines 1–6 are preserved on one piece of brown leather. For a color image see *Scrolls from the Dead Sea*, p. 83.

[15] Restored from Isa 10:34–11:1.

[16] There is a tear in the leather from here in lines 3 to 5. Before את there are no letters visible and the scribe leaves a wide space between words.

[17] The form of *mem* is often similar to *beth*.

[18] The noun is a *hapax legomenon*. From חלל, "to wound," "to pierce;" see *PssSol* 2:25–26. Not as probable is the root "to dance," from חול (as suggested by Wacholder and Abegg, p. 225, and Schiffman, *Reclaiming*, p. 346).

[19] See 11Q14 frg. 1 1.14.

[20] Frg. 8 may be seen as a composite of 4Q285 and 11Q14 (see notes) but restorations are highly speculative since the two texts differ in places.

[21] From 11Q14 frg. 1 2.2–3.

[22] See the note to 11Q14 frg. 1 2.3.

[23] From 11Q14 frg. 1 2.3–4.

2   [...]*tw* they will enter [...]

3   [...]*l* they will journey t[o ...]

4   [...] night[17] [...]

5   [...] upon him [...]

Frg. 7

1   [... as it is written in the Book of] Isaiah,[18] the Prophet: "And [they] will be cut down,

2   [the most massive of the forest with iron. And Lebanon, with its magnificence, will] fall. And a shoot will emerge from the Stump of Jesse,

3   [and an offshoot from his roots will bear fruit."[19] ...] the Sprout of David.[20] And they will enter into judgment with

4   [...]° and he[21] will cause him[22] to die, the Prince of the Congregation, the Spro[ut of][23]

5   [David[24] ... by affliction]s and by wounds.[25] And [the High] Priest will command

6   [... the s]lain [of] the Kittim[26] [...]*l*[...]

Frg. 8[27]

1   [. ... and he will bless them in the name of the God of Israel, and he will answer]

2   [and say] before [all the sons of I]srael; ["Blessed be you in the name of God Most High][28]

---

[17] Only reflection on how these fragments represent a similar thought allows that "night" may mean the night of rest after the final battle (see DJD 36, p. 238).

[18] A well-known formula.

[19] A quotation from Isa 10:34–11:1.

[20] Or "Branch of David." The Sprout of David appears five times in the Qumran Scrolls. See Abegg and Evans in *Qumran-Messianism*, pp. 197–98.

[21] "He" refers to the Prince of the Congregation.

[22] *Hip'il* (וְהֵמִיתוֹ, not וְהֵמִיתוּ, "and they will cause him to die"). "Him" refers to [the king of the] Kittim; see frg. 4 line 5. Most likely, the verb denotes death by sentence. Note *Isaiah Pesher 4* (4Q161 frgs. 8–10) interprets Isa 11:1–5 to refer to the judgment by a descendant of "David" who "will judge" all peoples (nations) by "his sword."

[23] Or "Bran[ch of]."

[24] The Prince of the Congregation will cause the king of the Kittim to die.

[25] From חלל, "to wound," "to pierce."

[26] Not in 11Q14.

[27] Frg. 8 may be seen as a composite of 4Q285 and 11Q14 (see notes).

[28] From 11Q14 frg. 1 2.3–4.

3 [   ] וברֿ[וֿ]ךֿ שם קודשו לֿ[עֿ]לֿמי עדֿ] וברוכים   וברוכים[

4 [כול מלאכי קודשו יברךֿ]²⁴ אתֿכֿם אל עֿ[ליון ויאר פניו אליכם²⁵ ויפתח]

5 [לכם את אוצרו הֿ[טֿובֿ [אשֿ]רֿ²⁶ בֿשמים לֿ[הוריד על ארצכם גשמי ברכה]

6 [טל ו]מֿטר²⁷ יֿו[רֿ]הֿ ומלקוֿ[שֿ] בעתו ולתֿתֿ] לכם פרי תנובות דגן]

7 [תירוש ויֿ]צֿהר²⁸ לרוב והארץֿ [תנו]בֿב לֿ[כם פרי עדנים ואכלתם]

8 [והדשנתֿ]מֿ²⁹ וֿאין משכלה [בֿ]אֿ[רצכֿ]מֿ ולוֿאֿ] מוחלה שדפון וירקון[³⁰

9 לוֿאֿ³¹ יראֿהֿ בתבואֿ[תיה וא[ין כֿוֿלֿ נגֿעֿ] ומכשול בעדתכם וחיה רעה שבתה[³²

10 מן הארץ ואין דב[ר בארצכֿ]מֿ³³ כיא אל עֿ[מכם ומלאכי קודשו מתיצבים בעדתכם ושם[³⁴

11 קודשו נקרא עֿ[ליכם³⁵   [°°° לֿ °°°]

12 לֿ[יֿ]חֿדֿ ובקרבכם]

Frg. 9

1 [שֿנה וכֿוֿ]לֿ

---

²⁴ The long restoration in lines 3 and 4 is from 11Q14 frg. 1 2.5–7.
²⁵ An echo from Num 6:24–25, the *Aaronic Blessing*.
²⁶ The restoration is from 11Q14 frg. 1 2.7–8.
²⁷ From 11Q14 frg. 1 2.8–9.
²⁸ The restoration in lines 6 and 7 is from 11Q14 frg. 1 2.9–10.
²⁹ The restoration in lines 7 and 8 is from 11Q14 frg. 1 2.10–11.
³⁰ From 11Q14 frg. 1 2.12.
³¹ The right margin might be visible.
³² From 11Q14 frg. 1 2.13.
³³ From 11Q14 frg. 1 2.14.
³⁴ From 11Q14 frg. 1 2.14–15. Additional evidence against assuming 4Q285 represents the same text as 11Q14 is the excessive length of line 10 (as noted in DJD 36, p. 241).
³⁵ From 11Q14 frg. 1 2.15.

3   [… and ble]ss[ed be his holy name for] ev[er]lasting eternity.[29] [And blessed be…. And blessed be]

4   [all the angels of his holiness.[30] May] God Mo[st Hi]gh [bless] you, [and may he shine his face toward you,[31] and may he open]

5   [for you his] good [treasure whi]ch[32] is in the heavens, to [cause to fall down on your land showers of blessing,]

6   [dew, and][33] rain, ea[r]ly and late rai[n] in its season, and to give [to you fruit, the produce of wheat,][34]

7   [new wine, and o]il[35] in plenty. And [may] the land [pro]duce for [you delicious fruits]. And may you eat]

8   [and may y]ou [be full.][36] And may there not be miscarriage[37] [in yo]ur l[and,] nor [sickness.] May [drought and blight][38]

9   not[39] be seen in [its] harvest[s. And may the]re [n]ot be any affliction [nor stumbling obstacle in your congregation, so[40] injurious beast(s)[41] ceased][42]

10   from the land. And may there not be pestile[nce in] your [land.][43] For God (is) wi[th you and the angels of his holiness are present in your congregation. And][44] may his holy [name]

11   be invoked ov[er you. …]°°° °*l* ° °°[…]

12   for a [com]munity.[45] And in your midst […]

Frg. 9

1   […] year and al[l …]

---

[29] See 1QS and 1QH^a 5.18.

[30] The long restoration in lines 3 and 4 is from 11Q14 frg. 1 2.5–7.

[31] An echo from Num 6:24–25, the Aaronic Blessing.

[32] From 11Q14 frg. 1 2.7–8.

[33] From 11Q14 frg. 1 2.8–9.

[34] Not "corn" (the British noun for "wheat").

[35] The restoration in lines 6 and 7 are from 11Q14 frg. 1 2.9–10.

[36] The restoration in lines 7 and 8 is from 11Q14 frg. 1 2.10–11.

[37] Not "miscarrying" (DJD 36, p. 243).

[38] From 11Q14 frg. 1 2.12.

[39] The margin might be preserved for lines 9–12.

[40] Hebrew *waw* can mean "and" or "so."

[41] Hebrew is singular but implies a plural: "beasts."

[42] From 11Q14 frg. 1 2.13. The past tense is a prophetic vision of a completed act.

[43] From 11Q14 frg. 1 2.14.

[44] From 11Q14 frg. 1 2.14–15.

[45] Heb. יחד or "community."

2   ‏[עת קץ‎³⁶‏ ל]‎

3   ‏[יֺם אשר]‎

4   ‏[וֺתֺוֺר]ה‎

Frg. 10

1   ‏[הֺ]‎

2   ‏[מֺתֺוֺך [ה]עדה]‎

3   ‏עוז]ב הוֺן ו[בֺצע]‎

4   ‏[וֺר ואכלתֺם אֺ]‎

5   ‏[להם קברי]ם‎

6   ‏[קֺ]]ל חלליה]ם‎

7   ‏ש[בי עוֺן‎³⁷‏ ישובו]‎

8   ‏[ברחמים ו]‎

9   ‏[וישׂ]ר]אל עוֺ]‎

10   ‏[ש ואׅ]‎³⁸

---

³⁶ See ‏עת קץ‎ in 4Q372 1.15.

³⁷ At Qumran, the expression is ‏שבי פשע‎; see that expression in CD MS A 2.5; CD MS B 20.17; 1QS 10.20; 1QHª 6.24, 10.9, 14.6; 4Q400 frg. 1 1.16; see the restoration in 4Q266 frgs. 1a–b line 22; 4Q299 frg. 71 line 1; and 4Q512 frgs. 70–71 line 2. Thus, ‏ש[בי עוֺן‎ is unique to 4Q285. 4Q285 retains elements of pre-Qumran documents.

³⁸ The bottom margin may be seen.

2 […] time[46] Endtime for[…]

3 […]*ym* which […]

4 […] and Tor[ah …]

Frg. 10[47]

1 […]*h*[…]

2 […] from the midst of [the] congregation […]

3 [… the one forsaki]ng wealth [and] gain […]

4 […]*wr* and it will devour them ᵓ[…]

5 […] for them grave[s …]

6 […]*q*[…]*l* the[ir] slain ones […]

7 [… those who r]eturn (from) iniquity will return […]

8 […] with compassion and […]

9 […] and Is[r]ael ῾*w*˚[…]

10 […]*š* and ᵓ[…]

---

[46] Or "season."
[47] Nitzan (*RQ* 16 [1993] 83) suggests frg. 10 mentions three subjects: wealth, burial, and repentance.

Hymns^a
11Q15

JAMES H. CHARLESWORTH with LEA BERKUZ[1]

Introduction

1. Contents

Hymns^a contains a hymn of praise to God for God's glory, works, and labors (frg. 1 line 5). The speaker acknowledges God's work in creating every spirit.

2. Texts and Edition

Hymns^a is preserved in 4 fragments. The fragments are unlined and dark brown. The hand is a developed Herodian formal script, or a late Herodian formal script, dating, on paleographic grounds, to 20–50 CE. The script is noticeably absent of the rounded characteristics of earlier hands.

3. Provenience and Relation to Other Jewish Writings

Fragments 1 and 2 make use of the Qumran expression "your elect ones" (frg.1 line 4 and frg. 2 line 4). This term, combined with the praise of God for God's works, follows typical Qumran theology reminiscent of the *Thanksgiving Hymns*. No other *termini technici* characteristic of Qumran, however, define the document. The hymnic qualities are well known at Qumran but are also established notably in the *Psalms of Solomon*.

4. Selected Bibliography

García Martínez, F., E. J. C. Tigchelaar and A. S. van der Woude. "15. 11QHymns^a." In *Qumran Cave 11.II: 11Q2–18, 11Q20–31*. DJD 23; Oxford, 1998, pp. 253–56, Pl. 29.The introduction is by Charlesworth. The text and translation is by Charlesworth with Berkuz.

---

[1] The introduction is by Charlesworth. The text and translation is by Charlesworth with Berkuz.

Hymns[a]
11Q15

Frg. 1

1 כ]ולנו[1] ב°[[2]

2 א]שׁ֯ר כוננו ידים̇[[3]

3]°כה ותראה מק°[[4]

4]בחיריכה[5] בשמותם ב֯[

5]כבודו ומעשיו ועמלו[6] ב֯[

6]אתה בראתה כול רוח[7] ל֯°°[(ו written above)

Frg. 2

1 משפ]טים °[

2]ר֯ם למע̇[שיכה

3] לשלח̇[

4] לעיני בחי֯֯ר[יכה

5]ר תבוא ע[

[1] For ולנו[in its entirety, see PAM 42.180. The *waw* and the *lamedh* have become separated from the rest of the fragment. DJD suggests the restoration כ]ולנו.
[2] DJD is correct to note that the second letter could possibly be an *ayin* or a *shin*. A *ṣade* may also be possible.
[3] DJD: ידיכ֯ה֯[. DJD also notes that ידים֯[is a possibility. The bottom stroke of the final *mem* on line four of PAM 44.003 is thicker than the proposed final *mem*. Its bottom is exactly the same as that of the *kaph* on line 2 and the one on line 3. Cf. Ex 15:17 (4Q14 6.40) and 4Q174 frgs. 1–3 and 21 1.3: כ֯֯וננו ידיכה.
[4] The edge of a stroke can be seen on the left edge of the fragment. Perhaps restore מקו֯]ם "place"; מקל֯]ות "branches"; or מקט֯]ר "incense."
[5] Ctr. DJD: בחדריכה[. What DJD restores as a *dalet* is far too narrow compared to *dalet* found on line 1 or line 5.
[6] Cf. Qoh 2:11: וּפָנִיתִי אֲנִי בְּכָל־מַעֲשַׂי שֶׁעָשׂוּ יָדַי וּבֶעָמָל שֶׁעָמַלְתִּי לַעֲשׂוֹת.
[7] Cf. 1QS 4.20.

Hymns[a]
11Q15

Frg. 1

1   [… a]ll of us *b*°[…]

2   [… wh]ich (your) hands established […]

3   […]°*kh* and you shall show[1] *mq*°[[2]…]

4   […] your elect ones[3] by their names *b*[…]

5   […] his glory and his works and his labor *b*[…]

6   […] you created every spirit and *l*°°[…]

Frg. 2

1   […] judgme]nts …]

2   […]*rm* for [your] wor[ks …]

3   […] to send forth […]

4   […] before the eyes of [your] elect one[s …]

5   […]*r* you shall come ʿ[…]

---

[1] Or "you shall show yourself;" the *nipʿal* 2nd masc. sing. of ראה. Other possibilities exist, including the *hipʿil* 2nd masc. sing. "you shall show" (see DJD 23, p. 254).

[2] Perhaps read and restore: "a pla[ce," "a refu[ge," "branc[hes," or "incen[se."

[3] This phrase is used in the 1QHᵃ 6.13, 26, and 10.15.

Frg. 3

1   [̊ פניכה ̊ ̊]

Frg. 4

1   וע[באזר]

Frg. 3

1   […]° your faces °°[…]

Frg. 4

1   […] by the ar[m of …]

Hymns^b
11Q16

JAMES H. CHARLESWORTH

Introduction

1. Contents

Hymns^b was originally published as one manuscript from three fragments in DJD 23.[1] In 1998, however, S. Talmon published three fragments that were discovered in Y. Yadin's archives. Talmon asked that these fragments be identified.[2] In 2001, H. Eshel suggested that Item 3 of Yadin's collection is an additional fragment of 11Q16 on the following grounds: coloration, similar character size, and a script dating to the same period. He theorized that these two fragments were lying on top of each other and were from different columns of the same scroll.[3] Further, these two fragments seem to contain a prayer akin to that in 4Q504–6.[4] Additional research is needed to decipher whether or not other fragments of this prayer exist.[5] Here they are published in an order similar to Eshel's suggestion: the fragment from DJD first and the Talmon fragment second. This prayer contains thanksgiving to God and mentions creation and apparently David's or Solomon's conquests.

2. Text and Edition

The script of fragment 1 is a Herodian hand and is marked by the "round" semiformal script. It conceivably dates from the first half of the first century CE. The leather of fragment 1 is lined and dark brown with a few dark spots; the consonants are distinctively small.[6] On PAM 44.006, fragment 1 is made up of three small fragments, joined together, and is 2.5 centimeters high by 2.8 centimeters wide. Fragment 2 is slightly larger (3.3 x 5cm) and is light brown with some gray. The fragment might be lined, or the scribe has maintained distinctly straight lines and even spacing. The hand is a Herodian formal script and dates to the first half of the first century CE.[7] It is possible that the same scribe copied both fragments; however, some consonants are formed differently.[8]

3. Provenience

Although there are no Qumran *termini technici* found in these fragments, a Qumran provenience is conceivable.[9] If H. Eshel's hypothesis is correct, a Qumran provenience seems likely, and supported by the numerous parallels with the *Hodayot*.[10]

4. Selected Bibliography

Eshel, H. "Three New Fragments From Qumran Cave 11." *DSD* 8/1 (2001) 1–8.

García Martínez, F., E. J. C. Tigchelaar and A. S. van der Woude. "16. 11QHymns^b." In *Qumran Cave 11.II: 11Q2–18, 11Q20–31.* DJD 23; Oxford, 1998, pp. 257–58, Pl. 29.

---

[1] F. García Martínez, E. J. C. Tigchelaar and A. S. van der Woude, "16. 11QHymns^b," in *Qumran Cave 11.II: 11Q2–18, 11Q20–31* (DJD 23; Oxford, 1998) p. 257.

[2] S. Talmon, "Fragments of Hebrew Writings Without Identifying Sigla of Provenance from the Literary Legacy of Yigael Yadin," *DSD* 5/2 (1998) 149–57.

[3] H. Eshel, "Three New Fragments From Qumran Cave 11," *DSD* 8/1 (2001) 5.

[4] H. Eshel, "Three New Fragments From Qumran Cave 11," 6.

[5] H. Eshel notes rumors of similar fragments in private collections.

[6] F. García Martínez, "Texts From Qumran Cave 11," in *The Dead Sea Scrolls: Forty Years of Research*, edited by D. Dimant and U. Rappaport (STDJ 10; Leiden, 1992) p. 24.

[7] The image was published in Talmon, "Fragments of Hebrew Writings Without Identifying Sigla of Provenance," 155. Also see DJD 36, Pl. 32.

[8] H. Eshel, "Three New Fragments From Qumran Cave 11," 5. See esp. note 19.

[9] The plene spelling of כיא in frg. 2 line 2, suggested to Talmon that "the fragment stems from Qumran." See Talmon in *DSD* 5/2 (1998) 156.

[10] See the notes to the text.

García Martínez, F. "Texts from Qumran Cave 11." In *The Dead Sea Scrolls: Forty Years of Research*, edited by D. Dimant and U. Rappaport. STDJ 10; Leiden, 1992, pp. 18–26.

Talmon, S. "Fragments of Hebrew Writings Without Identifying Sigla of Provenance From the Literary Legacy of Yigael Yadin." *DSD* 5/2 (1998) 149–57.

Talmon, S. "XQText B (=)11QHymns[b] frg. 2." In *Qumran Cave 4.XXVI: Cryptic Texts and Miscellanea, Part 1.* DJD 36; Oxford, 2000, pp. 487–89, Pl. 32.

Van der Ploeg, J. P. M. "Les manuscrits de la Grotte XI de Qumran." *RQ* 12/1 (1985) 3–15.

Hymns^b
11Q16

Frg. 1

1	[ה]ׄיׄ אתה יצרת¹[ה ׄ
2	[ׄ מעשיו בטרם³ כ]וׄל²
3	[ל] כלי⁵ באמתכה⁴[
4	[ם בטר]ותו ׄ[

Frg. 2⁶

1	[ ] ב[וט⁷
2	(VA[CAT) ו]בׄ[רציתה כיא⁸
3	[ממלכות ךׄ ויך⁹ או]יביו
4	[ותתן עוונותיו ׄ[
5	[ר]ׄשׁועו והון לו יה¹⁰[ה]
6	לו [וישתחוׄו] בידו
7	[ ] ל¹¹ׄׄ ׄ[ ]

---

¹ Cf. 1QH^a 7.35, 9.10, 18.24. See also 11Q15 1.6. Note also Isa 44:21:יִשְׂרָאֵל; Isa 64:7:וְיִשְׂרָאֵל כִּי עַבְדִּי־אַתָּה יְצַרְתִּיךָ עָבֶד־לִי אַתָּה יִשְׂרָאֵל לֹא תִנָּשֵׁנִי; Ps 74:17:אַתָּה יְצַרְתָּם; וְאַתָּה יְצַרְנוּ וּמַעֲשֵׂה יָדְךָ כֻּלָּנוּ קַיִץ וָחֹרֶף.

² According to DJD 23, the *lamedh* and *waw* are not visible on PAM 40.006; they are on a small piece which has not been photographed.

³ Cf. 1QH^a 5.25:וברטם נוסדו; 1QH^a 9.9; CD MS A 2.7:כול מעשיך בטרם בראתם עם צבא רוחיך.

⁴ The word באמת appears frequently with the 2nd masc. sing. suffix in the *Thanksgiving Hymns* (e.g., 7.36, 12.15, 15.29, 17.10, 18.19). See also 4Q428 frg. 10 line 6.

⁵ Perhaps with Van der Ploeg: בלי.

⁶ Talmon's "Item No. 3."

⁷ Ctr. Talmon: סוׄ[.

⁸ See Ps 149:4.

⁹ *Hip'il* impv. of נכה.

¹⁰ See Ps 112:3:הון ועשר בביתו.

¹¹ Perhaps restore כוׄל.

Hymns^b
11Q16

Frg. 1

1   […]°° you, you form[ed…]

2   [… a]ll his works before °[…]

3   […] in your truth, a vessel[1] for […]

4   […]°*wtw* befor[e …]

Frg. 2

1   […] goo[d …]

2   […. (VA]CAT) For you[2] took pleasure [in him[3] …]

3   […] his [ene]mies; and he smote the kingdoms […]

4   […]° his iniquities and you gave […]

5   [… it wil]l be for him. And treasure[4] and weal[th[5] …]

6   […] in his hand and they bowed down [to him …]

7   […] °°*l*[6]   […]

---

[1] Or "without."
[2] The subject is God.
[3] A King of Israel who "smote the kingdoms" may be the object, perhaps David or Solomon.
[4] Heb. הון.
[5] Heb. עושר.
[6] Perhaps: "all;" see frg. 1 line 2.

Dead Sea Scrolls[1]

List of Document Numbers, *Names of Documents,* and Volume Numbers

(when they have been published in this series)

CD *Damascus Document* **2**
Maslk *Angelic Liturgy* **4B**
Mas 1045–1350 and 1375 *A Joseph Apocryphon* **8A**
1QapGen *Genesis Apocryphon ar*
1QH[a] *Thanksgiving Hymns* **5A**
1QM *War Scroll* **2**
1QpHab *Habakkuk Pesher* **6B**
1QS *Rule of the Community* **1**
1Q1–13 *Biblical texts;* not included in PTSDSSP
1Q14 = 1QpMic *Micah Pesher 1* **6B**
1Q15 = 1QpZeph *Zephaniah Pesher 2* **6B**
1Q16 = 1QpPs68 *Psalm Pesher 2* **6B**
1Q17 = 1QJub[a] *Jubilees*
1Q18 = lQJub[b] *Jubilees*
1Q19a = 1Q19 = 1QNoah *Book of Noah* **8A**
1Q19b = 1Q19bis *Exaltation Hymn* **8A**
1Q20 = 1QapGen *Genesis Apocryphon* **8A**
1Q21 = 1QTLevi *Testament of Levi ar*
1Q22 = 1QDM *Sayings of Moses*
1Q23 *Book of Giants*[a]
1Q24 *Book of Giants*[b]*?*
1Q25 *Prophetic Apocryphon 2*
1Q26 *Instruction*
1Q27 = 1QMyst *Book of the Mysteries*
1Q28a = 1QSa *Rule of the Congregation* **1**
1Q28b = 1QSb *Blessings* **1**
1Q29 *Moses Apocryphon*[b]*?*
1Q29a *Two Spirits Treatise?*
1Q30 *Holy Messi[ah] Fragment*
1Q31 *Men of the Covenant Fragment*
1Q32 = 1QNJ *New Jerusalem? ar*
1Q33 = 1QM *War Scroll* **2**
1Q34–1Q34[bis] = 1QPr Fetes *Prayers for Festivals* **4A**

1Q35 = 1QH[b] *Thanksgiving Hymns* **5A**
1Q36 *Liturgical Fragment 1*
1Q37 *Elect of Israel Fragment*
1Q38 *Liturgical Fragment 2*
1Q39 *Liturgical Fragment 3*
1Q40 *Liturgical Fragment 4*
1Q41 *All the Land Fragment*
1Q42 *Famine Fragment*
1Q43 *All the Angel[s] Fragment*
1Q44 *Unidentified Fragments*
1Q45 *Poor Fragment*
1Q46 *Just Weight Fragment*
1Q47 *Unidentified Fragments*
1Q48 *Unidentified Fragments*
1Q49 *Your Strength Fragment*
1Q50 *Tree Fragment*
1Q51 *Eternal Fragment* **2**
1Q52 *Your Signs Fragment*
1Q53 *Worm Fragment*
1Q54 *Covenant of His Glory Fragment*
1Q55 *Nations Fragment*
1Q56 *Resting Place Fragment*
1Q57 *In Your Statutes Fragment*
1Q58 *[Is]rael Fragment 1*
1Q59 *Unidentified Fragments*
1Q60 *Unidentified Fragments*
1Q61 *Unidentified Fragments*
1Q62 *Moses Fragment 1*
1Q63 *On their Standards Fragment ar*
1Q64 *In the Bitterness Fragment ar*
1Q65 *[I]srael Fragment 2 ar*
1Q66 *Teacher Fragment ar*
1Q67 *Your Blotting Out Fragment ar*
1Q68 *Who is She? Fragment ar*
1Q69 *Evil Ones Fragment ar*
1Q70 *For a Song Fragment* **8A**
1Q70[bis] *He Who Brings in the Sheep* **8A**
1Q71–72 *Biblical texts;* not included in PTSDSSP

2Q1–17 *Biblical texts;* not included in PTSDSSP
2Q18 *Sirach*
2Q19 = 2QJub[a] *Jubilees*
2Q20 = 2QJub[b] *Jubilees*

2Q21 = 2QapMoses *Moses Apocryphon?*
2Q22 = 2QapDavid *David Apocryphon*
2Q23 = 2QapProph *Prophetic Apocryphon 1*
2Q24 = 2QJN *New Jerusalem ar*
2Q25 *Juridical Fragment* **2**
2Q26 = 2QEn Giants *Book of Giants ar*
2Q27 *Appointed Time Fragment* **8A**
2Q28 *Verdict Fragment* **2**
2Q29 *You Shall Say Fragment* **8A**
2Q30 *Yahweh Fragment* **8A**
2Q31 *Sword Fragment* **8A**
2Q32 *Unidentified Fragment* **8A**
2Q33 *Ninev[eh] Fragment*

3Q1–3 *Biblical texts;* not included in PTSDSSP
3Q4 = 3Qplsa *Isaiah Pesher 1* **6B**
3Q5 = 3QJub *Jubilees*
3Q6 = 3QHymn *Hymn of Praise* **5A**
3Q7 = 3QTJud? *Testament of Judah?*
3Q8 *Angel of Pea[ce] Fragment*
3Q9 *Our Congregation Fragment*
3Q10–11 *Unidentified Fragments*
3Q12 *Unidentified Fragments ar*
3Q13 *Unidentified Fragments ar*
3Q14 *Unidentified Fragments*
3Q14 frg. 8 *Genesis Apocryphon* **8A**
3Q15 *Copper Scroll*

4Q1–14 *Biblical texts;* not included in PTSDSSP
4Q15–16 = 4QExod[d–e] *Excerpted Exodus*
4Q17–36 *Biblical texts;* not included in PTSDSSP
4Q37–38 = 4QDeut[j,k,l] *Excerpted Deuteronomy*
4Q39–40 *Biblical texts;* not included in PTSDSSP
4Q41 = 4QDeut[n] *Excerpted Deuteronomy*
4Q42–43 *Biblical texts;* not included in PTSDSSP
4Q44 = 4QDeut[q] *Excerpted Deuteronomy*

---

[1] For further information, see E. Tov, *Revised Lists of the Texts from the Judean Desert* (Leiden, 2010).

4Q45–87 *Biblical texts;* not included in PTSDSSP

4Q88 = 4QPs^f *Non-Masoretic Psalms* **4A**

4Q89–122 *Biblical texts;* not included in PTSDSSP

4Q123 *Parabiblical Joshua paleo*

4Q124–125 *Unidentified Parabiblical Material paleo*

4Q126 *Unidentified Parabiblical Material gr*

4Q127 *Parabiblical Exodus gr*

4Q128–155 *Phylacteries and Mezuzot;* not included in PTSDSSP

4Q156 = 4QtgLev *Targum on Leviticus*

4Q157 = 4QtgJob *Targum on Job*

4Q158 = RP^a *Reworked Pentateuch^a*

4Q159 = 4QOr^a *Ordinances* **1**

4Q160 = 4QVisSamuel *Vision of Samuel*

4Q161 = 4QpIsa^a *Isaiah Pesher 4* **6B**

4Q162 = 4QpIsa^b *Isaiah Pesher 2* **6B**

4Q163 = 4QpIsa^c *Isaiah Pesher 3* **6B**

4Q164 = 4QpIsa^d *Isaiah Pesher 6* **6B**

4Q165 = 4QpIsa^e *Isaiah Pesher 5* **6B**

4Q166 = 4QpHos^a *Hosea Pesher 1* **6B**

4Q167 = 4QpHos^b *Hosea Pesher 2* **6B**

4Q168 = 4QpMic *Micah Pesher 2* **6B**

4Q169 = 4QpNah *Nahum Pesher* **6B**

4Q170 = 4QpZeph *Zephaniah Pesher 1* **6B**

4Q171 = 4QpPs37 and 45 *Psalm Pesher 1* **6B**

4Q172 = 4QpUnid *Unidentified Pesharim Fragments* **6B**

4Q173 = 4QpPs 118, 127, 129 *Psalm Pesher 3* **6B**

4Q173a *House of Stumbling Fragment* **6B**

4Q174 = 4QFlor *Florilegium* **6B**

4Q175 = 4QTest *Testimonia* **6B**

4Q176 = 4QTanh *Consolations* **6B**

4Q176, frgs. 19–21 = 4QJub? *Jubilees?*

4Q177 = 4QCat^a *Catena A* **6B**

4Q178 *Unidentified Fragments*

4Q179 = 4QapLam *PseudoLamentations*

4Q180–181 *Wicked and Holy* **2**

4Q182 = 4QCat^b *Catena B* **6B**

4Q183 *Pesher-Like Fragment* **6B**

4Q184 = 4QWiles *Dame Folly and Lady Wisdom*

4Q185 *A Sapiential Testament*

4Q186 *Horoscopes*

4Q187–195 Unused Numbers

4Q196 = 4QTob^a *Tobit ar*

4Q197 = 4QTob^b *Tobit ar*

4Q198 = 4QTob^c *Tobit ar*

4Q199 = 4QTob^d *Tobit ar*

4Q200 *Tobit Hebrew Fragment? heb*

4Q201 = 4QEn^a *Books of Enoch ar*

4Q202 = 4QEn^b *Books of Enoch ar*

4Q203 = 4QEn Giants, *Book of Giants, ar*

4Q204 = 4QEn^c *Books of Enoch ar*

4Q205 = 4QEn^d *Books of Enoch ar*

4Q206 = 4QEn^e *Books of Enoch ar*

4Q207 = 4QEn^f *Books of Enoch ar*

4Q208 = 4QEnastr^a *Books of Enoch ar*

4Q209 = 4QEnastr^b *Books of Enoch ar*

4Q210 = 4QEnastr^c *Books of Enoch ar*

4Q211 = 4QEnastr^d *Books of Enoch ar*

4Q212 = 4QEn^g *Books of Enoch ar*

4Q213 = 4QTLevi^a *Testament of Levi ar*

4Q213a = 4QTLevi^b *Testament of Levi ar*

4Q213b = 4QTLevi^c *Testament of Levi ar*

4Q214 = 4QTLevi^d *Testament of Levi ar*

4Q215 = 4QTNaph *Testament of Naphtali*

4Q215a *Time of Righteousness*

4Q216 = 4QJub^a *Jubilees*

4Q217 = 4QJub^b *Jubilees*

4Q218 = 4QJub^c *Jubilees*

4Q219 = 4QJub^d *Jubilees*

4Q220 = 4QJub^e *Jubilees*

4Q221 = 4QJub^f *Jubilees*

4Q222 = 4QJub^g *Jubilees*

4Q223 = 4QJub^h *Jubilees*

4Q224 = 4QJub^h? *Jubilees*

4Q225 = 4QPsJub^a *Pseudo-Jubilees*

4Q226 = 4QPsJub^b *Pseudo-Jubilees*

4Q227 = 4QPsJub^c? *Pseudo-Jubilees?*

4Q228 *Work with Citation of Jubilees*

4Q229 *Pseudepigraphic Work 1*

4Q230–231 *Catalogue of Spirits^a–b*

4Q232 = 4QJN *New Jerusalem?*

4Q233 *Fragments with Place Names*

4Q234 *Genesis 27:20–21 with Scribal Exercises*

4Q235 *Unidentified Nabatean Text*

4Q236 = 4QPs89 *A Form of Psalm 89* **4A**

4Q237 cancelled

4Q238 *Words of Judgment*

4Q239 *Pesher on the True Israel*

4Q240 *Commentary on Canticles?*

4Q241 cancelled

4Q242 = 4QPrNab *Prayer of Nabonidus ar*

4Q243–245 = 4QpsDan *PseudoDaniel ar*

4Q246 *Daniel Apocryphon ar*

4Q247 *Apocalypse of Weeks Pesher*

4Q248 *Historical Work A*

4Q249 = cryptA MSM *Midrash Sefer Moses*

4Q249a–i *Rule of the Congregation cryptA*

4Q249j *Biblical text;* not included in PTSDSSP

4Q249k–l *Text Quoting Leviticus cryptA*

4Q249m *Thanksgiving Hymns-like Text cryptA*

4Q249n *Liturgical Work E? cryptA*

4Q249o *Liturgical Work F? cryptA*

4Q249p *Prophecy? cryptA*

4Q249q *Planting Fragment cryptA*

4Q249r–z *Unidentified Cryptic A Texts*

4Q250 *Concerning Cultic Services A cryptA*

4Q250a *Concerning Cultic Services B? cryptA*

4Q250b *Related to Isaiah 11 cryptA*

4Q250c–j *Unidentified Cryptic A Texts*

4Q251 *Halakah A* **3**

4Q252–253 *Commentary on Genesis A–B* **6B**

4Q253a *Commentary on Malachi B* **6B**

4Q254–254a *Commentary on Genesis C–D* **6B**

4Q255–264 = 4QS MSS A–J *Rule of the Community* **1**

4Q264a *Halakah B* **3**

4Q265 = 4QSD *Miscellaneous Rules* **3**

4Q266 = 4QD^a *Damascus Document Fragments* **2/3**

4Q267 = 4QD^b *Damascus Document Fragments* **3**

4Q268 = 4QD^c *Damascus Document Fragments* **2/3**

4Q269 = 4QD^d *Damascus Document Fragments* **2/3**

4Q270 = 4QD^e *Damascus Document Fragments* **3**

4Q271 = 4QD^f *Damascus Document Fragments* **3**

4Q272 = 4QD^g *Damascus Document Fragments* **2/3**

4Q273 = 4QD^h *Damascus Document Fragments* **2/3**

4Q274 *Tohorot A*

4Q275 *Communal Ceremony*

4Q276 *Tohorot B*

4Q277 *Tohorot B*
4Q278 *Tohorot C*
4Q279 *Four Lots*
4Q280 *Curses*
4Q281a–f *Unidentified Fragments*
4Q282a–t *Unidentified Fragments*
4Q283 cancelled
4Q284 *Purification Liturgy*
4Q284a *Harvesting* **3**
4Q285 *Blessings of the High Priest 2* **5A**
4Q286–290 = 4QBer^{a-e} *Berakot*
4Q291–293 *Work with Prayers*
4Q294 *Sapiential-Didactic Work* C
4Q295–297 cancelled
4Q298 *Words to the Sons of Dawn* cryptA
4Q299–300 = Myst^{a-b} *Mysteries^{a-b}*
4Q301 = Myst^c? *Mysteries^c?*
4Q302 *Admonitory Parable*
4Q303–305 *Meditation on Creation A–C*
4Q306 *Men of People Who Err*
4Q307 *Sanctuary Text* **8A**
4Q308 *Sapiential Fragments?*
4Q309 *A Cursive Work ar*
4Q310 *An Aramaic Apocryphal Work ar*
4Q311 *Unidentified Fragment*
4Q312 *Hebrew Text in Phoenician Cursive*
4Q313 *Some Works of the Torah* **3**
4Q313a–b *Unidentified Cryptic A Texts*
4Q313c *Calendrical Document B cryptA*
4Q314–316 cancelled
4Q317 *Cryptic (Phases of the Moon)*
4Q318 *Zodiology and Brontology ar*
4Q319 *Otot*
4Q320 *Calendrical Document/Mishmarot A*
4Q321 *Calendrical Document/Mishmarot B*
4Q321a *Calendrical Document/Mishmarot C*
4Q322 *Mishmarot A*
4Q322a *Historical Work H?*
4Q323 *Mishmarot B*
4Q324 *Mishmarot C*
4Q324a *Mishmarot D*
4Q324b *Calendrical Document A?*
4Q324c *Mishmarot E*
4Q324d *Liturgical Calendar^a*
4Q324e *Liturgical Calenda^b*
4Q324f *Liturgical Calendar^c*
4Q324g *Calendrical Document F*

4Q324h *Calendrical Document G*
4Q324i *Mishmarot J*
4Q325 *Calendrical Document D*
4Q326 *Calendrical Document C*
4Q327 *Calendrical Document E*
4Q328 *Mishmarot F*
4Q329 *Mishmarot G*
4Q329a *Mishmarot H*
4Q330 *Mishmarot I*
4Q331 *Historical Work* C
4Q332 *Historical Work* D
4Q332a *Unidentified Text*
4Q333 *Historical Work* E
4Q334 *Ordo*
4Q335–336 *Astronomical Fragments?*
4Q337 *Calendrical Document E?*
4Q338 *Genealogical List*
4Q339 *List of False Prophets*
4Q340 *List of Netinim*
4Q341 *List of Proper Names*
4Q342 *Letter in Judeo-Aramaic*
4Q343 *Nabatean Letter*
4Q344 *Debt Acknowledgement*
4Q345 *Sale of Land 1 ar*
4Q346 *Sale of Land 2 ar*
4Q347 *Deed A ar*
4Q348 *Deed B heb?*
4Q349 cancelled
4Q350 *Account A gr*
4Q351 *Account of Cereal A sem*
4Q352 *Account of Cereal B sem*
4Q352a *Account A sem*
4Q353 *Account of Cereal or Liquid sem*
4Q354 *Account B sem*
4Q355 *Account C sem*
4Q356 *Account D sem*
4Q357 *Account E sem*
4Q358 *Account F sem*
4Q359 *Deed B ar*
4Q360 = 4QTher *Alphabetic Document*
4Q361 *Scribbles on Papyrus gr*
4Q362 *Cryptic Fragment 1*
4Q363 *Cryptic Fragment 2*
4Q363a *Cryptic Fragment 3*
4Q364–365 *Reworked Pentateuch^{b-c}*
4Q365 *Temple Scroll Source or Divergent Copy* **7**
4Q366–367 *Reworked Pentateuch^{d-e}*
4Q368 *Pentateuch Apocryphon A*
4Q369 *Prayer of Enosh?*
4Q370 *Admonitions Based on the Flood* **8A**
4Q371–373 *Narrative and Poetic Composition^{a-c}*

4Q373a *Narrative and Poetic Composition^d*
4Q374 *Exodus/Conquest Tradition*
4Q375 *Moses Apocryphon^a*
4Q376 *Moses Apocryphon^b?*
4Q377 *Pentateuch Apocryphon B*
4Q378–379 *Joshua Apocryphon^{a-b}*
4Q380–381 *Qumran Pseudepigraphic Psalms* **4A**
4Q382 *Parabiblical Kings*
4Q383 *Jeremiah Apocryphon A*
4Q384 *Jeremiah Apocryphon B?*
4Q385 *Pseudo-Ezekiel^a*
4Q385a *Jeremiah Apocryphon C^a*
4Q385b *Pseudo-Ezekiel^c*
4Q385c *Pseudo-Ezekiel: Unidentified Fragments*
4Q386 *Pseudo-Ezekiel^b*
4Q387 *Jeremiah Apocryphon C^b*
4Q387a *Jeremiah Apocryphon C^f*
4Q388 *Pseudo-Ezekiel^d*
4Q388a *Jeremiah Apocryphon C^c*
4Q389 *Jeremiah Apocryphon C^d*
4Q390 *Jeremiah Apocryphon C^e*
4Q391 *Pseudo-Ezekiel^e*
4Q392 *Works of God*
4Q393 *Communal Confession*
4Q394–399 = 4QMMT^{a-f} *Some Works of the Torah* **3**
4Q400–407 = 4QShirShabb^{a-h} *Angelic Liturgy* **4B**
4Q408 *Moses Apocryphon^c*
4Q409 *Liturgical Work A*
4Q410 *Vision and Interpretation*
4Q411 *Sapiential Hymn*
4Q412 *Sapiential-Didactic Work A*
4Q413 *Divine Providence*
4Q414 *Purification Ritual A*
4Q415 *Instruction^a*
4Q416 *Instruction^b*
4Q417 *Instruction^c*
4Q418 *Instruction^d*
4Q418a *Instruction^e*
4Q418b *Text with Quotation from Psalm 107?*
4Q418c *Instruction^f*
4Q419 *Instruction-like Composition*
4Q420–421 *Ways of Righteousness^{a-b}*
4Q422 *Genesis and Exodus Paraphrase*
4Q423 *Instruction^g*
4Q424 *Instruction-like Document*
4Q425 *Sapiential-Didactic Work B*
4Q426 *Sapiential-Hymnic Work A*
4Q427–432 = 4QH^{a-f} *Thanksgiving Hymns* **5A**
4Q433 *Hodayot-Like Text A* **5A**

4Q433a *Hodayot-Like Text B* **5A**
4Q434–438 *Barki Nafshi*$^{a–e}$
4Q439 *Poem Similar to the Thanksgiving Hymns* **5A**
4Q440 *Hodayot-Like Text C* **5A**
4Q440a *Hodayot-Like Text D* **5A**
4Q440b *Court of the Righteous [Ones]* **5A**
4Q441 *Individual Thanksgiving A*
4Q442 *Individual Thanksgiving B*
4Q443 *Personal Prayer*
4Q444 *Incantation*
4Q445 *Lament A*
4Q446 *Poetic Fragments A*
4Q447 *Poetic Fragments B*
4Q448 *Prayer for King Jonathan and Psalms*
4Q449 *Prayer A*
4Q450 *Prayer B?*
4Q451 *Prayer C*
4Q452 *Prayer D?*
4Q453 *Lament B*
4Q454 *Prayer E?*
4Q455 *Didactic Work*
4Q456 *Hallelujah*
4Q457a *Creation?*
4Q457b *Eschatological Hymn*
4Q458 *Narrative Work A*
4Q459 *Lebanon Fragment A*
4Q460 *Narrative Work and Prayer*
4Q461 *Narrative Work B*
4Q462 *Narrative Work C*
4Q463 *Narrative Work D*
4Q464 = 4QExpPat *Exposition on the Patriarchs*
4Q464a *Midwives to Pharaoh Fragment*
4Q464b *Unidentified Fragments*
4Q465 *Samson Text?*
4Q466 *Congregation of the Lord*
4Q467 *Text Mentioning 'Light to Jacob'*
4Q468a–c *Unidentified Fragments C*
4Q468d cancelled
4Q468e *Historical Work F*
4Q468f *Historical Work G*
4Q468g *Eschatological Work A?*
4Q468h cancelled
4Q468i *Sectarian Work?*
4Q468j *Unidentified Fragments*
4Q468k *Hymnic Text?*
4Q468l *Fragment Mentioning Qoh 1:8–9*
4Q468m–dd *Unidentified Fragments*
4Q469 *Narrative Work 1*
4Q470 *Zedekiah Fragment*
4Q471 *War Scroll-like Fragment B*

4Q471a *Polemical Fragment*
4Q471b *Self-Glorification Hymn*
4Q471c *Prayer Concerning God and Israel*
4Q472 *Eschatological Work B*
4Q472a *Halakah C* **3**
4Q473 *The Two Ways*
4Q474 *Rachel and Joseph Apocryphon* **8A**
4Q475 *Renewed Earth*
4Q476 *Liturgical Work B*
4Q476a *Liturgical Work C*
4Q477 *Rebukes*
4Q478 *Festivals Fragment*
4Q479 *David's Descendents*
4Q480 *Narrative Work F*
4Q481 *Mixed Kinds Fragments*
4Q481a *Elisha Apocryphon*
4Q481b *Narrative Work G*
4Q481c *Prayer for Money*
4Q481d *Red Ink Fragments*
4Q481e *Narrative Work H*
4Q482 *Jubilees?*
4Q483 *Jubilees or Genesis?*
4Q484 = 4QTJud? *Testament of Judah*
4Q485 *Prophetic Fragment*
4Q486 *Sapiential (?) Fragment A*
4Q487 *Sapiential (?) Fragment B*
4Q488 *They Contend Fragment* **8A**
4Q489 *Visionary Fragment* **8A**
4Q490 *Unidentified Fragment 20* **8A**
4Q491–496 = 4QM$^{a–f}$ *War Scroll* **2**
4Q497 *War Scroll-Like Fragment* **2**
4Q498 *Hymnic Fragment 1: "Like My Soul"* **5A**
4Q499 *Hymnic Fragment 2: Mentioning Nebo* **5A**
4Q500 *Benediction*
4Q501 *Laments*
4Q502 *So-Called Marriage Ritual*
4Q503 = 4QMorgen and Abendgebete *Daily Prayers* **4A**
4Q504–506 = 4QDibHam *Words of the Lights* **4A**
4Q507–509 = PrFetes$^{a–c}$ *Prayers for Festivals* **4A**
4Q510–511 = 4QShir$^{a–b}$ *Songs of the Master*
4Q512 *Purification Ritual B*
4Q513 = 4QOrd^{b} *Rules* **1**
4Q514 = 4QOrd^{c} *Purification Rule* **1**
4Q515 *Unidentified Fragment*
4Q516 *Haran Fragment*
4Q517 *Unidentified Fragment*
4Q518 *Unidentified Fragment*
4Q519 *Unidentified Fragment*
4Q520 *Unidentified Fragment*

4Q521 *On Resurrection*
4Q522 *Joshua Prophecy*
4Q523 *Jonathan*
4Q524 *Temple Scroll Source or Earlier Edition* **7**
4Q525 *Beatitudes*
4Q526 *Testament*
4Q527 *Liturgical Work D?*
4Q528 *Sapiential-Hymnic Work B*
4Q529 *Words of Michael ar*
4Q530 *Book of Giants^{b} ar*
4Q531 *Book of Giants^{c} ar*
4Q532 *Book of Giants^{d} ar*
4Q533 *Book of Giants ar*
4Q534 *Birth of Noah ar* **8A**
4Q535 *Birth of Noah ar* **8A**
4Q536 *Birth of Noah ar* **8A**
4Q537 = AJa *Apocryphon of Jacob ar*
4Q538 = AJu *Apocryphon of Judah ar*
4Q539 = AJo *Testament of Joseph ar*
4Q540 *Apocryphon of Levi ar*
4Q541 *Apocryphon of Levi ar*
4Q542 *Testament of Qahat ar*
4Q543–549 *Visions of Amram$^{a–g}$ ar*
4Q550 *Jews at the Persian Court ar*
4Q551 *Account ar*
4Q552–553a *Four Kingdoms$^{a–c}$ ar*
4Q554 = 4QJN^{a} *New Jerusalem ar*
4Q554a = 4QJN^{b} *New Jerusalem ar*
4Q555 = 4QJN^{c} *New Jerusalem ar*
4Q556 *Prophecy^{a} ar*
4Q556a *Prophecy^{b} ar*
4Q557 *Vision^{a} ar*
4Q558 *Vision^{b} ar*
4Q558a *Unidentified Fragments ar*
4Q559 *Biblical Chronology ar*
4Q560 *Magical Booklet ar*
4Q561 *Horoscope ar*
4Q562 *Unidentified Aramaic Fragment*
4Q563 *Wisdom Composition ar*
4Q564 *Unidentified Aramaic Fragment*
4Q565 *Vision?^{c} ar*
4Q566 *Prophecy?^{c} ar*
4Q567 *Unidentified Aramaic Fragment*
4Q568 *Prophecy^{d} ar*
4Q569 *Aramaic Proverbs*
4Q570 *Unidentified Aramaic Fragment*
4Q571 *Words of Michael ar*
4Q572 *Unidentified Aramaic Fragment*
4Q573 *Unidentified Aramaic Fragment*
4Q574 *Unidentified Aramaic Fragment*
4Q575 *Unidentified Aramaic Fragment*
4Q576 *Biblical text;* not included in PTSDSSP
4Q577 *Noah's Flood* **8A**
4Q578 *Historical Work B*
4Q579 *Hymnic Work?* **5A**

4Q580 *Testament ar*
4Q581 *Testament? ar*
4Q582 *Testament ar*
4Q583 *Prophecy ar*
4Q584a–x *Unidentified Aramaic Fragments*
4Q585a–D *Unidentified Aramaic Fragments*
4Q586a–n *Unidentified Aramaic Fragments*
4Q587 *Testament ar*
4Q588 *Words of Moses*
4Q589 *Blessings*

5Q1–8 *Biblical texts;* not included in PTSDSSP
5Q9 = 5QToponyms *Toponyms (Joshua Apocryphon?)*
5Q10 *Commentary on Malachi A* **6B**
5Q11 *Possible Fragment of the Rule of the Community* **1**
5Q12 = 5QD *Damascus Document* **2**
5Q13 *Sectarian Rule* **1**
5Q14 = 5QCurses *Curses*
5Q15 = 5QJN *New Jerusalem ar*
5Q16 *His Couches Fragment*
5Q17 *Jordan Fragment* or *Text with Torah Citations* **8A**
5Q18 *In Your Council Fragment* **8A**
5Q19 *Purification Fragment* **8A**
5Q20 *Lebanon Fragment B*
5Q21 *Unidentified Fragments*
5Q22 *Abraha[m] Fragment*
5Q23 *Land Fragment*
5Q24 *Upon You Fragment* **8A**
5Q25 *Sons of Jacob Apocryphon* **8A**

6Q1–7 *Biblical texts;* not included in PTSDSSP

6Q8 *Book of Giants ar*
6Q9 = 6QapSam/Kgs *Samuel–Kings Apocryphon*
6Q10 = 6QProph *Prophetic Text*
6Q11 = 6QAllegory *Allegory of the Vine*
6Q12 = 6QapProph *Prophetic Apocryphon 3*
6Q13 = 6QPriestProph *Priestly Prophecy*
6Q14 = 6QApoc *Apocalyptic Text ar*
6Q15 = 6QD *Damascus Document* **2**
6Q16 = 6QBen *Benediction 2* **5A**
6Q17 = 6QCal *Calendrical Document*
6Q18 = 6QHymn *Hymns* **5A**
6Q19 *Sons of Ham* **8A**
6Q20 *Deuteronomy?*
6Q21 *Prophetic Fragment*
6Q22 *Mose[s] Fragment 2* **8A**
6Q23 *Unidentified Aramaic Fragments (Words of Michael?)*
6Q24 *And Answer Fragment* **8A**
6Q25 *Unidentified Fragment*
6Q26 *M[en] of the House Fragment*
6Q27–28 *Unidentified Fragments 34–35* **8A**
6Q29 *With Silver Fragments* **8A**
6Q30 *[Congrega]tion of the Faithless Fragment*
6Q31–35 *Unidentified Fragments*

7Q1 *Biblical text;* not included in PTSDSSP
7Q2 *Letter of Jeremiah*
7Q3–19 *Greek Fragments*

8Q1–4 *Biblical texts;* not included in PTSDSSP

8Q5 = 8QHymn *A Hymn Concerning the "Mighty One"* **5A**

9Q1 *Unidentified Fragment*

10Q1 *Ostracon*

11Q1–4 *Biblical texts;* not included in PTSDSSP
11Q5 = 11QPs^a *Non-Masoretic Psalms* **4A**
11Q6 = 11QPs^b *Non-Masoretic Psalms* **4A**
11Q7–9 *Biblical texts;* not included in PTSDSSP
11Q10 = 11QtgJob *Targum on Job*
11Q11 = 11QPsAp^a *A Liturgy for Healing the Stricken* **4A**
11Q12 = 11QJub *Jubilees*
11Q13 = 11QMeleh *Melchizedek* **6B**
11Q14 *Blessings of the High Priest 1* **5A**
11Q15–16 *Hymns^{a–b}* **5A**
11Q17 = 11QShirShabb *Angelic Liturgy* **4B**
11Q18 = 11QJN *New Jerusalem ar*
11Q19 = 11QTemple^a *Temple Scroll* **7**
11Q20 = 11QTemple^b *Temple Scroll Edition Close to 11Q19* **7**
11Q21 *Temple Scroll–like Document* **7**
11Q22 *Unidentified Fragment*
11Q24–28 *Unidentified Fragments*
11Q29 *Rule of the Community Related Fragment*
11Q30 *Unidentified Fragments*

Dead Sea Scrolls

Names of Documents, (Document Numbers), and **Volume Numbers**
(when they have been published in this series)

Abraha[m] Fragment (5Q22)
Account (4Q350)
Account (4Q551)
Account A–F (4Q352a, 354–358)
Account of Cereal A–B (4Q351–352)
Account of Cereal or Liquid (4Q353)
Account of Money 1–4 (4Q355–358)
Act Regarding Ownership (4Q348)
Acts of a Greek King (4Q248)
Admonitions Based on the Flood
　(4Q370) **8A**
Admonitory Parable (4Q302)
Allegory of the Vine (6Q11)
All the Angel[s] Fragment (1Q43)
All the Land Fragment (1Q41)
Alphabetic Document (4Q360)
And Answer Fragment (6Q24) **8A**
Angel of Pea[ce] Fragment (3Q8)
Angelic Liturgy (Maslk) (4Q400–407),
　(11Q17) **4B**
Apocalypse (4Q489)
Apocalypse of Weeks Pesher (4Q247)
Apocalyptic Text (6Q14)
Apocryphon (4Q488)
Apocryphon of Jacob (4Q537)
Apocryphon of Joseph (4Q539)
Apocryphon of Judah (4Q538)
Apocryphon of Levi (4Q540–541)
Appointed Time Fragment (2Q27) **8A**
Aramaic Apocryphal Work (4Q310)
Astronomical Fragments? (4Q335–
　336)
Aramaic Proverbs (4Q569)
Barki Nafshi$^{a,\ b-e}$ (4Q434–438)
Beatitudes (4Q525)
Benediction 1 (4Q500)
Benediction 2 (6Q16) **5A**
Berakot (4Q286–290)
Biblical Chronology (4Q559)
Biblical Paraphrases (6Q19–20)
Birth of Noah (4Q534–536) **8A**
Blessings (1Q28b) **1**
Blessings (4Q589)
Blessings of the High Priest 1–2
　(11Q14, 4Q285) **5A**

Book of Giants (1Q23–24), (2Q26),
　(4Q203, 530–533), (6Q8)
Book of Noah (1Q19a) **8A**
Book of the Mysteries (1Q27)
Books of Enoch (4Q201–202, 204–
　212)
Calendrical Document A–G (4Q313c,
　324b, 324g–h, 325–326, 337),
　(6Q17)
Calendrical Document/Mishmarot A–C
　(4Q320–321a)
Catalogue of Spirits^{a-b} (4Q230–231)
Catena A–B (4Q177, 182) **6B**
Commentary on Canticles? (4Q240)
Commentary on Genesis A–D (4Q252–
　254) **6B**
Commentary on Malachi A (SQ 10) **6B**
Commentary on Malachi B (4Q253a)
　6B
Communal Ceremony (4Q275)
Communal Confession (4Q393)
Concerning Cultic Services A–B
　(4Q250, 250a)
*[Congrega]tion of the Faithless Frag-
　ment* (6Q30)
Congregation of the Lord (4Q466)
Consolations (4Q176) **6B**
Copper Scroll (3Q15)
Court of the Righteous [Ones]
　(4Q440b) **5A**
Covenant Fragment (1Q31)
Covenant of His Glory Fragment
　(1Q54)
Creation? (4Q457a)
Cryptic (Phases of the Moon) (4Q317)
Cryptic Fragment 1–3 (4Q362–363a)
Curses (4Q280), (5Q14)
Cursive Work (4Q309)
David's Descendents (4Q479)
Didactic Work A (4Q455)
Daily Prayers (4Q503) **4A**
Damascus Document (CD), (5Q12),
　(6Q15) **2**
Damascus Document Fragments
　(4Q266–273) **2/3**

Dame Folly and Lady Wisdom (4Q184)
Daniel Apocryphon (4Q246)
David Apocryphon (2Q22)
Day of Atonement Fragment (1Q34b)
Debt Acknowledgement (4Q344)
Decrees (4Q477)
Deed A–C (4Q347, 348, 359)
Deuteronomy? (6Q20)
Divine Providence (4Q413)
Elect of Israel Fragment (1Q37)
Elisha Apocryphon (4Q48la)
Eschatological Hymn (4Q457b)
Eschatological Work A–B (4Q468g,
　472)
Eternal Fragment (1Q51) **2**
Evil Ones Fragment (1Q69)
Exaltation Hymn (1Q19b) **8A**
Excerpted Deuteronomy (4Q37–38, 41,
　44)
Excerpted Exodus (4Q15–16)
Exodus/Conquest Tradition (4Q374)
Exposition on the Patriarchs (4Q464)
　6B
Famine Fragment (1Q42)
Festivals Fragment (4Q478)
Flood Fragment (4Q577)
Florilegium (4Q174) **6B**
For a Song Fragment (1Q70) **8A**
A Form of Psalm 89 (4Q236) **4A**
Four Kingdoms^{a-b} (4Q552–553)
Fragment Mentioning Elisha (4Q481a)
Fragment Mentioning Qoh 1:8–9
　(4Q468l)
Fragments of Rules for Liturgies?
　(4Q295–297) **3**
Fragments with Place Names (4Q233)
Genealogical List (4Q338)
*Genesis 27:20–21 with Scribal Exercis-
　es* (4Q234)
Genesis Apocryphon (1Q20=1QapGen,
　3Q14 frg. 8) **8A**
Genesis and Exodus Paraphrase
　(4Q422)
Grace After Meals (4Q434a)
Greek Fragments (7Q3–19)
Habakkuk Pesher (1QpHab) **6B**

Qumran Pseudepigraphic Psalms (4Q380–381) **4A**
Rachel and Joseph Apocryphon (4Q474) **8A**
Rebukes (4Q477)
Red Ink Fragments (4Q481d)
Related to Isaiah 11 (4Q250b)
Renewed Earth (4Q475)
Resting Place Fragment (1Q56)
Reworked Pentateuch^{a–e} (4Q158, 364–367)
Rule of the Community (1QS), (4Q255–264) **1**
Rule of the Community Related Fragment (11Q29)
Rule of the Congregation (1Q28a) **1**
Rule of the Congregation (4Q249a–i)
Rules (4Q513) **1**
Sale of Land 1–2 (4Q345–346)
Samson Text? (4Q465)
Samuel-Kings Apocryphon (6Q9)
Sanctuary Text (4Q307) **8A**
Sapiential-Didactic Work A–C (4Q294, 412, 425)
Sapiential Fragment A–B (4Q486–487)
Sapiential Fragments (4Q308)
Sapiential-Hymnic Work A (4Q426)
Sapiential-Hymnic Work B (4Q528)
Sapiential Testament (4Q185)
Sayings of Moses (1Q22)
Scribbles on Papyrus (4Q361)
Sectarian Rule (5Q13) **1**
Sectarian Work? (4Q468i)
Self-Glorification Hymn (1QH^a, 4Q427, 4Q471b, 4Q491) **5A**
Serekh Ha-Niddot (Menstrual Flow) (4Q284) **3**
Sirach (2Q18)
So-Called Marriage Ritual (4Q502)
Some Works of Torah (4Q394–399, 4Q313) **3**
Songs of the Master (4Q510–511)
Sons of Ham (6Q19) **8A**
Sons of Jacob Apocryphon (5Q25) **8A**
Sword Fragment (2Q31) **8A**

Targum on Job (4Q157), (1 1Q10)
Targum on Leviticus (4Q156)
Teacher Fragment (1Q66)
Temple Scroll (11Q19) **7**
Temple Scroll Edition Close to 11Q19 (11Q20) **7**
Temple Scroll-Like Document (11Q21) **7**
Temple Scroll Source or Divergent Copy (4Q365a) **7**
Temple Scroll Source or Earlier Edition (4Q524) **7**
Testament (4Q526, 580–582, 587)
Testament of Judah (3Q7), (4Q484)
Testament of Levi (1Q21), (4Q213–214)
Testament of Naphtali (4Q215)
Testament of Qahat (4Q542)
Testimonia (4Q175) **6B**
Text Mentioning 'Light to Jacob' (4Q467)
Text Quoting Leviticus (4Q249k–1)
Text with Quotation from Psalm 107? (4Q418b)
Thanksgiving Hymns (1QH^a, 1Q35), (4Q427–432) **5A**
They Contend Fragment (4Q488) **8A**
Three Tongues of Fire (4Q376)
Time of Righteousness (4Q215a)
Tobit (4Q196–199, 478)
Tobit Hebrew Fragment? (4Q200)
Tohorot A–C (4Q274, 276–278)
Toponyms (5Q9)
Tree Fragment (1Q50)
Two Spirits Treatise? (1Q29a)
Two Ways (4Q473)
Unidentified Aramaic Fragments (3Q12–13), (4Q558a, 562, 564, 567, 570, 572–575, 584a–x, 585a–D, 586a–n), (6Q23)
Unidentified Cryptic A Texts (4Q249r–z, 250c–j, 313a–c)
Unidentified Fragments (4Q464b) **6B**
Unidentified Fragments 12, 20, 34–35 (2Q32, 4Q490, 6Q27–28) **8A**

Unidentified Fragments (1Q44, 47–48, 59–61), (3Q10–11, 14), (4Q178, 281–282, 311, 468a–c, 468j, 468m–dd, 515, 517–520), (5Q21), (6Q25–26, 31), (9Q1), (11Q22–28, 30)
Unidentified Nabatean Text (4Q235)
Unidentified Parabiblical Material paleo (4Q124–125)
Unidentified Parabiblical Material gr (4Q126)
Unidentified Pesharim Fragments (4Q172) **6B**
Upon You Fragment (5Q24) **8A**
Verdict Fragment (2Q28) **2**
Vision^{a–c} (4Q557–558, 565)
Vision and Interpretation (4Q410)
Vision of Samuel (4Q160)
Visionary Fragment (4Q489) **8A**
Visions of Amram^{a–g} (4Q543–549)
War Scroll (1QM, 1Q33), (4Q491–496) **2**
War Scroll-Like Fragment (4Q497) **2**
War Scroll-Like Fragment B (4Q471)
Ways of Righteousness^{a–b} (4Q420–421)
Who is She? Fragment (1Q68)
Wicked and Holy (4Q180–181) **2**
Wisdom Composition (4Q563)
With Silver Fragments (6Q29) **8A**
Words of the Lights (4Q504–506) **4A**
Words of Michael (4Q529, 571)
Words of Moses (4Q588)
Words of Judgment (4Q238)
Words to the Sons of Dawn (4Q298)
Work with Citation of Jubilees (4Q228)
Work with Prayers (4Q291–293)
Works of God (4Q392)
Worm Fragment (1Q53)
Yahweh Fragment (2Q30) **8A**
You Shall Say Fragment (2Q29) **8A**
Your Blotting Out Fragment (1Q67)
Your Signs Fragment (1Q52)
Your Strength Fragment (1Q49)
Zedekiah Fragment (4Q470)
Zephaniah Pesher 1–2 (1Q15), (4Q170) **6B**
Zodiology and Brontology (4Q318)

Printed in the USA
CPSIA information can be obtained
at www.ICGtesting.com
LVHW081515191023
761572LV00011B/637